International Marketing

The Irwin Series in Marketing
Consulting Editor Gilbert A. Churchill, Jr.
University of Wisconsin, Madison

INTERNATIONAL MARKETING

Philip R. Cateora

Fellow, Academy of International Business

*Professor of Marketing and
International Business
University of Colorado*

Seventh Edition

IRWIN

Homewood, IL 60430
Boston, MA 02116

Cover illustration: John Craig

Sponsoring editor: Elizabeth MacDonell
Developmental editor: Ann Sass
Project editor: Waivah Clement
Production manager: Ann Cassady
Designer: Robyn Basquin
Compositor: Arcata Graphics/Kingsport
Printer: R. R. Donnelley & Sons Company

Library of Congress Cataloging-in-Publication Data

Cateora, Philip R.
    International marketing/Philip R. Cateora.—7th ed.
        Includes index. p.   cm.
        ISBN 0-256-07953-6
        ISBN 0-256-08397-5 (Int'l Student Ed.)
        1. Export marketing.   2. International business enterprises.
    I. Title.
    HF1009.5.C35   1990
    658.8'48—dc20   89–37430
                                        CIP

Printed in the United States of America
1 2 3 4 5 6 7 8 9 0 DO 6 5 4 3 2 1 0 9

To Nancy
and
Deborah, Phyllis, Hank,
and
Thomas

Preface

International Marketing has been the leading international marketing text since its introduction more than two decades ago.

The first edition of *International Marketing* pioneered the environmental/cultural approach to the study of international marketing. This new, innovative approach coincided with the dynamic changes occurring in U.S. businesses as many ventured into international markets for the first time and others expanded their international involvement beyond exporting. This seventh edition of *International Marketing* continues at the forefront of change by reflecting the current pervasiveness of world competition that has resulted in changing businesses' orientation from international marketing to a more encompassing global marketing.

At no other time in modern economic history have countries been more economically interdependent, have greater opportunities for international trade existed, or has the potential for greater global economic growth existed than now, the last decade of the 20th century. The future of business is global business. It is with the future that the seventh edition of *International Marketing* is concerned. As global economic growth occurs, understanding marketing in all cultures becomes increasingly important. Because the world is approaching an interdependent global market in the 21st century, the seventh edition of *International Marketing* has been revised to keep pace with the changes businesses face between now and the 21st century as they are confronted with the competitive consequences of such trends as Europe 1992, Russia and China's rapid shift from socialist-based economies to the free enterprise system, the changing economic role of the Pacific Rim countries, and the emerging economic importance of India and many Latin American countries.

Not all firms engaged in overseas marketing have a global perspective—nor do they need one. Some companies' foreign marketing is limited to marketing in one country; others market in a number of countries, treating each country as a separate market; and still others—the global enterprises—look for market segments with common needs and wants across political and economic boundaries. *International Marketing* addresses global issues that confront today's international marketer and presents concepts relevant to all international marketers, regardless of the extent of their international involvement.

From a marketing management view, the text emphasizes the strategic implications of marketing in different country cultures. Seven chapters address the cultural influences on marketing strategies; nine chapters present marketing management techniques and the adjustments necessary to accommodate cultural differences.

The text is designed to stimulate the reader's curiosity about management practices of companies seeking market opportunities outside the home country—to raise the reader's consciousness about the importance of viewing international marketing management strategies from a global perspective.

An environmental/cultural approach to international marketing permits a truly global orientation. The reader's horizons are not limited to any specific nation or to the particular ways of doing business in a single nation. Instead, the book provides an approach and framework for identifying and analyzing the important environmental uniqueness of any nation or global region. It helps to make readers aware of the importance of culture in marketing so when they are confronted with the task of marketing in a foreign milieu, the impact of crucial cultural issues will not be overlooked. The key to successful international marketing is adaptation; adapting to an ever-changing, mostly uncontrollable, and—to the inexperienced—frequently incomprehensible environment.

Although a global orientation is infused throughout this revised edition, export marketing is not overlooked. Issues specific to exporting are discussed where strategies applicable to exporting arise.

Structure of the Text

The text is divided into four parts. The first two chapters in **Part 1** introduce the environmental/cultural approach to international marketing and three international marketing management concepts—the Domestic Market Extension, the Multidomestic Market, and the Global Market. Global marketing as well as the other international marketing management concepts or orientations are discussed. Chapter 2 focuses on the global marketing environment and the challenges and opportunities confronting today's international marketer.

The seven chapters in **Part 2** present the cultural environment of international marketing. The effects of the cultural environment on global marketing are discussed in the context that cultural differences do not evaporate in a global orientation but must be recognized and, when necessary, accommodated if global marketing strategies are to be successful. Cross-cultural negotiations, the Export Trade Act of 1988, the United States–Canada Free Trade Agreement, Europe 1992, and the economic revitalization in Russia and China are only a few of the new and expanded topics discussed in these chapters. Geography and history are also included as important dimensions in understanding cultural and market differences among countries.

Part 3 has nine chapters on international marketing management. In addition to planning and organizing for international marketing, marketing research and sources of international market information are covered in Chapters 10 and 11. Chapters 12 and 13 focus on product management, reflecting the differences between consumer and industrial product development strategies and the growing importance in world markets for business services. Chapter 14 covers advertising and addresses the promotional element of the international marketing mix, and Chapter 15 discusses personal selling and personnel management. Price escalation and ways it is lessened, countertrade practices, and price strategies to employ when the dollar is strong or weak relative to foreign currencies are illustrative of the concepts presented in Chapter 16 on pricing. Chapter 17 takes the reader through the distribution process from the home country to the consumer in the target country market; Chapter 18 discusses in detail the special techniques of export operations.

Part 4 addresses the financial requirements of international marketing. The volatility of the value of world currencies plays a special role in international business today as does the ability to coordinate and control global marketing operations. Chapters 19 and 20 emphasize international finance and coordinating and controlling global operations.

Pedagogical Features of the Text

The text portion of the book provides a thorough coverage of the subject with specific emphasis on the planning and strategic problems confronting companies that market across cultural boundaries.

- Current, pithy, sometimes humorous, and always relevant examples in each chapter stimulate interest and increase understanding of the ideas,

concepts, and strategies presented and emphasize the importance of understanding cultural uniqueness found in many countries.
- Comprehensive questions and lists of relevant terms at the end of each chapter assist the student in reviewing the material presented and serve as the basis for class discussions.
- The boxed "incidents," another innovation of the first edition of *International Marketing*, have always been popular among students. The seventh edition includes more than 50 new incidents that provide insightful and often humorous examples of cultural differences while illustrating concepts presented in the text.

Cases

A selection of both short and long cases comprises Part 5. The short cases focus on a single problem that serves as the basis for a discussion of a specific concept or issue. The longer, more integrated cases are broader in scope and focus on more than one marketing management problem. The cases can be analyzed using the information provided, but they also lend themselves to more in-depth analysis that requires students to engage in additional research and data collection.

The Appendix is a guide for developing a comprehensive, strategic marketing plan. This detailed outline provides a format for developing a complete cultural and economic analysis of a country.

Acknowledgments

The success of a text depends on the contributions of many people—especially those who take the time to share their thoughtful criticisms and suggestions to improve the text. I appreciate the help of the many students and professors who have shared their opinions of past editions, and I welcome their suggestions on this and future editions of *International Marketing*.

Of the many contributors to the completion of this edition, no one has been more creative or enthusiastic than Nancy Cateora, without whose support and assistance this edition would never have been completed. To her I say thank you.

I wish also to acknowledge the helpful assistance of Scott Faulkenburg and Eugene Loui, who provided valuable research assistance and manuscript preparation. To the publishers and authors who permitted the reproduction of articles, cases, and other materials, I am also indebted.

Philip R. Cateora

Brief Contents

PART III
Global Marketing Management

PART IV
Corporate Contest of Marketing

Contents

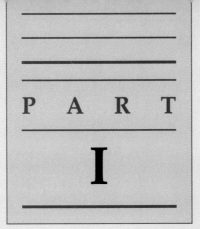

P A R T

I

An Overview

Chapters

CHAPTER 1

The Scope and Challenge of International Marketing

Never before in American history have U.S. businesses been so deeply involved in and affected by international trade. Four long-term trends are affecting U.S. businesses, small or large, domestic or international. The first trend is the internationalization of U.S. markets;[1] second, interdependence of world economies;[2] third, the emergence of international competitors from all over the world;[3] and fourth, the globalization of world markets.[4]

The world is rapidly becoming a one-world economic and market system. Whether or not a U.S. company wants to participate directly in international business, it cannot escape the effects of the ever-increasing number of American firms exporting, importing, and/or manufacturing abroad; the number of foreign-based firms operating in U.S. markets; and the increasing number of competitors for world markets.

[1] John J. Curran, "What Foreigners Will Buy Next," *Fortune*, February 13, 1989, pp. 94–97.

[2] Nigel M. Healey, "Danger in a 'Dormant' Crisis: The Debtors Are in a Worse Situation than Ever," *World Press Review*, January 1989, pp. 30–32.

[3] Louis Kraar, "Korea Tomorrow's Powerhouse," *Fortune*, August 15, 1988, pp. 75–81.

[4] For a continuation of the ideas Theodore Levitt presented in "The Globalization of Markets," *Harvard Business Review*, May–June, 1983, pp. 92–102, see From the Editor (Theodore Levitt), "The Pluralization of Consumption," *Harvard Business Review*, May–June 1988, pp. 7–8.

BOX 1–1
Internationalization of the U.S. Market

What happened to the microwave market in the United States? We invented the microwave oven, but Japan has over 52 percent of the market today. Of the four microwave makers gaining market share in 1985, only Litton is American. Among the six top U.S. sellers are the Japanese giants, Sanyo, Sharp, and Matsushita Electric. The microwave oven typifies the internationalization of U.S. markets. Consider the following list of events:

1945   Microwave cooking discovered by Raytheon (United States).
1947   Raytheon manufactured the first microwave oven for sale to restaurants and hotels.
1955   First microwaves are made by Tappan for consumer use.
1967   Amana introduces the microwave using standard household circuits.
1970   Litton enters the consumer market, sales top 100,000 units.
1977   Raytheon manufactures last magnetron tube in the United States. All production shifts to Japan.
1978   South Korea begins exporting microwaves to United States.
1979   Sanyo and Matsushita start manufacturing microwaves in the United States.
1980   Sharp starts manufacturing microwaves in the United States.
1983   Sanyo takes market lead from GE with 19 percent. Amana starts importing microwaves from the Far East.
1984   Japanese and Korean producers end the year with over 60 percent of U.S. market.
1984   GE decides to phase out U.S. production and buy microwaves from Japan and South Korea.
1985   Tappan begins importing small microwave ovens from Japan.
1986   Goldstar and Samsung, Korean-made microwave ovens, introduces deep price-cutting in U.S. markets.
1990   ?????

Source: Adapted from "Two Tough Contests: Microwave Ovens and Construction Equipment," *Dun's Business Month*, February 1985, p. 32, *Business Week*, August 26, 1985, p. 64, Ira C. Magaziner and Mark Patinkin, "Fast Heat: How Korea Won the Microwave War," *Harvard Business Review*, January–February 1989, pp. 83–92.

Today most business activities are global in scope. Finance, technology, research, capital and investment flows, production facilities, and marketing and distribution networks all have global dimensions.[5] Every business must be prepared to compete in an increasingly interdependent global

---

[5] For an interesting article on trade today, see Pat Choate and Juyne Linger, "Tailored Trade: Dealing with the World as It Is," *Harvard Business Review*, January–February 1988, pp. 86–93.

economic environment, and all business people must be aware of the effects of these trends when managing a multinational conglomerate or a domestic company that exports. As one international expert noted, "every American company is international, at least to the extent that its business performance is conditioned in part by events that occur abroad." Even companies which do not operate in the international arena are affected to some degree by the export-led growth in South Korea, the debt burden of Mexico, and the economic changes taking place in China.[6]

The internationalization of the U.S. market and the globalization of world markets have a profound impact on business operations. It is less and less possible for business to avoid the influence of the internationalization of the U.S. economy and the globalization of the world's markets. As competition for world markets intensifies, the number of companies operating solely in domestic markets will decrease. Or, to put it another way, the business of American business is international business.

Global business, multinational company, transnational, and *world enterprise* are all terms being used with greater frequency as significantly larger numbers of businesses become international both in philosophy and in scope of operations.[7] The challenge of international marketing is to develop strategic plans that are competitive as the globalization of markets intensifies.

THE INTERNATIONALIZATION OF U.S. BUSINESS

Current interest in international marketing can be explained by changing competitive structures coupled with shifts in demand characteristics in markets throughout the world. With the increasing globalization of markets, companies find they are unavoidably enmeshed with foreign customers, competitors, and suppliers even within their own borders.[8] They face competition on all fronts from domestic firms and from foreign firms. As one source reports, "the pianos at the Hilton and the Americana hotels are not Steinways but Yamahas as are the NBC organs that play background music for the 'Tonight Show.'" A significant portion (Exhibit 1–1) of all televisions, tape players, VCRs, apparel, and dinnerware sold in the United States is foreign made. Sony (Japan), Laura Ashley (Britain), Volkswagen (Germany), Norelco (Holland), Samsung (Korea), and Nescafé (Switzerland) are familiar brands in the United States, and, for U.S. industry,

---

[6] Ford S. Worthy, "What's Next for Business in China," *Fortune*, July 17, 1989, pp. 110–12.

[7] To discover how important international profits are to U.S. businesses, see "The 100 Largest U.S. Multinationals," *Forbes*, July 25, 1988, pp. 248–50.

[8] "Managing Now for the 1990s," *Fortune*, September 26, 1988, p. 45.

EXHIBIT 1–1   Percent of U.S. Market Held by Imported Products

Automobiles	44.3
Steel	26.2
Apparel	36.8
Footwear (nonrubber)	77.0
Machine tools	37.0
TV and video cameras	72.0
Telephone instruments	75.0
Automobile radios	45.0
Videotape recorders	99.0

SOURCE: Joseph M. Sakach, "Can We Compete?" *Business Marketing*, September 1987, p. 86; and "Back to Basics," *Business Week*, Special 1989 Bonus Issue, 1989, p. 17.

they are formidable opponents in a competitive struggle for U.S. and world markets.

Many familiar U.S. companies are now foreign controlled. When you shop for groceries at A&P supermarkets or buy Alka-Seltzer you are buying indirectly from a German company. Some well-known brands no longer owned by U.S. companies are Carnation (Swiss), Brooks Brothers clothing (Canada), and the all-American Smith and Wesson handgun which now is owned by a British firm. Travelodge, Saks Fifth Avenue, Keebler Cookies, and many more (see Exhibit 1–2) are currently owned or controlled by foreign multinational businesses.[9] In fact, foreign investment in the United

EXHIBIT 1–2   Foreign Acquisitions of U.S. Companies during the 1980s

U.S. Company	*Foreign Owner*
Pillsbury (Green Giant, Burger King, Haagen-Dazs)	British
Macmillan (publishing)	British
Firestone Rubber	Japan
G. Heileman Brewing (Colt 45)	Australia
CBS Records	Japan
Heublein (Smirnoff, Inglenook wine)	British
Chesebrough-Pond's (Vaseline)	Netherlands
Allied Stores (Ann Taylor, Jordan Marsh)	Canada
Carnation (Coffee-mate®, Friskies pet food)	Switzerland

SOURCE: Adapted from "Major Foreign Acquisitions of the 1980s," *Fortune*, February 13, 1989, p. 96.

[9] "The Selling of America (cont'd)," *Fortune*, May 22, 1988, pp. 54–64.

BOX 1–2
American-Made Products Yesterday—Today

Yesterday

Henry Ford built a 100-percent American-made automobile. Ford's Rouge plant in Dearborn, Michigan, was built in 1919 to turn out the country's first Model-Ts. The plant had its own steel mill, glass factory, and 32 other separate manufacturing plants under one roof. The only foreign element in a Model-T was rubber from Malaysia, and Henry Ford made a vain but valiant effort to grow rubber trees. Not until synthetic rubber in the 1940s did the Ford become 100 percent American. It was manufactured entirely in the Rouge plant, then the world's largest single industrial complex.

In the early 1960s things began to change. The last American-made Ford automobile rolled off the assembly line. About the same time, a memorandum from Henry Ford II set forth a new policy: "In order to further the growth of our worldwide operations, each purchasing activity of the company or an affiliated company should consider the selection of sources of supply not only in its own country but also sources located in other countries" or, to paraphrase: If it's cheaper abroad, get it abroad. Ford's memorandum was a harbinger of American business.

Today

World cars, assembled from all over the world and sold all over the world, are a fact. Ford's Festiva was designed in the United States, engineered by Mazda in Japan, and is being build by Kia in Korea principally for the American market.

Mercury Capri was designed by Ghia and Italdesign in Italy and is assembled in Australia, principally of Japanese components, for the American market.

Ford's new Probe was designed in the United States with input from Europe, engineered by Mazda, and assembled by Mazda in the Japanese automakers' Flat Rock, Michigan, plant.

Mercury Tracer has a Ford design, built on a Mazda platform in Hermosillo, Mexico, with a Ford engine manufactured in Mexico and other components from Taiwan.

Pontiac LeMans is a close cousin of the German-designed Opel Kadett but the LeMans is being built by Daewoo Motor Company in Korea. Volkswagen ships its Foxes from Brazil to sell in the United States.

Not to be forgotten is the Ford Escort, a truly world car. This best selling car in America and in the world is designed jointly by Ford of Europe and Ford of North America. It is built in 6 countries and sold in more than 30 others.

The American Honda Motor Company came to Marysville, Ohio, to build Honda motorcycles. It added production of Honda Accords and Civics for the U.S. market. The two-door Accord coupe, the first Honda to be manufactured exclusively in the United States, is exported to Japan and other countries.

Sources: Adapted from Nancy W. Hatton, "Born and Bred in the U.S.A.," *Detroit News*, March 12, 1983; and William Allan, "Ford Takes Lead in Producing World Cars," Scripps Howard News Service, March 26, 1988.

EXHIBIT 1–3   Some Big Players in the Global Game

Company*	Foreign Earnings as Percent of Total	Foreign Assets as Percent of Total
General Motors Corporation	54.0	23.4
Eastman Kodak Company	38.2	34.7
Digital Equipment Corporation	54.6	36.7
Coca-Cola Company	74.4	26.0
Goodyear Tire & Rubber Company	42.7	34.6
Johnson & Johnson	57.3	45.0
NCR Corporation	52.1	42.4
Gillette Company	63.9	61.5
H. J. Heinz Company	37.1	41.1
Avon Products, Inc.	49.4	27.2

* Company sales figures are for 1987.

SOURCE: "The 100 Largest U.S. Multinationals," *Forbes*, July 25, 1988, pp. 248–50.

States is in excess of $1.5 trillion of which $250 billion is in direct investment in companies. Investors from the United Kingdom (28 percent) and the Netherlands (20.1 percent) are the largest investors followed by Japan (12 percent), Canada (7.6 percent) and West Germany (6.8 percent).[10]

Once the private domain of U.S. businesses, the vast domestic market that provided them with an opportunity for continued growth must now be shared with a variety of foreign companies and products. Companies with only domestic markets have found it increasingly difficult to sustain customary rates of growth and many are seeking foreign markets to absorb surplus productive capacity. Companies with foreign operations find foreign earnings make an important overall contribution to total corporate profits; in fact, the return on foreign investments is frequently higher than on investments in the United States. The figures in Exhibit 1–3 illustrate that for some companies the profit generated on investments abroad, as well as the profit from foreign sales, are better than in the United States. Understandably, the opportunity for high profit margins is an important impetus for going international.

Companies that never ventured abroad until recently are now seeking foreign markets. Companies with existing foreign operations realize they must be more competitive to succeed against foreign multinationals. They have found it necessary to spend more money and time improving their marketing positions abroad because competition for these growing markets is intensifying. For the firm venturing into international marketing for

---

[10] "The Buying of America: Should We Be Worried?" *Business Week*, May 9, 1988, p. 36.

Two global products—Kentucky Fried Chicken and Coca-Cola promotion in Singapore. (Al Guiteras, Journalism Services, Inc.)

the first time and for those already experienced, the requirement is generally the same—a thorough and complete commitment to foreign markets and for many, new ways of operating.[11]

INTERNATIONAL MARKETING DEFINED

International marketing is the performance of business activities that direct the flow of a company's goods and services to consumers or users in more than one nation for a profit. The only difference in the definition of domestic marketing and international marketing is that the marketing activities take place in more than one country. This apparently minor difference accounts for the complexity and diversity found in international

---

[11] Jeremy Main, "The Winning Organization," *Fortune,* September 26, 1988, p. 50–60.

marketing operations. Marketing concepts, processes, and principles are universally applicable, and the marketer's task is the same whether doing business in Dimebox, Texas, or Dar es Salaam, Tanzania.[12] Businesses' goal is to make a profit by promoting, pricing, and distributing products for which there is a market. If this is the case, what is the difference between domestic and international marketing?

The answer lies not with different concepts of marketing but with the environment within which marketing plans must be implemented. The uniqueness of foreign marketing comes from the range of unfamiliar problems and the variety of strategies necessary to cope with different levels of uncertainty encountered in foreign markets. In short, international marketing is different from domestic marketing because of the different cultural influences involved and their potential impact on the successful implementation of marketing programs.

Competition, legal restraints, government controls, weather, fickle consumers, and any number of other uncontrollable elements can, and frequently do, affect the profitable outcome of good, sound marketing plans. Generally speaking, the marketer cannot control or influence these uncontrollable elements but instead must adjust or adapt to them in a manner consistent with a successful outcome. What makes marketing interesting is the challenge of molding the *controllable elements* of marketing decisions (product, price, promotion, and distribution) within the framework of the *uncontrollable elements* of the marketplace (competition, politics, laws, consumer behavior, level of technology, and so forth) in such a way that marketing objectives are achieved. Even though marketing principles and concepts are universally applicable, the environment within which the marketer must implement marketing plans can change dramatically from country to country. The difficulties created by different environments are the international marketer's primary concern.

THE INTERNATIONAL MARKETING TASK

The international marketer's task is more complicated than that of the domestic marketer because the international marketer must deal with at least two levels of uncontrollable uncertainty instead of one. Uncertainty is created by the uncontrollable elements of all business environments,

---

[12] For an interesting study on the applicability of marketing know-how in Third World countries, see Ishmael P. Akaah, Edward A. Riordan, and Kofi Q. Dadzie, "Applicability of Marketing Concepts and Management Activities in the Third World: An Empirical Investigation," *Journal of Business Research*, March 1988, pp. 133–48.

but each foreign country in which a company operates adds its own unique set of uncontrollables. Exhibit 1–4 illustrates the total environment of an international marketer. The inner circle depicts the controllable elements that constitute a marketer's decision area, the second circle encompasses those environmental elements at home that have some effect on foreign-operation decisions, and the outer circles represent the elements of the foreign environment for each foreign market within which the marketer operates. As the outer circles illustrate, each foreign market in which the company does business can (and usually does) present separate problems involving some or all of the uncontrollable elements. Thus, the more foreign markets in which a company operates, the greater the possible variety of

EXHIBIT 1–4   The International Marketing Task

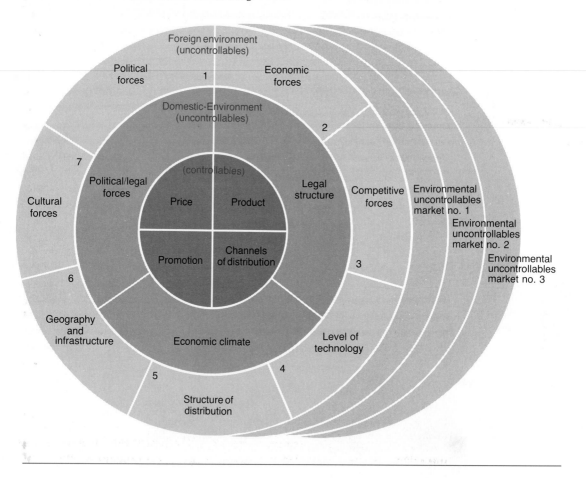

foreign environmental uncontrollables there are with which to contend. Frequently, a solution to a problem in country A is not applicable to a problem in country B.

Marketing Controllables

The successful manager constructs a marketing program designed for optimal adjustment to the uncertainty of the business climate. The inner circle in Exhibit 1–4 represents the area under control of the marketing manager. Assuming the necessary overall corporate resources, the marketing manager blends price, product, promotion, and channels-of-distribution activities to capitalize on anticipated demand. The controllable elements can be altered in the long run and, usually, in the short run, to adjust to changing market conditions or corporate objectives.

Represented by the outer circles surrounding market controllables are the levels of uncertainty created by the domestic and foreign environments. Although the marketer can blend a marketing mix from the controllable elements, the uncontrollables are just that and must be actively adapted to because their influence determines the ultimate outcome of the marketing effort.

Domestic Uncontrollables

The domestic environment illustrated in Exhibit 1–4 by the second circle includes elements that can have a direct effect on the success of a foreign venture including political forces, legal structure, and economic climate in the home country. A political decision involving domestic foreign policy can have a direct effect on a firm's international marketing success. For example, the U.S. government placed a total ban on trade with Libya to condemn Libyan support for terrorist attacks, imposed restrictions on the sales of computers and computer software to South Africa to protest apartheid, and placed a total ban on trade with Nicaragua whose actions "constitute an unusual and extraordinary threat to the national security of the United States." In each of these cases, the international marketing programs of such companies as IBM, Xerox, and Occidental Petroleum were restricted by domestic uncontrollables. The law permits the government to restrict foreign trade when such trade adversely affects the security or economy of the country or when such trade is in conflict with U.S. foreign policy.

The domestic economic climate is another important home-based uncontrollable variable with far-reaching effects on a company's competitive position in foreign markets. The capacity to invest in plants and facilities either in domestic or foreign markets is to a large extent a function of domestic economic vitality. It is generally true that capital tends to flow toward optimum use; however, capital must be generated before it can have mobility. Furthermore, if internal economic conditions deteriorate, restrictions against foreign investment and purchasing may be imposed to strengthen the domestic economy.

For a variety of economic reasons, the most pressing condition affecting U.S. international marketers in the mid-1980s was the relative strength of the dollar in world markets. Because the U.S. dollar's value was high compared to most foreign currencies, U.S. goods were expensive for foreign buyers. This gave a price advantage to foreign competitors by making American products relatively expensive and caused a downturn in export sales. By the end of the 1980s, the U.S. dollar had weakened compared to world currencies and U.S. products became bargains for foreign customers and export sales increased. For example, an English person who wanted to buy a $15 American-made product in 1984 when the exchange rate was £1 = $1.15 had to exchange £13 British pounds to get $15 U.S. By 1989, when the British pound equaled $1.74, that same $15 item would cost the British only £8.62.[13] Currency value, then, is one influence of the home environment's economy on the marketer's task. Inextricably entwined with the effects of the domestic environment are the constraints imposed by the environment of each foreign country.

Foreign Uncontrollables

Besides uncontrollable domestic elements, a significant source of uncertainty is the uncontrollable foreign business environments depicted in Exhibit 1–4 by the outer circles. A business operating in its home country undoubtedly feels comfortable in forecasting the business climate and adjusting business decisions to these elements. The process of evaluating the uncontrollable elements in an international marketing program, however, often involves substantial doses of cultural, political, and economic shock.

A business operating in a number of foreign countries might find polar extremes in political stability, class structure, and economic climate as critical elements in business decisions. The dynamic upheavals in some developing countries further illustrate the problems of dramatic change in cultural, political, and economic climates over relatively short periods of time. A case in point is China. It appeared to be rapidly opening up politically and economically until a student rally and hunger strike at Tiananmen Square in May 1989 and the subsequent June 3 crushing of the student demonstration caused a resurgence of political oppression.

---

[13] "Currency Trading," *The Wall Street Journal*, March 1, 1989, p. C10.

BOX 1–3
Just Because It Sells in Mexico Doesn't Mean It Will Sell Elsewhere in Latin America

Gerber, the baby-food company, is perplexed because their line of baby foods which have done well in other countries in Latin America, haven't done well in Brazil.

After eight years of trying, Gerber has not done well enough to justify continuing their Brazilian operation. They were never able to convince mothers to use baby food as an everyday feeding item. The Brazilian mother would use prepackaged baby food only when visiting or on a beach outing.

They failed in spite of an award-winning advertisement telling mothers they would have more time to show affection to their infants if they were not bent over sinks preparing food. The company underestimated a cultural factor: Brazilian mothers are not willing to accept the fact that prepared baby food is a good substitute for fresh food made by themselves or, more likely, by their live-in maids.

Source: "Brazil: Gerber Abandons a Baby-Food Market," *Business Week*, February 8, 1982, p. 45.

As a result, serious questions arose about China's continuation of the economic reforms that had been instituted by Deng Xiaoping.[14] At the time this is being written it is too early to forecast the final political and economic outcome of the student uprising. Nevertheless, in less than two months time from April to May 1989, foreign investor's enthusiasm for investment in China had turned to caution and withdrawal.[15] Such are the uncertainties of the uncontrollable political factors of international business.

The more significant elements in the uncontrollable international environment are shown in the outer circles of Exhibit 1–4. These factors include (1) political/legal forces, (2) economic forces, (3) competitive forces, (4) level of technology, (5) structure of distribution, (6) geography and infrastructure, and (7) cultural forces. They constitute the principal elements of uncertainty an international marketer must cope with in designing a marketing program. Each is discussed in some detail in subsequent chapters.

The problem of foreign uncertainty is further complicated by a frequently imposed "alien status" that increases the difficulty of properly assessing

---

[14] Ross Terrill, "China after Deng," *World Monitor*, July 1989, pp. 28–37.

[15] Alan Farnham," Ready to Ride Out China's Turmoil," *Fortune*, July 3, 1989, pp. 117–18.

BOX 1–4
Being Competitive in a Global Market

What we need in American industry is to establish more "citizens of the world" rather than citizens of the United States.

We've learned that we must understand and accept the importance of culture in doing business globally, but what can we really do? Here are a few suggestions:

Let's start adding Japanese-speaking people or people of Japanese ancestry to our payrolls—especially in sales and marketing.

Begin intensive cultural training programs for all your employees who have contact with non-U.S. companies.

Rethink your hiring practices to include language skills, world travel, and experience.

Make sure key employees who work with offshore companies have international work experience. You may even consider appointing a protocol officer, such as we have in our embassies.

Source: Adapted from Joseph M. Sakach, Jr., "Can We Compete?" *Business Marketing*, September 1987, pp. 88–89.

and forecasting the dynamic international business climate. There are two dimensions to the alien status of a foreign business; alien in that the business is controlled by foreigners and alien in that the culture of the host country is alien to the foreign company. The alien status of a business results in greater emphasis being placed on many of the uncontrollable elements than would be found with relation to those same elements in the domestic market.

The political environment offers the best example of the alien status. Domestic marketers must consider the political ramifications of their decisions although the consequences of this environmental element are generally minor. Even a noticeable change in government attitudes toward domestic business with a change of political parties is seldom serious. This certainly is not the case in a foreign country. The political environment can be extremely critical, and shifts in governments often mean sudden changes in attitudes that result in expropriation, expulsion, or major restrictions on operations. This is covered in Chapter 6 where the political considerations in assessing world markets are discussed. The fact is that the foreign company is *foreign* and thus always subject to the political whims of the government to a greater degree than a domestic firm.

Also a problem for some marketers attuned to one environment is the inability to easily recognize the potential impact of certain uncontrollable elements within another environment to which they have not been culturally acclimated. Road signs of danger and indicators of potential in a foreign

---

BOX 1–5
So, Jose Gomez-Meade—Are You Señor Gomez or Señor Meade?

In America, we try to get on a first-name basis quickly. In some countries, however, to do so makes you appear brash if not rude. The best policy is to use the last name with a proper and respectful title until specifically invited to do otherwise. But the problem doesn't end there because the "proper" last name can vary among cultures.

In Brazil and Portugal, people are addressed by their Christian names, along with the proper title or simply, Mr. so that Manuel Santos is Senor Manuel. In Spain and Spanish-heritage South America, it is not unusual to use a double surname from both the maternal and paternal family names. The last name is the main one, so that Jose Garcia-Alvarez is Senor Alvarez. In China, the first name is the surname, hence Premier Zhao Xiyang or Mr. Zhao, not Mr. Xiyang. The Egyptian President Nasser's real name was Gamal abdel-Nasser Hussein, the abdel-Nasser meaning literally "son of Nassar."

Source: Adapted from Lennie Copeland and Lewis Griggs, *Going International*, (New York: Random House, 1985), p. 158.

---

market may not always be read or interpreted accurately. The uncertainty of different foreign business environments creates the need for a close study of the operating environment within each new country. Different solutions to fundamentally identical marketing tasks are often in order and are generally the result of changes in the environment of the market. Thus, a strategy successful in one country can be rendered worthless in another by differences in political climate, stages of economic development, or other cultural variation.

ENVIRONMENTAL ADJUSTMENT NEEDED

To adjust and adapt a marketing program to foreign markets, marketers must be able to interpret effectively the influence and impact of each of the uncontrollable environmental elements on the marketing plan for each foreign market in which they hope to do business. In a broad sense, the uncontrollable elements constitute the culture; the difficulty facing the marketer in adjusting to the culture (i.e., uncontrollable elements of the marketplace) lies in recognizing their impact. In a domestic market the reaction to much of the uncontrollables' (cultural) impact on the marketer's activities is automatic. We are generally unaware of the various cultural influences that fill our lives; they are simply a part of our history. We react in a manner acceptable to our society without thinking about it because we are culturally responsive to our environment. The experiences we have gained throughout life have become second nature and serve as the basis for our behavior.

The task of cultural adjustment is, perhaps, the most challenging and important one confronting international marketers; they must adjust their marketing efforts to cultures to which they are not attuned. In dealing with unfamiliar markets, marketers must be aware of the frames of reference they are using in making their decisions or evaluating the potential of a market, because "judgments are derived from experience which is the result of the enculturative process." Once a frame of reference is established, it becomes an important factor in determining or modifying a marketer's reaction to situations—social and even nonsocial—especially if experience or knowledge of accustomed behavior is lacking.

When a marketer operates in other cultures, marketing attempts may fail because of unconscious responses based on frames of reference acceptable in one's own culture but unacceptable in different surroundings. Unless special efforts are made to determine local cultural meanings for every market, the marketer is likely to overlook the significance of certain behaviors or activities and proceed with plans that result in a negative or unwanted response.

For example, a Westerner must learn that white is a symbol of mourning in parts of the Far East, quite different from Western culture's white bridal gowns. Also, time-conscious Americans are not culturally prepared to understand the meaning of time to Latin Americans. These are cultural differences that must be learned to avoid misunderstandings that can lead to marketing failures. Such a failure actually occurred in the first situation when ignorance led to ineffective advertising on the part of an American firm; and the second misunderstanding resulted in lost sales when a "long waiting period" in the outer office of a Latin American customer was misinterpreted by an American sales executive. To avoid such errors, the foreign marketer should be aware of the principle of *marketing relativism, that is, marketing strategies and judgments are based on experience, and experience is interpreted by each marketer in terms of his or her own culture.* We take into the marketplace, at home or in a foreign country, frames of reference developed from past experiences that determine or modify our reactions to the situations we face.

Cultural conditioning is like an iceberg—we are not aware of nine tenths of it. In any study of the market systems of different peoples, their political and economic structures, religions, and other elements of culture, foreign marketers must constantly guard against measuring and assessing the markets against the fixed values and assumptions of their own cultures. They must take specific steps to make themselves aware of the home-cultural reference in their analyses and decision making.

SELF-REFERENCE CRITERION: AN OBSTACLE

The key to successful international marketing is adaptation to the environmental differences from one market to another. Adaptation is a conscious effort on the part of the international marketer to anticipate the influences of both the foreign and domestic uncontrollable environments on a marketing mix and then to adjust the marketing mix to minimize the effects.

The primary obstacle to success in international marketing is a person's **self-reference criterion** (SRC) in making decisions, that is, an unconscious reference to one's own cultural values, experiences, and knowledge as a basis for decisions. The SRC impedes the ability to assess a foreign market in its true light.

When confronted with a set of facts, we react spontaneously on the basis of knowledge assimilated over a lifetime; knowledge that is a product of the history of our culture. We seldom stop to think about a reaction, we react. Thus, when faced with a problem in another culture, the tendency is to react instinctively and refer to our SRC for a solution. Our reaction, however, is based on meanings, values, symbols, and behavior relevant to our own culture and usually different from those of the foreign culture. Such decisions are generally not valid.

To illustrate the impact of the SRC, consider misunderstandings that can occur about personal space between people of different cultures. In the United States, unrelated individuals keep a certain physical distance between themselves and others when talking or in groups. We do not consciously think about that distance; we just know what feels right without thinking. When someone is too close or too far away, we feel uncomfortable and either move further away or get closer to correct the distance—we are relying on our SRC. In some cultures the acceptable distance between individuals is substantially less than that comfortable to Americans. When Americans, unaware of another culture's acceptable distance, are approached too closely by foreigners, they unconsciously react by backing away to restore the proper distance (i.e., proper by American standards) and confusion results for both parties. Americans assume foreigners are pushy, while foreigners assume Americans are unfriendly and stand-offish. Both react to the values of their own SRCs making them all victims of a cultural misunderstanding.

Your SRC can prevent you from being aware that there are cultural differences or from recognizing the importance of those differences. Thus, you either fail to recognize the need to take action, you discount the cultural differences that exist among countries, or you react to a situation in a way offensive to your hosts. A common mistake made by Americans is to refuse food or drink when offered. In the United States, a polite refusal is certainly acceptable, but in Asia or the Middle East, a host is offended if you refuse hospitality. While you do not have to eat or drink much, you do have to accept the offering of hospitality. Understanding and dealing with the self-reference criterion are two of the more important facets in international marketing.

The SRC can influence an evaluation of the appropriateness of a domestically designed marketing mix for a foreign market. If U.S. marketers are not aware, they may evaluate a marketing mix on U.S. experiences (i.e., their SRC) without fully appreciating the cultural differences requiring adaptation. Esso, the brand name of a gasoline, was a successful name in the United States and would seem harmless enough for foreign countries; however, in Japan, the name phonetically means "stalled car"; not a desirable image for gasoline. Another example is "Pet" in Pet Milk. The name has been used for decades; yet in France, the word *pet* means, among other things, flatulence; again, not the image the company had in mind for its canned milk.[16] Both of these examples of real mistakes made by major companies stem from relying on SRC in making a decision. In U.S. culture, a person's SRC would not reveal a problem with either Esso or Pet; but, in international marketing, relying on one's SRC can produce an inadequately adapted marketing program that ends in failure.

The most effective way to control the influence of the SRC is to recognize its existence in our behavior. Although it is almost impossible for someone to learn every culture in depth and to be aware of every important difference, an awareness of the need to be sensitive to differences and to ask questions when doing business with another culture can avoid many of the mistakes of international marketing.[17]

Be aware, also, that not every activity within a marketing program is different from one country to another; there probably are more similarities than differences. Such similarities may lull the marketer into a false sense of apparent sameness. This apparent sameness, coupled with our SRC, is often the cause of international marketing problems. Undetected similarities do not cause problems; however, the one difference that goes undetected can create a marketing failure.

To avoid errors in business decisions, it is necessary to make a cross-cultural analysis isolating the SRC influences. The following steps are suggested as a framework for such an analysis.

Step 1. Define the business problem or goal in home-country cultural traits, habits, or norms.

Step 2. Define the business problem or goal in foreign cultural traits, habits, or norms. Make no value judgments.

---

[16] For a complete book on these and other mistakes in international business, see David A. Ricks, *Big Business Blunders* (Homewood, Ill.: Dow Jones-Irwin, 1983).

[17] Many answers and warnings on the problems of SRC can be found in Lennie Copeland and Lewis Griggs, *Going International* (New York: Random House, 1985).

Step 3. Isolate the SRC influence in the problem and examine it carefully to see how it complicates the problem.

Step 4. Redefine the problem without the SRC influence and solve for the optimum business goal situation.[18]

This approach requires an understanding of the culture of each foreign market as well as one's own culture. Surprisingly, understanding one's own culture may require additional study because much of the cultural influence on market behavior remains at a subconscious level and is not clearly defined.

BECOMING INTERNATIONAL

Once a company has decided to go international, it has to decide the way it will enter a foreign market and the degree of marketing involvement and commitment it is prepared to make. These decisions should reflect considerable study and analysis of market potential and company capabilities, a process not always followed. Many companies appear to grow into international marketing through a series of phased developments. They gradually change strategy and tactics as they become more involved. Others enter international marketing after much research, with long-range plans fully developed.[19]

Phases of International Marketing Involvement

Regardless of the means employed to gain entry into a foreign market, a company may, from a marketing viewpoint, make no market investment, that is, its marketing involvement may be limited to selling a product with little or no thought given to development of market control. Or a company may become totally involved and invest large sums of money and effort to capture and maintain a permanent, specific share of the market. In general, a business can be placed in at least one of five distinct but overlapping phases of international marketing involvement.

No Direct Foreign Marketing.   In this phase there is no active cultivation of customers outside national boundaries; this does not mean, however,

---

[18] James A. Lee, "Cultural Analysis in Overseas Operations," *Harvard Business Review,* March–April 1966, pp. 106–11.

[19] See, for example, "The Little Guys Are Making It Big Overseas," *Business Week,* February 27, 1989, pp. 94–96.

that the company's products do not reach foreign markets. Sales are often made to trading companies and other foreign customers who come directly to the firm. Or products reach foreign markets via domestic wholesalers or distributors who sell abroad on their own without explicit encouragement or even knowledge of the producer. An unsolicited order from a foreign buyer is often what piques the interest of a company to seek additional international sales.

2. **Infrequent Foreign Marketing.**   Temporary surpluses caused by variation in production levels or demand may result in infrequent marketing overseas. The surpluses are characterized by their temporary nature; therefore, sales to foreign markets are made as goods are available with little or no intention of maintaining continuous market representation. As domestic demand increases and absorbs surpluses, foreign sales activity is withdrawn. In this phase, there is little or no change in company organization or product lines.

3. **Regular Foreign Marketing.**   At this level, the firm has permanent productive capacity devoted to the production of goods to be marketed on a continuing basis in foreign markets. A firm may employ foreign or domestic overseas middlemen or it may have its own sales force or sales subsidiaries in important foreign markets. The primary focus for products presently being produced is to meet domestic market needs. Investments in marketing and management effort and in overseas manufacturing and/or assembly are generally begun in this phase. Further, some products may become specialized to meet the needs of individual foreign markets, pricing and profit policies tend to become equal with domestic business, and the company begins to become dependent on foreign profits.

4. **International Marketing.**   Companies in this phase are fully committed and involved in international marketing activities. Such companies seek markets throughout the world and sell products that are not surpluses from a saturated home market but a result of planned production for markets in various countries. This generally entails not only the marketing but also the production of goods throughout the world. At this point a company becomes an international or multinational marketing firm dependent on foreign revenues.

5. **Global Marketing.**   At the global marketing level, companies treat the world, including their home market, as one market. This is in contrast to the multinational or international company that views the world as a series of country markets, including their home market, with unique sets of market characteristics for which marketing strategies must be developed. A global company develops a strategy to reflect the existing commonalities

of market needs among many countries to maximize returns through global standardization of its business activities whenever it is cost effective.[20] Among U.S. firms there has been a noticeable increase in activity in foreign marketing involvement at all levels with an increasing number moving into the global marketing phase.[21]

Changes in International Orientation

Experience shows a significant change in the international orientation of a firm occurs when that company relies on foreign markets to absorb permanent production surpluses and comes to depend on foreign profits. Businesses usually move through the phases of international marketing involvement one at a time, but it is not unusual for a company to skip one or more phases. As a firm moves from one phase to another, the complexity and sophistication of international marketing activity tends to increase and the degree of internationalization to which management is philosophically committed tends to change. Such commitment affects the specific international strategies and decisions of the firm.

The international operations of businesses are reflecting the changing competitiveness brought about by the globalization of markets, interdependence of the world's economies, and the growing number of competing firms from developed and developing countries vying for the world's markets. *Global companies* and *global marketing* are terms frequently used to describe the scope of operations and marketing management orientation of these companies. Global markets are evolving for some products but do not yet exist for all products. There are still consumers in many countries and many products that reflect the differences in needs and wants and the different ways of satisfying these needs and wants based on cultural influences. As the 1990s begin, there are perhaps only a few global companies; however, a broader view of international marketing than has existed before is now evolving.

International Marketing Concepts

Although not articulated as such in current literature, it appears that the differences in the international orientation and approach to international markets that guide the international business activities of companies can

---

[20] James F. Bolt, "Global Competitors: Some Criteria for Success," *Business Horizons*, January–February 1988, pp. 34–41.

[21] Joann S. Lublin, "American Takeovers Soaring in Europe as Firms Position Themselves for 1992," *The Wall Street Journal*, January 17, 1989, p. A17.

be described by one of three orientations to international marketing management:

1. Domestic market extension concept.
2. Multidomestic market concept.
3. Global marketing concept.

It is to be expected that differences in the complexity and sophistication of a company's marketing activity depend on which of these orientations guides its operations. The ideas expressed in each of these concepts reflect the philosophical orientation that also can be associated with successive stages in the evolution of the international operations in a company. Among the many approaches describing the different orientations that evolve in a company as it moves through different phases of international marketing involvement from casual exporting to global marketing is the often quoted EPRG schema. The authors of this schema suggest that firms can be classified as having an ethnocentric, polycentric, regiocentric, or geocentric orientation (EPRG) depending on the international commitment of the firm. Further, the authors state that, "a key assumption underlying the EPRG framework is that the degree of internationalization to which management is committed or willing to move towards affects the specific international strategies and decision rules of the firm."[22] The EPRG schema is incorporated into the discussion of the three concepts that follows in that the philosophical orientations described by the EPRG schema help explain management's view when guided by one of the concepts.

The Domestic Market Extension Concept.   This orientation to international marketing is illustrated by the domestic company seeking sales extension of its domestic products into foreign markets. It views its international operations as secondary to and an extension of its domestic operations; the primary motive is to dispose of excess domestic production. Domestic business is its priority and foreign sales are seen as a profitable extension of domestic operations. Even though foreign markets may be vigorously pursued, the firm's orientation remains basically domestic. Its attitude toward international sales is typified by the belief that if it sells in Peoria it will sell anywhere else in the world. Minimal, if any, efforts are made to adapt the marketing mix to foreign markets; the firm's orientation is to market to foreign customers in the same manner the company markets to domestic customers. It seeks markets where demand is similar to the home market and its domestic product will be acceptable. This domestic market extension strategy can be very profitable; large and small exporting

---

[22] Yoram Wind, Susan P. Douglas, and Howard V. Perlmutter, "Guidelines for Developing International Marketing Strategy," *Journal of Marketing*, April 1973, pp. 14–23.

companies approach international marketing from this perspective.[23] Firms with this marketing approach are classified as ethnocentric in the EPRG schema.

2. **Multidomestic Market Concept.**   Once a company recognizes the importance of differences in overseas markets and the importance of offshore business to their organization, its orientation toward international business may shift to multidomestic market strategy. A company guided by this concept has a strong sense that country markets are vastly different (and they may be, depending on the product) and that market success requires an almost independent program for each country. Firms with this orientation market on a country-by-country basis with separate marketing strategies for each country.

Subsidiaries operate independently of one another in establishing marketing objectives and plans, and the domestic market and each of the country markets have separate marketing mixes with little interaction among them. Products are adapted for each market without coordination with other country markets; advertising campaigns are localized as are the pricing and distribution decisions. A company with this concept does not look for similarity among elements of the marketing mix that might respond to standardization; rather, it aims for adaptation to local country markets. Control is typically decentralized to reflect the belief that the uniqueness of each market requires local marketing input and control. Firms with this orientation would be classified in the EPRG schema as polycentric.

3. **Global Marketing Concept.**   A company guided by this orientation or philosophy is generally referred to as a global company, its marketing activity is global marketing, and its market coverage is the world. A company employing a global marketing strategy strives for efficiencies of scale by developing a standardized product, of dependable quality, to be sold at a reasonable price to a global market, that is, the same country market set throughout the world. Important to the global marketing concept is the premise that world markets are being "driven toward a converging commonalty"[24] seeking in much the same ways to satisfy their needs and desires. Thus, they constitute significant market segments with similar demands for the same product the world over. With this orientation a company attempts to standardize as much of the company effort as is practical on a worldwide basis. Some decisions are viewed as applicable

---

[23] For an article that strongly supports this concept, see Martin vanMesdag, "Winging It in Foreign Markets," *Harvard Business Review*, January–February 1987, pp. 71–74.

[24] Levitt, "Globalization," pp. 92–102.

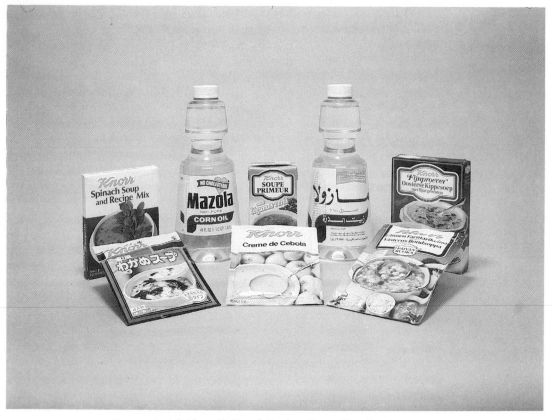

Knorr—A global brand? (Joseph Jacobson/Journalism Services, Inc.)

worldwide, while others require consideration of local influences. The world as a whole is viewed as the market and the firm develops a global marketing strategy. The global marketing company would fit the regiocentric or geocentric classifications of the EPRG schema.

Some early interpretations of global marketing focused narrowly on the standardization or globalization of product branding and/or advertising, and the concept of global marketing as an operating orientation was accepted or rejected on the basis of whether or not a global market existed. Reports abound of global marketing successes and failures.[25] The notion of global marketing is a more powerful idea if the scope of the concept is broadened beyond the idea of the existence of global markets. The global marketing concept views an entire set of country markets (whether

---

[25] Nathan Rosen and Jean Boddewyn, "U.S. Brands Abroad: An Empirical Study of Global Branding," *International Marketing Review* 6, no. 1, 1989, pp. 7–19.

the home market and only 1 other or the home market and 100 other countries) as a unit, examining the group as a market and developing a marketing plan that strives for standardization wherever it is cost and culturally effective. This might mean a company's global marketing plan has a standardized product but country specific advertising or a standardized theme in all countries with country or cultural specific appeals to a unique market characteristic, a standardized brand or image but adapted products to meet specific country needs, and so on. In other words, the marketing planning and marketing mix are approached from a global perspective and where feasible in the marketing mix, efficiencies of standardization are sought. Wherever cultural uniqueness dictates the need for adaptation of the product, its image, and so on, it is accommodated.

What is suggested as a global orientation is analogous to the normal operations of a U.S. domestic company. The entire United States is viewed as a single market—or if a company's objectives exclude some of the 50 states, then the states where they intend to market are viewed as a market unit. There are fewer uncontrollables to relate to among the 50 states but nevertheless the approach is to view the entire group of states as one market. The marketing mix is standardized for the entire market except where there are differences requiring adaptation for acceptance in the market. For example, automobiles have to be adapted to stricter emission controls in California than in the other 49 states, and fabric is heavier in men's winter suits destined for the northern and northeastern markets than for milder southern or western markets.

All companies, large or small, marketing to one country or to the entire world, should be guided by the global marketing concept. As the competitive environment facing U.S. businesses becomes more internationalized—and it surely will—the most effective orientation for all firms involved in marketing into another country will be a global orientation. This means operating as if all the country markets in a company's scope of operations (including the domestic market) are approachable as a single global market and standardizing the marketing mix where culturally feasible and cost effective.

We must acknowledge at least two dimensions to the question of global business: One side focuses on orientation of firms as just discussed; the other dimension of the question of global business is whether a global market exists as defined by Levitt.[26] In other words, do segments across several countries with similar needs and wants that can be satisfied with a single standardized product exist?

---

[26] For one company's approach to globalization, see "Electrolux's Global Approach to Markets and Corporate Finance," (Business International) *Management Europe*, September 26, 1988, pp. 10–16.

Although a company might visualize the world as a single market rather than as a series of country specific markets, to what extent the world has actually become a homogeneous market, (that is, a global market) is another question. These two dimensions of globalization should be separated. Regardless of the degree to which global markets exist, a company can benefit from a global orientation. The issues of whether marketing programs should be standardized or why they are localized are not as critical as the recognition that marketing planning processes need to be standardized.

Global Markets

Theodore Levitt's article, "The Globalization of Markets," has spawned a host of new references to marketing activities: global marketing, global business, global advertising, global brands, as well as serious discussions of the processes of international marketing.[27] Professor Levitt's premise is that world markets are being driven "toward a converging commonalty." Almost everyone everywhere wants all the things they have heard about, seen, or experienced via the new technologies. He sees substantial market segments with common needs, that is, a high quality, reasonably priced, standardized product. The "global corporation sells the same thing in the same way everywhere." Professor Levitt argues that segmenting international markets on political boundaries and customizing products and marketing strategies for country markets or on national or regional preferences are not cost effective. The company of the future, according to Levitt, will be a global company that views the world as one market to which it sells a global product. Competition in the future will require global marketing rather than international or multinational marketing.[28]

As with all new ideas, interpretations abound and discussions and debates flow. Professor Levitt's article has provoked many companies and marketing scholars to reexamine a fundamental idea that has prevailed for decades; that is, products and strategies must be adapted to the cultural needs of each country when marketing internationally. This approach is contrasted with a global orientation suggesting a commonality in marketing needs and thus a standardized product for all the world. While the need for cultural adaptation exists in many markets and for many products, the influence of mass communications in the world today and its influence

---

[27] Levitt, "Globalization," p. 92.

[28] For an interesting discussion of the differences between global and multinational marketing, see Gerald M. Hampton and Erwin Buske, "The Global Marketing Perspective," *Advances in International Marketing*, vol. 2, S. Tamer Cavusgil, ed. (Greenwich, Conn.: JAI Press, 1987), pp. 259–77.

on consumer wants and needs cannot be denied.[29] "Dallas," "Dynasty," "Miami Vice," instant news, and live broadcasts from halfway around the world are shown to hundreds of millions of potential consumers everywhere in the world. One study of the importance of cultural differences in marketing concluded:

> our investigation also demonstrated, however, that in a marketing world characterized by intensive communications, standardization, and the employment of similar decision technologies, cultural differences tend to diminish. Indeed, the process of globalization on the supply side has already begun.[30]

Certainly, the homogenizing effect of mass communications in the United States has eliminated many of the regional differences that once existed. As one sociological pundit noted about network TV, "When Johnny Carson wore a turtleneck sweater on the 'Tonight Show,' America followed the next day." It is difficult to deny the influences of mass media and communications on American tastes and consumer behavior. Based on American experiences, it seems reasonable to believe that people in other cultures exposed to the same influences will react similarly and that there is a converging commonalty of the world's needs and desires.

Does this mean markets are now global? The answer is yes, there are market segments in most countries with similar demands for the same product. Levi Strauss, Revlon, Toyota, Ford, McDonald's, and Coca-Cola are companies that sell a relatively standardized product throughout the world to market segments seeking the same products to satisfy their needs and desires.[31] Does this mean there is no need to be concerned with cultural differences when marketing in different countries? The answer is "it depends"; for some products adaptation is not necessary, but for other products more sensitive to cultural values, adaptation is still necessary. The issue of modification versus standardization of marketing effort cannot be answered as easily as yes or no.[32] The astute marketer always strives to present products that fulfill the perceived needs and wants of the consumer. Some products successful in one culture are equally acceptable in another; Pepsi-Cola is a good example. Other products demonstrate the vast differences in what is acceptable from one market to another.[33] Turkey

---

[29] Standardization does not fit in all markets as this article indicates: Joanne Lipman, "Marketers Turn Sour on Global Sales Pitch Harvard Guru Makes," *The Wall Street Journal*, May 12, 1988, p. 1.

[30] David K. Tse, Kam-hon Lee, Ilan Vertinsky, and Donald A. Wehrung, "Does Culture Matter? A Cross-Cultural Study of Executives' Choice, Decisiveness, and Risk Adjustment in International Marketing," *Journal of Marketing*, October 1988, p. 92.

[31] Ira C. Herbert, "Becoming One Big Market," *Export Today*, July–August 1987, p. 11.

[32] The issue of standardization versus modification is discussed in detail in the chapters covering the marketing mix.

[33] For several examples where globalization has not worked, see Lipman, "Marketers Turn Sour," p. 1.

testicles, wings, and necks, (considered gourmet fare in Taiwan and preferred to white meat which they consider disgusting) would probably
need some creative adaptation to sell for Thanksgiving dinner in Peoria,
Illinois.[34]

Marketing internationally should entail looking for market segments
with similar demands that can be satisfied with the same product, standardizing the components of the marketing mix that can be standardized,
and, where there are significant cultural differences that require parts of
the marketing mix to be culturally adapted, adapting. Throughout the
text, the question of adaptation versus standardization of products and
marketing effort, that is, global marketing, will be discussed.

ORIENTATION OF *INTERNATIONAL MARKETING*

Most problems encountered by the foreign marketer result from the strange-
ness of the environment within which marketing programs must be implemented. Success hinges, in part, on the ability to assess and adjust properly
to the impact of a strange environment. The successful international marketer possesses the best qualities of the sociologist, psychologist, diplomat,
lawyer, prophet, and businessperson.

In light of all the variables involved, with what should a text in foreign
marketing be concerned? It is the opinion of the author that a study of
foreign-marketing environments and their influences on the total marketing
process is of primary concern and is the most effective approach to a
meaningful presentation.

Consequently, the orientation of this text can best be described as an
environmental approach to international strategic marketing. By no means
is it intended to present principles of marketing; rather it is intended to
demonstrate the unique problems of international marketing. It attempts
to relate the foreign environment to the marketing process and to illustrate
the many ways in which the environment can influence the marketing
task. Although marketing principles are universally applicable, the environment within which the marketer must implement marketing plans can
change dramatically from country to country. It is with the difficulties
created by different environments that this text is primarily concerned.

Further, the text is concerned with any company marketing in or into
any other country or groups of countries however slight the involvement
or the method of involvement. Hence, this discussion of international
marketing ranges from the marketing and business practices of small export-

---

[34] James McGregor, "U.S. Turkey Exports Ruffle Feathers in Taiwan," *The Asian Wall Street
Journal Weekly,* November 21, 1988, p. 24.

ers like the Colorado-based company that generates more than 50 percent of its $40,000 annual sales of fish egg sorters in Canada, West Germany, and Australia[35] to a global company such as IBM that generates more than 63 percent of its $3.3 billion annual profit from the sales of multiple products to multiple country-market segments all over the world.[36]

The first section of *International Marketing* offers an overview of foreign marketing including a brief discussion of the economic and historical implications. The next section deals exclusively with the uncontrollable elements of the environment and their assessment followed by chapters dealing with world market patterns. Then problems of international marketing management are discussed, with a final section on the corporate context of marketing in international business. In each chapter, an attempt is made to illustrate the impact of the environment on the marketing process. Space prohibits an encyclopedic approach to all the issues; nevertheless, the author has tried to present sufficient detail so readers appreciate the real need to make a thorough analysis whenever the challenge arises. The text provides a framework for this task.

QUESTIONS

1. Define:
   SRC   controllable elements
   international marketing   marketing relativism✓
   foreign uncontrollables   alien status
   domestic uncontrollables

2. "The marketer's task is the same whether applied in Dimebox, Texas, or Dar es Salaam, Tanzania." Discuss.

3. How can the increased interest in international marketing on the part of U.S. firms be explained?

4. Discuss the four phases of international marketing involvement.

5. Discuss the conditions that have led to the development of global markets.

6. Differentiate between a global company and a multinational company.

7. Differentiate among the the three international marketing concepts.

8. Relate the three international marketing concepts to the EPRG schema.

---

[35] Mark Taige, "Weak Dollar Buoys Exports by Small Colorado Companies," *Denver Post,* July 11, 1988, p. 12.

[36] "The 100 Largest U.S. Multinationals," *Forbes,* July 25, 1988, p. 248.

CHAPTER

2

Global Business Environment

Trading among peoples and communities has taken place since before recorded time. Primitive people had a barter system, the early Greeks their agoras, the Romans their forums, and today we have shopping malls—all marketplaces. A market is a place where buyers and sellers come together to exchange goods. Each generation's marketplace has grown larger until we now live in an era of the global market. Each decade, through international trade, more of the goods of the world are brought to ever expanding global markets.

The emerging global economy in which we live brings us into world competition and adds significant advantages for both marketers and consumers. Marketers benefit from new markets opening and smaller markets growing large enough to become viable business opportunities. Consumers benefit by being able to select the lowest priced and widest range of goods produced anywhere in the world. More of the world's people, from the richest to the poorest, participate in the world's wealth through international trade.[1] As Exhibit 2–1 illustrates, world trade is an important economic activity to most countries. And, because of this economic importance,

---

[1] "Taiwan Steps Up Its Efforts to Open Markets to U.S. Products," *Business America*, January 30, 1989, p. 30.

EXHIBIT 2–1 Dependence on World Trade ($ millions)

	Exports	Imports	Balance
United States	$250.4	$424.1	−$173.7
Soviet Union	107.7	96.0	11.7
Japan	231.2	150.8	80.4
European Community*	953.5	955.1	−1.6
China	44.9	40.2	4.7

* Data includes trade between EC members.

SOURCE: Adapted from "The Superpower Contenders Compared," *The Wall Street Journal*, January 23, 1989, p. A8.

countries attempt to control international trade to their own advantage. As global competition intensifies, the protection of a country's market from foreign intrusion also gains momentum.[2]

This chapter includes a brief history of global trade activities in the United States and some theoretical concepts important to understanding the relationship between international trade and national economic policy. It also reviews available resources that facilitate conditions for fair trade among countries.

THE 20TH CENTURY

At no time in modern economic history have countries been more economically interdependent, have greater opportunities for international trade existed, or has the potential for increased demand existed than now, during the last decade of the 20th century. In the preceding 90 years, world economic development has been erratic. The first half of the century was marred by a major worldwide economic depression that occurred between two world wars and that all but destroyed most of the industrialized world. The last half of the century, while free of a world war, was marred by struggles between countries espousing the socialist Marxist approach and those following a democratic capitalist approach to economic development. As a result of this ideological split, traditional trade patterns were disrupted.

After World War II, as a means to dampen the spread of communism, the United States set out to infuse the ideal of capitalism throughout as much of the world as possible. The Marshall Plan to assist in rebuilding

---

[2] "Japan Facing Clashes with U.S., Others as Huge Trade Surplus Resumes Growth," *The Wall Street Journal*, January 10, 1989, A15.

Europe, financial and industrial development assistance to rebuild Japan, and funds channeled through the Agency for International Development and other groups designed to foster economic growth in the underdeveloped world were used to help create a strong world economy. Another significant trend during this period was the dissolution of colonial powers creating scores of new countries in Asia and Africa. With the striving of these countries to gain economic independence and the financial assistance offered by the United States, most of the non-Communist world's economies grew and new markets were created.[3]

The benefits from the foreign economic assistance given by the United States flowed both ways. For every dollar the United States invested in the economic development and rebuilding of other countries after World War II, hundreds of dollars more returned in the form of purchases of U.S. agricultural products, manufactured goods, and services. During this period of economic growth in the rest of the world, the United States experienced a major economic boom and an increased standard of living. Certainly a part of U.S. economic prosperity can be attributed to U.S. industry supplying the world demand created by economic growth. In short, we helped to make their economies stronger, and thus, enabled them to buy more from us.

In addition to U.S. economic assistance, a move toward international cooperation among trading nations was manifest in two forms, the General Agreement on Tariffs and Trade (GATT) and the creation of common markets or free-trade associations among groups of countries. The European Community (EC) and the European Free Trade Association (EFTA) are the best-known cooperative economic associations designed to promote international trade among member countries and mutual advantage in external trade.

Following World War I, international commerce ground to a halt because of high tariffs and other protectionist steps. Following the example set by the Smoot-Hawley Law (1930) that raised U.S. tariffs to a level that all but closed U.S. markets to foreign imports, most countries erected high tariff walls during the world depression to protect their limited markets. In the United States, average tariffs exceeded 60 percent in the early 1930s.

In an attempt to forestall such protectionism after World War II, the General Agreement on Tariffs and Trade (GATT) was negotiated as a voluntary association for the exchange of ideas to facilitate the mechanics of world trade.

GATT provided a framework within which negotiations among member nations encouraged trade and reduced tariffs and other trade restrictions.

---

[3] James Griffin, "The Decline of the Decline and Fall," *Fortune*, August 19, 1988, pp. 95–96.

The influence of GATT agreements reduced tariffs from that 1930 high to an average world tariff of 3 to 4 percent in the 1980s. By 1990, 94 countries were members of GATT and the Uruguay Round of GATT talks was well underway.[4]

From the 18th century through the first quarter of the 20th century, Great Britain was the undisputed leader in world trade. Then, world trade dominance passed to the United States. Not only did U.S. manufacturers export and import more merchandise than any other country but American companies also began to expand their scope of operations beyond the domestic market to become multinational companies.

WORLD TRADE AND U.S. MULTINATIONALS

The rapid growth of war-torn economies and previously underdeveloped countries, coupled with large-scale economic cooperation and assistance, led to new global marketing opportunities. Rising standards of living and broad-based consumer and industrial markets abroad created opportunities for American companies to expand exports and investment worldwide. During the 1950s, many U.S. companies that had never before marketed outside the United States began to export, and others made significant investments in marketing and production facilities overseas. The book value of U.S. direct foreign investment rose from $12 billion in 1950 to more than $276 billion by 1987.[5] By effectively linking their technological and managerial advantages with cheap overseas labor, U.S. multinational corporations (MNCs) increased their foreign earnings at a rate higher than was possible at home.

At the close of the 1960s, U.S. MNCs were facing major challenges on two fronts, direct investment and export markets. Large investments by U.S. businesses in Europe and Latin America heightened the concern of these countries about the growing domination of U.S. multinationals. The reaction in Latin American countries was to expropriate direct U.S. investments or to force the companies to sell controlling interests to nationals. In Europe, apprehension manifested itself in strong public demand to limit foreign investment. Concern that "Britain might become a satellite where there could be manufacturing but no determination of policy" led to specific guidelines for joint ventures between British and U.S. companies. In the European Community, U.S. multinationals were rebuffed in ways ranging from tight control over proposed joint ventures and regulations covering U.S. acquisitions of European firms to strong protectionist laws.

---

[4] "Uruguay Round: Mid-Term Review," *Business America*, January 16, 1989, pp. 2–4.

[5] *International Direct Investment*, 1988 Edition (Washington, D.C.: U.S. Department of Commerce), 1988, p. 17.

The threat felt by Europeans was best expressed in the popular book, *The American Challenge*, published in 1968, in which the French author, J. J. Servan-Schreiber, wrote:

> Fifteen years from now it is quite possible that the world's third greatest industrial power, just after the United States and Russia, will not be Europe but *American Industry in Europe*. Already, in the ninth year of the Common Market, this European market is basically American in organization.[6]

While Schreiber's prophecy of U.S. MNC domination of the world economy has not materialized, by examining Exhibit 2–2, the reader can see the reasons for concern.

Schreiber's prediction did not come true for many reasons, but, one of the more important reasons was that U.S. MNCs were confronted by a resurgence of competition from all over the world. The worldwide economic growth and rebuilding after World War II was beginning to surface in competition that challenged the supremacy of American industry. Competition arose on all fronts; Japan, Germany, most of the industrialized world, and many developing countries were competing for demand in their own countries and were looking for world markets as well. Countries once classified as less-developed were reclassified as newly industrialized countries or NICs. NICs such as Brazil, Mexico, South Korea, Taiwan, Singapore, and Hong Kong experienced rapid industrialization in selected industries and became aggressive world competitors in steel, shipbuilding, consumer electronics, automobiles, light aircraft, shoes, textiles, apparel, and so forth. In addition to NICs, developing countries such as Venezuela established state-owned enterprises (SOEs) that operate in neighboring countries. One Venezuelan-owned company has a subsidiary in Puerto Rico that produces canvas, cosmetics, chairs, and zippers; there are also Chilean and Colombian companies in Puerto Rico; in the state of Georgia, there is a Venezuelan company in agribusiness; and Bangladesh, the sixth largest exporter of garments to the United States, owns a mattress company also in Georgia.[7]

In short, economic power and potential became more evenly distributed among countries than was the case when Servan-Schreiber warned Europe about U.S. multinational domination. Instead, the U.S. position in world trade is now shared with MNCs from other countries. Exhibit 2–3 shows the dramatic change between 1963 and 1988. In 1963 the United States had 67 of the world's 100 largest industrial corporations; by 1986, that number had dropped to 48. Another dimension of world economic power, the balance of merchandise trade, reflects the changing role of the United

---

[6] J. J. Servan-Schreiber, *The American Challenge* (New York: Atheneum Publishers, 1968), p. 3.

[7] Valerie S. Koenig, "Made in Bangladesh Is a Label Americans May Be Seeing More of," *Business America*, April 15–29, 1988, p. 18.

EXHIBIT 2–2   Estimated U.S. Share of Certain Industries in France, West Germany, and Italy, Mid-1960s*

Percentages	Industries		
	France, 1963[†]	*West Germany*[‡]	*Italy, 1965*[§]
80 or more	Carbon black, razor blades and safety razors, synthetic rubber	Computers	Computers‖
60 to 79	Accounting machines, computers, electric razors, sewing machines		
50 to 59			Cosmetics
40 to 49	Electronic and statistical machinery,# telegraph and telephone equipment	Automobiles	
30 to 39	Elevators, tires, tractors, agricultural machinery	Petroleum	Pharmaceuticals
20 to 29	Machine tools, petroleum refining, refrigerators, washing machines		Soap, petroleum
5 to 19	Automobiles	Electrical-optics-toys,** food, machinery, vehicles-metal products[††]	Paper, tires

* Other estimates vary.
[†] Turnover figures.
[‡] Percentage of capital of public companies.
[§] Share in capital invested in industry (except where specified otherwise).
‖ Market share according to number of computers installed, 1969.
This includes computers, which were 75 percent.
** This includes computers, which were 84 percent.
†† This includes automobiles, which were 40 percent.

SOURCES: Data on France and West Germany adapted from Christopher Layton, *Trans-Atlantic Investments* (Boulogne-sur-Seine, France: The Atlantic Institute, 1966), p. 19, with additions on France and all data on Italy from Robert Hellman, *The Challenge to U.S. Dominance of the International Corporation* (New York: Dunellen, 1970), pp. 334, 100. Also see Mira Wilkins, *The Maturing of Multinational Enterprise: American Business Abroad from 1914 to 1970* (Cambridge, Mass: Harvard University Press, 1974), p. 404.

EXHIBIT 2–3 The World's 100 Largest Industrial Corporations, by Country of Origin

	1963	1979	1984	1988
United States	67	47	47	39
Germany	13	13	8	12
United Kingdom	7	7	5	5
France	4	11	5	9
Japan	3	7	12	15
Italy	2	3	3	4
Netherlands-United Kingdom	2	2	2	2
Netherlands	1	3	1	1
Switzerland	1	1	2	3
Canada	—	2	3	0
Belgium	—	1	1	1
Brazil	—	1	—	1
Mexico	—	1	1	1
Venezuela	—	1	1	0
South Korea	—	—	4	2
Argentina	—	—	1	0
Kuwait	—	—	1	1
Sweden	—	—	1	2
India	—	—	1	1
South Africa	—	—	1	0
Spain	—	—	—	1

SOURCES: Adapted from John Hein, "The World's Multinationals: A Global Challenge" Report No. 84 (New York: The Conference Board, 1981), p. 5; 1984 figures from "The World's Largest Industrial Corporations," *Fortune*, August 19, 1985, p. 179, "The 500 Largest U.S. Industrial Corporations," *Fortune*, April 29, 1985, pp. 266, 268; and for 1988 data: "The World's Biggest Industrial Corporations," *Fortune*, July 31, 1989, pp. 282–83.

States in world trade. From 1888 to 1971, the United States sold more to other countries than it bought from them; that is, the United States had a favorable balance of trade. But in 1971, a trade deficit, the first since 1888, of $2 billion grew to $26 billion in 1977 and soared to an estimated $137 billion in 1989.[8]

As Exhibit 2–1 illustrates, the United States' trade balance does not compare favorably with the trade balances of Japan, Germany, South Korea, and many other countries. Intense competition for world markets and U.S. demand for all sorts of imported products—automobiles, consumer electronics, appliances, computer printers, apparel, microwave ovens—continue to add to the deficits. For example, between 1970 and 1987, America's share of the United States market in phonographs dropped from 90 percent to 1 percent, in color TVs from 90 percent to 10 percent,

---

[8]"Will We Ever Close the Trade Gap?" *Business Week*, February 27, 1989, p. 87.

Container ships are important in trade among nations. (Tim McCabe/Journalism Services, Inc.)

in machine tools from 100 percent to about 35 percent, and in VCRs from 10 percent to 1 percent.[9] It is ironic that the economic problems facing the United States at the close of the 20th century are, in part, proof of the success of U.S. economic assistance programs. Those countries that benefited most from U.S. economic assistance are the competitors U.S. businesses now face in markets the world over, including the world's largest market, the United States.

---

[9] "Signs of Decline," *The Wall Street Journal*, November 14, 1988, p. R24.

BOX 2–1
The Globalization of the American Economy

America's involvement in the global economy has passed through two distinct periods: a development era during which the United States sought industrial self-sufficiency in the 18th and 19th centuries, and a free-trade era in the early and middle 20th century during which open trade was linked with prosperity. Now America has entered a third, more dangerous era—an age of global economic interdependence.

With surprising swiftness, the United States has shifted from relative economic self-sufficiency to global interdependence. In 1960 trade accounted for only 10 percent of the country's gross national product; by the mid-1980s, that figure had more than doubled. American farmers now sell 30 percent of their grain production overseas; 40 percent of U.S. farmland is devoted to crops for export. In fact, more U.S. farmland is used to feed the Japanese than there is Japanese farmland. American industry exports more than 20 percent of its manufacturing output, and one out of every six manufacturing jobs in the U.S. depends on foreign sales. More than 70 percent of American industry now faces stiff foreign competition within the U.S. market.

Source: Adapted from Pat Choate and Juyne Linger, "Tailored Trade: Dealing with the World as It Is," *Harvard Business Review*, January–February 1988, pp. 87–88.

This heightened competition for U.S. businesses is raising questions similar to those heard in Europe two decades ago; that is, how to maintain the competitive strength of American business, to avoid the domination of U.S. markets by foreign multinationals, and to forestall the buying of America.[10] Among the more important questions raised have been those concerning the ability of U.S. firms to compete in foreign markets and the fairness of international trade policies of some countries.[11] The United States, a strong advocate of free trade, is now confronted with the dilemma of how to encourage trading partners to reciprocate with open access to their markets without provoking increased protectionism. In fact, during the 1990s, the trading world as a whole faces problems arising from trade policies more atuned to the world economies of the 1950s through the 1980s than for today. Equalizing trade imbalances without

---

[10] Gene Koretz, "The Buying of America: Should We Be Worried?" *Business Week*, May 9, 1988, p. 36.

[11] For an interesting discussion of free trade, fair trade, and strategic trade, see Marc Levinson, "Is Strategic Trade Fair Trade?" *Across the Board*, June 1988, pp. 47–51.

BOX 2–2
Who Does Lead in the Number of Trade Barriers?

Mike Mansfield, the U.S. ambassador to Japan since 1977 says, "I think the Japanese market is more open than many Americans assume, and the American market is more closed than many Americans think." Well, is he correct or not? Many believe that the United States is the largest promoter of free trade. Actually, the United States, by design, has many nontarriff barriers against foreign goods. More imported, manufactured goods are subject to nontariff barriers in the United States than in many other nations. As a matter of fact, 34 percent of the products manufactured here are protected. The percentages for selected other countries are:

Italy	34%
France	32
United Kingdom	22
West Germany	20
Canada	10

And surprisingly, only 7 percent of Japan's manufactured goods are protected.

Sources: Adapted from Mike Mansfield, "Reexamining Our Trade Problems with Japan," *Express Magazine*, Fall 1988, p. 32; and Sak Onkvisit and John J. Shaw, "Marketing Barriers and International Trade," *Business Horizons*, May–June 1988, p. 64.

resorting to increased protectionism is a challenge.[12] An important concept in understanding trade among nations is a country's balance of payments.

BALANCE OF PAYMENTS

When countries trade, financial transactions among businesses or consumers of different nations occur. Products and services are exported and imported, monetary gifts are exchanged, investments are made, cash payments are made and cash receipts received, and vacation and foreign travel occurs. In short, over a period of time, there is a constant flow of money into and out of a country. The system of accounts that records a

---

[12] Philip Revzin, "As Trade Gap Closes, Partners of U.S. Face End of the Gravy Train," *The Wall Street Journal*, March 17, 1988, p. 1.

nation's international financial transactions is called its balance of payments.

A nation's balance-of-payments statement records all financial transactions between its residents and those of the rest of the world during a given period of time—usually one year. Because the balance-of-payments record is maintained on a double-entry bookkeeping system, it must always be in balance. As on an individual's financial statement, the assets and liabilities or the credits and debits must offset each other. And like an individual's statement, the fact that they balance does not mean a nation is in particularly good or poor financial condition. A balance of payments is a record of condition, not a determinant of condition. Each of the nation's financial transactions with other countries is reflected in its balance of payments.

A nation's balance of payments presents an overall view of its international economic position and is an important economic measure used by government agencies such as treasuries, central banks, and other authorities whose responsibility is to maintain external and internal economic stability. The overall state of the balance of payments has an effect on a country's trade policies, and its worldwide monetary value; it may influence such domestic economic policies as wages, employment, and investment. The state of a country's balance of payments affects the relative value of its currency and the ability of the country to acquire currencies of other nations. In international trade, countries continually assess the external positions and currency prospects of the countries with which they trade. As a consequence, a country's balance of payments also influences decisions of international businesses.

A balance of payments represents the difference between receipts from foreign countries on one side and payments to them on the other. On the plus side are export sales; money spent by foreign tourists; payments to the United States for insurance, transportation, and similar services; payments of dividends and interest on investments abroad; return of capital invested abroad; new foreign investments in the United States; and foreign government payments to the United States. On the minus side are costs

---

BOX 2–3
In Just Thirty-Three Years

News item February 1, 1957:
   Japan may soon get its long-awaited "people's car." Keita Goto, Japanese industrial tycoon, currently is preparing to manufacture 120 small four-wheel trucks a month. Then he will swing into . . . passenger vehicles . . .
   Source: From "Twenty-Five Years Ago," *Forbes*, February 1, 1981, p. 155.

of goods imported, spending by tourists overseas, new overseas investments, and the cost of foreign military and economic aid. A deficit results when international payments are greater than receipts. It can be reduced or eliminated by increasing a country's international receipts, (i.e., gain more exports or more tourists from abroad) and/or reducing expenditures in other countries.

A balance-of-payments statement includes three accounts: the current account—a record of all merchandise exports, imports, and services plus unilateral transfers of funds; the capital account—a record of direct investment, portfolio investment, and short-term capital movements to and from countries; and the official reserves account—a record of exports and imports of gold, increases or decreases in foreign exchange, and increases or decreases in liabilities to foreign central banks. Of the three, the current account is of primary interest to international business.[13]

Current Account

The current account is important because it includes all international trade and service accounts; that is, accounts for the value of all merchandise and services imported and exported and all receipts and payments from investments. Exhibit 2–4 gives the current account for the United States since 1978. Clearly, services, trade, and receipts from foreign investments (lines *2c* and *4c*) are important because they are positive and help to reduce the overall deficit in the current account (line *7*). The balance of trade reflected in the current account is an important factor in the U.S. economy for the 1990s.

Balance of Trade

The relationship between merchandise imports and exports (lines *1a* and *1b* in Exhibit 2–4) is referred to as the balance of merchandise trade or trade balance. If a country exports more goods than it imports, it has a favorable balance of trade; if it imports more goods than it exports, as did the United States in 1988, it has an unfavorable balance of trade as shown on line *1c*. Usually a country that has a negative balance of trade also has a negative balance of payments. Both the balance of trade and the balance of payments do not have to be negative; at times a country may have a favorable balance of trade and a negative balance of payments or vice versa. This was the case for the United States during the Korean

---

[13] "U.S. Prodding to Cut Trade Imbalance Is Stirring Hornets' Nest in South Korea," *The Wall Street Journal*, February 3, 1989, p. A10.

EXHIBIT 2–4 U.S. Current Account by Major Components, 1978–88 ($ billions)

	1978	1979	1980	1981	1982	1983	1984	1985	1986	1987	1988
1. Merchandise trade											
a. Exports	$142.1	$184.5	$224.3	$237.1	$211.2	$201.8	$219.9	$215.9	$224.0	$249.6	$319.9
b. Imports	176.0	212.0	249.7	265.1	247.6	268.9	332.4	338.1	368.5	409.9	446.4
c. Balance	−33.9	−27.5	−25.5	−28.0	−36.4	−67.1	−112.5	−122.2	−144.5	−160.3	−126.5
2. Business services											
a. Exports	27.1	31.2	37.0	42.4	42.3	42.3	44.3	46.2	51.8	59.4	69.1
b. Imports	23.7	27.2	29.4	32.3	33.0	35.8	42.3	47.2	51.0	58.0	63.2
c. Balance	+3.4	+4.0	+7.6	+10.1	+9.2	+6.6	+2.0	−1.0	+0.8	+1.4	+5.9
3. Other goods and services											
a. Exports	8.6	7.0	8.7	10.6	12.6	13.0	10.7	9.6	9.2	12.0	10.6
b. Imports	8.5	9.5	11.7	12.5	13.7	14.2	13.4	13.9	14.6	15.8	16.2
c. Balance	+0.1	−2.5	−3.0	−1.9	−1.1	−1.2	−2.7	−4.3	−5.4	−3.8	−5.6
4. International investment income											
a. Receipts	42.2	64.1	72.5	86.4	83.5	77.3	85.9	88.8	90.1	103.8	108.2
b. Payments	21.7	33.0	42.1	52.3	54.9	52.4	67.4	62.9	67.0	83.4	105.6
c. Balance	+20.6	+31.2	+30.4	+34.1	+28.6	+24.9	+18.5	+25.9	+23.1	+20.4	+2.6
5. Total goods and services											
a. Exports	220.0	286.8	342.5	376.5	349.6	334.4	360.8	360.6	375.0	424.8	507.8
b. Imports	229.9	281.7	333.0	362.2	349.3	371.2	455.6	460.7	498.6	565.3	629.6
c. Balance	−9.9	+5.1	+9.5	+14.3	+0.3	−36.8	−94.8	−100.1	−123.6	−140.5	−121.8
6. Net unilateral transfers	−5.6	−6.1	−7.6	−7.5	−9.0	−9.5	−12.2	−15.0	−15.3	−13.4	−13.6
7. Current account balance	−15.4	−1.0	+1.9	+6.9	−8.7	−46.2	−107.0	−115.1	−138.9	−153.9	−135.4

SOURCE: *Survey of Current Business* U.S. Department of Commerce, Bureau of Economic Analysis, June 1988, pp. 40–41 and March 1989, p. 40.

and Vietnam wars when there was a favorable balance of trade but a negative balance of payments. The imbalance was caused by heavy foreign aid assistance by the United States to other countries and the high cost of conducting the Korean and Vietnam wars.

Since 1970 the United States has had a favorable balance of trade in only three years. This means that for each year there was an unfavorable balance, the United States imported goods with a higher dollar value than the goods it exported. These imbalances resulted primarily from heavy U.S. demand for foreign petroleum, cars, industrial machinery, and other merchandise. Such imbalances have drastic effects on balance of trade, balance of payments, and, therefore, the value of local currency in the world marketplace.

Factors such as these eventually require adjustments in the balance of payments through changes in exchange rates, prices, and/or incomes. In short, once the wealth of a country whose expenditures exceed its income has been exhausted, that country, like an individual, must reduce its standard of living. If its residents do not do so voluntarily, the rate of exchange of its money for foreign monies declines; and through the medium of the foreign exchange market, the purchasing power of foreign goods is transferred from that country to another country. As U.S. deficits have continued to escalate, the exchange rate for dollars relative to currencies of other industrialized countries has declined. As can be seen in Exhibit 2–5, the dollar has fallen steadily against the major currencies of the world for a number of years.

This imbalance of trade is the overriding economic concern for the United States in the 1990s. The problem is to get the trade deficit back into balance or at least reduce the size of the deficit. Of the several proposals brought forward, most deal with the fairness of trade with some of our trading partners instead of reducing imports or adjusting other trade policies. Many feel that too many countries are allowed to trade freely in the United States without granting equal treatment to U.S. products in their countries. The trading partner with which we have the largest deficit, Japan, receives the most attention for not playing fair, that is, U.S. business sees the U.S. market as open to Japanese goods but Japan closed to U.S. goods.

EXHIBIT 2–5 What Would One U.S. Dollar Buy? (selected years)

	1985	*1986*	*1987*	*1988*	*1989*
British pound	.86	.69	.67	.54	.56
French franc	9.60	7.55	6.44	5.40	6.09
Japanese yen	250.23	200.87	159.54	123.32	125.80
Swiss franc	2.25	2.07	1.62	1.29	1.51

SOURCE: *The Wall Street Journal,* 1st trading day of January.

To address problems of fairness and the competitiveness of U.S. industry, the U.S. Congress passed a trade bill designed to assist U.S. exporters.

THE OMNIBUS TRADE AND COMPETITIVENESS ACT OF 1988[14]

Just as its name implies, the Omnibus Trade and Competitiveness Act of 1988 is many faceted, focusing on assisting businesses to be more competitive in world markets as well as correcting perceived injustices in trade practices.[15] The trade act was designed to deal with some of the problems discussed earlier—trade deficits, protectionism, and the overall fairness of our trading partners. Congressional concern centered around the issue that the United States, the world's largest economy, was open to Japan, Western Europe, and the newly industrializing countries of Asia but was closed out in parts of their markets.[16] In the opinion of some, the bill reflected the realization that we must "deal with our trading partners based on how they actually operate, not on how we want them to behave. Seventy-five percent of world trade is conducted by nations that reject, in practice, if not in theory, the free trade ideal."[17] These countries have accumulated vast trade surpluses while the United States has accumulated vast trade deficits. Some see the trade bill as a protectionist measure,[18] but the government sees it as a means of providing stronger tools to open foreign markets and to help U.S. exporters be more competitive.[19] The bill covers three areas considered critical in improving the U.S. trade position: improving access to foreign markets, assisting U.S. exporters to be more competitive, and providing relief to U.S. businesses affected by unfair trade activities.

Market Access.   There has been growing concern that U.S. business does not have the same access to foreign markets that foreign business has to

---

[14] This section is based, in part, on *The Omnibus Trade and Competitiveness Act of 1988* (Washington, D.C.: The International Division, U.S. Chamber of Commerce, 1988), p. 66.

[15] For an interesting point of view of why the trade bill will be ineffective, see "A Trade Bill Filled with Trade-Offs," *Business Week*, May 9, 1988, pp. 42–43.

[16] For an interesting review of Japanese-U.S. trade relations, see Robert Green and Trina L. Larsen, "Only Retaliation Will Open up Japan," *Harvard Business Review*, November–December 1987, pp. 22–28.

[17] Lewis Kaden and Lee Smith, "How to Get a Better Deal on Trade," *New York Times*, October 30, 1988, p. 12.

[18] "New U.S. Trade Bill Dismays France," *The Journal of Commerce*, October 6, 1988, p. 5A.

[19] Clayton Yeutter, "Asian Nations that Aren't Protectionist Have Little to Fear from U.S. Trade Law," *The Asian Wall Street Journal Weekly*, September 12, 1988, p. 13B.

U.S. markets. There are many barriers restricting or prohibiting goods from entering a foreign market: unnecessarily restrictive technical standards, compulsory distribution systems, customs barriers, tariffs, quotas, and restrictive licensing requirements are just a few. The act gives the president authority to deal with countries where specific barriers unfairly keep U.S. products from entering those countries' markets. If a country violates a trade agreement, the president can retaliate by restricting the country's products in U.S. markets. Under the previous law, the U.S. addressed unfair practices on an industry-by-industry basis, a lengthy and unwieldy procedure where when one barrier was removed, it was frequently replaced by another. In the 1988 act, the president has the authority to deal with generic or pervasive trade practices that restrict access across the border.[20]

Two other issues addressed under the market access section of the law are government procurement procedures and market access to telecommunications markets. Foreign government procurement procedures must not discriminate against U.S. firms; if they do, the president has the authority to impose a ban on U.S. government procurement of goods and services from that country.

Deregulation and the divestiture of American Telephone & Telegraph assured foreign telecommunications suppliers full access to the American market. By contrast, U.S. companies enjoy limited access to the major foreign telecommunications markets, most notably in Europe. The 1988 act clearly indicates that the United States regards telecommunications market access a top priority of U.S. trade policy and, when negotiation fails to open foreign markets, the government will take retaliatory action.

Export Expansion.   In addition to making foreign markets more accessible to U.S. goods, the 1988 act reflects an awareness that some problems with U.S. export competitiveness stemmed from impediments on trade imposed by U.S. regulations and export disincentives. Export controls, the Foreign Corrupt Practices Act (FCPA), and export promotion were specifically addressed. The new regulations facilitate and speed up the process for obtaining export licenses for products on the export control list. Much of the ambiguity in the FCPA was removed by clarifying the legality of most types of payments.[21] In addition, the act reaffirmed the government's role in the promotion of export trade in general, agricultural trade in particular, and continued financial assistance to small businesses engaged in exporting.

---

[20] "The New Trade Act: Tools for Exporters," *Business America*, October 24, 1988, pp. 2–6.

[21] See Chapter 6 for a complete discussion of the Foreign Corrupt Practices Act.

3. **Import Relief.**   Export trade is a two-way street; that is, we must be prepared to compete with imports in the home market if we force foreign markets to open to U.S. exports. The act provides a menu of remedies for U.S. businesses adversely affected by imports; it recognizes that foreign penetration of U.S. markets can cause serious competitive pressure, loss of market share and, occasionally, severe injury. Measures dealing with antidumping, countervailing duty, and intellectual property protection laws are designed to redress competitive advantages obtained by foreign companies through unfair trade practices. The act also provides temporary relief from competition to firms injured by fairly traded imports. Industries seriously injured by fairly traded imports can petition the government for temporary relief while they adjust to import competition and regain their competitive edge.[22]

The new trade bill was welcomed by many as long overdue. It will take time to tell if it meets its objective of opening foreign markets for U.S. exporters; for most of the provisions to be effective will require an administration and president willing to enforce them. Early indications are that some negotiations with the Japanese on beef and citrus quotas[23] have been positive as have negotiations to allow U.S. companies to bid on public construction projects.[24]

PROTECTIONISM

International business must face the reality that this is a world of tariffs, quotas, and nontariff barriers designed to protect a country's markets from intrusion by foreign companies. Although the General Agreement on Trade and Tariffs has been effective in reducing tariffs, countries still resort to protectionist measures. Nations utilize legal barriers, exchange barriers, and psychological barriers to restrain entry of unwanted goods. Businesses work together to establish private market barriers while the market structure itself may provide formidable barriers to imported goods.[25] The complex distribution system in Japan is a good example of a market structure creat-

---

[22] For a comprehensive summary of the major provisions of the act, see "Principal Features of the Omnibus Trade and Competitiveness Act of 1988," *Business America*, September 26, 1988, p. 6.

[23] "Japan Agrees to Open up Its Market to Imports of Beef, Citrus Products," *Business America*, July 4, 1988, p. 8–9.

[24] "The Trade Bill Proves It: A Little Pressure Goes a Long Way," *Business Week*, September 26, 1988, p. 65.

[25] "Despite Record Profits, Big Three Auto Firms Seek More Protection," *The Wall Street Journal*, January 24, 1989.

The trend of combining gasoline stations and mini markets spreads beyond the United States. (Rick Warner/Journalism Services, Inc.)

ing a barrier to trade. However, as effective as it is in keeping some products out of the market, in a legal sense it cannot be viewed as a trade barrier.[26]

Protection Logic and Illogic

Arguments to maintain gov't restrictions on trade (11)

Countless reasons are espoused by protectionists to maintain government restrictions on trade, but essentially all arguments can be classified as follows: (1) protection of an infant industry, (2) protection of the home market, (3) need to keep money at home, (4) encouragement of capital accumulation, (5) maintenance of the standard of living and real wages, (6) conservation of natural resources, (7) industrialization of a low-wage nation, (8) maintenance of employment and reduction of unemployment, (9) national defense, (10) increase of business size, and (11) retaliation and bargaining. Economists in general recognize as valid only the argu-

---

[26] For an interesting article on the folly of protectionism, see Robert Z. Lawrence and Robert E. Litan, "Why Protectionism Doesn't Pay," *Harvard Business Review*," May–June 1987, pp. 60–67.

BOX 2–4
The Japanese Market Is Open—If You Can Survive the Test

The protectionist Japanese set tough standards that products must pass before they can be imported. Porta-bote International of California attempted to sell their boat in Japan and encountered the following:

The president of the company knew he had a perfect product for Japan. Because storage space is at a premium in Japanese homes, he reasoned that the Japanese who loved fishing needed his boat—an $895 motorized or sailing craft that folds to four inches flat and can be carried on top of a car.

He turned to a Japanese distributor willing to test market his boat. Like most imported consumer products, the boat first had to clear Japanese safety tests. The president describes the test as "a veiled attempt to reject Porta-bote" and to protect domestic manufacturers. The Japanese Coast Guard filled one of the boats with 600 pounds of concrete and dropped it 20 feet into the water. The boat was examined for structural damage and then, to the amazement of the distributor who was snapping pictures, it was subjected to the same test twice more. The polypropylene boat held together and—ironically—the distributor used the photo to convince retailers of its strength and durability. The test was a success and the boat was allowed to enter the Japanese market.

Source: Adapted from Karen Berney, "Competing in Japan," *Nations Business*, October 1986, pp. 28–30.

ments for infant industry, national defense, and industrialization of under-developed countries. The resource conservation argument becomes increasingly valid in an era of environmental consciousness and worldwide shortages of raw materials and agricultural commodities.

There might be a case for *temporary* protection of markets with excess productive capacity or excess labor when such protection could facilitate an orderly transition. Unfortunately such protection becomes long term and contributes to industrial inefficiency while detracting from a nation's realistic adjustment to its world situation. Even the admission of these protectionist arguments is severely restricted and applies only in limited circumstances.

Most protectionists argue the need for tariffs on one of the three premises whether or not they are relevant to their products. Proponents are also likely to call on the maintenance-of-employment argument because it has substantial political appeal. When arguing for protection, the basic economic advantages of international trade are ignored. The fact that the consumer ultimately bears the cost of tariffs and other protective measures is conveniently overlooked. Sugar and textiles are good examples of pro-

EXHIBIT 2–6 The Price of Protectionism

Industry	Total Costs to Consumers (in $ millions)	Number of Jobs Saved	Cost per Job Saved
Textiles and apparel	$27,000	640,000	$ 42,000
Carbon steel	6,800	9,000	$750,000
Autos	5,800	55,000	$105,000
Dairy products	5,500	25,000	$220,000
Shipping	3,000	11,000	$270,000
Meat	1,800	11,000	$160,000

SOURCE: Michael McFadden, "Protectionism Can't Protect Jobs," FORTUNE, May 11, 1987, pp. 125.

tected industries in the United States which cannot be justified by any of the three arguments. U.S. sugar prices are artificially held higher than world prices for no sound economic reason. Looking at Exhibit 2–6, tariffs and quotas on textiles and apparel cost consumers $27 billion or $42,000 per job saved. Considering the average $12,000 salary in that industry, the case could be made that we would have been better off economically to not have saved the jobs but retired the 640,000 workers at a cost of less than $8 billion. In situations such as those shown in Exhibit 2–6, the net increase in costs constitutes a hidden tax consumers unknowingly pay.[27]

Trade Barriers

To encourage development of domestic industry and protect existing industry, governments may establish such barriers to trade as tariffs, quotas, boycotts, monetary barriers, nontariff barriers, and market barriers. Barriers are imposed against imports and foreign businesses as well. Even though the inspiration for such barriers may be economic or political, typically they are encouraged by local industry. Whether or not the barriers are economically logical, the fact is that they do exist.[28]

Tariffs. The tariff, simply defined, is a tax imposed by a government on goods entering at its borders. Tariffs are used as a revenue-generating

[27] Michael McFadden, "Protectionism Can't Protect Jobs," Fortune, May 11, 1987, pp. 121–28.

[28] For a comprehensive review of marketing barriers, see Sak Onkvisit and John J. Shaw, "Marketing Barriers in International Trade," Business Horizons, May–June 1988, pp. 64–72.

tax, to discourage the importation of goods, or both. In Mexico, for example, the tariff on foreign fabricated auto parts ranges from 60 to 80 percent of the item's value; this tariff is designed to protect local industry. In general, tariffs:

Increase   Inflationary pressures.
Special interests' privileges.
Government control and political considerations in economic matters.
The number of tariffs (they beget other tariffs).

Weaken   Balance-of-payments positions.
Supply-and-demand patterns.
International understanding (they can start trade wars).

Restrict   Manufacturers' supply sources.
Choices available to consumers.
Competition.

In addition, tariffs are arbitrary, discriminatory, and require constant administration and supervision. They are also often used as reprisals against protectionist measures of trading partners. In a dispute with the European Community over pasta export subsidies, the United States ordered a 40 percent increase in duties on European spaghetti and fancy pasta sold in gourmet groceries. The EC retaliated against U.S. walnuts and lemons; the United States then delayed a promised concession on semifinished steel. The great pasta war raged on as Europe increased tariffs on U.S. fertilizer, paper products, and beef tallow. The bickering involved several other industries before the Europeans backed down and reduced their pasta export subsidies.[29]

In addition to tariffs, governments restrict imports in a variety of other ways. Among them are restrictions on the quality of goods that may enter a country, sanitary and health requirements, methods of classifying and placing values on imports, and antidumping regulations, border taxes, and domestic subsidies. Nontariff barriers tend to gain importance as import duties are lowered. Some of the more frequently used barriers are quotas, embargoes or boycotts, and standards requirements. Exhibit 2–7 gives a complete list of nontariff barriers.

Quotas.   A quota is a specific numerical or dollar limit applied to a particular type of good. For example, there is a limit on imported television sets in Great Britain, German quotas on Japanese ball bearings, Italian

---

[29] Monica Langley, "Protectionist Attitudes Grow Stronger in Spite of Healthy Economy," *The Wall Street Journal*, May 16, 1988, p. 1.

EXHIBIT 2–7   Types of Nontariff Barriers

Specific Limitations on Trade:
   Quotas
   Import licensing requirements
   Proportion restrictions of foreign to domestic goods
   Minimum import price limits
   Embargoes
Customs and Administrative Entry Procedures:
   Valuation systems
   Antidumping practices
   Tariff classifications
   Documentation requirements
   Fees
Standards:
   Standard disparities
   Intergovernmental acceptances of testing methods and standards
   Packaging, labeling, marking standards
Governmental Participation in Trade:
   Government procurement policies
   Export subsidies
   Countervailing duties
   Domestic assistance programs
Charges on Imports:
   Prior import deposit requirements
   Administrative fees
   Special supplementary duties
   Import credit discriminations
   Variable levies
   Border taxes
Others:
   Voluntary export restraints
   Orderly marketing agreements

SOURCE: A. D. Cao, "Non-Tariff Barriers to U.S. Manufactured Exports," *The Columbia Journal of World Business,* Summer 1980, p. 94.

restrictions on Japanese motorcycles, Japanese quotas on citrus fruits, and U.S. quotas on textiles.[30] Quotas are designed to put an absolute restriction on the volume of specific items being imported into a country; they may also be linked with tariffs. Like tariffs, quotas tend to increase prices. For example, a U.S. honeydew melon—which is under a strict quota—retails for $40 in Tokyo.

---

[30] Julia Leung, "China's Textile Exports Falter as Quota, Production Problems Deter Some Buyers," *The Wall Street Journal,* September 12, 1988, p. 16.

Voluntary Export Restraint. Similar to quotas are the voluntary export restraints (VER). Common in textiles, clothing, steel, agriculture, and automobiles, the VER is an agreement between the importing country and the exporting country for a restriction on the volume of exports.[31] Japan has a VER on automobiles to the United States, that is, Japan has agreed to export a fixed number of automobiles annually. A VER is called voluntary in that the exporting country sets the limits; however, it is generally imposed under the threat of stiffer quotas and tariffs being set by the importing country if a VER is not established.[32]

Boycott. A government boycott is an absolute restriction against the purchase and importation of certain goods from other countries. A public boycott can be either formal or informal and may be government sponsored or sponsored by an industry. It is not unusual for the citizens of a country to boycott goods of other countries at the urging of their government or civic groups. Sometimes executives in a particular industry attempt to rouse public sympathy for that industry and induce a voluntary boycott against imported competitive goods. During the past decade, for example, the U.S. steel industry has been engaged in a campaign to urge steel users to purchase domestic steel products—solely because they are domestic.

An informal limitation, the Buy-American Act of 1933, was legislated as an antidepression measure. It is still on the books today. Interestingly, it is now under attack while other countries are initiating similar legislation and emphasizing their administration of nonlegislated buy-national policies. In the United Kingdom, for example, there is pressure not to buy imported capital goods; there is even pressure against buying goods made in the United Kingdom by foreign-owned corporations when similar goods are available from locally owned companies.

A particularly insidious type of boycott developed over a decade ago; the economic boycott used to achieve political ends. In 1978, some products were boycotted by a large number of countries over the issue of black rights. Arab countries and Israel boycott each other over the Palestine question. Cuba is boycotted by Brazil and South Korea because it supports revolutionary activities in both countries. Portugal is boycotted by a dozen African countries; Libya is boycotted by the United States over terrorist acts;[33] all communist countries are boycotted by Taiwan; the United States

---

[31] F. J. Clemens Boonekamp, "Voluntary Export Restraints," *Finance and Development*, December 1987, pp. 2–5.

[32] Makoto Kuroda, "Times Change: Thoughts on Japan's External Relations," *Speaking of Japan*, January 1989, pp. 14–18.

[33] "Qadhafi Said the U.S. Sanctions against Libya Won't Have Any Effect," *The Wall Street Journal*, January 10, 1986; and "Leaving Libya: U.S. Companies Are Dragging Their Feet," *Business Week*, January 27, 1986, p. 54.

[handwritten margin notes: 1801–1850, French economist, journalist, satirist, favored free trade, wrote against socialism]

BOX 2–5
A Word for Open Markets

Bastiat's century-old farcical letter to the French Chamber of Deputies points up the ultimate folly of tariffs and the advantages of utilizing the superior production advantage of others.

To the Chamber of Deputies:

We are subjected to the intolerable competition of a foreign rival, who enjoys such superior facilities for the production of light that he can *inundate* our *national market* at reduced price. This rival is no other than the sun. Our petition is to pass a law shutting up all windows, openings, and fissures through which the light of the sun is used to penetrate our dwellings, to the prejudice of the profitable manufacture we have been enabled to bestow on the country.

Signed: Candlestick Makers,
F. Bastiat

boycotts Nicaragua;[34] the list goes on and on. Whatever the cause, such trade dislocations are a great disservice to the world economy. However, they also point up the vitality of economic forces because they are widely ignored when it is more convenient to do so. South Africa trades openly with many of the countries boycotting it and covertly with others. One diplomat says, "Hypocrisy is the main ingredient on this continent . . . it's the market forces at play. Most African countries are so poor they can't afford to be moral in their transactions." A U.S. export administration act prohibits U.S. "persons" from supporting, furthering, or complying with boycotts not approved by the United States government. For many companies this poses further problems in their attempts to deal effectively with Arab countries whose boycott of Israel is not sanctioned.[35]

Monetary Barriers. A government can effectively regulate its international trade position by various forms of exchange-control restrictions. A government may enact such restrictions to preserve its balance-of-payment position or specifically for the advantage or encouragement of particular industries. There are three barriers to consider: blocked currency, differential exchange rates, and government approval requirements for securing for-

---

[34] "The Nicaragua Embargo: Multinationals Aren't Packing," *Business Week*, May 20, 1985, p. 66.

[35] "Sanctions Almost Never Work," *The Wall Street Journal*, August 19, 1985, p. 23.

BOX 2–6
Trade War Looming?

On New Year's Day 1989, the European Community imposed a health regulation barring imports of American and other beef produced from cattle fed
growth-inducing hormones, a practice not banned in the United States. In
return, the United States immediately retaliated with punitive 100 percent
tariffs on about $100 million worth of European products including canned
hams, tomatoes, coffee, and fruit juice.

The EC drew up a counterretaliation list that included punitive tariffs on
American canned corn, dried fruit, honey, and walnuts also worth about
$100 million.

The U.S. Department of Agriculture then considered whether or not to
ban all meat coming from Europe on grounds that hormones so dangerous
they are banned even in America were being injected by farmers in Europe
in defiance of European laws. Such a ban would cost Europe more than
$400 million a year in trade.

So how do we get out of an escalating trade war? Take the issue to GATT?
Maybe, but at the time this was written there wasn't even agreement on
what was to be arbitrated. The EC agreed to let GATT rule on whether it
has a right to impose a health rule that affects imports, but the United
States refused, saying that wasn't in question. For the Americans the issue
is whether the hormone ban is backed by the scientific evidence required
to make it a legal, health-based import curb. The United States offered to
submit the matter to a GATT scientific panel, but then the EC refused. It
admitted a lack of scientific evidence for the ban, but insisted it was free to
impose health rules demanded by public pressure, regardless of what scientists say.

"I expect we'll have more problems with Europe than with Japan . . . ,"
said Clayton Yeutter, a former U.S. trade representative.

Source: Adapted from Walter S. Mossberg, "Tensions between U.S., Europe Likely
to Dominate '89 Trade Agenda for Bush," *The Wall Street Journal,* January 3, 1989, p.
A12.

eign exchange. Blocked currency is used as a political weapon or as a
response to difficult balance-of-payment situations. In effect, blockage cuts
off all importing or all importing above a certain level. Blockage is accomplished by refusing to allow importers to exchange national currency for
the sellers' currency.[36]

The *differential exchange rate* is a particularly ingenious method of control-

---

[36] Companies have to be resourceful when blocked funds are a problem. See, for example,
"Successful Tactics for Managing Blocked Funds in Brazilian Subsidiaries," *Business Latin
America,* June 6, 1988, pp. 177–78.

ling imports. It encourages the importation of goods the government deems desirable and discourages importation of goods the government does not want. The essential mechanism requires the importer to pay varying amounts of domestic currency for foreign exchange with which to purchase products in different categories. For example, the exchange rate for a desirable category of goods might be one unit of domestic money for one unit of a specific foreign currency. For a less-desirable product, the rate might be two domestic currency units for one foreign unit. For an undesirable product, the rate might be three domestic units for one foreign unit. An importer of an undesired product has to pay three times as much for the foreign exchange as the importer of a desired product. This device has been used by several South American countries.

3. *Government approval to secure foreign exchange* is growing in importance. Most Latin American and East European countries require all foreign exchange transactions to be approved by a central minister. Thus, importers who want to buy a foreign good must apply for an exchange permit; that is, permission to exchange an amount of local currency for foreign currency. The exchange permit may also stipulate the rate of exchange, which can be an unfavorable rate depending on the desires of the government. In addition, the exchange permit may stipulate that the amount to be exchanged must be deposited in a local bank for a set period prior to the transfer of goods. For example, Brazil has at times required funds to be deposited 360 days prior to the import date. This is extremely restrictive because funds are out of circulation and subject to the ravages of inflation. Such policies cause major cash flow problems for the importer and greatly increase the price of imports. Needless to say, these currency-exchange barriers constitute a major deterrent to trade.

Standards. Nontariff barriers of this category include standards to protect health, safety, and product quality. The standards are sometimes used in an unduly stringent or discriminating way to restrict trade, but the sheer volume of regulations in this category is a problem in itself. Fruit content regulations for jam vary so much from country to country that one agricultural specialist says, "A jam exporter needs a computer to avoid one or another country's regulations." Plant and animal quarantine regulations serve an important function but often are used solely to keep out foreign products. Although all countries use standards to some extent, Japan has raised the process to the level of art. Differing standards is one of the major disagreements between the United States and Japan. The size of knotholes in plywood shipped to Japan can determine whether or not the shipment is accepted; a knothole too large and the shipment is rejected "because quality standards are not met."[37] American companies

---

[37] Marc Levinson, "Twelve Protectionist Traps," *Business Abroad*, March 1985, p. 28.

are often confronted by government standards that make it almost impossible to import any goods not tested in Japan. This is dramatically evident with autos. Before an American car can be sold in Japan, its government requires six volumes of documents on standards for each auto plus local testing of nearly every vehicle. This adds hundreds of dollars to the retail price of a U.S. car in Japan. In contrast, Japanese exports into the United States require only the manufacturer's label certifying the cars meet American safety standards. When costs to comply with standards and testing are coupled with the other taxes and additional costs, the Japanese price for a U.S. automobile can more than double the U.S. price—a $15,000 Ford Taurus costs about $33,000 in Japan.[38] Although most standards were not specifically intended to keep out imports, they do so by being so arbitrary or obtuse that importers become discouraged. Sweden, for example, insists on testing all foreign electrical appliances in its own labs, a costly and time-consuming bottleneck.

Not to be overlooked in this category are the Federal Drug Administration (FDA) requirements for the sale of pharmaceutical drugs in the United States. On the average, it takes 12 years of testing before a new drug product is licensed for sale in the United States. Although this precaution may not have been designed to limit the importation of pharmaceutical drugs, it does, in fact, do so.

Imports are not the only target of discrimination in international business. Many countries make it difficult or impossible to establish foreign production subsidiaries that might compete with local business. For years Japan held foreign investors at bay, and virtually no important industries in that country could be 100-percent foreign-owned. Japan has softened its regulations to allow more foreign countries to have some 100 percent-owned investments.[39] Many countries continue to require substantial local participation. Strict capital and profit repatriation rules can have almost identical effects. European countries have bristled at foreign mergers that would mean takeover of local companies; numerous major mergers have been stopped at the last minute by various national governments. Governments can easily exclude foreign goods from the marketplace by refusing to award public contracts to any plants or producers who have purchased foreign goods against the government's wishes.[40]

Foreign restrictions abound and the United States can be counted among those governments using restrictions. In fact, U.S. protectionism has been

---

[38] Yukicki Yanagishima, "Crawling through Japan's Car-Import Maze," *The Asian Wall Street Journal Weekly*, April 11, 1988, p. 16.

[39] Abraham Rotstein, "When the United States Was Canada's Japan," *Harvard Business Review*, January–February 1989, pp. 38–43.

[40] Masami Atarashi, "Survival Strategy: Challenges Facing Foreign Corporations in Japan," *Speaking of Japan* 9, no. 97 (January 1989), pp. 8–12.

BOX 2–7
Not Quite Blocked

. . . the mysterious market in which blocked accounts—funds trapped by government fiat within a given country—changed hands. There are billions of dollars worth of blocked accounts around the world, much of it owned by U.S. corporations. A buying-and-selling market exists to make use of these funds, sometimes in deals arranged directly between companies, sometimes through a bank as an intermediary. But often, buyer and seller are brought together by foreign-money brokers in a murky gray area. . . . Brokers tell of markdowns ranging from 2 to 50 percent, depending mostly on the eagerness of the seller.

The countries in which blocked funds are held range from underdeveloped nations such as Ghana and Zaire to fully industrialized ones like Italy and France. There are many degrees of blockage, from the mildest regulation of the outflow of money to ironclad embargoes. Some blockages last for a relatively short time. Others go on for years; U.S.-based multinational corporations have had accounts in Greece blocked since World War II. Many blockages, of course, stem from political upheavals or from a new regime coming into power. On the other hand, funds may be blocked because of a dispute between a company and the government over an issue far removed from currency regulations. Or the blockage may grow out of a wider problem, such as a nationwide shortage of foreign exchange or chronically weak domestic currencies. That is why blockage is most prevalent in underdeveloped countries, such as India and many younger African nations.

Source: "The Mysterious Market in Blocked Accounts." Reprinted with special permission of *Dun's Review*, October 1976. © 1976 by Dun & Bradstreet Publications Corporation.

growing rapidly. According to one source, approximately 45 percent of U.S. manufactured imports are subject to some form of nontariff barrier. On the other hand, Japan has only 22 percent of its imports subject to restrictions.[41] For over a decade, U.S. government officials have been arranging "voluntary" agreements with the Japanese steel industry to limit sales to the United States. Similar negotiations with the governments of major textile producers have limited textile imports into the United States.

In the 10 years before 1978, imported shoes captured 46 percent of the U.S. market, closing 300 American shoe factories. U.S. trade negotiators

[41] Vernon R. Alden, "The Trade Deficit: Stop Looking for Scapegoats," *Business Week*, April 8, 1985, p. 20.

were dispatched to Taiwan, South Korea, Spain, Brazil, and Uruguay to reach informal agreements that would restrain shoe exports to the United States.

Local Content Requirements.   A popular nontariff barrier is the requirement that a product must have local content before it can be sold within the importing country. Mexico requires foreign car manufacturers to use locally produced parts and materials equal to 50 percent of each vehicle's value.

Market Barriers

The location, size, and structure of a market may deter international goods from entering a given marketplace. Just as large companies in the domestic market tend to ignore villages and hamlets in their marketing plans, so companies engaged in international business are likely to overlook small markets when the vastly broader potential of larger ones remains untapped. A country may be denied the benefits of international trading because size or remote location make it unprofitable as a market. Distance and aggregate purchasing power or market potential for a given product are key considerations, but they too may be modified by the extent and level of competition within a country. One market may be relatively untapped while another is beyond consideration because competition has preempted it. Very lucrative markets may be closed to international competition because of cartels or other privately imposed market barriers.[42]

Even the habit patterns of consumers in world markets build market barriers. Companies are reluctant to enter markets with unfamiliar local customs and purchasing behavior because of the high possibility of failure. Inadequate channels of distribution also provide natural market barriers to companies wishing to operate at a mass-distribution level.

In the final analysis, natural market barriers are probably the more formidable deterrents to international trade. If markets appear to offer promise of great profits, most governmental, exchange, and psychological barriers can be surmounted by ingenious businesses. Even though countries tend to instigate barriers to trade, they appreciate the interdependence of the world's economies and thus strive to lower barriers in a controlled and equitable manner. The General Agreement on Tariffs and Trade is one such attempt by countries working together to promote world trade.

---

[42] "On Trade, the U.S. Sounds the Charge—and Comes Out Firing Blanks," *Business Week*, February 6, 1989, p. 45.

pudim

"DO SOMETHING. THAT FOREIGNER IS COMPET-
ING WITH ME."

The Colorado Daily, December 7, 1977, p. 6.

EASING TRADE RESTRICTIONS

Shrinking communication and transportation barriers throughout the world have focused attention in recent years on methods of breaking down barriers such as tariffs and boycotts between otherwise natural markets. Contributing to this desire for easier trade has been a high level of productive capacity of various nations, particularly the industrialized nations. If a firm or nation has adequate markets at home, it is not inclined to seek markets elsewhere; but, when the productive capacity outruns domestic consumption, there is a natural desire to extend the borders of the marketplace. Two major activities to ease trade restrictions have occurred in recent years: (1) development of trade and commercial treaties; and (2) the improvement of international monetary systems.

General Agreement on Tariffs and Trade

Historically, trade treaties were negotiated on a *bilateral* (between two nations) basis, with little attention given to relationships with other countries. Further, there was a tendency to raise barriers rather than extend markets and restore world trade. The United States and 22 other countries signed the General Agreement on Tariffs and Trade shortly after World War II. Although not all countries participated, this agreement paved the way for the first effective worldwide tariff agreement. The original agreement provided a process to reduce tariffs and created an agency to serve as watchdog over world trade. GATT's agency director and staff offer nations a forum for negotiating trade and related issues.[43] Member nations (94 in 1989) seek to resolve their trade disputes bilaterally; if that fails, special GATT panels are set up to recommend action. The panels are only advisory and have no enforcement powers.

The GATT treaty and subsequent meetings have produced agreements significantly reducing tariffs on a wide range of goods. Periodically member nations meet to reevaluate trade barriers and establish international codes designed to foster trade among members. In general, the agreement covers these basic elements: (1) trade shall be conducted on a nondiscriminatory basis; (2) protection shall be afforded domestic industries through customs tariff, not through such commercial measures as import quotas; and (3) consultation shall be the primary method used to solve global trade problems. Since GATT's inception, there have been seven "rounds" of intergovernmental tariff negotiations. The most recently completed was the Tokyo Round concluded in 1979. The Tokyo Round was the most comprehensive and far-reaching round undertaken by GATT. In addition to negotiating further tariff cuts, this round resulted in six major agreements on nontariff measures. These Codes, as they are often referred to, lay out new international rules for subsidies and countervailing measures, antidumping, government procurement, technical barriers to trade (standards), customs valuation, and import licensing.

The Tokyo Round made a good start at addressing a number of nontariff barriers that have become more serious in recent years. Despite the success of these past rounds, high tariffs have not disappeared entirely and nontariff barriers are still widely used. There are also areas that, until now, GATT has not addressed such as services, intellectual property rights, and investment.[44] As a consequence, the Uruguay Round (the eighth set of

---

[43] "EC, U.S. Head for New Trade Friction over the Meaning of 'Made in America,' " *The Wall Street Journal*, February 8, 1989, p. A19.

[44] Ann V. Morrison, "GATT's Seven Rounds of Trade Talks Span More than Thirty Years," *Business America*, July 7, 1986, pp. 8–13.

negotiations), was launched in 1987.[45] Specifically, GATT negotiations in this round are to address key areas of importance in international trade which are not now under the scope of GATT rules. For example, GATT rules do not apply to the international trade of services that represent an increasing percentage of international trade flows.[46] Similarly, GATT rules have little influence over government investment policies affecting international trade or on policies concerning the protection of intellectual property rights such as patents, trademarks, and copyrights. Agricultural trade is another area where GATT rules either do not apply or are not effective. Finally, the dispute settlement mechanism is seen to be increasingly ineffective at resolving conflicts among GATT members.[47]

GATT covers roughly 80 percent of world trade in merchandise but trade in services, agriculture, textiles, and investment and capital flows are excluded. Consequently, GATT only covers 5 to 7 percent of global economic activity.[48] The United States is especially interested in the talks on agriculture because most of the agricultural products in international trade are heavily subsidized by their governments.[49] The political power wielded by farmers in most countries has resulted in increased structures of subsidies and import restraints to protect them.[50] The Uruguay Round will not end until 1992 or later.

International Monetary Fund

Inadequate monetary reserves and unstable currencies are particularly vexing problems in world trade. So long as these conditions exist, world markets cannot develop and function as effectively as they should. To overcome these particular market barriers which plagued international trading before World War II, the International Monetary Fund (IMF) was formed. Among its objectives was the stabilization of foreign exchange rates and the establishment of freely convertible currencies. Later, the European Payments Union was formed to facilitate multinational payments. While the International Monetary Fund has some severe critics, most agree

---

[45] William C. Verity, "Uruguay Round: Opening World Markets," *Business America*, June 20, 1988, pp. 2–5.

[46] Robert J. Morris, "Trade in Services: U.S. Business' Stake in the New GATT Round," *Export Today*, July–August 1988, pp. 55–58.

[47] "U.S., E.C. Collide at GATT Review Over Agriculture," *Europe*, January–February 1989, pp. 14–15.

[48] Ann Morrison, "The Uruguay Round and the GATT: What They Are and What They Do," *Business America*, June 20, 1988, pp. 6–7.

[49] "A Look at GATT," *Harvard Business Review*, January–February 1988, p. 88.

[50] Michael W. S. Davenport, "Purchasing Power," *Look Japan*, February 1988, pp. 10–12.

Philadelphia Evening Bulletin

that it has performed a valuable service and at least partially achieved many of its objectives.

To cope with universally floating exchange rates, the IMF developed special drawing rights (SDRs), one of its more useful inventions. Because both gold and the U.S. dollar have lost their utility as the basic medium of financial exchange, most monetary statistics relate to SDRs rather than dollars. The SDR is, in effect, "paper gold" and represents an average base of value derived from the value of a group of major currencies. Rather than being denominated in the currency of any given country, trade contracts are written more frequently in SDRs because they are much less susceptible to exchange rate fluctuations. Even floating rates do not necessarily accurately reflect exchange relationships. Some countries permit their currencies to float cleanly without manipulation (clean float) while other nations systematically manipulate the value of their currency (dirty float), thus modifying the accuracy of the monetary marketplace.[51]

Although the motivation for economic and technical assistance in this unsettled age is undoubtedly more political than economic, the results have been to upgrade the economies of many nations and to bring many new, small, and underdeveloped nations into the world marketplace. Many of the developing nations represent potential growth markets of the future and should be considered in any evaluation of world markets.

---

[51] See Chapter 19 for a more detailed discussion of international financial management.

SUMMARY

Regardless of the theoretical approach used in defense of international trade, it is clear that the benefits from absolute or comparative advantage can accrue to any nation. Open markets are needed if world resources are to be developed and utilized in the most beneficial manner. It is true that there are circumstances when market protection may be needed and may be beneficial to national defense or the encouragement of infant industries in developing nations. The temptation, however, is always toward excessive market protection or, more correctly, excessive producer protection, because the consumer seldom benefits from such protection. Because free international markets can help underdeveloped countries become self-sufficient and because open markets provide new customers, most industrialized nations have, since World War II, cooperated in working toward freer trade. Such trade will always be partially threatened by various governmental and market barriers which exist or are created for the protection of local businesses, although the trend in the past few decades has been toward freer trade.

QUESTIONS

1. Define:
   GATT
   market mechanism
   exchange rate fluctuation
   current account √
   tariff √

   IMF √
   psychological market protection
   nontariff barriers
   VER √

2. Discuss the globalization of the U.S. economy.

3. Differentiate among the current account, balance of trade, and balance of payments.

4. Explain the role of price as a free market regulator.

5. "Theoretically, the market is an automatic, competitive, self-regulating mechanism which provides for the maximum consumer welfare and which best regulates the use of the factors of production." Explain.

6. Interview several local business people to determine their attitudes toward world trade. Further, learn if they buy or sell goods produced in foreign countries. Correlate the attitudes and report on your findings.

7. What is the role of profit in international trade? Does profit replace or complement the regulatory function of pricing? Discuss.

8. Why does the balance of payments always balance even though the balance of trade does not?

9. Enumerate the ways in which a nation can overcome an unfavorable balance of trade.

10. Support or refute each of the various arguments commonly used in support of tariffs.

11. France exports about 18 percent of its gross domestic product, neighboring Belgium exports 46 percent. What areas of economic policy are likely to be affected by such variations in exports?

12. Does widespread unemployment change the economic logic of protectionism?

13. Review the economic effects of major trade imbalances such as those caused by petroleum imports.

14. Discuss the main provisions of the Omnibus Trade and Competitiveness Act of 1988.

15. The Tokyo Round of GATT emphasized the reduction of nontariff barriers. How does the Uruguay Round differ?

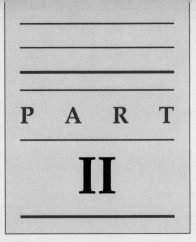

PART

II

The Cultural Environment of Global Marketing

Chapters

CHAPTER

3

Cultural Dynamics in Assessing Global Markets

Humans are born creatures of need. As they mature, *want* is added to need. Economic needs are spontaneous and, in their crudest sense, limited. Humans, like all living things, need a minimum of nourishment; like a few other living things, they need a type of shelter; and, unlike any other being, they need essential clothing. Economic *wants* however, are for nonessentials and, hence, are limitless. Unlike basic needs, wants are not spontaneous and not characteristic of the lower animals. They arise not from an inner desire for preservation of self or species but from a desire for satisfaction above absolute necessity. To satisfy their material needs and wants, humans consume.

The manner in which people consume, the priority of needs and the wants they attempt to satisfy, and the manner in which they satisfy them are functions of their culture which temper, mold, and dictate their style of living. Culture is the human-made part of human environment—the sum total of knowledge, beliefs, art, morals, laws, customs, and any other capabilities and habits acquired by humans as members of society. Culture is the "distinctive way of life of a group of people, their complete design for living"—a mosaic of human life.[1]

---

[1] James V. Wertsch, ed., *Culture, Communication, and Cognition* (New York: Cambridge University Press, 1985), p. 2.

Because culture deals with a group's design for living, it is pertinent to the study of marketing, especially foreign marketing. If you consider for a moment the scope of the marketing concept—the satisfaction of consumer needs and wants at a profit—it becomes apparent that the marketer must be a student of culture. What the marketer is constantly dealing with is the culture of the people (the market). When a promotional message is written, symbols recognizable and meaningful to the market (the culture) must be used. When designing a product, the style, uses, and other related marketing activities must be made culturally acceptable (i.e., acceptable to the present society) if they are to be operative and meaningful. In fact, culture is pervasive in all marketing activities—in pricing, promotion, channels of distribution, product, packaging, and styling—and the marketers's efforts actually become a part of the fabric of culture. The marketer's efforts are judged in a cultural context for acceptance, resistance, or rejection. How such efforts interact with a culture determines the degree of success or failure of the marketing effort.

BOX 3–1
Two Cultures Meet—At the Fast-Food Restaurant

McDonald's came to Singapore in 1980; one in the tourist section of Singapore and the other in People's Park, a chaotic bazaar in Chinatown where hundreds of hawkers shovel out Singapore's celebrated street food. Under a haze of charcoal smoke, People's Park is steamy and redolent, ringing with the noise of crashing dishes, sputtering fat, and bawling waiters. Its customers have a special appetite for entrails.

In McDonald's, a customer hears not Chinese music but a Ray Charles song. It is air conditioned, decor by plastic, with everything down to the floor tiles imported from the United States. Through McDonald's plate-glass window, flames are visible leaping under the woks of the Min Ho restaurant 30 feet away. A monkey sits on a table outside the open-ended kitchen eating peanuts. An old man washes dishes in a wooden tub while a youth pulls roasted ducks from a barrel-shaped oven. Baskets of noodles and vegetables are stacked here and there. Eels slither in a tank.

Here, in direct confrontation, are two great philosophies of fast-food. One uses the freezer, the computer, and the business school to manufacture a few simple dishes in less than 100 seconds. The other relies on the markets of Chinatown; the abacus; and a covey of cousins, aunts, and grandmothers to create a profusion of complicated dishes in a minute or two. McDonald's is fast for cook and customer, the other is fast for the customer, but not for the cook.

McDonald's has rhythm; at 9 A.M. spatulas are sharpened, tartar sauce cartridges are sanitized at 2 P.M., and reconstituted onion is mixed at 10 P.M. The grill beeps when it's time for the uniformed cook to flip a hamburger;

BOX 3–1 *(concluded)*

the bun toaster beeps when the buns are done; the fish-fillet cooking computer beeps when the fish is finished.

Across the alley, two cooks stand in fiery heat before six woks, furiously working six orders at once—plunging crabs into boiling oil, ladling chicken stock over steaming greens, pausing only to wipe the sweat off their arms. The menu has everything; flying foxes, furry bats, and, they boast, "If you want it, we will cook it."

The choice between the two fast-food restaurants comes down to a matter of taste. Two Americans from New York sit in the People's Park McDonald's eating Big Macs. Wouldn't they like to try some of this city's famous stall food?

"My wife has a weak stomach," says the husband. The wife responds, "I don't like Chinese food. The smell. I can't stand to see it prepared."

Over at the stall restaurant, two Chinese are having lunch. One has a plate of noodles fried with pig's intestines and the other a bowl of pig's-brain soup.

One comments, "Just a piece of meat between two pieces of bread, that's all a McDonald's is." "Here try some guts." The other savors a spoonful of pig's brains. "I've had a hamburger," he says. "I don't know. If I eat too much Western food, I get sick."

Source: Adapted from Barry Newman, "Singapore Fast-Food: Try Pig Intestines—or Maybe a Big Mac," *The Wall Street Journal*, January 20, 1981, p. 1.

The marketer's frame of reference must be that *markets are not (static), they become (change);* they are not static but change, expand, and contract in response to marketing effort, economic conditions, and other cultural influences. Markets and market behavior are part of a country's culture. One cannot truly understand how markets evolve or how they react to a marketer's effort without appreciating that markets are a result of culture. Markets are dynamic not only in response to economic change but also in response to changes in other aspects of the culture as well. Markets are living phenomena, expanding and contracting in response to cultural change. Markets are the result of the triune interaction of a marketer's efforts, economic conditions, and all other elements of the culture. Marketers are constantly in the process of adjusting their efforts to cultural demands of the market, but they are also acting as agents of change whenever the product or idea being marketed is innovative. Whatever the degree of acceptance in whatever level of culture, the use of something new is the beginning of cultural change and the marketer becomes a change agent.

This chapter's purpose is to heighten the reader's sensitivity to the dynamics of culture. By no means is it a treatise that can be referred to when seeking cultural information about a particular country; rather, it is designed to emphasize the need for study of each country's culture and to point up some of the more relevant aspects that should be examined. The chapter explores briefly the concept of culture related to foreign marketing, while subsequent chapters explore particular features of each of the cultural elements as they affect the marketing process.[2]

CULTURAL KNOWLEDGE

There are two classifications of knowledge about cultures a marketer must possess to cope with a different culture. One is factual knowledge about a culture that is usually obvious and must be learned. Different meanings of color, different tastes, and other traits indigenous to a culture are facts that a marketer can anticipate, study, and absorb. The other is interpretive knowledge, an ability to understand and to appreciate fully the nuances of different cultural traits and patterns. The meaning of time, attitudes toward other people and certain objects, the understanding of one's role in society, and meanings of life illustrate aspects of a culture that can differ considerably from one culture to another and which require more than factual knowledge to be fully appreciated.

Factual Knowledge

Frequently, factual knowledge has meaning as a straightforward fact about a culture but assumes additional significance when interpreted within the context of the culture. For example, that Mexico is 98 percent Roman Catholic is an important bit of factual knowledge. But equally important is what it means to be a Catholic within Mexican culture versus being Catholic in Spain or Italy. Each culture practices Catholicism in slightly different ways. For example, All Soul's Day is an important celebration among some Catholic countries; in Mexico, however, the celebration receives special emphasis that makes it different from most other Catholic countries. The Mexican observance is a unique combination of pagan (mostly Indian influence) and Catholic tradition. On the Day of the Dead, as All Soul's Day is called by many in Mexico, it is believed that the dead return to feast. Hence, many Mexicans visit the graves of their departed, taking the dead's favorite foods to place on the graves for them to enjoy. Prior to All Soul's Day, bakeries pile their shelves with bread shaped like bones and coffins, and candy stores sell sugar skulls and other special treats to commemorate the day. As the souls feast on the food, so do the living celebrants. Although the prayers, candles, and the

---

[2] For an interesting article on changing cultural behavior, see David Kolburn, ''Life's Little Luxuries,'' *Business Tokyo*, November 1987, pp. 26–28.

idea of the spirit of the soul are Catholic, the idea of the dead feasting is very pre-Christian Mexican. Thus, a Catholic in Mexico observes All Soul's Day quite differently from a Catholic in Spain. This interpretative, as well as factual, knowledge about a religion in Mexico is necessary to fully understand Mexican culture.[3]

Interpretative Knowledge

Interpretative knowledge requires a degree of insight that may best be described as a feeling. You must be able to project yourself into the situation. It is the kind of knowledge most dependent on past experience for interpretation and most frequently prone to misinterpretation if one's home-country frame of reference (SRC) is used. Ideally, the foreign marketer should possess both kinds of knowledge about a market. Generally, most facts about a particular culture can be learned by researching published material dealing with that culture. This effort can also transmit a small degree of empathy, but to appreciate the culture fully, it is necessary to live with the people for some time. Because this ideal solution is not practical for a marketer, other solutions are sought. Consultation and cooperation with bilingual nationals with marketing backgrounds is the most effective answer to the problem. This has the further advantage of helping the marketer acquire an increasing degree of empathy through association with people who understand the culture best—natives.

Cultural Sensitivity and Tolerance

The successful foreign marketer must become culturally sensitive—attuned to the nuances of culture so a new culture can be viewed objectively, evaluated, and appreciated. Cultural empathy must be cultivated; perhaps the most important step toward cultural empathy and objectivity is the recognition that cultures are not right or wrong, better or worse; they are simply different. For every amusing, annoying, peculiar, or repulsive cultural trait we find in a country, there is a similarly amusing, annoying, or repulsive trait others see in our culture. We find it peculiar that the Chinese eat dog while they find it peculiar that we buy packaged, processed dog food in supermarkets and keep dogs as pets. We bathe, perfume, and deodorize our bodies in a daily ritual which, in many cultures, is seen as compulsive, and we often become annoyed with those cultures

---

[3] Lawrence Rout, "To Understand Life in Mexico, Consider the Day of the Dead," *The Wall Street Journal*, November 4, 1981, p. 1. For a view of the celebration of All Saints Day see Roger Thurow, "Candlelit Cemeteries Come Alive during All Saints' Day in Poland," *The Wall Street Journal*, November 4, 1985, p. 25.

Youths in Aztec dress—Pyramids, Teotihuacan, Mexico. To understand people you must be aware of their cultural heritage.

less concerned with natural body odor. Just because a culture is different does not make it wrong. A marketer must guard against evaluating another culture in terms of his or her own cultural frame of reference. The more exotic the situation, the more sensitive, tolerant, and flexible one needs to be.

BOX 3–2
Cultures Just Different, Not Right or Wrong, Better or Worse

We must not make value judgments as to whether or not cultural behavior is good or bad, better or worse. There is no cultural right or wrong, just difference.

People around the world feel as strongly about their cultures as we do about ours. Every country thinks its culture is the best and for every foreign peculiarity that amuses us, there is an American peculiarity that amuses others. The Chinese tell American dog jokes, reflecting their amazement that we could feel the way we do about an animal that the Chinese consider better for eating than petting. And we're surprised by the French for taking their dogs to the finest restaurants, where they might be served at the table.

Source: Adapted from Lennie Copeland and Lewis Griggs, *Going International* (New York: Random House, 1985) p. 43.

It is necessary for a marketer to investigate the assumptions on which judgments are based, especially when the frames of reference are strictly from his or her own culture. Every person is a product of his or her own culture and instinctively evaluates foreign cultural patterns from their own perspectives. One major U.S. firm could have avoided a multimillion dollar mistake in Japan had it not relied on an American frame of reference assuming all Japanese homes had ovens in which to bake cakes made from the company's mixes. From the U.S. firm's perspective, it was unnecessary to ask if Japanese had home ovens; in fact, they had few ovens so attempts to market the product failed. As one expert warns, the success or failure of operations abroad depends on an awareness of the fundamental differences in cultures and the willingness to discard as excess baggage cultural elements of one's own culture.[4]

CULTURE AND ITS ELEMENTS

A point of departure in the study of cultural dynamics for assessing world markets is a brief discussion of the concept of culture. To many, the term *culture* implies a value judgment of another's way of life, knowledge, or social manners. A person is either cultured or uncultured, the difference being that the cultured person has acquired a certain ability in specialized fields of knowledge—usually in art, music, or literature plus good manners. Historians often use culture to mean those specific features of a civilization in which one society may have excelled; for example, Greek culture is associated with its art and literature. For the foreign marketer, these meanings of culture are much too narrow. The student of foreign marketing should approach an understanding of culture from the viewpoint of the anthropologist. Every group of people or society has a culture since culture is the entire social heritage of the human race—"the totality of the knowledge and practices, both intellectual and material of society . . . [it] embraces everything from food to dress, from household techniques to industrial techniques, from forms of politeness to mass media, from work rhythms to the learning of familiar rules."[5] Culture exists in New York, London, and Moscow just as it does among the Navajos, the South Sea islanders, or the aborigines of Australia.

It is imperative for foreign marketers to learn to appreciate the intricacies of cultures different from their own if they are to be effective in a foreign

---

[4] For an interesting discussion of the cultural differences between Chinese and Western people and marketing implications, see H. M. Oliver Yau, "Chinese Cultural Values: Their Dimensions and Marketing Implications," *European Journal of Marketing* 22, no. 5 (1988), pp. 44–56.

[5] Colette Guillaumin, "Culture and Cultures," *Cultures* 6, no. 1 (1979), p. 1.

market. A place to begin is to make a careful study of the elements of culture.[6]

Elements of Culture

The anthropologist studying culture as a science must investigate every aspect of a culture if an accurate, total picture is to emerge. To implement this goal, there has evolved a cultural scheme that defines the parts of culture. For the marketer, the same thoroughness is necessary if the marketing consequences of cultural differences within a foreign market are to be accurately assessed.

Culture includes every part of life. The scope of the term *culture* to the anthropologist is illustrated by the elements included within the meaning of the term. They are:

1. Material culture
   Technology
   Economics
2. Social institutions
   Social organization
   Education
   Political structures
3. Humans and the universe
   Belief systems
4. Aesthetics
   Graphic and plastic arts
   Folklore
   Music, drama, and dance
5. Language[7]

In the study of humanity's way of life, the anthropologist finds these five dimensions useful because they encompass all the activities of social heritage that constitute culture. They serve as a framework or pattern for the study and analysis of different cultures. Similarly, foreign marketers may find such a cultural scheme a useful framework in evaluating a marketing plan or in studying the potential of foreign markets.[8] All the elements are instrumental to some extent in the success or failure of a marketing effort because they constitute the environment within which the marketer

---

[6] John A. Reeder, "When West Meets East: Cultural Aspects of Doing Business in Asia," *Business Horizons,* January–February 1987, pp. 69–74.

[7] Melvin Herskovits, *Man and His Works* (New York: Alfred A. Knopf, 1952), p. 634.

[8] Lourdes Arizpe, "Culture in International Development," *Development: Journal of Sid,* no. 1 (1988), pp. 17–19.

operates. Furthermore, because we automatically react to many of these factors in our native culture, we must purposely learn them in another. Finally, these are the factors with which marketing efforts interact and that are basic in the understanding of the character of the marketing system of any society. Because the dimensions of culture influence the marketing process, it is necessary to study the implications of the differences of each one in any analysis of a specific foreign market. A brief examination of these elements illustrates the variety of ways marketing and culture are interwoven.

Material Culture.   Material culture is divided into two parts, technology and economics. Technology includes the techniques used in the creation of material goods; it is the technical know-how possessed by the people of a society. For example, the vast majority of U.S. citizens understand the simple concepts necessary to read gauges but in many countries of the world, this seemingly simple concept is not part of their common culture and is, therefore, a major technical limitation. Take, for example, this description of technology in the African country of Mauritania:

> The simple things are the ones that work best in the Sahel—an improved stove, fencing, planting trees in a row as windbreaks. . . . The advice and actions of aid donors, as well as the policies of Sahelian governments, were heavy with contradiction, poor planning, and mismanagement. . . . Outsiders brought in equipment requiring maintenance far beyond the skills of the native Sahelians. Pumps on wells broke down and were never repaired. Trucks and other vehicles sat abandoned for lack of repairs to fuel pumps and generators. Up until several years ago, there was only one elevator in all Mauritania, and the men who kept it running were in the front ranks of mechanical geniuses in the country.[9]

The level of technology ranges from that just described to the high level found in Germany or Switzerland. A culture's people have a level of technology that is manifest in many ways. Such concepts as preventative maintenance are foreign in many low-technology cultures. In the United States, Japan, Germany, or other countries with high levels of technology, the general population has a broad level of technical understanding that allows them to adapt and learn new technology more easily than in those countries with lower levels of technology. For example, simple repairs, preventative maintenance, and a general understanding of how things work all constitute a high level of technology. In China, one of the burdens of that country's economic growth is providing the general working population with a modest level of mechanical skills; that is, a level of technology.

Economics is the manner in which people employ their capabilities and

---

[9] Adapted from William S. Ellis, "Africa's Sahel—The Stricken Land," *National Geographic,* August 1987, p. 161.

BOX 3–3
Gaining Cultural Awareness in 17 and 18th-Century England—the Grand Tour

Gaining cultural awareness has been a centuries-old need for anyone involved in international relations. The term *Grand Tour*, first applied over three hundred years ago in England, was, by 1706, firmly established as the ideal preparation for soldiers, diplomats, and civil servants. It was seen as the best means of imparting to young men of fortune a modicum of taste and a knowledge of other countries. By the summer of 1785, there were an estimated 40,000 English on the Continent.

The Grand Tourist was expected to conduct a systematic survey of each country's language, history, geography, clothes, food, customs, politics, and laws. In particular, he was to study its most important buildings with their valuable contents, and he was encouraged to collect prints, paintings, drawings, and sculpture. All this could not be achieved in a few weeks and several years were to lapse before some tourists saw England's shores again. Vast sums of money were spent. At times touring was not the relatively secure affair of today. If the Grand Tourist managed to avoid the pirates of Dunkirk, he then had to run a gauntlet of highwaymen on Dutch roads, thieves in Italy and France, and marauding packs of disbanded soldiery everywhere, and the Inquisition in Spain, to say nothing of ravenous wolves and dogs.

He had to be self-contained; he carried with him not only the obligatory sword and pistols but also a box of medicines and other spices and condiments, a means of securing hotel rooms at night, and an overall to protect his clothes while in bed. At the end of these Grand Tours, many returned with as many as eight or nine hundred pieces of baggage. These collections of art, sculpture, and writings can be seen today in many of the mansions throughout the British Isles.

Source: Nigel Sale, *Historic Houses and Gardens of East Anglia* (Norwich, England: Jarrold Colour Publications, 1976), p. 1.

---

the resulting benefits. Included in the subject of economics are the production of goods and services, their distribution, consumption, means of exchange, and the income derived from the creation of utilities.

Material culture affects the level of demand, the quality and types of products demanded, and their functional features, as well as the means of production of these goods and their distribution. The marketing implications of the material culture of a country are obviously many. Electrical appliances will sell in England or France but have few buyers in countries where less than 1 percent of the homes have electricity. Even where electricity is available, economic characteristics, such as the level and distribution of income, may limit the desirability of products. Electric toothbrushes and electric carving knives are totally acceptable in the United States, but, in less-affluent countries, not only are they unattainable and probably unwanted, they would be a spectacular waste because disposable income could be spent more meaningfully on better houses, clothing, or food.[10]

Social Institutions.   Social organization, education, and political structures are concerned with the ways in which people relate to one another, organize their activities to live in harmony with one another, teach acceptable behavior to succeeding generations, and govern themselves. The positions of men and women in society, the family, social classes, group behavior, and age groups are interpreted differently within every culture. Each institution has an effect on marketing because each influences behavior, values, and the overall patterns of life. In cultures where the social organizations result in close-knit family units, for example, it is more effective to aim a promotion campaign at the family unit than at an individual family member.[11] Travel advertising in culturally divided Canada pictures a wife alone for the English audience but a man and wife together for the French segments of the population because the French are traditionally more closely bound by family ties.

The roles and status positions found within a society are influenced by the dictates of social organizations. A woman typically has overlapping family roles in most societies—wife, mother, grandparent, and/or child. Rules for each of these roles vary from culture to culture. Compare a U.S. housewife with a Swiss housewife; the Swiss considers washing dishes or cleaning floors as central to her role and rejects commercial appeals that emphasize saving time and effort in performing these household tasks. In fact, until 1987, a Swiss wife needed her husband's express permission to engage in any social, political, or economic activity. In one instance reported in the press, a female member of parliament was chosen to be the first woman in the seven-member Federal Council that governs Switzerland. However, before she could accept the job, she had to ask her husband's permission and, had he said no, she would have had to decline the position or break the law.[12]

The social institution of education affects literacy which affects marketing promotion. In countries with low literacy rates, conventional forms of printed promotion cannot be used successfully; therefore, more radio and movie advertising are employed in promotional strategy. Certain types

---

[10] "If You Are Queasy, Avoid India's Papers—And This Article," *The Wall Street Journal,* February 8, 1989, p. A1.

[11] For comparison of child rearing in Southeast Asia and its effect on behavior, see Peter Gosling, "As the Twig Is Bent," *Southeast Asia Business,* no. 11 (Fall 1986), pp. 42–45.

[12] "She'll Be President, Husband Allowing," *The Wall Street Journal,* March 19, 1985, p. 36.

BOX 3–4
Two Cultures, Two Barbies

Mattel's Barbie Doll has traveled all over the world. "Barbie Doll didn't do very well in Japan, however, until Mattel gave the manufacturing license to Takara, a Japanese toy and doll specialist. Takara did some marketing research and found that most Japanese disliked Barbie. Her breasts were far too big, her legs were exaggeratedly long. So Takara made the appropriate modifications of Barbie's anatomy, converted her California blue eyes to brown as well, and found instant success in the market.

What sells in America does not necessarily sell in Japan. In India it was a totally different story. Pity poor Barbie in India. She has no sari, and Ken has disappeared. But India loves this little doll just as she is, golden blonde, blue-eyed and leggy, if a bit plastic. A quarter century after she first charmed the hearts of little girls in the United States, Barbie has been selling like chapatis in New Delhi, Bombay, and Calcutta.

This Barbie is a precise copy of her American incarnation, right down to the design of her miniskirt, her lounger and end table set, her diary, and antique telephone.

At 236 rupees (around $18), a Barbie and her lounge furniture cost an equivalent of an average Indian's monthly income.

"Our research showed that nobody wanted an Indian-looking Barbie." Consumers do not want the adaptations popular in other markets where Barbie gets an Afro, a duskier shade, or a tiny kimono. They don't want her cooking plastic curry in an Indian-style townhouse. They don't want a caste mark on her forehead.

But the Indian market does have its peculiar demands. And that is leading to some lonely nights in the bubble bath for Barbie. Specifically, there is no place for a Ken doll in the market. Definitely not. The concept of a boyfriend may be too advanced in India where premarital relationships are frowned on and many wedding couples don't meet until their wedding day.

Source: Adapted from Erdener Kynak, "Global Marketing: Theory and Practice," *Journal of Global Marketing*, Fall–Winter, 1987, p. 18; and Suddt Chathakravarati, "Irate Phone Users Find Some Solace, but Legged Barbie Has No Such Luck," *The Wall Street Journal*, October 21, 1987, p. 28.

of political institutions hinder development of marketing organizations as well as the marketing of politically vulnerable products. Legal structures differ, too; certain business activities permitted in some European countries are forbidden in others.

Humanity and the Universe.   Within this category are religion, belief systems, superstitions, and their related power structures. The impact of religion on the value systems of a society and the effect of value systems on marketing must not be underestimated. Religion has considerable influence on people's habits, their outlooks on life, the products they buy, the way they buy them, even the newspapers they read. In Belgium and the Netherlands, the population is divided between Roman Catholics and Protestants and each group has its own newspapers. Logically enough, media selection can be based on the politics and/or religion of certain target market groups. Acceptance of certain types of food, clothing, and behavior are frequently affected by religion, and such influence can extend to the acceptance or rejection of promotional messages as well.[13] For example, in some countries, if too much attention to bodily functions were featured, advertisements would be judged immoral or improper and the products would be rejected.

Superstition plays a much larger role in a society's belief system in some parts of the world than it does in the United States. What might be considered by an American as mere superstition can be a critical aspect of a belief system in another culture. For example, in parts of Asia, ghosts, fortune-telling, palmistry, head-bump reading, phases of the moon, demons, and soothsayers are all integral parts of certain cultures. Astrologers are routinely called on in Thailand to determine the best location for a structure. The Thais insist that all wood in a new building must come from the same forest to prevent the boards from quarreling with each other. Houses should have an odd number of rooms for luck, and they should be one story because it is unlucky to have another's foot over your head.[14]

One incident reported in Malaysia involved mass hysteria from a fear of evil spirits. Most of the factory's laborers were involved, and production ground to a halt until a "bomoh" was called, a goat sacrificed, and its blood sprinkled on the factory floor; the goat was then roasted and eaten. The next day the hysteria was over and everyone was back at work.

It is easy to make light of superstitions in other cultures, but when doing business in these cultures, it can be an expensive mistake. To make a fuss about being born in the right year under the right phase of the moon and to rely heavily on handwriting and palm-reading experts as in Japan can be worrisome to a Westerner who seldom sees a 13th floor in a brand new building, refuses to walk under a ladder, or worries about the next seven years after breaking a mirror.

Aesthetics.   Closely interwoven with the effect of people and the universe are a culture's aesthetics; that is, the arts, folklore, music, drama, and dance. Aesthetics are of particular interest to the marketer because of

---

[13] Sid Astbury, "Port Rumors Vex Indonesia," *Advertising Age*, February 6, 1989, p. 32.

[14] Urban C. Lehner, "Cultures Clash in Dynamic South Korea as Nation Wrestles with Modernization," *The Asian Wall Street Journal Weekly*, September 12, 1988, p. 2.

their role in interpreting the symbolic meanings of various methods of artistic expression, color, and standards of beauty in each culture. The uniqueness of a culture can be spotted quickly in symbols having distinct meanings.

Without a culturally correct interpretation of a country's aesthetic values, a whole host of marketing problems can arise. Product styling must be aesthetically pleasing to be successful, as must advertisements and package designs. Insensitivity to aesthetic values can offend, create a negative impression, and, in general, render marketing efforts ineffective. Strong symbolic meanings may be overlooked if one is not familiar with a culture's aesthetic values. The Japanese, for example, revere the crane as being very lucky for it is said to live a thousand years; however, the use of the number four should be completely avoided since the word for four, *shi*, is also the Japanese word for death.[15] In the United States, the deer has a positive connotation, even overtones of masculinity when associated with hunting and the outdoors; in Brazil, the animal's name is the slang word for homosexual.

Language.   The importance of understanding the language of a country cannot be overestimated. The successful marketer must achieve expert communication; this requires a thorough understanding of the language as well as the ability to speak it. Advertising copywriters should be concerned less with obvious differences between languages and more with the idiomatic meanings expressed.

A dictionary translation is not the same as an idiomatic interpretation, and seldom will the dictionary translation suffice. A national food processor's familiar "Jolly Green Giant" translated into Arabic as "Intimidating Green Ogre," hardly the image the company sought to portray. Braniff Air Lines' advertising campaign designed to promote its plush leather seats urged customers to "fly on leather"; when translated for its Hispanic and Latin American customers, it told passengers to "fly naked." Possibly more interesting is Eastern Air Lines' "We Earn Our Wings Daily," the translation of which implied that its passengers often ended up dead.[16] Pepsi's familiar "Come Alive with Pepsi," when translated into German, conveyed the idea of coming alive from the grave, again not the intent of the original statement. Schweppes was not pleased with its tonic water translation into Italian: "Il Water" idiomatically means the bathroom. Carelessly translated advertising statements not only lose their intended meaning but also can suggest something very different, obscene, offensive, or just plain ridiculous. For example, in French-speaking countries, the trade-

---

[15] Nancy Hollander, "Cultural Considerations: Judging a Book by Its Cover," *Export Today*, July–August 1988, pp. 47–49.

[16] "Fast Times on Avenida Madison," *Business Week*, pp. 62–67.

BOX 3–5
Its Not the Gift that Counts, but How You Present It

Giving a gift in another country requires careful attention if it is to be done properly. Here are a few suggestions:

Japan:
Do not open a gift in front of a Japanese counterpart unless asked and do not expect the Japanese to open your gift.

Avoid ribbons and bows as part of gift wrapping. Bows as we know them are considered unattractive and ribbon colors can have different meanings.

Do not offer a gift depicting a fox or badger. The fox is the symbol of fertility; the badger, cunning.

Europe:
Avoid red roses and white flowers, even numbers, and the number 13. Do not wrap flowers in paper.

Do not risk the impression of bribery by spending too much on a gift.

Arab World:
Do not give a gift when you first meet someone. It may be interpreted as a bribe.

Do not let it appear that you contrived to present the gift when the recipient is alone. It looks bad unless you know the person well. Give the gift in front of others in less personal relationships.

Latin America:
Do not give a gift until after a somewhat personal relationship has developed unless it is given to express appreciation for hospitality.

Gifts should be given during social encounters, not in the course of business.

Avoid the colors black and purple, both are associated with the Catholic lenten season.

China:
Never make an issue of a gift presentation—publicly or privately.

Gifts should be presented privately, with the exception of collective ceremonial gifts at banquets.

Source: Adapted from "International Business Gift-Giving Customs," available from The Parker Pen Company, n.d.

mark toothpaste brand name, "Cue," was a crude slang expression for derriere. The intent of a major fountain pen company advertising in Latin America suffered in translation when the new ink was promoted to "help prevent unwanted pregnancies." The poster of an engineering company at a Russian trade show did not mean to promise that its oil well completion equipment was dandy for "improving a person's sex life."[17]

Of all the cultural elements a marketer should study to acquire some degree of empathy, language may be one of the most difficult to master, but the most important. Many believe that to appreciate fully the true meaning of a language it is necessary to live with the language for years. Whether or not this is the case, foreign marketers should never take it for granted that they are effectively communicating in another language. Until a marketer can master the vernacular, the aid of a national within the foreign country should be enlisted; even then, the problem of effective communications may still exist. One authority suggests a cultural translator, a person who translates not only among languages but also among different ways of thinking and among different cultures, as a means of overcoming the problem.[18]

Analysis of Elements

In an analysis of a potential market, it is advisable to consider the elements of the culture and evaluate each in light of how it could affect a proposed marketing program. Although some may not have a direct impact, others may be totally involved. As a broad generalization, it could be said that the more complete the marketing involvement or the more unique the product, the more need there is for thorough study of each cultural element. If a company is simply marketing an existing product in an already developed market, the need for studying the total culture is certainly less crucial than for the marketer involved in total marketing—from product development, through promotion, to the final selling.

While the analysis of each cultural element vis-à-vis a marketing program is a practical approach to ensure that each facet of a culture is included, it should not be forgotten that culture is a total picture, not a group of unrelated elements. Culture cannot be divided into separate parts and be fully understood. The facets of culture are intricately intertwined and cannot be viewed singly; they must be considered for their synergistic effects. The ultimate personal motives and interests of people are determined by all the interwoven facets of the culture rather than by the individual parts. While some specific cultural elements have a direct influence on individual marketing efforts and must be viewed individually in terms of their potential or real effect on marketing strategy, the whole of cultural elements is manifested in a broader sense on the basic cultural patterns. In a market the basic consumption patterns, that is, who buys, what they

---

[17] David A. Ricks, *Big Business Blunders* (Homewood, Ill: Dow Jones-Irwin, 1983).

[18] For other cultural blunders, see David A. Ricks, "International Business Blunders: An Update," *Business and Economics Review*, January–March 1988, pp. 11–14.

buy, frequency of purchases, sizes purchased, and so on, are established by cultural values of right and wrong, acceptable and unacceptable. The basic motives for consumption which help define fundamental needs and different forms of decision making have strong cultural underpinnings that are critical knowledge for the marketer. Exhibit 3–1 illustrates one approach to cross-cultural analysis of consumer behavior which should

---

EXHIBIT 3–1   Outline of Cross-cultural Analysis of Consumer Behavior

---

1. *Determine relevant motivations in the culture:*
   What needs are fulfilled with this product in the minds of members of the culture? How are these needs presently fulfilled? Do members of this culture readily recognize these needs?

2. *Determine characteristic behavior patterns:*
   What patterns are characteristic of purchasing behavior? What forms of division of labor exist within the family structure? How frequently are products of this type purchased? What size packages are normally purchased? Do any of these characteristic behaviors conflict with behavior expected for this product? How strongly ingrained are the behavior patterns that conflict with those needed for distribution of this product?

3. *Determine what broad cultural values are relevant to this product:*
   Are there strong values about work, morality, religion, family relations, and so on that relate to this product? Does this product connote attributes that are in conflict with these cultural values? Can conflicts with values be avoided by changing the product? Are there positive values in this culture with which the product can be identified?

4. *Determine characteristic forms of decision making:*
   Do members of the culture display a studied approach to decisions concerning innovations or an impulsive approach? What is the form of the decision process? On what information sources do members of the culture rely? Do members of the culture tend to be rigid or flexible in the acceptance of new ideas? What criteria do they use in evaluating alternatives?

5. *Evaluate promotion methods appropriate to the culture:*
   What role does advertising occupy in the culture? What themes, words, or illustrations are taboo? What language problems exist in present markets that cannot be translated into this culture? What types of salespeople are accepted by members of the culture? Are such salespeople available?

6. *Determine appropriate institutions for this product in the minds of the consumers:*
   What types of retailers and intermediary institutions are available? What services do these institutions offer that are expected by the consumer? What alternatives are available for obtaining services needed for the product but not offered by existing institutions? How are various types of retailers regarded by consumers? Will changes in distribution structure be readily accepted?

SOURCE: James F. Engel, Roger D. Blackwell, and Paul W. Miniard, *Consumer Behavior*, 5th ed. (Hinsdale, Ill.: Dryden Press, 1986), p. 399.

BOX 3–6
Ici on Parle Français

Frequently the conflict between a desire to borrow from another culture and at the same time the natural inclination not to pollute the culture by borrowing from others results in strange responses. France offers a good example of this conflict. On the one hand, the French accept with open arms such U.S. culture as TV's "Dynasty" and "Dallas," France's most watched programs, and the all-American gastronomic delight, the hamburger. At the same time, there is an uneasy feeling that accepting so much from America will somehow dilute the true French culture. Thus, in an attempt to somehow control cultural pollution, laws have been passed to forbid the use of foreign phrases in advertising. For example, the use of the word *hamburger* is forbidden; instead *bifteck hache* is required and for *show biz*, *industrie du spectacle* is the preferred term. While the demand for hamburger and U.S. TV shows cannot be stemmed, perhaps the language can be saved or, at least, that appears to be the logic.

   Source: "The New Refrain: Vive l'Amerique," *Time,* January 14, 1985, p. 40 , November 28, 1980.

identify those aspects of a culture that are critical in developing an effective marketing strategy.

   The different elements of culture have been emphasized but not its dynamic nature; cultures are not static but living processes. That change is constant seems paradoxical in that another important attribute of culture is that it is conservative and resists change. The dynamic character of culture is significant in assessing new markets even though changes occur in the face of resistance. In fact, any change in the currently accepted way of life meets with more initial resistance than acceptance.[19] Since the marketer is usually trying to introduce something completely new or to improve what is already in use, how cultures change and the manner in which resistance to change occurs should be thoroughly understood.

CULTURAL CHANGE

One view of culture sees it as the accumulation of a series of the best solutions to problems faced in common by members of a given society. In other words, culture is the means used in adjusting to the biological,

---

[19] Pierre Billard, "Europe Fights 'Americanization,'" *World Press Review,* October 1985, pp. 34–35.

BOX 3–7
And So, What Does Thanksgiving Mean to You?

If this is what foreigners know about Thanksgiving Day, how wrong
are we about their holidays? A variety of people in other countries were
asked what the Thanksgiving holiday meant in America. Here are some responses:

1. Americans arranged Thanksgiving Day to hail the election of Ronald
   Reagan, and they celebrate it by riding around in cars, putting pumpkins
   on their heads, and feasting on bread and wine.
2. "Indians?" asked a puzzled Hong Kong school teacher. "What do Indians
   have to do with Thanksgiving? Indians eat curry. Whoever heard of curried
   turkey?"
3. An eight-year-old Indian girl replied, "It is when Americans pray to their
   gods because they got so rich."
4. A cafe owner near the Trevi fountain in Rome said, "They are giving
   thanks for winning the Civil War."
5. A radio producer in Paris said, "Thanksgiving is the anniversary of the
   foundation of the federation of the United States."

Source: "Yes, Thanksgiving Day Is for Americans Only," United Press International.

environmental, psychological, and historical components of human existence. There are a variety of ways a society solves the problems created
by its existence. Accident has provided solutions to some problems; invention has solved many other problems; but more commonly, societies have
found answers by looking to other cultures from which they can borrow
ideas. Cultural borrowing is common to all cultures. Take, for example
the ubiquitous blue jeans. This garment has made its way into almost all
cultures. In fact, demand is so great in Eastern European countries that
Levi Strauss & Co. was invited by the East Germans to ship emergency supplies of its blue denim to satisfy the country's Christmas
holiday demand. Although each society has a few truly unique situations facing it, most problems confronting all societies are similar in
nature with circumstances altered for each particular environment and
culture.[20]

---

[20] An interesting article on cultural change among Japan's young is Elizabeth Rubinfien,
"In Japan's Weddings, the Bride's Father Just May Be a Rental," *The Wall Street Journal*,
March 28, 1989, p. A1.

Cultural Borrowing

Cultural borrowing is a responsible effort to borrow those cultural ways seen as helpful in the quest for better solutions to a society's particular problems. If what it does adopt is adapted to local needs, and once the adaptation becomes commonplace, it is passed on as cultural heritage. Thus, cultures unique in their own right are the result, in part, of borrowing from others. Consider, for example, American culture (United States) and the typical U.S. citizen who

> begins breakfast with an orange from the eastern Mediterranean, a cantaloupe from Persia, or perhaps a piece of African watermelon. . . . After his fruit and first coffee he goes on to waffles, cakes made by a Scandinavian technique from wheat domesticated in Asia Minor. Over these he pours maple syrup, invented by the Indians of the Eastern U.S. woodlands. As a side dish he may have the eggs of a species of bird domesticated in Indo-China, or thin strips of the flesh of an animal domesticated in Eastern Asia which have been salted and smoked by a process developed in northern Europe. . . . While smoking, he reads the news of the day, imprinted in characters invented by the ancient Semites upon a material invented in China by a process invented in Germany. As he absorbs the accounts of foreign troubles he will, if he is a good conservative citizen, thank a Hebrew deity in an Indo-European language that he is 100-percent American.[21]

Actually, the American just discussed was correct to assume that he or she was 100 percent American because each of the borrowed cultural facets has been adapted to fit his or her needs, molding them into uniquely American habits, foods, and customs. Americans behave as they do because of the dictates of their culture. Regardless of how or where solutions are found, once a particular pattern of action is judged acceptable by society, it becomes the approved way and is passed on and taught as part of the group's cultural heritage. Cultural heritage is one of the fundamental differences between humans and other animals. Culture is learned; societies pass on to succeeding generations solutions to problems, constantly building on and expanding the culture so that a wide range of behavior is possible. The point is, of course, that although much behavior is borrowed from other cultures, it is combined in a unique manner which becomes typical for a particular society. To the foreign marketer, this similar-but-different feature of cultures has important meaning in gaining cultural empathy.

---

[21] R. Linton, *The Study of Man* (New York: Appleton-Century-Crofts, 1936), p. 327.

Similarities: An Illusion

For the inexperienced marketer, the similar-but-different aspect of culture creates illusions of similarity that usually do not exist. Several nationalities can speak the same language or have similar race and heritage, but it does not follow that similarities exist in other respects; that a product acceptable to one culture will be readily acceptable to the other or that a promotional message that succeeds in one country will succeed in the other. Even though a people start with a common idea or approach, as is the case among English-speaking Americans and the British, cultural borrowing and assimilation to meet individual needs translate over time into quite distinct cultures. A common language does not guarantee a similar interpretation of even a word or phrase. Both the British and the

---

BOX 3–8
Are You Sure You're Not Talking about Beverly Hills?

After traveling 400 miles from Tokyo to one of Japan's most popular hot spa resorts, Mary decides she doesn't like bathing outdoors, especially with male company. She takes one dip in the steaming water, then springs up, clutching the edge of the tub. She glances indignantly at Harry, who sits relaxed, head back in the water, eyes closed.

Mary, an eight-month-old miniature spaniel, and Harry, a two-year-old Chihuahua, are spending a relaxing weekend at the Kinugawa Kokusai Hotel's "pets-only, mixed bathing" outdoor spa. After the bath, they will get a blow-dry, and then chow down on a low-fat dinner of boiled chicken and milk, at the same table as their owners.

Such are the lengths that Japanese pet lovers go to, to pamper their pooches. Pets are a $2 billion a year industry. Goods and services now available to Japan's 12 million dogs and cats include diapers, bikinis, dating services, yoga, and funerals.

After the prized pet passes on, a funeral service cremates the pet right outside the owner's door. "Pet Angel Service" sends a truck with a built-in incinerator and pink altar. The ceremony director instructs tearful owners to place flowers on the altar and a recorded woman's voice says "Thank you for taking care of me up till now."

For those interested in a more symbolic ritual, there is a planetarium-like dome in the basement of a Tokyo pet shop. Mourners gaze upward at a $520,000 computer-generated image of a galaxy, while music blares. A pulsing blob of light in a clear pyramid—meant to represent the pet's soul—shoots a spark of light into a star. "There," says the funeral director, "your pet has gone back to the land of stars."

Source: Adapted from Yumiko Ono, "Pampered Pooches Can Lap Up the Life of Luxury in Japan," *The Wall Street Journal*, September 2, 1988, p. 1.

American speak English, but their cultures are sufficiently different so that a single phrase has different meanings to each and can even be completely misunderstood. In England, one asks for a lift instead of an elevator and an American, when speaking of a bathroom, generally refers to a toilet, while in England a bathroom is a place to take a tub bath. Also, the English "hoover" a carpet whereas Americans vacuum.

Differences run much deeper than language differences, however. The approach to life, values, concepts of acceptable and unacceptable behavior, may all have a common heritage and may appear superficially to be the same. In reality, however, profound differences do exist. Among the Spanish-speaking Latin American countries, the problem becomes even more difficult because the idiom is unique to each country, and national pride tends to cause a mute rejection of any "foreign-Spanish" language. In some cases, an acceptable phrase or word in one country is not only unacceptable in another, it can very well be indecent or vulgar. In Spanish, *coger* is the verb "to catch," but in some countries, it also has a baser meaning.

Furthermore, it should not be assumed that differences exist only among national cultures. A single geopolitical boundary does not necessarily mean a single culture; Canada is divided culturally between its French and English heritages although it is politically one country. Within each culture there are many subcultures that can have marketing significance. A successful marketing strategy among the French Canadians may be certain failure among remaining Canadians.

Asians are frequently grouped together as if there were no cultural distinctions among Japanese, Koreans, and Chinese, to name but a few of the many ethnic groups in the Pacific region. Asia cannot be viewed as a homogeneous entity and the marketer must understand the subtle and not-so-subtle differences among Asian cultures.[22]

Even the United States has many subcultures that today, with mass communications and rapid travel, defy complete homogenization. It would be folly to suggest that the south is in all respects culturally the same as the northeastern or midwestern parts of the United States. The possible existence of more than one culture in a country, as well as subcultures, should be explored before a marketing plan is final.

Marketers must examine each country thoroughly in terms of the proposed products or services and never rely on an often-used axiom that if it sells in one country, it will surely sell in another. Although, as worldwide mass communications and increased economic and social interdependence of countries grow, similarities among countries will increase and common market behavior, wants, and needs will continue to develop. As the process

---

[22] Richard C. King, "Strategies for the Culture Factor," *Export Today*, November–December 1987, pp. 34–36.

occurs, the tendency will be to rely more on apparent similarities when they may not exist. A marketer is wise to remember that a culture borrows and then adapts and customizes to its own needs and idiosyncrasies.

The scope of culture is broad. It covers every aspect of behavior within a country. The task of foreign marketers is to adjust marketing strategies and plans to the needs of the culture in which they plan to operate. Whether innovations develop internally through invention, experimentation, or by accident, or are introduced from outside through a process of borrowing, cultural dynamics always seem to take on a positive and, at the same time, negative aspect.

Resistance to Change

A characteristic of human culture is that change occurs. That people's habits, tastes, styles, behavior, and values are not constant but are continually changing can be verified by reading 20-year-old magazines. This gradual cultural growth does not occur without some resistance. New methods, ideas, and products are held to be suspect before they are accepted, if ever, as the right way or thing.

The degree of resistance to new patterns varies; in some situations new elements are accepted completely and rapidly, and in others, resistance is so strong that acceptance is never forthcoming. Studies show the most important factor in determining what kind and how much of an innovation will be accepted is the degree of interest in the particular subject, as well as how drastically the new will change the old; that is, how disruptive the innovation will be to presently acceptable values and patterns of behavior. Observations indicate that those innovations most readily accepted are those holding the greatest interest within the society and those least disruptive. For example, rapid industrialization in parts of Europe has changed many long-honored attitudes involving time and working women. Today, there is an interest in ways to save time and make life more productive; the leisurely continental life is rapidly disappearing. With this time-consciousness has come the very rapid acceptance of many innovations which might have been resisted by most just a few years ago. Instant foods, laborsaving devices, McDonald's and other fast-food establishments, all supportive of a changing attitude toward work and time, are rapidly gaining acceptance.

Although a variety of innovations are completely and quickly accepted, others meet with firm resistance. India has been engaged in intensive population-control programs for over 20 years. But the process has not worked well and India's population remains among the highest in the world; it is forecasted to exceed 1.1 billion by the year 2000. Why has birth control not been accepted? Most attribute the failure to the nature of Indian culture. Among the influences that help to sustain the high

BOX 3–9
Selling Trivial Pursuit—Worldwide

Trivial Pursuit, originally a Canadian game, became a U.S. fad overnight. It was so successful that the game's inventors concluded that trivia could travel. They hired foreign-based journalists, teachers, and friends between jobs to write new versions in return for royalties. Going international wasn't easy for the game's owners. In the international pursuit of trivia, it pays to be careful. It is best, for example, not to ask the Dutch irreverent questions about their queen although questions about sex are just fine. In Britain, brainteasers about cricket are much preferred and the French love tests on grammar, nightlife, art, and literature as long as the questions are sophisticated. One rule transcends national boundaries: when it comes to religion, never be trivial.

There are 40 area guides, men and women, who write the foreign language editions of Trivial Pursuit. It was obvious from the start that a simple translation of the North American editions, which include special-interest versions of the game, would not work even though some questions could be retained for use in other countries.

Questions on Paris landmarks from the original game were obviously too easy for the French and those on British royalty that might challenge an American seemed insipid to Britons. American baseball questions had to go as did hundreds of questions about American national parks. As one Italian writer commented, "We know nothing of General Custer." Italians do know about the Vatican, spaghetti, vangole, and Milanese sports stars, but the questions must be phrased in a more trivial Italian way. For example, "What did Pope John XXIII tell the journalists who asked him how many people worked at the Vatican?" Answer: "About a half." Britons like to be asked, "In which sport might you find six Chinese men, a maiden, and a night watchman out with a duck?" Answer: "Cricket." And, "What does the Queen's telephonist say when she is putting the Queen Mother through to the Queen?" Answer: "Your Majesty. Her Majesty. Your Majesty." In the German edition, World War II is practically taboo as a subject for questions. "I would not ask, 'On which side did Hitler part his hair?' But, I would ask, 'On which side of the nose was Khrushchev's wart?'" Questions about East Germany are OK, and Italians don't seem to mind being asked about Mussolini. Some black humor is hard to resist; the one Nazi question teetering on the verge of inclusion in a pending German edition: "What ended 988 years before predicted?" Answer: "Hitler's 1,000 Year Reich."

Source: Adapted from Susan Carey, "Nations Have Quirks that Trivial Pursuit Just Can't Ignore," *The Wall Street Journal,* January 8, 1986, p. 1.

birthrate are early marriage, the Hindu religion's emphasis on bearing sons, dependence on children for security in old age, and a low level of education among the rural masses. All are important cultural patterns at variance with the concept of birth control. Acceptance of birth control would mean rejection of too many fundamental cultural concepts. For the Indian people, it is easier and more familiar to reject the new idea.

Japan is experiencing a revolution in the acceptance of Western ways, such as the world's most advanced electronically controlled commuter trains, television receivers, eating habits, and Western dress, but resistance is still strong to the reform of their archaic script.[23] Japan's "simplified" alphabet has 2,304 symbols, making the typewriter so complex that few Japanese have ever mastered it, yet suggestions for reform meet resistance. In fact, an influential Japanese magazine once published two articles denouncing any proposed change and further demanded that the characters which children must memorize as part of their education be increased from 1,850 to 3,000. In another instance, it appeared that modern Japanese were spurning the traditional arranged marriage, but evidence suggests that even though dating habits have changed and young people date freely, when it comes to marriage, they rely on parents to select their spouses.[24] Vigorous reaction to changes that affect cultural character is found in every society; changes that might alter that character most radically usually meet the strongest resistance.[25]

This process of change and the reactions to it are relevant to the marketer, whether operating at home or in a foreign culture, for marketing efforts are more often than not cultural innovations. As one anthropologist points out, "The market survey is but one attempt to study this problem of acceptance or rejection of an internal change . . . [and] in every attempt to introduce, in a foreign society, a new idea, a new technique, a new kind of goods, the question [of acceptance or rejection] must be faced."

Most cultures tend to be ethnocentric; that is, they have intense identification with the known and the familiar of their culture and tend to devalue the foreign and unknown of other cultures. Ethnocentrism complicates the process of cultural assimilation by producing feelings of superiority about one's own culture and, in varying degrees, generates attitudes that other cultures are inferior, barbaric, or at least, peculiar. Ethnocentric feelings generally give way if a new idea is considered necessary or particularly appealing.

---

[23] Shinya Nakata, "The Purchasing Behavior of Japanese Consumers," *Sumitomo Quarterly*, Summer 1988, pp. 12–15.

[24] For an interesting discussion of courting and marriage in Japan, see "Japan, Inc. Becomes a Marriage Broker," *The Wall Street Journal*, January 3, 1985, p. 16.

[25] For a thought-provoking discussion of a seldom discussed side of Japanese attitudes, see Henry Scott Stokes, "Lost Samurai: The Withered Soul of Postwar Japan," *Harper's*, October 1985, pp. 55–63.

Bicycles not automobiles create the rush hour in Canton, China. (Dave Brown/Journalism Services, Inc.)

There are many reasons cultures resist new ideas, techniques, or products. Even when an innovation is needed from the viewpoint of an objective observer, a culture may resist that innovation if the people lack an awareness of the need for it. If there is no perceived need within the culture, then there is no demand. Ideas may be rejected because local environmental conditions preclude functional use and thus useful acceptance, or they may be of such complex nature that they exceed the ability of the culture either to effectively use them or to understand them. Other innovations may be resisted because acceptance would require modification of important values, customs, or beliefs.

Imagine the problems facing the French government in mounting a campaign to persuade the French to drink apple or grape juice, or even water, in place of wine or other alcoholic beverages. Their concern is the high incidence of alcoholism in France, which has the highest per capita consumption of alcohol in the world. The French citizen—man, woman, and child—drinks 16 liters per year, twice U.S. per capita consumption. Success is possible only if values and customs can be changed. Such changes are especially difficult to accomplish in a country where many pour brandy into morning coffee, drink wine with a midmorning snack, and wash

---

BOX 3–10
Why Wouldn't You Buy Fang Fang Lipstick?

With more and more trade between China and the United States, one of
the problems facing the Chinese is the translation into English of Chinese
brand names. When translated, perfectly acceptable brand names to the
Chinese take on a somewhat different connotation. For example, they introduced a new sewing machine for the export market with the brand name
"Typical." When told that it was a bad name because it meant undistin-
guished, they replied that the United States had companies with similar
names, like "Standard Oil." Other brands that didn't translate well were:
"White Elephant Auto Parts," "Pansy Men's Clothing," "Junk Chemicals,"
and "Fang Fang Lipstick."

---

down lunch and dinner with two liters of wine. Add apertifs before meals
and brandy afterward, rare public water fountains, and bottled water that
costs more in a restaurant than beer or wine, and the scope of the problem
begins to emerge. As one Frenchman commented, "We French think tap
water is something to wash your hands in." This is not the first time the
government has attempted to change French drinking customs; a campaign
to get the French to drink milk failed. Perhaps grape juice will succeed
although the farmers and vintners who produce the "vins ordinaires"
will also resist the change, making the task all the more difficult.

All facets of a culture are interrelated, and when the acceptance of a
new idea necessitates the displacement of some other custom, threatens
its sanctity, or conflicts with tradition, the probability of rejection is greater.
Although cultures meet most newness with some resistance or rejection,
that resistance can be overcome. Cultures are dynamic and change occurs
when resistance slowly yields to acceptance so the basis for resistance
becomes unimportant or forgotten. Gradually there comes an awareness
of the need for change, ideas once too complex become less so because
of cultural gains in understanding, or an idea is restructured in a less
complex way, and so on.

Once a need is recognized, even the establishment may be unable to
prevent the acceptance of a new idea. For some ideas, solutions to problems,
or new products, resistance can be overcome in months; for others approval
may come only after decades or centuries.

An understanding of the process of acceptance of innovations is of crucial
importance to the marketer because many of the products or marketing
programs introduced into another culture encounter resistance. The marketer cannot wait centuries or even decades for acceptance but must gain
acceptance within the limits of financial resources and projected profitability
periods. Possible methods and insights are offered by social scientists who

are concerned with the concepts of planned social change. Historically, most cultural borrowing and the resulting change has occurred without a deliberate plan, but, increasingly, changes are occurring in societies as a result of purposeful attempts by some acceptable institution to bring about change; that is, planned change.

PLANNED CULTURAL CHANGE

The first step in bringing about planned change in a society is to determine which cultural factors conflict with an innovation creating resistance to its acceptance. The next step is an effort to change those factors from obstacles to acceptance into stimulants for change. The same deliberate approaches used by the social planner to gain acceptance for hybrid grains, better sanitation methods, improved farming techniques, or protein-rich diets among the peoples of underdeveloped societies can be adopted by marketers to achieve marketing goals.[26]

Marketers have two options when introducing an innovation to a culture. They can wait, or they can cause change. The former requires hopeful waiting for eventual cultural changes that prove their innovations of value to the culture; the latter involves introducing an idea or product and deliberately setting about to overcome resistance and to cause change that accelerates the rate of acceptance.

Obviously not all marketing efforts require change to be accepted. In fact, much successful and highly competitive marketing is accomplished by a *culturally congruent strategy*. Essentially this involves marketing products similar to ones already on the market in a manner as congruent as possible with existing cultural norms thereby minimizing resistance. However, when marketing programs depend on cultural change to be successful, a company may decide to leave acceptance to a *strategy of unplanned* change; that is, introduce a product and hope for the best. Or, a company may employ a *strategy of planned change*; that is, deliberately set out to change those aspects of the culture offering resistance to predetermined marketing goals. With the use of these last two strategies, the marketer becomes a change agent. Just introducing a product whose acceptance requires change begins the process of cultural change. An innovation that has advantages but requires a culture to learn new ways to benefit from these advantages establishes the basis for eventual cultural change. Both a strategy of unplanned change and a strategy of planned change produce cultural change. The fundamental difference is that unplanned change proceeds at its own pace whereas in planned change, the process of change is accelerated by the change agent. While culturally congruent strategy, strategy of un-

---

[26] For an interesting text on change agents, see Gerald Zaltman and Robert Duncan, *Strategies for Planned Change* (New York: John Wiley & Sons, 1979).

BOX 3–11
So You Think Chili Cook-Offs Are Peculiar?

White ants were out of season but caterpillars, locusts, and flying ants substituted nicely in a contest for cooks demonstrating how to feed a family of five for less than a dollar. First prize was a bicycle.

"I couldn't find white ants because there hasn't been enough rain. So I bought *Matsimbi* at the market," said a peasant farmer who produced the most exotic dish. The pièce de resistance was sauteed *Matsimbi*, yellow-and-black caterpillars four inches long, served with the national staple called *sadza*, ground-corn cooked into porridge. For dessert, the winner simmered the thick flesh and large seeds of wild oranges and sieved out the pulp to make a cheap and refreshing drink. She paid 60 cents for the caterpillars and 10 cents to have the corn ground. She picked the wild oranges in the bush.

Source: Associated Press release from Bomboshawa, Zimbabwe, October 1985.

---

planned change, and strategy of planned change are not clearly articulated in international business literature, the three situations occur. The marketer's efforts become part of the fabric of culture, planned or unplanned.

Take, for example, the change in diet that has occurred in Japan since the introduction of milk and bread soon after World War II. Most Japanese, who are predominantly fish eaters, have increased their intake of animal fat and protein to the point that fat and protein exceeded vegetable intake for the first time in 1981. As many McDonald's hamburgers are apt to be eaten in Japan as the traditional rice ball wrapped in edible seaweed. Along with a Westernized diet, many Japanese have become overweight. To counter this, the Japanese are buying low-calorie, low-fat foods to help shed excess weight and are flocking to health studios. All this began when U.S. occupation forces introduced bread, milk, and steak to Japanese culture. The effect on the Japanese was unintentional; nevertheless, change did occur. Had the intent been to introduce a new diet—that is, a strategy of planned change—specific steps could have been taken to identify resistance to dietary change and then to overcome these resistances, thus accelerating the process of change.

Marketing strategy is judged culturally in terms of acceptance, resistance, or rejection. How marketing efforts interact with a culture determine the degree of success or failure, but even failures leave their imprint on a culture. All too often marketers are not aware of the scope of their impact on a host culture.

The foreign marketer can function as a change agent and design a strategy to change certain aspects of a culture to overcome resistance to an innovative product. If a strategy of planned change is implemented, the marketer has some responsibility to determine the consequences of such action.

CONSEQUENCES OF AN INNOVATION

When product diffusion occurs, a process of social change may also occur. One issue frequently addressed concerns the consequences of the changes that happen within a social system as a result of adoption of an innovation. The marketer seeking product acceptance and diffusion may inadvertently bring about change which affects the very fabric of a social system. Consequences of diffusion of an innovation may be *functional or dysfunctional depending on whether the effects on the social system are desirable or undesirable.* In most instances, the marketer's concern is with perceived functional consequences—the positive benefits of product use. Indeed, in most situations, innovative products for which the marketer purposely sets out to gain cultural acceptance have minimal, if any, dysfunctional consequences, but that cannot be taken for granted.

On the surface, it would appear that the introduction of evaporated milk into the diet of babies in underdeveloped countries where protein deficiency is a health problem would have all the functional consequences of better nutrition and health, stronger and faster growth, and so forth. There is evidence, however, that in at least one situation, the dysfunctional consequences far exceeded the benefits. In Nicaragua, as the result of the introduction of evaporated milk, a significant number of babies annually are changed from breast-feeding to bottle feeding before the age of six months. In the United States, with appropriate refrigeration and sanitation standards, a similar pattern exists with no apparent negative consequences; but, in Nicaragua, where sanitation methods are inadequate, a substantial increase in dysentery, diarrhea, and a higher infant mortality rate have resulted. A change from breast-feeding to bottle feeding at an early age without complete understanding of purification by the users has caused dysfunctional consequences. This was the result of two factors: the impurity of the water used with the milk and loss of the natural immunity to childhood disease a mother's milk provides. To counteract this phenomenon, the Nicaraguan Ministry of Public Health and a U.S. agency have launched a program to deal with the control of dysentery and diarrhea in children. Milk marketers have responded positively to this and similar situations by altering their marketing programs substantially in an attempt to offset the dysfunctional consequences of using evaporated milk as a substitute for breast-feeding.[27]

Some may question their responsibility beyond product safety as far as the consequences of being change agents are concerned. The author's position is that the marketer has some responsibility for the results of marketing efforts whether intentional or not. Foreign marketers may cause

---

[27] For one opinion on the growing concern of the consequences of business actions, see Ellen Wallace, "European Business Ponders Its Social Role," *Christian Science Monitor*, May 21, 1987, p. 22.

cultural changes that can create dysfunctional consequences. If proper analysis indicates negative results can be anticipated from the acceptance of an innovation, it is the responsibility of the marketer to design programs not only to gain acceptance for a product but also to eliminate any negative cultural effects.

SUMMARY

A complete and thorough appreciation of the dimensions of culture may well be the single most important gain to a foreign marketer in the preparation of marketing plans and strategies. Marketers can control the product offered to a market—its promotion, price, and eventual distribution methods, but they have only limited control over the cultural environment within which these plans must be implemented. Because they cannot control all the influences on their marketing plans, they must attempt to anticipate the eventual effect of the uncontrollable elements and plan in such a way that these elements do not preclude the achievement of marketing objectives. They can also set about to effect changes that lead to quicker acceptance of their products or marketing programs. Planning marketing strategy in terms of the uncontrollable elements of a market is necessary in a domestic market as well, but when a company is operating internationally, the task is complicated by each new environment influenced by elements unfamiliar and sometimes unrecognizable to the marketer. For these reasons, special effort and study are needed to absorb enough understanding of the foreign culture to cope with the uncontrollable features. Perhaps it is safe to generalize that of all the tools the foreign marketer must have, those that help generate empathy for another culture are the most valuable. Each of the cultural elements is explored in depth in subsequent chapters. Specific attention is given to business customs, legal culture, and political culture in the following chapters.

QUESTIONS

1. Define:

cultural empathy	"cultured"
culture	"similar but different"
ethnocentrism	material culture
design for living	aesthetics
culturally congruent strategy	frame of reference
	cultural translator
strategy of unplanned change	functional innovation
	dysfunctional innovation
strategy of planned change	

2. Which role does the marketer play as a change agent?

3. Discuss the three cultural change strategies a foreign marketer can pursue.

4. "Culture is pervasive in all marketing activities." Discuss.

5. What is the importance of cultural empathy to foreign marketers? How do they acquire cultural empathy?

6. Why should a foreign marketer be concerned with the study of culture?

7. What is the popular definition of culture? What is the viewpoint of cultural anthropologists? What is the importance of the difference?

8. It is stated that members of a society borrow from other cultures to solve problems which they face in common. What does this mean? What is the significance to marketing?

9. "For the inexperienced marketer, the 'similar-but-different' aspect of culture creates an illusion of similarity that usually does not exist." Discuss and give examples.

10. Outline the elements of culture as seen by an anthropologist. How can a marketer use this "cultural scheme"?

11. What is material culture? What are its implications for marketing? Give examples.

12. Social institutions affect marketing in a variety of ways. Discuss, give examples.

13. Discuss the implications and meaning of the statement, "Markets are not, they become."

14. "Markets are the result of the triune interaction of a marketer's efforts, economic conditions, and all other elements of the culture." Comment.

15. What are some particularly troublesome problems caused by language in foreign marketing? Discuss.

16. Suppose you were requested to prepare a cultural analysis for a potential market, what would you do? Outline the steps and comment briefly on each.

17. Cultures are dynamic. How do they change? Are there cases where changes are not resisted but actually preferred? Explain. What is the relevance to marketing?

18. How can resistance to cultural change influence product introduction? Are there any similarities in domestic marketing? Explain, giving examples.

19. Prepare a cultural analysis for a specific country and product.

20. Innovations are described as being either functional or dysfunctional. Explain and give examples of each.

21. Defend the proposition that a MNC has no responsibility for the consequences of an innovation beyond the direct effects of the innovation such as the product's safety, performance, and so forth.

22. Find a product whose introduction into a foreign culture may cause dysfunctional consequences and describe how the consequences might be eliminated and the product still profitably introduced.

CHAPTER
4

Business Customs and Practices in Global Marketing

The trend in globalization of markets is reflected in the growing number of businesses moving toward uniformity in the manner in which they conduct international business. As global businesses interact, executives are exposed to differences in business practices which, in turn, change business behavior, just as cultures change when exposed to the ways of others. Methods that are an improvement over traditional ways are accepted and adapted to fit specific local business needs. Some suggest a world business culture is evolving and, indeed, that may be the case. However, to assume the trend toward similarities means differences in business behavior do not exist still is to court disaster.[1]

A lack of empathy for and knowledge of foreign business practices poses serious problems. Some business people plot their strategies with the idea that other business cultures are similar to their own and, as international business people become more cosmopolitan, similarities do evolve. But the misconception remains that business counterparts in other countries are moved by similar interests, motivations, and goals—that they "are just like us." Even though in some respects they may be just like us, the

---

[1] James S. Mortellaro, "Business across a Cultural Void," *Business Marketing*, February 1989, pp. 62–66.

differences that do exist—if not understood and responded to properly—can lead to frustration, miscommunication, and ultimately, failed business opportunities. A lack of understanding of the differences in business customs can create insurmountable barriers which prevent an otherwise acceptable product from ever reaching the final consumer.

A knowledge of the business culture, management attitudes, and business methods existing in a country and a willingness to accommodate the differences are important to success in an international market. Unless marketers remain flexible in their own attitudes by accepting differences in basic patterns of thinking, local business tempo, religious practices, political structure, and family loyalty, they are hampered, if not prevented, from reaching satisfactory conclusions to business transactions. In such situations, obstacles take many forms, but it is not unusual to have one negotiator's business proposition accepted over another's simply because "that one understands us."

An integral component of cultural environment is the manner in which people transact business. Business customs are as much a cultural element of a society as is the language. In fact, most of the cultural elements discussed in the preceding chapters are manifest in business customs. This chapter focuses on matters more specifically related to the business environment.[2] Besides an analysis of the need for adaptation and the complex problems of marketing in various business cultures, a review of the structural elements, attitudes, and behavior of international business processes is explored.

REQUIRED ADAPTATION

Adaptation is a key concept in international marketing, and willingness to adapt is a crucial attitude. Adaptation, or at least accommodation is required on small matters as well as large ones. In fact, the small, seemingly insignificant situations are often the most crucial. More than tolerance of an alien culture is required; there is a need for affirmative acceptance, that is, open tolerance of the concept "different but equal." Through such affirmative acceptance, adaptation becomes easier because empathy for another's point of view naturally leads to ideas for meeting cultural differences.

As a guide to adaptation, there are ten basic criteria that all who wish to deal with individuals, firms, or authorities in foreign countries should be able to meet. They are (1) open tolerance, (2) flexibility, (3) humility, (4) justice/fairness, (5) adjustability to varying tempos, (6) curiosity/interest,

---

[2] Vaso Knotts, "Cross-Cultural Management: Transformations and Adaptations," *Business Horizons,* January–February 1989, pp. 29–33.

(7) knowledge of the country, (8) liking for others, (9) ability to command respect, and (10) ability to integrate oneself into the environment. In short, add the quality of adaptability to the other qualities of a good executive for a composite of the perfect international marketer.

Degree of Adaptation

Adaptability and adaptation do not require business executives to forsake native ways or change to conform with local customs; rather, executives must be aware of local customs and be willing to accommodate those differences that can cause misunderstanding. Essential to effective adaptation is awareness of one's own culture and the recognition that differences in others can cause anxiety, frustration, and misunderstanding of the hosts' intentions. Also, the differences the host sees in the business executive can create the same potential for misunderstanding. The self-reference criterion (SRC) is especially operative in business customs. If we do not understand our foreign counterpart's customs, we are more likely to evaluate that person's behavior in terms of what is acceptable to us.

The key to adaptation is to remain American but to develop an understanding and willingness to accommodate differences that exist. A successful marketer knows: In Asia it is important to make points without winning arguments; criticism, even if asked for, can cause a host to "lose face."[3] In West Germany it is considered discourteous to use first names unless specifically invited to; always address a person as Herr, Frau, or Fraulein with the last name.[4] In Brazil do not be offended by the Brazilian inclination toward touching during conversation. Such a custom is not a violation of your personal space but the Brazilian way of greeting, emphasizing a point, or as a gesture of goodwill and friendship.[5]

A Chinese, West German, or Brazilian does not expect you to act like one of them. After all, you are not Chinese, German, or Brazilian, but American, and it would be foolish for an American to give up the ways which have contributed so notably to American success. It would be equally foolish for others to give up their native ways. When different cultures meet, open tolerance and a willingness to accommodate each other's differences are necessary. Once a marketer is aware of the possibility of cultural differences and the probable consequences of failure to adapt or accommo-

---

[3] See, for example, John A. Reeder, "When West Meets East: Cultural Aspects of Doing Business in Asia," *Business Horizons*, January–February 1987, pp. 69–74.

[4] Lennie Copeland, and Lewis Griggs, *Going International* (New York: Random House, 1985), p. 234.

[5] Phyllis A. Harrison, *Behaving Brazilian: A Comparison of Brazilian and North American Social Behavior* (Rowley, Mass.: Newbury House Publishing, 1983), p. 20.

BOX 4–1
Jokes Don't Travel Well

Cross-cultural humor has its pitfalls. What is funny to you may not be funny to others. Humor is cultural specific and, thus, rooted in people's shared experiences. Here is an example:

President Jimmy Carter was in Mexico to build bridges and mend fences. On live television President Carter and President Jose Lopez Portillo were giving speeches. In response to a comment by President Portillo, Carter said, "We both have beautiful and interesting wives, and we both run several kilometers every day. In fact, I first acquired my habit of running here in Mexico City. My first running course was from the Palace of Fine Arts to the Majestic Hotel where me and my family were staying. In the midst of the folklorico performance, I discovered that I was afflicted with Montezuma's Revenge." As it turned out, saying that he had Montezuma's Revenge was not funny at all. Editorials in Mexico and U.S. newspapers commented on the inappropriateness of the remark.

Most jokes, even though well intended, don't translate well. Sometimes a translator can help you out. One speaker, in describing his experience, said, "I began my speech with a joke that took me about two minutes to tell. Then my interpreter translated my story. About thirty seconds later the Japanese audience laughed loudly. I continued with my talk which seemed well received," he said, "but at the end, just to make sure, I asked the interpreter, 'How did you translate my joke so quickly?' The interpreter replied, 'Oh I didn't translate your story at all. I didn't understand it. I simply said our foreign speaker has just told a joke so would you all please laugh.'

Some international managers and negotiators argued that interpreters aren't necessary because English is the language of international business. This view is obviously not appreciated in most countries. The Japanese have a joke that goes, "What do you call a person that can speak two languages? Bilingual. What do you call a person that can speak three languages? Trilingual. What do you call a person that can speak one language? American." This may be funny to the Japanese, but is it to you?

Source: Robert T. Moran, "What's Funny to You May Not Be Funny to Other Cultures," *International Management*, July–August 1987, p. 74.

date, the seemingly endless variety of customs must be assessed.[6] Where does one begin, which customs should be absolutely adhered to, which others can be ignored? Fortunately, among the many obvious differences that exist between cultures, only a few are troubling.

---

[6] William W. Locke, "The Fatal Flaw: Hidden Cultural Differences," in David M. Andrus, D. Wayne Norvell, and Shalini V. Gogumalla, *International Marketing Management: A Reader* (Bessemer, Ala.: Colonial Press, 1988), pp. 68–73.

Imperatives, Adiaphora, and Exclusives

Business customs can be grouped into *imperatives*, customs that must be recognized and accommodated; *adiaphora*, customs to which adaptation is optional; and, *exclusives*, customs in which an outsider must not participate. An international marketer must appreciate the nuances of cultural imperative, cultural adiaphora, and cultural exclusives.

Cultural imperative refers to the business customs and expectations that must be met and conformed to if relationships are to be successful. Successful business people know the Chinese word *guan-xi*, the Japanese *nigen kankei*, or the Latin American *compadre*. All, one way or the other, refer to friendship, human relations, or attaining a level of trust. They also know there is no substitute for establishing *friendship* in some cultures before effective business negotiations can begin.

Friendship is not easily established and has to be developed and nurtured over time. Informal discussions, entertaining, mutual friends, contacts, and just spending time with others are ways *guan-xi, nigen kankei, compadre* and other trusting relationships are developed. In those cultures where friendships are a key to success, the businessperson should not slight the time required for their development. Friendship motivates local agents to make more sales and friendship helps establish the right relationship with end users leading to more sales over a longer period.[7] Naturally, after sales service, price, and the product must all be competitive but the marketer who has established *guan-xi, nigen kankei,* or *compadre* has the edge. Establishing friendship may seem a waste of time to a Westerner, but it is an important Asian and Latin American custom. It must be observed or one risks not earning trust and acceptance, the basic cultural prerequisites for developing and retaining effective business relationships.[8]

Cultural adiaphora relates to areas of behavior or to customs that cultural aliens may wish to conform to or participate in but that are not required. It is not particularly important but it is permissible to follow the custom in question; the majority of customs fit into this category. One need not adhere to local dress, greet another man with a kiss (a custom in some countries), or eat foods that disagree with the digestive system (so long as the refusal is gracious). On the other hand, a symbolic attempt to participate in adiaphora is not only acceptable but may also help to establish rapport. It demonstrates that the marketer has studied the culture. A Japanese does not expect a Westerner to bow and to understand the ritual of bowing among Japanese; yet, a symbolic bow indicates interest and

---

[7] "Cultivating Guan-xi (Personal Relationships) with Chinese Partners," *Business Marketing,* January 1987, pp. 62–66.

[8] "Guan-xi Is the Secret to Success for American Companies in Southern Taiwan," *Business America,* November 10, 1986, pp. 12–14.

BOX 4–2
MEISHI—Presenting a Business Card in Japan

In Japan the business card, or *Meishi*, is the executive's trademark. It is both a miniresume and a friendly deity which draws people together. No matter how many times you have talked with a businessperson by phone before you actually meet, business cannot really begin until you formally exchange cards.

The value of a *Meishi* cannot be overemphasized; up to 12 million are exchanged daily and a staggering 4.4 billion annually. As a consequence, there is a certain gamesmanship or etiquette that has evolved.

For example, the following instructions were given to Japanese business-people: First, have plenty of cards on hand when attending a large meeting of Japanese businesspersons. A participant must have at least 40 cards for each meeting. Participants often exchange cards more than once since the single exchange may not make a lasting impression. For a businessperson to make a call or receive a visitor without a card is like a Samurai going off to battle without his sword. It is bad form to greet someone and then, flipping through a card holder, apologize for being out of cards.

The card holder is also a mark of distinction. It should be of good quality and appropriate. A secretary may keep her cards in a handbag, but it makes a bad impression when a young executive pulls a card out of a cheap plastic case used for commuting tickets.

There are a variety of ways to present a card, depending on the giver's personality and style:

Crab style—held out between the index and middle fingers.
Pincer—clamped between the thumb and index finger.
Pointer—offered with the index finger pressed along the edge.
Upside down—the name is facing away from the recipient.
Platter fashion—served in the palm of the hand.

Not only is there a way to present a card, there is also a way of receiving a card. It makes a good impression to receive a card in both hands, especially when the other party is senior in age or status.

Source: Adapted from "Meishi," *Sumitomo Quarterly*, Autumn 1986, p. 3; and Shigeo Hirata, "In the Cards," *Business Tokyo*, October 1987, p. 59

some sensitivity to their culture which is acknowledged as a gesture of goodwill. It may well pave the way to a strong, trusting relationship.

Executives must also recognize certain *cultural exclusives;* that is, customs or behavior from which the foreigner is excluded. By concentrating on the wrong customs, one might ignore the more important cultural impera-tives which must be abided by or the cultural exclusives that must be avoided. Cultural adiaphora are the most visibly different customs and thus more tempting for the foreigner to try to adapt to when, in fact,

> **BOX 4–3**
> **The Eagle, an Exclusive in Mexico**
>
> According to legend, the site of the Aztec city of Tenochtitlán, now Mexico City, was revealed to its founders by an eagle bearing a snake in its claws and alighting on a cactus. That image is now the official seal of the country and appears on its flag. Thus, Mexican authorities were furious to discover their beloved eagle splattered with catsup by an interloper from north of the border: McDonald's.
>
> To commemorate Mexico's Flag Day, two Golden Arches outlets in Mexico City papered their trays with placemats embossed with a representation of the national emblem. Eagle-eyed government agents swooped down and confiscated the disrespectful placemats. A senior partner in McDonald's of Mexico explained, "Our intention was never to give offense. It was to help Mexicans learn about their culture."
>
> It is not always clear what symbols or what behavior patterns in a country are reserved exclusively for natives. In McDonald's case there is no question that the use of the eagle was considered among Mexicans as an exclusive for Mexicans only.
>
> Source: "Don't Drip on Me," *Time*, March 7, 1988, p. 45.

adaptation is unnecessary and, if overdone, unwelcome. A foreign manager needs to be perceptive enough to know when he or she is dealing with an imperative, an adiaphora, or an exclusive and have the adaptability to respond to each. There are not many imperatives or exclusives but most offensive behavior results from not recognizing them. When in doubt, rely on good manners and respect for those with whom you are associating.[9]

RELATIONSHIP BETWEEN CULTURE AND BUSINESS CUSTOMS

The behavior of business and the culture of a nation are inextricably intertwined. Culture not only establishes the criteria for day-to-day behavior but also forms general patterns of attitude and motivation. In the United States, for example, the historical perspective of individualism and "winning the West" today seem to manifest themselves as individual wealth or corporate profit being dominant measures of success. Japan's lack of frontiers and natural resources and its dependence on trade have focused individual and corporate success criteria on uniformity, subordination to the group, and society's ability to maintain high levels of employment.

---

[9] See, for example, Copeland and Griggs, *Going International*, pp. 156–72.

Celebrants leaving religious service, Indonesia. Religion—An important cultural element. (Al Guiteras/Journalism Services, Inc.)

The recent feudal background of southern Europe tends to emphasize maintenance of both individual and corporate power and authority, but blends those feudal concerns with paternalistic concern for minimal welfare for workers and other members of society. Various studies have identified North Americans as individualists; Japanese as consensus-oriented and committed to their group; and central and southern Europeans as elitists and rank conscious (these descriptions, of course, represent stereotyping and illustrate both the best and worst of that process). Spanish sociologist Travessi Anderes contrasts the hierarchical theological influence of the Roman Catholic way of thinking, where profits are considered almost sinful and individualism suspicious, with the Anglo-Saxon Protestant view that profit is the evidence of rational action by the all-important individual.

Executives, at least partially, are captives of their cultural heritages and cannot escape religious backgrounds, language heritage, or political and family ties. Business customs and daily habits are more likely to be those of one's own people. Such ethnocentrism causes problems when: (1) communicating with company headquarters, (2) adapting to local cultures, or (3) keeping up with political and economic change.

MODES OF DOING BUSINESS

Because of the diverse structures, management attitudes, and behavior encountered in international business, there is considerable latitude in methods of doing business. No matter how thoroughly prepared a marketer may be when approaching a foreign market, there is a certain amount of cultural shock when the uninitiated trader encounters actual business situations. In business transactions the international marketer becomes aware of the differences in contact level, communications emphasis, and tempo and formality of foreign businesses.[10] Ethical standards are likely to differ, as will the negotiation emphasis. In most countries, the foreign trader is also likely to encounter a fairly high degree of government involvement.

Sources and Level of Authority

Business size, ownership, and public accountability combine to influence the authority structure of business. The diversity characterizing each element naturally creates a diversity in each authority structure and therefore in the level of contact. Knowledge of authority patterns is essential to an international marketer to consummate successful negotiations in international trade. The international businessperson is confronted with a variety of authority patterns but most are a variation of three typical patterns: top-level management decisions; decentralized decisions; and committee or group decisions.

Top-level management decision making is generally found in those situations where family or close ownership gives absolute control to owners and where businesses are small enough to make such centralized decision making possible. In many European businesses, decision-making authority is guarded jealously by a few at the top who exercise tight centralized

---

[10] For an interesting discussion of differences between U.S. and Japanese negotiations, see Robert March "No-Nos in Negotiating with the Japanese," *Across the Board*, April 1989, pp. 44–51.

decision making. In many developing countries with a semifeudal, land-equals-power heritage, decision-making participation by middle management tends to be de-emphasized; decisions are made by dominant family members.

In Middle Eastern countries, the top man makes all decisions and prefers

---

BOX 4–4
Avoiding a Faux Pas When Visiting Japanese Business People—Adiaphora and Exclusives

So you are going to visit with foreign business representatives. Are there conversational topics that should be avoided? Are there topics that are safe? The answer depends on the culture. Some topics should be avoided (exclusives), that is, not generally discussed between foreigners because of the potential to offend or focus on issues embarrassing to those in the conversation. Other topics are acceptable (adiaphoria), that is, are generally not likely to lead to a confrontation, inadvertently offend, or be considered sensitive. In conversations with others from your own culture, such topics are generally obvious and thus avoided.

A memorandum distributed to U.S. attorneys who were to attend a national food and agricultural exposition in Kansas City offered some tips on making a good impression on Japanese delegates.

Adiaphora (safe topics of conversation):

1. How was your flight to Kansas City? Where are you staying?
2. Questions about Kansas City. Have you visited Kansas City before? Mention noteworthy attractions in Kansas City except as noted in number 9 below. Mention Kansas barbecue beef; ask them about their Kobie beef.
3. Discuss prior visits to the United States.
4. Discuss hobbies and sports.
5. Ask if they have seen the Japanese cherry trees in bloom in Washington, D.C. Comment on their beauty.
6. Discuss any trips you have made in Japan in recent years (avoid references to any pre-1965 visits).

Exclusives (topics to avoid):

1. Avoid a hard-sell of yourself or the firm. Minimize the use of I.
2. Avoid lengthy discussions of U.S./Japan trade problems.
3. Avoid discussions of politics, religion, sex, and military defense matters.
4. Avoid discussions of the role of the emperor in Japanese society.
5. Avoid discussions of the role of women. Do not ask about their wives. Most wives do not work outside the home and most probably will not be accompanying them on this trip.
6. Avoid discussions of vacations. The Japanese view long vacations as frivolous.

BOX 4–4 (*concluded*)

7. Do not mention competitors. Any mention of a competitor's name is one of the most offensive faux pas possible.
8. Avoid discussion of World War II and the Japanese occupation.
9. Avoid discussion of Harry S Truman. Do not suggest that while in Kansas City, they visit the Truman Library, the Truman home, or the Truman Sports Complex.
10. Do not refer to the Japanese or Japan as Orientals or the Orient. If you refer to their part of the world, call it Asia. Do not call the Japanese Asians or Orientals. They are simply Japanese, and they regard themselves as a special people set apart from all others.

Source: "Romancing the Japanese Market," *Harper's*, October 1985, pp. 20–22.

to deal only with other executives with decision-making powers (see Exhibit 4–1.) There, one always does business with an individual per se rather than an office or title.

Companies attempting to do business in the oil-rich markets of the Middle East are admonished to do business through an intermediary who knows the right people. One such intermediary, a Saudi Arabian, calls himself a "connector." His connecting seems to have paid off handsomely; he claims to have expedited sales totaling $11.5 billion with commissions to him of $575 million in six years. Although his earnings are unusual, his role is not. There are hundreds or perhaps thousands of contact makers flourishing in the Middle East and throughout the world.

As businesses grow and professional management develops, there is a shift toward decentralized management decision making. Decentralized decision making allows executives, at various levels of management, authority over their own functions. This mode is typical of large-scale businesses with highly developed management systems such as those found in the United States. A trader in the United States is likely to be dealing with middle management and title or position generally takes precedence over the individual holding the job.

Committee decision making is by group or consensus. Committees may operate on a centralized or decentralized basis, but the concept of committee management implies something quite different from the individualized functioning of top management and decentralized decision-making arrangements just discussed. Because Asian cultures and religions tend to emphasize harmony, it is not surprising that group decision making predominates there. Despite the emphasis on rank and hierarchy in Japanese social structure, business emphasizes group participation, group harmony, and group decision making—but at top management level.

The demands of these three types of authority systems on a marketer's

EXHIBIT 4–1   Differences in Mideastern and Western Management

Managerial Function	Mideastern Stereotype	Western Stereotype
Organizational design	Highly bureaucratic, over-centralized with power and authority at the top. Vague relationships. Ambiguous and unpredictable organization environments.	Less bureaucratic, more delegation of authority. Relatively decentralized structure.
Patterns of decision making	Ad hoc planning, decisions made at the highest level of management. Unwillingness to take high risk inherent in decision making.	Sophisticated planning techniques, modern tools of decision making, elaborate management information systems.
Performance evaluation and control	Informal control mechanisms, routine checks on performance. Lack of vigorous performance evaluation systems.	Fairly advanced control systems focusing on cost reduction and organizational effectiveness.
Personnel policies	Heavy reliance on personal contacts and getting individuals from the "right social origin" to fill major positions.	Sound personnel management policies. Candidate qualifications are usually the basis for selection decisions.
Leadership	Highly authoritarian tone, rigid instructions. Too many management directives.	Less emphasis on leader's personality, considerable weight on leader's style and performance.
Communication	The tone depends on the communicants. Social position, power, and family influence are ever-present factors. Chain of command must be followed rigidly. People relate to each other tightly and specifically. Friendships are intense and binding.	Stress usually on equality and a minimization of differences. People relate to each other loosely and generally. Friendships not intense and binding.
Management methods	Generally old and outdated.	Generally modern and more scientific.

SOURCE: M. K. Badawy, "Styles of Mideastern Managers," *California Management Review*, Spring 1980, p. 57. © 1980 by permission of the Regents.

> **BOX 4–5**
> **The Owner Is Busy**
>
> Except in special circumstances, even when local regulations permit, it is unwise to do business in the Arab market without a local partner or sponsor. He is the key figure to business success in the area and must accordingly be selected with great care. As a general rule, greater success is achieved with members of the established business families who, although they may demand a greater share of profit, have the contacts and experience required.
>
> Special care must taken to build a personal relationship with a partner or sponsor and he must be approached with the respect due to a person who is probably personally operating a multimillion dollar business enterprise. This often explains the long delays reported by businesspersons in seeking interviews; one would not expect an immediate interview with, for example, the chief executive of General Motors: and he is probably poorly paid compared to the profits earned by the successful Arab. Time is at a premium for him and he appreciates a comprehensive presentation of the proposed project. He often makes a decision quicker than thought possible in the West where board meetings and committees are involved.
>
> Source: Ian K. Hungton, "Doing Business in the Arab Middle East." © *World*, Peat, Marwick, Mitchell & Co.

ingenuity and adaptability are evident. In the case of the authoritative and delegated societies, the chief problem would be to identify the individual with authority. In the committee decision setup, it is necessary that every committee member be convinced of the merits of the proposition or product in question. The marketing approaches to each of these situations differ.

Management Objectives and Aspirations

The training and background, (i.e., cultural environment) of managers significantly affect their personal and business outlooks. Society as a whole establishes the social rank or status of management, and cultural background dictates patterns of aspiration and objectives among business people. These cultural influences affect the attitude of managers toward innovation, new products, and conducting business with foreigners. To fully understand another's management style, one must appreciate an individual's objectives and aspirations which are usually reflected in the goals of the business organization and in the practices that prevail within the company. In dealing with foreign business, a marketer must be particularly aware of the varying objectives and aspirations of management.

> **BOX 4–6**
> **Gaining Cultural Empathy the Japanese Way or The Frog in the Pond Doesn't Know about the Ocean**
>
> In the shade of bamboo and pines, at a company school far from their offices, Japanese executives gather to study management. In the morning, they hear lectures about Japanese architecture, American history, and the relationship between the Japanese and nature. In the afternoon, they break for exercise, standing in slippered feet, and stretching to the sky. And in the evenings, over sake and beer, they discuss the day's lessons in a class called "We Are One."
>
> Management training? Very much so. Knowledge of Japanese design and architecture may help a manager tailor products to consumer tastes. Classes such as "We Are One" reinforce Japan's emphasis on teamwork and human relationships as the cornerstones of good management.
>
> Perhaps most important, the classes force students to accept the existence and importance of the greater world within which the company must operate. "We learn about things like American history. I don't think any American business school would teach that," says a general manager of a major Japanese construction machinery firm.
>
> Jazz sessions and wine tastings leaven the menu of required case studies; the roster of guest speakers includes mountain climbers and artists as well as entrepreneurs and economists. "We have a saying in Japan, 'the frog in the pond doesn't know about the ocean.' We don't want our employees to become like that."
>
> Unlike the United States, where advanced business degrees are highly valued, Japanese companies prefer to recruit workers unencumbered by independent management theories. Thus, company schools are preferred for business education. "Companies start with the white cloth and then dye it into the colors they like," says a Japanese professor.
>
> Source: Adapted from Susan Chira, "Japanese Put Own Stamp on Training," *International Herald Tribune (London)*, August 6, 1985, p. 30.

Personal Goals.   In the United States, we emphasize profit or high wages while in other countries security, good personal life, acceptance, status, advancement, or power may be emphasized. Individual goals are highly personal in any country, so one cannot generalize to the extent of saying that managers in any one country always have a specific orientation.

Security and Mobility.   Personal security and job mobility relate directly to basic human motivation and therefore have widespread economic and social implications. The word *security* is somewhat ambiguous and this very ambiguity provides some clues to managerial variation. To some, security means good wages and the training and ability required for moving

BOX 4–7
You Don't Have to Be a Hollywood Star to Wear Dark Glasses

Arabs may even watch the pupils of your eyes to judge your responses to different topics.

A psychologist at the University of Chicago discovered that the pupil is a very sensitive indicator of how people respond to a situation. When you are interested in something, your pupils dilate; if I say something you don't like, they tend to contract. But the Arabs have known about the pupil response for hundreds if not thousands of years. Because people can't control the response of their eyes, which is a dead giveaway, many Arabs wear dark glasses, even indoors.

These are people reading the personal interaction on a second-to-second basis. By watching the pupils, they can respond rapidly to mood changes. That's one of the reasons why they use a closer conversational distance than Americans do. At about five feet, the normal distance between two Americans who are talking, we have a hard time following eye movement. But if you use an Arab distance, about two feet, you can watch the pupil of the eye.

Direct eye contact for an American is difficult to achieve since we are taught in the United States not to stare, not to look at the eyes that carefully. If you stare at someone, it is too intense, too sexy, or too hostile. It also may mean that we are not totally tuned-in to the situation. Maybe we should all wear dark glasses.

---

from company to company within the business hierarchy; for others, it means the security of lifetime positions with their companies; to still others, it means adequate retirement plans and other welfare benefits. In European companies, particularly in the countries that were late in industrializing such as France and Italy, there is a strong paternalistic orientation, and it is assumed that individuals will work for one company for the majority of their lives.

The cultures of Japan and other Eastern countries also incorporate paternalistic notions, and the employer feels full responsibility for guaranteeing employment security to personnel. Japan has no social security or welfare system similar to that of the United States, hence, the Japanese employee relies on the company for protection. When a company assumes the responsibility of lifetime security for its employees, it is not unusual for it to rely on temporary help for peak periods of employment. In Japan, about a third of the employees are maintained on "temporary status"; that is, they have no real job security and are paid significantly less than their fully employed counterparts.

It is safe to say that in most countries, businesses are more involved with the everyday lives of their employees than is the case in the United

States. This is either because of tradition, as in Japan, or law, as in many South American countries.

Personal Life.   For many individuals, a good personal life takes priority over profit, security, or any other goal. In his worldwide study of individual aspirations, David McClelland discovered that the culture of some countries stressed the virtue of a good personal life as being far more important than profit or achievement. The hedonistic outlook of ancient Greece explicitly included work as an undesirable factor that got in the way of the search for pleasure or a good personal life. Perhaps at least part of the standard of living that we enjoy in the United States today can be attributed to the hard-working Protestant ethic from which we derive much of our business heritage.[11]

To the Japanese, personal life is company life. Many Japanese workers regard their work as the most important part of their overall lives. Metaphorically speaking, such workers may even find themselves "working in a dream." The Japanese work ethic—maintenance of a sense of purpose—derives from company loyalty and frequently results in the Japanese employee maintaining identity with the corporation.[12]

Social Acceptance.   In some countries, acceptance by neighbors and fellow workers appears to be a predominant goal within business. The Asian outlook is reflected in the group decision making so important in Japan, and the Japanese place high importance on fitting in with their group. Group identification is so strong in Japan that when a worker is asked what he does for a living, he generally answers by telling you he works for Sumitomo or Mitsubishi or Matsushita rather than that he is a chauffeur, an engineer, or a chemist.

Power.   Although there is some power seeking by business managers throughout the world, power seems to be a more important motivating force in South American countries. In these countries, many business leaders are not only profit-oriented but also use their business positions to become social and political leaders.

Communications Emphasis

Probably no language readily translates into another, because the meanings of words differ widely among languages. Even though it is the basic communication tool of marketers trading in foreign lands, managers, particularly

---

[11] Richard Phalon, "Enjoy, Enjoy," *Forbes*, December 12, 1988, pp. 144–50.

[12] "Corporate Insignia," *Sumitomo Quarterly*, Autumn 1987, p. 3

from the United States, often fail to develop even a basic understanding of a language much less master the linguistic nuances that reveal unspoken attitudes and information.[13] One writer comments that "even a good interpreter doesn't solve the language problem." Besides conceptual differences between them, English and Japanese intertranslate badly by nature and structure. Seemingly similar business terms in English and Japanese often have different meanings. In fact, the Japanese language is so inherently vague that even the well-educated have difficulty communicating clearly among themselves. A communications authority on the Japanese language estimates that the Japanese are able to fully understand each other only about 85 percent of the time. No wonder they do not like their contracts written in the Japanese language. The Japanese prefer English-language contracts where words have specific meanings.[14]

The translation and interpretation of clearly worded statements and common usage is difficult enough, but when slang is added, the task is almost impossible. In an exchange between an American and a Chinese official, the American answered affirmatively to a Chinese proposal with, "It's a great idea, Mr. Li, but who's going to put wheels on it?" The interpreter, not wanting to admit he did not understand and thus lose face, turned to the Chinese official and said, "And now the American has made a proposal regarding the automobile industry."[15] The entire conversation was distracted by a simple misunderstanding of a slang expression.

The best policy when dealing in other languages, even with a skilled interpreter, is to stick to formal language patterns. When a businessperson uses slang phrases, he or she puts the interpreter in the uncomfortable position of guessing at meanings. Foreign language skills are critical in all negotiations, so it is imperative to seek the best possible personnel. Even then, especially in translations involving Asian languages, misunderstandings can occur.

Linguistic communication, no matter how imprecise, is explicit but much business communication depends on implicit messages that are not verbalized. E. T. Hall, professor of anthropology and, for decades, consultant to business and government on intercultural relations says, "In some cultures, messages are explicit; the words carry most of the information. In other cultures . . . less information is contained in the verbal part of the

[13] Leonard Nadler and Zeace Nadler, "Overcoming the Language Barrier," *Training and Development Journal,* June 1987, p. 108–11.

[14] Dyan Machan, "Ici On Parle Bottom-Line Responsibility," *Forbes,* February 8, 1988, p. 139.

[15] Francine C. Brevetti, "Hazards of Skimping on Skilled Chinese Interpreters," *The Asian Wall Street Journal,* June 13, 1988, p. 16.

> **BOX 4–8**
> **The Art of Lying or I Really Can't Say No**
>
> A Japanese professor says that the Japanese lie because they hate to say no and loathe confrontations. Real intentions (*honne* in Japanese) are disguised by a more agreeable smiling appearance (*tatemae*). A Japanese knows when he is being fobbed off with *tatemae*, but a foreigner may be taken in. In Japan, deviousness is an admired skill. A government minister faced with white-lying obstruction by another minister does not throw a tantrum. He understands.
>
> Source: "The Art of Lying," *World Press Review*, November 1985, p. 10.

message since more is in the context.[16] Hall divides cultures into high-context and low-context cultures. Communication in a high-context culture depends heavily on the context or nonverbal aspects of communication, whereas the low-context culture depends more on explicit, verbally expressed communications (see Exhibit 4–2). Managers in general probably function best at a low-context level because they are accustomed to reports, contracts, and other written communications.

In a low-context culture, one gets down to business very quickly. The high-context culture takes considerably longer to conduct business because the people have developed a need to know more about a businessperson before a relationship can develop. They simply do not know how to handle a low-context relationship with other people. Hall suggests that, "in the Middle East, if you aren't willing to take the time to sit down and have coffee with people, you have a problem. You must learn to wait and not be too eager to talk business. You can ask about the family or ask, 'how are you feeling?' but avoid too many personal questions about wives because people are apt to get suspicious. Learn to make what we call chit-chat. If you don't, you can't go to the next step. It's a little bit like a courtship,"—the preliminaries establish a firm foundation for a relationship.[17]

---

[16] E. T. Hall, "Learning the Arabs' Silent Language," *Psychology Today*, August 1979, pp. 45–53. Hall has several books that should be read by everyone involved in international business: *Beyond Culture* (New York: Anchor Press-Doubleday, 1976); *The Hidden Dimension* (New York: Doubleday, 1966); and *The Silent Language* (New York: Doubleday, 1959) and with Mildred R. Hall, *Hidden Differences: Doing Business with the Japanese* (Garden City, N.Y.: Anchor Press/Doubleday, 1987).

[17] For a detailed presentation of the differences in high- and low-context cultures, see Hall and Hall, *Hidden Differences*.

EXHIBIT 4–2   Contextual Background of Various Countries

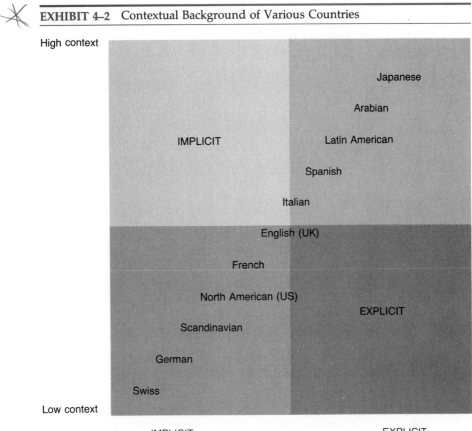

High context

IMPLICIT

Japanese

Arabian

Latin American

Spanish

Italian

English (UK)

French

North American (US)

EXPLICIT

Scandinavian

German

Swiss

Low context

IMPLICIT   EXPLICIT

Note: Patterned after E. T. Hall.

Even in low-context cultures, our communication is heavily dependent on our cultural context. Most of us are not aware of how dependent we are on the context, and, as Hall suggests, "since much of our culture operates outside our awareness, *frequently we don't even know what we know.*"

Probably every business person from America or other relatively low-context countries who has had dealings with counterparts in high-context countries can tell stories about the confusion on both sides because of the different perceptual frameworks of the communication process. It is not enough to master the basic language of a country; the astute marketer must also gain a mastery over the language of business as well as the silent languages of nuance and implication. Communication mastery, then, is not only the mastery of a language but also a mastery of customs. Such mastery can be developed only through long association.

BOX 4–9
You Say You Speak English?

The English speak English, North Americans speak English, but can we communicate? It is difficult unless you understand that in England:

Newspapers are sold at *book stalls*.

The *ground floor* is the main floor, while the first floor is what we call the second, and so on up the building.

An apartment house is a *block of flats*.

You will be putting your clothes not in a closet, but in a cupboard.

A closet usually refers to the W.C. or water closet which is the toilet.

When one of your British friends says she is going to "spend a penny," she is going to the ladies' room.

A *bathing dress* or *bathing costume* is what the British call a bathing suit, and for those who want to go shopping, it is essential to know that a *tunic* is a blouse; a *stud* is a collar button, nothing more; and garters are *suspenders*.

Suspenders are *braces*.

Formality and Tempo.   The breezy informality and haste that seem to characterize the American business relationship appear to be an American exclusive that business people from other countries not only fail to share but also fail to appreciate. This apparent informality, however, does not indicate a lack of commitment to the job. Comparing British and American business managers, an English executive commented about the American manager's compelling involvement in business, "At a cocktail party or a dinner, the American is still on duty."

Even though Northern Europeans seem to have picked up some American attitudes in recent years, do not count on them being "Americanized." As one writer says, "While using first names in business encounters is regarded as an American vice in many countries, nowhere is it found more offensive than in France." Formalities still reign in that country; those who work side by side for years still address one another with formal pronouns.

Haste and impatience are probably the most common mistakes of North Americans attempting to trade in the Middle East. Most Arabs do not like to embark on serious business discussions until they have had two or three opportunities to meet the individual they are dealing with; negotiations are likely to be prolonged. Even though Arabs may make rapid

> **BOX 4–9 (concluded)**
>
> If you want to buy a sweater, you should ask for a *jumper* or a *jersey* as the recognizable item will be marked in British clothing stores.
>
> A *ladder* is not used for climbing but refers to a run in a stocking.
>
> If you *called up* someone, it means to your British friend that you have drafted the person—probably for military service. To *ring someone up* is to telephone them.
>
> You put your packages in the *boot* of your car not the trunk.
>
> When you *table* something, you mean you want to discuss it, not postpone it as in the United States.
>
> *Queer* when used by a British person means only feeling funny.
>
> Any reference by you to an *M.D.* will probably not bring a doctor. The term means *mental deficient* in Britain.
>
> When the desk clerk asks what time you want to be *knocked up* in the morning, he is only referring to your wake-up call.
>
> A billion means a million million (1,000,000,000,000) and not a thousand million as in the United States.
>
> Sources: Adapted from Margaret Zellers, "How to Speak English," *Denver Post*, date unknown; and Copeland and Griggs, *Going International*, pp. 101–2.

decisions once they prepare to do so, they do not like to be rushed and they do not like deadlines. The managing partner of the Kuwait office of Peat, Marwick, Mitchell & Co. says of the "flying-visit" approach of many American businesspeople, "what in the West might be regarded as dynamic activity—the 'I've only got a day here' approach—may well be regarded here as merely rude."

Marketers who expect maximum success must be prepared to deal with foreign executives in ways that are acceptable to the foreigner. The Latin American depends greatly on friendships but establishes these friendships only in the South American way: slowly, over a considerable period of time. A typical Latin American is highly formal until a genuine relationship of respect and friendship is established. Even then the Latin American is slow to get down to business and will not be pushed. In keeping with the culture, *manana* is good enough. One facet of Latin American formality is that there is no involving business in personal life.

The Japanese are more likely to mix business and personal life but are also unharried in business relationships—so unharried, in fact, that Americans or Europeans are likely to lose patience and composure in dealing

---

BOX 4–10
When Being on Time Has Little Meaning—Will Atomic Clocks Help?

When you are in Rome and your watch reads 6:15, clocks on the Via Veneto offer a wide range of times. One says 1:35, another says 12:10, and a third says 6:05, and on the adjacent Via di Porta Pinciana, a clock points to 11:10. Hardly any clock works, says Carlo Ponzi, who is responsible for Rome's clocks. Time is irrelevant in Rome. Appointments aren't made for a certain hour but rather around a certain hour. Events begin at least a half an hour late, some complain they lose time by being punctual. Such quirks help you adjust to living in the Italian capital's time zones. You arrive 45 minutes late for 6:00 meetings and if anyone complains, you can blame the traffic: everyone does. But revolution is brewing. Soon the capital's clocks will be replaced with ones that are technologically avant-garde. Enhanced by quartz-time accuracy, they pick up radio signals from astronomical observatories that ensure they won't go wrong and will adjust automatically to winter or summer time. In effect, they will be linked to atomic clocks. What effect will the new clocks have on punctuality? Probably not much; Romans seem to care very little about their wayward clocks. Ponzi has no illusions about his planned time bomb. Asked if it will make the Romans more punctual, he replies: "Of course not, they will have just one less excuse for being late."

Source: Adapted from "In Italy's Capital, It's Time for a Change in Time," *The Wall Street Journal*, January 2, 1986, p. 8.

---

with the Japanese.[18] Japanese executives are exceedingly courteous but may, in fact, use courtesy and lavish treatment on guests as a future competitive weapon. The patient attitude is derived from indifference to the future, as explained in the following classic statement:

> The Japanese do not have any notion of time because they do not have any notion of self. Indeed, time exists only by reference to a term, or definite extent. But, according to the Japanese conception, there is no term, there is only continuous flow. There is no past, no future: time is what measures an action, or rather time is marked by the change of action.[19] It seems that time is an immense reservoir from which you can help yourself. Time belongs to nobody, it is at the disposal of everybody. Everybody can dip and the supply is inexhaustible. Time is what marks life, chiefly the psychological life, which is run, as it has been surmised, by all the others. To appropriate time would be to make it "mine." To direct time supposes a self. Time is simply the dimension in which

---

[18] Henry Eason, "In Japan, Make Haste Slowly," *Nation's Business*, May 1986, p. 48.

[19] Robert J. Brown, "Swatch vs. the Sundial: A Study in Different Attitudes toward Time," *International Management*, December 1987, p. 80.

Traditional Japanese and Western dress. Business customs often reflect the influence of more than one culture. (Journalism Services, Inc.)

the Japanese live; they do not own it. This is one explanation for not keeping appointments, set with so much eagerness and seriousness. Time possesses them, not the contrary. Since cultural concepts of time are dramatically different among most peoples of the world, U.S. marketers need to make a special effort to understand their foreign hosts' idea of time.[20]

P-time versus M-time.   Many of the differences between U.S. managers and those from other cultures center around the concept of time. North Americans are a more time-bound culture than Middle Eastern and Latin cultures. Our stereotype of those cultures is "they are always late" and their view of us is "you are always prompt." Neither statement is completely true though both contain some truth. What is true, however, is that we are a very time-oriented society—time is money to us—whereas, in other cultures, time is to be savored rather than spent.

Edward Hall defines two time systems in the world—monochronic and polychronic time.[21] M-time (monochronic) typifies most North Americans,

[20] "Maurice Bairy, "Japanese Ways," in *Doing Business in Japan*, ed. R. J. Ballon (Tokyo: Sophia University, 1967), p. 15. Reproduced by permission.

[21] Hall and Hall, *Hidden Differences*, pp. 16–18.

> **BOX 4–11**
> **How to Host Chinese Executives or, No Tossed Salads Please**
>
> Much is written about Americans doing business in China, but how about Chinese guests visiting the United States? How do we make their visits favorable? Some tips:
>
> - The higher the rank of the visitor, the more elaborate the VIP treatment. Not to host them properly according to status and position is a grave insult.
> - Plan their days and evenings; they like receptions, ceremonies, and dinners. The Chinese like to meet people with important titles and to receive recognition of their own status.
> - Hosting in a restaurant is considered more prestigious than being invited to a home.
> - If you serve a normal one- or two-course meal, explain that this is the American pattern of eating. The Chinese are used to 10 to 12 courses of food and may feel slighted by the meager offerings.
> - The Chinese do not care for Western tossed salads or marinated salads. They are not used to large quantities of beef or meat or wine, but they do enjoy scotch and soft drinks.
> - They enjoy sightseeing, taking pictures, and visiting economical discount stores to buy small mementos to take home for family and friends.
>
> Source: Adapted from Mark Magnier, "How to Host Chinese Executives." Reprinted from the *Journal of Commerce*, April 28, 1988, p. 5a.

Swiss, Germans, and Scandinavians. In these Western cultures, they tend to concentrate on one thing at a time. They divide time into small units and are concerned with promptness. M-time is used in a linear way and it is experienced as being almost tangible in that we save time, waste time, bide time, spend time, and lose time. Most low-context cultures operate on M-time.

P-time, or polychronic time, is more dominate in high-context cultures where the completion of a human transaction is emphasized more than holding to schedules. P-time is characterized by the simultaneous occurrence of many things and by "a great involvement with people." P-time allows for relationships to build and context to be absorbed as parts of high-context cultures.

One study comparing perceptions of punctuality in the United States and Brazil found that Brazilian timepieces were less reliable and public clocks less available than in the United States. Researchers also found that Brazilians more often described themselves as late arrivers, allowed greater flexibility in defining early and late, were less concerned about being late, and were more likely to blame external factors for their lateness than were Americans.[22]

The American desire to get straight to the point, to get down to business, and other indications of directness are all manifestations of M-time cultures. The P-time system gives rise to looser time schedules, deeper involvement with individuals and a wait-and-see-what-develops attitude. For example, two Latins conversing would likely opt to be late for their next appointments rather than abruptly terminate the conversation before it came to a natural conclusion.

P-time is characterized by a much looser notion of on time or late. Interruptions are routine; delays to be expected. It is not so much putting things off until *manana* but the concept that human activities are not expected to proceed like clockwork.[23]

Most cultures offer a mix of P-time and M-time behavior. Just as we all know people who are habitually late, some Latin Americans are routinely prompt. Cultures have a tendency, however, to be more P-time or M-time in regard to the role time plays. Some are similar to Japan where appointments are adhered to with the greatest M-time precision but P-time is followed once a meeting begins and with most other human interactions. The Japanese see U.S. businesspeople as too time-bound and driven by schedules and deadlines which thwart the easy development of friendships. The differences between M-time and P-time are reflected in a variety of ways throughout a culture.

When businesspeople from M-time and P-time meet, adjustments on both sides need to be made for a harmonious relationship. Often clarity can be gained by specifying tactfully, for example, whether a meeting is to be on Mexican time or American time. An American who has been working successfully with the Saudis for many years says he has learned to take plenty of things to do when he travels. Others schedule appointments in their offices so they can work until their P-time friend arrives. The important thing for the U.S. manager is to learn to adjust to P-time and avoid the anxiety and frustration that comes from being out of synchronization with local time.

Negotiation Emphasis

All the just discussed differences in business customs and culture come into play more frequently and may be more obvious in the negotiating process than any other aspect of business. The basic elements of business negotiations are the same in any country. They relate to the product, its

---

[22] Harrison, *Behaving Brazilian*, pp. 72–75.

[23] John C. Condon, *Good Neighbors* (Yarmouth, Me: Intercultural Press, Inc., 1985), pp. 65–66.

price and terms, services associated with the product, and, finally, friendship between vendors and customers.[24]

Simply stated, to negotiate is to confer, bargain, or discuss with a view toward reaching an agreement. It is a give-and-take discussion resulting in a mutually beneficial relationship. Most authorities on negotiating in the United States include three steps in the negotiating process: (1) positioning, that is, each party presents its position—its concept of the matter under negotiation, objectives, expectations, and preferences; (2) reflection, evaluation, and persuasion, that is, evaluation of the other's position to determine points of conflict, strengths and weaknesses, differences, and attempts to persuade the other side to accept one's position; and, (3) adjustment, that is, a series of reasonable adjustments by each party until a mutually acceptable agreement is reached or it is determined that a mutually acceptable agreement cannot be reached and negotiations are terminated.[25]

It is important to recognize that attitudes brought to the negotiating table by each individual are affected by many factors unknown to the other individuals and perhaps unrecognized by the individuals themselves. Each person represents the sum total of his or her background and environment. Attitudes, beliefs, schooling, social life, ideas of right and wrong, sensitivities, and economic problems affect his or her attitude toward the negotiation. Each negotiator's understanding and interpretation of what transpires in negotiating sessions is conditioned by his or her cultural background.

Along with sound business information, an important preparation for negotiating is to know as much about those with whom you are negotiating as possible. Equally important is knowing yourself, your prejudices, biases, attitudes, opinions, and beliefs. One standard rule in negotiating is "Know thyself" first, and, second, "Know thy opponent." The SRC of both parties can come to play here if care is not taken. The negotiating task is complicated and the risk of misunderstanding increases when negotiating with someone from another culture. The possibility of offending one another or misinterpreting each other's motives is especially high when one's SRC is the basis for assessing a situation.

Businesspeople must understand the cultural context of negotiations. An authoritative source on cross-cultural negotiating suggests one of the major difficulties in any cross-cultural negotiation is that expectations about the normal process of negotiations differ among cultures.[26] Establishing

---

[24] Neal W. Beckmann, *Negotiations* (Lexington, Mass.: Lexington Books, 1977), pp. 1–3.

[25] "Negotiating in Japan: Playing the Game by Japanese Rules," *Business International*, May 30, 1988, pp. 163–66.

[26] John L. Graham and Yoshihiro Sano, *Smart Bargaining: Doing Business with the Japanese*, 2d ed. (Cambridge, Mass.: Ballinger, 1989). This is an excellent book. Any person involved in international business should be familiar with its contents.

rapport and the degree of emphasis placed on each of the steps in the negotiating process by those involved in a negotiation are two important areas where differences can arise in cross-cultural negotiating.

Instead of a negotiating process with three steps as previously discussed, a fourth step, nontask sounding, is recommended. Cited is the need that exists in some cultures to establish rapport on a personal level before proceeding with actual business discussions. Knowing and trusting a person before doing business are soundly based in the norms of many cultures. Thus, establishing trust, understanding, and a harmonious relationship at the start of negotiations is necessary before a sound business relationship can develop. If a sound personal relationship is not achieved, a successful conclusion is more difficult, if not impossible, to attain. Cross-cultural negotiating, then, includes four steps: (1) nontask sounding or establishing rapport; (2) positioning; (3) reflection, evaluation, and persuasion; and (4) adjustment and agreement.

Obviously, U.S. business people do spend time establishing rapport. The difference is the extent and the process by which rapport is established. A fundamental difference between American culture and those who rely more heavily on personal relationships is one of attitude. An American is more apt to size up the other side within the context of discussing business, while those from other cultures prefer to accomplish this task before business-specific discussion begins.

An American thrives on getting the job done—getting down to business. In some cultures such an approach is considered brash or too aggressive and may create a sense of uncertainty. The Japanese, in fact, feel uncomfortable with Americans' urgency to get down to business *now*. Establishing rapport in many cultures is not achieved through the exchange of information related to the business of the meeting, as would probably be the case among U.S. negotiators, but rather focuses on getting to know the parties as individuals.[27]

Knowing your business associates becomes important in the resolution of future conflict.[28] Most businesspeople enter into agreements with the expectation of long-term relationships. Should difficulties arise in later years, an American has confidence in an ironclad contract to help solve differences and protect the company's rights. In cultures where contracts have less cultural importance than in the United States, the same level of security is reached only through strong personal relationships. These personal relationships serve as the basis for resolving disputes and ensuring continued harmony. Brazilians, for example, "cannot depend on a legal

---

[27] Mark Magnier, "Patience, Dedication, Key to Succeeding in Japan," *Journal of Commerce*, April 8, 1988, p. 5a.

[28] See also, John L. Graham, D. K. Kim, C. Y. Lin, and M. Robinson, "Buyer-Seller Negotiations Around the Pacific Rim," *Journal of Consumer Research*, June 1988, pp. 48–54.

BOX 4–12
When Yes Means No, or Maybe, or I Don't Know, or?

Once, my youngest child asked if we could go to the circus and my reply was "maybe." My older child asked the younger sibling, "What did he say?" The prompt reply, "He said NO!"

All cultures have ways to avoid saying "no" when they really mean "no." After all, arguments can be avoided, hurt feelings postponed, and so on. In some cultures, saying "no" is to be avoided at all costs—to say no is rude, offensive, and disrupts harmony. When the maintenance of long-lasting, stable personal relationships is of utmost importance, as in Japan, to say "no" is to be avoided because of the possible damage to a relationship. As a result, the Japanese have developed numerous euphemisms and paralinguistic behavior to express negation. To the unknowing American, who has been taught not to take "no" for an answer, the unwillingness to say "no" is often misinterpreted to mean that there is hope—the right argument or more forceful persuasion is all that is needed to get a "yes." But don't be mislead—the Japanese listen politely and when the American is finished respond with "hai." Literally it means "yes," but usually it only means, "I hear you." When a Japanese avoids saying yes or no clearly, it most likely means that he or she wishes to say no. Other replies that mean "no":

A vague "no."
Silence.
Leave the room with an apology.
Counter question.
Equivocation—making an excuse.
Yes, but . . .
Apology.
Delaying—"We will write a letter."
Let's think about it a little more.

Sources: Adapted from Mark Zimmerman, *How to Do Business with the Japanese* (New York: Random House, 1985), pp. 105–10; and Don R. McCreary, *Japanese–U.S. Business Negotiations* (New York: Praeger, 1986), pp. 61–66.

system to iron out conflicts, so they depend on personal relationships" as do the Japanese. The first step in the negotiating process, nontask sounding or establishing rapport, is often extended until an acceptable relationship is achieved. If the nontask sounding step is rushed and the parties who are seeking rapport are not satisfied that a positive personal relationship exists, a successful end to the negotiations may never occur. An impatient negotiator can force those involved to hurry past the nontask sounding step only to realize later that a successful solution to the negotiation is doomed.

A second difficulty that can occur in negotiations between cultures involves the emphasis and perceived importance of each of the four steps in the negotiation process. Americans tend to spend the most time on the third and fourth stages of negotiations reflecting a get-down-to-business style whereas others, such as the Japanese, spend more time in stages one and two. Conflict arises on both sides—the Japanese feel Americans are too anxious, and Americans feel too much time is being wasted in small talk.[29] An interesting comparison of Japanese and American business negotiation styles is illustrated in Exhibit 4–3.

Business customs have a vital influence on negotiations and the complexities of cross-cultural negotiations are much too involved to cover adequately here. The best advice when confronted with the prospect of doing business with associates from another culture is to prepare yourself by studying and understanding their negotiation styles as well as your own.[30]

BUSINESS ETHICS

The moral question of what is right and/or appropriate poses many dilemmas for domestic marketers. Even within a country, ethical standards are frequently not defined or always clear.[31] The problem of business ethics is infinitely more complex in the international marketplace because value judgments differ widely among culturally diverse groups. What is commonly accepted as right in one country may be completely unacceptable in another. Giving business gifts of high value, for example, is generally condemned in the United States, but in many countries of the world, gifts are not only accepted but also expected.

For U.S. businesses, bribery became a national issue during the mid-70s with public disclosure of political payoffs to foreign recipients by U.S. firms. At the time, there were no U.S. laws against paying bribes in foreign countries, but for publicly held corporations, the Securities and Exchange Commission's rules required accurate public reporting of all expenditures. Because the payoffs were not properly disclosed, many executives were faced with charges of violating SEC regulations.

The issue took on proportions greater than that of nondisclosure since it focused national attention on the basic question of ethics. The business community's defense was primarily that payoffs were a way of life through-

---

[29] "Negotiating in Japan: Playing the Game by Japanese Rules," *Business International*, May 30, 1988, pp. 163–66.

[30] An important study on cross-cultural negotiations among European countries is John L. Graham, N. Campbell, A. Jolibert, and H. G. Meissner, "Marketing Negotiations in France, Germany, the United Kingdom, and the United States," *Journal of Marketing*, April 1988, pp. 49–62.

[31] Damon Darlin, "Recruit Case Spotlights Fuzzy Japanese Ethics," *The Asian Wall Street Journal*, January 2, 1989, p. 1.

EXHIBIT 4–3 Summary of Japanese and American Business Negotiation Styles

Category	Japanese	Americans
Language	Most Japanese executives understand English, although interpreters are often used.	Americans have less time to formulate answers and observe Japanese nonverbal responses because of a lack of knowledge of Japanese.
Nonverbal behaviors	The Japanese interpersonal communication style includes less eye contact, fewer negative facial expressions, and more periods of silence.	American business people tend to "fill" silent periods with arguments or concessions.
Values	*Tatemae* is important. Vertical buyer/seller relationships with sellers depending on good will of buyers (*amae*) is typical.	Speaking one's mind is important. Buyer/seller relations are horizontal.
Four stages of business negotiations		
1. Nontask sounding	Considerable time and expense devoted to such efforts is the practice in Japan.	Relatively shorter periods are typical.
2. Task-related exchange of information	This is the most important step—high first offers with long explanations and in-depth clarification.	Information is given briefly and directly. "Fair" first offers are more typical.
3. Persuasion	Persuasion is accomplished primarily behind the scenes. Vertical status relations dictate bargaining outcomes.	The most important step: Minds are changed at the negotiation table and aggressive persuasive tactics used.
4. Concessions and agreement	Concessions are made only toward the end of negotiations—a holistic approach to decision making. Progress is difficult to measure for Americans.	Concessions and commitments are made throughout—a sequential approach to decision making.

SOURCE: John L. Graham, "A Hidden Cause of America's Trade Deficit with Japan," *Columbia Journal of World Business*, Fall 1981, p. 14.

BOX 4–13
The Hard Sell—Or Just Being Adaptable?

Anyone trying to sell in the international market will at some time be heard to complain that sales are too small and/or that it is too hard to sell certain kinds of products. Consider for example:

Russian consumer goods in the USA
Chilean wine in France
U.S. steel to the EC
Yugoslavian autos to the Japanese
Indian mangos to the Hawaiians
Jamaican bauxite anywhere in the world.

All these products are being sold throughout the world in an innovative way. The Jamaicans are successfully selling their bauxite to Europeans. They have no illusions about the difficulty of their task but with innovative financing, connections, and a willingness to barter, they are finding success.

In the same vein, a Brazilian firm, the largest farm-equipment manufacturer in South America, has tripled its sales to the depressed U.S. farm equipment market in the last three years. Prices are a factor to some degree, but more important, the firm made a commitment to the market at stable prices, not for equipment, but for parts. While U.S. farmers prefer U.S. equipment, they could care less as to the origin of the replacement parts. The Brazilian firm realized this and has profited as a result.

What all this points out is that international trade continues to grow as long as there are creative people to convert hard sales to opportunities and to try something new. The Japanese proverb notes: *"Merchants and Folding Screens Must Bend in Order to Stand."*

Source: John Freivalds, "The Hard Sell," *Foreign Trade*, August–September, 1985, p. 1.

out the world; if you didn't pay bribes, you didn't do business. Business persons illustrated their dilemma with the case of an aircraft company: What would you do when a $10 million payoff would assure a $200 million sale? In answering that question, it must be kept in mind that your foreign competition would be willing and able to pay and you would lose the sale and a $20 million profit. The difficulty with such a position is that even in those countries where bribery is practiced, it is not sanctioned. The statement, "Bribery is not condoned anywhere in the world, even in countries where it is a general practice," seems to reflect the consensus of those familiar with international business. The decision to pay a bribe creates a major conflict between what is ethical and proper and what is profitable and sometimes necessary for business. International payoffs are perceived by those involved as a means of accomplishing business goals.

The major complaint is that other countries do not have legislation as restrictive as the United States. It is especially interesting that in Italy and West Germany, where bribes are legal and can be deducted as a business expense, the laws clearly state they apply only to transactions outside the country.

The definition of bribery can range from the relatively innocuous payment of a few cents to a minor official or business manager to expedite the processing of papers or the loading of a truck, to the extreme of paying millions of dollars to a head of state to ensure a company preferential treatment.

Bribery—Variations on a Theme

Bribery must be defined because there appear to be limitless variations. First, the difference between bribery and extortion must be established. Voluntarily offered payments by someone seeking unlawful advantage is bribery; payments extracted under duress by someone in authority from a person seeking only what they are lawfully entitled to is extortion.[32] An example of extortion would be a finance minister of a country demanding heavy payments under the threat that millions of dollars of investment would be confiscated.

Another variation of bribery to consider is the difference between lubrication and subornation.[33] *Lubrication* involves a relatively small sum of cash, gift, or service made to a low-ranking official in a country where such offerings are not prohibited by law; the purpose of such a gift is to facilitate or expedite the normal, lawful performance of a duty by that official (a practice common in many countries of the world). *Subornation*, on the other hand, generally involves large sums of money, frequently not properly accounted for, designed to entice an official to commit an illegal act on behalf of the one paying the bribe. Lubrication payments accompany requests for a person to do a job more rapidly or more efficiently, whereas subornation is a request for officials to turn their heads, not do their jobs, or to break the law.

A third type of payment that can appear to be a bribe but may not be, is an agent's fee. When a businessperson is uncertain of a country's rules and regulations, an agent may be hired to represent the company in that country. This would be similar to hiring an agent in the United States;

---

[32] For an interesting account of apparent extortion by the president of a country, see Edward T. Pound, "Marcos Papers Said to Show Kickbacks," *The Wall Street Journal*, May 19, 1986, p. 30.

[33] Hans Schollhammer, "Ethics in an International Business Context," *MSU Business Topics*, Spring 1977, pp. 53–63.

for example, an attorney to file an appeal for a variance in a building code on the basis that the attorney will do a more efficient and thorough job than someone unfamiliar with such procedures.

Similar services may be requested of an agent in a foreign country when problems occur. However, if a part of that agent's fees is used to pay bribes, the intermediary's fees are being used unlawfully. Under U.S. law, an official who knows of an agent's intention to bribe may risk penalties of up to five years in jail. The Foreign Corrupt Practices Act (FCPA), prohibits U.S. businesses from paying bribes openly or using middlemen as conduits for a bribe when the U.S. official knows that part of the middle-man's payment will be used as a bribe.[34] There are many middlemen (attorneys, agents, distributors, and so forth) who function simply as conduits for illegal payments. The process is further complicated by legal codes that vary from country to country; what is illegal in one country is winked at in another and legal in a third. Further complicating the attitude toward bribery are the many contradictions that exist between proper behavior in the United States and improper behavior in another culture. For example, consider the following situations:

> Do you want to do business with the Defense Department? Perhaps you should hire a high-powered Washington lobbyist. The fees are outrageous, but the good ones have a reputation of getting things done.
>
> In Kuwait and Malaysia, there are similar agents available for hire. They, too, will charge you a king's ransom to help you sell your products.

The difference between these two situations in the minds of many is that under the FCPA law, you could go to jail for hiring the lobbyist in Kuwait or Malaysia, but you would not go to jail for hiring a lobbyist in Washington. The Foreign Corrupt Practices Act, a law passed in 1977, makes it illegal for an official to pay a fee to foreign government officials whether directly or through an agent when the official knows that the agent intends to use part of the payment for bribery. In no way should the reader assume that the Washington lobbyist is paying bribes. The point is that in both cases business is done through third parties; in one case, an illegal payment to an official is necessary to close a deal; in the other, personal influence is helpful in closing a deal.[35]

It is obvious from this discussion that the answer to the question of bribery is not an unqualified one. It is easy to generalize about the ethics of political payoffs and other types of payments; it is much more difficult to make the decision to withhold payment of money when the consequences

---

[34] See Chapter 6 for a detailed discussion of the Foreign Corrupt Practices Act.

[35] For an interesting view of ethical issues, see Verne E. Henderson, "Consulting on Ethical Issues," *Management Notes,* Arthur D. Little Management Education Institute, Fall 1986, pp. 4–19.

of not making the payment may affect the company's ability to do business profitably or at all. With the variety of ethical standards and levels of morality which exist in different cultures, the dilemma of ethics and pragmatism that faces international business cannot be resolved until more countries decide to deal effectively with the issue. Perhaps the U.S. stand on making bribery illegal is a step in that direction.

SUMMARY

Business customs and practices in different world markets vary so much that it is difficult to make valid generalizations about them; it is even difficult to classify the different kinds of business behavior that are encountered from nation to nation. The only safe generalizations are that business persons working in another country must be sensitive to the business environment and must be willing to adapt when necessary. Unfortunately, it is not always easy to know when such adaptation is necessary; in some instances adaptation is optional and, in others, it is actually undesirable. Understanding the culture you are entering is the only sound basis for planning.

Business behavior is derived in large part from the basic cultural environment in which the business operates; and as such, is subject to the extreme diversity encountered among various cultures and subcultures. Environmental considerations significantly affect the attitudes, behavior, and outlook of foreign business people. Motivational patterns of such business people depend in part on their personal backgrounds, their business positions, sources of authority, and their own personalities.

Varying motivational patterns inevitably affect methods of doing business in different countries. Marketers in some countries thrive on competition, while in others they do all possible to eliminate it. The authoritarian, centralized decision-making orientation in some nations contrasts sharply with democratic decentralization in others. International variation characterizes contact level, ethical orientation, negotiation outlook, and nearly every part of doing business. The foreign marketer can take no phase of business behavior for granted.

The new breed of international businessperson who has emerged in recent years appears to have a heightened sensitivity to cultural variations. Sensitivity, however, is not enough; the international trader must be constantly alert and prepared to adapt when necessary. One must always realize that, no matter how long in a country, the outsider is not a native; in many countries that person may always be treated as an outsider. Finally, one must avoid the critical mistake of assuming that a knowledge of one culture will provide acceptability in another.

QUESTIONS

1. Define:

cultural imperative	P-time
cultural adiaphora	M-time
cultural exclusive	subornation
stereotyping	eclectic borrowing
nontask sounding	silent language
FCPA	national character

2. "More than tolerance of an alien culture is required; there is a need for affirmative acceptance of the concept, 'different but equal.' " Elaborate.

3. "We should also bear in mind that in today's business-oriented world economy, the cultures themselves are being significantly affected by business activities and business practices." Comment.

4. "In dealing with foreign businesses, the marketer must be particularly aware of the varying objectives and aspirations of management." Explain.

5. Suggest ways in which persons might prepare themselves to handle unique business customs that may be encountered in a trip abroad.

6. Business customs and national customs are closely interrelated. In which ways would one expect the two areas to coincide and in which ways would they show differences? How could such areas of similarity and difference be identified?

7. Identify both local and foreign examples of cultural imperatives, adiaphora, and exclusives. Be prepared to explain why each example fits into the category you have selected.

8. Contrast the authority roles of top management in different societies. How do the different views of authority affect marketing activities?

9. Do the same for aspirational patterns.

10. What effects on business customs might be anticipated from the recent rapid increases in the level of international business activity?

11. Interview some foreign students to determine the types of cultural shock they encountered when they first came to your country.

12. Differentiate between:

Private ownership and family ownership	Decentralized and committee decision making

13. In which ways does the size of a customer's business affect business behavior?

14. Identify and explain five main patterns of business ownership.

15. Compare three decision-making authority patterns in international business.

16. Explore the various ways in which business customs can affect the structure of competition.

17. Why is it important that the business executive be alert to the significance of business customs?

18. Suggest some cautions that an individual from a high-context culture should take when dealing with someone from a low-context culture. Do the same from low- to high-context situations.

19. Political payoffs are a problem; how would you react if you faced the prospect of paying a bribe? If you knew that by not paying you would not be able to complete a $10-million contract?

20. Differentiate among the following:
    subornation   extortion
    lubrication   bribery

21. Why is nontask sounding important in cross-cultural negotiating? Discuss.

22. Discuss the steps in cross-cultural negotiations.

23. How does the emphasis on the four steps of negotiating differ between American and Japanese business people? Discuss.

24. Distinguish between P-time and M-time.

25. Discuss how a P-time person reacts differently from an M-time person in keeping an appointment.

READING

The following article is a classic. It was first published some 30 years ago, but these truths, like most cultural concepts, change slowly. Although some specifics may vary, the underlying message of sensitivity to nonverbal communication is timeless. Equally timeless seems to be the individual's capacity for blundering and insensitivity when dealing with foreign cultures.

The Silent Language in Overseas Business[*]

Edward T. Hall

With few exceptions, Americans are relative newcomers on the international business scene. Today, as in Mark Twain's time, we are all too often "innocents abroad," in an era when naïveté and blundering in foreign business dealings may have serious political repercussions.

When the American executive travels abroad to do business, he is frequently shocked to discover to what extent the many variables of foreign behavior and custom complicate his efforts. Although the American has recognized, certainly, that even the man next door has many minor traits which make him somewhat peculiar, for some reason he has failed to appreciate how different foreign business-men and their practices will seem to him.

He should understand that the various peoples around the world have worked out and integrated into their subconscious literally thousands of behavior patterns that they take for granted in each other.[†] Then, when the stranger enters, and behaves differently from the local norm, he often quite unintentionally insults, annoys, or amuses the native with whom he is attempting to do business. For example:

In the United States, a corporation executive knows what is meant when a client lets a month go by before replying to a business proposal. On the other hand, he senses an eagerness to do business if he is immediately ushered into the client's office. In both instances, he is reacting to subtle cues in the timing of interaction, cues which he depends on to chart his course of action.

Abroad, however, all this changes. The American executive learns that the Latin Americans are casual about time and that if he waits an hour in the outer office before seeing the Deputy Minister of Finance, it does not necessarily mean he is not getting anywhere. There people are so important that nobody can bear to tear himself away; because of the resultant interruptions and conversational detours, everybody is constantly getting behind. What the American does not know is the point at which the waiting becomes significant.

In another instance, after traveling 7,000 miles an American walks into the office of a highly recommended Arab businessman on whom he will have to depend completely. What he sees does not breed confidence. The office is reached by walking through a suspicious-looking coffeehouse in an old, dilapidated building situated in a crowded non-European section of town. The elevator, rising from dark, smelly corridors, is rickety and equally foul. When he gets to the office itself, he is shocked to find it small, crowded, and confused. Papers are stacked all over the desk and table tops—even scattered on the floor in irregular piles.

The Arab merchant he has come to see had met him at the airport the night before and sent his driver to the hotel this morning to pick him up. But now, after the American's rush, the Arab is tied up with something else. Even when they finally start talking business, there are constant interruptions. If the American

[†]For details see my book, *The Silent Language* (New York: Doubleday & Co., 1959).

is at all sensitive to his environment, everything around him signals, "What am I getting into?"

Before leaving home he was told that things would be different, but how different? The hotel is modern enough. The shops in the new part of town have many more American and European trade goods than he had anticipated. His first impression was that doing business in the Middle East would not present any new problems. Now he is beginning to have doubts. One minute everything looks familiar and he is on firm ground; the next, familiar landmarks are gone. His greatest problem is that so much assails his senses all at once that he does not know where to start looking for something that will tell him where he stands. He needs a frame of reference—a way of sorting out what is significant and relevant.

That is why it is so important for American businessmen to have a real understanding of the various social, cultural, and economic differences they will face when they attempt to do business in foreign countries. To help give some frame of reference, this article will map out a few areas of human activity that have largely been unstudied.

The topics I will discuss are certainly not presented as the last word on the subject, but they have proved to be highly reliable points at which to begin to gain an understanding of foreign cultures. While additional research will undoubtedly turn up other items just as relevant, at present I think the businessman can do well to begin by appreciating cultural differences in matters concerning the language of time, of space, of material possessions, of friendship patterns, and of agreements.

Language of Time

Everywhere in the world people use time to communicate with each other. There are different languages of time just as there are different spoken languages. The unspoken languages are informal; yet the rules governing their interpretation are surprisingly *ironbound.* In the United States, a delay in answering a communication can result from a large volume of business causing the request to be postponed until the backlog is cleared away, from poor organization, or possibly from technical complexity requiring deep analysis. But if the person awaiting the answer or decision rules out these reasons, then the delay means to him that the matter has low priority on the part of the other person—lack of interest. On the other hand, a similar delay in a foreign country may mean something altogether different. Thus:

In Ethiopia, the time required for a decision is directly proportional to its importance. This is so much the case that low-level bureaucrats there have a way of trying to elevate the prestige of their work by taking a long time to make up their minds. (Americans in that part of the world are innocently prone to downgrade their work in the local people's eyes by trying to speed things up).

In the Arab East, time does not generally include schedules as Americans know and use them. The time required to get something accomplished depends on the relationship. More important people get fast service from less important people, and conversely. Close relatives take absolute priority; nonrelatives are kept waiting.

In the United States, giving a person a deadline is a way of indicating the degree of urgency or relative importance of the work. But in the Middle East, the American runs into a cultural trap the minute he opens his mouth. "Mr. Aziz will have to make up his mind in a hurry because my board meets next week and I have to have an answer by then," is taken as indicating the American is overly demanding and is exerting undue pressure. "I am going to Damascus tomorrow morning and will have to have my car tonight," is a sure way to get the mechanic to stop work, because to give another person a deadline in this part of the world is to be rude, pushy, and demanding.

An Arab's evasiveness as to when something is going to happen does not mean he does not want to do business; it only means he is avoiding unpleasantness and is side-stepping possible commitments which he takes more seriously than we do. For example:

The Arabs themselves at times find it impossible to communicate even to each other that some processes cannot be hurried, and are controlled by built-in schedules. This is obvious enough to the Westerner but not to the Arab. A highly placed official in Baghdad precipitated a bitter family dispute because his nephew, a biochemist, could not speed up the complete analysis of the uncle's blood. He accused the nephew of putting other less important people before him and of not caring. Nothing could sway the uncle, who could not grasp the fact that there is such a thing as an *inherent* schedule.

With us, the more important an event is, the further ahead we schedule it, which is why we find it insulting to be asked to a party at the last minute. In planning future events with Arabs, it pays to hold the lead time to a week or less because other factors may intervene or take precedence.

Again, time spent waiting in an American's outer office is a sure indicator of what one person thinks of another or how important he feels the other's business to be. This is so much the case that most Americans cannot help getting angry after waiting 30 minutes; one may even feel such a delay is an insult, and will walk out. In Latin America, on the other hand, one learns that it does not mean anything to wait in an outer office. An American businessman with years of experience in Mexico once told me, "You know, I have spent two hours cooling my heels in an executive's outer office. It took me a long time to learn to keep my blood pressure down. Even now, I find it hard to convince myself they are still interested when they keep me waiting."

The Japanese handle time in ways which are almost inexplicable to the Western European and particularly the American. A delay of years with them does not mean that they have lost interest. It only means that they are building up to something. They have learned that Americans are vulnerable to long waits. One of them expressed it, "You Americans have one terrible weakness. If we make you wait long enough, you will agree to anything."

Indians of South Asia have an elastic view of time as compared to our own. Delays do not, therefore, have the same meaning to them. Nor does indefiniteness in pinpointing appointments mean that they are evasive. Two Americans meeting will say, "We should get together sometime," thereby setting a low priority on the meeting. The Indian who says, "Come over and see me, see me anytime," means just that.

Americans make a place at the table which may or may not mean a place made in the heart. But when the Indian makes a place in his time, it is yours to fill in every sense of the word if you realize that by so doing you have crossed a boundary and are now friends with him. The point of all this is that time communicates just as surely as do words and that the vocabulary of time is different around the world. The principle to be remembered is that time has different meanings in each country.

Language of Space

Like time, the language of space is different wherever one goes. The American businessman, familiar with the pattern of American corporate life, has no difficulty in appraising the relative importance of someone else, simply by noting the size of his office in relation to other offices around him:

Our pattern calls for the president or the chairman of the board to have the biggest office. The executive vice president will have the next largest, and so on down the line until you end up in the "bull pen." More important offices are usually located at the corners of buildings and on the upper floors. Executive suites will be on the top floor. The relative rank of vice presidents will be reflected in where they are placed along "executive row."

The French, on the other hand, are much more likely to lay out space as a network of connecting points of influence, activity, or interest. The French supervisor will ordinarily be found in the middle of his subordinates where he can control them.

Americans who are crowded will often feel that their status in the organization is suffering. As one would expect in the Arab world, the location of an office and its size constitute a poor index of the importance of the man who occupies it. What we experience as crowded, the Arab will often regard as spacious. The same is true in Spanish cultures. A Latin American official illustrated the Spanish view of this point while showing me around a plant. Opening the door to an 18-by-20-foot office in which seventeen clerks and their desks were placed, he said, "See, we have nice spacious offices. Lots of space for everyone."

The American will look at a Japanese room and remark how bare it is. Similarly, the Japanese look at our rooms and comment, "How bare!" Furniture in the American home tends to be placed along the walls (around the edge). Japanese have their charcoal pit where the family gathers in the *middle* of the room. The top floor of Japanese department stores is not reserved for the chief executive—it is the bargain roof!

In the Middle East and Latin America, the businessman is likely to feel left out in time and overcrowded in space. People get too close to him, lay their hands on him, and generally crowd his physical being. In Scandinavia and Germany, he feels more at home, but at the same time the people are a little cold and distant. It is space itself that conveys this feeling.

In the United States, because of our tendency to zone activities, nearness carries rights of familiarity so that the neighbor can borrow material possessions and invade time. This is not true in England. Propinquity entitles you to nothing. American Air Force personnel stationed there complain because they have to make an appointment for their children to play with the neighbor's child next door.

Conversation distance between two people is learned early in life by copying elders. Its controlling patterns operate almost totally unconsciously. In the United States, in contrast to many foreign countries, men avoid excessive touching. Regular business is conducted at distances such as 5 feet to 8 feet; highly personal business, 18 inches to 3 feet—not 2 or 3 inches.

In the United States, it is perfectly possible for an experienced executive to schedule the steps of negotiation in time and space so that most people feel comfortable about what is happening. Business transactions progress in stages from across the desk to beside the desk, to the coffee table, then on to the conference table, the luncheon table, or the golf course, or even into the home—all according to a complex set of hidden rules which we obey instinctively.

Even in the United States, however, an executive may slip when he moves into new and unfamiliar realms, when dealing with a new group, doing business with a new company, or moving to a new place in the industrial hierarchy. In a new country the danger is magnified. For example, in India it is considered improper to discuss business in the home on social occasions. One never invites a business acquaintance to the home for the purpose of furthering business aims. That would be a violation of sacred hospitality rules.

Language of Things

Americans are often contrasted with the rest of the world in terms of material possessions. We are accused of being materialistic, gadget crazy. And, as a matter of fact, we have developed material things for some very interesting reasons. Lacking a fixed class system and having an extremely mobile population, Americans have become highly sensitive to how others make use of material possessions. We use everything from clothes to houses as a highly evolved and complex means of ascertaining each other's status. Ours is a rapidly shifting system in which both styles and people move up or down. For example:

The Cadillac ad men feel that not only is it natural but quite insightful of them to show a picture of a Cadillac and a well-turned out gentleman in his early fifties opening the door. The caption underneath reads, "You already know a great deal about this man."

Following this same pattern, the head of a big union spends in excess of $100,000 furnishing his office so that the president of United States Steel cannot look down on him. Good materials, large space, and the proper surroundings signify that the people who occupy the premises are solid citizens, that they are dependable and successful.

The French, English, and the Germans have entirely different ways of using their material possessions. What stands for the height of dependability and respectability with the English would be old-fashioned and backward to us. The Japanese take pride in often inexpensive but tasteful arrangements that are used to produce the proper emotional setting.

Middle East businessmen look for something else—family, connections, friendship. They do not use the furnishings of their office as part of their status system; nor do they expect to impress a client by these means or to fool a banker into lending more money than he should. They like good things, too, but feel that they, as persons, should be known and not judged solely by what the public sees.

One of the most common criticisms of American relations abroad, both commercial and governmental, is that we usually think in terms of material things. "Money talks," says the American, who goes on talking the language of money abroad, in the belief that money talks the *same* language all over the world. A common practice in the United States is to try to buy loyalty with high salaries. In foreign countries, this maneuver almost never works, for money and material possessions stand for something different there than they do in America.

Language of Friendship

The American finds his friends next door and among those with whom he works. It has been noted that we take people up quickly and drop them just as quickly. Occasionally a friendship formed during schooldays will persist, but this is rare. For us there are few well-defined rules governing the obligations of friendship. It is difficult to say at which point our friendship gives way to business opportunism or pressure from above. In this we differ from many other people in the world. As a general rule, in foreign countries friendships are not formed as quickly as in the United States but go much deeper, last longer, and involve real obligations. For example:

It is important to stress that in the Middle East and Latin America your "friends" will not let you down. The fact that they personally are feeling the pinch is never an excuse for failing their friends. They are supposed to look out for your interests.

Friends and family around the world represent a sort of social insurance that would be difficult to find in the United States. We do not use our friends to help us out in disaster as much as we do as a means of getting ahead—or, at least, of getting the job done. The United States systems work by means of a series of closely tabulated favors and obligations carefully doled out where they will do the most good. And the least that we expect in exchange for a favor is gratitude.

The opposite is the case in India, where the friend's role is to "sense" a person's need and do something about it. The idea of reciprocity as we know it is unheard of. An American in India will have difficulty if he attempts to follow American friendship patterns. He gains nothing by extending himself in behalf of others, least of all gratitude, because the Indian assumes that what he does for others he does for the good of his own psyche. He will find it impossible to make friends quickly and is unlikely to allow sufficient time for friendships to ripen. He will also note that as he gets to know people better they may become more critical of him, a fact that he finds hard to take. What he does not know is that one sign of friendship is speaking one's mind.

Language of Agreements

While it is important for American businessmen abroad to understand the symbolic meanings of friendship rules, time, space, and material possessions, it is just as important for executives to know the rules for negotiating agreements in various countries. Even if they cannot be expected to know the details of each nation's commercial legal practices, just the awareness of and the expectation of the existence of differences will eliminate much complication.

Actually, no society can exist on a high commercial level without a highly developed working base on which agreements can rest. This base may be one or a combination of three types:

1. Rules that are spelled out technically as law or regulation.

2. Moral practices mutually agreed on and taught to the young as a set of principles.

3. Informal customs to which everyone conforms without being able to state the exact rules.

Some societies favor one, some another. Ours, particularly in the business world, lays heavy emphasis on the first variety. Few Americans will conduct any business nowadays without some written agreement or contract.

Varying from culture to culture will be the circumstances under which such rules apply. Americans consider that negotiations have more or less ceased when the contract is signed. With the Greeks, on the other hand, the contract is seen as a sort of way station on the route to negotiation that will cease only when the work is completed. The contract is nothing more than a charter for serious negotiations. In the Arab world, once a man's word is given in a particular kind of way, it is just as binding, if not more so, than most of our written contracts. The written contract, therefore, violates the Moslem's sensitivities and reflects on his honor. Unfortunately, the situation is now so hopelessly confused that neither system can be counted on to prevail consistently.

Informal patterns and unstated agreements often lead to untold difficulty in the cross-cultural situation. Take the case of the before-and-after patterns where there is a wide discrepancy between the American's expectations and those of the Arab:

In the United States, when you engage a specialist such as a lawyer or a doctor, require any standard service, or even take a taxi, you make several assumptions: (a) the charge will be fair; (b) it will be in proportion to the services rendered; and (c) it will bear a close relationship to the "going rate."

You wait until after the services are performed before asking what the tab will be. If the charge is too high in light of the above assumptions, you feel you have been cheated. You can complain, or can say nothing, pay up, and take your business elsewhere the next time.

As one would expect in the Middle East, basic differences emerge which lead to difficulty if not understood. For instance, when taking a cab in Beirut it is well to know the going rate as a point around which to bargain and for settling the charge, which must be fixed before engaging the cab.

If you have not fixed the rate *in advance*, there is a complete change and an entirely different set of rules will apply. According to these rules, the going rate plays no part whatsoever. The whole relationship is altered. The sky is the limit, and the customer has no kick coming. I have seen taxi drivers shouting at the top of their lungs, waving their arms, following a red-faced American with his head pulled down between his shoulders, demanding for a two-pound ride 10 Lebanese pounds which the American eventually had to pay.

It is difficult for the American to accommodate his frame of reference to the fact that what constitutes one thing to him, namely, a taxi ride, is to the Arab two very different operations involving two different sets of relationships and two sets of rules. The crucial factor is whether the bargaining is done at the beginning or end of the ride! As a matter of fact, you cannot bargain at the end. What the driver asks for he is entitled to!

One of the greatest difficulties Americans have abroad stems from the fact that we often think we have a commitment when we do not. The second complication on this same topic is the other side of the coin, that is when others think we have agreed to things that we have not. Our own failure to recognize binding obligations, plus our custom of setting organizational goals ahead of everything else, has put us in hot water far too often.

People sometimes do not keep agreements with us because we do not keep agreements with them. As a general rule, the American treats the agreement as something he may eventually have to break. Here are two examples:

Once while I was visiting an American post in Latin America, the Ambassador sent the Spanish version of a trade treaty down to his language officer with instructions to write in some "weasel words." To his dismay, he was told, "There are no weasel words in Spanish."

A personnel officer of a large corporation in Iran made an agreement with local employees that American employees would not receive preferential treatment. When the first American employee arrived, it was learned quickly that in the United States he had been covered by a variety of health plans that were not available to Iranians. And this led to immediate protests from the Iranians which were never satisfied. The personnel officer never really grasped the fact that he had violated an ironbound contract.

Certainly, this is the most important generalization to be drawn by American businessmen from this discussion of agreements: there are many times when we are vulnerable *even when judged by our own standards.* Many instances of actual sharp practices by American companies are well known abroad and are giving American business a bad name. The cure of such questionable behavior is simple. The companies concerned usually have it within their power to discharge offenders and to foster within their organization an atmosphere in which only honesty and fairness can thrive.

But the cure for ignorance of the social and legal rules which underlie business agreements is not so easy. This is because:

The subject is complex.

Little research has been conducted to determine the culturally different concepts of what is an agreement.

The people of each country think that their own code is the only one, and that everything else is dishonest.

Each code is different from our own; and the farther away one is traveling from Western Europe, the greater the difference is.

But the little that has already been learned about this subject indicates that as a problem it is not insoluble and will yield to research. Since it is probably one of the more relevant and immediately applicable areas of interest to modern business, it would certainly be advisable for companies with large foreign operations to sponsor some serious research in this vital field.

CHAPTER

5

Political Environment—A Special Problem

Permission to conduct business in any country is controlled by the government of the host country. The host government can and does control and restrict a foreign company's activities by encouraging and offering support, or by discouraging and banning, its activities—depending on the pleasure of the host.[1] Companies cannot pursue business interests as independent entities; each independent state has the recognized right to either grant or withhold permission to do business within its political boundaries. Further, the existence, functions, and ultimate success of foreign companies are tied to the overall goals of the economic, political, and social system of the host.[2] Thus, the political environment of a country is a special problem of immense importance for the international marketer.

National environments differ widely. Some countries are economically developed, some underdeveloped; some countries have an abundance of resources, others few or none; some countries are content with the status

---

[1] Shlomo Maital, ''Managing Risk: Were You Framed?'' *Across the Board,* January–February 1989, pp. 60–61.

[2] Humayun Akhter and Robert F. Lusch, ''Political Risk: A Structural Analysis,'' in *Advances in International Marketing,* vol. 2, S. Tamer Cavusgil, ed. (Greenwich, Conn.: JAI Press, 1987 pp. 81–101).

quo, others seek drastic changes to improve their relative positions in the world community. The important facts are that a government reacts to its environment by initiating and pursuing policies deemed necessary to solve the problems created by its particular environment. Reflected in its policies and attitudes toward foreign business are a government's ideas of how best to promote the national interest considering its own resources and political philosophy. The government is an integral part of every foreign business activity—a silent partner who has nearly total control. Therefore, the host country judges every business venture by standards as variable as there are nations, political philosophies, degrees of economic development, and environmental factors affecting human needs and wants.

Before a company commits itself to operating within a country, it should pay particular attention to assessing the dominant political climate. Such an assessment should cover at least the following: (1) the current form of government; (2) current political party system; (3) stability and permanency of government policy, and (4) the risks or encouragements to foreign business from political activity. The fundamental policies and attitudes toward foreign business differ drastically as a result of the different directions taken to achieve national goals. Errors are made by foreign marketers in not appraising correctly, if at all, the significance of the role of government in the success of their business ventures. This chapter explores some of the more salient political considerations in assessing world markets.

GOVERNMENT AND POLITICAL PARTY SYSTEMS

A realistic appraisal of the political climate begins with a thorough study of the basic structures of the government. Which type of government does the country have? Is it primarily a democracy, dictatorship, monarchy, socialist or communist state, or does it have tendencies toward any one of these forms of government? By knowing the form of government, the observer gains some insight into the impending business-political environment.[3]

Types of Governments

The type of government is determined by the procedure through which the citizens form and express their will and the extent to which their will controls the composition and policy of government.

---

[3] For an interesting approach suggesting that insights into a country's fundamental ideology can shed light on relationships between government and business, see George C. Lodge and Erza F. Vogel, *Ideology and National Competitiveness* (Boston: Harvard Business School Press, 1987), p. 164.

Most states can be classified as having either parliamentary or absolutist governments. Parliamentary governments can be further subdivided into either republics or constitutional monarchies, and absolutist governments include absolute monarchies and dictatorships.

Under parliamentary government, the people are consulted from time to time to ascertain the majority will; therefore, policies of the government theoretically reflect the majority opinion of the population. Under absolutist government, the ruling regime dictates government policy without specifically consulting the needs and wants of the people.

Political Parties

Under parliamentary government, public opinion is influential in forming policies, and political parties crystalize public opinion around definite legislative and administrative measures. The marketer should be concerned with political parties because of their influence on the attitudes of government toward business; and, more specifically, because they are instrumental in determining the role foreign business plays in the economy.

Political party systems within a government can be divided into four types: two-party system, multiparty system, single-party system, and dominant one-party system. The two-party system consists of two strong parties that typically succeed each other in control of the government. The two parties have different philosophies, and when they succeed one another, the impact on business and government relations can be more drastic on foreign firms than on domestic firms.

The government of Great Britain is a good example. An interview with a spokesperson for the British Labour Party pointed up some fundamental differences in attitude toward foreign business between the Labour and Conservative parties. The discussion involved how the Labour Party proposed to handle problems with the balance-of-payments when that party was in power and the spokesperson was the prime minister. It was made known there would be no hesitation about placing temporary limitations on imports of manufactured goods plus extending exchange controls if necessary. This approach was in direct contrast to the philosophy of the then-ruling Conservative Party which had been gradually liberalizing the controls on foreign businesses for several years. Later, when the Labour Party came to power, there were indeed some significant changes made; among them, a 15 percent surcharge on imports. When the Labour Party was later replaced by the Conservative Party, a liberalization of controls was instituted and the Conservative Party's policies were again put into place. A foreign firm doing business in Great Britain during this period see-sawed between the liberal trade policies of the Conservatives and the restrictive ones of the Liberals.

In the multiparty system, no single party is strong enough to gain control

Gate to Forbidden City on Tiananmen Square, Beijing, before student protests, 1989.

of the government, and the government is formed through coalitions of various parties. In contrast to the two-party system, the multiparty system has frequent and continuous changes of coalition parties because the longevity of each coalition is dependent on the cooperation of each one of its partners—all of whom are typically at philosophical odds. The multiparty system with all its problems is best typified by Italy. Other modern governments with multiparty systems are Germany, France, Belgium, the Netherlands, and Israel.

In contrast to the multiparty system is the single-party system with one political party dominating to such an extent that no other party has any chance of gaining control in an election. Such situations generally exist in young countries early in the development of a parliamentary system. For a young country in the throes of economic development, a sound one-party system may provide a degree of stability and continuity of development that is necessary, or at least helpful, for steady growth. As they advance, significant changes occur and a multiparty system generally develops.

Mexico is a good example of a single-party system that has existed for more than 40 years but is now beginning to develop into a multiparty system. The PRI Party (revolutionary party) was virtually guaranteed election in every national vote. Open elections were held, but the opposing PAN Party's slate of candidates seldom pulled more than a nominal vote. In the 1988 election, however, the PRI won by only a thin margin. The closeness of the election may be the first sign of a true multiparty system developing in Mexico.[4]

The fourth political party system is a very different version of the one-party political system. In this type, the dominant party actively quells any true opposition and inhibits the growth and normal operations of other parties. Instead of the dominant party having the support of the majority in open and free competition, all competition is severely restricted, and the controlling party gets support because no effective opposition is permitted. Instead of the dominant one-party system developing into a two-party or multiparty system, it generally becomes a dictatorship.

Knowledge of Party Philosophy

Particularly important to the marketer is the prevailing attitude of government toward foreign business. Equally important are all the basic philosophies of parties represented within the country since any one of them might come into power and alter prevailing attitudes. In addition, it is important to study the overall political system of a country because each party's philosophy can have a significant effect on the general direction of the political policies of government. It is not unusual for a winning party in an election to consider the policies advocated by the other party or parties. In a multiparty system, this is usually more the case than the exception since a coalition is required to form a government.

Even in a single-party system, as in Mexico where the PRI Party is always in power, attitudes and philosophies of the other parties remain important. As the opposing party's support becomes stronger, it has more influence in the government. The growing strength of the PAN Party in the early 1960s resulted in electoral reform that assured it some representation in the Chamber of Deputies. Having almost won the presidency in 1988 means even more influence for this opposition group.

Changes in political parties that head a government generally mean changes in policy so that the operation of foreign businesses is more in line with the philosophy of the new party. In some instances, a new political party at the helm can result in action as severe as nationalization or expropriation of an industry; however, the usual results are tightening or lessening of various government controls. For example, the change in the Chinese government that occurred with the death of Chairman Mao Zedong has resulted in easing the restrictions on foreign business to the extent that wholly owned branches and subsidiaries are allowed in the country.[5]

---

[4] Stephen Baker, "For Solinas, The Real Campaign Is Just Beginning," *Business Week,* December 5, 1988, p. 48.

[5] "China's Reformers Say: Let a Thousand Businesses Bloom," *Business Week,* April 11, 1988, pp. 70–71.

The Permanency of Government Policy

Foreign businesses find the stability or instability of government policies within the countries in which they operate of prime importance. One misconception about changes of government whether by elections, power struggles, or coups is that the change always means high levels of political risk. What is much more important than change of government is the continuity of the set of rules or code of behavior that continues regardless of which government is in power. Frequent changes in governments do not necessarily mean changes in the climate for foreign business. At the same time, radical changes in policies may occur in the most stable governments.

India is an example of a country where there have been changes in policies within a government that has been in power for over 30 years. Over the last 10 years, its policies have vacillated from hostility toward foreign investment to encouragement. In 1978 India put such strong demands on foreign businesses that Coca-Cola and IBM chose to leave the market rather than comply with new policies. Ten years later, attitudes changed and not only did India welcome the importing of a variety of technical goods but the government also encouraged investment and development.[6]

Jamaica is another high-risk country; there, a new set of rules comes with every change in government. Italy, on the other hand, has had the most changes in governments of any European country, yet the foreign investment climate has been favorable because the rules have stayed the same. In Ghana, one of the poorest countries in Africa, military and civilian governments with ideologies on the left, the right, and the center have come and gone over the last 20 years. Yet Kaiser Aluminum has not only survived it all but has also made handsome profits.[7]

The most drastic changes in government-business relations can occur when one type of government is replaced by another. In many instances retaliation against "exploiting foreign businesses" becomes the political battle cry of the reform government. Thus, foreign business becomes the scapegoat against which both social discontent and national frustrations can be aimed. Once in power, the reform government can create a public image of success and spectacular accomplishment by instituting reprisals against foreign "exploiters."

Although government policy may alter the potential of some markets, foreign investments can be profitable under any government as long as

---

[6] "PepsiCo's Entry into India Has Lessons for Other MNCs," *Business ASIA*, October 3, 1988, pp. 319–20.

[7] Seamus G. Connolly, *Finding, Entering, and Succeeding in a Foreign Market* (Englewood Cliffs, N.J.: Prentice-Hall, 1987), p. 274.

there is some long-run predictability and stability. For example, PepsiCo operated profitably in the Soviet Union under one of the more extreme political systems. Years before the era of *glasnost* and *perestroika* in the late 1980s, PepsiCo established a very profitable business with Russia by exchanging Pepsi syrup for Russian vodka.

Unpredictable and drastic shifts in government tactics deter investments. The rise to power of an unpredictable, radical reform government seems to worsen the investment climate and to deter new investment more than government corruption or hostility toward specific foreign businesses.[8] It was reported that billions of dollars' worth of business decisions were halted as multinational executives in France and around the world tried to determine what the stunning presidential victory of socialist François Mitterrand meant for foreign business. Although the government under Giscard d'Estaing had Europe's most formidable array of government controls on business, that situation was predictable, whereas Mitterrand's policies were unknown. Similarly, the uncertainty in China arising from the government's hardline response to the May 1989 student rebellion in Beijing[9] caused many multinationals to reexamine their investment plans.[10] Businesses find these kinds of uncertainty difficult to deal with.

In summary, a firm assessing the political climate of a foreign government should consider existing governmental philosophy as well as the long-range direction of its political development whenever possible. The latter requires a knowledge of the various political parties and their attitudes toward business and government, and, more important, their attitudes toward foreign business and government.

Nationalism

Although shifts in political parties and types of government philosophies may cause instability and changes in government-business relations, the wave of intensive economic nationalism that is spreading throughout the world may prove to be the most critical political factor affecting international business for the remainder of this century. If not properly coped with, this militant nationalism, which "has as one of its central aims, the preservation of national economic autonomy," may make the early history of nationalism and foreign investment pall by comparison.

---

[8] Xiao-Hong Sun and Peter D. Bennett, "The Effect of Political Events on Foreign Direct Investment in Marketing," *Journal of Global Marketing,* Spring 1988, pp. 7–27.

[9] "Seven Days in May: A Beijing Diary," *Business Week,* June 5, 1989, p. 46.

[10] "Has Beijing Burned Its Bridges with Business?" *Business Week,* June 19, 1989, pp. 32–33.

> **BOX 5–1**
> **Economic Revolution—Marxist or Nationalist?**
>
> The Chief of the Joint Staff of the Peruvian military says:
> "We are fighting for the dignity and sovereignty of Peru. How can we, in this country, accept that the rich should grow richer and the poor grow poorer? Shouldn't the foreign companies be ashamed to reap high profits when a great part of the population lacks the necessities of life? We want to fight against unpardonable privileges of the oligarchy and we are determined to use all our energies to crush those who oppose the indispensable change in Peru's social structure. . . . Our revolution is not Marxist. It is nationalist."
>
> Source: Peter Nehemkis, "Latin America: Testing Ground for International Business," © by The Regents of the University of California. Reprinted from *California Management Review* 13, no. 4, p. 90, by permission of The Regents.

For a state to survive more than a fleeting historical moment, it must enjoy the loyalty of most of its residents. In other words, most residents must identify their interest more with the preservation of the sovereignty of the state in which they reside than with any other. Some would call this *personal identification* or *loyalty nationalism*; others, *patriotism*.

To understand the conflicts and pressures inherent in the international movement of capital, skills, technology, and goals, an appreciation for the essential nature of nationalism and the cluster of interests represented in that notion is needed. Regardless of the objectivity of one's view, it is necessary to appreciate that no nation-state, however secure, will tolerate unlimited penetration by a foreign company into its market and economy if control of management is in another country. This is especially true if the decisions made are perceived as insensitive to the social/economic priorities of the host country.

Concern over the position of foreign investment in a country must be seen from the perspective of the host country to be appreciated. Consider the situation in Canada where a strong feeling among Canadians is that too much of their economy is dominated by U.S. investors. By the early 1980s, the majority of the ownership of Canada's oil industry was held by U.S. companies. U.S. companies also own 32 percent of the pulp and paper industry; 36 percent of the mining and smelting industry; and 39 percent of manufacturing as a whole. Of the 100 largest companies in Canada, 37 are U.S. owned or controlled. Many Canadian citizens consider these figures intolerable and are concerned about the involvement of foreign business in the economy of their country.

Even in the United States, where foreign ownership of U.S. business is relatively small compared with Canada, there is growing concern among legislative officials and citizens that too much of U.S. industry is controlled

---

BOX 5–2
Once an American Always an American

"For us IBM is a European company," said the European Community President Jacques Delors. Little wonder. Once an ugly American, IBM is straining to show that it's as European as its competitors. The company seizes every opportunity to push that message on EC officials.

IBM makes a good case. Its European sales of $19.3 million are four times the computer revenues of its nearest rival, Siemens. IBM produces locally 92 percent of what it sells in Europe—more than any other outsider and probably as much as or more than its indigenous competition. The company is France's sixth biggest exporter and its research facilities in Europe create high-technology jobs. The contrast with Japanese "screwdriver" assembly plants couldn't be starker.

Suspicions still abound. Britain nixed an IBM networking deal with British Telecommunications. IBM is kept out of the European chipmaking consortia and there is resentment against it being a part of Esprit, a European multicompany research project. Commented Jacques Stern, the chairman of Bull, a French telecommunications company, "only European naïveté allows IBM into Esprit. Who owns IBM's research? Where do the profits go?" Stern asks. "IBM never has been and never will be a European company."

Source: Adapted from "IBM Is More European than Well, Most Anybody," *Business Week*, September 19, 1988, p. 148.

---

by foreigners. A survey of attitudes indicated that "80 percent of Americans . . . would like to limit foreign buying, and 40 percent want to halt it all together."[11]

As nation-states are challenged by the multinational corporations, it gives rise to xenophobic economic nationalism in developing nations as well as in developed ones. One reason given for this attitude by both developed and underdeveloped countries is concern over the control and protection of the nation's sovereignty.

We are accustomed to the idea of rigid regulation of investments and even expropriation in underdeveloped countries, but the idea of economic nationalism among developed Western nations seems unusual. However, the United States, which customarily has had an open-door policy toward investments, (in fact, until recently holding seminars to encourage foreign investment) has been offering resistance and raising questions about skyrocketing foreign investment.[12]

The effects of nationalism on the multinational company are the same

---

[11] "The Selling of America (Cont'd)," *Fortune*, May 23, 1988, p. 54.

[12] "Cheap Dollars Come Home: Foreign Buying May Boost Stocks and Create Jobs, but Legislators Worry about Outside Control," *Christian Science Monitor*, March 21, 1988, p. 1.

whether the country is industrialized or among the lesser developed nations. Most variation would be in degree of intensity, but all countries demand control of profits and borrowing within the host country, control of impact on local companies (i.e., curtailment of imports in favor of locally made products, and pushing of exports of locally made products), control over foreign investment in established and locally owned business, local ownership of equity, in part at least, by nationals, and the replacement of expatriate management by local citizens.

Strong feelings of nationalism, changes in governments, and shifts in political parties all lead to conditions which create unstable relations between governments and foreign businesses.[13] The following discussion deals with the political risks confronting an MNC.

CONFISCATION, EXPROPRIATION, DOMESTICATION, AND OTHER RISKS

Risks resulting from the political implications of a company's activities can range from confiscation, the most severe, through many lesser but still significant government activities such as exchange controls, import restrictions, price controls, and labor policy. Confiscation, expropriation, domestication, or nationalization of foreign investments are the most severe government actions taken against foreign investors.[14] While these terms are frequently used interchangeably, there are subtle but important differences among them.

Confiscation occurs when a foreign investment is taken over by a government without any reimbursement. Expropriation occurs when a foreign investment is taken over by a government but some form of reimbursement is made. The reimbursement may not be the full value of the investment from the viewpoint of the company being expropriated, but, nonetheless, some attempt to reimburse the foreign investor is made. Expropriation also implies that even though reimbursement was made, the original owners of the company did not willingly sell.

While confiscation and expropriation deal with the taking of property, *nationalization* technically refers to ownership by the government. A firm's property may be expropriated and subsequently turned over to the private sector within the country, or it may be confiscated or expropriated and operated by the government. In the latter situation, it is correct to say that the business was nationalized. Generally, nationalization affects an entire industry rather than a single company. For example, the British

---

[13] Charles R. Kennedy, Jr., "Political Risk Management: A Portfolio Planning Model," *Business Horizons*, November–December 1988, pp. 26–33.

[14] For an account of a recent threat of expropriation by the Peruvian government in 1986, see "Garcia Dusts off an Old Ploy: Expropriation," *Business Week*, January 13, 1986, p. 50.

nationalized the railways, that is, railroads in Britain are owned and operated by the British government; the French government nationalized all banks.

Domestication is defined as that process whereby a government, by various means, forces a foreign-held corporation to relinquish control to nationals, including actual ownership, on several fronts. This process is discussed in more detail later in the chapter. Each of the politically and/or economically inspired sanctions against foreign business is sufficiently important and occurs with enough frequency to require the special consideration of foreign marketers; in most foreign business ventures, one or all of these risks are incurred to some degree and must be accepted as political realities of the environment when marketing overseas.

Confiscation and Expropriation

Confiscation and expropriation of foreign business are probably the most frequently used and most critical politically induced risks of foreign business. Modern economic history is replete with cases of confiscation and expropriation. Some better-known examples are Mexico's takeover of the foreign-owned railway system in 1937 and the oil industry in 1938; Guatemala's takeover of foreign-owned banana plantations in 1953; the Cuban confiscation and nationalization of all industry in 1960; Brazil's takeover of U.S.-owned electrical power plants; the 1973 expropriation and nationalization of the Cerro holdings by the government of Peru; Iranian confiscation of foreign investments in 1979; and France's nationalization of banks in 1983. The World Bank reported that since 1960, a total of 1,535 firms from 22 different capital-exporting countries have been expropriated in 511 separate actions by 76 nations.

The motivation of a country that expropriates investment is frequently couched in deep sentiments of nationalism. Why does a nation feel that it must seize foreign investment? Many reasons are given, but basically such actions stem from the belief (valid or not) that the country's national goals and self-interest can best be served by government or national ownership rather than by foreign control of a particular industry.

Confiscation is especially alluring to many underdeveloped countries. One observer noted that because all confiscation requires is a decree by the government, it is relatively easy—dirt cheap; in fact, it costs nothing at all. Further, confiscation seems to transfer national wealth and property from foreign to local hands rapidly and with a minimum of continuing problems. However, history shows foreign business investments generally are reluctant to return to a country after assets have been confiscated.[15]

---

[15] Anthony Spaeth and Ajay Singh, "Coca-Cola and Du Pont Test Attitude of India Toward Foreign Investment," *The Wall Street Journal*, May 26, 1989, p. A8.

There is also increasing evidence to show that another firm's problems are not necessarily seen as one's own. As we become a more market-oriented world society, the rules are changing. Greater economic competition (economic survival) is increasing the number of multinationals willing to risk dealing with radical governments for a foothold in a foreign market. Just two years after the revolutionary government of Iran confiscated a substantial portion of foreign investment, European and Japanese auto manufacturers were negotiating with the Iranian government for the right to assemble cars and trucks there.[16]

Expropriation is typically justified on grounds that the industry is critical to national defense, national sovereignty, national wealth and/or national economic growth, and thus the nation's interests require that the industry not be controlled by a foreigner. Certain industries are more susceptible to expropriation than others; public utilities are a frequent target since it is universally believed they are critical to economic growth as well as being instrumental in defense capabilities. Mining, oil, and other natural resources are also particularly vulnerable since the nation's wealth is at stake. Other industries basic to the country's economy can be just as vulnerable. Another justification for expropriation is the strong feeling that foreign businesses typically exploit the national wealth of the host country, taking everything from the country and giving nothing in return.

Government takeover does not always mean total loss for the foreign investor; in some cases, the government reimburses the investor for the value of losses. The reimbursement is seldom felt to be equitable by the foreign owner, but there is less stigma attached to such government action if some payment is made.

Some authorities see future risks of confiscation and expropriation lessening for three reasons. One, governments are coming to realize investment is necessary for desired growth potential. Furthermore, past experience has shown that government or local ownership does not always yield the desired results; in some cases, an industry has faltered and its contribution to the national economy has decreased after expropriation. A second fact that may alter future attempts at confiscation and expropriation is the more stringent economic pressure being levied against offending nations by the country of the affected firm when equitable reimbursement is not made. Although in the opinion of one international legal authority, "the traditional international rules on property protection are outdated . . . international law is indifferent to expropriation of aliens." The third

---

[16] Tony Horwitz, "Iran-Iraq Truce Lures Firms Eager to Profit on Postwar Rebuilding," *The Wall Street Journal*, November 30, 1988, p. 1.

BOX 5–3
Expropriation Means Loss?—Depends on the View

The meaning of failure is confused by a basic difference in investment philosophy. One writer explains:

"The United States investors view their foreign investment prospectively—they look at the investment today and project various inputs in the future that can contribute to the value of the total investment. On the other hand, many Latin American hosts view an investment 'historically'—they look back at what the investor has already exacted from his investment and therefore value his present-day investment at a much lower figure. These diverse views of valuation result in the initial positions (investor's and host's) being far apart."

Even the Anaconda and Kennecott expropriations in Chile cannot really be described as failures if one considers the profits gained since the early 1900s, before the companies were finally expropriated. A true failure is a company which shows a net loss from its Latin American ventures—and these are very few.

Source: Jon B. Utley, "Doing Business with Latin Nationalists," *Harvard Business Review* 51, no. 1, p. 80.

reason is that investing firms are trying to make themselves indispensable and less vulnerable in a host country. Such activities include encouraging nationals to invest in the business venture, training nationals for important management positions, borrowing capital from local or third-country banks to which the host government is indebted, and generally attempting to erase the constant suspicion that the foreign firm is somehow exploiting the host country.[17]

Although the threat of confiscation or expropriation may be abating, it still persists and is of prime significance as a political risk in doing business abroad. Another, and perhaps more insidious, way for a government to take over a company is a process of systematically restricting a company and forcing step-by-step liquidation, thus forcing the investment into the hands of nationals. This domestication of business ownership is not the only problem; control of marketing activities creates many problems for the international marketer.[18]

---

[17] Kate Bertrand, "Real-Life Risky Business," *Business Marketing*, January 1987, pp. 49–53.

[18] For a complete discussion of host country control over marketing mix variables, see Humayun Akhter and Robert F. Lusch, "Political Risk and the Evolution of the Control of Foreign Business: Equity, Earnings, and the Marketing Mix," *Journal of Global Marketing*, Spring 1988, pp. 109–27.

Domestication

Increasingly, more host countries are attempting to transfer control of foreign investment to national ownership and bring the firm's activities in line with national interests through *domestication*.[19]

Rather than outright confiscation or expropriation, concern over foreign investment is manifested more subtly in the gradual encroachment on the freedom to operate within the country. In essence, governments seek to *domesticate* the foreign investor rather than confiscate or expropriate. Domestication entails:

A transfer of ownership in part or totally to nationals.

The promotion of a large number of nationals to higher levels of management.

Greater decision-making powers resting with nationals.

A greater number of component products locally produced.

Specific export regulations designed to dictate participation in world markets.

Effects of Government-Initiated Domestication.   The effects of government-initiated domestication of a foreign firm can be disastrous; in fact, the effect can be the same as confiscation. Consider an established foreign investor with 100 percent ownership of a firm facing an ultimatum to sell 51 percent or more of that ownership to local nationals by a specific date. Even if local capital were available, it would be almost impossible to sell the stock at a fair, equitable price since prospective purchasers know a forced sale means they can negotiate the price to an expropriative level and the foreign investor has no recourse. Even when equity is sold at reasonable prices, a basic conflict of interest between the foreign investor and the national stockholder frequently arises. A forced sale is generally made to a small group interested in an immediate return on investment rather than the reinvestment of profits necessary for continued market development and capital growth.

Equally calamitous can be government directives requiring a certain percentage of top-level management to be nationals. Unless nationals willing to follow corporate guidelines are appointed to fill these positions, companies are unable to maintain control over their investments. In many instances companies have no adequately trained nationals within the company to transfer to higher level positions, so they must seek others outside the business. They then find few available who have the depth of experience

---

[19] Parts of this section are from Philip R. Cateora, "The Multinational Enterprise and Nationalism," *MSU Business Topics* 19, no. 2.

necessary, and the competition for those few is fierce. Equally troublesome is the fact that new owners may force the hiring of "loyal" nationals with little capability for the positions and more interest in protecting the personal interests of the national stockholder than in implementing long-term corporate plans. In either case, personnel in executive positions are unable or unwilling to make decisions commensurate with positions they hold.

Further complications and costly problems come with requirements that supplies, raw materials, and perhaps component parts be purchased locally. In most cases, when a government requires raw materials and supplies be of local origin, they are not readily or economically available. The intent of the government, in fact, is to force the foreign owner to create local demand, thus stimulating local production. The company then finds that not only are supplies unavailable but to create local supplies they must also provide the primary investment capital for local industries, as well as train and provide necessary expertise. With established supply sources, experience, and/or local financing completely lacking, the foreign investor must find ways (frequently at enormous expense and time lapse) of producing locally.[20]

Foreign investors of the future face dramatically changing conditions directly affecting their interest in foreign countries. Unless a multinational investor exhibits concern with the host-country's national goals, animosity toward foreign investment will continue to show itself in government-initiated domestication, confiscation, or expropriation. To avoid the economic pitfalls of these policies, global investment strategies should reflect a social awareness of local needs and wants. The investment must be designed to become a fully integrated part of the domestic economy.

Economic Risks

Most foreign businesses abroad are faced with less drastic risks than confiscation, expropriation, or domestication. More common are a series of economic restraints that can be almost as costly and are frequently imposed with little warning. These economic risks may be imposed under the banner of national security, protection of infant industry, protection of scarce foreign exchange, or as taxes to raise revenue.

Exchange Controls.   Exchange controls stem from shortages of foreign exchange held by a country. When a nation faces shortages of foreign exchange, controls may be leveled over all movements of capital or, selec-

---

[20] William A. Stoever, "India: The Long, Slow Road to Liberalization," *Business Horizons,* January–February 1988, pp. 42–46.

tively, against the most politically vulnerable companies to conserve the supply of foreign exchange for the most essential uses. A recurrent problem for the foreign investor is getting profits and investments into the currency of the home country.

Exchange controls are also extended to products by applying a system of multiple exchange rates to regulate trade in specific commodities classified as necessities or luxuries. Necessary products are placed in the most favorable (low) exchange categories, while luxuries are heavily penalized with high foreign-exchange rates. Venezuela, for example, has a three-tiered exchange rate system to protect scarce foreign reserves. For essential imports and approved debt payments, dollars can be purchased from Venezuelan government banks at 7.5 bolivars (Bs) per dollar, at 14.5 Bs for most trade and capital flows, and at the current floating rates (32.6 Bs at the time the three-tiered system was established) for unapproved transactions including travel abroad. Depending on the transaction, the bolivar has a value in U.S. dollars of 13.3 cents for essential goods, 6.8 cents for nonessential goods, and 3.1 cents for unapproved transactions.[21]

In countries with especially scarce foreign exchange, earnings as well as capital repatriation have been frozen for considerable periods of time. For example, capital must remain in Chile for 36 months before it is eligible for repatriation and 10 years if the investment was made with debt originating in Chile. In addition, to force companies to reinvest rather than repatriate capital, some governments force companies to buy government bonds. In Peru, companies with sales of more than $100,000 must buy treasury investment bonds for an amount equal to 30 percent of taxable profits. The bonds generally mature in three years and pay interest at the Central Bank's minimum rate, well below the rate of inflation.[22]

Currency convertibility is a continuing problem since most countries maintain regulations for control of currency and, in the event an economy should suffer an economic setback or foreign exchange reserves suffer severely, the controls on convertibility are imposed quickly.

Local Content Requirements.   In addition to restricting imports of essential supplies to force local purchase, countries often require a portion of any product sold within the country to have local content; that is, to contain locally made parts. This is often imposed on foreign companies that assemble products from foreign-made components. Mexico, for example, has a 60 percent local content requirement for all automobiles assembled there. Local content requirements are not restricted just to Third World

---

[21] "Capsule Guides to Exchange Controls in Latin America," *Business Latin America,* July 11, 1988, p. 222.

[22] "Peru's Latest Measures Hit MNCs Again with Forced Investment," *Business Latin America,* May 4, 1987, p. 142.

countries. The European Community has a 45 percent local content requirement for "screwdriver operations," a name often given foreign-owned
assemblers.[23]

Import Restrictions.   Selective restrictions on the import of raw materials,
machines, and spare parts are fairly common strategies to force foreign
industry to purchase more supplies within the host country and thereby
create markets for local industry. One such move by the Brazilian government required that before issuing an import permit for parts not made
in Brazil, a 360-day import deposit was required prior to importation of
the goods. The net result was at least a 50 percent increase in import
costs to that particular firm. Although this is done in an attempt to support
the development of domestic industry, the result is often to hamstring
and sometimes interrupt the operations of established industries.[24] The
problem becomes critical when there are no adequately developed sources
of supply within the country.

Tax Controls.   Taxes must be classified as a political risk when used as
a means of controlling foreign investments. In such cases, they are raised
without warning and in violation of formal agreements. A squeeze on
profits results from raising taxes significantly as a business becomes established. In those underdeveloped countries where the economy is constantly
threatened with a shortage of funds, unreasonable taxation of successful
foreign investments appears to be the handiest and quickest means of
finding operating funds.

Price Controls.   Essential products that command considerable public interest, such as drugs, medicines, food, gasoline, and cars are often subjected
to price controls. Such controls applied during inflationary periods can
be used by a government to control the cost of living. They also may be
used to force foreign companies to sell equity to local interests. A side
effect to the local economy can be to slow or even stop capital investment.
Price controls can be especially devastating to investment in a country
that has high rates of inflation such as Brazil. For example, local bottlers
of Coca-Cola delayed planned annual investments of over $150 million
because margins were squeezed by price controls. Even though a price
increase of 14 percent was granted, it fell short of the 50 percent needed
to keep up with inflation.[25]

---

[23] "The Europeans Start to Play a Little Rough," *Business Week*, February 9, 1987, p. 47.

[24] "Brazil Unveils First Take on New Industrial Plan but Export Zones in Doubt," *Business
Latin America*, August 15, 1988, p. 262.

[25] "Foreigners Boost Investments in Brazil despite Its Daunting Economic Problems," *The
Wall Street Journal*, October 26, 1988, p. 18.

Labor Problems. In many countries, labor unions have strong government support which they use effectively in obtaining special concessions from business. Layoffs may be forbidden; profits may have to be shared; and an extraordinary number of services may have to be provided. In fact, in many countries, foreign firms are considered fair game for the demands of the domestic labor supply.

In France, the belief in full employment is almost religious in fervor; layoffs of any size, especially by foreign-owned companies, are regarded as national crises. When, as a result of cutbacks in demand, both General Motors and Remington Rand attempted to lay off workers in their French plants, the French minister of industry reprimanded them and stated he would not allow "certain isolated enterprises to practice an irresponsible policy that does not respect the social contract linking a financially powerful enterprise to the labor it employs." Although both General Motors and Remington Rand were privately assured that the minister's remarks were for public consumption, the reaction is indicative of the relationship between government and labor in many countries. The same conditions that forced General Motors and Remington Rand to lay off workers were causing domestic French industry to lay off personnel also, but apparently that situation went unnoticed by the government.

Another labor problem is the restriction on entry into a country of key technicians. To force the hiring of nationals, some countries do not provide work permits for technically trained personnel regardless of whether or not similar talents are available within the country. When they do provide the permit, it is limited to a short period during which the foreigner is to train a local for the position.[26]

Political Sanctions

In addition to economic risks, politically motivated risks can prove costly. Increasingly, companies are caught in the crossfire of political disputes between countries or between political factions within a country. Companies may be used as weapons against a political opponent or they may simply be the victims of political sanctions one country imposes on another. In the one case, violence against a multinational may be used to force a government to react; and in the other, one government may impose trade restrictions against another country to force a change in the country's behavior and the multinational unwittingly suffers.

Violence.   Although not government-initiated, violence is another related risk for multinational companies to consider in assessing the political vul-

---

[26] Ali M. Fatemi et al., "Influences of Social and Political Factors on U.S. Multinational Firms," *Business Journal*, Fall 1987, pp. 8–14.

nerability of their activities.[27] Violence against governments as well as against multinational firms is increasing. In fact, between 1970 and 1984, there were more than 5,000 violent acts recorded, of which over 50 percent were directed toward businesses. Losses reached $500 million or more in material damage, ransoms paid in abductions, and funds taken in robberies.[28] Moreover, thousands of business executives and personnel were held hostage, wounded, or killed.[29] Frequently, violence is directed to embarrass a government and its relationship with multinational firms; it forces the government to take action against the multinational to placate the groups who have instigated the violence. In other cases, kidnappings and robbery are used to generate funds to finance the goals of terrorists. Precautions taken to guard against acts of violence range from insurance against kidnappings to elaborate security measures including defensive driving lessons for foreign personnel.[30]

Political Reprisals.   Unlike acts of violence that directly involve a multinational in a political dispute, political reprisals involve disputes between countries, and damage to the MNC is not purposely intended. For political reasons, one country may boycott another thereby stopping all trade between countries. In 1985 the U.S. government imposed a boycott against Nicaragua and requests for export permits by U.S. companies and Nicaraguan customers were denied. In this case, all business was prohibited. In other cases, only strategic goods may be restricted. The U.S. government frequently restricts trade in goods designated as strategic. (See Chapter 18 for a complete discussion of U.S. trade restrictions.) Social issues may also be a basis for restricting trade to a country. South Africa has been a focal point for many countries that want to force the South African government to stop the practice of apartheid.[31] Some companies have voluntarily imposed trade restrictions on South Africa as a corporate social-responsibility statement.[32]

In addition to lost business, companies caught in such political infighting may also be considered high-risk suppliers. The United States frequently uses economic boycotts as a political weapon. So much so that one of the most frequent criticisms of U.S. firms is that they are not dependable

---

[27] Brian O'Reilly, "Business Copes with Terrorism," *Fortune*, January 6, 1986, pp. 47–55.

[28] "Multinational Firms Act to Protect Overseas Workers from Terrorism," *The Wall Street Journal*, April 29, 1986, p. 3.

[29] "Terrorism: A Threat to Global Firms," *The Journal of Commerce*, April 26, 1988, p. 9a.

[30] Robert S. Greenberger and John Walcott, "More U.S. Firms, Individuals Targeted as Terrorism Spreads in Latin America," *The Wall Street Journal*, February 8, 1989, p. A18.

[31] Robert Rolfe, "South Africa: The Next Wave of Pullouts," *International Management*, April 1988, pp. 43–51.

[32] David Beaty and O. Harari, "Investment and Disinvestment from South Africa: A Reappraisal," *California Management Review*, Summer 1987, pp. 31–50.

because no one knows when the U.S. government will prohibit U.S. companies to trade. Another major political weapon used by the United States government is the trade sanction that is questionable in its effectiveness.

ENCOURAGING FOREIGN INVESTMENT

Many governments encourage foreign investment. In fact, within the same country, some foreign businesses fall prey to politically induced harassments while others may be placed under a government umbrella of protection and preferential treatment. The difference lies in the evaluation of a company's contribution to the nation's self-interest.

Foreign Governments

The most important reason to encourage foreign investment is that it affords the most rapid means of providing necessary goods and services. Actually, foreign investment can be instrumental in accelerating the development of an economy. Many countries are coming to realize that foreign investment, properly controlled, need never be discouraged because the benefits outweigh most of the disadvantages involved.

One underdeveloped country has openly invited investors literally to take over the industrialization of that country. The many inducements include tax exemptions, protection against competing imports, unimpeded movement of capital and profits, and a multitude of other concessions. Naturally, direct contribution to the economy is necessary for the special treatment. Colombia's most recent 10-year development plan allows for special considerations to foreign investors, including income-tax exemptions up to 100 percent, providing the company's "sole business is the development of a basic industry necessary for Colombia's development."

Along with direct encouragement from the host country, an American company can receive assistance from the U.S. government. The intent is to encourage investment by helping to minimize and shift some of the risks from foreign political considerations.

U.S. Government

The U.S. government is motivated for economic as well as political reasons to encourage American firms to seek business opportunities in other countries. This has resulted in a variety of services and inducements to encourage

American firms to go overseas. The assistance can be divided into two areas: activities designed to create favorable climates for foreign investment, and activities designed to assist day-to-day operations and encourage exports.[33]

Part of the government's efforts to create favorable climates for overseas investment are the various activities designed to minimize some of the more troublesome politically motivated risks of doing business abroad. The government provides assistance against risks from deliberate activities of foreign governments such as losses arising from confiscation, expropriation, revolutions, war, and the inability to transfer profits and capital because of exchange restrictions.

Government support in minimizing political risks comes in at least two ways. One is through various agencies which offer guarantees against specific types of risks. In essence, the government provides the means for a foreign investor to purchase insurance against a particular risk. Another means of help covers the most severe political risk, confiscation; limitations have been placed on the granting of U.S. aid to those countries that have seized American-controlled property without equitable restitution.

The Export-Import Bank (Eximbank) is a U.S. government agency whose purpose is to underwrite international trade and investment activities of American firms. Through the Foreign Credit Insurance Association (FCIA), an agency of the Eximbank, an exporter can insure against nonpayment of a buyer's obligation due to commercial or political reasons.[34]

The Eximbank also provides for guarantees against political risks. For a cost of 0.5 percent per year of the guarantee coverage, a foreign investor can get coverage in selected countries of up to 95 percent of loss because of political risks. Those insurable risks include inconvertibility, war, confiscation, civil disturbances, and the cancellation or restriction of export or import licenses.

The Agency for International Development (AID), in conjunction with its aid to underdeveloped countries, has provisions for limited protection in support of "essential" projects in approved countries and for approved products. The costs of coverage are similar to those of the Eximbank, and coverage extends to the basic political risks of convertibility, confiscation or expropriation, and war.

A broader risk insurance coverage was provided in 1969 when the Foreign Assistance Act authorized creation of the Overseas Private Investment

[33] An excellent guide to the various assistance programs offered by the U.S. government can be found in "Where to Get Export Assistance," *Business America*, May 22, 1989, p. 16.

[34] John A. Hanson, "Reducing the Risks of Exporting: The Government Can Help," *Export Today*, July–August 1988, pp. 62–63.

Corporation (OPIC) to provide "political-risk insurance for companies investing in less developed countries."[35]

In addition to government-sponsored insurance against political risk, there are private sources from which political risk insurance can be purchased.[36] Lloyd's of London provided NBC-TV protection against potential loss in 1988 for the Olympic Games in Seoul, Korea. Unfortunately, the loss NBC incurred was from poor viewer ratings not covered by insurance.

MARKET CONCESSION AND FOREIGN INVESTMENT

Rather than expropriate or impose restrictions on a foreign company after it enters a market, an increasing number of foreign-exchange-poor countries are requiring foreign investors to commit to specific contributions to the country's economic development goals prior to granting the foreign company permission to enter the market. Before being granted permission to enter the market and be allowed to repatriate future profits and/or capital, companies have had to agree to make specific contributions that are designed, in one way or the other, to conserve foreign exchange, create local employment, transfer technology, generate export sales, and/or stimulate growth and development of local industry.

India, for example, has vacillated between encouraging and discouraging foreign investment over the last 30 years; today India seeks foreign investment under specific conditions.[37] The arrangement PepsiCo made with India permitting PepsiCo to make and sell Pepsi-Cola is a good example of the conditions a foreign investor must meet to gain entrance into a foreign market.

Specifically, PepsiCo has entered into a joint venture with Indian partners owning approximately 60 percent of the venture while PepsiCo owns the remaining 40 percent. The joint venture comprises four divisions:

1. An agricultural research center to develop high-yielding, disease-resistant seed varieties for fruits, vegetables, and grains for sale to local farmers.
2. A potato and grain processing unit that turns 25,000 tons of potatoes and 5,000 tons of grain into ready-to-serve snacks for the domestic market.

---

[35] Ibrahim F. I. Shihata, "Encouraging International Corporate Investment: The Role of the Multilateral Investment Guarantee Agency," *Columbia Journal of World Business*, Spring 1988, p. 19.

[36] "Political Risk Market Grows," *Journal of Commerce*, July 18, 1988, p. 14a.

[37] Cheryl McQueen, "Liberal Economic Policies and Steady Growth Are Luring More American Companies to India," *Business America*, October 10, 1988, pp. 14–18.

3. A fruit and vegetable processing unit to process 80,000 tons of tomatoes, pears, mangoes, and apples into pulp and concentrates for export.
4. A soft-drink concentrate plant to supply Indian bottlers with soft-drink concentrates including the concentrate for Pepsi-Cola. The joint venture does not bottle any soft drinks itself. It only produces concentrate to sell to Indian bottling plants. This is not unusual for PepsiCo because the majority of Pepsi-Cola drinks are produced by independently owned bottling plants.

The conditions the joint venture agreed to were as follows: First, exports must be equivalent to 50 percent of total factory production costs. Of foreign sales, 80 percent must be products the venture makes and the other 20 percent must be agricultural and food products the joint venture buys from small-scale producers. These conditions will be imposed for ten years. Second, no dividends or capital may be repatriated until the export obligation is fulfilled. Third, the joint venture will have to generate five times as much foreign currency from exports as it spends on imports. Until the foreign-exchange rates are achieved, PepsiCo will not be permitted to repatriate any profits. Fourth, soft-drink concentrate sales cannot exceed 25 percent of total sales for the joint venture.[38] The joint venture is expected to create 1,000 jobs and give work to about 15,000 farmers.[39]

For all this, PepsiCo gets a 40 percent ownership in a joint venture that has profit potential from concentrate sales and food processing. The future reward, however, is access to India's potentially huge soft-drink market. A population of 800 million drinks about 2.4 billion bottles of soft drinks annually. This is an annual average of just 3 bottles of carbonated drink per person, against neighboring Pakistan's 13.[40] The growth potential is enormous if one considers that in parts of the world, the per capita consumption is several hundred bottles per year.

The conditions India imposed on the PepsiCo investment are probably among the most stringent, and other countries are following a similar trend. For example, Russia has implemented a law authorizing joint ventures but, under the law, the foreign companies cannot take profits out of the country in dollars unless the venture itself earns hard currency.[41] Joint ventures in China often have similar provisions as do investments in many Latin American countries.

---

[38] "PepsiCo's Entry into India," pp. 319–20.

[39] "PepsiCo Accepts Tough Conditions for the Right to Sell Cola in India," *The Wall Street Journal*, September 20, 1988, p. 42.

[40] "Pepsi Deal Aids India's Farmers," *Journal of Commerce*, October 5, 1988, p. 6a.

[41] "American Pizza Purveyors in Moscow Say It's Just a Slice of Things to Come," *The Wall Street Journal*, April 13, 1988, p. 24.

BOX 5-4
Coke's Got a Secret—And They Aren't Going to Tell

For 91 years, the formula for making Coca-Cola had been a closely guarded secret. Then the government of India ordered Coca-Cola to disclose it or cease operations in that country. A secret ingredient called 7-X supposedly gives Coke its distinctive flavor. The government's minister for industry told the Indian parliament that Coca-Cola's Indian branch would have to transfer 60 percent of its equity shares to Indians and hand over its know-how by April 1978, or shut down. Indian sales account for less than 1 percent of Coca-Cola's worldwide sales. The potential market, however, in India, a country of 800 million, is tremendous.

The government refused to let the branch import the necessary ingredients, and Coke—once as abundant as bottled drinking water sold in almost every Indian town of more than 50,000—packed up their bags and left the country. The minister for industry said Indian scientists had developed a concentrate for a substitute soft drink, and he expected Indian bottlers to take advantage of this new development. "The minister feels the activities of Coca-Cola in India 'furnish a classic example of how multinational corporations operating in a low-priority, high-profit area in a developing country attain run-away growth and, in the absence of alertness on the part of the government concerned, can trifle with the weaker indigenous industry in the process.'" Coke said they wouldn't give up the formula and India said they had to leave.

By 1988 Coke had negotiated a deal to go back to India without having to reveal the formula.

Source: Adapted from "Coca-Cola Ordered by India to Disclose Formula for Drink," *The Wall Street Journal*, August 13, 1977, p. 11; "Indians Want Coke Know-How," *New York Times*, August 10, 1977; and Ranjan Das, "Impact of Host Government Regulations on MNC Operation: Learning from Third World Countries," *Columbia Journal of World Business*, Spring 1981, p. 89; and James R. Schiffman, "Coca-Cola Seeking to Re-Enter Huge Indian Market after 11 Years," *The Asian Wall Street Journal*, November 21, 1988, p. 23.

ASSESSING POLITICAL VULNERABILITY

Some products appear to be more politically vulnerable than others; that is, because of particular circumstances, they receive special government attention, either favorable or unfavorable depending on the product.

It is not unusual for countries seeking investments in high-priority industries to exempt investors from corporate taxes for several years and from customs duties and surcharges on machinery and equipment. Countries may also give investors priorities in financing from local banks and protection from foreign competition through quotas or increased duties on imported goods.

Political vulnerability can also lead to labor agitation, public regulations, price fixing, allocation quotas, expropriation, regulation, and control, or other forms of government harassment if an investment or product is considered nonessential, undesirable, or in competition with host country enterprises. Philco and RCA corporations are good examples of companies producing politically vulnerable products. Their efforts to manufacture digital chips were halted by the Brazilian government for the benefit of local firms. Philco and RCA both made investments to manufacture digital chips in Brazil. But, by the time they were ready to begin selling chips to Brazilian firms, the government issued an order requiring all digital chips used in Brazil to be manufactured only by Brazilian-owned companies. The Brazilian government has continued systematically to push foreign MNCs out of the computer and telecommunications market and replace them with Brazilian companies.[42]

Politically Sensitive Products

There are at least as many reasons for a product's political vulnerability as there are political philosophies, economic variations, and cultural differences. Unfortunately, there are no guidelines a marketer can follow to determine whether or not a product will be subject to political attention. By answering the following questions, a marketer may detect clues to a product's vulnerability.

1. Is the availability of supply of the product ever subject to important political debates (sugar, salt, gasoline, public utilities, medicines, foodstuffs)?
2. Do other industries depend on the production of the product (cement, power machine tools, construction machinery, steel)?
3. Is the product considered socially or economically essential (key drugs, laboratory equipment, medicines)?
4. Is the product essential to agricultural industries (farm tools and machinery, crops, fertilizers, seed)?
5. Does the product affect national defense capabilities (transportation industry, communications)?
6. Does the product include important components that would be available from local sources and that otherwise would not be used as effectively (labor, skills, materials)?
7. Is there local competition or potential local competition from manufacturers in the near future (small, low-investment manufacturing)?

---

[42] For an interesting article on competition and host government intervention, see Chan W. Kim, "Competition and the Management of Host Government Intervention," *Sloan Management Review*, Spring 1987, pp. 33–39.

8. Does the product relate to channels of mass communication media (newsprint, radio equipment)?
9. Is the product primarily a service?
10. Does the use of the product, or its design, rest on some legal requirements?
11. Is the product potentially dangerous to the user (explosives, drugs)?
12. Does the product induce a net drain on scarce foreign exchange?[43]

Depending on how these questions are answered and the particular philosophy of those in power at the time, a company might expect to receive favorable political attention if it contributed to the achievement of national goals or, conversely, unfavorable attention if it were nonessential in view of current national needs. For products judged nonessential, the risk would be great, but for those thought to be making an important contribution, encouragement and special considerations could be available.

Forecasting Political Risk

In addition to quantitative measures of political vulnerability, a growing number of firms are employing more systematic methods of measuring political risk. *Political risk assessment* is an attempt to forecast political instability and thus alter the rules of the game under which a firm makes its decision to enter a market. It helps management identify and evaluate political events and their potential influence on current and future international business decisions.[44] Political risk assessment can:

Help managers decide if risk insurance is necessary.

Devise an intelligence network and an early warning system.

Help managers develop contingency plans for unfavorable future political events.

Build a database of past political events for each country in which the corporation conducts business for use by corporate management.

Interpret the data gathered by its intelligence network to advise and forewarn corporate decision makers about political and economic situations.[45]

[43] Richard D. Robinson, "The Challenge of the Underdeveloped National Market," *Journal of Marketing*, October 1961, pp. 24–25. Reprinted from *Journal of Marketing*, published by the American Marketing Association.

[44] For a complete discussion of political risk analysis, see David M. Raddock, *Assessing Corporate Political Risk* (Totowa, N.J.: Roowman and Littlefield, 1986), p. 212.

[45] Francis M. Jeffries, "Political Risk Analysis," *Export Today*, Summer 1985, pp. 61–63.

The Great Wall in China—An early political statement.

There are a variety of methods used to measure political risk. They range from having in-house political analysts to using external sources that specialize in analyzing political risk. Presently, all methods are far from being perfected; however, the very fact a company attempts to systematically examine the problem is significant.[46]

For a marketer doing business in a foreign country, a necessary part of any market analysis is an assessment of the probable political consequences of a marketing plan—some marketing activities are more susceptible to political considerations than others. Basically, it boils down to evaluating the essential nature of the immediate activity.[47] The following section explores ways businesses can reduce political vulnerability.

---

[46] For more information on political risk assessment, see William P. Kelly, "Political Risk Assessment: Half the Equation," in *Global Risk Assessments* (Riverside, Cal.: Global Risk Assessments, 1985).

[47] "How MNCs Are Aligning Country-Risk Assessment with Bottom-Line Concerns," *Business International*, June 1, 1987, pp. 169–70.

REDUCING POLITICAL VULNERABILITY

Even though a company cannot directly control or alter the political environment of the country within which it operates, there are measures that can lessen the degree of susceptibility of a specific business venture to politically induced risks.

Foreign investors frequently are accused of exploiting a country's wealth at the expense of the national population and for the sole benefit of the foreign investor. This attitude is best summed up in a statement made by a recent president of Peru: "We have had massive foreign investment for decades but Peru has not achieved development. Foreign capital will now have to meet government social goals."

These charges are not wholly unsupported by past experiences, but today's enlightened investor is seeking a return on investments commensurate with the risk involved. To achieve such returns, hostile and generally unfounded fears must be overcome; countries, especially the less developed, fear foreign investment for many reasons. They fear the multinationals' interest is only to exploit their labor, markets, or raw materials and to leave nothing behind except the wealthy who become wealthier.

Good Corporate Citizenship

As long as fears of this sort persist, the political climate for foreign investors continues to be hostile. Are there ways of allaying these fears? A list of suggestions made some 20 years ago is still appropriate for a company that intends to be a good corporate citizen and thereby minimize its political vulnerability. A company is advised to remember:

1. It is a guest in the country and should act accordingly.
2. The profits of an enterprise are not solely any company's; the local national employees and the economy of the country should also benefit.
3. It is not wise to try to win over new customers by completely Americanizing them.
4. Although English is an accepted language overseas, a fluency in the language of the international customer goes far in making sales and cementing good public relations.
5. It should try to contribute to the country's economy and culture with worthwhile public projects.
6. It should train its executives and their families to act appropriately in the foreign environment.
7. It is best not to conduct business from the United States but to staff foreign offices with competent nationals and supervise the operation from home.

Manifestations of these suggestions include such examples as Pepsi-Cola sponsoring opera and ballet in Argentina; Procter & Gamble, IBM, and others supporting educational programs in Asia; Gulf Oil fighting smallpox in Nigeria; General Electric providing music in hospitals and jails; Xerox Corporation sponsoring "Sesame Street" in Latin America, and Cargill funding agricultural research in Brazil.

Many companies survive even the most hostile environments; through their operating methods, they have been able to minimize their political vulnerability. Sears, Roebuck & Co., for example, has a favorable image throughout Latin America, and thus is able to survive wave after wave of nationalistic attack. Sears developed its favorable image in a variety of ways, including a successful profit-sharing program. It voluntarily offers profit participation to all employees, and today employees and their families are among Sears' most ardent defenders.

In addition, Sears has pioneered programs to develop local industry. It has, as corporate policy, a program to buy at least 20 percent of all merchandise sold in its stores from local manufacturers; today, Sears is operating closer to 90 percent. The results of such policy are that Sears buys from over a thousand local sources throughout Latin America, suppliers who owe their very existence to Sears' activities. It is estimated that some 400 companies have been founded directly on the basis of Sears' guarantees of markets.

Although many of those interested in doing business overseas may not feel they can go as far as Sears, there is certainly much to be said for attempting to become more closely identified with the ideals and desires of the host country.[48] To do so might render a marketer's activities and products less politically vulnerable; and although it would not eliminate all the risks of the political environment, it might reduce the likelihood and frequency of some politically motivated risks.[49]

In spite of efforts at being good citizens, responsive to their various publics (see Exhibit 5–1), new modes of investment which render the venture less risky initially may be the only long-range solutions to hostile political environments.[50]

Strategies to Lessen Political Risk

In addition to corporate activities focused on the social and economic goals of the host country and good corporate citizenship, MNCs can use other strategies to minimize political vulnerability and risk.

---

[48] "European Business Ponders Its Social Role," *The Christian Science Monitor,* May 21, 1987, p. 22.

[49] "How Green Is Your Company?" *International Management,* January 1989, pp. 24–27.

[50] S. Prakash Sethi and K.A.N. Luther, "Political Risk Analysis and Direct Foreign Investment," *California Management Review,* Winter 1986, pp. 57–68.

EXHIBIT 5–1 The MNCs Publics and Issues

Publics	Issues*
Church	Nationalism
Labor	Industrial democracy
Suppliers	Environment protection
Customers	Energy and raw materials
Competitors	Taxes
Pressure groups	Incentives and restrictions
Stockholders	Investment approvals and permits
Academia	Personnel relations
General public	Attracting personnel
Minority groups	Mergers and acquisitions
Public media	Money and credit
Governments and agencies	Legitimacy
Conservationists	Prices and profits
Financial community	Image (company and product)
	Consumerism
	Women's liberation
	Union relations
	Equal opportunities

* The issues do not correspond with the publics listed.

SOURCE: Adapted from "How Embattled MNCs Can Devise Strategies for External Affairs," *Business International,* December 12, 1975, p. 394.

Joint Ventures. Typically less susceptible to political harassment, joint ventures can be with either locals or other third-country multinational companies; in both cases, a company's financial exposure is limited. A joint venture with locals helps minimize anti-MNC feelings, and a joint venture with another MNC adds the additional bargaining power of a third country.

Expanding the Investment Base. To include several investors and banks in financing any investment in the host country is another strategy. This has the advantage of engaging the power of the banks whenever any kind of government takeover or harassment is threatened. This strategy becomes especially powerful if the banks have made loans to the host country; if the government threatens expropriation or other types of takeover, the financing bank has substantial power with the government.

Marketing and Distribution. Controlling distribution in world markets can be used effectively if an investment should be expropriated; the host country would then lose access to world markets. This has proved especially useful for MNCs in the extractive industries where world markets for iron ore, copper, and so forth are crucial to the success of the investment. Peru found that when Marcona Mining Company was expropriated, the country lost access to iron-ore markets around the world and ultimately had to deal with Marcona on a much more favorable basis than first thought possible.

Licensing. A strategy some firms find that eliminates almost all risks is to license technology for a fee. It can be effective in situations where the technology is unique and the risk is high. Of course, there is some risk assumed because the licensee can refuse to pay the required fees but continue to use the technology.

The strategies just discussed can be effective in forestalling or minimizing the effect of a total takeover. However, in those cases where an investment is being domesticated by the host country, the most likely long-range solution is planned phasing out, that is, planned domestication. While this idea is not a favorite business practice, the alternative of government-initiated domestication can be as disastrous as confiscation. As a feasible response to rising nationalism, planned domestication is a system that can be profitable and politically acceptable to the host country as well as profitable and operationally expedient for the foreign investor.

Planned Domestication: An Alternative[51]

Planned domestication is, in essence, a gradual process of participating with nationals in all phases of company operations. Initial investment planning would include steps to:

1. Sell equity to nationals at fair prices over a number of years.
2. Prepare nationals for top decison-making positions.
3. Integrate local companies (where feasible) into worldwide marketing programs.
4. Develop local companies as sources of supply.
5. Put on a sound economic base or make unnecessary any government concessions initially needed for successful investment.

Initial investment planning provides for eventual sale of a significant interest (perhaps even controlling interest) to nationals and incorporation of national economic needs and national managerial talent into the business as quickly as possible. Such a policy is more likely to result in reasonable control remaining with the parent company even though nationals would hold important positions in management and ownership. Company-trained

---

[51] Both planned domestication and *predetermined domestication* are used to refer to the process of a gradual disinvestment of multinational assets in a host country. In early editions of *International Marketing*, the term *predetermined domestication* was used exclusively.

nationals would be more likely to have a strong corporate point of view rather than a national perspective.

Local suppliers developed over a period of time could ultimately handle a significant portion of total needs, thus meeting government demands for local content. Further, a sound, sensible plan to sell ownership over a number of years would ensure a fair and equitable return on investment in addition to encouraging ownership throughout the populace. Finally, if government concessions and incentives essential in early stages of investment were rendered economically unnecessary, the company's political vulnerability would be lessened considerably.

A good example of planned domestication is the Singer Company's recently initiated policy to systematically share ownership with local investors of many of its Asian operations to avert confrontations with host governments. Most Asian governments require some local participation even though they do allow exceptions. Singer feels that planned domestication is a wise move because companies that have not taken early steps to share ownership have had to "accept final terms they didn't like." Singer's policy is to domesticate their investments while they "have some discretion about the partner and price." Transfer of ownership is made through sales to employees, to the public, and to other business partners. Even though planned domestication may not be the ideal investment plan, it is a practical, workable alternative to government-initiated domestication or expropriation.

Political Payoffs

One approach to dealing with political vulnerability is the political payoff—attempting to lessen political risks by paying those in power to intervene on behalf of the multinational company. Political payoffs or bribery have been used to lessen the negative effects of a variety of problems. Paying heads of state to avoid confiscatory taxes or expulsion, paying fees to agents to ensure the acceptance of sales contracts, and providing monetary encouragement to an assortment of people whose actions can affect the effectiveness of a company's programs are decisions that frequently confront multinational managers and raise ethical questions.[52]

As discussed in Chapter 4, bribery poses problems for the marketer both in the home country and the host country. It is illegal by U.S. law for a U.S. citizen to pay a bribe. Just as important is the fact that even though bribery is supposedly customary in a host country, if the bribe is exposed, the host country does not condone it regardless of the circum-

---

[52] Matt Miller, "Manila Filing Says Westinghouse Used Bribes to Win Plant Contract," *The Asian Wall Street Journal*, February 13, 1989, p. 14.

BOX 5–5
The Loser Wins When Mah-Jongg and Bribery Meet

A fashionable way of disguising bribes, payoffs, or gifts in both business and political circles in Japan is to purposely lose when playing Mah-Jongg or golf. If you can lose skillfully, your services may be in demand. Losing at Mah-Jongg and golf are classic examples of indirect but preferred ways the Japanese use when it comes to greasing palms.

Mah-Jongg is a Chinese table game played with ivory tiles, having rules similar to gin rummy. Gambling is a minor crime in Japan whereas bribery is a major one. To skirt the law, Japanese business people invite officials or others to a discreet high-class restaurant or club that provides a salon for private Mah-Jongg games. Executives of the host company bring along young employees noted for their abilities to deftly lead their opponent to a successful win at a substantial loss for themselves. If your guests prefer golf to Mah-Jongg, no problem. They can have a golf game with the company's "reverse pro," that is, a duffer who specializes in hooking and slicing his way to sure defeat.

Source: Adapted from "Those Who Lose Really Win in Japan; the Fine Art of Mah-Jongg as Bribery," *The Wall Street Journal*, January 20, 1984, p. 28.

---

stances. In most instances where parties to payoffs have been exposed, both the United States and host-country citizens have received punishment. There may be short-run benefits to political payoffs, but, in the long run, the risk appears to be sufficiently high that it should be avoided.[53]

MANAGING EXTERNAL AFFAIRS

Regardless of how well multinational companies lessen political vulnerability through investment and business decisions, a problem they all face is one of public image. Reading the popular press in the United States, or anywhere in the world, could lead one to believe that almost everything evil is caused by multinational companies and that any good acts they do are self-serving. In other words, on top of everything else, MNCs have a bad press—a poor image—and based on a recent study of U.S.-owned MNCs, most do not have a specific worldwide external affairs program to deal with the problem. There is growing concern over this

---

[53] Steven A. Meyerowitz, "Treading the Line between Grease and Bribery," *Business Marketing*, January 1987, pp. 92–95.

issue and many companies have begun specific actions to improve their public images.

Several issues involved shape the external affairs programs, or absence thereof, of multinational companies. One important consideration is whether to maintain a low profile and react to criticisms as they develop or to actively meet and perhaps forestall challenges before they develop. Advocates of a low profile support their position on the basis that it is better to attract minimum attention and avoid criticism. Further, they feel that a company that attracts attention might also attract political harassment and the potential for violence against the company and employees. Those who support a more active external affairs program suggest that ignoring the public image of MNCs allows the public image to get worse instead of better; that by not being active in their public pronouncements and actions, MNCs are always on the defensive, never having the opportunity to present positive achievements of the company. Further, there is little evidence of the effectiveness of being passive and maintaining a low profile.[54]

The United Nations, Andean Common Market, and EC have strong public opinions about multinational companies that affect the present as well as the future potential environment for the MNC. In addition, private organizations such as international trade unions and the very active international trade secretariats have specific opinions about the MNCs and their roles relative to their specific interest groups. Some of the private groups can cause major problems. An example is the Third World Working Group, which published a report alleging that an international milk company and others were mass murderers of babies in less-developed countries as a result of their advertising and marketing. The company sued the Third World Working Group and ultimately won; but the public relations cost was high.[55]

One suggestion for managing external affairs effectively is to be certain that those in government are aware that the MNC's investment contributes to the economic, social, or human development of the country. Government–MNC relations are generally positive if a foreign investment (1) improves the balance of payments by increasing exports or reducing imports through import substitution; (2) uses locally produced resources; (3) transfers capital, technology, and/or skills; (5) creates jobs; and, (6) makes tax contributions.[56]

An external affairs program, however well designed and executed, is

---

[54] Jessica Skelly, "A Code of Conduct for the American Partners," *Across the Board*, December 1988, pp. 37–38.

[55] "Boycotts: Activists' Group Resumes Fight against Nestlé, Adds American Home Products," Associated Press News Release, October 5, 1988.

[56] Seamus G. Connolly, *Finding, Entering, and Succeeding in a Foreign Market* (Englewood Cliffs, N.J.: Prentice-Hall, 1987), p. 76.

never better than the behavior of the company. Most companies today strive to become good corporate citizens in their host countries; but because of overheated feelings of nationalism or political parties seeking publicity or scapegoats for their own failures, the negative aspects of MNCs, whether true or false, are the ones which frequently reach the public. The only effective defense for the multinational company is to actively tell its own story. As one authority states, "Passivity is passé. It is high time for a high profile."

SUMMARY

Vital to every marketer's assessment of a foreign market is an appreciation for the political environment of the country within which he or she plans to operate. Government involvement in business activities, especially foreign-controlled business, is generally much greater than business is accustomed to in the United States. The foreign firm must strive to make its activities politically acceptable, or it may be subjected to a variety of politically condoned harassments. In addition to the harassments that can be imposed by a government, the foreign marketer frequently faces the problem of uncertainty of continuity in government policy. As governments change political philosophies, a marketing firm accepted under one administration may find that its activities are completely undesirable under another. The U.S. government may aid American business in its foreign operations; and for those companies a country considers vital to achieving national economic goals, the host country often provides an umbrella of protection not extended to others. An unfamiliar or hostile political environment does not necessarily preclude success for a foreign marketer if the marketer's plans are such that the company becomes a local economic asset.

QUESTIONS

1. Define: *Rule of people*
   parliamentary government
   absolutist government *Rule of*
   expropriation *firm w/ Regime*
   external affairs *public image*
   political risk assessment

   confiscation *firm w/o Reim*
   currency convertibility *Readily to convert*
   political vulnerability *products*
   domestication *Relinquish control*
   planned domestication

2. Why would a country rather domesticate than expropriate?

3. How can government-initiated domestication be tantamount to confiscation?

4. Discuss planned domestication as an alternative investment plan.

5. "A crucial fact when doing business in a foreign country is that permission to conduct business is controlled by the government of the host country." Comment.

6. What are the main factors to consider in assessing the dominant political climate within a country?

7. Why is a working knowledge of party philosophy so important in a political assessment of a market? Discuss.

8. What are the most common causes of instability in governments? Discuss.

9. Discuss how governmental instability can affect marketing.

10. What are the most frequently encountered political risks in foreign business? Discuss.

11. Expropriation is considered a major risk of foreign business. Discuss ways in which this particular type of risk has been minimized somewhat as a result of company activities. Explain how these risks have been minimized by the activities of the U.S. government.

12. How do exchange controls impede foreign business? Discuss.

13. How do foreign governments encourage foreign investment? Discuss.

14. How does the U.S. government encourage foreign investment? Spell out the implications in foreign marketing.

15. Discuss measures a company might take to lessen its political vulnerability.

16. Why do less-developed countries fear foreign investment? Is there any evidence that these attitudes are changing? Are there steps a company can take to lessen these fears? Discuss.

17. Select a country and analyze it politically from a marketing viewpoint.

18. The text suggests that violence is a politically motivated risk of international business. Comment.

19. Exhibit 5–1 lists the various publics and issues frequently confronting a multinational; add as many more as you can to the lists.

CHAPTER

6

The International Legal Environment

Among the many components of a marketer's operating environment and an integral part of a country's culture are the laws that govern business activities. The marketer is confronted with as many different legal environments as there are countries; furthermore, in commercial transactions between countries, the problem of determining which country's legal system has jurisdiction must be faced. Because no single, uniform international commercial law governing foreign business transactions exists, the legal environment for foreign marketers takes on added importance.[1]

The legal systems of the world are so disparate and complex that it is beyond the scope of this text to explore the laws of each country individually. There are, however, legal problems common to most international marketing transactions that must be given special attention when operating abroad.

A summary of these potential problems is found in a checklist by *Business International;* it was compiled as an aid in developing awareness of the legal problems of foreign marketing. The list includes elements related to marketing that are most prone to legal difficulty:

---

[1] Nicholas D. Kristof, "What's the Law in China? It's No Secret (Finally)," *New York Times,* November 20, 1988, p. 11.

Prone to (legal) difficulty.

1. Rules of competition on (a) collusion, (b) discrimination against certain buyers, (c) promotional methods, (d) variable pricing, (e) exclusive territory agreement.
2. Retail price maintenance laws.
3. Cancellation of distributor or wholesaler agreements.
4. Product quality laws and controls.
5. Packaging laws.
6. Warranty and after-sales exposure.
7. Price controls, limitations on markups, or markdowns.
8. Patents, trademarks, and copyright laws and practices.[2]

This list is not a definitive compilation of all possible legal problems; it deals only with those problems peculiar to marketing. Marketers must also be concerned with laws that apply to business in general. This chapter provides a broad view of the international legal environment with the hope that the reader appreciates the need for knowledge of all legal systems likely to be encountered and the necessity of securing expert legal advice when doing business in a foreign country.

BASES FOR LEGAL SYSTEMS

4 systems

The legal systems of the world are based on four common heritages—Islamic law[3] derived from the interpretation of the Koran and found in Pakistan, Iran, and other Islamic states; socialist law[4] derived from the Marxist-socialist system and found in Russia, China, and other Marxist socialist states; common law derived from English law and found in England, the United States, Canada, and other countries that at one time have been under English influence; and civil or code law, derived from Roman law and found in the remaining non-Islamic and non-Marxist countries. The differences among these four systems are of more than theoretical importance because due process of law may vary considerably among these various legal systems. Although a country's laws may be based on one of the four legal systems, its individual interpretation may vary significantly, from a fundamentalist interpretation of Islamic law as found in Pakistan to a combination of several legal systems found in the United States where both common and code law are reflected in the legal system.[5]

---

[2] "201 Checklists—Decision Making in International Operations," *Business International,* 1980, pp. 243–44.

[3] Hasan Moinuddin, *The Charter of the Islamic Conference and Legal Framework on Economic Cooperation Among Its Member States* (Oxford: Clarendon Press, 1987), pp. 1–12.

[4] John N. Hazard, *Communists and Their Law* (Chicago: University of Chicago Press, 1969) pp. 1–9.

[5] Nabil A. Saleh, *Unlawful Gain and Legitimate Profit in Islamic Law* (Cambridge: Cambridge University Press, 1986), pp. 8–32.

Islamic and Socialist Law

The basis for the Shari'ah (Islamic law) is interpretation of the Koran. It encompasses religious duties and obligations as well as the secular aspects of law regulating human acts. Broadly speaking, Islamic law defines a complete system that prescribes specific patterns of social and economic behavior for all individuals. It includes issues such as property rights, economic decision making, and types of economic freedom. The overriding objective of the Islamic system is social justice.[6] Among the most unique aspects of Islamic law is the prohibition against the payment of interest. The Islamic law of contracts states that any given transaction should be devoid of *riba*, defined as the unlawful advantage by way of excess or deferment; that is, interest or usury.[7] Prohibition against the payment of interest impacts most severely on banking practices; however, payment for the use of money occurs through an ingenious compromise developed by some Islamic banks. Instead of an interest-bearing loan, banks finance trade by buying some of the borrower's stock which it sells back to the company at a higher price. The size of the markup is determined by the amount and maturity of the loan and the credit worthiness of the borrower, all traditional yardsticks for determining interest rates. This practice is frowned on by strict fundamentalists, but it is practiced and is an example of the way the strictness of Islamic law can be reconciled with the laws of non-Islamic legal systems.[8]

Socialist law is based on the fundamental tenets of the Marxist-socialist state. Whereas Islamic law is distinguished by concepts clustered around a core concept of the role of holy writ, that is, the Koran, Marxist-socialist law clusters around the core concept of economic, political, and social policies of a Marxist-socialist state.[9]

Marxist-socialist countries are generally those which formerly had laws derived from the Roman or code law system. Some of the characteristics of Roman law have been preserved within their legal systems. Although much of the terminology and other similarities of code law have been retained in socialist law, the basic premise on which socialist law is based is that "law, according to Marxist-socialist tenets, is strictly subordinate to prevailing economic conditions."[10] Thus, the words *property, contract,* and *arbitration* denote different realities because of the collectivization of the means of production and state planning. As socialist countries become

---

[6] Mohsin S. Khan, "Islamic Interest Free Banking," *IMF Fund Papers,* March 1988, pp. 1–3.

[7] Moinuddin, *The Charter of the Islamic Conference,* pp. 115–18.

[8] Jason Nisse, "No Interest?" *The Banker,* October 1987, pp. 35–44.

[9] Hazard, *Communists and Their Law,* pp. 519–31.

[10] Rene David and John E. C. Brierley, *Major Legal Systems in the World Today* (London: The Free Press, 1968) p. 18.

Government official in Saudi Arabia. Local laws govern business activities.
(Gregory Murphey/Journalism Services, Inc.)

more directly involved in trade with non-Marxist countries, laws governing ownership, contracts, and other business realities have been developed to reconcile the differences between socialist law and the common or code law that prevails in most of the industrialized world. China, for example, has had to pass laws covering the protection of intellectual property rights, clarifying ownership rights in joint ventures, and other pieces of commercial legislation necessary for international business. Even within existing laws, the interpretation is influenced by the basic tenets of the Marxist-socialist state. For example, China has no law protecting trade secrets. The only means of protecting licensed technology is by contract. However, the terms of the contract and the period of confidentiality are frequent issues of contention because existing Chinese law generally limits the term of technology import contracts to ten years. After this period, the Chinese insist that the licensee be allowed to continue to use the technology free of charge.[11]

Common and Code Law

The basis for common law is tradition, past practices, and legal precedents set by the courts through interpretations of statutes, legal legislation, and past rulings. Common law seeks "interpretation through the past decisions

---

[11] T. K. Chang, "Selling to China: A Practical Legal Guide," *Export Today*, March–April 1988, pp. 43–47.

of higher courts which interpret the same statutes or apply established and customary principles of law to a similar set of facts.[12]

Code law is based on an all-inclusive system of written rules (codes) of law. Under code law, the legal system is generally divided into three separate codes: commercial, civil, and criminal. Common law is recognized as not being all-inclusive, while code law is considered complete as a result of catchall provisions found in most code-law systems. For example, under the commercial code in a code-law country, the law governing contracts is made inclusive with the statement that "a person performing a contract shall do so in conformity with good faith as determined by custom and good morals."[13] Although code law is considered all-inclusive, it is apparent from the foregoing statement that some broad interpretations are necessary to include everything under the existing code.

Commercial law can vary in meaning between common-law and code-law countries; under common law, commercial disputes are subject to laws that may be applied to either civil or commercial disputes because there is no specific recognition of commercial problems as such. Code law differs in that there is a separate code specifically designed for business. The commercial code has precedence over other codes when matters of business are before the court. The provision results from historical recognition that the legal problems of merchants are often unique and thus should have special status under the law.

Steps are being taken in common-law countries to codify commercial law even though the primary basis of commercial law is common law, that is, precedents set by court decisions. An example of the new uniformity and a measure of codification is the acceptance of the Uniform Commercial Code by most states in the United States. Even though U.S. commercial law has been codified to some extent under the Uniform Commercial Code, the philosophy of interpretation is anchored in common law. Similar strides toward a unified commercial code have been made in England.

As we discuss later in the section on protection of intellectual property rights, laws governing intellectual property rights offer the most striking differences between common-law and code-law systems.[14] Under common law, ownership is established by use; under code law, ownership is determined by registration.

In some code-law countries, certain agreements may not be enforceable unless properly notarized or registered; whereas in a common-law country,

---

[12] Leslie Llewellyn Lewis, ed., *The Dartnell International Trade Handbook*, 1st ed. (Chicago: The Dartnell Corporation, 1963), p. 513.

[13] Ibid.

[14] Industrial property rights and intellectual property rights are used interchangeably. The more common term used today is *intellectual property rights* to refer to patents, copyrights, trademarks, and so forth.

the same agreement may be binding so long as proof of the agreement can be established.

Although every country has elements of both common and code law, the differences in interpretations between common- and code-law systems regarding contracts, sales agreements, and other legal issues are significant enough that an international marketer familiar with only one system must enlist the aid of legal counsel for the most basic legal questions.

An illustration of where fundamental differences in the two systems can cause such difficulty is in the performance of a contract. Under common law in the United States, it is fairly clear that impossibility of performance does not necessarily excuse compliance with the provisions of a contract unless it is impossible to comply for reasons of an act of God, such as some extraordinary happening of nature not reasonably anticipated by either party of a contract. Hence, floods, lightning, earthquakes, and similar occurrences are generally considered acts of God. Under code law, acts of God are not limited solely to acts of nature but are extended to include "unavoidable interferences with performance, whether resulting from forces of nature or unforeseeable human acts," including such things as labor strikes and riots.[15]

Consider the following situations: A contract was entered into to deliver a specific quantity of cloth. In one case, before delivery could be made by the seller, an earthquake caused the destruction of the cloth, and compliance was then impossible. In a second case, pipes in the sprinkler system where the material was stored froze and broke, spilling water on the cloth and destroying it. In each case, loss of the merchandise was sustained and delivery could not be made. The question is whether the parties in these cases were absolved of their obligations under the contract because of the impossibility of delivery. The answer depends on the system of law invoked.

In the first situation, the earthquake would be considered an act of God under both common and code law and impossibility of performance would excuse compliance under the contract. In the second situation, courts in common-law countries would probably rule that the bursting of the water pipes did not constitute an act of God if it happened in a climate where freezing could be expected. Therefore, impossibility of delivery would not necessarily excuse compliance with the provisions of the contract. In code-law countries where the scope of impossibility of performance is extended considerably, the destruction might very well be ruled an act of God, and thus release from compliance with the contract could be obtained. When entering a contract with Eastern European countries, there are two sensitive areas to consider when wording a detailed act of God statement. One involves the phrase "act of God." Eastern European

---

[15] Lewis, *Trade Handbook*, p. 533.

negotiators prefer "act of nature," and for all practical purposes, the meaning is the same. The other area of sensitivity concerns strikes. Eastern European negotiators tend to look on labor disruptions as issues readily resolved by their Western partners by meeting workers' demands.

The international marketer must be especially concerned with the differences among Islamic, socialist, common-law, and code-law systems when operating between countries using different systems; the rights of the principals of a contract or some other legal document under one law may be significantly different from the rights under the other. It should be kept in mind that there can also be differences between the laws of two countries whose laws are based on the same legal system. Thus, the problem of the marketer is not only one of appreciating the significance of the basis for the law in a particular country—whether or not it is an Islamic, socialist, common-law, or code-law country—but also one of anticipating the different laws regulating business regardless of the legal system of the country.

JURISDICTION IN INTERNATIONAL LEGAL DISPUTES

Another problem of international marketing is determining whose legal system has jurisdiction when commercial disputes arise. A frequent error is to assume that disputes between citizens of different nations are adjudicated under some supranational system of laws. Unfortunately, there is no judicial body to deal with legal commercial problems arising between citizens of different countries.

In the everyday discussions of foreign business, it is often implied that there exists a body of international law to which all foreign trade activities are subject. There is no such body of international law. The confusion probably stems from the existence of international courts, such as the World Court at The Hague and the International Court of Justice, the principal judicial organ of the United Nations. These courts are operative in international disputes between sovereign nations of the world rather than between private citizens.

Legal disputes can arise in three situations: (1) between governments; (2) between a company and a government; and, (3) between two companies. Disputes between governments can be adjudicated by the World Court whereas the other two situations must be handled either in the courts of the country of one of the parties involved or through arbitration. Unless a commercial dispute involves a national issue between states, it is not handled by the International Court of Justice or any similar world court.[16]

---

[16] "Asia's Export Upstarts Face High Winds from Washington," *Business Week*, November 7, 1988, pp. 52–53.

Because there is no body of rules concerned solely with international commercial transactions, no "international commercial law," the foreign marketer must look to the legal system of each country involved—the laws of the home country, and/or the laws of the countries within which business is conducted. This, then, is the added dimension of the legal environment that becomes significant in foreign marketing. Every country has its own legal system to which the foreign marketer's operations must be tailored.

When international commercial disputes must be settled under the laws of one of the countries concerned, the paramount question in a dispute is which law governs. Jurisdiction over private, international legal disputes is generally determined in one of three ways: (1) on the basis of jurisdictional clauses included in contracts; (2) on the basis of where a contract was entered into; or (3) on the basis of where the provisions of the contract were performed.

The most clear-cut decision can be made when the contracts or legal documents supporting a business transaction state clearly whose law is to prevail. In fact, it is advisable to include a jurisdictional clause in all contracts to avoid the problem of determining jurisdiction after a dispute arises. In most cases, a clause similar to the following establishes jurisdiction in the event of future disagreements:

> That the parties hereby agree that the agreement is made in Colorado, USA, and that any question regarding this agreement shall be governed by the law of the state of Colorado, USA.

In this clause, it is agreed that should a dispute arise, the laws of the state of Colorado would be invoked. If the complaint were brought in the court of another country, it is probable that the same Colorado law would govern the decision. Cooperation and a definite desire to be judicious in foreign legal problems have led to the practice of foreign courts judging disputes on the basis of the law of another country or state whenever applicable. Thus, if an injured party from Colorado brings suit in the courts of Mexico against a Mexican over a contract which included the preceding clause, it would not be unusual for the Mexican courts to decide on the basis of Colorado law. This is assuming, of course, it was recognized that Colorado law prevailed in this dispute either as a result of a prior agreement by the parties or on some other basis.

A jurisdictional clause, however, does not always solve the legal problem of which laws should be invoked. Even with a specific clause establishing jurisdiction, if the contractual events are not entered into or executed within the state indicated, courts have been known to disregard the jurisdictional clause and apply different rules in determining which law governs. In cases where there is no jurisdictional clause, or where such a clause is not effective, decisions are sometimes arrived at on the basis of where the contract was entered into. In such disputes, the laws of the country or state where the contract was created prevail. Other legal disagreements are sometimes settled on the basis of where the provisions of the contract were performed. The laws of the country where the business transaction was actually carried out are invoked in judging a dispute. In all cases where there is no jurisdictional clause, the governing legal system is determined by one of these two methods. Because there is no clear-cut procedure concerning who has jurisdiction, and the laws of one country may typically be more favorable than another, it is probably wise to include a clause stipulating whose laws are to govern in all agreements. In most cases, courts uphold these clauses provided substantial acceptance or performance of the agreement has actually occurred within the designated state.[17]

LEGAL RECOURSE IN RESOLVING INTERNATIONAL DISPUTES

When it becomes apparent that the settlement of a dispute cannot be resolved on a private basis, the foreign marketer must resort to more resolute action. Many international business people prefer a settlement through arbitration rather than to sue a foreign company.

Problems with Litigation

Lawsuits in public courts are avoided for many reasons. Most observers of litigation between citizens of different countries believe that almost all victories are spurious because the cost, frustrating delays, and extended aggravation which these cases produce are more oppressive by far than any matter of comparable size. The best advice is to seek a settlement, if possible, rather than sue. other frequent deterrents to litigation are:

1. Fear of creating a poor image and damaging public relations.
2. Fear of unfair treatment in a foreign court. (Although not intentional, there is justifiable fear that a lawsuit can result in unfair treatment since the decision could be made by either a jury or judge not well versed in trade problems and the intricacies of international business transactions.)
3. Difficulty in collecting a judgment that may otherwise have been collected in a mutually agreed settlement through arbitration.
4. The relatively high cost and time required when bringing legal action.
5. Loss of confidentiality.

One authority suggests that the settlement of every dispute should follow three steps: first, try to placate the injured party; if this does not work,

---

[17] For a summary of the legal issues discussed in this section, see David Scalise, "Export Agreements that Work," *Export Today*, July–August 1987, pp. 41–46.

arbitrate; and finally, litigate. The final step is typically taken only when all other methods fail. Actually, this advice is probably wise whether one is involved in an international dispute or a domestic one.

Arbitration

Because of the pitfalls of litigation, the majority of international commercial disputes are resolved by arbitration. The usual arbitration procedure is for the parties involved to select a disinterested and informed party or parties as referee to determine the merits of the case and make a judgment that both parties agree to honor. In actual practice, however, formal rules and procedures are established for entering into an arbitration agreement.

Tribunals for Arbitration.   Although the preceding informal method of arbitration is workable, most arbitration is conducted under the auspices of one of the more formal domestic and international arbitration groups organized specifically to facilitate the mediation of commercial disputes. These groups have experienced arbitrators available and formal rules for the process of arbitration and, in most countries, the decisions reached in formal mediation are enforceable under the law.

Among the formal arbitration organizations are:

1. The Inter-American Commercial Arbitration Commission, which conducts arbitration in disputes between the businesses of 21 American republics, including the United States.
2. The Canadian-American Commercial Arbitration Commission, which functions in disputes between Canadian and U.S. businesses.
3. The London Court of Arbitration, which is restricted to those cases that can be legally arbitrated in England. Decisions by the London Court of Arbitration are enforceable under English law and English courts.
4. The American Arbitration Association was one of the early arbitration tribunals organized in the United States and was originally concerned only with disputes within the United States. Later, however, its activities were expanded worldwide.
5. The International Chamber of Commerce, which is an affiliation of Chambers of Commerce of many of the world's nations. With its worldwide scope, it has established a Court of Arbitration whose rules are used in conducting arbitration.

International Chamber of Commerce.   The procedures used by formal arbitration organizations are similar. Arbitration under the rules of the International Chamber of Commerce (ICC) affords an excellent example of how most organizations operate. When an initial request for arbitration is received, the chamber first attempts a conciliation between the disputants. If this fails, the process of arbitration is started. The plaintiff and the defendant select one person each from among acceptable arbitrators to defend their case, and the ICC Court of Arbitration appoints a third member, generally chosen from a list of distinguished lawyers, jurists, and/or professors.

The arbitrators arrange for a meeting with both parties; after hearing each side present its case, the ICC members make a decision and an award. The history of ICC effectiveness in arbitration has been spectacular; of the scores of decisions recorded, only a few have been rejected by the litigants. Of the decisions rejected, all but one have had the arbitration decision upheld in the courts when further litigation was pursued.

An example of a case that involved arbitration by the ICC concerned a contract between an English business and a Japanese manufacturer; the English business agreed to buy 100,000 plastic dolls for 80 cents each. On the strength of the contract, the English business sold the entire lot at $1.40 per doll. Before the dolls were delivered, the Japanese manufacturer had a strike; the settlement of the strike increased costs and the English business was informed that the delivery price of the dolls had increased from 80 cents to $1.50 each. The English business maintained that the Japanese firm had committed to make delivery at 80 cents and should deliver at that price. Each side was convinced that it was right. The Japanese, accustomed to code law, felt that the strike was beyond control, was an act of God, and thus compliance with the original provisions of the contract was excused. The English, accustomed to common law, did not accept the Japanese reasons for not complying because they considered a strike the normal course of doing business and not an act of God. The dispute could not be settled except through litigation or arbitration. They chose arbitration; the ICC appointed a Scandinavian Supreme Court justice who heard both sides and ruled that the two parties would share proportionately in the loss. The case was settled to the satisfaction of both parties, and costly litigation was avoided. Most arbitration is successful, but it must be emphasized that the success of arbitration depends on the willingness of both parties to accept the arbitrator's rulings.

Arbitration Clauses. Most authorities recommend that contracts and other legal documents include clauses specifying the use of arbitration in case of dispute. Unless a provision for arbitration of any dispute is incorporated as part of a contract, the likelihood of securing agreement for arbitration after a dispute arises is reduced. In fact, attempts to refer a dispute to arbitration after disagreement arises, frequently fail because one party or the other is unwilling to agree on the form or place of arbitration.

The following is an example of an arbitration clause suggested by the International Chamber of Commerce for inclusion in all legal documents where arbitration may be necessary.

All disputes arising in connection with the present contract shall be finally settled under the rules of conciliation and arbitration of the International Chamber of Commerce by one or more arbitrators appointed in accordance with the said rules.

The inclusion of an arbitration clause in a contract can avert problems, but sometimes enforcing arbitration agreements even when made prior to a dispute can be difficult.

Enforcement of Arbitration Clauses

Arbitration clauses generally require agreement on two counts: (1) the parties agree to arbitrate in case of a dispute according to the rules and procedures of some arbitration tribunal; (2) they agree to abide by the awards resulting from the arbitration. Difficulty arises when the parties to a contract fail to honor the agreements. Companies may refuse to name arbitrators, refuse to arbitrate, or after arbitration awards are made, they may refuse to honor the award. In most countries, arbitration clauses are recognized by the courts and are enforceable by law within those countries.

Over seventy countries have signed a U.S. Convention on the Recognition and Enforcement of Foreign Arbitral Awards, also known as the New York Convention, that binds them to uphold foreign arbitration awards. Previously, a winning party had to sue to enforce a foreign award; under the New York Convention, the courts of the signatory countries automatically uphold foreign arbitral awards issued in member countries. The United States has a federal arbitration law that recognizes the legality of arbitration clauses and establishes the necessary legal procedures to enforce such clauses.

In addition to the New York Convention, the United States has signed the Inter-American Convention on International Arbitration, to which many Latin American countries are party. However, ratification by the U.S. Senate, while expected, was still pending when this edition went to press. The United States is also party to a number of bilateral agreements containing clauses providing for enforcement of arbitral awards.[18]

Experience suggests that arbitration awards or judgments confirming arbitration clauses in contracts are generally enforceable in most foreign courts. This is true even in countries where binding national laws are not in existence. Since laws and procedures vary from country to country, arbitration can be used as a sort of "legal esperanto" to bridge the gap between differing legal systems.[19]

---

[18] Daniel M. Price, "The Arbitration Advantage," *Export Today*, July–August 1988, pp. 58–61.

[19] Thomas Peele and Marsha A. Cohan, "Dispute Resolution in China," *The China Business Review*, September–October 1988, pp. 46–49.

PROTECTION OF INTELLECTUAL PROPERTY RIGHTS—
A SPECIAL PROBLEM

Companies spend thousands of dollars establishing product brand names or trademarks to symbolize quality and a host of other product features designed to entice customers to buy their brands to the exclusion of all others. Millions of dollars are spent on research to develop industrial properties such as products, processes, designs, and formulas that provide companies with advantages over their competitors. Such intellectual or industrial properties are among the more valuable assets a company may possess. Names such as Kodak, Coca-Cola, Gucci, or rights to processes like xerography, or the production of nylon or cellophane are invaluable. Normally property rights can be legally protected to prevent other companies from infringing on such assets.[20] Companies must, however, keep a constant vigil for piracy and counterfeiting.[21]

Estimates are that more than 10 million fake Swiss timepieces carrying famous brand names such as Cartier and Rolex are sold every year netting illegal profits of at least $500 million. Although difficult to pinpoint, lost sales from the unauthorized use of U.S. patents, trademarks, and copyrights amount to about $20 billion annually. That translates into nearly 750,000 lost jobs. Software is an especially attractive target for pirates because it is costly to develop but cheap to reproduce. Unauthorized U.S. software that sells for $500 in this country can be purchased for less than $10 in areas of the Far East.[22] Counterfeit trade has risen to the point that several countries including the United States, the European Community, and Canada are seeking a change in GATT rules that would impose severe penalties against countries permitting the manufacture and sale of pirated goods.[23] Counterfeit and pirated goods come from a wide range of industries—apparel, automotive parts, agricultural chemicals, pharmaceuticals, books, records, films, and computer software to name a few.

Inadequate Protection

The failure to protect intellectual or industrial property rights adequately in the world marketplace can lead to the legal loss of these rights in potentially profitable markets. Because patents, processes, trademarks, and copy-

---

[20] For an interesting article on how IBM protects its intellectual property from infringement, see Gunter Hauptman, "Intellectual Property Rights," *International Marketing Review*, Spring 1987, pp. 61–64.

[21] "NICs Make Progress but Do not Make Grade on Intellectual Property," *Business International*, May 23, 1988, p. 155.

[22] Eileen Hill, "The Administration Is Working to Improve Worldwide Protection of One of Our Most Valuable Trade Assets: Intellectual Property," *Business America*, July 21, 1986, pp. 9–11.

[23] C. William Verity, "Uruguay Round," *Business America*, June 20, 1988, p. 3.

BOX 6–1
Time Runs out in Miami

Miami was not the place to be for anyone wearing a $40 Rolex watch. While the media and agents of the U.S. Customs Service and U.S. Secret Service looked on, a steam roller flattened 17,000 counterfeit watches falsely bearing the names Rolex, Patek Fillippe, Corum, Concorde, and Piaget.

The watches, valued at more than $620,000 even as fakes, were seized by Customs Service and Secret Service agents during the climax of their Operation Stopwatch case. Operation Stopwatch was initiated when supposedly high-priced watches, primarily Rolex, began appearing with price tags of $20 to $40 at flea markets and street vendors' racks throughout southeastern Florida. They same watches fetch $5 to $10 in Hong Kong where they are made. Agents arrested 26 persons on charges of trafficking in counterfeit merchandise; all 26 were convicted. According to customs officials, more than 10 million counterfeit watches are sold each year based on estimates by Swiss watch manufacturers. The watches are only a piece of the multibillion dollar worldwide trade in counterfeit goods.

Source: Adapted from "Time Runs out for Fake Watches," *The Journal of Commerce,* November 14, 1988, p. 4a.

---

rights are valuable in all countries, some companies have found that their assets have been appropriated and profitably exploited in foreign countries without license or reimbursement. Further, they often learn not only that other firms are producing and selling their products or using their trademarks, but also that the foreign companies are the rightful owners in the countries where they are operating.[24]

There have been many cases where companies have legally lost the rights to trademarks and have had to buy back these rights or pay royalties for their use. One of the most unusual cases involved a U.S. citizen residing in Mexico who registered in Mexico, a code-law country, the brand names and trademarks of some 40 companies. Included were such well-known names as "Carter's Little Liver Pills" and "Bromo Seltzer." Although most of the companies were able to regain control of their brand names, the procedure required lengthy litigation and considerable help from the U.S. government. If the culprit had not been so blatant in pirating 40 such well-known brands, he could have been successful.

It is not uncommon to find situations where manufacturers have licensed local companies to produce products in return for a royalty only to have

---

[24] Guy C. Smith, "Protecting Intellectual Property Rights Abroad: Pointers for U.S. Exporters," *Business America,* November 21, 1988, pp. 14–15.

BOX 6–2
When the Counterfeit Is Better than the Original, Which One Is Genuine?

When the West German maker of Comtesse-brand high-fashion leather goods decided to do some manufacturing in Hong Kong, it was in for a surprise. In its leased factory space were 10 large boxes left behind by the previous tenant. Inside the boxes were thousands and thousands of Comtesse labels, all fake. The previous tenant had been a Comtesse counterfeiter. Rolls of trademarked labels are so perfectly copied and so commonly available in Hong Kong that some manufacturers buy their own faked labels in street stalls when they run low. Hong Kong copiers specialize in luxury goods—Seiko and Rolex watches, Lacoste shirts, Celine bags, Hermes scarves, and fake labels.

   Tough laws to control such piracy are being enacted by many countries who fear that foreign manufacturers will stop licensing technology if piracy and counterfeiting are not controlled. Taiwan, previously noted for its lax attitude toward piracy, is responding to pressure from the United States and other countries to control counterfeiting. Year-long prison terms were given to two Taipei businessmen for pirating the 10-volume, 15-million-word *Concise Encyclopaedia Britannica.* Over 56,000 bindings and thousands of completed volumes of the encyclopaedia were seized and destroyed. Despite stronger enforcement of existing laws, piracy and counterfeiting still cost U.S. businesses between $43 and $61 billion annually.

   Sources: Adapted from Anthony Spaeth, "Hong Kong Counterfeit Trade Thrives but Faked Brands Arouse Genuine Ire," *The Wall Street Journal,* October 29, 1980, p. 35; and "Encyclopaedia Britannica Hails Favorable Piracy Case Verdict," *The Journal of Commerce,* September 26, 1988, p. 4a.

royalty payments stopped a short time later. When inquiries about the stopped royalty payments are made, the licensor is told that the particular process is no longer being used. Further inquiry finds the process has been changed minimally and the licensee continues to produce the product without paying the royalty. In most instances, the pirating of processes can be avoided by carefully drawn agreements between the licensee and the licensor.

   The problems of inadequate protective measures taken by the owners of valuable assets stem from a variety of causes. One of the more frequent errors is assuming that since the company has established rights in the United States, it will be protected around the world or that rightful ownership can be established should the need arise. Such was the case with McDonald's (the hamburger franchise) in Japan. Its "Golden Arches" trademark was registered by an enterprising Japanese. Only after a lengthy and costly legal action was McDonald's able to regain the exclusive right to use the trademark in Japan. McDonald's now has a very active program to protect its trademarks.[25] Many businesses fail to understand that most countries do not follow the common-law principle that ownership is established by prior use, or that registration and legal ownership in one country does not necessarily mean ownership in another.

Prior Use versus Registration

In the United States, a common-law country, ownership of intellectual property rights is established by prior use—whoever can establish first use is typically considered the rightful owner. In fact, before trademarks and brand names can be registered, they must actually be in use. In many code-law countries, however, ownership is established by registration rather than by prior use—the first to register a trademark or other property right is considered the rightful owner. Therefore, a company that believes it can always establish ownership in another country by proving it used the trademark or brand name first is wrong and risks the loss of these assets. It is best to protect intellectual property rights through registration.

To further complicate the problem, countries frequently change their laws from a typical common-law basis to code law. For example, Canada, a common-law country, has changed its patent laws to give priority to registration over prior invention as a means of establishing rights to a patent. The United States is also considering such a move. In negotiations to strengthen intellectual property rights protection in Japan and Europe, U.S. negotiators have indicated a willingness to change from the long-standing prior-use principle to recognizing first registration as the determiner of ownership of a patent.[26]

Avoiding the possible loss of intellectual property rights that may be profitable either for the company to sell directly or to license others to produce and sell in foreign markets is generally a matter of properly registering them within these countries. This task can be facilitated by several international conventions which provide for simultaneous registration in member countries.

International Conventions

Many countries participate in international conventions designed for mutual recognition and protection of intellectual property rights. There are three major international conventions. They are:

---

[25] "McDonald's Wages Its 'Mc' Battle Worldwide," Associated Press, April 25, 1988.

[26] Eduardo Lachica, "U.S. Is Offering to Revise Its Patent Code if Other Countries Agree to Reciprocate," *The Wall Street Journal*, June 15, 1988, p. 19.

1. The International Convention for the Protection of Industrial Property, commonly referred to as the *Paris Union*, comprises a group of 94 nations, including the United States, that have agreed to recognize the rights of all members in the protection of trademarks, patents, and other property rights. Registration in one of the member countries ensures the same protection afforded by the home country in all the member countries.

2. The Inter-American Convention includes most of the Latin American nations and the United States. It provides protection similar to that afforded by the Paris Union.

3. The Madrid Arrangement established the Bureau for International Registration of Trademarks. There are some 26 member countries in Europe that have agreed to automatic trademark protection for all members. Even though the United States is not a participant of the Madrid Arrangement, if a subsidiary of a U.S. company is located in one of the member nations, the subsidiary could file through the membership of its host country and thereby provide protection in all 26 countries for the U.S. company.

In addition to these three agreements; two new multicountry patent arrangements have streamlined patent procedures in Europe. The Patent Cooperation Treaty (PCT) facilitates the application of patents among its 28 member countries. It provides comprehensive coverage in that a single application filed in the United States supplies the interested party with an international search report on other patents to help evaluate whether or not to seek protection in each of the countries cooperating under the PCT.

The European Patent Convention (EPC) establishes a regional patent system allowing any nationality to file a single international application for a European patent. Once the patent is approved, the patent has the same effect as a national patent in each individual country designated on the application.[27]

Once a trademark, patent, or other intellectual property right is registered, most countries require that these rights be worked and properly policed. The United States is one of the few countries where a patent can be held by an individual throughout the duration of the patent period without being manufactured and sold. Other countries feel that in exchange for the monopoly provided by a patent, the holder must share the product with the citizens of the country. Hence, if patents are not produced within a specified period, usually from one to five years (the average is three years), the patent reverts to public domain. This is also true for trademarks;

---

[27] Thomas J. Maronick, "European Patent Laws and Decisions: Implications for Multinational Marketing Strategy," *International Marketing Review*, Summer 1988, pp. 31–40.

products bearing the registered mark must be sold within the country, or the company may forfeit its right to a particular trademark. McDonald's was confronted with that problem in Venezuela. Even though the Mc-Donald's trademark was properly registered in that code-law country, the company did not use it for more than two years. Under Venezuelan law, a trademark must be used within two years or it is lost. Thus, a Venezuelan-owned "Mr. McDonald's," with accompanying golden arches, is operating in Venezuela. The U.S. McDonald's Corporation faces a potentially costly legal battle if it decides to challenge the Venezuelan company. Individual countries expect companies to actively police their intellectual property by bringing to court any violators. Policing can be a difficult task, with success depending in large measure on the cooperation of the country within which the infringement or piracy takes place.[28]

COMMERCIAL LAW WITHIN COUNTRIES

When marketers are doing business in more than one country, they must remain alert to the different legal systems. This problem is especially troublesome for the marketer who formulates a common marketing plan to be implemented in several countries. Although differences in languages and customs may be negated, legal differences between countries may still prevent a standardized marketing program.[29]

Marketing Laws

All countries have laws regulating marketing activities in promotion, product development, labeling, pricing, and channels of distribution. In some, there may be only a few laws with lax enforcement; in others, there may be detailed, complicated rules to follow that are stringently enforced. Even when different countries have laws covering the same activities, there are frequently vast differences in enforcement and interpretation among those countries. Laws governing sales promotions in the European Community offer good examples of the diversity that can exist among countries.

In Austria premium offers to consumers come under the discount law that prohibits any cash reductions that give preferential treatment to different groups of customers. Because most premium offers would result in discriminatory treatment of buyers, they normally are not allowed. Pre-

---

[28] "NICs Make Progress," p. 155.

[29] See for example, Mushtaq, Luqmani, Ugar, Yavas and Zahir, Quraeshi "Advertising in Saudi Arabia: Content and Regulation," *International Marketing Review*, Volume 6, Number 1 (1989), pp. 59–72.

Free market in Leshan, China. Laws in China have changed to allow free markets.

mium offers in Finland are allowed with considerable scope as long as the word *free* is not used and consumers are not coerced into buying products. France also regulates premium offers which are, for all practical purposes, illegal because it is illegal to sell for less than cost price or to offer a customer a gift or premium conditional on the purchase of another product. Furthermore, a manufacturer or retailer cannot offer products different from the kind regularly offered (i.e., a detergent manufacturer cannot offer clothing or kitchen utensils; the typical cereal premiums would be completely illegal under this law). West German law covering promotion in general is about as stringent as can be found. In fact, the laws are so voluminous and complicated that any advertiser contemplating a promotional campaign should consult a lawyer. Most kinds of promotion are allowed but with severe restrictions.

Another major stumbling block confronting those attempting to advertise across national boundaries is the various laws concerning product *comparison,* a natural and effective means of expression. In Germany, comparisons in advertisements are always subject to the competitor's ability to go to the courts and ask for proof of any implied or stated superiority. In Canada, the rulings are even more stringent; all claims and statements must be examined to ensure that any representation to the public is not false or misleading. Such representation can be made verbally in selling or contained in or on anything that comes to the attention of the public (such as product labels, inserts in products, or any other form of advertising including what may be expressed in a sales letter). Courts have been directed by the law to take into account in determining whether a representation is false or misleading the "general impression" conveyed by the representation as well as its literal meaning. The courts are expected to apply the *credulous person standard*, which means that if any reasonable person could possibly misunderstand the representation, the representation is misleading. In essence puffery, an acceptable practice in the United States, could be interpreted in Canada as false and misleading advertising. Thus, a statement such as "the strongest drive shaft in Canada" would be judged misleading unless the advertiser had absolute evidence that the drive shaft was stronger than any other drive shaft for sale in Canada.

The examples illustrate the diversity of laws found among countries. These differences are apparent not only in advertising but also in pricing, sales agreements, and other commercial activities. A frequent marketing approach to Europe is to consider the continent as a unified market. The problems created by differences in laws among countries are no less pronounced there than the difficulties that arise from the differences found in social customs, taste, and economies.

There is some hope, especially among the European Community, of having a common commercial code. This has not yet been achieved and those U.S. companies that have operated under the erroneous belief that the Common Market is truly common in all respects have had spectacular failures. Although the EC is a beautiful picture of economic cooperation, for the marketer it is still a matter of dealing with 12 different countries, cultures, and languages, as well as 12 different legal systems. The EC has set a goal to achieve barrier-free movement of people, goods, services, and capital within the community by 1992. If this complete integration is achieved, many of the current legal and trade differences will be eliminated.[30]

Antitrust—an Evolving Issue

With the exception of the United States, antitrust laws have been either nonexistent or unenforced in most of the world's countries for the better part of the 20th century. However, by the 1970s, the European Community began to actively enforce its antitrust laws patterned after those in the United States. Price discrimination, supply restrictions, and full-line forcing are areas in which the European Court of Justice has dealt severe penalties. For example, Michelin was fined $700,000 for operating a system of discrimi

---

[30] "Europe without Borders: Answer to Some Questions," *Europe*, October 1988, pp. 15–17.

natory rebates to Dutch tire dealers. Similar penalties have been assessed against such major companies as United Brands Co. for price discrimination and F. Hoffmann-LaRoche and Company for noncost-justified fidelity discounts to its dealers.[31]

Even developing countries are becoming more concerned with antitrust problems. While antitrust is commonly considered a preoccupation of developed nations, there has been a substantial increase in concern over restraint of trade among developing countries. In the industrialized world, restraint of trade has typically meant restraint of competition, and, in most instances, refers to restrictions imposed on competition between independent companies. Developing nations see intracorporate limitations imposed by a parent company on its subsidiary within their country as the major violation of free trade. Thus, restraint of trade is more an interpretation of their concern with a parent multinational firm restraining the competitive activities of its subsidiary within the country. In all these situations, the multinational firm is confronted with various interpretations of antitrust. To confuse the marketer further, its activities in one country may inadvertently lead to antitrust violations in another.

U.S. LAWS APPLY IN HOST COUNTRIES

Leaving the political boundaries of a home country does not exempt a business from home-country laws. Regardless of the nation where business is done, a U.S. citizen is subject to certain laws of the United States. What is illegal for an American business at home can also be illegal by U.S. laws in foreign jurisdictions. U.S. laws cover business practices related to ethics, national security, and some antitrust considerations. All governments are concerned with protecting their political and economic interests domestically and internationally; thus, any activity or action, wherever it occurs, that threatens security is subject to government control.[32]

Laws that prohibit participating in unauthorized boycotts like the Arab boycott, trading with an enemy of the United States, or participating in a commercial venture that adversely affects the U.S. economy apply to U.S. businesses regardless of where they operate. Thus, at any given time, a U.S. citizen in a foreign country must look not only at the laws of the host country, but simultaneously at the rules of the home sovereign.

The question of jurisdiction of U.S. law over acts committed outside the territorial limits of the country has been settled by the courts through

---

[31] The Department of Justice has recently published draft antitrust guidelines for international operations; see Robert H. Brumley, "How Antitrust Law Affects International Joint Ventures," *Business America*, November 21, 1988, pp. 3–5.

[32] Walter J. Olson, "Export Administration Act of 1985," *Business America*, September 2, 1985, pp. 2–5.

application of a long-established principle of international law, "objective theory of jurisdiction." This concept holds that even if an act is committed outside the territorial jurisdiction of U.S. courts, those courts can nevertheless have jurisdiction if the act produces effects within the home country.[33]

Any activity by a U.S. firm considered by U.S. courts to affect national security or to damage U.S. foreign or domestic commerce is subject to U.S. law.[34] The only exception may be that action would not be taken if the violation occurred as a result of enforced compliance with local law. Two areas that are most troublesome to U.S. firms are issues involving national security and antitrust. In both instances, questions of the extraterritoriality of U.S. law are frequently raised by host countries.

Foreign Corrupt Practices Act

The Foreign Corrupt Practices Act (FCPA) makes it illegal for companies to pay bribes to foreign officials, candidates, or political parties. Stiff penalties can be assessed against company officials, directors, employees, or agents found guilty of paying a bribe or of knowingly participating in or authorizing the payment of a bribe. As we discussed in the chapter on business customs, bribery is a custom of business in many countries; different types of bribes range from lubrication to extortion.

The original FCPA lacked clarity and early interpretations were extremely narrow and confusing. Even simple payments to expedite activities (grease) were considered illegal. Another troubling part of the law for U.S. executives was the provision that executives could be held liable for bribes paid by anyone in their organizations, including agents in the foreign country, if they had any "reason to know." Many U.S. firms restricted their agents from business as usual for fear the agents were paying bribes. A general reaction to this law from those knowledgeable about international business is that U.S. businesses are at a disadvantage in international business transactions in those cases where bribery payments are customary. The debate continues as to whether the FCPA makes U.S. business less able to compete. Some studies show that it has little effect while others seem to suggest some disadvantage for U.S. companies competing in those countries where bribery is seemingly a way of business.[35] The truth probably lies somewhere in between.

---

[33] Andre Simons, "Foreign Trade and Antitrust Laws," *Business Topics*, Summer 1962, p. 27.

[34] Terrance R. Murphy, "Technology Transfer Update," *Export Today*, Summer 1985, pp. 65–66.

[35] Mark E. Haskens and Robert N. Holt, "FCPA and RICO," *Export Trade*, Summer 1986, pp. 61–69.

BOX 6–3
Whatever You Call It—It's Still a Bribe

U.S. expressions such as *bribe* or *payoff* all sound a little stiff and cold. In some countries, the terms for the same activities have a little more character.*
For example:

Country	Term	Translation
Japan	Kuroi kiri	Black mist
Germany	Schmiergeld	Grease money
Latin America	El soborno	Payoff
Mexico	La mordida	The bite
Middle East	Baksheesh	Tip, gratuity
France	Pot-de-vin	Jug of wine
East Africa	Chai	Tea
Italy	Bustarella	Little envelope

* Other terms are *wairo* (Japan), *dash* (Nigeria), and *backhander* (India).

All attempts to amend the original law and correct the causes of confusion were unsuccessful until 1988. The Omnibus Trade and Competitiveness Act of 1988 amended the FCPA and reduced the potential liability of corporate officers from "have reason to know" to "know of or authorize" illegal payments. In addition, if it is customary in the culture, the law permits small (grease or lubrication) payments made to encourage officials to complete routine government actions such as processing paper, stamping visas, and scheduling inspections.[36] Clearly, U.S. businesses have learned to live with the law; the consensus is that most comply in good faith. With the recent amendments to the FCPA, two of the most troubling provisions of the law have been modified and some of the earlier confusion and lack of clarity erased.[37]

National Security Laws

U.S. firms, their foreign subsidiaries, or foreign firms who are licensees of U.S. technology cannot sell a product to a country where the sale is considered, by the U.S. government, to affect national security.[38] U.S. multinational firms with foreign-based subsidiaries or joint ventures with

---

[36] The Omnibus Trade and Competitiveness Act of 1988 (Washington, D.C.: International Division, U.S. Chamber of Commerce, 1988), p. 32.

[37] "The New Trade Act: Tools for Exporters," *Business America*, October 24, 1988, p. 3.

[38] See Chapter 16 for a complete discussion of export controls.

BOX 6–4
Turnabout Is Fair Play

Japanese knitwear makers want their government to take tough action against South Korean clothing companies they accuse of dumping products in Japan. They allege that Korean manufacturers are dumping, selling below cost, as a way to steal the market from domestic producers. Japanese makers want the government to investigate and then force Korea to stop this practice. The ministry of International Trade and Industry (MITI) says other industries are beginning to talk of import competition problems; among them are makers of synthetic fibers, cotton yarns, cement, and even companies producing semiconductors, tape recorders and stereo equipment.

Japan also advances the argument that it often heard from the United States; that Korea, as an exporting country, has a commitment to the world trade system and should not violate "orderly marketing principles." Says a MITI representative, "We are trying to deepen their understanding of the effect Korean export policies have on the Japanese market."

Americans might find certain irony in the current spat: It wasn't so long ago that U.S. companies were leveling accusations against the very Japanese industries that are now up in arms.

"I wonder if the old proverb applies: History repeats itself," say Aichi Tamori, deputy director of MITI. Indeed the foreign minister who led Japan's handling of trade disputes with the United States says, "I hear myself making the same argument I heard from the U.S." during two and a half tough years of trade talks.

Japan might not have any more success with the NICs than the United States did with Japan as these countries follow the path that Japan once followed.

Source: Adapted from Damon Darling, "Japanese Manufacturers Fighting Back as Asian Rivals Invade Domestic Market," *The Wall Street Journal*, December 5, 1988, p. A10.

---

host-country companies often find they are inadvertently involved with host-country trade that puts the U.S. firm in violation of U.S. law. For example, the Fruehauf Corporation was caught in the middle when its French subsidiary signed a $20-million contract with the People's Republic of China. At that time, the United States was not trading with China, and any U.S. firm that did was in violation of the Trading with the Enemy Act. Fruehauf (U.S.) canceled the contract, but the French government intervened, legally seized the French subsidiary, and the deal went through without U.S. Fruehauf involvement. Since the Fruehauf case, relations between the United States and China have improved considerably and these two nations are trading extensively. Yet, a U.S. company or any of its joint ventures or licensees cannot sell products to China or any other country without special permission from the U.S. government. The United States successfully blocked the sale of French telecommunications equipment to China that included licensed U.S. technology because of its fear that the equipment would have military use.

The consequences of violation of this law can be severe: fines, prison sentences, and in the case of foreign companies, economic sanctions. Toshiba Machine Tool Company of Japan sold the Soviet Union milling machines to make ultraquiet submarine propellers. However, the technology for the milling machines was licensed to the Japanese company by a U.S. company and sale to Russia was forbidden. Besides sanctions taken against Toshiba in Japan for violation of Japanese law, the U.S. Trade Bill of 1988 specifically banned all government purchases from Toshiba Corporation, parent of Toshiba Machine Company, for three years. The estimated losses annually are about 3 percent of the company's total exports to the United States.[39] Protection of U.S. technology that has either national security or economic implications is an ongoing activity of the U.S. government.[40]

U.S. Antitrust Laws

Antitrust enforcement has two purposes in international commerce. The first is to protect American consumers by ensuring that they benefit from products and ideas produced by foreign competitors as well as by domestic competitors. Competition from foreign producers is important when imports are, or could be, a major source of a product or when a domestic industry is dominated by a single firm. This becomes relevant in many joint ventures, particularly if the joint venture creates a situation where a U.S. firm entering a joint venture with a foreign competitor restricts competition for the U.S. parent in the U.S. market. The second purpose of antitrust legislation is to protect American export and investment opportunities against any privately imposed restrictions. The concern is that all U.S.-based firms engaged in the export of goods, services, or capital should be allowed to compete on merit and not be shut out by restrictions imposed by bigger or less-principled competitors.

The questions of jurisdiction and how U.S. antitrust laws apply are frequently asked but only vaguely answered. The basis for determination

[39] "New Japanese Council Hopes to Defuse U.S.-Japan Trade Tensions," *Business International,* August 29, 1988, p. 274.

[40] "America's Domestic and International Role in Protecting the Free World's High Technology," *Business America,* January 18, 1988, pp. 7–9.

> **BOX 6–5**
> **ET Go Home—Extra-Territorial, That Is**
>
>   The United States and Europe are embroiled in serious conflict over an issue with the unlikely code letters of E. T. The name refers not to "The Extraterrestrial," but rather to the Extra Territorial concerns raised by the U.S. government's export control policies. President Reagan's decision to exercise foreign-policy controls after the military takeover in Poland triggered a dispute between the United States and Europe over a Soviet gas pipeline. European governments objected because the administration insisted on applying U.S. laws not only to American companies, but also to their foreign-based subsidiaries and foreign companies under license to U.S. firms. The European protest document stated that it was neither justifiable nor acceptable for the U.S. government to impose U.S. law and policy on other friendly countries which have their own policy views and wish to make their own decisions with respect to restrictions, if any, that may be imposed on trade with third countries.
>
>   The U.S. government forbid Caterpillar Tractor Company and other equipment manufacturers from selling pipeline-laying equipment to the Russians. A General Electric licensee in France was also restricted from selling the Russians gas-pumping equipment necessary for the natural gas pipeline. The U.S. government felt that it was strategically important for Russia not to complete the natural gas pipeline to Europe. The general consensus was that once this natural gas pipeline was complete, Europe would be too closely tied to Russia, thereby weakening U.S. influence in Europe.

ultimately rests with the interpretation of Sections I and II of the Sherman Act; Section I states that "every contract, combination . . . or conspiracy in restraint of trade or commerce among the several states or with foreign nations is hereby declared to be illegal"; Section II makes it a violation to "monopolize, or attempt to monopolize, or combine or conspire with any other person or persons, to monopolize any part of the trade or commerce among the several states, or with foreign nations."

The Justice Department recognizes that application of U.S. antitrust laws to overseas activities raises some difficult questions of jurisdiction. It recognizes that U.S. antitrust-law enforcement should not interfere unnecessarily with the sovereign interest of a foreign nation. At the same time, however, the Antitrust Division is committed to control foreign transactions at home or abroad which have a substantial and foreseeable effect on U.S. commerce. When such business practices occur, there is no question in the Antitrust Division of the Department of Justice that U.S. laws apply.

> **BOX 6–5** (*concluded*)
>
> The Russian pipeline incident is just one of many incidents where U.S. law is applied in other countries. Not only does it create problems among governments, but the companies involved also suffer.
>
> Caterpillar Tractor Company estimates that it lost $90 million in sales as a direct result of the sanctions as well as being barred from bidding on a subsequent $200 million Soviet project. Sanctions such as these make customers feel that U.S. businesses are not dependable; thus, when other sources are available, U.S. companies are at a competitive disadvantage. As one Caterpillar executive commented, "How many times is a country going to be burned by a U.S. company before it finally buys from someone else?"
>
> From the U.S. viewpoint, steps need to be taken to curtail the flow of U.S. technology to the Soviet Union. It is felt that export controls have been allowed to deteriorate resulting in a major leakage of Western technology to the Soviet Union which boosted its military buildup and saved the Soviets millions of dollars in research-and-development costs. There is no easy answer to using export controls; as one congressmen noted, "This is a genuine dilemma, we have to be more competitive but we have certain national security and foreign policy objectives."
>
> Sources: Adapted from Bailey Morris, "ET Go Home: U.S.-European Crisis Threatens over Extra-Territoriality Issue," *Europe*, July–August 1983, pp. 22–24; and "Moscow Yawns as the U.S. Lobbies for Trade," *Business Week*, July 29, 1985, pp. 38–39.

Extraterritoriality of U.S. Laws[41]

Heads of state do not like the idea of possible interference with their national policies, and frequently the multinational firm is caught in the middle. The issue is especially important to U.S. multinational firms since the long arm of U.S. legal jurisdiction causes anxiety for heads of state in Europe, Canada, and Latin America. These governments fear the influence of American government policy on their economies through U.S. multinationals.

With all due respect to the Justice Department's commitment to protect commerce within the United States, the extraterritorial application of U.S. antitrust laws creates major problems for international companies in the United States and elsewhere. The problems are twofold: (1) the kinds of

---

[41] Steve Hirsch, "Export Policy Faces New Congress: Europeans Oppose Extraterritoriality," *Europe*, January–February 1985, pp. 16–17.

activities imposed by foreign countries such as joint ventures, licensing requirements, and joint research may be subject to antitrust review. Frequently in these situations, companies are caught between the host government requiring joint ventures to do business within the country and the U.S. Justice Department restricting or forbidding such ventures because of their U.S. anticompetitive effects. (2) The extraterritorial application of antitrust laws can and does cause problems with host countries who are incensed at the influence of U.S. law within their boundaries. Host countries see this influence as further evidence of U.S. interference. When the intent of any kind of overseas activity is to restrain trade, there is no question about the appropriateness of applying U.S. laws. There is some question, however, when the intent is not to restrain trade but simply to conclude a reasonable business transaction.

There is growing concern among international marketers about the effects of antitrust enforcement by the U.S. government beyond its borders. Outright purchases, mergers, licensing, and joint ventures with foreign firms have been on the increase in recent years, sparking considerable interest within the antitrust department. As a result, jurisdictional issues have become more and more crucial because they raise the question of how and when a country's laws can be enforced outside its political boundaries.

A reasonable question is, if the government encourages U.S. firms to become multinational in operation, then shouldn't the government take a closer look at antitrust legislation designed to control the actions of *domestic* companies which may not be appropriate in terms of worldwide business practices?

Adding to the confusion are the many foreign countries that are adopting laws similar to the U.S. antitrust laws designed to regulate antitrust activities within the country and, in some instances, to reduce the effect of U.S. competition.

SUMMARY

Foreign business faces a multitude of problems in its efforts to develop a successful marketing program. Not the least of these problems are the varying legal systems of the world and their effect on business transactions. Just as political climate, cultural differences, local geography, different business customs, and the stage of economic development must be taken into account, so must such legal questions as jurisdictional and legal recourse in disputes, protection of industrial property rights, extended U.S. law enforcement, and enforcement of antitrust legislation by U.S. and foreign governments. A primary marketing task is to develop a plan that will be enhanced or at least not adversely affected by these and other environmental elements. The myriad questions created by different laws and different legal systems indicate that the most prudent path to follow at all stages of foreign marketing operations is one that leads to competent counsel well versed in the intricacies of the international legal environment.

QUESTIONS

1 & 4

past decisions   written rules   KoRan

1. Differentiate between common law, code law, and Islamic law. Show how the differences may affect marketing activities.

2. How does the international marketer determine which legal system will have jurisdiction when legal disputes arise?

3. Discuss the state of international commercial law. *no body of law to follow*

4. Discuss the limitations of jurisdictional clauses in contracts.

5. What is the "objective theory of jurisdiction"? How does it apply to a firm doing business within a foreign country?

6. Discuss some of the reasons why it is probably best to seek an out-of-court settlement in international commercial legal disputes rather than to sue.

poor image
unfair treatment
diff. in collecting
high cost & time
loss of confidence

Placate
Arbitrate
Litigate

7. Illustrate the procedure generally followed in international commercial disputes when settled under the auspices of a formal arbitration tribunal.

8. What are intellectual property rights? Why should a company in international marketing take special steps to protect them?

9. In many code-law countries, ownership of intellectual property rights is established by registration rather than prior use. Comment.

10. Discuss the advantages to the international marketer arising from the existence of the various international conventions on trademarks, patents, and copyrights.

11. "The legal environment of the foreign marketer takes on an added dimension of importance since there is no single uniform international commercial law which governs foreign business transactions." Comment.

12. What is the *credulous person standard* in advertising and what is its importance in international marketing?

13. Differentiate between the European Patent Convention (EPC) and the Patent Cooperation Treaty (PCT) in their effectiveness in protecting industrial property rights.

pg 199

14. "In the industrialized world, restraint of trade has typically meant restraint of competition, and, in most instances, refers to restrictions

imposed on competition between independent companies." Developing countries view restraint of trade differently. Comment.

15. Discuss why the U.S. Justice Department has become more active in enforcing the Sherman Antitrust law against U.S. multinationals. Which kinds of problems does this create in foreign countries?

16. Discuss the recent changes in the FCPA made in the Omnibus Trade and Competitiveness Act of 1988.

CHAPTER

7

Geography and History—The Foundation of Cultural Understanding

The serious student of a country's culture studies its geography and history. One cannot completely understand the culture of a country without understanding the geographical characteristics to which that culture has had to adapt and to which it must continuously respond, as well as the historical events shaping that society in its cultural evolution. Broad forces that influence the cultural development of a country or society come both from within and from the outside. Culture can be defined as a society's program for survival, the accepted basis for responding to external and internal events.

Marketers can learn about a current culture but without the foundation of geographical and historical knowledge, they cannot expect to understand and explain completely a society's behavior and fundamental attitudes. This chapter discusses how geography and history affect behavior and why they should be taken into account when examining the environmental aspects of marketing in another country.

GEOGRAPHY AND GLOBAL MARKETS

Geography, the study of the earth's surface, climate, continents, countries, peoples, industries, and resources is an element of the uncontrollable environment that confronts the marketer but which receives little attention.

There is a tendency to study the manifestations of the effect of climate, topography, and available resources rather than to study the geographical factors as important causal agents in the marketing environment. The physical character of a nation is perhaps the principal and broadest determinant of both the characteristics of a society and the means by which that society undertakes to supply its needs. Thus, the study of geography is important for the student of marketing when evaluating marketing and its environment.

This section discusses the important geographic characteristics that affect markets and the marketer's need to consider these when examining the environmental aspects of marketing. By examining the world as a whole we acquaint readers with the broad scope of world markets and the effects of geographic diversity on the economic profiles of various nations. A secondary purpose is to provide the student of international marketing with a greater awareness of the world, its complexities, and its diversities; an awareness that can mean the difference between success and failure in marketing ventures.

Climate and topography are examined as facets of the broader and more important elements of geography. A brief look at the earth's resources and population—the building blocks of world markets—and world trade routes completes the presentation on geography and global markets.

Climate and Topography

As elements of geography, the physical terrain and climate of a country are important environmental considerations when appraising a market. The effect of these geographical features on marketing ranges from the obvious influences on product adaptation to more profound influences on the development of marketing systems.

Altitude, humidity, and temperature extremes are all climatic features that affect the uses and functions of products and equipment. Products that perform well in temperate zones may deteriorate rapidly or require special cooling or lubrication to function adequately in tropical zones. In the Sahara Desert manufacturers have found that construction equipment used in the United States required extensive modifications to cope with the intense heat and dust. Within even a single national market, climate can be sufficiently diverse to require major adjustments. In Ghana, a product adaptable to the entire market must operate effectively in extreme desert heat and low humidity and in tropical rain forests with consistently high humidity.

South America represents an extreme but well-defined example of the importance of geography in marketing considerations. The economic and social systems there can be explained partly in terms of the geographical characteristics of the area.

Steam train and Great Wall of China. China's geography—formidable barrier to economic growth. (Sophie Taubert/Journalism Services, Inc.)

South America is a continent 4,500 miles long and 3,000 miles wide at its broadest point. Two thirds of it is comparable to Africa in its climate, 48 percent of its total area is made up of forest and jungle, and only 5 percent is arable.

Mountain ranges cover the west coast for 4,500 miles with an average height of 13,000 feet and a width of 300 to 400 miles. This is a natural, formidable barrier which has precluded the establishment of commercial routes between the Pacific and the Atlantic coasts. Building railroads and highways across the United States was a monumental task, but cannot compare to the requirements of building a railroad from northeast Brazil to the Peruvian West through jungles and mountains.

Once the Andes are surmounted, the Amazon basin of 2 million square miles lies ahead. It is the world's greatest rain forest, almost uninhabitable and impenetrable. Through it runs the Amazon, the world's second largest river which, with its tributaries, has almost 40,000 miles of navigable water. On the east coast is another mountain range covering almost the entire coast of Brazil, with an average height of 4,000 feet.[1]

---

[1] For an interesting article on economic development and the Amazon rain forest, see "Will the Planet Pay the Price for Third World Debt?" *Business Week*, October 24, 1988, p. 88.

BOX 7–1
Climate and Success

A major food processing company had production problems after it built a pineapple cannery at the delta of a river in Mexico. It built the pineapple plantation upstream and planned to barge the ripe fruit downstream for canning, load them directly on ocean liners, and ship them to the company's various markets. When the pineapples were ripe, however, the company found itself in trouble: crop maturity coincided with the flood stage of the river. The current in the river during this period was far too strong to permit the backhauling of barges upstream; the plan for transporting the fruit on barges could not be implemented. With no alternative means of transport, the company was forced to close the operation. The new equipment was sold for 5 percent of original cost to a Mexican group who immediately relocated the cannery. A seemingly simple, harmless oversight of weather and navigation conditions was the primary cause for major losses to the company.

Source: David Ricks, *Big Business Blunders: Mistakes in Multinational Marketing* (Homewood, Ill.: Richard D. Irwin, 1983), p. 4.

South America presents a geographic picture of natural barriers that inhibit national growth, trade, and communication. It is a vast land area with a population concentration on the outer periphery and an isolated and almost uninhabited interior. The major cities of South American countries are within 200 miles of the coast, but even the cities are often separated from each other by inadequate roads and poor communication. Thus, national unity and an equal degree of economic development are nearly impossible. Many citizens of South America are so isolated they do not recognize themselves as part of the nation that claims their citizenship. Geography has always separated South America into secluded communities.

Another characteristic of Latin American countries is the population concentration in major cities. In almost every case, a high percentage of the total population of each country lives in a few isolated metropolitan centers with most of the wealth, education, and power. The surrounding rural areas remain almost unchanged from one generation to the next, with most of the people existing at subsistence levels. In many areas, even the language of the rural people is not the same as that of metropolitan residents.[2] Such circumstances rarely result in homogeneous markets.

---

[2] This discussion is based in part on a monograph of Herbert V. Prochnow, "Economic, Political, and Social Trends in Latin America" (Chicago: First National Bank of Chicago, n.d.).

Colombia has four major population centers separated from one another by high mountains. Even today these mountain ranges are a major barrier to travel. The air time from Bogotá to Medellin, the third largest city in Colombia, is 30 minutes; by highway, the same trip takes 10 to 12 hours. One president declared that before he left office, an improved highway would be built and that he planned to drive the distance in six or seven hours. Because of the physical isolation, each center has a different dialect, style of living, and population characteristics; even the climates are different. From a marketing view, the four centers constitute four distinctly different markets.

The geography of Latin America has extremes, but a study of geography reveals that many areas in the world have extreme topographic and climatic variations. Consider, for example, the physical and/or climatic variations that exist within such countries as China, the Soviet Union, and India.

In Canada, one observer notes that vast distances and extreme winter weather have a major influence on distribution. Reorder points and safety stock levels must be higher than normally expected for given inventories because large cities like Montreal can be isolated suddenly and completely by heavy snowfalls.[3] At such times, delivery delays of three to four days are common. Additionally, shipment delays can result from a shortage of insulated railcars and trucks, and the high cost of heating railcars on long hauls in extreme weather can add 10 percent or more to a company's freight bill. Imagine the formidable problems of appraising market potential or devising a marketing mix that would successfully reconcile the diversities in such situations.

Rolls-Royce found that fully armor-plated cars from England required extensive body work and renovations after a short time in Canada. It was not the cold that demolished the cars but the salted sand spread to keep the streets passable throughout the four or five months of virtually continuous snow. The fenders were corroded and rusted, the doorside panels likewise, and the oil system leaked. While this may be an extreme and isolated case, it illustrates the harshness of a climate and the need to consider such elements in product development.

Geographic hurdles are not insurmountable but they must be recognized as having a direct effect on marketing and the related activities of communications and distribution. Furthermore, there may be indirect effects from the geographical ramifications on society and culture that are ultimately reflected in marketing activities. Many of the peculiarities of a country (i.e., peculiar to the foreigner) would be better understood and anticipated if its geography were studied more closely.

The effect of natural barriers on market development is also important.

---

[3] Peter M. Banting et al., "Canadian Distribution Is Different," *International Journal of Physical Distribution*, February 1972, p. 76.

BOX 7–2
Geography, Infrastructure, and Level of Technology—Why Won't the Cars and Buses Run?

Geography, infrastructure, and level of technology of a market are important uncontrollable elements to which products must be adapted. Here are two incidents where they were not properly accounted for:

General Motors of Canada sold 25,000 Chevrolet Malibus to Iraq. However, they were mechanically unfit for Iraq's hot, dusty climate. When the Malibus hit Baghdad's roads and streets their air filters choked on the dust and their transmissions labored in the heat and traffic. GM tripled to 36 its full-time engineers and mechanics in Baghdad where they installed supplementary air filters and changed clutches. Iraq refused to take any more cars until the 13,500 already delivered were repaired properly.

In Egypt, the problem was with buses whose diesel engines were so loud and noisy that they were nicknamed the "Voice of America." All 600 buses had to have replacement mufflers for urban use. But that wasn't all. In less than a year, performance was so bad that their failure became a source of embarrassment and irritation to Egyptian and U.S. officials. According to a transportation engineering firm, the trouble stemmed from a failure to anticipate how roughly they would be used. "With a few changes to meet American air pollution control standards, they would probably last for years on American roads with American drivers and American maintenance," said one engineer. "But, in Egypt, the driving conditions are appalling, the drivers are untrained and reckless, and the concept of maintenance is to ignore it until the bus breaks down. Buses routinely must carry double the load they were meant for. Whoever approved the original specifications should have known that."

Sources: "GM Runs into a Middle-East Crisis: It's Too Hot and Dusty in Baghdad," *The Wall Street Journal*, February 23, 1982, p. 29; and "Egypt Angered, Not Aided, by Gift of U.S. Buses," *Los Angeles Times*, January 12, 1982.

Because of the ease of distribution, coastal cities or cities situated on navigable waterways are more likely to be trading centers than are landlocked cities. Cities not near natural physical transportation routes generally are isolated from one another even within the same country. Consequently, when planning distribution systems, natural barriers may dictate distribution points rather than actual miles.

In discussing distribution in Africa, one marketer pointed out that a shipment from Mombasa on the Kenya east coast to Freetown on the bulge of West Africa could require more time than a shipment from New York or London to Kenya over established freight routes.

In Ecuador, the road conditions are such that it is almost impossible to drive a car from the port of Guayaquil to the capital of Quito only 200 miles away. Contrast this to the more economically advanced countries where formidable mountain barriers have been overcome. A case in point is the 7.2-mile tunnel which cuts through the base of Mont Blanc in the Alps. This highway tunnel brings Rome and Paris 125 miles closer and provides a year-round route between Geneva and Turin of only 170 miles. Before the tunnel opened, it was a trip of nearly 500 miles when snow closed the highway over the Alps. After decades of consideration, a tunnel under the English Channel between Britain and France is scheduled to open in 1993. In its first year it is expected to carry more than 17 million short tons of freight and 30.7 million people.[4]

As countries expand their economies, natural barriers are adapted to instead of being overcome; the task of surmounting natural barriers is left to more affluent generations. Thus, geography is of great importance in underdeveloped countries where societies have not had the time or economic capability to overcome such obstacles.

Of the world's 20 poorest countries, climate and topography contribute significantly to their plight. As one report suggested, each of the 20 countries has a slim margin between subsistence and disaster:

> all exist in a fragile tropical environment which had been upset by the growing pressure of people. Without irrigation and water management, they are afflicted by droughts, floods, soil erosion, and creeping deserts, which reduce the long-term fertility of the land. Disasters such as drought intensify the malnutrition and ill health of the people, and endemic diseases undermine their vitality. Their poverty, harsh climate, and isolation all make it harder to exploit their resources, especially minerals. The sun, a valuable source of cheap energy, is presently a curse, sapping their vigor while they are forced to use relatively conventional forms of energy.[5]

The poverty of these countries is reflected in their economies which, as measured by their gross domestic products, have grown over a 20-year period at an average annual rate of 0.7 percent compared with the 2.9 percent for developing countries as a group. Climate and geography are not the only causes of their economic woes; politics is also a contributor. Ethiopia's civil war has been raging for more than 25 years, and the conflict has caused a terrible diversion of human and material resources from the war against hunger. In 1988 there was a deficit of 1.5 million tons of food and, unless hostilities cease, food shortages of 7 million tons are projected by the end of the century. It is estimated that relief groups can deliver no more than 2 million tons a year under ideal conditions.[6]

---

[4] "Eurotunnel of Love?" *Business Week*, February 27, 1989, p. 56.

[5] Desiree French "Poorest of the Poor," *Forbes*, July 20, 1981, p. 38.

[6] "The Politics of Starvation," *World Press Review*, May 1988, p. 64.

Resources

The availability of minerals and the ability to generate energy are the foundations of modern technology. The location of the earth's resources as well as available sources of energy are geographical accidents, and the world's nations are not equally endowed; nor does a nation's demand for a particular mineral or energy source necessarily coincide with domestic supply.

Energy is necessary to power the machinery of modern production and to extract and process the resources necessary to produce the goods of economic prosperity. In much of the underdeveloped world, human labor provides the preponderance of energy. The principal supplements to human energy are animals, wood, fossil fuel, nuclear power, and to a lesser and more experimental extent, the ocean's tides, geothermal power, and the sun. Of all the energy sources, petroleum usage is increasing most rapidly because of its versatility and the ease with which it is stored and transported.

Many countries that were self-sufficient during much of their early economic growth have become net importers of petroleum during the past 25 years and continue to become increasingly dependent on foreign sources. A spectacular example is the United States, which was almost completely self-sufficient until 1942, became a major importer by 1950, and by 1980 was importing over 50 percent of its annual requirements. If present rates of consumption continue, predictions are that the United States will be importing over 70 percent of its needs by the year 2000.

Only since World War II has concern for the limitless availability of seemingly inexhaustible supplies become a prominent factor. The dramatic increase in economic growth in the industrialized world and the push for industrialization in the remaining world has put tremendous pressure on the earth's resources; at the beginning of the 1980s, predictions of exhausted resources threatened many of the necessary building blocks of economic growth and development. Unfortunately, once exhausted a mineral deposit is gone forever; petroleum, the premium fossil fuel used in energy creation, is rapidly approaching exhaustion according to all current predictions.

As an environmental consideration in world marketing, the location, quality, and availability of resources will affect the pattern of world economic development and trade for at least the remainder of the century. This factor must be weighed carefully by astute international marketers in making worldwide international investment decisions. In addition to the raw materials of industrialization, there must be an available and economically feasible energy supply to successfully transform resources into usable products.

Because of the great disparity in the location of the earth's resources, there is world trade between those who do not have all they need and

---

BOX 7–3
How Many Slaves Work for You?

A healthy, hard-working person can produce just enough energy to keep a 100-watt bulb burning. This may seem unimportant, but it is a humbling reminder that muscle power is really very puny. . . .

Supplementary energy now exceeds muscle energy in every part of our lives from food production to recreation. It is like a gang of silent slaves who labor continually and uncomplainingly to feed, clothe, and maintain us. The energy comes, of course, from mineral resources such as coal, oil, and uranium, not from real slaves, but everyone on the earth now has "energy slaves." . . . In India the total supplementary energy produced is equivalent to the work of 15 slaves, each working an eight-hour day, for every man, woman, and child. In South America everyone has approximately 30 "energy slaves"; in Japan, 75; Russia, 120; Europe, 150; and in the United States and Canada, a huge 300. The concept of "energy slaves" demonstrates how utterly dependent the world has become on mineral resources. If the "slaves" were to strike (which means if the supplies ran out), the world's peoples could not keep themselves alive and healthy. Reverting to muscle power alone would bring starvation, famine, and pestilence. Nature would quickly reduce the population.

Source: Brian J. Skinner, *Earth Resources*, 2d ed., © 1976, pp. 3–4. Reprinted by permission of Prentice-Hall, Inc., Englewood Cliffs, N.J.

---

those who have more than they need and are willing to sell. Importers of most of the resources are industrial nations with insufficient domestic supplies. Aluminum is a good example; Australia, Guinea, and Brazil account for over 65 percent of the world's reserves, and one country, the United States, consumes 35 percent of all aluminum produced. Of the 20 items listed in Exhibit 7–1, the United States has major reserves in only 5, but consumes 20 percent or more of the world's total of 16 of the 20 items.

Aside from the geographical unevenness in which most resources occur, the continuing availability of supply is a matter of grave concern. For many minerals, consumption is multiplying at an alarming rate. As populations grow, more minerals are required, and with improvement in the general welfare and economic level, per capital consumption further accelerates demand. The result is an increasing growth rate which portends near exhaustion of most known reserves within this century. Exhibit 7–1 presents two possible rates of depletion. Column *A* presents the known reserves and column *B* gives the number of years known global reserves will last at current rates of consumption. Assuming increased population growth and an increasing rate of per capital consumption, column *D* shows the remaining years of supply when consumption grows at projected rates.

EXHIBIT 7-1 Reserves, Projected Consumption, and Principal Producers and Consumers of Selected Nonrenewable Resources

Resource	(A) Known Global Reserves, 1985*	(B) Static Index Years†	(C) Probable Annual Projected Rate of Growth (percent)‡	(D) Amount Used 1983–2000§	(E) Amount of Reserves Left in the Year 2000‖
Aluminum	4,420 million m.t.	244	4.0	395 million m.t.	4,025 million m.t.
Chromium	1,165 million s.t.	354	4.4	74 million s.t.	1,091 million s.t.
Coal	987 billion s.t.	224	NA	75 billion s.t.	912 billion s.t.**
Cobalt	8,000 million lbs.	169	3.7	1,200 million lbs.	6,800 million lbs.
Copper	340 million m.t.	35	2.7	168 million m.t.	172 million m.t.
Gold	1,280 million T.oz.	32	1.8	674 million T.oz.	606 million T.oz.
Iron	72 billion s.t.	157	2.4	10 billion s.t.	62 million s.t.
Lead	95 million m.t.	18	1.8	61 million m.t.	34 million m.t.
Manganese	1,000 million s.t.	114	1.4	169 million s.t.	831 million s.t.
Mercury	4 million fl.	18	1.4	3.6 million fl.	309 thousand fl.
Molybdenum	12 billion lbs.	80	2.5	3.6 billion lbs.	8,500 billion lbs.
Natural gas	3,400 trillion cu.ft.	63	NA	918 trillion cu.ft.*	2,482 trillion cu.ft.**
Nickel	58 million s.t.	57	3.0	18 million s.t.	40 million s.t.
Petroleum	700 billion bbls.	32	NA	366 billion bbls.*	334 billion bbls.**
Platinum group#	1,000 million T.oz.	143	2.1	130 million T.oz.	870 million T.oz.
Silver	7,830 million T.oz.	32	2.1	5,400 million T.oz.	2,430 million T.oz.
Tin	3,060 thousand m.t.	14	1.0	3,930 thousand m.t.	—
Tungsten	2,800 thousand m.t.	57	2.9	967 thousand m.t.	1,833 thousand m.t.
Zinc	170 million m.t.	25	2.0	129 million m.t.	41 million m.t.

* Data are from U.S. Bureau of Mines, *Mineral Facts and Problems, 1985* (Washington, D.C.: U.S. Government Printing Office, 1985), m.t. = metric ton, s.t. = short ton, lbs = pounds, T.oz. = Troy ounce, fl. = flask, ft. = feet, bbls. = barrels. Data for coal, natural gas, and petroleum are from *International Energy Annual 1984*, Energy Information Administration (Washington, D.C.: U.S. Government Printing Office, 1985).

† The number of years known global reserves will last at current global consumption. Calculated by dividing known reserves (column A) by the current annual consumption (*Mineral Facts and Problems, 1985*).

‡ SOURCE: *Mineral Facts and Problems, 1985*.

§ SOURCE: *Mineral Facts and Problems, 1985*. Amount of reserves used between 1983–2000 at the annual projected rate of growth.

‖ Amount of reserves remaining in the year 2000 (column A − column D).

Platinum group includes platinum, palladium, iridium, osmium, rhodium, and ruthenium.

** Based on 1984 annual consumption.

At an annual projected growth rate of 1.4 percent, known reserves of mercury at present rates of consumption (column *B*) will almost be depleted by the year 2000. Continuing exploration will turn up new reserves, but even if reserves are doubled, the extended availability of mercury is limited. Petroleum and natural gas, two major sources of energy needed for production, are also in short supply. Petroleum supplies at present usage rates will be reduced by more than half by 2000. Costs will also be affected as reserves diminish.

Some of the most critical shortages involve strategic materials such as cobalt, tantalum, and tungsten, a scarcity further aggravated by political instability. Over the next two decades the probability of continued political upheavals that can interrupt the supply of strategic materials is very high. This is a major concern for many multinationalists who must resort to stockpiling as protection from sudden stoppage of supplies.

One possible source of scarce minerals still untapped can be found in the ocean floors. Undersea mining, currently uneconomical, may provide the world with new reserves of scarce minerals. At the bottom of the Pacific are fields thousands of miles long containing the world's largest reserves of nickel, copper, cobalt, and magnesium. Nodules containing these minerals have been estimated to total 10 billion tons of rich ore, with 10 million new tons formed every year. Similar fields of ore-rich nodules exist in all the world's oceans and seas.

This undersea wealth of minerals will not be easy to exploit because of a variety of obstacles to rapid commercialization. The cost of undersea mining (higher than traditional mining), disputes over ownership of minerals outside territorial waters, and the potential for upsetting the sensitive ocean ecosystem are current barriers to economical exploitation. Yet, like other natural barriers, these too will eventually be overcome as world demand increases and current reserves dwindle.

Whatever mathematics are used to determine known reserves, and even if the projections in Exhibit 7–1 were doubled, there is no question that the availability of resources is, and will continue to be, a major environmental consideration in international marketing with intense political and economic ramifications.

World Population Trends

While not the only determinant, sheer numbers of people are significant in appraising potential consumer demand. Current population, rates of growth, age levels, and rural/urban population distribution are closely related to today's demand for various categories of goods. Changes in the composition and distribution of population among the world's countries during the next 40 years will profoundly affect future demand.

Exhibit 7–2 presents the population by major areas and the percentage

EXHIBIT 7–2   World Population by Major Areas, Years to Double, and Life Expectancy

	1950 (millions)	1985 (millions)	Years to Double	Life Expectancy 1985 (years)	2000 (millions)
World	2,515.0	4,842.0	43	60	6,123.0
Africa	219.0	553.0	23	49	877.0
Asia	1,380.0	2,824.0	45	49	3,544.0
North America	166.0	263.0	80	74	298.0
Latin America	164.0	406.0	32	64	550.0
Europe (including USSR)	572.0	771.0	118	72	824.0
Oceania	12.6	25.0	49	68	30.0

* Estimate.

SOURCE: *World Population Prospects* (New York: United Nations, 1986).

change between 1985 and 2000. Recent estimates claim there are over 4.7 billion people in the world. At current growth rates, there will be more than 6 billion by the year 2000. Exhibit 7–2 illustrates dramatically that population in less-developed countries is going to increase most rapidly; and it is these poor nations that are least able to support such population increases. Kenya is a good example of what is happening to many developing countries. The average number of children born to a woman in Kenya is now eight; when that is combined with a declining infant mortality rate, the country's population could quadruple almost overnight, increasing from 20 million in 1986 to 83 million in 2000. Kenya's present economic growth rate will not support the demands created by such growth.

Population Distribution.   In addition to rapid growth, the distribution of population is shifting from the industrial nations of the Northern Hemisphere to the developing nations of the Southern Hemisphere. By the end of this century, population in developed areas is expected to increase by about 200 million whereas the developing areas of Africa, Asia, and Latin America are expected to increase by 3 billion. By the year 2025, the World Bank predicts over four fifths of the world's population will be concentrated in developing countries.

Rural/Urban Shifts.   A relatively recent phenomenon is a pronounced shift of the world's population from rural to urban areas. In the early 1800s, less than 3.5 percent of the world's people were living in cities of 20,000 or more and less than 2 percent in cities of 100,000 or more. The real beginning of worldwide urbanization started in Europe with the Industrial Revolution (about 1760); by the 1950s, over 20 percent of the people of the world lived in cities of 20,000 or more.

Today, more than 35 percent of the world's people are urbanites and

---

BOX 7–4
The Peso Was Devalued Where?—New Mexico?

Geography has never been the strong suit of Americans. To prove the point, consider New Mexico. A proud member of the union since 1912, the name sounds vaguely alien. This leads to problems—just where is New Mexico anyway?

The state tourism magazine has been collecting anecdotes that speak to this extraterritorial image. The best of these geographic gaffes:

- A young man from New Mexico who applied to Harvard Business School got this reply: "Since you are an 'international' candidate, you must first take a test proving your proficiency in English."
- A Texas woman talking to a New Mexico county courthouse telephone operator inquired: "If it's Friday in Texas, will it be Friday in New Mexico?"
- An upstate New York man applied for social security numbers for his two daughters. He was told they weren't eligible because they were born in New Mexico.
- A Florida resident was taken ill during a New Mexico vacation and received treatment in a clinic in Tierra Amarilla. Medicare refused reimbursement and replied, "medical expenses incurred outside the United States are not payable."
- A couple moved from Florida to New Mexico and notified Mastercard of their new address and were informed: "Since we do not mail any credit cards out of the continental U.S.A., we must temporarily cancel your account."
- A New Yorker commented to an X-ray technician during an examination that he was retiring to New Mexico. "That's wonderful," came the reply, "you should do well there now that they have devalued the peso."

Source: Adapted from Eugene Carlson, "See the Map; See the U.S.; See New Mexico; No, NEW Mexico." Reprinted by permission of *The Wall Street Journal*, © Dow Jones & Company, Inc.; November 17, 1986, p. 35. All rights reserved.

---

the trend away from rural areas is accelerating. Current trends in urban, rural, and total population are illustrated for selected regions in Exhibit 7–3. Regardless of the level of their economic development, the rise in urban population in all regions is extraordinary. Between 1975 and 1985, urban population in developing countries increased by 155 percent on top of a growth of 311 percent between 1950 and 1975.

By 2025, it is estimated that more than 60 percent of the world's population will live in urban areas compared with the current 39 percent, and at least 60 cities will have populations of 5 million or more. Mexico City, now the world's third largest city (18.7 million in 1985) is expected to be the world's largest with a population of 31 million inhabitants by the year 2000.

EXHIBIT 7–3   Percentage of the Population in Urban Areas by Region

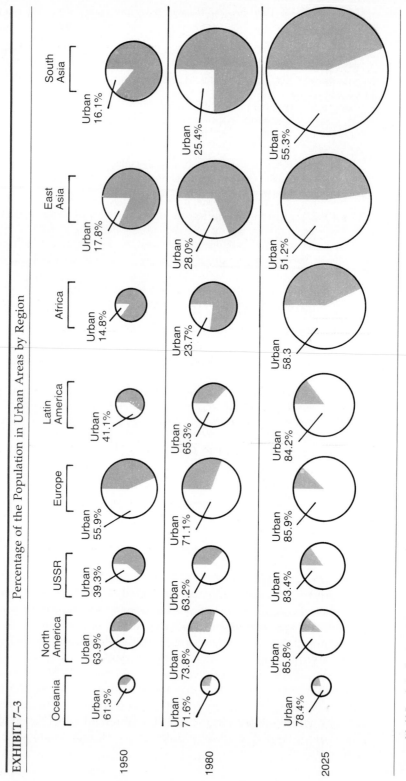

SOURCE: *World Population Prospects* (New York: United Nations, 1986), pp. 140–80.

EXHIBIT 7–4   The World's Largest Urban Areas (1986) and Projections to the Year 2000

Rank and Urban Area (1986) (millions)		Rank and Urban Area (2000) (millions)	
1. Tokyo/Yokohama	18.82	1. Mexico City	25.82
2. Mexico City	17.30	2. Sao Paulo	23.97
3. Sao Paulo	15.88	3. Tokyo/Yokohama	20.22
4. New York	15.64	4. Calcutta	16.53
5. Shanghai	11.96	5. Greater Bombay	16.00
6. Calcutta	10.95	6. New York	15.78
7. Buenos Aires	10.88	7. Shanghai	14.30
8. Rio de Janeiro	10.37	8. Seoul	13.77
9. London	10.36	9. Teheran	13.58
10. Seoul	10.28	10. Rio de Janeiro	13.26
11. Greater Bombay	10.07	11. Jakarta	13.25
12. Los Angeles	10.05	12. Delhi	13.24
13. Osaka/Kobe	9.45	13. Buenos Aires	13.18
14. Beijing	9.25	14. Karachi	12.00
15. Moscow	8.97	15. Beijing	11.17

SOURCE: *Prospects of World Urbanization* (New York: United Nations, 1987), pp. 25–26.

The growing migration of people from rural to urban areas is largely a result of a desire for greater access to sources of education, health care, and improved job opportunities. These attractions can be considerable to individual families, for once in the city, perhaps three out of four migrants make economic gains. Income can roughly triple for an unskilled laborer with a move to an urban area. The family income of a manual worker in urban Brazil is almost five times that of a farm laborer in a rural area.

Industries also benefit from concentrations of laborers and consumers. Large cities provide big, differentiated labor markets and the exploitation of economies of scale for water supplies, electric power, health services, food distribution and other social services made possible in large urban centers.

Although there are some benefits from urban growth and migrants experience some relative improvement in their living standards, intense urban growth without commensurate investment in services eventually leads to profound problems. Slums populated with unskilled workers living hand to mouth puts excessive pressure on sanitation systems, water supplies, and other social services. At some point, the disadvantages of unregulated urban growth begin to outweigh the advantages for all concerned.

Consider conditions that exist in Mexico City today. Over 14,000 tons of garbage are produced every day but only 8,000 tons are processed; the rest is dumped in landfills or left to rot in the open. More than 2 million families have no running water or sewage facilities in their homes. Sewage facilities are so overtaxed that tons of waste are left in gutters or vacant lots where it dries and is blown into the atmosphere. The problem is so severe, one Mexico City newspaper reported, "If fecal matter were fluorescent, the city wouldn't need lights." This is a grim picture of a city that is at the same time one of the most beautiful and sophisticated in Latin America. Vast numbers of migrants tax the ability of any city to provide adequate services. If Mexico City is unable to cope with its present size, imagine conditions in 2000 when it will be the world's largest city with over 30 million inhabitants.

Many fear that as we approach 2000, the bulging cities will become fertile fields for social unrest unless conditions in urban areas are improved. Prospects for improvement are not encouraging because most of the growth will take place in developing countries already economically strained. Further, there is little progress in controlling birth rates.

Increasing Unemployment. Rapid population increases without commensurate economic development create other difficulties.[7] Among the most pressing are the number of new jobs needed to accommodate the flood of people entering the labor pool. In the 1970s, 200 million people entered the labor market in the Third World; by the turn of the century, an additional 700 million will be of working age.[8] The International Labor Organization (ILO) estimated that 1 billion jobs must be created worldwide by the end of the century.

Kenya is one of the world's fastest-growing countries, and currently creates jobs at an unprecedented rate of 5 percent a year. This provides 70,000 new jobs annually, but is far short of full employment for the million people leaving primary school every year. In Botswana, where 30,000 people enter the job market each year, there are only 5,000 new jobs created annually. Already an estimated 500 million Third World people are unemployed or underemployed. The ability to create enough jobs to keep pace with population growth is only one problem of uncontrolled growth. Providing enough to eat is another.

World Food Production. Having enough food to eat depends on a country's ability to produce sufficient quantities, ability to buy food from sources when it is not self-sufficient, and the ability physically to distribute food when the need arises. The world produces enough food to provide adequate diets for all its 4.7 billion people yet famine exists in the world, most notably in Africa. Long-term drought, economic weakness, inefficient distri-

---

[7] Steve Mufson, "Little Is Being Done to Control Explosive Growth of Africa's Population, Posing Future Threat," *The Wall Street Journal*, July 31, 1985, p. 24.

[8] "Population and Power Preparing for Change," *The Wall Street Journal*, June 6, 1988, p. 1.

BOX 7–5
Two Different Worlds

France

For more than a decade various French governments have tried to stop the dramatic decline in the nation's population growth rate by encouraging families to have more than two children. For the past 10 years, the French have had 1.9 children per family, well under the 2.1 figure considered necessary to prevent a drastic reduction in current population. If the decline in the growth rate is not halted, France will become underpopulated, underproductive, and top-heavy with senior citizens who will overtax the social security system. The latest incentive to be offered is a proposed law to pay 24,000 francs, about $3,000, to couples producing a third child. Critics of the bill contend that financial incentives will not be successful because all past financial incentives have failed.

Nigeria

Christiana Nzeakor's eyes twinkle when she remembers her initiation into the Society of Those Whom God Has Blessed, a club for women who have had 10 pregnancies. The society members made a circle around Christiana and her husband Bernard and said blessings over a goat he supplied. The husbands wrapped the live goat around Mrs. Nzeakor's waist. Then Mr. Nzeakor slaughtered the animal and everyone ate goat and kola nuts and drank palm wine.

It is said that if a husband doesn't perform this ceremony, his wife can't have more children. Happily, Mrs. Nzeakor had two more children making her husband the proud father of, as he puts it, 24 or 25 children from his three wives.

The World Bank calls population growth the single greatest long-term threat to Africa's economic development, but that concern hasn't reached villages like this. Here children are considered blessings for women and financial assets to subsistence farmers. "The number of children one has is something to show off. It is a status symbol," says the family planning coordinator for Imo state where the village is located.

Sources: "Be Fruitful and Multiply," *Europe*, January–February 1984, p. 4; and adapted from "Little Is Being Done to Control Explosive Growth of Africa's Population, Posing Future Threat," *The Wall Street Journal*, July 31, 1985, p. 24.

bution and civil unrest have created conditions that have led to tens of thousands of people starving.[9]

Unfortunately, even countries with impressive economic growth have not been able to keep pace with population growth. In Zambia, agricultu-

---

[9] "Horn of Famine," *World Press Review*, August 1988, p. 41.

BOX 7–6
Global Trivia: A Test for the Worldly Wise

Test your knowledge of life around the globe with this quiz taken from the new "Not-So-Trivial-Game" designed by Runzheimer International "for thinking professionals." This consulting firm based in Rochester, Wisconsin, specializes in studies of travel and living costs around the world. Circle your answer to each of the questions then see the answers. If you get 10 or more correct, you are a world-class traveler, probably a member of the 100,000-mile club—or just a good gamesperson.

1. What country prohibits the sale of imported bananas?
   (a) Kuwait (b) South Africa (c) Greece
2. For each vehicle-mile traveled, what country has the highest pedestrian death rate?
   (a) Poland (b) United States (c) Germany (FRG)
3. The longest river in the world is:
   (a) The Amazon (b) The Nile (c) The Volga
4. Which city has the largest seaport in the world?
   (a) London (b) New York (c) Rotterdam
5. What is a rack rate?
   (a) The rib section of a slaughtered animal (b) The undiscounted price of a hotel room (c) A degree of torture
6. The Japanese drive on which side of the road?
   (a) The left (b) The right (c) Alternate sides every other day

---

ral output increases 2.8 percent a year but the population increases 3.5 percent a year. As a result, per capita food consumption declines. While Egypt was building the Aswan High Dam to irrigate land capable of sustaining 4 million people, the number of Egyptians grew by 10 million.

As the human race approaches 5 billion, the seas are being depleted of fish, forests are shrinking, meadowlands are being grazed to exhaustion, and one fifth of all arable land is losing its fertility through soil erosion. In the Sahara Desert, years of drought have pushed the desert southward, sometimes at the rate of 93 miles a year.

Controlling Population Growth.   Faced with the ominous consequences of the population explosion, it would seem logical for countries to take appropriate steps to reduce growth to manageable rates, but procreation is one of the most culturally sensitive uncontrollables worldwide. Economics, self-esteem, religion, politics, and education all play a critical role in attitudes about family size.

The prerequisites to population control are adequate incomes, higher

---

BOX 7-6 (concluded)

7. Kuala Lumpur means:
   (a) Hello (b) Goodbye (c) Muddy River
8. When you are in a Flughafen, you are at an airport in what country?
   (a) Norway (b) Germany (FRG) (c) Luxembourg
9. Among the countries of the world, how does the People's Republic of China rank in terms of area?
   (a) Second largest (b) Third largest (c) Tenth largest
10. Of which country is Harare the capital?
    (a) Zaire (b) Zambia (c) Zimbabwe
11. Romaji is:
    (a) Used to bring out the delicate taste of squid (b) Used to translate the Japanese language into Roman (Latin) letters (c) The Kentucky Derby winner kidnapped from an Irish stud farm
12. What is the currency of Malaysia?
    (a) Baht (b) Ringgit (c) Rupee
13. Which country uses the dollar as its national currency?
    (a) Panama (b) Liberia (c) South Africa

Global Trivia—Answers: 13 b, 12 b, 11 b, 10 c, 9 a, 8 b, 7 c, 6 a, 5 b, 4 c, 3 b, 2 a, 1 c.

Source: Adapted from "Global Trivia: A Test for the Worldly Wise," *Across the Board*, September 1985, p. 77. Reproduced by permission of The Conference Board and Runzheimer International, a Rochester, Wisconsin-based management consulting firm specializing in travel and living costs.

---

literacy levels, education for women, better hygiene, universal access to health care, improved nutrition, and, perhaps most important, a change in basic cultural beliefs toward the importance of large families. Unfortunately, progress in providing improved conditions and changing beliefs is hampered by the increasingly heavy demand placed on institutions responsible for change and improvement.[10]

In many cultures, a man's prestige, alive and dead, depends on the number of his progeny, and a family's only wealth is its children. Many religions discourage or ban family planning and thus serve as a deterrent to control. Nigeria, for example, has a strong Moslem tradition in the north and a strong Roman Catholic tradition in the east, and both faiths favor large families. Most traditional religions in Africa encourage large families; in fact, the principal deity for many is the goddess of land and fertility.[11]

---

[10] "Shlomo Reutlinger," Food Security and Poverty in LDCs," *Finance and Development*, December 1985, pp. 7–13.

[11] Mufson, "Little Is Being Done," p. 24.

EXHIBIT 7–5   Composition of U.S. Foreign Trade (equalizing imbalances)

IMPORTS

Oil, Petroleum Products
Bananas, Spices
Copper, Mercury, Coffee
Mohogany, Chrome, Zinc
Tungsten, Rubber, Hides
and Skins, Tin, Tea
Tungoil, Manganese
Bauxite, Newsprint
Cane Sugar, Pepper
Coconut Oil
Wines and Spirits
Wood Pulp, Diamonds, Nickel, Lead
Manufactured Goods
Semimanufactured Goods
Autos

EXPORTS

Apples   Wheat

Lumber

Paper and
Paperboard

Wheat   Meat   Agricultural
                                    machinery

Soybeans   Books

Canned fruits   Wheat   Steel
and vegetables   Corn   Automobiles
                            Meat   and parts   Coal
Paints

Beef   Industrial machinery

Photographic   Tobacco
goods

Aircraft   Cigarettes

Petroleum
refining   Sulfur   Cotton
products   Goods

Cotton

Cottonseed cake   Naval stores
and meal

SOURCE: W. S. and E. S. Woytinsky, *World Population and Production,* rev. ed. (New York: The Twentieth Century Fund, 1953), p. 183; *Yearbook of International Trade Statistics* (New York: United Nations Publishing Series, 1986).

Population control is also seen as a political issue. Overpopulation and the resulting problems have been labeled by some as an imperialist myth to support a devious plot by rich countries to keep Third World population down and maintain the developed world's dominance of the globe. Instead of seeking ways to reduce population growth, some politicians encourage growth as the most vital asset of poor countries. As long as such attitudes prevail, it will be extremely difficult, if not impossible, to control population.

Developed World Population Is Declining.   While the developing world faces rapidly growing population, it is estimated that the Western industrialized world's population will decline. Birthrates in Western Europe have been decreasing since the early or mid-1960s; women are choosing careers instead of children, and working couples elect to continue a free-spending life-style. As a result of these and other contemporary factors, populations in many countries have dropped below the rate necessary to maintain present population levels. West Germany's native population has been falling steadily since 1972 to 57 million in 1981 and will fall to 52 million by the year 2000. In 1964, the fertility rate was over 2.5, but the present fertility rate is down to 1.4. The populations of France, Sweden, Switzerland, and Belgium are all expected to begin dropping within a few years. Austria, Norway, Denmark, and several other nations are now at about zero population growth and probably will slip to the minus side in another decade or so. See Exhibit 7–6 for the 11 highest population-growth areas and the countries with zero population growth.

These trends worry government officials; population decreases do not always produce positive results. The German government has raised family

---

EXHIBIT 7–6   The World's 11 Fastest Growing Areas versus 11 Areas with No Growth

Annual Growth Rate (percent)	*Annual Growth Rate (percent)*
1. Qatar (6.8)	1. Federal Republic of Germany (−.2)
2. Bolivia (6.3)	2. Austria (.0)
3. United Arab Emirates (6.1)	3. Denmark (.0)
4. Kuwait (5.5)	4. German Democratic Republic (.0)
5. Oman (4.7)	5. Vatican City (.0)
6. Bahrain (4.4)	6. Hungary (.0)
7. Saudi Arabia (4.2)	7. Lebanon (.0)
8. Kenya (4.1)	8. Luxembourg (.0)
9. Macau (4.0)	9. Sweden (.1)
10. Libya (3.9)	10. Switzerland (.1)
11. Vanuatu (3.9)	11. United Kingdom (.1)

SOURCE: *World Population Prospects* (New York: United Nations, 1986), pp. 44–45.

allowances, particularly for second and third children, and substantially liberalized maternity leave pay. Sweden has increased child allowances and lengthened maternity/paternity leaves, and the Swedish parliament has ordered a major study of the reasons for recent low fertility rates. Other West European governments have taken similar steps. Many businesses also are beginning to watch demographic developments with concern (see Exhibit 7–7). For example, the Nestlé Company has been looking for markets outside Europe because of these trends.

The economic fallout of a declining population has many ramifications. Businesses find their domestic market shrinking for items such as maternity and infant goods, school equipment, and selected durables. This leads to reduced production and worker layoffs that affect living standards. Europe has a special problem because of the increasing percentage of elderly people who must be supported by shrinking numbers of active workers. The elderly require higher government outlays for health care and hospitals, special housing and nursing homes, and pension and welfare assistance, but the work force that supports these costs is dwindling. In

EXHIBIT 7–7   A Comparison of 20 Countries

Country	Population (000)	GNP per person U.S. Dollars	Life Expectancy Male	Female
Australia	15,698	$10,840	71.6	78.6
Belgium	9,903	8,450	70.2	77.0
Brazil	135,564	1,640	60.9	66.0
Canada	25,426	13,670	72.3	79.3
France	54,621	9,550	70.6	78.7
Federal Republic of Germany	60,877	10,940	70.4	77.2
India	758,927	250	55.6	55.2
Italy	57,300	11,330	74.3	79.7
Japan	120,742	6,520	71.2	78.0
Netherlands	14,500	9,180	72.7	79.5
New Zealand	3,318	7,310	70.7	77.0
Norway	4,142	13,890	72.6	79.5
Philippines	54,498	600	60.2	63.7
South Africa	32,392	2,010	51.8	55.2
Sri Lanka	16,205	370	67.0	70.0
Sweden	8,351	11,890	73.4	79.4
Turkey	49,289	1,130	60.0	83.3
United Arab Emirates	1,327	19,120	65.4	69.8
United Kingdom	56,125	8,390	70.7	76.9
United States	238,020	16,400	70.6	78.1

SOURCE: Data for 1985 and 1986 from *World Population Prospects* (New York: United Nations, 1986), and *World Bank Atlas*, 1987 (Oxford: International Bank for Reconstruction and Development, 1987).

addition, a shortage of skilled workers is anticipated in these countries because of the decreasing population. The trends of increasing population in the developing world with substantial shifts from rural to urban areas and declining birthrates in the industrialized world will have profound effects on the state of world business and world economic conditions by 2000. And, while world population is increasing, multinational firms could see world markets decreasing on a relative basis since the monied world is losing numbers and poor nations are gaining numbers. Even though population size is important in marketing, the people must have a means to buy to be an effective market.

WORLD TRADE ROUTES

Major world trade routes have developed among the most industrialized countries of the world—Europe, North America and Japan. It might be said that world trade routes bind the world together, minimizing distance, natural barriers, lack of resources, and the fundamental differences between peoples and economies. Early trade routes were, of course, overland; later came sea routes and, finally, air routes to connect countries. Trade routes represent the attempts of the world's countries to overcome economic and social imbalances created in part by the influence of geography.

A careful comparison among world population figures in Exhibit 7–2, world trade figures in Exhibit 7–8, and the world map, Exhibit 7–9, graphically illustrates just how small the percentage is of the world's land mass

---

BOX 7–7
New Zealand, Australia—Next Door?

Many New Zealand sales are lost because Americans think of Australia and New Zealand as one market and ask one Australia-based representative to serve both. This is about the same air mileage-wise as having one representative for Albuquerque and Pittsburgh. New Zealand is not as close to Australia as many Americans think. Auckland is 1,343 air miles from Sydney (Albuquerque and Pittsburgh are 1,308 air miles apart). Many U.S. firms have granted agency distributor or other representative rights covering New Zealand to companies located in Australia, but the American Consulate in Auckland says many such Australian companies often do not know the New Zealand markets or do not make reasonable efforts to sell the U.S. product there. In addition, shipments incur additional costs by being routed through Australia, and payment complications sometimes ensue because of the different Australian and New Zealand currency values.

Source: "Marketing News," date unknown.

EXHIBIT 7–8   15 Leading World-Trading Countries (in $ millions)*

Country	Imports			Exports	
	Total Exports/ Imports for Ranking	U.S. Dollar Value of Total Imports	Percent Total Sales by Leading Supplier	U.S. Dollar Value of Total Exports	Percent Total Sales to Leading Customer
United States	$593,259	$381,362	22.4% Japan	$211,897	20.6% Canada
Federal Republic of Germany	432,051	189,647	11.6 Netherlands	242,404	11.9 France
Japan	328,505	119,424	22.2 United States	209,081	38.9 United States
France	246,925	127,854	19.5 Federal Republic of Germany	119,071	16.1 Federal Republic of Germany
United Kingdom	232,103	125,449	16.5 Federal Republic of Germany	106,654	14.2 United States
USSR	186,070	88,906	11.4 German Democratic Republic	97,164	11.5 German Democratic Republic
Italy	197,590	99.775	20.5 Federal Republic of Germany	97,815	18.1 Federal Republic of Germany

and population that accounts for the majority of trade. It is no surprise that the major sea lanes and the most developed highway and rail systems link these major trade areas. The more economically developed a country, the better developed the surface transportation infrastructure is to support trade.

Although air freight is not extremely important as a percentage of total freight transportation, an interesting comparison between surface routes and air routes is air service to the world's less industrialized countries. Although air routes are the heaviest between points in the major industrial centers, they are also heavy to points in less-developed countries. The obvious reason is that for areas not located on navigable waters or where the investment in railroads and effective highways is not yet feasible, air service is often the best answer. Air communications have made otherwise isolated parts of the world reasonably accessible.

EXHIBIT 7–8 *(concluded)*

	Imports			Exports	
Country	Total Exports/ Imports for Ranking	U.S. Dollar Value of Total Imports	Percent Total Sales by Leading Supplier	U.S. Dollar Value of Total Exports	Percent Total Sales to Leading Customer
Canada	164,086	79,836	68.3 United States	84,250	77.1 United States
Netherlands	143,862	75,580	26.4 Federal Republic of Germany	68,282	28.4 Federal Republic of Germany
Belgium/ Luxembourg	136,673	68,024	23.3 Federal Republic of Germany	68,649	19.7 Federal Republic of Germany
Switzerland	78,722	41,188	33.0 Federal Republic of Germany	37,534	21.1 Federal Republic of Germany
Sweden	69,611	32,493	20.5 Federal Republic of Germany	37,118	11.5 Federal Republic of Germany
Spain	82,211	35,055	9.8 United States	27,156	18.0 France
Australia	45,388	24,340	21.9 Japan	21,048	24.7 Japan
Austria	49,310	26,793	44.0 Federal Republic of Germany	22,517	32.7 Federal Republic of Germany

* Order determined by total dollar value of imports and exports.

SOURCE: *1986 International Trade Statistics Yearbook* (New York: United Nations, 1988).

HISTORICAL PERSPECTIVE IN GLOBAL BUSINESS

To understand, explain, and appreciate a people's image of itself and the fundamental attitudes and unconscious fears that are often reflected in its view of foreign cultures, it is necessary to study the culture as it is now as well as to understand culture as it was; that is, a country's history. All cultures are dynamic and reveal their characteristics not

EXHIBIT 7–9   Map of the World

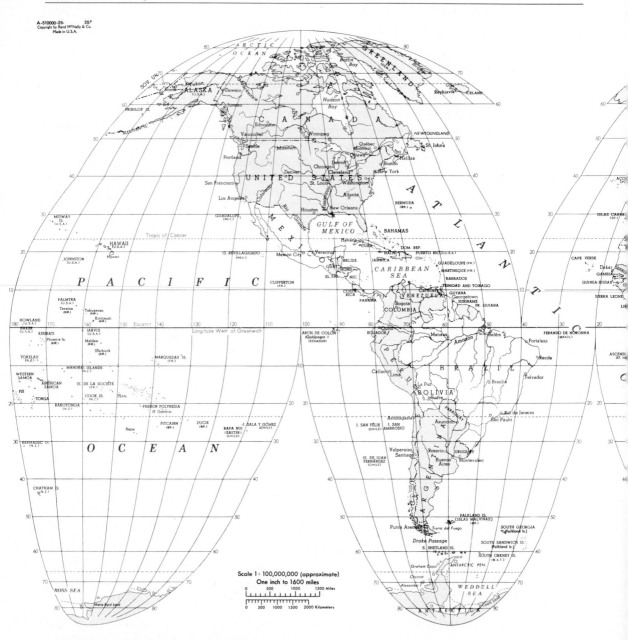

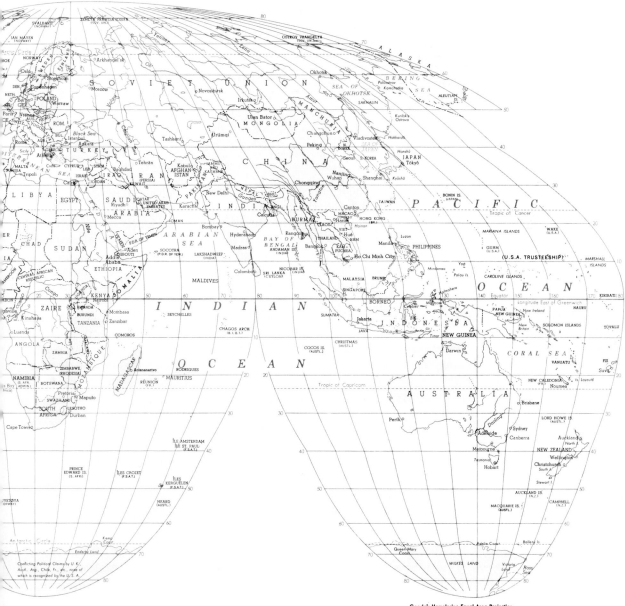

Goode's Homolosine Equal Area Projection

simultaneously but successively over time. To see them flat is not to see them at all. A snapshot view will miss the sense of direction and movement; it will fail to distinguish what is old from what is new, the elements of continuity from the appearance of change.[12]

An awareness of the history of a country is particularly effective for understanding attitudes about the role of government and business, the relations between managers and the managed, the sources of management authority, and attitudes toward foreign MNCs. History is what helps define a nation's "mission," how it perceives its neighbors, and how it sees its place in the world.[13]

History and Contemporary Behavior

Unless you have a historical sense of the many changes that have buffeted Japan, the isolation before the coming of Admiral Perry in 1853, the threat of domination by colonial powers, the rise of new social classes, Western influences, the humiliation of World War II, and involvement in the international community, it is difficult to fully understand its contemporary behavior.[14] Why do the Japanaese have such strong loyalty toward their companies? Why is the loyalty found among participants in the Japanese distribution systems so difficult for an outsider to develop? Why are decisions made by consensus? Answers to such questions can be explained in part by some sense of Japanese history.

Loyalty to family, to country, to company, to social groups and the strong drive to cooperate, to work together for a common cause permeate many facets of Japanese behavior and have historical roots that date back for hundreds of years. Loyalty and service, a sense of responsibility, and respect for discipline, training, and artistry have been stressed since ancient times as necessary for stability and order. Confuscian philosophy emphasizing the basic virtue of loyalty "of friend to friend, of wife to husband, of child to parent, of brother to brother, but, above all, of subject to lord" i.e., to country, has been taught throughout Japan's history.[15] A fundamental premise of Japanese ideology reflects the importance of cooperation for the collective good. Japanese achieve consensus by agreeing that all

---

[12] Susan Strange, *Paths to International Political Economy* (London: George Allen and Unwin, 1984), p. 23.

[13] David M. Raddock, *Assessing Corporate Political Risk* (Totowa, N.J.: Rowman and Littlefield, 1986) pp. 59–60.

[14] Ezra Vogel, "Japan: Adaptive Communitarianism," in *Ideology and National Competitiveness*, ed. George C. Lodge and Ezra P. Vogel (Boston: Harvard Business School Press, 1987) pp. 140–44.

[15] Ibid.

will unite against outside pressures which threaten the collective good. A historical perspective gives the foreigner in Japan a basis on which to begin developing cultural sensitivity and to better understand contemporary behavior.

History Is Subjective

History is important in understanding why a country behaves as it does, but history from whose viewpoint? Historical events are always viewed from one's own biases and thus, what is recorded by one historian may not be what another records, especially if the historians are from different cultures. Historians are traditionally objective but few can help filtering events through their own cultural biases.[16]

A crucial element in understanding any nation's business and political culture is the subjective perception of its history. Why do Mexicans have a love/hate relationship toward the United States? Why are Mexicans required to have majority ownership in most foreign investments? Why did dictator General Porfirio Diaz lament, "Poor Mexico, so far from God, so near the United States"? Because Mexicans see the United States as a threat to their political, economic, and cultural independence. To most citizens in the United States, the causes for such feelings are a mystery. After all, the United States has always been Mexico's good neighbor. Most would agree with President John F. Kennedy's proclamation during a visit to Mexico, "Geography has made us neighbors, tradition has made us friends." North Americans may be surprised to learn that most Mexicans "felt it more accurate to say 'Geography has made us closer, tradition has made us far apart.' "[17]

North Americans feel they have been good neighbors. They see the Monroe Doctrine as protection for Latin America from European colonization and the intervention of Europe in the governments of the Western Hemisphere. Latin Americans tend to see the Monroe Doctrine as an offensive expression of U.S. influence in Latin America. Or to put it another way, "Europe keep your hands off, Latin American is only for the United States."

United States Marines sing with pride of their exploits "from the halls of Montezuma to the shores of Tripoli." To the Mexican, the "halls of

---

[16] A very good example of revisionist history is occurring among some historians in Japan in writing about World War II. See, for example, "Japan Revisionists Tackle Ideas Much As Westerners Do," *The Wall Street Journal*, September 8, 1988, p. 20; and "Changed History: More Japanese Deny Nation Was Aggressor During World War II," *The Wall Street Journal*, September 8, 1988, p. 1.

[17] John C. Condon, *Good Neighbors* (Yarmouth, Maine: Intercultural Press, Inc., 1985) p. xvii.

BOX 7–8
Europe 1992—Can Italy Adjust?

In an integrated Europe, Italians must change their business style.

In heaven, the old joke goes, the police are British, the cooks are French, the lovers are Italian, and it is all organized by Germans. In hell, the police are French, the cooks are British, the lovers are German, and it is all organized by the Italians.

The move toward greater unification of the common market in 1992 is causing soul searching all over Europe. Britons are reexamining their long ambivalent ideas about the continent. The French are eagerly spreading out from their home base across Europe, Germans are realizing they're going to have to let the French and others onto their long protected turf.

Perhaps nowhere else is the soul-searching and anxiety so deep as it is in Italy. Italians know the chaos of daily life in Naples and the ingenious organization of the Italian Parliament, the Italian Post Office, Italian banks, and the Italian construction industry can't long survive unhindred competition from the ingeniously organized Germans. To win in 1992, Italians are going to have to mend their ways. "In Naples," says an executive while running a red light with the rest of the traffic in the middle of town, "traffic signals are advisory. Much remains to be done and quickly. We spend the same amount per capita on the post office as in France or Germany. But in Germany, a letter arrives the next day, where here it takes a week or three weeks, or

Montezuma" is remembered as U.S. troops marching all the way to the center of Mexico City and extracting as tribute 890,000 square miles that included Texas, New Mexico, Arizona, and California.[18] Los Ninos Heroes (the boy heroes), who resisted U.S. troops, wrapped themselves in Mexican flags, and jumped to their deaths rather than surrender, are remembered by a prominent monument at the entrance of Chaptultepec Park. Most U.S. citizens probably do not know of the boy heroes of Chaptultepec Park but every Mexcian can recount the heroism of Los Ninos Heroes and the loss of Mexican territory to the United States.[19]

The Mexican Revolution, which overthrew dictator Diaz and launched the modern Mexican state, is particularly remembered for the expulsion of foreigners, especially North American businessmen who were the most visible of the wealthy and influential entrepreneurs in Mexico.[20]

---

[18] Condon, *Good Neighbors,* pp. 1–16.

[19] Those interested in knowing more about Mexico, its history, and culture should read Alan Riding, *Distant Neighbors: A Portrait of the Mexicans* (New York: First Vantage Books, 1986), p. 563.

[20] See also Jorge I. Dominquez, "Revolution and Flexibility in Mexico," *Ideology and National Competitiveness,* pp. 272–80.

BOX 7–8 *(concluded)*

sometimes it never arrives at all. Naples was organized by Italians. It has three times as many garbagemen as Paris and three times as much uncollected garbage on the streets."

At a dingy downtown Naples branch of the Banco di Naploi, 37 customers crowd around a cluttered wooden countertop. Behind it only 2 of the 11 bank employees present are dealing with the public. A request to cash a $20 traveller's check evokes a blank stare. The clerk goes to an office to ask a supervisor, returns to hunt under the counter for a thick book of forms, struggles with them, leaves twice more to get approval, goes upstairs to photocopy the customer's passport, and finally hands over a hand-written chit. This is to be exchanged for money at the second counter. Getting there requires more elbow bumping. Eventually, 26,320 lire are turned over. The transaction takes 32 minutes.

Three streets away, the main branch of U.S.'s Citi-Bank Italia has installed a revolutionary device, a barrier behind which customers line up to wait for an available teller. The tellers even have computers, and a supervisor sits only four feet away. Here, a $20 traveller's check becomes 26,320 lire in one minute and 15 seconds.

Source: Adapted from Philip Revzin, "Italians Must Change Their Business Style in Integrated Europe," *The Wall Street Journal*, November 21, 1988, p. 1.

Manifest Destiny and the Monroe Doctrine were accepted as the basis for U.S. foreign policy during much of the 19th and 20th centuries. Manifest Destiny, in its broadest interpretation, meant that Americans were a chosen people ordained by God to create a model society. More specifically, it referred to the desires of American expansionists in the 1840s to extend the U.S. boundaries from the Atlantic to the Pacific. The idea of Manifest Destiny was used to justify U.S. annexation of Texas, Oregon, New Mexico, and California and later, U.S. involvement in Cuba, Alaska, Hawaii, and the Philippines.

The Monroe Doctrine, a cornerstone of U.S. foreign policy, was enunciated by President James Monroe in a public statement proclaiming three basic dicta: no further European colonization in the New World, abstention of the United States from European political affairs, and nonintervention of European governments in the governments of the Western Hemisphere.

After 1870 interpretation of the Monroe Doctrine became increasingly broad. In 1881 its principles were evoked in discussing the development of an interoceanic canal across the Isthmus of Panama. The Monroe Doctrine was further applied by Theodore Roosevelt with what became known as the Roosevelt Corollary to the Monroe Doctrine. The corollary stated that not only would the United States prohibit non-American intervention in Latin American affairs but it would also police the area and guarantee

BOX 7–9
History and Motivation

How do you motivate a nation to make sacrifices in the name of industrialization? You call on history. In 1931 Stalin offered this persuasive rationale for the Russian people to make sacrifices.

"Those who fall behind get beaten. But we do not want to be beaten. No, we refuse to be beaten. One feature of the history of old Russia was the continual beatings she suffered because of her backwardness. She was beaten by the Mongol Khans. She was beaten by the Turkish beys, she was beaten by the Swedish feudal lords. She was beaten by the Polish and Lithuanian gentry. She was beaten by the British and French capitalists. She was beaten by the Japanese barons. All beat her—because of her backwardness, because of her military backwardness, cultural backwardness, political backwardness, industrial backwardness, agricultural backwardness."

Stalin struck a responsive chord in appealing to the desire to escape backwardness and gain international respect. This may go a long way in explaining Soviet attitudes toward the West—attitudes that were manifest in business as well as political and military relationships since World War II.

Source: Adapted from David M. Raddock, *Assessing Corporate Political Risk* (Totowa, N.J.: Rowman and Littlefield, 1986), pp. 59–60.

that Latin American nations met their international obligations. The corollary sanctioning American intervention was applied in 1905 when Roosevelt forced the Dominican Republic to accept the appointment of an American economic advisor who quickly became the financial director of the small state; it was used in the acquisition of the Panama Canal Zone from Colombia, and the formation of a provisional government in Cuba in 1906.

According to U.S. history, these Latin American adventures were a justifiable part of our foreign policy; to Latin Americans, they were unwelcome intrusions in Latin American affairs. The way historical events are recorded and interpreted in one culture can differ substantially from the way those same events are recorded and interpreted in another. A comparison of histories goes a long way in explaining the differences in outlooks and behavior of people on both sides of the border. Many Mexicans believe that their "good neighbor" to the north is not reluctant to throw its weight around when it wants something. There are suspicions that self-interest is the primary motivation in good relations with Mexico, whether it be fear of Fidel Castro 25 years ago or eagerness for Mexican oil today.[21]

---

[21] Condon, *Good Neighbors*, pp. 1–16.

Battleship Maine at Havana, Cuba. Late 19th century U.S. political and military intervention in Latin America affects present attitudes about the United States. (Journalism Services, Inc.)

By seeing history from a Latin American's perspective, it is understandable how a national leader, under adverse economic conditions, can point a finger at the United States or a U.S. MNC and evoke a special emotional, popular reaction that would divert attention away from the government in power.[22] The leader might be cheered for expropriation or confiscation of a foreign investment, even though the investment was making an important contribution to the economy. To understand a country's attitudes, prejudices, and fears, it is necessary to look beyond the surface or current events to the inner subtleties of the country's entire past for clues.[23]

SUMMARY

One British authority admonishes foreign marketers to study the world until "the mere mention of a town, country, or river enables it to be picked out immediately on the map." Although it may not be necessary for the student of foreign marketing to memorize the world map to that extent, a prospective international marketer should be reasonably familiar with the world, its climate, and topographic differences. Otherwise, the important marketing characteristics of geography could be completely overlooked when marketing in another country. The need for geographical

---

[22] Raddock, *Assessing Corporate Political Risk*, p. 36.

[23] Riding, *Distant Neighbors*, p. xi.

and historical knowledge goes deeper than being able to locate continents and their countries. For someone who has never been in a tropical rain forest with an annual rainfall of at least 60 inches and sometimes more than 200 inches, it is difficult to anticipate the need for protection against high humidity, or to anticipate the difficult problems caused by dehydration in constant 100 degrees plus heat in the Sahara region. Without a historical understanding of a culture, the attitudes within the marketplace may not be understood.

Aside from the simpler and more obvious ramifications of climate and topography, there are complex geographical and historical influences on the development of the general economy and society of a country. In this case, the need for studying geography and history is to provide the marketer with an understanding of why a country has developed as it has rather than as a guide for adapting marketing plans. Geography and history are two of the environments of foreign marketing that should be understood and that must be included in foreign marketing plans to a degree commensurate with their influence on marketing effort.

QUESTIONS

1. Study the data in Exhibit 7–1 and briefly discuss the long-term prospects for industrialization of an underdeveloped country with a high population growth and minimum resources.

2. Why study geography in international marketing? Discuss.

3. Pick a country and show how employment and topography affect marketing within the country.

4. Discuss the bases of world trade. Give examples illustrating the different bases.

5. The marketer "should also examine the more complex effect of geography on general market characteristics, distribution systems, and the state of the economy." Comment.

6. The world population pattern trend is shifting from rural to urban areas. Discuss the marketing ramifications.

7. Select a country with a stable population and one with a rapidly growing population. Contrast the marketing implications of these two situations.

8. "The basis of world trade can be simply stated as the result of equalizing an imbalance in the needs and wants of society on one hand and its supply of goods on the other." Explain.

9. How do differences in people constitute a basis for trade?

10. World trade routes bind the world together." Discuss.

11. Why are air routes so important in less-developed countries? Illustrate your answer with examples.

12. What are the marketing ramifications of the population projections for the year 2000 in the developing world?

13. How does an understanding of history help an international marketer?

14. Why is there a love/hate relationship between Mexico and the United States? Discuss.

15. Discuss how an American's interpretation of Manifest Destiny and the Monroe Doctrine might differ from a Latin American's.

CHAPTER

8

Multinational Market Groups

Two important economic cooperation agreements created in the 1980s will have far reaching influence on world trade in the 1990s: the Single European Act (1987)[1] and the United States and Canada Free-Trade Agreement (1989).[2] Economic cooperation has been an international byword since the conclusion of World War II when the European Economic Community, now officially known as the European Community, was created. Many countries banded together in various multinational economic market groups seeking the benefits of economic cooperation. To date none has been as successful as the European Community.[3]

The passage of the Single European Act and the United States and Canada Free-Trade Agreement demonstrates a renewed interest in economic cooperation, while increasing concern about the effect of such cooperation on global competition. Governments and businesses are concerned that

---

[1] Richard I. Kirkland, Jr., "Outsider's Guide to Europe in 1992," *Fortune,* October 24, 1988, pp. 121–27.

[2] For details of the agreement see "Summary of the U.S.-Canada Free-Trade Agreement," *Export Today,* November–December 1987, pp. 57–61; and Glenn R. Reichardt, "Free Trade Agreement," *Global Trade,* April 1988, pp. 36–37.

[3] Tim Dickson, "Delors Leads E.C. toward 1992," *Europe,* January–February 1989, pp. 32–33.

Europe, 1992. A unified Europe will become one of the world's largest markets. (Journalism Services, Inc.)

Europe 1992 might become Fortress Europe[4] and the U.S.-Canadian market and the East Asia Market will become regional trading blocs with no trade restrictions internally and borders protected from outsiders.[5] Whatever the future reality, global companies must realize that economic cooperation is growing and multinational market groups are important environmental factors in the decade of the 1990s.[6]

Essentially, a multinational market is created when a number of individual countries agree to take positive steps to reduce trade and tariff barriers among the participating countries. Organizational form varies widely among market groups, but the universal orientation of such multinational cooperation is economic benefit for the participants. Sometimes political and social benefits accrue, but the dominant motive for affiliation remains economic.

Economic integration through customs unions relates directly to the marketing function of business. Such cooperation facilitates the marketing

---

[4] Steven Greenhouse, "The Growing Fear of Fortress Europe," *New York Times*, October 23, 1988, p. 1c.

[5] "Trade Bloc Protectionism Forecast," *The Journal of Commerce*, October 7, 1988, p. 3a.

[6] Rosalind Rachid, "Caribbean Fears Reduction in Access to EC after '92," *The Journal of Commerce*, December 5, 1988, p. 3a.

of one country's goods in another country and facilitates the acquisition of lower-priced goods produced elsewhere. Development of multinational markets and their success are partly functions of the stage of economic development of the participating countries; as nations expand their productive capacities, they also need to expand the boundaries of their markets. Without mass marketing facilities and mass markets, modern mass production capacity (or the surplus productive capacity of relatively inefficient nations) cannot be successfully utilized.

The European Community is the foremost example of economic cooperation and the world's largest multinational market. Other multinational markets are the Central American Common Market, the British Commonwealth of Nations, the Council for Mutual Economic Assistance, the Afro-Asian Organization for Economic Cooperation, and the more recently created Latin American Integration Association.[7]

Multinational market groups form large markets that provide potentially significant opportunities for international business. Although it may not be feasible to market into each of a number of separate nations, economic union of those nations may offer a logical market. Be alert to the marketing implications of multinational market developments reviewed in this chapter; the impact of such market groupings in world business is greater than ever anticipated in the early days of the markets in question.

LA RAISON D'ÊTRE

The Right to be

Successful economic union requires favorable economic, political, social, and geographic factors as a basis for success. Major flaws in any one factor could destroy a union unless the other factors provide sufficient strength to overcome the weaknesses. In general, the advantages of economic union must be clear cut and significant, and the benefits must greatly outweigh the disadvantages before nations forgo any part of their sovereignty. Often a strong threat to the economic or political security of a nation is needed to provide the impetus for cooperation.

Economic Factors

Every type of economic union shares the development and enlargement of market opportunities as a basic orientation; usually markets are enlarged through preferential tariff treatment for participating members or common

---

[7] The Latin American Integration Association replaced the Latin American Free Trade Association in 1980. For a discussion of the causes for the change see, "New Latin American Association Carries on Traditions of LAFTA, with Some Important Differences," *Business America*, April 6, 1981, p. 15.

tariff barriers against outsiders. Enlarged, protected markets stimulate internal economic development by providing assured outlets and preferential treatment for goods produced within the customs union. Consumers benefit from lower internal tariff barriers among the participating countries. In many cases, external as well as internal barriers are reduced because of the greater economic security afforded domestic producers by the enlarged market.

Nations with complementary economic bases are least likely to encounter frictions in the development and operation of a common market unit. The European Community includes countries with diverse agricultural bases, different industries, and different natural resources. It is significant that most of the problems the European Community has encountered concern agricultural products where several countries have significant productive capability and national producers who desire protection. For example, reportedly to protect the British poultry industry from a poultry virus on the continent, the British banned French poultry. In unrelated incidents, the French banned Italian wine and the Irish banned all poultry and eggs from other member countries. In each of the cases, the underlying reasons were more a desire to protect local markets than to protect health. The European Commission entered the dispute and charged all countries involved with violations of EC regulations. With the recent addition of Greece, Spain, and Portugal, economic issues arising from economic disparity among member nations will intensify as the full integration of Europe 1992 takes place.[8] There is also an increasingly expressed concern by outsiders that protectionism is the goal of Europe 1992.[9]

Productive inequities are likely to be a major stumbling block in the success of such nearly homogeneous markets as the Central American Common Market (CACM) countries. One advantage that Latin countries have is an economic base that is not yet highly developed. A major orientation of CACM, so far, has been to encourage different member countries to follow different industrial lines. Protecting markets from exploitation by foreign companies was also an important factor in development of the CACM.

The demise of the Latin American Free Trade Association (LAFTA) in 1980 was caused, in part, by its economically stronger members not allowing for the needs of the weaker ones. The new Latin American Integration Association (LAIA), which replaces LAFTA, permits more flexibility in bilateral agreements and less rigid operational rules. Most attempts at common markets which do not work as well as expected can count economic incompatibility as the major reason.

---

[8] See, for example, "The Supereconomy Stirs in a Web of Self-Interest," and "Far Side of Integration May Fuel Fatal Backlash," *Insight*, June 20, 1988, pp. 10–17.

[9] "EC's Auto Plan Would Keep Japan at Bay: 1992 Unification Effort Smacks of Protectionism," *The Wall Street Journal*, October 27, 1988, p. A18.

Political Factors

Political amenability among countries is another basic requisite for development of a supranational market arrangement. Participating countries must have comparable aspirations and general compatibility before they will give up any part of their national sovereignty. State sovereignty is one of the most cherished possessions of any nation and relinquished only for a promise of significant improvement of the national position through cooperation.

Economic considerations provide the basic catalyst for the formation of a customs union group, but political elements are equally important. The uniting of the original European Community countries was partially a response to the outside threat of Russia's great political and economic power; the countries of Western Europe were willing to settle their family squabbles to present a unified front to the Russian bear.

One of the chief arguments for the admission of Spain and Portugal to the EC was that their participation would help stabilize their governments and stay the threat of communism in those countries. The EC's united front is also evident from time to time in negotiations between the EC and the United States. A basic premise of the European Community is that it will gradually develop into a political as well as economic union. There exists now an agreement for European Political Cooperation (EPC). The tenets of the EPC, which are included in the Single European Act, commit the 12 EC member states to consult and cooperate on foreign policy issues and to work toward coordinated positions and joint actions. Its aim is to maximize the influence of the EC in international affairs through a single, coherent European approach.[10]

Geographic Proximity

Although it is not absolutely imperative that cooperating members of a customs union have geographical proximity, such closeness facilitates the functioning of a common market. Transportation networks basic to any marketing system are likely to be interrelated and well developed when countries are close together. Countries that are widely separated geographically have a major barrier to overcome in attempting economic fusion.

Social Factors

Cultural similarity can ease the shock of economic cooperation with other countries. The more similar the cultures, the more likely a market is to succeed because members understand the outlook and viewpoints of their

---

[10] "EC Assesses Half-Way Mark of 1992 Plan," *Europe,* January–February 1989, pp. 47–48.

colleagues. Although there is great cultural diversity in the European Community, key members share a long-established Christian heritage. They are also commonly aware of being European.

Language, as a part of culture, did not create as much a barrier for European Community countries as was expected. Initially there were seven major languages, but such linguistic diversity did not impede trade because European businesses historically have been multilingual. Nearly every educated European can do business in at least two or three languages; thus, in every relationship, there is likely to be a linguistic common ground. However, when the number of countries expanded beyond the original seven, language difficulties began to complicate the process. With the 12 member nations, language has become a greater problem because EC rules require translation to be available for all languages at official meetings. An official meeting now requires 30 interpreters to be able to intertranslate all 12 languages.[11]

PATTERNS OF MULTINATIONAL COOPERATION

Multinational market groups take several forms, varying significantly in the degree of cooperation, dependence, and interrelationship among participating nations. The United States provides a common external trade barrier for all states and a free flow of labor and capital from one state or region to another. These U.S. characteristics also represent the principal characteristics of a full, economically integrated union. There are also political unions not completely integrated economically. In some nations, various regions or states have the power to limit entry of products from other states through tariffs. In the United States, there is a minor amount of product exclusion (milk and some agricultural products) but internal tariffs are prohibited by the Constitution.

This section examines five arrangements for regional economic integration: regional cooperation for development plans, free-trade area arrangements, customs union programs, common market arrangements, and semi-political unions.

Regional Cooperation Groups

One multinational market group that has developed in recent years is the Regional Cooperation for Development (RCD). In the RCD arrangement, several governments agree to participate jointly with business in developing basic industries beneficial to each economy. Each country makes

---

[11] Karen Elliot House, "Europe's Global Clout Is Limited by Divisions 1992 Can't Paper Over," *The Wall Street Journal*, February 13, 1989, p. 1.

an advance commitment to participate in the financing of new joint-venture projects and to purchase a specified share of the output of the production facilities developed.

In one RCD, Colombia and Venezuela are cooperating to build a hydro-electric generating plant on the Orinoco River. They are sharing jointly in the construction and will share in the electricity produced.

Regional cooperation groups differ from common markets in that there is no elimination or lowering of tariffs or structuring of external tariffs. In a sense they are simply joint ventures of various governments cooperating with private business to develop new facilities. Such cooperation, however, is likely to presage fuller multinational developments.

The Association of South East Asian Nations (ASEAN) has established foreign investment rules and a program for complementary sectorial development of various industries.[12]

Indonesia and Malaysia, for example, have been allocated urea production; Singapore, heavy diesel engines; the Philippines, superphosphates; and Thailand, soda ash. The economic ministry has developed an extensive list of future projects for intragroup cooperation. ASEAN falls somewhere between a regional cooperation group and a free-trade area because it also has a specific program for reducing tariffs and nontrade barriers within the group.

Free-Trade Area

The key function of a free-trade area (FTA) is to provide a mass market without barriers that impede the flow of goods and services among participating member countries. Essentially, a free-trade area is created to reduce or eliminate customs duties and nontariff trade barriers among partner countries.

Although a free-trade area does not establish common external trade barriers and customs duties and does not provide for a free flow of labor and capital within countries as a common market does, there are increased communication and cooperation on economic issues. The central agency acts as a clearinghouse when the countries decide to upgrade the area to greater cooperative efforts.

Latin America works within the Latin American Integration Association (LAIA). The United States-Canada Free-Trade Area, ratified by the United States in 1988 and Canada in 1989, is the newest free-trade area.[13] The

---

[12] Richard J. Buczynski, "American Investment Abroad: The ASEAN Option," *Business America*, February 1, 1988, p. 7–8.

[13] Louis Kraar, "North America's New Trade Punch," *Fortune*, May 22, 1989, pp. 123–27.

BOX 8–1
Pure German Sausage Brings out Wurst in European Community

A widespread suspicion among many Europeans is that many of the local country regulations are simply disguised trade restrictions. There has been a concerted effort on the part of the EC Commission to eliminate trade barriers and make the EC a true common market. The problem becomes one of deciding when restrictions are really protection of health and tradition or just more roadblocks. Consider the case for bratwurst.

At Eduard Kluehspies's snack bar in a corner of the Viktualienmarkt in Munich, the talk has turned to sausage, but not the plump and juicy bratwurst, brockwurst, or currywurst that are served together with a slice of bread and a dollop of sweet Bavarian mustard. Today, the regulars are contemplating something that is totally indigestible—something less than pure German wurst.

The European Community is upset about stringent German rules that define what may or may not be put into sausage. For generations, Germans have insisted in keeping their sausage more or less pure by limiting the amount of nonmeat additives such as vegetable fat and protein. But EC bureaucrats and other European sausage-makers see the regulations as a clever German ploy to keep out imports, and they are demanding change. This causes dismay among the beer-drinking regulars at the snack bar. "I'd rather eat my dog," says one grumpy local.

Not only wurst but beer, which Bavarians call "liquid bread," is under attack. The EC had to go to court to get Germany to drop its Reinheitsgebot, a medieval decree stipulating that beer may be brewed only with malt, hops, water and yeast. It kept the beer "pure" and just incidentally kept most other beers out of Germany.

Source: Adapted from Peter Gumbel, "Pure German Sausage Brings out Wurst in European Community," *The Wall Street Journal*, September 9, 1985, p. 24.

United States is also involved in a FTA with Israel. The European Free Trade Association (EFTA), among the better-known free-trade areas, has been expanded to include the member nations of the European Community. The newly structured 17-country EFTA is a larger market than the United States and Canada, exceeding 350 million consumers. EC countries operate as a free-trade area with other members of EFTA while they continue to operate as a common market among themselves.

Full Customs Union

The customs union represents the next stage in the development of cooperation. The customs union enjoys the free-trade association's reduced or eliminated internal tariffs and a common external tariff on products imported from countries outside the union. The union is a logical stage of development in the transition from free-trade area to a common market. The Benelux nations have been participants in a customs union dating back to 1921. Other customs unions exist between France and Monaco, Italy and San Marino, and Switzerland and Liechtenstein.

Common Market

The common market builds on the reduction or elimination of internal tariffs and the development of a common external tariff structure characteristic of the preceding class of economic integration. It adds the further elements of free flow of capital and labor from country to country. Thus, a common market is a common marketplace for goods as well as for services (including labor) and for capital. It is a *unified economy* and lacks only political unity to become a nation. The common market may establish further objectives and additional devices to assure effective economic integration.

The Treaty of Rome which established the European Community called for common external tariffs and the gradual elimination of intramarket tariffs, quotas, and other trade barriers—both now in effect. The treaty also called for elimination of restrictions on the movement of services, labor, and capital; prohibition of cartels; coordinated monetary and fiscal policies; common agricultural policies; use of common investment funds for regional industrial development; and similar rules for wage and welfare payments.

The founders of the European Community intended to be a truly common market; so much so that economic integration must eventually be supplemented by political integration to accomplish the objectives completely. In such an arrangement, members of the European Community will become truly interdependent members of a supranational community. The objectives of the original Treaty of Rome have yet to be completely fulfilled. Although there have been great strides made toward full economic integration, barriers still exist. The purpose of the Single European Act is to achieve a unified market by 1992.[14]

Latin America boasts two common markets, the Central American Common Market and the Andean Common Market. Both have roughly similar goals and seek eventual full economic integration. The CACM provides a successful example of cooperation in normally individualistic Latin America. It pioneered the unique feature called *sectorial development;* its governing body formally allocates production authority for certain manufactured products to individual member countries. In this way, the group has encouraged

---

[14] Shawn Tully, "The Coming Boom in Europe," *Fortune*, April 10, 1989, pp. 108–14.

". . . COMMON MARKET, HELL! . . . THAT'S A SUPERMARKET . . ."

With Permission of The Denver Post *and Conrad.*

development of a number of industries by guaranteeing the entire CACM market to a single producer.

Africa has had a wide variety of proposed economic unions including one common market, the Economic Community of West African States (ECOWAS). Its 15 members have a population of some 130 million people. The record of economic integration efforts in Africa has been dismal; despite such experience, ECOWAS has scheduled full customs union integration by 1990 including elimination of internal duties and a common external tariff wall.

Political Union

Political union of economic affairs may be voluntary or enforced; but regardless of the motivation, such union ultimately depends on economic logic for success.

The Commonwealth of Nations. *Time* magazine has commented that:

the Commonwealth of Nations is clearly impossible. Except for the colonial past, its 18 member nations—five white, nine black, four brown—have nothing, not even wealth, in common. They are divided by almost every possible denominator: color, geography, education, culture, nationalism, and economic interests. And so, before each meeting of the Commonwealth Prime Ministers in London, logical men quite logically predict its collapse. They are always wrong. The Commonwealth not only staggers through but it keeps growing.

The British Commonwealth is a completely voluntary organization providing for the loosest possible relationship that could still be classified as economic integration. Still, its membership covers one fourth of the earth's land mass, contains one fourth of the world's people, and carries on within its confines one third of the world's trade. Despite its size, the bonds holding together the Commonwealth are hard to visualize. One Whitehall official has commented that "I am not sure that all this scrutinizing is a good thing. The Commonwealth is something that may disappear if you stare at it too hard." Although it is technically neither a legal nor a political conglomeration, the Commonwealth can best be classified as a political union based on economic history and a sense of tradition. One authority comments that the real binding forces are the English language and parliamentary democracy. The Commonwealth does not share the common internal tariff structure which characterizes the weakest of the other forms of economic integration. Even the bilateral trade preferences between the United Kingdom and the individual commonwealths were largely dissipated when Britain entered the EC.

Despite its loose bonds and its informal relationship, the Commonwealth still exists as an example of one form of politically based economic integration and cooperation.

Enforced Political Union.   Reacting to the popularity and exceptional success of the Marshall Plan in Western Europe, Joseph Stalin established the Council for Mutual Economic Assistance (COMECON). Although it is centrally controlled and more tightly organized than the Commonwealth, COMECON has not approached any of the other methods of economic integration in effectiveness. COMECON has been, in part, an agency for the exploitation of its member countries; because of the satellites' defensiveness, it has not been an effective union.[15]

A recent COMECON summit (1988) indicated that member states were upset about intrablock pricing, the lack of currency convertibility, and slow economic growth.[16] COMECON as a trade group has been ineffective and reliant on forced cooperation rather than consensus. The future does not look much brighter although under the principles of *perestroika*, mem-

[15] "Two Great Experiments: Perestroika and 1992," *World Press Review*, January 1989, p. 24.

[16] "COMECON Summit: No Agreement Reached," *Business Eastern Europe*, July 18, 1988, pp. 225–26.

bers of COMECON have been guaranteed that the output of some enterprises will be purchased outright rather than traded to the State and others will receive the essential components to turn out needed goods.[17] Heavy debt plagues COMECON countries and the future looks much like the past: continued reliance within the bloc on bilateral trade, no currency convertibility among members and slow economic growth.[18]

Except for the poltical pressures involved, COMECON can be said to have failed as an agency for economic integration because its member countries do not meet the basic requisites for effective union and because it has failed to establish agencies that permit mutual benefit. The Eastern European economies are not complementary; language and cultural barriers exist, and the satellite countries are unwilling to give up what sovereignty they do possess.

MULTINATIONAL MARKET GROUPS TODAY

The following pages summarize only basic information about the world's major market groups. Their names and compositions change frequently, but the number of groups attests to the vitality of the multinational market group movement which seems to be the dominant theme of international trade in the late 20th century.

Europe

Nearly every multinational market grouping is found in Europe and all have functioned with varying degrees of success (see Exhibits 8–1 and 8–2). The most successful has been the EC; its progress has been punctuated by extremes of optimism and pessimism relative to its future potential.

European Community.   The European Community was created as a result of three treaties, the European Coal and Steel Community, the European Economic Community, and the European Atomic Energy Community. These three treaties are incorporated within the European Community and serve as the community's constitution. They provide a policy framework and empower the commission and the Council of Ministers to pass laws to carry out EC policy. The community uses three legal instruments: (1) regulations binding the member states directly and having the same strength as national laws; (2) directives also binding the member states

---

[17] "Soviet Program Sets 1989–90 State Orders," *Business Eastern Europe*, October 31, 1988, pp. 345–46.

[18] "E.C.–COMECON Links: No Guarantees of More Trade," *Business Eastern Europe*, August 19, 1988, pp. 273–74.

EXHIBIT 8–1   European Market Groups

Association	Member	Population (millions)	GDP (U.S. $ billions)	GDP per Capita (U.S. $)	Imports (U.S. $ millions)
European Community (EC)	Belgium	9.9	$ 79.1	$ 7,985	$ 55,561
	Luxembourg	0.4	3.6	9,826	—
	Denmark	5.1	58.1	11,336	17,986
	France	54.6	510.3	9,343	107,588
	Germany	61.0	625.0	10,266	157,597
	Ireland	3.6	18.4	5,098	10,049
	Italy	57.1	358.7	6,259	88,593
	United Kingdom	56.1	454.5	8,069	109,415
	Netherlands	14.5	125.0	8,620	65,212
	Greece	9.9	33.4	3,382	10,138
	Spain	38.6	164.3	4,262	30,067
	Portugal	10.2	20.7	2,026	7,650
European Free Trade Association (EFTA)	Austria	7.6	66.1	8,805	26,793
	Iceland	0.2	2.7	10,959	904
	Norway	4.2	58.4	14,092	14,519
	Portugal	10.2	20.7	2,026	7,650
	Sweden	8.4	100.2	12,203	28,538
	Switzerland	6.4	92.8	14,555	30,626
EC and EFTA Associates	Finland	4.9	54.1	11,064	13,226
	Spain	38.6	164.3	4,262	30,067
	Turkey	49.3	52.7	1,069	11,340

SOURCE: *National Account Statistics: Analysis of Main Aggregates, 1985* (New York: United Nations, 1988); *Demographic Yearbook, 1985* (New York: United Nations, 1987); and *1986 International Trade Statistics Yearbook*, vol. 1 (New York: United Nations, 1988).

but allowing them to choose the means of execution; and, (3) decisions addressed to a government, an enterprise, or an individual, binding the parties named.

Of all the multinational market groups, none is more secure in its cooperation or more important economically than the European Community. From its beginning, it has successfully made progress toward achieving the ultimate goal of complete economic integration. However, it is easy to be confused in evaluating the progress of the EC through information in the public press. Journalism seems to thrive on bad news, so many of the articles about the community focus on its problems, limitations, disputes, lack of cohesiveness, and limited progress. There is no denying that problems exist, but it is important for the international marketer not to minimize the real power of the European Community. Despite its problems, the community exists as a functional entity exerting a major force in commercial affairs. Its court system has overriding powers in many

Exhibit 8–2   The European Economic Region: EC, EFTA, and Associates

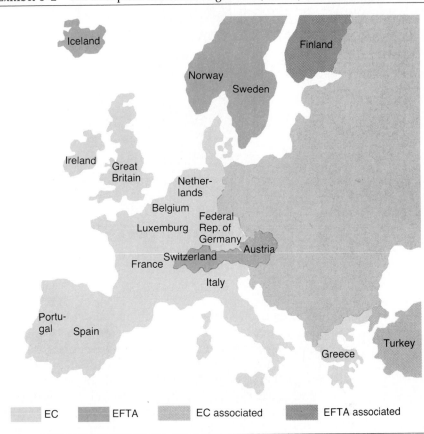

| EC | EFTA | EC associated | EFTA associated |

areas of litigation; common tariff walls protect the market against production outside its borders; internal tariffs among the countries have been reduced. The European Community negotiates as a single entity in matters of world trade and politics, and has become the voice of Europe in international discussions. There is no denying the importance of EC's policies in such broad areas as environment and energy where detailed programs have been developed. And with the commitments made in the Single European Act, further integration and success are assured.

The Single European Act—Europe 1992.   Europe without borders, Fortress Europe, and Europe 1992 refer to the Single European Act—the latest and most significant agreement among the countries in the European Community to move further toward the original goal of complete economic and political integration. Implementation of the provisions of the Treaty of Rome was to occur in stages, to reduce and eventually terminate all

*European Community Headquarters Building,
Brussels, Belgium. (Journalism Services, Inc.)*

tariffs and other trade restrictions, and to gradually advance complete political and economic integration, a United States of Europe.

Many, including Europeans, had little hope for the success of the European Common Market because of the problems that would be created by integration and the level of national sovereignty that would have to be conceded to the community.[19] There were, after all, 1,000 years of economic separatism to overcome. Their skepticism has proved wrong. Today, many marvel at how far the European Community has come even though there is much left to do. The Single European Act is designed to bring the European Community closer to its ultimate goal; that is, the elimination of all barriers to trade and the free movement of capital and labor.

There are still formidable obstacles to overcome. The European Common Market is very uncommon; there are language differences, individual national interests, political differences, and centuries-old restrictions designed to protect local national markets. The habit of protectionism and the resulting variety of standards must be addressed. Historically, standards have been used to effectively limit market access. For example, Germany protected its beer market from foreign beer with a purity law requiring beer sold in Germany to be brewed from only water, hops, malt, and yeast. Italy protected its pasta market by requiring that pasta be made only from durum wheat.

---

[19] Kirkland, "Outsider's Guide to Europe," pp. 124–27.

Under the Single European Act there eventually will be single European standards; however, the time and money to convert to one single standard is overwhelming in the short run. Technical standards for electrical products are an example of the problems the EC faces before complete integration is a reality: Twenty-nine different types of electrical outlets, 10 kinds of plugs, and 12 kinds of cords are used by EC member countries. The estimated cost for all EC countries to change their wiring systems and electrical standards to a single European standard is 80 billion European Currency Units (ECUs).[20] Until the ultimate goal of uniform Eurostandards for health, safety, technical, and other areas can be reached, the Single European Act policy of harmonization, or mutual recognition, will be observed.

Under harmonization, essential requirements for protection of health, safety, the environment, and product standards will be established. Once these are harmonized and EC-wide essential requirements have been met, each member state will be expected to recognize the adequacy of each others' national standards for nonessential characteristics. There are exceptions to mutual recognition, especially in the area of health, but ostensibly, this policy reduces standards as a barrier to trade.[21]

The European Commission, the EC's executive body, published a white paper that outlines almost 300 pieces of legislation designed to remove physical, technical, and fiscal barriers between member states to achieve full integration.[22] It provides for the elimination of border controls with corresponding strengthening of external border controls, the unification of technical regulations on product standards, procedures to bring national value added and excise tax systems among member countries closer together, and free migration of the population. In addition to dismantling the existing barriers, the white paper proposes a wide range of new commercial policies, some extremely controversial.[23] The most controversial policies are free capital market, deregulation of financial services, and the opening of government purchases and contracts to nondomestic companies.

As of the beginning of 1989, over one third of the 300 proposals outlined in the commission's white paper have been presented and adopted. A single customs document replacing 70 forms required for transborder shipments to member countries was one of the first and most welcome

---

[20] Sherry Buchanan, "Europlug: Its Day Is a Long Way Off," *International Herald Tribune,* June 30, 1988, p. 9.

[21] Patrick W. Cooke and Donald R. Mackay, "The New EC Approach to Harmonization of Standards and Certification," *Business America,* August 1, 1988, pp. 8–9.

[22] "The European Community Comes of Age with Its Single Market," *Business International,* June 27, 1988, pp. 193–94.

[23] "1992 Is upon Us," *International Management,* January 1988, pp. 44–46.

BOX 8–2
Oh, Life Would Be Easier if We Only Had a Europlug

Those of you who have traveled Europe know of the frustration of electrical plugs, different electrical voltages, and other annoyances of international travel. But consider the cost to consumers and the inefficiency of production for a company that wishes to sell electrical appliances in the European "Common" Market.

Philips, the electrical appliance manufacturer, has to produce 12 kinds of irons to serve just its European market. The problem is that Europe does not have a universal standard. The ends of irons bristle with different plugs for different countries. Some have three prongs, others two; prongs protrude straight or angled, round or rectangular, fat, thin, and sometimes sheathed. There are circular plug faces, squares, pentagons and hexagons. Some are perforated and some are notched. One French plug has a niche like a keyhold; British plugs carry fuses.

Europe's plugs and sockets are balkanized partly because different countries have different voltages and cycles. But the variety of standards also has other causes, such as protecting local manufacturers. Estimated cost for lack of universal standards is between $60 and $80 billion a year or nearly 3 percent of the EC's total output of goods and services.

Source: Adapted from "Philips Finds Obstacles to Intra-Europe Trade Are Costly, Inefficient," *The Wall Street Journal*, August 7, 1985, p. 1.

---

reforms.[24] By the end of 1989, it is expected that over 90 percent of the 300 pieces of proposed legislation will have been presented to the Council of Ministers for consideration and adoption.[25] How rapidly they will be adopted and whether or not the 1992 deadline will be met is open to debate.

Some of the proposals may be too far reaching to overcome "archaic, nationalistic" reactions. Although most Europeans accept the rationale behind the single market, few fully understand its ramifications of free movement of labor, shared social programs, new and strange tax systems, and shared professional standards. The consumer who prefers "pure British milk" as the supermarket sign reads, or the French farmers who burned Spanish trucks carrying early season strawberries (a south of France monopoly before Spain became an EC member) may be less than enthusiastic about a single Europe.[26] Even though all proposals may not be met by

---

[24] "Progress Report on Europe's Single Internal Market," *Europe*, April 1987, p. 32.

[25] "Study Analyzes Impact of 1992 Internal Market," *Europe*, May 1988, pp. 18–19.

[26] "Community's Goal: A State of Oneness," and "The Supereconomy Stirs in a Web of Self-interest," *Insight*, June 20, 1988, pp. 8–11.

1992, the program for unification has built up a momentum that probably cannot be reversed.[27]

EC Authority Strengthened.   Over the years, the community has gained an increasing amount of authority over its member states. The community's institutions (the commission, the Council of Ministers, the European Parliament, and the Court of Justice) and their decision-making processes distinguish it from other international cooperative organizations. The institutions have legal status and extensive powers in fields covered by common policies. The institutions are the support structure of the integration process leading toward a federal system. Community institutions have the power to make decisions and execute policies in specific areas. They form a federal pattern with executive, parliamentary, and judicial branches.

The European Commission.   The 17-member commission initiates policy and supervises its observance by member states. It proposes and supervises execution of laws and policies. The commission has a president and four vice presidents; each of its members is appointed for a four-year term by mutual agreement of EC governments. Commission members act only in the interest of the EC. They may not receive instructions from any national government and are subject to the supervision of the European Parliament. Their responsibilities are to ensure that EC rules and the principles of the common market are respected. They can propose legislation and are charged with the task of implementing EC policies. The commission initiated the white paper on EC integration and proposed the Single European Act to the Council of Ministers.

Council of Ministers.   The Council of Ministers, which is composed of a minister from each member country, passes laws based on commission proposals. Because the council is the decision-making body of the EC, it is their responsibility to debate and decide which proposals of the Single European Act to accept as binding on EC members. In concert with the commission's white paper, the Single European Act included the first and only amendment of the original Paris Treaty that streamlined decision making. Under provisions in the act, the council can enact into law many of the proposals in the white paper by majority vote instead of the unanimity formerly required. However, proposals for changes in tax rates on products and services still require a unanimous vote. Requiring only a majority vote by the council for passage of reforms is seen as a necessary change if Europe 1992 is to be a reality.[28]

---

[27] "Europe without Borders: Answers to Some Questions," *Europe*, October 1988, pp. 15–17.

[28] Richard Gwyn, "The Spark for a New Mediterranean Miracle," *World Press Review*, March 1989, pp. 22–23.

The European Parliament.   With 518 members elected every five years by universal suffrage, the European Parliament is mainly a consultative body which passes on most community legislation with limited but gradually increasing budgetary powers. Since introduction of the Single European Act, modest new powers have been conferred on parliament. Previously it was consulted on day-to-day legislation, but the new rules of the Single European Act give parliament greater powers.[29] After legislation has gone through two readings, parliament has the right on the second reading to put forward detailed alterations and amendments that, if accepted by the commission, can be rejected only by the member states and a unanimous vote of the Council of Ministers. Parliament can now influence legislation but it does not have the power to initiate legislation. The commission has the sole power of initiative and the council plays the major role in making decisions. However, the parliament has the power to dismiss the commission by a two-thirds majority and it has budgetary powers that allow it to take part in major decisions on EC expenditures.

The Court of Justice.   Consisting of 13 judges, the Court of Justice is the community's supreme court. Its first responsibility is challenging any measures incompatible with the Treaty of Rome when they are adopted by the commission, council, or national governments. Its second responsibility is passing judgment, at the request of a national court, on interpretation or validity of points of EC law. The court's decisions are final and cannot be appealed in national courts. The Court of Justice has increased its presence in the last decade and has become very important in enforcing community laws and regulations.

Court decisions are binding on EC members; through its judgments and interpretations, the court is helping to create a body of truly EC law that will apply to all EC institutions, member states, national courts, and private citizens.[30] Judgments of the court, in the field of EC law, overrule those of national courts. In a recent case, the court overruled the German purity law for beer that had been in force since 1516 and was considered the world's oldest health regulation. The Court of Justice declared the ban by the Federal Republic of Germany on all beers that included any ingredient other than water, hops, malt, and yeast (thereby barring all foreign brews) to be illegal. The court ruled that the German law violates EC competition rules and cannot be used to restrict imports of foreign beer into Germany.[31]

---

[29] "E.C. Treaty Reform Gives New Power to Parliament," *Europe*, March 1988, pp. 32–33.

[30] Sandra J. Thompson, "The Making of an Internal Market Directive: The European Community's Legislative Process," *Business America*, August 1, 1988, pp. 12–14.

[31] Heinz Peter Dietrich, "Court Overrules Purity Law for Beer in Germany," *Europe*, April 1987, p. 20.

THE AMERICAS

The United States of America and the Economic Commission for Latin America have played major roles in the development of various market groups in the Americas (see Exhibit 8–3). Progress has been slow because of the low level of development and the political instability that have characterized Latin American nations.[32] Nevertheless, interest in economic cooperation has increased between the United States and Canada and in Latin America.

United States–Canada Free-Trade Area

The world's largest bilateral trade is between the United States and Canada. Bilateral trade in goods exceeded $166 billion in 1987. U.S. exports to Canada exceeded its exports to the entire EC ($62 billion in 1988) and more than double those to Japan. Canada accounts for 20 percent of all U.S. imports and the United States accounts for almost 70 percent of Canadian imports.[33] Despite this unique commercial relationship, tariff and other trade barriers have hindered even greater commercial activity. With the final ratification by Canada of the free-trade agreement, the world's largest free-trade area stretching from the Rio Grande to the Arctic Circle was brought into existence.

This free-trade agreement creates a single, continental commercial market for all goods and most services. The agreement between the United States and Canada is not a customs union such as the European Community; no economic or political union of any kind is involved. It provides for the eventual elimination of tariffs and other trade barriers.[34]

This comprehensive agreement removes barriers to trade and investment for most industrial, agricultural, and service sectors.[35] The tariffs are being removed in stages. Effective January 1, 1989, products were assigned into three categories for tariff removal: (1) immediate elimination; (2) five equal cuts of 20 percent a year; and, (3) ten equal cuts of 10 percent a year.

---

[32] Nigel M. Healey, "Danger in a Dormant Crisis: The Debtors Are in a Worse Situation than Ever," *World Press Review*, January 1989, p. 30.

[33] Ann H. Hughes, "United States and Canada Form World's Largest Free-Trade Area," *Business America*, January 3, 1989, pp. 2–5.

[34] William H. Cavitt, "Your Market Is About to Grow by 10 Percent; Are You Ready?" *Business America*, November 7, 1988, pp. 12–13.

[35] Negotiations for the U.S.-Canada Free-Trade Area were begun in 1986, and an agreement in principle was reached in 1987; it was ratified by the U.S. Congress in 1988, and by the Canadian Parliament in 1989.

Other trade barriers such as quotas, embargoes, border crossings for business personnel, protection of intellectual property, and restrictions on financial services are being phased out as rapidly as possible.[36]

Special attention has been given to ensure that the benefits of the agreement accrue to the United States and Canada only. Preferred tariff treatment under the agreement for products incorporating third-country materials will be based on specific changes in tariff classification. For the most part, third-country products or component parts imported into one country cannot be reexported to the other tariff free. Generally, imported articles are required to incur at least 50 percent of their manufacturing costs in the United States and/or Canada to enjoy tariff-free classification.[37]

The United States–Canada Free-Trade Agreement and Europe 1992 have raised fears among other trading nations that regional economic groupings will lead to protectionism. One European economist expressed the opinion that a Fortress America has been created and that the world is moving into a system of trading blocs.[38] The Japanese in particular fear being closed out of the world's two largest markets,[39] the EC and U.S.–Canada, as a result of regional trade agreements even though the creation of such regional trade agreements is permitted under GATT regulations.[40] There are suggestions that the United States and Japan should enter into a free-trade pact[41] to lessen trade differences between the two nations and provide for a stronger trade position vis-à-vis Europe 1992.[42] Whatever the outcome, global trading patterns will be altered in the years ahead because of the economic impact of the integration of the EC into a free internal market and the United States–Canada Free-Trade Agreement.[43] International marketers must assess the implications of these two events on business strategies.[44] Some of the strategic implications are discussed in a later section.

---

[36] Robin Gaines, "FTA Provides Vehicle for Driving into the Future," *Business America,* January 30, 1989, p. 5.

[37] For a brief review of other provisions of this comprehensive agreement, see "U.S.-Canada Free Trade Agreement," *Business America,* October 26, 1987, pp. 2–8.

[38] "A Giant Step Closer to North America Inc.," *Business Week,* December 5, 1988, p. 44–45.

[39] Sir John Whitehead, "Mutual Responsibilities: Growing Roles in the World Economy for Japan and the EC," *Speaking of Japan* 9, no. 97 (January 1989), pp. 19–23.

[40] A. E. Cjullison, "Japan to Protest Regional Groupings," *Journal of Commerce,* May 31, 1988, p. 1.

[41] Ernest H. Pregg, "Next, A Free-Trade Pact with Japan," *The Wall Street Journal,* August 12, 1988, p. 14.

[42] Greenhouse, "The Growing Fear of Fortress Europe," p. 3–1.

[43] Hideo Sato, "Protecting Open Markets," *Look Japan,* February 1988, p. 3.

[44] Kate Bertrand, "Scrambling for 1992," *Business Marketing,* February 1989, pp. 49–59.

Latin American Economic Cooperation

Several of the Latin American market groups shown in Exhibit 8–3 have had varying degrees of success. The first and most ambitious of the Latin American associations, the Latin American Free Trade Association (LAFTA), was not as successful as anticipated and was replaced in 1980 by LAIA. LAIA, the Caribbean Community and Common Market (CARICOM) and the Andean Common Market (ANCOM) have had measured success while the Central American Common Market has suffered because of hostilities among member countries. Honduras, for example, withdrew from CARICOM over disputes with El Salvador. On the whole, a general lack of cooperation has continued to plague this association.

The Andean Common Market. The Andean Pact, as it is generally referred to, continues to survive conflicts similar to CARICOM's. Although considerable progress has been made in ANCOM's internal economic aid and sectorial programs, excessive restrictions on foreign investments have caused dissension. Chile withdrew in 1976 and Peru threatened to leave the Andean Pact if changes were not made in the controversial Decision 24 rule. This rule stipulated that foreign companies were limited to the repatriation of only 20 percent of direct investment capital and could not participate in the expanded Andean market unless they agreed to convert to "mixed" or "national" status by taking on government partners. Although foreign companies had 15 years to comply with mixed or national status, 15 percent local capital was required from the onset and the 15-year countdown for transformation began at the date the company originally entered the country. Thus, for many companies, mixed or national status had to occur immediately. Most MNCs refused to meet the requirements and limited their activity to local country markets.

In 1987 Andean Pact nations agreed on important changes to the founding Treaty of Cartegena. When implemented, the changes will ensure greater flexibility in the rules affecting traders and investors in the Andean region. Decision 24 was modified by Decision 220. Decision 220 allows each nation broader latitude to regulate foreign investment in accordance with its own laws. Transformation from foreign to mixed or national ownership is still required if a company wants to profit from intra-Andean tariff and trade benefits but the phase-in period has been expanded to 30 years. The countdown for transformation begins when new or existing contracts are signed to reflect the changes in Decision 220. In addition, Decision 220 permits earnings remittances to be determined by each country.[45]

Other changes along with changes in foreign investment requirements,

---

[45] "How Colombia Plans to Ease Foreign Investment Rules Following Changes in ANCOM," *Business Latin America*, July 13, 1987, pp. 217–23.

EXHIBIT 8–3   Latin American Market Groups

Association	Member	Population (millions)	GDP (U.S. $ billions)	GDP per Capita (U.S. $)	Imports (U.S. $ millions)
Andrean Common Market (ANCOM)	Bolivia	6.4	$ 6.3	$ 984	$ 417
	Colombia	28.6	34.2	1,191	4,131
	Ecuador	9.4	16.0	1,704	1,716
	Peru	19.7	14.4	731	1,881
	Venezuela	17.3	49.6	2,864	7,418
	Panama (Associate)	2.2	4.9	2,238	1,383
Central Common Market (CACM)	Guatemala	8.0	11.1	1,398	1,154
	El Salvador	4.8	5.7	1,032	892
	Costa Rica	2.6	3.8	1,467	993
	Nicaragua	3.3	4.4	1,331	775
	Honduras	4.4	3.5	796	8,132
Caribbean Community and Common Market (CARICOM)	Antigua and Barbuda	0.08	0.2	2,188	132
	Barbados	0.30	1.2	4,862	607
	Belize	0.20	0.2	1,196	128
	Dominica	0.07	0.1	1,211	55
	Grenada	0.10	0.1	857	56
	Guyana	0.80	0.5	485	436
	Jamaica	2.40	2.0	867	1,144
	Montserrat	0.01	0.04	3,083	—
	St. Kitts-Nevis Anguilla	0.04	0.1	1,226	44
	St. Lucia	0.10	0.1	1,277	129
	St. Vincent	0.10	0.1	981	57
	Trinidad-Tobago	1.20	7.6	6,378	1,526
Latin American Integration Association (LAIA)	Argentina	30.6	65.9	2,157	3,814
	Bolivia	6.4	6.3	984	417
	Brazil	135.6	226.8	1,673	15,209
	Chile	12.1	16.0	1,329	2,964
	Colombia	28.6	177.5	1,191	4,131
	Ecuador	9.4	16.0	1,704	1,716
	Mexico	78.5	177.5	2,247	11,254
	Paraguay	3.7	5.8	1,577	586
	Peru	19.7	14.4	731	1,881
	Uruguay	3.0	5.1	1,678	708
	Venezuela	17.3	49.0	2,864	7,418

SOURCE: *National Account Statistics: Analysis of Main Aggregates*, 1985 (New York: United Nations, 1988); *Demographic Yearbook, 1985* (New York: United Nations, 1987) and *1986 International Trade Statistics Yearbook*, vol. 1 (New York: United Nations, 1988).

are designed to relaunch programs for economic integration of the six member nations. The immediate elimination of intra-Andean tariffs and a common external tariff are important changes that will encourage more trade within pact countries and away from third countries.[46]

Latin America Integration Association.   Similar economic disagreements among member nations led to the dismantling of LAFTA and the creation of the new Latin America Integration Association (LAIA). The original 11 members of LAFTA signed an accord to create the new organization in 1980. The long-term goal of LAIA (like LAFTA) is the establishment, in a gradual and progressive manner, of a Latin American Common Market. In the initial stages, this consists of an area of economic preferences and not a free-trade area.

One of the more important aspects of the new treaty is the differential treatment of member countries according to their level of economic development. To avoid the big country bias for which LAFTA was criticized, there are three recognized levels under the LAIA framework: the more-developed countries (MDCs) including Argentina, Brazil, and Mexico; the less-developed countries (LDCs)—Chile, Colombia, Venezuela, Peru, Paraguay; and the least-developed countries (LLDCs)—Bolivia, Ecuador, and Uruguay. The differential benefits are designated for the LLDCs and the LDCs by application of the "principle of nonreciprocal treatment" when they signed their bilateral trade arrangements with the MDCs. The LLDCs are to receive most-favored nation treatment, thereby receiving the same rights other LAIA countries have obtained through their bilateral treaties. These changes in the new organization were designed to permit the less economically developed members of the group to participate more fully.

Most observers believe the changes in LAIA have led to improved economic relations among its members. Negotiations among member countries have lowered duties on selected products and eased trade tensions over such trade barriers as quotas, local content requirements, and import licenses.[47]

Flexibility in regional trading made possible under LAIA agreements has resulted in companies operating in LAIA countries in ways few imagined possible when LAIA was first created. New ways to source imports, often more cheaply than under LAFTA, and the opening of new export markets are seen as two of the most important benefits MNCs derive from the creation of LAIA.[48]

---

[46] Herbert A. Lindow, "The Andean Pact Relaunched: Implications for the United States," *Business America*, October 12, 1987, pp. 112–13.

[47] "LAIA Starts New Round of Tariff Cuts," *Business Latin America*, October 24, 1988, p. 335.

[48] "LAIA Bilateral Deals Can Open New Markets with One-Shot Concessions, *Business Latin America*, June 12, 1985, pp. 187, 191.

Caribbean Community Market.   The Caribbean Free Trade Association tasted the fruits of success and opted for even stronger management, forming the Caribbean Community Market (CARICOM) which initially included the more-developed countries and was expected to incorporate less-developed members also. Despite high expectations for success when CARICOM was developed in 1973, it has not lived up to expectations. It still survives, but the extent of its overall achievements and its current standing among the Caribbean nations is disappointing. The organization is weakened by the continued economic problems confronting its Caribbean members. Most of the Caribbean members have had a short history free of commonwealth status which makes them reluctant to give up any of their recently acquired political freedom to a regional organization.

The major contribution of the Latin American market groups to international market theory is the concept of sectorial development. In this arrangement, different sectors of business, such as metalworking, are studied by the sectorial commissions which assigns various segments of the industry to different countries for development. They then hold common-market monopolies on the goods they are producing. The result is a series of agreements which provide for marketing and sharing on a complementary basis among LAIA members.

Africa

Africa's multinational market development activities can be characterized by a great deal of activity but little progress. Including bilateral agreements, an estimated 200 economic arrangements exist between African countries (see Exhibit 8–4). Despite the large numbers and assortment of paper organizations, there has been little progress in actual economic integration. This is understandable in light of the political instability that has characterized Africa in the last decades and the unstable economic base on which Africa has had to build. The United Nations Economic Commission for Africa (ECA) has held numerous conferences but has been hampered by governmental inexperience, undeveloped resources, labor problems, and chronic product shortages. It has managed to sponsor an African Development Bank, which began making loans against a $250 million capital in 1967. ECA is also working to induce African members to develop modern customs services and to adopt the Brussels tariff nomenclature, a standard in the Western world.

Political sovereignty is a new enough phenomenon to most African nations that they are reluctant to relinquish any part of it without specific and tangible benefits in return. However, André Simmons cited the major problem in his study of economic integration of Africa. When the population and income factors are combined in a country of 2 million inhabitants with an annual income of about $100 per capita, it has an aggregate purchas-

EXHIBIT 8–4   African Market Groups

Association	Member	Population (millions)	GDP (U.S. $ billions)	GDP per Capita (U.S. $)	Imports (U.S. $ millions)
	Benin	3.9	$ 1.1	$ 269	$ 476
	Burkina Faso	6.6	1.1	171	291
	Cameroon	10.1	10.2	1,030	1,107
	Central African Republic	2.6	0.6	249	123
	Chad	5.0	0.6	128	172
	People's Republic of the Congo	1.7	2.1	1,189	744
Afro-Malagasy	Côte d'Ivoire	9.5	6.6	705	1,314
Economic	Gabon	1.2	3.8	3,280	686
Union	Mali	8.2	0.6	71	402
	Mauritania	1.9	0.6	334	246
	Niger	6.1	1.8	293	466
	Senegal	6.4	2.6	410	1,010
	Togo	3.0	0.7	242	271
	Ethiopia	43.4	5.3	122	989
	Kenya	20.3	5.8	280	1,456
East Africa	Sudan	21.6	5.7	263	1,355
Customs	Tanzania	21.7	6.4	285	867
Union	Uganda	15.5	0.5	31	371
	Zambia	6.7	2.6	390	1,000
	Algeria	21.7	55.7	2,564	9,813
Maghreb	Libya	3.6	28.9	8,018	7,176
Economic	Tunisia	7.1	8.2	1,160	2,597
Community	Morocco	21.9	11.9	542	3,850
	Egypt	48.5	64.1	1,365	9,961
Casablanca	Ghana	13.6	1.1	508	1,016
Group	Guinea	6.1	0.1	391	52
	Morocco	21.9	0.1	542	3,850
	Benin	3.9	1.1	269	476
	Burkina-Faso	6.6	1.1	71	291
	Cape Verde	0.3	0.1	325	72
	Côte d'Ivoire	9.5	6.6	705	1,314
	Gambia	0.6	0.2	309	—
Economic	Ghana	13.5	6.9	508	1,016
Community of	Guinea	6.1	2.4	391	52
West African	Guinea-Bissau	0.9	0.1	62	—
States	Liberia	2.2	0.8	370	363
(ECOWAS)	Mali	8.2	0.5	71	402
	Mauritania	1.9	0.6	334	246
	Niger	6.1	1.8	293	466
	Nigeria	95.2	59.5	625	5,808

EXHIBIT 8–4 (concluded)

Association	Member	Population (millions)	GDP (U.S. $ billions)	GDP per Capita (U.S. $)	Imports (U.S. $ millions)
	Senegal	6.4	2.6	410	1,010
	Togo	3.0	0.7	242	271
West Africa	Burkina-Faso	6.6	1.1	71	291
Economic	Côte d' Ivoire	9.5	6.6	705	1,314
Community	Mali	8.2	0.5	71	402
(CEAO)	Mauritania	1.9	0.6	334	246
	Niger	6.1	1.8	293	466
	Senegal	6.4	2.6	410	1,010
Customs and	Cameroon	10.1	10.2	1,030	1,107
Economic	Central African				
Union of	Republic	2.6	0.6	241	123
Central Africa	People's Republic	1.7	2.1	1,189	744
(CEUCA)	of the Congo				
	Gabon	1.2	3.8	3,280	686

SOURCE: *National Account Statistics: Analysis of Main Aggregates, 1985* (New York: United Nations, 1988); *Demographic Yearbook, 1985.* (New York: United Nations, 1987); and *1986 International Trade Statistics Yearbook,* vol. 1 (New York: United Nations, 1988).

ing power similar to that of a U.S. community of 50,000 people. He suggests that no one would consider an economic unit of that size economically viable. Somehow, sovereignty, history, and tribal pride maintain such nations.

Two approaches are being employed to integrate Africa. First are attempts to bring together a few (three or four) nations into close economic relationships emphasizing economic growth in the industrial sector. The second approach involves more grandiose schemes grouping a large number of nations (perhaps 12 to 15) and is designed to bring about cooperation in nearly all areas of economic activity, including transportation, education, labor, natural resources, agriculture, and industrial development.

The Economic Community of West African States, ECOWAS, is the most recent and ambitious of the African regional cooperative groups. ECOWAS has an aggregate gross national product (GNP) of more than $28 million, and the 14-nation group hopes to achieve full economic integration soon. Experts suggest that the economic domination by Nigeria (64 percent of all the market's exports) may create internal strains that cannot be repaired. Yet, of all the attempts at economic integration among African states, ECOWAS seems to have the best chance of succeeding. A number of African organizations, including the East African Community, have attempted to organize regional cooperative trading programs. The East

African Community, established in 1967, was considered by many to have some reasonable chance of succeeding; however, a dispute between Kenya and Tanzania, two major member states, led to closing of their borders to one another and the eventual demise of the organization in 1977. Of the many economic groups organized, ECOWAS has been the only one to survive to date. It is safe to say that among all the world's regional integration schemes, African attempts have been the least successful.

Middle East

Less developed than Europe to begin with, the Middle East has been slower in the formation of successfully functioning multinational market groups. Some progress is now being made toward the development of freer trade. (See Exhibit 8–5). Countries belonging to the Arab Common Market set a goal of free internal trade by 1974 but did not make it; they are planning to equalize external tariffs at some later date. A new variety of economic cooperation has been pioneered through Regional Cooperation for Development, formed by Pakistan, Iran, and Turkey, which had made impressive strides in encouraging basic industrial production in those countries until the revolution in Iran ended any economic activity. So far, the

EXHIBIT 8–5   Middle and Far East Market Groups

Association	Member	Population (millions)	GDP (U.S. $ billions)	GDP per Capita (U.S. $)	Imports (U.S. $ millions)
Arab Common Market	Iraq	15.9	$ 46.8	$ 2,942	$11,043
	Kuwait	1.7	19.8	10,902	6,901
	Jordan	3.5	4.1	1,157	2,593
	Syria	10.3	20.3	1,929	3,967
	Egypt	48.5	64.1	1,365	9,961
Regional Cooperative for Development	Pakistan	96.2	33.1	330	5,890
	Iran	44.2	168.1	3,766	13,422
	Turkey	49.3	52.7	1,069	11,340
Association of South East Asian Nations (ASEAN)	Brunei	0.2	3.0	12,847	621
	Indonesia	163.4	85.1	511	10,259
	Malaysia	15.6	31.2	2,008	13,953
	Singapore	2.6	17.5	6,843	25,461
	Philippines	54.4	32.8	602	5,445
	Thailand	51.3	38.3	746	9,243

SOURCE: *National Account Statistics: Analysis of Main Aggregates, 1985* (New York: United Nations, 1988); *Demographic Yearbook, 1985* (New York: United Nations, 1987); and *1986 International Trade Statistics Yearbook*, vol. 1 (New York: United Nations, 1988).

RCD has not succeeded in lowering or eliminating tariffs or in building a common external tariff wall. Continued political turmoil has slowed economic cooperation among Middle East countries.

Asia

About one third of the world's population (even excluding China) lives in Asia and the Far East, but this massive population produces less than 2 percent of the world's industrial output. The United Nations Economic Commission for Asia and the Far East (ECAFE) has worked diligently to strengthen the Asian market through development of multinational market groups. It also formed the Asian Industrial Development Council, dedicated to the development of trade and commercial arrangements and multicountry joint ventures to speed the industrialization of Asia. It has created the Asian Development Bank, which has been in full operation since 1966 and has an authorized capital of $1 billion (a third of which is subscribed to by European and North American countries). Despite the low volume of trade in the area, Asia has a heritage of international trading, and one third of its international trade has been on an interregional basis. This, coupled with the fact that many Asian nations are members of the British Commonwealth and already have established working relationships, makes the future of multinational economic organizations promising.

The Association of Southeast Asian Nations (ASEAN) is the primary multinational group in Asia. The goals of the group are economic integration and cooperation through a complementary industry program, preferential trading including reduced tariff and nontariff barriers, guaranteed member access to markets throughout the community, and harmonized investment incentives.[49] ASEAN countries offer opportunities for U.S. investment and they serve as a growing market. Like all multinational market groups, ASEAN has experienced many problems and false starts in attempting to unify their combined economies.[50]

One problem is the small amount of interarea trade because of similar exports and similar national assets. All ASEAN nations except Singapore have an abundance of labor and an underdeveloped economic infrastructure.[51] Nevertheless, a long list of products is covered by preferential trading agreements and the group has weathered some extreme economic disagreements and disappointments when proposed sectorial investment projects did not materialize.

[49] Edwin A. Finn, Jr., "Taking the Tigers Off the Dole," *Forbes*, January 23, 1989, p. 70.

[50] George Paine, Linda Droker, and Joan Sitnik, "ASEAN Economic Dialogue Returns to Washington," *Business America*, February 1, 1988, pp. 2–6.

[51] Aurelio Periquet, "Asian Integration—Realizing ASEAN's Full Potential," *Speaking of Japan*, April 1989, pages 19–24.

FUTURE MULTINATIONAL MARKET GROUPS?

With the advent of Europe 1992, the United States–Canada Free-Trade Agreement, and the general concern that these two formidable market groups may be the forerunners of regional trading blocs, there is speculation about other future alliances.[52] Most may never materialize because of economic, cultural, and political diversities; however, as we have seen in the European Community, if the economic needs are strong enough, centuries of mutual animosity and cultural uniqueness can be subverted for economic growth and prosperity.

The United States, Japan, Hong Kong, Taiwan and China are frequently discussed as a likely multinational market group, as are Canada, the United States, and Mexico. Reasons for cooperative trade agreements among these speculative alliances vary substantially. A Japan–United States trade link reflects three lines of reasoning: First is defensive and results from the preoccupation with an internal unified EC market and the fear that reciprocity means a closed market to the United States and Japan. The second line of reasoning sees a United States–Japan free-trade agreement as a less political way to handle the growing number of trade disputes between the two countries. Greater harmony between the two industrial countries is more apt to be realized within the confines of a free-trade agreement.

The third point is a more complex extension of the second in that the more complex issues of trade have yet to be resolved but will become increasingly troublesome. Successful resolution of problems of the protection of intellectual property, government procurements, and regulatory issues within Japan requires a broader economic relationship than now exists.[53] Antidumping and the growing resistance in the United States to Japanese direct investment further complicate the reality of a free-trade agreement.

The likelihood of a Japan–United States free-trade agreement materializing is at best years, if not decades, away.[54] No formal talks have taken place although informal studies addressing the feasibility of such a pact are underway. Further, a Japan–United States free-trade agreement raises the question of United States and Japanese trade relationships with the other nations in the Pacific Rim. From the U.S. perspective, the stabilization of trade in Asia, as the smaller, newly industrialized countries become more economically forceful, is welcome. Former Treasury Secretary James Baker proposed that a Pacific Rim economic policy coordination group include the United States, Japan, and the four newly industrializing coun-

---

[52] Claudia Bosett, "A Political Lovefest in Asia," *The Asian Wall Street Journal,* January 9, 1989, p. 10.

[53] Preeg, "Next, a Free-Trade Pact with Japan?" p. 14.

[54] Karen Elliot House, "Though Rich, Japan Is Poor in Many Elements of Global Leadership," *The Wall Street Journal,* January 30, 1989, p. 1.

tries, South Korea, Taiwan, Hong Kong, and Singapore. Although only in the discussion stage when Baker became Secretary of State, such a proposal has support from the Japanese.[55]

Another more speculative trade group centers around the political and economic unification of China, Taiwan, and Hong Kong. Although politically at odds, the economies of these three countries are becoming more integrated with substantial trade through Hong Kong. As trade between Taiwan and China increases and they become more economically interdependent, and when Hong Kong reverts to China in 1997, the prospects of a China–Hong Kong–Taiwan economic alliance may not be out of the question despite political differences between China and Taiwan. Each one's strengths—China's labor, Taiwan's manufacturing experience and skills, and Hong Kong's financial clout—can combine to create a formidable market and industrial competitor.[56] Because China and Taiwan have no formal diplomatic ties, trade between the two is informal and indirect, in and out of China through Hong Kong. Indirect annual trade between the two is more than $2 billion and indirect investment in China by Taiwanese is approximately $100 million.

Perhaps the most far-reaching suggestion for a North American free-trade agreement is an alliance among Canada, the United States, and Mexico. This relationship has been discussed at various times by U.S. spokespersons but almost always dismissed by the Mexicans and Canadians.[57] However, two events may make such an agreement feasible. The United States–Canada Free-Trade Agreement concerns Mexico in that United States–Mexican trade could be affected. Mexico's economic situation may force the government to reluctantly pursue such an alliance as the only way to resolve growing economic problems and social tensions that will worsen unless there is economic improvement.[58]

Despite the disparity between Mexico's economy and the two other countries', there are sound reasons why such an alliance makes economic sense. Canada is a sophisticated industrial economy, resource rich, but with a small population and domestic market. Mexico, on the other hand, desperately needs investment, technology, exports, and other economic reinforcement to spur its economy. Even though Mexico has an abundance of oil and a rapidly growing population, the number of new workers is increasing faster than its economy can create new jobs. The United States needs resources (especially oil), a source of new laborers to augment the

---

[55] "U.S. Japan Trade Pact May Make Sense," *The Wall Street Journal,* September 12, 1988, p. 1.

[56] "Asia's New Fire-Breather," *Business Week,* October 10, 1988, pp. 54–56.

[57] Larry Rohter, "Mexico Leery of North American Common Market," *New York Times,* November 25, 1988, p. 10c.

[58] Richard Lawrence, "Mexico Weighs Trade Pacts with the U.S.," *Journal of Commerce,* October 31, 1988, p. 4a.

decreasing size of the U.S. labor pool, and, of course, markets. The three need each other to compete more effectively in world markets, and they need mutual assurances that their already dominate trading positions in each other's markets are safe from protectionist pressures. A North American free-trade agreement would create a market with a population of 355 million, 10 percent more than the EC, and include the fastest-growing country in North America—Mexico.[59]

Both Canada and Mexico have serious concerns about the loss of sovereignty and potential for cultural domination by the United States in a North American free-trade association. Mexico is suspicious that the United States has designs on Mexico's resources and productive capacity and that neither Canada nor the United States is prepared to accept millions of Mexican migrants crossing their borders to work in factories and farms.

Despite the reservations held by all three countries, their cultural and economic diversity, and the resistance among political groups in all three, the time may be right for the three countries to join a North American free-trade association to compete in a global economy dominated by regional trading blocs.[60]

STRATEGIC IMPLICATIONS FOR MARKETING

The complexion of the entire world marketplace has been changed significantly by the coalition of nations into multinational market groups. To international business firms, multinational groups spell opportunity in bold letters through access to greatly enlarged markets with reduced or abolished country-by-country tariff barriers and restrictions. Production, financing, labor, and marketing decisions are affected by the remapping of the world into market groups.

As the goals of Europe 1992 and the United States–Canada Free-Trade Agreement are reached, new marketing opportunities are created; so are new problems. World competition will intensify as businesses become stronger and more experienced in dealing with large market groups. European and non-European multinationals are preparing to deal with the changes in competition in a fully integrated Europe.[61] In an integrated Europe, U.S. multinationals may have an initial advantage over expanded European firms because U.S. businesses are more experienced in marketing to large, diverse markets and are accustomed to looking at Europe as

---

[59] "North America into the Year 2000," *Business International,* October 3, 1988, pp. 301–4.

[60] "Will North America Follow Europe's Lead?" *The Wall Street Journal,* September 26, 1988, p. 1.

[61] William C. Verity, "U.S. Business Needs to Prepare Now for Europe's Single Internal Market," *Business America,* August 1, 1988, pp. 2–5.

one market.[62] That advantage, however, is only temporary as mergers, acquisitions, and joint ventures consolidate operations of European firms in anticipation of the benefits of Europe 1992. International managers will still be confronted by individual national markets with the same problems of language, customs, and instability even though they are packaged under the umbrella of a common market. However, as barriers come down and multicountry markets truly are treated as one common market, a global market will be one notch closer to reality.

Multinational trade alliances also cause businesses to be closed out of many markets. If a company is unwilling to produce within a market area, if may lose access to the entire market or face restrictions in the quantity it can sell. Japan currently has problems exporting autos and TVs to the European Community. Italy, Spain, and France have been effective in restricting Japanese auto sales in their countries and are looking for ways to continue to restrict Japanese imports when barriers across borders are eliminated.[63]

Regulation of business activities has been intensified throughout multinational market groups; each group now has management and administrative bodies specifically concerned with business. In the process of structuring markets, rules and regulations common to the group are often more sophisticated than those of the individual countries. Many non-EC countries see such activities as creating a Fortress Europe, and in effect, making marketing entry into Europe 1992 more difficult than entering the 12 member countries individually. Despite the problems and complexities of dealing with the new markets, the overriding message to the international marketer continues to be opportunity and profit potential for the astute.

Opportunities

Economic integration creates large mass markets for the marketer. Many national markets, too small to bother with individually, take on new dimensions and significance when combined with markets from cooperating countries. Large markets are particularly important to businesses accustomed to mass production and mass distribution because of the economies of scale and marketing efficiencies that can be achieved. In highly competitive markets, the benefits derived from enhanced efficiencies are often passed along as lower prices which lead to increased purchasing power.

---

[62] "Will the New Europe Cut U.S. Giants Down to Size?" *Business Week*, December 12, 1988, p. 55.

[63] "E.C.'s Proposed Car Policy Aims to Keep Japan Companies at Bay," *The Asian Wall Street Journal Weekly*, October 31, 1988, p. 10.

BOX 8–3
Wouldn't It Be Easier if You Spoke Only One Language?

Language is a major problem of economic unity since EC regulations require that when any one of the official languages is used at a meeting, interpretation into the others must be available on demand. The official languages include English, Danish, Dutch, French, German, Italian, Greek, Spanish, and Portuguese. This variety of languages causes major problems with the interpreting services. Interpreters for English, French, and German are relatively easy to find. But Danish, Dutch, and Italian interpreters come at a premium and finding a Greek interpreter is nearly impossible. It is further complicated because the Greek interpreter must be able to translate any of the other nine languages into Greek. Not only is the Greek language difficult, but it is spoken fluently in combination with other languages by very few people, even Greeks. The interpreting service director said, "We began recruiting Greek interpreters three years before Greece joined the Economic Community and so far we haven't been very successful." She was able to find nine interpreters to translate into Greek and six others to translate out of Greek. But finding anyone who could turn Greek into Danish seems virtually impossible.

Suppose you can't find an interpreter who can translate Danish into Greek. What do you do? One solution is to double-relay your interpretation. For example, one interpreter would translate Danish into German; this would be picked up by another one who could translate German into French; a third would then turn the French into Greek. Most interpreters dislike the relay system; major problems can develop if one interpreter errs. The second interpreter then simply spreads the mistake. With the addition of more languages, double-relays as standard practice would make discussions at certain meetings totally incomprehensible.

Even further in the future lies the possibility that Turkey will join the EC. The interpreters simply shake their heads at the thought of having to find Turkish interpreters. "Impossible," one official mutters under his breath.

Source: Adapted from David Brand, "In Brussels Today, a Great Dane Is One Who Knows Greek," *The Wall Street Journal*, January 12, 1981, p. 1.

Most multinational groups have coordinated programs to foster economic growth as part of their cooperative effort. Such programs work to the advantage of marketers by increasing purchasing power, improving regional infrastructure, and fostering economic development. Expected changes resulting from the U.S.–Canada Free-Trade Agreement and a single Europe serve as good examples of the benefits arising from multinational market groups.

Despite the problems that are sure to occur because of integration, the economic benefits from free trade within the EC and the United States and Canada can be enormous.

BOX 8–4
What Europe 1992 Will Mean to One Company

Philips is a prime example of how reforms in customs procedures and product standards will help the bottom line for MNCs in Europe. Like many multinationals, it has long operated without much regard to national borders. Giant assembly plants take in components from Philips factories across Europe and dispatch finished products to distribution centers by way of a vast trucking network. A television factory in Belgium gets tubes from Germany, transistors from France, and plastics from Italy while electronic components are made in another factory in Belgium.

In theory, Philip's system of centralized manufacturing should be a model of efficiency; in practice, frontiers have made it cumbersome and expensive. On average, trucks spend 30 percent of their travel time idling in lines at customs posts. Factories can never be sure that supplies will arrive on time. To avoid shutting down an assembly line when shipments are late, factories keep extra stock on hand. Philip's inventories are now worth some $7 billion, or 23 percent of annual sales, compared to around 14 percent for producers in the United States and Japan who can count on punctual deliveries.

By the end of 1989, Philip's trucks were allowed to roll past customs posts without stopping. The company simply sent customs information to authorities in each member state via computer. Philips saved about $100 million in 1988 by cutting inventories, closing warehouses, and reducing clerical staff. By 1992, the savings are expected to exceed $300 million a year.

As local standards vanish under Europe 1992, Philip's plan to shrink its vast number of different variations of washing machines, hairdryers, fluorescent light bulbs, and above all, TV sets—a crucial $3 billion a year business. Europe now has two standards for television reception. To make matters worse, Germany, Italy, and Denmark imposed different norms for radio interference ostensibly to ensure against TV's audio signal blocking shortwave radio reception in passing police cars.

To meet such standards, Philip's plant in Belgium turns out seven types of TV sets equipped with different tuners, semiconductors, and even plugs. A staff of 70 engineers does nothing but adjust new models to local requirements. Assembly lines are revamped weekly to produce TVs for different countries. All told, the extra costs of meeting national standards comes to $20 million a year, including $8 million for the assortment of components and $2 million for the array of plugs. Philips is now preparing to streamline production thanks in part to a recent European Community directive harmonizing regulations for radio interference.

Source: Adapted from Shawn Tully, "Europe Gets Ready for 1992," *Fortune*, February 1, 1988, p. 83. © 1988 Time Inc. All rights reserved.

In Canada and the United States, the largest savings result from the lowering of prices for goods and services. Once all Canadian tariffs are eliminated, the cost of U.S. exports to Canadian business and consumers will have been reduced over $2.3 billion per year. Conversely, U.S. business and consumers will save over $650 million per year on imports from Canada. Initially, Canada will benefit more than the United States; studies estimate that Canada's GNP will be higher by 2 to 5 percent because of the agreement. The effect on the U.S. GNP will be smaller but increased U.S. and Canadian sales to each other are projected at more than $25 billion over five years.[64]

Savings within the EC will be even more spectacular because each of the 12 countries has had its own set of barriers; thus, companies that attempted to sell in all 12 countries were confronted with a fragmented picture of a dozen separate markets. One study showed that the EC loses at least $250 billion a year as a result of market barriers that impede productivity and competitiveness. Quotas, border restrictions, and excessive documentation alone are estimated to cost nearly 7 percent of the value of goods traded annually; in essence, a tax comparable to the average tariff existing on all trade among industrialized countries.

Another major savings will result from the billions of dollars wasted in developing different versions of products to meet a hodgepodge of national standards. Philips and other European companies invested a total of $20 billion to develop a common switching system for Europe's 10 different telephone networks. This compares with $3 billion spent in the United States for a common system and $1.5 billion in Japan for a single system.[65]

Advertising is another area where the costs are much higher today than they will be when Europe 1992 eliminates variations in rules and regulations. Kellogg Company in Europe must prepare several versions of their television commercial for Kellogg's Corn Flakes to comply with different national broadcast regulations governing advertising. Uniform standards for television commercials will make it possible for Kellogg to use the same spot, with voice-overs, across Europe.[66]

Studies show that EC's gross domestic product (GDP) will increase by 5 percent, 5 million new jobs will be created, and as much as a 6 percent drop in consumer prices will result from the cost savings and competition brought about by the reforms in Europe 1992. With a market size and

---

[64] William H. Cavitt, "Your Market Is About to Grow," pp. 12–14.

[65] Cees Bruynes, "Europe in 1992 and beyond: Philips Looks to the Future," *Europe,* October 1988, pp. 18–20.

[66] "1992: Europe Becomes One," *Advertising Age,* July 11, 1988, p. 46.

export trade comparable to the United States–Canada market, as the EC's GDP approaches that of the United States and Canada, the European Community could replace the United States as the world's largest market.[67]

Market Barriers

The initial aim of a multinational market is to protect the businesses that operate within its borders. An expressed goal is to give an advantage to the companies within the market in their dealings with other countries of the market group. Analysis of the intraregional and international trade patterns of the market groups indicates that such goals have been achieved. Trade does increase among member nations and decrease with nonmember nations. When Greece joined the EC, imports from other EC countries increased while those from the United States decreased.

Local preferences certainly spell trouble for the exporter located outside the market. Companies willing to invest in production facilities in multinational markets may be benefited by such protection as they become a part of the market. Exporters, however, are in a considerably weaker position. This prospect confronts many U.S. exporters faced with the possible need to invest in Europe to protect their export markets as Europe 1992 approaches.[68] The possibility of increased market barriers to the EC and the expanded U.S.-Canadian market is troubling for MNCs as well.

The prospect of Europe as one unified internal market has many countries concerned about the EC becoming Fortress Europe—free trade within but highly protectionist to all others.[69] In fact, there is considerable concern that reactions to Europe 1992 by other major trading countries will lead to the creation of regional trading blocs in Europe, East Asia, and North America.[70] The United States–Canada Free-Trade Agreement is seen as a possible trading bloc that could also have protectionist barriers. If such regional trading blocs evolve, the fear is that external tariffs among trading blocs will further close out nontrading bloc members.[71]

---

[67] Sandra Vandermerwe and Marc-Andre L'Huiller, "Euro-Consumers in 1992," *Business Horizons*, January–February 1989, pp. 34–40.

[68] "Should Small U.S. Exporters Take the Big Plunge?" *Business Week*, December 12, 1988, pp. 64–68.

[69] Walter S. Mossberg, "As EC Markets Unite, U.S. Exporters Face New Trade Barriers," *The Wall Street Journal*, January 19, 1989, p. 1.

[70] William Armbuster, "Trade Bloc Protectionism Forecast," *Journal of Commerce*, October 7, 1988, p. 3a.

[71] Margaret Tuder, and Diana Federman, "Switzerland Fears Being Left in the Dust as Europe Prepares for 1992 Unification," *The Wall Street Journal*, August 8, 1988, p. 12.

The European Commission strongly denies such possibilities and insists that access by outsiders to their common market will not become more difficult than it is now. Nevertheless, there is concern in many countries, especially Japan. In recent trade talks with European Commission members, the Japanese envoy expressed concern that "the removal of barriers to internal EC trade could be accompanied by moves to keep out imports from non-EC members." These same concerns were also expressed by the United States and the six-member European Free Trade Association.[72] Are rules being drafted under the Single European Act that will deny foreign financial institutions, automakers, and others equal market access to Europe?[73] It is too early to know whether or not such fears will materialize. However, one point is known; the EC will require equal treatment for EC firms in other countries.[74]

Reciprocity is an important part of the trade policy of Europe 1992. If a country does not open its markets to an EC firm, it cannot expect to have access to the EC market.[75] Europeans see reciprocity as a fair and equitable way of allowing foreign companies to participate in the European market without erecting trade barriers while at the same time giving Europeans equal access to foreign markets. There are strong feelings that the Japanese market is not equally accessible to foreign firms and reciprocity addresses such inequities.[76] The community will not grant trade concessions to Japan if Japan fails to reciprocate for European exporters. The desire by some Europeans to force reciprocity on the Japanese was best explained by one who observed, "This time the game will not pit Japan against an individual European country, to be picked off, as was often the case in the past," and now there will be 12 countries with which to deal.[77] Reciprocity is to be directed to all outsiders. A French government-sponsored advertisement on TV captured the European attitude. As the advertisement opens, "a skinny French boxer is squaring off to battle a giant American football player and a menacing Japanese sumo wrestler. Suddenly 11 buddies—the rest of the EC, of course—rush to his side, and the aggressors turn away."[78]

---

[72] "Japan Urges E.C. Not to Close Market after 1992," *Europe,* July–August 1988, pp. 26–27.

[73] "Europe Could Become the New Trade Villain," *The Wall Street Journal,* August 1, 1988, p. 1.

[74] Richard L. Hudson, "Europe Is Girding for an Invasion by Manufacturers from Japan," *The Asian Wall Street Journal,* February 6, 1989, p. 5.

[75] "Laying the Foundation for a Great Wall of Europe," *Business Week,* August 1, 1988, pp. 40–41.

[76] Maryann N. Keller, "Two-Way Street," *World Monitor,* October 1988, pp. 86–87.

[77] William Pfaff, "Look Out, America, Europe Is Coming," *International Herald Tribune,* June 23, 1988, p. 8.

[78] Kirkland, "Outsider's Guide to Europe," p. 122.

BOX 8–5
How to Compete in Japan

Michelin has done well for itself in Japan by doing business as the Japanese do. Its U.S. plants supply 14 percent of Japan's tire imports. Nihon Michelin Tire Company has grown to the point where it accounts for half of all Japan's radial tire imports. And tires produced in the United States provide a hefty share of Michelin's total.

"We will remain committed to doing business in this market like our Japanese friends. We're not here like any other importer. Our goals are not the same. Our competitors are the Japanese." Besides supplying auto companies, Michelin sells tires to Japan's four motorcycle makers, all the leading truck and bus manufacturers, most of the country's construction and farm equipment manufacturing machinery producers, and to the Tokyo monorail. It now holds 8 percent of the entire Japanese auto tire market despite the fact that it never has built a tire plant in Japan.

Experts cite several reasons for Michelin's success. One, it quotes the delivery price right to the automaker's assembly plant and it quotes its price in yen—the same as Japanese competitors! Two, the company has developed a nationwide warehousing capability that enables it to meet the growing demands of the Japanese replacement tire market as well as the just-in-time delivery requirements of the Japanese industry. Three, Michelin's five non-Japanese staff members—including the new president—are proficient in Japanese. Four, its worldwide production base of 54 factories in 12 countries on three continents enables it to supply original equipment customers with identical products from different countries of origin. Five, it has benefited from the Japanese predilection for prestigious status-oriented products.

Source: "Michelin Has Done Well for Itself by Doing Business as Japanese Do," *Journal of Commerce,* April 25, 1988, p. 1c.

Even though the United States–Canada Free-Trade Agreement does not have a reciprocity clause, it contains safeguards to prevent products of third countries from being shipped through one of the free-trade agreement parties to avoid tariffs. The agreement contains rules of origin to prevent such products from profiting from the benefits of free-trade agreement tariff elimination. A crucial decision for MNCs is whether or not to invest within market groups to secure access to other member countries. However, investment within the EC is not a guarantee of access to the entire market unless the home country of the MNC is willing to offer European companies the same privileges.[79]

---

[79] "Writing the New Rules for Europe's Merger Game," *Business Week,* February 6, 1989, pp. 48–49.

Competition

European companies are merging with nonmember companies to get a foothold in the EC. Swiss-based Nestlé has bought Rowntree, a United Kingdom candy maker, and Britone, the Italian food conglomerate, to strengthen their ties to EC market firms.[80] European banking is also going through a stage of mergers. In one 18-month period, 400 banks and finance firms merged, took stock in one another or devised joint marketing ventures to sell stocks, mutual funds, insurance, or other financial instruments. These mergers are viewed as necessary to compete with Japanese, U.S., and Swiss financial institutions.

In short, EC, European, Japanese, and American firms are preparing for a major assault on a unified EC. But, can one European market sustain so much competition? There may be too many competitors and too much capacity for a unified Europe.[81] Does Europe need six mass-marketed auto makers when the United States sustains only three? Does an integrated Europe need 12 airlines? The probability is that before 2000 there will be fewer competitors in Europe than in 1992. The only certainty is that the primary effect of the internal market program will be to increase the competitive pressures companies face.[82]

Marketing Mix Implications

Companies are already adjusting their marketing mix strategies to reflect anticipated market differences in Europe 1992 and to benefit from the cost savings that might be forthcoming. Colgate-Palmolive Company, for example, has adapted its Colgate toothpaste into a single formula for sale across Europe at one price. Currently the brand sells at different prices in various parts of Europe. When this occurs, there is the possibility that lower-priced goods will find their way into higher-priced markets. Bededas Shower Gel, for example, is priced in the middle of the market in West Germany and as a high-priced product in the United Kingdom. Occasionally such parallel imports have arrived at United Kingdom retailers from West Germany. Such incidents will increase under Europe 1992, unless companies standardize their pricing policies for all of Europe.

In addition to initiating uniform pricing policies, companies are reducing

---

[80] "Swiss Go on a European Shopping Spree," *The Wall Street Journal*, August, 31, 1988, p. 18.

[81] A report from several European newspapers on Europe 1992 gives the reader a feeling of different attitudes about the EC. All are under the broad title "One Europe." *World Press Review*, January 1989, pp. 13–19.

[82] "Executive Focus Europe," *Business Europe*, December 7, 1987, p. 8.

the number of brands they produce to focus advertising and promotion efforts. For example, Nestlé's current three brands of yogurt in the EC will be reduced to a single brand.[83]

A major benefit from an integrated Europe is competition at the retail level. Europe lacks an integrated and competitive distribution system which supports small and midsize outlets. The elimination of borders could result in increased competition among retailers and the creation of Europewide distribution channels. Retail giants like France's Carrefour and Germany's Aldi group are planning huge hypermarkets with big advertising budgets. This could spell the slow death of shopkeepers and midsize retailers which today dominate most European countries.[84]

SUMMARY

The experience of the multinational market groups developed since World War II points up both the possible successes and the hazards such groups encounter. The various attempts at economic cooperation represent varying degrees of success and failure, but, almost without regard to their degree of success, the economic market groups have created great excitement among marketers.

Economic benefits possible through cooperation relate to more efficient marketing and production: marketing efficiency is effected through the development of mass markets, encouragement of competition, the improvement of personal income, and various psychological market factors. Production efficiency derives from specialization, mass production for mass markets, and the free movement of the factors of production. Economic integration also tends to foster political harmony among the countries involved; such harmony leads to stability, which is beneficial to the marketer.

The marketing implications of multinational market groups may be studied from the standpoint of firms located inside the market or of firms located outside which wish to sell the markets. For each viewpoint the problems and opportunities are somewhat different; but regardless of the location of the marketer, multinational market groups do provide great opportunity for the creative marketer who wishes to expand volume. Market groupings make it economically feasible to enter new markets and to employ new marketing strategies that could not be applied to the smaller markets represented by individual countries.

The success of the European Community and the creation of the United

---

[83] "1992: Europe Becomes One," p. 46.

[84] "Reshaping Europe, 1992 and beyond," *Business Week*, December 12, 1988, pp. 48–51.

States–Canada Free–Trade Area suggest the growing importance of economic cooperation and integration. Such development will continue to challenge the international marketer by providing continually growing market opportunities.

QUESTIONS

1. Define:

   OECD

   United States–Canada Free-
   Trade Agreement ✓

   COMECON ✓

   harmonization

   Decision 220

   Single European Act ✓

   reciprocity

   sectorial program

2. Elaborate on the problems and benefits for international marketers from multinational market groups.

3. Explain the political role of multinational market groups. Identify the factors on which one may judge the potential success or failure of a multinational market group.

4. Explain the marketing implications of the factors contributing to the successful development of a multinational market group.

5. Imagine that the United States was composed of many separate countries with individual trade barrires. What marketing effects might one visualize?

6. Discuss the possible types of arrangements for regional economic integration.

7. Differentiate between a free-trade area and a common market. Explain the marketing implication of the differences.

8. It seems obvious that the founders of the European Community intended it to be a truly common market; so much so that economic integration must obviously be supplemented by political integration to accomplish these objectives. Discuss.

9. The European Commission, the Council of Ministers, and the Court of Justice of the EC have gained power in the last decade. Comment.

10. Select any three countries which might have some logical basis for establishing a multinational market organization (such as Canada, the United States, and Mexico). Identify the various problems that would be encountered in forming multinational market groups of such countries.

11. U.S. exports to the European Community are expected to decline in future years. What marketing actions may a company take to counteract such changes?

12. "Because they are dynamic and because they have great growth possibilities, the multinational markets are likely to be especially rough and tumble for the external business." Discuss.

13. Differentiate between a full customs union and a political union.

14. Which actions must be taken by business to cope with limitations imposed by sectorial programs?

15. Why have African nations had such difficulty in forming effective economic unions?

16. Discuss the implications of Europe 1992 on marketing strategy in Europe.

17. Discuss the United States–Canada Free-Trade Agreement.

18. Discuss the strategic marketing implications of the United States–Canada Free-Trade Agreement.

19. How is the concept of reciprocity linked to protectionism?

20. What are some of the possibilities for other multinational marketing groups forming? Discuss the implications to global marketing if these groups should develop.

CHAPTER

9

Developing Markets and Market Behavior

The world's economies are changing rapidly and most are experiencing some degree of industrialization, urbanization, rising productivity, higher personal incomes, and technological progress although not all at the same level or rate of development. Few nations are content with the economic status quo; instead, they seek economic growth, increased standards of living, and an opportunity for the good life. Nothing exemplifies the striving for economic growth and prosperity more than China's Open Door policy and Russia's more recent policy of *glasnost* (openness) and *perestroika* (restructuring).[1] Both countries are setting aside past policies of economic self-sufficiency and political isolation in exchange for economic growth, improved standards of living, and a more commanding position in the global marketplace. These two new arrivals to world trade are only a part of the dynamic growth that is taking place in global economies.[2]

Taiwan, Hong Kong, Singapore, South Korea, Brazil, Argentina, and India are some of the other countries at various stages of economic develop-

---

[1] Those interested in learning more about the basis for political and economic changes occurring in Russia should begin by reading Mikhail Gorbachev, *Perestroika* (New York: Harper & Row, 1987).

[2] "Tactics for the Russian Front," *Business Marketing*, January 1989, pp. 42–49.

ment that, coupled with the projected growth of the developed world, will contribute to the rising demand for goods and services. Markets are dynamic, developing entities reflecting the changing lifestyles of a culture—they are becoming different, larger, more demanding. Old stereotypes, traditions, and habits are being cast aside or tempered, and new patterns of consumer behavior are emerging. Instant tortilla meal is consumed in Guatemala, hot dogs and hamburgers in France; supermarkets are displacing specialty stores and market vendors in many countries. Continual and rapid changes are so much the rule in today's markets that change must be recognized and viewed as a critical environmental factor.

Opportunities for the marketer are afforded through continuous increases in demand in more-industrialized countries and in emerging demand in less-developed countries. If marketing efforts are made to coincide with the developmental goals of the host country, prime opportunities await marketers in these less-developed countries where three quarters of humanity live. Further, in more advanced economies, consumer lifestyles are changing as the country's economy moves from one level of economic development to another. The impact on market characteristics is often sudden, causing rapid change in the degree and/or kinds of market demands. Failure to keep abreast of these changes and differences and their implications can end in costly disappointment. This chapter explores economic development and changing market patterns that can create opportunities for those companies prepared to enter the global marketplace.

MARKETING AND ECONOMIC DEVELOPMENT

The economic level of a country is the single most important environmental element to which the foreign marketer must adjust the marketing task in a developing market. The stage of economic growth within a country affects the attitudes toward foreign business activity, the demand for goods, distribution systems found within a country, and, indeed, the entire marketing process. Growth forces successful marketing to achieve the zenith of the marketing concept. In static economies, consumption patterns become rigid and marketing is typically nothing more than a supply effort. In a dynamic economy consumption patterns change rapidly, marketing is constantly faced with the challenge of detecting and providing for new levels of consumption, and marketing efforts must be matched with ever-changing market needs and wants. Certainly a nation's economy and its dynamic nature must be paramount in the evaluation of any potential market, domestic or foreign.

As part of the world marketing environment to which the marketer must be attuned, economic development presents a two-sided challenge. First, a study of the general aspects of economic development is necessary

---

BOX 9–1
Market Potential in LDCs Depends on What You Have to Sell

Market potential frequently depends on how you see opportunity. There is an old story about two salesmen, one successful and the other not so successful, who visited the same country. The less successful salesman arrives and sees everyone is without shoes. He telexes his company, "No market, poverty rampant, they don't even have shoes." The other arrives, surveys the situation, and telexes his company, "Send 500,000 pairs of shoes, everyone needs shoes."

Most people look at rural India and only see misery. The president of a manufacturer of turnkey solar-cell module plants sees opportunity. He explains, "In India there are 500,000 villages with populations between 500 and 8,000 that don't have electric power." The cost of electrifying those villages the usual way—tying them to a national power grid—would be astronomical; but, a solar-panel system for the minimal electricity needs of each village could mean about $20 billion a year in business.

Photovoltaics, the most advanced form of solar technology, is a market of the future in the United States. But in the Third World, the future is now. Most technologies begin in the U.S. market and are then exported. But there is no U.S. market now for photovoltaics so companies go overseas. The Third World is the only game in town.

The same is true of many other advanced technologies. The Third World is a huge market for the West in everything from aircraft and heavy construction to communications equipment. Overall, U.S. companies sold $59 billion worth of manufactured goods to developing nations in 1982, fully 40 percent of American exports. The 94 nations the World Bank classes as "developing" now have a total gross domestic product of more than $2.4 trillion, almost as much as the United States GDP.

What makes the developing world the only game in town for advanced-technology firms is the changing nature of development. The Third World is looking for smaller, localized technology that will allow it to leap into the modern era without disturbing its labor-intensive societies. Totally computerized automation can sometimes be more hindrance than help because it throws people out of work.

Source: Adapted from Stephen Kindel and Robert Teitelman, "If Only . . ." *Forbes*, August 29, 1983, p. 8.

---

to gain empathy for the economic climate within developing countries. A country's economic goals, marketing's assigned role in such expectations, and marketing's actual role must be examined to appreciate the environment that faces a foreign marketer in a developing country.

Second, the state of economic development should be studied with respect to market potential including the present level of economic achievement and the economy's growth potential. The current level of economic development dictates the kind and degree of market potential that exists, while a knowledge of the dynamism of the economy allows the marketer to prepare for dramatic economic shifts. To begin, a definition of economic development is in order.[3]

Stages of Economic Development

Economic development is generally understood to mean an increase in national production that results in an increase in the average per capita gross domestic product. An increase in average per capita GDP alone, however, is not sufficient to denote the implied or expected meaning of economic development. Besides an increase in average per capita GDP, most interpretations of the concept imply a widespread distribution of the increased income as well. Economic development, as commonly defined today, also tends to mean *rapid growth*—improvements achieved "in decades rather than centuries."

One frequently used model for classifying countries by stage of development is that presented by Walt Rostow. He identified five stages of development—growth is the movement from one stage to another, and countries in the first three stages are considered to be underdeveloped. Briefly, the stages are:

Stage 1:   The traditional society.   Countries in this stage lack the capability of significantly increasing the level of productivity. There is a marked absence of systematic application of the methods of modern science and technology. Literacy is low as well as other types of social overhead.

Stage 2:   The preconditions for take-off.   This second stage includes those societies in the process of transition to the take-off stage. During this period, the advances of modern science are beginning to be applied in agriculture and production. The development of transportation, communications, power, education, health, and other public undertakings are begun in a small but important way.

Stage 3:   The take-off.   At this stage, countries achieve a growth pattern which becomes a normal condition. Human resources and social overhead have been developed to sustain steady development. Agricultural and industrial modernization lead to rapid expansion in these areas.

---

[3] Jeremy Main, "How to Make Poor Countries Rich," *Fortune*, January 16, 1989, pp. 101–6.

Spice Merchants. Pakistan. (Journalism Services, Inc.)

Stage 4:   The drive to maturity.   After take-off, sustained progress is maintained and the economy seeks to extend modern technology to all fronts of economic activity. The economy takes on international involvement. In this stage, an economy demonstrates that it has the technological and entrepreneurial skills to produce not everything, but anything it chooses to produce.

Stage 5:   The age of high mass consumption.   The age of high mass consumption leads to shifts in the leading economic sectors toward durable consumers' goods and services. Real income per capita rises to the point where a very large number of people have significant amounts of discretionary income.[4]

---

[4] Walt W. Rostow, *The Stages of Economic Growth,* 2d ed. (London: Cambridge University Press, 1971), p. 10. For an interesting contrast to Rostow's stages of industrial development, see Leslie M. Dawson, "Multinational Strategic Planning for Third World Markets," *Journal of Global Marketing,* Spring 1988, pp. 29–49.

For purposes of this chapter, the terms *less-developed, underdeveloped,* and so forth, refer to countries whose economies would fall in one of Rostow's first three categories. To quantify this degree of development, it is frequently the practice to arbitrarily place all those economies with less than $300 to $700 annual per capita income in the underdeveloped category. A range of this level classifies many of the nations of Asia, Africa, Latin America, and Southern and Eastern Europe as underdeveloped. Under the preceding conditions, the category of "developing country" comprises those underdeveloped countries that are taking steps to move from a lower stage to a higher one with some degree of success. The author realizes, of course, that such an approach in identifying underdeveloped countries has its faults, but it serves in the ensuing discussion.

Several developing countries have experienced relatively rapid industrial growth during the last two decades. They have grown more rapidly than most LDCs and have experienced improvement in their general economic well-being. These newly industrialized countries (NICs) do not fit the traditional mold of developing countries.[5] Their GNP per capita generally exceeds $1,500 and, further, their rapid industrialization includes locally owned companies as well as several joint ventures with foreign MNCs. The majority of the manufactured products are exported and include such items as clothing, athletic and rubber footwear, and electronics. Exhibit 9–1 provides a startling picture of economic progress among LDCs.

Brazil, the eighth largest economy in the capitalist world, is an example of the growing importance of NICs in world trade exporting everything from alcohol to carbon steel. Brazilian orange juice, poultry, soybeans, and weapons (Brazil is the world's sixth largest weapons exporter) compete with the United States for foreign markets.[6] Embraer, the Brazilian aircraft manufacturer, provides a substantial portion of the commuter aircraft used in the United States. Even in automobile production, Brazil is a world player; it ships more than 200,000 cars, trucks, and buses to Third World countries. Further, it competes in the United States for the low-priced car market.[7]

Among the other NICs, South Korea, Taiwan, Hong Kong, and Singapore have had such rapid growth and export performance that they are discussed as the "Four Tigers" of Southeast Asia. These four countries have become major world competitors as well as major suppliers of many products to

---

[5] NICs include Brazil, Mexico, South Korea, Taiwan, Singapore, and Hong Kong.

[6] For an interesting discussion of the growing importance of developing countries, see Heidi Vernon-Wortzel and Lawrence H. Wortzel, "Globalizing Strategies for Multinationals from Developing Countries," *Columbia Journal of World Business,* Spring 1988, pp. 27–35.

[7] "Brazil Challenges Japan and South Korea for Export Markets in Low-Price Autos," *The Wall Street Journal,* March 13, 1986, p. 28.

EXHIBIT 9–1   LDC Exports Boom

In only fifteen years, LDC exports swelled 1,100 percent. But look at the compositional change: manufactured goods and fuels now account for a far greater proportion of exports than foodstuffs and minerals.

Export earnings
of developing countries

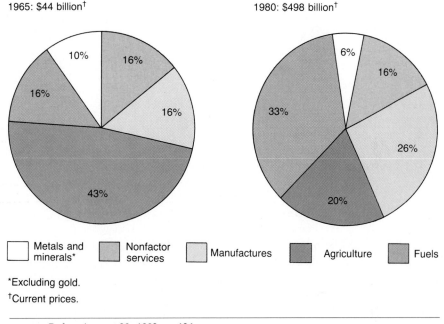

1965: $44 billion[†]   1980: $498 billion[†]

Metals and minerals*   Nonfactor services   Manufactures   Agriculture   Fuels

*Excluding gold.
[†]Current prices.

SOURCE: *Forbes*, August 29, 1983, p. 126.

the United States and Japan.[8] Unlike Brazil and Mexico, they have not had an enormous foreign debt to hold them back economically and, as a result, personal incomes have increased over the last decade to the point that they are becoming major markets for industrial and consumer goods.[9] They also differ economically from Mexico and Brazil in that much of their initial industrial growth was as assemblers of products for U.S. and

---

[8]"Can Asia's Four Tigers Be Tamed?" *Business Week*, February 15, 1988, pp. 46–50.

[9]*The Other Path: The Invisible Revolution* (New York: Harper & Row, 1988) by Hernando de Soto is causing many to reexamine the economic approach to growth in developing countries. For a brief summary and review, see Ronald Bailey, "The Right Path," *Forbes*, January 23, 1989, pp. 80–81.

EXHIBIT 9–2   Economic Indicators—Selected Countries

	Population (millions)	$Billion GDP	Per Capita National Income	Average Hourly Wage	TVs (000)	Computers (000)	Energy KH per Capita
United States	240.1	$4,168.9	$15,621	$9.53	145,037	12,350	6,694
Japan	121.4	1,576.6	11,248	7.52	30,250	5,750	2,600
Brazil	141.5	270.9	1,716	—	36,000	—	484
Mexico	81.0	127.5	1,734	0.90	9,490	—	1,174
China	1,072.2	263.4	226	0.15	9,950	—	485
Hong Kong	5.6	37.4	6,200	1.41	1,312	34	1,169
South Korea	42.6	77.7	1,793	1.31	10,100	258	1,130
Singapore	2.6	17.3	—	1.65	485	—	5,385
Taiwan	19.6	70.5	2,780	2.18	6,085	18	—
India	772.7	185.9	158	—	5,000	450	178

SOURCE: "Indicators of Market Size for 117 Countries." *Business International*, June 1988, pp. 12–18.

Japanese companies.[10] Now, they are developing their own product lines and are competing with U.S. and Japanese firms that they also supply with products. Samsung, Hyundai, and Lucky-Goldstar are becoming familiar names in automobiles, microwaves, televisions, and other Korean products in the United States.[11] See Exhibit 9–2 for a comparison of NICs with other countries.

Infrastructure and Development

One indicator of economic development is the extent of social overhead capital or infrastructure within the economy. Infrastructure represents those types of capital goods that serve the activities of many industries. Included in a country's infrastructure are support facilities such as paved roads, railroads, seaports, communications networks, and energy supplies—all necessary to support production and marketing. The quality of infrastructure directly affects a country's economic growth potential and the ability of an enterprise to engage effectively in business.

Infrastructure is a crucial component of the uncontrollable elements fac-

---

[10] Raj Aggarwal, "Foreign Operations of Singapore Industrial Firms: A Study of Emerging Multinationals from a Newly Industrializing Country,' *Asia Pacific Economies: Promises and Challenges*, Research in International Business and Management, vol. 6, M. J. Dutta, ed. (Greenwich, Conn.: JAI Press, 1988) part B, pp. 253–65.

[11] Andrew Tanzer, "Samsung: South Korea Marchs to Its Own Drummer," *Forbes*, May 16, 1988, pp. 84–89.

BOX 9–2
Infrastructure

India

Animals in India provide 30,000 MW of power, more than the 29,000 MW provided by electricity.

Because the slaughter of cattle is banned in almost all states in the country, India has the highest cattle population in the world—perhaps as many as 360 million. Bullocks are used for plowing fields, turning waterwheels, working crushers and threshers, and above all for hauling carts. The number of bullock carts has doubled to 15 million since India's independence in 1947. Bullocks haul more tonnage than the entire railway system (though over a much shorter distance); in many parts of rural India they are the only practical means of moving things about.

As a bonus, India's cattle produces enormous quantities of dung, which is used both as farmyard manure and when dried in cakes as household fuel. Some studies suggest that these forms of energy are the equivalent of another 10,000 MW.

Source: Adapted from "Bullock Manure," *The Economist*, London, October 17, 1981, p. 88.

---

ing marketers. Without adequate transportation facilities, for example, a marketer's distribution costs can increase substantially, and the ability to reach certain segments of the market may be impaired. In fact, a market's full potential may never be realized because of an inadequate infrastructure. To a marketer, the key issues in evaluating the importance of infrastructure concern the types necessary for profitable trade and the impact on a firm's ability to market effectively if a country's infrastructure is underdeveloped. In addition to the social overhead capital type of infrastructure described, business efficiency is also affected by the presence of financial and commercial service infrastructure such as advertising agencies, warehousing storage facilities, credit and banking facilities, marketing research agencies, and quality-level specialized middlemen found within a country. Generally speaking, the less developed a country is, the less adequate the infrastructure is for conducting business.

As trade develops, a country's infrastructure typically expands to meet the needs of the expanding economy. There is some question of whether effective marketing increases the pace of infrastructure development or whether an expanded infrastructure leads to more effective marketing. Most probably, infrastructure and effective economic development and marketing activity increase concurrently although never progressing at the same pace. Certainly companies still market with an inadequate infrastructure, but it is usually necessary to modify the offerings and approach

EXHIBIT 9–3   Infrastructure—Selected Countries

Country	Highways (paved km)	Railways (km)	Trucks and Buses in Use (000)	Electricity Production (kwh billion)	Newspaper Sales (000)
United States	6,221,000	778,000	34,995	2,367	62,415
Brazil	1,411,600*	30,000	1,144	139	5,094
Japan	1,123,300	53,500	16,146	602	68,142
Colombia	78,200*	3,700	328	27	1,105
Germany	482,000	31,711	1,535	373	25,103
Kenya	64,600*	2,700	87	2	220
Mexico	218,600*	25,000	2,103	82	10,212
Spain	318,549	15,344	1,504	115	2,978

*Includes unpaved and paved.

SOURCES: *International Marketing Data and Statistics, 13th ed.* (London: Euromonitor Publications, 1988).

to meet existing levels. A significant portion of the capital spent by developing countries is on the expansion of their infrastructure. (See Exhibit 9–3.)

When infrastructure does not develop with an expanding population and economy, countries begin to lose economic development ground. Conditions can develop where a country produces commodities for export but cannot export them because of inadequacies of the infrastructure. For example, Zimbabwe expanded the agricultural sector of its economy to the point that it had excess agricultural products for export. However, of the 1.5 million tons of maize available for export, only a third could be moved to ports because the rolling stock for railroads was so inadequate.

This problem is not unique to LDCs; even NICs must struggle with inadequate support services. Mexico's economy has been throttled by its archaic transport system; some observers estimate that the system will grind to a halt if the economy grows at an expected 7 to 9 percent a year. Roads and seaports are inadequate, and the railroad system has seen little modernization since the 1910 revolution. If it were not for Mexico's highway system (although it, too, is inadequate), the economy would have already come to a halt. Mexico's highways have consistently carried more freight than the railroads.

Objectives of Developing Countries

A thorough assessment of economic development and marketing should begin with a brief review of the basic facts and objectives of economic development. To be capable of adjusting to a foreign economic environ-

---

BOX 9–3
Doing Business in the Third World—Unilever's Approach

Unilever operates in 40 Third-World countries; sales in Africa, Asia, and Latin America contributed more than a fifth of the company's $20 billion plus sales. Its core products are soaps, detergents, margarine, and other inexpensive edible oils that are bought frequently and in small amounts.

Unilever has targeted rural consumers as a prime constituency. As these consumers enter the cash economy, among the first items they want are the soaps, cooking oils, and simple packaged foods that Unilever sells. The market is huge. In India, for example, agricultural workers account for 75 percent of total consumption of manufactured consumer goods.

Careful scrutiny is given to the actual use of Unilever products by consumers. For example, when executives noticed that women in India and the Far East traditionally relied on soap to wash clothing, the firm developed a detergent bar that could be used by hand. In Africa and Asia, Unilever subsidiaries are actively engaged in business ventures to create durable infrastructures in agricultural regions. The aim is to raise the overall standard of living, thus stimulating demand for company products. Although the perspective is long-term, the payoff can be immediate: Unilever's Indian subsidiary preserved an important part of its business by launching a campaign to improve animal husbandry methods and revive a flagging dairy industry near the company's milk-processing plant.

Local raw materials are used when possible to reduce overhead and stimulate local industry and thus local markets. One Kenyan subsidiary slashed the cost of importing chemicals from Europe by altering its detergent formula to make use of abundant nearby stocks of soda ash. To overcome a costly local shortage of palm oil, company scientists adapted a number of previously neglected indigenous oils for use in the manufacture of soaps. This eliminated the need for imports, lowered the cost of manufacturing, and helped to support the local economy and Unilever's markets.

Source: Adapted from "Building Sales in LDCs: Unilever's Tailor-Made Approach to Marketing," *Business International*, April 26, 1985, pp. 129–30.

---

ment, an international marketer must be able to answer questions such as: (1) What are the objectives of the developing nations? (2) What role is marketing assigned, if any, in economic growth plans? (3) What contribution must marketing make, whether overtly planned or not, for a country to grow successfully? (4) Which of the prevailing attitudes might hamper marketing strategies, development, and growth? and (5) How can the market potential, present and future, be assessed?

Industrialization in the fundamental objective of most developing countries, although for an appreciation of its impact on a nation's people, economic growth must be viewed as a means to an end rather than as the

---

BOX 9–4
Electronic Gadgetry Isn't Worth Much to People Who a Need a Good Charcoal Stove

In this age of high technology, we sometimes forget there are parts of the world where low-tech might make the most efficient product. How valuable is American and Japanese technology to people in developing countries? The poor cousins of the family of nations often wind up with inappropriate, wasteful technology instead of basic tools they can effectively use.

For example, the $40 million French-financed airport at the Tanzanian capital of Dar es Salaam has all the modern airport trappings—air-conditioning, video monitors, and a loudspeaker system. Yet, a huge percentage of the Tanzanian population can't afford to fly anywhere. The nation is so poor few people have electricity, much less air-conditioning and many flights in Tanzania are routinely canceled because of a chronic fuel shortage. Which leads to the key question: Isn't there technology from the United States, Europe, or Japan that would be of more value to the average Tanzanian than a video-display monitor telling about canceled plane flights that he couldn't afford to take anyway?

Of course, and it is the most basic kind of technology: better backhoes, stoves that use 50 percent less charcoal, hydraulic palm oil presses, simple wheelchairs, a substitute for cement, a pedal-operated cassava grinder, or a way to store milk for five days in a village with no electricity. It is these things, not super-computers and jet ports, that spell progress to the poor of the world.

The simplest ideas often have the greatest impact and local people often know best how to apply them. A local school principal in Kenya had an idea. He imported a little basic technology, adapted it to village needs, and came up with something of vital importance to his village, something others had tried and failed to develop: a better charcoal-burning stove.

Source: "The Case of Low-Tech," *The Wall Street Journal,* November 14, 1988, pg. R50.

---

end itself. Certainly, most countries see in economic growth the achievement of social as well as economic goals. Better education, better and more effective government, elimination of many social inequities, and improvements in moral and ethical responsibilities are some of the expectations of developing countries. Thus, economic growth is not measured solely in economic goals but also in social achievements. Because foreign marketers are outsiders, it is often assumed their presence is limiting the attainment of these objectives. This can result in political and government harassment and, sometimes, consumer boycott of goods. The widespread fear and resentment of foreign control of an economy commonly leads to the adoption of policies and actions that retard rather than facilitate

economic progress. Though marketing's crucial role is often not appreciated, foreign enterprise and marketing can play a significant role in helping
countries achieve their growth objectives.

Marketing's Contribution Neglected

How important is marketing to the achievement of the preceding goals?
Unfortunately, marketing (or distribution) is not always considered meaningful to those responsible for planning. Economic planners frequently
are more production- than marketing-oriented and tend to ignore or regard
distribution as an inferior economic activity. Given such attitudes, economic
plans generally are more concerned with the problems of production,
investment, and finance than the problems of efficiency of distribution.

There is a strongly held opinion (albeit wrong) that an economic system
must first have the capacity to produce before the level of consumption
and distribution becomes a problem. With this concept in mind, one developing nation invested $20 million in a fertilizer plant without making
provisions for the sale and distribution of the product. After a few weeks
of production, the plant accumulated a huge inventory it was unable to
distribute effectively. Marketing problems had been ignored with the result
that the plant had excess inventory and had to stop production while a
severe shortage of fertilizer existed in a nearby area. The country had
production capability but the product could not be distributed.

Why Marketing Is Neglected.   Lack of concern for distribution and economic planning extends to the technical assistance offered by developed
countries as well. The United States, for example, has ignored many of
the problems of distribution or marketing in its technical assistance programs for underdeveloped countries. Of the several explanations for such
an orientation, the first is that concern for production seems more practical
than concern for consumption in an underdeveloped country. Second,
many cultures view marketing as a wasteful activity and those engaged
in marketing as parasites. The utility of advertising, product planning,
and innovation is constantly questioned in even the most mature economic
systems.

Third, the cultural or traditional rigidity found in the distribution structure of many countries has caused neglect of the distribution problem.
The intangible nature of marketing fosters general neglect; it is difficult
to quantify marketing benefits compared to production. Furthermore, of
all the skills, those in marketing may be the most difficult to transfer
from one economy to another. Machines can be built in the United States
and used in Egypt, but a marketing plan or system adequate for the U.S.
market usually is inappropriate in another culture. One authority noted
that production or technical know-how is about 100 percent transferrable

Old and new in Beijing, China. Notice the "Walkman" worn by the man on the right.
(Journalism Services, Inc.)

to Mexico from the United States, but marketing know-how is only 20
percent transferrable. Even if marketing skills were 100 percent transferrable, they could not be applied efficiently in many of the developing
countries because the distribution and *economic infrastructure* necessary to
implement marketing programs are not available. Imagine marketing where
there is production but no disposable income, no storage, transportation
available only to the wrong markets, and no middlemen and facilitating
agents to participate in the flow of goods from the manufacturer to the
consumer. When such conditions exist in developing markets, marketing
and economic progress are retarded.

Marketing's Contributions.   Walt Rostow notes that if the process of modernization is to continue in developing nations, distribution and the entire
process of widening the market will lead the way. Marketing is an economy's arbitrator between productive capacity and consumer demand. The
marketing process is the critical element in effectively utilizing production
resulting from economic growth; it can create a balance between higher
production and higher consumption. Effective marketing not only improves
the lifestyle and well-being of people in a specific economy, it also upgrades
world markets; after all, a developed country's best customer is another
developed country.

BOX 9–5
Junk, New Measure of Economic Development

"For U.S. entrepreneurs going to strange foreign countries, junk studies can be very suggestive. Junk tends to be a leading economic indicator.

According to Dr. Richard N. Farmer, "Most economic data is erroneous for reasons beyond the control of statisticians."

In quest of knowledge, Farmer has roamed the junkyards of at least 10 countries.

"Every country," he maintains, "is in at least one of five junk and trash development cycles," which he labels:

1. Nothing gets used. Mainly because the natives don't have the skill to make use of junk. Characteristic of primitive and remote tribes of desert nomads. Per capita income of less than $50 per year.
2. Everything gets used indicative of rudimentary skills in reusing old materials. Nothing is thrown away for good. Ingenuity develops. Autos are totally stripped. Per capita income up to $200.
3. Piling up phase. Low-grade materials show up in junkyards and about the countryside: broken bottles, cement fragments, occasional tires, leaking bottles, and autos almost, but not quite totally, stripped.

    "Labor, particularly skilled labor, is being drawn off into more productive pursuits, so cars begin to have bits and pieces of hard-to-get things left on them." The junkyard "comes into its own."
4. The Age of Affluence. Usable trash accumulates. Lots of bottles, cans, tires, occasional abandoned cars. Useful stuff appears such as copper piping, two-by-fours, wire. Per capita income up to $1,200. Influential people talk about ecology. Trash no longer an asset but a costly burden.
5. Total Affluence. Per capita income up to $2,500 or more. Trash becomes a major public issue. Abandoned cars, throw-away containers, piles of paper become problems.

Source: John Cunniff, "Junk Pile Analyzation Gives Clues to Economic Conditions of Countries," Associated Press.

Although marketing may be considered a passive function, it is instrumental in laying the groundwork for effective distribution. Most underdeveloped countries have an inefficient, outrageously high-cost market structure in which those engaged in marketing barely manage to survive. Further, because of inadequate distribution networks, products cannot be distributed efficiently beyond major cities.[12] In China, for example,

---

[12] Ford S. Worthy, "Why There's Still Promise in China," *Fortune,* February 22, 1989, pp. 95–100.

most of the 1 billion potential consumers are not accessible because of a poor or nonexistent distribution network. The consumer market in China is probably limited to no more than 20 percent of those who live in the more affluent cities.

What is happening in China is an excellent example of how marketing contributes to the development of a distribution system. The free-market policy established about 10 years ago at first resulted only in outlets for locally grown produce and other good products. Some 10 years later a free market distribution system is developing. One study notes that when the distribution system was state-owned, people in different provinces could not take advantage of product availability that might exist in other provinces. But with free market retailing, enterprising retailers travel from province to province in search of merchandise that is either unavailable at home or can be purchased more cheaply than at home. Numerous enterprising middlemen are buying products in one location at one price and selling them in another for a higher price. Cigarettes bought in Shanghai for 1 yuan per pack can be sold to a wholesaler in another city for 1.5 yuan and then sold at retail for 2 yuan. The study reports many retailers also perform wholesale functions and provide for the distribution of goods from one area to another.[13]

An efficient distribution system matches production capacity and resources with consumer needs, wants, and purchasing power. To eliminate some of the inefficiencies that sap the economies of underdeveloped countries, a fully developed distribution system with adequate financing of the distribution of goods must be allowed to evolve. If the market is allowed to develop without interference and controls from government, an effective distribution system evolves.

Another important contribution of marketing to less-developed economies is the growth or spread of a money economy. With money instead of barter as a medium of trade, a society can develop a wider choice in consumption opportunity. Because the range of available products generally increases as marketing grows, people are exposed to a greater variety of goods. The possibility of acquiring these goods has a stimulating effect on the self-discipline and motivation of the people; instead of labor meaning subsistence living, as in many backward economies, it becomes the means of obtaining a more satisfying list of wants.

Finally, marketing contributes to the development of standards for economic behavior, integrity, and product and service reliability. A population

---

[13] For a very interesting study on the evolving free market system in China, see Heidi Vernon-Wortzel and Lawrence H. Wortzel, "The Emergence of Free Market Retailing in the People's Republic of China: Promises and Consequences," *California Management Review,* Spring 1987, pp. 59–76.

struggling for survival tends to overlook the importance of private ownership of personal property. Business needs standards of integrity, honesty, expertise and quality if it is to expand. Thus, as business develops in scope and size, it fosters the development of these characteristics. Sears, Roebuck, for example, has been credited with making a significant economic contribution to its host countries. The opening of a Sears store results in making customers more cognizant of value, in forcing consumer credit, in changing attitudes toward the customer, store clerks, suppliers, and merchandise. Sear's growth has spawned the creation of new local businesses with higher standards of expertise, quality, and delivery to supply the store with goods. Sears has advanced the science of management in many countries.

In short, marketing is instrumental in economic development. This economic development, in turn, increases the standard of living for a culture thereby improving the lives of the populace.

MARKETING IN A DEVELOPING COUNTRY

In making a market appraisal, the economic level of a country must be reviewed to determine which marketplace limitations be accounted for and adjusted to in marketing plans and strategies.

A marketer cannot superimpose a sophisticated marketing program on an underdeveloped economy. Marketing effort must be keyed to each situation: it is a job of custom tailoring for each set of circumstances. A promotional program for a population 90 percent illiterate is vastly different from a program for a population that is 90 percent literate. Pricing in a subsistence market poses different problems than pricing in an affluent society. The distribution structure should provide an efficient method of matching productive capacity with available demand. An efficient marketing program is one that provides for optimum utility at a single point in time, given a specific set of circumstances. In evaluating the potential in a developing country, the marketer must make an assessment of the existing level of marketing development within the country.

Level of Marketing Development

The level of the marketing function roughly parallels the stages of economic development. Exhibit 9–4 illustrates various stages of the marketing process as they develop in a growing economy. The table is a static model representing an idealized evolutionary process. Economic cooperation and assistance; technological change; and political, social, and cultural factors can and do cause significant deviations in the evolutionary process. However,

EXHIBIT 9-4   Evolution of the Marketing Process

Stage	Substage	Examples	Marketing Functions	Marketing Institutions	Channel Control	Primary Orientation	Resources Employed	Comments
Agricultural and raw materials (Mk.(f) = prod.)*	Self-sufficient	Nomadic or hunting tribes	None	None	Traditional authority	Subsistence	Labor Land	Labor intensive No organized markets
	Surplus commodity producer	Agricultural economy—such as coffee, bananas	Exchange	Small-scale merchants, traders, fairs, export-import	Traditional authority	Entrepreneurial Commercial	Labor Land	Labor and land intensive Product specialization Local markets Import oriented
Manufacturing (Mk.(f) = prod.)	Small scale	Cottage industry	Exchange Physical distribution	Merchants, wholesalers, export-import	Middlemen	Entrepreneurial Financial	Labor Land Technology Transportation	Labor intensive Product standardization and grading Regional and export markets Import oriented
	Mass production	U.S. economy 1885-1914	Demand creation Physical distribution	Merchants, wholesalers, traders, and specialized institutions	Producer	Production and finance	Labor Land Technology Transportation Capital	Capital intensive Product differentiation National, regional, and export markets
Marketing (Prod.(f) = mk.)	Commercial—transition	U.S. economy 1915-1929	Demand creation Physical distribution Market information	Large-scale and chain retailers Increase in specialized middlemen	Producer	Entrepreneurial Commercial	Labor Land Technology Transportation Capital Communication	Capital intensive Changes in structure of distribution National, regional and export markets
	Mass distribution	U.S. economy 1950 to present	Demand creation Physical distribution Market information Market and product planning, development	Integrated channels of distribution Increase in specialized middlemen	Producer Retailer	Marketing	Labor Land Technology Transportation Capital Communication	Capital and land intensive Rapid product innovation National, regional, and export markets

* Mk.(f) = prod.: Marketing is a function of production.

the table focuses on the logic and interdependence of marketing and economic development. The more developed an economy, the greater the variety of marketing functions demanded, and the more sophisticated and specialized the institutions become to perform marketing functions.

Perhaps the most strikingly obvious illustration of the relationship between marketing development and the stage of economic development of a country can be found in the evolution of the channel structure. One study found that with increasing economic development:

1. More-developed countries have more levels of distribution, more specialty stores and supermarkets, more department stores, and more stores in rural areas.
2. The influence of the foreign import agent declines.
3. Manufacturer-wholesaler-retailer functions become separated.
4. Wholesaler functions approximate those in North America.
5. The financing function of wholesalers declines and wholesale markup increases.
6. The number of small stores declines and the size of the average store increases.
7. The role of the peddler and itinerant trader and the importance of the open-garden fair declines.
8. Retail margins improve.[14]

Advertising agencies, facilities for marketing research, repair services, specialized consumer financing agencies, and storage and warehousing facilities are supportive facilitating agencies created to serve the particular needs of expanded markets and economies. It is important to remember that these institutions do not come about automatically, nor does the necessary marketing institution simply appear. Part of the marketer's task when studying an economy is to determine what in the foreign environment will be useful and how much adjustment will be necessary to carry out stated objectives. In some less-developed countries it may be up to the marketer to institute the foundations of a modern marketing system.

The limitation of Exhibit 9–4 in evaluating the market system of a particular country stems from the fact that the marketing system is in a constant state of flux. To expect neat, precise progression through each successive growth stage, as in the geological sciences, is to oversimplify the dynamic nature of marketing development.

---

[14] George Wadinambiaratchi, "Channels of Distribution in Developing Economies," *Business Quarterly*, Winter 1965, pp. 74–82. Reprints of this article in its entirety may be obtained from *The Business Quarterly*, School of Business Administration, The University of Western Ontario, London 72, Canada.

BOX 9–6
Those Wealthy Japanese?—The Myth of the Japanese Middle Class

Meet Akira Chizuka, a member of Japan's middle class. He spends almost three hours a day commuting to and from his job like millions of employees living around Tokyo. At 34, he makes $33,000 a year but budgets nearly half of his $1,615 monthly take-home pay for rent and utilities for the three bedroom, 484-square-foot apartment he shares with his wife. He and his wife save about $150 a month, hardly enough to generate a 20 percent down payment on a house. The Chizukas will be in their forties before they have even enough for a 10 percent down payment, assuming they can find a 90 percent mortgage.

Most Japanese take great comfort in their self-image, which carries with it the belief that nearly all Japanese are sharing equally in their country's enormous success. Yet despite four decades of hard work and sacrifice, the typical Japanese family's quality of life lags far behind that of its American and Western European counterparts. There is a wide gap between the myth and reality of owning a home. Even though Parisians and New Yorkers are finding it much harder to buy houses or apartments than their parents did, there is no question that they live better than most Tokyoites.

While the average American home covers 1,583 square feet and a typical European dwelling is more than 1,050 square feet, Japanese make do with 925 square feet. The basic U.S. family averages 2.2 automobiles. Comparable households in the European community average 1.3 cars; in Japan, it is 0.88.

As any Japanese will tell you, their nation is a land rich in income, but less rich in wealth. Tokyo is a city of tiny "rabbit hutches" in part because land and tax policies make it difficult to build larger homes. Prices on most things in Japan are outrageous by American standards, often as a result of deliberate government policies. While Americans spend 17 percent of their incomes on food, the average Japanese spend 25 percent, in part because tariffs and subsidies punish cheaper imports. Sirloin steak in six times the U.S. price, grapefruit seven times, and rice ten times. Japanese button-makers say they can sell buttons for 40 percent more than in the United States, in part because laws protecting small Mom and Pop stores and middlemen add layers of markups. Japan's middle class is not really middle class by anyone else's standards.

A worker on the Toyota assembly line sweats to make better cars for America, but countless laws and taxes make it difficult to buy that same car, to afford the gasoline to run it, and even to drive it on decent roads. No wonder many Japanese business people transferred to the United States discover they like the standard of living and are reluctant to leave.

Sources: "The Japan as Number One Myth," *The Wall Street Journal*, September 2, 1986, p. 30, and "Myth of the Japanese Middle Class," *Business Week*, September 12, 1988, pp. 49–52.

One significant factor in evaluating a developing market is the influence of borrowed technology on the acceleration of market development. Examples can be found of countries or areas of countries that have been propelled from the 18th century to the 20th century in the span of two decades. In such cases, a country might spend a relatively short time at any given stage, bypass stages completely, or telescope several stages into one. In fact, the marketing structures within many developing countries are simultaneously at many stages; it would not be unusual to find traditional marketing retail outlets functioning side-by-side with advanced, modern markets. This is true especially in food retailing where a large segment of the population buys food from small specialty stores while the same economy supports modern supermarkets equal to any found in the United States.

Influence of Import Orientation

The source of manufactured goods can condition and influence the characteristics and development of a country's market system. A strong dependence on imported manufactured goods is reflected in the structure of the market and general business practices frequently found in developing countries.

Some of the differences between foreign-based market systems and domestic-based systems result from two factors: First, the foreign-based market system creates a seller's market; and second, the source of supply is limited and controlled by a few importers. The entire marketing system develops around the philosophy of selling a limited supply of goods at high prices to a small number of affluent customers. Market penetration or a developed system of mass distribution is not necessary since demand exceeds supply and, in most cases, the customer seeks the supply. This, of course, is in contrast to the mass consumption-distribution philosophy of domestic-based systems which prevails in industrialized nations such as the United States. In these cases, it is generally a buyer's market, and supply can be increased or decreased within a given range. This creates a need to penetrate the market and push the goods out to the consumer, resulting in a highly developed system of intermediaries. One authority notes that an import-oriented market system usually works backwards:

> Consumers, retailers, and other intermediaries are always seeking goods. This results from the tendency of importers to throttle the flow of goods, and from this sporadic and uneven flow of imports, inventory hoarding as a means of

checking the market can be achieved at relatively low cost, and is obviously justified because of its lucrative and speculative yields.[15]

This import-oriented philosophy manifests itself in much of the activity and behavior in marketing. An interesting anecdote told by an authority on Brazil concerned a bank which had ordered piggy banks for a local promotion. The promotion went better than expected so the banker placed a reorder of an amount three times the original. The local manufacturer immediately increased the price and, despite arguments that pointed out reduced production costs and other supply-cost factors involved, could not be dissuaded from this move. The entire notion of economies of scale in production and the use of price as a demand stimulus is contrary to the traditional beliefs in an import-oriented market. The manufacturers were going on the theory that with demand up, the price also had to go up. A one-deal mentality of pricing at retail and wholesale levels exists because in an import-oriented market, goods come in at a landed price and pricing from there on is simply an assessment of demand and diminishing supply. Thus, variations in manufacturing costs are of little concern; each shipment is a deal, and when that is gone the merchant waits for another good deal, basing the price of each deal on the landed cost and assessment of demand and supply at that time.

An import-oriented philosophy also affects the development of intermediaries and the functions they perform. Most distribution systems are local with national distribution being of little importance since it is contrary to the import-oriented philosophy. The relationship between the importer and any middleman in the market-place is considerably different from that found in domestic-based manufacturing or mass-marketing systems. The idea of a channel as a chain of intermediaries performing specific activities and each selling to a smaller unit beneath it until the chain reaches the ultimate consumer is relatively unknown. In an import-oriented economy, an intermediary may not sell to a specific link in the channel but to a range of other intermediaries. Some simultaneously assume all the different functions—importing, wholesaling, semiwholesaling, and retailing—while other middlemen are so specialized that a high degree of division of labor is created. Such tasks as financing, storage, trucking, shipping, packaging, and breaking bulk may each have to be performed by separate agencies, resulting in extremely high-cost distribution.

Besides different operating procedures, an import-oriented market dominated by an importer-wholesaler system may present special public relations problems that obstruct the goals of a marketer attempting to substitute

---

[15] A. A. Sherbini, "Import-Oriented Marketing Mechanisms." *MSU Business Topics,* Spring 1968, p. 71. Reprinted by permission of the publisher, the Bureau of Business and Economic Research, Division of Research, Graduate School of Business Administration, Michigan State University.

locally manufactured products for imported ones or making a total market commitment in the country.[16] The major point of contention is the threat posed by the foreign marketer who, with a mass-marketing philosophy, attempts to control the distribution process to the point where consumption causes shifts in the location and control of many marketing activities and functions.

> In an import-oriented marketing system, the locus (of market activities and functions) lies near the consumer end of the marketing channel. Many marketing functions such as sorting and assorting, selling, storage and warehousing, advertising and promotion, and financing are performed by wholesale and retail intermediaries.
>
> But the establishment of domestic manufacturing of the import substitution type (or mass-marketers) invariably shifts the locus of marketing functions to the production end of the channel. This is particularly true of advertising and promotion, standardization and grading, and storage and warehousing.[17]

This shift is seen as altering the position of the local importer-wholesalers from a dominant position in the marketplace to a secondary one. Because it threatens their very existence, resistance to changes in the locus of marketing functions is intense. Resistance may cause outright competitive warfare, bargaining, or eventual government intervention on behalf of the domestic importer-wholesaler.

In addition to problems resulting from a country having an import-oriented market system, developing nations seldom have a significant middle-income class—the market consists mainly of the very wealthy and the very poor. This creates some interesting demand characteristics which must be considered in planning and estimating market potential.

Demand in a Less-Developed Country

Estimating market potential in less-developed countries involves myriad challenges. Most of the difficulty stems from economic dualism; that is, the coexistence of modern and traditional sectors within the economy. The modern sector is centered in the capital city and has jet airports, international hotels, new factories, and a small Westernized middle class. Along with this modern sector is a traditional sector containing the remainder of the country's population. Although the traditional sector is very

---

[16] The assumption here and throughout the book is that the foreign marketer enters a market with the intent of making a full commitment, that is, establishing market objectives and maintaining a continuous market representation, with broad distribution and market penetration. This approach is taken regardless of whether the products marketed are manufactured within the political boundaries of the country or are imported.

[17] Sherbini, "Marketing Mechanisms," p. 72.

close geographically, it is centuries away in production and consumerism. This dual economy affects the size of the market and, in many countries, creates two distinct marketing levels. Because they are substantially different and require different approaches for marketing success, they cannot be combined into a single market estimate. The modern sector demands products and services similar to those found in any industrialized Western country while the traditional sector demands items more indigenous and basic to subsistence. As one authority on India's market observed, "A rural Indian can live a very sound life without many products. Toothpaste, sugar, coffee, washing soap, bathing soap, kerosene are all bare necessities of life to those who live in semiurban and urban areas, but rural Indians have less to spend so they search out substitutes for the 'bare necessities.' "[18]

In an import-oriented economy, the modern sector presents a highly segmented, thin market and the importer tends to specialize in the unique needs of a relatively narrow range of customers.

> Thus the aggregate demand for a "given product" often consists of many thin and heterogeneous demand schedules that are not necessarily additive.
>
> The demand for even a simple product such as imported sardines sometimes reflects a high degree of consumer attachment to certain product attributes; for example, shape and type of tin, sauce packed or oil packed, flavor, and price. Foreign exporters who sell in worldwide markets generally find it economically feasible to cater to thin domestic market segments in the developing countries.[19]

For a company desirous of developing a long-term market commitment within a country, it may be economically impossible to serve all the thin market segments, and a single segment may be too small to warrant a substantial market investment.

The traditional sector may offer the greatest potential for a company willing to change from production orientation to marketing orientation. Briefly, this means that a company begins producing products geared to the investment, production, and distribution needs of the traditional sector rather than selling what has already been accepted in a more modern market. This can require substantial changes in marketing strategies and tactics: penetration pricing as a means to market cultivation, new distribution practices devised to place products economically throughout the market, redesigned products more fitting to the lifestyle of the traditional sector, and/or changes in promotional objectives. Products designed for industrialized Western markets may be unknown or unusable in the traditional sectors of a developing nation. Since product design must be geared

---

[18] Y. A. Verma, "Marketing in Rural India," *Management International Review* 10, no. 4 (1980), p. 47.

[19] Ibid.

to the basic wants of the population, promotion must create primary demand, acquainting the market with the attributes of a "new" product. Besides changes in market strategies, this market orientation approach could necessitate a longer investment period before profitability occurs.

Less-Developed Countries and Long-Range Potential

The growth of tomorrow's markets will include expansion in industrialized countries and the development of the traditional side of less-developed nations, as well as continued expansion of the modern sectors of such countries. In fact, the greatest long-range potential is found in growth in the traditional sector, realizing that a profit may require not only a change in orientation but also a willingness to invest time and effort for longer periods. The development of demand in a traditional market sector means higher marketing costs initially, compromises in marketing methods, and sometimes redesigning products; in other words, market investment today is necessary to produce profits tomorrow. The companies that will benefit in the future from emerging markets such as China and Russia are the ones that invest when it is not easy or profitable.

In some of the less-developed countries, it may be up to the marketer to institute the very foundations of a modern marketing system, thereby gaining a foothold in an economy that will some day be highly profitable. *The price paid for entering in the early stages of development may be lower initial returns on investment, but the price paid for waiting until the market becomes profitable may be a blocked market with no opportunity for entry.* Once a country gains momentum in development, feelings of nationalism run high, and there is a tendency to give preferential treatment to those foreign companies that helped in its development while closing doors to all others. The political price a company must be willing to pay for entry into a less-developed country market is one of entering when most of the benefits of the company's activities will be enjoyed by the host country. Once profitability is assured, many companies want into the market.

Some companies are currently designing products specifically for the needs of traditional sectors of less-developed countries with the long-range hope of being established when the sectors gain greater affluence.

SOCIALIST COUNTRIES—A SPECIAL CASE

The socialist countries of Eastern Europe,[20] Russia, and China constitute a market of increasing importance for nonsocialist nations. While Western Europe, Canada, and Japan have been trading with these countries for

---

[20] Bulgaria, Czechoslovakia, German Democratic Republic, Hungary, Poland, and Romania.

several decades, the easing of tensions among the USSR, the People's Republic of China, and the United States has led to increased sales activity by U.S. firms in these developing markets. Contrasting political systems and economic philosophies account for major differences in the trade characteristics of Eastern and Western countries. Within a nonsocialist economy, supply and demand are the most important determinants of price. In socialist countries, national goals for economic development are more crucial determinants of pricing policies than are market conditions. Further, because of centralized planning, most trade is conducted by state trading organizations rather than by individual, profit-oriented end-users as in most nonsocialist economies. Suppliers rarely negotiate directly with the final user of a product. In most instances, the selling process in socialist-based economies is done through hard-driving negotiations between the seller and a trading company representative. Everything from price to delivery times to supplies is negotiated as a total package. This requires different marketing strategies and tactics than those a U.S. marketer recognizes as traditional. Purchase patterns and demand estimations are different; promotion and advertising must be approached differently; and methods of payments and the demand for certain classes of goods are different. Potential demand for industrial goods and some consumer goods is so great and business practices are so different that the problems associated with marketing need special attention.

China and Russia—Departing from Strict Socialism

Of the socialist countries, China and Russia are rapidly moving toward dual economic systems that embrace socialism along with many tenets of capitalism. China has led the way toward a balance between the rigid economic planning of socialist doctrine and the free-enterprise system of capitalism. The initiation of the Four Modernizations program in China has brought profound changes in every sector of the Chinese economy.[21]

Almost 10 years after the start of China's transformation from a strict socialist economy, Russia embarked on a policy of openness *(glasnost)* and restructuring *(perestroika)* of their economy. It appears as if Russia is emulating many of China's development policies; easing restrictions on direct foreign investment, allowing direct contact between foreign sellers of industrial goods and end-users, allowing limited access to consumer markets, allowing free markets to develop on a limited basis, making changes in the legal structure to facilitate interaction with foreign businesses, and creating special economic zones for foreign investment.

---

[21] "Reunderstanding Capitalism," *Beijing Review*, November 14–20, 1988, pp. 22–26.

China. The economic and social changes that have occurred in China since 1978 when that country began actively seeking economic ties with the industrialized world have been dramatic. China's gross national product has grown at an annual rate of over 8 percent; if the trend continues (quadrupling industrial and agricultural output by the year 2000), the goal set in 1980 can surely be reached.[22] Over 60,000 free market areas provide outlets for marketing the output of goods and services from private, free enterprise production. Within these free market areas the number of retailing establishments has grown from approximately 10,000 in 1980 to over 6 million in 1985.[23] Joint ventures between foreign MNCs and Chinese partners manufacture a long list of products ranging from Jeeps (Chrysler) to chewing gum (Leaf Inc., manufacturers of Good and Plenty bubble gum).[24] Guangdong, China's most prosperous exporting province, shipped $5.5 billion in goods in 1987 and has attracted $5.3 billion in foreign investment, 60 percent of the country's total.[25]

Economic reform and growth have not evolved smoothly or without frustration for the Chinese or foreign investors. Chinese agencies and bureaucrats, experienced in a centrally planned economy, have had to adjust to the new capitalistic reforms and to learn, by trial and error, how to manage foreign investors eager to tap China's billion consumers. New laws regarding profit, exchange rates, ownership, legal redress, all necessary when dealing with foreign investment and trade, had to be written and interpreted.

At times the Chinese have moved slowly and cautiously and, when there were too many projects to digest at one time, have retrenched or interrupted their development until the rate of economic growth could be adjusted to a more acceptable level. Despite its unevenness, China has made enormous progress and foreign businesses that have mastered the four Ps (product, preparation, persistence, and patience) are succeeding. China is still a socialist country that is slowly evolving into a hybrid, balancing socialist Marxist principles with selected attributes of a capitalistic economic system. Each year since the end of the Cultural Revolution, the Chinese market opens wider and it becomes easier for foreigners to

[22] Shahid Javed Burki, "Reform and Growth in China," *Finance and Development*, December 1988, pp. 46–49.

[23] For a comprehensive review of emerging retailing in China, see Vernon-Wortzel and Wortzel, "The Emergence of Free Market Retailing," pp. 59–76.

[24] Dinah Lee, "Beijing Opens the Door to Bubble Gum and Band-Aids," *Business Week*, August 8, 1988, p. 40.

[25] "China's Reformers Say: Let a Thousand Businesses Bloom," *Business Week*, April 11, 1988, pp. 70–71.

Vegetable vendor, Xian, China. Free markets in China are popular because they often have more and fresher fresh vegetables than state-owned stores. (Journalism Services, Inc.)

do business.[26] This trend will continue so long as the Chinese need assistance in reaching their industrialization goals.[27] Demand for foreign investment will vary with the various stages of industrialization. Box 9–7 illustrates the changes in consumer markets that are occurring in China today.

As it industrializes, China has the potential of becoming one of the world's largest markets as well as a major world competitor. However, the political trauma created by a too rapid move toward capitalism and demands for democratic reforms may have caused delay in China's economic development goals. What was rapidly becoming an economic boom and virtual unlimited opportunity for foreign investment was suddenly disrupted in 1989 by the uncertainty of political upheaval brought about by the confrontation between students and the military at Tiananmen Square.[28] Despite the political turmoil and the jockeying for power that took place among China's leaders after the riots were quelled, the official government word was that China's door was still open to foreign capital and technology. Even though Western businesses continued to be optimistic about the future of investment in China, there was no doubt that the

---

[26] Milton R. Larson, "Exporting Private Enterprise to Developing Communist Countries: A Case Study on China," *Columbia Journal of World Business,* Spring 1988, pp. 79–90.

[27] Jim Abrams, "Ten Years of Reform: China Learns the Successes, Failures of Capitalism," Associated Press Release, November 29, 1988.

[28] Dori Jones Yang, Dinah Lee, and William Holstein, "The Great Leap Backward," *Business Week,* June 19, 1989, pp. 29–32.

BOX 9–7
Capitalism Comes to China

All of China wants TVs, and at the Beijing Television Factory, monthly output has soared 30 percent since deputy manager Jin Zhaogui began offering piece-rate bonuses for each set produced above target. Jin, a plant hero who discovered bonuses after attending a course on Western-style management, is elated about the resulting $81,000 increase in his profits.

In the countryside near Canton, now called Guangzhou, a young peasant named Huang Peilin invites a visitor into his new two-story detached house, filled with new furniture. To earn the money to move his family out of a two-room hovel, Huang raised chickens, ducks, and geese as a sideline to his work as a veterinarian. A decade ago, he could have been jailed for such daring.

Source: Adapted from "Capitalism in China," *Business Week*, January 14, 1985, p. 53.

---

rate of economic development had been dampened. Most MNCs put major investment decisions on hold because they felt political and economic uncertainty would prevail for the near future; perhaps, even until after the leadership struggle which would be sure to come when 84-year-old Deng Xiaoping dies or relinquishes his political power.[29] In the history of the economic development of China, this incident will probably be no more than a footnote since, in the author's opinion, China will be a major world economic power in the 21st century.

Russia. Many U.S. businesses have long regarded the Russian market as too complicated and inaccessible to be included among important international markets. Between U.S. government restrictions on the sale of strategic commodities and Russia's policy of economic self-sufficiency and political isolation, there was, until recently, a limited demand for a limited number of products.[30] Consequently, most MNCs found the Russian market unattractive until General Secretary Mikhail Gorbachev's 1987 decision to restructure the Russian economy created a more favorable climate for trade. Like the Chinese experience, initial changes were halting and tenuous. However, Russia has liberalized foreign trade laws much more quickly than has China. Before the changes brought about by Secretary Gorbachev,

---

[29] Ford S. Worthy, "What's Next For Business in China," *Fortune*, July 17, 1989, pp. 110–12.

[30] George Black, "Big Business for U.S. Business in the USSR," *Business Marketing*, November 1988, pp. 69–80.

the Ministry of Foreign Trade had a monopoly on foreign trade, all of which was conducted through a single ministry.

The new Soviet law on state enterprise authorized more than 100 state ministries, enterprises, and cooperatives to deal directly with foreign companies and to enter into direct business relationships. New directives involving joint ventures were also established.[31] Initially, these rules required at least 51 percent ownership by the Soviets, profits to be distributed according to ownership, strict limits on the repatriation of profits, and a governing board to be chaired by a Russian citizen.[32] However, less than a year after the first law was passed, a Soviet government resolution liberalized trade relations further. Joint venture rules were amended to allow foreigners to own majority stakes, a non-Soviet could direct the venture, and duties were lowered or eliminated on equipment imported by joint ventures.

In addition, all Soviet state-owned and private companies were allowed to establish direct import-export operations eliminating the need to go through one of the ministries of trade.[33] One Swedish Trade Council adviser feels that the prevailing attitude is best summarized by the Russian advice to "not just read our decrees; everything's flexible, everything's negotiable."[34] At the rate Russia is opening opportunities for foreign investments and trade, it will not be long until they have reached the level of the Chinese.

Glasnost and *perestroika* also appear to mean an increase in consumer goods production and that joint ventures to provide a greater variety of consumer goods will be encouraged. Joint ventures for fast-food franchises (Pizza Hut)[35] and automated lines for bottling and packaging milk (Tetra Pak AB of Sweden) have recently been authorized.[36] Similar to the Chinese market where no more than 20 percent of urban residents are in a viable consumer market, only a small portion of the 300 million Soviets are potential consumers. Estimates place the size of the consumer market at approximately $30 billion per year, although there is a large underground economy that may boost the total considerably.[37]

---

[31] Wallace H. Johnson, "Entering the Soviet Marketplace: If at First You Don't Succeed . . . ," *Export Today*, September–October 1988, pp. 19–22.

[32] "All that's Glasnost Does Not Glitter," *U.S. News & World Reports*, April 4, 1988, pp. 50–53.

[33] Peter Gumbel, "Soviets to Devalue Ruble by 50%, Alter Tariffs to Boost Economy," *The Wall Street Journal*, December 12, 1988, p. A7.

[34] "All that's Glasnost Does Not Glitter," p. 53.

[35] "PepsiCo's Pizza Hut Signs Agreement for Soviet Venture: McDonald's Next?" *The Wall Street Journal*, Septebmer 18, 1987, p. 29.

[36] "TVs Replace Tanks in Some Soviet Plants," *The Wall Street Journal*, December 6, 1988, p. A16.

[37] Dinah Lee, "The U.S. in China: Letting a New Caution Bloom," *Business Week*, January 30, 1989, p. 47.

Estimating Demand

A marketer encounters the first major problem in socialist countries with the first step in appraising a potential market, estimating demand. Meaningful economic data are infrequently published and economic plans, the most meaningful indicator of industrial goods demand, are considered state secrets. There is no published market research such as can be found in the West and marketing research, by Western standards, is unknown. Thus, a marketer cannot forecast future demand but simply must wait for a request for goods. Even if reliable economic statistics were available, they would be of little use in demand assessments because the basic buying decisions are not determined by marketing forces familiar to Western exporters. Buying decisions are determined by long-range economic plans and only products included in those plans are purchased.

In such circumstances, how can a market be assessed for market potential, trends, and consumption patterns? The only data available are the successive five-year plans which, if fully analyzed, contain helpful information such as: when and for what purposes currency will be allocated; priorities for particular products, services, and projects; internal and external potential competition and logistics.[38] Equally important to assessing the market are personal contacts within the country developed through past business transactions, exploratory visits to the country, and attendance at trade fairs and exhibitions.

Recent five-year plans revealed that some Eastern European countries are responding to consumer demands for products such as wristwatches, washing machines, and refrigerators. Even though such demands will not result in importing these consumer goods, it will create a demand for production know-how, technology, and equipment to produce them.

Another problem in estimating demand is the general lack of a profit motive in communist-socialist countries. In planning export sales to Western countries, the marketer can promote sales to the decision maker on the basis of what the product will do for the decision maker's profits since it can be assumed the buyer is largely motivated by and evaluated on profits. For socialist decision makers controlled by centralized economic plans, a marketer cannot be certain what besides profits affects demand and purchase decisions. The situation is further complicated by the difficulty in describing products except in cost savings, even though the product is not necessarily being evaluated on that basis. Consequently, estimating demand involves conjecture and reliance on the meager data available. Even with little data, some insights into the characteristics of trade are possible. As would be expected in a country dedicated to rapid industrializa-

---

[38] Rian Matthews, "Selling to Eastern Europe," *Countertrade and Barter*, June–July 1987, pp. 30–34.

tion, industrial goods necessary for growth and development are in greatest demand. Increasingly, demand includes entire manufacturing plants delivered on a turn-key basis. For example, Poland purchased from the West industrial plants valued at over $100 million to produce tractors, harvesting machines, electronics and data processing equipment, and chemicals.

Communications Process

The communication process has changed dramatically with the opening of China and Russia to foreign investment; it is now possible to deal directly with the end-user in many cases. In other socialist countries, marketers have problems finding out who affects decisions regarding their products and getting their messages to those persons. Yet, even though negotiations for a final sale may be conducted between the seller and a state-controlled buying organization, it cannot be assumed that the end-user has no say in such negotiations.[39] The fact is that the degree of influence end-users have within the socialist bloc varies among countries. Some governments permit recommendations for a specific product although they generally go through channels to the foreign trade organization responsible for making the purchase and the seller may never have any face-to-face meetings with the end-user. As a result, it is essential to try to communicate with others beyond those with whom the marketer is trading or negotiating because of the inaccessibility of the end-user in many countries and the uncertainty of when an end-user may be influential in a decision.

Modern communication methods continue to improve dramatically in socialist countries. Newspapers, outdoor advertising, industry-related magazines, and even direct mail are available in all of the communist-socialist countries and are a viable means of communicating product data. In several of the countries, consumer goods can be advertised on television, radio, and in newspapers. In Russia, time can be purchased on television and in general magazines. Pepsi-Cola International became the first advertiser to buy commercial time on Soviet television, two one-minute commercials featuring singer Michael Jackson with Russian voice-overs.[40] In Poland advertising on television and radio is available although all television and radio advertising is broadcast together in a single block. China has commercial television, catalogs, and advertising in U.S. journals distributed in China to get the message to potential buyers. Posters advertising products ranging from Japanese televisions to Coca-Cola can be seen in Beijing as well as in the Chinese countryside.

---

[39] "The Deal of the Decade May Get Done in Moscow," *Business Week*, February 27, 1989, pp. 54–55.

[40] "Pepsi Buys 5 Ad Spots on Soviet TV," Associated Press Wire Service, May 5, 1988.

BOX 9–8
Future Consumer Markets in Russia

Next time you start worrying about the high cost of living, pause a moment—and thank your lucky stars you're not a Russian.

The average wage earner works:

Nearly three times as long to buy a loaf of white bread as the American worker.
Three times as long to buy a cut of beef for dinner.
Six times as long to buy a bottle of vodka or gin.
Ten times as long to buy a dozen eggs.

If you're a housewife, you would probably have to do your washing with a machine that has a hand wringer. Seventy percent of all washing machines in the Soviet Union have hand wringers.

Apartment dwellers (including those on the fourth floor) must share their bathroom and kitchen facilities with their neighbors—and these rooms are usually on the ground floor. Even in the large Soviet cities, about 25 percent of new apartments are not equipped with running water or other plumbing conveniences. And taking national averages, the Soviet family enjoys only one third the living area of an American family the same size.

The average American worker can buy a 19-inch TV, priced at about $400, with 165 hours of work. The Russian must work 1,169 hours to buy an equivalent set, which has a price tag of—hold your breath—$1,323.

Automobiles? "These are clearly out of the reach of the average person" in the Soviet Union. It costs a Russian 43.3 months of work—over 3½ years' salary even if he or she buys nothing else in that time—to acquire a Soviet version of the small Fiat car. An American wage earner, however, could buy it with 4.4 months of work.

Source: "Economic Aspects of Life in the USSR," North Atlantic Treaty Organization.

Shortages of Convertible Currency

Currencies of socialist countries are inconvertible; that is, socialist governments do not permit residents or nonresidents to purchase or sell their currency. Russian law forbids the ruble to go in or out of Russia and so the ruble is not convertible into any other currency on foreign-exchange markets.[41] Thus, a product sold to Russia is not paid for in rubles but in a convertible currency that Russia has earned by selling a Russian product outside Soviet-bloc countries. Just as a planned economy affects the types of goods imported, the scarcity of convertible currencies—usually available

---

[41] Richard I. Kirkland, Jr., "Why Russia Is Still in the Red," *Fortune*, January 30, 1989, pp. 173–175.

only for priority goods designated by the current economic plan—affects price negotiations. This shortage of currency has resulted in heavy reliance on countertrade—the exchange of goods for other goods—in socialist-bloc trade. Every marketer should be prepared for negotiations that encompass payment which may include goods as part of the asking price.[42] The author's research indicates that over 40 percent of trade with socialist countries is, in total or in part, paid for by other goods. Early in negotiations, or more frequently toward the end, the socialist-bloc buyer stipulates that the final price will be paid in part or in total with goods produced by them.[43]

U.S. marketers are often at a disadvantage because few have experience in countertrading. The competition, however, notably Western Europe and Japan, is willing to include countertrade in negotiations. The Japanese supply the Soviets with mining and logging equipment in trade for coal and timber. France, Germany, and Italy have built pipelines in Eastern Europe in return for future delivery of natural gas. The Japanese sell petrochemical manufacturing plants to the Chinese on a buy-back arrangement where Japan receives some of the output of the plant as partial payment for construction costs. Pepsi-Cola trades bottling equipment and Pepsi-Cola syrup for vodka in Russia and for wine in Romania and Hungary.

The complete range of countertrade transactions—straight barter to buy-back arrangements—is utilized in trade with socialist countries: and is a major factor in effective competition in these countries. One businessman's advice for successful Russian trade applies to all socialist countries, "If you can buy something from them, you should . . . otherwise, you should combine with other companies that can use Russian [exports], say timber, or ore, or any other of the many raw materials Russia has for export."[44] In other words, go prepared to create the convertible currency from the goods that will be offered to you as payment.

In summary, trading with most socialist countries involves sales made to government trading companies, demand that is determined by an economic plan not by market conditions, and finally, nonconvertible currencies that dictate countertrade as an important aspect of marketing. Although China and Russia are correctly classified as socialist countries, many of the market characteristics of a socialist economy discussed here do not apply as the two countries move further away from strict adherence to socialist-marxist economic doctrines and adopt many of the economic principles of capitalism.

---

[42] Countertrade as a pricing tool is discussed in Chapter 16.

[43] Karen Elliott House, "Domestic Burdens Limit Global Role of Beijing, Moscow," *The Asian Wall Street Journal*, February 13, 1989, p. 1.

[44] "An Interview with Armand Hammer, U.S. Soviet Trade: The Long March from Lenin to Gorbachev," *Export Today*, September–October 1988, p. 25.

CHANGING MARKET BEHAVIOR AND POTENTIAL

As a country develops, profound changes occur that affect its people. Incomes change, population concentrations shift, expectations for a better life adjust to higher levels, new infrastructures evolve, social capital investments are made, and foreign and domestic companies seek new markets or expand their positions in existing markets. All of this results in changes in market behavior and potential.

Markets evolve from the interaction of the economy, the culture, and the marketing efforts of companies. Exhibit 9–5 presents some of the market differences which occur throughout the world. The real meaning of less-developed versus developed nations becomes apparent when Exhibit 9–5 is examined carefully.

Consider, for example, the differences between France and India. Per capita GDP in France is more than 40 times greater than in India and,

EXHIBIT 9–5 Market Indicators for Selected Countries

	(A) *Market Growth* *percent Change* *1981–1986*	(B) *GDP* *per* *Capita*	(C) *Cars* *in Use (000)*	(D) *TVs in* *Use (000)*	(E) *Telephones* *in Use (000)*	(F) *Energy* *Consumption* *per Capita*
USA	8.4	15,621	132,108	145,037	106,239	6,694
Argentina	NA	2,157	220	1,300	585	920
Australia	12.3	9,019	6,842	6,000	1,187	4,591
Brazil	24.3	1,673	952	15,500	8,536	484
Canada	9.8	11,472	11,118	15,300	10,468	6,937
China	44.9	226	182	9,950	NA	485
France	9.1	9,343	20,800	369	29,374	3,923
Germany	5.3	10,558	26,099	22,908	23,630	4,024
India	41.3	215	1,128	5,000	2,667	178
Indonesia	32.7	460	956	4,900	503	179
Italy	7.1	6,340	21,500	14,521	15,601	2,303
Japan	12.3	11,248	27,845	30,250	44,967	2,600
Mexico	41.5	2,247	2,103	9,490	5,411	1,174
Poland	13.7	1,691	3,426	229	3,648	4,494
South Korea	42.4	1,793	557	10,100	4,810	1,130
Spain	11.8	4,262	8,874	258	12,820	2,180
U.K.	6.6	8,069	16,055	457	29,061	4,760
USSR	11.9	4,268	9,996	308	26,667	5,977

SOURCE: "Indicators of Market Size for 117 Countries," *Business International*, June 1988, pp. 12–18. *International Marketing Data and Statistics* (London: Euromonitor Publications, 13 ed. 1988). *European Marketing Data and Statistics* (London: Euromonitor Publications, 24 ed. 1988). *National Accounts Statistics-Analysis of Main Aggregates, 1985* (New York: United Nations, 1988), pp. 217–24. *Energy Statistics Yearbook* (New York: United Nations, 1988), pp. 2–31.

BOX 9–9
Third World Faces up to Progress

Much of the marketing challenge in the developing world, which is not used to consumer products, is just to get consumers to use the product and to offer it in the right sizes. Because many Latin American consumers can't afford a 7-ounce bottle of shampoo, Gillette sells it in half-ounce plastic bubbles. In Brazil, Gillette sells Right Guard in plastic squeeze bottles instead of metal cans.

But the toughest task for Gillette is convincing Third World men to shave. The company recently began dispatching portable theaters to remote villages—Gillette calls them mobile propaganda units—to show movies and commercials that tout daily shaving. In South African and Indonesian versions, a bewildered bearded man enters a locker room where clean-shaven friends show him how to shave. In the Mexican film, a handsome sheriff is tracking bandits who have kidnapped a woman. He pauses on the trail to shave every morning. The camera lingers as he snaps a double-edged blade into his razor, lathers his face and strokes it carefully. In the end, of course, the smooth-faced sheriff gets the woman. In other places, Gillette agents with an over-sized shaving brush and a mug of shaving cream lather up and shave a villager while others watch. Plastic razors are then distributed free and blades—which must be bought—are left with the local storekeeper.

Once they shave, Gillette introduces them to shaving cream. Gillette discovered a while back that only 8 percent of Mexican men who shave use shaving cream. The rest soften their beards with soapy water or just plain water, neither of which Gillette sells. Today 13 percent of Guadalajaran men use shaving cream and Gillette is planning to sell its new product, Prestobarba, (Spanish for "quick shave") in the rest of Mexico, Colombia, and Brazil. In Guadalajara they introduced plastic tubs of shaving cream that sell for half the price of aerosol.

From packaging blades so that they can be sold one at a time to educating the unshaven about the joys of a smooth face Gillette is pursuing a growth strategy.

Source: Adapted from David Wessel, "Gillette Keys Sales to Third World Taste," *The Wall Street Journal,* January 23, 1986, pp. 30.

---

with the exception of TVs, ownership of automobiles, telephones, and energy consumption ranges from 4 to 20 times greater in France. While ownership of automobiles, TVs, and telephones may not be considered the good life by some, they are indicators of wealth and the figures in Exhibit 9–6 clearly illustrate the disparity that exists between countries.

Even though economic opulence or a lack of it varies from country to country, most world markets are continually expanding. Column A of Exhibit 9–5 is an indicator of market growth based on average percentage growth over a five-year period of various indicators such as the consump-

EXHIBIT 9–6   Living Standards in Selected Countries

| Country | Rooms per Dwelling | Persons per Room | Percent of Households | | |
			Piped Water	Flush Toilets	Electric Lighting
Brazil	4.6	1.1	55%	28%	70%
Chile	2.9	1.6	70	59	88
Costa Rica	4.1	1.4	88	60	73
El Salvador	1.7	3.5	32	28	38
Ethiopia	2.0	2.6	83	(NA)	62
Guatemala	2.4	2.7	21	15	34
Hong Kong	3.1	0.5	98	78	90
Indonesia	3.3	1.2	12	22	43
Japan	4.6	0.7	93	46	98
Peru	2.4	2.3	32	36	44
Saudia Arabia	3.1	1.9	46	26	56
Singapore	2.1	2.3	92	80	97
Sri Lanka	2.2	2.5	13	16	22
United States	5.3	0.5	99	99	99

SOURCE: *International Marketing Data and Statistics*, 13th ed. (London: Euromonitor Publications, 1988).

tion of energy, steel, cement, trucks, buses, and automobiles. An interesting point is that countries with the highest market growth are the developing countries. For example, the United Kingdom has a market growth percentage of 6.6, while Brazil has 24.3. The indicators in Exhibit 9–6 illustrate the disparities between the rich and poor that exist in many countries and the potential for improvement and growth of living standards of world markets.

As living standards improve, consumer attitudes and consumption patterns change. In Spain, for example, traditional consumption patterns are shifting as more women work outside of their homes. Retail outlets are changing in response to consumer demands for longer hours and convenience of shopping with better service, ease of access, and proximity to home. The trend is toward hypermarkets and department stores; the traditional practice of shopping at small specialty stores is in decline. Purchasing priorities are also changing with more emphasis on quality than price, and service is more in demand as a component of a purchase.[45] Wherever economies are growing, one can expect changes in consumption patterns and the emergence of trends in market behavior.[46]

[45] "Marketing Strategies in a Changing Spain," *Business Europe,* July 26, 1985, pp. 234–35.

[46] For other examples, see "Affluent Asian Markets Prompt New Questions: Can West Meet East?" *Business International,* January 25, 1985, pp. 25–26.

BOX 9–10

Minutes of Worktime Required to Purchase:

Minutes of Worktime Required to Purchase:

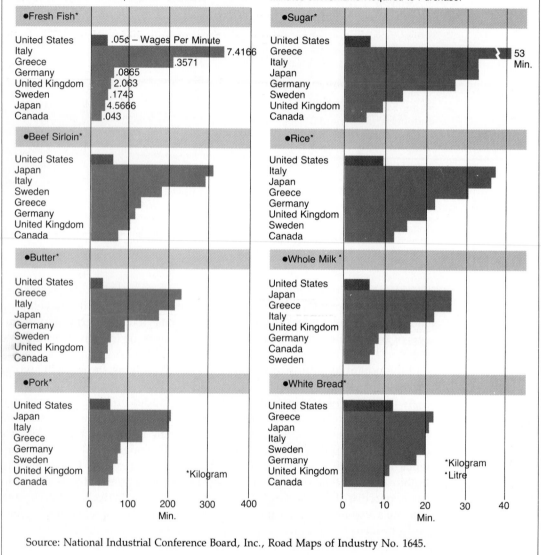

● Fresh Fish*

United States	.05¢ – Wages Per Minute
Italy	7.4166
Greece	.3571
Germany	.0865
United Kingdom	2.063
Sweden	.1743
Japan	4.5666
Canada	.043

● Sugar*

United States	
Greece	53 Min.
Italy	
Japan	
Germany	
Sweden	
United Kingdom	
Canada	

● Beef Sirloin*

United States
Japan
Italy
Sweden
Greece
Germany
United Kingdom
Canada

● Rice*

United States
Italy
Japan
Greece
Germany
United Kingdom
Sweden
Canada

● Butter*

United States
Greece
Italy
Japan
Germany
Sweden
United Kingdom
Canada

● Whole Milk*

United States
Japan
Greece
Italy
United Kingdom
Germany
Canada
Sweden

● Pork*

United States
Japan
Italy
Greece
Germany
Sweden
United Kingdom
Canada

*Kilogram

● White Bread*

United States
Greece
Japan
Italy
Sweden
Germany
United Kingdom
Canada

*Kilogram
*Litre

```
0      100     200     300     400
            Min.
```

```
0        10       20       30      40
                 Min.
```

Source: National Industrial Conference Board, Inc., Road Maps of Industry No. 1645.

SUMMARY

Over the last 30 years, the scope and level of technical and economic growth have enabled some nations to advance their standards of living by two centuries. As a nation develops, its capacity to produce develops pressures, typically in the distribution structure. Emphasis by the marketer must be on developing marketing systems designed to utilize to the utmost the economic level of development. The impact of social and economic trends will continue to be felt in many countries during the next decade causing significant changes in distribution systems, personal shopping habits, and consumer demand. China and Russia are undergoing rapid political-economic changes and the easing of political tensions in the last decade has opened many of the socialist-bloc nations to selected foreign marketing. Although there are still special problems in these countries, they are promising markets for a broad range of products. The continued growth of these trends requires foreign marketers to constantly evaluate the dynamic aspects of a market, because many of today's market facts will likely be tomorrow's historical myths.

QUESTIONS

1. Define the following terms:
   underdeveloped
   economic development
   NICs *(newly industrialized country)*

2. It is possible for an economy to experience economic growth as measured by total GNP without a commensurate rise in the standard of living. Discuss fully.

3. Why do technical assistance programs of more affluent nations typically ignore the distribution problem or relegate it to a minor role in development planning? Explain.

4. Discuss each of the stages of evolution in the marketing process. Illustrate each stage with a particular country.

5. As a country progresses from one economic stage to another, what in general are the marketing effects?

6. Locate a country in the agricultural and raw material stage of economic development and discuss what changes will occur in marketing when it passes to a manufacturing stage.

7. What are the consequences of each stage of marketing development on the potential for industrial goods within a country? For consumer goods?

8. Discuss the significance of economic development to international marketing. Why is the knowledge of economic development of importance in assessing the world marketing environment? Discuss.

9. Select one country in each of the five stages of economic development. For each country, outline the basic existing marketing institutions and show how their stages of development differ. Explain why.

10. Why should economic development be studied by a foreign marketer? Discuss.

11. The infrastructure is important to the economic growth of an economy. Comment.

12. What are the objectives of economically developing countries? How do these objectives relate to marketing? Comment.

13. What is marketing's role in economic development? Discuss marketing's contributions to economic development.

14. Discuss the problems a marketer might encounter when considering the socialist-communist countries as a market.

15. Why do the socialist-communist countries demand countertrade when they buy? What problems do marketers face when confronted with a countertrade?

16. The needs and wants of a market and the ability to satisfy them are the result of the triune interaction of the economy, culture, and the marketing efforts of businesses. Comment.

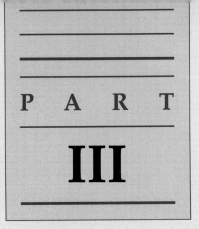

PART

III

Global Marketing Management

Chapters

CHAPTER

10

Global Marketing Management—Planning and Organization

How can the information confronting an international marketer be focused on the task of marketing a product internationally? The most effective approach to managing and utilizing such information is careful planning and an organizational structure designed to facilitate the needs of international marketing.

Interestingly, not all international firms use strategic planning nor are all structured to reflect the special problems of international business.[1] However, as involvement deepens and firms are faced with uncertainties caused by rapid environmental changes in markets, competition, resource availability, fluctuating foreign currencies, shifting political alignments, and/or the complexities of expansion into multiple markets, formal corporate-level strategic planning and organizational restructuring are generally adopted. Strategic planning is a major trend among U.S. multinationals. A study of *Fortune* 500 firms found 90 percent of responding firms surveyed engaged to some degree in long-range planning. The most interesting finding was that two fifths had begun such activities only recently.

Strategic planning and the development of an organizational structure

---

[1] Susan A. Mohrman and Ian I. Mitroff, "Business Not as Usual," *Training and Development Journal,* June 1987, pp. 37–43.

BOX 10–1
The Global Enterprise—A Definition

A new day is dawning for the Global Enterprise. International competition requires it. The concept of Global Enterprise can be seen taking shape as an entity able to outmaneuver and respond to the demands of the marketplace far more quickly than its multinational predecessors. MNCs, as their name implies, recognize national boundaries and cultures, cater to real or perceived needs of national markets, and tailor products to the preferences of different countries. Their internal reward and control systems usually focus more closely on local performance than overall performance of the company.

The truly Global Enterprise discards notions of national markets and instead views the entire world as its local sphere of activity. Unlike a centralized entity with market-based subsidiaries, the Global Enterprise is a network of various management, manufacturing, marketing, and resource "nodes." These nodes are organized to provide a market or market sphere with products at the lowest cost and with the shortest delivery times. Node managers have great latitude in responding to local business changes, and on occasion deal directly with their counterpart nodes for problem resolutions.

Multinational corporations are likely candidates to become Global Enterprises. Yet, a company need not be a multinational to achieve this desired end. Small, growing companies may find the absence of a larger multinational structure that needs to be changed or dismantled much to their advantage.

For all who would aspire to become a Global Enterprise, the time to begin planning for the transition is now. Only then will they be prepared to confront new sources of competition on truly global terms.

Source: Adapted from Daniel F. Hefler, Jr., "The Dawn of the Global Enterprise," *Journal of Business Strategy*, Winter 1984, pp. 86–87.

---

are interrelated. A specific organizational structure can shape and affect the planning and decision processes while the planning processes are affecting the organizational structure. As a company intensifies its international involvement and becomes a global company, the organizational structure changes to reflect the different coordination, communication, and operational demands of a global orientation.[2]

Reorganizing, reforming, restructuring, and regrouping are increasingly necessary as firms become aware of the need for more comprehensive planning and organizational structure to accommodate the complexities of global marketing operations. Domestic bias in an organizational structure quickly becomes apparent when a substantial portion of a firm's profits are generated internationally and it is confronted with intensive competi-

---

[2] Kenichi Ohmae, "Getting Back to Strategy," *Harvard Business Review*, November–December 1988, pp. 149–56.

tion; then the inadequate planning and lines of communication become highly visible.[3]

This chapter discusses global marketing management, strategic planning for international marketing, and alternative market-entry strategies; it also identifies the elements that contribute to effective international or global organization. Because the focus of this chapter is on the role of marketing in an international organization, it stresses strategic planning and organization for effective global marketing.

GLOBAL MARKETING MANAGEMENT

The two central tasks of global marketing management are determining the firm's overall global strategy and shaping the organization to achieve company goals and objectives. Company organization, the orientation of management, and the firm's objectives are important in determining the level of international integration of the company. *Global, multinational, international, and foreign marketing,* are terms used loosely and liberally to denote an international orientation. As discussed in Chapter 1, a company's international orientation can be included in one of three operating concepts: (1) under the Domestic Market Extension Concept foreign markets are extensions of the domestic market and the domestic marketing mix is extended, as is, to foreign markets; (2) with the Multidomestic Market Concept each country is viewed as being culturally unique and an adapted marketing mix for each country market is developed; and (3) with the Global Market Concept the world is the market and wherever cost and culturally effective, a standardized marketing mix is developed for entire sets of country markets (whether the home market and only one other or the home market and 100 other countries). Although standardization is sought in a global strategy, cultural differences are not ignored and adaptations are made if such differences prove critical to the marketing success of the program.[4]

Global versus International Marketing Management

How does global marketing management differ from international marketing management or, for that matter, marketing management? As Exhibit 10–1 shows, the difference is primarily in orientation. Global marketing

---

[3] Christopher A. Bartlett and Sumantra Ghoshal, "Organizing for Worldwide Effectiveness: The Transnational Solution," *California Management Review,* Fall 1988, pp. 54–74.

[4] For a comprehensive discussion of different approaches to global strategy, see Sumantra Ghoshal, "Global Strategy: An Organizing Framework," *Strategic Management Journal,* October 1987, pp. 425–40.

EXHIBIT 10–1   A Comparison of Assumptions About Global and Multinational Companies

	Multinational Companies	*Global Companies*
Product Life Cycle	Products are in different stages of the product life cycle in each nation.	Global product life cycles. All consumers want the most advanced products.
Design	Adjustments to products initially designed for domestic markets.	International performance criteria considered during design stage.
Adaptation	Product adaptation is necessary in markets characterized by national differences.	Products are adapted to global wants and needs. Restrained concern for product suitability.
Market Segmentation	Segments reflect differences. Customized products for each segment.	Segments reflect between group similarities. Group similar segments together.
	Many customized markets.	Fewer standardized markets.
	Acceptance of regional/national differences.	Expansion of segments into worldwide proportions.
Competition	Domestic/national competitive relationships.	Ability to compete in national markets is affected by a firm's global position.
Production	Standardization limited by requirements to adapt products to national tastes.	Globally standardized production. Adaptations are handled through modular designs.
The Consumer	Preferences reflect national differences.	Global convergence of consumer wants and needs.
Product	Products differentiated on the basis of design, features, functions, style, and image.	Emphasis on value enhancing distinction.
Price	Consumers willing to pay more for a customized product.	Consumers prefer a globally standardized good if it carries a lower price.
Promotion	National product image, sensitive to national needs.	Global product image, sensitive to national differences and global needs.
Place	National distribution channels.	Global standardization of distribution.

SOURCE: Adapted with the authors' permission from Gerald M. Hampton and Erwin Buske, "The Global Marketing Perspective," *Advances in International Marketing*, vol. 2, S. Tamer Cavusgil, ed. (Greenwich, Conn.: JAI Press, 1987), pp. 265–66.

Market differences do exist. Two cultures—two tastes: Jalapeños peppers in Mexico and Camembert cheese in France.

management is guided by the global marketing concept viewing the world as one market. It "is based on cross-cultural similarities instead of cross-cultural differences."[5] International marketing management is based on the premise of cross-cultural differences and is guided by the belief that each foreign market requires its own culturally adapted marketing strategy.[6]

As discussed in earlier chapters, there is some debate as to the extent of global markets today. A reasonable question concerns whether a global marketing strategy is possible only when a completely standardized marketing mix can be achieved. Keep in mind that a global marketing strategy as used in this text and the globalization of markets are two separate although interrelated ideas. One has to do with efficiency of operations and competitiveness, the other with the homogeneity of demand across cultures. A global marketing strategy can be cost effective and competitively advantageous without absolute homogeneity in global market demand because standardization across markets is sought wherever possible. As international competition intensifies, successful international firms are guided by the global market concept. "The big issue today is not whether to go global but how to tailor the global marketing concept to fit each business and how to make it work."[7]

---

[5] Rita Martenson, "Is Standardization of Marketing Feasible in Culture-Bound Industries? A European Case Study," *International Marketing Review,* Autumn 1987, pp. 7–16.

[6] J. J. Boddewyn, Robin Soehl, and Jacques Picard, "Standardization in International Marketing: Is Ted Levitt in Fact Right?" *Business Horizons,* November–December 1986, pp. 69–75.

[7] John A. Quelch and Edward J. Hoff, "Customizing Global Marketing," *Harvard Business Review,* May–June 1986, pp. 59–68.

Benefits of a Global Orientation

Why globalize? Several benefits are derived from globalization and standardization of the marketing mix. Economies of scale in production and marketing are the most frequently cited benefits. Black & Decker Manufacturing Company (electrical hand tools, appliances, and other consumer products) realized significant production cost savings when they adopted a global strategy. They were able to reduce not only the number of motor sizes for the European market from 260 to only 8 but also 15 different models to 8. Savings in the standardization of advertising can also be substantial. Colgate-Palmolive Company introduced its Colgate tartar-control toothpaste in over 40 countries, each of which could choose one of two ads. The company estimates that for every country where the same commercial runs, it saves $1 to $2 million in production costs.[8]

Transfer of experience and know-how across countries through improved coordination and integration of marketing activities is also cited as a benefit of globalization.[9] Unilever, N.V. successfully introduced two global brands originally developed by two subsidiaries. Their South African subsidiary developed Impulse body spray and a European branch developed a detergent that cleaned effectively in European hard water. These are examples of how coordination and transfer of know-how from a local market to a world market can be achieved.

Another benefit derived from globalization is a uniform global image. Global recognition of brand names and/or corporate logos accelerate new product introductions and increase the efficiency and effectiveness of advertising. Uniform global images are increasingly important as satellite communications spread throughout the world. Philips International, an electronics manufacturer, had enormous impact with a global product image when it sponsored the soccer World Cup—the same advertisement was seen in 44 countries with voice-over translations in six languages.[10]

Control and coordination of operations is also an often-mentioned benefit. It is easy to imagine the difference in controlling one or two worldwide advertising projects in 40 countries versus 40 different country-specific advertisements. The same quality standards, promotional campaigns, product inventories, and spare parts inventories are easier to control and manage with a global strategy than with a multidomestic strategy.

Without doubt, cultural differences do not always permit standardization.

---

[8] Joanne Lipman, "Marketers Turn Sour on Global Sales Pitch Harvard Guru Makes," *The Wall Street Journal*, May 12, 1988, p. 17.

[9] Ralf Thomas Kreutzer, "Marketing-Mix Standardization: An Integrated Approach in Global Marketing," *European Journal of Marketing*, 22, 10 (1988), pp. 19–29.

[10] John Marcom, Jr., "Cable and Satellites Are Opening Europe to TV Commercials," *The Wall Street Journal*, December 27, 1987, p. 1.

BOX 10–2
The Meaning of Global Business—Coca-Cola around the World

The Coca-Cola Company has been an international company for most of its corporate existence; today it exhibits all the trappings of a global company. Coca-Cola leads in soft drink sales around the world; it outsells Pepsi-Cola, its closest rival, by more than three to one outside North America. Coca-Cola earned more money in 1988 from soft drinks in Japan than it did in the United States even with a record year in the United States. Japan produced about $350 million dollars in operating income compared with $324 million in the United States.

   The executive suite of Coca-Cola reflects their global reach: Cuban-born Roberto Goizueta is chairman and chief executive officer; Iowa native Donald Keough is president; and German Klaus M. Halle is president of the international division. These men truly view the world as their market. They can tick off country by country per capita consumption figures as easily as they pop the tops on soft drink cans: In the United States, 274 eight-ounce servings of Coca-Cola products for every man, woman, and child; Australia 177; Germany 155; Japan 89; Great Britain 63; and Thailand 26. They become giddy thinking about the possibilities of Thais drinking as much soda as Texans or Indonesians; currently their population of 180 million in a hot, humid climate drinks only 3.2 servings of Coke per year. The market potential is a marketer's dream that only seems to become more grandiose when thoughts turn to China with an annual consumption of just 0.2 of a serving for each of its 1 billion people. "If we could get per capita in China up to what we have in Australia (around 177) we could have another whole Coca-Cola Company just in China!" Who is their competition? Goizueta says "sometimes competition is Pepsi, sometimes it is water, sometimes it is wine."

   Source: Adapted from Richard W. Stevenson, "Having Won Japan, Coca-Cola Sets Sights on Asia, Europe," *New York Times*, March 15, 1988, p. 5.

Government and trade restrictions, differences in the availability of media, differences in customer interests and response patterns, and the whole host of cultural differences presented in earlier chapters preclude complete standardization of a global marketing mix.[11] Nevertheless, the trend is toward similarities in consumer behavior among market segments all over the world. Tomorrow's competitive leader in world marketing will be the company guided by the global marketing concept.[12]

---

[11] For a detailed discussion of the benefits and barriers to globalization, see Susan P. Douglas and Samuel C. Craig, "Global Marketing Myopia," *Journal of Marketing Management* 2, no. 2 (1986), pp. 155–69.

[12] Sandra M. Huszagh, Richard J. Fox and Ellen Day, "Global Marketing: An Empirical Investigation," *Columbia Journal of World Business*, Vol. 20, No. 4, pp. 31–43.

3M Corporation's decision to reorganize into a global company illustrates some of the benefits cited as well as how a global marketing strategy can be a mixture of standardized and adapted elements. In the early 1980s, 3M Corporation faced mounting competition in its major markets for its magnetic audio/video products. Once the traditional leader in North America and Europe, 3M had lost significant market share in those markets; in Japan, it lagged behind competitors by a significant margin. 3M's approach had been to treat country markets as different segments with no uniformity in packaging across country markets and little coordination and communication among subsidiary personnel. A study revealed that there was a proliferation of brands with homogeneous packaging which was contributing to consumers' inability to distinguish one product from another. Further, an analysis of consumer preferences confirmed that trends in the marketplace were consistent across national boundaries, reinforcing the importance of developing a distinctive and consistent image for 3M products on a global basis.

3M developed a global strategy and introduced a global brand identity and packaging for the entire line of magnetic media products. The package was designed to communicate the Scotch™ brand quality to a variety of markets. It was fashioned so that it could be used for all the division's products (the firm's first uniform package) and in all markets (packages had differed from country to country). To communicate the design change to consumers, 3M launched a major global advertising campaign for the new logo. Because both print and television advertisements heavily emphasized the logo, the ads were easier to adapt to different country markets. Foreign language versions of the commercial were produced in Japanese, German, Spanish, and Italian, and theme music was tailored to reflect national taste. In addition, packaging and advertising standardization mechanisms to improve communication and coordination between the parent and foreign subsidiaries were also set in place.

The result of this global effort was that 3M achieved its goals in all three major markets; it recovered the lead in Europe and North America and dramatically increased its market share in Japan. In addition to boosting volume and market share, the program helped reduce the cost of marketing through the use of a unified packaging system. Global marketing also made a marked difference in accelerating product launch on a global scale. For example, a high-grade super VHS videotape was introduced in Japan one month, and in the United States three months later; it appeared in Europe only six months after its introduction in Japan. In the past, it would have been impossible to get effective media coverage and introduce a new 3M product in all its markets in such a short time span.[13]

---

[13] "3M's Global Marketing Plan: How a New Package Helped Its Worldwide Reorganization," *Business International*, July 13, 1987, pp. 217–18.

STRATEGIC PLANNING

Strategic planning is a systematized way of relating to the future. It is an attempt to manage the effects of external, uncontrollable factors on the firm's strengths, weaknesses, objectives, and goals to attain a desired end. Further, it is a commitment of resources to a country market to achieve specific goals. In other words, planning is the job of making things happen that may not have otherwise occurred.[14]

The question that needs addressing is whether or not there is a difference between strategic planning for a domestic company and for an international company. The principles of planning are not in themselves different, but the intricacies of the operating environments of the MNC (host country, home, and corporate environments), its organizational structure, and the task of controlling a multicountry operation create differences in the complexity and process of international planning.

Strategic planning allows for rapid growth of the international function, changing markets, increasing competition, and the ever varying challenges of different national markets. The plan must blend the changing parameters of external country environments with corporate objectives and capabilities to develop a sound, workable marketing program. A strategic plan commits corporate resources to products and markets to increase competitiveness and profits.

Planning relates to the formulation of goals and methods of accomplishing them, so it is both a process and a philosophy. Structurally, planning may be viewed as corporate, strategic, and/or tactical. International planning at the corporate level is essentially long-term, incorporating generalized goals for the enterprise as a whole. Strategic planning is conducted at the highest levels of management and deals with long- and short-term goals of the company, while tactical planning or market planning pertains to specific actions and to the allocation of resources used to implement strategic planning goals in specific markets.

A major advantage to a MNC involved in strategic planning is the discipline imposed by the process. An international marketer who has gone through the planning process has a framework for analyzing marketing problems and opportunities and a basis for coordinating information from different country markets. The process of planning may be as important as the plan itself because it forces decision makers to examine all factors that can affect the success of a marketing program and involves those who will be responsible for its implementation. When Massey-Ferguson Incorporated—Canada's farm implement producer—completes a strategic planning program, the final product represents the efforts of 200 managers

---

[14] Donald V. Shiner, "Marketing's Role in Strategic and Tactical Planning," *Journal of European Marketing* 22, no. 5 (1988), pp. 23–31.

worldwide, combining input from field operating managers and senior management alike. Another key to successful planning is evaluating company objectives, including an assessment of management's commitment and philosophical orientation to international business.[15]

Company Objectives and Resources

Evaluation of a company's objectives and resources is crucial in all stages of planning for international operations. Each new market entered can require a complete evaluation—including existing commitments, relative to the parent company's objectives and resources. As markets grow increasingly competitive, as companies find new opportunities, and as the cost of entering foreign markets increases, companies need such planning.

Defining objectives clarifies the orientation of the domestic and international divisions, permitting consistent policies. A lack of well-defined objectives has found companies rushing into promising foreign markets only to find activities that conflict with or detract from the companies' primary objectives.

Foreign market opportunities do not always parallel corporate objectives; it may be necessary to change the objectives, alter the scale of international plans, or abandon them.[16] One market may offer immediate profit but have a poor long-run outlook while another may offer the reverse. Only when corporate objectives are clear can such differences be reconciled effectively.

International Commitment

The strategic planning approach taken by an international firm affects the degree of internationalization to which management is philosophically committed. Such commitment affects the specific international strategies and decisions of the firm. After company objectives have been identified, management needs to determine whether it is prepared to make the level of commitment required for successful international operations—commitment in terms of dollars to be invested, personnel for managing the interna-

---

[15] For a contrary view on the value of planning, see Bronislaw J. Verhage and Eric Waarts, "Marketing Planning for Improved Performance: A Comparative Analysis," *International Marketing Review,* Summer 1988, pp. 20–30.

[16] For an insightful study on the importance of strategic planning for Third World markets, see Leslie M. Dawson, "Multinational Strategic Planning for Third World Markets," *Journal of Global Marketing,* Spring 1988, pp. 29–49.

> **BOX 10–3**
> **Common Mistakes of Beginning International Marketers**
>
> 1. *Mistake:* Failure to obtain qualified export counseling and to develop a master international marketing plan before starting an export business.
>   *Correction:* Get qualified outside guidance.
> 2. *Mistake:* Insufficient commitment by top management to overcome the initial difficulties and financial requirements of exporting.
>   *Correction:* Take a long-range view and establish a good foundation or don't get involved.
> 3. *Mistake:* Insufficient care in selecting overseas agents or distributors.
>   *Correction:* Conduct a personal evaluation of the personnel handling your account, the distributor's facilities, and the management methods employed. Remember, your foreign distributor's reputation is your company's reputation wherever he represents you.
> 4. *Mistake:* Chasing orders from around the world instead of establishing a basis for profitable operations and orderly growth.
>   *Correction:* Concentrate efforts in one or two geographical areas at a time, then move on to the next selected geographical area.
> 5. *Mistake:* Neglecting export business when the U.S. market booms.
>   *Correction:* Make a long-term commitment to export business and don't neglect it or relegate it to a secondary place when the home market booms.
> 6. *Mistake:* Failure to treat international distributors on an equal basis with domestic counterparts.
>   *Correction:* Don't isolate your export distributors from domestic programs. Expand institutional advertising campaigns, special discount offers, sales

tional organization, and determination to stay in the market long enough to realize a return on these investments.

The degree of commitment to an international marketing cause affects the extent of a company's involvement. A company uncertain of its prospects is likely to enter a market timidly using inefficient marketing methods, channels, or organizational forms, thus setting the stage for the failure of a venture that might have succeeded with full commitment and support by the parent company. Occasionally casual market entry is successful, but more often than not, market success requires long-term commitment.

ALTERNATIVE MARKET-ENTRY STRATEGIES

When a company makes the commitment to go international, it must choose an entry strategy. This decision should reflect an analysis of market potential, company capabilities, and the degree of marketing involvement

BOX 10–3 (*continued*)

incentive programs, special credit-term programs and so forth, to include foreign distributors as equal partners. Otherwise, you run the risk of destroying the vitality of overseas marketing efforts.

7. *Mistake:* Unwillingness to modify products to meet regulations or cultural preferences of other countries.

   Correction: Modifications necessary to be legal and locally competitive are best made at the factory. If modifications are not made at the factory, the distributor must make them—usually at greater costs and, perhaps, not as well. As a result, the added cost may make your account less attractive for the distributor and less profitable for you.

8. *Mistake:* Failure to print services, sales, and warranty messages in locally understood languages.

   Correction: Print all instructions, sales messages, and warranties in the local language. Just think how it would be if operating instructions on your new camera were in Japanese.

9. *Mistake:* Failure to consider use of an export management company or other marketing intermediary.

   Correction: If the company does not have the personnel or capital to invest in experienced export staff, engage an appropriate intermediary.

10. *Mistake:* Failure to consider licensing or joint-venture agreements.

    Correction: A licensing or joint-venture agreement may be a simple, profitable way to overcome problems of import restrictions, insufficient personnel/financial resources, or a too limited product line in an otherwise profitable overseas market.

Source: Adapted from the "Twelve Most Common Mistakes of New-to-Export Firms," *Business America* December 7, 1987, pp. 14–15.

and commitment management is prepared to make. A company's approach to foreign marketing can require minimal investment and be limited to infrequent exporting with little thought given to market development. Or, a company can make large investments of capital and management effort to capture and maintain a permanent, specific share of world markets. Both approaches are profitable.

Even though companies begin with modest export involvement, experience and expansion into larger numbers of foreign markets increases the number of entry strategies used. There are a variety of foreign market entry strategies from which to choose. Each has particular advantages and shortcomings depending on company strengths and weaknesses, the degree of commitment the company is willing or able to make, and market characteristics.

Exporting

A company might decide to enter the international arena by exporting from the home country. This means of foreign market development is the easiest and most common approach employed by companies taking their first international step because the risks of financial loss can be minimized. Exporting is a common approach for the mature international company as well.[17] Some of America's largest companies engage in exporting as their major market-entry method. Generally, early motives are to skim the cream from the market or gain business to absorb overhead. Even though such motives might appear opportunistic, exporting is a sound and permanent form of operating in international marketing.[18] The mechanics of exporting and the different middlemen available to facilitate the exporting process are discussed in detail in Chapters 17 and 18.

Licensing

A means of establishing a foothold in foreign markets without large capital outlays is licensing. Patent rights, trademark rights, and the rights to use technological processes are granted in foreign licensing. It is a favorite strategy for small and medium-sized companies although by no means limited to such companies. Not many confine their foreign operations to licensing alone; it is generally viewed as a supplement to exporting or manufacturing rather than the only means of entry into foreign markets. The advantages of licensing are many: when capital is scarce, when import restrictions forbid other means of entry, when a country is sensitive to foreign ownership, or when it is necessary to protect patents and trademarks against cancellation for nonuse. Although this may be the least profitable way of entering a market, the risks and headaches are less than for direct investments; it is a legitimate means of capitalizing on a foreign market.

Determining the value of the property to be licensed is a key issue for international executives involved with licensing. For many companies, putting a price tag on intellectual property is a haphazard affair.[19] Pricing methods range from a systematic analysis by the licensee to determine potential profitability (follow the 25 percent rule, that is, take up to 25 percent of the pretax profit) to charging what the market will bear. In some cases, laws restrict the amount of royalties that can be paid. In

---

[17] Catherine N. Axinn, "Export Performance: Do Managerial Perceptions Make a Difference?" *International Marketing Review*, Summer 1988, pp. 61–71.

[18] Michael Stoff, "The Secret of Small Business Exporting," *Export Today*, September–October 1987, pp. 54–55.

[19] "How Licensing Executives Put a Price Tag on Technology Assets," *Business International*, September 21, 1987, pp. 297–98.

BOX 10–4
Competing with the Japanese and the Company Town

We are all familiar with Toyotas, one of the more popular Japanese automobiles sold in the United States. But how much do we know about their production?

Toyota City—the actual name of the home for Toyota—leads Japan in production of automobiles. Over 3.6 million automobiles, trucks, and busses are produced there each year.

An absolute monarch, Toyota organizes everything in Toyota City. It is easy for a Toyota employee to buy a Toyota. Repayments are deducted from salaries. As for housing, young workers straight from technical school live three to a room in company dormitories. After five years, they may claim a room for themselves. The rent meanwhile is deducted from their salaries. Eventually, Toyota employees can move on to an apartment where the longest they may stay is 10 years. Toyota Homes then invites them to choose one of its seven models of prefabricated homes. The payments are deducted from their salaries.

Toyota provides everything for recreation: an athletic stadium, an Olympic-sized swimming pool, gymnasiums, and six sport grounds. Every year, Toyota organizes its own Olympics in which the company's teams vie with one another.

For everything else inhabitants rely on Seikyo, the Toyota cooperative group. Besides its supermarkets, the cooperative operates dozens of sales outlets, supplies canteens, stocks vending machines, and distributes gasoline. It hires out wedding dresses and sells headstones for graves. Large purchases can be made on credit which can be deducted from employees' salaries.

So how do the workers feel about this? One 40-year-old married Japanese worker with three children says, "I should feel completely at home in the company. Something went wrong, however. I was immediately marked because I refused to do overtime. I am a sports enthusiast and I want to have my evenings free." He managed to have just that, but at the price of remaining in the lowest job category. "Management pushes you to buy and then holds you to debt," he says. "If you agree to do overtime, it is often because the basic wage is not enough to maintain living standards. In any case, most employees are tamed. They identify with the company."

Source: Adapted from "The Steel Cocoon," *World Press Review*, November 1988, p. 58.

Brazil, for example, royalties for technology are limited to 1 to 5 percent of net sales and for trademarks to 1 percent of net sales.[20]

Licensing in international business may take several forms; licenses may be granted for production processes, for the use of a trade name, or for

---

[20] Ibid., p. 298.

Quick restaurant, Europe. Fast food franchises are not limited to the U.S. market. (N'Diaye/ Journalism Services, Inc.)

the distribution of imported products. In some circumstances, licensing provides an ideal entry into foreign countries that otherwise block non-domestic enterprises. Licenses may be closely controlled or autonomous and permit expansion without great capital or personnel commitment if licensees have the requisite capabilities. Not all licensing experiences are successful because of the burden of finding, supervising, and inspiring licensees. Licensing, however, does provide the basis for many success stories in various businesses.

Franchising

form of exporting

Franchising is a rapidly growing form of licensing in which the franchiser provides a standard package of products, systems, and management services, and the franchisee provides market knowledge, capital, and personal involvement in management. The combination of skills permits flexibility in dealing with local market conditions and yet provides the parent firm with a reasonable degree of control. The franchiser can follow through on marketing of the products to the point of final sale. It is an important form of vertical market integration. Potentially, the franchise system provides an effective blending of skill centralization and operational decentralization, and has become an increasingly important form of international marketing.[21]

Prior to 1970, international franchising was not a major activity. A survey by the International Franchising Association revealed only 14 percent of its member firms had franchises out of the United States and the majority of those were in Canada. By the 1980s, more than 15,000 franchises of U.S. firms were located in countries throughout the world. These franchises included soft drinks, motels, retailing, fast foods, car rentals, automotive services, and recreational services.

3 Joint Ventures

A company may decide to share management with one or more collaborating foreign firms and enter into a joint venture for a variety of reasons. Joint ventures as a means of engaging in international business have accelerated sharply during the past 20 years. As in the case of licensing, one of the strongest reasons for entering joint ventures is the substantial reduction of political and economic risks by the amount of the partner's contributions to the venture. Also, many countries, especially less-developed ones, require joint ventures as a means of foreign investment. A joint venture can be attractive to an international marketer: (1) when it enables a company to utilize the specialized skills of a local partner; (2) when it allows the marketer to gain access to a partner's local distribution system; (3) when a company seeks to enter a market where wholly owned activities are prohibited; and (4) when the firm lacks the capital or personnel capabilities to expand its international activities otherwise.[22]

There are some objections to this means of developing a foreign market. The principal fear is loss of absolute control and perhaps loss of freedom of action in the production and marketing operations. Regardless of the shortcomings, joint ventures are increasing; for many countries, they are frequently the only means of direct investment still open.[23] China and Russia have liberalized their joint-venture laws to make this an attractive

---

[21] Emi Hayashi, "Franchising Fever: The Growth Business of the 1990s," *Export Today*, April 1989, pp. 22–25.

[22] Ghazi M. Habih and John J. Burnett, "An Assessment of Channel Behaviour in an Alternative Structural Arrangement: The International Joint Venture," *International Marketing Review*, Vol. 6, No. 3, 1989, pp. 7–20.

[23] For an excellent article on joint ventures in developing countries, see Anthony J. F. O'Reilly, "Establishing Successful Joint Ventures in Developing Nations: A CEO's Perspective," *Columbia Journal of World Business*, Spring 1988, pp. 65–71.

way for Western businesses to enter those countries. Warner-Lambert Company recently signed a $5 million joint-venture contract with the People's Republic of China to produce and market chewing gums and candies. The joint venture—Harbin Warner-Lambert Confectionery Company, Ltd.—will produce Dentyne chewing gum, Halls cough drops, and Fruitfuls center-filled candies for both the domestic market and export. Warner-Lambert is providing the production equipment and technology while China provides the land, the building, and some equipment.[24]

Nearly all companies active in world trade participate in at least one joint venture somewhere; many number their joint ventures in the dozens. A recent Conference Board study indicates that the 40 percent of Fortune 500 companies with more than $100 million in sales were engaged in one or more international joint ventures.

There is no one reason for the increase in joint ventures. Commitment to joint venture depends on the type of market, the country in which the company plans to do business, and the basis for the business. The Conference Board study revealed a variety of reasons for companies trying joint ventures. Among the important reasons listed were:

1. Attractive new markets for companies in mature home markets.
2. The need to deal with rising economic nationalism, especially important in Third World countries where many require local participation for any investment.
3. The need for new raw materials, important for politically sensitive extractive industries seeking new sources of raw materials and a means of passing along the heightened economic risk of new business ventures. (In the face of worldwide inflation, political instability, terrorism, and other uncertainties, many companies believe a local partner will lessen such risks.)
4. Provide an exporting base from a region; when a partner is in a common market association, a joint venture with a partner in one country eases the task of exporting to all other common market members. (For example, a joint venture with a partner in a Central American country would probably make it easier to export to member countries in the Latin American Integration Association [formerly Latin American Free Trade Area] than if exports were made from a non-LAIA member country.)
5. To sell technology; of the five reasons for joint ventures, selling technology is the least important; but in many countries, a joint venture with a local partner is necessary to sell or license technology.[25]

A more recent reason for joint ventures has been sparked by the anticipation of Europe 1992; that is, the full integration of Europe. There has

---

[24] "Warner-Lambert in Chinese Venture," *Export Today,* May–June 1988, p. 70.

[25] Are Foreign Partners Good for U.S. Companies?" *Business Week,* May 28, 1984, pp. 58–59.

EXHIBIT 10–2   Why Joint Venture?

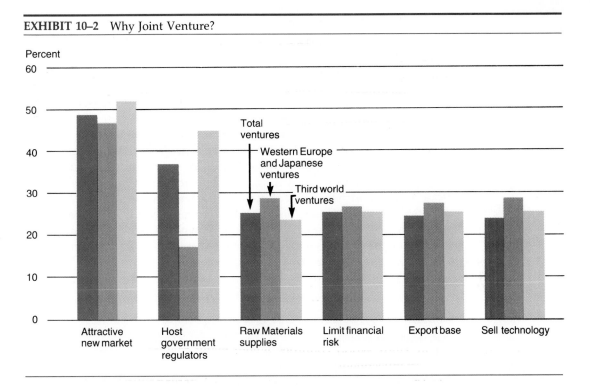

SOURCE: Allen R. Janger, *Organization of International Joint Ventures*, Report No. 787 (New York: The Conference Board), p. 3.

been a rash of buy-outs, mergers, and joint ventures among companies positioning themselves to compete in Europe 1992, a market that will rival the United States in size and potential. Whirlpool Corporation, number two in market share in the United States, and Philips, number two in Europe, have formed an appliance joint venture that positions Whirlpool as a contender for the top rung in the world appliance industry. This move gives Whirlpool a major position in the expanding European market.[26]

Exhibit 10–2 illustrates the varied components that make up joint ventures in Western Europe, Japan, and Third World countries. Attractive new markets are important for both Western Europe and Third World countries; however, the next most important reason for joint ventures is to overcome host country regulations. (This, of course, is most predominant in the Third World.) There are numerous legal methods of joining companies together, but the joint-venture form is essentially a merger or partnership of two or more participating companies which have joined forces for marketing, financing, and/or managerial reasons.

---

[26] "Whirlpool Plots the Invasion of Europe," *Business Week*, September 5, 1988, p. 70.

Joint ventures should be differentiated from minority holdings by a MNC in a local firm. Three definite factors are associated with joint ventures: (1) There is an acknowledged intent by the partners to share in the management of the joint venture. (2) Joint ventures are partnerships between legally incorporated entities such as companies, chartered organizations, or governments; and not between individuals. (3) Equity positions are held by each of the partners.

Foreign government restriction of ownership of joint ventures has intensified in recent years. For example, Venezuela publishes a list of companies in which foreign partners cannot have over 20 percent interest; India specifies maximum foreign participation at 40 percent in many industries; Nigeria has a long list of business enterprises reserved exclusively for Nigerian ownership, plus a second list in which foreign equity is limited to 40 percent. Japan has carefully limited foreign ownership and has been restrictive about joint ventures with non-Japanese companies. Recently, however, it has permitted more international joint ventures.

BOX 10–5
Ten Ways to Control a 50–50 Joint Venture Abroad

1. Issue two kinds of stock—voting and nonvoting—that divide the profits evenly but give a majority vote to the U.S. side.
2. Arrange the deal 49–49 with 2 percent in the hands of a third party friendly to the U.S. side.
3. Provide in the bylaws that the U.S. side has a majority of directors.
4. Have the bylaws stipulate that the U.S. directors (even though equal in number with the partner's directors) appoint the management.
5. Have the bylaws provide that in the case of a tie vote, the position of the U.S. side prevails.
6. Arrange a 50–50 deal, but with a management contract awarded to the U.S. investor.
7. Arrange a contract for the entire output of the jointly owned producing facility to be sold to a U.S.-controlled marketing company. The marketing company should get what it wants from the producing company.
8. A modification of number 7: give 51 percent of the producing company to the local partner in exchange for 51 percent of the selling company.
9. Satisfy the pressure for 50 percent local ownership by putting the local 50 percent in the hands of a local insurance company that has no interest in management.
10. Better yet, spread the local 50 percent over a multitude of shareholders. Kaiser in Brazil has thousands of local shareholders.

Source: Reprinted from "75 Management Checklists for Foreign Operations" with permission of the publisher, Business International Corporation (New York).

Marketing Motives.   Market access is the chief marketing reason for joint ventures; nearly all developing countries, and many developed countries, require at least some degree of local participation of firms operating in their country. Foreign automobile makers were completely closed out of Japan for years, but finally entered the market through joint ventures.

Mergers with companies that have well-established local distribution may provide rapid market entry. American companies first entering Europe found inadequate distribution facilities and insufficient local capital for expansion, so they formed partnerships and provided needed funds to strengthen the local middlemen. Local firms possessed market information and marketing know-how which would have taken years for a foreign company to acquire. Such participation minimizes the risk of market failure, speeds the marketing effort, and strengthens the market.

Financial and Personnel Advantages.   Merger through joint venture may provide tax advantages, funds, or access to local capital markets and combine the resources and fund-raising capabilities of companies. As a low-cost method of keeping up with the growing requirements of their international clients, advertising agencies have employed the joint-venture method of expansion extensively in the last decade.

The worldwide shortage of capable management personnel has been another reason for mergers. Numerous joint ventures have been worked out so that nationals with managerial ability could be acquired. In some countries it is almost impossible to gain effective distribution without joining forces with firms which have already developed large sales forces or distribution networks.[27]

Consortia

The consortium and syndicate are similar to the joint venture and could be classified as such except for two unique characteristics: (1) they typically involve a large number of participants; and (2) they frequently operate in a country or market in which none of the participants is currently active. Consortia are developed for pooling financial and managerial resources and to lessen risks. Often, huge construction projects are built under a consortium arrangement in which major contractors with different specialties form a separate company specifically to negotiate for and produce one job. One firm usually acts as the lead firm or the newly formed

---

[27] "Two Plus Two Equals One: Ford and VW Consolidate in Brazil and Argentina," *Business Latin America*, January 19, 1987, pp. 17–18.

BOX 10–6
Liquid Tide—Where Do You Come From?

Research and development are becoming an international process for more and more American, European, and Japanese companies. As competition grows and national differences diminish for products from cars to computers to consumer goods, companies scour the world for technology. Today's objective is technology that can be applied worldwide.

Procter & Gamble Co. introduced Tide in 1946. Tide represented American technology at work. P&G researchers found chemicals that would get clothes cleaner even in hard water and developed the first synthetic detergent. P&G's new liquid Tide has a distinctly international heritage. A new ingredient that helps suspend dirt in wash water came from the company's research center in Cincinnati but the formula for liquid Tide's cleaning agents was developed by P&G technicians in Japan. Ingredients that fight the mineral salts present in hard water came from P&G's scientists in Brussels. Ideas and technologies to develop liquid Tide were drawn from around the world.

Liquid Tide, the first detergent without phosphates, cleans as well as phosphate detergents. Tide's cleaning agents were formulated in Japan because Japanese consumers wash their clothes in colder water (around 70 degrees F) than do consumers in the United States (about 95 degrees F) and Europe (160 degrees F). Because Japanese cleaning agents must work harder to get clothes clean, the technology is especially advanced there. Liquid Tide's water-softening ingredients which enable its cleaning agents to work better were developed in P&G's Brussels laboratories because water in Europe averages more than twice the metal content of typical U.S. water. The new result is a successful new liquid Tide that can get clothes clean in cold, hard water. It has become an overnight success in the United States.

Source: Adapted from Paul Ingrassina, "Industry Is Shopping Abroad for Good Ideas to Apply to Products," *The Wall Street Journal*, April 29, 1985, p. 1.

corporation may exist quite independently of its originators. A somewhat different example of a consortium is the American Trade Consortium, Inc. organized to give participating U.S. companies, including RJR Nabisco, Eastman Kodak Company, Johnson and Johnson, Ford Motor Company and others, a strong base to jointly negotiate a trade agreement with Soviet authorities. The group hopes to steer its way around some of the obstacles of doing business in Russia by concluding a trade agreement that will act as a framework for any joint ventures the members agree to form individually in Russia. The major purpose for this consortium is to negotiate trade agreements on behalf of its members with Soviet officials from various state agencies and ministries. The consortium is expected to facilitate coordination of major projects that require multibureaucratic approval and to be more efficient than individual negotiations would be.[28]

Manufacturing

A fourth and major means of foreign market development is manufacturing within the foreign country. This strategy is employed when the demand justifies the investment involved. A company may manufacture locally to capitalize on low-cost labor, avoid high import taxes, reduce the high costs of transportation to market, gain access to raw materials, and/or as a means of gaining entry into other markets. For example, the only way to avoid high tariffs imposed on an outsider by countries of the European Community may be to invest in one of the countries and thereby gain entry into the others. This has become especially important as Europe moves toward full integration, as many anticipate that after 1992 Europe will move toward greater protectionism.[29] Generally, when a company makes production investments outside its home country, markets are serviced in the country where the manufacturing facilities are located. They also service markets in other countries and sometimes exports back to the home country.

Many U.S. manufacturing firms have found lower labor and manufacturing costs and facilities outside the country make it possible to export to the United States at prices lower than manufacturing those same products at home. The *maquiladoras* in Mexico are a case in point: by sending parts to Mexican plants for assembly, manufacturers can save substantially on labor costs.[30] An International Trade Commission report indicates that for most U.S. industries domestic hourly wages, including fringe benefits, are four to five times greater than those of the typical foreign assembly sites in Mexico.[31] Offshore production is important for most of the world's manufacturing companies including those in Japan. To increase price competitiveness in the United States, Japanese companies are making invest-

---

[28] Peter Gumbel, "American Companies Form a Consortium to Cope with Soviet Trade Bureaucracy," *The Wall Street Journal*, April 14, 1988, p. 25.

[29] "Why GE Took a European Bride," *Business Week*, January 30, 1989, pp. 28–29.

[30] See Chapter 18 for a complete discussion on *maquiladoras* and other offshore operations.

[31] "New U.S. Study Deflates Criticism of Offshore Production," *Business Latin America*, February 15, 1988, p. 50.

ments to manufacture in Mexico.[32] Major companies seeking lower labor costs offshore is no longer an unusual strategy. Japanese firms manufacture throughout Southeast Asia to service markets in Japan and elsewhere, as do many American firms.[33] In fact, most television sets sold in the United States by domestic companies are not manufactured totally in America.

Management Contract

Quite a different kind of arrangement is the management contract where a management company agrees to manage some or all functions of another company's operations in return for management fees, a share of the profits, and sometimes an option to purchase stock in the company at a given price. The management contract can assure operating control in joint ventures or consortia or be used when a company wishes to gain an immediate return for services rendered. A company that has been expropriated or "purchased" by a local government may be able to maintain a profitable position by consenting to operate the enterprise through a management contract. It often permits participation in a foreign venture without capital risk or investment and is a major tool for maintaining managerial control in situations where governments require nationals to own a majority of stock interest.

Regardless of the alternative market-entry strategies used or the number of countries where a company markets, operating without some overall integrating process can result in spotty world marketing performance. The complexities encountered in multinational marketing make it difficult to coordinate worldwide product and marketing strategies concurrently without a planning process that focuses simultaneously on a broad range of environments.

THE PLANNING PROCESS

Whether a company is marketing in several countries or is entering a foreign market for the first time, planning is a major factor of success. The first-time foreign marketer must decide what products to develop, in which markets, and with what level of resource commitment. For the company already committed, the key decisions involve allocating effort

---

[32] "Japanese Companies Target Mexico's In-Bond Sector to Gain Cost and Trade Edge," *Business Latin America*, November 7, 1988, p. 350.

[33] "How Maquiladora Production Fits into Global Strategy of Japan's Kyocera Corp," *Business Latin America*, November 14, 1988, pp. 358–59.

and resources among countries and product, deciding on new markets to develop or old ones to withdrawn from, and which products to develop or drop. Guidelines and systematic procedures are essential for evaluating international opportunities and risks and for developing strategic plans to take advantage of such opportunities. The process illustrated in Exhibit 10–3 offers a systematic guide to planning for the multinational firm operating in several countries.

Phase 1—Preliminary Analysis and Screening: Matching Company/Country Needs. Whether a company is new to international marketing or heavily involved, an evaluation of potential markets is the first step in the planning process. A critical first question in the international planning

---

EXHIBIT 10–3   International Planning Process

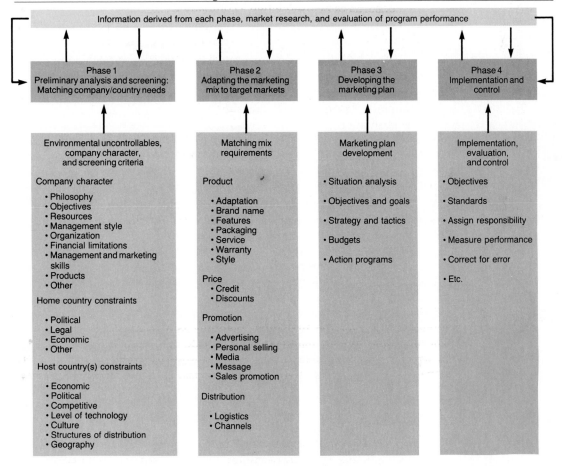

Information derived from each phase, market research, and evaluation of program performance

Phase 1 Preliminary analysis and screening: Matching company/country needs	Phase 2 Adapting the marketing mix to target markets	Phase 3 Developing the marketing plan	Phase 4 Implementation and control

Environmental uncontrollables, company character, and screening criteria	Matching mix requirements	Marketing plan development	Implementation, evaluation, and control
Company character	**Product**	• Situation analysis	• Objectives
• Philosophy	• Adaptation	• Objectives and goals	• Standards
• Objectives	• Brand name		
• Resources	• Features	• Strategy and tactics	• Assign responsibility
• Management style	• Packaging		
• Organization	• Service	• Budgets	• Measure performance
• Financial limitations	• Warranty		
• Management and marketing skills	• Style	• Action programs	• Correct for error
• Products	**Price**		• Etc.
• Other	• Credit		
Home country constraints	• Discounts		
• Political	**Promotion**		
• Legal			
• Economic	• Advertising		
• Other	• Personal selling		
	• Media		
Host country(s) constraints	• Message		
	• Sales promotion		
• Economic			
• Political	**Distribution**		
• Competitive			
• Level of technology	• Logistics		
• Culture	• Channels		
• Structures of distribution			
• Geography			

process is deciding in which existing country market to make a market investment. A company's strengths and weaknesses, products, philosophies, and objectives must be matched with a country's constraining factors as well as limitations and potential. In the first part of the planning process, countries are analyzed and screened to eliminate those that do not offer sufficient potential for further consideration.

The next step is to establish screening criteria against which prospective countries can be evaluated. These criteria are ascertained by an analysis of company objectives, resources, and other corporate capabilities and limitations. It is important to determine the reasons for entering a foreign market and the returns expected from such an investment. A company's commitment to international business and objectives for going international are important in establishing evaluation criteria. A company guided by the Global Market Concept looks for commonalities among markets and opportunities for standardization, whereas a company guided by the Domestic Market Extension Concept seeks markets that accept the domestic marketing mix as implemented in the home market. Minimum market potential, minimum profit, return on investment, acceptable competitive levels, standards of political stability, acceptable legal requirements, and other measures appropriate for the company's products are examples of the evaluation criteria to be established.

Once evaluation criteria are set, a complete analysis of the environment within which a company plans to operate is made. The environment consists of the uncontrollable elements discussed earlier and includes both home-country and host-county restraints, marketing objectives, and any other company limitations or strengths that exist at the beginning of each planning period. Although an understanding of uncontrollable environments is important in domestic market planning, the task is more complex in foreign marketing because each country under consideration presents the foreign marketer with a different set of unfamiliar environmental constraints. It is this stage in the planning process that more than anything else distinguishes international from domestic marketing planning.

The results of Phase 1 provide the marketer with the basic information necessary to: (1) evaluate the potential of a proposed country market; (2) identify problems that would eliminate the country from further consideration; (3) identify environmental elements which need further analysis; (4) determine which part of the marketing mix can be standardized for global companies or which parts of and how the marketing mix must be adapted to meet local market needs; and (5) develop and implement a marketing action plan.

Information generated in Phase 1 helps a company avoid the mistakes that plagued Radio Shack Corporation, a leading merchandiser of consumer electronic equipment in the United States, when it first went international. Radio Shack's early attempts at international marketing in Western Europe

BOX 10–7
Standardized versus Localized Marketing Plans

Many market conditions would preclude the standardization of marketing plans. Because national identity can influence buyers, many manufacturers understand the importance of having country identity both with the manufacture of a product and in advertising. For example, buy American is a very important issue in certain parts of the United States. Conversely, some products associated with particular countries such as wine or fine cameras may have greater market demand when associated with the foreign home country rather than a local market. In addition, national taste preferences differ for some kinds of products from market to market. For example, in Britain, gelatin desserts are preferred in solid wafer or cake form while in the United States and other parts of the world, they are sold as a powder. Germans are accustomed to buying salad dressing in tubes.

While some market conditions prevent standardization, other conditions would certainly encourage standardizing worldwide marketing plans. Some products actually lend themselves to standardization. This is certainly true for cola beverages and gasoline, as well as many fast foods and hotel services. Most of these are standardized although there are some exceptions. Kentucky Fried Chicken is prepared differently in Malaysia than in other parts of the world. The parent company was opposed to any changes because they have attempted to standardize their product line throughout their markets. However, after a comprehensive survey they succumbed to local cultural taste preferences. The change required that the chicken be cooked to a firm texture instead of the standard soft texture. The Malaysians considered a firm chicken to be fresh and a soft texture to have been frozen and not fresh. Packaging, prices, and distribution methods may also be standardized across markets.* Although Kentucky Fried Chicken did adapt the preparation of firm chicken, the company continued to follow a global orientation for all other parts of the marketing mix, standardizing where possible.

*From David Zielenziger, "Fast-Food Chains Flocking to Malaysia to Tap Expanding Consumer Market," *The Asian Wall Street Journal,* June 1, 1981, p. 15.

resulted in a series of costly mistakes that could have been avoided had it properly analyzed the uncontrollable elements of the countries targeted for the first attempt at multinational marketing. The company staged its first Christmas promotion for December 25 in Holland, unaware that the Dutch celebrate St. Nicholas Day and gift giving on December 6. Legal problems in various countries interfered with some of their plans; they were unaware that most European countries have laws prohibiting the sale of citizen-band radios, one of the company's most lucrative U.S. products and one they expected to sell in Europe. A free flashlight promotion in German stores was promptly stopped by German courts because giveaways violate German sales laws. In Belgium, the company overlooked a law requiring a government tax stamp on all window signs, and poorly selected store sites resulted in many of the new stores closing shortly after opening.[34]

With the analysis in Phase 1 completed, the decision maker faces the more specific task of selecting country target markets, identifying problems and opportunities in these markets, and beginning the process of creating marketing programs.

Phase 2—Adapting the Marketing Mix to Target Markets.   A more detailed examination of the components of the marketing mix is the purpose of Phase 2. When target markets are selected, the market mix must be evaluated in light of the data generated in Phase 1. In which ways can the product, promotion, price, and distribution be standardized and in which ways must they be adapted to meet target market requirements? Incorrect decisions at this point lead to costly mistakes through efficiency loss from lack of standardization; products inappropriate for the intended market; and/or costly mistakes in improper pricing, advertising, and promotional blunders. The primary goal of Phase 2 is to decide on a marketing mix adjusted to the cultural constraints imposed by the uncontrollable elements of the environment that effectively achieve corporate objectives and goals.

An example of the type of analysis done in Phase 2 is the process used by the Nestlé Company. Each product manager has a country fact book that includes much of the information suggested in Phase 1. The country fact book analyzes in detail a variety of culturally related questions. In Germany, the product manager for coffee must furnish answers to a number of questions: How does a German rank coffee in the hierarchy of consumer products? Is Germany a high or a low per capita consumption market? (These facts alone can be of enormous consequence. In Sweden the annual per capita consumption of coffee is 18 pounds, while in Japan it's half a gram!) How is coffee used—in bean form, ground, or powdered? If it is ground, how is it brewed? Which coffee is preferred—Brazilian Santos blended with Colombian coffee, or robusta from the Ivory Coast? Is it roasted? Do the people prefer dark roasted or blond coffee? (The color of Nestlé's soluble coffee must resemble as closely as possible the color of the coffee consumed in the country.) As a result of the answers to these and other questions, Nestlé produces 200 types of instant coffee, from the dark robust espresso preferred in Latin countries to the lighter blends popular in the United States. Almost $50 million a year is spent in four research laboratories around the world experimenting with new shadings

---

[34] David Ricks, *Big Business Blunders: Mistakes in Multinational Marketing* (Homewood, Ill.: Richard D. Irwin, 1983) p. 36.

in color, aroma, and flavor.[35] Do the Germans drink coffee after lunch or with their breakfast? Do they take it black or with cream or milk? Do they drink coffee in the evening? Do they sweeten it? (In France, the answer is clear: in the morning, coffee with milk; at noon, black coffee— i.e., two totally different coffees.) At what age do people begin drinking coffee? Is it a traditional beverage, as in France, or is it a form of rebellion among the young as in England where coffee drinking has been taken up in defiance of tea-drinking parents, or a gift as in Japan? There is a coffee boom in tea-drinking Japan were Nescafé is considered a luxury gift item; instead of chocolates and flowers, Nescafé is toted in fancy containers to dinners and birthday parties. With such depth of information, the product manager can evaluate the marketing mix in terms of the information in the country fact book.

Phase 2 also permits the marketer to determine possibilities for standardization. By grouping all countries together and looking at similarities, market characteristics that can be standardized become evident.

Frequently, the results of the analysis in Phase 2 indicate that the marketing mix would require such drastic adaptation that a decision not to enter a particular market is made. For example, a product may have to be reduced in physical size to fit the needs of the market, but the additional manufacturing cost of a smaller size may be too high to justify market entry. Also the price required to show a profit might be too high for a majority of the market to afford. If there is no way to reduce the price, sales potential at the higher price may be too low to justify entry.

On the other hand, additional research in this phase may provide information that can suggest ways to standardize marketing programs among two or more country markets. This was the case for Nestlé when research revealed that young coffee drinkers in England and Japan had identical motivations. As a result, Nestlé now uses principally the same message in both markets.

The answers to three major questions are generated in Phase 2: (1) Which elements of the marketing mix can be standardized and where is standardization not culturally possible? (2) Which cultural/environmental adaptations are necessary for successful acceptance of the marketing mix? And (3) will adaptation costs allow profitable market entry? Based on the results in Phase 2, a second screening of countries may take place with some countries dropped from further consideration. The next phase in the planning process is development of a marketing plan.

Phase 3—Developing the Marketing Plan.   At this stage of the planning process, a marketing plan is developed for the target market—whether a

---

[35] Shawn Tully, "Nestlé Shows How to Gobble Markets," *Fortune*, January 16, 1989, p. 75.

single country or a global market set. It begins with a situation analysis and culminates in a specific action program for the market. The specific plan establishes what is to be done, by whom, how it is to be done, and when. Included are budgets and sales and profit expectations. Just as in Phase 2, a decision not to enter a specific market may be made if it is determined that company marketing objectives and goals cannot be met.

Phase 4—Implementation and Control.   A go decision in Phase 3 triggers implementation of specific plans and anticipation of successful marketing. However, the planning process does not end at this point. All marketing plans require coordination and control (Phase 4) during the period of implementation. Many businesses do not control marketing plans as thoroughly as they could even though they could increase their success with continuous monitoring and control. An evaluation and control system requires performance objectives for successive time intervals covering the duration of the plan, a means of measuring against predetermined stan-

---

BOX 10–8
The VW Beetle—The First Global Product?

Much has been written recently about global marketing and global products. The general idea is that a global product is well-built, serves a recognizable purpose, is dependable, and inexpensive. Perhaps the global product has been around for over 50 years. In the mid-1930s the people's car or Volkswagen was driven for the first time. The car of infinite popularity, the Beetle, celebrated its 50th anniversary in 1985. There were over 20 million produced, rivaling the Model T Ford, at only 15 million.

The Beetle proved to be a successful car in almost every country in the world. It was first built in 1935, but World War II broke out before it was popularized. After the war (where it served as Germany's equivalent to the Jeep), the Beetle caught the fancy of American buyers and nearly 5 million were sold. It even became a movie star; painted with a racing stripe and the number 53, it became "Herbie" and starred in a series of Walt Disney movies beginning with *The Love Bug* and finally ending with *Herbie Goes Bananas*. Americans haven't been able to buy Beetles since 1980, but they are produced in Mexico and Brazil for the Latin American market at a fraction of the original production numbers—400 a day compared to 5,500 a day in 1971. The Beetle provided basic transportation that was dependable and inexpensive. The Beetle sounds much like the global product so many articles are written about today.

Source: "Volkswagen Beetle: The Ubiquitous Bug Turns 50," *The Wall Street Journal*, October 18, 1985, p. 34.

dards, plus the flexibility to take corrective action, that is, to bring the plan back on track should standards of performance fall short. As discussed in Chapter 20, a global orientation facilitates the difficult but extremely important tasks of coordinating and controlling an international marketing plan. The complexities of operating internationally make coordination and control a critical part of management responsibility in international marketing.

While the model is presented as a series of sequential phases, the planning process is a dynamic, continuous set of interacting variables with information continuously building among phases. The phases outline a crucial path to be followed for effective, systematic planning.

Although the model depicts a global company operating in multiple country markets, it is equally applicable for a company interested in a single country. Phases 1 and 2 are completed for each country being considered, and Phases 3 and 4 are developed individually for the target market whether it consists of a single country or a series of separate country markets. A global company uses the same process but integrates planning and information to serve as many markets as feasible and then concentrates on a global market set in Phases 3 and 4.

Utilizing a strategic planning process encourages the decision maker to consider all variables that affect the success of a company's plan. Furthermore, it provides the basis for viewing all country markets and their interrelationships as an integrated global unit. By following the guidelines presented in the Appendix, "The Country Notebook—A Guide for Developing a Marketing Plan," the international marketer can put the strategic planning process into operation.[36]

As a company expands into larger numbers of foreign markets with several products, it becomes more difficult to efficiently manage all products across all markets. Strategic marketing planning helps the marketer focus on all the variables to be considered for successful global marketing. Regardless of which of the three strategies (domestic market extension, multidomestic, or global) a company chooses, rigorous information gathering, analysis, and planning are necessary for successful marketing. In addition to determining the firm's overall global strategy, international marketing management includes shaping the organization to achieve that strategy.[37] As companies expand their global reach and become concerned with strategic planning, the issue of an effective organization surfaces.

---

[36] Students engaged in class projects involving a country analysis should see the Appendix for a set of guidelines on developing cultural, economic, and market analyses of a country.

[37] "Can Maytag Clean up around the World?" *Business Week,* January 30, 1989, pp. 86–87.

ORGANIZATIONAL STRATEGY

An international marketing plan should optimize the resources committed to stated company objectives. The organizational plan must include the type of organizational arrangements to be used, the mode and timing of entry, and the scope and location of responsibility. The localization of decision-making authority and the degree of autonomy at each level of decision making are crucial decisions in the planning stage. Even though a planner spends time and effort developing a coordinated global marketing strategy, the plan is no better than its implementation. Multinational headquarters must rely on subsidiaries throughout the world for implementation of the plan. Many ambitious multinational plans meet with less than full success because of confused lines of authority, poor communications, and lack of cooperation between headquarters and subsidiary organizations.[38]

Responsibility for each marketing function must be assigned or the company could lose flexibility and decisiveness in the crucial early months in foreign markets. If lines of authority are clearly defined, then the equally important lines of communication usually function smoothly.

Enough flexibility must be planned into an organization to account for contingencies that inevitably arise. Companies in international partnerships have sometimes found their partners lacked the capital or the ability to cope with growing market potential and were forced to buy out unsatisfactory partners at exorbitant prices or to contend with an unsatisfactory operation. Because of the dynamic nature of international business, some executives tend to think in short-run terms even though long-range planning is crucial to continuing successful operations. In as short a period as five years, a business situation can change completely or a business relationship can undergo a total transformation.

Organizational arrangements employed in international marketing are difficult to categorize. Nearly every company has its own modification of a standard organizational pattern. Some firms profess to have one kind of organization when an analysis of their operations reveals an altogether different organizational setup.

In building an organization, important considerations include the level of policy decisions, length of chain of command, staff support, source of natural and personnel resources, degree of control, centralization, and the type or level of marketing involvement. Such considerations provide the general orientation for the international marketing organization which can be analyzed in terms of geography, function, and product.

---

[38] For an interesting approach used by Beech Aircraft Corporation to enhance communications, see "International Team Marketing," *The Conference Board's Management Briefing: Marketing,* Vol. 4, No. 1, February–March 1989, pp. 1–2.

BOX 10–9
Anheuser-Busch Goes International but Not with Budweiser

Anheuser-Busch made a decision to begin distributing its beer in Europe's largest beer markets: Great Britain, Germany, and France. Distribution agreements were made with some of Europe's largest brewers but there was one hitch—they can't use the brand name Budweiser in Europe.

In 1911 Anheuser-Busch purchased American rights to the name and recipe for the beer from the brewers of Budweis in Czechoslovakia. The Czechs sold the United States rights but held on to all rights in Europe. Budweis' Budweiser brand beer is available in Europe so the U.S. beer is sold under the brand name of *Anheuser-Busch*.

Source: From "Bitte, Herr Ober, ein Anheuser-Busch!" *World Business Weekly*, June 22, 1981, p. 42.

A company may be organized by product lines but have geographical subdivisions under the product categories. Both may be supplemented by functional staff support. Exhibit 10–4 shows such a combination. Modifications of this basic combination arrangement are used by a majority of large companies doing business internationally.

Structural Basis

International marketing organizations are usually structured around one of three alternatives: global product divisions responsible for the sales of their products throughout the world; geographical divisions responsible for all products and functions within a given geographical area; and, a matrix organization consisting of either of these arrangements with a centralized functional staff, or a combination of area operations and global product management.[39]

Companies that adopt the global product division structure are generally experiencing rapid growth and have broad, diverse product lines.[40] Geographic structures work best when a close relationship with national and local governments is important. The matrix form—the most expensive of the three organizational structures—is growing in popularity with compa-

---

[39] James F. Bolt, "Global Competitors: Some Criteria for Success," *Business Horizons*, January–February 1988, pp. 38–39.

[40] "Colgate-Palmolive Realigns Staff in Europe in Advance of 1992," *Journal of Commerce*, September 26, 1988, p. 5.

EXHIBIT 10–4 Schematic Marketing Organization Plan Combining Product, Geographic, and Functional Approaches

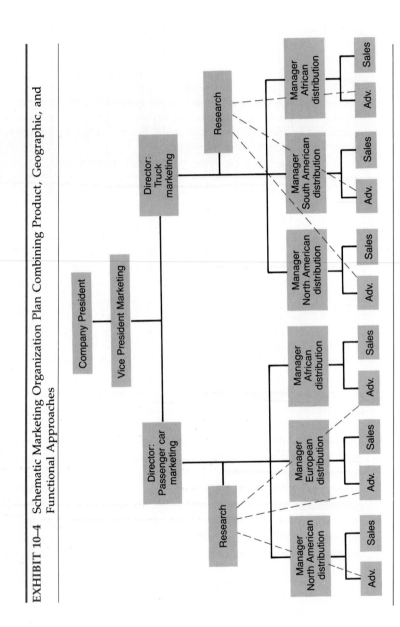

BOX 10–10
Just Getting Started

Soviet manufacturers are now awake to the need for marketing abroad but have only taken the first few steps away from the bed. Moscow opened a 13-day Soviet Export Goods Exposition in New York. The show offered products ranging from Russian Crown Sables to fashions by Moscow's All Union Fashion House. Kamchatka crab legs competed for attention with a 10,000-ton icebreaker.

The Expo also showed Soviet officials where they have some work to do on market research and sales. Some Soviets refused orders from American retailers because orders were not large enough, not understanding the principle of test-marketing a product before making a large investment.

The Soviets knew that Americans loved home appliances, so they brought their best hi-fi stereo equipment only to discover that phonographs are losing ground to cassette and compact disc players.

Asked the price of a prototype, steamlined Soviet automobile, the display attendant said there was no price. "Why do you keep asking me questions for which there are no answers?" he asked.

"I can honestly say we are in the Stone Age in advertising," said a Soviet official at the show.

The Soviet Union has begun a special program to educate its people at international business schools.

Source: Adapted from Robert Ebiscah, "Bolshevik Business," Associated Press News Release December 27, 1988.

nies as they reorganize for global competition. Eastman Kodak Company shifted from a functional organization to a matrix system based on business units. The traditional manufacturing, marketing, and R&D divisions have been replaced by 19 product-based business units with geographical responsibility.[41] NCR Corporation (formerly National Cash Register) is another firm whose reorganization reflects the need to build a truly global management structure. NCR, a multinational company for almost 100 years, operated for most of that time with an emphasis on domestic business; everything else was grouped into what was referred to as "the overseas business."

Such a restrictive view of international business has been replaced with a global perspective and an organization that includes five marketing groups, four international, and one national.[42] As multinational companies

---

[41] "Kodak's Matrix System Focuses on Product Business Units," *Business International*, July 18, 1988, pp. 221–22.

[42] Norman A. Cocke, "NCR Corporation: 100 Years of International Trade," *Export Today*, Fall 1986, pp. 17–20.

face increasing competitive pressure to develop global strategies, adapting the corporate organization to match global objectives is crucial. The rules for doing business in a global market are changing and the organizational structure must change to reflect new opportunities and levels of competitiveness.[43]

Locus of Decision

Considerations of where decisions will be made, by whom, and by which method constitute a major element of organizational strategy. Management policy must be explicit about which decisions are to be made at corporate headquarters, which at international headquarters, which at regional levels, and which at national or even local levels. Most companies also limit the amount of money to be spent at each level. Decision levels for determination of policy, strategy, and tactical decisions must be established. Tactical decisions normally should be made at the lowest possible level without country-by-country duplication. If a tactical decision applies to several countries, it probably should be made at the regional level, but if it applies to only one country, it should be made at the national level.

When U.S. expatriate managers and foreign national managers are working together either in a training or working capacity, it is especially important to delineate the areas of decision-making responsibility for each party. Predetermination of the final decision-making authority among product managers, functional managers, and line managers also can lessen possible conflict.

When determining the locus of decision, the method of decision making to be employed should also be considered. Europeans tend to have one fairly highly placed executive make decisions autonomously. Americans are more likely to delegate decision making to a lower level of management and use various committee arrangements. Japanese are noted for their *ringi* type of decision which calls for consensus.

Centralized versus Decentralized Organizations

An infinite number of organizational patterns of *headquarters activities* of multinational firms exist, but most fit into one of three categories: centralized, regionalized, or decentralized organizations. The fact that all of the systems are used indicates that each has certain advantages and disadvantages. Chief advantages of centralization are the availability of experts at one location, the ability to exercise a high degree of control on both the

---

[43] Mohrman and Mitroff, "Business Not as Usual," p. 37.

planning and implementation phases, and the centralization of all records and information.

Companies often shift from one pattern to another to gain temporary advantages. Franklin Mint Corporation moved its international division from Philadelphia to London to facilitate expansion of the firm's overseas sales. Four years later, having succeeded in establishing its international base, the parent company moved its offices back to Philadelphia so marketing and planning personnel could be in closer contact with parent-company management. Now the company uses what it calls a satellite organizational arrangement for its branches. Each established branch takes responsibility for new branches in adjacent countries until they are well established. This system allows support from experienced executives in a similar market during critical start-up periods.

Some companies effect extreme decentralization by selecting competent managers and giving them full responsibility for national or regional operations. These executives are in direct day-to-day contact with the market but lack a broad company view, which can mean partial loss of control for the parent company. Massey Ferguson has nine major market subsidiaries, each operating quasi-independently. All are run by nationals with the support of an "export" subsidiary in Toronto to provide staff support and maintain contact. Phillips Lamp, the fourth largest industrial company outside the United States, operated as a loosely run collection of national companies for 14 years after formation of the European Community. Its decentralized organizational approach is considered to have seriously hampered company growth before the organization was centralized and tightened to take advantage of Britain's entry into the EC.

Square D Company, a manufacturer of over 18,000 electrical distribution and control products, has developed an interesting combination approach. Prior to its reorganization, senior management at corporate headquarters controlled international strategy. The overall strategy was for U.S. corporate headquarters to direct manufacturing subsidiaries to sell U.S. products overseas. Communications between managers in the United States and overseas subsidiaries were infrequent, and foreign subsidiaries lacked line authority to execute timely strategic plans. Although Square D had a strong international network of manufacturing facilities and sales offices, the corporate organization provided inadequate linkages to take advantage of that network. As a result, the company tried to sell U.S. products without sufficient sensitivity to regional market requirements. This fragmented international organization dominated by domestic operations became increasingly inadequate as global competition intensified.

The reorganization focused on improving coordination and communications among the various regions. It was based on a global management structure, with a product/regional matrix encompassing three business units (distribution equipment, power equipment, and controls) and five regional segments (the United States, Asia Pacific, Canada, Europe, and

Latin America). By creating an organizational structure emphasizing global line responsibilities and cooperation between the corporate office and operations at all management levels, Square D has improved communications of market level information to the business unit responsible for manufacturing.[44] The trend seems to be toward regionalized and/or decentralized systems designed to combine the control and expertise of a central organization with the close contact of a decentralized organization.[45]

In many cases, whether or not a company's formal organizational structure is centralized or decentralized, the informal organization reflects some aspect of all organizational systems. This is especially true relative to the locus of decision making. Studies show that even though product decisions may be highly centralized, subsidiaries may have a substantial amount of local influence in pricing, advertising, and distribution decisions. If a product is culturally sensitive, the decisions are more apt to be decentralized.

SUMMARY

Market-oriented firms are finding greater competitiveness in world markets makes it essential to assume a global perspective in organizational structure. Increasingly, company objectives, structure of the market, and the competitive environment require the greater efficiencies found in standardizing across all markets whenever feasible. Organizing for marketing may be complicated even for one country, but, when a company is doing business internationally, the problems are multiplied. A global marketing perspective helps focus company objectives in an integrated pattern instead of a fragmented one. Company objectives vary from market to market and from time to time; the structure of international markets also changes periodically and from country to country, and the competitive, governmental and economic parameters affecting organization are in a constant state of flux. These variations require the international marketing executive to be especially flexible and creative in orientation and organizing organization for international marketing.

Level, type, and extent of control are relevant organizational determinants given prime consideration in the marketing approach to international organization. This chapter considers international organization first from the viewpoint of the parent company arrangements that are used in directing the world marketing operation. Second, it considers the various arrange-

---

[44] "Global Organization: Square D Unites Managers to Compete Globally," *Business International,* September 21, 1987, pp. 297–302.

[45] See, for example, Jeremy Main, "The Winning Organization," *Fortune,* September 26, 1988, pp. 50–60.

ments that may be used in the actual operations of the worldwide marketing activity, including a variety of alternatives of owned or external organizations which may be subject to tight or loose control, depending on the wishes of management. Many international marketers utilize several different organizational structures, and may be classed as having a conglomerate organizational pattern.

Change, adaptation, and restructuring are ever-present needs within growing companies operating in constantly changing markets, so organization for international marketing should be built around dynamic elements of the marketplace.

QUESTIONS

1. Define:

   managing agent   multidomestic market
   joint venture   concept
   domestic market extension   global market concept
      concept

2. Define strategic planning. How is strategic planning different for international marketing than domestic marketing?

3. Discuss the benefits to a MNC of accepting the global market concept.

4. The relationship between corporate organization structure and strategic planning is both intimate and powerful. Discuss.

5. In Phases 1 and 2 of the international planning process, countries may be dropped from further consideration as potential markets. Discuss some of the conditions in each phase that may exist in a country that would lead a marketer to exclude a country.

6. Assume that you are the director of international marketing for a company producing refrigerators. Select one country in Latin America and one in Europe and develop screening criteria to use in evaluating the two countries. Make any additional assumptions that are necessary about your company.

7. "The dichotomy typically drawn between export marketing and overseas marketing is partly fictional; from a marketing standpoint, they are but alternative methods of capitalizing on foreign market opportunities." Discuss.

8. Review the parameters complicating international marketing organization.

9. How will entry into a developed foreign market differ from entry into a relatively untapped market?

10. What is the value of the marketing approach to international organization?

11. How do governments influence the organizational pattern of companies in international business?

12. Formulate a general rule for deciding where international business decisions should be made.

13. Explain the popularity of joint ventures.

14. Compare the organizational implications of joint ventures versus licensing.

CHAPTER

11

Researching Global Markets

A study of international marketing blunders leads to one conclusion—the majority of mistakes made could have been avoided if the decision maker had better knowledge of the market. The broader the scope of a company's international operations, the more critical information becomes for making successful decisions. The quality of information available to a foreign marketer varies from uninformed opinion (i.e., the marketer's SRC or self-reference criterion), to thoroughly researched fact. The purpose of marketing research is to provide the most accurate and reliable data possible within the limits imposed by time, cost, and the present state of the art. The measure of the competent researcher is the ability to utilize the most sophisticated and adequate techniques and methods available within these limits.

Marketing research is the *systematic gathering, recording, and analyzing of data to provide information useful in marketing decision making*. When operating in foreign markets, the need for thorough information as a substitute for uninformed opinion is equally as important as it is in domestic marketing.

International marketing research and *marketing research* are synonymous since research is basically the same whether applied in Hoboken, New Jersey, or Colombo, Sri Lanka.

Generally, the tools and techniques for research remain the same in foreign and domestic marketing, but the environments within which they are applied are different, thus creating difficulty. Rather than acquiring new and exotic methods of research, the international marketing researcher must develop the ability for imaginative and deft application of tried and tested techniques in sometimes totally strange milieus. The mechanical problems of implementing foreign marketing research might vary from country to country, but the overall objectives for foreign and domestic marketing research are basically the same—to answer questions with current, valid information that a marketer can use to design and implement successful marketing programs. Within a foreign environment, the frequently differing emphasis on the kinds of information needed, the often limited variety of tools and techniques applicable, and the difficulty of implementing the research process constitute the challenges facing most international marketing researchers.[1]

This chapter deals with the operational problems encountered in gathering information in foreign countries for use by international marketers. Emphasis is on those elements of data generation that usually prove especially troublesome in conducting research in an environment other than the United States. There is also a summary of secondary sources available through public and private agencies followed by a section on multinational marketing information systems.

BREADTH AND SCOPE OF INTERNATIONAL MARKETING RESEARCH

A basic difference between domestic and foreign market research is the broader scope necessary for foreign research. Research can be divided into three types based on information needs. These are: (1) general information about the country, area, and/or market; (2) specific information used to solve problems arising in advertising, pricing, distribution, and product development; and (3) the forecasting of future marketing requirements by anticipating social, economic, and consumer trends within specific markets or countries. In domestic operations, the marketing research department is usually responsible only for the second type because other departments are responsible for such activities as business and economic research.

In international marketing research, the researcher's activities are frequently much broader than those of a domestic marketer and often involve all types of information essential to conducting business abroad.[2] A foreign market researcher is routinely expected to provide all the information rele-

---

[1] For a complete discussion of marketing research in foreign environments, see Susan P. Douglas and C. Samuel Craig, *International Marketing Research* (Englewood Cliffs, N.J.: Prentice-Hall, 1983).

[2] For an interesting comparison of domestic and international research, see Kjell Gronhaug and John L. Graham, "International Marketing Research Revisited," in *Advances in International Marketing*, vol. 2, S. Tamer Cavusgil, ed. (Greenwich, Conn.: JAI Press, 1987), pp. 121–37.

vant to the question of a firm entering a new market—political stability of the country, cultural attributes, geographical characteristics, market characteristics, and projections of potential economic growth. In addition, a foreign market research department might also be expected to be the source of information necessary to compensate for lack of empathy within a strange environment, probable language deficiencies, and the lack of day-to-day market contact normally maintained in the home market. Unisys Corporation's planning steps call for collecting and assessing data in three major categories: (1) environmental conditions, (2) divisional assessment, and (3) review of strategies. The environmental conditions section includes:

1. Economic: General data on growth of the economy, inflation, business cycle trends, and the like; profitability analysis for the division's products; specific industry economic studies; analysis of overseas economies; and key economic indicators for the United States and major foreign countries.
2. Sociological and political climate: A general noneconomic review of conditions affecting the division's business. In addition to the more obvious subjects, it also covers ecology, safety, leisure time, and their potential impact on the division's business and so on.
3. Overview of market conditions: A detailed analysis of market conditions the division faces by market segment, including international.
4. Summary of the technological environment: A summary of the "state of the art" technology as it relates to the divison's business. It, too, is carefully broken down by product segments.
5. A last section reviews competitors' market shares, methods of market segmentation, products, and apparent strategies on an international scope.[3]

Such in-depth information is necessary for a sound marketing decision. For the domestic marketer, most such information has been acquired after years of experience with a single market; but, in foreign markets, this basic information must be gathered for each new market.[4]

There is a basic difference between information ideally needed and that which is collectible and/or used. Many firms engaged in foreign marketing do not make decisions with the benefit of the information listed. Cost, time, and the human elements are critical variables. Some firms have neither the appreciation for information nor adequate time or money for implementation of research. As a firm becomes more committed to foreign marketing and the cost of possible failure increases, greater emphasis is placed on research. Consequently, a global firm is or should be engaged

---

[3] *Corporate External Affairs* (New York: Business International, December 1975), p. 142.

[4] For an idea of the kind of information exporters prefer, see Van R. Wood and Jerry R. Goolsby, "Foreign Market Information Preferences of Established U.S. Exporters," *International Marketing Review*, Winter 1987, pp. 43–52.

in the most sophisticated and exhaustive kinds of research activities, while the infrequent or part-time exporter has less concern.

In addition to the degree of need, the cost of research must be considered. When the cost of research, the business risk involved, and the probable profit potential of markets are incompatible, a decision for research may lead to minimal commitment. The cost of original research can outweigh the value of information gathered and must be evaluated accordingly. Less costly secondary information is also available; for example, many export agencies provide information as part of their services to exporters. This type of secondary data is a part of the total research effort. When considering foreign-market information needs, two questions arise: (1) What are the procedures and problems of collecting data? And (2) who should collect the data?

BOX 11–1
Are Instincts Better than Marketing Research?

When Sony Corporation researched the market for a lightweight portable cassette player, the research showed that consumers would not buy a tape recorder that did not record. Company Chairman Akio Morita decided to introduce the Walkman anyway and the rest is history. Today it is one of Sony's most successful products.

Japanese companies use market surveys but they trust their instincts first. Japanese executives put much more faith in information they get directly from wholesalers and retailers in the distribution channels. A good example is Canon's decision on a new U.S. distribution strategy. The company's senior management became concerned about U.S. camera sales. Other product lines were doing well but Canon sales had lost ground to the chief competitor, Minolta. Canon finally decided it needed its own sales subsidiary because its distributor, Bell & Howell Company, wouldn't give additional support for the Canon line. Senior managers didn't use broad surveys of consumers or retailers to make this decision. They sent three managers to the United States to look into the problem and changed strategies based on their observations.

Canon's head of the U.S. team spent almost six weeks visiting camera stores and other retail outlets across the United States. On entering a store, the Japanese manager would act as if he was just a customer browsing around. By asking simple questions like, "What cameras do you stock?" he could assess whether the dealer was enthusiastic or indifferent about the Canon line. Based on their research, Canon changed their distribution strategy. They dropped drugstores and other discount outlets to sell exclusively through speciality dealers serving an upscale, high-quality niche just below Nikon's targeted segment.

Source: Adapted from Johny K. Johansson, and Ikujiro Nonaka, "Marketing Research the Japanese Way," *Harvard Business Review*, May–June 1987, pp. 16–22.

THE RESEARCH PROCESS

A marketing research study is always a compromise imposed by limits of time, cost, and the present state of the art; that is, every study would have the possibility of being more accurate and reliable if there had been more time to design and conduct the study, more money to spend, and if the techniques of research were without imperfection. Obviously such conditions will never exist. Nevertheless, the researcher must always strive for the most accurate and reliable information within existing limits and constraints. A key to successful research is a systematic and orderly approach to the collection and analysis of data. Whether a research program is conducted in New York or Bogotá, Colombia, the research process should always proceed along the following steps:

1. Define the research problem and establish research objectives.
2. Determine the sources of information to fulfill the research objectives.
3. Gather the relevant data from secondary and/or primary sources.
4. Analyze, interpret, and present the results.

The researcher's task is to execute each of these steps with maximum objectivity and accuracy within the limitations of cost, time, and ability.

Although the steps in a research program are similar for all countries, variations and problems in implementation occur because of differences in cultural and economic development. Subsequent sections illustrate some frequently encountered problems of the international market researcher. It must be emphasized that these problems vary from country to country. While the problems of research in England or Canada may be similar to those in the United States, research in Germany, South Africa, or Mexico may offer a multitude of very different and difficult distinctions from one another.[5] These distinctions become apparent with the first step in the research process—formulation of the problem.

Defining the Problem and Establishing Research Objectives

The first step in the research process is to define the research problem and establish specific research objectives. The major difficulty here is translating the business problem into a research problem with a set of specific, researchable objectives. This initial stage of research frequently goes amiss because of improper definition. Researchers often embark on the research process with only a vague grasp of the total problem.

---

[5] For an interesting articulation of these problems, see John Monaco, "Overcoming the Obstacles to International Research," *Marketing News*, August 29, 1988, p. 12.

This first step in research is more critical in foreign markets since an unfamiliar environment tends to cloud problem definition. Researchers either fail to anticipate the influence of the local culture on the problem or fail to identify the self-reference criterion and treat the problem definition as if it were in the researcher's home environment. A student of international marketing reads of foreign business failures from what appears to be a simple error and wonders why the company did not conduct research. In many of those cases, research was conducted, but the questions asked were more appropriate for the U.S. market than for the foreign one. Isolating the self-reference criterion is a crucial step in the problem formulation stage of international marketing research.

Other difficulties in foreign research stem from failure to establish problem limits broad enough to include all relevant variables. Information on a far greater range of factors is necessary to offset the unfamiliar cultural background of the foreign market. Consider proposed research concerning consumption patterns and attitudes about hot milk-based drinks. In the United Kingdom, hot milk-based drinks are considered to have sleep-inducing, restful, and relaxing properties and are traditionally consumed prior to bedtime. People in Thailand, however, drink the same milk-based drinks in the morning on the way to work and see them as being invigorating, energy-giving, and stimulating. If one's only experience is the United States, the picture is further clouded since hot milk-based drinks are frequently associated with cold weather either in the morning or evening and for different reasons at each time of day. The market researcher must be certain that the problem definition is sufficiently broad to cover the whole range of response possibilities and not be clouded by his or her self-reference criterion.

Once the problem is adequately defined and research objectives established, the researcher must determine the availability of the information needed. If the data are available—if they have been collected by some other agency—the researcher should then consult these secondary sources. If no data are available, or the secondary sources appear inadequate, it is necessary to begin the collection of primary data.

PROBLEMS OF THE AVAILABILITY AND USE OF SECONDARY DATA

The breadth of many foreign marketing research studies and the marketer's lack of familiarity with a country's basic socioeconomic and cultural data result in considerable demand for information generally available from secondary sources in the United States. Unfortunately, such data are not as available in foreign markets. The U.S. government provides comprehensive statistics for the United States. Periodic censuses of U.S. population, housing, business, and agriculture have been taken, in some cases, for over 100 years. Commercial sources, trade associations, management groups, and state and local governments also provide the researcher with additional sources of detailed U.S. market information.

Few foreign countries can match data available in the United States; data collection has only recently begun in many countries. However, data collection is improving substantially through the efforts of organizations such as the United Nations and the Organization for Economic Cooperation and Development (OECD). As a country becomes more involved in international business, a greater interest in basic data and better collection methods develops.

Availability of Data.   Among the three critical shortcomings of secondary data on foreign markets is the paucity of detailed data for many market areas. Much of the secondary data an American marketer is accustomed to having about United States markets is just not available for many countries. Detailed data on the numbers of wholesalers, retailers, manufacturers, and facilitating services, for example, are unavailable for many parts of the world as are data on population and income. This appears to be true even for the most developed nations.

Reliability of Data.   Available data may not have the level of reliability necessary for confident decision making for many reasons. Official statistics are sometimes too optimistic, reflecting national pride rather than practical reality, while tax structures and fear of the tax collector often adversely affect data. Although not unique to them, less-developed countries lacking well-defined marketing infrastructures are particularly prone to be both overly optimistic and unreliable in reporting relevant economic data about their countries. As one researcher noted, Saudi Arabian statistics are almost as fluid "as the nation's shifting sands." An American survey team verified that 60 million frozen chickens had been imported into Saudi Arabia in 1975 although official figures reported only 10 million. A Japanese company found that 40,000 air conditioners had actually been imported but official figures were underestimated by 30,000 units. Whether errors of such magnitude are intentional or simply the result of sloppy record-keeping is not always clear.

In the case of the European Community (EC), tax policies can affect the accuracy of reported data. Production statistics are frequently inaccurate because these countries collect taxes on domestic sales. Thus, companies have been known to shave their production statistics a bit to match the sales reported to tax authorities. Conversely, foreign trade statistics may be blown up slightly because each country in the EC grants some form of export subsidy. Errors of this type are critical for a marketer who relies on secondary data for forecasting or estimating market demand.

Researchers should always have a healthy degree of skepticism about secondary data regardless of the source. The economics department of

BOX 11–2
International Data: Caveat Emptor

The statistics used . . . are subject to more than the usual number of caveats and qualifications concerning comparability than are usually attached to economic data. Statistics on income and consumption were drawn from national-accounts data published regularly by the United Nations and the Organization for Economic Cooperation and Development. These data, designed to provide a "comprehensive statistical statement about the economic activity of a country," are compiled from surveys sent to each of the participating countries (118 nations were surveyed by the UN). However, despite efforts by the UN and the OECD to present the data on a comparable basis, differences among various countries concerning definitions, accounting practices, and recording methods persist. In Germany, for instance, consumer expenditures are estimated largely on the basis of the turnover tax, while in the United Kingdom, tax-receipt data are frequently supplemented by household surveys and production data.

Even if data-gathering techniques in each country were standardized, definitional differences would still remain. These differences are relatively minor except in a few cases; for example, Germany classifies the purchase of a television set as an expenditure for "recreation and entertainment," while the same expenditure falls into the "furniture, furnishings, and household equipment" classification in the United States.

While income and consumption expenditures consist primarily of cash transactions, there are several important exceptions. Both income and expenditures include the monetary value of food, clothing, and shelter received in lieu of wages. Also included are imputed rents on owner-occupied dwellings, in addition to actual rents paid by tenants. Wages and salaries, which make up the largest share of consumer income, include employer contributions to social security systems, private pension plans, life and casualty insurance plans, and family allowance programs. Consumer expenditures include medical services even though the recipient may make only partial payment; if, however, the same services are subsidized wholly by public funds, the transaction is listed as a government rather than a consumer expenditure.

Expenditures, as defined by both the UN and the OECD, include consumption outlays by households (including individuals living alone) and private nonprofit organizations. The latter include churches, schools, hospitals, foundations, fraternal organizations, trade unions, and other groups which furnish services to households free of charge or at prices that do not cover costs.

Source: David Bauer, "The Dimensions of Consumer Markets Abroad," *The Conference Board Record*, reprinted with permission.

the respected Organizaton of Economic Cooperation and Development (OECD) is one of the world's oldest sources of multinational economic data. For the most part, OECD data are among the most accurate to be found; yet it sometimes has been criticized for adjusting forecasts to the official line of its member governments. In fact, several years ago, it was charged that economic reports were so heavily weighed in favor of its wishful-thinking government members that an economic upturn was being forecast when, in fact, world economic conditions were already reflecting a downturn. In this incident, the OECD research staff was able to resist pressures so that accurate data were ultimately reported.

Comparability of Data.   The last problem involves the comparability and current of available data. In the United States, current sources of reliable and valid estimates of socioeconomic factors and business indicators are readily available. In other countries, especially those less-developed, data can be many years out of date as well as having been collected on an infrequent and unpredictable schedule. Naturally, the rapid change in socioeconomic features being experienced in many of these countries makes the problem of currency a vital one. Further, even though many countries are now gathering reliable data, there are generally no historical series with which to compare the current information.

A related problem is the manner in which data are collected and reported. Too frequently, data are reported in different categories or in categories much too broad to be of specific value. The term *supermarket*, for example, has a variety of meanings around the world. In Japan a supermarket is quite different from its American counterpart. The Japanese supermarkets are usually establishments in large cities occupying two- or three-story structures; they sell foodstuffs, daily necessities, and clothing on respective floors. Some even sell furniture, electric home appliances, stationery, and sporting goods and have a restaurant. General merchandise stores, shopping centers, and department stores are different from stores of the same name in the United States. These differences add to the difficulty of trying to understand the structure of the Japanese retail industry as well as differences in other countries.[6] The next section lists specific agencies that are sources of secondary data on foreign markets.

Validating Secondary Data.   The possibility of the shortcomings discussed here should be considered when using any source of information. Many countries have the same high standards of collection and preparation of data generally found in the United States but secondary data from any

---

[6] Shinya Nakata, "Retailing: Variety of Means and the Conglo-Merchants," *Sumitomo Quarterly*, Winter 1987, pp. 16–18.

source, including the United States, must be checked and interpreted carefully. As a practical matter, the following questions should be asked to effectively judge the reliability of data sources:

1. Who collected the data? Would there be any reason for purposely misrepresenting the facts?
2. For what purpose were the data collected?
3. How were the data collected? (methodology)
4. Are the data internally consistent and logical in light of known data sources or market factors?

In general, the availability and accuracy of recorded secondary data increase as the level of economic development increases. There are many exceptions; India is at a lower level of economic development than many Latin American countries but has more accurate and complete development of government-collected data.

Fortunately, interest in collecting quality statistical data rises as countries realize the value of extensive and accurate national statistics for orderly economic growth. This interest to improve the quality of national statistics has resulted in remarkable improvement in the availability of data over the last 20 years.

Corner shop, Bucharest, Rumania. Who knows the real sales volume? Secondary data sources of retail sales are often not accurate. (V. Ivanov/Journalism Services, Inc.)

SOURCES OF SECONDARY DATA

For almost any marketing research project, an analysis of avai
ary information is a useful and inexpensive first step. Alt
are information gaps, particularly for detailed market information, the
situation on data availability and reliability is improving. The principal
agencies that collect and publish information useful in international business are presented here, with some notations of selected publications.

U.S. Government.   The U.S. government actively promotes the expansion
of U.S. business into international trade. In the process of keeping U.S.
businesses informed of foreign opportunity, the U.S. government generates
a considerable amount of general and specific market data for use by
international market analysts. Although information is available from a
number of agencies of the U.S. government, the principal source of information is the Department of Commerce which makes its services available
to U.S. business in a variety of ways. First, information and assistance
are available either through personal consultation in Washington, D.C.,
or through any of the field offices of the International Trade Administration
(ITA) of the Department of Commerce located in key cities in the United
States. Second, the Department of Commerce works closely with trade
associations, chambers of commerce, and other interested associations in
providing information, consultation, and assistance in developing international commerce. Third, the department publishes a wide range of information available to interested persons at nominal cost.

   1. *Foreign Trade Report*, FT 410: U.S. exports—commodity by country.
The FT 410 provides a statistical record of all merchandise shipped from
the United States to foreign countries, including both quantity and dollar
value of these exports to each country during the month covered by the
report. Additionally, it contains cumulative export statistics from the first
of the calendar year. From this report, you can learn which of more than
150 countries have bought any of more than 3,000 U.S. products. By checking the FT 410 over a period of three or four years, one can determine
which countries have the largest and most consistent markets for specific
products.

   2. *International economic indicators:* Quarterly reports providing basic data
on the economy of the United States and seven other principal industrial
countries. Statistics included are gross national product, industrial production, trade, prices, finance, and labor. This report measures changes in
key competitive indicators and highlights economic prospects and recent
trends in the eight countries.

   3. *Market share reports:* An annual publication prepared from special computer runs shows U.S. participation in foreign markets for manufactured
products during the last five-year period. The 88 reports in a country's

series represent import values for U.S. and eight other leading suppliers and the U.S. percentage share for about 900 manufactured products.

4. *International marketing information series:* Publications that focus on foreign market opportunities for U.S. suppliers. This series is designed to assemble under a common format a diverse group of publications and reports available to the U.S. business community. The following publications are made available on a continuing basis under this program:

  a. Global market surveys. Extensive foreign market research is conducted on target industries and target business opportunities identified by the Commerce Department. Findings are developed into global market surveys. Each survey condenses foreign market research conducted in 15 or more nations into individual country market summaries.

  b. Country market sectoral surveys. These in-depth reports cover the most promising U.S. export opportunities in a single foreign country. About 15 leading industrial sectors usually are included. Surveys currently available deal with Brazil, Nigeria, Venezuela, Indonesia, and Japan.

  c. Overseas Business Reports (OBR). These reports provide basic background data for business people who are evaluating various export markets or are considering entering new areas. They include both developing and industrialized countries.

  d. Foreign economic trends and their implications in the United States. This series gives in-depth reviews of current business conditions, current and near-term prospects, and the latest available data on the gross national product, foreign trade, wage and price indexes, unemployment rates, and construction starts.

  e. *Business America* (formerly *Commerce America*). The Department of Commerce's principal periodical, a weekly news magazine, provides an up-to-date source of worldwide business activity covering topics of general interest and new developments in world and domestic commerce.

5. *Trade Opportunities Program (TOP):* Overseas trade opportunities, private and government, are transmitted to the TOP computers through various American embassies and councils. U.S. business firms can indicate the product or products they wish to export and the types of opportunities desired (direct sales and representation) in countries of interest. The TOP computer matches the foreign buyer's agent's or distributor's product interest with the U.S. subscriber's interest. When a match occurs, a trade opportunity notice is mailed to the U.S. business subscriber.

6. *Commercial Information Management System (CIMS):* CIMS is a new computer system linking the Department of Commerce to worldwide resources. It enhances the ability of commerce officers to assist exporters in overseas markets by providing detailed information on a more timely basis than the hard copy of past years that frequently was a year or more out of date before it became available. CIMS, an interactive system, dramatically shortens the time it takes to move information from foreign markets to international trade specialists at the department's district offices. Interested exporters contact a trade specialist who queries the CIMS data base about specific criteria such as country, product, industry, and marketing information. CIMS then constructs a package of information drawing from all parts of the system's data base. The system's information base is continually refined because new data are added to the data base as they are collected.[7]

In addition, the Department of Commerce provides a host of other information services. Exhibit 11–1 indicates the scope of information available through the Department of Commerce.[8] Besides the material available through the Department of Commerce, consultation and information are available from a variety of other U.S. agencies. For example, the Department of State, Bureau of the Census, and the Department of Agriculture can provide valuable assistance in the form of services and information for an American business interested in international operations.[9]

International Organizations.   A number of international organizations provide information and statistics on international markets. The *Statistical Yearbook,* an annual publication of the United Nations, provides comprehensive social and economic data for more than 250 countries around the world. Many regional organizations, such as the Organization for Economic Cooperation and Development (OECD), Pan American Union, and the European Community publish information statistics and market studies relating to their respective regions.

Chambers of Commerce.   In addition to government and organizational publications, many foreign countries maintain chamber-of-commerce offices in the United States functioning as permanent trade missions. These foreign chambers of commerce generally have research libraries available and are knowledgeable regarding further sources of information on specific products or marketing problems. There are also American chambers in most major trading cities of the world. Often the American Chamber of Commerce in Paris can give more current information and lists of potential business contacts in France than are available from any other source. A listing of chambers of commerce and other government and nongovernment agencies can be found in *A Directory of Foreign Organizations for Trade*

---

[7] Beverly Wolpert, "Commerce Department Arms Exporters with Up-to-Date Global Market Research" and "How to Use CIMS," *Global Trade,* June 1988, pp. 19–20.

[8] For a useful guide to the uses of these data in marketing research, see "A Step-by-Step Approach to Market Research," *Business America,* March 16, 1987, pp. 10–12.

[9] "Roadmap to Export Services," *Business America,* September 12, 1988, pp. 10–15.

EXHIBIT 11–1 Department of Commerce Information Sources

FAST — MATCH

A quick, easy way to match your international business requirements to the appropriate government programs or services designed to satisfy those needs

If you are seeking information regarding ⇨

Use ⬇

	Potential markets	Market research*	District sales leads	Agents/distributors	License	Credit analysis	Financial assistance	Risk insurance	Tax incentives
Foreign Trade Statistics (FT—410)	•	•							
Global Market Surveys	•	•							
Foreign Market Reports	•	•							
Market Share Reports	•	•							
Foreign Economic Trends	•	•							
Business America	•	•	•	•	•				
Commercial Exhibitions	+	+	•	•	•				
Overseas Business Reports (OBR)		•					•	•	
Overseas Private Investment Corporation		•							
Commerce Business Daily			•						
New Product Information Service			•	•	•				
Trade Opportunity Program (TOP)			•	•	•				
Industry Trade Lists			•	•	•				
Special Trade Lists			•	•	•				
Export Mailing List Service (EMLS)			•	•	•				
Agent/Distributor Service (ADS)				•					
World Traders Data Reports (WTDR)						•			
Export-Import Bank							•	•	
Foreign Credit Insurance Assoc. (FCIA)								•	
Domestic International Sales Corporation (DISC)							•		•

*Foreign trade outlook market profiles; industry trends; distribution and sales channels; transportation facilities; local business practices and customs; investment criteria; import procedures and trade regulations; and industrial property rights.

⁺ Research material developed regarding a planned exhibition and released to support promotional activities. Cost of services may be obtained from Commerce District Offices.

SOURCE: Department of Commerce, International Trade Administration (Washington, D.C.).

and Investment Promotion published by the U.S. Department of Commerce. The U.S. Chamber of Commerce publication, *Foreign Commerce Handbook: Basic Information and a Guide to Sources*, is an excellent reference source for foreign trade information.

Trade, Business, and Service Organizations.   Foreign trade associations are particularly good sources of information on specific products or product lines. Many associations perform special studies or continuing services in collecting comprehensive statistical data for a specific product group or industry. Although some information is proprietary in nature and available only to members of an association, nonmembers frequently have access to it under certain conditions. Up-to-date membership lists providing potential customers or competitors are often available to anyone requesting them, and a listing of foreign trade associations is usually annotated at the end of a specific *Trade List*.

Foreign service industries also supply valuable sources of information useful in international business. Service companies—such as commercial and investment banks, international advertising agencies, foreign-based research firms, economic research institutes, foreign carriers, shipping agencies, and freight forwarders—generally regard the furnishing of current, reliable information as part of their service function. The banking industry in foreign countries is particularly useful as a source of information on current local economic situations. The Chase Manhattan Bank in New York periodically publishes a newsletter on such subjects as the European Community. There are several good independently published reports on techniques, trends, forecasts, and other such current data. Many foreign banks publish periodic or special review newsletters relating to the local economy, providing a firsthand analysis of the economic situation of specific foreign countries. For example, the Kretiet Bank in Brussels published *Belgium, Key to the Common Market* and the Banco National Commercio Exterior in Mexico published *Mexico Facts, Figures, Trends*. Even though these publications are sometimes available without charge, they usually must be translated.

A number of research agencies specializing in detailed information on foreign markets provide information services on a subscription basis. A listing of commercial and investment banks in foreign countries, as well as a detailed list of special-purpose research institutes, can be found in *The Europa Yearbook*. At the end of this chapter is a list of sources of information that are helpful and available for purchase or subscription. Many can be found in major libraries.[10]

---

[10] For an interesting insight into creative uses by the Japanese of secondary information much of which is available in public libraries, see Alan K. Engel, "Number One in Competitor Intelligence," *Across the Board*, December 1987, pp. 43–47.

PROBLEMS OF GATHERING PRIMARY DATA

When there are no adequate sources of secondary data, the market researcher must collect primary data. The problems of foreign primary-data collection are different from those in the United States only in degree. The most significant factor affecting the success of a survey hinges on the willingness of respondents to provide the desired information, or their ability to articulate what they know; that is, the ability of the researcher to get unwilling respondents to provide correct and truthful information.[11]

Cultural differences offer the best explanation for the unwillingness or the inability of many to respond to research surveys. In some countries, the husband not only earns the money but also dictates exactly how it is to be spent. Because the husband controls the spending, it is he and not the wife who should be questioned to determine preferences and demand for many consumer goods. In such a situation, the resarcher may not properly identify the correct source of information and may also find varying degrees of unwillingness to answer personal gender-related inquiries.[12]

Unwillingness to Respond

Citizens of many countries do not feel the same legal and moral obligations to pay their taxes as we do in the United States. Tax evasion is an accepted practice for many and a source of pride for the more adept. Where such an attitude exists, taxes are arbitrarily assessed by the government and anyone asking questions about any topic from which tax assessment could be inferred is immediately suspected of being a tax agent and provided with incomplete or misleading information. One of the problems reported by the government of India in a recent population census was the underreporting of tenants by landlords trying to hide the actual number of people living in houses and flats. The landlords had been subletting accommodations illegally and were concealing their activities from the tax department.

In the United States, publicly held corporations are compelled by the Securities and Exchange Commission (SEC) to disclose certain operating figures on a periodic basis. In many European countries, such information is seldom if ever released and then most reluctantly. Attempts to enlist the cooperation of merchants in setting up a store sample for shelf inventory

---

[11] Yusuf A. Choudhry, "Pitfalls in International Marketing Research: Are You Speaking French Like a Spanish Cow?" *Akron Business and Economic Review,* Winter 1986, pp. 18–28.

[12] For a discussion of this problem in Saudi Arabia, see Cecil Tuncalp, "The Marketing Research Scene in Saudi Arabia, *European Journal of Marketing* 22, no. 5 (1988), pp. 15–22.

and sales information ran into strong resistance because of suspicions and a tradition of competitive secrecy. The resistance was overcome by the researcher's willingness to approach the problem step-by-step. As the retailer gained confidence in the researcher and realized the value of the data gathered, more and more necessary information was provided. Besides the reluctance of businesses to respond to surveys, local politicians in underdeveloped countries may interfere with studies in the belief they might be subversive and must be stopped or hindered. A few moments with local politicians can prevent days of delay.

In some cultures, women would never consent to an interview by a male or any stranger.[13] A French-Canadian woman does not like to be questioned and is likely to be reticent; she prefers privacy for herself and her family. In some societies, a man would certainly consider it beneath his dignity to discuss shaving habits or brand preference in personal clothing with anyone; and most emphatically not with a female interviewer. The growing resistance to surveys everywhere is a result of the misuse of interviewing by door-to-door salespeople claiming to be doing marketing research when, in fact, they are selling household items.

The paucity of available information may also stem from the inability of the respondent to articulate the answer. The ability to express attitudes and opinions about any product depends on the respondent's ability to recognize the usefulness and value of such a product. It is difficult for a respondent to formulate needs, attitudes, and opinions about goods whose use may not be understood, that have never been available, or that are not in common use within the community. In fact, it may be impossible for someone who has known only iceboxes to express accurate feelings or provide any reasonable information about purchase intentions, likes, or dislikes concerning electric refrigerators. Under these circumstances, the creative capabilities of the foreign marketing researcher undergo thorough testing.[14]

Although cultural differences may make survey research more difficult to conduct, it is possible. In some communities, it is necessary to enlist the aid of locally prominent people to open otherwise closed doors; in other situations, professional people and local students have been used as interviewers because of their knowledge of the market. As with most of the problems of collecting primary data, the difficulties are not insurmountable to a researcher aware of their existence.

---

[13] Naresh K. Malhotra, "A Methodology for Measuring Consumer Preferences in Developing Countries," *International Marketing Review*, Autumn 1988, pp. 52–64.

[14] Graham J. Hooley, David Shipley, and Natalie Krieger, "A Method for Modelling Consumer Perceptions of Country of Origin," *International Marketing Review*, Autumn 1988, pp. 67–76.

Sampling in Field Surveys

The greatest problem of sampling stems from the lack of adequate detail of population characteristics and available lists from which to draw meaningful samples. If current, reliable lists are not available, sampling becomes more complex and generally less reliable. In many countries, telephone directories, cross-index street directories, census tract and block data, and detailed social and economic characteristics of the population being studied are not available on a current basis if at all. The researcher has to estimate characteristics and population parameters, sometimes with little basic data on which to build an accurate estimate.

To add to the confusion, in some South American, Mexican, and Asian cities, street maps are unavailable, and, in some Asian metropolitan areas, streets are not identified nor are houses numbered. In contrast, one of the easier aspects of research in Japan is that names and addresses are normally available from the local *Inhabitants Register* compiled by the city or town government.

The adequacy of sampling techniques is also affected by a lack of detailed social and economic information. Without an age breakdown, for example, the researcher can never be certain of a representative sample requiring an age criterion, because there is no basis of comparison with the age distribution in the sample. A lack of detailed information does not prevent the use of sampling, it just makes it more difficult. In place of probability techniques, many researchers in such situations rely on convenient samples taken in marketplaces and other public gathering places. The danger in that solution comes from the differences in the respondents found at public gathering places. Due to the practice of *purdah*, for example, shopping mall interviews in Saudi Arabia would produce an all-male sample.

The effectiveness of various methods of communication (mail, telephone, and personal interview) in surveys is limited. In many countries telephone ownership is extremely low, making telephone surveys virtually worthless unless the survey is intended to cover only the wealthy. In Sri Lanka, fewer than 3 percent of the residents—only the wealthy—have telephones. Even if the respondent has a telephone, the researcher may still not be able to complete a call. It is estimated that in Cairo 50 percent of the telephone lines can be out of service at the same time, and 75 percent of all dialed calls fail to get through on the first attempt.

Inadequate mailing lists and poor postal service are more problems for the market researcher using mail to conduct research. In Nicaragua, delays of weeks in delivery are not unusual, and expected returns are lowered considerably because a letter can be mailed only at a post office. In addition to potentially poor mail service within countries is the extended length of time required for delivery and return when a mail survey is conducted from another country. Surface delivery can require three weeks or longer between some points on the globe, and although airmail reduces this time drastically, it also increases costs considerably.

The problems of sampling can best be summarized by one authority in Saudi Arabia who commented: "It is a formidable, if not impossible, task to draw probabilistic samples in Saudi Arabia. The sampling difficulties are so acute that nonprobabilistic sampling becomes a necessary evil."[15] He continues by listing all the problems encountered in drawing a random sample.

- There is no officially recognized census of population.
- Other listings that can serve as sampling frames do not exist.
- Telephone directories tend to be incomplete and out of date.
- Voter registration lists do not exist.
- Accurate maps of population centers are not available. Thus, cluster (area) samples cannot be taken.

He concludes that convenience sampling is the only alternative. The conditions described do not exist in all countries but they do illustrate why the collection of primary data requires creative applications of research techniques.

Cross-Cultural Studies—A Special Problem

As companies become global marketers and seek to standardize various parts of the marketing mix across several countries, cross-cultural studies become more important. A company needs to determine whether standardization or adaptation of the marketing mix is appropriate. Thus, market characteristics across diverse cultures must be compared for similarities and differences before a company proceeds with a global marketing strategy. The research difficulties discussed thus far have addressed problems of conducting research within a culture. When engaging in cross-cultural studies, many of these same problems further complicate the difficulty of cross-cultural comparisons. To complete a cross-cultural study done on perceived risk in the United States and Mexico, differences in survey methods, respondent selection, and interviewing techniques were required.[16] In the U.S. portion of the study, a telephone criss-cross directory was used to identify income areas from which streets were randomly selected; then, from the selected streets, one household was randomly picked for a telephone interview. Mexico does not have a source comparable

---

[15] Tuncalp, "The Marketing Research Scene," p. 18.

[16] Robert J. Hoover, Robert T. Green, and Joe Saeger, "A Cross-National Study of Perceived Risk," *Journal of Marketing*, July 1978, pp. 102–8.

Girl with turquoise paryak, India. Cross-cultural research must reflect different cultural norms. (Rich Clark/Journalism Services, Inc.)

to the criss-cross directory and it is estimated that 60 percent or more of the upper-middle and upper-class families in the city have unlisted telephone numbers. And since Mexican respondents are also reluctant to give information to strangers over the telephone, the research had to be designed differently. First, local, knowledgeable professionals were hired to identify upper-middle and upper-class residential sections of the city; from these sections, a sample of blocks was randomly chosen, and interviewers were instructed to begin at a randomly selected corner of each block to contact every third house for an interview.

The adaptations necessary to complete this cross-national study serve as good examples of the need for resourcefulness in international marketing research. However, it also raises a serious question about the reliability of data gathered in cross-national research. There is evidence that insufficient attention is given not only to nonsampling errors and other problems that can exist in improperly conducted cross-cultural studies but also to the appropriateness of consumer research measures that have not been tested in cross-cultural contexts.[17]

One study of the cross-cultural comparison of consumer research measures concluded that "the same scales may have different reliabilities in different cultures, and that the same scales may exhibit different reliabilities when used by the same individual in evaluating products from different cultures."[18] They warn against using simple comparisons of research results in cross-national marketing and that cross-cultural research data comparisons should be attempted only after accounting for necessary adjustments for possible variability. Researchers are addressing these and other problems, and methodologies are being evaluated as to their applicability for cross-cultural studies.[19]

Language and Comprehension

The most universal survey sampling problem in foreign countries is the language barrier. Differences in idiom and the difficulty of exact translation create problems in eliciting the specific information desired and in interpreting the respondents' answers. Equivalent concepts may not exist in all languages. *Family*, for example, has different connotations in different countries. In the United States, it generally means only the parents and children. In Italy and many Latin countries it could mean the parents, children, grandparents, uncles, aunts, cousins, and so forth. The meaning of names for family members can have different meanings depending on the context within which they are used. In the Indian culture, uncle and aunt are different for the maternal and paternal sides of the family. The concept of *affection* is a universal idea but the manner in which it is manifest in each culture may differ. Kissing, an expression of affection in the West, is alien to many Eastern cultures and even taboo in some.[20] The obvious solution of having questionnaires prepared or reviewed by someone fluent

---

[17] Harry L. Davis, Susan P. Douglas, and Alvin J. Silk, "Measuring Unreliability: A Hidden Threat to Cross-National Marketing Research?" *Journal of Marketing*, Spring 1981, pp. 98–108.

[18] Ravi Parameswaran and Attila Yaprak, "A Cross-National Comparison of Consumer Research Measures," *Journal of International Business Studies*, Spring 1987, p. 45.

[19] Emmanuel J. Cheron, Thomas C. Padgett, and Walter A. Woods, "A Method for Cross-Cultural Comparisons for Global Strategies," *Journal of Global Marketing*, Winter 1987, pp. 31–51.

[20] Choudhry, "Pitfalls in International Marketing Research," pp. 21, 24.

BOX 11–3
Stumble in Japan or Do Marketing Research First

If you are going to do business in another culture, you must know your market. Marketing research would have helped avoid most of the problems these companies had.

A baby powder company fretted about the relatively low demand for baby powder until it did some research on how the Japanese live. In their small homes, mothers fear powder will fly around and get into their spotlessly clean kitchens. The company had to settle for selling its product in flat boxes with powder puffs so that mothers could apply it sparingly. Adults won't use it at all. They wash and rinse themselves before soaking in hot baths—after which powder makes them feel dirty again.

A cake mix company designed a mix to be prepared in electric rice cookers which all the Japanese have rather than in ovens which few have. The product flopped. Why? The Japanese take pride in the purity of their rice which they thought would be contaminated by cake flavors. It was like asking an English housewife to make coffee in her teapot.

One company that was ready to launch a new peanut-packed chocolate bar aimed at giving teenagers quick energy while cramming for exams found out in time that a Japanese old wives' tale held that eating chocolate with peanuts can give one a nosebleed. The product was never marketed.

Source: From "Learning How to Please the Baffling Japanese," *Fortune*, October 5, 1981, p. 122.

---

in the language is frequently overlooked. In one such case, a German respondent was asked the number of "washers" (washing machines) produced in West Germany for a particular year; the reply reflected the production of the flat metal disk.

A researcher cannot assume that a translation into one language will suffice in all areas where that language is spoken. Such was the case when the author was in Mexico and requested a translation of the word *outlet*, as in "retail outlet," to be used in Venezuela. It was read by Venezuelans to mean an electrical outlet, an outlet of a river into an ocean, and the passageway into a patio. Needless to say, the responses were useless although interesting.

Literacy poses yet another problem; in some less-developed countries with low literacy rates, written questionnaires are completely useless. Within countries, too, the problem of dialects and different languages can make a national questionnaire survey impractical. In India, there are 14 official languages and considerably more unofficial ones.

One suggestion designed to deal with semantic problems in questionnaires is to use *back translation*, that is, have material translated from one language into another language, then have a third party translate it back into the original. This pinpoints misinterpretations and misunderstandings before they reach the public. A soft drink company wanted to use a very successful Australian advertising theme, "Baby, it's cold inside," in Hong Kong. They had the theme translated from English into Cantonese by one translator and then retranslated by another from Cantonese into English where the statement came out, "Small Mosquito, on the inside it is very cold." Although "small mosquito" is the colloquial expression for small child in Hong Kong, the intended meaning was lost in translation.

Back translation may not always assure that an accurate translation has been made because translators may not know the most commonly used idiom. A parallel translation is suggested as an alternative. In this process, more than two translators are used to make a translation and the results are compared, differences are discussed, and the most appropriate selected. A third suggestion, a hybrid of back translation, is called "decentering." Decentering is a successive iteration process of translation and retranslation of a questionnaire, each time by a different translator. The process is as follows: an English version is translated into French and then translated back to English by a different translator. The two English versions are compared and where there are differences, the original English version is modified and the process is repeated. If there are differences between the two English versions, the original English version of the second iteration is modified and the process of translation and back translation is repeated. The process continues to be repeated until an English version can be translated into French and back translated, by a different translator, into the same English. In this process, wording of the original instrument undergoes a change and the version that is finally used and "its translation have equally comprehensive and equivalent terminologies in both languages."[21] Regardless of the procedure used, proper translation of a questionnaire is of critical importance to successful research design.

Because of cultural and national differences, confusion can just as well be the problem of the researcher as the respondent. One classic misunderstanding which occurred in a *Reader's Digest* study of consumer behavior in Western Europe resulted in the report that France and West Germany consumed more spaghetti than did Italy. This rather curious and erroneous finding resulted from questions that asked about purchases of "packaged and branded spaghetti." Italians buy their spaghetti in bulk, the French and West Germans buy branded and packaged spaghetti. Since the Italians buy little branded or packaged spaghetti, the results underreported spaghetti purchases by Italians. However, the real question is what the researcher wanted to find out. Had the goal of the research been to determine how much branded and packaged spaghetti was purchased, the results

---

[21] Ibid., p. 25.

BOX 11–4
Hanged or Suspended—It's a Matter of Translation

Be sure that your English original is as clear and unambiguous as possible. An American executive based abroad received a cable about his daughter, a college student in the States: "Daughter hanged for crimes committed in youth." Traced through various translations, the original turned out to be: "Daughter suspended for minor offense." Make the distinction between your hanging and your suspension clear to your translators.

Source: Donnella Ruiz, *Business America Colorado*, January 1982, p. 7.

would have been correct. However, because the goal was to know about total spaghetti consumption, the data were incorrect. Researchers must always verify that they are asking the right question.

Modifications in marketing research methods must be made to obtain the desired information for decision making, but the quality of results need not be slighted. Indeed, the reason for modification is to ensure results that are usable even though methods of application are different. It is the modifications that give the assurance that full communication occurs, which, after all, is the cornerstone of a good survey.

PROBLEMS IN ANALYZING AND INTERPRETING RESEARCH INFORMATION

Once data have been collected, the final steps are the analysis and interpretation of findings in light of the stated marketing problem. Both secondary and primary data collected by the market researcher are subject to the many limitations just discussed. In any final analysis, the researcher must take into consideration these factors and, in spite of their limitations, produce meaningful guides for management.

The meaning of words, the consumer's attitude toward a product, the interviewer's attitude, or the interview situation can distort research findings. Just as culture and tradition influence the willingness to give information, they also influence the information given. Accepting information at face value in foreign markets is an imprudent practice. Newspaper circulation figures, readership and listenership studies, retail outlet figures, and sales volume can all be distorted through local business practice. To cope with such disparities, the foreign market researcher must possess three talents to generate meaningful marketing information.

First, the researcher must possess a high degree of cultural understanding of the market in which research is being conducted. In order to analyze research findings, social customs, semantics, current attitudes, and business customs of a society or a subsegment of a society must be clearly understood.

Second, a creative talent for adapting research findings is necessary. A researcher in foreign markets often flies by the seat of the pants and is called on to produce results under the most difficult circumstances. Ingenuity and resourcefulness, willingness to use "catch as catch can" methods to get facts, patience, a sense of humor, and a willingness to be guided by original research findings even when they conflict with popular opinion or prior assumptions are all considered prime assets in foreign marketing research.

Third, a skeptical attitude in handling both primary and secondary data is helpful. It might be necessary to check a newspaper press run over a period of time to get accurate circulation figures, or deflate or inflate reported consumer income in some areas by 25 to 50 percent on the basis of observable socioeconomic characteristics.

These essential traits suggest that a foreign marketing researcher should be a foreign national or should be advised by a foreign national who can accurately appraise the data collected in light of the local environment, thus validating secondary as well as primary data.

ESTIMATING MARKET DEMAND

In assessing current product demand and forecasting future demand, reliable historical data are required. As previously noted, the quality and availability of secondary data frequently are inadequate; nevertheless, estimates of market size must be attempted to plan effectively.[22] Despite limita-

---

[22] Nicolas Papadopoulos, "Inventory, Taxonomy, and Assessment of Methods for International Market Selection," *International Marketing Review*, Autumn 1988, pp. 38–49.

tions, there are approaches to demand estimation usable with minimum information. The success of these approaches relies on the ability of the researcher to find meaningful substitutes or approximations for the needed economic and demographic relationships. Some of the necessary but frequently unavailable statistics for assessing market opportunity and estimating demand for a product are current trends in market demand. When the desired statistics are not available, a close approximation can be made using local production figures plus imports with adjustments for exports and current inventory levels. These data are more readily available because they are commonly reported by international organizations such as the United Nations. Once approximations for sales trends are established, historical series can be used as the basis for projection of growth. In any straight extrapolation, however, the estimator assumes that the trends of the immediate past will continue into the future. In a rapidly developing economy, extrapolated figures may not be valid and must be adjusted accordingly.

Another possible technique is to estimate by *analogy*. This assumes that demand for a product develops in much the same way in all countries as comparable economic development occurs in each country. First, a relationship must be established between the item to be estimated and a measurable variable in a country that is to serve as the basis for the analogy. Once a known relationship is established, the estimator then attempts to draw an analogy between the known situation and the country in question. For example, suppose a company wanted to estimate the market growth potential for a beverage in country X, for which it had inadequate sales figures, but the company had excellent beverage data for neighboring country Y. In country Y it is known that per capita consumption increases at a predictable ratio as per capita gross domestic product (GDP) increases. If per capita GDP is known for country X, per capita consumption for the beverage can be estimated using the relationships established in country Y. Caution must be used with analogy because the method assumes that factors other than the variable used (in this example GDP) are similar in both countries, such as the same tastes, taxes, prices, selling methods, availability of products, consumption patterns, and so forth. Despite the apparent drawbacks to analogy, it is useful where data are limited.[23]

Income elasticity, which measures the relationship between personal or family income changes and demand for a product, can be used in market-demand forecasting. In income-elasticity ratios, the sensitivity of demand for a product to income changes is measured. The elasticity coefficient is determined by dividing the percentage change in the quantity of a product demanded by the percentage change in income. With a result of less than

---

[23] Essam Mahmoud and Gillian Rice, "Use of Analytical Techniques in International Marketing," *International Marketing Review*, Autumn 1988, pp. 7–12.

one, it is said that the income-demand relationship is relatively inelastic and, conversely, if the result is greater than one, the relationship is elastic. As income increases, the demand for a product increases at a rate proportionately higher than income increases. For example, if income coefficient elasticity for recreation is 1.20, it implies that for each 1 percent change in income, the demand for recreation could be expected to increase by 1.2 percent; or if the coefficient is 0.8, then for each 1 percent change in income, demand for recreation could be expected to increase only 0.8 percent. The relationship also occurs when income decreases, although the rate of decrease might be greater than when income increases. Income elasticity can be very useful, too, in predicting growth in demand for a particular product or product group.

The major problem of this method is that the data necessary to establish elasticities may not be available. However, in many countries, income elasticities for products have been determined and it is possible to use the analogy method described (with all the caveats mentioned) to make estimates for those countries. Income elasticity measurements only give an indication of change in demand as income changes and do not provide the researcher with any estimate of total demand for the product.

As is the case in all methods described in this section, income elasticity measurements are no substitute for original market research when it is economically feasible and time permits. As more adequate data sources become available, as would be the situation in most of the economically developed countries, more technically advanced techniques like multiple regression analysis or input-output analysis can be used.

RESPONSIBILITY FOR CONDUCTING MARKETING RESEARCH

Depending on size and degree of involvement in foreign marketing, a company in need of foreign market research can rely on an outside foreign-based agency or on a domestic company with a branch within the country in question. It can conduct research using its own facilities or employ a combination of its own research force with the assistance of an outside agency.

In many companies, an executive is specifically assigned the research function in foreign operations; he or she selects the research method and works closely with foreign management, staff specialists, and outside research agencies. Other companies maintain separate research departments for foreign operations or assign a full-time research analyst to this activity. For many companies, a separate department is too costly; the diversity of markets would require a large department to provide a skilled analyst for each area or region of international business operations.

A trend toward decentralization of the research function is apparent.

In terms of efficiency, it appears that local analysts are able to provide information more rapidly and accurately than a staff research department. The obvious advantage to decentralization of the research function is that control of the research function rests in hands closer to the market. Field personnel, resident managers, and customers generally have a more intimate knowledge of the subtleties of the market and an appreciation of the diversity that characterizes most foreign markets. The disadvantage of decentralized research management is possible ineffective communications with staff-level executives. If a company wants to use a professional marketing research firm, many are available. Most major advertising agencies and many research firms have established branch offices worldwide. There also has been a healthy growth in foreign-based research and consulting firms.[24]

MULTINATIONAL MARKETING INFORMATION SYSTEMS

Increased marketing activity by domestic and multinational firms has generated not only more data but also a greater awareness of its need. In addition to the changes in the quantity and type of information needed, there has been an increase in competent agencies (many of them subsidiaries of U.S. marketing research firms) whose primary functions are to gather data. As firms become established, and their information needs shift from those necessary to make initial market investment decisions to those necessary for continuous operation, there is a growing demand for continuous sources of information both at the country operational level and at the worldwide corporate level. However, as the abundance of information increases, it reaches a point of "information overload" and requires some systematic method of storing, interpreting, and analyzing data.

A company shift from decisions involving market entry to those involved in managing and controlling a number of differnt growing foreign markets requires greater emphasis on *a continuous system designed to generate, store, catalogue, and analyze information from sources within the firm and external to the firm for use as the basis of worldwide and country-oriented decision making.* In short, companies have a need for a *Multinational Marketing Information System* (MMIS).

Conceptually, an MMIS embodies the same principal as any information system, that is, an interacting complex of persons, machines, and procedures designed to generate an orderly flow of relevant information and to bring all the flows of recorded information into a unified whole for decision making.[25] The only differences from a domestic marketing informa-

---

[24] E. D. Jaffe, "Multinational Marketing Intelligence: An Information Requirement Model," *Management International Review* 19, no. 2 (1979), pp. 53–60.

[25] For further discussion of information systems see Refik Culpan, "Integration of Information Systems and Strategic Planning: A Critical Appraisal," *Business Journal*, Fall 1987, pp. 15–19.

tion system are (1) scope—an MMIS covers more than one country—and (2) in levels of information—an MMIS operates at each country level with perhaps substantial differences among country systems and at a worldwide level encompassing an entire international operation. The system (see Exhibit 11–2) includes a subsystem for each country designed for operational decision making—a country-level marketing information system. Each country system also provides information to a Multinational Marketing Information System designed to provide for corporate control and strategic long-range planning decisions. In developing an MMIS, it is necessary to design an adequate CMIS (Country Marketing Information System) for each country/market. Because of the vast differences among a company's various markets, each country/market CMIS will probably have different data requirements. Once a CMIS is set for each country/market, then an overall MMIS for the worldwide operation is designed. Each level of management has substantially different data needs because country/market systems are designed to provide information for day-to-day operations while the MMIS is concerned with broader issues of control and long-range strategic planning. However, the country/market CMIS data are not only used for daily operations but also are ultimately transmitted to the MMIS to be included in overall planning decisions. Some of the most challenging tasks facing the developer of the MMIS are determining the kinds of data and the depth of detail necessary and analyzing how it should be processed. This implies that models for decision making have been thought through and are sufficiently specific to be functional.

An MMIS can be designed as a basic system that provides only a source of information or as a highly sophisticated system that includes specific

EXHIBIT 11–2   Multinational Marketing Information System

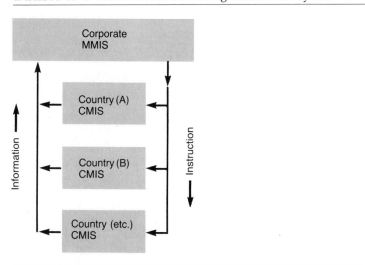

decision models. Experience has shown that success is greater when a company begins with a basic system and continues perfecting it to the desired level of sophistication.

In the development of any information system, there are some problems that can be avoided with the proper approach. It is important to appreciate that the same market information system cannot serve all levels of management. As discussed earlier, this is especially true for an MMIS since top management at worldwide corporate levels needs information to make strategic and control decisions while country-level management needs information for operational decisions. Another problem to avoid is a plethora of detail and too broad a range of information: too much information is as bad as too little, and information overload is one of the most frequent reasons given for the underutilization of an information system. The decision maker needs an information system designed to reduce masses of raw data into usable forms. Finally, unless familiar with the scope of the marketing problem, a decision maker may be unable to appreciate the kind of information needed and therefore be unable to use the more sophisticated data a CMIS can provide. Adequate familiarization with the output of a system is mandatory or it may be rejected in its entirety as overwhelming. The masses of raw data generated as a company becomes more involved in a country market, and as a multinational company's breadth of operation expands, require intelligent analysis and interpretation to arrive at more competitive decisions. An MMIS could be the answer.

REFERENCES

The following research sources are commonly found in the business or reference section of most libraries, a good place to find sources of secondary data on international marketing.

Abstracts, Bibliographies, and Indexes

Business International. Master Key Index. New York: Business International. Quarterly; covers *Business International* publications.[26]

Business Periodical Index. New York: H. W. Wilson, 1958—. Monthly with quarterly and annual cumulations. Arranged alphabetically by subject.

Business Index. Menlo Park, Calif.: Information Access Corporation, 1979—. Monthly cumulation on a 16-mm computer-output microfilm.

---

[26] An excellent information service is *Business International,* which also publishes *Business Europe, Business Asia, Business Latin America,* and *Business China.*

Indexes articles, reviews, news, and other related material of interest to the business community.

Encyclopedia of Geographic Information Sources. Companion volume to *Encyclopedia of Business Information Sources.* Detroit: Gale Research, 1988. Listings by foreign country cover basic sources for statistics, directories, guides for doing business, and so on.

Flud, Leonard M. "Foreign Intelligence from U.S. Sources," Chapter 8 in *Competitor Intelligence.* New York: John Wiley & Sons, 1985, pp. 249–95. An excellent bibliography of sources of marketing information for most of the world's countries.

F & S Index International and F & S Europe. Cleveland: Predicasts. Monthly with quarterly and annual cumulations. Indexes foreign companies and product, and industry information with emphasis on sources giving data or statistics.

International Business References Sources by Cynthia C. Ryans, Lexington, Mass.: Lexington Books, 1983. A comprehensive bibliography of reference books.

The International Executive. American Graduate School of International Management. (Thunderbird) Tempe, Ariz. Quarterly annotated bibliography. Reviews over 195 publications. All articles are on international business topics.

Sources of European Economic Information. 3d ed. Compiled by Cambridge Information and Research Services Ltd., Cambridge, U.K.: Gower Publishing Co. Ltd., 1983. Alphabetical by country with a separate index listing sources by subject and country.

Statistics Europe: Sources for Social, Economic, and Market Research. 5th ed. Joan M. Harvey, U.K.: CBD Research Ltd./Gale Research, 1987. Arranged by country.

Wall Street Journal Index. Princeton, N.J.: Dow Jones, 1956—. Monthly with annual cumulations. Compiled from the final eastern edition. Divided into two sections: Corporate News and General News by broad subject headings.

J. W. O'Brien and S. R. Wasserman, eds. *Statistics Sources.* 11th ed. Detroit: Gale Research, 1988. Subject guide to data on industrial, business, social, educational, financial, and other topics for the United States and other countries.

Sources of Marketing Statistics

Business International, Worldwide Economic Indicators. New York. Annual; economic, demographic, trade, and other statistics.

Consumer Europe. London: Euromonitor Publications. Annual; marketing indicators and trends for various markets.

European Marketing Data and Statistics. London: Euromonitor Publications. Annual. 24th ed., 1988/89.

International Labour Office. Yearbook of Labour Statistics. Geneva. Annual; current statistics in its *Bulletin of Labour Statistics.*

International Marketing Data and Statistics. London: Euromonitor Publications, Ltd. Annual; covers the Americas, Asia, Africa, and Australasia. Includes data on retail and wholesale sales, living standards, and general consumer marketing data.

International Monetary Fund. *International Financial Statistics.* Monthly; statistics on exchange rate, international liquidity, money and bank statistics, interest, prices, production, and so on.

The Markets of Asia/Pacific: Thailand, Taiwan, Peoples Republic of China, Hong Kong, South Korea, The Philippines, Indonesia, Singapore, and Malaysia. London: The Asia Pacific Centre, Ltd., New York: Facts on File, various years. An excellent source for data on prices, retail sales, consumer purchases, and other country information.

Retail Trade International, Vol. 1., United Kingdom; Vol. 2, Europe; and Vol. 3, The Americas, Africa, Asia, and Oceania Europe. London: Euromonitor Publications, 1980. Data on consumer purchase patterns by product, retail store type. Some prices, middleman markups, and other data.

Statistical Yearbook for Latin America. United Nations: Economic Commission for Latin America. Updated by *Statistical Bulletin for Latin America.*

SUMMARY

The basic objective of the market research function is providing management with information for more accurate decison making. This objective is the same for domestic and international marketing. In foreign marketing research, however, achieving that objective presents some problems not encountered on the domestic front.

Consumer attitudes about providing information to a researcher are culturally conditioned. Foreign market information surveys must be carefully designed to elicit the desired data and at the same time not offend the respondent's sense of privacy. Besides the cultural and managerial constraints involved in gathering information for primary data, many foreign markets have inadequate and/or unreliable bases of secondary information.

Three generalizations can be made about the direction and rate of growth of marketing research in foreign marketing. First, both home-based and foreign management are increasingly aware of and accept the importance of marketing research's role in decision making. Second, there is a current trend toward the decentralization of the research function to put control closer to the area being studied. Third, the most sophisticated tools and techniques are being adapted to foreign information gathering with increasing success. So successful, in fact, that it has become necessary to develop structured information systems to appreciate and utilize effectively the mass of information available.

QUESTIONS

1. Define and show the significance to international marketing:

   international marketing research
   research process
   comparability and currency of data
   overseas business reports
   CIMS

   MMIS
   back translation
   income elasticity
   analogy
   parallel translation
   decentering

2. Discuss how the shift from making "market entry" decisions to "continuous operations" decisions creates a need for different types of information and data. What assistance does an MMIS provide?

3. Using a hypothetical situation, illustrate how an MMIS might be established and how it would be used at different levels.

4. Discuss the breadth and scope of international marketing research. Why is international marketing research generally broader in scope than domestic marketing research?

5. The measure of a competent researcher is the ability to utilize the most sophisticated and adequate techniques and methods available within these limits [of time, cost, and the present state of the arts]. Comment.

6. What is the task of the international market researcher? How is it complicated by the foreign environment?

7. Discuss the stages of the research process in relation to the problems encountered. Give examples.

8. Why is the formulation of the research problem difficult in foreign market research?

9. Discuss the problems of gathering secondary data in foreign markets.

10. "In many cultures, personal information is inviolably *private* and absolutely not to be discussed with strangers." Discuss.

11. What are some problems created by language and the ability to comprehend in collecting primary data? How can a foreign market researcher overcome these difficulties?

12. Sampling offers some major problems in market research. Discuss.

13. Select a country. From secondary sources compile the following information for at least a 10-year period prior to the present:

Principal imports	Chief of state
Principal exports	Major cities and population
Gross national product	Principal agricultural crop

14. "The foreign market researcher must possess three essential capabilities to generate meaningful marketing information." Discuss.

15. Discuss the growing need for an MMIS system.

16. Discuss how "decentering" is used to get an accurate translation of a questionnaire.

CHAPTER

12

Developing Consumer Products for Global Markets

A key theme in international marketing management is the globalization of markets and its impact on the firm's strategies and marketing mix. Implicit in the development of any marketing program is the question, "Which products should we sell?" For the company with a domestic market extension orientation, the answer generally is, "whatever we are selling in the United States." The company with a multidomestic market orientation develops different products to fit the uniqueness of each country market and the global company ignores frontiers and seeks commonalities in needs among sets of country markets and responds with a global product. Regardless of the strategy followed, each country market must be examined thoroughly. To do otherwise means a firm risks marketing poorly conceived products in incorrectly defined markets with an inappropriate marketing effort.[1]

For larger firms the trend is toward becoming global in orientation and strategy, but many other firms approach new markets with products that

---

[1] For an interesting study of marketing mix standardization, see Ralf Thomas Kreutzer, "Marketing-Mix Standardization: An Integrated Approach to Global Marketing," *European Journal of Marketing* 22, no. 10 (1988), pp. 19–30.

have been successfully marketed elsewhere.[2] Product adaptation is as important a task in a smaller firm's marketing effort as it is for global companies. As competition for world markets intensifies and as market preferences become more global, selling what is produced for the domestic market in the same manner as it is sold at home proves to be increasingly less effective. Some products cannot be sold at all in foreign markets without modification, others may be sold as is but their acceptance is greatly enhanced when they are tailored more specifically to market needs. In a competitive struggle, products that meet the needs and wants of a market at an affordable price should be the goal of any marketing firm.[3] For some product category groups and some country markets, this means differentiated products for each market, but other product groups and country market segments do well competitively with a global or standardized product.

This chapter explores some of the relevant issues facing an international marketer when planning and developing consumer products for global markets. The questions about product planning and development range from the obvious—which product to sell—to the more complex—when and how products should be adapted for different markets, if at all.

GLOBAL MARKETS AND PRODUCT DEVELOPMENT

There is a recurring debate relative to product planning and development. It focuses on the question of standardized or global products marketed worldwide versus differentiated products adapted, or even redesigned, for each culturally unique market. Those with strong production and unit cost orientation advocate standardization while others, perhaps more culturally sensitive, propose a different product for each market.[4]

Underlying the arguments offered by the proponents of standardized products is the premise that global communications and other worldwide socializing forces have fostered a homogenization of tastes, needs, and values in a significant sector of the population across all cultures. This has resulted in a large global market with similar needs and wants that demands the same reasonably priced products of good quality and reliability.[5] In support of this argument, a study of MNCs found that

[2] Alecia Swasy, "After Early Stumbles, P&G Is Making Inroads Overseas," *The Wall Street Journal,* February 9, 1989, p. B1.

[3] See, for example, Jeryl M. Whitelock, "Global Marketing and the Case for International Product Standardization," *European Journal of Marketing* 21, no. 9 (1987), pp. 32–44.

[4] For an interesting article, see Roberto Friedmann, "Psychological Meaning of Products: A Simplification of the Standardization vs. Adaptation Debate," *Columbia Journal of World Business,* Summer 1986, pp. 97–104.

[5] Pradeep A. Rau and John F. Preble, "Standardization of Marketing Strategy by Multinationals," *International Marketing Review,* Autumn 1987, pp. 18–27.

BOX 12–1
The Muppets Go Global

"One of the interesting things about puppetry and our work is that it crosses cultural lines. . . . We are known around the world."

It's no idle statement. The "Muppet Show" is truly a world product, now seen on TV screens in over 100 countries and dubbed in 15 languages. The three Muppet movies have played in nearly 60 countries. The TV series "Fraggle Rock" reached 96 countries in 13 different languages. Hansen's "Big Bird" adapted perfectly to cultural environments around the world. In Arabic-speaking countries, Big Bird became the big camel; in Latin America, a big parrot; in the Philippines, a tortoise; in West Germany, a big brown bear.

"You can link up the entire world in television which you could not do five years ago. All of the sudden you can link everybody up."

Source: Adapted from Alan Bunce, "The Muppets Take the World," *World Monitor*, January 1989, pp. 44–50.

---

products targeted for urban markets in less-developed countries needed few changes from products sold to urban markets in developed countries. Thus, "modern products usually fit into the lifestyles of urban consumers wherever they are."[6] A study done for Electrolux, the consumer appliance marketer, found more similarity across national markets for some products than across market segments in the same national market. The growth of the global consumer means that differentiating markets by sociological category rather than by geography may show that "preferences of consumers in midtown Manhattan are more similar to those in central Milan than in the Bronx . . . Yuppies in New York need the same dishwashers as yuppies in Paris, or parents in Rome make similar demands on a washing machine as do parents in Toledo."[7]

Standardization of products leads to production economies and other savings that permit profits at prices attractive to the global market. Although recognizing cultural variations, advocates of standardization believe that price, quality, and reliability will offset any differential advantage of a culturally adapted product. They strongly suggest future competitiveness demands a strategy of standardization rather than differentiation.[8]

---

[6] John S. Hill and Richard R. Still, "Effects of Urbanization on Multinational Product Planning: Markets in Lesser-Developed Countries," *Columbia Journal of World Marketing*, Summer 1984, p. 62.

[7] "Electrolux's Global Approach to Markets and Corporate Finance," *Management Europe*, September 26, 1988, p. 11.

[8] Marina Specht, "Henkel Thinks Pan-Europe," *Advertising Age*, January 30, 1989, p. 44.

Those who hold the opposing view stress the importance of cultural variations which dictate the need to differentiate products to accommodate the uniqueness of social and cultural norms found among countries. They stress product adaptation to reflect cultural differences.

The issue cannot be resolved with a simple either/or decision. Cost-revenue analyses need to be done and decisions made in the hard, cold light of profitability. There is no question that significant cost savings can be realized from standardized products, packages, brand names, and promotional messages; but this makes sense only if there is adequate demand for the standardized product: costs must be balanced with demand. On the other hand, if the cost of an individualized product when evaluated against price/demand characteristics within a market exceeds potential profit, then other alternatives, including not marketing the product at all, must be considered.

The continual conflict between differentiation to accommodate small-market segments and standardization to reduce unit costs can be settled only when the marketer's evaluation identifies "when there are market differences sufficient to justify the loss of standardization," and when sufficient demand exists to offset increases in cost. The issue of standardized worldwide product and marketing programs versus programs tailored to accommodate unique cultural differences can be resolved with a sound marketing analysis and a profitability study of both approaches.

To differentiate for the sake of differentiation is not a solution; realistic business practice requires a company to strive for uniformity in its marketing mix whenever and wherever possible. Economies of production, better planning, more effective control, and better use of creative managerial personnel are the advantages of standardization. In contrast, a company with multiple products scattered around the world and different management practices in each nation dissipates managerial intensity and focus.[9]

Nevertheless, there are reasons a company may choose to adapt a product to local markets or, in some cases, be forced to adapt. Some marketers simply prefer to sell an adapted version of what they sell at home in a foreign market rather than make the necessary investment to develop a standardized product. Some countries have laws and other requirements making it mandatory to adapt a product to their specific markets. Adaptation may also make some products more attractive to a local market than an undifferentiated standardized product. For example, this description of rice cookers explains:

> The product concept, cooking rice in an electric cooker, is the same around the world, but because of local preferences, the marketing has to be modified

---

[9] Sudhir H. Kale, "A Strategic Approach to International Segmentation," *International Marketing Review*, Summer 1987, pp. 60–70.

Refreshment stands similar to this one in Mexico are found throughout Latin America.
At this stand, five fruit drinks are sold for every bottle of soft drink.

locally. Japanese like warm, sticky rice; Chinese like loose, warm, or cool fried rice; and people in the Middle East like theirs crisply burnt, warm, or cool.

These preferences require that the cooking technology also be modified. In the Middle East, a higher temperature is needed to burn the rice. In China, a different thermostat must be installed so cooking temperatures can be varied from sizzling hot to warm. Even the product application, how it is used by the consumer, would vary, because while the Chinese keep the cooker out of view in the kitchen, the Japanese have theirs in full view in the dining room. Thus, two design considerations must be accounted for, one utilitarian, the other decorative.[10]

These differences in use patterns for rice cookers would result in different marketing responses depending on a company's operating orientation. The company with a domestic market extension orientation would simply sell whatever rice cooker sold in the home market. The multidomestic market oriented firm would market at least three different models of rice cookers, each specially designed for each of the three markets. The approach taken by a global company would be to standardize where possible and

---

[10] John Thackray, "Much Ado about Global Markets," *Across the Board*, April 1985, p. 46. Published by The Conference Board.

adapt where necessary. For example, perhaps it would be possible to design one rice cooker that would be cost effective and culturally acceptable in each of the three markets.

Rather than arbitrarily assume the need for three different rice cookers, the problem could be approached from a global perspective; that is, to look for similarities lending themselves to standardization and, where cultural differences dictate changes necessary for product acceptance, adapt. With the rice cooker, it appears only two features really differ, the need for attractiveness because the Japanese keep their cookers in full view and the three thermostatic settings necessary for the different cooking temperatures. One attractively designed cooker with a thermostat adjustable to the different cooking temperature ranges could possibly be developed to satisfy the needs in each of the three markets and thus to become a standardized product. Products are not devoid of cultural influences although some products, such as wristwatches (the entire world is on a 24-hour day) may be culturally the same worldwide; others, such as rice cookers, are influenced by cultural preferences.

Global Brands

Hand in hand with global products are global brands. One of the objectives of global companies is to establish a world brand identification even when is not possible to have a standardized product. In addition to the substantial cost savings, a global brand gives the company a uniform worldwide image that enhances efficiency and cost savings when introducing other products associated with the brand name. A recent study of brand name recognition in Western Europe, Japan, and the United States reported that the three most powerful brand names were Coca-Cola, IBM, and Sony. Of the 40 corporate brand names that registered most strongly with the respondents, 17 were from the United States, 14 European, and 9 Japanese. As the marketplace becomes more competitive and more globalized, products with the strongest brand image have the best opportunity of gaining the largest market share.[11]

PRODUCTS AND CULTURE

To appreciate the complexity of standardized versus adapted products, one needs to understand how cultural influences are interwoven with the perceived value and importance a market places on a product. A product

---

[11] Barry N. Rosen, Jean J. Boddlewyn, and Ernst A. Louis, "U.S. Brands Abroad: An Empirical Study of Global Branding," *International Marketing Review*, Vol. 6, No. 1, 1989, pp. 7–19.

BOX 12–2
Hot Milk for Cold Cereal Changing Eating Habits

The instructions on the box say: Pour into a bowl, add milk, preferably cold milk, and sugar to taste. Eat. This step-by-step recipe for preparing a bowl of corn flakes is a key weapon in Kellogg Company's eight-year, increasingly successful campaign to get the croissant-munching French to eat American-style breakfasts. As with any form of new product, Kellogg has had to overcome ingrained habits. More than 30 percent of French adults skip breakfast entirely. Others have a cup of coffee or cafe au lait and a slice of bread with chocolate spread or they grab a croissant and coffee while standing up at a bar on their way to work. Market research shows that of those who eat cereal for breakfast, a staggering 40 percent pour on warm milk.

So in addition to instructions on the box, Kellogg's French television ads always show milk being poured from a transparent glass pitcher, traditionally used for cold milk here, instead of an opaque procelain jug, reserved for the hot milk usually added to the morning's coffee.

The hot milk problem, however, isn't nearly as crucial to Kellogg as the general no breakfast problem and the residual anticorn bias. Corn came to French farms only after World War II and more than 80 percent of what is grown here is fed to pigs and chickens. Kellogg estimates sales will grow by 25 percent this year and each of the next four years. Even this rapid growth leaves France well down the list of cereal-eating countries: Last year while the French ate 10 ounces of cereal per capita, West Germans were eating 23 ounces, Americans 9 pounds, the British 12 pounds, and the champion Australians 13 pounds.

"I have no idea what warm milk on Corn Flakes tastes like," says the head of Kellogg's French unit. "It can't do much for the crunchiness though." A Kellogg spokeswoman says, "Small markets like France where cereal is a new idea, are challenges. We look at it as a market with tremendous potential."

Source: Adapted from Philip Revzin, "While Americans Take to Croissants, Kellogg Pushes Corn Flakes on France," *The Wall Street Journal*, November 11, 1986, p. 4.

---

is more than a physical item; it is a bundle of satisfactions (or utilities) the buyer receives. That includes its form, taste, color, odor, and texture, how it functions in use, the package, the label, the warranty, manufacturer's and retailer's servicing, the confidence or prestige enjoyed by the brand, the manufacturer's reputation, and any other symbolic utility received from possession or use of the goods. In short, the market relates to more than a product's physical form and primary function.[12]

---

[12] Joanne Lipman, "Lowe Marschalk Takes Braun World-Wide," *The Wall Street Journal*, March 8, 1989, p. B4.

BOX 12–3
McDonald's Cheeseburger—A Diet Food?

One key to success in international marketing is to adapt your marketing program and product to the needs of the market. McDonald's sells hamburgers in Australia to one segment of the market as a low-calorie food. Here is an excerpt from a McDonald's advertisement appearing in a leading women's magazine in Australia.

Low Calorie Counter

If you are counting calories (or kilojoules) come to our counter. Here's a meal that will fit into your diet and it's food you can really enjoy.
Cheeseburger, french fries (reg. serv.), black coffee—527 calories—less than a third of what the average woman uses each day.
Above is a well-balanced, low-calorie (kilojoule), nutritious meal. We believe any McDonald's menu combination makes a significant contribution to your nutritional requirements. We want you to enjoy good food and enjoy it in good health. *Come to our counter and see how our figures can help your figure.*

Source: *The Australian Women's Weekly.*

Much of the importance of these other benefits are imputed by the values and customs within a culture. In other words, a product is the sum of the physical and psychological satisfactions it provides the user.

Its physical attributes generally are required to create the primary function of the product. The primary function of an automobile, for example, is to move passengers from point A to point B. This ability requires a motor, transmission, and other physical features to achieve its primary purpose. The physical features or primary function of an automobile are generally in demand in all cultures where there is a desire to move from one point to another other than by foot or animal power. Few changes to the physical attributes of a product are required when moving from one culture to another. However, an automobile has a bundle of psychological features as important in providing consumer satisfaction as its physical features. Within a specific culture, other automobile features (color, size, design, brand name) have little to do with its primary function, the movement from point A to B, but do add value to the satisfaction received.

Depending on cultural values and customs, these features have complex symbolic meanings denoting status, taste, achievement, aspiration, material value, and a host of other psychological attributes that make a product acceptable and help create the bundle of satisfactions received. The meaning and value imputed to these psychological attributes can vary among cultures and are perceived as negative or positive.[13] To maximize the bundle of satisfactions received and to create positive product attributes rather than negative ones, adaptation of the nonphysical features of a product may be necessary.

For example, Coca-Cola, frequently touted as a global product, found it had to change one product name from Diet Coke to Coke Light when it was introduced in Japan. Japanese women do not like to admit they are dieting; further, the idea of diet implies sickness or medicine. So, instead of emphasizing weight loss, "figure maintenance" is stressed.

Adaptation may require changes of any one or all of the psychological aspects of a product. A close study of the meaning of a product shows to what extent the culture determines an individual's perception of what a product is and what satisfaction that product provides.

The adoption of some products can be affected as much by how the product concept conflicts with norms, values, and behavior patterns as its physical or mechanical attributes. For example, introduction of a new product into a culture that does not perceive a need for such an item can conflict with established norms; locally accepted values can be upset by introducing personal care items into a culture that prefers body functions remain private; assuming too high a level of sophistication in product usage may overlook local behavior patterns. As one authority states:

> In short, it is not just lack of money, nor even differences in the natural environment, that constitutes major barriers to the acceptance of new products and new ways of behaving. A novelty always comes up against a closely integrated cultural pattern, and it is primarily this that determines whether, when, how, and in what form it gets adopted. Insurance has been difficult to introduce into Moslem countries, because the pious could claim that it partook of both usury and gambling, both explicitly vetoed in the Koran. The Japanese have always found all body jewelry repugnant. The Scots have a decided resistance to pork and all its associated products, apparently from days long ago when such taboos were decided by fundamentalist interpretations of the Bible. Filter cigarettes have failed in at least one Asian country because the local life expectancy of 29 years hardly places many people in the age-bracket most prone to fears of lung cancer—even supposing that they shared the Western attitudes about death.[14]

When analyzing a product for a second market, the extent of adaptation required depends on cultural differences in product use and perception between the market the product was originally developed for and the new market. The greater these cultural differences between the two mar-

---

[13] For an interesting report on such differences in Europe, see Janette Martin, "Beyond 1992: Lifestyle Is Key," *Advertising Age*, July 11, 1988, p. 57.

[14] D. E. Allen, "Anthropological Insights into Customer Behavior," *European Journal of Marketing 5*, no. 3, p. 54.

kets, the greater the extent of adaptation necessary. Examples are typically given about cultures other than American but the need for cultural adaptation is often necessary when a foreign company markets a product in the United States. For example, a major Japanese cosmetic company, Shiseido, attempted to break into the U.S. cosmetic market with the same products sold in Japan. After introducing them in more than 800 U.S. stores, they realized that American's taste in cosmetics is very different from Japan's. The major problem was that Shiseido's makeup required a time-consuming series of steps, a point that does not bother Japanese women. Success was attained after designing a new line of cosmetics as easy to use as American products.[15]

Another example of this involves an undisputed American leader in cake mixes which tacitly admitted failure in the English market by closing down operations after five unsuccessful years. Taking its most successful mixes in the U.S. market, the company introduced them into the British market. A considerable amount of time, money, and effort was expended to introduce its variety of cake mixes to this new market. Hindsight provides several probable causes for the company's failure. Traditionalism was certainly among the most important. The British eat most of their cake with tea instead of dinner and have always preferred dry sponge cake, which is easy to handle; the fancy, iced cakes favored in the United States were the type introduced. Fancy, iced cakes are accepted in Britain, but they are considered extra special and purchased from a bakery or made with much effort and care at home. The company introduced what it thought to be an easy cake mix. This easy cake mix was considered a slight to domestic duties. Homemakers felt guilty about not even cracking an egg, and there was suspicion that dried eggs and milk were not as good as fresh ones. Therefore, when the occasion called for a fancy cake, an easy cake mix was simply not good enough. Ironically, this same company had faced almost identical problems, which they eventually overcame, when introducing new easy cake mixes on the U.S. market. There was initial concern about the quality of mixes and the resulting effect on the homemaker's reputation as a baker. Even today there remains the feeling that "scratch" cakes are of special quality and significance and should be made for extra-important occasions. This, in spite of the fact that the uniform quality of results from almost all mixes and the wide variety of flavors certainly equal, if not exceed, the ability of most to bake from scratch.

Such a cultural phenomenon apparently exists in other cultures as well. When instant cake mixes were introduced in Japan, the consumers' response was less than enthusiastic. Not only do Japanese reserve cakes

---

[15] Brian Dumaine, "Japan's Next Push in U.S. Markets," *Fortune*, September 26, 1988, p. 138.

for special occasions, they prefer they be beautifully wrapped and pur-chased in pastry shops. The acceptance of instant cakes was further compli-cated by another cultural difference—most Japanese homes do not have ovens.[16]

The problems of adapting a product to sell abroad are similar to those associated with the introduction of a new product at home. Products are not measured solely by their physical specifications; the nature of the new product is in what it does to and for the customer—"to his habits, his tastes, and his patterns of life."[17] The problems illustrated in the cake mix example have little to do with the physical product or the user's ability to make effective use of it, but more with the fact that acceptance and use of the cake mixes would have required upsetting behavior patterns considered correct or ideal.

What significance, outside the intended use, might a product have in a different culture? When product acceptance requires changes in patterns of life, habits, tastes, the understanding of new ideas, acceptance of the difficult to believe, or the acquisition of completely new tastes or habits, special emphasis must be used to overcome natural resistance to change.

Innovative Products and Adaptation

An important first step in adapting a product to a foreign market is to determine the degree of newness perceived by the intended market. How people react to newness and how *new* a product is to a market must be understood. In evaluating the newness of a product, the international marketer must be aware that many products successful in the United States, having reached the maturity or even decline stage in their life cycles, may be perceived as new in another country or culture and, thus, must be treated as innovations. From a sociological viewpoint, any idea perceived as new by a group of people is an innovation. Whether or not a group accepts an innovation and the time it takes depends on its character-istics. Products new to a social system are innovations, and knowledge about the diffusion (i.e., the process by which innovation spreads) of innovations is helpful in developing a successful product strategy. Market-ing strategies can guide and control to a considerable extent the rate and extent of new product diffusion because successful new product diffusion is dependent on the ability to communicate relevant product information and new product attributes.

---

[16] Larry J. Rosenberg, "Deciphering the Japanese Cultural Code," *International Marketing Review*, Autumn 1986, p. 54.

[17] Chester Wason, "What Is New about a New Product?" *Journal of Marketing*, July 1960, pp. 52–56.

A critical factor in the newness of a product is its effect on established patterns of consumption and behavior. In the preceding cake mix example, the fancy, iced cake mix was a product that required acceptance of the "difficult to believe," that is, that dried eggs and milk are as good in cake as the fresh products; and the "acquisition of new ideas," that is, that easy-to-bake fancy cakes are not a slight to one's domestic integrity. In this case, two important aspects of consumer behavior were directly affected by the product, and the product innovation met with sufficient resistance to convince the company to leave the market. Had the company studied the target market before introducing the product, perhaps it could have avoided the failure. Another U.S. cake mix company entered the British market but carefully eliminated most of the newness of the product. Instead of introducing the most popular American cake mixes, the company asked 500 British housewives to bake their favorite cake. Since the majority baked a simple, very popular dry sponge cake, the company brought to the market a similar easy mix and gained 30 to 35 percent of the British cake-mix market.

The sponge cake mix represented familiar tastes and habits that could be translated into a convenience item, and it did not infringe on the emotional aspects of preparing a fancy product for special occasions. Consequently, after a short period of time, the second company's product gained acceptance.

The goal of a foreign marketer is to gain product acceptance by the largest number of consumers in the market in the shortest span of time. However, as discussed in Chapter 4 and as many of the examples cited have illustrated, new products are not always readily accepted by a culture; indeed, they often meet resistance. Although they may ultimately be accepted, the time it takes for a culture to learn new ways, to learn to accept a new product, are of critical importance to the marketer since planning reflects a time frame for investment and profitability. If a marketer invests with the expectation that a venture will break even in three years and it takes seven to gain profitable volume, the effort may have to be prematurely abandoned. The question comes to mind whether or not the probable rate of acceptance can be predicted before committing resources and, more critically, if the probable rate of acceptance is too slow, whether it can be accelerated. In both cases, the answer is a qualified yes. Answers to these questions come from examining the work done in diffusion research—research on the process by which "innovations spread to the members of a social system."[18]

---

[18] Everett M. Rogers, *Diffusion of Innovations,* 3d ed. (New York: Free Press, 1983), pp. 211–38.

> **BOX 12–4**
> **Four in a Package Has Got to Be Better than Three**
>
> A leading U.S. golf ball manufacturer targeted Japan as an important new market by virtue of the expanding popularity of golf in that nation. Special packaging in sets of four was developed for export although golf balls are generally packaged in sets of 3, 6, or 12 for domestic consumption. The company's sales were well below anticipated volume. Researchers eventually targeted packaging in fours as a primary factor for lagging sales. *Four is the number of death in Japan.*

Diffusion of Innovations

Everett Rogers notes that "crucial elements in the diffusion of new ideas are (1) an innovation, (2) which is communicated through certain channels, (3) over time, (4) among the members of a social system." Rogers continues with the statement that it is the element of time that differentiates diffusion from other types of communications research. The goals of the diffusion researcher and the marketer are to shorten the time lag between introduction of an idea or product and its widespread adoption.

Rogers gives ample evidence of the fact that product innovations have a varying rate of acceptance. Some diffuse from introduction to widespread use in a few years, others take decades. Microwave ovens, introduced in the United States initially in the 1950s, have only recently reached widespread acceptance; whereas the contraceptive pill was introduced during that same period and gained acceptance in a few years. In the field of education, modern math took only 5 years to diffuse through U.S. schools while the idea of kindergartens took nearly 50 years to gain total acceptance. There is also a growing body of evidence that the understanding of diffusion theory may provide ways in which the process of diffusion can be accelerated. Knowledge of this process may provide the foreign marketer with the ability to assess the time it takes for a product to diffuse before it is necessary to make a financial commitment. It also focuses the marketer's attention on features of a product that provoke resistance, thereby providing an opportunity to minimize resistance and hasten product acceptance. At least three extraneous variables affect the rate of diffusion of an object: the degree of perceived newness, the perceived attributes of the innovation, and the method used to communicate the idea. Each variable has a bearing on consumer reaction to a new product and the time needed for acceptance. An understanding of these variables can produce better product strategies for the international marketer.

Degree of Newness

As perceived by the market, varying degrees of newness categorize all new products. Within each category myriad reactions affect the rate of diffusion. In giving a name to these categories, one might think of (1) congruent innovations, (2) continuous innovations, (3) dynamically continuous innovations, and (4) discontinuous innovations.

1. A *congruent* innovation is actually not an innovation at all because it causes absolutely no disruption of established consumption patterns. The product concept is accepted by the culture and the innovativeness is typically one of introducing variety and quality or functional features, style, or perhaps an exact duplicate of an already existing product—exact in the sense that the market perceives no newness, such as cane sugar versus beet sugar.

2. A *continuous* innovation has the least disruptive influence on established consumption patterns. Alteration of a product is almost always involved rather than the creation of a new product. Generally the alterations result in better use patterns—perceived improvement in the satisfaction derived from its use. In some segments of the market, a continuous innovation may be more disruptive than in others. Examples include: fluoride toothpaste, menthol cigarettes, and annual automobile model changeovers.

3. A *dynamically continuous* innovation has more disruptive effects than a continuous innovation, although it generally does not involve new consumption patterns. It may mean the creation of a new product or considerable alteration of an existing one designed to fulfill new needs arising from changes in lifestyles or new expectations brought about by change. It is generally disruptive and therefore resisted because old patterns of behavior must change if consumers are to accept and perceive the value of the dynamically continuous innovation. Examples include: electric toothbrushes, electric haircurlers, central air conditioning, and frozen dinners.

4. A *discontinuous* innovation involves the establishment of new consumption patterns and the creation of previously unknown products. It introduces an idea or behavior pattern where there was none before. Examples include: television, the computer, the automobile, and microwave ovens.[19]

Most innovation in the U.S. economy is of a continuous nature. However, a product that could be described as a continuous innovation in the U.S. market could be a dynamically continuous innovation, if not a discontinuous innovation, in many industrialized nations of the world. For example, when the cake mix was first introduced into the American economy, it was a dynamically continuous innovation. However, with time it overcame

---

[19] Thomas S. Robertson, "The New Product Diffusion Process," in *American Marketing Association Proceedings*, ed. Bernard A. Marvin (Chicago: American Marketing Association, June 1969), p. 81.

BOX 12–5
Déjà Vu or We Will Get It Right Someday

Campbell entered a joint venture with a Brazilian company to produce and market soups. After fiscal losses of $1.2 million, the Campbell Soup Company announced it would stop producing and selling canned soup in Brazil.

What went wrong for Campbell in soup-conscious Brazil? Campbell's offerings—mostly vegetable and beef combinations in extra-large cans—failed to catch on. Brazilian housewives seemed to prefer the dehydrated products of competitors such as Knorr and Maggi, which they used as a soup starter, adding their own flair and extra ingredients. If one bought Campbell's soup, it was usually to put aside for an emergency, "like when she was late coming home from a party."

A comprehensive, in-depth study revealed that the Brazilian housewife felt she was not fulfilling her role as homemaker if she served her family a soup she could not call her own.

This was the second failure for the Campbell Soup Company. Fifteen years earlier, it introduced canned soup into another soup-eating market. The introduction in England was also a loser for a number of years. One of the problems then was the difference between the condensed soup which Campbell introduced and which was unknown to the English market and the more familiar "full-strength," ready-to-eat soup to which the English market was accustomed. The company failed to appreciate the market's lack of familiarity with the preparation of condensed soups. The English housewife opened a can of condensed Campbell soup and heated it without the necessary can of water. No wonder it tasted too strong and spicy.

In each case, the company failed to appreciate the need to adapt the marketing program to the market. For Brazil, behavior patterns and attitudes about roles had to be changed or accounted for in the marketing program; and for the English, market knowledge, that is, the consumers' ability to properly prepare the product, had to be developed.

Sources: "The $30 Million Lesson," *Sales Management*, March 1, 1967, pp. 31–38; "Brazil: Campbell Soup Fails to Make It to the Table," *Business Week*, October 12, 1981, p. 66; and "How Big Advertisers Flopped in Brazil," *Advertising Age*, July 5, 1982, p. 18.

resistance, consumption and behavior patterns changed, and it was accepted in the U.S. market. Indeed, there are many continuous innovations involving the cake mix itself, such as the introduction of new flavors, changes in package size, elimination of dried eggs in favor of fresh eggs, and so on. That same cake mix, now a part of U.S. eating habits, is a congruent innovation when a new brand is offered on the U.S. market. If it is offered in a new, unqiue flavor, it is a continuous innovation; if it is introduced at the same time into a market unfamiliar with cake mixes, it is a dynamically continuous innovation. That same product also could be classified as a discontinuous innovation in a market that had no previous knowledge of cakes. In all cases, we are dealing basically with a cake mix, but in acceptance and marketing success, we are dealing with people, their feelings, and their perception of the product.

Continuing with the previous example, the second U.S. cake mix company that entered the British market with a sponge cake had, in fact, changed the product innovation from a dynamically continuous innovation to a continuous innovation by altering the cake in the mix from a fancy cake to an already accepted dry sponge cake. Thus, one advantage of analyzing a product's degree of innovativeness is to determine what may alter the degree of newness to gain quicker acceptance. Even a tractor must be modified to meet local needs and uses if it is to be accepted in place of an ox-drawn plow.

The time the diffusion process takes, that is, the time it takes for an innovation to be adopted by a majority in the marketplace, is of prime importance to a marketer. Generally speaking, the more disruptive the innovation, the longer the diffusion process takes.

The extent of a product's diffusion and its rate of diffusion are partly functions of the particular product's attributes. Each innovation has characteristics by which it can be described, and each person's perception of these characteristics can be utilized in explaining the differences in perceived newness of an innovation. These attributes can also be utilized in predicting the rate of adoption, and the adjustment of these attributes or product adaptation can lead to changes in consumer perception and thus to altered rates of diffusion. Emphasis given to product adaptation for local cultural norms and the overall brand image created are critical marketing decision areas.[20]

PHYSICAL OR MANDATORY REQUIREMENTS AND ADAPTATION

There are a variety of ways a product may have to be changed to meet physical or mandatory requirements of a new market. These range from simple package changes to total redesign of the physical core product. Some changes are obvious with relatively little analysis; a cursory examination of a country will uncover the need to rewire electrical goods for a different voltage system, simplify a product when the local level of technology is not high, or print multilingual labels when required by law. Other necessary changes may surface only after careful study of an intended market.

---

[20] Ibid., p. 84.

BOX 12–6
Shoe Comfort Really Depends on the Conditions

Part of the tremendous success of the Japanese in the Saudi market rests on their effectiveness in implementing a strategy of product adaptation, specifically producing goods to satisfy the unique needs of the Saudi market. Not all marketers have such foresight. For instance, the famous United Kingdom-made Clark brand shoes are sold in Saudi Arabia. In spite of their reputation for comfort, they are not suitable to the hot and humid Saudi climate. They usually contain thick crepe-rubber soles and their upper-soles are made out of thick leather that causes sweating feet. Furthermore, their style is not suited to the needs of the Saudi consumers who prefer to wear open sandals.

Source: Ugur Yavas and Secil Tuncalp, "Exporting to Saudi Arabia: The Power of the 'Made in' Label," *International Marketing Review,* Autumn–Winter 1984, p. 44.

Legal, economic, technological, and climatic requirements of the local marketplace often dictate product adaptation; specific package sizes and safety and quality standards are usually set by laws that vary among countries. If per capita incomes are low, the number of units per package may have to be reduced from the typical quantities offered in the United States to make the product more affordable. To accommodate lower-income markets, razor blades, cigarettes, chewing gum, and other multiple pack items are often sold singly or two to a pack instead of the 10 or 20 customary in the United States. If the concept of preventive maintenance is unfamiliar to an intended market, product simplification and maintenance-free features may be mandatory for successful product performance. General Motors of Canada experienced major problems with several thousand Chevrolet automobiles shipped to Iraq; it was quickly discovered they were unfit for the hot, dusty climate. Supplementary air filters and different clutches had to be added to adjust for the problem. Even crackers have to be packaged in special tins for humid areas and many product features adjusted for hostile climates.

The less economically developed a market is the greater degree of change a product may need for acceptance. One study found only 1 in 10 products could be marketed in developing countries without modification of some sort. Of the modifications made, nearly 25 percent were mandatory; the other modifications were made to accommodate variations in cultures.[21] Because most products sold abroad by international companies origi-

---

[21] John S. Hill and Richard R. Still, "Adapting Products to LDC Tastes," *Harvard Business Review,* March–April 1984, pp. 92–101.

nate in home markets and most require some form of modification, companies need a systematic process to identify which product needs adaptation.

PRODUCT LIFE CYCLE AND ADAPTATION

Even between markets with few cultural differences, substantial adaptation can be necessary if the product is in a different stage of its life cycle in each market. The product life cycle and the marketing mix are interrelated;

BOX 12–7
Failure—Then Success but Only after Adaptation

General Foods' Tang, the orange juice substitute that the astronauts took into space, is a major contributor to General Foods' foreign earnings. This was not always the case. Success came only after Tang was adapted to local market conditions. First attempts to market Tang involved packaging the orange-flavored powdered product in a glass jar and promoting it as a convenient breakfast "drink of the astronauts."

The Germans didn't like the name and the British didn't like the taste. In Latin America, few countries have the breakfast-eating habit and Brazil is the world's largest fresh orange juice exporter.

Yet, success came and Tang swept through country after country, in most cases creating a market where none existed before. This was a result of renaming, reformulating, repackaging, and repositioning the product for different markets.

In West Germany, the drink was renamed *Seefrisch;* in Britain, Tang was given a more tart flavor. The Tang sold in Latin America is not the same one sold in the United States. There Tang is sold specially sweetened, premixed, and ready to drink in a bright one-liter pouch in five different flavors: orange, passion fruit, peach, lemon, and pineapple.

Tang's traditional breakfast time positioning has been altered in most countries into a mealtime or throughout-the-day beverage because few Latin Americans sit down to cornflakes, eggs, and juice in the morning.

Tang's TV campaign typically focuses on happy families sitting around the table at mealtime enjoying Tang's good taste accompanied by a catchy jingle. In an Argentinian commercial, the neighbors drop by and bring their own Tang, thereby making everyone even happier.

In Brazil Tang promotes flavor and fun. "Perhaps the only reasonable reason to buy Tang is that it's convenient, but God forbid we should try to sell it as being easier than squeezing your own oranges," commented a Brazilian product manager.

Sources: Adapted from Laurel Wentz, "How General Foods Beat the Odds with Tang," *Advertising Age,* July 4, 1983, p. m–18; and "Ad Agencies and Big Concerns Debate World Brands Value," *The Wall Street Journal,* June 14, 1984, p. 27.

a product in a mature stage of its life cycle in one market can have unwanted and/or unknown attributes in a market where the product is perceived as new and thus in its introductory stage. Marketing history is replete with examples of mature products in one market being introduced in another and failing. An example is Campbell Soup's introduction of concensed soups in England; they were rejected until the market "learned" that condensed soups were as good as "full-strength" soups. After 20 years of success with the instant camera, Polaroid introduced the Model 20 "Swinger" Land Camera to a mature U.S. market in 1965. The Swinger was designed to place Polaroid, for the first time, in the mass market for inexpensive cameras. The Swinger capitalized on the established reputation of Polaroid and its concept of instant photography and was very successful.

After a phenomenally successful introduction in the United States, Polaroid introduced the Swinger into the French market using its successful U.S. marketing program. The Swinger was Polaroid's first product in France and a spectacular failure. Polaroid withdrew the product, changed the marketing approach, and successfully reintroduced it.

What happened? As far as the French market was concerned, the Swinger and its concept of instant photography were unknown. In short, the product was in the introductory stage of its life cycle and the marketing effort required adaptation of the marketing program designed for the mature U.S. market. The major problem was a lack of awareness of the concept of instant photography. A company study done after the poor showing in the initial introduction found that only 5 percent of the French market was familiar with instant photography whereas, in the United States, over 85 percent were knowledgeable about the concept. What Polaroid failed to appreciate was the 20 years of development and use of instant photography that was lacking in France. The French consumer did not perceive any "bundle of satisfaction" from this new product. Certainly an important approach in analyzing products for foreign markets is determining the stage of the product's life cycle. All subsequent marketing plans must then include adaptations necessary to correspond to the stage of the product life cycle in the new market.

PRODUCT ALTERNATIVES

When a company plans to enter a market in another country, careful consideration must be given to whether or not the present product lines will prove adequate in a new culture. Will they sell in quantities large enough and at prices high enough to be profitable? If not, what other alternatives are available? The marketer has at least three viable alternatives when entering a new market: (1) sell the same product presently sold in the home market (Domestic Market Extension Strategy); (2) adapt existing products to the tastes and specific needs in each new country market

Global brands. Brand competition for washing powders in a Swiss hypermarket.

(Multidomestic Market Strategy): or (3) develop a standardized product for all markets (Global Market Strategy).

An important issue in choosing which alternative to use is whether or not a company is starting from scratch (i.e., no existing products to market abroad), or whether it has products already established in various country markets. For a company starting fresh, the prudent alternative is to develop a global product. If the company has several products that have evolved over time in various foreign markets, then the task is one of repositioning the existing products into global products.

The success of these alternatives depends on the product and the fundamental need it fulfills, its characteristic, its perception within the culture, and the associated costs of each program. To know that foreign markets are different and that different product strategies may be needed is one thing; to know when adaptation of your product line and marketing program is necessary is another and more complicated problem.

SCREENING PRODUCTS FOR ADAPTATION

Evaluating a product for marketing in another country requires a systematic method of screening products to determine if there are cultural resistances to overcome and/or physical or mandatory changes necessary for product acceptance. Only when the psychological (or cultural) and physical dimensions of the product, as determined by the country market, are known can the decision for adaptation be made. Products can be screened on two different bases by using the Analysis of Characteristics of Innovations to determine if there are cultural-perceptual reasons why a product will be better accepted if adapted; and/or Analysis of Product Components to determine if there are mandatory or physical reasons why a product must be adapted.

Analysis of Characteristics of Innovations

Earlier, we discussed the idea that the more innovative a product is perceived to be, the more difficult it is to gain market acceptance. The perception of innovation can often be changed if the marketer understands the perceptual framework of the consumer.

Attributes of a product that cause market resistance to its acceptance and affect the rate of acceptance can be determined if a product is analyzed by the five characteristics of an innovation: (1) relative advantage: the perceived marginal value of the new product relative to the old; (2) compatibility: its compatibility with acceptable behavior, norms, values, and so forth; (3) complexity: the degree of complexity associated with product use; (4) trialability: the degree of economic and/or social risk associated with product use; and, (5) observability: the ease with which the product benefits can be communicated.[22] In general, it can be postulated that the rate of diffusion is positively related to relative advantage, compatibility, trialability, and observability but negatively related to complexity.

By analyzing a product within these five dimensions, a marketer can often uncover perceptions held by the market which, if left unchanged, would slow product acceptance. Conversely, if these perceptions are identified and changed, the marketer may be able to accelerate product acceptance.

The evaluator must remember it is the perception of product characteristics by the potential adopter, not the marketer, that is crucial to the evaluation. A market analyst's self-reference criterion may cause a perceptual bias when interpreting the characteristics of a product. Thus, instead of evaluating product characteristics from the foreign user's frame of reference, it is analyzed from the marketer's frame of reference, leading to a misinterpretation of the cultural importance.

Once the analysis has been made, some of the perceived newness or cause for resistance can be minimized through adroit marketing. The more congruent with current cultural values perceptions of the product can be, the less the probable resistance and the more rapid the diffusion or acceptance of the product. A product frequently can be modified physically

---

[22] See Rogers, *Diffusion of Innovations*, pp. 211–38, for a discussion of the characteristics of an innovation.

BOX 12–8
The Secret of Enjoying Them Is to Imagine You're Eating A Dog

On the culinary round in Seoul in 1988, there was good news and bad. Which was which, however, depended on how one saw the neighbor's Chihuahua.

The South Korean capital shut down hundreds of dog meat restaurants during the 1988 Olympics following a barrage of bad foreign press, much of it prompted by British animal rights groups.

To the rescue came Lee Kyung Sam determined to fill the dog meat vacuum with snails; they fit with the Olympic theme of national development. And, advanced countries seemed to be where people eat snails. "I think Korea is the first country at this economic level to eat snails."

The hitch to Lee's plan was that most Koreans found the idea of dining on snails disgusting. "Snails? To eat? That's creepy."

At the meat market in downtown Seoul, shoppers can find snakes, sea slugs, hairy red sea creatures, and hunks of dog with the paws attached— but nothing like land snails. "Most Koreans' stomachs turn when they think of eating snails," said Lee.

Lee saw limitless possibilities: snail sphaghetti, snail shish kebab, snail salad, Korean-style snails, snail snacks at street stalls, and on and on.

Source: Adapted from: Susan Moffat, "The Secret to Enjoying Them Is to Imagine You're Eating a Dog," *The Wall Street Journal*, September 8, 1988, p. 29.

---

to improve its relative advantage over competing products, enhance its compatibility with cultural values, and even minimize its complexity. Its relative advantage and compatibility also can be enhanced and some degree of complexity lessened through advertising efforts. Small sizes, samples, packaging, and product demonstrations are all sales promotion efforts that can be used to alter the characteristics of an innovative product and accelerate its rate of adoption.

The marketer must recognize not only the degree of innovativeness a product possesses in relation to each culture, but marketing efforts must reflect an understanding of the importance of innovativeness to product acceptance and adoption. One of the values of analyzing characteristics of innovations is that it focuses the efforts of the marketer on those issues that influence the acceptance of a product concept. It is possible to accentuate the positive attributes of an innovation, thus changing the market's perception to a more positive and, therefore, acceptable attitude.[23]

---

[23] For an interesting study of the diffusion of an innovation, see G. A. Lancaster and C. T. Taylor, "A Study of Diffusion of Innovations in Respect to the High-Speed Train," *European Journal of Marketing* 22, no. 3, (1988), pp. 21–47.

The potential of communicating product innovations can be illustrated with some hypothetical questions about the cake mix example used earlier: Would the company have had the same results if it had analyzed the cake mix as an innovation and then set out to make the idea a more acceptable one? What would have been the result, for example, if the introduction had been the traditional sponge cake which required minimal communication to gain acceptance? Or, in offering the market a fancy cake mix, what if the company had set out to convince the market of the advantages of that type of cake over the traditional, thus enhancing its relative advantage? The company could also have set out to promote advantages of the "new" cake mix over the old traditional cake so that it would have seemed more compatible with present behavior. There are many "what ifs" to be asked; "what if it had communicated the product's ease of trialability and observability to allay fears as to quality, taste, flavor, and ease of preparation?" In retrospect, the answers to these questions are of little value to the cake mix company but they illustrate to the marketer the value of viewing a product in terms of innovation and characteristic analysis and then communicating a positive product picture to the new market. Frequently, the cause of failure for a U.S. marketer abroad is not inadequate marketing practices but failure to employ the right marketing practices against the correct problems.

Analysis of Product Components

In addition to cultural resistance to product acceptance which may require adaptation, physical attributes can influence the acceptance or rejection of a product. A product is multidimensional, and the sum of all its features determines the bundle of satisfactions received by the consumer. To identify all the possible ways a product may be adapted to a new market, it helps to separate its many dimensions into three distinct components as illustrated in Exhibit 12–1, the Product Component Model. The core component, packaging component, and support services component include all a product's tangible and intangible elements and provide the bundle of utilities the market receives from use of the product. By analyzing a product along the dimensions of its three components, the marketer focuses on different levels of product adaptation.

The Core Component. This component consists of the physical product, its design features, and all its functional features. Major adjustments in the core component may be costly because a change in the physical product can affect production processes and thus require additional capital investment. There are, however, minor changes that may be important in bringing a product in line with local needs. For example, Campbell Soup changed their condensed canned soups to full strength to be competitive in a market

EXHIBIT 12–1   Product Component Model

Core Component

1. product
2. design
3. Functional features

Packaging Component

1. Trademark
2. Brand name
3. Price
4. Quality
5. Package
6. Styling

Support Serv Comp.

1. Deliveries
2. Warranty
3. Spare parts
4. Repair & maint.
5. Installation
6. Instruction

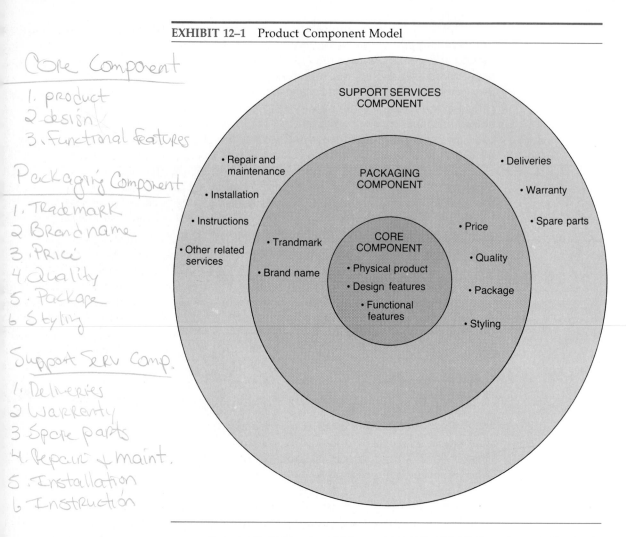

SUPPORT SERVICES
COMPONENT

PACKAGING
COMPONENT

CORE
COMPONENT

- Repair and maintenance
- Installation
- Instructions
- Other related services
- Trandmark
- Brand name
- Deliveries
- Warranty
- Spare parts
- Price
- Quality
- Package
- Styling
- Physical product
- Design features
- Functional features

SOURCE: For a detailed discussion of this concept, see Franklin R. Root, *Strategic Planning for Export Marketing* (Scranton, Pa.: International Textbook Company, 1964), chap. 3.

where condensed soup was unfamiliar. For the Brazilian market, where fresh orange juice is plentiful, General Foods changed the flavor of its presweetened powdered juice substitute, Tang, from the traditional orange to passion fruit and other flavors. Changing flavor or fragrance is often necessary to bring a product more in line with what is expected in a culture. Household cleansers with the traditional pine odor and hints of ammonia or chlorine popular in U.S. markets were not successful when introduced in Japan. Many Japanese sleep on the floor on futons with their heads close to the surface they have cleaned so a citrus fragrance was more pleasing.[24]

Functional features can be added or eliminated depending on the market. In markets where hot water is not commonly available, washing machines have heaters as a functional feature. In other markets, automatic soap and bleach dispensers may be eliminated to cut costs and/or to minimize repair problems. Additional changes may be necessary to meet safety and electrical standards or other mandatory requirements. The physical product and all its functional features should be examined as potential candidates for adaptation.

The Packaging Component.   The packaging component includes style features, packaging, labeling, trademarks, brand name, quality, price, and all other aspects of a product's package. As with the core component, the importance of each of these elements in the eyes of the consumer depends on the need that the product is designed to serve. Packaging components frequently require both discretionary and mandatory changes. For example, some countries require labels to be printed in more than one language while others forbid the use of any foreign language. Elements in the packaging component may incorporate symbols which convey an unintended meaning and thus must be changed. One company's red-circle trademark was popular in some countries but was rejected in parts of Asia where it conjured up images of the Japanese flag. Yellow flowers used in another company trademark were rejected in Mexico where a yellow flower symbolizes death or disrespect.

The classic example of misinterpreted symbols was experienced by a well-known baby-food producer that introduced small jars of baby food in Africa complete with labels featuring a picture of a baby. The company was aghast to find that consumers were absolutely horrified—they thought the jars contained ground-up babies. It is easy to forget that in low-literacy countries, pictures and symbols are taken quite literally for instructions and information.

Care must be taken to ensure that corporate trademarks and other parts of the packaging component do not have unacceptable symbolic meanings. Particular attention should be given to translations of brand names and colors used in packaging. White, the color for purity in Western countries, is the color for mourning in others. When Coca-Cola went to China, translators chose characters that sounded like Coca-Cola, but to the Chinese they read, "bite the wax tadpole."

There are countless reasons why a company might have to adapt a product's package. In some countries, specific bottle, can, and package

---

[24] "Adapting for Success," *Business Tokyo*, October 1987, p. 26.

sizes are stipulated by law as are measurement units. If a country uses the metric system, it will probably require that weights and measurements conform to the metric system. Such descriptive words as "giant" or "jumbo" on a package or label may be illegal. High humidity and/or the need for long shelf life because of extended distribution systems may dictate that extra-heavy packaging be used for some products. As is frequently mentioned, the Japanese attitudes about quality include the packaging of a product. A poorly packaged product conveys an impression of poor quality to the Japanese. It is also important to determine if the packaging has other uses to the market. Again in Japan, Lever Brothers sells Lux soap in stylish boxes because in Japan more than half of all soap cakes are purchased during the two gift-giving seasons.[25] Size of the package is also a factor that may make a difference in success in Japan. Soft drinks are sold in smaller size cans than in the United States to accommodate the smaller Japanese hand.[26]

Labeling laws vary from country to country and do not seem to follow any predictable pattern. In Saudi Arabia, for example, product names must be specific. "Hot Chili" will not do, it must be "Spiced Hot Chili." Prices are required to be printed on the labels in Venezuela, but in Chile, it is illegal to put prices on labels or in any way suggest retail prices. Coca-Cola ran into a legal problem in Brazil with its Diet Coke. Brazilian law interprets *diet* to have medicinal qualities. Under the law, producers must give daily recommended consumption on the label of all medicines. Coke had to get special approval to get around this restriction.

Marketers must examine each of the elements of the packaging component to be certain that this part of the product conveys the appropriate meaning and value to a new market. Otherwise they may be caught short as was the U.S. soft-drink company that incorporated six-pointed stars as decoration on its package labels. Only when investigating why sales were weak did they find they had inadvertently offended some of their Arab customers who interpreted the stars as symbolizing pro-Israeli sentiments.

The Support Services Component. Included in this component are repair and maintenance, instructions, installation, warranties, deliveries, and the availability of spare parts. Many otherwise successful marketing programs have ultimately failed because little attention was given to this product component. Repair and maintenance are especially difficult problems in developing countries. In the United States, a consumer has the option of

---

[25] Agostino Mauriello, "Japan: U.S. Companies Who Do Their Homework Find Success," *Global Trade*, July 1987, p. 38.

[26] Richard C. King, "Learning from the Competition: Strategies for the Culture Factor," *Export Today*, November–December 1987, p. 35.

BOX 12–9
Adapting a Foreign Product for the U.S. Market, or If It Sells in Germany, Will It Sell in Wyoming?

Companies with successful products in foreign markets frequently look to the United States for market growth. But, products successful in foreign markets are not necessarily successful in the U.S. without adaptation.

Procter & Gamble makes several different formulations of Ariel, the top-selling brand of concentrated powder detergent in Europe. After seven years of strong foreign sales, P&G introduced Ariel in Wyoming and several other Western states.

The U.S. formula is different than the German one because it must work at lower water temperatures and produce greater sudsing and faster performance than the Ariel sold in Germany. In Germany, the typical washload is presoaked at 95 degrees for an hour and then washed at 140 to 200 degrees in front-load machines holding three and one-half gallons of water. In the United States there is no presoaking and a load is washed for 10 minutes at 95 degrees in machines holding 17 gallons of water. U.S. customers also expect more suds.

Even package labels differ in more than language. Because European consumers seem intently interested in how Ariel works, the label for foreign markets goes into great detail about chemical formulations and water temperatures. Not so for the Ariel in the United States; Americans are less interested in the nuts and bolts of how it works and more concerned with the end result. It's "ring around the collar" that's important in the United States.

Source: Adapted from "New Foreign Products Pour into U.S. Markets in Increasing Numbers," *The Wall Street Journal,* November 11, 1982, p. 1.

company service as well as a score of competitve service retailers ready to repair and maintain anything from automobiles to lawn mowers. Equally available are repair parts from company-owned or licensed outlets or the local hardware store. Consumers in a developing country and many developed countries may not have even one of the possibilities for repair and maintenance available in the United States.

In some countries, the concept of routine maintenance or preventive maintenance is not a part of the culture. As a result, products may have to be adjusted to require less frequent maintenance and special attention given to features that may be taken for granted in the United States.

Literacy rates and educational levels of a country may require a firm to change a product's instructions. A simple term in one country may be incomprehensible in another. In rural Africa, for example, the consumer had trouble understanding that Vaseline Intensive Care lotion is absorbed into the skin. Absorbed was changed to soaks into and the confusion was eliminated. The Brazilians have successfully overcome low literacy and technical skills of users of the sophisticated military tanks it sells to Third World countries by including videocassette players and television tapes with detailed repair instructions as part of the standard instruction package. They also minimize spare parts problems by using standardized, "off-the-shelf" parts available throughout the world.

While it may seem obvious to translate all instructions into the language of the market, many firms overlook such a basic point. "Do Not Step Here," "Danger," or "Use No Oil" have little meaning to an Arab unfamiliar with the English language.[27]

The Product Component Model can be a useful guide to examine adaptation requirements of products destined for foreign markets. A product should be carefully evaluated on each of the three components for mandatory and discretionary changes that may be needed.

SUMMARY

The growing globalization of markets that gives rise to standardization must be balanced with the continuing need to assess all markets for those differences that might require adaptation for successful acceptance. Each product must be viewed in light of how it is perceived by each culture with which it comes in contact. What is acceptable and comfortable within one group may be radically new and resisted within others depending on the experiences and perceptions of each group. Understanding that an established product in one culture may be considered an innovation in another is critical in planning and developing consumer products for foreign markets. Analyzing a product as an innovation and using the Product Component Model may provide the marketer with important leads for adaptation.

QUESTIONS

1. Terms: Define and show the significance to international marketing:
   product diffusion   global brands
   dynamically continuous   trialability
      innovation   innovation
   Product Component Model   relative advantage

2. Debate the issue of global versus adapted products for the international marketer.

---

[27] For a complete list of steps in product adaptation, see "How to Prepare Your Product for Export," *Business-America*, May 25, 1987, pp. 10–11.

3. Discuss product alternatives and the three marketing strategies: Domestic market extension, multidomestic markets, and global market strategies.

4. Discuss the different promotional/product strategies available to an international marketer.

5. Assume you are deciding to "go international," and outline the steps you would take to help you decide on a product line.

6. Products can be adapted physically and culturally for foreign markets. Discuss.

7. What are the three major components of a product? Discuss their importance to product adaptation.

8. How can a knowledge of the diffusion of innovations help a product manager plan international investments?

9. Old products (that is, old in the U.S. market) may be innovations in a foreign market. Discuss fully.

10. ". . . if the product sells in Dallas, it will sell in Tokyo or Berlin." Comment.

11. How can a country with a per capita GNP of $100 be a potential market for consumer goods? What kinds of goods would probably be in demand? Discuss.

12. Discuss the four types of innovations. Give examples of a product that would be considered by the U.S. market as one type of innovation but a different type in another market. Support your choice.

13. Discuss the characteristics of an innovation that can account for differential diffusion rates.

14. Give an example of how a foreign marketer can use knowledge of the characteristics of innovations in product adaptation decisions.

CHAPTER

13

Marketing Industrial Products and Business Services

There are more similarities in marketing industrial products across country markets than differences. The issue of global markets, whether they exist or not, has greater relevance to consumer goods. Photocopy machines are sold in Saudia Arabia for the same reason as in the United States—to make photocopies. There are, of course, occasions for adaptation—the photocopy machine may need adaptation to accommodate different paper sizes found in some countries, different electrical power supplies, and so on. The inherent nature of industrial goods and the similarities in motives among industrial goods consumers, however, creates a market where product and marketing mix standardization is more commonplace than for consumer goods.[1]

Two fundamental factors account for greater market similarities among industrial goods customers than consumer goods customers. First is the inherent nature of the product; industrial products are those goods and services used in the process of creating other goods and services. Consumer goods are in their final form and are consumed by individuals. And second,

---

[1] Ellen Day, Richard J. Fox, and Sandra M. Huszagh, "Segmenting the Global Market for Industrial Goods: Issues and Implications," *International Marketing Review*, Autumn 1988, pp. 14–26.

the motive or intent of the user differs; industrial consumers are seeking profit while the ultimate consumer is seeking self-satisfaction. These factors manifest themselves in specific buying patterns, demand characteristics, and selling techniques for industrial goods. They also account for the level of predictability of customer demands within industrial goods markets.

Marketing concepts and principles are the same when dealing with industrial or consumer goods; however, the tactics used to implement marketing programs and the degree of emphasis applied to the various components of the marketing mix vary. Whether a company is marketing at home or abroad, the differences between industrial and consumer markets merit special consideration. A marketing approach to an industrial goods customer is generally different than the marketing approach to a consumer goods buyer because they are buying for different reasons.

In addition to problems created by cultural, legal, political, and other environmental differences among countries, two significant trends to consider in the marketing of industrial goods are (1) rapidly growing demand for industrial goods throughout the world, and (2) global competition from Western Europe, Japan, and a host of developing countries from Asia to Latin America.[2] The successful industrial goods manufacturing firm cannot expect to be sought out by buyers; instead, the firm must compete with the many eager and relatively new competitors actively selling to increasingly demanding customers. Industrial marketers face the same competitive intensity as do consumer goods companies: competition in the U.S. market from U.S. and foreign firms and competition for foreign markets from other U.S. firms as well as foreign firms. A global approach to marketing is the key to competitive success whether marketing consumer or industrial goods to the world's growing markets.

Growth is occurring not only in the sale of tangible industrial goods but also in the sale of intangibles or business services. Rapid economic growth, active competition, and a lack of a ready pool of highly skilled technicians and experts in many developing countries have created a steadily growing international market for business services ranging from marketing research to engineering assistance.

This chapter discusses the special problems in marketing industrial goods and business services internationally, the increased competition and demand for industrial goods and business services, and their implications for the global marketer.

---

[2] "Organizing for International Success," *Distribution*, October 1988, pp. 48–54.

THE INDUSTRIAL PRODUCT

Because an industrial product is purchased for business use and thus sought, not as an entity in itself, but as part of a total process, the buyer values service, dependability, quality, performance, and cost. In foreign markets, these features are complicated for the marketer by the differences between countries. Cultural and environmental variations place different emphasis on service, dependability, quality, performance, and cost. One such complicating factor is the degree of industrial development reached by each country.

Stages of Economic Development

Perhaps the most significant environmental factor affecting the industrial goods market is the degree of industrialization. Although generalizing about countries is an imprudent practice, the degree of economic development in a country can be used as a rough gauge of market characteristics for industrial goods. Regardless of the degree, demand for industrial products exists, but different levels of development typically result in changes in demand and kinds or quality of industrial goods sought.

Since industrial goods are products for industry, there is a logical relationship between the degree of economic development and the character of demand for industrial goods found within a country. One authority suggests that nations can be classified into five stages of development. This classification is essentially a production-oriented approach to economic development in contrast to the marketing-oriented approach used in Chapter 12. Although the development of productive facilities parallels the evolution of the marketing process, emphasis in this section is on the development of manufacturing as the basis for industrial products demand rather than development of the marketing process. A production orientation is helpful because at each stage some broad generalizations can be made about the level of development and the industrial market within the country.

The first stage of development is really a preindustrial or commercial stage with little or no manufacturing and an economy almost wholly based on the exploitation of raw materials and agricultural products. The demand for industrial products is confined to a limited range of goods used in the simple production of the country's resources, that is, the industrial machinery, equipment, and goods required in the production of these resources. During this stage, a transportation system develops that creates a market for highly specialized and expensive construction equipment that must be imported.

The second stage reflects the development of primary manufacturing concerned with the partial processing of raw materials and resources which

---

BOX 13–1
Unfair Trade or Poor Marketing?

"The main reason Japanese goods are attracting so many customers both outside and inside the United States has to do with the intrinsic appeal of the products." For example, Mitsubishi led the way in this country with large-screen television sets. American TV manufacturers have yet to catch up. Japanese electronics continue to excel. Nissan got the jump in the production of sport cars that also served family purposes. The Japanese are even demonstrating abilities no one thought they had in designing women's clothing.

It's nonsense to say the Japanese have an advantage because of low labor costs. Wages are now comparable.

The kingpins of American industries have been concentrating on corporate acquisitions instead of on production. Takeovers and mergers have supplanted the requirements of the marketplace. Brain power, which ought to be going in to competitive thinking, has been going into stock market strategies, bank arrangements, and corporate restructuring. Industry is being run increasingly by financial wizards rather than by industrial experts.

Why do we lag behind? The technology for VCRs was developed in the United States but the Japanese control manufacturing of 90 percent of all VCRs. Semiconductors are another prime example where the Japanese have beat out the Americans. When U.S. companies were standing pat with 64K chips, Japan was moving ahead with its demonstrably superior 256K chip. The Japanese manufacturers did this by upgrading their facilities, creating even higher levels of state-of-the-art products, increasing productivity, and lowering their prices.

SOURCE: Adapted from Norman Cousins, "Japan Wins in Business Because U.S. Isn't Trying," *Christian Science Monitor*, December 8, 1988, p. 73.

---

in stage one were shipped in raw form. At this level demands are for the machinery and other industrial goods necessary for processing raw materials prior to exportation. For example, in Kenya, a trade mission reports the need for empty jute bags, sulphur in lumps, bleaching powder, alum for a sugar factory, and fertilizers for a plantation.

The third stage of development is characterized by the growth of manufacturing facilities for nondurable and semidurable consumer goods. Generally, the industries are small local manufacturers of consumer goods having relative mass appeal. In such cases, the demand for industrial products extends to entire factories and the supplies necessary to support manufacturing. Liberia is a country at this stage of development. The Liberian Development Corporation has been focusing attention on developing small- and medium-size industries, such as shoe factories and battery and nail manufacturing. This degree of industrialization requires machinery and equipment to build and equip the factories and the supplies to keep them operating. Liberia's chief imports from the United States are construction and mining equipment, motor vehicles and parts, metal structures and parts, and manufactured rubber goods. In some cases, countries at the third stage are good markets for used plants; that is, plants deemed obsolete in more economically advanced countries but adequate in size and modest enough in cost to fit the needs of a developing country. A used alkaline plant dismantled in Canada and shipped to India was in operation at a cost of $4 million; the estimated cost of a new plant was in excess of $10 million. A used cement plant sent to Venezuela from the United States cost $30 million against $50 to $60 million for a new one.

A country at stage four is a well-industrialized economy. This stage reflects the production of capital goods as well as consumer goods, including products such as automobiles, refrigerators, and machinery. Even though the country produces some industrial goods it still needs to import more specialized and heavy capital equipment not yet produced there but necessary for domestic industry. Many countries that were classified in stages two or three only a few years ago have achieved rapid industrialization in key industries. These newly industrialized countries (NICs) are strong markets for industrial goods to fuel their rapidly expanding automobile, electronic, shipbuilding, and other manufacturing enterprises. South Korea, an example of a country in this situation, not only has manufacturers of automobile parts and automobiles sold all over the world, but also steel making and shipbuilding to name a few key industries.[3] South Korea is not yet self-sufficient in industrial tools and many of the component parts necessary in the operations of these industries. Korea's five automakers expect to double production by 1993 and are building new plants to achieve that goal. They are also building steel mills to supply the steel. Over a two-year period, Korean companies invested $2.5 billion in semiconductors as well as launching entirely new industries such as aircraft and robotics.[4] Such intense industry makes South Korea a growing market for all classes of industrial goods.[5]

This stage of development also can be accompanied by a rapid growth of consumer demand creating markets for consumer goods in addition to an increase in demand for industrial goods as manufacturing firms develop to produce for the home market. As a country moves from the fourth to the fifth stage of development, many of the industrial goods that have been purchased from others are produced domestically. The fifth stage of economic development signifies complete industrialization and generally indicates world leadership in the production of a large variety

---

[3] David Halberstam, "Japan All Over Again," *Business Month*, February 1988, pp. 60–63.

[4] "Korea," *Business Week*, September 5, 1988, pp. 44–50.

[5] Julie Skur Hill, "Asia's Little Dragons," *Advertising Age*, November 9, 1988, p. 104.

of goods. Countries that have achieved this level typically compete world-wide for markets for both their consumer and industrial goods. Even though a country is completely industrialized, a demand still exists within it for industrial goods from other countries. Characteristic of a high degree of industrialization is a tendency to specialize in the production of certain goods rather than including everything an industrialized nation would need. Such specialization creates intense competition with domestic industries as well as with foreign industries.

Japan, the United States, and West Germany have all reached the fifth stage of industrial development; although they are industrialized economies, there is still the need to import goods. Countries in this category are markets for the latest technology as well as less sophisticated products that can be produced more economically in other countries. Demand is found for telecommunication equipment, computer chips, electronic testing equipment, scientific controlling and measuring equipment as well as fork lifts and lathes. However, products on the cutting edge of technology and goods produced in the most cost effective manner are the important differential advantages for companies competing for market demand in countries in the fifth stage.

Success in a fiercely competitive global market for industrial goods depends on building an edge in science and technology. The industrialization of many countries in stages one to four creates enormous demand for goods produced by firms in the most advanced stages of technical development.[6] For example, the Asian worker who can wire 120 integrated circuits for semiconductor chips in one hour is being phased out by automated machines that wire 640 circuits in an hour. As technology develops, countries that have been relying on cheap labor for a competitive advantage have to shift to more sophisticated machines, thus creating markets for products from more technologically advanced countries.

Although each stage of industrial development appears clear cut, most countries are actually in a state of economic and industrial flux striving for greater and more rapid economic growth. As one observer noted: "Don't expect to sell an automation feature in places where people till their fields by hand. On the other hand, don't underestimate the newly awakening nations. The term *underdeveloped* can be very deceiving." Along with most other less-developed countries, India has, or is seeking, the latest technology.[7] A country such as South Korea can move from being a war-ruined country to become a major world competitor in a matter of decades.

---

[6] Stuart Gannes, "The Good News about U.S. R&D," *Fortune*, February 1, 1988, pp. 48–56.

[7] "Suddenly U.S. Business Is Banging on India's Door," *Business Week*, June 13, 1985, pp. 54–55.

Countries can jump several stages of development as they industrialize and become markets for the latest technology. Technology is the key to economic growth and the ability to compete in global markets. As precision robots and digital control systems take over the factory floor, manufacturing is becoming more science-oriented and access to inexpensive labor and raw materials is becoming less important. Another way to classify countries is on the basis of their ability to use technology. One economist suggests a grouping of countries and/or companies on their ability to use modern technology because that ability is becoming widely recognized as a factor in "economic growth and in the international competitiveness of countries and companies."[8]

In level one, the lowest stage, are those countries and companies not capable of making use of modern technology. Stage two countries and companies have the ability to use modern technology and to reach international standards of quality and performance but do not make new contributions to technology. Many NICs fit this category; they are effective users of technology but not developers. In stage three not only are they effective users of technologies but they also are innovative in application and often push the use of the technology to its highest level of efficiency. Although moving rapidly into stage four, Japan is probably the best example of a country at stage three of technological capability. Many of the successful products that put Japan in the lead depend on the technology they have creatively adapted. The technology for electronically recording television programs was developed in the United States for use in commercial television; the Japanese adapted the technology to a home appliance, the VCR, and now dominate a multibillion dollar consumer market.

Stage four countries and companies are those whose technology in a field at a given moment is the most advanced, those considered by others as the world standard by which to measure their own strengths. The United States, West Germany, England, and Japan all have areas where they lead in a particular technology. Just as in the stages of economic development described earlier, participants may be at more than one stage of technological capability. Further, companies and countries may move up the scale or regress, as new technologies are developed. Where a country fits on the technology scale can reveal much about its demand for industrial goods.[9]

Regardless of the level of industrialization, there is a fascination for the latest technology in many Third World countries whether or not the technology can be used effectively. One of the challenges facing the international marketer selling to developing countries is how to deal with a country

---

[8] Otto Hieronymi, "The Domestic and International Impact of National Electronics Policies," *Siemens Review*, June 1988, p. 35.

[9] Ibid., pp. 35–36.

seeking the most up-to-date technology when there is reason to doubt its ability to absorb the high technology. The marketer is faced with the dilemma of losing a sale if the company refuses the order because the buyer cannot effectively use the technology, or making the sale and being blamed for failures when the technology cannot be properly utilized. One international authority suggests that the marketer assess the level of technology needed, and sell the proper technology with the appropriate service-support systems including necessary training in product use and maintenance.

Not all segments of a nation's economy are at the same stage of development. An economy may operate at several levels of industrial development at once, but one degree of development is more prominent than another. The rate of industrialization in many Third World nations is occurring rapidly despite gaps within the various economies.

A major exception is the acceptance and ability to use the most up-to-date technology in computer and communications technology. There is a worldwide demand for the latest computer technology as well as the latest communications equipment. One of the world's fastest-growing industrial markets is in telecommunications, and presently, the United States is the world's leader with every country a viable market.

Political and National Implications

The political and national implications affecting the demand for industrial goods must be kept in mind when studying industrial markets. Industrialization is typically a national issue, and industrial goods are the fodder for industrial growth; consequently, purchasing motives and patterns can have political overtones both internally and internationally. Industrial goods frequently are counted among the implements of economic warfare, and a market can be turned into a battlefield of international political aspirations of foreign powers. The stage of economic development achieved often reflects significant internal political changes in addition to increased demand for industrial goods. In fact, at certain stages of development, the govenment is, in reality, the customer for most industrial goods.

Product Design

Besides the effect economic development has on the demand for kinds of goods, it also affects product development. Each stage of industrial advancement requires a greater degree of sophistication in necessary equipment because the general technological proficiency of a country is tied closely to its economic development. A country in the early stages of industrialization does not have an adequate pool of trained technicians, nor has the general level of technical abilities reached a significant degree of achievement. Therefore, the adequacy of a product must be considered in relation to the environment within which it will be operated rather than solely on the basis of technical efficiency. Equipment that requires a high degree of technical skill to operate, maintain, or repair can be inadequate in a country that lacks a pool of technically skilled labor.

Industrial marketers must keep in mind that industrial goods are ultimately evaluated on the basis of their contribution to profit or the improvement of the production process of the buyer. Consequently, products designed to meet the needs of individual industrial users are critical for competitive advantage. Certainly this is more the case today when there is competition from industrial goods producers such as Germany, France, and Japan. When there was little competition, a U.S. manufacturer could sell a machine designed for a 40,000-unit production run to a foreign company needing a machine with only one quarter that capacity. But, with competitors from other countries willing to offer a machine with the desired capacity at competitive prices, how can U.S. companies compete? Ironically, U.S. companies in the domestic market are very consumer oriented, producing what the market wants; yet, in foreign marketing, they are highly production oriented. As global competition increases, U.S. companies must become more marketing oriented to survive.

The problem of overengineered and overpriced products may not only be a problem for U.S. manufacturers in developing markets but also in U.S. markets. Product simplicity has contributed to the popularity of foreign-made products in the United States. Although less sophisticated than American-made, the products are easier to use, frequently more reliable, and cheaper.

Toyota and Nissan successfully introduced lightweight forklift trucks for $15,000 when U.S. manufacturers were focusing on heavy sophisticated forklift trucks costing $30,000 each. The foreign-made trucks cost less, were easier to maintain and service, and easier to operate. German and Japanese suppliers, which have about 35 percent of the machine-tool market in the United States, offer U.S. buyers machine tools that are less sophisticated and less technologically advanced than U.S. machine tools. This translates into lower prices, less expensive repair, and, because they are simpler to operate, lower cost, less-skilled labor.[10]

In light of today's competition, a company must consider the nature of its market and the adequacy of the design of its products for each market. Effective competition in global markets means that products must meet the requirements of the customer.[11] Success depends on giving each

---

[10] Lynn Adkins, "The Import Wave, Toughest Test for U.S. Business," *Dun's Business Month*, February 1985, pp. 30–33.

[11] "France 1985: The Focus Is on Haute Technologie," *France*, Fall 1985, pp. 22–26.

market the kind of products it needs and wants, technologically advanced products for some and less sophisticated for others. One of the strengths of the Japanese as world competitors is their willingness to adapt products to the target market.

Concept of Quality.   Industrial marketers frequently misinterpret the concept of quality. Good quality as interpreted by a highly industrialized market is not the same when interpreted by standards of less-industrialized nations. For example, an African government had been buying hand-operated dusters to distribute pesticides in cotton fields; the dusters were loaned to individual farmers. The duster supplied was a finely machined device requiring regular oiling and good care. But the fact that this duster turned more easily than any other on the market was relatively unimportant to the farmers. Furthermore, the requirement for careful oiling and care simply meant that in a relatively short time, the machines froze up and broke. The result? The local government went back to an older type of French duster that was heavy, turned with difficulty, and gave a poorer distribution of dust, but which lasted longer because it required less care and lubrication. In this situation, the French machine possessed more relevant quality features and, therefore, in marketing terms, possessed the higher quality.

It must be kept in mind that the concept of quality is not an absolute measure but one relative to use patterns and/or predetermined standards. Best quality is best because the product adheres exactly to specified standards that have been determined by expected use of the product. Since use patterns are frequently different from one economy to another, standards vary so that superior quality in one country falls short of superior quality as determined by needs in another country.

Variations in Product Features.   The design and quality of a product must be viewed from all aspects of use. Extreme variations in climate create problems in designing equipment that is universally operable. Products that function effectively in the United States may require major design changes to operate as well in the hot, dry Sahara region or the humid, tropical rain forests of Latin America. Trucks designed to travel the superhighways of the United States almost surely will experience operational difficulties in the mountainous regions of Latin America on roads that closely resemble jeep trails. Many variations must be considered if manufacturers are to make products functional for far-flung markets.

Service, Replacement Parts, and Standards

Effective competition abroad not only requires proper product design but also effective service, prompt deliveries, and the ability to furnish spare and replacement parts without delay. In the highly competitive European community, for example, it is imperative to give the same kind of service a domestic company or EC company can give. One U.S. export management firm warned that U.S. business may be too apathetic about Europe, treating it as a subsidiary market not worthy of "spending time to develop." It cites the case "of an American firm with a $3 million potential sale in Europe which did not even give engineering support to its representatives when the same sale in the States would have brought out all the troops."

For many technical products, the willingness of the seller to provide installation and training may be the deciding factor in accepting one company's product over another's.[12] Korean and other Asian businesspersons are frank in admitting they prefer to buy from American firms but the Japanese get the business because of service. Frequently heard tales of conflicts between U.S. and foreign firms over assistance buyers expect from the seller are indicative of the problems of after-sales service and support. A Korean businessman related his experiences with an American engineer and some Japanese engineers typifying the situation: The Korean electronic firm purchased semiconductor-chip-making equipment for a plant expansion. The American engineer responsible for installing the equipment was slow in completing the installation; he stopped work at five o'clock and would not work on weekends. Japanese engineers installing other equipment understood the urgency of getting the factory up and running; they came in and worked day and night until the job was finished without being asked.

Unfortunately this is not an isolated case; Hyundai Motor Company bought two multimillion dollar presses to stamp body parts for cars. The "presses arrived late, the engineers took much longer than promised to set up the machines, and Hyundai had to pay the Americans extra to get the machines to work right." The impact of such problems translates into lost business for U.S. firms. Samsung Electronics Company, Korea's largest chip maker, used U.S. equipment for 75 percent of their first memory-chip plant. When it outfitted its most recent chip plant, it bought 75 percent of the equipment from Japan.[13]

Technical training is rapidly becoming a major after-sales service when selling technical products in countries that demand the latest technology but do not always have trained personnel. China demands the most advanced technical equipment but frequently has unqualified people responsible for products they do not understand. Heavy emphasis on training programs and self-teaching materials to help overcome the common lack

---

[12] "Good Follow-up Is Vital to Export Success," *Business America*, October 26, 1987, pp. 14–15.

[13] Stephen Kreider Yoder, "U.S. Failure to Compete Irks the Koreans," *The Wall Street Journal*, January 6, 1989, p. A8.

of skills to operate technical equipment is a necessary part of the after-sales service package in much of the developing world.

A recent study of international users of heavy construction equipment revealed that, next to the manufacturer's reputation, quick delivery of replacement parts was of major importance in purchasing construction equipment. Furthermore, 70 percent of those questioned indicated they bought parts not made by the original manufacturer of the equipment because of the difficulty of getting original parts. Smaller importers complain of U.S. exporting firms not responding to orders or responding only after extensive delay. It sometimes appears the importance of timely availability of spare parts to sustain a market is forgotten by American exporters; frequently, orders for replacement parts are ignored. When companies are responsive, the rewards are significant. U.S. chemical production equipment manufacturers dominate sales in Mexico because, according to the International Trade Administration, they deliver quickly. The ready availability of parts and services provided by U.S. marketers can give them a competitive edge.[14]

Some foreign marketers also may be forgoing the opportunity of participating in a lucrative aftermarket. Certain kinds of machine tools use up five times their original value in replacement parts during an average lifespan and thus represent an even greater market. One international machine tool company has capitalized on the need for direct service and available parts by changing its distribution system from the "normal" to one of stressing rapid service and readily available parts. Instead of selling through independent distributors as most machine tool manufacturers in foreign markets do, this company has established a series of company stores and service centers similar to those found in the United States. As a result of the change, the company stands ready to render service through its system of local stores while most competitors dispatch service people from their home-based factories. Service people are kept on tap for rapid service calls in each of its network of local stores, and each store keeps a large stock of standard parts available for immediate delivery. The net result of meeting industrial needs quickly is keeping the company among the top suppliers in foreign sales of machine tools.

Two relatively new services, international small package door-to-door express air services and international toll-free telephone service between a rapidly growing number of countries and the United States, have helped speed up the delivery of parts and made after-sales technical service almost instantly available. Technical advice is only a toll-free call away and parts are air-expressed immediately to the customer. Not only does this approach

---

[14] "A Big Selling Feature for Exporters: The Assurance of After-Sales Services," *Business America*, February 15, 1988, pp. 19–20.

> **BOX 13-2**
> **Now This Is What You Call Service!**
>
> Maschinenfabrik Augsburg-Nürnberg (MAN) the West German commercial vehicle and machinery group, has won a $109 million, two-year contract to provide trucks and backup services to the Iraqi-Jordanian Overland Transport Company. The order is for 400 60-metric-ton trucks to operate along the highways linking the Jordanian port of Aqaba with Iraq.
>
> MAN won the deal against competition from most of the major European commercial vehicle manufacturers. Company executives attribute their success to the firm's offer of extensive backup services. While most of the bidders could provide drivers for their trucks, few could match MAN's promise of mobile repair workshops, water supply facilities, and a drivers' camp complete with butcher shop and dispensary.
>
> Source: "MAN Lands an Iraqi-Jordanian Deal," *World Business Weekly*, August 24, 1981, p. 19. Reprinted by permission of the *Financial Times*, London.

improve service standards but it also is often more cost effective than maintaining an office in a country even though linguists must be hired to answer calls. The cost of opening and staffing an office and maintaining a parts inventory can exceed several hundred thousand dollars annually.[15]

Universal Standards

A lack of universal standards is another problem in the international sales of industrial products. The United states has two major areas of concern for the industrial goods exporter: One is a lack of common standards for highly specialized equipment manufacturing, such as machine tools and computers, and the other is in the use of the inch-pound[16] or English system of measurement.[17] Domestically the use of the inch-pound and the lack of a universal manufacturing standard are minor problems, but they have serious consequences when affected products are scheduled for export. Conflicting standards are encountered in test methods for materials and equipment, quality control systems, and machine specifications. In the telecommunications industry, the vast differences of standards

---

[15] Elaine Santoro, "Telemarketing Globalized," *Direct Marketing*, June 1987, p. 195.

[16] "Memo to U.S. Computer Makers: Standardize or Else," *Business Week*, October 3, 1988, p. 34.

[17] Also referred to as the *foot* or *yard-pound* system.

BOX 13–3
Japan Eyes the Auto-Service Market

As the Mideast automobile market expands, so too does demand for spare parts, gas station equipment, tires, repair-shop tools, and mechanical services. Japanese motor vehicle manufacturers have been quick to see the potential of this market and have begun training auto mechanics all over the region in the art of auto repair. In the latest such venture, Toyota, Nissan and Honda have announced plans to help Libya set up service shops in 44 towns and cities.

Toyota will soon send three experts to Libya to give technical advice on building a repair shop in Tripoli, and five Libyans will go to Japan in August for training in motor-servicing techniques. Honda will also send auto experts to Libya, while Nissan will train Libyan mechanics at its service centers in Athens as well as in Japan.

The automakers are counting on the service market not only to provide a lucrative sidelight to the main business of selling cars but also to boost Mideast demand for Japanese vehicles. The region is now Japan's second-largest market for automobile sales, but it is way behind the number one market—the United States. If Mideast mechanics are trained to service Japanese cars, the reasoning goes, people in the market for a new car are more likely to choose a brand they know they can have repaired locally.

Source: "Japan Eyes the Auto-Service Market," *World Business Weekly*, June 22, 1981, p. 19. Reprinted by permission of the *Financial Times*, London.

---

among countries create enormous problems for expansion of that industry.

Efforts at universal standardization are being made through international organizations dedicated to the creation of international standards; for example, the International Electrotechnical Commission (IEC) is concerned with standard specifications for electrical equipment for machine tools. Another international organization interested in the development of world standards is the International Organization of Standardization (ISO). In the United States, conversion to the metric system and acceptance of international standards have been slow. Congress and industry have dragged their feet for fear conversion would be too costly. As American industry sales are accounted for more and more by foreign customers on the metric system, the cost of dealying standardization mounts. Measurement-sensitive products account for one half to two thirds of U.S. exports, and if the European Community bars nonmetric imports as expected, many U.S. products will lose access to that market just as the EC is on the threshold of economic expansion. To spur U.S. industry into action, the 1988 Trade Act states that the metric system is the preferred system of weights and

BOX 13–4
In the European Community, Standards a Must for Telecommunications

The EC Commission predicts that by the year 2000, telecommunications may grow more than threefold to 7 percent of the Common Market's gross domestic product, topping autos as the biggest industrial sector. Seven of the world's top 13 telephone-switch makers are European. But obstacles abound—there is little or no standardization. Here is some trivia about Europe's telephone system.

In Spain the busy signal is three pips a second; in Denmark, it's two. French telephone numbers are seven digits long; Italian numbers are almost any length. West German phones run on 60 volts of electricity; elsewhere, it is 48. The list of differences goes on and on; only 30 percent of the technical specifications involved in phone systems are common from one country to the next. In telephones, as in much else in Europe, each country goes its own way.

Technical conflicts abound. Each national telephone authority sets different technical requirements for equipment to enter its market. One representative from an electronics company estimates that an average of 50 to 100 labor-years of costly software engineering are needed to rework computerized exchange equipment for each additional European country his company enters.

Technical differences serve political ends. The idiosyncratic specifications in each country protect local equipment makers from foreign competition which suits many European governments and companies just fine.

Source: Adapted from "European Officials Push Idea of Standardizing Telecommunications—But Some Makers Resist," *The Wall Street Journal*, April 10, 1985, p. 28.

measures for the United States and calls for a preference in government purchasing for metric products. It also requires federal agencies to use the metric system exclusively in grants, procurements and all other business-related activities by 1992. The Defense Department now requires metric specifications for all new weapons systems.[18] Perhaps these two efforts will push U.S. industry to adopt the metric system.[19] It is hard to believe that the only two countries not officially on the metric system are Burma and the United States. It is becoming increasingly evident that the United States must change or be left behind.

---

[18] "The Defense Department Throws Its Weight Behind the Metric System," *Business Week*, April 11, 1988, p. 123.

[19] "Metric Transition: Help for U.S. Exporters," *Business America*, September 26, 1988, pp. 2–5.

CHANNEL STRATEGY

A multitude of channel alternatives are available to the foreign marketer of industrial goods. American firms distribute in three ways: through American-based export middlemen; through foreign-based middlemen; and through company-managed and -organized sales forces.[20] Companies can use any combination of these three distribution systems or only one, depending on the extent of their involvement in foreign marketing, their organization, production facilities, and financial status. In each category, several kinds of institutions are available for use, or several kinds of company-owned sales organizations are utilized.

The type of distribution employed depends on company size, level of market commitment, and market conditions (finance, middlemen, political climate, and so forth). The use of domestic-based exporters is probably adequate for small companies without extensive acumen in foreign operations or for a firm that prefers a minimum of involvement in foreign sales. Those companies that intend to become truly international in scope and are totally committed to foreign marketing need the more direct methods available. The decision to deal with an agent or distributor or to set up an independent sales organization is influenced by many factors—availability of adequate middlemen, finances, desired control of sales, character of the product. The successful use of entirely different methods of distribution by two large companies serves as an illustration. A leading manufacturer of machine tools established its own sales distribution points throughout Europe. The decision was based on the competitive need to provide rapid service for its equipment and on a desire to participate in the lucrative parts market associated with the use of its products. This method of distribution was the most suitable for the company's circumstances.

In contrast, a leading manufacturer of farm and earth-moving equipment changed from direct distribution through company-owned sales subsidiaries to the use of independent local distributors. It was decided that independent local distributors would provide this company with a stronger, more economical organization that was far more stable for its products which were sensitive to economic shifts. Particularly in smaller markets, a local distributor would be better able to weather economic ups and downs by carrying complementary products. Furthermore, the manufacturer felt that a local distributor would be more effective than its own sales organization because it would have better market knowledge and would eliminate the normal break-in period required by company-owned operations. A final point—through the use of local distributors, the company could exploit markets too small to support a company sales organization but needing the services available from locally based distribution points.

---

[20] For a complete discussion, see Chapters 17 and 18.

In today's buyer's market unless a company can provide after-sales service, including prompt delivery, repair, and adequate supplies of replacement parts, a direct sales force may not be effective. The representative
or agent who handles many lines from a small office is slowly losing
ground to the engineering firm that can prepare technical bids and stock
spare parts. The evolving market pattern indicates that the company that
plans a long-range program abroad and wishes to remain competitive
has to select full-service distributors or organize its own sales unit to include
a complete stock of parts and full-service facilities. Since agents do not
normally provide much in the way of extra services, a company that utilizes
agents in its distribution system must arrange for additional services
through other channels.[21]

International trade fairs and trade centers found throughout major market
areas of the world may also be considered methods of distribution. Although these fairs provide a means for the introduction of new products
or an introduction into new markets, thereby helping to establish trade
relations, they are primarily classified as promotional activities and are
discussed in the following section on promotion.

PROMOTING INDUSTRIAL PRODUCTS

The promotional problems encountered by foreign industrial marketers
are little different from the problems faced by domestic marketers. Until
recently there was a paucity of specialized advertising media in many
countries; but, in the last decade, especially in Western Europe and to
some extent in Eastern Europe, Russia, and China, specialized industrial
media have developed to provide the industrial marketer with a means
of communicating with potential customers. In addition to the advertising
that would normally take place in print media, many industrial markets
can also be reached through catalogs, direct mail, and trade fairs which
are important promotional media in international industrial marketing.

Industrial Trade Fairs and Trade Centers

For industrial advertisers, one of the most powerful international media
is the trade show or trade fair. Products and product demonstrations almost
automatically surmount all communications barriers. As part of the U.S.

[21] For an interesting case for direct marketing, see "Marketing Strategies: Adapting a U.S.
Sales Approach to Penetrate the U.K. Market," *Business International*, September 14, 1987,
p. 289.

BOX 13–5
Now That's a "Classy" Turn Down

The Chinese are very polite and frequently their responses reflect the traditional exaggerated courtesy and honorific behavior of the academic Chinese. A rejection slip from a Beijing economic journal, received recently by a British writer, was couched in these flowing terms:

"We have read your manuscript with boundless delight. If we were to publish your paper it would be impossible for us to publish any work of a lower standard. And as it is unthinkable that, in the next thousand years, we shall see its equal, we are, to our regret, compelled to return your divine composition, and beg you a thousand times to overlook our short sight and timidity."

Source: "Atlantic Monthly, Please Take Note," *World Business Weekly*, December 15, 1981, p. 43.

Department of Commerce's international promotion activities, the federal government sponsors trade fairs in many cities around the world.[22]

In addition to trade fairs sponsored by governments, a number of private firms sponsor their own, including a flying fair using converted jet airliners as exhibition halls, a floating fair using ships as showrooms, and fairs sponsored by international trade and professional associations.

Trade fairs date back in history to the time when most trade was centered at markets or fairs. Today's international fairs are generally government-sponsored attempts to facilitate foreign trade. Governments often sponsor within their countries international trade fairs that are open to domestic and foreign exhibitors. They also sponsor fairs and trade centers in other countries to facilitate foreign trade for their domestic industries.

Fairs provide the facilities for a manufacturer to exhibit and demonstrate products to potential users. They are an opportunity to create sales and establish relationships with agents and distributors that can lead to more permanent distribution channels in foreign markets. Thirty-nine American firms participated in a seven-day electronics production equipment exhibition in Osaka, Japan, and came home with $1.6 million in confirmed orders and estimates for the following year of $10.1 million. Five of the companies were seeking Far Eastern agent/distributors through the show and each was able to sign a representative before the show closed. Trade fairs are scheduled periodically and any interested manufacturer can reserve space to exhibit goods.[23]

---

[22] "Taking Advantage of Trade Fairs for Maximum Sales Impact," *Business International*, October 12, 1987, pp. 321–22.

[23] "World Trade Fair Schedule for 1986," *Business America*, January 16, 1986, pp. 2–24.

The American government has also established permanent trade centers where products from various American industries are exhibited for specific time periods. There are 17 permanent U.S. trade centers in industrial centers such as London, Frankfurt, Milan, Bangkok, Stockholm, Tokyo, and Rome. The trade center functions in the same manner as a trade fair except that the former is permanent and operates the year-round with 8 to 10 shows a year. In conjunction with the trade centers, the Commerce Department offers manufacturers seeking business overseas the opportunity to have their products presented to potential buyers on a videotape and thus gain greater exposure.[24]

PRICING AND COMPETITION

One of the outgrowths of rapidly growing world markets for industrial goods is the considerable price competition among those vying for this expanding market. The problem is compounded by aggressive competition from suppliers and by the political involvement of governments of some manufacturers. As mentioned earlier, industrial goods are often the cannon fodder of economic wars being waged to win the political allegiance of underdeveloped countries. As a result, foreign marketers are sometimes confronted with impossible price competition because prices are shaded by a foreign government for political rather than economic reasons. Today, India, Brazil, or any underdeveloped and industrializing nation can buy Russian-made machinery and equipment at prices at least 50 percent lower than those charged by American manufacturers for similar goods. Such political price competition cannot be overcome by private industry.

American manufacturers also face other kinds of price problems abroad. It has been charged that they are pricing themselves out of the market and they follow too conservative a policy with regard to price and credit. Reports from India indicate that despite their booming market for machine tools, selling American products is difficult, if not impossible, because of the manufacturer's insistence on payment in dollars. Soviet bloc nations and our Western European competitors are not making this mistake.

European concerns offer liberal credit terms and payment in almost any of the world's currencies, while U.S. manufacturers are hesitant about granting credit and usually demand payment in dollars. Price alone is not always the sole determinant in purchasing decisions. In fact, some Venezuelan firms reportedly have indicated a willingness to pay 30 to 40 percent more for U.S. industrial products than for European products if

---

[24] For a detailed article on combining exporting and exhibiting in trade shows, see Daniel C. Bello, and Hiram C. Barksdale, Jr., "Exporting at Industrial Trade Shows," *Industrial Marketing Management*, no. 15, 1986, pp. 197–206.

adequate credit was available: presumably this is because of the better quality image of U.S. products. However, U.S. industrial goods are also being challenged on this front now by other competitors. One Department of Commerce study revealed that the demand for U.S. goods in Ecuador was extremely high, but, the trend was for Ecuadorians to buy from suppliers who offered the best payment terms rather than the lowest price.[25]

Price-Quality Relationship

A price-quality relationship plagues the U.S. manufacturer. Standard quality requirements of industrial products sold in the American market that require commensurately higher prices may be completely out of line for the needs of many of the underdeveloped growth markets of the world. Rather than question if American manufacturers are pricing themselves out of world markets, it may be more appropriate to ask whether or not they are advancing themselves out of some world markets with products of extremely high quality. When companies pay labor $15 or more per hour, labor-saving features in a product make sense, but not when the going rate of pay is $1.50 per day as in India. One Indian observer commented that the purchase of modern equipment in the West is often justified purely in labor-saving terms. But with an adult population of 326 million and an official urban unemployment rate of 15 million, the last thing India needs is labor-saving equipment. In fact, India is having serious reservations about highly automated industry. The country has embarked on a program to scale down many industries that could be labor intensive. The labor minister suggested that by converting to a cottage industry, a highly automated match company currently employing 15,000 workers could create 250,000 new jobs immediately.

Labor-saving features in a product have little value when time has limited value and labor is plentiful. Also of little value is the ability of machinery to hold close tolerances where people are not quality-control conscious, where production runs in the American volume sense do not exist, and where skillful workers cost so little it is affordable for them to take their time to do what amounts to selective fits in assembly and repair work. This does not mean there is no interest in quality or cost in developing countries like India, but that the achievement of low cost and good quality in these countries is not through high-production, high-precision equipment, and minimum labor cost, but through the use of skillful labor under close supervision with a minimum of the most versatile low-cost equipment adequate for the job. Hence, for the company that wants to market its

---

industrial goods in some countries, it may be necessary to design products for the export market with fewer functional features to lower the price and thereby compete effectively on price.

Countertrading—A Pricing Tool

Of growing importance in Eastern European countries, Russia, the People's Republic of China, and many less-developed countries, is a sale paid for with something other than currencies. *Countertrade* is the inclusive term used to describe transactions where all or partial payment is made in kind rather than cash.[26] There was a significant increase in countertrade transactions during the late 1960s through the 1980s. This is primarily the result of shortages of hard currencies available to industrializing nations. For Communist countries, purchases from non-Communist suppliers must be made with monies earned from Western nations; and the less-developed countries' (LDCs) inflation-ridden or weak currencies are insufficient to meet all the demands of industrialization. In all situations, hard currencies are reserved for top-priority purchases while goods of less importance, as well as some top-priority needs, are being purchased with some form of countertrade.

Willingness to accept countertrades is an important competitive price advantage. U.S. equipment companies, unwilling to countertrade, frequently lose out to other countries.[27] Barter, the basic countertrade, has been used in foreign trade since the beginning of economic history. After World War I, economically devastated countries resorted to barter to cope with financial crises in the aftermath of the war. During the worldwide depression of the 1930s, barter was again revived as a means of trade, and Germany proved a most effective user of barter in rebuilding after World War I. Again, since the early 1980s barter is on the upswing. Shortages of hard currencies characteristic of developing countries and the enormous foreign debt of some, mean that many need good credit terms or a willingness on the part of the seller to countertrade.[28] Much of the trade with China, for example, is paid for with countertrade.[29]

---

[26] There are a variety of terms used to describe the transactions that the author classifies as countertrades. In order not to further confuse the issue and to help standardize terminology, I have used the terms developed by Business International Corporation.

[27] For an interesting study on British attitudes toward countertrade see David Shipley and Bill Neale, "Industrial Barter and Countertrade," *Industrial Marketing Management*, no. 16 (1987), pp. 1–8.

[28] Countertrades are discussed in-depth in Chapter 16.

[29] Noel Fletcher and Gregory S. Johnson, "Chinese Offer Swap: Coal for Engines." *Journal of Commerce*, April 15, 1988, p. 1.

BUSINESS SERVICES AS A PRODUCT

When we think of foreign trade, manufactured products generally come to mind. That view is rapidly changing as business services gain a greater share of world trade. Accounting services, advertising, consulting, construction, insurance, movie and TV films, auto rentals, hotel services, financial services, and many other similar intangible products are included in the category of business services as products.[30] See Exhibit 13–1 for some definitions of different services. International trade in services is becoming more important in the economies of the United States and other countries; it is the fastest growing sector of international trade. It is estimated that services account for about one fourth of the value of all international trade.

EXHIBIT 13–1   Services: Some Definitions

The service account in the balance of payments has been described as "a composite of many dissimilar types of transactions." Yet, these have a common denominator because they involve selling or buying part of the output of the United States and its trading partners, or providing a return on United States capital invested abroad in a previous period, or on foreign capital invested in this country.

The largest single category, *investment income*, represents payments and receipts of income on direct investments and other internationally held private and government assets, including bank and commercial loans. *Travel and transportation*, the second largest item, includes all expenditures connected with the international movement of people and goods, such as passenger fares and freight. It also includes expenditures on goods and services made by travelers outside their countries of residence.

Fees and royalties consist of payments by both firms and individuals for the use of technology, intangible property, and managerial services. *Military transfers* reflect provision of goods and services to foreign governments under United States military sales contracts. On the payments side, *defense expenditures* include goods and services purchased abroad by both the Department of Defense and United States military personnel. *Other services* show payments and receipts on private services such as construction, finance and insurance, as well as on government services not covered elsewhere (such as foreign expenditures by nonmilitary agencies and personnel).

Not included under services are private remittances, government grants, and other unilateral transfers—although these are often grouped with services under the heading of "invisibles." Merchandise trade and invisibles together constitute the so-called current-account transactions, the net balance of which is the broadest measure of the United States balance-of-payments position.

SOURCE: John Hein, "International Trade in Services," *World Business Perspective* no. 75 (October 1983), p. 2.

---

[30] "Service Exports: The Silent Revolution," *Export Today*, April 1989, pages 5–8.

Growth of U.S. Business Services

The United States' exports of services are one fifth as large as merchandise exports. In 1988 U.S. exports of business services reached an estimated $69 billion. These figures are the ones reported in the balance of payments which omits several categories of services.[31] Omitted services include advertising, accounting, management consulting, legal services, most insurance, and probably most of the new computer and communications services. Ironically, those services omitted are the fastest growing. Services trade may be underestimated in balance-of-payments figures by as much as 50 percent. If such is the case, U.S. services trade is probably in excess of $100 billion.

The economic importance of services trade to the United States has resulted in the Trade and Tariff Act of 1984 mandating the Commerce Department to establish a Service Industries Development Program. An essential element of this program is a reporting system that is to be expanded to include statistics on exports and imports of services, receipts, employment, and wages paid by service firms. Also included are explicit mandates for negotiations with U.S. trading partners to remedy rapidly expanding trade barriers. The single biggest impediment to trade in services, especially the expansion of high-technology services, is the lack of the necessary trade machinery to handle the increases of services trade as they occur.[32]

U.S. Multinational Services Expand

Initially, most U.S. service companies became international to service their U.S. clients—travelers and American tourists. Accounting and advertising firms were among the earlier companies to establish branches or acquire local affiliations abroad to serve their multinational clients. Hotels and auto rental agencies followed the business traveler and tourist to fill their needs. However, it quickly became apparent that the expansion of international business throughout the world created a market for international service companies whether the MNCs were American, European, Japanese, or Brazilian. By the 1970s, there was a noticeable trend of service companies seeking business other than serving their home-country clients.

H & R Block, Inc., the income-tax preparation firm, has about 6,000 offices worldwide and is a good example of a company that made the transition from serving U.S. expatriates to serving local customers. Entry

---

[31] "U.S. Trade Facts," *Business America*, May 22, 1989, p. 12.

[32] Robert J. Morris, "Trade in Services: U.S. Business' Stake in the New GATT Round," *Export Today*, July–August 1988, pp. 55–57.

BOX 13–6
Garbage Collection an International Service?

The service industry in the United States has a bright future with a variety of services to sell. Ten thousand house-hungry Londoners signed up for more than $500 million of mortgages. A Wall Street subsidiary of Salomon Brothers has European executives eager to get a package from Amsterdam to Atlanta. Increasingly, they are turning to Federal Express, a Memphis company whose international revenues have been doubling every year since it began operating overseas. That is only part of the story, there are many services we don't hear about. For example, national-based Hospital Corporation of America, the biggest operator of private hospitals in the United States, has acquired 28 hospitals abroad and signed contracts to operate 9 others.

In Japan ServiceMaster of the United States is showing those masters of industry quality control a few things about improving productivity and cutting costs when it comes to scrubbing floors and washing laundry. ServiceMaster has in the past few years launched more than 500 home cleaning franchises in Japan and won contracts to do the housekeeping for 40 hospitals.

Having persuaded hundreds of local governments in the United States to contract out street cleaning and trash collection, $2-billion-a-year Waste Management, Inc. is cleaning up in Argentina, Saudi Arabia, and Australia. Fred Weinert, chief of the garbage king's international division, thinks revenues can grow 25 percent a year over the next five years. "Our main competitive advantage is our experience," he says. The company has a $155 million contract in Saudi Arabia to collect garbage.

Source: Adapted from Richard I. Kirkland, Jr., "The Bright Future of Service Exports," *Fortune*, June 8, 1987, pp. 32 and 38.

into Latin America began with target countries being selected on the basis of how many U.S. citizens were residing in an area. After a short time, the scope of operations was expanded and the same methodology used to prepare U.S. tax returns for expatriates was applied to the local market.[33]

Price Waterhouse & Company, one of the largest U.S. accounting firms, has made a significant commitment in the People's Republic of China because of its expectation of the future importance of that country as a market. There are several reasons why Price Waterhouse sees expansion in China as important. First, it is necessary to be in China to properly service its many multinational clients located there. Second, China's accounting practices and management techniques did not advance during the Mao period so there is an opportunity to help the Chinese meet the

---

[33] How H & R Block Took the Plunge into Latin America," *Business Latin America*, April 10, 1985, p. 118.

demands being created by their open-door policy for investment and industrial growth. Third, for foreign companies to be willing to make investments there, China must develop a rational system for taxing the earnings from these investments. Finally, there appear to be long-term opportunities for auditing Chinese enterprises and for providing broad consulting services.[34] The expansion into international markets is not restricted to American firms. From Germany, Britain, Japan, and Brazil tough new competitors are moving into the market for business and personal services. Governments are also taking notice of the growth of this industry and protectionism and other barriers to unrestricted trade are beginning to emerge to create an environment not too dissimilar from that facing a merchandise trader. When the EC fully integrates in 1992, opportunities for service industry growth will improve but the issue of restrictions for those outside the EC have yet to be resolved.[35]

Market Environment for Business Services

Service firms face most of the same environmental constraints and problems confronting merchandise traders. Protectionism, control of transborder data flows, competition, and the protection of trademarks, processes, and patents are possibly the most important problems confronting the MNC in today's international services market.

Protectionism.   The most serious threat to the continued expansion of international services trade is protectionism. The growth of international services has been so rapid during the last decade it has drawn the attention of domestic companies and governments. As a result, direct and indirect trade barriers have been imposed to restrict foreign companies from domestic markets. Every reason, from the protection of infant industries to national security, has been used to justify some of the restrictive practices. A list of more than 2,000 instances of barriers to the free flow of services among nations was recently compiled by the U.S. government.[36] In the Uruguay Round of GATT, the United States is stressing the elimination of trade barriers, the protection of intellectual property, and market access for service industries.[37] Service exports currently are not accorded the

---

[34] Mark Stevens, "Price Waterhouse's Orient Express," *Across the Board*, July–August 1985, p. 23.

[35] Jonathan D. Aronson and Albert Bressand, "Services in Europe: A Policy for the '90s," *Europe*, January–February 1987, pp. 25–27.

[36] Merriam Mashatt, "The FTA Sets International Precedent in Service Trade," *Business America*, January 30, 1989, pp. 8–9.

[37] C. William Verity, "Uruguay Round," *Business America*, June 20, 1988, pp. 2–7.

same treatment as manufactured goods in either the United States or other countries' laws and regulations.[38]

A study of U.S. service firms reported that the most frequently encountered barriers to trade were restrictions on the right to conduct business in a country or to have complete ownership of investments; restrictions on repatriation of royalties, fees, and profits; discriminatory tax policies; and barriers to transborder data flows.

Transborder Data Flow.   Restrictions on transborder data flows are potentially the most damaging to both the communications industry and other MNCs who rely on data transfers across borders to conduct business. Some countries impose tariffs on the transmission of data and many others are passing laws forcing companies to open their computer files to inspection by government agencies.[39]

Most countries have a variety of laws to deal with the processing and electronic transmission of data across borders. There is intense concern about how to deal with this relatively new technology. In some cases, concern stems from not understanding how best to tax transborder data flows and, in other cases, there is concern over the protection of individual rights when personal data are involved. By far the greatest concern most countries have, although often unstated, is the desire to inhibit the activities of multinationals to protect local industry.

Restrictions, however, are not all generated by host countries. A study released by the Commerce Department reveals that our international information service firms are hemmed in by restrictions from the U.S. government as well as from abroad. Three major barriers encountered abroad by data base and data processing firms are discrimination by government telecommunications agencies, transborder data flow restrictions, and foreign exchange controls.[40]

The biggest domestic headache is U.S. export control processes. Getting through the U.S. export-license maze is by far the greatest domestic barrier firms face in selling services abroad. Not only is it time-consuming to get permission to do business abroad, it is frequently not clear which of many U.S. agencies are involved in approving requests. If data from data

---

[38] Stephen Barlas, "Service Exporters Spell Relief 'GATT,'" *Business Marketing,* January 1987, pp. 58–61.

[39] For a comprehensive review of this and other problems, see Rajan Chandran, Arvind Phatak, and Rakesh Sambharya, "Transborder Data Flows: Implications for Multinational Corporations," *Business Horizons,* November–December 1987, pp. 74–82.

[40] For a comprehensive study of the regulation of data flows, see "Regulating International Data Transmission: The Impact on Managing International Business," Report no. 852, *The Conference Board,* 1984, p. 23.

bases involving foreign activities are to be transmitted, there is always the question of national security to resolve.[41]

Competition.   As mentioned earlier, competition in all phases of the services industry is increasing as host-country markets are invaded by many foreign firms. Telecommunications, advertising, software development, construction, and hotels face major competition from Europe, Japan, and many NICs. Brazil and India are important software developers exporting sophisticated software to European and U.S. companies. The fastest growing services sector with the most severe competition is the telecommunications, electronic data processing and analysis, and transmission industries.[42] Because communications and all its related industries have national security implications, government monopolies are frequently among the major competitors. Despite growing global competition for export and domestic markets, the United States remains the world's largest producer and exporter of services.[43]

Protection of Intellectual Property.   Another form of competition difficult to combat is pirated trademarks, processes, and patents. Computer design and software, trademarks, brand names, and other intellectual properties are easy to duplicate and difficult to protect. The protection of intellectual property rights is a major problem in the services industries. Countries seldom have adequate—or any—legislation; any laws they do have are extremely difficult to enforce.[44] The Omnibus Trade and Competitiveness Act of 1988 addresses the issue of protecting intellectual property and the measures proposed benefit both goods and services firms.[45] Computer software is one of the most frequently pirated products. Estimates are that U.S. firms lose between $1 and 3 billion annually to piracy. Protection for software generally comes only with vigilance and continuous upgrading of the quality of the software.[46]

Prerecorded music and TV and movie films from the United States are popular the world over; with the ease of duplication, a major problem is

---

[41] U.S. Industry Identifies Top Trade Barriers to Information Services," *Business International,* May 3, 1985, pp. 139–40.

[42] "Outlook Is Brightening for Service Exports," *Business America,* March 30, 1987, pp. 5–6.

[43] Brant W. Free, "U.S. Services Are on the Competitive Edge," *Business America,* May 9, 1988, pp. 26–27.

[44] For a comprehensive review of services trade and some of the inherent problems, see Marc Levinson, "Unfettering Trade in Services," *Across the Board,* April 1987, pp. 24–31.

[45] *The Omnibus Trade and Competitiveness Act of 1988,* The International Division of the U.S. Chamber of Commerce, Washington, D.C. 1988, pp. 39–41.

[46] "What Apple Does to Catch and Convict High Tech Pirates," *Business International,* January 18, 1985, p. 17.

piracy. There is no accurate way of determining the exact amount of pirated sales, but it is estimated to be in the hundreds of millions of dollars annually.[47]

SUMMARY

Industrial goods face fewer challenges in global marketing because the inherent concepts and principles are the same in dealing with industrial and consumer goods. Even so, tactics and emphasis vary. Global competition has risen to the point that industrial goods marketers must pay close attention to the needs of each market in terms of its level of economic and technological development. Companies which adapt their products to the variety of differing needs are the ones that should be the most effective in the marketplace. Industrial markets are lucrative and continue to grow as more countries strive for at least a semblance of industrial self-sufficiency.

One of the fastest growing areas of industrial marketing is business services. This segment of marketing involves all countries at every level of development; even the least-developed countries are seeking computer technologies and sophisticated data banks to aid them in advancing their economies. It is also an area subject to protectionism and privacy.

QUESTIONS

1. Define the following terms and show their significance to international marketing:

   inch-pound system   universal standards
   trade centers   service
   trade fairs   countertrades
   price-quality relationship

2. What are the differences between consumer and industrial goods and what are the implications for international marketing? Discuss.

3. Discuss how the various stages of economic development affect the demand for industrial goods.

4. "Industrialization is typically a national issue, and industrial goods are the fodder for industrial growth." Comment.

5. "The adequacy of a product must be considered in relation to the general environment within which it will be operated rather than solely

---

[47] 'That's Entertainment,'' *Business America,* August 5, 1985, pp. 20–21.

on the basis of technical efficiency." Discuss the implications of this statement.

6. Why hasn't the United States been more helpful in setting universal standards for industrial equipment? Do you feel that the argument is economically sound? Discuss.

7. What role do service, replacement parts, and standards play in competition in foreign marketing? Illustrate.

8. Discuss the part industrial trade fairs and trade centers play in international marketing of industrial goods. What is the difference between industrial trade fairs and trade centers?

9. Discuss some of the more pertinent problems in pricing industrial goods.

10. What is the price-quality relationship? How does this affect a U.S. firm's comparative position in world markets?

11. Select several countries, each at a different stage of economic development, and illustrate how the stage affects demand for industrial goods.

12. England has almost completed the process of shifting from the inch-pound system to the metric system. What effect do you think this will have on the traditional U.S. reluctance to such a change? Discuss the economic implications of such a move.

13. Discuss the importance of international business services to total U.S. export trade. How do most U.S. service companies become international?

14. Discuss the international market environment for international business services.

CHAPTER

14

The Global Advertising and Promotion Effort

Once a product is developed to meet target market needs and is properly priced and distributed, the intended customers must be informed of the product's availability and value. Advertising and promotion are basic activities in an international company's marketing mix. A well-designed promotion mix includes advertising, sales promotion, personal selling, and public relations which are mutually reinforcing and focused on a common objective. Of all the elements of the marketing mix, decisions involving advertising are the ones most often affected by cultural differences among country markets. Consumers reflect their culture, its style, feelings, value systems, attitudes, beliefs, and perceptions.[1] Because advertising's function is to "interpret or translate the need/want satisfying qualities of product and services in terms of consumer needs, wants, desires, and aspirations," the emotional appeals, symbols, persuasive approaches and other characteristics of an advertisement must coincide with cultural norms to be effective.[2]

---

[1] Jae W. Hong, Aydin Muderrisoglu, and George M. Zinkhan, "Cultural Differences and Advertising Expression: A Comparative Content Analysis of Japanese and U.S. Magazine Advertising," *Journal of Advertising* 16, no. 1 (1987), p. 55.

[2] S. Watson Dunn and Arnold M. Barban, *Advertising* (Hinsdale, Ill.: The Dryden Press, 1986), p. 99.

Reconciling an international advertising and sales promotion effort with the cultural uniqueness of markets is the challenge confronting the international or global marketer. The basic framework and concepts of international promotion are essentially the same wherever employed. Five steps are involved: (1) determine the promotional mix (the blend of advertising, personal selling, and sales promotions) by national or global markets; (2) determine the extent of worldwide standardization; (3) develop the most effective messages; (4) select effective media; and (5) establish the necessary controls to assist in achieving worldwide marketing objectives. After a review of some of the global trends that might impact international advertising, we consider global versus modified advertising and survey other problems and challenges for international marketers, including basic creative strategy, media planning and selection, sales promotions, and the communications process.

GLOBAL ADVERTISING

Intense competition for world markets and the increasing sophistication of foreign consumers have led to a need for more sophisticated advertising strategies. Increased costs, problems of coordinating advertising programs in multiple countries, and a desire for a common worldwide company or product image have caused MNCs to seek greater control and efficiency without sacrificing local responsiveness. In the quest for more effective and responsive promotion programs, policies covering centralized or decentralized authority; use of single or multiple foreign or domestic agencies; appropriation and allocation procedures; copy, media, and research are all being examined. One of the most widely debated policy areas pertains to the degree of advertising variation necessary from country to country. One view sees advertising customized for each country or region because every country is seen as posing a special problem. Executives with this viewpoint argue that the only way to achieve adequate and relevant advertising is to develop separate campaigns for each country. At the other extreme are those who suggest that advertising should be standardized for all markets of the world overlooking regional differences altogether.

Debate on the merits of standardization compared to modification of international advertising has been going on for decades.[3] Theodore Levitt's article, "The Globalization of Markets," caused many companies to examine their international strategies and to adopt a global marketing strategy.[4]

---

[3] See, for example, pp. 533–34 of the first edition of this text, *International Marketing* (Homewood, Ill.: Richard D. Irwin, Inc., 1966).

[4] Theodore Levitt, "The Globalization of Markets," *Harvard Business Review*, May–June 1983, pp. 92–102.

Pepsi-Cola and Coca-Cola promote worldwide. (Left: Rick Warner/Journalism Services, Inc.) (Right: N'Diaye/Journalism Services, Inc.)

He postulated the existence and growth of the global consumer with similar needs and wants and advocated that international marketers should operate as if the world were one large market, ignoring superficial regional and national differences. Without discussing the merits of Levitt's arguments, there is evidence that companies may have overcompensated for cultural differences and modified advertising and marketing programs for each national market without exploring the possibilities of a worldwide, standardized marketing mix. After decades of following country-specific marketing programs, companies had as many different product variations, brand names, and advertising programs as countries in which they did business.

A case in point is the Gillette Company that sells 800 products in more than 200 countries. Gillette has a consistent worldwide image as a masculine, sports-oriented company, but its products have no such consistent image. Its razors, blades, toiletries, and cosmetics are known by many different names. Trac II blades in the United States are more widely known worldwide as G-II, and Atra blades are called Contour in Europe and Asia. Silkience hair conditioner is known as Soyance in France, Sientel in Italy, and Silkience in Germany.[5] Whether or not a global brand name could have been chosen for Gillette's many existing products is speculative. However, Gillette's current corporate philosophy of globalization provides for an umbrella statement, "Gillette, the Best a Man Can Get," in all advertisements for men's toiletries products in the hope of providing some common image.[6]

A similar situation exists for Unilever N.V. that sells a cleaning liquid called Vif in Switzerland, Viss in Germany, Jif in Britain and Greece, and Cif in France.[7] This situation is a result of Unilever marketing separately to each of these countries. At this point, it would be difficult for Gillette or Unilever to standardize their brand names since each brand is established in its market. Yet, with such a diversity of brand names it is not hard to imagine the problem of coordination and control and the potential competitive disadvantage against a company that has global brand recognition.

As discussed earlier, there is a fundamental difference between a multidomestic marketing strategy and a global marketing strategy. One is based on the premise that all markets are culturally different and a company must adapt marketing programs to accommodate the differences, whereas the other assumes similarities as well as differences and standardizes where there are similarities but adapts where culturally required. Further, it may be possible to standardize some parts of the marketing mix and not others. Also, the same standardized products may be marketed globally but, because of differences in cultures, have a different appeal in different markets.

Parker Pen Company, for example, sells the same pen in all markets but advertising differs dramatically from country to country. Print ads in Germany simply show the Parker pen held in a hand that is writing a headline—"This is how you write with precision." In the United Kingdom, where it is the brand leader, the exotic processes used to make pens, such as gently polishing the gold nibs with walnut chips, is emphasized. In the United States, the ad campaign's theme is status and image. The headlines in the ad are, "You walk into a boardroom and everyone's naked. Here's how to tell who's boss," and "There are times when it has to be a Parker." The company considers the different themes necessary because of the different product images and different customer motives in each market. On the other hand, their most expensive Duofold Centennial pen (about $200), created to coincide with the company's 100th anniver-

---

[5] "Gillette Finds World-Brand Image Elusive," *Advertising Age*, June 25, 1984, p. 50.

[6] "Gillette: $80M to Rebuild Image," *Advertising Age*, October 31, 1988, p. 1.

[7] John R. Marcom, "Cable and Satellites Are Opening Europe to TV Commercials," *The Wall Street Journal*, December 22, 1987, p. 1.

sary and targeted for an upscale market in each country, is advertised the same throughout the world. The advertising theme is designed to convey a statement about the company as well as the pricey new product.[8]

A global perspective directs products and advertising toward worldwide markets rather than multiple national markets. The seasoned international marketer or advertiser realizes the decision for standardization or modification depends more on motivational patterns than geography. Advertising must relate to motivation; if people in different markets buy similar products for significantly different reasons, advertising must focus on these differences. On the other hand, when markets react to similar stimuli, it is not necessary to vary advertising messages for the sake of variation. Because there are few situations where either position alone is clearly the best, most companies compromise with pattern advertising.

Pattern Advertising

As discussed earlier in the chapter on product development, a product is more than a physical item; it is a bundle of satisfactions the buyer receives. This package of satisfactions or utilities includes the primary function of the product along with many other benefits imputed by the values and customs of the culture. Different cultures often seek the same value or benefits from the primary function of a product, that is, the ability of an automobile to get from point A to point B, a camera to take a picture, or a wristwatch to tell time. But, while agreeing on the benefit of the primary function of a product, other features and psychological attributes of the item can have significantly different importance.

Consider the different market-perceived needs for a camera. In the United States, excellent pictures with easy, foolproof operation are expected by most of the market; in Germany and Japan, a camera must take excellent pictures but the camera must also be state-of-the-art in design. In Africa, where penetration of cameras is less than 20 percent of the households, the concept of picture-taking must be sold. In all three markets, excellent pictures are expected (i.e., the primary function of a camera is demanded) but the additional utility or satisfaction derived from a camera differs among cultures. There are many products that produce these different expectations beyond the common benefit sought by all. Thus, many companies follow a strategy of pattern standardization, a global advertising strategy with a standardized basic message allowing some degree of modification to meet local situations. In this way, some economies of standardization can be realized while specific cultural differences are accommodated.

---

[8] Kevin Cote, "Parker Pen Finds Black Ink," *Advertising Age*, July 13, 1987, p. 49.

BOX 14–1
Selling Levi's around the World

Levi's are sold in more than 70 countries with different cultural and political aspects affecting advertising appeals. Here are some of the appeals used:

In Europe, TV commercials have a super-sexy appeal.

In the United Kingdom, ads emphasize that Levi's are an American brand and star an all-American hero, the cowboy, in fantasy wild west settings.

In Japan, local jeans companies had already positioned themselves as American. To differentiate Levi's, the company positioned themselves as *legendary* American jeans with commercials themed "Heroes Wear Levi's" featuring clips of cult figures like James Dean. The Japanese responded—awareness of Levi's in Japan went from 35 percent to 95 percent as a result of this campaign.

In Brazil, the market is strongly influenced by fashion trends emanating from the Continent rather than America. Thus, the ads for Brazil are filmed in Paris featuring young people, cool amidst a wild Parisian traffic scene.

In Australia, commercials were designed to build brand awareness with product benefits. The lines "fit looks tight, doesn't feel tight, can feel comfortable all night" and "a legend doesn't come apart at the seams" highlighted Levi's quality image and "since 1850 Levi jeans have handled everything from bucking broncos . . ." stressed Levi's unique positioning.

Source: Adapted from "Exporting a Legend," *International Advertiser*, November–December 1981, pp. 2–3.

Levi Strauss and Company changed from all localized ads to a pattern advertising strategy where the broad outlines of the campaign are given but the details are not. The Seven-Up Company advertises in dozens of countries with a policy that allows variation in specific detail to suit local market conditions. Certain elements of Seven-Up advertising remain constant in every country; the Seven-Up logotype; the basic color combination; the Seven-Up bottle crown; and fundamental point-of-purchase units such as illuminated plastic signs, metal tackers, and brand signs. Libby is another company that has successfully standardized advertising themes from country to country through effective techniques. The Libby, McNeil & Libby commercial, used by subsidiaries throughout the world, features a clown, pantomime, and the simple story of the clown enjoying Libby food products. A study to determine the standardized versus localized advertising campaigns of U.S. firms revealed that the majority (66 percent) utilized a combination of localized and standardized advertising (pattern advertising); 36 percent used all modified advertising, and only 8 percent used all standardized advertising.[9]

Global Advertising and World Brands

Global brands generally are the result of a company that elects to be guided by a global marketing strategy. Global brands carry the same name, same design, and same creative strategy everywhere in the world; Coca-Cola, Pepsi-Cola, McDonalds, and Revlon are a few of the global brands. Even when cultural differences make it ineffective to have a standardized advertising program or a standardized product, a company may have a world brand. Nescafé, the world brand for Nestlé Company's instant coffee, is used throught the world even though advertising messages and formulation (dark roast and light roast) vary to suit cultural differences. In Japan and the United Kingdom, advertising reflects each country's preference for tea; in France, Germany, and Brazil, cultural preferences for ground coffee call for a different advertising message and formulation. Even in this situation, however, there is some standardization; all advertisements have one common emotional link: "Whatever good coffee means to you and however you like to serve it, Nescafé has a coffee for you."[10]

Some global companies have successfully capitalized on the worldwide popularity of pop music stars in their global advertisements. Michael Jackson is featured in Pepsi-Cola advertisements used all over the world including Russia. PepsiCo was the first company to buy commercial time on Soviet television and it used the global advertisement featuring Michael Jackson. A Russian voice-over translated the commercial but Michael Jackson was not translated.[11] Tina Turner has also been featured in global advertisements for Pepsi; when bottlers wanted to localize the commercial, Pepsi designed a generic version. They shot a videotape in which Tina was performing alone on stage but it appeared as if she were singing to someone. The tape was then sent to various countries where a local star was later dubbed in, appearing to be singing a duet with Tina.[12]

---

[9] Robert E. Hite and Cynthia Fraser, "International Advertising Strategies of Multinational Corporations," *Journal of Advertising Research*, August–September 1988, p. 16.

[10] Gordon L. Link, "Global Advertising: An Update," *Journal of Consumer Marketing*, Spring 1988, p. 72.

[11] "Pepsi Buys 5 Ad Spots on Soviet TV," *Denver Post* Wire Services, May 5, 1988.

[12] "Global Marketing Campaigns with a Local Touch," *Business International*, July 4, 1988, p. 210.

The debate between advocates of strict standardized advertising and those who support locally modified promotions will doubtless continue. The author cannot support either extreme position since he believes neither approach is always correct. Some products in certain countries can be promoted most effectively with a standardized approach while others require a localized, modified program to be successful. As discussed in Chapter 12, markets are constantly changing and in the process of becoming more alike, but the world is still far from being a homogeneous market with common needs and wants for all products. Myriad obstacles to strict standardization remain. Nevertheless, the lack of commonality among markets should not deter a marketer from being guided by a global strategy; that is, a marketing philosophy that directs products and advertising toward a worldwide rather than a local or regional market, seeking standardization where possible, and modifying where necessary.

CREATIVE CHALLENGES

The growing intensity of international competition coupled with the complexity of marketing multinationally demand that the international advertiser function at the absolute highest creative level. Advertisers from around the world have developed their skills and abilities to the point that advertisements from different countries reveal basic similarities and a growing level of sophistication. To complicate matters further, boundaries are placed on creativity by legal, language, cultural, media, production, and cost limitations.

Legal and Tax Considerations

Some countries regulate advertising more closely than others; this requires modification of the creative approach from country to country. Laws pertaining to advertising may restrict the amount spent on advertising, media used, type of product advertised, manner in which price may be advertised, type of copy and illustration material used, and other aspects of the advertising program. In Germany, for example, it is against the law to use comparative terminology. An advertiser cannot say that one soap gets clothes cleaner than another because the statement implies that other products do not get clothes clean. Advertisers live under the threat of immediate lawsuit from competitors if they claim their brand is best. Similar restrictions on language exist in most European countries; in Italy, even common words—deodorant and perspiration—are banned from television.[13]

---

[13] See, for example, J. J. Boddewyn, "The Global Spread of Advertising Regulation," *MSU Business Topics*, Spring 1981, pp. 5–13.

BOX 14–2
If It Wasn't for the Law

If there were no differences in country laws, one of the major obstacles to standardized advertising programs would be eliminated. Consider this sample of country laws that make a standardized advertisement almost impossible.

* In the United Kingdom, the Marlboro cowboy is outlawed, as are a chuck wagon and a lit campfire—if there is a campfire or chuck wagon, there is a cowboy nearby. British law prohibits all ads that portray heroic figures in cigarette ads since they might have special appeal and encourage people to start smoking.
* A 30-second Kellogg cereal commercial produced for British TV would have to have the following alterations to be acceptable in Europe:

   Reference to iron and vitamins would have to be deleted in the Netherlands.
   A child wearing a Kellogg's T-shirt would be edited out in France where children are forbidden from endorsing products on TV.
   In Germany the line, "Kellogg makes their cornflakes the best they've ever been" would be cut because of rules against making competitive claims.
   After alterations, the 30-second commercial would be about five seconds long.

* In Austria, where children are not permitted in commercials, some advertisers have resorted to hiring dwarfs or using animated drawings of children.
* A survey of 40 countries revealed that 11 require preclearance for children's advertising. War toys, presweetened cereals, candy and gum, children's magazines, and video games are all restricted in advertisements in one way or another. Well over 20 of the 40 nations surveyed restricted comparison advertisements or promotions that use well-known, popular, or fictional characters.

Source: Adapted from: "Country's Different Ad Rules Are Problem for Global Firms," *The Wall Street Journal*, September 27, 1984, p. 27; "EEC Media Experts Push for New Limits on Pan-Europe Ads," *Advertising Age*, January 30, 1984, p. 52; and "Advertising to Children: 17 Nations Consider Setting Controls," *Business International*, August 3, 1984, pp. 243–44.

In Kuwait the government-controlled TV network allows only 32 minutes of advertising per day and this in the evenings. Commercials are controlled to exclude superlative descriptions, indecent words, fearful or shocking shots, indecent clothing or dancing, contests, hatred or revenge shots, and attacks on competition. It is also illegal to advertise cigarettes, lighters, pharmaceuticals, alcohol, airlines, and chocolates or other candy.

Some countries have special taxes that apply to advertising which might restrict creative freedom in media selection. The tax structure in Austria best illustrates how advertising taxation can distort media choice by changing the cost ratios of various media. In federal states, with the exception of Bergenland and Tyrol, there is a 10 percent tax on ad insertions. For posters, there is a 10–30 percent tax according to state and municipality. Radio advertising carries a 10 percent tax, except in Tyrol where it is 20 percent. In Salzburg, Steiermark, Karnten, and Voralbert, there is no tax. There is a uniform ad tax of 10 percent throughout the country on television. Cinema advertising has a 10 percent tax in Vienna, 20 percent in Bergenland, and 30 percent in Steiermark. There is no cinema tax in the other federal states.

The Monopolies Commission in England has accused the Procter & Gamble Co. and Unilever of creating a monopoly (duopoly?) situation by spending nearly one fourth of their revenues on advertising. The companies were also criticized for earning too much. New taxes and restrictions on advertising have been introduced and some are passed nearly every year in countries that have traditionally imposed minimal restrictions on advertising and free competition. The variations between countries in interpreting what constitutes acceptable, honest advertising causes most problems. What is acceptable in one country may be deemed false and misleading in another. Legal and tax considerations are a major deterrent to complete standardization of advertising.

Language Limitations

Language is one of the major barriers to effective communication through advertising. The problem involves the different languages of different countries, different languages or dialects within one country, and the subtler problems of linguistic nuance and vernacular.[14]

Incautious handling of language has created problems in nearly every country. Some automotive examples suffice. Chrysler Corporation was nearly laughed out of Spain when it translated the U.S. theme advertising, "Dart Is Power." To the Spanish, the phrase implied that buyers sought but lacked sexual vigor. Ford floundered on the linguistic problems of number; in many languages the word *company* is plural rather than singular, as in English. "Ford Have Something for It" trumpeted one headline in English. Ford goofed again when it named its low-cost "Third World" truck *Fiera*, which means "ugly old woman" in Spanish. Market research showed that American Motor's *Matador* name meant virility and excitement, but when the car was introduced in Puerto Rico it was discovered that the word meant "killer"—"an unfortunate choice for Puerto Rico which has an unusually high traffic fatality rate." One Middle Eastern country

---

[14] "Linguistic Divide Key to Belgian Nation," *Europe*, March–April, 1984, pp. 34–35.

BOX 14–3
A European Consumer?

"The day you find a product labeled 'Made in Europe,' send it to me and I'll frame it as an historic document." So speaks the head of a French advertising agency.

"Europe?" questions another. "It's a concept, no more. Certainly, we advertise all over the continent, but it's a lot more difficult than it is in the United States. Do you know how many languages there are here?" (In the Common Market alone, there are six languages: English, French, German, Italian, Danish, and Dutch, not counting Flemish, Luxembourgois, Gaelic, or the various—and numerous—regional dialects.)

"A Europroduct?" asks another ad agency man. "What's that? The only one I know of that's acceptable anywhere is a Eurocheque. Money is one of the few things that can be internationalized."

Source: Barbara Farnsworth, "Advertising in Europe," © European Community. Reprinted with permission. All rights reserved.

advertisement featured an automobile's new suspension system that, in translation, said the car was "suspended from the ceiling." Since there are at least 30 dialects among Arab countries, there is ample room for error. What may appear as the most obvious translation can come out wrong. "A whole new *range* of products" in a German advertisement came out as "a whole new *stove* of products."[15]

Low literacy in many countries seriously impedes communications and calls for greater creativity and use of verbal media. Multiple languages within a country or advertising area provide another problem for the advertiser. Even a tiny country such as Switzerland has three separate languages. The melting-pot character of the Israeli population accounts for some 50 languages. A Jerusalem commentator says that even though Hebrew "has become a negotiable instrument of daily speech, this has yet to be converted into advertising idiom."

Language translation encounters innumerable barriers that impede effective, idiomatic translation and thereby hamper communication. This is especially apparent in advertising materials. Abstraction, terse writing, and word economy, the most effective tools of the advertiser, pose problems for translators. Communication is impeded by the great diversity of cultural heritage and education which exists within countries and which causes varying interpretations of even single sentences and simple concepts. Some companies have tried to solve the translation problem by hiring foreign

---

[15] "Ten Rules to Live by and Sell by Overseas," *Sales and Marketing Management*, April 2, 1984, p. 64.

translators who live in the United States, but this usually is not satisfactory; both the language and the translator change so the expatriate in the United States is often out of touch after a few years. Everyday words have different meanings in different cultures. Even pronunciation causes problems: Wm. Wrigley, Jr. Company had trouble selling Spearmint gum in Germany until it changed the spelling to Speermint. Seeking universally pronounceable brand names, that company selected the brand Yusi for an inexpensive gum to market in low-income countries.[16]

Cultural Diversity

The problems of communicating to people in diverse cultures is one of the great creative challenges in advertising. Communication is more difficult because cultural factors largely determine the way various phenomena are perceived. If the perceptual framework is different, perception of the message itself differs.

International marketers are becoming accustomed to the problems of adapting from culture to culture. Knowledge of differing symbolisms of colors is a basic part of the international marketer's encyclopedia. An astute marketer knows that white in Europe is associated with purity but in Asia it is commonly associated with death. The marketer must also be sophisticated enough to know that the presence of black in the West or white in Eastern countries does not automatically connote death. Color is a small part of the communications package, but if the symbolism in each culture is understood, the marketer has an educated choice of using or not using various colors.

Knowledge of cultural diversity must encompass the total advertising project. General Mills had two problems with one product. When it introduced instant cake mixes in the United States and England, it had the problem of overcoming the homemaker's guilt feelings. When General Mills introduced instant cake mixes in Japan, the problem changed; cakes were not commonly eaten in Japan. There was no guilt feeling associated with the instant cakes, but the homemaker was concerned about failing. She wanted the cake mix as complete as possible. In testing TV commercials promoting the notion that making cake is as easy as making rice, General Mills learned it was offending the Japanese homemaker who believes the preparation of rice requires great skill.

Existing perceptions based on tradition and heritage are often hard to overcome. Marketing researchers in Hong Kong found that cheese is associated with Yeung-Yen (foreigners) and rejected by the Chinese. The concept of cooling and heating the body is important in Chinese thinking; malted

---

[16] For an excellent discussion of language and marketing, see Vern Terpstra, *The Cultural Environment of International Business* (Cincinnati: South-Western Publishing, 1984), chap. 1.

BOX 14–4
Where the Commercial Is the Program

There are around 775 radio stations in Mexico, 57 of these in Mexico City (30 AM, 27 FM). Radio covers 83 percent of Mexico; 95 percent of Mexico City. There are close to 9 million radio households in the country and 2,715,000 in Mexico City.

Mexicans consider radio an excellent medium because of the high market penetration. But program ratings are low. To make an impact, the advertiser has to buy a large number of stations and spots. It is not unusual for a liquor advertiser to buy 40 spots per day on 32 stations in Mexico City alone—a total of 200 spots per week per station.

There are only two stations in Mexico that carry continuous programming for 15 to 25 minutes. On most stations, there are 24 minutes of commercial time per hour, and two commercial minutes per break with approximately 11 breaks per hour. As such, the entertainment on Mexican radio is so fragmented that listeners change stations constantly and never become attached to one program, announcer, or station.

Needless to say advertising clutter is tremendous. The usual commercial length is 30 seconds; the longest is 60 and the shortest, 10.

Source: Adapted from Erika Engels Levine, "Commercial Radio in Latin America," *International Advertiser*, January–February 1982, p. 27.

---

milk is considered heating, while fresh milk is cooling; brandy is sustaining, whiskey harmful. A soap commercial featuring a man touching a woman's skin while she bathed, a theme used in the United States, would be rejected in Japan; the idea of a man being in the same bathroom with a female would be taboo.[17]

As though it were not enough for advertisers to be concerned with differences among nations, they find subcultures within a country require attention as well. In Hong Kong, for example, there are 10 different patterns of breakfast eating. The youth of a country almost always constitutes a different consuming culture from the older people, and urban dwellers differ significantly from rural dwellers. Besides these differences, there is the problem of changing traditions. In all countries, people of all ages, urban or rural, cling to their heritage to a certain degree but are willing

---

[17] For a discussion of cultural differences and advertising in Japan, see Barbara Mueller, "Reflections of Culture: An Analysis of Japanese and American Advertising Appeals," *Journal of Advertising Research*, June–July 1987, pp. 51–59. And Sumio Okahashi, "The Myth of Universality—Cultural Differences between the United States and Japan," *Speaking of Japan*, February 1989, p. 1–4.

to change some areas of behavior. A few years ago, it was unthinkable to try to market coffee in Japan, but it has become the fashionable drink for younger people and urban dwellers who like to think of themselves as European and sophisticated. Coffee drinking in Japan was introduced with instant coffee and there is virtually no market for anything else.[18]

Media Limitations

Media are discussed at length later, so here we mention only that limitations on creative strategy imposed by media may diminish the role of advertising in the promotional program and may force marketers to emphasize other elements of the marketing mix.

A marketer's creativity is certainly challenged when a television commercial is limited to 10 showings a year with no two exposures closer than 10 days, as is the case in Italy. Creative advertisers in some countries have even developed their own media for overcoming media limitations. In some African countries, advertisers run boats up and down the rivers playing popular music and broadcasting commercials into the bush as they travel.

Production and Cost Limitations

Creativity is especially important when a budget is small or where there are severe production limitations; poor quality printing and the lack of high-grade paper are simple examples. The necessity for low-cost reproduction in small markets poses another problem in many countries. For example, hand-painted billboards must be used instead of printed sheets because the limited number of billboards does not warrant the production of printed sheets.

The cost of reaching different market segments can become almost prohibitive in some instances. In Hong Kong, for example, it is imperative that ads run in both English and Chinese. Even if the market being sought is Chinese, English must be used so Orientals know the product is not inferior and being advertised only to Asians. To continue the Far Eastern example, advertisers in Bangkok must use English, Chinese, and Thai languages. In Singapore, besides English and Chinese, Malay and Tamil are necessary if the market is to be reached. Translations alone impose significant cost and production burdens for the advertiser.

---

[18] For an interesting study of advertising in South Korea see Kyung-il Ghymn, "Advertising in Korea at the Crossroads of Maturity," *Marketing Education: Challenges, Opportunities and Solutions*, Western Marketing Educator's Association 1989 Conference Proceedings, 1989, pp. 58–61.

Outdoor advertising, Shanghai, China. Many companies promote in China in anticipation of future demand.

The various restrictions to advertising creativity can be seen as insurmountable impediments to a standardized worldwide promotional campaign. Or, as the ultimate creative challenge for an advertiser; that is, to develop a promotional campaign that communicates across country markets, is informative, and persuasive. There are many internationally known advertising agencies that feel they can successfully surmount the obstacles encountered when creating a standardized, global advertising campaign.[19]

In reflecting on what a marketer is trying to achieve through advertising, it is clear that an arbitrary position strictly in favor of either modification or standardization is wrong; rather, the position must be to communicate a relevant message to the target market. If a promotion communicates

---

[19] Laurel Wentz, ''1992 to Breed Global Brands,'' *Advertising Age*, April 24, 1989, p. 44.

effectively in multiple-country markets, then standardize; otherwise, mod-ify. It is the message a market receives that generates sales, not whether an advertisement is standardized or modified.[20]

MEDIA PLANNING AND ANALYSIS

Tactical Considerations

Although nearly every sizable nation essentially has the same kinds of media, there are a number of specific considerations, problems, and differences encountered from one nation to another. The primary areas an advertiser must consider in international advertising are the availability, cost, and coverage of the media. Local variations and lack of market data provide fertile areas for additional attention.

Imagine the ingenuity required of advertisers who confront the following situations:

1. TV commercials are sandwiched together in a string of 10 to 50 commercials within one station break in Brazil.
2. In many countries, national coverage means using as many as 40 to 50 different media.
3. Specialized media reach small segments of the market only. In the Netherlands, there are Catholic, Protestant, Socialist, neutral, and other specialized broadcasting systems.
4. In Germany, TV scheduling for an entire year must be arranged by August 30 of the preceding year, and there is no guarantee that commercials intended for summer viewing will not be run in the middle of winter.[21]

Many of these European restrictions may be eliminated in 1992 when the EC becomes more integrated. Another factor that has caused some reduction of restrictions on television is the competition government-owned media receive from private and satellite companies. The number of government-owned stations has increased and restrictions on advertising have been lessened.

Availability.   One of the contrasts of international advertising is that some countries have too few advertising media and others have too many. In some countries, certain advertising media are forbidden by government

---

[20] Rolf T. Kreutzer, "Marketing Mix Standardisation: An Integrated Approach in Global Marketing," *European Journal of Marketing*, Vol. 22, No. 10, 1988, pp. 19–30.

[21] For other examples of the diversity of rules and regulations, see "Murdoch's Sky Channel Beams Strong Signal across Europe," *International Management*, March 1985, p. 49.

edict to accept some advertising materials. Such restrictions are most prevalent in radio and television broadcasting. In many countries there are too few magazines and newspapers to run all the advertising offered to them. Conversely, some nations segment the market with so many newspapers that the advertiser cannot gain effective coverage at a reasonable cost. Gilberto Sozzani, head of an Italian advertising agency, comments about his country: "One fundamental rule. You cannot buy what you want." Additional information on availability is discussed in a later section on specific media.

Cost. Media prices are susceptible to negotiation in most countries. Agency space discounts are often split with the client to bring down the cost of media. The advertiser may find the cost of reaching a prospect through advertising depends on the agent's bargaining ability. The per-contract cost varies widely from country to country. One study showed the cost of reacing a thousand readers in 11 different European countries ranged from $1.58 in Belgium to $5.91 in Italy; in women's service magazines, the page cost per thousand circulation ranged from $2.51 in Denmark to $10.87 in West Germany.

A recent five-year study of advertising costs in nine major foreign markets indicated that costs were increasing at a rate of 10 to 15 percent each year, a rate considerably higher than the cost increases in U.S. media. In some markets, shortages of advertising time on commercial television have caused substantial price increases. In Britain, prices escalate on a bidding system. They do not have fixed rate cards; instead, there is a preempt system. A company can book a spot at "$57,000, but if someone comes along and pays more, the higher bidder gets it."[22]

Coverage. Closely akin to the cost dilemma is the problem of coverage. Two points are particularly important: one relates to the difficulty of reaching certain sectors of the population with advertising and the other to the lack of information on coverage. In many world marketplaces, a wide variety of media must be used to reach the majority of the markets. In some countries, large numbers of separate media have divided markets into uneconomical advertising segments.[23] With some exceptions, a majority of the native population of less-developed countries cannot be reached readily through the medium of advertising. In Brazil, an exception, television is an important medium with a huge audience. One network, in fact, can reach 90 percent of Brazil's more than 17 million TV households.[24]

---

[22] Tim Harper, "U.K. Eyes New Channel to Ease Demand, Prices," *Advertising Age*, May 16, 1988, p. 68.

[23] "India's Many Voices," *World Press Review*, September 1985, p. 58.

[24] Julia Michaels, "Brazilian Creatives Mix Avant Garde, Sentiment," *Advertising Age*, April 13, 1987, p. 64.

BOX 14-5
The Wash Bucket They Understand!

One noted advertising executive in Mexico comments that ads that are successful in Mexico might be considered too simple or unsophisticated in the United States or Europe but they do work well in Mexico.

He offers an example to illustrate his point. Ariel, the largest-selling detergent in Mexico, successfully used a campaign which put the detergent into a washtub. In the TV ad, the suds rotate in a washtub which turns into a washing machine. Following the promotional dialogue, the clothes are taken out spanking clean.

He stresses that to the Mexican viewer the bucket is the washer. "We deal with people who still do their daily wash in a washtub. But they can relate to the luxury of a washing machine. What the ad says is that no matter what you wash your clothes in, Ariel gets them clean."

Source: Adapted from Laurie M. Kassman, "Ed Noble's Mexican Mastery," *International Advertiser*, November–December 1980, p. 35.

Verification of circulation or coverage figures is a difficult task. Even the fact that many countries have organizations similar to the Audit Bureau of Circulation does not assure accurate circulation and audience data. For example, the president of the Mexican National Advertisers Association charged that newspaper circulation figures are "grossly exaggerated." He suggested that "As a rule agencies divide these figures in two and take the result with a grain of salt."[25] Radio and television audiences are always difficult to measure, but, at least in most countries, geographic coverage is known. Not so in Brazil where privately owned transmitters are under contract to broadcasting stations. When transcription contracts are shifted from station to station, a station may advise agencies of its increased audience resulting from a new pact with the owner of a transmitter while the station with the old contract does not mention the shift, thus giving rise to ghost audiences. Private companies gather and disseminate audience and cost data but do not guarantee accuracy.

Lack of Market Data.   Even where advertising coverage can be measured with some accuracy, there are still questions about the composition of the market reached. Lack of available market data seems to characterize most international markets; advertisers should have information on income, age, and geographic distribution, but even such basic data seems chronically elusive. If adequate market data were available, they would show not

---

[25] "Successful Advertisement: Global Vision and a Latin Touch," *Advertising Age*, February 6, 1985, p. 43.

only the great variation in the audiences of different periodicals and broadcast media, but also the great diversity and variations that exist from country to country. Often even a small nation has a dozen or more subcultures within its borders. The advertiser is confounded with the problem of selecting media to provide coverage for an entire market.

Media Patterns

Perhaps the dominant pattern in the arena of world advertising is the proliferation of advertising media. Some countries have more media than their economy or population can adequately support. However, many countries have been long underdeveloped in terms of commercial mass communication media. Additional magazines, newspapers, and radio and television stations will be a boon to most advertisers.

In response to the trend toward worldwide advertising campaigns, major networks are selling advertising space on movie films and television shows that are distributed internationally. The British Broadcasting Corporation (BBC), in cooperation with Gillette, has developed and distributed a series of 26 sports programs to television stations throughout the world. Each program, called a "Gillette World Sports Special," includes references to Gillette products. CBS is offering U.S. advertisers prime-time space on Chinese and Brazilian networks in conjunction with the sale of U.S. TV programs. If global syndication of TV network programs continues to increase, important new precedents in media patterns will emerge.[26]

Specific Media Information

An attempt to evaluate specific characteristics of each medium is beyond the scope of this discussion. Furthermore, such information would quickly become outdated because of the rapid changes in the international advertising media field. It may be interesting, however, to examine some of the particularly unique international characteristics of various advertising media. In most instances, the major implications of each variation may be discerned from the data presented.

Newspapers.   The newspaper industry is suffering in some countries from lack of competition and choking because of it in others. Most U.S. cities have just two major daily newspapers but, in many countries, there are

---

[26] For a list of the top world advertisers, how much they spend, and worldwide media costs, see Nancy Griges, "Global Marketing and Media: Unilever Top Spender Outside U.S.," *Advertising Age*, December 14, 1988, pp. 53–65.

so many newspapers an advertiser has trouble reaching even partial market coverage. Uruguay with a population of only three million, has 21 daily newspapers with a combined circulation of 533,000. Imagine the complexity of trying to reach 500,000 households through the newspaper medium in Uruguay. In Turkey, in addition to the problem of selecting from some 380 newspapers, the advertiser must also be concerned with the political position of the newspapers used so the product's reputation is not harmed through affiliations with unpopular positions.

In contrast, Japan has five national daily newspapers; the largest, *Asahi*, has a circulation of almost 7 million, reaching 85 percent of all politicians and government officials, 81 percent of all business people, 44 percent of the nation's college graduates, and nearly 40 percent of households with incomes in the upper-middle range. Unfortunately, the complications of producing a Japanese-language newspaper are such that the newspaper contains just 16 to 20 pages. Connections are necessary to buy advertising space; *Asahi* has been known to turn down over a million dollars a month in advertising revenue.

Newspapers customarily list timeliness and short lead time for advertisements as one of their major advantages, yet in an international context that, too, changes. In many countries there is a long time lag before an advertisement can be run in a newspaper. In India paper shortages require ads be booked up to six months before their desired publication. An advertising executive reports a similar condition in Indonesia: "The situation at the newspapers is almost indescribable. Because of a lack of paper, the bigger newspapers are constantly short of advertising space and this means that you have to bribe the administration every time you want to run an ad." Furthermore, newspapers simply cannot be made larger to accommodate the increase in advertising demand. One newspaper publisher indicated that because of equipment limitations it is impossible to print more than 12 pages daily; thus, when advertising demand exceeds the space allocated for advertising, some are postponed.

Policies regarding separation between editorial and advertising content in newspapers provide another basis for contrast on the international scene. In some countries, it is possible to buy editorial space for advertising and promotional purposes. The news columns are for sale not only to the government but to anyone who has the price. Mexican newspapers often run paid ads as though they were editorial material, even on the front page. Since there is no indication that the space is paid for, it is impossible to tell exactly how much advertising appears in a given newspaper. The government, along with private industry, helps publishers pay reporters by handing out a monthly stipend to reporters on a given beat. Foreign newspapers cannot be considered homogeneous advertising entities so the advertiser must exert considerable judgment in spending international advertising dollars in newspapers.

Magazines.   The use of foreign national consumer magazines by international advertisers has been notably low because of many problems. Few magazines have large circulations or provide dependable circulation figures. Technical magazines are used rather extensively to promote export goods; but, as in the case of newspapers, paper shortages cause placement problems. One British agency manager says, "Can you imagine what it feels like to be a media planner here when the largest magazine accepts up to twice as many advertisements as it has space to run them in? Then they decide what advertisements will go in just before going to press by means of a raffle." Such local practices may be key items favoring the growth of so-called international media which attempt to serve many nations. Many U.S. publications are publishing overseas editions. *Reader's Digest* international editions, published in more than 20 languages, have been joined by a variety of other American print media ranging from *Playboy* to *Scientific American*. These media offer alternative choices to U.S. MNCs as well as to local advertisers.[27] Advertisers accustomed to the broad assortment of magazines published in economically advanced countries may have to reassess media strategies involving magazines as they shift their attention from country to country. The media void could shift media usage and force a company to change its entire promotion mix as well as affect distribution channels and market coverage.

Radio and Television.   Possibly because of their inherent entertainment value, radio and television have become major communications media in most nations. Most populous areas have television broadcasting facilities. In some markets, such as Japan, television has become almost a national obsession and thus finds tremendous audiences for its advertisers. Radio has been relegated to a subordinate position in the media race in countries where television facilities are well developed. In many countries, however, radio is a particularly important and vital advertising medium because it is the only one reaching large segments of the population.

Television and radio advertising availability varies between countries. Three patterns are discernible; competitive commercial broadcasting, commercial monopolies, and noncommercial broadcasting. Countries with free competitive commercial radio and television normally encourage competition and have minimal broadcast regulations. Local or national monopolies are granted by the government in other countries; individual stations or networks may then accept radio commercials according to rules established by the government. In some countries, commercial monopolies may accept all the advertising they wish; in others, only spot advertising is permissible

---

[27] For a list of these media and prices, see, "Advertising Age's Global Media Lineup," *Advertising Age,* December 14, 1988, p. 54.

and programs may not be sponsored. In other countries, live commercials are not permitted; in still others, commercial stations must compete for audiences against the government's noncommercial broadcasting network.

In some countries, no commercial radio or television is permitted, but several of the traditional noncommercial countries have changed their policies in recent years because television production is so expensive. Until recently France limited commercials to a daily total of 18 minutes of advertisements but extended the time limit to 12 minutes per hour per channel. For years agencies had to book space a year in advance; now, space can be reserved up to 12 days before air time.[28] Germany permits only 20 minutes a day for commercials and runs them bunched together between 6 P.M. and 8 P.M. daily, except Sundays and holidays. Not only is the time segment for commercials controlled, so are content and audience. For example, the Quebec, Canada, government passed a bill completely banning television advertising directed toward children and all commercials that urge people to borrow money; further, the beer/liquor industry has been told that advertising can no longer imply people enjoy themselves if they drink.

Although commercial programming is limited, people in most countries have an opportunity to hear or view commercial radio and television. Entrepreneurs in the radio-television field have discovered audiences in commercially restricted countries are hungry for commercial television and radio, and that marketers are eager to bring their messages into these countries. Because of both business and public demand for more programming, countries that have not allowed private broadcast media have changed their laws in recent years to allow privately owned broadcasting stations. Italy, which had no private/local radio or TV until 1976, currently has some 300 privately owned stations. In countries where advertising has not been permitted on government-owned stations, there has been some softening of restrictions, allowing limited amounts of air time for commercials. In Belgium, advertising is allowed on state-controlled radio and television, but television advertising is concentrated in time slots at the beginning and end of evening programs.

Satellite and Cable TV.   Of increasing importance in TV advertising are the growth and development of satellite TV broadcasting. Sky Channel, a United Kingdom-based commercial satellite television station, beams its programs and advertising into most of Europe via cable TV subscribers. New technology now permits households to receive broadcasts directly from the satellite via a dish the "size of a dinner plate" costing about

---

[28] Joshua Jampol, "French Politics Focus on TV Ad Regulations," *Advertising Age,* August 15, 1988, p. 43.

$350.[29] This innovation adds greater coverage and the ability to reach all of Europe with a single message. The expansion of TV coverage will challenge the creativity of advertisers and put greater emphasis on global, standardized messages.

Both advertisers and governments are concerned about the impact of satellite TV. Governments are concerned because they see further loss of control of their airways and "American cultural imperialism." With "Dallas" and "Dynasty" already long-running hits on conventional TV, French and German officials in particular fear that lowbrow game shows, sitcoms, and soap operas from the United States will crush domestic producers.[30] However, most governments are reducing restrictions, adding TV satellites of their own, and privatizing many government-owned channels in an attempt to attract more commercial revenue and provide independent broadcasters with greater competition.[31]

The reality of satellite TV provides the means to have truly global advertising. This raises the question of the effectiveness of standardized advertising versus locally produced ads. Problems of different languages and laws raise doubts about the effectiveness of pan-European ads. In European satellite broadcasting, English is the preferred language for programming because the satellites must cover a territory with 12 languages and 17 national borders. A study done on Sky Channel viewers indicated that the English-language programs are unacceptable for many. Germans watch the English-language programs for about a minute before deciding they have the wrong station.[32] European programming is developing, but slowly. One of the reasons for using U.S. programming is that producing quality programs for each country is too costly. One approach to language differences and the production costs of programming is a six-part series called "Eurocops." It is a police series in which each country produces one episode based in the country with their own police, in their own style and with their own problems. Each broadcaster provides the episode produced in his country to the other five. The five are then dubbed into the local language and broadcast locally. The idea is to produce European programming but at a much lower cost per country than if each country had to produce all six shows. There is no question that cable, satellites, privatization, and the advent of Europe 1992 will revolutionize broadcasting and create greater demand for global advertising.[33]

---

[29] "Sky TV Rates Down to Earth," *Advertising Age,* October 24, 1988, p. 64.

[30] "European Satellite TV: Just So Much Pie in the Sky?" *Business Week,* October 24, 1988, p. 40.

[31] Raymond Snoddy, "The Changing Face of European TV," *Europe,* April 1988, p. 26.

[32] Ibid., p. 28.

[33] Ibid., p. 26.

Lack of reliable audience data is another major problem in international marketing via radio and television. Measurement of radio and television audiences is always a precarious business even with highly developed techniques. In most countries, audience measurement is either unaudited or existing auditing associations are ineffective. Despite the paucity of audience data, many advertisers use radio and television extensively. Advertisers justify their inclusion in the media schedule on the inherent logic favoring the use of these media, or defend their use on the basis of sales results.[34]

Direct Mail.   Direct mail is a viable medium in many countries. It is especially important when other media are not available. As is often the case in international marketing, even such a fundamental medium is subject to some odd and novel quirks. For example, in Chile, direct mail is virtually eliminated as an effective medium because the sender pays only part of the mailing fee; the letter carrier must collect additional postage for every item delivered. Obviously, advertisers cannot afford to alienate customers by forcing them to pay for unsolicited advertisements. Despite some limitations with direct mail, many companies have found it a meaningful way to reach their markets.[35] For example, The Reader's Digest Association has used direct mail advertising in Mexico to successfully market its magazines.

In Southeast Asian markets where print media are scarce, direct mail is considered one of the most effective ways to reach those responsible for making industrial goods purchases, although a problem in Asia, as well as other parts of the world, is accurate mailing lists.[36] Industrial advertisers are heavy mail users and rely on catalogs and sales sheets to generate large volumes of international business.

Other Media.   Restrictions on traditional media or their availability cause advertisers to call on lesser media for the solution of particular local-county problems. The cinema is an important medium in many countries as are billboards and other forms of outside advertising. Billboards are especially useful in countries with high illiteracy rates.

In Haiti, sound trucks equipped with powerful loudspeakers provide an effective and widespread advertising medium. Private contractors own

---

[34] John M. Eger, "Global Television: An Executive Overview," *Columbia Journal of World Business,* Fall 1987, pp. 5–10.

[35] Tom Eisenhart, "Savvy Mailers Tap Foreign Markets," *Business Marketing,* September 1988, pp. 55–56.

[36] "The Far East: A Good List Is Hard to Find," *Business Marketing,* September 1988, pp. 62–64.

the equipment and sell advertising space much as a radio station would. This medium combats the problems of illiteracy, lack of radio and television set ownership, and limited print media circulation.

SALES PROMOTION

Other than advertising, personal selling, and publicity, all marketing activities that stimulate consumer purchases and improve retailer or middlemen effectiveness and cooperation are sales promotions. Cents-off, in-store demonstrations, samples, coupons, gifts, product tie-ins, contests, sweepstakes, sponsorship of special events such as concerts and fairs, and point-of-purchase displays are types of sales promotion devices designed to supplement advertising and personal selling in the promotional mix.[37]

Sales promotions are short-term efforts directed to the consumer and/or retailer to achieve such specific objectives as: (1) consumer-product trial and/or immediate purchase; (2) consumer introduction to the store; (3) gaining retail point-of-purchase displays; (4) encouraging stores to stock the product; and (5) supporting and augmenting advertising and personal sales efforts. An example of sales promotion is the African cigarette manufacturer who, in addition to regular advertising, sponsors musical groups, river explorations, and participates in local fairs in attempts to make the public aware of the product. In a similar vein, R. J. Reynolds (tobacco) entered into an agreement with a European clothing manufacturer to carry a silhouette of its camel on a designer collection of clothing as a sales promotion effort for both.

In markets where the consumer is hard to reach because of media limitations, the percentage of the promotional budget allocated to sales promotions may have to be increased. In some less-developed countries, sales promotions constitute the major portion of the promotional effort in rural and less accessible parts of the market. For example, in parts of Latin America, a portion of the advertising-sales budget for both Pepsi-Cola and Coca-Cola is spent on carnival trucks which make frequent trips to outlying villages to promote their products. When a carnival truck makes a stop in a village, it may show a movie or provide some other kind of entertainment; the price of admission is an unopened bottle of the product purchased from the local retailer. The unopened bottle is to be exchanged for a cold bottle plus a coupon for another bottle. This promotional effort tends to stimulate sales and encourages local retailers, given prior notice of the carnival truck's arrival, to stock the product. Nearly 100 percent

---

[37] "Advertising Alternatives: Gifts, Premiums, and Competitions," *Business International*, July 11, 1988, pp. 218.

> **BOX 14–6**
> **Mobile Cinema in Kenya**
>
> The most expensive 30-second spot availabile in Kenya isn't heard on TV, radio, or in a movie theater, but in an open field on a collapsible screen.
>
> Called mobile cinema, this unusual advertising medium brings free vintage Western and comedy films to the isolated populations of Kenya. Each mobile cinema company operates 26 show circuits that travel monthly from the fields just outside Nairobi to the relatively inaccessible tracts in northern and western Kenya.
>
> Mobile cinema is the only opportunity most advertisers have to present visual messages to Kenya's rural population because posters and other outdoor boards are illegal.
>
> Source: Antony Shugaar, "Ads Take High Road in Kenya, on Cinema," *Advertising Age,* April 11, 1983, p. 35.

coverage of retailers in the village is achieved with this type of promotion. In other situations, village stores may be given free samples, have the outsides of their stores painted, or receive clock signs in attempts to promote sales.

An especially effective promotional tool is product sampling when the product concept is new to a market. For example, Crayola crayons were not known outside the United States; colored pencils and markers are more popular than crayons in other countries. Crayola Products distributed samples of the product and sponsored special activities such as a youth race in Bermuda and coloring contests in Singapore, Saudi Arabia, Hong Kong, and hundreds of cities elsewhere to help make its products more familiar to consumers in foreign markets.[38]

As is true in advertising, the success of a promotion may depend on local adaptation. Major constraints are imposed by local laws which may not permit premiums or free gifts to be given.[39] Some countries' laws control the amount of discount given at retail, others require permits for all sales promotions, and in at least one country, no competitor is permitted to spend more on a sales promotion than any other company selling the product. Effective sales promotions can enhance the advertising and personal selling efforts and, in some instances, may be effective substitutes when environmental constraints prevent full utilization of advertising.

---

[38] "Crayolas Color the World," *Global Trade*, February 1987, pp. 10–11.

[39] For a list of regulatory constraints in 20 countries, see "Regulations Regarding Premiums, Gifts, and Competitions in Selected Countries," *Business International*, July 11, 1988, pp. 216–17. For a more comprehensive coverage of regulations in 42 countries see J. J. Boddewyn, *Premiums, Gifts, and Competitions* (New York: International Advertising Association, 1988).

GLOBAL ADVERTISING AND THE COMMUNICATIONS PROCESS

Promotional activities (advertising, personal selling, sales promotions, and public relations) are basically a communications process. All the attendant problems of developing an effective promotional strategy in domestic marketing plus all the cultural problems just discussed must be overcome to have a successful international promotional program. A major consideration for foreign marketers is to ascertain that all constraints (cultural diversity, media limitations, legal problems, and so forth) are controlled so the right message is communicated to and received by prospective consumers. International communications may fail for a variety of reasons: a message may not get through because of media inadequacy; the message may be received by the intended audience but not be understood because of different cultural interpretations; or, the message may reach the intended audience and be understood but have no effect because the marketer did not correctly assess the needs and wants of the target market.

The effectiveness of promotional strategy can be jeopardized by so many factors that a marketer must be certain no influences are overlooked. Those international executives who understand the communications process are better equipped to manage the diversity they face in developing an international promotional program.

In the communications process, each of the seven identifiable segments can ultimately affect the accuracy of the process. As illustrated in Exhibit 14–1, the process consists of (1) an information source—an international marketing executive with a product message to communicate; (2) encoding—the message from the source converted into effective symbolism for transmission to a receiver; (3) a message channel—the sales force and/or advertising media which conveys the encoded message to the intended receiver; (4) decoding—the interpretation by the receiver of the symbolism transmitted from the information source; (5) receiver—consumer action by those who receive the message and are the target for the thought transmitted; (6) feedback—information about the effectiveness of the message which flows from the receiver (the intended target) back to the information source for evaluation of the effectiveness of the process; and, to complete the process, (7) noise—uncontrollable and unpredictable influences such as competitive activities and confusion detracting from the process and affecting any or all of the other six steps. Unfortunately, the process is not as simple as just sending a message via a medium to a receiver and being certain that the intended message sent is the same one perceived by the receiver. In Exhibit 14–1, the communications-process steps are encased in Cultural Context A and Cultural Context B to illustrate the influences complicating the process when the message is encoded in one culture and decoded in another. If not properly considered, the different cultural contexts can increase the probability of misunderstanding.

Most promotional misfires or mistakes in international marketing are

EXHIBIT 14–1   The International Communications Process

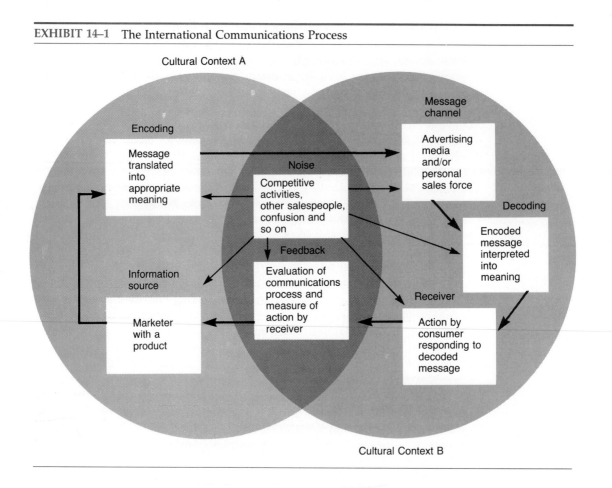

Cultural Context A

Cultural Context B

attributable to one or several of these steps not properly reflecting cultural influences and/or a general lack of knowledge about the target market. A review of some of the points discussed in this chapter serves to illustrate this point. The information source is a marketer with a product to sell to a specific target market. The product message to be conveyed should reflect the needs and wants of the target market; however, as many previous examples have illustrated, the marketer's perception of market needs and actual market needs do not always coincide. This is especially true when the marketer relies more on the self-reference criterion (SRC) than on effective research. It can never be assumed that "if it sells well in one country, it will sell in another!" Bicycles designed and sold in the United States to consumers fulfilling recreational-exercise needs are not as effectively sold for the same reasons in a market where the primary use of the bicycle is transportation. Cavity-reducing fluoride toothpastes sell well in the United States where healthy teeth are perceived as important, but they have limited appeal in markets such as Great Britain and the French areas of Canada where the reason for buying toothpaste is breath control. From the onset of the communications process, if basic needs are incorrectly defined, communications fail because an incorrect or meaningless message is received even though the remaining steps in the process are executed properly.

The encoding step causes problems even with a proper message. At this step such factors as color, values, beliefs, and tastes can cause the international marketer to symbolize incorrectly the message. For example, the marketer wants the product to convey coolness so the color green is used; however, people in the tropics might decode green as dangerous or associate it with disease. Another example of the encoding process misfiring was a perfume presented against a backdrop of rain which, for Europeans, symbolized a clean, cool, refreshing image, but to Africans was a symbol of fertility. The ad prompted many viewers to ask if the perfume was effective against infertility.

In the United States, the Marlboro man sells a lot of cigarettes but in Hong Kong, the appeal failed. The Hong Kong consumers are urbane and increasingly affluent buyers, so they saw little charm in riding around in the hot sun all day. The basic need or want can be correctly identified but the encoding step in the communications process may render the result ineffective.

Message channels must be carefully selected if an encoded message is to reach the consumer. Media problems are generally thought of in terms of the difficulty in getting a message to the intended market. Problems of literacy, media availability, and types of media create problems in the communications process at this step. Errors such as using television as a

---

BOX 14–7
What's in a Name?

If you are going to do business in Europe, you should become familiar with *Firenze, 's Gravenhage, Hellas, Helsingfors, Kobenhavn, Koln, Munchen, Norge, Osterreich, Polska, Praha, Sverige,* and *Warszawa.* They are countries and cities we know as Florence, the Hague, Greece, Helsinki, Copenhagen, Cologne, Munich, Norway, Austria, Poland, Prague, Sweden, and Warsaw.

You can imagine how those same names have been converted into other languages! In French, just as one example, Austria is *l'Autriche,* Belgium is *la Belgique,* England *l'Angleterre,* Germany *l'Allemagne,* London *Londres,* The Netherlands *Les Pays-Bas,* and Spain *l'Espagne.*

Source: Howard G. Sawyer, "If It's Mardi, This Must Be la Belgique, or, What We Do to Each Other's Names." Reprinted from *Industrial Marketing,* July 1977, p. 133, by Crain Communications, Inc., Chicago.

medium when only a small percentage of an intended market is exposed to TV or using print media for a channel of communications when the majority of the intended users cannot read are examples of ineffective media channel selection in the communications process.[40]

Decoding problems are generally created by improper encoding, causing such errors as Pepsi's "Come Alive" slogan which decoded as "Come out of the grave," and Chevrolet's brand name for the Nova model which decoded into Spanish as *No Va!*—meaning, "it doesn't go." In a Nigerian ad, a platinum blonde sitting next to the driver of a Renault was intended to enhance the image of the product but she was perceived as not respectable and so created a feeling of shame. Decoding errors may also occur accidentally. Such was the case with Colgate-Palmolive's selection of the brand name Cue for a toothpaste. The brand name was not intended to have any symbolism; nevertheless, it was decoded by the French into a pornographic word. In some cases, the intended symbolism has no meaning to the decoder. One soft drink manufacturer's advertisement promised a thirst-quenching reward based on the concepts "Glacier Fresh" or "Avalanche of Taste" in a part of the world where wintry mountain temperatures are an unknown experience. Errors at the receiver end of the process generally result from a combination of factors: an improper message resulting from incorrect knowledge of use patterns, poor encoding producing a meaningless message, poor media selection that does not get the message to the receiver, or inaccurate decoding by the receiver so that the message is garbled or incorrect.

Finally, the feedback step of the communications process is important as a check on the effectiveness of the other steps. Companies that do not measure their communications efforts are apt to allow errors of source, encoding, media selection, decoding, or receiver to continue longer than necessary. In fact, a proper feedback system allows a company to correct errors before substantial damage occurs.

In addition to the problems inherent in the steps outlined, the effectiveness of the communications process can be impaired by *noise*. Noise comprises all other external influences such as competitive advertising, other sales personnel, and confusion at the receiving end which can detract from the ultimate effectiveness of the communications. Noise is a disruptive force interfering with the process at any step and is frequently beyond the control of the sender or the receiver. The significance is that one or all steps in the process, cultural factors, or the marketer's SRC, can affect the ultimate success of the communication. For example, the message, encoding, media, and the intended receiver can be designed perfectly

---

[40] Examples of issues that can cause problems in the communications process can be found in Mushtaq Luqmani, Ugur Yavas, and Zahir Quraeshi, "Advertising in Saudi Arabia: Content and Regulation," *International Marketing Review*, Vol. 6, No. 1, 1989, pp. 59–72.

BOX 14-8
Some Advertising Misses and Near-Misses

Fortunately some culturally incorrect ads are caught before they get into print. Here are some that were stopped in time.

An American cleansing-product manufacturer developed some commercials that showed people tossing hats around in jest. One advertisement had a green hat landing on a male model's head. It was pointed out to the advertiser that among the Chinese a green hat signifies that the male in question has an unfaithful wife.[*]

A U.S. luggage manufacturer came up with the idea of designing a Middle East advertising campaign around an illustration showing its suitcases being flown aloft by a magic carpet. A pretest showed that the Arab audience thought it was an advertisement for Samsonite *Carpets.*[†]

The foregoing ads were caught in time, these weren't.

Parker Pen Company translated a counter display card for its brand of ink which had been very successful in the United States. The card said, "Avoid Embarrassment—use Quink." The Spanish translation, "Evite embarazos—use Quink," unfortunately meant idiomatically "Avoid Pregnancy—use Quink."[‡]

A British ad agency thought the Fiat 127 Palio (a sporty automobile) was a nice bit of goods with a shapely rear end and, for the English audience, coined the slogan: "If it were a lady, it would get its bottom pinched." There were 21 individual complaints about the ad along with one letter with 34 indignant feminist signatures. The ad was considered "offensive" and "tantamount to inciting sexual molestation." The agency disagreed saying it thought the advertisement would "generally be interpreted as a humorous allusion to the Italian origin of the car." Shows you how wrong you can be.[§]

An ad in which a Nigerian praised a glass of beer, holding it in his left hand, conveyed a sign of homosexuality to his countrymen. ∥

Sources: [*] "Be Sure Not to Wear a Green Hat if You Visit in Hong Kong," *The Wall Street Journal*, May 10, 1979, p. 1.

[†] "How to Sell Success in the Middle East," *International Management*, October 1981, p. 61.

[‡] Oscar S. Cornejo, "Avoid Embarrassments in Latin America," *International Advertiser*, May–June 1981, p. 12.

[§] "An Ad with a (humorous) Italian Accent," *World Business Weekly*, April 21, 1980, p. 39.

∥ "African Advertising Expands," *World Press Review*, February 1984, p. 48.

but the inability of the receiver to decode may render the final message inoperative. In designing an international promotional strategy, the international marketer can effectively use this model as a guide to help assure all potential constraints and problems are considered so that the final communication received and the action taken corresponds with the intent of the source.

THE ADVERTISING AGENCY

Just as manufacturing firms have become international, U.S., Japanese, and European advertising agencies are expanding internationally to provide sophisticated agency assistance worldwide. Local agencies have also expanded as the demand for advertising services by MNCs has developed. Thus, the international marketer has a variety of alternatives available. In most commercially significant countries, an advertiser has the opportunity to employ (1) a local domestic agency, (2) its company-owned agency, or (3) one of the multinational advertising agencies with local branches. There are strengths and weaknesses with each. A local domestic agency may provide a company with the best cultural interpretation in situations where local modification is sought, but the level of sophistication can be weak. Another drawback of local agencies is the difficulty of coordinating a worldwide campaign. One drawback of the company-owned agency is the possible loss of local input when it is located outside the area and has little contact within the host country. The best compromise is the multinational agency with local branches because it has the sophistication of a major agency with local representation. Further, the multinational agency with local branches is better able to provide a coordinated worldwide advertising campaign. This has become especially important for firms doing business in Europe as Europe 1992 approaches.[41] With the interest in global or standardized advertising, agencies have expanded to provide worldwide representation. Many companies with a global orientation employ one, or perhaps two, agencies to represent them worldwide.

Compensation arrangements for advertising agencies throughout the world are based on the U.S. system of 15 percent commissions. However, agency commission patterns throughout the world are not as consistent as they are in the United States; in some countries, agency commissions vary from medium to medium. Services provided by advertising agencies also vary greatly but few foreign agencies offer the full services found in U.S. agencies.

Even a sophisticated business function such as advertising may find it is involved in unique practices. In some parts of the world, advertisers often pay for the promotion with the product advertised rather than with cash. Kickbacks on agency commissions are prevalent in some parts of the world and account in part for the low profitability of international advertising agencies. In Mexico, India, and Greece, the advertiser returns half the media commissions to the agencies. In many of the developing countries, long-term credit is used to attract clients. Venezuela has a rather highly developed advertising agency system, yet 120 days is the *average*

---

[41] "1992 Means Restructuring," *Advertising Age*, October 3, 1988, p. 64.

BOX 14–9
The Soaps in Brazil Sell Cereal, Too

The good news is that the Kellogg Company has no competition in the breakfast cereal market in Brazil. The bad news is that Brazilians don't eat breakfast. The answer is advertising *in* a soap opera—*in* not *on.* Generally, Brazilians do what the people in *novelas* (what they call soaps in Brazil) do.[*] Both millionaire and peasant watch the soaps faithfully four times daily at 5:00, 7:00, 8:30, and 9:30.[†]

Brazil's wildly popular prime-time soaps have a subplot few viewers are aware of—consumer product advertising built right into the script. One TV network covers an estimated 25 to 30 percent of the cost of its elaborately produced *novelas* by inserting the products of a dozen or more major advertisers into each of the six-month-long soaps. There are regular advertisements, too, but many products are deftly integrated into the plot.

For example, when jailed suspect Ze Brandao was acquitted of murder charges, he headed straight home to drink a glass of Tang with his family. In another scene, Olivia, the maid, happily cut her employer's lawn while enumerating the selling points of the lawn mower.

One character, Jose Wilder, the Bohemian son of a rich, dominating mother, drives a Ford, sells Atari Video games at his electronics store, and plays Pac-Man.

The character rides his bicycle—pedaling carefully so the brand name shows—to withdraw money for his wedding, using a much advertised bank card. Learning the woman he loves is an impostor, he confronts her friend at a shoe store, pausing in his quest for the truth only long enough to ask, "What's that?" as he points to a yellow plastic boot. The friend explains it is the latest style already the rage in the United States and Europe, and sure to be bought by everyone in Brazil this season. The butler cleans with Johnson's Wax, the lead actor owns a Star Wars-like robot that falls madly in love with a Braun mixer. Oh yes, Kellogg's cereal is eaten for breakfast with a short statement of how healthy it is to eat breakfast. And so it goes throughout the soap to a point where the actors do so much merchandising it's amazing there is time for the story plot.

How effective are these hidden commercials? Atari's Brazilian manufacturer wanted to strike back at cheaper pirate videogames that were cutting into Atari cartridge sales and damaging Atari consoles. So a scene was created in which a woman takes her defective Atari console into Jose Wilder's electronics store. He examines it, says the guarantee doesn't apply because she used a cartridge not compatible with the system, and explains how harmful that is. Within a week, real store managers reported a violent drop in sales of pirate cartridges.

Sources: [*] "Kellogg Awakens New Habit," *Advertising Age,* July 5, 1984, p. 25.
[†] "Brazil's TV Boom," *World Press Review,* October 1984, p. 61.
[‡] "Soap Operas Slip Sales Pitches into Scripts," *Advertising Age,* July 5, 1984, p. 24.

time between the agency's payment to the media and the client's payment. Some agencies actually negotiate agency contracts on the size of the kickback and the duration of the credit extension. Such policies are bound to result in less-effective selection and, therefore, less-effective advertising effort than choosing an agency on merit alone.

The task of selecting and maintaining international advertising agencies is not easy. The comprehensive services of American agencies may be one reason so many firms seek branch offices of these firms.

INTERNATIONAL CONTROL OF ADVERTISING

Consumer criticisms of advertising are not a phenomenon of the U.S. market. Consumer concern with the standards and believability of advertising may have spread around the world more swiftly than have many marketing techniques. A study of a representative sample of European consumers indicated that only half believed advertisements gave consumers any useful information, 6 out of 10 believed that advertising meant higher prices (if a product is heavily advertised, it often sells for more than brands that are seldom or never advertised), nearly 8 out of 10 believed advertising often made them buy things they did not really need, and that ads were often deceptive about product quality. In Hong Kong, Colombia, and Brazil advertising fared much better than in Europe. The non-Europeans praised advertising as a way to obtain valuable information about products; most Brazilians consider ads entertaining and enjoyable.[42]

European Community officials are under increasing pressure to establish communitywide controls on advertising as cable and satellite broadcasting expands. Deception in advertising is a major issue since most member countries have different interpretations of what constitutes a misleading advertisement. Demands for regulation of advertising aimed at young consumers is a trend appearing in both industrialized and developing countries. A survey by the International Advertising Association lists 17 countries where there is a specific focus by consumer organizations for controls on advertising to children. Advertising is attacked as conducive to harmful consumption patterns and antagonistic toward traditional family values.

Besides advertising deception, other common standards sought are to:

- Reach agreement on the allowable volume of TV advertising and make general the practice of advertising in blocks.
- Limit the volume of sponsored programs and provide for clear distinctions between ads and programs.

---

[42] Ronald Alsop, "Advertisers Find the Climate Less Hostile Outside the U.S.," *The Wall Street Journal*, December 10, 1987, p. 29.

• Limit testimonials and comparative ads.
• Forbid the interruption of children's programs with ads.
• Ban ads for tobacco, alcohol, and certain pharmaceutical products.[43]

Advertising regulations are not limited to Europe; there is an enhanced awareness of the expansion of mass communications and the perceived need to effect greater control in developing countries as well. Malaysia consistently regulates TV advertising to control the effect of the "excesses of Western ways." The government has become so concerned that it will not allow "Western cultural images" to appear in TV commercials. No bare shoulders or exposed armpits are allowed, no touching or kissing, no sexy clothing, and no blue jeans. These are just a few of the prohibitions spelled out in a 41-page advertising code that the Malaysian government has been adding to for more than 10 years.

The advertising industry is sufficiently concerned with the negative attitudes of consumers and governments and with the poor practices of some advertisers that the International Advertising Association and other national and international industry groups have developed a variety of self-regulating codes. Sponsors of these codes feel that unless the advertisers themselves come up with an effective framework for control, governments will intervene. This threat of government intervention has spurred interest groups in Europe to develop codes to ensure that the majority of ads conform to standards set for "honesty, truth, and decency." In those countries where the credibility of advertising is questioned and in those where the consumerism movement exists, the creativity of the advertiser is challenged.

In many countries, there is a feeling that advertising and especially TV advertising is too powerful and persuades consumers to buy what they do not need. Certainly this is an issue that has been debated in the United States for many years.

SUMMARY

Global advertisers face unique legal, language, media, and production limitations in every market that must be considered when designing a promotional mix. As the world and its markets become more sophisticated, there is greater emphasis on global marketing strategy. The current debate among marketers is the effectiveness of standardized versus modified advertising for culturally varied markets. And, as competition increases and

---

[43] "EEC Media Experts Push for New Limits on Pan-Europe Ads," *Advertising Age*, January 30, 1984, p. 52.

markets expand, greater emphasis is being placed on global brands and/or image recognition.

The most logical conclusion seems to be that, when buying motives and company objectives are the same for various countries, the advertising orientation can be the same. When they vary from nation to nation, the advertising effort will have to reflect these variations. In any case, variety in media availability, coverage, and effectiveness will have to be taken into consideration in the advertiser's plans. If common appeals are used, they may have to be presented by a radio broadcast in one country, by cinema in another, and by television in still a third.

A skilled advertising practitioner must be sensitive to the environment and alert to new facts about the market. It is also essential for success in international advertising endeavors to pay close attention to the communications process and the steps involved.

QUESTIONS

1. Define:

international media	sales promotion
promotion mix	communications process
noise	encoding

2. "Perhaps advertising is the side of international marketing with the greatest similarities from country to country throughout the world. Paradoxically, despite its many similarities, it may also be credited with the greatest number of unique problems in international marketing." Discuss.

3. Discuss the difference between advertising strategy when a company follows a multidomestic strategy rather than a global market strategy.

4. Someone once commented that advertising is America's greatest export. Discuss.

5. With satellite TV able to reach many countries, discuss how a company can use satellite TV and deal effectively with different languages, different cultures, and different legal systems.

6. Outline some of the major problems confronting an international advertiser.

7. Defend either side of the proposition that advertising can be standardized for all countries.

8. Review the basic areas of advertising regulation. Are such regulations purely foreign phenomena?

9. How can advertisers overcome the problems of low literacy in their markets?

10. What special media problems confront the international advertiser?

11. Discuss the reason for pattern advertising.

12. Discuss the advantages and problems in using satellite TV advertising in Europe or in any other group of countries.

13. Will the ability to broadcast advertisements over TV satellites increase or decrease the need for standardization of advertisements? What are the problems associated with satellite broadcasting? Comment.

14. "In many world marketplaces, a wide variety of media must be used to reach the majority of the market." Explain.

15. Cinema advertising is unimportant in the United States but a major medium in such countries as Austria. Why?

16. "Foreign newspapers cannot be considered homogeneous advertising entities." Elaborate.

17. Borrow a foreign magazine from the library. Compare the foreign advertising to that in an American magazine.

18. What is sales promotion and how is it used in international marketing?

19. Show how the communications process can help an international marketer avoid problems in international advertising.

20. Take each of the steps of the communications process and give an example of how cultural differences can affect the final message received.

21. Discuss the problems created because the communications process is initiated in one cultural context and ends in another.

22. What is the importance of feedback in the communications process? Of noise?

CHAPTER

15

Personal Selling and Personnel Management

The increasing competitiveness of international markets demands that companies take direct responsibility for the management of marketing personnel in foreign markets if marketing objectives are to be attained. The personnel involved are those with direct and continuing responsibility for international marketing activities including personnel in the home office. This chapter is concerned with those responsible for marketing management and direct field assignments; specifically, personnel who make up the international sales force and their managers. The sales force comprises the bulk of people employed in foreign positions and deals most directly with middlemen and the public in foreign markets.

The personnel requirements and organizational structure of the international marketing function present some interesting variations. The tasks of building, training, compensating, and motivating an international marketing group generate unique problems at every stage of management and development. This chapter discusses some of the alternatives and problems a firm faces when managing local and company personnel in foreign countries.

SOURCES OF MARKETING AND SALES PERSONNEL

The number of marketing management personnel assigned in foreign countries varies according to the operation; generally, it is not large. For a given country, it may include only the marketing manager for that country; or, for a larger operation, it may include a marketing manager, an advertising manager, a sales manager, and someone in charge of middleman relations.[1]

The sales force itself is by far the largest personnel requirement abroad for most companies, and includes three types: (1) the expatriate salesperson working in a foreign country; (2) the foreign salesperson working at home for a foreign company; and (3) the cosmopolitan salesperson, a special sort of expatriate who works in various countries. These types are identified for analytical purposes and refer to individuals, but a given company may employ all three types in any single foreign operation.

Expatriates

The number of expatriate personnel is declining as the volume of world trade increases and as more companies use foreign nationals to fill marketing positions. However, when products are highly technical, or where selling requires an extensive background of information and applications, an expatriate sales force may be the best choice.

The expatriate salesperson may have the advantages of greater technical training, better knowledge of the company and its product line, and proven dependability and effectiveness. Because they are not natives, expatriates sometime add to the prestige of the product line in the eyes of foreign customers.[2]

Chief disadvantages of an expatriate sales force are high cost, cultural and legal barriers, and the limited numbers of high caliber personnel willing to live abroad for extended periods.[3] U.S. companies are finding it difficult to persuade outstanding employees to take overseas posts at a time when companies are relying more heavily on such experience. Employees are reluctant to go abroad for many reasons: Some find it difficult to uproot families for a two- or three-year assignment; increasing numbers of dual-career couples often require finding suitable jobs for spouses; and many executives believe such assignments impede their subsequent promotions

---

[1] Sherry Buchanan, "Overseas Assignments: Mobility vs. Continuity," *International Herald Tribune,* June 23, 1988, p. 11.

[2] Elisa Herr, "High Cost Workers," *Business Tokyo,* October 1987, p. 62.

[3] "The Care and Feeding of Your American Management," *International Management,* October 1987, pp. 112–14.

at home. Companies with well-planned career development programs have the least difficulty. The problem stems from the participants' belief that out of sight is out of mind so they fear the loss of their corporate visibility.

Expatriates are committed to foreign assignments for varying lengths of time, from a few weeks or months to a lifetime. Some expatriates have one-time assignments (which may last for years) after which they are returned to the parent company; others are essentially professional expatriates working abroad in country after country. Still another expatriate assignment is a career-long assignment to a given country or region; this is likely to lead to assimilation of the expatriate into the foreign culture to such an extent that the person may more closely resemble a foreign national than an expatriate. Marketing personnel on expatriate status are likely to cost a company a great deal more than foreign nationals, so a company must be certain of their effectiveness.[4]

Foreign Nationals

The historical preference for using expatriate managers from the home-office country is gradually giving way to a preference for foreign nationals. At the sales level, the picture is clearly biased in favor of the foreign national. Most companies with sales forces abroad use foreign nationals because they transcend both cultural and legal barriers. Furthermore, companies are finding more qualified foreign personnel available; their salaries and selling expenses are less than for expatriates. Recent studies report the percentage of executive and technical positions held overseas by U.S. citizens continues to fall from a high of 85 percent to a current 45 percent as more companies rely on local personnel. PepsiCo, for example, reduced its expatriate work force by 50 percent between 1985 and 1988.[5]

Cosmopolitan Personnel

The growing internationalization of business breeds a cosmopolitan expatriate from country A working for a company headquartered in country B, in country C, or in countries C, D, E, and so on. Such third-country arrangements are most likely found at management levels and infrequently at the sales level. Development of cosmopolitan executives reflects not only a growing internationalization of business but also acknowledges

[4] An interesting viewpoint on expatriate effectiveness is Stephen Kobrin, "Are Multinationals Better after the Yankees Go Home?" *The Wall Street Journal,* May 8, 1989, p. B14.

[5] "When in Rome, Let the Romans Do It," *The Wall Street Journal* May 3, 1988, p. 1.

BOX 15–1
Lack of Commitment

America has never depended on foreign trade for survival. As late as 1985, U.S. imports were only about 9 percent of the gross national product. Contrast this with Japan, which imports 85 percent of its total energy requirements and all of its oil. Life in the United States would be possible, though uncomfortable, without any external trade.

American managers simply are not willing to make the considerable effort and personal sacrifices to penetrate distant markets. American managers are "too fat and lazy" to compete with hard-driving, dedicated foreign producers. That comment contrasts with the thoughts of the resident manager of a large Japanese firm in Brazil. He had only experienced one month of what would be a typical three-to-five-year assignment. A conversation with him went like this:

Q: "How do you like Brazil?"
A: "I hate it!"
Q: "Are your wife and children happy here?"
A: "No, they're miserable!"
Q: "Will you stay for the full three-to-five years?"
A: "Of course!"

When a Japanese manager is given a foreign assignment by the company with which he will spend his entire career, he will make the necessary commitment and sacrifice to see the job through. It is his duty to the company, co-workers and to Japan. When the local manager of a U.S.–Japan joint venture in Tokyo was asked how long he felt his American counterpart would be willing to stay in Japan, his quick reply was "no more than six weeks."

It seems fair to say that a major reason U.S. businesspersons are not doing well in Asian, European, and South American markets is they really don't want to succeed.

The truth is, deep down in their hearts, typical Yankee businesspeople would rather stay at home. One executive of a large multinational company said "When all is said and done, I'd stick with my Beautyrest mattress, our his-and-hers Cadillacs, and a juicy Texas steak." For this man and many like him, be it ever so humble, there is no place like home.

Source: Adapted from Arthur M. Whitehill, "America's Trade Deficit: The Human Problems," *Business Horizons,* January–February 1988, pp. 18–19.

that personnel skills and motivations are not the exclusive property of one nation. At one time, Burroughs Corporation's Italian company was run by a Frenchman, the Swiss company by a Dane, the German company by an Englishman, the French company by a Swiss, the Venezuelan company by an Argentinian, and the Danish company by a Dutchman.

HOST-COUNTRY RESTRICTIONS

The flexibility of selecting expatriate U.S. nationals or local nationals has been complicated in recent years by changes in attitude by many governments toward foreign workers. Many countries are exhibiting concern with foreign corporate domination and are tightening investment controls, limiting foreign companies to specific industries, restricting nonnational personnel, and exerting other controls to reduce the influence of the foreign investor. In seeking ways to maximize benefits from foreign investment, many countries increasingly insist on more locals being hired at the management level. Over the last few decades, this has consistently reduced the opportunities for sending home-country personnel to management positions in a foreign country. A study of U.S. MNCs revealed that 66 percent regarded the assignment of an American to a foreign job as a temporary measure to fill an immediate and special need.

Many countries have specific laws limiting work permits for foreigners to positions that cannot be filled by a national. Further, the law usually limits such permits to a period just long enough to train a local for that specific position. Thus, MNCs must staff more positions with locals and be more selective about the home-country nationals sent abroad.[6] This fundamental change in the attitude of host countries toward foreign employees has had a profound effect on the entire personnel management process. For example, in situations where a firm has been forced to hire a local, the title may be similar (e.g., a foreign country national comptroller versus a U.S. comptroller), but the skill level is quite dissimilar. This requires adjustments in supervisory and control methods as well as organizational responsibility to accommodate personnel with limited skills. The most profound effect has been felt by U.S. citizens; in earlier years, many lower-management positions abroad could be staffed with less-experienced personnel who gained the necessary training to eventually assume top-level positions in these countries. Most countries, including the United States, control the number of foreign managers allowed to work or train within their borders. In one year the United States Immigration Service rejected 37 out of 40 applications from European chefs the Marriott Corporation wanted to bring to the United States for management training.[7]

U.S. companies find they must send only the more experienced personnel abroad.[8] Historically, there had been a scarcity of highly skilled foreign

[6] Vineeta Anand, "Firms Ship Fewer Executives Abroad," *Global Trade and Exports*, February 1987, p. 27.

[7] John Huey, "Executive Immigrants Find Maze of Rules Hindering Entry to U.S." *The Wall Street Journal*, June 26, 1985, p. 29.

[8] "Finding Local Executives: Peruvian Business School Is a Good Training Ground," *Business Latin America*, February 6, 1985, pp. 44–45.

BOX 15–2
It's Still Work

"In my judgment foreign service is not exciting *per se*. I really don't find much in the way of added stimulation coming to work in the morning in Brussels than I did in California, New York, or any other place."

Source: An American executive.

---

managers; however, this has become less of a problem as the pool of experienced managers trained by the world's largest MNCs grows each year. A recent Conference Board study reported 60 percent of the firms surveyed felt the supply of local management adequate. Further, 35 percent stated they were hiring greater numbers of locals for management jobs.

MANAGING INTERNATIONAL PERSONNEL

Several vital questions arise when attempting to manage in other cultures. How much does a different culture affect management practices, processes, and concepts used in the United States? Will practices that work well in the United States be equally effective when customs, values, and lifestyles differ? Transferring management practices to other cultures without concern for their exportability is no less vulnerable to major error than assuming a product successful in the United States will be successful in other countries. Management concepts are influenced by cultural diversity and must be evaluated in local norms. Whether or not any single management practice needs adapting depends on the culture.[9]

Differences in Cultural Values Affect Management Practices

Because of the unlimited cultural diversity in the values, attitudes, and beliefs affecting management practice, only those fundamental premises on which U.S. management practices are based are presented here for comparison. International managers must analyze the management practices normally used to assess their transferability to another culture. The purpose of this section is to heighten the reader's awareness of the need

---

[9] Faye Rice, "Should You Work for a Foreigner?" *Fortune*, August 1, 1988, pp. 123–34.

BOX 15–3
Now This Is Salesmanship

G. and J. Greenhall Distillers of Warrington and the *Export Times* of London sponsored the Vladivar Vodka Incredible Export Award to honor British capitalistic ingenuity. Here are some of the winners.

1. *Tom-toms to Nigeria:* The Premier Drum Company of Leicester won first prize with their sale of four shipments of tom-toms to Nigeria, including complete kits for the Nigerian Police Band and the country's top band (Dr. Victor Oliyia and his all-star orchestra). Premier also sold maracas to South America and xylophones to Cuba.
2. *Oil to the Arabs:* Second place went to Permaflex Ltd. of Stoke-on-Trent, which exports £50,000 of petroleum a year to the Arab states in the form of lighter fluid.
3. *Sand to Abu Dhabi:* Eastern Sands and Refractories of Cambridge shipped 1,800 tons of sand to sand-rich Abu Dhabi, which needed sand grains of a special shape for water filtration.
4. *Snowplow to Arabia:* The defense force of the Arab sheikhdom of Dubai purchased from Bunce Ltd. of Ashbury, Wiltshire, one snowplow. It is to be used to clear sand from remote roads.
5. *Coals to Newcastle:* Timothy Dexter (1747–1806), an American merchant prince and eccentric who once published a book without punctuation actually sent a shipload of coal to Newcastle, known as a center for shipping coal *out*. The coal arrived just as Newcastle was paralyzed by a coal strike and there was a shortage of fuel for the citizenry. Dexter came away with enormous profits.
6. *Peking ducks to China:* Cherry Valley Duck Farms signed a 10-year contract in Canton to sell British-bred Peking ducks to a farm at Tai Ling Shan, China.

---

for adaptation of management rather than to present a complete discussion of U.S. culture and management behavior.[10]

There are many divergent views on the most important ideas on which normative U.S. cultural concepts are based. Those that occur most frequently in discussions of cross-cultural evaluations are represented by the following: (1) "master of destiny" viewpoint; (2) independent enterprise—the instrument of social action; (3) personnel selection on merit; (4) decisions based on objective analysis; (5) wide sharing in decision making; and (6) never-ending quest for improvement.

---

[10] Amanda Bennett, "American Culture Is Often a Puzzle for Foreign Managers in the U.S.," *The Wall Street Journal*, February 12, 1986, p. 29.

The *master of destiny* philosophy underlies much of U.S. management thought and is a belief held by many in our culture. Simply stated: people can substantially influence the future; we are in control of our own destinies. This viewpoint also reflects the attitude that although luck may influence an individual's future, on balance, persistence, hard work, a commitment to fulfill expectations, and effective use of time give people control of their destinies. Many cultures have a fatalistic approach to life—*individual* destiny is determined by a higher order and what happens cannot be controlled.

In the United States, approaches to planning, control, supervision, commitment, motivation, scheduling, and deadlines are all influenced by the concept that individuals can control their futures. In cultures with more fatalistic beliefs, these good business practices may be followed but concern for the final outcome is different. After all, if one believes the future is determined by an uncontrollable higher order, then what difference does effort really make?[11]

The acceptance of the idea that *independent enterprise* is an *instrument for social action* is the fundamental concept of U.S. corporations. A corporation is recognized as an entity that has rules, continuity of existence, and is a separate and vital social institution. This recognition of the corporation as an entity can result in strong feelings of obligation to serve the company. In fact, the enterprise can take priority over personal preferences and social obligations because it is viewed as an entity that must be protected and developed.[12] This concept ties into the master-of-destiny concept in that for a company to work and for individuals to control their destinies, they must feel a strong obligation to fulfill the requirements necessary to the success of the enterprise. Indeed, the company may take precedence over family, friends, or other activities which might detract from what is best for the company.[13] Among cultures where employees have special corporate allegiance, the Japanese are best known for their lifelong commitment to their companies.

American management theory rests on the assumption that each member of an organization will give primary efforts to performing assigned tasks in the interests of that organization. Thus, in the United States an enterprise takes precedence and receives loyalty and the willingness to conform to its managerial systems. This is in sharp contrast to the attitudes held by

---

[11] Mark Mendenhall and Gary Oddou, "Acculturation Profiles of Expatriate Managers: Implications for Cross-Cultural Training Programs," *Columbia Journal of World Business*, Winter 1986, pp. 73–79.

[12] Phyllis Birnbaum, "What Makes Salaryman Run?" *Across the Board*, June 1988, pp. 14–21.

[13] Antonio Grimaldi, "Interpreting Popular Culture: The Missing Link between Local Labor and International Management," *Columbia Journal of World Business*, Winter 1986, pp. 67–72.

Latin Americans who feel strongly that personal relationships are more important in daily life than the corporation.[14]

Consistent with the view that individuals control their own destinies is the belief that *personnel selection is made on merit*. The selection, promotion, motivation, or dismissal of personnel by U.S. managers emphasizes the need to select the best-qualified persons for jobs, retaining them as long as their performance meets standards of expectations, and continuing the opportunity for upward mobility as long as those standards are met. Indeed, the belief that anyone can become the corporate president prevails among management personnel within the United States. Such presumptions lead to the belief that striving and making accomplishments will be rewarded, and conversely, the failure to do so will be penalized. The penalty for poor performance could be, and often is, dismissal. The reward and penalty scheme is a major basis for motivating U.S. personnel. In other cultures where friendship or family ties may be more important than the vitality of the organization, the criteria for selection, organization, and motivation are substantially different from those in U.S. companies. In some cultures, organizations expand to accommodate the maximum number of friends and relatives. Further, if one knows that promotions are made on the basis of personal ties and friendships rather than on merit, a fundamental motivating lever is lost.

The very strong belief in the United States that business *decisions are based on objective analysis* and that managers strive to be more scientific has a profound effect on the U.S. manager's attitudes toward objectivity in decision making and accuracy of data. While judgment and intuition are important criteria for making decisions, most U.S. managers believe decisions must be supported and based on accurate and relevant information. This scientific approach is not necessarily the premise on which foreign executives base decisions. In fact, the infallibility of the judgment of a key executive in many foreign cultures may be more important in the decision process than any other single factor. If one accepts scientific management as a fundamental basis for decision making, then attitudes toward accuracy and promptness in reporting data, availability and openness of data to all levels within the corporation, and the willingness to express even unpopular judgments become important characteristics of the business process. Thus, in U.S. business, great emphasis is placed on the collection and free flow of information to all levels within the organization and on frankness of expression in the evaluation of business opinions or decisions. In other cultures, such high value on factual and rational support for decisions is not important; the accuracy of data and even the proper

---

[14] For an interesting comparison of U.S., Japanese, Mexican, and Chinese managers' style, see Lane Kelley, Arthur Whatley, and Reginald Worthley, "Assessing the Effects of Culture on Managerial Attitudes: A Three-Culture Test," *Journal of International Business Studies*, Summer 1987, pp. 17–31.

reporting of data are not prime prerequisites. Further, existing data frequently are for the eyes of a select few. The frankness of expression and openness in dealing with data characteristic of U.S. businesses do not fit easily into some cultures.

Compatible with the views that one controls one's own destiny and that advancement is based on merit is the prevailing idea of *wide sharing in decision making.* Although decision making is not truly a democratic process in U.S. businesses, there is a strong belief that individuals in an organization require and, indeed, need the responsibility of making decisions for continued development. Thus, decision making is frequently decentralized and the ability, as well as the responsibility of making decisions, are pushed down to lower ranks of management. In this way, employees have an opportunity to grow with responsibility and to prove their abilities. In many cultures, decisions are highly centralized, in part, because of the belief that only a few in the company have the right or the ability to make decisions. In the Middle East, for example, only top executives make decisions.

Finally, all of these concepts culminate in a *never-ending quest for improvement.* The United States has always been a relatively activist society; in many walks of life, the prevailing question is: "Can it be done better?" Thus management concepts reflect the belief that change is not only normal but also necessary, that no aspects are sacred or above improvement. In fact, the merit on which one achieves advancement is frequently tied to one's ability to make improvements. Results are what count; if practices must change to achieve results, then change is in order. In other cultures, the strength and power of those in command frequently rest not on change but on the premise that the status quo demands stable structure. To suggest improvement implies that those in power have failed; for someone in a lower position to suggest change would be viewed as a threat to another's private domain rather than the suggestion of an alert and dynamic individual.[15]

The views expressed here pervade much of what is considered U.S. management technique. They are part of our SRC and affect our management attitudes and must be considered by the international marketer when developing and managing an international marketing force.

Recruiting and Selecting International Personnel

To recruit and select personnel for international positions effectively, management must define precisely what is expected of its people. A formal job description can aid management in expressing those desires both for

---

[15] Robert T. Moran, "Japan's Remarkable Ability to Adapt to the Real World," *International Management,* May 1988, p. 77.

> **BOX 15–4**
> **So You Want to Own a Car in Japan**
>
> If you're staying in Japan awhile and thinking about buying a car, forget
> it. Owning a car in this country isn't a sensible proposition. Although cars
> are cheaper in Japan than in the United States, the money-saving factor
> ends there.
>
> To register a car in Japan, you first must show proof of a parking space,
> which will cost as much as $400 per month. Registration costs $800, and it
> must be renewed every two years, along with an inspection that costs an
> additional $800. Highway tolls average $5 for every seven miles, and some
> bridge tolls are as high as $40 one way. Gasoline costs about $4.50 a gallon.
>
> Source: Adapted from "Get Around Like the Japanese," *International Living*, October
> 1988, p. 3.

long-range needs as well as current needs. In addition to descriptions
for each marketing position, the criteria should include special requirements
indigenous to various countries.

People operating in the home country need only the attributes of effective
salespersons while a transnational manager can require skills and attitudes
that would challenge a diplomat. Personnel requirements for various positions vary considerably, but despite the range of differences, some basic
requisites leading to effective performance should be considered because
effective executives and salespeople, regardless of where they are operating,
share certain characteristics. Special personal characteristics, skills, and
orientations are demanded for international operations.

Maturity is a prime requisite for expatriate and cosmopolitan personnel.
Managers and sales personnel working abroad typically must work more
independently than their domestic counterparts. The company must have
confidence in the ability of its personnel to make decisions and commitments without constant recourse to the home office or they cannot be
individually effective.

International personnel require a kind of *emotional stability* not demanded
in domestic positions. Regardless of location, these people are living in
cultures dissimilar to their own; to some extent they are always under
scrutiny, and always aware that they are official representatives of the
company abroad. They need a sensitivity to behavioral variations in different countries but cannot be so hypersensitive that their behavior is adversely
affected. Finally, managers or salespeople operating in foreign countries
need *considerable breadth of knowledge of many subjects both on and off the job.*
The ability to speak several languages is always preferable.

In addition to the intangible skills necessary in handling interpersonal
relationships, international marketers must also be effective salespeople.

BOX 15–5
Model Latin-American Manager

Although selecting a manager to head a Latin American operation depends on a firm's specific needs at a particular time, most companies have a good idea of the characteristics they would most like to find in an ideal candidate. Firms say the four leading traits, in order of importance, are flexibility, empathy with the environment (defined by one company as the ability to understand and operate in a Latin environment and enjoy it), the desire to take on change, and self-confidence.

The list includes many other desirable attributes. Knowing the language—Spanish in the bulk of Latin America or Portuguese in Brazil—is considered very important by almost all companies, although a strong minority believes this skill can be mastered after the person gets to the country. Next in line come such traits as the ability to recognize and develop the skills of others, generate enthusiasm, and achieve results within budget limits. Other companies stress the need for an individual who can deal with local regulatory bodies, can think in a disciplined and logical manner, and is energetic and persistent.

Other corporate checklists cite an aggressive person with a feel for strategic thinking and the high moral standards necessary to withstand the temptation of corruption in many Latin American countries. Other sought-after traits include the ability to confront conflicts, take action without being asked, and identify key issues in a disagreement.

All companies want strong managers who can lead and influence people—staff, clients, government officials, and shareholders. The ideal choice should also be endowed with strong entrepreneurial drive, be efficiency oriented and strive for high performance. Companies also agree that personality definitely gets the edge over technical skills. One MNC explains: "In Europe, our top requirement would be strategic planning abilities; in Latin America we need a person who can fit in the environment."

Source: "Companies Offer Tips on How to Select Managers for Latin American Subs." Reprinted from p. 266 of the August 29, 1981 issue of *Business Latin America* (BL), with the permission of the publisher, Business International Corporation (New York).

Every marketing person in a foreign position is directly involved in the selling effort and must possess a sales sense that cuts through personal, cultural, and language differences and deals effectively with the selling situation.

The marketer who expects to be effective in the international marketplace needs to have a *favorable outlook on an international assignment*. People who do not genuinely like what they are doing and where they are doing it stand little chance of success. Failures usually are the result of overselling

> **BOX 15–6**
> **The View from the Other Side**
>
> The globalization of U.S. markets means that more foreign managers are coming to the United States to live. The problem of cultural adaptation and adjustment is no less a problem for them than for Americans going to their countries to live. Here are a few observations from the other side—from foreigners in the United States.
>
> "There are no small eggs in America," says a Dutchman, "There are only jumbo, extra large, large, and medium." This is no country for humility.
>
> "If you are not aggressive, you're not noticed." "For a foreigner to succeed in the United States . . . he needs to be more aggressive than in his own culture because Americans expect that."
>
> Young Japanese have difficulty addressing American superiors in a manner that shows self-confidence and an air of competence. The essential elements are posture and eye contact, but the Japanese simply cannot stand up straight, puff up their chests, look the Americans in the eyes, and talk at the same time.
>
> Schedules and deadlines are taken very seriously. How quickly one does a job is often as important as how well one does the job. Japanese, who are experts at being members of teams, need help in learning to compete, take initiative, and develop leadership skills.
>
> A Latin American has to refrain from the sort of socializing he would do in Latin countries, where rapport comes before deal making. "Here that is not necessary," he says. "You can even do business with someone you do not like." He still feels uncomfortable launching right into business, but Americans become frustrated when they think they are wasting time.
>
> Americans say, "Come on over sometime," but the foreigner learns—perhaps after an awkward visit—that this is not really an invitation.
>
> "Living alone in the United States is very sad, so much loneliness. Of course, living alone in Japan is also lonely, but in this country we can't speak English so fluently, so it is difficult to find a friend. I miss my boyfriend. I miss my parents. I miss my close friends."
>
> Adapted from Lennie Copeland, "Managing in the Melting Pot," *Across the Board*, June 1986, pp. 52–59.

the assignment, showing the bright side of the picture, and not warning about the bleak side.

An international salesperson must have a high level of adaptability whether working in a foreign country or at home. Expatriates working in a foreign country must be particularly sensitive to the habits of the market; those working at home for a foreign company must adapt to the requirements and ways of the parent company.

Successful adaptation in international affairs is based on a combination of attitude and effort. A careful study of the customs of the market country should be initiated before the marketer arrives in a country, and should continue as long as there are facets of the culture that are not clear. One useful approach is to listen to the advice of national and foreign business people operating in that country. Cultural empathy is clearly a part of basic orientation because it is unlikely that anyone can be effective if antagonistic or confused about the environment.

The personal characteristics, skills, and orientation which identify the potentially effective person have been labeled in many different ways. Each person studying the field has a preferred list of characteristics, yet rising above all the characteristics there is an intangible something that some people have referred to as a "sixth sense." This implies that regardless of the individual attributes, there is a certain blend of personal characteristics, skills, and orientation that is hard to pinpoint and which may differ from individual to individual, but produces the most effective overseas personnel.[16]

Getting the right person to handle the job is a primary function of personnel management. It becomes especially important in the selection of home-country nationals to work for foreign companies within their home country. Most less-developed countries and many European countries have stringent laws protecting workers' rights. These laws are specific as to penalties for the dismissal of employees. Venezuela has the most stringent dismissal legislation: with more than three months of service in the same firm, a worker gets severance pay amounting to one-month's pay at severance notice plus 15-days' pay for every month of service exceeding eight months plus an additional 15-days' pay for each year employed. Further, after an employee is dismissed, the law requires that person be replaced within 30 days at the same salary. Colombia and Brazil have similar laws that make employee dismissal a high-cost proposition.

The Gender Bias in International Business

What are the opportunities for women in international business? Should women represent U.S. firms abroad? These and similar questions are more frequently asked as U.S. companies become more internationalized and as more women move up the management ranks domestically and seek career-related international assignments.[17] Unfortunately, the gender bias toward women managers that exists in many countries creates a hesitancy among U.S. MNCs to offer women international assignments.[18]

---

[16] Rosalie L. Tung, "Expatriate Assignments: Enhancing Success and Minimizing Failure," *Academy of Management Executive*, 1, no. 2 (1987), pp. 117–26.

[17] "High-Tech Women at the Top," *Across the Board*, July–August 1988, pp. 11–17.

[18] David Nye, "The Female Expat's Promise," *Across the Board*, February 1988, pp. 38–43.

BOX 15–7
Women Negotiators—A U.S. Whammy for Some

Adapting to cultural differences is not only necessary for Americans—it is necessary for other nations, too. Other cultures have to understand our cultural differences and adapt if they are to be successful. About half of the 100 professional staff members at the Office of the U.S. Trade Representative are women who play prominent roles in U.S. trade negotiations. If the foreign negotiator from a male-dominated culture is not prepared, confusion prevails and opportunities are lost.

In many Latin American, Middle Eastern, and Asian countries, women are not in the upper levels of government and management. When Americans send female negotiators, the host country male negotiators have a hard time adapting to the cultural differences. Unless foreign negotiators are prepared for the shock of having to do business with women, they can be thrown off balance.

During a round of textile negotiations with an Asian country, the Asians led an all-male team against an American all-female team. The American recalled: "We were being pretty tough, politely stonewalling them. Suddenly their delegation leader threw a temper tantrum. He shouted that he didn't like the position we were taking, said our arguments reminded him of dealings with his wife." A recess was called. The outburst apparently caused the foreign negotiator to lose face among his colleagues.

The negotiations concerned a quota to determine the number of cotton shirts and blouses the Asian government could ship to the United States. In the end, the foreign negotiators settled for a lower quota than the United States was prepared to grant. The Asian lost not only his cool but hundreds of thousands of dollars in U.S. sales by his country's apparel producers.

Confusion prevailed as to just how they should react to women. Should they react as they would to women in their country, as foreign women, as American women, or as representatives of the U.S. government? Being culturally insensitive and unwilling to accommodate to cultural differences can deal unsuspecting negotiators a double whammy—skilled U.S. negotiators to whom they do not react effectively because of their own cultural biases.

Adapted from Clyde H. Farnsworth, "For U.S., Women Win More than Their Quota of Trade Negotiations," *International Herald*, July 5, 1988, p. 1.

In many cultures—Asian, Arab, Latin American, and even some European—women are not typically found in upper levels of management. Traditional roles in male-dominated societies are often translated into minimal business opportunities for women. This cultural bias raises questions about the effectiveness of women in establishing successful relationships with host country associates. An often asked question is whether it is appropriate to send a woman to conduct business with foreign customers.

To some it appears logical that if women are not accepted in managerial roles within their own cultures, a foreign woman would not be any more acceptable. Such are the arguments offered when international business positions are denied women.[19]

It is a fact that men and women are treated very differently in some cultures. In Saudi Arabia, for example, women are segregated, expected to wear veils, and forbidden even to drive.[20] Evidence suggests, however, that prejudice toward foreign women executives may be exaggerated and that the treatment local women receive in their own cultures is not necessarily an indicator of how a foreign businesswoman is treated.

When a company gives management responsibility and authority to someone, a large measure of the respect initially shown that person is the result of respect for the firm. When a woman manager receives the strong backing of her firm, she usually receives the respect commensurate with the position she holds and the firm she represents. Thus, resistance to her as a female either does not materialize or is less severe than anticipated.[21] Even in those cultures where a female would not ordinarily be a manager, foreign female executives benefit, at least initially, from the status, respect, and importance attributed to the firms they represent. In Japan where Japanese women rarely achieve even lower-level management positions, representatives of U.S. firms are seen first as Americans, second as representatives of firms, and then as males or females.[22] Once business negotiations begin, the willingness of a business host to engage in business transactions and the respect shown to a foreign business person grows or diminishes depending on the business skills he or she demonstrates, regardless of gender.[23]

Rather than accept conventional wisdom that women cannot do business in a particular country, study the culture and examine what the obstacles and opportunities actually are. Although everyone conducting business in another culture should be aware of the local business customs that help develop a successful business relationship, female executives may have to learn an added subset of customs that are uniquely important.

Certain customs require a different response from females than males. For example, in Middle Eastern countries, custom may dictate that women

[19] Jolie Solomon, "Women, Minorities and Foreign Postings," *The Wall Street Journal*, June 2, 1989, p. B1.

[20] "Saudi Arabia's Conservative Car Rules Lead to a Lack of Drive among Women," *The Wall Street Journal*, May 27, 1986, p. 32.

[21] Nancy Adler, "Pacific Basin Manager: A Gaijin, Not a Woman," *Human Resource Management*, Summer 1987, pp. 169–92.

[22] Lennie Copeland and Lewis Griggs, *Going International* (New York: Random House, 1985) p. 220.

[23] Nancy J. Adler, "How They Educated Their Companies," *Across the Board*, February 1988, p. 42.

be segregated in social settings and/or in business gatherings. Thus, acceptance in one setting does not guarantee acceptance in the other. As with all business people, a woman must know and adapt to the different settings or risk creating a major faux pas. For example, after a day of business meetings the female vice president of a U.S. firm was invited to dinner at the home of a Saudi businessman, and, upon entering the home, was escorted to a room set aside for women. Feeling that she was not being accorded the proper status (she was head of the American delegation), she crashed the dinner in the men's dining room. Dinner and business discussion ended abruptly.[24] Had she been sensitive to local custom, the incident could have been avoided by declining the dinner invitation and telling her male counterparts to proceed without her until meetings resumed the next day.

To ease the entrance of women into cultures where female executives are not customary, companies must not only forewarn foreign clients that women will represent them but also inform clients of their representatives' qualifications, their authority to act for the company, and top management's confidence in them. For a woman to suddenly appear as a representative of a company would only add confusion to the problem of cultural shock that arises from conducting business with women. As world markets become more internationalized and as international competition intensifies, U.S. companies need to be represented by the most capable personnel available; it seems shortsighted to limit the talent pool simply because of gender.[25]

Training and Motivating International Personnel

The nature of a training program depends largely on whether expatriate or foreign personnel are being trained for overseas positions. Training for the expatriates focuses on the customs and special foreign sales problems that will be encountered, while foreign national personnel require greater emphasis on the company, its products, technical information, and selling methods. In training either type of personnel, the sales training activity is burdened with problems stemming from long-established behavior and attitudes. Foreign nationals cling to habits continually reinforced by local culture and expatriates are captives of their own habits and patterns as well. Before any training can be effective, open-minded attitudes must be established.

Continual training may be more important in foreign markets than

---

[24] Nye, "The Female Expat's Promise," p. 41.

[25] Monci Jo Williams, "Women Beat the Corporate Game," *Fortune*, September 12, 1988, pp. 128–38.

BOX 15–8
Japanese Boot Camp—Preparing for Sales in America

It is no secret that NEC Corporation, a giant Japanese computer company, is making a vigorous assault on the world's computer and communications markets. Behind the scenes in NEC's rapid globalization, the company has a kind of permanent boot camp with elaborate training exercises to prepare NEC managers for overseas battle.

The training is not entirely grim. It includes lessons in table manners, cocktail party chit chat, and English language jokes. But most of it deals with the nitty-gritty of business. At NEC's Institute for International Studies, six middle managers spend Saturdays learning how to negotiate with non-Japanese. For three hours at a stretch they face each other across a negotiating table in a fierce game of bargaining. The participants are drilled in the tired cliches of American negotiating slang so they know all about "going in cold," "shooting from the hip," and "beating around the bush."

At this campuslike NEC facility, 14 younger staffers arrive with suitcases for a 12 hour-a-day course in English conversation. The course is so intense that teachers are replaced every few days. The students have to pay a fine every time they speak Japanese.

In another of the institute's 162 courses, 24 wives of NEC managers who are headed overseas begin a three-day introduction to life as expatriates. The anxiety in the room is palpable and the women worry about their futures and their children. Education overseas can be a serious headache says the lecturer but it also gives your child a chance to be a child of the 21st century. The students practice public speaking and learn how to write letters to the editor.

The ultimate aim of the course? "The graduate should smell like soy sauce when he is talking with Japanese clients and smell like butter when he is with foreigners" says Mr. Kira, referring to a traditional Japanese belief that Westerners give off a faint smell of butter.

Contrast the Japanese experience with the following policy of a large American electronics firm: "Let people become good engineers first and then prepare them, if they need, to go overseas."

"The problem is they never really do train them," reports a dean of an engineering college. "The training program consists of an intensive nine-day Japanese-language course that, in the words of one company executive, 'teaches you the basic pleasantries.' "

Another Fortune 500 company's globalization program for senior executives involves a week of management training, two weeks spent visiting plants in this country and overseas and then follow-up project work.

Source: Adapted from Bernard Wysocki, Jr., "Japanese Executives Going Overseas Take Anti-Shock Courses," *The Wall Street Journal*, January 12, 1987, p. 1; and "High-Technology Lip Service," *U.S. News and World Report*, December 26, 1988, pp. 112–14.

in domestic ones because of the lack of routine contact with the parent company and its marketing personnel. One aspect of training is frequently overlooked; home office personnel dealing with international marketing operations need training designed to make them responsive to the needs of the foreign operations. In most companies, the requisite sensitivities are expected to be developed by osmosis in the process of dealing with foreign affairs; a few companies send home-office personnel abroad periodically to increase their awareness of the problems of the foreign operations.

Although the stages in the development of an overseas management team are the same as those in domestic marketing, there are vast differences in the approaches used and the problems encountered in accomplishing these steps in the world market. Motivation is especially complicated because the firm is dealing with different cultures, different sources, different philosophies—and always dealing with individuals.[26]

Marketing is a business function requiring high motivation regardless of the location of the practitioner. Marketing managers and sales managers typically work hard, travel extensively, and have day-to-day challenges. Selling is hard, competitive work wherever undertaken and a constant flow of inspiration is needed to keep personnel functioning at an optimal level. National differences must always be considered in motivating the marketing force. One company found its sales people were losing respect and had low motivation because they did not have girls to pour tea for customers in the Japanese branch offices. The company learned that when male personnel served tea, they felt they lost face; tea girls were authorized for all branches.

Communications are also important in maintaining high levels of motivation; foreign managers need to know the home office is interested in their operations; and, in turn, they want to know what is happening in the parent country. Everyone performs better when well informed.

Because promotion and the opportunity to improve status are important motivators, a company needs to make the opportunities for growth within the firm clear. One of the greatest fears of expatriate managers is that they will be forgotten by the home office; such fears can be easily allayed.

Because the cultural differences reviewed in earlier chapters affect the motivational patterns of a sales force, a manager must be extremely sensitive to the personal behavior patterns of employees. Individual incentives which work effectively in the United States can fail completely in other cultures. For example, with Japan's emphasis on paternalism and collectivism and its system of lifetime employment and seniority, motivation through indi-

---

[26] For an interesting perspective on training from the Japanese view, see Hidesuke Nagashima, "Building Japanese Managers," *Japan Update*, Spring 1986, pp. 16–19.

Walking Buddha, Malaysia. International salespeople know that religious beliefs often influence the selling situation. (Al Guiteras/Journalism Services, Inc.)

vidual incentive does not work because the Japanese employee seems to derive the greatest satisfaction from being a comfortable member of a group. Thus, an offer of financial reward for outstanding work could be turned down because the employee would prefer not to appear different from peers and possibly attract their resentment. Blending company sales objectives and the personal objectives of the salespeople and other employees is a task worthy of the most skilled manager. The U.S. manager must be constantly aware that many of the techniques used to motivate U.S. personnel and their responses to these techniques are based on six basic cultural premises discussed earlier. Therefore, each method used to motivate a foreigner should be examined for cultural compatibility.[27]

---

[27] To learn how two different management styles can be blended, see John Holusha, "Two Cultures but One Assembly Line," *International Herald Tribune*, June 9, 1988, p. 6.

PREPARING U.S. PERSONNEL FOR
FOREIGN ASSIGNMENTS

Estimates of the annual cost of sending and supporting a manager and the family in a foreign assignment range from 150 to 475 percent of base salary. The costs in money as well as morale increase substantially if the expatriate requests a return home before completing the normal tour of duty (a normal stay is two to four years). In addition, if repatriation into domestic operations is not successful and the employee leaves the company, an indeterminately high cost in low morale and loss of experienced personnel results. To ameliorate these problems, international personnel management has increased planning for expatriate personnel to move abroad, remain abroad, and then return to the home country. The planning process must begin prior to the selection of those who go abroad and extend to their specific assignments after returning home. Selection, training, compensation, and career development policies (including repatriation) should reflect the unique problems of managing the expatriate.

Besides the job-related criteria for a specific position, the typical candidate for an international assignment is married, has two school-aged children, is expected to stay overseas three years, and has the potential for promotion into higher management levels. These characteristics of the typical selectee are the basis of most of the difficulties associated with getting the best of the qualified to go overseas, keeping them there, and assimilating them on their return.

Overcoming Reluctance to Accept a
Foreign Assignment

Concerns for career and family are the most frequently mentioned reasons for a manager to refuse a foreign assignment. The most important career-related reservation is the fear that a two- or three-year absence will adversely affect opportunities for advancement. This "out of sight, out of mind" fear is closely linked to the problems of repatriation. Without evidence of advance planning to protect career development, better qualified and ambitious personnel may decline the offer to go abroad. However, if candidates for expatriate assignments are picked thoughtfully and returned to the home office at the right moment and rewarded for good performance with subsequent promotions at home, companies find recruiting of executives for international assignments eased.

Even though the career development question may be adequately answered with proper planning, concern for family may interfere with many accepting an assignment abroad. Initially, most potential candidates are worried about uprooting a family and settling into a strange environment. Questions about the education of the children, isolation from family and

BOX 15–9
The Risks of a Foreign Assignment

You have been offered a job overseas—are there any risks involved? The answer, "It depends." In some companies, an overseas assignment is absolutely necessary for advancement up the management ladder above a certain level. At one stage in a person's career, there is no other way to get as much and as varied experience as you get on a foreign assignment. At Ford Motor Company, for example, foreign experience is part of your learning curve and, if you are to grow as an executive, you must spend time abroad. When you return, you understand the global picture and can make better decisions. With other companies, overseas experience may be considered unimportant and you could lose out at home. Consider the following situation:

A $65,000-a-year marketing executive employed by a major diversified consumer-products company had yearned for a foreign assignment since he joined the company. Six years after joining the company and learning the product lines, he was sent to the Far East where he got consistently good reviews for his work. His initial compensation package was worth $90,000 and included the cost of housing for him and his wife (who had an overseas position with another U.S. firm), a car, driver, and a full-time maid. It was great until he returned and found there was no position for him at home.

To make matters worse, there had been enormous turnover among the senior managers he had been reporting to in the company's domestic operations. He came back to a situation where there was no job and where he no longer knew anyone. He found he was without contacts within the company. He was getting paid but had no serious assignment. Unfortunately, this situation is not unusual. The best protection: Keep in touch with someone high enough in the company to look out for your best interests. Some companies provide such a "godfather," others don't, so it is up to you.

Source: Adapted from "Weigh the Risks First on That Job Abroad," *U.S. News & World Report,* December 2, 1985, p. 82.

friends, proper medical and health care, and, in some countries, the potential for violence reflect the misgivings a family faced with relocating in a foreign country.[28] Special compensaton packages have been the typical way to deal with this problem. A hardship allowance, allowances to cover special educational requirements that frequently include private schools,

---

[28] For an account of what firms are doing as protection against terrorism, see "Multinational Firms Act to Protect Overseas Workers from Terrorism," *The Wall Street Journal,* April 29, 1986, p. 31; and "How U.S. Executives Dodge Terrorism Abroad," *Business Week,* May 12, 1986, p. 41.

housing allowances, and extended all-expense-paid vacations are part of compensation packages designed to overcome family-related problems with an overseas assignment. Ironically, the solution to one problem creates a later problem when that family returns to the United States and must give up those extra compensation benefits used to induce them to accept the position.[29]

Reducing the Rate of Early Returns

Once the employee and family accept the assignment abroad, the next problem is keeping them there for the assigned time. The attrition rate of those selected for overseas positions can be very high. One firm with a hospital management contract experienced an annualized failure rate of 120 percent—not high when compared with the construction contractor who started out in Saudi Arabia with 155 Americans and was down to 65 after only two months (annualized, an attrition rate of 368 percent).

The most important reasons a growing number of companies are including an evaluation of an *employee's family* among selection criteria are the high cost of sending an expatriate abroad, and increasing evidence that unsuccessful family adjustment is the single most important reason for expatriate dissatisfaction and the resultant request for return home. In fact, a study of personnel directors of over 300 international firms found that the inability of the manager's spouse to adjust to a different physical or cultural environment was the primary reason for an expatriate's failure to function effectively in a foreign assignment.

Dissatisfaction is caused by the stress and trauma of adjusting to new and often strange cultures. The employee has less trouble adjusting than family members; an expatriate moves in a familiar environment even abroad and is often isolated from the cultural differences that create problems for the rest of the family. Family members have far greater daily exposure to the new culture but are seldom given assistance in adjusting. Family members frequently cannot be employed and, in many cultures, female members of the family face severe social restrictions.[30] In Saudi Arabia, for example, the female's role is strictly dictated. In one situation, a woman's hemline offended a religious official who, in protest, sprayed black paint on her legs. In short, the greater problems of cultural shock befall the family. Certainly any recruiting and selection procedure should include an evaluation of the family's ability to adjust.

---

[29] Mark E. Mendenhall and Gary Oddou, "The Overseas Assignment: A Practical Look," *Business Horizons*, September–October 1988, pp. 78–84.

[30] Peter Blunt, "Cultural Consequences for Organization Change in a Southeast Asian State: Brunei," *Academy of Management Executive*, II, no. 3 (1988), pp. 235–40.

Families that have the potential and the personality traits that would enable them to adjust to a different environment may still become dissatisfied with living abroad if they are not properly prepared for the new assignment. More and more companies realize the need for cross-cultural training to prepare families for their new homes. One- to two-day briefings to two- to three-week intensive programs that include all members of the family are provided to help assimilation into new cultures. Language training, films, discussions, and lectures on cultural differences, potential problems, and stress areas in adjusting to a new way of life are provided to minimize the frustration of the initial cultural shock.[31] This cultural training helps a family anticipate problems and eases adjustment. Once the family is abroad, some companies even provide a local ombudsman (someone experienced in the country) to whom members can take their problems and get immediate assistance. Although the cost of preparing a family for an overseas assignment may appear high, consider that one company estimates the measurable cost of one prematurely returned family could cover cross-cultural training for 300 to 500 families. Companies that do not prepare employees and their families for the cultural shock have the highest incidence of premature return to the United States.[32] For those assignments abroad which are successful, the next hurdle confronting the expatriate and family is coming home or repatriation.

Successful Expatriate Repatriation

A Conference Board study reported that many firms have sophisticated plans for executives going overseas but few have comprehensive programs to deal with the return home.

Low morale and a growing amount of attrition among returning expatriates have many reasons. Some complaints and problems are family related, others are career related. The family-related problems generally deal with financial and lifestyle readjustments. Some expatriates find that in spite of higher compensation programs their net worths have not increased, and the inflation of intervening years makes it impossible to buy a home comparable to the one they sold on leaving. The hardship compensation programs used to induce the executive to go abroad also create readjustment

---

[31] One especially effective series of film/videos useful for the manager and the family is *Going International*. There are four programs in the series, ''Bridging the Culture Gap,'' ''Managing the Overseas Assignment,'' ''Beyond Culture Shock,'' and ''Welcome Home Stranger.'' With each film, leader's and user's guides are available to make maximum use of each program. For information contact: Copeland Griggs Productions, 3454 Sacramento Street, San Francisco, CA 94118, (415) 921-4410.

[32] George Anders, ''What Price Lunch? The Big Mac Index Provides a Quick Guide to Currency Values,'' *The Wall Street Journal*, September 23, 1988, p. 30R.

problems on the return home. Such compensation benefits frequently permitted the family to live at a much higher level abroad than at home (for example, yard boys, chauffeurs, domestic help, and so forth). Because most compensation benefits are withdrawn when employees return to the home country, their standard of living decreases and they must readjust. Another objection to returning to the United States is the location of the new assignment; the new location often is not viewed as desirable as the location before the foreign tour. Unfortunately, little can be done to ameliorate these kinds of problems short of transferring the managers to other foreign locations. It is being repeatedly suggested that the problem of dissatisfaction with compensation and benefits can be reduced by reducing benefits. Rather than provide the family abroad with hardship payments, some companies are considering reducing payments on the premise that the assignment abroad is an integral requirement for growth, development, and advancement within the firm. Even though family dissatisfaction may cause stress within the family on returning home, the problem is not as severe as career-related complaints.

A returning expatriate's dissatisfaction with the perceived future is usually the reason many resign their positions after returning to the United States. The problem is not unique to U.S. citizens; Japanese companies have similar difficulties with their personnel. The most frequently heard complaint involves the lack of a detailed plan for the expatriate's career when returning home. New home-country assignments are frequently mundane and do not reflect the experience gained or the challenges met during foreign assignment. Some feel their time out of the mainstream of corporate affairs has made them technically obsolete and thus ineffective in competing immediately on return. Finally, there is some loss of status requiring ego adjustment when an executive returns home. As discussed earlier, overseas assignments are most successfully filled by independent, mature self-starters. The expatriate executive enjoyed a certain degree of autonomy, independence, and power with all the perquisites of office not generally afforded in comparable positions domestically. Many find it difficult to adjust to being just another middle manager at home. In short, returning expatriates have a series of personal and career-related questions to anticipate with anxiety back at corporate headquarters. Companies with the least amount of returnee attrition differ from those with the highest attrition in one significant way—personal career planning for the expatriate.[33]

Expatriate career planning begins with the decision to send the person abroad. The initial transfer abroad should be made in the context of a long-term company career plan. Under these cirumstances, the individual

---

[33] Rosalie L. Tung, "Career Issues in International Assignments," *Academy of Management Executive*, August 1988, pp. 241–44.

knows not only the importance of the foreign assignment but also when to expect to return and at what level. Near the end of the foreign assignment, the process for repatriation is begun.

The critical aspect of the return home is to keep the executive completely informed: proposed return time, new assignment and whether it is interim or permanent, new responsibilities, and future prospects. In short, the returnees should know where they are going and what they will be doing next month and several years ahead. To provide such a program requires considerable preparation prior to the assignment. The most effective solution to handling international personnel management is probably reflected in corporate attitudes toward the long-term importance of foreign assignments.[34] If it is understood that foreign corporate experience is a necessary prerequisite for growth and promotion within the company, many of the problems faced today with foreign assignments would be eliminated. As all employees—management, office staff, blue-collar workers—develop a multinational outlook, as the company effectively prepares employees for overseas assignments, and if expectations for management jobs are high, most of the problems discussed will be substantially eased. Although this discussion has been directed primarily toward U.S. personnel, it is equally applicable and important for the assignment of foreign personnel in the United States.[35]

Developing Cultural Awareness

Throughout the text, the need to adapt to the local culture has been stressed over and over. Developing cultural sensitivity is necessary for all international marketers. Personnel can be selected with great care, but, if they do not possess or are not given the opportunity to develop some understanding of the culture to which they are being assigned, there is every chance they will develop culture shock, inadvertently alienate those with whom they come in contact in the new culture, and/or make all the cultural mistakes discussed in this text. As the world becomes more interdependent and as companies become more dependent on foreign earnings, there is a growing concern within many companies for developing cultural awareness.

Just as we remark that someone has achieved good social skills (i.e., an ability to remain poised and be in control under all social situations), so good cultural skills can be developed. These skills serve a similar function

---

[34] Robert T. Moran, "Corporations Tragically Waste Overseas Experience," *International Management*, January 1988, p. 74.

[35] To see the problems from the view of foreigners coming to the United States, see Lennie Copeland, "Managing in the Melting Pot," *Across the Board*, June 1986, pp. 52–59.

in varying cultural situations; they provide the individual with the ability to relate to a different culture even when the individual is unfamiliar with the details of that particular culture. Cultural skills can be learned just as social skills can be learned. People with cultural skills can: (1) communicate respect and convey verbally and nonverbally a positive regard and sincere interest in people and their culture; (2) tolerate ambiguity and cope with cultural differences and the frustration that frequently develops when things are different and circumstances change; (3) display empathy by understanding other people's needs and differences from *their* point of view; (4) be nonjudgmental by not judging the behavior of others on their own value standards; (5) recognize and control the SRC, that is, recognize their own culture and values as an influence on their perceptions, evaluations, and judgment in a situation; (6) laugh things off; a good sense of humor helps when frustration levels rise and things do not work as planned.

Compensating

Developing an equitable and functional compensation plan that combines balance, consistent motivation, and flexibility is extremely challenging in international operations. This is especially true when a company operates in a number of countries, when it has individuals who work in a number of countries, or when the force is composed of expatriate and foreign personnel. Fringe benefits play a major role in many countries. Those working in high-tax countries prefer liberal expense accounts and fringe benefits which are nontaxable instead of direct income subject to high taxes. Fringe-benefit costs are high in Europe ranging from 35 to 60 percent of salary.

Pay can be a significant factor in making it difficult for a person to be repatriated. Often, those returning home realize they have been making considerably more money with a lower cost of living in the overseas market; returning to the home country means a cut in pay and a cut in standard of living.

Conglomerate operations that include domestic and foreign personnel cause the greatest problems in compensation planning. Expatriates tend to compare their compensation with what they would have received at the home office; at the same time, foreign personnel and expatriate personnel are likely to compare notes on salary. Although any differences in the compensation level may easily and logically be explained, the group receiving the lower amount almost always feels aggrieved and mistreated.

Short-term assignments for expatriates further complicate the compensation issue, particularly when the short-term assignments extend into a longer time. In general, short-term assignments involve payments of overseas premiums (sometimes called *separation allowances* if the family does

BOX 15–10
The Eyes Have It!

Cultural differences abound in eye contact between individuals. In the United States we have been taught to look someone directly in the eye when speaking or being spoken to. In other cultures, looking someone in the eye may be considered disrespectful. For example:

In Japan a person who looks a subordinate in the eye is felt to be judgmental and punitive, while someone who looks his superior in the eye is assumed to be hostile.

Arabs like eye contact but their eyes seem to dart about much more than Americans; unfortunately, Americans don't trust shifty eyed people.

Brazilians look people in the eye even more consistently than Americans. Americans tend to maintain intermittent rather than sustained eye contact during a conversation and find the steady Brazilian gaze more staring and very disconcerting. The only exception is when people of different age and status converse, then the less powerful person looks down and away. This downcast gaze is a sign of lower status and not evasiveness or deceit.

Source: Adapted from Lennie Copeland and Lewis Griggs, *Going International* (New York: Random House, 1985), pp. 111–12; and Phyllis A. Harrison, *Behaving Brazilian* (Rowley, Mass.: Newbury House Publishers, 1983), pp. 23–24.

not go along), all excess expenses, and allowances for tax differentials. Longer assignments can include home-leave benefits or travel allowances for the spouse. Many companies estimate that these expenses equal approximately the base compensation of the employees.

Besides rewarding an individual's contribution to the firm, a compensation program can be used effectively to recruit, develop, motivate, or retain personnel. Most recommendations for developing a compensation program suggest that a program focus on whichever one of these purposes fits the needs in the particular situation. If all four purposes are targeted, it can result in unwieldy programs that have become completely unmanageable for many. International compensation programs also provide additional payments for hardship locations and special inducements to reluctant personnel to accept overseas employment and to remain in the position. Fringe benefit costs for an annual base salary of $40,000 can range from $138,300 in Canada to $427,800 in Nigeria for a three-year period.[36]

An important trend questions the need for expatriates to fill foreign positions. Many companies now feel that the increase in the number and quality of managers in other countries means many positions being filled

[36] "Tokyo Still Most Expensive City," *Business International*, July 11, 1988, p. 214.

by expatriates could be filled by nationals and/or third-country nationals who would require lower compensation packages. Several major U.S. multinationals, PepsiCo, Black & Decker Mfg. Company, and Hewlett-Packard Company, have established policies to minimize the number of expatriate personnel they post abroad.[37] With more emphasis being placed on the development of third-country nationals and locals for managerial positions, companies find they can reduce compensation packages.

Adapting Personal Selling Skills to Global Markets

An international sales force is composed of personnel from the parent company, foreign nationals directed by a foreign sales or domestic sales manager operating abroad, or a group of individuals from both the parent company and the country in which business is being sought. Although the trend for large companies is to hire nationals to conduct sales, the home-country salesperson remains important for a vast number of companies.

Communications and the art of persuasion, knowledge of the customer and product, the ability to close a sale, and after-sale service are all necessary for successful selling. These attributes are sought when hiring an experienced person and are taught to new employees. Since culture impacts on the international sales effort just as it does on international advertising and promotion, cultural adaptation needs to be included in sales training programs. Selling is communication. Unless the salesperson can communicate effectively in different cultural settings, the sales process is thwarted.

Effective communications is understanding the nuances of the spoken language as well as the silent language discussed in the chapter about business customs. If the salesperson does not know a Japanese "yes" often means "no" but that in China a "no" often means "yes," confusion will result. Perhaps more important than language nuances are the meanings of different silent languages spoken by people from different cultures. They may think they are understanding one another when, in fact, they are misinterpreting one another. For example:

> An American visits a Saudi official to convince him to expedite permits for equipment being brought into the country. The Saudi offers the American coffee which is politely refused (he had been drinking coffee all morning at the hotel while planning the visit), he sits down and crosses his legs exposing the sole of his shoe, he passes the documents to the Saudi with his left hand, inquires after the Saudi's wife, and emphasizes the urgency of getting the needed permits.

In less than three minutes, the American unwittingly offends the Saudi five times. He refused his host's hospitality, showed disrespect, used an

---

[37] "When in Rome, Let the Romans Do It," p. 1.

"unclean" hand, implied an unintended familial familiarity, and displayed impatience with his host. The American had no intention of offending his host and probably was not aware of the rudeness of his behavior. The Saudi might forgive his American guest for being ignorant of local custom, but the forgiven salesperson is in a weakened position.

Knowing your customer in international sales means more than knowing your customer's product needs; it includes knowing your customer's culture. One international consultant suggests five rules of thumb for successful selling abroad. (1) Be prepared and do your homework. Learn about the host's culture, values, geography, artists, musicians, religion, and political structure. In short, do as complete a cultural analysis as possible to avoid cultural mistakes. (2) Slow down. Americans are slaves to the clock. Time is money to an American but, in many countries, emphasis on time implies unfriendliness, arrogance, and untrustworthiness. (3) Develop relationships and trust before getting down to business. In many countries, business is not done until a feeling of trust has developed. (4) Learn the language, its nuances, the idiom or get a good interpreter. There are just too many ways to miscommunicate. (5) Respect the culture. Manners are important, you are the guest so respect what your host considers important.[38]

Anyone being sent into another culture as a salesperson or company representative should receive training to develop the cultural skills discussed. In addition, they should receive specific schooling on the customs, values, and social and political institutions of the host country. There are a variety of organizations involved in intercultural training and many companies are doing inhouse training as well.[39]

SUMMARY

An effective international personnel force constitutes one of the international marketer's greatest concerns. The company sales force represents the major alternative method of organizing a company for foreign distribution and, as such, is on the front line of a marketing organization.

The role of marketers in both domestic and foreign markets is rapidly changing, along with the composition of international managerial and sales forces. Such forces have many unique requirements which are being filled by expatriates, foreign nationals, cosmopolitan personnel, or a combi-

---

[38] This section draws heavily on Lennie Copeland, "The Art of International Selling," *Business America*, June 25, 1984, pp. 2–7; and the Parker Pen Company, "Do's and Taboos Around the World," (Elmsford, N.Y.: The Benjamin Company, 1985).

[39] For a comprehensive source on cultural differences and business see Copeland and Griggs, *Going International*.

nation of the three. In recent years, the pattern of development has been to place more emphasis on the foreign personnel operating in their own lands. This, in turn, has highlighted the importance of adapting U.S. managerial techniques to local needs.

The development of an effective marketing organization calls for careful recruiting, selecting, training, motivating, and compensating of expatriate personnel and their families to ensure maximization of a company's return on its personnel expenditures. The most practical method of maintaining an efficient international marketing force is careful, concerned planning at all stages of career development.

QUESTIONS

1. Define:

   expatriate   "master of destiny" viewpoint
   cosmopolitan personnel   cultural skills
   line and staff organization

2. Why may it be difficult to adhere to set job criteria in selecting foreign personnel? What compensating actions might be necessary?

3. Why does the conglomerate sales force cause special compensation problems? Suggest some alternative solutions.

4. Under which circumstances should expatriate salespeople be utilized?

5. Discuss the problems that might be encountered in having an expatriate sales manager supervising foreign salespeople.

6. "To some extent, the exigencies of the personnel situation will dictate the approach to overseas sales organization." Discuss.

7. How do legal factors affect international sales management?

8. How does the sales force relate to company organization? To channels of distribution?

9. "It is costly to maintain an international sales force." Comment.

10. Adaptability and maturity are traits needed by all salespeople. Why should they be singled out as especially important for international salespeople?

11. Can a person develop good cultural skills? Discuss.

12. Describe the six attributes of a person with good cultural skills.

13. Discuss the gender bias in international business.

14. What are some important steps to take to ensure the successful entrance of women into international business? Discuss.

15. Interview a local company that has a foreign sales operation. Draw an organization chart for the sales function and explain why that particular structure was used by that company.

16. Evaluate the three major sources of mutinational personnel.

17. Which factors complicate the task of motivating the foreign sales force?

18. Discuss how the "master of destiny" viewpoint would affect attitudes of an American and a Mexican toward job promotion. Give an example.

19. Discuss the basic ideas on which U.S. management practices are based.

20. Why do companies include an evaluation of an employee's family among selection critera?

21. Discuss how a family can affect the entire process of selecting personnel for foreign assignment.

22. "Concerns for career and family are the most frequently mentioned reasons for a manager to refuse a foreign assignment." Why?

23. Discuss and give examples of why returning U.S. expatriates are dissatisfied. How can these problems be overcome?

CHAPTER

16

Pricing for Global Markets

Global marketing, Europe 1992, increased competition from NICs, and offshore production contribute to the importance of pricing as a competitive factor. As competition for the world's markets becomes more intense, price is increasingly important as a competitive tool. Whether exporting or managing overseas operations, the international marketing manager is ultimately responsible for establishing price policies for a company's international operations. Within the range of prices allowed by the market, competition, and various government regulations, the manager may also be responsible for setting and attempting to control the actual prices for goods as they are traded in different markets. Each market adds new problems and variables to be considered; differing tariffs, costs, attitudes, inflation, currency fluctuations, and methods of price quotation contribute to confounding the marketing executive.

This chapter focuses on pricing considerations of particular significance in the international marketplace. Basic policy questions related to the special cost, market, and competitive factors in foreign markets are reviewed. Consideration is given to price escalation and its control as well as the problems and policies associated with price fixing on business, government, and international levels, and mention is made of some of the mechanics of international price quotation. The considerations in this chapter are relevant to all firms doing business internationally.

PRICING POLICY

Expediency

Active marketing in several countries compounds the number of pricing problems and variables relating to price policy. Unless a firm has a clearly thought-out, explicitly defined price policy, prices are established by expediency rather than design. Pricing activity is affected by the country in which business is being conducted, the type of product, variations in competitive conditions, and other strategic factors. Price and terms cannot be based on domestic criteria alone.[1]

Pricing Objectives

Profit #1 objective

Two choices are available to a company in setting its price policy: Pricing can be viewed as an active instrument for the accomplishment of marketing objectives, or considered as a static element in business decisions. If the former viewpoint is followed, the company uses prices to accomplish certain objectives relative to a target return or profit from overseas operations or for the accomplishment of a target volume of market share. If the second approach is used, the company is likely content to sell what it can in overseas markets and look on this as bonus volume. The second alternative is inadequate for enterprises with operations in foreign countries; it is more likely to be the viewpoint of a firm that exports only and places a low priority on foreign business. Profit is by far the most important of the pricing objectives. When U.S. and Canadian international businesses were asked to rate several factors important in price setting on a scale of one to five, total profits received an average rating of 4.7, followed by return on investment (4.41), market share (4.13), total sales volume (4.06), and liquidity ranking the lowest (2.19).

A company's policies may emphasize control over final prices or the net price received by the business. In the latter case, the producer may not attempt to control the price at which the product is ultimately sold; in the former, price is considered an important strategic element of the marketing mix so the company wants to retain all possible control over the end price. Firms that followed a price control policy in their domestic business found they were unable to control end prices in foreign markets, and so reoriented their thinking to "mill net pricing," that is, prices received for goods when shipped from the plant.

Price control is a many-faceted activity. End prices charged to consumers must be controlled if a marketer is to reach the desired level of market penetration. Profits and profit margins must be maintained and controlled

---

[1] S. Tamer Cavusgil, "Unraveling the Mystique of Export Pricing," *Business Horizons*, May–June 1988, pp. 54–63.

country by country, and product by product, for each type of transaction. Competition within a company must be controlled so that different divisions, subsidiaries, or branches of a company are not undercutting each other thus depriving the company as a whole of profits. Lack of control and effective management of prices results in the emergence of parallel imports (sometimes called a gray market) that upset price levels within a country.

Parallel Imports

Parallel imports develop when importers buy products from distributors in one country and sell them in another to distributors who are not part of the manufacturer's regular distribution system. This practice is lucrative when wide margins exist between prices for the same products in different countries. A variety of conditions can create the profitable opportunity for a parallel market.

Variations in the value of currencies between countries frequently lead to conditions that make parallel imports profitable. When the dollar was high relative to the West German mark, Cabbage Patch dolls were purchased from German distributors at what amounted to a discount and resold in the United States. Purposefully restricting the supply of a product in a market is another practice that can cause abnormally high prices and thus make a parallel market lucrative. Such was the case with the Mercedes-Benz automobile whose supply was limited in the United States. Americans could buy a Mercedes-Benz in Germany for $12,000 when it sold in the United States for $24,000. The gray market that evolved in Mercedes-Benz automobiles was partially supplied by Americans returning to the United States with cars they could sell for double the price they paid in Germany. This situation persisted until the relative value of the dollar to the mark weakened and the price differential created by limited distribution evaporated.

Pricing policies that permit large price differentials between country markets is another condition conducive to the creation of parallel markets. Japanese merchants have long maintained very high prices for consumer products sold within the Japanese market. As a result, prices for Japanese products sold in other countries are often lower than they are in Japan. For example, Japanese can buy Canon cameras from New York catalogue retailers and have them shipped to Japan for a price below that of the camera purchased in Japan.[2] In addition to the higher prices for products at home, the rising value of the yen makes these price differentials even

---

[2] Robert E. Weigand, "Back Door Imports Should Be Banned," *New York Times*, May 1, 1988, p. 2.

> **BOX 16–1**
> **VWs at Luxury Prices—The Dane Curse Where VW's Cost $35,000**
>
> You may think you pay enough for your car and gas, but the poor people in Denmark literally get robbed by the government. A gallon of premium leaded gas is $4, but that is not the reason that there are so many econoboxes here. Car taxes are calculated like this: Take the price of the car and add the general 22 percent sales tax, and then pay the 105 percent special car tax on the first $3,200 and 180 percent on the rest.
>
> In real world U.S. dollar prices, this means a VW Golf GTI is $35,000; a Toyota MR2—$44,000; a BMW 735I—$130,000; a Mercedes-Benz 560 SEL— a cool $248,000. The best-selling car, a Corolla in its cheapest hatchback version with no extras whatsoever costs $18,000. Shocked? The Fiero V6 has a calculated price of $61,000. This is in a country where average income is $1,628 a month with an income tax of 51–68 percent.
>
> Source: Adapted from "The Dane Curse," *Road and Track*, August 1988, p. 15.

wider. For example, when the New York price for Panasonic cordless telephones was $59.95, they cost $152 in Tokyo and when the Sony Walkman was $89, it was $165.23 in Tokyo.

Foreign companies doing business in Japan generally follow the same pattern of high prices for the products they sell in Japan, thus creating an opportunity for parallel markets in their products also. Eastman Kodak prices its film higher in Japan than in other parts of Asia. Enterprising merchants buy Kodak film in South Korea for a discount and resell it in Japan at 25 percent less than the authorized Japanese Kodak dealers. For the same reason, Coca-Cola syrup imported from Los Angeles is cheaper than that purchased through normal channels in Japan.[3]

The possibility of a parallel market occurs whenever price differences are greater than the cost of transportation between two markets. In Europe, because of differing taxes and competitive price structures, prices for the same product vary between countries. When this occurs, it is not unusual for companies to find themselves competing in one country with their own products imported from a country with lower prices.

Perfume and designer brands such as Gucci and Cartier are especially prone to gray markets. To maintain the image of quality and exclusivity, prices for such products traditionally include high profit margins at each level of distribution, differential prices among markets, and limited quanti-

---

[3] "Now, Japan Is Feeling the Heat from the Gray Market," *Business Week,* March 14, 1988, pp. 50–51.

BOX 16–2
Who Sets Prices?

Pricing problems in international operations are a source of concern to executives with varying and diverse management responsibilities. The international division vice president is concerned with the effect of pricing on divisional profits; the regional manager is concerned with the impact that policies on intercorporate and local market pricing will have in his geographic area; the subsidiary manager tries to operate on a profitable basis within the policy limitations on intercorporate transfer, export, and local market pricing imposed on him. The director of international marketing wants a price that will be competitive in the marketplace; the controller and the treasurer want prices that will be profitable; and the manufacturing director wants prices that will give longer production runs with evenly distributed plant loads for more efficient operations. The tax manager looks at the implications of pricing policy on the total tax burden to the corporation and tax-deferral opportunities; and the lawyer is concerned with pricing policies and practices that may lead to antitrust or restriction-of-trade violations. Even domestic product managers have an interest in transfer prices to the international division or to overseas units.

Source: *Solving International Pricing Problems*, p. 3. Reprinted with permission of the publisher, Business International Corp. (New York).

ties, as well as distribution restricted to upscale retailers. In the United States, wholesale prices for exclusive brands of fragrances are often 25 percent more than wholesale prices in other countries. These are the ideal conditions for a lucrative gray market for unauthorized dealers in other countries who buy more than they need at wholesale prices lower than U.S. wholesalers pay. They then sell the excess at a profit to unauthorized U.S. retailers, but at a lower price than the retailer would have to pay to an authorized U.S. distributor.

To prevent parallel markets from developing when such marketing and pricing strategies are used, companies must maintain strong control systems.[4] These control systems are difficult to maintain and there remains the suspicion that some companies are less concerned with controlling gray markets than they claim. For example, in 1986 French perfume exported directly to Panamanian distributors totaled $40 million. At that rate, Panama's per capita consumption of perfume was 35 times that of the United States.[5]

---

[4] "Gray-Market Victim, Heal Thyself," *Business Week*, November 7, 1988, p. 196.

[5] "There's Nothing Black-and-White about the Gray Market," *Business Week*, November 7, 1988, p. 172.

Another complicated area of pricing policy relates to the objectives sought in intracompany sales, that is, sales between a parent company and a subsidiary, from one subsidiary to another, or from a foreign subsidiary to a parent company. Intracorporate pricing objectives relate to minimization of tax burdens and duties, repatriation of profits, profit balancing among units, and, of course, maximizing profit. The continuing growth and proliferation of marketing activities and organizational arrangements make it imperative to establish corporate policies and procedures for handling intracompany pricing that meet these requirements. Intracorporate pricing policy and strategy are discussed later in this chapter.

Approaches to International Pricing

Whether the orientation is toward control over end prices or over net prices, company policy relates to the net price received. Both cost and market considerations are important; a company cannot sell goods below cost of production and cannot sell goods at a price unacceptable in the marketplace. Firms unfamiliar with overseas marketing and many firms producing industrial goods orient their pricing solely on a cost basis. Firms that employ pricing as part of the strategic mix, however, are aware of such alternatives as market segmentation from country to country or market to market, competitive pricing in the marketplace, and other market-oriented pricing factors.

Firms that orient their price thinking around cost must determine whether to use variable-cost or full-cost pricing in costing their goods. In variable-cost pricing, the firm is concerned only with the marginal or incremental cost of producing goods to be sold in overseas markets. Such firms regard foreign sales as bonus sales and assume that any return over their variable cost makes a contribution to net profit. These firms may be able to price most competitively in foreign markets; but, because they are selling products abroad at lower net prices than they are selling them in the domestic market, they may be subject to charges of dumping. In that case, they open themselves to antidumping tariffs or penalties which take away from their competitive advantage. Companies following the full-cost pricing philosophy insist that no unit of a similar product is different from any other unit in terms of cost and that each unit bears its full share of the total fixed and variable cost.

In domestic marketing, both variable-cost and full-cost policies are followed. An international firm that uses variable-cost pricing must ultimately decide if it is a marketer exporting from one country into another or a global marketer. If the firm regards itself as a global marketer, it is more likely to think of full-cost pricing for all markets. There remains the question of whether pricing should be below full costs if it increases profits and there is no other access to certain markets. These are all policy questions to be resolved by the firm.

Leasing in International Markets

Leasing

An increasingly important selling technique to alleviate high prices and capital shortages for capital equipment is the leasing system. The concept of equipment leasing has become increasingly important as a means of selling capital equipment in overseas markets. In fact, it is estimated that $50 billion worth (original cost) of U.S.-and foreign-made equipment are on lease in Western Europe.

The system of leasing used by industrial exporters is similar to the typical lease contracts used in the United States. Terms of the leases usually run one to five years, with payment made monthly or annually; included in the rental fee are servicing, repairs, and spare parts. Just as contracts for domestic and overseas leasing arrangements are similar, so are the basic motivations and the shortcomings. For example:

1. Leasing opens the door to a large segment of nominally financed foreign firms that can be sold on a lease but might be unable to buy for cash.
2. Leasing can ease the problems of selling new, experimental equipment, since less risk is involved for the users.
3. Leasing helps guarantee better maintenance and service on overseas equipment.
4. Equipment leased and in use helps to sell other companies in that country.
5. Lease revenue tends to be more stable over a period of time than direct sales would be.

The disadvantages or shortcomings take on an international flavor. Besides the inherent disadvantages of leasing, some problems are compounded by international relationships. In a country beset with inflation, lease contracts that include maintenance and supply parts, as most do, can lead to heavy losses toward the end of the contract period. Further, countries where leasing is most attractive are those where spiraling inflation is most likely to occur. The added problems of currency devaluation, expropriation, or other political risks are operative longer than if the sale of the same equipment is made outright. In the light of these perils, there is greater risk in leasing than outright sale; however, there is a definite trend toward increased use of this method of selling internationally.

COST FACTORS

Regardless of the strategic factors involved and the company's orientation to market pricing, every price must be set with cost considerations in mind. At a minimum, prices over a long run must cover full costs for a business to survive. Full costs do not have to be covered in every market as long as total company sales cover all costs in international marketing.

In the case of intracorporate transfers, such transfers may be based solely on direct production costs (variable costs only) or may include profit plus general administrative costs, research and development costs, and so forth. In determining producer company overhead, management must not include factors which would raise foreign prices to the point that sales volume is reduced. Sometimes domestic marketing sales and advertising costs are included in the basic price of the goods, but because such costs are reincurred in the foreign markets, they should not be included in basic cost determination.

Widely fluctuating costs of raw materials and supplies and equally widely fluctuating exchange rates have become especially important in recent years and have forced increased emphasis on pricing.

A number of other costs unique to international marketing or exaggerated in international marketing should be borne in mind by the pricing executive. These costs include taxes and tariffs, inflation, exchange rate fluctuations, middlemen, and transportation costs.

Taxes and Tariffs

"Nothing is surer than death and taxes" has a particularly familiar ring to the ears of the international trader because taxes include tariffs, and tariffs are one of the most pervasive features of international trading. Taxes and tariffs affect the ultimate consumer price for a product, and, in most instances, the consumer bears the burden of both. Sometimes, however, the consumer benefits when manufacturers selling goods in foreign countries reduce their net return to gain access on a competitive footing to a foreign market. Absorbed or passed on, taxes and tariffs must be considered by the international businessperson.

A tariff, or duty, is a special form of taxation, and, like other forms of taxes, may be levied for the purpose of protecting a market or for increasing government revenue. A tariff is a fee charged when goods are brought into a country from another country. The level of tariff is typically expressed as the rate of duty and may be levied as specific, ad valorem, or a combination. A *specific* duty is a flat charge per physical unit imported, such as 15 cents per bushel of rye. *Ad valorem* duties are levied as a percentage of the value of the goods imported, such as 20 percent of the value of imported watches. *Combination* tariffs include both a specific and an ad valorem charge, such as $1 per camera plus 10 percent of its value.

Tariffs and other forms of import taxes serve to discriminate against all foreign goods. Fees for import certificates or for other administrative processing can assume such levels that they are, in fact, import taxes. Many countries have purchase or excise taxes which apply to various categories of goods, value added or turnover taxes which apply as the product goes through a channel of distribution, and retail sales taxes. Such taxes increase the end price of goods but, in general, do not discriminate against foreign goods. Tariffs are the primary discriminatory tax which must be taken into account in reckoning with foreign competition.

Inflation

The effect of inflation on cost must be accounted for. In countries with rapid inflation or exchange variation, selling price must be related to the cost of goods sold and the cost of replacing the items. Goods are often sold below their cost of replacement plus overhead and sometimes are sold below replacement cost. In these instances, the company would be better off not to sell the products at all. When payment is likely to be delayed for several months or is worked out on a long-term contract, inflationary factors must be figured into the price. Inflation and lack of control over price were instrumental in the unsuccessful new product launch in Brazil by the H. J. Heinz Company; after only two years, they withdrew from the market. Misunderstandings with the local partner resulted in a new fruit-based drink being sold to retailers on consignment; that is, they did not pay until the product was sold. Faced with a 300 percent plus rate of inflation, just a week's delay in payment eroded profit margins substantially.[6]

Soaring inflation in many developing countries (Latin America in particular) makes widespread price controls a constant threat. Prices have virtually been frozen since 1988 in Mexico; and, with inflation spiraling in Brazil, price controls could be imposed at any time. Because inflation and price controls imposed by a country are beyond the control of companies, they use a variety of techniques to inflate the selling price to compensate for inflation pressure and price controls. They may charge for extra services, inflate costs in transfer pricing, break up products into components and price each component separately, or require the purchase of two or more products simultaneously and refuse to deliver one product unless the purchaser also agrees to take another, more expensive item along with it.[7]

Exchange-Rate Fluctuations

At one time, world trade contracts could be easily written and payment was specified in a relatively stable currency. The American dollar was the standard and all transactions could be related to the dollar. Now that

---

[6] Julia Michaels, "Why Heinz Went Sour in Brazil," *Advertising Age*, December 5, 1988, p. 61.

[7] "Seven Ways to Get an Edge in the Pricing Tug of War," *Business Latin America*, September 12, 1988, p. 284.

High operating costs of small speciality stores like these in Mexico and Thailand lead to high retail prices. (Ingrid Johnsson/Journalism Services, Inc.)

all major currencies are floating freely relative to one another, no one is quite sure of the value of *any* currency in the future. Increasingly, companies are insisting that transactions be written in terms of the vendor company's national currency, and forward hedging is becoming more common. Companies active in international business are more aware of currency fluctuations but have yet to find a better method of protecting themselves against currency fluctuations. If exchange rates are not carefully considered in long-term contracts, companies can find themselves unwittingly giving

---

BOX 16–3
Everybody Wins in a Japanese/USSR Countertrade

Trading without hard currencies leads to some convoluted transactions. One proposal combines direct and third-country trade. A Japanese trading company's proposal is to buy used, surplus refrigerated railroad cars in Japan cheap, and sell them to the Trans-Siberian Railroad which has a shortage of such cars. The cars would be used to haul fish from Soviet Pacific fisheries to China via Mongolia. The Chinese would process the fish and sell it in the United States. The cars would be used to haul cheap Mongolian pork for shipment to Japan from Chinese or Soviet Far East ports. The Siberian railroad would not need cash to pay for the cars; it would pay the trading company by shipping the fish and pork free until the cars are paid for in transportation charges. Everybody wins: The Japanese make a profit on used, refrigerated railroad cars and get a source of cheap pork; the Russians and Chinese get products to market and a new source of hard currency.

Source: Bradley K. Martin, "Japanese Seek to Be Moscow's Middlemen," *The Wall Street Journal*, July 13, 1984, p. 18.

15 to 20 percent discounts. The added cost incurred as exchange rates fluctuate on a day-to-day basis must be taken into account, especially where there is a significant time lapse between signing the order and delivery of the goods. Exchange-rate differentials mount up. Hewlett-Packard gained nearly half a million dollars additional profit through exchange-rate fluctuations in one year. Nestlé lost a million dollars in six months while other companies have lost and gained even larger amounts.[8]

Varying Currency Values

In addition to the risks from exchange rate variations, other risks result from changing values of a country's currency relative to other currencies. Consider the situation in Germany for a purchaser of U.S. manufactured goods during the 1980s. During this period the value of the U.S. dollar to the German mark went from very strong ($1 U.S. to 2.69 DM in 1982) to a weaker position in 1989 ($1 U.S. to 1.95 DM). A strong dollar produces price resistance because it takes a large quantity of local currency to buy a U.S. dollar. Conversely, when the U.S. dollar is weak, demand for U.S. goods increases because fewer units of German currency are needed to buy a U.S. dollar. Each additional market in which a company operates adds to the problem. Currency-exchange rate swings are considered by many global companies to be a major trade barrier.[9] For a company with long-range plans calling for continued operation in foreign markets and yet wanting to remain price competitive, price strategies need to reflect variations in currency values.

When the value of the dollar is weak relative to the buyer's currency (i.e., it takes fewer units of the foreign currency to buy a dollar), companies generally employ cost-plus pricing. To remain price competitive when the dollar is strong (i.e., when it takes more units of the foreign currency to buy a dollar), companies must find ways to offset the higher price caused by currency values. Exhibit 16–1 focuses on the different price strategies a company might employ under a weak or strong domestic currency.

Innumerable cost variables can be identified depending on the market, the product, and the situation. The cost, for example, of reaching a market with relatively small potential may be high. Intense competition in certain world markets raises the cost or lowers the margins available to world business. Even small things like payoffs to local officials can introduce unexpected cost to the unwary entrepreneur. Only experience in a given

---

[8] Methods used to minimize exchange rate risks are discussed in detail in Chapter 19.

[9] George Melloan, "Global Manufacturing Is an Intricate Game," *The Wall Street Journal,* November 29, 1988, p. A19.

EXHIBIT 16–1   Export Strategies under Varying Currency Conditions

When Domestic Currency is *WEAK . . .*	*When Domestic Currency is* *STRONG . . .*
• Stress price benefits	• Engage in nonprice competition by improving quality, delivery and after-sale service
• Expand product line and add more costly features	• Improve productivity and engage in vigorous cost reduction
• Shift sourcing and manufacturing to domestic market	• Shift sourcing and manufacturing overseas
• Exploit export opportunities in all markets	• Give priority to exports to relatively strong-currency countries
• Conduct conventional cash-for-goods trade	• Deal in countertrade with weak-currency countries
• Use full-costing approach, but use marginal-cost pricing to penetrate new/competitive markets	• Trim profit margins and use marginal-cost pricing
• Speed repatriation of foreign-earned income and collections	• Keep the foreign-earned income in host country, slow collections
• Minimize expenditures in local, host country currency	• Maximize expenditures in local, host country currency
• Buy needed services (advertising, insurance, transportation, etc.) in domestic market	• Buy needed services abroad and pay for them in local currencies
• Minimize local borrowing	• Borrow money needed for expansion in local market
• Bill foreign customers in domestic currency	• Bill foreign customers in their own currency

SOURCE: S. Tamur Cavusgil, "Unraveling the Mystique of Export Pricing," *Business Horizons*, May–June 1988, Figure 2, p. 58.

---

marketplace provides the basis for compensating for cost differences in different markets. With experience, a firm that prices on a cost basis operates in a realm of reasonably measurable factors.

Middleman and Transportation Costs

Channel length and marketing patterns vary widely, but in most countries, channels are longer and middleman margins higher than is customary in the United States. The diversity of channels used to reach markets and the lack of standardized middleman markups leave many producers unaware of the ultimate price of a product.

Besides channel diversity, the fully integrated marketer operating abroad faces various unanticipated costs because marketing and distribution channel infrastructures are underdeveloped in so many countries. The marketer also can incur added expenses for warehousing and handling of small shipments, and may have to bear increased financing costs when dealing with underfinanced middlemen.

Because no convenient source of data on middleman costs is available, the international marketer must rely on experience and marketing research to discover what middleman costs will be. For example, the Campbell Soup Company found its middleman and physical distribution costs in the United Kingdom were 30 percent higher than in the United States. Extra costs were incurred because soup was purchased in small quantities—English grocers typically purchase 24-can cases of *assorted* soups (each case being hand-packed for shipment). In the United States, typical purchase units are 48-can cases of one soup purchased by dozens, hundreds, or carloads. The purchase habits in Europe forced the company to an extra wholesale level in its channel to facilitate handling small orders. Purchase frequency patterns also run up billing and order costs; both wholesalers and retailers purchase two or three times as often as their U.S. counterparts. Sales-call costs become virtually prohibitive. These and other distribution cost factors not only caused the company to change its price and price patterns but also forced a complete restructuring of the channel system.

Exporting also incurs increased transportation costs when moving goods from one country to another. If the goods go over water, there are additional costs for insurance, packing, and handling not generally added to locally produced goods. Such costs add yet another burden because import tariffs in many countries are based on the landed cost that includes transportation, insurance, and shipping charges.

Long distribution channels, tariffs, transportation costs, and other costs associated with international marketing combine to escalate the final price to a level considerably higher than in the domestic market. A case in point is the pacemaker for heart patients that sells for $2,100 in the United States. The Japanese distribution system plus extra tariffs add substantially to the final price. As one executive of a U.S. pacemaker manufacturer realized, "The ailing Japanese wouldn't be able to get the product cheap. If and when the devices entered Japan," he was told, "they would first have to go through an importer, then to the company with primary responsibility for sales and service, then to a secondary and even a tertiary local distributor, and finally to the hospital." Markups at each of these levels result in the $2,100 pacemaker selling for over $4,000 in Japan. Inflation fueled by such costs results in one of the major pricing obstacles facing the multinational marketer—price escalation.

PRICE ESCALATION

People traveling abroad are often surprised to find that goods relatively inexpensive in their home country are priced outrageously higher in other countries. Because of the natural tendency to assume such prices are a result of profiteering, manufacturers often resolve to begin exporting to crack these new foreign markets.

Excess profits exist, in fact, but more often the added costs are the cause of the disproportionate difference in price, here termed *price escalation*. Specifically, the term relates to situations where ultimate prices are raised by shipping cost, tariffs, longer channels of distribution, larger middlemen margins, special taxes, and exchange-rate fluctuations. During most of the 1980s, the strength of the dollar against most of the world's currencies has had a profound effect on the price of goods imported from the United States. The effect of dollar value can add to the price escalation of products.

Sample Effects of Price Escalation

Exhibit 16–2 illustrates some of the possible effects these factors may have on the end price of a consumer item. Because costs and tariffs vary so widely from country to country, a hypothetical but realistic example is used. It assumes (1) that a constant net price is received by the manufacturer; (2) that all domestic transportation costs are absorbed by the various middlemen and reflected in their margins; and (3) that the foreign middlemen have the same margins as the domestic middlemen. In some instances, foreign middleman margins are lower, but it is equally probable that these margins could be greater. In fact, in many instances, middlemen use higher wholesale and retail margins for foreign goods than for similar domestic goods.

Notice that the retail prices in Exhibit 16–2 range widely, illustrating the difficulty of price control by manufacturers in overseas retail markets. No matter how much the manufacturer may wish to market a product in a foreign country for a price equivalent to $10 U.S., there is little opportunity for such control. Even assuming the most optimistic conditions of foreign example 1, the producer would need to cut net by more than one third to absorb freight and tariff costs if the goods are to be priced the same in both foreign and domestic markets. Price escalation is everywhere; a man's dress shirt that sells for $40 in the United States retails for $80 in Caracas, and a bottle of Cutty Sark Scotch whiskey that retails for $25 in the United States sells for more than $90 in Japan. One study of European housewares provides numerous examples of price escalation. A $20 U.S. electric can opener is priced in Milan at $70, a $35 U.S. automatic toaster is priced at $80 in France.

EXHIBIT 16–2   Sample Causes and Effects of Price Escalation

	Domestic Example	Foreign Example 1: Assuming the Same Channels with Wholesaler Importing Directly	Foreign Example 2: Importer and Same Margins and Channels	Foreign Example 3: Same as 2 but with 10 Percent Cumulative Turnover Tax
Manufacturing net	$ 5.00	$ 5.00	$ 5.00	$ 5.00
Transport, c.i.f.	n.a.	1.10	1.10	1.10
Tariff (20 percent c.i.f. value)	n.a.	1.22	1.22	1.22
Importer pays	n.a.	n.a.	7.32	7.32
Importer margin when sold to wholesaler (25 percent) on cost	n.a.	n.a.	1.83	1.83
				+0.73 turnover tax
Wholesaler pays landed cost	5.00	7.32	9.15	2.56
				=9.88
				3.29
				+0.99 turnover tax
Wholesaler margin (33⅓ percent on cost)	1.67	2.44	3.05	=4.28
Retailer pays	6.67	9.76	12.20	14.16
				7.08
				+1.42 turnover tax
Retail margin (50 percent on cost)	3.34	4.88	6.10	=8.50
Retail price	10.01	14.64	18.30	22.66

Notes: a. All figures in U.S. dollars.
b. The exhibit assumes that all domestic transportation costs are absorbed by the middleman.
c. Transportation, tariffs, and middleman margins vary from country to country, but for purposes of comparison, only a few of the possible variations are shown.

Strategic Approaches to Lessening Price Escalation

Several strategic approaches are employed to counteract the problem of price differentials. Here are some of the more frequently used:

1. High tariffs can often be reduced by lowering the net price for goods sold in foreign markets. Because tariffs are generally on an ad valorem basis, companies use marginal-cost pricing instead of full-cost pricing to lower the selling price and thus offset some of the tariffs. This may not be an acceptable alternative if the importing country views this as dumping and levies countervailing tariffs that nullify the intended price advantage.

2. The manufacturer may go into overseas production to remain competitive in foreign markets. One of the more important reasons for manufacturing in a third country is an attempt to lower the effects of price escalation. As discussed in Chapter 18, the popularity of offshore production in customs-privileged areas is caused by the need to reduce the cost of manufacturing to offset price escalation. The impact can be profound if you consider that the hourly cost of skilled labor in a Mexican *maquiladora* is 81 cents an hour including benefits.[10] At comparable plants in Hong Kong, labor costs are $1.50 and in Singapore, $1.62; the minimum wage in the United States is $3.35 per hour. Further, most of the workers in these offshore plants are more skilled than a minimum-wage earner in the United States. In comparing the costs of manufacturing microwave ovens in the United States and Korea, General Electric Company found substantial differences. A typical microwave oven cost GE $218 to manufacture compared to $155 for Samsung, a Korean manufacturer. A breakdown of costs revealed that assembly labor cost GE $8 per oven, and the Korean firm only 63 cents. Overhead labor for supervision, maintenance, and setup was $30 per GE oven and 73 cents for the Korean company. The largest area of difference was for line and central management; that came to $20 per oven for GE versus two cents for Samsung. Perhaps the most disturbing finding was that Korean laborers delivered more for less cost. GE produced four units per person whereas the Korean company produced nine.[11]

3. Shorter channels may keep prices under control. The process of eliminating middlemen is as costly in international markets as in domestic markets, and although channels may be shortened, marketing functions are not eliminated so marketing costs are not necessarily reduced. Many countries levy a *value added tax* on goods as they pass through channels; each time goods change hands, they are taxed. The tax may be cumulative or noncumulative. The cumulative value added tax is based on total selling

---

[10] "Will the New Maquiladoras Build a Better Mañana?" *Business Week*, November 14, 1988, p. 102.

[11] Ira C. Magaziner and Mark Patinkin, "Fast Heat: How Korea Won the Microwave War," *Harvard Business Review*, January–February 1989, p. 89.

> **BOX 16–4**
> **Now These Are High Prices!**
>
> The finest Matsuzaka prize beef is only 100,000 yen a kilo. Matsuzaka beef is well-known for its astronomical prices. The beef that fetched the highest price at auction doubled last year's and topped 26.01 million yen ($203,000 U.S. dollars) for one cow. If you are interested, Isetan will have 50 kilograms of that steer on sale by reservation only at 100,000 yen ($780) a kilo. Talk about bargains!
>
> If beef is so high, what about land prices? The city of Mitaka, a suburb of Tokyo, recently built a pedestrian overpass two meters wide and 47 meters long. Total job cost was 95.34 million yen ($744,845). Now here is the kick in the pants: cost of land—92.70 million yen ($724,220), cost of construction—2.64 million yen ($20,625).
>
> Source: Adapted from "Data Box Short Takes." *Look Japan*, February 1988, pp. 34 and 35.

price and is assessed each time the goods change hands. Obviously, in countries where value added tax is cumulative, tax alone provides a special incentive for developing short distribution channels. In the latter case, tax is paid only on the difference between the middleman's cost and selling price.

4. Eliminating costly functional features or even lowering overall product quality is another method of minimizing price escalation. For U.S. manufactured products, the quality and additional features required for the more-developed home market may not be necessary in countries that have not attained the same level of development or consumer demand. Elimination of such features or changing the quality may lower manufacturing costs and thus lessen escalation of costs when the product is exported.

5. When tariffs account for a large part of price escalation, as they often do, seeking tariff reclassification can lower the tariff rate. Often products can be classified in a different and lower customs classification. For example, an American company selling data communications equipment in Australia faced a 25 percent tariff which affected the price competitiveness of its products. Seeking relief, it persuaded the Australian government to change the classification for the type of products the company sells from "computer equipment" (25 percent tariff) to "telecommunication equipment" (38 percent tariff).[12] Like many products, this company's products could be legally classified under either category. The way a product can be classified varies among countries; therefore, a thorough investigation of tariff schedules

---

[12] "Exporting Pays Off," *Business America*, August 17, 1987, p. 12.

and classification criteria is an important way to lessen cost escalation in exporting.

6. It may be possible to modify a product to qualify for a lower tariff rate within a tariff classification. Within a tariff classification, there are often differential rates between fully assembled, ready-to-use products and those requiring some assembly, further processing, the addition of locally manufactured component parts, or other activities that add value to the product and can be performed within the foreign country. A ready-to-operate piece of machinery with a 20 percent tariff may be subject to only a 12 percent tariff when imported unassembled. One of the more important activities in foreign-trade zones, as described in the next section, is the assembly of imported goods using local and, frequently, lower-priced labor. This usually qualifies a product for a lower tariff and sometimes even a lower total cost of manufacturing for the finished product.[13]

7. Shipping in bulk and repackaging in a foreign-trade zone can also result in lower tariffs. Consider, for example, tequila entering the United States. In containers of one gallon or less, the duty is $2.27 per proof gallon, whereas for larger containers the duty is only $1.25. If the cost of rebottling is less then $1.02 per proof gallon, and it probably would be, considerable saving could result.[14]

Using Foreign-Trade Zones to Lessen Price Escalation

Some countries have established foreign or free-trade zones (FTZ) or free ports to facilitate international trade. There are more than 300 of these facilities in operation throughout the world where imported goods can be stored or processed. In a free port or FTZ, payment of import duties is postponed until the product leaves the FTZ area and enters the country. A FTZ is in essence a tax-free enclave and not considered part of the country as far as import regulations are concerned. When an item leaves a FTZ and is officially imported into the host country of the FTZ, all duties and regulations are imposed.

Price escalation resulting from the layers of taxes, duties, surcharges, freight charges, and so forth, can be controlled by utilizing free-trade zones. The benefits of FTZs permit many of these added charges to be avoided, reduced, or deferred so that the final price is more competitive. One of the more important benefits of the FTZ in controlling prices is

---

[13] John Adams, Jr., "Foreign Trade Zones: How Competitive Are They?" *Export Today*, February 1989, pp. 46–48.

[14] While this example reflects U.S. tariffs, similar benefits can accrue to FTZ users in other countries. For other examples, see Wade Ferguson, "Using Foreign Trade Zones to Reduce Costs," *International Journal of Physical Distribution and Materials Management*, no. 1 (1987), pp. 47–53.

the exemption from duties on labor and overhead costs incurred in the FTZ in assessing the value of goods.

By shipping unassembled goods to a FTZ in an importing country, a marketer can lower costs in a variety of ways:

1. Tariffs may be lower because duties are typically assessed at a lower rate for unassembled than assembled goods.
2. If labor costs are lower in the importing country, substantial savings may be realized in the final product cost.
3. Ocean transportation rates are affected by weight and volume, thus, unassembled goods may qualify for lower freight rates.
4. If local content, such as packaging or component parts can be used in the final assembly, there may be a further reduction of tariffs.

All in all, a FTZ is an important method for controlling price escalation. Incidentally, all the advantages offered by a FTZ for an exporter are also advantages for an importer. Over 100 FTZs in the United States are used by U.S. importers to help lower their cost of imported goods.[15]

Dumping

A logical outgrowth of a market policy in international business are goods priced at widely differing prices in various markets. The market and economic logic of such a policy can hardly be disputed, but the practice itself is often classified as dumping; as such, it is likely to be the subject of strong legislation. *Dumping* is defined differently by various economists. One approach classifies international shipments as dumped if the products are sold below their cost of production. The other characterizes dumping as selling goods in a foreign market below the price of the same goods in the home market. Even rate-cutting on cargo shipping has been called dumping. Laws may invoke both definitions to plug all possible loopholes. The *Exporters' Encyclopedia* summarizes dumping legislation in most countries. Its description of the situation in Norway reflects the scope of provisions used to make the laws as inclusive as possible. Note especially the provisions for calculating subsidies in determining prices.

> Dumping and Countervailing Duty: The law authorizes the imposition of a dumping duty when goods are sold at a price lower than the normal export price or less than the cost in the country of origin increased by a reasonable amount for the cost of sales and profits; and when this is likely to be prejudicial to the economic activity of the country. A countervailing duty may be imposed on foreign goods benefiting from subsidies in production, export, or transport.[16]

---

[15] For an interesting report on a Kansas City FTZ see Carlos M. Navarro, "Former Limestone Mine Houses Kansas City Foreign-Trade Zone," *Journal of Commerce*, September 22, 1988, p. 3a.

[16] From "Norway," in *Exporter's Encyclopedia*, published annually by Dun & Bradstreet, New York.

BOX 16–5
Foreign-Trade Zones, What Do They Do?

Foreign-trade zones exist in almost every country in the world with over 100 in the United States. Both U.S. and foreign companies use them to postpone the payment of tariffs on products re-exported out. Here are a few examples of what goes on in a free-trade zone.

- A Canadian company assembles electronic teaching machines using cabinets from Italy; electronics from Taiwan, Korea, and Japan; and labor from the United States, for export to Colombia and Peru.
- A major U.S. company manufactures typewriters from domestic and foreign components, for both domestic and export markets.
- A European-based medical supply company manufactures kidney dialysis machines and sterile tubing, using raw material from West Germany, U.S. labor, and exporting 30 percent to Scandinavia.
- A Japanese firm manufactures motorcycles, jet-skis, and three-wheel all-terrain vehicles for import as well as export to Canada, Latin America, and Europe.
- A major electronics firm warehouses, tests, repairs, and scraps electronic components.
- An American oil refinery produces gasoline, jet fuel, synthetic natural gas, and carbon dioxide.
- A U.S. women's clothing manufacturer cuts and sews imported fabric for import and export.
- A major Japanese firm manufacturers trucks with domestic and foreign components completely replacing previous imports with U.S. production.

In all of these cases, the tariffs are postponed while these products remain in the FTZ; many of these products qualify for a lower tariff as unassembled goods than they would if they were imported fully assembled and ready to use.

Source: Adapted from Lewis E. Leibowitz, "An Overview of Foreign Trade Zones," *Europe*, Winter–Spring 1987, p. 12.

Before antidumping laws can be invoked, it must be shown not only that prices are lower in the importing country but also that producers in the importing country are being *directly* harmed by the dumping.

In the 1960s and 1970s, dumping was hardly an issue because world markets were strong. As the decade of the 1980s began, dumping became a major issue for a large number of industries. Excess production capacity relative to home-country demand caused many companies to price their goods on a marginal cost basis figuring that any contribution above variable cost was beneficial to company profits. In a classic case of dumping, prices are maintained in the home country market and reduced in foreign markets. For example, the European Community charged that differences in prices between Japan and EC countries ranged from 4.8 to 86 percent. To correct for this dumping activity, a special import duty of 33.4 percent was imposed on Japanese computer printers.[17]

Tighter government enforcement of dumping legislation is causing international marketers to seek new routes around such legislation. Some of the strategies include subsidies by governments to exporting companies, kickbacks to purchasers, and model-year changes to permit discounting. Assembly in the importing country is another way companies attempt to lower prices and avoid dumping charges. However, these screwdriver plants, as they are often called, are subject to dumping charges if the price differentials reflect more than the cost savings that result from assembly in the importing country. The EC imposed a $27 to $58 dumping duty on a Japanese firm that assembled and sold electronic typewriters in the EC. The firm was charged with valuing imported parts for assembly below cost.[18] The increased concern and enforcement in the European Community reflects the changing attitudes among all countries toward dumping. The EC has had antidumping legislation from its inception, but the first antidumping duties ever imposed were on Taiwanese bicycle chains in 1976. Since then, the Department of Trade of the EC has imposed duties on a variety of products.

The U.S. market also is becoming more sensitive to dumping than it has been in the recent past.[19] Changes in U.S. law have enhanced the authority of the Commerce Department to prevent circumvention of antidumping duties and countervailing duties that have been imposed on a country for dumping. Previously when an order was issued to apply antidumping and countervailing duties on products, companies charged with the violation would get around the order by slightly altering the product or doing minor assembly in the United States or a third country. This created the illusion of a different product not subject to the antidumping order. The new authority of the Department of Commerce closes many such loopholes.[20] Another loophole used in price competition is government subsidies.

Subsidies have long been unacceptable devices used by governments to aid exporters. Increasingly protectionist attitudes have caused the United States to add countervailing duties when government subsidies are involved. For example, the United States imposed countervailing duties of

---

[17] "EC Acts against Japanese Dumping of Computer Printers," *Europe*, July–August 1988, p. 51.

[18] Julie Wolf, "EC May Fine Japanese Firms for Dumping," *The Asian Wall Street Journal*, March 14, 1988, p. 11.

[19] Gleen R. Reichardt and Elisabeth Salchow, "Risk of Antidumping Penalties Rises," *Global Trade*, February 1988, p. 42.

[20] "Principal Features of the Omnibus Trade and Competitiveness Act of 1988," *Business America*, September 26, 1988, p. 6.

BOX 16–6
Dirt Bikes Run around Dumping Laws

Harley-Davidson Motor Company charged last week that its major Japanese competitors are using the auto market "model-year" concept as a ploy to evade U.S. antidumping laws. . . .

"Our information shows that there were more than 1 million excess Japanese motorcycle inventories here . . . To sell these, the Japanese cut prices even further than their already low U.S. prices," Harley said. "This practice of predatory price cutting was not followed in Japan or other such major markets as France, Italy, and West Germany."

Harley-Davidson, the last American company with a niche in the motorcycle market, said motorcycle makers don't have model years like the auto industry. Japanese makers, it charged, copied the auto industry's practice of discounting prior year model prices simply as a means of moving inventories once demand for motorcycles turned soft.

According to Harley-Davidson estimates, the Japanese makers charge as much as 139 percent for the same motorcycle in Japan and some European countries as they do in the United States.

Source: "Harley-Davidson Cites Japanese Pricing Ploys." Reprinted with permission, from the June 1977 issue of *Advertising Age*. Copyright 1977 by Crain Communications Inc.

19.6 percent for cotton yarn and 15.8 percent for scissors imported from Brazil. Exported scissors had received exemption from Brazilian industrial products tax, value-added tax, and income tax. Cotton yarn had benefited from preferential government financing, and regional investment incentives provided for building plants in remote areas of northeastern Brazil. The pressure of higher duties eventually forced Brazil to eliminate the subsidies and the U.S. government correspondingly reduced the countervailing duties.

Kickbacks are another device used to get around antidumping legislation. In the case of Japanese television tubes imported into the United States, the export price matched the Japanese price (thus counteracting any possible notion of dumping), but the producer provided under-the-table payments to the importer. Zenith officials charged that nearly every television set brought into the United States in the late 1970s benefited from such kickbacks, much to the detriment of Zenith and other domestic companies.

Model-year discounts that make price variations possible from country to country have also come to the attention of antidumping authorities. The model-year device works this way: an exported item is designated as the previous year's model and discounted in the foreign country but still sold at the current model-year prices in the home country. These dumping devices are cheerfully winked at in times of soft world competition, but receive careful attention when competition is intense and antidumping commissions take a hard line against subterfuge.

ADMINISTERED PRICING

Administered pricing relates to attempts to establish prices for an entire market. Such prices may be arranged through the cooperation of competitors; through national, state, or local governments; or by international agreement. The legality of administered pricing arrangements of various kinds differs from country to country and from time to time. A country may condone price fixing for foreign markets but condemn it for the domestic market.

In general, the end goal of all administered pricing activities is to reduce the impact of price competition or eliminate it. Price fixing by business is not viewed as acceptable procedure (at least in the domestic market), but when governments enter the field of price administration, they presume to do it for the general welfare to lessen the effects of "destructive" competition.

The point when competition becomes destructive depends largely on the country in question. To the Japanese, excessive competition is *any* competition in the home market that disturbs the existing balance of trade or gives rise to market disruptions. Few countries apply more rigorous standards in judging competition as excessive than Japan, but no country favors or permits totally free competition. Economists, the traditional champions of pure competition, acknowledge that perfect competition is unlikely and agree that some form of workable competition must be developed.

Price Setting by Industry Groups

The pervasiveness of price-fixing attempts in business is reflected by the diversity of the language of administered prices; pricing arrangements are known as agreements, arrangements, combines, conspiracies, cartels, communities of profit, profit pools, patent licensing, trade associations, price leadership, customary pricing, or informal interfirm agreements. The arrangements themselves range from the completely informal with no spoken or acknowledged agreement to highly formalized and structured arrangements. Any type of price-fixing arrangement can be adapted to international business; but of all the forms mentioned, the three most directly associated with international marketing are patent licensing, cartels, and trade associations.

Patent Licensing Agreements.   In industries where technological innovation is especially important, patent or process agreements are the most common type of international combination. In most countries, patent licensing agreements are legally acceptable because the owner of the patent is granting an exclusive license to someone in another country to produce the product. By contractual definition, the patent holder can control territorial boundaries and, because of the monopoly, can control pricing. Often such arrangements go beyond a specific licensing agreement to include a gentlemen's agreement to give their foreign counterparts first rights on patents and new developments. Such arrangements can lead to national monopolies that significantly restrict competition and thereby raise product prices. Like so many other agreements related to restricting competition, the legality of patent licensing agreements is difficult to discuss outside the context of a specific situation. Patent licensing arrangements have been an important factor in international marketing in the past and continue to be important despite numerous restrictions.

Cartels.   A cartel exists when various companies producing similar products work together to control markets for the types of goods they produce. Generally, a cartel involves more than a patent licensing agreement and endows the participants with greater power. The cartel association may use formal agreements to set prices, establish levels of production and sales for the participating companies, allocate market territories, and even redistribute profits. In some instances, the cartel organization itself takes over the entire selling function, sells the goods of all the producers, and distributes the profits.

The economic role of cartels is highly debatable, but their proponents argue that they eliminate cut-throat competition and "rationalize" business, permitting greater technical progress and lower prices to consumers. However, in the view of most experts, it is doubtful that the consumer benefits very often from cartels.

Cartels are often thought of as peculiar to Europe, but U.S. companies have participated in international cartels as have producers from nearly every country at one time or another. Country cartels seem to exhibit a marked tenacity for survival despite attempts to regulate them.

The Organization of Petroleum Exporting Countries (OPEC) is probably the best-known international cartel. Their power in controlling the price of oil resulted from the amount of oil production they controlled. In the early 70s when OPEC members provided the industrial world with 67 percent of its oil, OPEC was able to quadruple the price of oil. The sudden rise in price from $10 or $12 a barrel to $50 or more a barrel was a major factor in throwing the world into a major recession. Non-OPEC oil exporting countries benefited from the price increase while net importers of foreign oil suffered economic downturns. Among Third World countries, those producing oil prospered while oil importers suffered economically from the high prices. Much of the Third World debt that now exists had its start with the rapid rise in oil prices. One important aspect of cartels is their inability to maintain control for indefinite periods. Greed by a cartel member and other problems generally weaken the control of the cartel. OPEC's unity began to dissolve because of a glut in the supply of oil. Member nations were violating production quotas, users were taking effective steps for conservation, and new sources of oil production by non-OPEC members were developed. In 1988 the West's energy needs provided by OPEC countries had dropped to about 38 percent and prices that were at a $40 per barrel high in 1980 tumbled to about $16 in 1989.[21]

Japanese companies may participate in cartels called *recession cartels* with the explicit permission of the Trade Ministry (MITI). These confer all cartel benefits and are considered essential to survival for industries with highly leveraged debt financing and in which surplus workers cannot easily be terminated. They are used when market prices are below the average cost of production, a term that leaves considerable room for interpretation. Recession cartels create dilemmas for foreign producers; they almost have to join recession cartels to participate in the market but may violate home-country laws in the process.

Although American companies are usually embarrassed by their participation in cartels, companies from other countries are not particularly concerned; perhaps, because it pays so well. A worldwide uranium cartel drove world prices from $6 a pound to more than $40 a pound within a three-year period. Gulf Oil was a major participant in that cartel; the company representatives presumably helped draw up the cartel's rules. U.S. congressional hearings into that cartel had such severe repercussions that the Canadian finance minister urged President Carter to terminate the investigations. The Canadian government itself had helped set up the cartel to protect Canadian miners from "predatory tactics of American uranium producers."

The legality of cartels at present is not clearly delineated. Domestic cartelization is illegal in the United States, and the European Community has provisions for controlling cartels. The United States, however, does permit firms to take cartel-like actions in foreign, but not domestic, markets. Increasingly, it has become apparent that many governments have concluded they cannot ignore or destroy cartels completely, so they have chosen to establish ground rules and regulatory agencies to oversee the cartel-like activities of businesses within their jurisdiction.

Trade Associations.   The very term *trade association* is so broad it is almost meaningless. Trade associations may exist as hard, tight cartels or merely

---

[21] "For the Oil Companies, 'Downstream Is Mainstream,' " *Business Week,* January 9, 1989, p. 100.

Fresh farm eggs on sale in a French hypermarket. Hypermarkets helped erode retail price controls in Europe.

informal trade organizations having nothing to do with pricing, market share, or levels of production. In many countries, trade associations gather information about prices and transactions within a given industry. Such associations have the general goal of protecting and maintaining the pricing structure most generally acceptable to industry members. In the early 1930s, the National Industrial Recovery Act gave broad powers to U.S. trade associations for this activity. Since the act was declared unconstitutional, trade associations in the United States have been enjoined by antitrust laws from playing a significant role in pricing. This is not the case in other industrial nations; manufacturers' associations frequently represent 90 to 100 percent of an industry. The association is a club one must join for access to customers and suppliers. It may handle industrywide labor negotiations and is often capable of influencing government decisions relating to the industry.

Government-Influenced Pricing

Companies doing business in foreign countries encounter a number of different types of government price setting. To control prices, governments may establish margins, set prices and floors or ceilings, restrict price changes, compete in the market, grant subsidies, and act as a purchasing monopsony or selling monopoly. The government may also influence prices by permitting, or even encouraging, business to collude in setting manipulative prices.

1.

Establishing Margins.   Middlemen sometimes are required to mark up their goods by a government-dictated margin and may not be permitted to deviate significantly from that margin. Even manufacturers may be subject to dictated margins, with the government specifying the amount goods may be marked up over cost. Both types of margin setting are encountered in Norway, for example, where the government sets maximum ranges but permits some price cutting.

2.

Setting Price Floors and Ceilings.   Numerous methods of setting price floors and ceilings are employed in different countries. Some have laws dictating that goods cannot be sold below their cost plus a government-stipulated markup. Price ceilings imposed by government also are not uncommon in the world marketplace. Bread, rice, milk, and other food staples are often subject to price ceilings.

Some governments use rather innovative ways to set price floors and ceilings. Argentina established a temporary price freeze to help restrain inflation; rather than remove the freeze, the government took steps to encourage competition but maintained price control on monopolistic or oligopolistic industries. Tariffs on some products were lowered to help set a ceiling price; on cigarettes, for example, the tariff was reduced to 5 percent. The logic was that cigarettes are particularly price sensitive and a lower price in foreign brands would keep domestic brand prices from rising. Such price controls are used in countries suffering from inflation and other economic problems.[22]

3.

Restricting Price Changes.   Regardless of the level of economic development of the countries they are in, international marketers are likely to find they cannot change prices without government permission or at least giving official notification. In some countries, such as India and Spain, price changes for a wide range of products are regulated. American business may chafe at such regulation, but a close look reminds marketers that the U.S. marketplace is not completely free of price change restrictions.

Although not designed primarily to limit freedom in changing prices, tax laws of various nations sometimes affect prices charged on final products and tend to restrict price changing. This is particularly true in the case of intercorporate transfers where changeovers from one pricing system to another can bring on retroactive tax penalties or higher taxes because of excessive profits.

---

[22] "Foreigners Boost Investments in Brazil Despite Its Daunting Economic Problems," *The Wall Street Journal*, October 26, 1988, p. 18.

4

Competing in the Market. Governments frequently compete directly in the marketplace to control prices. For example, three U.S. companies raised aluminum ingot prices by one half cent a pound; within days, the U.S. government announced it would release 200,000 to 300,000 tons of aluminum from its strategic stockpile. Shortly afterward the companies reevaluated the situation and rolled back prices to the original level. The continuing activity of the U.S. government in wheat and other commodities also has the effect of regulating prices through direct government competition.

In countries where the government owns a large share of productive assets, the government is a major competitor in the market. Some government-owned businesses, such as Italy's ENI, compete in both the domestic and international markets.

5

Creating Subsidies. Government subsidies may permit companies to reduce the prices of their goods in world competition, but they also involve the government in the pricing picture. Subsidies may be direct or indirect. To encourage the development of an industry, a nation may pay a producer of shoes a direct subsidy of 50 cents per pair. That industry then may be able to compete more effectively in the local market against imported shoes because it can sell its shoes 50 cents cheaper than it normally would. It also can compete more effectively in foreign markets because of its subsidy.

An indirect subsidy is created when a nonexported component is subsidized and the component then becomes part of an exported product. A tentmaker, for example, may buy canvas made of subsidized cotton. GATT agreements tend to outlaw direct export subsidies but do not normally prohibit indirect subsidies. However, in the Uruguay Round of the current GATT negotiations, agricultural subsidies are included as a major point of negotiation.[23]

6

Government Monopolies. Government agencies in socialized countries may act as sole sellers for certain products at the domestic and import-export levels. The Soviet Union, for example, handles its international sales through Amtorg, a government trading agency.

Like a private monopolist, the government has price authority when acting as a monopoly. Sometimes a government steps into a chaotic market situation and attempts to bring order by purchasing and selling the entire output of an industry. The Brazilian government, for example, sponsors the Brazilian Coffee Institute (IBC), a clearinghouse that handles all Brazil's international sales of raw coffee beans. Like other monopolies, the IBC has learned that falsely inflated prices invite competition. As a result of monopoly-induced price increases, the coffee market has been so favorable that production was encouraged in French West Africa, Mexico, Guatemala,

---

[23] "Uruguay Round: Mid-Term Review," *Business America*, January 16, 1989, pp. 2–4.

Indonesia, and other countries not historically important as producers. A few decades ago Brazil supplied approximately 80 percent of the world's coffee; at present, it sells less than 40 percent of the coffee in the world marketplace.

Negotiating with Monopsonies.   The word *monopsony* implies that there is only one buyer in a given market. In a monopsonistic situation, the buyer had great bargaining power and may play off a variety of suppliers to secure the most advantageous price and terms.

Monopsonistic purchasing by a government can be especially troublesome for international marketers. They not only have to compete with firms from many countries but also play by rules designed by the customers. For example, a company may be unable to vary prices on the open market to meet local situations because some countries pay only the *lowest price offered to any customer anywhere.* Cutting of margins in any area may require cutting margins on all government sales to those countries.

East European countries have become particularly adept at taking advantage of their monopsonistic position by tying purchases to forced sales of their own goods. One way is to insist on countertrade purchases requiring a vendor to accept a certain amount of goods produced in the East European

---

BOX 16–7
Not All Products Can Be Countertraded

One of the reasons countertrades arise when doing business with a country is the shortage of hard currency to buy the goods. Obviously, a product offered in a countertrade does not have a ready world market, otherwise the product would be sold on the world market for hard currency. Thus, Polish hams and sausages received by McDonnell Douglas Corporation, pink and orange telephone rotaries received by GTE Corporation, Algerian wine accepted by Caterpillar and served in its cafeterias are all evidence of the difficulty of disposing of countertraded goods and the low-market value of the goods so offered.

Some countries have elaborate rules on exactly what can be used for countertrade. In Ecuador, for example, petroleum and by-products, frozen shrimp, tuna, other fish and fish meal, instant coffee, cacao and derivatives, and green beans are expressly prohibited from being used for countertrade. Bananas may be used for barter but only in new markets. Because Ecuador's production of other goods is limited, countertrade is limited.

Source: "Countertrade Caveats," *Business Latin America*, April 18, 1984, p. 128, and "The Booming World of Countertrade," *Dun's Business Month*, January 1984, p. 78.

country in payment. Countertrade lessens the pressure on the balance-of-payments but may leave the vendor with unwanted goods to dispose of elsewhere. The volume of countertrade depends directly on the bargaining power of each party. Trade ratios range from 10 to 30 percent of the value of the imported goods but sometimes have matched or even exceeded the total value of the imports.

International Agreements

Governments of producing and consuming countries seem to play an ever-increasing role in the establishment of international prices for certain basic commodities. There are, for example, an international coffee agreement, an international cocoa agreement, and an international sugar agreement. The world price of wheat has long been at least partially determined by negotiations between national governments.

Despite the pressures of business, government, and international price agreements, most marketers still have wide latitude in their pricing decisions for most products and markets.

COUNTERTRADES

Today an international company must include in its market pricing tool kit some understanding of countertrading.[24] Although cash is the preferred method of payment, countertrades are becoming an important part of trade with Eastern Europe, China, and to a varying degree some Latin American and African nations.[25] The key problems in successfully consummating countertrade transactions are (1) accurately establishing the market value of the goods being offered and (2) disposing of the bartered goods once they are received. Most countertrades judged unsuccessful are the result of one or both of the problems cited not being properly solved.

---

[24] A variety of terms are used to describe the transactions the author classifies as countertrades. In order not to further confuse the issue and to help standardize terminology, he has used the terms developed by Business International Corporation. A comprehensive report on countertrades can be found in Sandra M. Huszagh and Hiram C. Barksdale, "International Barter and Countertrade: An Exploratory Study," *Journal of the Academy of Marketing Science*, Spring 1986, pp. 21–28.

[25] Louis Kraar, "How to Sell to Cashless Buyers," *Fortune*, November 7, 1988, pp. 147–54.

Types of Countertrade

Countertrade includes four distinct transactions: barter, compensation deals, counterpurchase, and buy-back.[26]

Barter is the direct exchange of goods between two parties in a transaction. One of the largest barter deals to date involved Occidental Petroleum Corporation's agreement to ship superphosphoric acid to the Soviet Union for ammonia urea and potash under a 2-year, $20-billion deal. No money changed hands nor were any third parties involved. Obviously, in a barter transaction, the seller (Occidental Petroleum) must be able to dispose of the goods at a net price equal to the expected selling price in a regular, for-cash transaction. Further, during the negotiation stage of a barter deal, the seller must have some knowledge of the market and the price for the items offered in trade. In the Russian barter trade example, the price and a market for the ammonia urea and potash were established since Occidental could use the products in its operations. But bartered goods can range from hams to iron pellets, mineral water, furniture, or olive oil—all somewhat more difficult to establish a price and market for when customers are needed. Because of the almost limitless range of goods and quality grades possible and a lack of expertise or information necessary, sellers rely on barter houses to provide information and find potential buyers for goods received. Another possibility is the use of a switch trader, an outsider who switches the traded goods to a third country where a market exists.

Compensation deals involve payment in goods and in cash. A seller delivers lathes to a buyer in Venezuela and receives 70 percent of the payment in convertible currency and 30 percent in tanned hides and wool. In an actual deal, General Motors Corporation sold $12 million worth of locomotives and diesel engines to Yugoslavia and took cash and $4 million in Yugoslavian cutting tools as payment.

An advantage of a compensation deal over barter is the immediate cash settlement of a portion of the bill; the remainder of the cash is generated after successful sale of the goods received. If the company has a use for the goods received, the process is relatively simple and uncomplicated. On the other hand, if the seller has to rely on a third party to find a buyer, the cost involved must be anticipated in the original compensation negotiation if the net proceeds to the seller are to be equal to the market price.

Counterpurchase is probably the most frequently used type of countertrade. For this trade, two contracts are negotiated. The seller agrees to

---

[26] *Switch trading, parallel trades, offset trades,* and *clearing agreements* are other terms used to describe countertrade, but they are only variations of the four types mentioned here. For a description, see Stephen S. Cohen and John Zysman, "Countertrade, Offsets, Barter, and Buybacks," *California Management Review,* Winter 1986, pp. 41–56.

BOX 16–8
Some Examples of Countertrade

- Under Indonesia's counterpurchase policy, all foreign companies awarded government contracts for construction projects and major procurements must undertake to export specified Indonesian products, other than oil or natural gas, equivalent to the total foreign currency value of the equipment and materials, they import into Indonesia. The export of Indonesian products purchased under these arrangements to a third country is permitted only if the third country is a new market for such products.
- The Malaysian-owned rubber trading company, Sime Darby, is said to have worked out a barter deal with Mexican tire manufacturers under which the Mexican firms paid Sime Darby's New York-based agency for Malaysian rubber with cocoa beans. Sime Darby, New York, in turn, resold the cocoa beans to confectionery manufacturers in the United States.
- The United States aerospace company McConnell Douglas Corporation is reported to have sold aircraft to Romania in return for canned ham "which the firm's staff is expected to munch its way through at the company's canteen for years to come."

---

sell a product at a set price to a buyer and receives payment in cash. However, the first contract is contingent on a second contract that is an agreement by the original seller to buy goods from the buyer for the total monetary amount involved in the first contract or for a set percentage of that amount. This arrangement provides the seller with more flexibility than the compensation deal since there is generally a time period—6 to 12 months or longer—for completion of the second contract.[27] During the time that markets are sought for the goods in the second contract, the seller has received full payment for the original sale. Further, the goods to be purchased in the second contract are generally of greater variety than those offered in a compensation deal. Even greater flexibility is offered when the second contract is nonspecific, that is, the books on sales and purchases need to be cleared only at certain intervals. The seller is obligated to generate enough purchases to keep the books balanced or clear between purchases and sales.

These *offset trades*, as they are sometimes called, are becoming more prevalent among economically weak countries. Several variations of a counterpurchase or offset have developed to make it more economical

---

[27] For an illustration of this see, Marion Cotter, "Countertrade Technique Lands Boeing Big Order," *Journal of Commerce*, January 12, 1988, p. 1.

<table>
<tr><td>

BOX 16–9
Cuttlefish—Who Wants Cuttlefish?

For effective international pricing you need a working knowledge of counter-trade. You can almost bet that with certain countries something other than money will be offered in a deal. Here's what happened to a Denver business-man.

The businessman figured he would make about $1 million on the deal, a $2.5 million contract with the Republic of China. He started looking for a loan to pay expenses; ten Denver banks turned him down. The problem: his deal had a catch—instead of cash the Chinese wanted to pay him in cuttlefish.

"A lot of countries don't pay money," he says, "They pay in countertrade of commodities." He had only started his company two years before and this type of deal was new to him. The banks found it hilarious. "I saw dollars, the bankers saw fish," he says. "One banker said he had never heard anything so ridiculous in his life."

After it was too late, he found there were banks with experience in counter-trading deals that might have approved his financing. He also learned he could have instantly sold the cuttlefish in Indonesia. But it was too late. "I lost out on a fine deal because I did not know how to handle it, I didn't know anything about countertrade."

Source: Adapted from "Going Global," *Denver Business,* April 1988, p. 44.
</td></tr>
</table>

for the selling company. For example, the Lockheed Corporation goes sofar as to build up offset trade credits before a counterpurchase deal is made. Knowing that some type of countertrade would have to be accepted to make maritime aircraft sales to Korea, they actively sought the opportunity to assist in the sale of Hyundai personal computers even though there was no guarantee that Korea would actually buy aircraft from them. Lockheed has been involved in countertrades for over 20 years; during that time countertrade agreements have totaled over $1.3 billion and have included everything from tomato paste to rugs, textiles, and automotive parts.[28]

McDonnell Douglas Corporation is another company that actively engages in counterpurchases. A $100 million sale of DC-9s to Yugoslavia required McDonnell Douglas to sell or buy $25 million in Yugoslavian goods. Some of their commitment to Yugoslavia was settled by buying

---

[28] "Lockheed Barters for a Deal," *Sales and Marketing Management,* September 1987, pp. 40–42.

Yugoslavian equipment for its own use, but it also sold such items as hams, iron castings, rubber bumper guards, and transmission towers to others. McDonnell Douglas held showings for department store buyers to sell glassware and leather goods to fulfill their counterpurchase agreement. Twice a year, company officials meet to claim credits for sales and clear the books in fulfillment of their counterpurchase agreement.[29]

Product buy-back agreement is the last of the four countertrade transactions. This type of agreement is made when the sale involves goods or services that produce other goods and services, that is, production plant, production equipment, or technology. The buy-back agreement usually involves one of two situations: the seller agrees to accept as partial payment a certain portion of the output or the seller receives full price initially but agrees to buy back a certain portion of the output. For example, one U.S. farm equipment manufacturer sold a tractor plant to Poland and was paid part in hard currency and the balance in Polish-built tractors. In another situation, General Motors Corporation bought autos from Brazil in partial payment for building an automobile manufacturing plant there. Levi Strauss and Company is taking Hungarian blue jeans, which it will sell abroad, in exchange for setting up a jeans factory near Budapest. A major drawback to product buy-back agreements comes when the seller finds that the products bought back are in competition with its own similarly produced goods. On the other hand, some have found that a product buy-back agreement provides them with a supplemental source in an area of the world where there is demand but where there is no available supply.[30]

U.S. Firms Reluctant to Countertrade

Countertrade transactions are definitely on the increase in world trade. Some estimates of countertrade in international trade go as high as 30 percent. More conservative estimates place the amount closer to 20 percent. Regardless, a significant amount of all international trade now involves some type of countertrade transaction; this percentage is predicted to increase substantially in the near future. Much of that increase will come in trading with Third World countries; in fact, some require countertrades of some sort with all foreign trade.[31] India requires all foreign compa-

---

[29] Stephen S. Cohen and John Zysman, "Countertrade, Offsets, Barter, and Buybacks," pp. 41–56.

[30] Raj Aggarwal, "International Business through Barter and Countertrade," *Long-Range Planning*, Vol. 22, No. 3, June, 1989, pp. 75–81.

[31] Samuel Rabino and Kirit Shah, "Countertrade and Penetration of LDC's Markets," *Columbia Journal of World Business*, Winter 1987, pp. 31–37.

EXHIBIT 16–3   Why Purchasers Impose Countertrade Obligations

---

To Preserve Hard Currency. Countries with nonconvertible currencies look to countertrade as a way of guaranteeing that hard currency expenditures (for foreign imports) are offset by hard currency (generated by the foreign party's obligation to purchase domestic goods).

To Improve Balance of Trade. Nations whose exports to the West have not kept pace with imports increasingly rely on countertrade as a means to balance bilateral trade ledgers.

To Gain Access to New Markets. As a nonmarket or developing country increases its production of exportable goods, it often lacks a sophisticated marketing channel to sell the goods to the West for hard currency. By imposing countertrade demands, foreign trade organizations utilize the marketing organizations and expertise of Western companies to market their goods for them.

To Upgrade Manufacturing Capabilities. By entering compensation arrangements under which foreign (usually Western) firms provide plant and equipment and buy back resultant products, the trade organizations of less-developed countries can enlist Western technical cooperation in upgrading industrial facilities.

To Maintain Prices of Export Goods. Countertrade can be used as a means to dispose of goods at prices that the market would not bear under cash-for-goods terms. Although the Western seller absorbs the added cost by inflating the price of the original sale, the nominal price of the counterpurchased goods is maintained, and the seller need not concede what the value of the goods would be in the world supply and demand market. Conversely, if the world price for a commodity is artificially high, such as the price for crude oil, a country can barter its oil for Western goods (e.g., weapons) so that the real "price" the Western partner pays is below the world price.

SOURCE: Leo G. B. Welt, "Countertrade? Better than No Trade," *Export Today*, Spring 1985, p. 54.

---

nies trading with State Trading Corporations to engage in countertrades. Countertrade arrangements are involved in an estimated 50 percent or more of all international trade with Communist-bloc and Third World countries.

Western European and Japanese firms have the longest history of countertrade because of their trading experience with Eastern Europe. U.S. firms have been slow to accept countertrade, preferring to lose a sale rather than become involved in an unfamiliar situation. In fact, a recent survey of several hundred U.S. firms involved in international trade indicated that a majority would refuse a countertrade offer. This attitude seems to stem from inexperience and, as one respondent candidly replied, "We don't need the hassle. We have enough business without it." Regardless of prevailing U.S. attitudes, demands for countertrade will increase and many firms will find they have little choice but to cope with hassles or problems of countertrade to be competitive in world markets. As Exhibit

16–3 illustrates, countertrade will continue to be important in the future.[32]

While many U.S. firms shun barter or countertrade arrangements, others are profitably involved. Certainly one of the more interesting trades involves Pepsi-Cola which has barter arrangements with Russia and Romania. Pepsi-Cola sells cola concentrate to produce Pepsi-Cola and receives vodka (sold under the brand name *Stolichnaya)* from Russia and bottled wines (sold under the brand name *Premiat)* from Romania as full payment. From all indications, this has been a very profitable arrangement for Russia, Romania, and Pepsi-Cola.

Problems of Countertrading

The crucial problem confronting a seller in a countertrade negotiation is determining the value and potential demand of the goods offered. Frequently there is inadequate time to conduct a market analysis; in fact, it is not unusual to have sales negotiations almost completed before countertrade is introduced as a requirement in the transaction.

Although such problems can be difficult to deal with, they can be minimized with some preparation. In most cases where losses have occurred in countertrades, the seller has been unprepared to negotiate in anything other than cash. Some preliminary research should be done in anticipation of being confronted with a countertrade proposal. Countries with a history of countertrading are easily identified and the products most likely to be offered in a countertrade can be quickly ascertained. For a company trading with Third World countries or Communist countries, these facts and some background on handling countertrades should be a part of every pricing tool kit. Once goods are acquired, they can be passed along to institutions that assist companies in selling barter goods.

Barter houses specialize in trading goods acquired through barter arrangements and are the primary outside source of aid for companies beset by the uncertainty of a countertrade. Barter houses, most of which are found in Europe, can find a market for bartered goods but the time required can put a financial strain on a company because capital is tied up longer than in normal transactions. A solution to this problem would be for a company to seek loans to tide it over until sales are completed.

In the United States, companies are being developed to assist with bartered goods and their financing. Citibank has created a countertrade department to allow the bank to act as a consultant as well as to provide financing for countertrades. A New York company, Universal Trading Exchange, acts as a clearinghouse for bartered goods. Members can trade products

---

[32] For an interesting study of attitudes on the importance of countertrades, see David Shipley and Bill Neale, "Countertrade: Reactive or Proactive?" *Journal of Business Research,* June 1988, pp. 327–35.

BOX 16–10
"Dallas" Arrives in China

Three hundred million Chinese have the opportunity to see such U.S. television programs as "The People's Court" and "Dallas" as a result of a barter deal between a Shanghai-based television network and Lorimar-Telepictures Corporation. The movie, television, and advertising company expects to show its television programs on the Shanghai network in return for advertising time on the network. Under the barter arrangement, Lorimar will trade a variety of U.S. TV programs and concert tours of rock bands for advertising time on Chinese TV networks. Lorimar expects to get its profits from reselling the advertising time to U.S. and European companies that want to advertise in China. Lorimar expects this arrangement to produce "solid profits" after about two years.

Source: Adapted from "Lorimar to Supply Shows for TV Network in China," *The Wall Street Journal*, December 5, 1987, p. 10.

---

of unequal value with other members or they have the option of settling accounts in cash. It is estimated that there are now about 500 barter exchanges in the United States.[33]

Barter houses serve a vital role in countertrade but for companies with a large percentage of their business involving barter, a third party is not always the answer. Some companies have organized their own in-house trading groups to provide the assistance needed to effectively deal in countertrades. One such inside group, perhaps a forerunner of many to come, is Motors Trading Company, a wholly owned subsidiary of General Motors Corporation. It is designed to develop markets for GM products in countries where cash deals or capital investments are not practical. General Motors has countertrade deals with 20 countries accounting for more than 50 percent of all the business it does with Eastern-bloc nations. General Electric Co., McDonnell Douglas, and several other major U.S. corporations have recently established their own special departments to help dispose of countertraded goods. In many situations, these companies have been able to deal with countertrades when the competition has been less flexible, thus enabling them to consummate a transaction not possible for the competitor to handle successfully.

There are many examples of companies losing sales to competitors who were willing to enter into countertrade agreements. For example, a U.S. oil-field equipment manufacturer claims it submitted the lowest dollar bid in an Egyptian offer but lost the sale to a bidder who offered a counter

---

[33] "Better Barter?" *Fortune*, February 18, 1985, p. 105.

purchase arrangement. Incidentally, the successful company was Japanese with a sizable trading company established to dispose of the Egyptian goods received in the counterpurchase arrangement. The pressure for countertrading is increasing as a result of the oil glut and the apparent weakening of OPEC. After a period of discipline within OPEC, barter surfaced as a method of circumventing production quotas. For example, an OPEC member has excess oil it cannot sell at OPEC prices, but it does not want to openly violate OPEC regulations, so an arrangement is made to purchase a ship for $5 million with the requirement that the shipbuilder take $5 million worth of oil in payment. On paper, the member is abiding by OPEC obligations. Further, the oil can be discounted by having the shipbuilder inflate the ship's price thereby discounting the oil price. There is so much pressure to trade oil for goods that several oil-producing countries, including Saudi Arabia, have signed barter accords which move toward institutionalizing barter as a way to sell otherwise unwanted oil production for the industrial goods these countries need.[34]

One experienced countertrader suggests the following factors be considered before entering into a countertrade agreement. (1) Is it the only way the order can be secured? (2) Is there a ready market for the goods bartered? (3) Can the countertrade portion be kept to a minimum? (4) Can the exporter handle the negotiations alone or are experts needed? (5) Has the exporter increased the contract price to cover the cost of barter? (6) Has the would-be barterer considered exchange-control regulations which require payment for exports to places outside scheduled territories? (7) Are the goods offered in exchange subject to import control?

Some authorities suggest that companies should have a defined countertrade strategy as part of their marketing strategy rather than be caught unprepared when confronted with a countertrade proposition.[35] Most companies have a reactive strategy, that is, they use countertrade when they believe it is the only way to make a sale.[36] Even when these companies include countertrade as a permanent feature of their operations, they use it to react to a sales demand rather than using countertrade as an aggressive marketing tool for expansion.

A proactive countertrade strategy may be the most effective for global companies that market to developing and Communist-bloc countries because the demand for countertrade arrangements is most often a significant part of any purchases they make. Companies with a proactive strategy make a commitment to use countertrade aggressively as a marketing and

---

[34] For an interesting perspective on countertrade as a financial tool see Jay Hernandize, "Alternative Financing Options Win More Sales," *Export Today*, November–December 1987, pp. 54–56.

[35] For a comprehensive coverage of countertrading see C. G. Alexandrides and Barbara Bowers, *Countertrade: Policies, Strategies, and Tactics*, (New York: John Wiley & Sons, 1987).

[36] C. G. Alexandrides and Barbara Bowers, "The American Way to Countertrade," *Countertrade and Barter*, February–March 1988, p. 48.

pricing tool. They see countertrades as an opportunity to expand markets rather than as an inconvenient reaction to market demands. The vast market potential of China and Russia depend on countertrades for many of the goods necessary for their industrialization. Companies not prepared to seek this business with a proactive countertrade strategy will miss important market opportunities.[37]

INTRACOMPANY PRICING STRATEGY

As companies increase the number of worldwide subsidiaries, joint ventures, company-owned distributing systems, and other marketing arrangements, the price charged to different affiliates becomes a preeminent question. Prices of goods transferred from operations or sales units in one country to a company's units elsewhere may be adjusted to enhance the ultimate profit of the company as a whole. The benefits are:

1. Lowering duty costs by shipping goods into high-tariff countries at minimal transfer prices so duty base and duty are low.
2. Reduction of income taxes in high-tax countries by overpricing goods transferred to units in such countries; profits are eliminated and shifted to low-tax countries. Such profit shifting may also be used for "dressing up" financial statements by increasing reported profits in countries where borrowing and other financing are undertaken.
3. Facilitation of dividend repatriation. When dividend repatriation is curtailed by government policy, invisible income may be taken out in the form of high prices for products or components shipped to units in that country.

The tax and financial manipulation possibilities of transfer pricing have not been overlooked by government authorities. As multinational firms gain increasing prominence on the world marketing scene, national governments are becoming increasingly restrictive and paying special attention to transfer pricing in tax audits. The overall objectives of the intracompany pricing system include: (1) maximizing profits for the corporation as a whole, (2) facilitating parent-company control, and (3) offering management at all levels, both in the product divisions and in the international divisions, an adequate basis for maintaining, developing, and receiving credit for their own profitability. Transfer prices that are too low are unsatisfactory to the product divisions because their overall results look poor; prices that are too high make the international operations look bad and limit the effectiveness of foreign managers.

Part of an effective pricing system is recognition of the complexity of pricing and an awareness of variations in local conditions. Pricing policies of the parent company should be such that the international divisions

---

[37] For an example of the importance of countertrade in Russia, see Nancy Giges, "Lada Sales Driving Coke Forward in Soviet Union," *Advertising Age*, May 16, 1988, p. 69.

maintain ultimate market initiative and have final profit responsibility for their operations. One recent study of intracorporate pricing showed conclusively that "setting up transfer prices remains the absolute prerogative of the parent company executives regardless of the firm's nationality." The systems should be simple enough so that all participants in the decision and transfer can understand how prices were established. Finally, the intracorporate pricing system should employ sound accounting techniques and be defensible to the tax authorities of the countries involved. All of these factors argue against a single uniform price or even a uniform pricing system for all international operations.

Four arrangements for pricing goods for intracompany transfer are:

1. Sales at the local manufacturing cost plus a standard markup.
2. Sales at the cost of the most efficient producer in the company plus a standard markup.
3. Sales at negotiated prices.
4. Arm's-length sales using the same prices as quoted to independent customers.

Of the four, the arm's-length transfer is most acceptable to tax authorities and most likely to be acceptable to foreign divisions, but the appropriate basis for intracompany transfers depends on the nature of the subsidiaries and market conditions. Sometimes inappropriate pricing policies can completely knock a product out of the market even though it might contribute significantly to the profitability of the company as a whole. For example, an item with a factory cost of $100 is transferred to the international divison at $120 with an additional cost of $10 involved in the export; assume competition limits the international selling price to $135. The sale might be rejected because a $5 profit reflects only a 3.7 percent return on sales. The total profit to the corporation, however, will be $25, or 18.5 percent *if all* the profit to the corporation were taken into account. Thus what appears to be an unprofitable sale becomes a highly profitable one when viewed from the overall corporate perspective.

PRICE QUOTATIONS

In quoting the price of goods for international sale, a contract may include specific price elements affecting the price, such as credit, sales terms, and transportation. Parties to the transaction must be certain that the quotation settled on appropriately locates responsibility for the goods during transportation and spells out who pays transportation charges and from what point. Price quotations must also specify the currency to be used, credit terms, and the type of documentation required. Finally, the price quotation and contract should define quantity and quality. A quantity definition might be necessary because different countries use different units of measurement. In specifying a ton, for example, the contract should identify it as a metric or an English ton, and as a long or short ton.

Furthermore, there should be complete agreement on quality standards to be used in evaluating the product. The international trader must review all terms of the contract; failure to do so may have the effect of modifying prices even though such a change was not intended.

SUMMARY

Pricing is one of the most complicated decision areas encountered by international marketers. Rather than deal with one set of market conditions, one group of competitors, one set of cost factors, and one set of government regulations, international marketers must take all these factors into account, not only for each country in which they are operating, but sometimes for each market within a country. Market prices at the consumer level are much more difficult to control in international than in domestic marketing, but the international marketer must still approach the pricing task on a basis of objectives and policy, leaving enough flexibility for tactical price movements. Pricing in the international marketplace requires a combination of intimate knowledge of market costs and regulations, infinite patience for detail, and a shrewd sense of market strategy.

QUESTIONS

1. Define:

dumping	administered pricing
buy-back	compensation deal
countervailing duty	cartel
subsidy	monopsony
countertrade	FTZ
parallel imports	

2. Discuss the causes and solutions of parallel imports and their effect on price.

3. Why is it so difficult to control consumer prices when selling overseas?

4. Explain the concept of "price escalation" and tell why it can mislead an international marketer.

5. What are the causes of price escalation? Do they differ for exports and goods produced and sold in a foreign country?

6. Why is it seldom feasible for a company to absorb the high cost of international transportation and reduce the net price received?

7. Price escalation is a major pricing problem for the international marketer. How can this problem be counteracted? Discuss.

8. Changing currency values have an impact on export strategies. Discuss.

9. "Regardless of the strategic factors involved and the company's orienta-

tion to market pricing, every price must be set with cost considerations in mind." Discuss.

10. "Price fixing by business is not generally viewed as an acceptable procedure (at least in the domestic market); but when governments enter the field of price administration, they presume to do it for the general welfare to lessen the effects of 'destructive' competition." Discuss.

11. Do value added taxes discriminate against imported goods?

12. Explain specific tariffs, ad valorem tariffs, and combination tariffs.

13. Suggest an approach a marketer may follow in adjusting prices to accommodate exchange-rate fluctuations.

14. Explain the effects of indirect competition and how they may be overcome.

15. Why has dumping become such an issue in recent years?

16. Cartels seem to rise phoenixlike after they have been destroyed. Why are they so appealing to business?

17. Develop a cartel policy for the United States.

18. Discuss the various ways in which governments set prices. Why do they engage in such activities?

19. Discuss the alternative objectives possible in setting prices for intracompany sales.

20. Why do governments so carefully scrutinize intracompany pricing arrangements?

21. Why are costs so difficult to assess in marketing internationally?

22. Discuss why countertrading is on the increase.

23. Discuss the major problems facing a company that is countertrading.

24. If a country you are trading with has a shortage of hard currency, how should you prepare to negotiate price?

25. Of the four types of countertrades discussed in the text, which is the most beneficial to the seller? Explain.

26. Why should a "knowledge of countertrades be part of an international marketer's pricing tool kit"? Discuss.

27. Discuss the various reasons purchasers impose countertrade obligations on buyers.

28. Discuss how FTZs can be used to help reduce price escalation.

29. Why is a proactive countertrade policy good business in some countries?

30. Differentiate between a proactive and reactive countertrade policy.

CHAPTER

17

The International Distribution System

The influence of the globalization of markets extends beyond global brands, products, and advertising to include distribution. Global brand and global product efficiencies achieved through global market strategy can be severely limited if products reach the target market through inefficient distribution systems. Although the global marketer seeks the most effective and direct distribution network, choices are limited by the existing distribution structures within a country market or markets.[1] In some markets, the distribution system is multilayered, complex, and difficult for new marketers to penetrate. In Japan the dozen middlemen between the marketer and the end users increase the cost of selling to a prohibitive level.[2]

At the other extreme are many developing countries with a paucity of specialized middlemen except in major urban areas. Those that do exist are often small with traditionally high margins. In China, for example, the often quoted 1 billion person market is, in reality, fewer than 20 percent

---

[1] For a comprehensive study of uses of existing channels by U.S. companies and implications of channel choice, see Eirn Anderson and Anne T. Coughlan, "International Market Entry and Expansion vs. Independent or Integrated Channels of Distribution," *Journal of Marketing,* January 1987, pp. 71–82.

[2] Karen Berney, "Competing in Japan," *Nation's Business,* October 1986, p. 29.

of the population of the most affluent cities. Lack of personal income is certainly one reason for the relatively small size of this market but distribution inadequacies limit marketers in reaching all those who have adequate incomes.[3] In both extremes, the difficulty of developing an efficient channel from existing middlemen plus the high cost of distribution may nullify efficiencies achieved in other parts of the marketing mix.

Some important trends in distribution systems will lead to their eventual globalization. That is, there is greater commonality than disparity among middlemen in different countries. United States-based Southland Corporation's 7-Eleven Stores are replacing many of the traditional mom-and-pop stores that have dominated a significant part of Japan's retail food distribution. In Spain, 7-Eleven and Campsa, the Spanish gasoline monopoly, opened 200 7-Eleven minimarkets at Campsa service stations.[4] Hypermarkets, a retailing innovation developed in France, have expanded beyond French borders to other European countries and to the United States. These huge stores, supplied with computerized inventories, may spell a slow death for small shops and midsize retailers which today account for 80 percent of sales in southern Europe. Discount, home repair, self-service, and supermarkets are mass merchandising concepts gradually spreading all over the world.

In anticipation of Europe 1992, national and international retailing networks are developing throughout the world.[5] European integration, global brands, globalized media communications, consumers who expect rational and predictable product assortments, and global companies anxious for their products to be distibuted in the most efficient manner are factors driving a growing number of traditional distibution channel members to greater efficiencies and competitiveness. Many are developing into transnational, if not global, operations.[6] Global products require integrated, efficient distribution systems to achieve maximum effectiveness.

In every country, communist or capitalist, and in every market, urban or rural, rich or poor, all consumer and industrial products eventually go through a distribution process. The process includes the physical handling and distribution of goods, the passage of ownership, and—most important from the standpoint of marketing strategy—the buying and selling negotiations between middlemen, producers, and consumers.

This chapter discusses the basic points to consider in making a channel

---

[3] "Laying the Foundation for the Great Mall of China," *Business Week,* January 25, 1988, p. 68.

[4] Kevin Cote, "European Advertisers Prepare for 1992," *Europe,* September 1988, p. 19.

[5] John Rossant, Peter Galuszka and Stanley Reed, "The Race to Stock Europe's Common Supermarket," *International Business,* June 26, 1989, pp. 80–82.

[6] Ron Beyma, "U.S., European Retailers Are Becoming More Transnational," *Europe,* January–February 1989, p. 20.

decision: (1) available alternative middlemen; (2) locating, selecting, motivating, and terminating middlemen; and (3) controlling the channel process.

CHANNEL OF DISTRIBUTION ALTERNATIVES

In preceding chapters, product development, pricing, and promotion issues have been discussed. To complete the components of the marketing mix and to get the product to the target market, channels of distribution must be developed. Every country or target market area presents the international marketer with unique middlemen and distribution patterns. The challenge for the international marketer is to forge channels from available middlemen that effectively meet the needs of the target market within the constraints imposed by company policies and resources.

Exhibit 17–1 shows some of the many possible channel-of-distribution alternatives. The arrows show those to whom the producer and each of the middlemen may sell. The channel process includes all activities beginning with the manufacturer and ending with the final consumer. Further,

EXHIBIT 17–1   International Channel-of-Distribution Alternatives

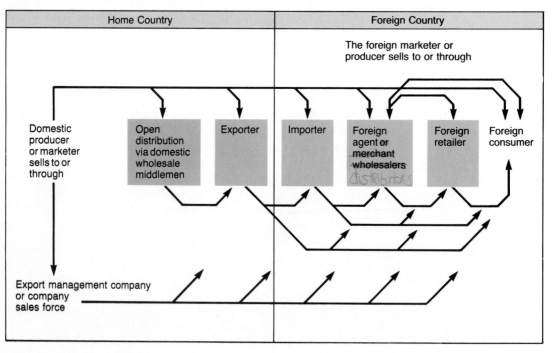

the ultimate goal is to ensure that target markets receive the product in a manner that leads to customer satisfaction. This means the seller must exert influence over two sets of channels, one in the home country and one in the market country. In the home country, the seller must have an organization (generally the international marketing division of the company) to deal with the channel members necessary to move goods between countries. In the foreign country, the seller must also supervise the channels that supply the product to the end user. Ideally, the company wants to control or be involved in the process all the way through the various channels to the final user. To do less may result in unsatisfactory distribution and failure in reaching marketing objectives. In practice, however, such involvement throughout the channel process is not always practical or cost effective. As a consequence, channel member selection and effective controls are high priorities in the distribution process.

A host of policy and strategy questions confronts the international marketing manager. The policies and problems are not in themselves very different from those encountered in domestic distribution, but the solutions differ because of different market patterns and channel alternatives.

The international marketer needs a clear understanding of market characteristics and must have established operating policies before beginning the selection of channel middlemen. The following factors should be addressed prior to the selection process:

1. Specific marketing goals, expressed in terms of volume, market share, and profit margin requirements.
2. Specific financial and personal commitments to the development of international distribution.
3. Questions of control, length of channels, terms of sale, and channel ownership.

Once these points are established, the process of selecting among alternative middlemen to forge the best channel can begin.

FACTORS AFFECTING CHOICE OF CHANNELS

Marketers must get their goods into the hands of consumers and must choose between handling all distribution or turning part or all of it over to various middlemen. Distribution channels vary depending on market size, competition, and available distribution intermediaries.

Key elements in distribution decisions include: (1) functions performed by middlemen (and the effectiveness with which each is performed), (2) cost of their services, (3) their availability, and (4) extent of control which the manufacturer can exert over middlemen activities.

Although the overall marketing strategy of the firm must embody the company's profit goals in the short and long run, the channel strategy itself is considered to have six specific strategic goals. These goals can be characterized as the six Cs of channel strategy—cost, capital, control, coverage, character, and continuity.

In forging the overall channel-of-distribution strategy, each of the six Cs must be considered in building an economical, effective distribution organization. This must be done within the long-range channel policies of the company, which in turn must fit the firm's overall marketing program.

Cost

Two kinds of channel cost are encountered: the capital or investment cost of developing the channel and the continuing cost of maintaining it. The latter can be in the form of direct expenditure for the maintenance

---

BOX 17-1
Corner Store—On Every Corner

MILAN—Via Padova is an ordinary busy street near the outskirts of Milan. In a six-block area, from Piazza Loreto to Via Mamiani, there are two PAM supermarkets and 41 other food stores.

Of these small stores, seven are *alimentari* or *drougherie*—that is, traditional grocery stores. The others are bakeries, fruit and vegetable stores, milk stores; delicatessens, and butchers. But because of the complex licensing laws and a natural love of variety, a customer can buy vermouth from the milk store, canned goods from the fruit and vegetable store, fresh meat from the delicatessen, and eggs from the butcher.

The average number of clients for each retail food outlet in Italy is 130. The official figures dip as low as 82 in Sardegna and climb to 174 in Lombardy.

Dr. Allessandro Borrini, who is advertising manager for UPIM and SMA, both part of the Rinascente network, points out that these figures become even lower when the government method for reaching them—dividing population, including the newborn, by outlets—is considered.

"It is closer to reality to say there are, as a high average, 30 families per food outlet. There are perhaps less, since they don't count *ambulanti* (pushcarts), of which there are thousands, as outlets or small markets."

Supermarkets must be seen against this background. The law is weighted for the protection of thousands of small food outlets, and Italian supermarket operators run into inexorable difficulties.

"It is the nature of a supermarket to be part of a chain," says Dr. Borrini, "but it is prohibitively difficult to get building permits."

Source: Elspeth Durie, "Italian Supers: Up Against the Little Guy." Reprinted with permission from the September 1977 issue of *Advertising Age.* © 1977 by Crain Communications, Inc.

BOX 17–2
Sales Discipline Breaking Down

German retailers are subject to a bewildering array of restrictive laws and codes of practice. The law on the timing of sales dates back to 1909 and the Discount Law was enacted in the 20s.

In practice, the system is breaking down. Retailers openly exceed the limit of twice-yearly end-of-season winter and summer sales by holding interim sales. Clearance sales are theoretically subject to written requests and local chamber of commerce approval. There is no provision for spur-of-the-moment markdowns. Needless to say, retailers are flouting the regulations. Local chambers of commerce, charged with enforcing the nationwide sales dates, also seem to have given up fining offending stores.

Also breaking down in practice is the German system of designated specialty stores. Sports goods retailers have been fighting to prevent coffee retailers, who already feature brief "loss-leader" sales with watches and textiles, from offering skis and other sports equipment. Legal action is also being taken against the Metro discount chain for selling Cartier watches and personal computers below recommended retail prices.

It is now suggested that retailers may be deliberately provoking legal action from speciality store associations to get publicity. Their sensational loss-leaders are offered for only a short period and, in fact, may no longer be available by the time a court order is obtained.

Source: "Sales Discipline Breaking Down," *Business Europe*, April 27, 1984, p. 132.

of the company's selling force or in the form of the margins, markup, or commission of various middlemen handling the goods. Marketing costs (the bulk of which is channel cost) must be considered the entire difference between the factory price of the goods and the price the customer ultimately pays for the merchandise. The costs of middlemen include transporting and storing the goods; breaking bulk; handling the paperwork; handling credit; and local advertising, sales representation, and negotiations.

Many companies have thought they could perform distribution miracles at low cost by assuming middlemen functions but have been forced to rethink or restructure their channels of distribution when their cost-saving dreams were not realized.

One study found that of five different channels, including selling to an affiliate, a consumer goods firm selling directly to a distributor in a country was the most profitable. The least profitable was exporting directly to retailers in a country.[7]

---

[7] Warren J. Bilkey, "Variables Associated with Export Profitability," presented at the 1980 Annual Conference of the Academy of International Business, New Orleans.

Despite the old truism that you can eliminate middlemen but you cannot eliminate their functions or cost, creative marketing does permit channel cost savings in many circumstances. Some marketers have found, in fact, that they can reduce cost by using shorter channels. Mexico's largest producer of radio and television sets has built annual sales of $36 million on its ability to sell goods at a low price because it eliminated middlemen, established its own wholesalers, and kept margins low. Conversely, many firms accustomed to using their own sales forces in large-volume domestic markets have found they must lengthen channels of distribution to keep costs in line with foreign markets.

Capital Requirement

The financial ramifications of a distribution policy are often overlooked. Two critical elements are capital requirement and cash-flow patterns associated with using a particular type of middleman. Maximum investment is usually required when a company establishes its own internal channels, its own sales force. Use of distributors or dealers may lessen the cash investment, but manufacturers often provide initial inventories on consignment, loan, floor plan, or other arrangement. Agent middlemen may require no investment but are sometimes subsidized by the company during an introductory period. Agents, of course, do not provide any cash flow to the producer until transactions with the ultimate buyers are consummated. Distributors and dealers provide immediate cash flow when they purchase the products.

Control

Companies often involve themselves deeply in the distribution of their own goods to improve control of their marketing destinies. It is generally conceded that the company's own sales force permits maximum control even though it imposes additional cost. Each type of channel arrangement, indeed each specific middleman, has a different level of susceptibility to control. As channels of distribution grow longer, the ability to control price, volume, promotion methods, and type of outlets is diminished. Some companies give up any attempt to control the end destiny of their products and are satisfied to place the goods in the hands of a middleman who passes them on for international distribution. Such a company cannot know where its product is going, what volume of sales can be expected, or the future of the international portion of its business.[8]

---

[8] Julia Michaels, "Why Heinz Went Sour in Brazil," *Advertising Age*, December 5, 1988, p. 61.

4. Coverage

Another major goal is full-market coverage to (1) gain the optimum volume of sales obtainable in each market, (2) secure a reasonable market share, and (3) attain satisfactory market penetration. Coverage may be assessed on geographic or other market segments. Adequate market coverage may require changes in distribution systems from country to country or time to time. Coverage is difficult to develop both in highly developed areas and in sparse markets; the former because of heavy competition and the latter because of inadequate channels.

Many companies do not attempt full-market coverage but seek significant penetration in major population centers. In some countries, two or three cities constitute the majority of the national buying power. For instance, 60 percent of the Japanese population lives in the Tokyo-Nagoya-Osaka market area which essentially functions as one massive city.

Coverage also includes the concept of full representation for all lines a company wishes to sell within a given market. Sometimes middlemen take on more lucrative parts of a line but neglect or refuse to handle other products that the manufacturer wants to emphasize. Without full-line coverage, a manufacturer can be seriously crippled in building profitable distribution. A company may prefer a nice, clean channel arrangement utilizing only one major type of distribution; but, to achieve coverage, it may have to use all available channels. A company, therefore, may have to use many different channels; its own sales force in one country, manufacturers' agent channels in another, and merchant wholesalers in still another.[9]

5. Character

The channel-of-distribution system selected must fit the character of the company and the markets in which it is doing business. Some obvious product requirements, often the first considered, relate to perishability or bulk of the product, complexity of sale, sales service required, and value of the product. Matching the character of the producer and middleman may be a more difficult task; sometimes meshing the two characters is so impossible companies have given up markets rather than compromise company standards. In other instances, company standards have been adhered to and local channel characteristics ignored with resulting distribution disasters.[10]

---

[9] "U.S. Companies Face Tough Task: Cracking the Japanese Market," *Journal of Commerce*, September 19, 1988, p. 9a.

[10] Shinya Nakata, "'Complicated and Inefficient,' or 'Tailored to Consumers' Needs'?" *Sumitomo Quarterly*, Summer 1987, pp. 10–13.

Channel commanders must be aware that channel patterns change; they cannot assume that once a channel has been developed to fit the character of both company and market that no more need be done. Great Britain, for example, has epitomized distribution through specialty-type middlemen; distributors, wholesalers, and retailers, in fact, all middlemen have traditionally worked within narrow product specialty areas. In recent years, however, there has been a trend toward broader lines, conglomerate merchandising, and mass marketing. The firm that neglects the growth of self-service, scrambled merchandising, or discounting may find it has lost large segments of its market because its channels no longer reflect the character of the market.

Continuity

Channels of distribution often pose longevity problems. Most agent middlemen firms tend to be small institutions. When one individual retires or moves out of a line of business, the company may find it has lost its distribution in that area. Wholesalers and especially retailers are not noted for their continuity in business either. Most middlemen have little loyalty to their vendors. They handle brands in good times when the line is making money, but quickly reject such products within a season or a year if they fail to produce during that period. Distributors and dealers are probably the most loyal middlemen, but even with them, manufacturers must attempt to build brand loyalty downstream in a channel lest middlemen shift allegiance to other companies or other inducements.

If a channel is to perform consistently well, it must have continuity, and this reason alone has prompted some companies to develop their own company-controlled distribution organizations. One American company in a highly competitive field of producers from Germany, England, and the Netherlands lost middlemen accounting for nearly 50 percent of its volume in Latin America within a year. The reason for the loss was more readily discovered than remedied. Two major competitors had simultaneously hit on methods of squeezing the U.S. firm out of the market. One, marketing a broad product line, forced distributors to drop the U.S. company's narrow line if they wished to continue as distributors of the broader line. The other company purchased an interest in several large distributors who carried the U.S. company's products. The U.S. company found that within a year it had lost over one quarter of its foreign distribution system. Such maneuvers in the United States would have been in violation of several laws covering unfair competition, lessening competition, and so forth, but many countries do not have antimonopoly laws and such activities are perfectly legal. Effective channels must be protected to ensure continuity.

DISTRIBUTION PATTERNS

International marketers need to have a general awareness of the patterns of distribution that confront them in world marketplaces. Nearly every international trading firm is forced by the structure of the market to use at least some middlemen in the distribution arrangement. It is all too easy to conclude that because the structural arrangements of foreign and domestic distribution seem alike, foreign channels are the same or similar to domestic channels of the same name. This is misleading. Only when the varied intricacies of actual distribution patterns are understood can the complexity of the distribution task be appreciated. The following description should dispel false notions or at least convey a sense of the variety of world distribution patterns.

General Patterns

Generalizing about internal distribution channel patterns of various countries throughout the world is almost as difficult as generalizing about behavior patterns of people throughout the world. There are certain patterns of similarity among distribution channels, and an understanding of the basic distribution alternatives lends a skeletal understanding of choices in all countries.

Despite similarities, marketing channels are not the same throughout the world. Marketing methods taken for granted in the United States are rare in many countries. One pattern that recurs in studies of various countries is that middlemen in most countries are predominantly very large or very small. The middle-sized wholesalers and retailers in the United States are unable to survive at either level in many economies.

Middlemen Services. Service attitudes of tradespeople vary sharply at both the retail and wholesale levels from country to country. In Egypt, for example, the primary purpose of the simple trading system is to handle the physical distribution of available goods. On the other hand, because there are so many tradespeople in India, margins are low and there is a continuing battle for customer preference. Both wholesalers and retailers try to offer extra services to make their goods attractive to consumers.

Line Breadth. Every nation has a distinct pattern relative to the breadth of line carried by wholesalers and retailers. The distribution system of some countries seems to be characterized by middlemen who carry or can get everything. In others, every middleman seems to be a specialist dealing only in extremely narrow lines. In the United States, a specialization appears to increase with firm size; in other countries, there is an inverse relationship.

Government regulations in some countries limit the breadth of line that can be carried by middlemen. Norway has specific licensing requirements for middlemen; and in Italy, there is municipal discretion over the lines to be handled. In the city of Milan a dairy store may sell boiled eggs or boiled rice with oil but may not sell boiled eggs with butter or boiled rice with tomato sauce. (Contrast this practice with the more modern outlook in some states in the United States, where for years grocery stores have been able to sell warm but not cold beer.) In selling a wide variety of products in many countries, Proctor & Gamble has encountered a host of restrictions that require continuous adaptation on its part. In Italy, for example, stores need a license for every product category they sell; there-fore, some sell only soaps and others sell only detergents. Imagine the effect on distribution costs when specific merchandising ordinances vary considerably from city to city. The end result has been a general stifling of progress in the distributive trades, discouragement of more advanced merchandising techniques, and the granting of a premium to inefficient practices.

Costs and Margins.   Cost levels and middleman margins vary widely from country to country depending on the level of competition; services offered; efficiencies or inefficiencies of scale; and geographic and turnover factors related to market size, purchasing power, tradition, and other basic determinants. In Italy, the political potency of small middlemen has kept direct competition to a minimum and costs high. In India, competition in large cities is so intense that costs are low and margins thin; but, in rural areas, the lack of capital has permitted the few traders with capital to gain monopolies with consequent high prices and wide margins. In most developing countries, manufacturers do not bear much of the market-ing burden but shift such functions as credit, storage, shipping, market development, and even research directly to the channel of distribution.

Channel Length.   Some correlation may be found in the stage of economic development and the length of marketing channels. In every country, of course, channels are likely to be shorter for industrial goods and for high-priced consumer goods than for low-priced products. In general, there is an inverse relationship between channel length and the size of the purchase. Even Korea and Japan, which have notoriously long distribution channels, have found that market development has had a major impact on shortening distribution channels. Such flattening of the distribution system eventually eliminates middlemen and therefore some markups; the consumer eventu-ally benefits from the greater efficiencies created by larger markets.[11]

Combination wholesaler-retailer or semi-wholesalers exist in many coun-

---

[11] "Levi Strauss Moves Closer to Its Distributors," *Business Europe*, March 15, 1985, p. 81.

tries, adding one or two links to the length of the distribution chain. Channels in the United States and in Russia are shorter than in most countries. In the United States, length is shortened by efficiencies of scale; in Russia, channels are shortened by administrative edict. This shortening often results in distribution inefficiencies because goods may not be available when or where needed.[12]

Nonexistent Channels. One of the things companies discover about international channel-of-distribution patterns is that in most countries adequate market coverage through a simple channel of distribution is nearly impossible. In many instances, appropriate channels do not exist; in others, parts of a channel system are available but others parts are not. Several distinct distribution channels must be established to reach different segments of a market; channels suitable for distribution in urban areas seldom provide adequate rural coverage. Companies often have to depart from their customary channel patterns to gain distribution. For example, Proctor & Gamble, well-known for its mass merchandising in the United States and a mass merchandising pioneer in Europe, sells soap and other products though door-to-door salespeople in the Philippines and other developing countries.

Japanese and American ingenuity triumphed again when Bristol-Myers Company and its Japanese joint-venture partner created a unique door-to-door program. One of their efforts is a combination door-to-door and consignment scheme. The Japanese householder is induced to accept, on consignment, a box including a variety of dentrifices, analgesics, and other home remedies. About every six months, a salesperson returns to replenish the collection and collect for the products that have been used. Who says there are no new marketing ideas under the sun?

Blocked Channels. International marketers are often blocked from using the channel of their choice. Blockage can be the result of competitors' already established lines in the various channels, trade associations or cartels having closed certain channels, or customary marketing patterns precluding market acceptance of still another middleman. Finally, a major reason for blockage is politics.

Competition for the few available middlemen in most of the world marketplaces creates extreme difficulties for the marketer seeking an outlet for a product. Blockages are intensified in international business because the number of middlemen available is small and the number of potential suppliers is large relative to the market size in most countries. Companies suffer through spotty distribution for extended periods of time because they simply cannot gain entry through existing channels and cannot afford

---

[12] "Moving toward Direct Distribution," *Business International*, April 5, 1985, p. 107.

to establish new ones. One manufacturer found he was absolutely prevented from entering European markets because every middleman who logically could handle his product was either financially tied to a competitor or had long-term relationships or commitments to competitors.[13]

Sometimes competition for distribution has been so intense that businessmen have established trade associations, cartels, or other regulatory groups to divide the market and eliminate new competition.

Associations of middlemen sometimes restrict the number of distribution alternatives available to a producer. Druggists in many countries have inhibited distribution of a wide range of goods through any retail outlets except drugstores. The drugstores, in turn, have been supplied by a relatively small number of wholesalers who have long-established relationships with their suppliers. Thus, through a combination of competition and association, a producer may be kept out of the market completely.

Blocked channels can be opened. Sometimes the company hoping to enter a market can buy equity in middlemen and assure itself of market entry. United Fruit Company, for example, found the only way it could gain satisfactory distribution in Europe was to purchase distributors. A blocked company may simply "buy distribution" by offering extremely wide margins, contract bonuses, or other forms of cash settlement to middlemen who take on their line.

Distribution in Japan has been long considered the most effective nontariff barrier to the Japanese market; it is the epitome of blocked channels. The distribution system is different enough from U.S. or European counterparts to give an advantage to domestic competitors.[14] One authority suggests that the Japanese system is characterized by three layers: (1) a structure dominated by many small wholesalers dealing with many small retailers; (2) unique trade customs; and (3) a philosophy shaped by a unique culture.[15]

It is not unusual for consumer goods to go through three or four intermediaries before reaching the consumer—producer to primary, secondary, regional, and local wholesaler, and finally to retailer to consumer. The high degree of fragmentation and specialization makes it difficult to go direct and thus forces a manufacturer to rely on middlemen with an elaborate set of trade customs. Since most retailers have limited access to capital, sales are generally made on a consignment basis with credits extending to several months. To facilitate the financing function and to competitively tie retailers to wholesalers, there is an elaborate rebate system with an

---

[13] Damon Darlin, "Shelf Control: 'Papa-Mama' Stores in Japan Wield Power to Hold Back Imports," The *Wall Street Journal*, November 14, 1988, p. 1.

[14] Vernon R. Alden, "Who Says You Can't Crack Japanese Markets?" *Harvard Business Review*, January–February 1987, pp. 52–56.

[15] For a complete discussion of these characteristics and Japanese distribution, see Mitsuaki Shimaguchi and Larry J. Rosenberg, "Demystifying Japanese Distribution," *Columbia Journal of World Business*, Spring 1979.

BOX 17–3
Evolving Middlemen—The Higgler

Although most Latin American countries consider smuggling a criminal offense, this informal trade is being regarded with increasing approval.

"Smugglers see themselves as valiant entrepreneurs who defy the restrictions on international trade being imposed by their countries. They are the heroes of capitalism," declares a Brazilian senator and former planning minister in a recent interview with a Brazilian newspaper.

In some countries, governments have become convinced it is better to accept unofficial trade and glean some benefit from it than continue prosecuting it. In Jamaica, smuggling has grown so that the prime minister became a staunch advocate of free trade, legalized the activity as a way of levying taxes and allaying the demand for foreign exchange in the black market. Smugglers in Jamaica have now been granted professional status and are called ICI—Independent Commercial Importers.

The great majority of Jamaica's 13,000 ICIs are women known as "higglers" who benefit from a special government exchange rate to go shopping abroad. When the higglers come home laden with bags of shoes, bottles, dresses, and other consumer goods, they come right in the country's front door. They even have two professional associations to defend their interests to authorities.

In Dominica, another Caribbean island, the government now relies on smugglers to boost the country's exports. Known as "hucksters," these unofficial businessmen buy fruits and vegetables from the island farmers, truck them to port, and ship them to Barbados or the nearby French colonies for sale. The government even donated a house to serve as a headquarters for the Hucksters Association. The hucksters are considered important to Dominica's economy because they bring in much needed hard currency and the island's 10,000 farmers depended on them to sell their farm surpluses.

Smugglers are considered as an escape valve for modernization in many countries. In Colombia, for instance, there are so many "San Andresitos," as the smugglers are known there, that the government has opted to look the other way and not dismantle street stalls. An estimated 35,000 establishments in the country are engaged exclusively in selling smuggled products.

Much of this economic activity is not reported for taxes. Thus, the reported gross national products (GNPs) in many of the countries is lower than it really is. This informal economy, sometimes referred to as underground economy, is considered to account for a large percentage of the GNP in many countries. In Peru, the informal or underground economy accounts for about 40 percent of the GNP and 60 percent of all hours worked. Smuggling, of course, is only one part of the underground economy.

Source: Adapted from "The Higglers," *World Press Review*, November 1988, pp. 48–49; and "Even Central Banks Do It," *World Press Review*, November 1988, p. 49.

estimated 500 variations. These and other inefficiencies in the system render the cost of Japanese consumer goods among the highest in the world and are major contributors to the high cost of living in Japan.[16] In addition, manufacturers use promissory notes with extended due dates (for periods as long as six months) to finance wholesalers and retailers. Storage facilities for inventories are limited so delivery is frequent and each order transaction small. Intermediaries receive a host of displays, advertising, management education programs, in-store demonstrations, and other dealer aids which strengthen the relationship with dealers.

Coupled with the close ties created by trade customs and the long structure of Japanese distribution channels is a unique philosophy that emphasizes loyalty, harmony, and friendship. Thus, long-term dealer/supplier relationships are difficult to change as long as each party perceives economic advantage. The advantage, then, is to the traditional partner, the insider. This is not to say that foreign firms are unsuccessful in penetrating Japan's blocked channels.[17] The key to success is understanding the environment and seeking local assistance. One of the advantages of entering a joint venture with a Japanese firm is immediate access to the Japanese distribution system.[18]

Stocking and Servicing. The high cost of credit, danger of loss through inflation, lack of capital, and other concerns cause foreign middlemen in many countries to carry inadequate inventories, resulting in out-of-stock conditions and sales lost to competitors. Physical distribution lags intensify this problem so that, in many cases, the manufacturer must provide local warehousing or extend long credit to encourage middlemen to carry large inventories. Considerable ingenuity, assistance and, perhaps, pressure are required to induce middlemen in most countries to carry adequate or even minimal inventories.

The services required or desired by manufacturers may be quite dissimilar from those middlemen are willing or able to furnish. Because middlemen are unable to extend adequate credit to their customers, the selling company itself may have to take on the credit burden. In most nations, middlemen are notoriously disinterested in promoting or selling individual items of merchandise; the manufacturer then must provide adequate inducement to the middlemen or undertake much of the promotion and selling effort.

Power and Competition. The structure of wholesaling, a cluster of extremely large middlemen at one end of a scale and a mass of small middlemen at the the other end, provides the basis for an interesting study in

---

[16] "Japan's Master of Retailing," *World Press Review*, January 1989, p. 52.

[17] See, for example, Vernon R. Alden, "Who Says You Can't Crack Japanese Markets?" *Harvard Business Review*, January–February 1987, pp. 52–56.

[18] Urban C. Lehner, "U.S. Pushing Japan to Liberalize Its Retail Distribution Network," *The Asian Wall Street Journal Weekly*, August 22, 1988, p. 7.

contrasts. Large-small patterns seem to exemplify wholesaling in many countries. In Malaysia, for example, fewer than a dozen (European) merchant houses handle over half the import trade while hundreds of local trading companies handle the balance. In Israel, there are some 1,500 wholesalers; most are small except Hamashbir Hamerkazi, the giant Israeli wholesaler. This firm handles all kinds of products and has full or partial ownership in 12 major industrial firms; it reportedly handles approximately one fifth the wholesaling volume of Israel. Such giant wholesalers are major factors in the political and competitive lives of their countries. Their power lies in their financial, wholesaling, and manufacturing interests within the country.

There appears to be a worldwide trend toward more vertical integration from the wholesale or retail level back to manufacturing. Such a development is of great concern to marketers who have been dependent on wholesalers to handle their products because they often find the channel blocked by the wholesaler handling its own custom-manufactured products. In India, outside companies have a hard time gaining distribution because the large wholesalers, by providing financial and marketing services, have such an entrenched position that they obtain monopsonistic power (the market condition that exists when there is only one buyer).

Another development in the wholesale market that tends to concentrate distribution power in the hands of a relatively small number of wholesalers is the development of voluntary chains sponsored by wholesalers. According to a government study in Britain, one third of the soft goods wholesalers have set up voluntary retail chains that handle nearly three fourths of the volume in those goods.

The financial power of large wholesalers affects the geographic distribution patterns they undertake. In Japan, Israel, and Australia, nearly all major wholesalers operate on a nationwide basis. In sharp contrast are countries such as Italy, Turkey, and Egypt, where government regulations, scattered markets, and poor transportation facilities have limited the growth of national wholesalers. A marketer must contact many middlemen to establish distribution.

Services and Efficiency. A wholesaler is never considered a strong, hard-selling middleman, but in some countries, wholesalers and some distributors perform minimal selling functions. The oft-repeated complaint that wholesalers do an inadequate job of selling merchandise does have exceptions. In some countries where there are strong national distributors, there is usually a high level of selling; in fact, wholesalers in some such countries utilize their position in pressure selling; in production-oriented socialist states such as Yugoslavia, wholesalers have taken over the selling function from manufacturers.

Most wholesalers offer credit, but the high cost of money in many countries keeps inventories at minimal levels and reorder service is slow. Inflation may serve as a countervailing force when wholesalers (or retailers)

BOX 17–4
Selling Do-It-Yourself Lumber and Hardware Stores to the Europeans

Wickes Corporation, the home improvement materials retailer, has 45 home-improvement centers in Belgium, Holland, England, and West Germany. It is considered to be one of the most successful retailing ventures ever launched in foreign markets by a U.S. company. It is also one of the corporation's most profitable divisions, earning 30 percent on assets. However, it was not all that easy at first. They had to overcome:

Tradition.   Until Wickes entered Europe, "Supermarkets of hardware and lumber" for do-it-yourselfers were unknown. Most such supplies were sold to professionals in "trade-only stores." Europeans didn't "do-it-themselves."

Competition and resistance.   In several cities, local sellers of building materials persuaded their friendly burgomasters or relatives on town councils to reject or stall the company's applications for permission to open stores.

Bureaucratic delays.   There was confusion over the company's designation as a retailer of building materials rather than the more normal wholesaler. At one point, they were authorized to sell hammers to the public but not nails.

Supplier cartels.   Manufacturer's cartels were reluctant to supply Wickes for fear that the traditional stores would retaliate against the cartels.

They managed to overcome all the obstacles and things are more normal, (i.e., competition from European imitators is now their main problem). In Holland, the locally owned Gamma chain has 58 stores to Wickes' 18; in Belgium, Grand Bazaar has 35 to Wickes' 9; in Germany, OBI chain has 56 stores to 10, and so on.

Source: Adapted from John Quirt, "Wickes Corp.'s Retailing Triumph in Europe," *Fortune*, August 13, 1979, pp. 178–84.

purchase in larger-than-normal quantities to establish a supply of merchandise before price increases.

Retail Patterns

Retailing shows even greater diversity in its structure than does wholesaling. In some countries, such as Italy and Morocco, retailing is composed largely of specialty houses carrying narrow lines. In other countries such as Finland, most retailers carry a more general line of merchandise. Retail size is represented at one end by Japan's giant Mitsukoshi Ltd., which reportedly enjoys the patronage of more than 100,000 customers every day. The other extreme is represented in the market of Ibadan, Nigeria, where some 3,000 one- or two-person stalls serve not many more customers.

Size Patterns.   The extremes in size in retailing are similar to those that predominate in the wholesaling field. Exhibit 17–2 dramatically illustrates some of the basic retailing relationships. Effective interpretation requires analysis of per capita consumption expenditures, average total sales per retail store, and number of customers per retail store. The statistics alone do not tell the whole story; imagine how much wider the spread would be if other less-developed countries of the world were considered. Imagine, too, the impact of such variation on wholesale structure and channel policy. The retail structure and the problems it engenders cause real difficulties for the international marketing firm selling consumer goods. Large dominant middlemen are approachable, but there is no adequate channel of

EXHIBIT 17–2   Retail Patterns in 18 Countries

Country	Population (millions)	GDP per Capita	Consumption per Capita	Number of Retailers
Argentina	30	4,314	3,623	445,800
Belgium	10	8,754	7,534	121,700
Colombia	28	1,424	871	500
France	55	9,962	8,196	604,000
West Germany	61	10,684	7,648	401,300
Greece	10	3,871	2,814	164,000
India	738	242	175	450,000
Ireland	3	5,077	3,356	33,850
Italy	58	6,122	4,403	1,029,200
Japan	120	8,973	5,724	1,628,600
Republic of Korea	40	1,754	1,213	637,700
Malaysia	13	1,781	932	80,175
Mexico	77	2,346	1,423	463,612
Netherlands	14	9,616	6,190	143,200
Panama	2	2,102	1,016	6,611
Philippines	53	786	461	327,573
United Kingdom	56	8,495	5,906	343,600
United States	236	13,152	8,043	1,855,100

SOURCES: Population data taken from: *Population and Vital Statistics Report* (New York: United Nations 1985); GDP per capita data from: *National Accounts Statistics: Analysis of Main Aggregates* (New York: United Nations, 1985). Consumption data from: *Worldwide Economic Indicators* (New York: Business International Corp., 1985). Retailing data from: *International Marketing Data and Statistics 13th ed., 1988/89* and *European Marketing Data and Statistics 24th ed, 1988/89* (London: Euromonitor Publications Ltd.).

Modern supermarket and traditional food store in Mexico. MNCs must adapt their distribution strategies to reflect the traditional and modern distribution systems that exist side by side in many developing markets.

distribution through which to make an effective marketing presentation to small retailers who, in the aggregate, handle a great volume of sales. Consider the problems in Italy where official figures show there are 865,000 retail stores or one store for every 66 Italians. Of the 340,000 food stores, fewer than 1,500 can be classified as large. Thus, middlemen are critical to achieve adequate distribution in Italy.

Change.   Retailing around the world has been in a state of active ferment for some years. The rate of change appears to be directly related to the stage and speed of economic development in the countries concerned, but even the least developed countries are experiencing dramatic changes. Self-service retailing has grown at an overwhelming rate throughout the world. Supermarkets of one variety or another are blossoming in developed and underdeveloped countries alike. Discount houses have taken increasing shares of the market in countries where such activity is legal.[19] Automatic vending and mail-order trends are being set around the world; in both fields, the United States has been eclipsed by fast-moving business people in other countries.[20]

Change appears to be the key word in the food industry which is marked by highly developed voluntary chains, multiple chain stores, consumer co-ops, supermarkets, mail-order houses, and convenience stores. In fact, the fastest growing retailers in Japan are the convenience stores. 7-Eleven, the U.S. convenience store, has opened over 3,349 franchised stores in

---

[19] Bill Kelley, "The New Wave from Europe," *Sales And Marketing Management*, November 1987, pp. 45–50.

[20] Madhav P. Kacker, "The Metamorphosis of European Retailing," *European Journal of Marketing* 20, no. 8 (1988), pp. 15–22.

BOX 17–5
What Time Did You Say the Store Opens?

On Friday evenings, shops in Rome are now allowed to stay open until 9 P.M., an hour or more later than before. This modest attempt at deregulation has met with widespread opposition from storekeepers. The Rome Friday-evening dispute is just one knot in a tight tangle of retail trade rules.

A shopper is confronted with a jungle of regulated opening schedules that vary according to the kind of store, according to the season, and often from city to city. You can enter a food shop and ask for raw ham, an excellent Italian product, but if it's Thursday afternoon, you won't be able to get it because Thursday afternoons this sort of store is allowed to sell only cooked food. Some clothing shops are closed on Monday morning; others are closed on Saturday afternoon. Fish dealers demanded and got the right to close Monday mornings, butchers now want to close Monday afternoons rather than on Thursday afternoons. Most shops close for up to three hours in midday, but food stores open earlier in the morning and reopen later in the afternoon. Both hairdressers and barbershops are closed on Sunday and Monday. On other days, barbershops close at midday like most other stores. Hairdressers don't, but they open later in the morning and close earlier in the afternoon, a schedule similar to that of hotel barbershops.

The only exception, tourist resorts, where most restrictions are waived during the high season. In cities, on the other hand, many shops close down in August along with quite a few that are supposed to stay open. The few stores open in August often hike their prices and unload poor quality goods.

Retailers dread the prospect of somebody else's store staying open while theirs is shut. Powerful shopkeepers' associations have been created to keep politicians aware of their demands—keep everybody closed by law.

Source: Leo J. Wollemborg, "Italy a Shopper's Paradise? Read On," *The Wall Street Journal*, July 1, 1985, p. 12.

Japan.[21] Franchising is not limited to convenience stores and fast-foods; major franchisers include soft drinks, automotive services, automobile rentals, and hotels and motels.

Automation is also an important change occurring in retailing. It is now a reality in Europe as retailers seek greater efficiency to offset increasing price competition. An estimated $2 billion was spent by 1990 for electronic point-of-purchase systems. Bar coding of merchandise, electronic inventory control between manufacturers and retailer, and electronic funds transfer at the point of sale are becoming realities among major European retailers.[22]

---

[21] Shinichi Sano, "Japan's 7-Eleven Franchises Face Early Burnout," *The Asian Wall Street Journal*, August 22, 1988, p. 14.

[22] "You Can't Market Variety," *Forbes*, July 27, 1987, pp. 82–83.

Self-Service. Started in the United States in 1930, self-service had only a few early imitators in other parts of the world. Sweden and Germany, for example, opened self-service stores in 1938. Since the end of World War II, however, self-service has been a major element in world retailing. Because of the larger unit size, share of sales has grown even more rapidly. The effect on a manufacturer's marketing policy has been little short of revolutionary. Just a few years ago, a company selling food had to have literally hundreds of salespeople; now many companies have cut back their sales forces to the small number required to deal with wholesalers and self-service chains. The small grocers are never visited by these salespeople and must now seek out merchandise themselves through wholesalers. Some companies, such as Britain's Beechams, have developed various sales forces to deal with the different types of outlets; one force for grocery chains, one for large supermarkets, one for wholesalers, and one for the small retailers.

Direct Marketing. Selling directly to the consumer through the mail, by telephone, or door-to-door is certainly most highly developed in the United States. Although some countries are just beginning, there is a decided trend toward direct sales almost everywhere. Direct marketing sales totaled $10 billion in West Germany, $22.4 billion in Japan, and over $3 billion each in France and the United Kingdom.[23]

Products sold through direct marketing include books, insurance, general merchandise, electronic gear, home furnishings, housewares, and cosmetics. Avon Products, Inc. the cosmetics firm, has an Asian sales force of 10,000 and its door-to-door sales are more than $200 million. Changing lifestyles, acceptance of credit cards, and improved postal and telephone services in many countries assist in the growing trend of direct marketing.[24] The growth in direct marketing has been so pronounced that consumer protection laws controlling the commercial use of mailing lists are becoming commonplace.[25]

Resistance to Change. Such developments as consolidation of middlemen, larger store size, self-service, and discounting have not gone unnoticed by small merchants; distribution is enmeshed in a battle between politically powerful independent retailers and wholesalers and economically powerful chain discount and department stores.[26] In many cases, it

---

[23] For a brief survey of the growth of direct marketing see Sean Milmo, "Direct Marketers in Europe Planning Regional Operations," *Business Marketing,* September 1988, pp. 20–24.

[24] Elaine Santoro, "Telemarketing Globalized," *Direct Marketing,* June 1987, pp. 102–10.

[25] Tom Eisenhart, "Savvy Mailers Tap Foreign Markets," *Business Marketing,* September 1988, pp. 55–65.

[26] "Tough German Law on Loss Leading Likely," *Business Europe,* March 29, 1985, p. 97.

BOX 17–6
**When Is a Supermarket not a Supermarket but a Department Store, or
Maybe Even a Shopping Center?**

"When people of other countries, especially Americans try to understand
the structure of the Japanese retail industry, the first thing that puzzles
them is the name used to designate the various kinds of retail businesses.
When they hear the word *supermarket*, they probably call to mind a self-
service grocery store dealing mainly in foodstuffs and housed in an independent, single store structure with a spacious parking lot."

A supermarket in Japan, however, is quite different from that picture.
What the Japanese call supermarkets are usually establishments in large
cities, occupying two- or three-story structures and sometimes four- or five-
story structures. They sell foodstuffs, daily necessities, and clothing on respective floors. Some even sell furniture, electric home appliances, stationary,
and sporting goods, and have a restaurant section. In Japan, the four- or
five-story supermarkets stocked with a variety of goods, are sometimes called
a GMS (general merchandise store). However, this is different from the American GMS, typical examples of which are Sears, Roebuck & Company and
J. C. Penney Company. The merchandise lines of American GMS's are mainly
nonfood items—apparel, household goods, and furniture. Essential to the
Japanese GMS are self-service sales of food stuffs and daily necessities. Considerably different from the department store in America and Europe, the
Japanese department store emphasizes foodstuffs and operates a restaurant
on the premises. It crams into an eight or nine-story building as many kinds
of merchandise as possible.

When Japanese say shopping center, they normally mean a building in
which many specialty shops are housed. These differences also bewilder
Japanese who go to America and see that retail outlets described by a certain
name are not the same as a store in Japan that bears the same generic
name. Writing about Sears Roebuck department stores, Japanese newspapers
were at a loss as to the proper generic name for them. They settled on a
word that literally means *popular department store*, a term that does not convey
a clear concept to the Japanese.

Source: Shinya Nakata, "Retailing: Variety of Means and the Conglo-Merchants,"
Sumitomo Quarterly, Winter 1987, p. 16.

is the manufacturers who get caught in the middle of this battle. If they
avoid the large-volume retailers, these retailers turn to other sources, and
the manufacturers have lost a portion of the market. If they move to the
large-volume outlets, they are likely to be scorned by small-scale middlemen
and lose that market segment.

In some countries, small but numerous independent merchants seem
to be waging an effective delaying battle against discounting. In Italy, a

new retail outlet must obtain a license from a municipal board composed of well-entrenched local tradespeople hardly ready to welcome new competition. In a two-year period, some 200 applicants seeking to establish supermarkets in Milan were able to secure only 10 new licenses. In Belgium, national legislation does not permit new department stores to be opened in towns of less than 50,000, and any store that employs as few as five persons is considered a department store. In Norway and Sweden, potential entrepreneurs must serve a long apprenticeship in the business before they are considered for licensing.

Even in such a progressive country as Japan, supermarkets and chains have run into formidable opposition. One chain of medium-sized supermarkets was unable to open at a newly constructed location because local opposition invoked a national "large retail store law" that forces chains to negotiate with local merchants about days, hours, and store size. In this particular case, local retailers had pushed for a prefectural local government law and had it passed while the store was being built. Nevertheless, Japanese supermarkets number over 5,000 and account for 12–14 percent of retail grocery sales.

It appears in many cases that governments have placed a premium on retailing inefficiency to support politically powerful merchants. Taxes are a favorite restrictive tool of the small retailer groups to penalize the discounter or self-service store. Even health and sanitary regulations are called into play to hamper large-scale retailing. Milk in Switzerland, for example, may not be sold with other merchandise; because supermarkets cannot handle this product, small dairy product retailers flourish.

Nationalism has been a major force limiting the introduction of mass merchandising techniques by foreign firms. Unilever, for example, found consumers in Turkey were chafing under the exorbitant prices charged by monopolistic local tradesmen, so it purchased a fleet of vans and introduced mobile supermarkets to the countryside. The reaction was swift and certain; local merchants found their monopolies evaporating, contacted the government, and within a matter of months, Unilever was out of the Turkish retailing picture. Through a joint venture, Safeway attempted to introduce a series of supermarkets in Japan, but as soon as plans were announced, nationalistic groups seized on this as a major cause. The resulting furor caused parliamentary debate on the subject and Safeway discreetly withdrew.

Opposition to retail innovation prevails everywhere, yet in the face of all the restrictions and hindrances, self-service, discount merchandising, and large-scale chains continue to grow because they offer the consumer a broad range of quality brand products at advantageous prices. Ultimately the consumer does prevail.

Franchising.   The same factors that spurred the growth of franchising in the U.S. domestic economy have led to its growth in foreign markets.

Franchising is an attractive form of corporate organization for companies wishing to expand quickly with low capital investment. The franchising system combines the knowledge of the franchiser with the local knowledge and entrepreneurial spirit of the franchisee. Foreign laws and regulations are not overly restrictive toward franchising because it tends to foster local ownership, operations, and employment.[27]

More than 300 U.S. franchising companies operate almost 32,000 outlets in foreign countries; Canada is the dominant market with Japan and the United Kingdom second and third in importance.[28] U.S. franchisers operate in most of the world.

Fast foods were among the first U.S. industries to franchise abroad and they continue to expand rapidly in countries from Latin America to Asia.[29] Most major U.S. fast-food companies such as McDonald's, Pizza Hut, and Kentucky Fried Chicken have investments offshore. Some are having a profound effect on traditional businesses. In England, for example, it is estimated that annual franchised sales of fast foods is nearly $2 billion which accounts for 30 percent of all foods eaten outside the home there.[30]

GOVERNMENT-AFFILIATED MIDDLEMEN

Marketers must deal with governments in every country of the world. Products, services, and commodities for the government's own use are always procured through government purchasing offices at federal, regional, and local levels. As more and more social services are undertaken by governments, the level of government purchasing activity escalates. In the Netherlands, the state's purchasing office deals with more than 10,000 suppliers in 20 countries. About one third of the products purchased by that agency are produced outside the Netherlands; 90 percent of foreign purchases are handled through the Dutch representatives. The other 10 percent are purchased directly from producing companies. In planned economies of Eastern Europe, most import-export activity is handled by government agencies. In the Soviet Union, for example, 50 foreign trading offices are part of the Ministry of Foreign Trade. Each has its own organization and is responsible for an exclusive product specialty. These organiza-

---

[27] "U.S. Franchising Industry Promotes Increased Domestic and International Business Activity," *Business America*, March 3, 1986, pp. 11–13.

[28] "Franchising Abroad Is Hot—Perhaps Too Hot," *The Wall Street Journal*, April 25, 1988, p. 27.

[29] "Franchisers Find a Welcome in Japan," *Sales and Marketing Management*, September 1987, p. 32.

[30] Joann Lublin, "U.S. Franchisers Learn Britain Isn't Easy," *The Wall Street Journal*, August 16, 1988, p. 18.

tions, in turn, are represented by government-owned foreign trading companies. The Amtorg Trading Corporation is responsible for handling exports and imports between the United States and the Soviet Union. Most countries have specialized trading organizations handling one specific type of product (such as electrical machinery) and some deal directly without any Amtorg-type clearing agency.

Various patterns of representation are employed in dealing with government-affiliated middlemen—the company may deal directly with the government agency or may use an agent middleman. Only rarely are merchant middlemen employed to handle goods for sale to or through government agencies. In some countries, a foreign company or agent may deal only with the foreign trading organization; in turn, it attempts to represent the interests of the company to customers in that country. Such arrangements offer little control over the selling effort and are generally unsatisfactory.

In countries such as Poland, Czechoslovakia, Hungary, and Bulgaria, companies may hire an exclusive agent who deals with foreign trading organizations and also represents the product to the foreign consumer or user. In this arrangement, the foreign trading organization is merely involved in handling the permits and paperwork, leaving the marketing to the agent.

ALTERNATIVE MIDDLEMAN CHOICES

Once the market has clarified company objectives and policies, the selection of specific intermediaries necessary to develop a channel must be made. In all instances involving middlemen external to the company, only two basic types of middlemen are available: agent middlemen who directly represent the principal rather than themselves and merchant middlemen who take title to the goods and buy and sell on their own account. The distinction between agent and merchant middlemen is an important one because a manufacturer's control of the distribution process can be affected by the choice of one or the other.

Agent middlemen work on a commission and arrange for sales in the foreign country, but do not take title to the merchandise. The manufacturer establishes policy guidelines and prices and requires its agents to provide sales records and customer information. In some cases, an agent middleman works from the company's office resulting in a close working relationship.

Because merchant middlemen actually take title to the manufacturer's goods, they tend to be less controllable than agent middlemen. Merchant middlemen provide a variety of import and export wholesaling functions involving purchasing for their own account and selling in other countries. The merchant middleman bears the majority of trading risks for all products handled. Because merchant middlemen are primarily concerned with sales and profit margins on their merchandise, they are frequently criticized for not always representing the best interests of a manufacturer. Unless they have a franchise or a strong and profitable brand, merchant middlemen seek goods from any source and are likely to have low brand loyalty. Ease of contact, minimized credit risk, and elimination of all merchandise handling outside the United States are some of the advantages of using merchant middlemen.

Middlemen are not clear-cut, precise, easily defined entities. It is exceptional to find a firm that represents one of the pure types identified here. Thus intimate knowledge of middlemen functions is especially important in international activity because misleading titles can easily fool a marketer unable to look beyond mere names. What functions, for example, are performed by the British middleman called a *stockist* or, for that matter, an exporter or importer? One exporter may, in fact, be an agent middleman, whereas another is a merchant. Many, if not most, international middlemen wear several hats and can be clearly identified only in the context of their relationship with a specific firm. One company, for example, engages in both importing and exporting; acts both as an agent and a merchant middleman; operates from offices in the United States, Germany, and Great Britain; provides financial services; and acts as a freight forwarder. It would be difficult to put this company into an appropriate pigeonhole. Many firms work in a single capacity, but the conglomerate type of middleman described here is a major force in some parts of international business.

Only by analyzing middlemen functions in skeletal simplicity can the nature of the channels be determined. Three alternatives are presented: first, middlemen physically located in the manufacturer's home country; next, middlemen located in foreign countries; and finally, a company-owned system.

Home Country Middlemen

Home country or domestic middlemen are located in the same country as the producing firm and provide marketing services from a domestic base. By selecting domestic middlemen as intermediaries in the distribution processes, companies are leaving the responsibility of managing foreign market distribution to others. They must accept the marketing effort and channel selection offered by these middlemen. Domestic middlemen offer many advantages to companies with small international sales volume—those inexperienced with foreign markets, not wanting to become immediately involved with the complexities of international marketing, and not wanting to sell abroad with minimum financial and management commitment. A major trade-off for using domestic middlemen is that the marketer has less control over the entire process than if foreign middlemen are used. Domestic middlemen are most likely to be used when the marketer is uncertain and/or desires to minimize financial and management investment. A brief discussion of the more frequently used domestic middlemen follows.

Export Management Company.   The export management company (EMC) is a particularly important agent middleman for firms with relatively small international volume or for those that do not want to involve their own personnel in the international function. EMC firms range in size from one person upward to 100 and handle about 10 percent of the manufactured goods exported. Whether handling 5 clients or 100, the stock in trade of the EMC is personalized service. Typically, the EMC becomes an integral part of the marketing operations of the client companies. Working under the name of the manufacturers, the EMC functions as a low-cost, independent marketing department with direct responsibility to the parent firm. The working relationship is so close that customers seldom realize they are not dealing directly with the export department of the company. (See Exhibit 17–3.)

EXHIBIT 17–3   How Does an EMC Operate?

Most export management companies offer a wide range of services and assistance, including:

Researching foreign markets for a client's products.

Traveling overseas to determine the best method of distributing the product.

Appointing distributors or commission representatives as needed in individual foreign countries, frequently within an already existing overseas network created for similar goods.

Exhibiting the client's products at international trade shows, such as U.S. Department of Commerce-sponsored commercial exhibitons at trade fairs and U.S. Export Development Offices around the world.

Handling the routine details in getting the product to the foreign customer—export declarations, shipping and customs documentation, insurance, banking, and instructions for special export packing and marking.

Granting the customary finance terms to the trade abroad and assuring payment to the manufacturer of the product.

Preparing advertising and sales literature in cooperation with the manufacturer and adapting it to overseas requirements for use in personal contacts with foreign buyers.

Corresponding in the necessary foreign languages.

Making sure that goods being shipped are suitable for local conditions, and meet overseas legal and trade norms, including labeling, packaging, purity, and electrical characteristics.

Advising on overseas patent and trademark protection requirement.

SOURCE: "The Export Management Company," U.S. Dept. of commerce, Washington, D.C.

The EMC provides many services for the manufacturer; in all instances, however, the main functions are contact with foreign customers (sometimes through an EMC's own foreign branches) and negotiations for sales.[31] An EMC's specialization in a given field often makes it possible to offer a level of service that could not be attained by the manufacturer without years of groundwork.[32]

The EMC may take full or partial responsibility for promotion of the goods; credit arrangements; physical handling; market research; and information on financial, patent, and licensing matters. The EMC depends on commissions for compensation, but may also receive a retainer and various other fees.

Two of the chief advantages of using EMCs are (1) minimum investment on the part of the company to get into international markets, and (2) no company personnel or major expenditure of managerial effort. The result, in effect, is an extension of the market for the firm with negligible financial or personnel commitments.

The major disadvantage is that EMCs can seldom afford to make the kind of market investment needed to establish deep distribution for products because they must have immediate sales payout to survive. Such a situation does not offer the market advantages gained by a company that can afford to use company personnel. Carefully selected EMCs can do an excellent job, but the manufacturer must remember the EMC is dependent on sales volume for compensation and probably will not push the manufacturer's line if it is spread too thinly, generates too small a volume from a given principal, or cannot operate profitably in the short run. Then the EMC becomes an order taker and not the desired substitute for an international marketing department.

Trading Companies.   Trading companies have a long and honorable history as important intermediaries in the development of trade between nations. Trading companies accumulate, transport, and distribute goods from many countries. In concept, the trading company has changed little in hundreds of years.

Trading companies were important in the colonial movement and continue to be important in trade with developing countries. The English Hudson's Bay Company and East India Company were the trading vehicles of the 16th, 17th, and 18th centuries. The United Africa Company (now a subsidiary of Unilever), formed in 1929 by joining several existing trading

---

[31] The EMC was formerly known as a Combination Export Manager (CEM).

[32] A detailed explanation of the EMC and other middlemen can be found in "Basic Question: To Export Yourself or to Hire Someone to Do It for You?" *Business America*, April 27, 1987, pp. 14–17.

BOX 17–7

Mitsubishi—A Giant Japanese Industrial, Trading, and Banking Conglomerate, Annual Sales in Billions of Dollars

Trading:

Mitsubishi Corp.	$68.3

Oil:

Mitsubishi Oil	$6.5

Autos:

Mitsubishi Motors	$5.4

Foods:

Kirin Brewery	$4.2

Cement, glass, paper:

Asahi Glass	$2.3
Mitsubishi Mining & Cement	1.2
Mitsubishi Paper Mills	0.7

Metals:

Mitsubishi Metal	$1.6
Mitsubishi Steel	0.4
Mitsubishi Aluminum	0.4

Transport:

Nippon Yusen Kaisha	$2.8
Mitsubishi Warehouse and Transportation	0.3

Banking:

Mitsubishi Bank	$84.1 (assets)
Mitsubishi Trust & Banking	18.9 (assets)

Electrical and optical equipment:

Mitsubishi Electric	$6.0
Nippon Kogaku	0.6

Machinery, ships, arms:

Mitsubishi Heavy Industries	$6.5
Mitsubishi Kakoki Kaisha	0.2

Real estate and construction:

Mitsubishi Estate	$0.7
Mitsubishi Construction	0.4

Banking:

Mitsubishi Bank— branches	$4,000 (assets)
Mitsubishi Trust & Banking	600 (assets)
Mitsubishi Bank of California	500 (assets)

Chemicals, fibers:

Mitsubishi Chemical Industries	$3.9
Mitsubishi Petrochemical	2.0

Trading:

Mitsubishi International	$13,900
Koppel Inc.—grain elevators and shipping	465
RJM Co.—steel wholesaler, 2/3-owned	11

Marketing:

Mitsubishi cars and trucks (Imported by Chrysler)	$743
Nikon cameras, optical equipment (Imported by Nippon Kogaku subsidiary)	156
Semiconductors and computers (Imported by Mitsubishi Electronics America)	18
Kirin beer (Imported by wholly-owned distributor)	3

Manufacturing, other investments:

Amorient Petroleum—50% owned Filling stations	$257
Fletcher Oil & Refining—20% owned Oil refining	200
Mitsubishi Electric Sales America TV sets, video equipment	130
Chino mine—1/3 owned Copper mining	130
Mitsubishi Aircraft International Corporate aircraft	90
Palmco Coconut and palm oil refining	59
Bonaventure Hotel—Los Angeles— 50% owned	48
ATR Wire & Cable—20% owned Steel tire cord	25

BOX 17–7 *(continued)*

Mitsubishi Gas Chemical	0.9	MHI Corrugating Machinery	
Mitsubishi Rayon	0.9	—50% owned	10
Mitsubishi Monsanto Chemical	0.7	Dosanko Foods—40% owned	2
Mitsubishi Plastic Industries	0.4	Fast-food chain	
Insurance:			
Meiji Mutual Life	$3.5 (premium	MIC Petroleum	0
Insurance	income)	Oil exploration	
Tokio Marine & Fire	2.5 (premium		
Insurance	income)		

companies, has a series of department stores, retail grocery stores, and automobile agencies throughout the African continent.

The rise of Middle Eastern countries as consumer markets emphasizes the importance of trading companies in reaching unique markets. Patterns vary widely, many local companies are built around families who have been merchants in the Middle East for generations.

The British firm; Gray MacKenzie and Company, is typical of companies operating in the Middle East. It has some 70 salespersons and handles consumer products ranging from toiletries to Mercury outboard motors and Scotch whiskey. The key advantage to this type of trading company is that it covers the entire Middle East. Some companies prefer to deal with the strongest trading company they can find in each country.

Large, established trading companies generally are located in developed countries selling manufactured goods to developing countries and buying back their raw materials and unprocessed goods. Quite a different pattern is encountered with Japanese trading companies that were formed about 1700 to facilitate distribution of goods within the country. They later developed into companies emphasizing the importing of goods into Japan. Their current role is that of merchant importers and exporters with operations around the world. Some 300 are engaged in foreign and domestic trade through 2,000 branch offices outside Japan and handle over $300 billion (U.S.) in trading volume annually. They perform five major functions: the importing and exporting functions per se, financing, development of joint ventures, technical assistance and advice, and production of goods.

For companies seeking entrance to the complicated Japanese distribution system, the Japanese trading company offers one of the easiest routes to success. The omnipresent trading companies virtually control distribution through all levels of channels in Japan. Many companies have experienced greater success selling consumer goods through trading companies than through other types of middlemen. Since trading companies may control many of the distributors and maintain broad distribution channels, they provide the best means for intensive coverage of the market.[33]

An increasingly important part of trading company business consists of sales to markets in countries other than Japan; third nation or offshore deals make up a growing part of trading company business. Mitsui and Company, for example, helps export American grain to Europe. Nissho-Iwai Corporation arranges for athletic shoes to be manufactured in South Korea and Taiwan for Nike Inc. of Beaverton, Oregon. The nine largest Japanese trading companies have sales to other nations in excess of 10.6 percent of their combined sales. Do not think of Japanese trading companies as a means to only Japanese markets.

Because they are efficient in foreign marketing, and because they sometimes encourage small producers to enter international markets, foreign trading companies are generally favored by their governments. Brazil, for example, passed a law in the early 1970s giving trading companies a variety of tax advantages; by 1978, 40 trading companies had been formed. One of the chief advantages of the Brazilian arrangement is the loans trading companies receive to purchase local products that the trading companies then market abroad. These companies have been a major factor in facilitating and enlarging Brazilian exports of manufactured goods.

U.S. Export Trading Companies.[34]   The Export Trading Company Act of 1982 (ETC) allowed producers of similar products to form export trading companies. A major goal of the ETC Act was to increase U.S. exports by encouraging more efficient export trade services to producers and suppliers to improve the availability of trade finance; and to remove antitrust disincentives to export activities. By providing U.S. businesses with an opportunity to obtain antitrust preclearance for specified export activities, the ETC Act creates a more favorable environment for the formation of joint export ventures. Through such joint ventures, U.S. firms can take advantage of economies of scale, spread risk, and pool their expertise. In addition, through joint selling arrangements, domestic competitors can avoid inter-firm rivalry in foreign markets. Prior to the passage of the ETC Act, competing companies could not engage in joint exporting efforts without possible violation of antitrust provisions. The only other way that competing firms

---

[33] For an insightful discussion of trading companies, see Takeo Kikkawa, "How and Why Did Sogo Shosha (General Trading Companies) Develop in Japan?" *Aoyama Business Review* no. 13, (March 1988), pp. 47–63.

[34] For a complete report on ETCs, see "Export Trading Companies," *Business America,* October 12, 1987, pp. 2–9.

could avoid possible antitrust violations was to join a Webb-Pomerene export association (WPEA). However, WPEA rules on antitrust are not as clear as those under the ETC Act which permits the issuance of specific antitrust exemption certificates prior to the formation of an ETC.[35] The other important provision of the ETC Act is to permit bank holding companies to own ETCs. Prior to the ETC Act, banks were not permitted to own commercial enterprises. Immediately after passage of the ETC Act, several major companies (General Electric, Sears Roebuck, K mart and others) announced the development of export trading companies. In most cases, these export firms did not require the protection of the ETC Act since they initially operated independently of other enterprises. They provided international sales for U.S. companies to a limited extent, but, primarily they operated as trading companies for their own products. To date, initial growth expectations have been elusive for some of the major U.S. trading companies. On the other hand, U.S. trading companies designed to provide sales services for the parent company and other customers are gradually becoming an important means of gaining access to foreign markets. The economies of scale an ETC provides for the small- or medium-sized firm are important reasons to use an ETC as one of the various methods of international distribution.[36]

Complementary Marketers.   Companies with marketing facilities or contacts in different countries with excess marketing capacity or a desire for a broader product line sometimes take on additional lines for international distribution; although the generic name for such activities is complementary marketing, it is commonly called *piggybacking*. General Electric Company has been distributing merchandise for other suppliers for many years. They accept products that are noncompetitive but complementary and that add to the basic distribution strength of the company itself. Singer Sewing Machine Company emphasizes products closely allied to its own; they piggyback fabrics, patterns, notions, and thread.

Most piggyback arrangements are undertaken when a firm wants to fill out its product line or keep its distribution channels for seasonal items functioning throughout the year. Companies may work either on an agency or merchant basis, but the greatest volume of piggyback business is handled on an ownership (merchant) purchase-resale arrangement.

The selection process for new products for piggyback distribution must answer the following questions: (1) Is the product related to the product

---

[35] For an illustration of an exemption certificate application, see John Steiner, "Export Trading Companies: Antitrust Protection for U.S. Exporters," *Export Today*, January–February 1988, pp. 42–49.

[36] Donald G. Howard, "The Export Trading Company Act of 1982: Does It Lay the Foundation for the Development of American Sogo Shoshas?" *Journal of Global Marketing*, Vol. 2(3) 1989, pp. 49–70.

BOX 17–8
Marketing in the People's Republic of China

As the Chinese market opens to consumer goods, new ways of marketing are being tried. Advertising in China is still a far cry from Madison Avenue. You can't claim to be number one in commercials, it goes against the moral system where everyone is equal. Because foreign products are new to China, multinationals advertise to increase consumer awareness more than to battle each other for the same slice of the marketing pie. Ads are more literal and instructive than in the West. Nescafé's TV commercials, for instance, teach viewers how to make a cup of instant coffee.

Censorship can be a problem. Lever Brothers has been forced to delay its Lux soap TV ads because Shanghai authorities found samba dancers in skimpy beaded outfits appearing in the background. McDonnell Douglas Corporation had to revise its TV ads because officials in Beijing objected to footage of a plane flying into a map of China, a national symbol the Chinese don't want commercialized.

Simple promotions can be a better way to reach potential customers. When Lever Brothers launched its Shield soap in China, they asked consumers to guess the number of soap bars inside a transparent box displayed in a Canton department store. The grand prize was a color TV. The contest drew more than 500,000 entries, five times the number Lever Brothers expected.

Selling is an alien concept to the Chinese who are accustomed to "all they could make they could sell." There is no incentive to get out and hustle

---

line, and does it contribute to it? (2) Does the product fit the sales and distribution channel presently employed? (3) Is there an adequate margin to make the undertaking worthwhile? (4) Will the product find market acceptance and profitable volume? If these requirements are met, piggybacking can be a logical way of increasing volume and profit for both the carrier and the piggybacker.

Manufacturer's Export Agent.   The manufacturer's export agent (MEA) is an individual agent middleman or an agent middleman firm providing a selling service for manufacturers. Unlike the EMC, the MEA does not serve as the producer's export department but has a short-term relationship, covers only one or two markets, and operates on a straight commission basis. Thus, a manufacturer would be likely to deal with only one EMC but numerous MEAs. Another principal difference is that MEAs do business in their own names rather than in the name of the client.

Within a limited scope of operation, the MEAs provide services similar to those of the EMC, but for an internationally minded firm, their chief shortcoming is the lack of wide market coverage and an ongoing market relationship.

BOX 17–8 *(continued)*

for sales. A manager of a Chinese consumer products company was once asked by a Chinese distributor to slow down because he had achieved his annual sales goal and was afraid his superiors would require him to meet a higher target the following year.

Multinationals must work through an inefficient state control system of wholesalers and retailers. Chinese distributors often sell competitors' products and even refuse to reveal inventory levels to their suppliers. Many manufacturers in China don't even bother making deliveries to retailers. But that is changing as Coke and Pepsi escalate their distribution duel. When both companies started out in China, customers bicycled up to bottling plants to pick up their soda. "Factories were only production houses. They left the merchandise in the warehouse and waited for you to come and buy." Now Coke and Pepsi have set up direct distribution, investing heavily in trucks and refrigerators for retailers.

Multinationals sometimes find that socialism and salesmanship clash. Since commissions are forbidden in China, the only incentives a company can offer top salespeople are banquets, ribbons, and T-shirts. "Right now we are operating on pride" says a multinational manager.

Source: Adapted from "Laying the Foundation for the Great Mall of China," *Business Week,* January 25, 1988, pp. 68–69.

Broker.   The term *broker* is a catchall for a variety of middlemen performing low-cost agent services. The term is typically applied to import-export brokers who provide the intermediary function of bringing buyers and sellers together and who do not have a continuing relationship with their clients. Most brokers operate in the bulky goods of the commodity field and specialize in one or more commodity types for which they maintain contact with major producers and purchasers throughout the world.

Other brokers specialize in individual countries rather than in commodities and offer specialized knowledge of trading regulations and markets of the countries in which they deal.

Buying Offices.   A variety of agent middlemen may be classified simply as buyers or buyers for export. Their common denominator is a primary function of seeking and purchasing merchandise on request from principals; as such, they do not provide a selling service. In fact, their chief emphasis is on flexibility and the ability to find merchandise from any source. They do not often become involved in continuing relationships with domestic suppliers and do not provide a continuing source of representation. The buyer, however, is a good avenue for sales, and as long as the price, merchandise, and terms are right, may continue to buy from one firm over a period of years. Unfortunately, from a distribution control stand-point, the supplier firm's role is essentially passive.

Selling Groups.   Several types of arrangements have been developed in which various manufacturers or producers cooperate in a joint attempt to sell their merchandise abroad. This may take the form of complementary exporting or of selling to a business combine such as a Webb-Pomerene export association. Both are considered agency arrangements when the exporting is done on a fee or commission basis.

When business firms have unused marketing or export capacity, they sometimes share their facilities with companies having complementary but noncompeting lines. Complementary exporting or piggybacking is cov-ered at length earlier in the domestic middlemen section of this chapter.

Webb-Pomerene Export Associations (WPEA).   WPEAs constitute an-other major form of group exporting. The Webb-Pomerene Act of 1918 made it possible for American business firms to join forces in export activi-ties without being subject to the Sherman Antitrust Act. WPEAs cannot participate in cartels or other international agreements that would reduce competition in the United States, but can offer four major benefits: (1) reduction of export costs, (2) demand expansion through promotion, (3) trade barrier reductions, and (4) improvement of trade terms through bilat-eral bargaining. Additionally, WPEAs set prices, standardize products, and arrange for disposal of surplus products.

The mode of operation of the WPEA determines its place in the corporate organization. The association may: (1) limit itself to publicity, advertising, and information dissemination; (2) handle export procedures for its mem-bers but perform only an order-filling function; (3) act as a selling agent, promoting merchandise, negotiating sales, dividing orders among associa-tion members, and arranging for shipment; or (4) purchase products from corporate members under terms and proportional allotments agreed on by the membership, then act as a merchant wholesaler to market the products in foreign countries.

Although they account for less than 5 percent of U.S. exports, WPEAs include some of America's blue-chip companies in agricultural products, chemical and raw materials, forest products, pulp and paper, textiles, rubber products, motion pictures, and television.

Foreign Sales Corporation (FSC).   A FSC is an important type of selling organization that can be created by an exporter to benefit from U.S. tax incentives designed to encourage U.S. exports. Although not technically a selling group such as the WPEA, the FSC is an important benefit available for small and medium-size exporters. Further, a FSC can be a means of distribution for manufacturers because FSC has the authority to buy on its own account for export.

A FSC (pronounced fisk) is a sales corporation set up in a foreign country or U.S. possession that can obtain a corporate tax exemption on a portion of the earnings generated by the sale or lease of export property. FSCs can be formed by manufacturers and export groups. A FSC can function as a principal, buying and selling for its own account, or as a commission agent. It can be related to a manufacturing parent or can be an independent merchant or broker.

Shared FSCs are also permitted; 25 or fewer unrelated exporters can own and operate a shared FSC. A trade association can sponsor a shared FSC for its members. Banks alone or in conjunction with other banks, private businesses (such as export management companies and shippers) and state or regional government agencies can sponsor FSCs. Several states and regional associations are sponsoring FSCs as a way of promoting export trade in their regions.[37]

Domestic International Sales Corporation (DISC). The DISC was replaced by the FSC which was also designated as a tax incentive program for exports. Since its inception in 1972, the DISC was challenged as a direct violation of GATT rules on export subsidies. After prolonged dispute, the U.S. government replaced DISC with FSC (1985) whose tax incentives are more consistent with GATT rules.

Norazi Agent.   Norazi agents are unique middlemen who specialize in shady or difficult transactions. They deal in contraband materials, such as radioactive products or war materials, and in providing strategic goods to countries closed to normal trading channels. The Norazi is also likely to be engaged in black-market currency operations as well as trade in untaxed liquor, narcotics, industrial espionage, and other illicit traffic.

Although they are called agents, the Norazi is not limited to an agent-type transaction. If the profit picture is exceptionally large, the Norazi change from merchant to agent or agent to merchant, whichever is most advantageous. Despite the unsavory trade of Norazi agents, they have a reputation for dealing ethically with their clients. This is mandatory because neither client nor agent works on the basis of written contracts nor has recourse to justice through the court system. The Norazi exists because tariffs, import taxes, import/export restrictions, and excise taxes make illegal movements of goods more profitable than legal movements. In Uruguay, for example, the legal cost of a package of U.S. cigarettes is $1.40 (U.S.), but it sells for $0.50 on the black market. Argentina estimates that it loses over $43 million (U.S.) a year in cigarette taxes alone because of smuggling from Uruguay. In Argentina a smuggled Japanese camera can be bought for about half the price of the camera coming through official channels. As a top-ranking official commented, "Contrabanding has a major impact of the economies of Latin nations."

---

[37] John J. Korbel, Amin B. Hassam, and Richard M. Hammer, "Lower Your Taxes while Lowering the Trade Deficit," *Price Waterhouse Review*, no. 2, (1987), pp. 29–38.

The volume of business transacted by Norazi is unknown but its activities have reached such a proportion that a counterforce called Inter-Respol has been organized to combat contrabanding on an international basis. Respol of Chile, for example, recently confiscated $100,000 worth of Japanese radio and television sets being flown into Chile from Panama. The Norazi is not without representation in the halls of government; for example, in Bolivia a group called the Union of Minority Businessmen speaks openly in favor of the smuggling trade. It has communicated its story so well that one government official says, "Smuggling is a social and economic necessity since it allows people to guy goods at lower prices."

That most manufacturers do not need or desire the services of Norazi agents is indeed fortunate; they are difficult to contact and their fees or markups are extremely high.

Export Merchants.   Export merchants are essentially domestic wholesalers operating in foreign markets. As such, they operate much like the domestic wholesaler. Specifically, they purchase goods from a large number of manufacturers, ship them to foreign countries, and take full responsibility for their marketing. Sometimes they utilize their own organizations, but, more commonly, they sell through middlemen. They may carry competing lines, have full control over prices, and maintain little loyalty to suppliers although they continue to handle products as long as they are profitable. Most tend to specialize in a given field.

Export Jobbers.   Export jobbers are similar to domestic drop-shippers or desk jobbers; they are, in fact, often called export drop-shippers. They deal with bulky goods or raw materials and do not take physical possession of the goods but assume responsibility for arranging transportation. Export jobbers represent only themselves and typically buy or sell goods only when they have completed both sides of a transaction. Because they work on a job-lot basis, they do not provide a particularly attractive distribution alternative for most producers.

Exhibit 17–4 summarizes information pertaining to the major kinds of domestic middlemen operating in foreign markets. No attempt is made to generalize about rates of commission, markup, or pay because so many factors influence compensation. Services offered or demanded, market structure, volume, and product type are some of the key determinants. The data represent the predominant patterns of operations; however, individual middlemen of a given type may vary in their operations.

Foreign Country Middlemen

The variety of agent and merchant middlemen in most countries is not too dissimilar to those in the United States. An international marketer seeking greater control over the distribution process may elect to deal

EXHIBIT 17–4   Characteristics of Domestic Middlemen Serving Overseas Markets

Type of Duties	Agent						Merchant			
	EMC	MEA	Broker	Buying Offices	Selling Groups	Norazi	Export Merchant	Export Jobber	Importers and Trading Companies	Complementary Marketers
Take title	No	No	No	No	No	Yes	Yes	Yes	Yes	Yes
Take possession	Yes	Yes	No	Yes	Yes	Yes	Yes	No	Yes	Yes
Continuing relationship	Yes	Yes	No	Yes	Yes	No	No	Yes	Yes	Yes
Share of foreign output	All	All	Any	Small	All	Small	Any	Small	Any	Most
Degree of control by principal	Fair	Fair	Nil	Nil	Good	Nil	None	None	Nil	Fair
Price authority	Advisory	Advisory	Yes (at market level)	Yes (to buy)	Advisory	Yes	Yes	Yes	No	Some
Represent buyer or seller	Seller	Seller	Either	Buyer	Seller	Both	Self	Self	Self	Self
Number of principals	Few—many	Few—many	Many	Small	Few	Several per transaction	Many sources	Many sources	Many sources	One per product
Arrange shipping	Yes	Yes	Not usually	Yes	Yes	Yes	Yes	Yes	Yes	Yes
Type of goods	Manufactured goods and commodities	Staples and commodities	Staples and commodities	Staples and commodities	Complementary to their own lines	Contraband	Manufactured goods	Bulky and raw materials	Manufactured goods	Complementary to line
Breadth of line	Specialty—wide	All types of staples	All types of staples	Retail goods	Narrow	n.a.	Broad	Broad	Broad	Narrow
Handle competitive lines	No	No	Yes	Yes—utilizes many sources	No	Yes	Yes	Yes	Yes	No
Extent of promotion and selling effort	Good	Good	One shot	n.a.	Good	Nil	Nil	Nil	Good	Good
Extend credit to principal	Occasionally	Occasionally	Seldom	Seldom	Seldom	No	Occasionally	Seldom	Seldom	Seldom
Market information	Fair	Fair	Price and market conditions	For principal not for manufacturer	Good	No	Nil	Nil	Fair	Good

Note: n.a. = not available.

directly with middlemen in the foreign market. They gain the advantage of shorter channels and deal with middlemen in constant contact with the market. As with all middlemen, particularly those working at a distance, effectiveness is directly dependent on the selection of middlemen and on the degree of control the manufacturer can and/or will exert.[38]

Using foreign country middlemen moves the manufacturer closer to the market and involves the company more closely with problems of language, physical distribution, communications, and financing. Foreign middlemen may be agents or merchants; they may be associated with the parent company to varying degrees; or they may be temporarily hired for special purposes. Some of the more important foreign country middlemen are manufacturer's representatives and foreign distributors.

Manufacturer's Representatives. Manufacturer's representatives are agent middlemen who take responsibility for a producer's goods in a city, regional market area, entire country, or several adjacent countries. When responsible for an entire country, the middleman is often called a sole agent. As in the United States, the well-chosen, well-motivated, well-controlled manufacturer's representative can provide excellent market coverage for the manufacturer in certain circumstances. The manufacturer's representative is widely used in distribution of industrial goods overseas and is an excellent representative for any type of manufactured consumer goods.

Foreign manufacturers' representatives have a variety of titles, including sales agent, resident sales agent, exclusive agent, commission agent, and indent agent. They take no credit, exchange, or market risk but deal strictly as field sales representatives. They do not arrange for shipping or for handling and usually do not take physical possession. Manufacturers who wish the type of control and intensive market coverage their own sales force would afford, but who cannot field one, may find the manufacturer's representative a satisfactory choice.

Distributors. A foreign distributor is a merchant middleman. This intermediary often has exclusive sales rights in a specific country and works in close cooperation with the manufacturer. The distributor has a relatively high degree of dependence on the supplier companies, and arrangements are likely to be on a long-run, continuous basis. Often distributor-manufacturer relationships are formalized through franchises or ownership arrangements. Working through distributors permits the manufacturer a reasonable degree of control over prices, promotional effort, inventory, servicing,

---

[38] For a discussion of Saudi middlemen, see Ugur S. Yavas, Tamer Cavusgil, and Secil Tuncalp, "Assessments of Selected Foreign Suppliers by Saudi Importers: Implications for Exporters," *Journal of Business Research*, no. 15 (1987), pp. 237–46.

and other distribution functions. If a line is profitable for distributors, they can be depended on to handle it in a manner closely approximating the desires of the manufacturer.[39]

Brokers.   Like the export broker discussed in an earlier section, brokers are agents who deal largely in commodities and food products. The foreign brokers are typically part of small brokerage firms operating in one country or in a few contiguous countries. Their strength is in having good continuing relationships with customers and providing speedy market coverage at a low cost.

Managing Agents and Compradors.   A managing agent conducts business within a foreign nation under an exclusive contract arrangement with the parent company. The managing agent in some cases invests in the operation and in most instances operates under a contract with the managed company. Compensation is usually on the basis of cost plus a specified percentage of the profits of the managed company.[40]

In Far Eastern countries, managing agents are likely to be called *compradors,* and are used because of their initimate knowledge of the obscure and enigmatic customs and languages of the importing country. Few of the true general-manager type of compradors are still in operation, but there is a tendency for other kinds of foreign middlemen to expand their functions to accommodate small manufacturers.

Dealers.   Generally speaking, anyone who has a continuing relationship with a supplier in buying and selling goods is considered a dealer. More specifically, dealers are middlemen selling industrial goods or durable consumer goods direct to customers; dealers are the last step in the channel of distribution. Dealers have continuing, close working relationships with their suppliers and exclusive selling rights for their producer's products within a given geographic area. Finally, they derive a large portion of their sales volume from the products of a single supplier firm. Usually a dealer is an independent merchant middleman, but sometimes the supplier company has an equity in its dealers.

Some of the best examples of dealer operations are found in the farm equipment, earth-moving, and automotive industries. These categories include Massey Ferguson, with a vast, worldwide network of dealers; Caterpiller Tractor Company, with dealers in every major city of the world; and the various automobile companies.

---

[39] Evelyn A. Sprada, "Distributors: Key to Sales Success," *Export Today*, Winter–Spring 1987, pp. 33–36.

[40] See, for example, Jeffrey B. Johnson, "Marketing in India," *Business America*, June 10, 1985, p. 9.

EXHIBIT 17–5 Characteristics of Middlemen in Foreign Countries

Type of Duties	Agent					Merchant		
	Broker	Manufacturer's Representative	Managing Agent	Comprador	Distributor	Dealer	Import Jobber	Wholesaler and Retailer
Take title	No	No	No	No	Yes	Yes	Yes	Yes
Take possession	No	Seldom	Seldom	Yes	Yes	Yes	Yes	Yes
Continuing relationship	No	Often	With buyer, not seller	Yes	Yes	Yes	No	Usually not
Share of foreign output	Small	All or part for one area	n.a.	All one area	All, for certain countries	Assignment area	Small	Very small
Degree of control by principal	Low	Fair	None	Fair	High	High	Low	Nil
Price authority	Nil	Nil	Nil	Partial	Partial	Partial	Full	Full
Represent buyer or seller	Either	Seller	Buyer	Seller	Seller	Seller	Self	Self
Number of principals	Many	Few	Many	Few	Small	Few major	Many	Many
Arrange shipping	No	No	No	No	No	No	No	No
Type of goods	Commodity and food	Manufactured goods	All types manufactured goods	Manufactured goods	Manufactured goods	Manufactured goods	Manufactured goods	Manufactured consumer goods
Breadth of line	Broad	Allied lines	Broad	Varies	Narrow to broad	Narrow	Narrow to broad	Narrow to broad
Handle competitive lines	Yes	No	Yes	No	No	No	Yes	Yes
Extent of promotion and selling effort	Nil	Fair	Nil	Fair	Fair	Good	Nil	Nil usually
Extend credit to principal	No	No	No	Sometimes	Sometimes	No	No	No
Market information	Nil	Good	Nil	Good	Fair	Good	Nil	Nil

Note: n.a. = not available.

Import Jobbers. Import jobbers purchase goods directly from the manufacturer. They sell to wholesalers and retailers and to industrial customers. The import jobber is also known as an import house or an import merchant. Import jobbers differ from distributors mainly in that they do not have exclusive territorial rights. In a given port or country, one manufacturer may sell to several import jobbers.

Wholesalers and Retailers. Large and small wholesalers and retailers alike engage in direct importing both for their own outlets and for further redistribution to smaller middlemen. The combination retailer-wholesaler is more important in foreign countries than in the United States. It is not at all uncommon to find most of the larger retailers in any city wholesaling their goods to local shops and dealers.[41]

Exhibit 17–5 summarizes the characteristics of the middlemen found in foreign countries. These are generalizations and the reader needs to be alert to export country variation.

COMPANY DISTRIBUTION ABROAD

Although the company's own selling force is not considered part of a channel of distribution *per se*, it should be because the foreign marketing arm of the company is sufficiently independent that it often must be dealt with as if it were an independent channel. It also substitutes for or supplements independent channels of distribution. Companies undertake development of their own overseas marketing organizations for two reasons: (1) to increase volume of sales and (2) to increase control over the distribution system. The two activities should combine to give the company greater profitability and stability but sometimes the company finds it loses volume when it gives up established distribution channels and encounters intense competition from former distributors and middlemen. Though it may take two to five years before a new operation reaches the break-even point, many companies have found that establishing their own internal distribution channel has been the most satisfactory way of reaching certain major markets.

Increasingly, companies serious about the long-term relationship in a market tend to develop their own distribution systems whenever economically possible.

Companies that want to establish their own marketing structures abroad may employ salespeople to report directly to the home office or establish sales branches or subsidiaries abroad. Some have utilized the joint-venture

[41] Shinya Nakata, "Limited Distribution Channels and Exclusive Wholesale Stores," *Sumitomo Quarterly*, Autumn 1987, pp. 10–12.

plan, or have merged with or purchased former middlemen to develop their own foreign marketing systems.

Rather than set up new sales offices or branches, some companies have chosen to utilize their own missionary sales force which, like its domestic counterpart, has the responsibility for making customer contact and sales presentations and for providing follow-up service. The actual physical distribution of the product is handled through an assortment of wholesalers or other middlemen.[42]

LOCATING, SELECTING, AND MOTIVATING CHANNEL MEMBERS

The actual process of building channels for international distribution is seldom easy and many companies have been stopped in their efforts to develop international markets by their inability to construct a satisfactory system of channels.

Despite the chaotic condition of international distribution channels, international marketers can follow a logical procedure in developing channels. After general policy guides are established, marketers need to develop criteria for the selection of specific middlemen. Construction of the middleman network includes seeking out potential middlemen, selecting those who fit the company's requirements, and establishing working relationships with them.

In international marketing, the channel-building process is hardly routine. The closer the company wants to get to the consumer in its channel contact, the larger the sales force required. If a company is content with finding an exclusive importer or selling agent for a given country, channel building may not be too difficult; but if it goes down to the level of subwholesaler or the retailer, it is taking on a tremendous task and must have an internal staff capable of supporting such an effort.

Locating Middlemen

The search for prospective middlemen should begin with study of the market and determination of criteria to be used in evaluating middlemen servicing that market. The company's broad policy guidelines should be followed, but expect expediency to override policy at times. The checklist of criteria differs according to the type of middlemen being used and the nature of their relationship with the company. Basically, such lists are

---

[42] "Meeting the Competition: Burroughs Taps New Channel for Sales to Tough Markets," *Business International,* July 26, 1985, p. 233.

built around four subject areas: (1) productivity or volume, (2) financial strength, (3) managerial stability and capability, and (4) the nature and reputation of the business. Emphasis is usually placed on either the actual or potential productivity of the middleman.

Setting policies and making checklists are easy; the real task is implementing them. The major problems are locating information to aid in the selection and choice of specific middlemen and discovering middlemen available to handle one's merchandise. Firms seeking overseas representation should compile a list of middlemen from such sources as: (1) The U.S. Department of Commerce; (2) commercially published directories; (3) foreign consulates; (4) chamber-of-commerce groups located abroad; (5) other manufacturers producing similar but noncompetitive goods; (6) middlemen associations; (7) business publications; (8) management consultants; and (9) carriers—particularly airlines.[43]

Selecting Middlemen

Finding prospective middlemen is less a problem than determining which of them can perform satisfactorily. Most prospects are hampered by low volume or low potential volume, many underfinanced, and some simply cannot be trusted. In many cases, when a manufacturer is not well known abroad, the reputation of the middleman becomes the reputation of the manufacturer, so a poor choice at this point can be devastating.

Screening. The screening and selection process itself should follow this sequence: (1) a letter including product information and distributor requirements in the native language to each prospective middleman; (2) a follow-up to the best respondents for more specific information concerning lines handled, territory covered, size of firm, number of salespeople, and other background information; (3) check of credit and references from other clients and customers of the prospective middleman; and (4) if possible, a personal check of the most promising firms.

One source suggests the only way to select a middleman is to go personally to the country and talk to ultimate users of your product to find whom they consider to be the best distributors. Visit each one before selecting the one to represent you; look for one with a key man who will take the new line of equipment to his heart and make it his personal objective to make the sale of that line a success. Further, this exporter stresses that if you cannot sign one of the two or three customer-recommended distributors, it might be better not to have a distributor in that

---

[43] "Finding a Distributor Takes Planning and Skill: A BI Checklist," *Business International*, March 8, 1985, p. 74.

BOX 17–9
Local Laws and Distribution Agreements

Exporters should watch out for local laws that have these features:

* Require that any private international commercial agreement be controlled by local law.
* Prohibit a local distributor or agent from waiving its rights in a contract.
* Prohibit or impede termination of contracts for other than "just cause"— as defined by local law.
* Classify local agents as "employees," subject to all the protection of labor law, especially regarding rules for dismissal.
* Turn a customer into a distributor by construing an "implicit distribution agreement."
* Specify high termination compensation related to an agent's longevity, past earnings, goodwill, or investment in the product line.
* Require an unreasonable notice period before termination.
* Construe a refusal to renew an agreement as "unjust termination."
* Require release by an old agent before a new one may be appointed.
* Mandate lengthy dispute-resolution procedures that an unhappy representative can use to delay appointment of a new agent.
* Limit post-termination restrictions on a distributor.
* Extend such protection even to nonexclusive distributor agreements.

Companies report that these countries make it particularly difficult to get out of distribution agreements: Belgium, Costa Rica, Denmark, the Netherlands, Norway, Puerto Rico, Sweden, Venezuela, and under certain circumstances, France and Germany.

Source: Reprinted by permission of the publisher, Business International Corporation, New York. "What the Worst Laws Say," *Business International*, July 12, 1985, p. 218.

country because having a worthless one costs you time and money every year and may cut you out when you finally find a good one.

The Agreement.[44]   Once a potential middleman has been found and evaluated, there remains the task of detailing the arrangements with that middleman. So far the company has been in a buying position; now it must shift into a selling and negotiating position to convince the middleman to handle the goods and accept a distribution agreement that is workable for the company. Agreements must spell out specific responsibilities of

---

[44] John T. Masterson, Jr., "Drafting International Distributorship and Sales Representative Agreements," *Business America*, November 21, 1988, pp. 8–9.

the manufacturer and the middleman including an annual sales minimum. The sales minimum serves as a basis for evaluation of the distributor and failure to meet sales minimums may give the exporter the right of termination.[45]

Some experienced exporters recommend that initial contracts be signed for one year only. If the first year's performance is satisfactory, they should be reviewed for renewal for a longer period. This permits easier termination, and more important, after a year of working together in the market, a more workable arrangement generally can be agreed on. At this point, success depends on a good product and company reputation; a skilled negotiator or salesperson; and an intimate knowledge of the market, the middleman, and the environment within which they work.[46]

Motivating Middlemen

Once middlemen are selected, a promotional program must be started to maintain high-level interest in the manufacturer's products. A larger proportion of the advertising budget must be devoted to channel communications than in the United States because there are so many small middlemen to be contacted. Consumer advertising is of no avail unless the goods are actually available. Furthermore, few companies operating in international business have the strong brand image in foreign environments that they have in their own country. In most countries, retailers and wholesalers are only minimally brand conscious, and yet, to a large degree, they control the success or failure of products in their countries. Witness the phenomenal acceptance of *produits libres* (generic products) introduced by *Carrefour*, France's large *hypermarche* and *supermarche* operator.

The level of distribution and the importance of the individual middleman to the company determine the activities undertaken to keep the middleman alert. On all levels there is a clear correlation between the middleman's motivation and sales volume. The hundreds of motivational techniques that can be employed to maintain middleman interest and support for the product may be grouped into five categories: financial rewards, psychological rewards, communications, company support, and corporate rapport.[47]

Obviously, financial rewards must be adequate for any middleman to

---

[45] "How to Avoid Pitfalls with LA Distributor and Agent Agreements," *Business Latin America,* June 13, 1988, pp. 187–88.

[46] For a survey of different rules and regulations, protection and termination indemnities for Latin American countries, see "Distributor and Agent Agreements in Latin America," *Business Latin America,* June 13, 1988, pp. 188–89.

[47] Evelyn Sprada, "Distributors: The Management Phase," *Export Today,* January–February 1988, pp. 37–40.

carry and promote a company's products. Margins or commissions must be set to meet the needs of the middleman and may vary according to the volume of sales and the level of services offered. Without a combination of adequate margin and adequate volume, a middleman cannot afford to give much attention to a product.

Being human, middlemen and their salespeople also need psychological rewards and recognition for the jobs they are doing. For most business people throughout the world, a trip to the United States or to the parent company's home or regional office is a great honor. The American company has been pictured as the business with all the answers so foreign associates are likely to be particularly flattered if it seeks their advice. Publicity in company media and local newspapers also builds esteem and involvement among foreign middlemen.

In all instances, the company should maintain a continuing flow of communication in the form of letters, newsletters, and periodicals to all its middlemen. The more personal these are, the better. One study of exporters indicated that the more intense the contact between the manufacturer and the distributor, the better the performance from the distributor. More and better contact naturally leads to less conflict and a smoother working relationship. One factor that was partly responsible for the success of Smith, Kline, and French in building their own channels for Contac was a monthly periodical specifically published for the 1,200 wholesale salespeople dealing in their product.

A company can support its middlemen by offering advantageous credit terms, adequate product information, technical assistance, and product service. Such support helps build the distributor's confidence in the product and in their own ability to produce results.

Finally, considerable attention must be paid to the establishment of close rapport between the company and its middlemen. In addition to methods noted earlier, a company should be certain the conflicts that arise are handled skillfully and diplomatically. The American business person is often perceived abroad as insensitive and impersonal, but this image can be overcome if the people representing the company make special efforts at diplomacy. Bear in mind that all over the world business is a personal and vital thing to the people involved.

Terminating Middlemen

When middlemen do not perform up to standards or when market situations change requiring a company to structure its distribution differently, it may be necessary to terminate relationships with certain middlemen or certain types of middlemen. In the United States, it is usually a simple action regardless of the type of middlemen—agent, merchant, or employee; they are simply dismissed. However, in other parts of the world, the middleman typically has some legal protection that makes it difficult to terminate relationships. In Norway, for example, manufacturers must usually have evidence of negligence on the part of the agents they seek to replace. Even if they succeed in dismissing an agent, they are likely to have to repay the agent for investments made in establishing customer contacts and creating goodwill. Recent court decisions have confirmed the customary practice of giving the dismissed agent indemnity equal to one year's commissions. Such restrictions may destroy a company's marketing plans and may make distribution difficult for firms that have merged. In some countries, an agent cannot be dismissed without going through an arbitration board to determine whether the relationship should be ended. Some companies make all middlemen contracts for one year, but, in a few instances, termination under these contracts has been contested. Competent local legal advice is a vital prerequisite to writing contracts with middlemen in any country. But as many experienced international marketers know, the best rule is to avoid the need to terminate distributors by screening all prospective middlemen carefully. A poorly chosen distributor may not only fail to live up to expectations but may also adversely affect future business and prospects in the country.[48]

Controlling Middlemen

The extreme length of channels typically used in international distribution makes control of middlemen particularly difficult. Some companies solve this problem by establishing their own distribution systems; others issue franchises or exclusive distributorships in an effort to maintain control through the first stages of the channels. Until the various world markets are more highly developed, most international marketers cannot expect to exert a high degree of control over their international distribution operations. Although control is difficult, a company that succeeds in controlling distribution channels is most likely to be a successful international marketer. Indeed, the desire for control is a major reason companies initiate their own distribution systems in domestic as well as in international business.

All control systems, of course, originate in corporate plans and goals. Marketing objectives must be spelled out both internally and to middlemen as explicitly as possible. Standards of performance should include sales volume objective, market share in each market, inventory turnover ratio, number of accounts per area, growth objective, price stability objective, and quality of publicity. Obviously the more specific the standards of

---

[48] Ovidio M. Giberga, "The Legal Pitfalls of Negotiating with Foreign Agents," *Business America*, July 21, 1986, pp. 2–5.

performance, the easier they are to administer. Ease of administration, however, should not be confused with control.

Control over the system and control over middlemen are necessary in international business. The first relates to control over the distribution channel *system* per se. This implies overall controls for the entire system to be certain operations are within the cost and market coverage objectives. The specifics of distribution must also be controlled since pricing margins, transshipping, and other specific elements affect the overall system. Some manufacturers have lost control through "secondary wholesaling" when rebuffed discounters have secured their products through unauthorized outlets. A company's goods intended for one country are sometimes diverted through distributors to another country where they compete with existing retail or wholesale organizations. A manufacturer may find some of the toughest competition from its own products that have been diverted through other countries or manufactured by subsidiaries and exported or bootlegged into markets the parent would prefer to reserve. Such action can directly conflict with exclusive arrangements made with distributors in other countries and may undermine the entire distribution system by harming relationships between manfacturers and their channels.

The second type of control is at the middleman level. When possible, the parent company should know (and to a certain degree control) the activities of middlemen in respect to their volume of sales, market coverage, services offered, prices, advertising, payment of bills, and even profit. All levels of the distribution system cannot be controlled to the same degree or by the same methods, but quotas, reports, and personal visits by company representatives can be effective in managing middleman activities at any level of the channel.

When control fails and the best interests of the company are not being met, the middleman must be terminated. As mentioned earlier, middleman separations can be painful and expensive in other countries. American business is free to hire and fire middlemen with relative abandon unless specific contractual relationships to the contrary exist. In most other countries of the world, however, there is an implied obligation to middlemen who have incurred expenses or helped build distribution.

SUMMARY

From the foregoing discussion, it is evident that the international marketer has a broad range of alternatives for developing an economical, efficient, high-volume international distribution system. To the uninitiated, however, the variety may be overwhelming.

Careful analysis of the functions performed suggests more similarity than difference between international and domestic distribution systems; in both cases there are three primary alternatives of using agent middlemen, merchant middlemen, or a company's own sales and distribution system. In many instances, all three types of middlemen are employed on the international scene, and channel structure may vary from nation to nation or from continent to continent. The neophyte company in international marketing can gain strength from the knowledge that information and advice are available relative to the structuring of international distribution systems and that many well-developed and capable middleman firms exist for the international distribution of goods. Within the past decade, international middlemen have become more numerous, more reliable, more sophisticated, and more readily available to marketers in all countries. Such growth and development offer an ever-wider range of possibilities for entering foreign markets, but the international business person should remember that it is just as easy for competitors.

QUESTIONS

1. Define:
   distribution structure 570 WPEA 604
   distribution channel 572 DISC 605
   facilitating agency   FSCs 604
   EMC 596

2. Discuss how the globalization of markets, especially Europe 1992, will affect retail distribution.

3. To what extent, and in what ways, do the functions of domestic middlemen differ from their foreign counterparts?

4. Why is the EMC sometimes called an independent export department?

5. Can facilitating agencies be called a part of the channel of distribution? Explain.

6. Discuss how physical distribution relates to channel policy and how they affect one another.

7. Explain how and why distribution channels are affected as they are when the stage of development of an economy improves.

8. In what circumstances is the use of an EMC logical?

9. Predict whether the Norazi agent is likely to grow or decline in importance.

10. Discuss the possible antitrust ramification of WPEAs.

11. In which circumstances are trading companies likely to be used?

12. How is distribution-channel structure affected by increasing emphasis

on the government as a customer and by the existence of state trading agencies?

13. Review the key variables which affect the marketer's choice of distribution channels.

14. Account, as best you can, for the differences in channel patterns which might be encountered in a highly developed country and an underdeveloped country.

15. One of the first things companies discover about international channels-of-distribution patterns is that in most countries it is nearly impossible to gain adequate market coverage through a simple channel-of-distribution plan. Discuss.

16. Discuss the various methods of overcoming blocked channels.

17. Review the six Cs of channel strategy and show their interrelationships.

18. What strategy might be employed to distribute goods effectively in the dichotomous small-large middleman pattern which characterizes merchant middlemen in most countries?

19. Discuss the economic implications of assessing termination penalties or restricting the termination of middlemen. Do you foresee such restrictions in the United States?

20. FSCs have replaced DISCs. What are FSCs and why have they replaced DISCs?

21. Discuss why Japanese distribution channels can be the epitome of blocked channels.

22. What are the two most important provisions of the Export Trading Act of 1982?

23. Why are WPEAs considered more risky from an antitrust perspective than are ETCs?

CHAPTER

18

Export Trade Mechanics and Logistics

Exporting is an essential function of all international business from the smallest company marketing in a single country to global marketers. Goods manufactured in one country, destined for markets in another, must be moved across their borders to complete the process. Most countries control the movement of goods crossing their borders whether leaving (exporting) or entering (importing). Required documents, terms of payment, tariff systems, and other barriers to the free flow of goods between independent sovereigns are requirements unique to export marketing that must be considered by the export marketer. Export mechanics are sometimes considered the essence of foreign marketing, and although their importance cannot be minimized, they must not be viewed as the primary task of global marketing. Successful marketing requires the selection of a target market, designing an appropriate product, establishing a price, planning a promotional program, developing a distribution channel, and delivering the goods to the final consumer. When operating internationally, the successful marketing plan also includes the mechanics of exporting and the physical movement of the product to country markets. The rules and regulations that cover the exportation of goods and the physical movement of those goods between countries are the special concerns of this chapter.

REGULATIONS AND RESTRICTIONS OF EXPORTING

All countries impose some form of regulation and restriction on the exporting and importing of goods; restrictions are placed on the movement of goods in foreign markets for many reasons. Export regulations can be designed to conserve scarce goods for home consumption or to control the flow of strategic goods to actual or potential enemies. Import regulations may be imposed to protect health, conserve foreign exchange, serve as economic reprisals, protect home industry, or provide revenue in the form of tariffs. To comply with various regulations, the exporter may have to acquire licenses or permits from the home country and ascertain that the potential customer has the necessary permits for importing goods.[1]

U.S. Export Controls

Although the United States requires no formal or special license to engage in exporting as a business, permission or a license to export a product may be required in certain situations depending on the commodity and its destination. Most items requiring special permission or a license for exportation are under the control of the Department of Commerce. Other departments or agencies responsible for goods not under the control of the Department of Commerce are: (1) Department of State for arms and implements of war; (2) Atomic Energy Commission for atomic and fissionable energy material; (3) U.S. Department of the Treasury for gold and silver coins; (4) Department of Justice for narcotic drugs; (5) U.S. Federal Power Commission for natural gas and electric energy; and (6) Department of the Interior for endangered wildlife. For all products not controlled by one of the agencies listed, the marketer needs to consult the Department of Commerce to determine whether a specific license to export is required.

Export licensing controls administered by the Department of Commerce apply to (1) exports of commodities and technical data from the United States; (2) reexports of U.S.-origin commodities and technical data from a foreign destination to another foreign destination; (3) U.S.-origin parts and components used in foreign countries to manufacture foreign products for exports; and (4) in some instances, foreign products made from U.S.-origin technical data.[2]

All regulations imposed by the Department of Commerce are published

---

[1] For a complete review of export and import barriers to trade, see Sak Onkvisit and John J. Shaw, "Marketing Barriers in International Trade," *Business Horizons,* May–June 1988, pp. 64–72.

[2] "The New Bureau of Export Administration," *Business America,* February 29, 1988, pp. 2–26.

in the *Export Administration Regulations,* periodically revised and supplemented by the *Current Export Bulletin.* The respective department or bureau should be contacted for current control regulations since specific products controlled change frequently.

Types of Licenses.   Except for U.S. territories and possessions and, in most cases, Canada, products exported from the United States require export licenses. The first step in the export licensing process is to determine whether a product requires a general or a validated license. This depends on what is being exported, where it is going, the end use, and the final user.[3]

1. A general license permits exportation of certain commodities with nothing more than a declaration of the type of product and its destination. It is not necessary to submit a formal application or receive written authorization to ship products under a general license; goods can be shipped by merely inserting the correct general license symbol on the shipper's export declaration.

2. A validated license is a specific document authorizing exportation within specific limitations; it is issued only on formal application. Application for a validated license must be made in accordance with procedures set forth in the *Export Administration Regulations.*

Most commodities can be exported from the United States to free-world countries under a general license, but a validated license is required when exporting strategic goods and when exporting to unfriendly countries. Two factors determine whether a validated or general license is required—the country of destination and the type of commodity. For reasons of national security, short supply, or foreign policy, the United States controls the export of certain commodities and technical data to certain countries. For example, shotgun shells can be shipped to Japan under a general license, but for foreign-policy reasons, a validated license is required when shotgun shells or any other product used to enforce apartheid are shipped to South Africa. In this case, the country of destination determines the type of license. On the other hand, Western red cedar logs and/or lumber require a validated license for shipment to all countries including Canada. The fact that Western red cedar, the commodity, is considered in short supply determines the type of license.[4]

An exporter must consult the *Commodity Control List* and *Country Groups Supplement* of the *Export Administration Regulations* to determine whether a validated or general license is required for shipment of a particular commodity to a specific country.

---

[3] "Export Licensing from 'A' to 'Z,'" *Business America,* February 29, 1988, pp. 12–16.

[4] Cecil Hunt, "Some Advice on Export Controls—An Imaginary but Practical Discourse," *Business America,* November 21, 1988, pp. 16–18.

EXHIBIT 18–1   Examples of Commodity Control List Export Regulations

---

4997B Viruses or viroids for human, veterinary, plant, or laboratory use, except hog cholera and attentuated or inactivated systems.
Controls for ECCN 4997B

Unit: Report in "$ value."
Validated License Required: Country Groups QSTVWYZ.
GLV $ Value Limit: $0 for all destinations.
Processing Code: CM.
Reason for Control: National security.
Special Licenses Available: See Part 373.

6899G Other rubber and rubber products, n.e.s.
Controls for ECCN 6899G

Unit: Report in "$ value."
Validated License Required: Country Groups S and Z.
GLV $ Value Limit: General license *GLV* not applicable; however, another general license may apply.
Processing Code: CM.
Reason for Control: Foreign policy.
Special Licenses Available: None.
Special South Africa and Namibia Controls: A validated license is required for export of tires to the Republic of South Africa and Namibia if intended for delivery to, or for use by or for military or police entities in these destinations, or for use in servicing equipment owned, controlled or used by or for these entities. See § 385.4(a).

SOURCE: Export Administration Regulations, Commodity Control List, U.S. Department of Commerce.

All countries of the world except Canada are classified into seven groups designated by the symbols Q, S, T, V, W, Y, and Z depending on the degree of export restriction. Group Z countries–North Korea, Vietnam, Cuba, and Cambodia (formerly Kampuchea between 1976 and 1989)–and Group S (Libya) countries have the most stringent license requirements; a validated license is required for the shipment of most commodities. Exhibit 18–1 is a copy of the control regulations of two different commodity categories from the Commodity Control List. In one case, a validated license is required; in the other, only countries in groups S and Z require validated licenses. Whether a commodity destined for a country other than one in group Z requires a validated license depends on its scarcity and/or its strategic qualities.[5]

The Commodity Control List classifies products according to their avail-

---

[5] William B. Filbert, "The Licensing Process: Getting the Export License," *Export Today,* February 1989, pp. 60–63.

ability for export. Exporting scarce or strategic goods to specific countries may be prohibited altogether or restricted in quantity. If a validated license is required, the exporter must obtain the appropriate license before export shipment is allowed.

Other Export Documents.   In addition to a validated license and an antidiversion clause, certain shipments must be supported by documents supplied by the prospective purchaser or the government of the country of destination. An International Import Certificate certifies that the exported products will be disposed of responsibly in the designated country. This form is ordinarily obtained by the importer from his or her government.

The Statement of Ultimate Consignee and Purchaser is written assurance that the foreign purchaser of the goods will not resell or dispose of the goods in a manner contrary to the terms of the export license under which the goods were originally exported. The exporter has to send the statement to the foreign importer for completion.

One of the major complaints about exporting rules is the lack of speed with which licenses are granted. Export controls are considered to be one of the reasons many U.S. companies hesitate to export, and, U.S. competitors consider the U.S. system of export controls one of their best marketing tools. U.S. companies can falter and lose sales because export controls delay shipments and increase costs.[6] Aware of such charges, the Department of Commerce has instituted several changes to expedite completion of export licenses in an effort to increase exports.[7]

ELAIN and STELA.   Two innovations designed to cut through the paperwork and time necessary to acquire export licenses are the Export License Application and Information Network (ELAIN) and the System for Tracking Export License Applications (STELA). Once exporters have authorization, they will be able to submit license applications electronically to ELAIN, via the CompuServe network, for all commodities—except supercomputers—for all free-world destinations. When approved, licensing decisions will be electronically conveyed back to exporters via the same electronic network.

STELA is the Department of Commerce's computerized voice answering service that provides exporters with information on the status of their export license applications. In addition to telling an exporter exactly where an application is in the system and how long it has been there, STELA can also give an exporter authority to ship goods for those applications approved without conditions. ELAIN and STELA are among several

---

[6] Thomas D. Matty, "Export Control Changes Continue to Cause Problems for Exporters," *Global Trade*, October 1988, pp. 18–19.

[7] An article that traces the steps in acquiring export licenses is Lora F. McClure, "Making It out of the Country: Negotiating the Export Licensing Process," *Export Today*, November–December 1987, pp. 10–14.

changes that have enabled the Department of Commerce to reduce in-house processing times from an average of 46 days for free-world destinations in 1984 to just 14 days by the end of 1987. In fact, the average license processing time for trade with COCOM members, our most trusted trading partners, is now five days or less.[8]

Harmonized System.   The Export Trade Act of 1988 authorized the United States to participate with most of the trading nations of the world in the Harmonized Commodity Description and Coding System—Harmonized System for short.[9] Approximately 12 years ago, the United States and its trading partners began working on a new and more efficient goods classification system. Under the old system, a product could be given one code when imported, another when exported and various other codes in foreign countries. So many different systems complicated the preparation of documents, hampered the analysis of trade data, created uncertainty in the negotiation and interpretation of trade agreements, impeded the development of standardized forms, and slowed the use of electronic data processing in international transactions. The new system, implemented in 1988, assigns all products a six-digit code used by participating countries for both imported and exported goods.[10] A common goods classification system eliminates many of the problems that arise from nonstandardized systems; when fully implemented, this common system will accelerate the exporting process.[11]

Import Restrictions

In any analysis of the feasibility of exporting to a foreign country, it is necessary to examine the export restrictions of the home country as well as the import restrictions and regulations of the foreign country. Although the responsibility of import restrictions would rest with the importer, they are an important consideration to the exporter in terms of the feasibility of conducting business with a particular foreign customer.

There are many types of trade restrictions besides the major impediment of import duties imposed by the foreign country. A few examples of the 30 basic barriers to exporting considered important by *Business International*

---

[8] "The Electronic Age of Export Licensing: 'Elain' Joins Stela to Cut Processing Time," *Business America*, February 29, 1988, pp. 7–11.

[9] The goal for implementation of the Harmonized System was January 1, 1988. However, the United States was not authorized by the Omnibus Trade and Competitiveness Act of 1988 to participate until January 1, 1989.

[10] Laura Malt, "Exporters Sing the Blues as Code Date Passes," *Business Marketing*, February 1988, pp. 26–28.

[11] Dale O. Torrence, "New Tariff Code Streamlines Global Trading System," *Business America*, November 23, 1987, pp. 2–5.

BOX 18–1
Prison Terms for Illegally Exporting Goods to Russia

Two company executives were given prison terms; one for one year and two years for the other plus five years probation for both and $10,000 fines each for illegally shipping a sophisticated krypton laser system and a seismometer to Russia.

The equipment was sent to an intermediate party in Germany with the intention of final shipment to Russia. U.S. Customs agents intercepted the shipment in Munich during a raid of a firm called Sciencecare. The agents substituted 700 pounds of concrete for the devices and included a short personal message for Soviet scientists that said only: "(expletive) you." They then arrested the American executives. The two could have received seven-year prison terms but the lighter sentences reflected their cooperation in the investigation of other companies and individuals suspected of making illegal shipments of technology.

Source: Associated Press News Release, "High-Tech Leak Report Cites Englewood Operation," May 2, 1984.

include: (1) import licenses, quotas, and other quantitative restrictions; (2) currency restrictions and allocation of exchange at unfavorable rates on payments for imports; (3) devaluation; (4) prohibitive prior import deposits, prohibition of collection-basis sales, and insistence on cash letters of credit; (5) arbitrarily short periods in which to apply for import licenses; and (6) delays resulting from pressure on overworked officials or from competitors' influence on susceptible officials. The most frequently encountered trade restrictions are tariffs, exchange permits, quotas, import licenses, boycotts, standards, and voluntary agreements. The various market barriers that exist among members of the European Community create a major impediment to trade. One study of 20,000 EC firms indicated that the most troublesome barriers were administrative roadblocks, frontier delays, and capital controls. The proposal for a single, united EC market by 1992 specifically addresses the elimination of such barriers among member countries. At the same time, the question arises as to whether or not the European Community as a unit will increase its protectionist barriers toward nonmember countries.[12]

Tariffs.   Tariffs are the taxes or customs duties levied against goods imported from another country. All countries have tariffs for the purpose

---

[12] "The Single Market: Fertile Ground for Protectionist Bloc?" *Business International*, June 27, 1988, pp. 195–96.

of raising revenue and protecting home industries from the competition of foreign-produced goods. Tariff rates are based on value or quantity or a combination of both. In the United States, for example, the types of custom duties used are classified as (1) ad valorem duties based on a percentage of the determined value of the imported goods; (2) specific duties, a stipulated amount per unit weight or some other measure of quantity; and (3) a compound duty which combines both specific and ad valorem taxes on a particular item, that is, a tax per pound plus a percentage of value (ad valorem). Because tariffs frequently change, published tariff schedules for every country are available to the exporter on a current basis.

Exchange Permits.   Especially troublesome to exporters are exchange restrictions placed on the flow of currency by some foreign countries. To conserve scarce foreign exchange and alleviate balance-of-payment difficulties, many countries impose restrictions on the amount of their currency they will exchange for the currency of another country. In effect, they ration the amount of currency available to pay for imports. Exchange controls may be applied in general to all commodities, or as is frequently the case, a country may employ a system of multiple exchange rates based on the type of import. Essential products might have a very favorable exchange rate while nonessentials or luxuries would have a less favorable rate of exchange. In some cases, no exchange permits would be issued for certain classes of commodities.

In countries that use exchange controls, the usual procedure is for the importer to apply to the control agency of the importing country for an import permit; if the control agency approves the request, an import license is issued. On presentation to the proper government agency, the import license can be used to have local currency exchanged for the currency of the seller.

Receiving an import license or even an exchange permit is not a guarantee that a seller can exchange local currency for the currency of the seller. If local currency is in short supply, a chronic problem in some countries, other means of acquiring home-country currency are necessary. For example, in a transaction between the government of Colombia and a U.S. truck manufacturer, there was a scarcity of U.S. currency to exchange for the 1,000 vehicles Colombia wanted to purchase. The problem was solved through a series of exchanges. Colombia had a surplus of coffee that the truck manufacturer accepted and traded in Europe for sugar; the sugar was traded for pig iron, and finally the pig iron for U.S. dollars.

This somewhat complicated but effective transaction has become more common. As discussed in earlier chapters, countertrade deals are often a

---

BOX 18–2
No Korean Noodles Due to Sugar Quotas—What's the Connection?

Lemon curd is trapped in Los Angeles, Korean noodles are stuck in Seattle, chocolate glazes for tortes languish in Baltimore, and in New York, there are more than 20,000 kosher pizzas from Israel that can't get off the boat. Why? U.S. sugar quotas.

Here's an explanation although it doesn't make much sense. Hundreds of food products imported freely for years are suddenly barred from the United States because the government is seeking to protect the powerful domestic sugar industry. The U.S. government issued an emergency proclamation putting import quotas on food containing high concentrations of sugar such as sweetened cocoa, pancake and flour mixes, and other blended foods. The reason for the quotas? Sugar. The government believes food products made with sugar are being imported so that the sugar can be extracted and then sold on the U.S. market. There is a powerful incentive for this, at 21 cents a pound in New York, U.S. raw sugar sells at nearly seven times the price of world sugar which can't be freely traded. Unfortunately, the restricted product categories had a miscellaneous grouping, "other edible preparations," that included the pizzas and Korean noodles.

Source: "Why Israeli Pizzas and Korean Noodles Find Door Slammed," *The Wall Street Journal,* April 23, 1985, p. 1.

---

result of the inability to convert local currency into home-country currency and/or the refusal of a government to issue foreign exchange.[13]

Quotas.   Countries may also impose limitations on the quantity of certain goods imported during a specific period. These quotas may be applied to imports from specific countries or from all foreign sources in general. The United States, for example, has specific quotas for importing sugar, wheat, cotton, tobacco, and rice; in the case of some of these items, there are limitations on the amount imported from specific countries as well.[14]

Quotas are set for a variety of reasons; the most important is to protect domestic industry and to conserve foreign exchange. Some importing countries also set quotas to ensure an equitable distribution of a major market among friendly countries.

---

[13] For a summary of exchange controls in all major countries, see "Capsule Guide to Exchange Controls, part I, *Business International,* February 8, 1988, pp. 36–37; and "Capsule Guide to Exchange Controls, Latin America," *Business Latin America,* July 11, 1988, pp. 220–23.

[14] Paul Magnusson, "U.S. Consumers, and the Caribbean, Are Getting a Sour Deal on Sugar," *Business Week,* May 8, 1989, p. 41.

Import Licenses. As a means of regulating the flow of exchange and the quantity of a particular imported commodity, countries often require import licenses. The fundamental difference between quotas and import licenses as a means of controlling imports is the greater flexibility of import licenses over quotas. Quotas permit importing until the quota is filled, whereas licensing limits quantities on a case-by-case basis.

Boycott. A boycott is an absolute restriction against trade with a country, or trade of specific goods. Countries can refuse to trade (buy or sell) with other countries; for example, Arab nations have a boycott on trade with Israel. Boycotts sanctioned by the United States must be honored by American firms; however, if a U.S. company participates in an unauthorized boycott, it may be fined for violating the U.S. antiboycott law. The Arab nations' boycott of Israel puts U.S. multinationals in a delicate position. Arab nations refuse to do business with companies that trade with Israel and may even demand that a company assure them none of the products it sells is from Israel. If an American firm refuses to trade with Israel to do business with an Arab nation, or in any other way participates in the Arab nation boycott, it may face stiff fines. Boycotts are the most restrictive because they permit no trade, whereas other types of restrictions permit some trade.

Standards. Like many nontariff barriers, standards have legitimacy. Health standards, safety standards, and product quality standards are necessary to protect the consuming public, and imported goods are required to comply with local laws. Unfortunately, standards can also be used to slow down or restrict the procedures for importing to the point that the additional time and cost required to comply becomes, in effect, a trade restriction. Safety standards are a good example. Most countries have safety standards for electrical appliances. They require that imported electrical products meet local standards; certainly a reasonable requirement. However, the restrictiveness of safety standards can be escalated to the level of an absolute trade barrier by manipulating the procedures used to determine if products meet the standards. The simplest process for the importing nation is to accept the safety standard verification used by the exporting country, for example, Underwriters Laboratories in the United States. If the product is certified for sale in the United States and, if U.S. standards are the same as the importing country's, then U.S. standards and certification are accepted and no further testing is necessary. Most countries not interested in using standards as a trade barrier follow such a practice.[15]

The extreme situation occurs when the importing nation does not accept the same certification procedure required by the exporting nation but de-

---

[15] John Hayes, "Who Sets the Standards?" *Forbes*, April 17, 1989, pp. 110–112.

BOX 18–3
The United States Supports Free Trade—Or Does It?

There is much written about the trade problems between the United States and Japan. The impression frequently conveyed is that the United States is a free open market and Japan's market is riddled with trade restrictions. Neither impression is completely true. The United States engages in trade restrictions, too. One estimate is that over 25 percent of all manufactured goods sold in the United States are affected by trade barriers. The cost to U.S. consumers is $50 billion more than if there were no restrictions Consider a sample of U.S. trade restrictions.

Quotas: Sugar quotas imposed by the United States result in a pound of sugar costing 10 cents in Canada versus 35 cents in the United States. There are quotas with all major apparel-producing nations and on steel with the European Community and Japan: specific quotas have existed on imported peanuts since 1953.

Tariffs: Tariffs average 26 percent of the value of imported clothing, 49 percent on imported motorcycles, and 25 percent on imported ceramic tiles.

Local manufacture: To qualify for U.S. copyright protection, books and periodicals published in the United States must be printed and bound in the United States.

Shipping: Foreign ships are barred from carrying passengers or freight between any two U.S. ports.

Source: Adapted from "As Free-Trade Bastion, U.S. Isn't Half as Pure as Many People Think," *The Wall Street Journal*, November 1, 1985, p. 1.

mands all testing be done in the importing country. Even more restrictive is the requirement that each item be tested instead of accepting batch testing. When such is the case, the effect is the same as a boycott. Until recently, Japan required all electrical consumer products to be tested in Japan or tested in the United States by Japanese officials.[16] Japan now accepts the Underwriters Laboratories' safety tests; however, medical supplies and agricultural products still must be tested in Japan.[17]

Voluntary Agreements. Foreign restrictions of all kinds abound and the United States can be counted among those governments using restrictions.

---

[16] Rahul Jacob, "Export Barriers the U.S. Hates Most," *Fortune*, February 27, 1989, pp. 88–89.

[17] Kazuo Nukazawa, "Japan and the USA: Wrangling toward Reciprocity," *Harvard Business Review*, May–June 1988, pp. 42–52.

For over a decade, U.S. government officials have been arranging "voluntary" agreements with the Japanese steel industry to limit sales to the United States. Similar negotiations with the governments of major textile producers have limited textile imports into the United States.

In the 10 years prior to 1978, imported shoes captured 46 percent of the U.S. market, closing 300 American shoe factories. U.S. trade negotiators were dispatched to Taiwan, South Korea, Spain, Brazil, and Uruguay to reach informal agreements that would restrain shoe exports to the United States. Voluntary agreements on automobiles imported from Japan were expected to be lifted in 1985 after six years. However, political concern in the United States over the growing trade deficits with Japan provoked Japan to agree to extend voluntary quotas on automobiles beyond 1985. As a result of Japan's voluntary agreement to restrict automobile sales in the United States, average prices for Japanese autos are estimated at $2,500 more and domestic automobiles $1,000 more than they would otherwise have been without the quotas.[18]

Other Restrictions.   Restrictions may be imposed on imports of harmful products, drugs, medicines, and immoral products and literature. Products must also comply with government standards set for health, sanitation, packaging, and labeling. For example, in the Netherlands all imported hen and duck eggs must be marked in indelible ink with the country of origin; in Spain, imported condensed milk must be labeled to show fat content if it is less than 8 percent fat; and in Mexico, all animals imported from the United States must be accompanied by a sanitary certificate issued by an approved veterinary inspector and a visa secured from a Mexican consulate.

Failure to comply with these regulations can result in severe fines and penalities. Because requirements vary for each country and change frequently, regulations for all countries must be consulted individually and on a current basis. *Overseas Business Reports,* issued periodically by the Department of Commerce, provide the foreign marketer with the most recent foreign trade regulations of each country as well as U.S. regulations regarding each country.[19]

While sanitation certificates, content labeling, and other such regulations serve a legitimate purpose, countries can effectively limit imports by using such restrictions as additional trade barriers. Most of the economically developed world encourages foreign trade and works through GATT to reduce tariffs to a reasonable rate. Yet, in times of economic recession,

---

[18] "Japan's Quotas on Cars: A Loss for Consumers," *The Wall Street Journal,* February 14, 1986, p. 21.

[19] For an interesting article on some unique trade barriers, see Marc Levinson, "Twelve Protectionist Traps," *Across the Board,* September 1985, pp. 24–28.

BOX 18–4
A Few Examples of Nontariff Barriers

France—prohibits all whiskey advertising and levies huge taxes on grain-based spirits; forbids walnut imports before September 25 to exclude Italy's early crop; uses customs slowdowns to stop refrigerators at the border; burdens foreign automobiles with special insurance rates; has a state monopoly on phosphates; excludes Dutch cheese by prohibiting ingredients typically used in the Netherlands; charges a special transportation fee on foreign wine.

Italy—has slowed Volkswagen imports by a special tax; raises the cost of Bavarian milk by requiring Italian inspection at the time of production; has a state monopoly on matches and alcoholic beverages; covertly seeks bids on government projects only from national firms.

Germany—requires the use of *German* architects on all construction by German firms; prohibits the import of high-lead gasoline needed by French- and Italian-made cars; has strict packaging requirements that keep out most foreign foodstuffs; prohibits the use of preservatives and artificial flavorings in imported food; limits coal-derived fuel consumption to the northern part of the country.

Britain—gives loyalty rebate to steel users who have not purchased imported steel in six months; requires a costly "air worthiness" certificate for all imported aircraft; bans coal imports.

Japan—refuses to accept U.S. certification that American pharmaceutical exports are safe; requires that importer-distributors of foreign autos submit each car shipped to painstaking emissions-testing rather than, say, 1 out of every 10.

The list is endless, and every country is involved.

Source: Author's compilation.

---

countries revert to a protectionist philosophy and seek ways to restrict the importing of goods. Nontariff barriers have become one of the most potent ways for a country to restrict trade and still appear to comply with the spirit of GATT agreements.[20]

CUSTOMS-PRIVILEGED FACILITIES

To facilitate export trade, countries designate areas within their borders as customs-privileged areas, that is, areas where goods can be imported for storage or processing with tariffs postponed until the products leave

---

[20] A comprehensive briefing on the ongoing Uruguay round of GATT negotiations is in "Uruguay Round: Opening World Markets," *Business America*, June 20, 1988, pp. 2–7.

Special Economic Zone, Shenzhen, China. China's 1979 economic development program established Special Economic Zones as a means of attracting foreign capital and technology. In 10 years, Shenzhen's population grew from 30,000 to over 1 million.

the designated area. Foreign-trade zones, free ports, and in-bond arrangements are all types of customs-privileged facilities that countries use to promote foreign trade.

Foreign-Trade Zones

Most countries have foreign- or free-trade zones (FTZs) that improve the efficiency of foreign trade for the export marketer.[21] Most FTZs function much the same way regardless of the host country.[22] In the United States

---

[21] John Adams, Jr., "Foreign Trade Zones: How Competitive Are They?" *Export Today,* February 1989, pp. 46–48.

[22] See Chapter 16 for a discussion on using FTZs to help reduce price escalation.

FTZs extend their services to thousands of firms engaged in a spectrum of international trade-related activities ranging from distribution to assembly and manufacturing.[23] More than 100 foreign-trade zones are located throughout the United States, including New York, New Orleans, San Francisco, Seattle, Toledo, Honolulu, Mayaques (Puerto Rico), Kansas City, Little Rock, and Sault St. Marie. Goods subject to U.S. custom duties can be landed in these zones for storage or such processing as repackaging, cleaning, and grading before being brought into the United States or reexported to another country. In situations where goods are imported into the United States to be combined with American-made goods and reexported, the importer or exporter can avoid payment of U.S. import duties on the foreign portion and eliminate the complications of applying for a "drawback," that is, a request for a refund from the government of 99 percent of the duties paid on imports later reexported. Other benefits for companies utilizing foreign-trade zones include: (1) lower insurance costs due to the greater security required in FTZs; (2) more working capital since duties are deferred until goods leave the zone; (3) the opportunity to stockpile products when quotas are filled or while waiting for ideal market conditions; (4) significant savings on goods or materials rejected, damaged, or scrapped for which no duties are assessed; and (5) exemption from paying duties on labor and overhead costs which are excluded in determining the value of the goods when incurred in a FTZ.

Offshore Assembly *(Maquiladoras)*

Maquiladoras, in-bond companies, or twin plants are names given to a special type of customs-privileged facility that originated in Mexico in the early 1970s. It has since expanded to other countries with abundant, low-cost labor. In China, a variation of the *maquiladora* is the Economic Trade Zone (ETZ). Hourly manufacturing labor costs in Mexico and China are very low compared with the U.S. minimum wage; average per capita labor costs, including benefits, run between $32 and $60 per month in Mexico and between $60 and $95 per month in China.[24] Higher labor costs in the United States and other countries have led MNCs to search worldwide for low-cost labor. In most in-bond arrangements, special tax privileges are part of the process. Even though in-bond operations vary from country to country, the original

---

[23] For a comprehensive study of the role of FTZs in global marketing see, Patriya S. Tansuhaj and James W. Gentry, "Firm Differences in Perceptions of the Facilitating Role of Foreign Trade Zones in Global Marketing and Logistics," *Journal of International Business Studies,* Spring 1987, pp. 19–33.

[24] "The Chinese Workforce," *China Business Review,* May–June 1988, p. 51.

arrangement between Mexico and the United States still remains the most typical.[25]

In 1971 the Mexican and U.S. governments established an in-bond program that created a favorable opportunity for U.S. companies to utilize abundant, low-cost Mexican labor.[26]

The Mexican government allows U.S. processing, packaging, assembling and/or repair plants located in the in-bond area to import parts and processed materials without import taxes provided the finished products are reexported to the United States or to another foreign country. In turn, the U.S. government permits the reimportation of the packaged, processed, assembled, or repaired goods with a reasonably *low* import tariff applied only to the value added while in Mexico. Originally goods processed in *maquiladoras* could not be sold in Mexico without first being shipped back to the United States and reimported at regular Mexican tariffs. However, Mexican law was recently changed to allow *maquiladoras* the right to sell their products in Mexico if they use some Mexican raw materials. Similar changes have occurred in other countries that make in-bond arrangements increasingly important to MNCs.[27] More than 1,100 U.S. companies in electronics, health care, automotive parts, furniture, clothing, and toy manufacturing participate in the in-bond program in Mexico. RCA's TV chassis assembly plant employs 600 and is the largest *maquiladora* in Mexico.[28]

Information about foreign-trade zones, free ports, and similar customs-privileged facilities abroad may be obtained from the Foreign-Trade Zone Board, U.S. Department of Commerce.

EXPORT DOCUMENTS

Each export shipment requires various documents to satisfy government regulations controlling exporting as well as to meet requirements for international commercial payment transactions. The most frequently required documents are export declarations, consular invoices or certificates of origin, bills of lading, commercial invoices, and insurance certificates. In addition, documents such as import licenses, export licenses, packing lists, and inspection certificates for agricultural products are often necessary.

---

[25] For a detailed report on the economies of using *maquiladoras*, see the U.S. International Trade Commission report: *The U.S.–Mexican Border Industrialization Program: Use and Economic Impact of TSUS Items 806.3 and 807.0*, Washington, D.C.: Government Printing Office, January 1988, p. 500.

[26] Vineeta Anand, "Mexican Border Plants Support U.S. Trade," *Global Trade*, June 1987, pp. 34–35.

[27] Haskel Knight, "Lower Cost Production: The Maquiladora Alternative," *Export Today* July–August 1988, pp. 21–23.

[28] "Will the New Maquiladoras Build a Better Mañana?" *Business Week*, November 14, 1988, pp. 102–3.

The paperwork involved in successfully completing a transaction is considered by many to be the greatest of all nontariff trade barriers. There are 125 different types of documents in regular or special use in more than 1,000 different forms. A single shipment may require over 50 documents and can involve as many as 28 different parties and government agencies or require as few as five. Generally, preparation of documents can be handled routinely, but their importance should not be minimized; incomplete or improperly prepared documents lead to delays in shipment. In some countries, penalties, fines, or even confiscation of goods result from errors in some of these documents. Export documents are the result of requirements imposed by the exporting government, of requirements set by commercial procedures established in foreign trade, and, in some cases, of the supporting import documents required by the foreign government. Principal export documents are as follows:

Export Declaration. To maintain a statistical measure of the quantity of goods shipped abroad and to provide a means of determining whether regulations are being met, most countries require shipments abroad to be accompanied by an export declaration. Usually such a declaration, presented at the port of exit, includes the names and addresses of the principals involved, the destination of the goods, a full description of the goods, and their declared value. When manufacturers are exporting from the United States, Customs and the Department of Commerce require an export declaration for all shipments. If specific licenses are required to ship a particular commodity, the export license must be presented with the export declaration for proper certification. It thus serves as the principal means of control for regulatory agencies of the U.S. government.

Consular Invoice or Certificate of Origin. Not all countries require consular invoices, but those that do are typically very exacting about the manner in which the invoices are prepared. Proper forms must be obtained from the country's consulate and returned with two to eight copies in the language of the country along with copies of other required documents (e.g., import license, commercial invoice, and/or bill of lading) before certification is granted. The consular invoice probably produces the most red tape and is the most exacting to complete. Preparation of the document should be handled with extreme care because fines are levied for any errors uncovered. In most countries, the fine is shared with whomever finds it so few errors go undetected.

Bill of Lading. The bill of lading is the most important document required to establish legal ownership and facilitate financial transactions. It serves the following purposes: (1) as a contract for shipment between the carrier and shipper, (2) as a receipt from the carrier for shipment, and (3) as a certificate of ownership or title to the goods. Bills of lading are issued in the form of straight bills, which are nonnegotiable and are delivered directly to a consignee, or order bills, which are negotiable instruments. Bills of lading frequently are referred to as being either *clean* or *foul*. A clean bill of lading means the items presented to the carrier for shipment were properly packaged and clear of apparent damage when received; a foul bill of lading means the shipment was received in damaged condition and the damage is noted on the bill of lading.

Commercial Invoice.   Every international transaction requires a commercial invoice, that is, a bill or statement for the goods sold. This document often serves several purposes in that some countries require a copy for customs clearance, plus it is one of the financial documents required in international commercial payments.

Insurance Policy or Certificate.   The risks of shipment due to political or economic unrest in some countries, and the possibility of damage from sea and weather, make it absolutely necessary to have adequate insurance covering loss due to damage, war, or riots. Typically the method of payment or terms of sale require insurance on the goods so few export shipments are uninsured. The insurance policy or certificate of insurance is considered a key document in export trade.

Licenses.   Export or import licenses are additional documents frequently required in export trade. In those cases where import licenses are required by the country of entry, a copy of the license or license number is usually required to obtain a consular invoice. Whenever a commodity requires an export license, it must be obtained before an export declaration can be properly certified.

Others.   Sanitary and health inspection certificates attesting to the absence of disease and pests may be required for certain agricultural products before a country allows goods to enter its borders. Packing lists with correct weights are also required in some cases.[29]

TERMS OF SALE

Terms of sale or trade terms differ somewhat in international marketing from those used in the United States. In U.S. domestic trade, it is customary to ship FOB factory, freight collect, prepaid, and/or COD. International trade terms often sound similar to those used in domestic business but

---

[29] "Know Your Import and Export Documentation," *Distribution*, October 1988, pp. 92–93.

generally have different meanings. International terms indicate how buyer and seller divide risks and obligations and, therefore, the costs of specific kinds of international trade transactions. When quoting prices, it is important to make them meaningful. The most commonly used international trade terms include:

CIF—(cost, insurance, freight) to a named overseas port of import. A CIF quote is more meaningful to the overseas buyer because it includes the costs of goods, insurance, and all transportation and miscellaneous charges to the named place of debarkation.

C&F—(cost and freight) to named overseas port. The price includes the cost of the goods and transportation costs to the named place of debarkation. The cost of insurance is borne by the buyer.

FAS—(free alongside) at a named U.S. port of export. The price includes cost of goods and charges for delivery of the goods alongside the shipping vessel. The buyer is responsible for the cost of loading onto the vessel, transportation, and insurance.

FOB—(free on board) at a named inland point of origin; at a named port of exportation; or a named vessel and port of export. The price includes the cost of the goods and delivery to the place named.

EX—(named port of origin). The price quoted covers costs only at the point of origin (example, EX Factory). All other charges are the buyer's concern.

A complete list of terms and their definitions can be found in *Incoterms,* a booklet published by the International Chamber of Commerce, 801 Second Avenue, Suite 1204, New York, NY 10017. It is important for the exporter to understand exactly the meanings of terms used in quotations. A simple misunderstanding regarding delivery terms may prevent the exporter from meeting contractual obligations or make that person responsible for shipping costs he or she did not intend to incur. Exhibit 18–2 indicates who is responsible for a variety of costs under various terms.

PACKING AND MARKING

Special packing and marking requirements must be considered for those shipments destined to be transported over water, subject to excessive handling, or destined for parts of the world with extreme climate. Packing adequate for domestic shipments often falls short for goods subject to the conditions mentioned. Protection against rough handling, moisture, temperature extremes, and pilferage may require heavy crating which increases total packing costs as well as freight rates because of increased weight and size. Since some countries determine import duties on gross weight, packing can add a significant amount to import fees. To avoid

EXHIBIT 18–2 Who's Responsible for Costs under Various Terms?

Cost Items/Terms	FOB (Free on Board) Inland Carrier at Factory	FOB (Free on Board) Inland Carrier at Point of Shipment	FAS (Free Along Side) Vessel or Plane at Port of Shipment	CIF (Cost, Insurance, Freight) at Port of Destination
Export packing*	Buyer	Seller	Seller	Seller
Inland freight	Buyer	Seller	Seller	Seller
Port charges	Buyer	Buyer	Seller	Seller
Forwarder's fee	Buyer	Buyer	Buyer	Seller
Consular fee	Buyer	Buyer	Buyer	Buyer†
Loading on vessel or plane	Buyer	Buyer	Buyer	Seller
Ocean freight	Buyer	Buyer	Buyer	Seller
Cargo insurance	Buyer	Buyer	Buyer	Seller
Customs duties	Buyer	Buyer	Buyer	Buyer
Ownership of goods passes	When goods onboard an inland carrier (truck, rail, etc.) or in hands of inland carrier	When goods unloaded by inland carrier	When goods alongside carrier, in hands of air or ocean carrier	When goods on board air or ocean carrier at port of shipment

* Who absorbs export packing? This charge should be clearly agreed on. Charges are sometimes controversial.
† The seller has responsibility to arrange for consular invoices (and other documents requested by buyer's government). According to official definitions, buyer pays fees, but sometimes as a matter of practice, seller includes in quotations.

the extremes of too much or too little packing, the marketer should consult export brokers, export freight forwarders, or other specialists.

All countries have some import regulations for marking goods and containers; noncompliance can result in severe penalties. Recently announced Peruvian regulations require all foreign products imported into Peru to bear a brand name, country of origin, and an expiration date clearly inscribed on the product. In case of imported wearing apparel, shoes, electric appliances, automotive parts, liquors, and soft drinks, the name and tax identity card number of the importer must also be added. Peruvian customs refuse clearance of foreign products not fulfilling these requirements, and the importer has to reship the goods within 60 days of the customs appraisal date or they are seized and auctioned as abandoned goods. Further, goods already in Peru must also meet the provisions of the decree or be subject to public auction.

The exporter should be particularly careful that all marking on the container conforms exactly to the data on the export documents as well because discrepancies are often interpreted by customs officials as an attempt to defraud. A basic source of information for American exporters is the Department of Commerce pamphlet series entitled *Preparing Shipment to (Country)* which details the necessary export documents and pertinent U.S. and foreign government regulations for labeling, marking, packing, and customs procedures.[30]

EXPORT SHIPPING

Whenever and however title to goods is transferred, those goods must be transported. Shipping goods to another country presents some important differences from shipping to a domestic location. The goods can be out of the shipper's control for longer periods of time than in domestic distribution; more shipping and collections documents are required; packing must be suitable; and shipping insurance coverage is necessarily more extensive. The task is to match each order of goods to the shipping modes best suited for swift, safe, and economical delivery. Ocean shipping, air freight, air express, and parcel post are all possibilities; however, ocean shipping is usually the least expensive method and the most frequently used for heavy bulk shipments. For certain categories of goods, air freight can be the most economical and certainly the speediest.[31]

Shipping costs are an important factor in a product's price in export marketing; the transportation mode must be selected in terms of the total

---

[30] For help and guidance through the maze of rules and regulations, see "Tools of the Export Trade," *Business America*, October 28, 1985, pp. 2–5.

[31] "The Export Express: Don't Miss the Boat," *Distribution*, October 1987, p. 71.

impact on cost. One estimate is that logistics account for between 19 and 23 percent of the total cost of a finished product sold internationally. In ocean shipping one of the important innovations in reducing or controlling the high cost of transportation is the use of containerization. Containerized shipments, in place of the traditional bulk handling of full loads or breakbulk operations, has resulted in intermodal transport between inland points, reduced costs, and simplified handling of international shipments.[32]

With increased use of containerization, rail container service had developed in many countries to provide the international shipper with door-to-door movement of goods under seal originating and terminating inland. This eliminates several loadings, unloadings, and changes of carriers and reduces costs substantially as illustrated in Exhibit 18–3, although such savings are not always possible for all types of cargo. Containerized cargo handling also reduces damage and pilferage in transit.

For many commodities of high unit value and low weight and volume, international air freight has become an important method of shipping. Air freight has shown the fastest growth rate for freight transportation even though it accounts for only a fraction of total international shipments. Depending on the point of origin, the destination, the commodity, and size of shipment, air freight can cost two to five times surface charges for general cargo. Some cost reduction is realized through reduced packing requirements, paperwork, insurance, and the cost of money tied up in inventory, but usually not enough to offset the higher rates charged for air freight. The key to air freight is time saving; if the commodity has high unit value or high inventory costs, or if there is concern with delivery time, air freight can be a justifiable alternative. Many products moving in foreign markets meet the requirements. The top 10 commodities shipped by air are:

1. Newspapers, magazines, periodicals, books, and catalogs.
2. Industrial and agricultural machinery.
3. Personal effects.
4. Electrical equipment and appliances.
5. Surface vehicles and parts.
6. Printed matter.
7. Chemicals, drugs, and pharmaceuticals.
8. Clothing.
9. Cloth and textiles.
10. Baby poultry.

Despite the high cost, air freight's speed and flexibility make it a viable alternative in many export shipping decisions.

Even though the selection of transportation mode has an important bearing on the cost of export shipping, it is not the only cost involved in

---

[32] "International Logistics: Passport to Profits," *Distribution*, October 1987, pp. 12–20.

EXHIBIT 18–3   Examples of Distribution Costs from Paris to Denver via New York (U.S. dollars per metric ton)

Conventional Cargo Handling	Commodity A per Metric Ton	Commodity B per Metric Ton
Domestic carrier	$ 0.95	$ 0.95
Inland warehouse, 1 month including handling and delivery	12.14	12.14
Transport to port	12.78	12.78
Ship's agent	1.89	5.18
Port forwarder	0.97	2.66
Port warehouse (average 4 days) including handling	2.92	2.92
Stevedore	3.93	5.70
Sea carrier	21.67	80.70
Stevedore + port warehouse	6.32	6.32
Ship's agent	0.94	2.59
Port forwarder	0.79	0.79
Inland transport	46.64	46.64
Unloading	11.50	11.50
Totals	123.44	190.87

Containerized Cargo Handling	Commodity A per Metric Ton	Commodity B per Metric Ton
Domestic carrier	$ 0.95	$ 0.95
Inland warehouse, 1 month including handling and delivery	12.14	12.14
Transport to port	5.97	5.97
Ship's agent	1.69	4.65
Port forwarder	0.87	2.39
Stevedore	1.60	1.60
Sea carrier	23.07	78.35
Stevedore + port warehouse	6.32	6.32
Ship's agent	0.85	2.32
Forwarder	0.79	0.79
Inland transport	33.45	35.49
Unloading	11.50	11.50
Totals	99.20	162.47

Note: Commodity A = Industrial cooking oil in 10-gallon containers (low-tariff cargo).
Commodity B = Industrial chemicals, harmless (high-tariff cargo).

the physical movement of goods from point of origin to ultimate market. Indeed, the selection of mode, the location of inventory, warehouses, and so forth, all figure in the cost of the physical movement of goods. A narrow solution to physical movement of goods is the selection of transportation; a broader application is the concept of logistics management or physical distribution.

LOGISTICS

When a company is primarily an exporter from a single country to a single market, the typical approach to the physical movement of goods is the selection of a dependable mode of transportation which ensures safe arrival of the goods within a reasonable time for a reasonable carrier cost.[33] However, as a company becomes global, such a solution to the movement of products could prove costly and highly inefficient for seller and buyer.[34] At one point in the growth and expansion of an international firm, costs other than transportation are such that an optimal cost solution to the physical movement of goods cannot be achieved without thinking of the physical distribution process as an integrated system. When a foreign marketer begins producing and selling in more than one country and becomes a global marketer, it is time to consider the concept of logistics management, that is, a total systems approach to management of the distribution process that includes all activities involved in physically moving raw material, in-process inventory, and finished goods inventory from the point of origin to point of use or consumption.[35]

Interdependence of Physical Distribution Activities

Distribution viewed as a system involves more than physical movement. At least five major activities are involved plus the ever-important considerations of customer service and contractual obligation.

1. *Facility locations:* Where should plant, warehouses, and depots be located?
2. *Inventory allocation:* Where should inventory be located and in what quantities?
3. *Transportation:* What mode or modes of transport should be used? Lease or buy?
4. *Communications:* A distribution system must work in both directions— material flowing one way and information the other.
5. *Unitization:* How should the products be packaged and wrapped so that economies of movement and storage may be achieved?[36]

The physical distribution concept recognizes that the costs of each activity are interdependent and a decision involving one affects the cost and effi-

---

[33] "Global Logistics," *Distribution*, October 1988, pp. 26–32.

[34] "Organizing for International Success," *Distribution*, October 1988, pp. 48–54.

[35] David L. Anderson, "International Logistics Strategies for the 1980s," *International Journal of Physical Distribution and Materials Management* 15, no. 4 (1985), pp. 5–19.

[36] Martin Christopher, "Logistics in its Marketing Context," *European Journal of Marketing* 6, no. 2 (1972), p. 118.

Canal boats, Suzhou, China; horse cart, Kashmir; and high speed train, Europe. Getting the product to market can mean multitransportation modes. (Lower left: Rich Clark/Journalism Services, Inc.; (Lower right: N'Diaye/ Journalism Services, Inc.)

ciency of one or all others. In fact, because of their interdependence, there are an infinite number of "total costs" for the sum of each of the different activity costs. (*Total cost* of the system is defined as the sum of the costs of all these activities.) The idea of interdependence can be illustrated by the classic example of air freight. Exhibit 18–4 is a hypothetical

EXHIBIT 18-4   Cost Comparison between Air Freight and Ocean Shipping of Spare Parts—Europe to the United States

	Air	Ocean
Packing	$ 19.57	$ 37.99
Transportation to port of departure, handling	23.79	21.87
Freight	233.72	120.50
Transportation from port of destination, handling	52.19	45.67
Import duties	227.19	230.26
Insurance	2.69	6.52
Total cost of transportation	$ 559.15	$ 462.81
Number of days in transit	4 days	30 days
Cost of capital tied up in transit	$ 2.30	$ 12.66
Total cost transportation	561.45	475.47
Cost of goods	1,474.06	1,474.06
Total cost	2,035.51	1,949.53
Cost difference	$ 85.98	—
Time savings	26 days	—

SOURCE: Adapted from Felix Wentworth, Martin Christopher, Gordon Wills, and Bernard J. La Londe, *Managing International Distribution* (New York: AMACOM, American Management Association, 1979), p. 262.

illustration of a shipment of spare parts from Europe to the United States using two different modes of transportation—ocean freight and the more expensive air freight. When total costs are calculated, air freight is just slightly more costly than ocean freight. However, when the 26 days in time savings are considered, air freight could prove considerably less costly. One cost not included in the illustration is the potential cost of U.S. storage and warehousing that would be necessary with ocean freight to provide the same level of customer service by both systems. When total costs are calculated, air freight may be less costly because it is possible to reduce inventory investment, use less protective packaging, make one local destination delivery instead of two, and eliminate a warehouse. These overall savings more than offset the higher freight rate for air shipment.

Another example involves a large multinational firm with facilities and customers the world over. This firm shipped parts from its U.S. Midwest plant to the nearest East Coast port, then by water route around the Cape of Good Hope (Africa), and finally to its plants in Asia taking 14 weeks. Substantial inventory was maintained in Asia as a safeguard against uncertain water-borne deliveries. The transportation carrier costs were the least expensive available; however, delivery delays and unreliable service caused the firm to make emergency air shipments to keep production lines going. Air shipment costs rose to 70 percent of the total transport bill. An analysis of the problem in the physical distribution system showed that costs could be lowered by using higher cost motor carriers to truck

BOX 18–5
Coors Beer Flies to Tokyo

"This whole beer lift came about," explained the VP of physical distribution, "because Asahi-brewed Coors was such a big hit with Japanese beer drinkers. Asahi just couldn't keep up with demand and asked Coors to help by exporting beer from Golden."

Asahi Brewers, Ltd., brews Coors and Coors Light brands under license from Adolph Coors Company, the United States' fifth largest beer company of Golden, Colorado. After only 10 months, sales exceeded expectations by more than 100 percent. Asahi needed extra Coors to get through the summer season.

So on June 4, Coors Transportation Company, the brewery's trucking subsidiary, began hauling truckloads of beer to Denver's Stapleton International Airport. The trucks were met by Boeing 747–200 series freighters flown by Flying Tigers. In all, 15 plane loads of beer, weighing 3 million pounds, were airlifted to Japan. That is the equivalent of more than 60 trailer truck loads flown across the Pacific.

At first, Coor's international transportation analysts thought they would use ocean freight. That was ruled out by the urgency of getting the beer to Japan for the peak summer months and the quality concerns of both Coors and Asahi—Coors beer would not stand up under the hot, humid conditions on a long sea voyage.

What does the future hold? Will Coors continue to ship beer by air to Tokyo? Asahi thinks shortages will continue and another seasonal airlift will be necessary next summer if the Japanese continue to quench their thirst with Coors' golden brew.

Source: Adapted from "International Strategies: Adolph Coors," *Distribution*, October 1988, p. 66.

the parts to West Coast ports, then ship them by sea. Transit time was reduced, delivery reliability improved, inventory quantities in Asia lowered, and emergency air shipments eliminated. The new distribution system produced an annual savings of $60,000. Obviously, a cost difference will not always be the case, but the examples serve to illustrate the interdependence of the various activities in the physical distribution mix and the total cost. A change of transportation mode affected a change in packaging and handling, inventory costs, warehousing time and cost, and delivery charges.

The concept of physical distribution is the achievement of optimum (lowest) system cost consistent with customer service objectives of the firm. If the activities in the physical distribution system are viewed separately without consideration of their interdependence, the final cost of distribution and quality of service rendered may be suboptimized.[37] Distribution problems confronting the international marketer are compounded by additional variables and costs that are also interdependent and must be included in the total physical distribution decision. As the international firm broadens the scope of its operations, the additional variables and costs become more crucial in their effect on the efficiency of the distribution system.

Effect of Environment on Physical Distribution Costs

One of the most consistent variables to be dealt with is the physical environment or geography. Environmental differences encountered in foreign marketing place an extra burden on the process of physical distribution. The environmental differences that confront a company with one U.S. manufacturing plant selling in two geographical regions in the United States are substantially different from those of a company with a manufacturing plant in one country selling in two different countries. The company operating on an international front must deal with several currencies, several sets of laws, sometimes indefinable taxes, varied local transportation costs, and different warehousing systems. In the Netherlands, Belgium, and Italy, there is no limit on the time goods can be left in a bonded warehouse without paying import taxes, but in Germany and France, there is a limit. In the United States, transportation tariffs are set by the ICC and all tariffs are on file resulting in uniform tariffs to all. This is not so in Europe where transportation rates are negotiated in open competition and prices may vary from day to day. To further confuse the situation, door-to-door delivery and ship unloading costs can vary substantially from port to port in Europe.

For MNCs, one of the major benefits of the European Community's unification plans for 1992 will be the elimination of transportation barriers among member countries. Instead of approaching Europe on a country-by-country basis, after 1992 a centralized logistics network will be the most efficient distribution system for a unified market.[38] Even before 1992, there were improvements in the amount of paperwork necessary when transporting goods between borders. The introduction of the Single Administrative Document (SAD) has reduced the number of documents from approximately 35 to 1 two-page document.[39]

---

[37] For a complete discussion of the breadth and scope of physical distribution management, see James R. Stock and Douglas M. Lambert, "Physical Distribution Management in International Marketing," reprinted in David M. Andrus et al. *International Marketing Management: A Reader* (Bessemer, Ala.: Colonial Press, 1988), pp. 278–91.

[38] "Europhobia or Europhoria?" *Distribution*, October 1988, pp. 38–46.

[39] "Europe without Borders: Answers to Some Questions," *Europe*, October 1988, pp. 15–17.

BOX 18–6
When Is a Car a Truck or a Truck a Car?

Chrysler officials were miffed about Japan's fastest-growing class of imports in the United States: four-wheel drive, sport-utility vehicles that include the Toyota 4Runner, Isuzu Trooper, and Suzuki Samurai. Some 230,000 such Japanese vehicles were imported into the United States, capturing nearly a third of the $10 billion market. These vehicles are aimed squarely at the Jeep, America's best-known maker of four-wheel drives.

All Japanese four-wheel drives are imported into the United States without backseats. That way, they are able to qualify as trucks instead of cars, thereby avoiding Japan's voluntary limit of 2.3 million passenger-car imports into the United States. As trucks they simply pay a duty and roll onto America's docks.

Trucks? True, the Japanese vehicles don't have backseats when they are imported but they do have carpeting, ash trays, air-conditioning, vents, and stereo speakers in the back. Most even have rear seat mounts so that backseats—imported separately—can be quickly and easily installed by U.S. dealers.

This is not unlike the 1960s subterfuge the Japanese engaged in when they dodged U.S. truck tariffs by importing pickup trucks as "truck parts." They imported the trucks without the box on the back and once the trucks were in the United States the boxes—again imported separately—were simply bolted on.

As one official stated, "close the door and they come through the window. Close the window and they come through the door."

Source: Adapted from Edwin A. Finn, Jr., "Look, Ma, No Back Seats," *Forbes*, February 22, 1988, p. 91.

The flexibility and cost of the physical distribution activity also are affected by increasing pressure brought about by local governments as policies are expanded to encompass greater economic development. An individual logistics orientation could help minimize the adverse effects of government policy changes on worldwide distribution systems. Further, planning and location of production facilities are drawn into consideration of physical distribution systems. Some governments offer lucrative inducements for plant locations in their countries, but a company must look at the effect of that specific plant location on their marketwide physical distribution cost both with the inducement and without. A country that gives tariff protection, tax privileges, government financing, and favorable exchange rates can also take away those advantages after capital investments have been made. Evaluating the alternatives in a logistics system context could reveal impending problems with potential restrictions on inventory levels, taxes, and controls on imports, quotas, and tariffs. Certainly the typical pattern is for governments to change their policies toward foreign companies as it suits their natural internal policy development goals. All these factors must be accounted for in physical distribution because they are all interdependent and affect the total cost of distribution. A physical distribution system can aid in minimizing that total cost.[40]

Benefits of Physical Distribution Systems

There are other benefits to a physical distribution system besides cost advantages. An effective physical distribution system can result in optimal inventory levels and, in multiplant operations, optimal production capacity, both of which result in better use of working capital. In making plant-location decisions, a company with a physical distribution system can readily assess operating costs of alternative plant locations to serve various markets. For example, suppose a company is assessing the advantage of building a plant in Italy to supply markets there that are presently being sourced from Great Britain or West Germany.

> At the headquarters in New York, the logistics planning group is asked to examine this proposal. The logistics group takes five-year sales forecasts for all national markets and, using a linear programming model, calculates estimates of the minimum total variable cost of producing and shipping products from all plants to all markets. Two calculations are made, one assuming the new Italian plant is already "on stream," and the other assuming the British and West German plants are used to serve the Italian market. The study includes, of course, an estimate of the added investment to equip the proposed Italian plant, hire and train new workers, and put it on stream.[41]

With this information, company managers can now examine this decision's effect on the operating costs of the entire distribution system.

A physical distribution system may also result in better (more dependable) delivery service to the market; when products are produced at different locations, companies are able to quickly determine the most economical source for a particular customer. As companies expand into multinational markets and source these markets from multinational production facilities, they are increasingly confronted with cost variables that make it imperative to employ a total systems approach to the management of the distribution process to achieve efficient operation. Finally, a physical distribution system can render the natural obstructions created by geography less economically critical for the multinational marketer.

---

[40] Felix Wentworth, Martin Christopher, Gordon Wills, and Bernard J. La Londe, *Managing International Distribution* (New York: AMACOM, American Management Association, 1979), p. 262.

[41] Robert E. McGarrah, "Logistics for the International Manufacturer," *Harvard Business Review,* March–April 1966, p. 165.

THE FOREIGN-FREIGHT FORWARDER

An indispensable agent for an exporting firm that cannot afford an in-house specialist to handle paperwork and other export trade mechanics is the foreign-freight forwarder. Foreign-freight forwarders are licensed by the Federal Maritime Commission and arrange for the shipment of goods as agents for the exporter.[42] Even in large companies with active export departments capable of handling documentation, a forwarder is useful as a shipment coordinator at the port of export or at the destination port. Besides arranging for complete shipping documentation, the full-service foreign-freight forwarder provides information and advice on routing and scheduling, rates and related charges, consular and licensing requirements, labeling requirements, and export restrictions. Further, the agent offers shipping insurance, warehouse storage, packing and containerization, and ocean cargo or air freight space. Both large and small shippers find freight forwarders' wide range of services useful and well worth the fees normally charged. In fact, for many shipments, forwarders may save on freight charges if they are able to consolidate shipments into larger, more economical quantities. Experienced exporters regard the foreign-freight forwarder as an important addition to in-house specialists.[43]

SUMMARY

An awareness of the mechanics of export trade is indispensable to the foreign marketer who engages in exporting goods from one country to another. Although most marketing techniques are open to interpretation and creative application, the mechanics of exporting are very exact; there is little room for interpretation or improvisation with the requirements of export licenses, quotas, tariffs, export documents, packing, marketing, and the various uses of commercial payments. The very nature of the regulations and restrictions surrounding importing and exporting can lead to frequent and rapid change. In handling the mechanics of export trade successfully, the manufacturer must keep abreast of all foreign and domestic changes in requirements and regulations pertaining to the product involved. For firms unable to maintain their own export staffs, foreign-freight forwarders can handle many details for a nominal fee.

With paperwork completed, the physical movement of goods must be considered. Transportation mode affects total product cost because of the

---

[42] Robert Vidrick, "How to Choose and Use an International Freight Forwarder," *Distribution*, October 1988, pp. 78–84.

[43] "The Role of the Freight Forwarder," *American Import/Export Global Trade*, March 1988, pp. 16–27.

varying requirements of packing, inventory levels, time requirements, perishability, unit cost, damage and pilfering losses, and customer service. Transportation for each product must be assessed in view of the interdependent nature of all these factors. To assure optimum distribution at minimal cost, a physical distribution system determines everything from plant location to final customer delivery in terms of the most efficient use of capital investment, resources, production, inventory, packing, and transportation.

QUESTIONS

1. Define and show the significance to international marketing of the following terms:

commodity control list	FAS
general license	foul bill of lading
commodity classifications	*maquiladora*
validated license	clean bill of lading
exchange permits	logistics
Foreign-Trade Zone	physical distribution
ad valorem duty	systems
harmonized system	ELAIN and STELA

2. Explain the reasoning behind the various regulations and restrictions imposed on the exportation and importation of goods.

3. Define the two licenses required for exporting goods from the United States.

4. What determines the type of license needed for exportation? Discuss.

5. Discuss the most frequently encountered trade restrictions.

6. What is the purpose of an import license? Discuss.

7. Explain free-trade zones and illustrate how they may be used by an exporter. By an importer. How do free-zones differ from bonded warehouses?

8. How do in-bond areas differ from foreign-trade zones? How would an international marketer use an in-bond area?

9. Explain each of the following export documents
   a. Bill of lading
   b. Counselor invoice or certificate of origin
   c. Commercial invoice
   d. Insurance certificate

10. What are the differences between a straight bill of lading and order bill of lading? What are the differences between a clean bill of lading and foul bill of lading?

11. Why would an exporter use the services of a foreign-freight forwarder? Discuss.

12. Besides cost advantages, what are the other benefits of a physical distribution system?

13. Discuss customs-privileged facilities. How are they used?

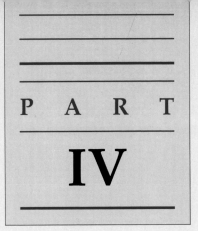

PART

IV

Corporate Context of Marketing

Chapters

CHAPTER

19

Financial Requirement for Global Marketing

Marketing and finance are inextricably intertwined with overall corporate planning, goals, and objectives; policies and decisions in each have a profound effect on the others. Without proper financial support, marketing activities cannot attain their ultimate potential; and, in turn, without adequate cash flows and profits generated by marketing activities, corporate ability to achieve full growth and development potential is limited. It is generally thought that financial considerations are the primary domain of the finance officer, but as any international marketer can attest, the financier's concerns are also those of the marketer.

Marketers have an intense interest in financial functions because money is the basic tool for facilitating marketing activities. Effective financial arrangements significantly strengthen competitive marketing positions. With adequate monetary resources at their disposal, marketing managers can effect greater profits by lowering costs or by increasing sales volume. Adequate profits by lowering costs or by increasing sales volume. Adequate inventories can be maintained if funds are available—a critical variable in international business where restocking can take months. The business with plentiful purchasing power usually can buy merchandise more cheaply by buying directly or in quantity, or have access to an array of sources by being able to pay cash. Plentiful money can permit a marketer to build the most effective marketing channels for the firm—regardless of cost.

Furthermore, advertising can be treated as a capital expenditure if adequate funds are available. Ability to finance customer purchases is another business-building, competitive activity often denied to underfinanced companies.[1]

As a company moves more deeply into the international arena, the interdependence of marketing and financial activities increases and places greater financial demands on the company. Two areas of impact are: (1) the increased need for working capital, and (2) the enhanced financial risk resulting from fluctuating foreign exchange. This chapter emphasizes the financial requirements of international marketing; it considers the need for increased funds, the sources of those funds, and the increased financial risk and methods of minimizing the risks. The entire treatment is concerned less with the mechanics of international finance than with the strategic marketing implications related to finance.

CAPITAL NEEDS FOR INTERNATIONAL MARKETING

Distance, time lags, tariffs, taxes, financial participation requirements, exchange restrictions, fluctuating monetary values, and adequate local financial strength are all elements differentiating the problems of financing international marketing activities from those related to domestic marketing. Effective management of the financial functions of marketing can be a strategic factor affecting profits and having great impact on the company's ability to develop marketing channels.

Time lags caused by distance and crossing international borders add cost elements to international marketing that make cash-flow planning especially important. Even in a relatively simple transaction, money may be tied up for months while goods are being shipped from one part of the world to another; customs clearance may add days, weeks, or months; payment may be held up while the international payment documents are being transferred from one nation to another; and breakage, commercial disputes, or governmental restrictions can add further delay. Nearly every international transaction encounters some kind of time lag during which marketing financing must be provided. Financial time lags exist even when a company is dealing with its own subsidiaries or branches in overseas operations.

Besides greater demands for working capital, the international marketer may have to make long-term capital investments as well. In some instances, markets are closed to a foreign business unless all or some portion of

---

[1] For a complete discussion of the role of financial management in international business, see "New Directions and Tactics in Financial Management," *Business International*, September 12, 1988, pp. 281–92.

the product is manufactured locally. Thus, international marketing activities frequently require supplemental financing for (1) working capital and (2) capital investment.

Working Capital Requirements

Because of time lags, shippings costs, duties, higher start-up costs, inventory cost, market penetration costs, and increased financial needs for trade and channel credit, foreign operations typically require larger amounts of working capital than domestic activities operating at the same volume levels. Travel costs alone can consume working capital funds; in one instance, a U.S. firm discovered it was spending more on travel in a foreign market than on salaries.

Start-up Costs.   Larger amounts of working capital are frequently required to cover the start-up cost of a company entering new international markets. Such costs can come as a surprise to the firm accustomed to operating in a familiar domestic market. A firm may find it must pay for information assumed or acquired without cost in the home country. Also part of start-up costs are legal fees, establishing an office, purchase of licenses, and so on. Marketing research can become an major expense, particularly if a company has to research three or four countries before embarking on a business enterprise in any one of them.

Inventory.   The marketer's effectiveness in managing inventories can have considerable impact on the financial requirements of this function. Adequate servicing of overseas markets frequently requires goods to be inventoried in several locations; one company that uses two factory warehouses for the entire United States needed six foreign distribution points that together handled less merchandise than either U.S. outlet.

Slower transportation and longer distances when shipping over water mean inventory turnover can be lengthened considerably over the customary time for domestic operations. Add loading and unloading time and the time in transit for an overseas shipment from a Midwest manufacturer in the United States to Europe and transit time can take as much as two months or longer. If your product is entering a congested port such as La Guaira in Venezuela, there may be a month's delay just for unloading. The additional time required for delivery increases the capital requirements needed to finance inventories.

An entirely new type of inventory financing requirement is sometimes foisted on the marketer forced to accept countertrade goods to close a transaction with a currency-short country or forced to buy back goods as part of a financing package for capital equipment. Unless the goods are readily disposable, the company may find itself carrying them for significant periods of time before markets are found.

Because goods offered in countertrade seldom have a readily available market (otherwise there would be no need to offer them in countertrade), marketers must warehouse the goods, incur the expense of marketing them, or discount them to get them out of inventory. Any one of these situations increases inventory costs.

Market Penetration Costs

A variety of costs is associated with market penetration. In many cases these costs are higher, relative to sales, in foreign markets than in U.S. markets, thereby increasing the capital needs for international marketing.

Promotion and advertising costs are similar in domestic and foreign markets except they are generally higher relative to actual sales. Markets are smaller, media usually more expensive, and multiple media generally required; these and similar factors increase investment needs.

Manufacturers of durable goods have found they often must provide funds for service facilities before their products are accepted. Japanese automakers met with little success in the United States until they provided funds for adequate service facilities and expanded spare parts inventories.

It is never inexpensive to establish a channel of distribution, but again, the complications of international distribution can require extra large channel investments. Foreign middlemen are seldom adequately financed and may require extensive long-term credit if they are to carry adequate inventories and offer their customers adequate credit.

Channel credit requirements have surprised many American firms. Most of the world's middlemen are dreadfully underfinanced, and if they are to buy goods in economical quantities, interim credit must be provided by the producers. The international finance director of a machinery and equipment company says he expects increasing foreign sales volume to require additional working capital to "support from 50 percent to 75 percent of the sales increase."

The American firm's competitive position may be weaker in the world markets than in domestic markets because of the number of competitors vying for customers in certain product lines. One U.S. company that marketed insecticides in Spain through seven local distributors found that within less than three years, six of those distributors had been purchased, or partially purchased, by competitive firms thus blocking the initial supplier's distribution. The company found similar situations in Latin America, South Africa, Australia, and southern Europe. To retain a competitive position, the company in question was virtually forced to make major investments in buying distributors throughout the world. While many of these ventures are profitable, it requires huge infusions of funds to maintain market position. In the home market, such investments would probably have been unnecesary.

Credit is becoming as important to export sales as the price of a product. Credit and payment terms have become major weapons of international competition in the global marketplace. Historically, U.S. business has been reluctant to offer advantageous credit terms to foreign buyers; despite this, strong product preferences internationally have permitted U.S. businesses to thrive. Such conditions no longer prevail since extended credit terms have become an important factor in selling. Moderate-size foreign exchange reserves and the willingness of West German, British, and Japanese competitors to offer favorable credit terms have increasingly put U.S. businesses at a disadvantage in international markets unless comparable credit terms are available. In fact, one of Japan's chief advantages over U.S. competitors is its excellent pipeline of low-cost loans to boost its exports.[2]

The fact that U.S. businesses are changing their attitudes toward issuing credit is supported by the evidence that most firms' export accounts receivable have shown substantial increases in the past few years. Many firms are using open accounts rather than cash payment as the basic means of extending credit.

Accounts-receivable financing imposes great strains on international working capital. Both middlemen and industrial customers have learned they are in a position to pressure manufacturers into continuously longer and longer credit extensions because credit terms are such an important marketing weapon in the battle for competitive position in international markets. Marketing and product advantages are being offset by more advantageous financial terms from competing foreign suppliers. To get goods into the channel of distribution, marketers may have to compensate for the middlemen's lack of capital by providing consignment merchandise, floor-plan financing, or long-term credit. Without such financial assistance, most foreign middlemen cannot handle adequate inventories.

A decade or two ago, international marketers had little concern about credit because terms tended to be cash in advance. Many small agricultural marketers or exporters continue to rely on these terms; but, in today's intensely competitive world marketplace, no major marketer can afford a cash-only posture. Middlemen may require both extensive and intensive credit availability to develop the type of distribution systems requisite to large-scale marketing. A major arena of credit competition demands provision of long-term credit for major capital goods purchases. All three types—consumer, trade, and industrial markets—may make extreme credit demands on company resources.

---

[2] Alan Cohen, "Improved Financing for U.S. Exports: A New Year's Assessment," *Export Today*, January–February 1988, p. 13.

Capital Investment

Some markets are closed to foreign businesses unless they produce goods locally. The French government, for example, gave notice to Ford Motor Company that if it expected to keep its large volume of sales in France, it had to produce there; Ford prudently agreed to build its next European plant in France. In such cases, the production facility itself is a crucial element to market entry and may be considered part of the marketing system because market requirements alone dictated the expenditure. In addition, such marketing facilities as warehouses, shipping docks, retail stores, and sales offices, all require significant capital investment in physical facilities. In considering financial implications, the cost of the production facility as well as costs of marketing facilities may logically be related to marketing as a cost of market entry.

An important financial issue facing the international marketer is the availability and source of capital to finance the additional working capital needed. Besides a company's own resources, there are a variety of public funds available.

SOURCES OF GOVERNMENT FUNDS FOR INTERNATIONAL MARKETING OPERATIONS

Working capital for international marketing operations is usually derived from the assets of the company engaging in international trade or exporting. However, private external sources may be used for financing inventory, accounts receivable, construction of physical facilities, and other financing needs. Public sources of funds are likely to play a more important role in financing marketing operations internationally than they do domestically. A number of supranational agencies are engaged in financing international development and marketing activities, plus the foreign marketer may turn to foreign, national, state, and local governments for various kinds of financial assistance.[3]

The great majority of sources of public funds for international business are oriented to industrial development activities. Some agencies, however, interpret industrial development broadly and make funds available for a wide range of business activities.

Export-Import Bank.   Eximbank is the primary U.S. government agency in the business of providing funds for international trade and investment. The Eximbank has long been the major source of U.S. government credit

---

[3] Carol Stitt, "Exporting to the Developing World: The World Bank and Project Finance," *Export Today*, February 1989, pp. 50–54.

BOX 19–1
Living with Inflation

What would you do if we had an inflation rate that increased a $20 restaurant tab in one year to $680, a 3,400 percent change? Such was the case in Bolivia between 1984 and 1985. Here is the way some survive.

When Edgar Miranda gets his monthly teacher's pay of 25 million pesos, he hasn't a moment to lose. Every hour pesos drop in value. So, while his wife rushes to market to lay in a month's supply of rice and noodles, he is off with the rest of the pesos to change them into black-market dollars. Why the rush? Look at what happens to the value of a peso relative to a dollar. The day he was paid 25 million pesos, a dollar cost 500,000 pesos so his salary would have bought $50. A few days later, the rate was at 900,000 per dollar and he would have received $27. The only strategy is to convert pesos to dollars as quickly as possible. What happens then when you want to buy something with pesos and need to convert dollars to pesos? There is a strategy for that, too. Mrs. Miranda wants to change $5 to buy fruit and vegetables for dinner. She goes to town, slows down in traffic and shouts, "What's your price?" at a group of youths on the curb. Within seconds, the price of a dollar rises from 800,000 pesos to 830,000. By the time she reaches the corner, she is hearing 850,000. That is a 6.25 percent increase in less than a block. She buys at the highest price only to find out that had she waited one day longer she could have gotten 950,000. Of course, the price of fruit and vegetables probably went up proportionately. So goes a day in the life of a Bolivian.

The situation in Brazil is not much better; a 500 cruzado bill with a value of $36 (U.S.) was worth only $4 (U.S.) 18 months later. One system used to beat the inflation rate is to keep money in the "over." Available in all banks, the "over" is a 24-hour deposit in Treasury bonds whose interest rate is indexed to the rate of inflation. It is estimated that $35 billion or 13.5 percent of the value of the country's output of goods and services is traded in the "over" each night.

Source: Adapted from Everett G. Martin, "Amid Wild Inflation, Bolivians Concentrate on Swapping Currency," *The Wall Street Journal*, August 13, 1985, p. 1; and "Wealthy Brazilians Deal with Inflation with a Lot of Fancy Financial Footwork," *The Wall Street Journal*, April 20, 1988, p. 17.

for American exporters. The Eximbank has carved out a role in the financing of costly capital equipment, major overseas projects, and less expensive products that are normally financed through short- and medium-term repayment periods. The bank devotes a large percentage of its resources to supporting exports to developing countries, reflecting, in part, their greater need for credit with which to purchase goods and services.[4]

---

[4] Cohen, "Improved Financing for U.S. Exports, pp. 13–14.

The Eximbank supports exports through four major financial programs. First is its direct-credit facility used to finance products and projects requiring long-term repayment periods from 5 to 15 years. Large mining, industrial, and infrastructure projects, as well as such big-ticket products as commercial jet aircraft are included in this program.

A second Eximbank program is its bank guarantees and export credit insurance operations. Commercial bank guarantees assure repayment to U.S. banks engaged in financing U.S. exports. Closely related is the Eximbank's export credit insurance program FCIA (Foreign Credit Insurance Association) that offers insurance covering credit risks of an exporter.[5] FCIA is discussed in more detail later in this chapter.

The third program is a discount-loan facility that makes it possible for U.S. commercial banks to extend fixed-rate export credits. Under this program, a commercial bank is able to borrow from Eximbank up to 85 percent of the amount of a fixed-rate loan it has extended to a foreign buyer of U.S. exports.

The newest program offered by Eximbank is its working-capital guarantee program. Businesses often need working capital assistance before they need financing for export sales. Eximbank guarantees working capital loans that would not be made commercially without the guarantee. Loan funds are used to purchase materials, products, services, and labor for production of goods or services for current or future export sales. Loan funds may also be used for foreign business development such as marketing activities, trade fair participation, or other promotional activities. Funds cannot be used to pay existing debts.

All Eximbank programs operate as loan guarantee programs. Loans are made through commercial banks and guaranteed by Eximbank. Thus the U.S. exporter is able to deal directly with his or her own commercial bank whose efforts are supported indirectly by the U.S. agency.[6]

Agency for International Development (AID). This agency provides loans and grants to Third World nations for both developmental and foreign policy reasons. Developmental loans are extended to support recipient-country development in key economic sectors in agriculture and nutrition, health, training and education, and energy. Foreign policy loans are extended to developing countries and are used to pay for imports needed to run their economies. A significant portion of each loan or grant is used to finance American exports. Specific opportunities for product exports through AID are reported through two publications: *AID-Financial Export Opportunities* and *Procurement Information Bulletin.*

---

[5] Francis X. Boylan, "Exchange Blockage Risk: An Insurance Overview," *Export Today,* March, 1986, pp. 41–45.

[6] For information on these and other Eximbank programs, contact Marketing Department, Eximbank, 811 Vermont Avenue NW, Washington, D.C. 20571.

Overseas Private Investment Corporation (OPIC).   Although best known as a U.S. agency whose major job is to provide insurance against lost due to specific noncommercial international operating risks, OPIC does engage in direct loans for development projects. These loans are to be spent for U.S. projects in LDCs and for goods purchased from the United States. OPIC programs provide financing for U.S. exports in three ways: First, U.S. capital equipment and other products are financed by the agency through its own direct lending and through guarantees on bank credits. Second, the distributorship program supports the strengthening of foreign distributors that buy American products. Loans are made for physical expansion of the foreign distributor's facilities with direct credits and guarantees of bank loans with long-term repayment schedules. Third, OPIC's leasing program provides loans and guarantees to buy American equipment for leasing in foreign countries to U.S.-owned or -managed overseas leasing firms.

Eurodollar Market.   The Eurodollar market is one of the more important sources of debt capital available to the MNC. The term *Eurodollar* refers to a deposit liability banked outside the United States, that is, dollars banked in Germany or any country other than the United States. While the Eurodollar market refers to dollars, the Eurodollar market includes other national currencies banked outside their country of origin. Because the Eurodollar market includes other than U.S. currencies, it is sometimes referred to as the Eurocurrency market even though the predominant currency is the U.S. dollar. These currencies serve as a ready source of cash that holding banks can use as an asset on which a dollar-denominated loan can be made to someone else. This is an important source of funds for financing world trade. In 1986, the estimated gross size of the Eurocurrency was in excess of $1,300 billion. Similar markets in Asia and the Caribbean consist of national currencies deposited in banks outside the country of origin.

Debt-Equity Swaps.   An increasingly common source of funds for companies operating in countries with high external debt, are *debt-equity swaps.* As discussed in Chapter 9, cooperating banks wanting to lower their debt portfolios, and countries wanting to lower their debt burdens without using scarce foreign exchange, participate in favorable debt-equity swaps with multinational companies.[7] For the MNC, this may be a way to finance business activity in a country at discount rates. Debt-equity swaps have been used to finance joint ventures, to acquire working capital,[8] to buy

---

[7] "Deals that Are Making a Dent in Third World Debt," *Business Week.* October 3, 1988, pp. 111–12.

[8] "Bank/MNC Joint Venture Uses Chile's Swap Program in Forging Mega-Deal," *Business Latin America,* October 3, 1988, p. 315.

raw materials and to invest in new facilities.[9] Savings in debt swaps can be substantial.[10] For example, Swift-Armour S. A. Argentina, a wholly-owned subsidiary of Campbell Soup Company, undertook a deal to expand its facilities in Argentina. It needed the equivalent of $41 million (U.S.) in Argentine australs (Argentine currency) for the expansion of its plant. Swift purchased $63 million dollars of Argentina's debt from a U.S. bank for $25 million. Swift then presented the notes to the Argentine central bank that redeemed them for the equivalent of $41 million (U.S.) in Argentine australs. So, for an outlay of $25 million, Swift was able to acquire the equivalent of $41 million in australs. In this case all won; instead of writing off $63 million of bad debt, the bank was able to realize $25 million, Argentina was able to reduce its foreign debt by $63 million, and Swift was able to save $16 million.[11]

FOREIGN COMMERCIAL PAYMENTS

The sale of goods in other countries is further complicated by additional risks encountered when dealing with foreign customers. There are risks from inadequate credit reports on customers; problems of currency exchange controls, distance, and different legal systems; and the cost and difficulty of collecting delinquent accounts which require a different emphasis on payment systems utilized. In U.S. domestic trade, the typical payment procedure for established customers is an open account—the goods are delivered and the customers is billed on an end-of-the-month basis. The most frequently used term of payment in foreign commercial transactions for both export and import sales is a letter of credit, followed closely in importance by commercial dollar drafts or bills of exchange drawn by the seller on the buyer. Internationally, open accounts are reserved for well-established customers, and cash in advance is required of only the poorest credit risks or when the character of the merchandise is such that incompletion of the contract may result in heavy loss. Because of the time required for shipment of goods from one country to another, advance payment of cash is an unusually costly burden for a potential customer and places the seller at a definite competitive disadvantage.

Terms of sale are typically arranged between the buyer and seller at the time of the sale. Type of merchandise, the amount of money involved,

---

[9] "How One MNC Negotiated a Debt Swap in Honduras as Part of Acquisition Deal," *Business Latin America*, July 11, 1988, pp. 218–19.

[10] "Bank/MNC Joint Venture Uses Chile's Swap Program in Foreign Mega-Deal" *Business International*, October 31, 1988, p. 342.

[11] "Debt-Equity Conversions; How MNCs Tap Swap Market to Reduce Investment Costs," *Business Latin America*, September 12, 1988, p. 285.

business custom, the credit rating of the buyer, the country of the buyer, whether the buyer is a new or old customer, are items to be considered in establishing the terms of sale. The four basic payment arrangements, (1) letters of credit, (2) bills of exchange, (3) cash in advance, and (4) open accounts, are discussed in this section.

Letters of Credit

Most American exports are handled by export letters of credit opened in favor of the seller by the buyer. Letters of credit shift the buyer's credit risk to the bank issuing the letter of credit. When a letter of credit is employed, the seller ordinarily can draw a draft against the bank issuing the credit and receive dollars by presenting proper shipping documents. Except for cash in advance, letters of credit afford the greatest degree of protection for the seller.[12]

The procedure for a letter of credit begins with completion of the contract when the buyer goes to a local bank and arranges for the issuance of a letter of credit; the buyer's bank then notifies its correspondent bank in the seller's country that the letter has been issued. After meeting the requirements set forth in the letter of credit, the seller can draw a draft against the credit (in effect, the bank issuing the letter) for payment of the goods. The precise conditions of the letter of credit are detailed in it and usually also require presentation of certain documents with the draft before the correspondent bank will honor it. The documents usually required are: (1) commercial invoice, (2) consular invoice (when requested), (3) clean bill of lading, and (4) insurance policy or certificate.

Letters of credit can be revocable or irrevocable. Irrevocable means that once the credit has been accepted by the seller, it cannot be altered in any way by the buyer without permission of the seller. Added protection is gained if the buyer is required to confirm the letter of credit through a U.S. bank. This irrevocable, confirmed letter of credit means that a U.S. bank accepts responsibility to pay regardless of the financial situation of the buyer or foreign bank. From the seller's viewpoint, this eliminates the foreign political risk and replaces the commercial risk of the buyer's bank with that of the confirming bank. Payment against a confirmed letter of credit is assured by the confirming bank. As soon as the documents are presented to the bank, the seller receives payment.[13]

---

[12] Steven A Meyerowittz, "Selling Abroad: Making Sure You Get Paid," *Business Marketing,* February 1988, pp. 68–74.

[13] For a complete discussion on the use of a letter of credit and warnings about potential pitfalls, see Andre H. Friedman, "Let the Exporter Beware," *Export Today,* Summer 1986, pp. 35–45.

The international department of a major U.S. bank cautions that a letter of credit is not a guarantee of repayment to the seller. Rather, payment is tendered only if the seller complies exactly with the terms of the letter of credit.[14] Since all letters of credit must be exact in the terms and considerations, it is important for the exporter to check the terms of the letter carefully to be certain that all necessary documents have been acquired and properly completed. Some of the more frequent discrepancies found in documents that cause delay in honoring drafts or letters of credit include:

surance defects such as inadequate coverage, no endorsement or counrsignature, and a dating later than the bill of lading.

-lading defects include the bill lacking an "on board" endorsement, nature of carrier, missing an endorsement or failing to specify freight.

dit defects arise if it has expired or is exceeded by the invoice hen including unauthorized charges or disproportionate

late to missing signatures, failure to designate terms F, CIF, FAS) as stipulated in the letter of credit.

with documents that are missing, staledated, or

Bills o

mmercial payment form is sight or time ellers on foreign buyers. In letters of s is involved, but in the use of bills assumes all risk until the actual ure is for the seller to draw a necessary documents to the se. nts required are principally the sam. of the draft, the U.S. bank forwards it with to a correspondent bank in the buyer's country, presented with the draft for acceptance and immediat t. With acceptance of the draft, the buyer receives the propen d bill of lading that is used to acquire the goods from the carr.

Bills of exchange or dollar drafts have one of three time periods—sight, arrival, or date. A sight draft requires acceptance and payment on presenta-

---

[14] Parts of this section are taken from "International Trade Finance Services—Collections, Letters of Credit, Acceptances," Worldwide Banking Department, The First National Bank of Chicago.

BOX 19–2
A Letter-of-Credit Transaction

Here is what typically happens when payment is made by an irrevocable
letter of credit confirmed by a U.S. bank.

1. After you and your customer agree on the terms of sale, the customer
   arranges for his or her bank to open a letter of credit. (Delays may be
   encountered if, for example, the buyer has "insufficient funds." In many
   developing countries, foreign currencies, such as the U.S. dollar, may
   be scarce.)
2. The buyer's bank prepares an irrevocable letter of credit, including all
   instructions.
3. The buyer's bank sends the irrevocable letter of credit to a U.S. bank
   requesting confirmation. (Foreign banks with more than one U.S. correspondent bank generally select the nearest one to the exporter.)
4. The U.S. bank prepares a letter of confirmation to forward to you, along
   with the irrevocable letter of credit.
5. You review carefully all conditions in the letter of credit, in particular,
   shipping dates. If you cannot comply, alert your customer at once. (Your
   freight forwarder can help advise you.)
6. You arrange with your freight forwarder to deliver your goods to the
   appropriate port or airport. If the forwarder is to present the documents
   to the bank (a wise move for new-to-export firms), the forwarder will
   need copies of the letter of credit.
7. After the goods are loaded, the forwarder completes the necessary documents (or transmits the information to you).
8. You (or your forwarder) present documents indicating full compliance
   to the U.S. bank.
9. The bank reviews the documents. If they are in order, it issues you a
   check. The documents are airmailed to the buyer's bank for review and
   transmitted to the buyer.
10. The buyer (or agent) gets the documents which may be needed to claim
    the goods.

Source: "A Basic Guide to Exporting," U.S. Department of Commerce, International
Trade Administration, Washington, D.C.

---

tion of the draft and often before arrival of the goods. An arrival draft
requires payment be made on arrival of the goods. Unlike the other two,
a date draft has an exact date for payment and in no way is affected by
the movement of the goods. There may be time designations placed on
sight and arrival drafts stipulating a fixed number of days after acceptance
when the obligation must be paid. Usually this period is 30 to 120 days,
thus providing a means of extending credit to the foreign buyer.

Dollar drafts have advantages for the seller because an accepted draft

disadv.

frequently can be discounted at a bank for immediate payment. Banks, however, usually discount drafts only with recourse; that is, if the draft is not honored by the buyer, the bank returns it to the seller for payment. An accepted draft is firmer evidence in the case of default and subsequent litigation than an open account would be.

Cash in Advance

The volume of business handled on a cash-in-advance basis is not large. Cash places unpopular burdens on the customer and typically is used when credit is doubtful, when exchange restrictions within the country of destination are such that the return of funds from abroad may be delayed for an unreasonable period, or when the American exporter for any reason is unwilling to sell on credit terms.

Although payment in advance is infrequently employed, partial payment (from 25 to 50 percent) in advance is not unusual when the character of the merchandise is such that an incomplete contract can result in heavy loss. For example, complicated machinery or equipment manufactured to specification or special design would necessitate advance payment which would be, in fact, a nonrefundable deposit.

Open Accounts

Sales on open accounts are not generally made in foreign trade except to customers of long standing with excellent credit reputations or to a subsidiary or branch of the exporter. Open accounts obviously leave sellers in a position where most of the problems of international commercial finance work to their disadvantage. It is generally recommended that sales on open account not be made when it is the practice of the trade to use some other method, when special merchandise is ordered, when shipping is hazardous, when the country of the importer imposes difficult exchange restrictions, or when political unrest requires additional caution.[15]

FINANCIAL RISK AND RISK MANAGEMENT

Several types of financial risk are encountered in international marketing; the major problems include commercial, political, and foreign exchange risk. Some risks are similar to domestic risks although usually intensified

---

[15] For an interesting article on the risks associated with different payment terms, see Bob Letovsky, "Setting Competitive Payment Terms: A Balancing Act for Exporters," *Export Today*, May–June 1988, pp. 25–28.

while others are uniquely international. Every business should deal with the fact of risk through a structured risk-management program. Such a program may call for assuming risks, engaging in some type of risk avoidance, and/or initiating risk-shifting behavior.

Commercial Risk

Commercial risks are handled essentially as normal credit risks encountered in day-to-day business. They include solvency, default, or refusal to pay bills. The major risk is competition which can only be dealt with through consistently effective management and marketing. One unique risk encountered by the international marketer involves financial adjustments. Such risk is encountered when a controversy arises about the quality of goods delivered (but not accepted), a dispute over contract terms, or any other disagreement over which payment is withheld. For example, one company shipped several hundred tons of dehydrated potatoes to a distributor in Germany. The distributor tested the shipment and declared it to be below acceptable taste and texture standards (not explicitly established). The alternatives for the exporter of reducing the price, reselling the potatoes, or shipping them home again, each involved considerable cost. Although there is less risk of substantial loss in the adjustment situation, it is possible for the selling company to have large sums of money tied up for relatively long periods of time until the client accepts the controversial goods, if ever. In some cases, goods must be returned or remanufactured, and in other instances, contracts may be modified to alleviate the controversies. All such problems are uninsurable and costly.

Political Risk

Political risk is related to the problems of war or revolution, currency inconvertibility, expropriation or expulsion, and restriction or cancellation of import licenses. One of the most frequently encountered political risks arises when a country refuses to allow local currency to be converted to any other currency. This often happens when countries are experiencing economic difficulties and want to conserve scarce supplies of hard currencies; that is, currencies that are easily exchangeable for goods or other currencies.[16] For example, when someone in Brazil wants to purchase goods from a company in another country, the seller would probably not accept payment in the Brazilian crezado because its value is being

---

[16] Brazil's Export Engine Is Starting to Sputter," *Business Week*, November 14, 1988, p. 84.

eroded daily as a result of annual inflation of nearly 1,000 percent.[17] The Brazilian has to convert crezados into a hard currency, the U.S. dollar, British pound, French franc, or any other currency that is freely accepted for payment by most of the world.

The Brazilian government also wants to acquire hard currencies to pay off debts owed to other countries and to use when it needs to buy strategic goods from other countries. So, when Brazil runs short of hard currencies, the government is reluctant to exchange cruzados for scarce hard currencies to use for purchases outside Brazil. Thus, the government also frequently blocks a company from converting profits earned in Brazil into hard currencies. When funds are blocked, a company's profits cannot leave the country or be converted into safer hard currencies; unless profits are protected, inflation can seriously erode their value.[18] At times it is not possible to avoid political risks, so marketers must be prepared to handle them or give up doing business in risky markets.[19] Some types of political risk are insurable by agencies mentioned in the risk management section that follows.

Foreign-Exchange Risk

Floating exchange rates of the world's major currencies have forced all marketers to be especially aware of exchange-rate fluctuations and the need to compensate for them in their financial planning. Eastman Kodak Company reported that exchange-rate losses during the early 1980s amounted to about $3.5 billion. To counter such losses, Kodak's business units and overseas offices have received extensive briefing on foreign-exchange planning; further, all decisions involving foreign exchange are carefully analyzed for foreign-exchange impact.[20] Before rates were permitted to float, devaluations of major currencies were infrequent and usually could be anticipated; as illustrated in Exhibit 19–1, however, exchange-rate fluctuations in the float system occur daily.

Until 1973 and the demise of the Bretton Woods Agreement, the international monetary system operated in an environment of quasi-fixed exchange rates pegged to a gold exchange standard. During the time of the Bretton Woods Agreement, the exchange rate for the most industrialized countries'

---

[17] The cruziero was replaced by the cruzado in 1986 as part of a wage and price freeze. The cruzado was created by dropping three zeros off the old cruziero.

[18] "Blocked Funds Management: Ten Innovative Strategies for Getting Your Money Out," *Business Latin America*, September 12, 1988, p. 283.

[19] Roger Cohen, "Brazil Imposes Plan to Quash Hyperinflation," *The Wall Street Journal*, January 16, 1989, p. A6.

[20] Christopher J. Chipello, "The Market Watcher," *The Wall Street Journal*, September 23, 1988, p. 25R.

EXHIBIT 19–1 Exchange Rates of Major Currencies against the Dollar, 1967–1987 (percentage deviations with respect to dollar parities of October 1967 monthly average of daily figures*)

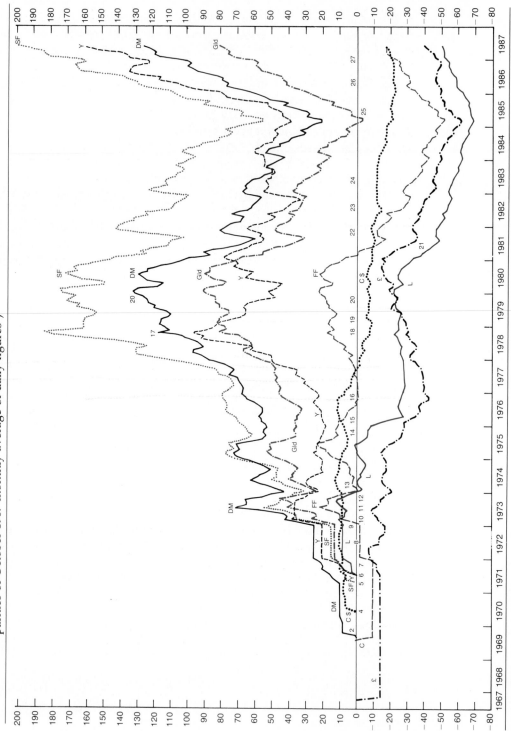

SOURCE: *OECD Economic Outlook* (June 1987), p. 137.

BOX 19–3
If You Can't Get Dollars Will Beans Do?

The Third World represents a huge market but it is tough to crack because of a lack of hard currency to spend. Barter is a major tactic used by company managers who believe it is important to get into these markets early because of their potential 10 to 15 years from now. Here are a few of the ways companies get their money back.

PepsiCo does a lot of countertrade. Their world trade corporation helps generate foreign exchange that enables soft-drink bottlers to buy concentrate. In Mexico, Pepsi's largest soft-drink market, the company bought a locally owned pineapple canning factory and found U.S. buyers for its products; it has also backed a frozen broccoli operation. The Sudan bottlers pay for their concentrate with sesame seeds, while Tanzania provides sisalls used for making rope. Nicaragua still sips Pepsi because the U.S. company has generated exports of sesame seeds and molasses.

To sell copiers and printers in Brazil, Xerox Corporation exports Brazilian steel to Europe and venetian blinds to the United States worth $100 million annually. To close a sale of a million dollars in telephone switching equipment, one communications company agreed to take payment in ginger. The company hired a commodity broker to advise on how much ginger to demand (two tons) and to help convert the brown root into dollars. H. J. Heinz Company has moved into Zimbabwe by buying a stake in a family-owned manufacturer of edible oils and soap. The company introduced Michigan pea beans (kidney beans) which are baked and canned for local consumption and exported into neighboring Botswana. They're also shipped in bulk to Britain. Already most of the original $17 million investment has come back in cash by selling canned beans all over the world. Baked beans are a Sunday dinner treat in Zimbabwe and Botswana.

Source: Adapted from Louis Kraar, "How to Sell to Cashless Buyers," *Fortune*, November 7, 1988, pp. 147–52.

currencies was relatively stable and fluctuations were infrequent and small. Thus, a firm's transactions in foreign currencies were fairly secure in terms of exchange rates to other currencies. Since 1973 a system of floating exchange rates has evolved, producing a heightened volatility in the prices of currencies. With world inflation, the swings of currencies have intensified since the late 1970s. Exhibit 19–1 shows the variations in OECD country currencies between 1967 and 1987. It is not hard to imagine the foreign-exchange risk problems of MNCs that had large amounts in accounts receivable in Japanese yen, German marks, British pounds, or French francs during this period. Depending on the specific time span, a firm could stand to lose substantial sums of money from too much exposure to fluctuating currencies. The variations in currencies have put severe

World currencies. Global companies must plan for financial riaks arising from economic inflation, varying exchange rates, and inconvertibility of local currency. (Mike Kidulich/Journalism Services, Inc.)

strains on multinational company income streams and have resulted in major concern over the extent of *transaction exposure.*

Transaction exposure occurs at any time a company has assets denominated in some currency other than that of its home country and expects to convert the foreign currency to its home currency to realize a profit. When a U.S. company sells in a foreign country, it sometimes must accept payment in the buyer's currency to be competitive. The seller then has to exchange the currency received for dollars. Between the time price is agreed on and payment actually received and converted to dollars, the company's transaction is exposed to exchange rate fluctuations, that is, the company experiences transaction exposure. As an example, suppose that on February 6, a U.S. company contracts to sell 100 gross of western shirts to a Japanese buyer for a total price of 20 million yen. The sale price is based on an exchange rate of $0.004944 (U.S.) per yen and the U.S. seller expects to realize $98,880 (20 million ¥ × 0.004944 = $98,880) in payment. The Japanese buyer has demanded the sale be quoted in yen. When the company enters the contract for the sale, it has incurred transaction exposure; that is, until it closes the sale and converts the yen to dollars it is running the risk of a loss (if the exchange rate of dollar per yen is lower when the company exchanges the yen for dollars). During the time of the exposure—between February 6, and July 6 of the same year when payment is received—the exchange rate of the U.S. dollar changed from \$0.004944/yen to \$0.004379/yen. Based on the exchange rate existing at the time the company receives the 20 million yen and converts the yen to dollars, the company would receive only \$87,580 (U.S.) (20 million ¥ × \$0.004379 = \$87,580) in exchange, thereby losing \$11,300 over the anticipated sales value of \$98,880.[21]

In long-term transactions (even those of two or three years) exchange rate fluctuations can have extreme effects and at times can far exceed the profitability of a given transaction. Consider the following example of the cost of money in a strongly fluctuating money market.

July 22, 1987	U.S. firm borrows 10,000,000 pound sterling. Interest rate: 14 percent. Exchange rate: 1 pound sterling = \$1.5990 U.S. Company secures \$15,990,000.
July 21, 1988	U.S. firm owes \$11,400,000 pound sterling. Exchange rate: 1 pound sterling = \$1.7093 U.S. Company requires \$19,486,020.
Transaction cost	\$3,496,020 to use \$15,990,000 for 1 year. 21.86 percent effective cost of money for 1 year.

Because of exchange rate exposure, a loan that was expected to cost 14 percent increased to a rate of 21.86 percent, certainly a substantial increase in the cost of doing business.

Transaction exposure occurs when a company:

1. Has assets in one currency that it expects to convert to another to realize a profit.
2. Has assets denominated in one currency that must be converted into another at some expected value.
3. Borrows money in one currency that, when repaid, must be exchanged to make repayment.
4. Purchases goods for resale in one currency, sells them in another, and needs to convert the proceeds into a third currency to realize planned profits.

A large MNC might encounter several of all of these situations in the course of normal business activity.[22] Should the extent of risk be large, most firms try to minimize it. The most obvious way is to demand payment

---

[21] The company could receive a windfall profit if the dollar exchange rate were higher at the time of the final exchange. Had the rate gone to \$0.005110 (U.S.) per yen, then the company would have made a windfall gain of \$3,320. Since most companies are not interested in speculation but in the protection of their expected profits, the fear of a loss is much greater than the expectation of a gain and thus they may prefer to protect themselves against a loss at the expense of potential windfall gain.

[22] Michael R. Sesit, "By Trading Currencies, Kodak's Eric R. Nelson Saves the Firm Millions," *The Wall Street Journal*, March 5, 1985, p. 1.

in the home-country currency, but competitively that is not always possible. When a company demands payment in home-country currency, the exchange risk is shifted to the buyer who is then similarly exposed. In a fluctuating exchange market such as the one that has existed since the early 1970s, there is a tendency for each party in a transaction to attempt to shift the exchange risk to the other. Thus demand for payment in the seller's currency may not always be possible. More formal methods of risk avoidance are discussed in the following section on financial risk management.

MANAGING FINANCIAL RISKS

When financial risks become too high, companies either stop doing business in high-risk situations or seek ways to minimize potential loss. There are various tools available to manage risk although none provides perfect protection.

Commercial and political risks are insurable through a variety of U.S. government agencies. The principal agencies are: (1) Overseas Private Investment Corporation (OPIC); (2) The Foreign Credit Insurance Association (FCIA); and (3) the Export-Import Bank (Eximbank). OPIC and the Eximbank provide insurance against noncommercial losses arising from political activities such as expropriation, war, revolution, inconvertibility of currency, and insurrection. OPIC's emphasis is on developing countries while Eximbank provides assistance for almost all nations considered friendly to the United States. In addition, Eximbank participates with the FCIA to provide insurance against failure to receive payment and other commercial losses.

Protection against risks resulting from exchange rate fluctuations is not available from any government agency. It comes only from effective financial risk management. Some companies avoid risks by refusing to enter transactions not denominated in home-country currency, others accept the consequences of currency oscillations as a condition of doing business. And increasingly, a large number shift the risk to a third party by hedging.[23]

Hedging

Hedging in money is essentially no different from any other kind of hedging in the marketplace. It consists of forward sale for dollars of a currency in danger of devaluation.

---

[23] See, for example, Chuck C. Y. Kwok, "Hedging Foreign Exchange Exposures: Independent vs. Integrative Approaches," *Journal of International Business Studies*, Summer 1987, pp. 35–51.

Referring to the earlier illustration of the U.S. company that sold 100 gross of western shirts to a Japanese buyer and lost $11,300 as a result of an adverse change in the value of the yen, there are several steps that might have been taken to avoid or minimize such a loss. Had the Japanese not insisted on paying in yen, the seller could have received payment in dollars and not suffered any loss, or the seller could have included a clause in the contract stipulating an adjustment if the currency value changed more than a stipulated amount. Another possibility would have been to increase the selling price by some percentage in anticipation of a potential loss. None of these steps are usual in a highly competitive market. One other alternative is to hedge the risk even though hedging does not ensure complete protection. Since trading in foreign-exchange futures was begun by the International Monetary Market (IMM) in Chicago, there has been a viable opportunity to buy futures contracts in most of the world's major currencies either directly in the money market or through the international trade division of a major bank.

The same techniques used to buy futures in wheat, soybeans, and cattle can be used to reduce risks associated with fluctuations in the values of currencies. The process consists of offsetting risk incurred in the actual sale with buying a futures contract in that currency. Continuing the previous example, had the company engaged in a hedge either through its bank or with a direct purchase of a contract on the IMM, it could have covered all or most of its risk.

Suppose that on February 6 when the company sold the shirts for 20 million yen with delivery for May and payment on July 6 (of the same year) the company decided to hedge the risk using Japanese yen futures. To do this, it would be necessary to make two transactions in the futures market. On February 6, an August 5 futures contract for 20 million yen is sold at a price of $0.004995 (U.S.) per yen.[24] In other words, the company promises to deliver 20 million yen to the market on August 5. The value of this contract in U.S. dollars is 20 million times the futures price of $0.004995 for a total of $99,900; that is, for the 20 million yen they agreed to sell August 5 they expect to receive $99,900 (U.S.). At this point, the company is said to be short in the futures market since there has been a sale of yen which will not be received until later.

On July 6, when the company receives the 20 million yen from the buyer of the western shirts, another contract to buy 20 million yen on the futures market is made to offset the earlier futures contract which comes due August 5. On this transaction, the buyers pay $0.004429 (U.S.) yen for a total cost of $88,580 to be delivered on August 5. At this point, the gain or loss on the actual sale should be offset with a gain or loss on

---

[24] An August 5 futures was purchased to ensure some degree of safety because there was no guarantee that the payment would be received exactly on July 6. Had the company wanted to, the futures contract could have been made for July 6.

the two futures contracts. Exhibit 19–2 summarizes the transactions and shows that the yen's value decreased during the 5 months of exposure and the company lost $11,300 when the yen received from the actual sale of shirts were exchanged for dollars. However, on the futures contracts, the company realized a $11,320 gain which can be used to balance the $11,300 loss and pay commissions for the transactions, thereby protecting the original sales price of $98,880.

Had the value of the yen increased during the time of exposure, the original contract would have generated a windfall profit and the futures contract would have generated a loss. In such circumstances, the windfall gains would have been used to offset the loss in the futures contracts. The reason a company hedges is that increases or decreases in the value of currency cannot be predicted and, since companies are typically not in the business of speculation, they forgo potential windfall profits for protection of their normal business profits.

Hedging does not always afford complete protection against price changes; nor is it always as simple as the preceding illustration indicated. Sometimes factors operate to prevent a hedge from offering complete protection or providing the small profit as was illustrated. The primary reason for there being no perfect hedge (i.e., where the spot and future yields would be the same) is that the spread between the spot and futures markets does not always move at the same rate. The two prices may move in the same direction but at different degrees and different rates of speed. Thus a company which hedges can receive an unexpected profit or incur an unexpected loss. However, in situations where exchange rates are fluctuating, the profits or losses are comparatively smaller than they would have been without a hedge.[25]

Foreign-Exchange Options

In addition to buying foreign-exchange futures to hedge against exchange risk, the international marketer has the alternative of buying foreign-exchange options. An option is an agreement between two parties in which one party grants the other the *right*, but *not* the obligation, to buy or sell foreign exchange under specific conditions. With a futures contract, there is an *obligation* to buy or sell foreign exchange. The foreign currency option market functions in much the same manner as options for commodities or stocks. Although using options to hedge can often be more expensive

---

[25] For a complete discussion of financial risk management see, David K. Eiteman and Arthur I. Stonehill, *Multinational Business Finance*, 5th ed. (Reading, Mass: Addison-Wesley, 1987). For complete discussion of the International Monetary Market, see *Understanding Futures in Foreign Exchange* (Chicago: International Monetary Market Division of Chicago Mercantile Exchange, 1979), p. 40.

EXHIBIT 19-2 A Short Hedge—U.S. Company Selling to a Japanese Firm

	Spot Market Transactions		Future Market Transactions	
February 6	U.S. company agrees to sell 100 gross of western shirts to a Japanese retailer for 20 million yen for delivery in May, with payment due July 6. Current spot market for yen is $0.004944 (U.S.)/yen	$98,880	To hedge the risk of a falling price for yen, the company sells August 5, yen contracts for $0.004995 (U.S.)/yen and receives a credit (20 million ¥ times $0.004995 =) for	$99,900
July 6 (same year)	U.S. company receives 20 million yen and exchanges the yen for dollars at the current price of $0.004379 (U.S.)/ yen to receive	$87,580	The U.S. company completes the hedge by buying August 5 yen contracts for $0.004429 (U.S.)/yen (20 million ¥ times $0.004429 =)	$88,580
	The company realized a *loss* due to decreasing value of the yen during the time of exposure. $98,880 − 87,580 =	($11,300)	The company realized a gain in the futures market with which to offset the loss in the spot market. $99,900 − 88,580 =	$11,320

Note: The $11,320 gain in the futures market less the $11,300 loss in the spot-market transactions left the company with a slight gain of $20. After commissions are paid, there will be a slight loss on this transaction.

than buying futures contracts, there are circumstances when it would be better to hedge with options. Because hedging with futures contracts or with options is a complicated financial process, the international department of a major bank should be consulted.

BOX 19–4
Hedging with Call Options

Conceptually, hedging is done with the intent of minimizing the risk of exchange exposure; in so doing, opportunities for windfall profits are offset by potential loss. Using an option in hedging can allow the hedger to benefit from favorable exchange rate changes with a predictable downside risk.

Consider a hypothetical example of a U.S. importer buying machinery from Germany. The importer knows the bill will come due in three months, when he must pay the German producer of the machinery DM 31 million, or $10 million, say, at a spot exchange rate of DM 3.10 per U.S. dollar. To hedge against adverse movement in the exchange rate, the importer pays a $200,000 premium to buy a European call option that gives him the right to buy in three months DM 31 million at a striking price of DM 3.10 per U.S. dollar. (For simplicity, it is assumed that the striking price and the spot exchange rate when the option is purchased are the same, and the option can only be exercised on the maturity date of the contract.) Three of the possible outcomes after three months are:

1. The *DM appreciates from DM 3.10/$ to DM 3.00/$*. Without the option, the U.S. importer would have to pay $10.3 million, that is the DM 31 million owed to the German producer converted into dollars at the new spot rate of DM 3.00/$. By exercising the option, the U.S. importer instead pays $10 million for the DM 31 million. Hedging with the option cost $200,000 for the premium but saved $300,000. (Figures are rounded to the nearest $100,000. For simplicity the interest forgone on the $200,000 premium does not appear in the calculations.)

2. The *DM depreciates from DM 3.10/$ to DM 3.20/$*. The U.S. importer pays $9.7 million (DM 31 million converted into dollars at the new spot rate of DM 3.20/$), or $300,000 less than the amount calculated on the basis of the initial spot rate. The option is not exercised because doing so would mean paying $10 million rather than $9.7 million for the needed deutsche marks. Hedging with the option thus cost $200,000 for the premium; because there was no obligation to exercise the option, the importer was able to benefit from the $300,000 decline in the cost of the machinery as a result of the depreciation of the deutsche mark.

3. The *DM remains unchanged at DM 3.10/$*. The U.S. importer is indifferent between exercising and not exercising the option, because in either case the machinery costs $10 million. There are neither gains nor losses on account of exchange rate movement, but there is a cost of $200,000 for the premium.

The decision to exercise the option depends on whether the foreign currency in question appreciates or depreciates relative to the striking price. If the deutsche mark appreciates, the call option would be exercised because the option allows its holder to buy the needed foreign currency at a more favorable

BOX 19–4 *(concluded)*

exchange rate. The option would not be exercised if the deutsche mark depreciates because it would then be cheaper to buy the currency at the new spot rate than at the striking price. Unlike a forward or future contract, the option allows the importer to take advantage of the depreciating foreign currency by simply not exercising the option, although he incurs the "insurance" cost of the option's premium. By using the foreign currency option to hedge, the importer cannot, however, lose more than the premium; options thus limit the downside risk from exchange rate movements while allowing the contract holder to profit from any favorable exchange rate changes.

Source: "Foreign Currency Call Options: An Example," *Finance and Development,* December 1985, p. 40.

European Currency Units

Some of the volatility of European currencies can be minimized by denominating contracts in the European Currency Unit (ECU). The ECU, originally introduced in 1975 as the European Unit of Account, represents a composite of 10 European currencies, Exhibit 19–3. The ECU was developed to promote monetary stability among European currencies. Intended originally as a unit of account for central banks of EC-member countries and as a unit of account for all EC budgetary purposes, it gradually grew as a private payment medium. The ECU is freely convertible into all major currencies and is used to price, invoice, and settle transactions involving

---

EXHIBIT 19–3   European Currency Unit

European Community Currencies are Included in the ECU "Basket" in the Following Amounts (Based on February 1989 ECU Value of $1.13144 U.S.)*

0.719 German mark	34.519%
0.0878 Pound sterling	13.723
1.31 French francs	18.409
140 Italian lire	9.181
0.256 Dutch guilder	10.865
{ 3.71 Belgian francs	
{ 0.14 Luxembourg francs }	8.846
0.219 Danish krone	2.697
0.00871 Irish punt	1.098
1.15 Greek drachmas	.662
	100%

*In September 1989, the Spanish (peseto) and Portuguese (escudo) were added to the ECU basket. Amounts unknown when the text was published.

SOURCE: Ralph Mehnert, "The ECU 'For Beginners'," *Europe,* April 1989, pp. 20–22.

goods and services.[26] Credit cards, traveler's checks, and customer accounts in ECUs are also available.[27]

The major advantage of the ECU is the stability relative to any one of the major European currencies. Since there is relative stability, contracts denominated by ECUs have potentially less financial risk than contracts denominated in any one of the currencies included in the determination of the ECU. Future contracts for ECUs can be purchased making the ECU available for forward buying and hedging. Because it is used in customer accounts and other consumer financial transactions among Europeans, some see the ECU as a forerunner of the accepted currency of the European Community.[28]

UNBLOCKING PROFITS

International marketing executives are plagued with a problem unknown to their domestic counterparts; they must not only sell the goods but also find ways to repatriate payment for the goods and profits from operations to the parent company. Countries have long controlled the holding and purchasing of currency within their borders. Due to the global debt crisis that has plagued the world since the mid-1970s, the controls have spread as developing countries have tried to allocate scarce dollars and other so-called hard currencies to specific imports or to pay interest on foreign debt.

The result is that MNCs often have problems repatriating their profits. These blocked funds include both capital repatriation and the repatriation from the sale of goods. Solutions include bartering, third-country (three-way) trading without the use of financial exchange, and switch trading. One English company sold $5 million worth of airplanes to Brazil and was paid entirely in coffee. Often, part of the selling price of goods can be repatriated directly with the balance being bartered. Vendors may find themselves in businesses they do not particularly enjoy; however, they can find help in specialized barter brokers. In switch trading, three or more parties are generally involved, one from each of the countries that have bilateral payment agreements with one or more of the other countries involved. When funds are blocked, the money may be repatriated through the export of goods from the foreign country to the parent country.[29]

---

[26] "One Currency, One Central Bank?" *Business International,* June 27, 1988, p. 204.

[27] "Exchange Risk: The ECU Alternative," *Countertrade and Barter,* April–May 1988, pp. 26–30.

[28] Peter Norman, "E.C. Studies Ways Toward Monetary and Economic Union," *Europe,* March 1989, pp. 18–19, and Philip Revzin, "Pressure Builds for Common European Currency," *The Wall Street Journal,* April 28, 1989.

[29] "Managing Money in Brazil: Techniques for Moving Blocked Funds Offshore," *Business Latin America,* January 25, 1988, p. 27.

BOX 19–5
Talk about Markup!

For $47,000 you can get a $10,000 U.S. car in South Korea.

One of the complaints of many of America's trading partners is that U.S. products carry too heavy a tax burden when they're sold in other countries. Real sticker shock can be found in South Korea. Here is what a $10,000 imported car costs once all taxes, tariffs, and special levies are made.

Manufacturer's delivery price	$10,000
Customs duties	4,000
Defense tax	250
Consumption tax	6,160
Defense tax on consumption tax	1,848
Valued added tax	6,048
Dealer acquisition tax	4,246
Customs clearance fee and dealer mark-up	3,255
Registration tax	2,148
Customer acquisition tax	5,371
Subway bonds	3,800
Total	$47,126

By contrast, the Hyundai Excel retails in Korea for $7,982 plus $412 in fees and taxes and $190 in Subway Bonds.

Source: Adapted from "The Three Tigers Article," *Business Week*, February 15, 1988, p. 47.

Columbia Pictures Industries, Inc., filmed *Sheena* in Kenya to use up blocked funds generated by its parent Coca-Cola Co.'s soft-drink operation. PepsiCo, Inc. exports wine to the United States from Romania, Bulgaria, and Hungary and vodka from Russia in exchange for sales of Pepsi-Cola to those countries. Since the Chinese market has opened, many firms have found they must trade goods to repatriate profits. One manufacturer of coal-fired stoves produces stoves in China for sale there and then converts profits into export credits. The export credits are then used to buy Chinese goods for export; done properly, it enables the exporter to realize profits from Chinese sales in hard currency.[30]

A multinational firm may also have the option of allocating profit to a variety of locations outside a country through internal accounting procedures. Profit may be taken in a country in which the goods are sold, in a country in which they are produced, in the headquarters country, or perhaps, in yet another country. Profits may be allocated to provide maxi-

---

[30] Paula L. Green, "U.S. Firm to Take Rugs in Return for Stoves It Makes in China," *Journal of Commerce*, October 17, 1988. p. 4a.

BOX 19–6
Unblocking Profits

Corporations often go to great lengths to get around foreign-exchange controls, one of the oldest games in international finance, and one of the riskiest. It also has become one of the most widely played. Here are a few examples of some of the more creative approaches.

- *Take to the air:* A Frenchman straps on a money belt loaded with French francs given to him by a multinational company operating in France. He hang glides over the Swiss border so he can get Swiss francs to deposit in a Swiss bank account.
- *Threaten:* A pharmaceutical company based in New York threatened Brazilian officials that if they did not release funds, the company would not be able to buy the imports necessary to protect Brazilian chickens from disease. It worked; Brazil came back with double what the company requested.
- *Reinvest:* Rather than try to repatriate $30 to $40 million from liquidated Brazilian assets, one chemical company reinvested in a polyester film factory.
- *And then, sometimes nothing works:* The international manager of a French chemical firm once had to accept Romanian trucks as payment for an oil sale to Morocco. He couldn't sell the trucks so they were traded for oranges. He could not sell the oranges either. "It was a business without end: we couldn't get any money," he said.

Source: Adapted from Michael R. Sesit, "Funds Blocked Abroad by Exchange Controls Plague Big Companies," *The Wall Street Journal,* December 3, 1984, p. 1.

mum profit for the subsidiary or for the corporation as a whole. By taking profits in a country with low tax rates, for example, the net profit after taxes can be optimized. The marketer may want to take the profits in countries with sound currencies or where the funds are needed to finance further operations.[31]

Profit can be allocated through manipulation of prices charged for goods exchanged internationally or through allocation of expenses; the marketing manager's salary, for example, may be charged off to the operation expenses of any of the countries involved in the production or distribution chain. To bring profits to the home company, the parent may charge its subsidiary licensing fees, franchise fees, or may allocate increasing portions of home-office expenses to the subunit. Such decisions generally are made at the corporate level.

Obviously there are other financial alternatives to repatriation. The com-

---

[31] John Frisbie, "Balancing Foreign Exchange," *China Business Review,* March–April 1988, pp. 24–28.

pany having trouble repatriating funds may choose to reinvest in other local enterprises or expand operations in the country. Sometimes if a company has stockholders in the foreign country it simply pays out dividends directly from the parent company.

SUMMARY

Although it is not their formal domain, marketing executives should be acquainted with the requirements, sources, problems, and opportunities associated with the financing of international marketing operations. The financial needs of international marketing differ considerably from those of the domestic market. Most specifically, the international marketer must be prepared to invest larger-than-normal amounts of working capital in inventories, receivables, channel financing, and consumer credit. It is possible that market entry may require capital financing of production facilities for purely marketing reasons. International marketers need to be willing to undertake additional financial burdens if they are to operate successfully in foreign countries. Indeed, adequate financing may spell the difference between success and failure in foreign operations. The willingness of marketers to carry adequate inventories in strategic locations or to provide consumer or channel credit that they would not be likely to furnish in their home country may be key elements in market development.

Financial risks associated with international marketing are greater than those encountered domestically, but such risk-taking is necessary for effective operations. Many companies have been so conservative in their credit and payment terms that they have succeeded in alienating foreign customers. These risks, as well as those of exchange availability or fluctuation and the various political risks, can be accommodated in an effective financial risk management program.

QUESTIONS

1. Define:

transaction exposure	AID
Eximbank	ECUs
OPIC	Debt-Equity Swaps
Eurodollars	hard currency

2. Explain why marketers should be concerned with the financial considerations associated with international business.

3. Explain how a debt-equity swap works for a MNC that wants to make an investment in a country.

4. Identify the financial requirements for marketing internationally most likely to concern the domestic marketer.

5. Discuss the differences between financial requirements for export marketers and for overseas marketing operations.

6. What are the extra working capital requirements of the international marketer?

7. Review some of the ways financial requirements can be reduced by variations in marketing policies or strategies.

8. In which ways are marketing financial requirements of exporters different from those of full-scale international marketers?

9. What significance do government sources of funds have for marketers?

10. Discuss the importance of Eximbank and its services which facilitate international marketing activities.

11. "The principles of international credit are basically no different from those of domestic credit." Elaborate.

12. Compare the advantages and disadvantages of bills of exchange and letters of credit.

13. Review the types of financial risk involved in international operations and discuss how each may be reduced.

14. Using exchange data in *The Wall Street Journal* on a date assigned by the instructor, calculate the foreign exchange gain or loss on this transaction: a U.S. firm borrows 5 million Swiss francs one year before the assigned date, converts those to U.S. dollars, pays 9 percent interest per annum. How many dollars will be required to repay the loan and interest?

15. Define and give an example of a company that has a transaction exposure.

16. In which four situations does transaction rate exposure occur? Give an example of each.

17. Discuss the ways a company can reduce exchange risk.

18. Discuss the ways a company can reduce the risk of exchange rate fluctuations. Give examples of each.

19. What is the European Currency Unit (ECU) and how might it be used in managing financial risks?

20. What is the value of options in hedging?

CHAPTER

20

Coordinating and Controlling Global Marketing Operations

Whether a company's marketing strategy is multidomestic or global, it is unlikely to achieve expected goals without effective coordination and control of marketing operations. The larger a company becomes, the more critical the decisions are and the more difficult they are to control. The complexities encountered by multinational marketers with global or multidomestic strategies are a result of multinational, multicultural, and frequently, multimanaged operations. The more diverse the international operations, the greater the need to establish a system to control them.

For companies pursuing a global strategy, the expected efficiencies and benefits of globalization depend on global control. Implicit in a global marketing strategy is standardization of the marketing mix which should produce a system to control market activities in numerous markets. Such control is critical to the success of a global strategy. A global marketer gains a competitive advantage through a coordinated strategy that includes all the countries in which it operates. A global product may be designed in which it operates. A global product may be designed in a European country, with components manufactured in Taiwan and Korea, assembled in Canada or Mexico, and "sold as a standard model in Brazil and as a model fully loaded with options in the United States."[1] Global enterprises

---

[1] John J. Dyment, "Strategies and Management Controls for Global Corporations," *Journal of Business Strategy*, Spring 1987, p. 20.

need control systems that can monitor performances across national borders and ensure that global objectives are achieved.

Coordination and control are no less important for the company guided by a multidomestic market strategy. The control of marketing activities within each country market and control among country markets are essential in achieving corporate goals and objectives. Few business firms control all domestic functions or activities as completely as they should; still fewer firms have adequate control of their international activities. There are many uncontrollable factors that preclude exercising total control, but continuous coordination and effective managerial control are prime requisites for successful marketing operations. Time lags, cultural lags, communication lags, and varying country-market objectives contribute to the difficulty of establishing and managing an effective system of control for international marketing operations.

To perform consistently at an optimum profit level, all forms of international organization, centralized or decentralized, require a functioning coordination and control system for each area. Pricing policies, personnel utilization, channel and physical distribution arrangement, advertising, market evaluation, selling arrangements, and the products themselves benefit from well-implemented coordination and control systems.

Establishment of a comprehensive system is not an easy task; a system which adequately controls the operations of one company may overcontrol the activities of a second or undercontrol those of another. The key is the balance between central and local control. As a company shifts from a multidomestic market strategy to a global strategy, the company must make systems decisions rather than let each country-specific subsidiary make individual decisions.[2] This chapter addresses coordination and control and identifies specific areas of marketing control for international operations.

CONTROL AS A MANAGEMENT TOOL

Control means to direct, regulate, or manage. Controlling is the very essence of management and implies a means of measuring accomplished events against set standards. Control also implies that corrective action can and will be taken to realign operations on a schedule that allows a firm to achieve stated objectives. Before there can be any meaningful control, however, plans and organizational structure must be clear, complete, and integrated.

---

[2] Peter F. Drucker, one of the most thoughtful and insightful authorities on business management, discusses the changing world competitive structure and its impact on the operations of multinationals in ''The Changing Multinational,'' *The Wall Street Journal*, January 15, 1986. This editorial column is well worth the time to read carefully.

Ronald McDonald, Tokyo. Maintaining a global image requires effective control. (Rick Warner/Journalism Services, Inc.)

To accomplish overall objectives, the interdependence and interaction of the many marketing functions as well as the full business spectrum require all segments to attain individual goals. Control is the system used to effectively monitor business activities, measure deviations from standards, and signal those in command to adjust wayward operations to bring them back on course. A business can operate without formal control systems; indeed, a small business with few levels of management where all operations are concentrated, easily seen, and monitored, can frequently function without a formal system. But as the complexity of a business's operation builds, the ability to function efficiently without formal control lessens.

Reflecting on material covered in earlier chapters, the problems and futility of attempts to manage an international company without adequate control procedures can be appreciated. Ironically, even today, international business activities frequently receive inadequate coordination or control from top management. Such neglect results from the markedly different orientation to these functions in domestic and foreign operations, and because a company has no real interest in permanent foreign-market development, goods are exported with little thought or follow-up. Overseas business is often turned over to an export manager who runs an almost autonomous operation with no coordinating or controlling strings attached. In such cases, the parent companies appear to be content with less-than-optimal overseas profits because they are not sufficiently committed to international operations to exert effective control. Inadequate control also results from inadequately designed systems; but, ultimately, inadequate control results from a lack of commitment. As companies remain in international programs and as these programs become more profitable, they realize that efficiently managed operations require a formal control system. This realization can come as profits from the international division are affected, or more frequently, by the surfacing of a whole host of inefficiencies and intracompany conflicts that arise from inadequate controls. Inefficiencies result from corporate divisions in different countries being in competition with one another and from poorly managed customer services. Exhibit 20–1 lists some of the recurring problems that surface because of inadequate controls. In each situation, the problem arises because some phase of the business was not functioning as planned or expected. A

BOX 20–1
How Nestlé Plans for Control

Nestlé begins the annual marketing planning process with each subsidiary preparing a general fact book giving home country details and a product fact book for each of the major products the subsidiary sells. The general fact book provides a format for gathering information on factors that may affect the subsidiary's marketing activities such as population composition and trends, economic climate, industry outlook, competition, and marketing legislation. The product fact book contains—again in standardized format—specific information about each product such as total market size and segments, market shares and trends, consumers' habits and attitudes.

Using the fact book as a starting point, subsidiary managers then propose both one-year and six-year marketing plans in an internationally uniform format. In addition to detailed figure work, the annual plan has a qualitative part that is essential. It not only interprets the figure work but also discusses and justifies actions planned for the coming year, identifies critical success factors, spells out responsibilities and deadlines for implementation, and establishes yardsticks for performance measurement.

Source: Ralph Z. Sorenson and Ulrich E. Wiechmann, "How Multinationals View Marketing Standardization," *Harvard Business Review*, May/June 1975, Copyright © 1975 by the President and Fellows of Harvard College; all rights reserved, p. 166.

EXHIBIT 20–1   Control Problems

Indicators	*Characteristics*
Conflicts among divisions or subsidiaries over territories or customers in the field.	Most common when a company is expanding into new geographic areas. Also caused by the introduction of new products abroad and acquisitions or mergers.
Failure of foreign operations to grow in accordance with plans and expectations.	May only apply to overall sales in a particular area, or to a particular product line. Obviously more acute if one's share of the market is falling even when sales are increasing.
Lack of financial control over operations abroad.	Related to the company's philosophy of centralization versus decentralization and the degree to which authority is delegated to managers overseas. Further complicated by foreign tax laws and accounting conventions.
Duplication of administrative personnel and services.	Most common when product lines go abroad as extensions of independent domestic divisions, or when major acquisitions are made.
Underutilization of manufacturing or distribution facilities abroad.	Often occurs when various product lines extend operations abroad independent of each other, or when consolidation does not take place after a merger.
Duplication of sales offices and specialized field salespersons.	Common within corporations selling technical products such as specialty chemicals or electronic equipment.
A proliferation of relatively small legal entities and/or operating units within a country or geographical area.	Often results from establishing a new subsidiary each time a domestic division enters a new foreign country, until five, six, or even more function side by side.
A proliferation of distributors.	Overlapping coverage and conflicting interests.
An increase in complaints relating to customer service abroad.	Often a symptom that field marketing personnel do not have a coordinated approach to handling a common customer.

SOURCE: J. W. Widing, Jr., "Reorganizing Your Worldwide Business," *Harvard Business Review* 51, no. 3, p. 155.

system of controls attempts to monitor functions and measure deviations, allowing management to take necessary corrective action before overall objectives are impaired.

The process of developing a control system for a firm operating in several countries is further complicated by multinational and multicultural involvement. All involvements produce special factors which affect the design of the control system and a manager's ability to cope with them.

DEVELOPING A GLOBAL CONTROL SYSTEM

International marketing plans are among the most complex to adapt to a control system. This complexity can be attributed to the differences arising from the multinational, multicultural, and multimanagerial nature of international business. In addition to typical control development problems found in domestic business, the design of an effective global control system is plagued by rapidly shifting political, cultural, and economic factors.

Unique Factors in Global Control

One of the crucial aspects affecting control processes is the diversity inherent in global markets. Market size, labor costs, currency value differences, legal structures, political structures, social features, and cultural factors all lend complication to the task of developing effective marketing programs and to controlling them. Because of the diversity, each division seeks specific plans reflecting local situations for each major product and major market. Divisions feel the need to function autonomously with plans, priorities, products, and so forth, reflecting their unique cultural demands; yet from a global strategy perspective, these units are highly interdependent. In developing global marketing strategy, all activities of foreign subsidiaries must be blended to achieve a single corporate goal. The final global strategy is an agglomeration of programs of each functioning unit toward a single objective. Global management control must be reconciled with national initiative and central direction versus local accountability. Consumers may prefer a global product but their choice is academic if the global company is unable to build and control a viable base from which to supply them.[3] These continuing conflicts between the country/cultural needs of each operating unit and the overall corporate objectives need to be reflected in a control system.

Physical distance separating countries and management is another impor-

---

[3] "The Issue Globalists Don't Talk About," *International Management*, September 1987, pp. 37–42.

tant consideration in the design of a control system. As companies grow and as physical distances separating headquarters management and the worldwide operations increase, the time, expense and potential error in communications affect the flexibility and speed with which changes in worldwide plans can be implemented and problems detected.

Control implies an ability to take corrective action if operations need adjustments. However, foreign operations are frequently faced with *uncontrollable factors* that influence the outcome of an operation, but over which local and/or international headquarters have little or no control. Outside stockholders with objectives different from those of the company, government regulations, and home-country goals are all uncontrollable factors that can affect the ultimate success of a program but cannot be influenced by management.

Another factor to consider in planning a control system is the inadequacy of data available in many parts of the world. As discussed in Chapter 11, the inaccuracy and lack of completeness of economic and industrial data affect control. Goals and plans developed in many markets cannot reflect true potential because the information used to set the goals was inaccurate. Thus, controls established to monitor plans formulated on the basis of inaccurate data are not workable. Further, because of economic planning by host countries and the instability of political and economic goals, it is difficult to make economic forecasts on which to base marketing plans. Government economic plans that change rapidly can affect the results of even the most carefully drawn marketing programs. A control process, therefore, must be sufficiently flexible to compensate for the inaccuracy and instability of the data on which plans are based.

A company's management philosophy and organization, whether *centralized* or *decentralized,* has a major effect on the development of a control system. Both those who argue in favor of centralized management and decentralized management use the factors just discussed as the basis for their positions. For example, centralized management advocates defend their position on the grounds that diversity, distance, inadequate data, and so forth, create such control problems that effective control can be assured only if handled centrally. Those in favor of decentralization support their position on the same basis suggesting that the problems outlined make centralized decision making unworkable because it lacks sufficient flexibility to permit immediate reaction to local problems. Conversely, those who argue for centralized control suggest that the conditions discussed have the potential for wasteful duplication of efforts and that the attainment of efficiency and ultimate maximization of worldwide profits can only be achieved through tight central decision making. Advocates of decentralization claim strong central management frequently means constant delays in reaching decisions; that instead of the central bureaucracy reacting to meaningful differences at the local level, they ultimately react only to capital budgets and profitability, the primary tools of control. Critics contend that as centralized management becomes more highly struc-

---

BOX 20–2
Recapturing American Competitiveness?

When a national research firm read a list of 10 things that affected their lifestyles to workers in the United States, Europe, and Japan, the Americans listed their childrens' education, family life, and health as their top concerns. The most satisfaction, they said, came from family life, friends and relatives, and childrens' education. Work ranked eighth in importance and seventh in satisfaction.

    Among Europeans, by contrast, work ranked as the fourth most important aspect in their lives and the sixth most satisfying. And to the Japanese, work is second in importance only to health and the fourth most satisfying. Concludes the research firm: "The American commitment to the work ethic may be a thing of the past."

    Source: "Labor Letter," *The Wall Street Journal,* June 28, 1988, p. 1.

---

tured, knowledge of the local situation is lost. This, of course, can produce errors that give rise to the question: "Why didn't someone ask a local?"

    Regardless of the philosophy employed, the control system must be designed in a way that minimizes problems with either management philosophy. For a highly centralized management, the control system must permit effective communications between headquarters and the local decision maker so local input and contribution is not adversely affected; in a decentralized organization, the control system should assure that local autonomy does not reach the point where global corporate efforts are jeopardized because of a lack of a common objective. This type of conflict can occur when companies move rapidly to a global, centrally controlled strategy and lose the participation of local managers. Many attribute Procter & Gamble's loss of market position for its disposable diapers as the result of a lack of coordination and control between the company's goal of a pan-European marketing effort and local country subsidiaries. A French brand manager was quoted as saying, "As soon as it was known that I would be principally working with the European Pampers manager and not the subsidiary general manager, my local support dried up." [4] Responsibility was eventually returned to the subsidiaries, but not before P&G had lost market share and initiative. The optimal balance between centralization and decentralization is difficult to achieve because the two forces are driving the multinational simultaneously in both directions. P&G has subsequently adopted an approach dubbed the "Eurobrand concept" to achieve cooperation. In this "lead country" system, the subsidiary having

---

[4] Ibid., p. 42.

the most experience with an important brand, or the most commitment and resources, is given the responsibility to coordinate its marketing throughout Europe.

Eastman Kodak has addressed the problem with a compensation system that encourages working for the common good. The pay of all key managers, the country general manager, the regional general manager, and the worldwide business unit manager, is based on the same numbers. If the annual operating plan for Germany says that X amount of a particular product will be produced and sold and Y profit will be earned, those are everyone's goals. This approach makes the European and German general managers just as responsible for delivering performance on that product as is the business unit manager who "owns" it.[5] Both P&G and Kodak are focusing on achieving a balance between paying too much or too little attention to local details.

Regardless of the steps taken to compensate for some of the unique factors confronting attempts for effective control, there seems to be continual conflict between those in the home office and those in the field. The dichotomy that exists between headquarters and subsidiary managers is similar to what traditionally exists in any organization between staff and line personnel; that is, neither believes the other understands his or her own problems and, as a consequence, cooperation and communication sometimes suffer. This problem is exacerbated by the distance, culture, language, and differences in nationality that are found in international marketing.

This conflict was highlighted in a study questioning headquarters and subsidiary personnel on what each considered to be the most pressing problems they faced.[6] Interestingly enough, some of the worst problems had to do with internal subsidiary headquarters relations rather than external environmental conditions. Central office managers' principal concerns fell into three categories. (1) A shortage of qualified persons to staff the international operations; the issue here was the expressed difficulty in finding qualified local managers for subsidiaries. (2) Subsidiary managers who had deficiencies in planning and marketing know-how; major concerns here were subsidiary managers too preoccupied with operational problems and without a long-range, worldwide perspective. As a consequence, the company lacked marketing competence at the subsidiary level. (3) Shortcomings in the communications and control processes of the multinational operation.

In contrast, subsidiary personnel's major concerns dealt with:

---

[5] "Kodak's Matrix System Focuses on Product Business Units," *Business International*, July 18, 1988, p. 222.

[6] Ulrich E. Wiechmann and Louis G. Pringle, "Problems that Plague Multinational Marketers," *Harvard Business Review*, July–August 1979, pp. 118–24.

1. Two many constraints imposed by headquarters. They thought they had too little autonomy and were required to produce excessive paperwork to satisfy headquarters control and information requirements that were never effectively used by headquarters.
2. Too little attention was given by headquarters to local differences. Many believed that headquarters had a domestic bias and as a consequence was insensitive to foreign market requirements. There was also belief that a heavy emphasis on standardization of marketing programs led to a disregard for subsidiary personnel's input in planning or marketing programs.
3. Inadequate information from headquarters. In this situation, they believed that while they were required to provide information to headquarters, very little useful information flowed back from headquarters that would be beneficial in their decision-making processes. They thought central headquarters spent a great deal of time and effort collecting information but paid little attention to the dissemination of information.[7]

These conflicts are in many respects inevitable. It is natural for subsidiaries to want less control, more authority, and fewer reports, and more local differentiation in operations. At the same time, it is equally natural to expect those who attempt to manage extended worldwide operations to require greater reporting to facilitate control and more centralized standardization. These conflicting needs can lead to misunderstanding if *proper control methods* are not utilized.

The key to effective management is the ability to guide the company toward achievement of worldwide objectives without stifling the initiative of local operations. To reach these goals, effective international control systems must contend with all the problems found in domestic business plus additional obstacles unique to international business. In developing an international control system, the unique factors discussed affect specifically each step of the control sequence.

Control Seqeunce

There are two prerequisites to a control system: plans and organizational structure. The process of control begins with expected objectives; therefore, specific plans must precede development of the control system. Further, controls require that someone have the responsibility to implement action when operations are "out of control" and need to be corrected. Before adequate control can be established, lines of authority and responsibility

---

[7] For an interesting discussion of lack of information flows, see "The Bhopal Legacy: MNCs Need to Weigh Centralization vs. Control," *Business International*, January 4, 1985, p. 1.

must be developed within the organization. Assuming plans are established and responsibility assigned, a control system follows a logical sequence of steps beginning with objectives reflecting marketing plans and ending with responsibility for someone to initiate corrective action when needed. Exhibit 20–2 shows the relationship and dynamic nature of the seven steps of a control sequence. Whether controlling international marketing operations or domestic operations, a control system begins with (1) establishing objectives, then (2) selecting the control methods, (3) setting standards, (4) determining location of responsibility, (5) establishing a communications system, (6) devising a method for evaluating and reviewing results, and (7) establishing a method to initiate effective action where and when needed. Each step can be influenced by the unique factors outlined in the previous section.

Establish Objectives.   Newcomers in international marketing are liable to have unformed ideas about their precise objectives in entering international competition. Lack of a sharply defined objective is not totally unacceptable, but it can prove a hazard if substituted for realistic goals and objectives that might be accomplished through adequate planning and a comprehensive control system. Management must outline explicitly in advance general objectives and specific short- and long-term objectives for the international operation. Unless these are determined at the outset, management cannot know which resources are required or which gains

EXHIBIT 20–2

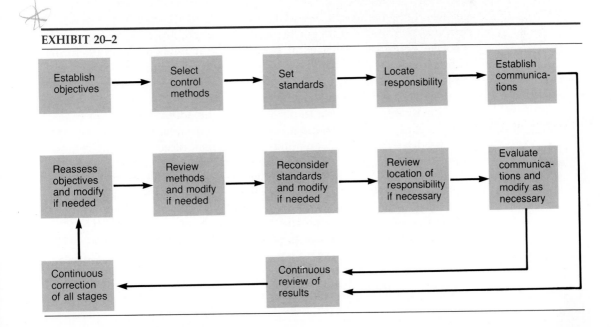

are expected. Without knowing objectives, company standards cannot be established and planned control is impossible.

Companies with a variety of far-flung subordinate organizations often fail to communicate adequately about firm objectives and the goals for specific operating units. Unless statements of objectives are conveyed explicitly, they have little relevance to subordinates. Objective statements should identify overall company goals so everyone concerned knows where the company is going, and they should provide specific details of operational objectives to the persons in charge. Statements may include specific, explicit goals such as the attainment of a given market share or specific dollar level of sales or profit or may spell out less-tangible goals such as increasing product visibility, developing channel structure, or improving product and company image. It is advantageous to be as concrete as possible in communicating objectives, but inclusion of abstract objectives lends perspective. After the general and operational objectives are established, management should select the basic method or methods of coordination and control most likely to be effective in a given circumstance.

Select Control Method.   Direct or indirect controls are the basic alternatives relevant to overseas marketing operations. Methods of direct control include contractual arrangements and ownership participation. Indirect control may rely on communications or competition. The extent and degree of control can vary widely for both control methods.

Formal contractual arrangements can provide a positive and direct mechanism for controlling overseas operations but not the control; specific contract provisions are needed for effective control. Two of the more common control arrangements utilize quotas and license requirements. Even though both may require specific performance, contractual provisions cannot always be enforced. Contractual provisions can rely on elaborate formal administrative mechanisms or depend solely on voluntary compliance, but the parent company may need to turn to alternative marketing arrangements if contractual requirements are not met.

When a company is able to participate in the administration (or at least policy setting) of its international representatives, a large degree of control is assured. Ownership, even a minority interest, often offers a substantial opportunity for control through ownership participation in management.

Set Standards.   Before a control mechanism can work effectively, an objective-based set of standards must be adopted to measure progress. Standards should be expressed as explicitly as possible, and need not be limited to financial or cost matters. Standards of achievement for the marketing task can be set concerning profits, sales volume, establishment of channels of distribution, achieving entry into a given foreign market, or some other relevant measure.

Revenue and the expense budgets should be included in the company's standards for overseas operations. Companies unfamiliar with overseas operations should immediately establish expense budgets to help appraise costs and make realistic plans. Expense budgets typically are understated while revenue plans have a tendency to work the other way. Companies frequently find from projecting domestic figures that they have understated expenses and overstated anticipated revenues. Continuing research and analysis of budget and accomplishment standards should be undertaken early to permit realistic standard setting. Standards must be established at all levels of operation and must be reviewed sequentially by each higher level to determine if they are realistic and consonant with the company's world goals.

Locate Responsibility.   The complexities of international organization make it difficult to locate the *ultimate* responsibility for overseas operation, and assignment of responsibility sometimes involves much coordination. Different departments or functional areas of the parent company must be aware of what is going on in other functional areas. Companies organized by product line need greater coordination of efforts in international than in domestic markets. Firms organized for international operations on a national basis need to establish liaison and coordination links among the various nations in which they have trading activities. Whenever possible, primary responsibility should be located with one person who can coordinate the efforts of others to permit centralized action and control. In no case should someone be given responsibility that is not in line with the authority delegated to that person.

Establish Communication System.   A reporting and control system is a company's central nervous system necessary for accumulating data and disseminating messages calling for action. Informal communication systems can be adequate in domestic marketing, but in international business, it is imperative that an organized and systematic information system be developed to provide for a continuous flow of data for central office analysis and decision.

Information collection and dispersion can be costly activities, so the communication system must be carefully geared to just the right level of reporting. Too much information wastes executive time, too little fails to give an adequate basis for control. Analyzing data from the reporting system must not consume so much of a manager's time that there is no time left for actual management of the operation. Because of improving communications technology, the tendency seems to be to ask for too much information, much of which has no apparent or real purpose. Besides being time consuming for those in the field, it risks denigrating the value of reporting. One country manager warned, "You must have good reasons for asking for greater amounts of data. Otherwise you run the danger of various forms of noncompliance, including misinformation."[8]

Language and communication breakdowns occur not only between companies and customers but also between managers. Both outgoing and incoming communications must be thoroughly comprehensible to the recipient to be effective. Since the conceptual frameworks of various managers differ, there may be a loss of communication even with words that seem understandable. Such conceptual problems are most likely to occur when dealing with abstractions, such as "good customer relations," or "prompt delivery." Communications should be kept in concrete terms.

A key element of the communications system is an apparatus for collecting information. Rather than just one method for collecting information, a company should collect data from a variety of sources using periodic inquiry, automatic collection, company records, and field audits. Regardless of the makeup of a foreign operation, a company should gather data from field personnel, foreign agents, local marketing researchers, and customers. A company may also rely on a variety of automatic reporting systems including customer guarantee cards and routine reports by field sales personnel or middlemen. All these routine reporting systems should be evaluated periodically to determine if they are economical, flexible, accurate, and, most important, provide the necessary information for the control process. Field audits by headquarters personnel can add insights into a company's foreign problems and opportunities. Such visits can be determined by the number and kind of problems encountered, the value and profit potential in the area, the cost of such visits, and the capability of the local managers or representatives. Trips abroad, frequently looked on by local managers as more of a burden than a benefit, should be handled by experienced personnel who know what to look for and who have developed a capacity to listen to local problems.

Physical facilities for handling international communications are becoming more sophisticated each year. International communications systems incorporating leased circuits, radios, teleprinters, and satellite communications systems permitting instantaneous transmission have all facilitated communications over long distances. Information inputs also provide direct access to computers from any place in the world and permit real-time systems of management allowing home-office personnel to participate in or observe operations as they occur. As impressive as these technological advancements in communications are, they are meaningless unless there are parallel conceptual breakthroughs that facilitate meaningful use of the masses of information being transmitted internationally.

---

[8] The problem of information and communication is addressed in "Global Organization: Square D Unites Managers to Compete Globally," *Business International*, September 21, 1987, pp. 297–299.

Evaluate Results and Make Corrections.   Evaluation of results and initiation of corrective action to modify defective programs are the final steps of the control sequence. Information gathered from the field must be compared with established operational standards and objectives. If the results do not meet expectations, corrective action can be taken, or the standards and objectives can be modified. In international marketing, there is a special likelihood of a significant lag between the time corrective action is initiated and the time it is completed. While such a time lag is understandable in view of the distance, cultural variations, and organizational problems involved, it is particularly important that evaluation and correction be continuing activities. A company should establish, whenever possible, contingency plans in advance and prestructured action patterns that are employable on short notice to meet fast-changing market conditions. The control sequence as discussed has no ending; it is an ongoing cycle of establishing, evaluating, reestablishing, and reevaluating.[9]

Analytical Problems of Control

Whether dealing with branch, subsidiary, joint venture, or franchise organizational arrangements, the individual responsible for establishing coordination and control systems finds numerous problems requiring analysis and harmonization with company objectives. Each of the alternatives has a variety of solutions, none generally superior, but each offering specific advantages in unique circumstances. The system must be designed within the framework of the organizational structure, goals, level of maturity, and working relationship that has been established. The success of an operation can depend as much on the evaluation system and the control system selected as on the realities of the situation.

The basis of measurement is critical in measuring profit as well as in measuring sales volume. Even the approach to measuring a simple thing like volume must be given careful analysis. If volume goals are set in terms of dollars, then inflation, monetary fluctuation, and price modification beyond the control of the manager can affect results. Measurement of the number of units, tonnage, or some other physical measure is not necessarily correlated with the end goal of profit. Transfer pricing policies, inventory procedures (LIFO versus FIFO), and the way that exchange rate fluctuations are handled also greatly affect operating results.

Profits can be distorted significantly depending on where the parent company wishes to allocate earnings for tax or other purposes. Profits can be located in any facet of the multinational company and can be vari-

---

[9] For an interesting discussion of global strategy and organization and control, see Sumantra Ghoshal, "Global Strategy: An Organizing Framework," *Strategic Management Journal* 8, 1987, pp. 425–440.

ously allocated to subfunctions; for example, in a vertically integrated oil company, profit could be located at the production phase, the refining phase, or the distribution phase, or could be allocated in some mix predetermined by the corporate headquarters. Another profit question pertains to short- versus long-term profits; a manager might maximize short-term profits and receive bonuses and praise while jeopardizing long-term profits.

All of these questions relate directly to the level and extent of authority, responsibility, and control. The location and identification of profit centers should be subjected to careful analysis as should the appropriate level of control and the amount of reporting demanded from any level of the marketing system. Typically, no single system is adequate for a large company with different types of organizational relationships and market situations; therefore, the coordination and control system requires continuous analysis to assure that it is functioning in the manner for which it was designed.[10]

AREAS OF CONTROL

Because international marketing costs have a tendency to get out of line, they require special emphasis; markets are small, transportation and communication are difficult, and auditing procedures often inadequate. Even the costs of operating the international division at the home office can easily escalate. The areas of international marketing control are similar to the domestic, but control systems and objectives can be quite different. To facilitate analysis, the international marketing manager may evaluate control activities from the viewpoint of volume, product, channel of distribution, promotion, personnel, or profit control mechanisms.

Volume Control

Measurement of sales volume is one of the most convenient control mechanisms available. The ease of securing aggregate weekly, monthly, or quarterly sales figures makes comparison with forecasts simple and provides management with a periodic check of subsidiary progress and sales by product line. Sales volume depends on the intensity of the marketing efforts, so the individual responsible can determine whether promotional expenditures and sales effort are appropriate to potential returns. That person should also be able to control profit levels through judicious care in other areas of marketing.

Detailed sales reports provide information on sales market by market,

---

[10] See, for example, "Colgate-Palmolive Realigns Staff in Europe in Advance of 1992," *Journal of Commerce*, September 26, 1988, p. 5a.

product by product, and by gross margin category. They give sales breakdowns to subsidiaries or other related companies and may identify government or other large-volume purchases.

Market share information should also be gathered on a regular basis so
that management can have both absolute and relative bases of control.

Price Control

Both price cutting and excessively high prices jeopardize a company's
market position. Management should receive regular reports of prices actually being collected and should be alert to the possibility of subsidiaries
or middlemen competing against each other on a price basis. Such price
competition can be beneficial to the winner, but it is detrimental to the
company as a whole. Also, multinational customers are aware of prices
in different countries and frequently demand the lowest international price.

Despite tariffs, transportation, and local market conditions which modify
actual prices, central management should always retain basic control over
prices. To provide competitive flexibility, management may establish price
ranges for foreign markets and require transactions negotiated at different
prices to be reported immediately. This reporting lessens the number of
such sales and permits decentralization of the pricing function without
full loss of control. Regardless of the level of operation or the type of
middlemen involved, price information is needed for effective home-office
control.

Product Control

Domestic marketing managers must be certain that a product is suitable
for the market and delivered to customers in good condition. A product
or brand image is directly dependent on a customer's experiences with
the product and the firm. Foreign customers are more likely than domestic
customers to indict all products of a particular firm if they have a bad
encounter with one; products of the foreign producer are, so to speak,
"on trial" at all times—in such cases, indeed, in all cases, product quality
control is crucial.

Often product image is more important than the product itself, and
good quality alone is not enough to overcome a poor image. A single
company cannot by itself overcome a poor industrywide or nationwide
product image. The Japanese government, for instance, helped its industries overcome the reputation for shoddy, imitative products by enforcing
rigid government standards and inspection of export goods. No company
should expect less of its products.

Domestic marketers cannot always foresee whether their products will
be suitable for a foreign country, but effective communication and control

systems can provide information about product and product-line decisions. Without an adequate feedback mechanism, a manager may not be able to identify the cause of purchaser dissatisfaction. Other product hazards that must be controlled are: (1) excess damage that can be spotted through a well-organized control system; (2) pre-and post-sale servicing not measuring up to necessary standards; and (3) quality risk when an product is produced by a foreign subsidiary, a licensee, or franchisee that can be minimized through adequate control systems. Only close control can assure management that the product's brand image will be preserved.[11]

4   Promotion Control

Advertising and personal selling should be subject to the same broad range of control systems and mechanisms applied in domestic markets. The advertising function may be organized and developed centrally or decentralized. As discussed in Chapter 14, campaigns may be standardized for all markets or locally developed; whether standardized or not, all advertising needs control. In fact, the success of an advertising program may depend more on how well the campaign is being controlled than on whether or not it is standardized.[12] The home office particularly needs to know it is communicating effectively in all markets and corporatewide objectives are being met throughout the world. Personal selling cannot be directed from the home office, but it certainly can and should be managed.[12]

5   Channel Control

The primary measure of a middleman's effectiveness is the volume of purchases from the company, but such information does not provide adequate detail on whether the distributor is maintaining reasonable prices or is functioning effectively in the areas of sales and service. Because middlemen will not or cannot provide objective information about themselves, continuing customer research is the only way of getting adequate feedback on the level of sales representation, speed of filling orders, quality of post-sale service, and other distributor functions. If volume and marketing-share goals are not being met, the entire distribution setup should be reviewed to determine if it is causing the market problems.

Supervision and control of distribution channels require standards that differ from those in domestic trade. A company may have little decision latitude in foreign distribution-channel policy with less opportunity to

---

[11] Judith Zaichkowsky, "A Global Look at Consumer Involvement and Use of Products," *International Marketing Review,* Volume 6 Number 1, 1989, pp. 20–34.

[12] Dean Peebles, "Executive Insights Don't Write Off Global Advertising: A Commentary," *International Marketing Review,* Volume 6 Number 1, 1989, pp. 73–78.

Global brands. Effective control of promotion, price, brand, and product is critical in a global marketing strategy. (Joseph Jacobson/Journalism Services, Inc.)

manage and control these channels. For example, restricting the number of outlets for merchandise can cause problems because middlemen structures may not permit exclusive or restricted distribution. A company accustomed to a small number of middlemen may find itself confronted with an entirely different control system in supervising a large number of dissimilar outlets. And the caliber of middlemen is hard to control because there often are no middlemen who meet normal predetermined standards.

Since sales volumes are often too low to permit extensive control mechanisms, many manufacturers are content with less control in overseas markets, but such laxity can destroy the effectiveness of a distribution system. For example, it was discovered quite by accident that a British franchisee of packaging machinery was making nearly one third of its quota through sales in another franchisee's territory on the Continent. This discovery highlighted both inadequate territorial control and an inadequate sales quota system.

Marketing Personnel Control

Personnel is a vital ingredient to the success of a marketing program. Home-office management must always be concerned with top-level marketing management in each country; increasingly companies are taking greater interest in all marketing personnel, including hiring, management development, and compensation. Performance reports are accumulated on a regular basis, and records of managers in different parts of the world are routinely compared as a method of spotting managerial deficiencies. Companies

---

BOX 20–3
Out of Control—Or Necessary?

It would certainly make it easier if there could be only one brand name for a product throughout the world. For some companies like Coca-Cola and Pepsi-Cola it is possible but others have to adapt to local customs. Gillette, the razor blade company, has found it necessary to have different brand names in different countries.

Atra, Gillette's swivel-head razor, is called *Contour* in most of Europe and Latin America. The same product is sold as an *Acta* in Japan. Although it has no meaning, the word was chosen because of "the cultural effectiveness of a snappy first syllable and an 'a' at the end of the word."

The use of different names violates the old Gillette gospel of "one sight, one sound, one sell." That dictum fell when it was found that sales of Right Guard deodorant were flagging in Italy because the name was practically unpronounceable in Italian.

Gillette itself goes under different names in different countries, selling *Nacet* blades in the Middle East and *Minora* products in Africa and Latin America. In Eastern Europe, the company's products carry trademarks of *Mem* while in Indonesia they are *Rubie* and *Goal*.

Source: *Associated Press* News report, August 1980.

---

using tight control with marketing personnel have encountered considerable resistance from field managers but maintain the practice because it has proved successful.[13]

Profit Control

The goal of a corporation is generally to maximize worldwide *net* profits. Profit reports can communicate to management the overall health of subsidiary operations and current market conditions. They may also function effectively as trend reports to provide overall management guidance. Because profit is the ultimate goal of all marketing activity, the ultimate measure of success is in terms of profit. And although profit measures managerial effectiveness, success in building volume, maintaining margins, and controlling costs, success in all does not guarantee profit. Indeed, profit as a simple, concrete idea does not easily fit in an international business framework.

Some companies reinvest all profits and count their operations most successful. Obviously, any corporation must establish its own methodology

---

[13] For a different view, see an interview with the chairman of British Petroleum of America, "Global in Our Outlook on Life" *MIT Management*, Spring 1988, pp. 21–25.

BOX 20–4
Government Control

Socialist governments have found that one of their chief problems in maintaining control over the businesses they direct. Problems are sometimes aggravated in a mixed economy such as that of Egypt, where private business and socialized firms exist side by side.

The success of the flourishing general merchandise business of one *Mohamed X* in Cairo agitated government planners, so they established a subsidized store directly across the street from his place of business. The subsidized store purchased all it wanted of goods at reduced government prices; this imposed a distinct threat to the entrepreneur across the street. The private store owner, however, was a student of human nature and quickly made a bargain with the operator of the one-man government store. The former would purchase all of the merchandise from the latter, who could then fulfill his sales quotas and get his sales commission and not be troubled with the problems of keeping the store. Each morning when the government truck delivered the supplies, the government-store manager diverted them across the street, collected the day's receipts, and spent his day in leisure.

Officials from the Ministry of Supplies were delighted that the new store had become so successful so quickly. Eventually supervisors made a field investigation and discovered what was happening. Rather than report the situation to their superiors and show their own possible negligence, they approved the arrangement so everyone could continue doing business as usual.

Source: Related by Mohamed Khalil to the author.

for measuring and controlling profits. One of the critical decisions in profit management is determination of where the profits will be taken, so ultimate profit control must be at the home-office level. Another home-office decision is whether profits are to be maximized in the short or long term. Control is a much broader concept than accounting and applies to all areas of the marketing operation. Control in most areas of marketing is more difficult and expensive in world markets than in domestic markets, and each of the control areas mentioned earlier is closely related to *all* the others; effective control systems in one area add little benefit unless all others are effective also. The requirements of close control and its resulting difficulties pose an ever-present dilemma for international marketers.

HOME-OFFICE RESPONSIBILITY

Although responsibility for international operations may be delegated to a chief international officer, the ultimate responsibility for the success or failure of an international enterprise falls on the chief operating officer of

BOX 20–5
When Is It Overcontrol or How About the 25 Cents Spent for Parking?

In the past, corporate headquarters often permitted overseas subsidiaries to be run as independent fiefdoms. Today, subsidiary managers must have strong relationships to corporate staff. An extreme example of this is the new CEO who required that the major product-line controllers within each operating division travel monthly to corporate headquarters for a formal presentation to the CEO and his corporate financial staff.

One executive of the firm interviewed by BI said that all work in his department effectively ceases for three full days each month while staff members prepare and rehearse this presentation. He also expressed the irony of the fact that, at one of these sessions, he was questioned in depth about an $11,000 item—part of a several-million-dollar report—by the CEO, who is responsible for running a multibillion-dollar MNC.

Source: "Corporate Staffs Are Playing Greater Role in Control of the MNC." Reprinted from *Business International*, April 3, 1981, pp. 106–7 with the permission of the publisher, Business International Corporation (New York).

the company. Because of this primary responsibility, home-office management needs to exercise just the right degree of control over affiliated international organizations. Control functions must be carefully assigned at a level where they can be most appropriately implemented. At a minimum, the home office must make basic policy decisions, major fund allocations, and executive selections.

The trend in international management thinking is shifting from decentralized control toward some balance between complete decentralization and complete centralization. Full decentralization has not proved consistently reliable, and communications and information-handling technology have developed to a point where home-office control is more feasible. Yet, full centralization has its detractors also. The major criticism of centralized decision making is the lack of responsiveness to local conditions. A reasonable reply to this issue is for a decision to be made centrally if control and standardization are critical factors, or locally if local market conditions are of major importance. Or as one authority states, "think globally and act locally."[14] Whatever the argument, corporate staffs are assuming greater responsibility in the control process.

---

[14] Christopher A. Bartlett and Sumantra Ghoshal, "Organizing for Worldwide Effectiveness: The Transnational Solution," *California Management Review*, Fall 1988, p. 73.

SUMMARY

In organizations, as in individuals, self-control is at least partly a function of maturity. Many companies new to global operations reason that the need for flexibility, the complexity of international organization, and the differences in operations from country to country justify neglect of coordination and control systems. However, companies that have been most successful in global operations have learned that control systems can be developed to handle most situations. Controlling marketing operations is always difficult, but it is especially so in international operations. All marketing areas can be coordinated and controlled through a basic control sequence. The planning stage of the control sequence includes establishing objectives, selecting control methods, setting up standards, and locating responsibility. Ideally, all four of these activities should be undertaken before a firm ever ventures into international marketing operations. Such control can be accomplished, however, through analysis of the firm's specific organizational structure as it affects control mechanism and determination of the exact areas in which control is desired. Coupling this information with a basic knowledge of the control sequence should result in an effective program of coordination and control.

The profitability of a global operation depends directly on the relationship between sales volume, the cost of producing the goods, and the cost of marketing or distribution. All four items—profit, volume, production cost, and marketing cost—are subject to control. Any effective program for coordinating and controlling world marketing operations requires special attention to the functions of price, promotion, product, and distribution channels. International information systems help maintain communications, then a continual review of results, with subsequent corrections and modifications, is required. These are the concepts relevant to coordination and control of global marketing operations.

QUESTIONS

1. Define:
   volume control
   feedback
   field audit

2. What barriers make controlling an international operation more difficult than controlling domestic marketing activities?

3. How do company objectives relate to control systems?

4. "To minimize losses, management must be especially control conscious when it is engaging in the overseas business for some reason other than direct short-run profit." Explain.

5. Discuss the basic requisites of an effective control system.

6. Review the relative advantages of centralized and decentralized systems for controlling international marketing operations.

7. Develop a control system for a marketing program using autonomous foreign franchises to market a domestic product.

8. Review the control sequence.

9. Explain the importance of "timing" standards and controls.

10. Visit a firm with international sales or marketing activity. Compare their control system with one which you develop for them. Explain the differences.

11. Discuss the difficulties associated with field audits.

12. How can a company be certain its control system fits its organization and objectives?

13. Controlling is the very essence of management. Explain.

14. Discuss how the unique factors in international control affect the control process. Give examples.

APPENDIX

The Country Notebook—A Guide for Developing a Marketing Plan

The first stage in the planning process is a preliminary country analysis. The marketer needs basic information to: (1) evaluate a country-market's potential; (2) identify problems that would eliminate a country from further consideration; (3) identify aspects of the country's environment that need further study; (4) evaluate the components of the marketing mix for possible adaptation; and (5) develop a strategic marketing plan. One further use of the information collected in the preliminary analysis is as a basis for a country notebook.

Many companies, large and small, have a *country notebook* for each country in which they do business. The country notebook contains information a marketer should be aware of when making decisions involving a specific country-market. As new information is collected, the country notebook is continually updated by the country or product manager. Whenever a marketing decision is made involving a country, the country notebook is the first data base consulted. New product introductions, changes in advertising programs, and other marketing program decisions begin with the country notebook. It also serves as a quick introduction for new personnel assuming responsibility for a country-market.

This section presents four separate guidelines for collection and analysis of market data and preparation of a country notebook: (1) guideline for cultural analysis; (2) guideline for economic analysis; (3) guideline for a market audit and competitive analysis; and (4) guideline for a preliminary marketing plan. These guidelines suggest the kinds of information a marketer can gather to enhance planning.

The points in each of the guidelines are general. They are designed to provide direction to areas to explore for relevant data. In each guideline, specific points must be adapted to reflect a company's products. The decision as to the appropriateness of specific data and the depth of coverage depends on company objectives, product characteristics, and the country-market. Some points in the guidelines are unimportant for some countries and/or some products and should be ignored. Preceding chapters of this book provide specific content suggestions for the topics in each guideline.

I. GUIDELINE FOR CULTURAL ANALYSIS

The data suggested in the cultural analysis include informaton that helps the marketer make market planning decisions. However, its application extends beyond product/market analysis to an important source of information for someone interested in understanding business customs and other important cultural features of the country.

The information in this analysis must be more than a collection of facts. Whoever is responsible for the preparation of this section should attempt to interpret the meaning of cultural information. That is, how does the information help in understanding the effect on the market? For example, the fact that almost all the populations of Italy and Mexico are Catholic is an interesting statistic but not nearly as useful as understanding the effect of Catholicism on values, beliefs, and other aspects of market behavior. Even though both countries are predominantly Catholic, the influence of their individual and unique interpretation and practice of Catholicism can result in important differences in market behavior.

Guidelines for Cultural Analysis

    I. Introduction
       Include short profiles of the company, the product to be exported, and the country with which you wish to trade.
    II. Brief Discussion of the Country's Relevant History
    III. Geographical Setting
      A. Location
      B. Climate
      C. Topography
      D. Minerals and resources
      E. Surface transportation
        1. Modes
        2. Availability
        3. Usage rates
        4. Ports
      F. Communication systems
        1. Types
        2. Availability
        3. Usage rates
    IV. Social Institutions
      A. Family
        1. The nuclear family
        2. The extended family

        3. Dynamics of the family
           a. Parental roles
           b. Marriage and courtship
        4. Female/male roles (Are they changing or static?)
    B. Education
        1. The role of education in society
           a. Primary education (quality, levels of development, etc.)
           b. Secondary education (quality, levels of development, etc.)
           c. Higher education (quality, levels of development, etc.)
        2. Literacy rates
    C. Political system
        1. Political structure
        2. Political parties
        3. Stability of government
        4. Special taxes
        5. Role of local government
    D. Legal system
        1. Organization of the judiciary system
        2. Code, common socialist or Islamic-law country
        3. Participation in patents, trademarks, and other conventions
    E. Social organizations
        1. Group behavior
        2. Social classes
        3. Clubs, other organizations
        4. Race, ethnicity, and subcultures
    F. Business customs and practices
  V. Humans and the Universe: Philosophy and Religion
    A. Belief systems
    B. The church
        1. Orthodox doctrines and structures
        2. Relationship with the people
        3. Which religions are prominent?
        4. Membership of each religion
        5. Are there any powerful or influential cults?
    C. Aesthetics
        1. Visual arts (plastics, graphics, public art, colors, etc.)
        2. Music
        3. Drama, ballet, and other performing arts
        4. Folklore and relevant symbols
 VI. Living Conditions
    A. Diet and nutrition
        1. Meat and vegetable consumption rates
        2. Typical meals
        3. Malnutrition rates
    B. Housing
        1. Types of housing available
        2. Do most people own or rent?
        3. Do most people live in one-family dwellings or with other families?
    C. Working conditions
        1. Employer-employee relations

     2. Employee participation
     3. Salaries and benefits
   D. Clothing
     1. National dress
     2. Types of clothing worn at work
   E. Recreation, sports, and other leisure activities
     1. Types available and in demand
     2. Percentage of income spent on such activities
VII. Language
   A. Official language(s)
   B. Spoken versus written language(s)
   C. Dialects
VIII. Executive Summary

   After completing the research for this section, prepare a *two-page* (maximum length) summary of the major points. The purpose of an executive summary is to give the reader a brief glance at the critical points of your report. Those aspects of the culture a reader should know to do business in the country but would not be expected to know or would find different based on his or her SRC should be included in this summary.

IX. Sources of Information
X. Appendixes

II. GUIDELINE FOR ECONOMIC ANALYSIS

The reader may find the data collected for the economic analysis guideline are more straightforward than for the cultural analysis guideline. There are two broad categories of information in this guideline: general economic data that serve as a basis for an evaluation of the economic soundness of a country; and, information on channels of distribution and media availability. As mentioned earlier, the guideline focuses only on broad categories of data and must be adapted to particular company/product needs.

Guideline for Economic Analysis

  I. Introduction
 II. Population
   A. Total
     1. Growth rates
     2. Number of live births
     3. Birth rates
   B. Distribution of population
     1. Age
     2. Sex
     3. Geographic areas (urban, suburban, and rural density and concentration)

    4. Immigration rates and patterns

    5. Ethnic groups

III. Economic Statistics and Activity

  A. Gross national product (GNP or GDP)

    1. Total

    2. Rate of growth (real GNP or GDP)

  B. Personal income per capita

  C. Average family income   70   **3.4**

  D. Distribution of wealth

    1. Income classes

    2. Proportion of the population in each class

    3. Is the distribution distorted?

  E. Principal industries

    1. What proportion of the GNP does each industry contribute?

    2. Ratio of private to publicly owned industries

  F. Foreign investment

    1. Opportunities?

    2. Which industries?

  G. International trade statistics

    1. Major exports

      a. Dollar value

      b. Trends

    2. Major imports

      a. Dollar value

      b. Trends

    3. Balance of payments situation

      a. Surplus or deficit?

      b. Recent trends

    4. Exchange rates

      a. Single or multiple exchange rates

      b. Current rate of exchange

      c. Trends

  H. Trade restrictions

    1. Embargoes

    2. Quotas

    3. Import taxes

    4. Tariffs

    5. Licensing

    6. Custom duties

  I. Extent of economic activity not included in cash income activities

    1. Countertrades

      a. Products generally offered for countertrading

      b. Types of countertrades requested (i.e., barter, counterpurchase, etc.)

    2. Foreign aid received

  J. Labor force

    1. Size

    2. Unemployment rates

  K. Inflation rates

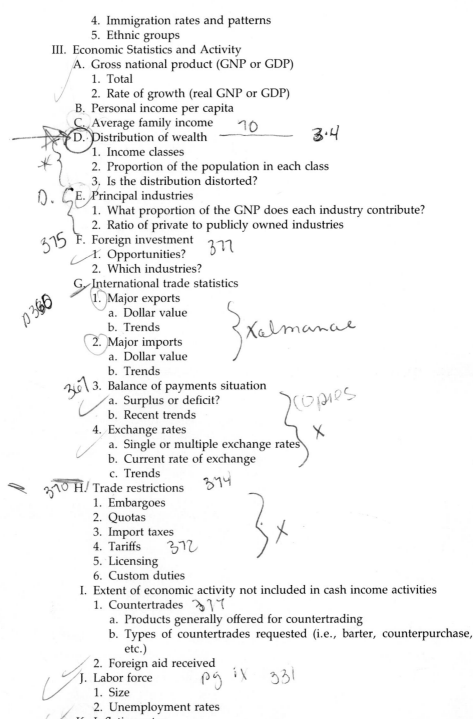

IV. Developments in Science and Technology
   A. Current technology available (computers, machinery, tools, etc.)
   B. Percentage of GNP invested in research and development
   C. Technological skills of the labor force and general population
V. Channels of Distribution
   A. Middlemen
      1. Availability
      2. Services offered
      3. Customary markups for various classes of goods
         a. Wholesale
         b. Retail
      4. Retailers
         a. Number of retailers
         b. Typical size of retail outlets
         c. Method of operation (cash-credit)
         d. Scale of operation (large-small)
         e. Role of chain stores, department stores, and specialty shops
      5. Wholesale middlemen
         a. Number and size
         b. Method of operation (cost-credit)
   B. Penetration of urban and rural markets
   C. Facilities available
   D. Credit availability
VI. Media
   A. Availability of media
   B. Costs
      1. Television
      2. Radio
      3. Print
      4. Other media (cinema, outdoor, etc.)
   C. Agency assistance
   D. Coverage of various media
   E. Percentage of population reached by each of the media
VII. Executive Summary
   After completing the research for this report, prepare a two-page (maximum) summary of the major economic points.
VIII. Sources of Information
IX. Appendixes

III. GUIDELINE FOR A MARKET AUDIT AND COMPETITIVE MARKET ANALYSIS

Of the guidelines presented, this is the most product or brand specific. Information in the other guidelines is general in nature focusing on product categories, whereas data in this one are brand specific and are used to determine competitive market conditions and market potential.

Two different components of the planning process are reflected in this guideline.

Information in Parts I and II serve as the basis for an evaluation of the product/brand in a specific market country. Information in this guideline provides an estimate of market potential and an evaluation of the strengths and weaknesses of competitive marketing effort. The data generated in this step are used to determine the extent of adaptation of the company's marketing mix necessary for successful market entry and to develop the final step, the action plan.

The detailed information needed to complete this guideline is not necessarily available without conducting a thorough marketing research investigation. Thus, another purpose of this part of the country notebook is to identify the correct questions to ask in a formal market study.

Guideline for a Market Audit and Competitive Market Analysis

I. Introduction

II. The Product

   A. Evaluate the product as an innovation as it is perceived by the intended market
      1. Relative advantage
      2. Compatibility
      3. Complexity
      4. Trialability
      5. Observability
   B. Major problems and resistances to product acceptance based on the preceding evaluation. (See Chapter 12 for a discussion of this topic.)

III. The Market

   A. Describe the market(s) in which the product is to be sold
      1. Geographical region(s)
      2. Forms of transportation and communication available in that (those) region(s)
      3. Consumer buying habits
         a. Product-use patterns
         b. Product feature preferences
         c. Shopping habits
      4. Distribution of the product
         a. Typical retail outlets
         b. Product sales by other middlemen
      5. Advertising and promotion
         a. Advertising media usually used to reach your target market(s)
         b. Sales promotions customarily used (sampling, coupons, etc.)
      6. Pricing strategy
         a. Customary markups
         b. Types of discounts available
   B. Compare and contrast your product and the competition's product(s)
      1. Competitor's product(s)
         a. Brand name
         b. Features
         c. Package

        2. Competitor's prices
        3. Competitor's promotion and advertising methods
        4. Competitor's distribution channels
   C. Market size
        1. Estimate industry sales for the planning year
        2. Estimate sales for your company for the planning year
   D. Government participation in the marketplace
        1. Agencies that can help you
        2. Regulations you must follow
IV. Executive Summary
   Based on your analysis of the market, briefly summarize (two-page maximum) the major problems and opportunities requiring attention in your marketing mix.
V. Sources of Information
VI. Appendixes

IV. GUIDELINE FOR A PRELIMINARY MARKETING PLAN

Information gathered in Guidelines I through III serves as the basis for developing a marketing plan for your product/brand in a target market. How the problems and opportunities that surfaced in the preceding steps are overcome and/or exploited to produce maximum sales/profits are presented here. The action plan reflects, in your judgment, the most effective means of marketing your product in a country market. Budgets, expected profits and/or losses, and additional resources necessary to implement the proposed plan are also presented.

  I. The Marketing Plan
   A. Marketing objectives
      1. Target market(s) (specific description of the market)
      2. Expected sales 19__
      3. Profit expectations 19__
      4. Market penetration and coverage
   B. Product adaptation—Using the extended product model as your guide, indicate how your product can be adapted for the market. (See Chapter 12.)
      1. Core component
      2. Packaging component
      3. Support services components
   C. Promotion
      1. Advertising
         a. Objectives
         b. Media mix
         c. Message
         d. Costs
      2. Sales promotions
         a. Objectives
         b. Coupons

      c. Premiums
      d. Costs
   3. Personal selling
   4. Other promotional methods
D. Distribution: from origin to destination
   1. Mode selection: advantages/disadvantages of each mode
      a. Railroads
      b. Air carriers
      c. Ocean carriers
      d. Motor carriers
   2. Port selection
      a. Origin port
      b. Destination port
   3. Packing
      a. Marking and labeling regulations
      b. Containerization
      c. Costs
   4. Insurance claims
   5. Documentation required
      a. Bill of lading
      b. Dock receipt
      c. Air bill
      d. Commercial invoice
      e. Pro forma invoice
      f. Shipper's export declaration
      g. Statement of origin
      h. Special documentation *Packify List*
   6. Freight forwarder
   If your company does not have a transportation or traffic management
   department, then consider using a freight forwarder. There are distinct
   advantages and disadvantages to hiring one.
   7. Destination point
      a. Warehousing available
      b. Wholesalers available
      c. Retail outlets available
      d. Import/export agents available
   8. Retail distribution
      a. Types of retailers
      b. Retail margins
E. Price
   1. Cost of the shipment of goods
   2. Transportation costs
   3. Handling expenses
      a. Pier charges
      b. Wharfage fees
      c. Loading and unloading charges
   4. Insurance costs

        5. Customs duties
        6. Import taxes and value added tax
        7. Wholesale and retail markups and discounts
        8. Company's gross margins
        9. Retail price
    F. Terms of sale
        1. EX WORKS, FOB, FAS, C&F, CIF
        2. Advantages/disadvantages of each
    G. Methods of payment
        1. Cash in advance
        2. Open accounts
        3. Consignment sales
        4. Sight, time, or date drafts
        5. Letters of credit
II. Pro Forma Financial Statements and Budgets
    A. Marketing budget
        1. Selling expense
        2. Advertising/promotion expense
        3. Distribution expense
        4. Product cost
        5. Other costs
    B. Pro forma annual profit and loss statement (first year and fifth year)
III. Resource Requirements
    A. Finances
    B. Personnel
    C. Production capacity
IV. Executive Summary
    After completing the research for this report, prepare a two-page (maximum) summary of the major points of your successful marketing plan.
V. Sources of Information
VI. Appendixes

The intricacies of international operations and the complexity of the environment within which the international marketer must operate create an extraordinary demand for information. When operating in foreign markets, the need for thorough information as a substitute for uninformed opinion is equally as important as it is in domestic marketing. Sources of information needed to develop the country notebook and answer other marketing questions are discussed in Chapter 11.

SUMMARY

Market-oriented firms build strategic market plans around company objectives, markets, and the competitive environment. Planning for marketing can be complicated even for one country, but when a company is doing business internationally, the problems are multiplied. Company objectives may vary from market to market and from time to time; the structure of international markets also changes periodically and from country to country, and the competitive, governmental, and economic parameters affecting market planning are in a constant state of flux. These variations require international marketing executives to be specially flexible and creative in their approach to strategic marketing planning.

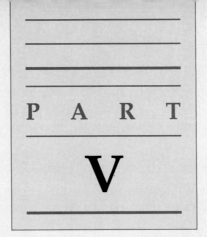

P A R T

V

Cases

Sections

Case 1–1

WHEN IS A COMPANY GLOBAL?

Listen to four senior executives of the world's largest firms with extensive holdings outside their home countries speak:

Company A: "We are a global firm. We distribute our products in about 100 countries. We manufacture in over 17 countries and do research and development in 3 countries. We look at all new investment projects—both domestic and overseas—using exactly the same criteria."

The executive from company A tells us that most of the key posts in company A's subsidiaries are held by home-country nationals. Whenever replacements for these people are sought, it is the practice, if not the policy, to "look next to you at the head office" and "pick someone (usually a home-country national) you know and trust."

Company B: "We are a global firm. Only 1 percent of the personnel in our office companies are non-nationals. Most of these are U.S. executives on temporary assignments. In all major markets, the affiliate's managing director is of the local nationality."

The executive from company B does not hide the fact that there are very few non-Americans in the key posts at headquarters. The few who are there are "so Americanized" that their foreign nationality literally has no meaning. The explanation for this paucity of non-Americans seems reasonable enough: "You can't find good foreigners who are willing to live in the United States, where our headquarters are located. American executives are more mobile. In addition, Americans have the drive and initiative we like. In fact, the European nationals would prefer to report

to an American rather than to some other European."

Company C: "We are a global firm. Our product division executives have worldwide product responsibility. As our organizational charts show, the United States is just one region on a par with Europe, Latin America, or Africa, in each product division."

The executive from company C goes on to explain that the worldwide product-division concept is rather difficult to implement. The senior executives in charge of these divisions have little overseas experience. They have been promoted from domestic posts and tend to view foreign consumer needs "as really basically the same as ours." Also, product-division executives tend to focus on the domestic market because the domestic market is larger and generates more revenue than the fragmented European markets. The rewards are for global performance, but the strategy is to focus on domestic. The executive's colleagues say "one pays attention to what one understands—and our senior executives simply do not understand what happens overseas and really do not trust foreign executives in key positions here or overseas."

Company D (European): "We are a global firm. We have at least 18 nationalities represented at our headquarters. Most senior executives speak at least two languages. About 30 percent of our staff at headquarters are foreigners."

The executive from the European company D begins by explaining that since the voting shareholders must by law come from the home country, the home-country's interests must be given careful consideration. In the final analysis the executive insists: "We are proud of our nationality; we shouldn't be ashamed of it," and cites examples of the previous reluctance of headquarters to use home-country ideas overseas, to their detriment—especially in their U.S. subsidiary. "Our country produces good executives, who tend to stay with us a long time. It is harder to keep executives from the United States."

Source: This case first appeared in the fifth edition of *International Marketing* and it is adapted from Howard V. Perlmutter, "The Tortuous Evolution of the Multinational Corporation," *Columbia Journal of World Business*, January–February 1969, pp. 9–10.

QUESTIONS

1. Discuss the degree of international involvement of each of the companies.
2. Which is a global country? Why?
3. Write a definition of a global country.

Case 1–2

THE MULTINATIONAL—SAINT OR SINNER?

Critics of multinational companies contend they are, among other things, exploitive, disruptive of local culture, purveyors of social unrest, and so forth. As one critic is reported to have said:

> It's time to monitor the multinationals. . . . They are everywhere. Shutting down plants and fleeing to low-wage havens. Violating workers' rights. Ignoring health and environmental responsibilities. Undermining third-world development. Aided and abetted by favorable government policies, while avoiding taxes.[1]

---

[1] "Multinational Monitor," June 1984 as quoted in Ann McKinstry Micou, "The Invisible Hand at Work in Developing Countries," *Across the Board*, March 1985, p. 8.

Is there nothing positive that can be said about multinational companies? You answer that question. Listed below are seven prejudices against multinationals excerpted from a recent report of the President's Task Force on International Private Enterprise. Evaluate each prejudice and write a short report refuting or supporting the prejudice with documented examples.

> **Prejudice 1:** No matter how small or large, international private enterprises (IPEs) do not owe their allegiance to the countries in which they transact business. Their main interest is the global integration of production and sales, not achieving host-country industrial goals. They pose the threat of economic hegemony which is sanctioned (if not encouraged) by developed-country governments.

Prejudice 2: International companies are large economic units that can exert enormous power in and over local markets. Their capacity to transfer resources and knowledge for production gives them monopolistic positions that inhibit local business development and contribute little to the local economy.

Prejudice 3: Developing countries are dependent upon a limited group of IPEs for product development and technology. As a result, the developing countries are at a disadvantage and have little negotiating leverage.

Prejudice 4: Foreign private enterprises seek investments in developing countries in order to reap excessive profits.

Prejudice 5: The business practices of large companies are abusive. Direct government intervention in negotiations, ownership, and regulation is the only way to protect developing-country societies and to force IPEs to make positive contributions to development.

Prejudice 6: Even though an expanding private sector may result in more rapid economic growth, the benefits generated will be unfairly and unequally distributed, to the disadvantage of the majority of the people.

Prejudice 7: As an instrument of industrialized-country policies, international private enterprises will neither share technology, research, and development facilities nor transfer such facilities to developing countries. The payment for such technology is excessive. The goal is to keep developing countries dependent on IPE suppliers.

Source: Adapted from Ann McKinstry Micou, "The Indivisible Hand at Work in Developing Countries," *Across the Board*, March, 1985, pp. 16–17.

Case 1–3

SELLING U.S. ICE CREAM IN KOREA

Effect of Controllable and Uncontrollable Factors

The call from Hong Kong was intriguing: Go to South Korea and be the franchisee of an American premium ice cream to capitalize on the Koreans' new disposable income and their growing appetite for Western fast-food products.

Within six months of my application, the government granted me permission to bring the ice cream, Hobson's, to Seoul with only two nontariff trade conditions: Make my ice cream in Korea after a year of operation and at the same time take on a Korean partner who had at least a 25 percent stake in the company.

I agreed, and chose Itaewon for my site, figuring that between the Korean bar girls and the U.S. Army up the road it would give me a good cross-section of East and West.

Necessary Ingredient

Almost a half year after start up, I still think it's a timely idea but it certainly hasn't been easy pickings. The Korean bar girls, for instance, think my ice cream is too expensive, and Koreans in general are highly suspicious of new products. Government red tape is horrendous and foreigners are not welcome.

But because internationalization and economic progress are hard to separate, Seoul is coming to accept foreigners and their products as a necessary ingredient for their own growth.

The irony, however, is that Korean intransigence is not the only problem a Yankee entrepreneur faces here: Washington trade-bashing can take its toll as well. The U.S. government has been pressuring this country to raise the value of the won, to make Korean exports more expensive and U.S. imports less. On top of this is Congress's omnibus trade bill, which forces Korea to open its markets or face punitive sanctions on its own exports to the U.S. Although these efforts are designed to help American traders like me, I have seen all too often how the best laid political plans can actually make it more difficult for us to maintain a foothold in these countries.

In fairness it also must be said that some American companies bring this on themselves. Evidence indicates that American companies are badly outclassed by their failure to take Asian markets seriously and a tendency to follow the laws of least resistance by concentrating on selling within the borders of the United States.

American companies have tried to cheat by getting Congress to force not only Korea, but also Japan, Hong Kong, Singapore and other countries to raise the value of their currency. Those forces are now driving the won to a value of 590 to 600 won for one dollar by this year's end, when just two years ago $1 would buy 890 won. I thus find myself importing more dollars (16 percent since October 1987) just to stay even with my earlier projections when it was 800 won to the dollar. In other words it has cost me 16 percent more dollars just to get started operating, and this

was the margin I was hoping I could apply toward profits. Any price increase to recoup losses risks pricing my ice cream out of the Korean market.

Another result of exchange-rate jiggling is inflation. This is a byproduct of the won's strengthening against the dollar, reflected in the many outside investment dollars trying to find a home in Korea's currency and stock market.

Consequently everything comes with a price tag that equals or exceeds what one can buy in the United States. On top of this are import taxes, tariffs and nontariff barriers on imported capital goods and, in my case, finished ice cream. Duties, for example, range from 20 to 38 percent additional money.

U.S. trade bullying also fans the flames of anti-Americanism here, and American business pays for that. Even though Washington has some legitimate gripes about closed Korean markets, Koreans feel that they're being pushed around and that the United States doesn't recognize the great strides they have made. For me this resentment has translated into vandalism of my store-front property, such as knocked-down signs, broken patio tables and chairs, pane-glass windows smeared with soda and dirt, and even human feces left on my doorstep. It also manifests itself by Koreans staying away from buying my ice cream.

The Korean bureaucracy seems to share the suspicion of foreigners trying to do business here. When I made arrangements for the arrival of my first ice cream shipment into Pusan a month before the scheduled opening of my store, the authorities informed me that they couldn't care less about my ice cream and that I was illegally in the country. The upshot was my lawyers spent three weeks trying to persuade some second-echelon bureaucrat that I was here under valid reasons, to no avail. Desperate, and a day away from packing my bags and buying a one-way ticket to

California, I called the one friend I have in government. By a one-in-a-thousand chance, he knew the second-echelon bureaucrat and was able to clear away his mental block about me.

But this was a fluke. I have no doubt that the mental block was the Korean dairy farmers complaining about foreign imports of ice cream, which in turn is part of the bigger picture of pressure that Korean agriculture is receiving from U.S. trade negotiators to open its market.

Nevertheless, there has been some progress. In June 1987 the American Chamber of Commerce here wrote in its annual summary of trade issues that "access to the Korean market is one of the most frustrating issues faced by American companies in Korea." A year and a half later, however, the chamber wrote that "1988 has been a good year for the Korean economy and American business in Korea. U.S. exports to Korea have increased approximately 40 percent over 1987. As 1988 progressed, the Korean government took significant steps to open the market providing much broader accesss for American business."

The question now is whether American companies can take advantage of the "much broader access" into the Korean market. This will not be easy, for American business is not what it used to be. Woo Choong Kim, founder of the Daewoo business empire, has said: "In the old days, Americans worked hard to challenge new frontiers. But as their economy got mature, they became more interested in nice houses, jogging, and having a good time than in doing business. How can you compete without dedication? It is not the management system that is not working in American companies, it is the people not working hard."

Indeed even outgoing Commerce Secretary William Verity recently admitted that although Americans are great at coming up with new inventions, they "are not good at getting them into products to be sold."

Establishing a Beachhead

For example, Korean executives were almost throwing machine-tool and welding-machine orders at American companies—with the U.S. concerns dropping the ball almost every time. The reasons given by Koreans were various: inflexibilty about the terms of a contract, poor service, or just plain not trying hard enough (e.g., not working on Saturdays). The one American company that did measure up was Varian Associates. Its management team projected that the bulk of world manufacturing will be done in Asia in years to come and that right now U.S. companies are missing out on Asia's rush to outfit the factories building more and more of the world's cars, computers, and fast-food plants.

Varian installed 18 Korean nationals and several expatriates in a Seoul office to market their equipment and match Japanese service. Unlike other American companies, Varian has accommodated the Korean culture and way of doing business by establishing a beachhead presence in one of the world's fastest growing markets.

I myself have learned that it is important to be here and to learn their ways. In doing so, we help each other. The Korean company I chose to do business with, for example, will learn from me an ice cream-making technology and formula that enhances its competitiveness in that industry at home and abroad. I, in turn, will learn from my partner how to be competitive in Korea. What neither of us needs is a U.S. Congress trying to make its balance sheets add up nicely by rigging the currency in a way that hurts the very entrepreneurs it is supposed to help, fans the flames of anti-Americanism, and could lead to a trade war where nobody wins.

EXHIBIT 1   The International Marketing Task

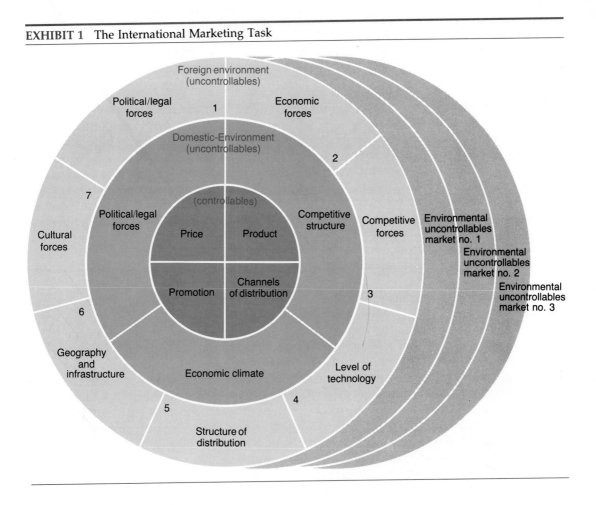

As a guide use Exhibit 1 described in Chapter 1 and do the following:

1. Identify each of the domestic and foreign uncontrollable elements that U.S. ice cream encountered in Korea.

2. Describe how problems encountered with each uncontrollable element may have been avoided or compensated for had the element been recognized in the planning stage.

3. Identify other problems U.S. ice cream may encounter in the future.

Source: Adapted from Jay R. Tunney, "U.S. Ice Cream Fares Poorly in Korea," *The Asian Wall Street Journal Weekly*, February 13, 1989, p. 13.

Case 1–4

HARVEY WALLBANGER POPCORN

Harvey Wallbanger, president of Harvey Wallbanger Popcorn, Inc., entered the popcorn market in 1972. He is considered the person most responsible for creating a gourmet popcorn market in the United States. His claim to fame is that his corn is lighter, fluffier, tenderer, and bigger than ordinary popcorn. He also boasts that his popcorn has fewer hard, unpopped kernels than competitive products.

Harvey's company sells popcorn to several markets:

1. Unpopped corn sold to food stores for the consumer to take home. There are several companion products—flavored seasoning, cooking oil—and a variety of different size packages including a sealed cooking bag with popcorn, oil, and flavoring for use in a microwave oven.

2. Bulk popcorn is sold to concessionaires such as movie theaters and sports arenas.

3. Franchising the Harvey Wallbanger Popcorn Shoppe, a gourmet popcorn store, is a new venture. He has 20 company-owned stores and 120 licensed stores. Franchises of popcorn shops have been successful in the United States but are considered a fad and only do well in shopping malls and other high-traffic locations. Consumption of popcorn is, however, a staple in U.S. snack diets. Gourmet popcorn stores handle a large variety of flavors; sour cream and onion, cheese and spice flavors, and jalapeño, are popular additions to the traditional salted, buttered variety. Also included are the various caramel-flavored and other sweet flavors including watermelon, chocolate, Amaretto, and cherry licorice.

4. The company is testing a concept of leasing popping equipment to supermarkets to make fresh popcorn for on-premise consumption as well as to take home. For gourmet popcorn shops, he has machines that can pop 320 gallons of corn in an hour and cook up to 20 seasoned flavors or seven sweet flavors in the same time. He leases a smaller version of these machines to large supermarkets; the few he has in a test market are proving successful. The idea fits in with the move by larger supermarkets to add gourmet foods, delis, and other up-scale attractions for customers.

5. His newest venture is fresh-popped corn packaged in foil bags for distribution through food stores and wherever corn chips, potato chips, and other snacks are sold. The company sells regular popcorn plus a line of flavored gourmet popcorn. He is experimenting with a new flavor, vinegar and salt, reminiscent of fish and chips for this packaged goods market.

Problem

Wallbanger spent six months in England and was surprised that the British ate practically no popcorn yet consumed large amounts of other snacks while they drank beer. The only popcorn he could find, besides some stale bagged corn in supermarkets, was caramel corn which wasn't very popular. Wallbanger believes there is a great opportunity in the United Kingdom. The British are big snackers, they visit pubs on a frequent basis, and they are great TV watchers. He wants to explore the possibility of expanding into England. At the moment, he is thinking about exporting his franchise gourmet-shop operation and licensing stores to sell his brand of popcorn. Although he is open to suggestions of other possibilities, he is sure, as he told his board of directors, that "Harvey Wallbanger Popcorn will have a major investment in the United Kingdom within two years." As his staff assistant, you have been selected to do a preliminary evaluation of the opportunities and problems of selling popcorn in England.

Wallbanger gathered some information on the English market while he was there. He has given you that information and has asked you to give him your best judgment on: (1) of all the ways the company sells popcorn, which one or more ways should they attempt to enter the British market? (2) what are some of the major problems and opportunities the company might experience in England? and (3) what is the potential market for popcorn both shortrun and long term? You have three weeks to present your report to Mr. Wallbanger. You know if you do a good job and the company does go to England, you will probably be in charge of the new venture.

The English Market

Here is some of the information Wallbanger collected about the English market:

The British make a distinction between "savory" or spicy, salty snacks and "sweet" snacks. Savory or salty snacks in Britain include a wide variety of flavored potato crisps, extruded cheese snacks like Bugles, and salted peanuts.[1] Snacking on potato crisps or salted peanuts while drinking beer, especially in pubs, is very traditional social behavior. Nut snacks are purchased as a companion product

EXHIBIT 1 Savory Snack Sales by Outlet	
Supermarkets and grocers	40%
Public houses and off-license	25
Confectionery, tobacconists, newsagents	13
Variety stores	6
Others	16

to beer and they are bought in pubs and in grocery stores for home consumption.

As Exhibit 1 shows, 40 percent of all savory snacks are purchased at grocers and supermarkets while 25 percent are purchased in public houses and off-license establishments.[2] More important, 50 percent of all nuts are purchased in grocery stores, 24 percent are purchased in pubs, and 6 percent in off-license houses. Sixty-five percent of all beer purchased on premises is in pubs (brewery-owned and free), 21 percent in private clubs, and 11 percent in off-license. (See Exhibits 2 and 3 for more detailed data.)

Many of the snack-food distributors are also owners of off-license houses and pubs. "KPs," the best-selling beer nut, is manufactured by a brewer that also owns pubs. Forty-five percent of all pubs are owned by breweries who typically do not carry competing products. Most products sold in brewery-owned or licensed pubs are distributed exclusively by the brewery.

Savory snacks include potato crisps, extruded snacks, and nuts. There are 20,700,000 households in England in which an annual average of 159,000 tons of savory snacks, or 7.7 kilograms per household are consumed. (This compares to 2.7 kilograms per household in France.)

Prepackaged nuts have traditionally been

---

[1] In Great Britain, U.S. potato chips are called potato crisps or just crisps, and what we know as french fries are known as chips.

[2] Off license shops sell take-home alcoholic beverages.

EXHIBIT 2 Savory Snacks

Total Consumption (000s tonnes) = (1,000 kilograms)					
1975	1976	1977	1978	1979	1980
137.2	142.7	135.9	142.1	152.6	159.0

Consumption per Household
(kilograms)

	1975	1979	1983	1985
United Kingdom	7.2	7.7	10.0	12.0
Germany	—	5.0	—	—
France	—	2.7	—	—

Distributors
(percent value)

	Crisps	Extruded Snacks	Nuts
Grocers	49	60	50
CTNs*	12	20	7
Off-license	3	2	6
Pubs	14	5	24
Clubs	7	1	4
Other	15	12	8
Total	100	100	100

Consumption by Type
(000s tonnes)

		Percent of Market
Crisps	104.6	60%
Extruded Snacks	25.3	14
Nuts	31.2	20
Savory Bisquits	13.5	6
	174.6	100%

* CTNs are shops selling confectionary, tobacco goods, and newspapers.

marketed and consumed as a snack to go with beer. In England, to the predominantly male pub-goer, it has been considered manly to consume a fair number of pints of beer. Since eating any salty snack tends to increase thirst that leads to increased beer consumption, the wise pub owner has always made salty snack foods available.

The total savory snack food industry in Britain was $1.1 billion for 1985, and grew to over $1.7 billion by 1990.

Popcorn is available in England, but it is usually candied, similar to Cracker Jacks, and sold in small boxes at the cinema. Fresh, hot, buttered, and salted popcorn is a relatively new product concept in Britain.

One problem in positioning popcorn as a savory snack is its possible comparison with caramel corn. Butterkist, the most popular brand of caramel corn, is essentially a sweet snack and the British tend not to mix sweet with savory. Fortunately, caramel-flavored

EXHIBIT 3

Alcoholic Drinks—Take-Home Sales
(percent value)

Off-licenses	45%
Supermarkets	32
Superstores	5
Grocers	7
CTNs	4
Other	7
Total	100%

Beer
(percent value)

Off-License Sales of Beer		All Beer	
Major brewery chains	18%	Brewery owned bars	45%
Other specialists	30	Free bars	20
Multiple grocers	25	Clubs	21
Cooperatives	10	Off-licenses	11
Independent grocers	17		
Total	100%	Total	100%

sweet popcorn products are not particularly popular in the United Kingdom, so this resistance may be minimal.

The favorite snack of the British are crisps which account for 60 percent of all savory snacks sold in the United Kingdom. They do not snack with television as is the case in the United states, but they do snack while drinking beer, visiting bingo halls, and at all sporting events. In all these situations, regular or flavored crisps and salted nuts are favorites.

Case 1–5

FASTENERS, INC.—EQUAL OPPORTUNITY FOR WOMEN IN THE INTERNATIONAL DIVISION

Fasteners, Inc. manufactures a complete line of industrial fasteners used in the manufacture of almost all products. For example, a typical telephone uses 78 fasteners, a gas range 150, and a refrigerator 211. The appliance industry alone uses some 5 billion fasteners a year. Fasteners, Inc. makes several thousand different types and sizes of spring steel, plastic, and threaded fasteners, and snap and steel retaining rings. They also design and produce special-order fasteners to fit the particular needs of a manufacturer. The market for fasteners consists, quite literally, of any manufacturer who produces a product that might be assembled and held together in any way other than welding, soldering, or gluing. Total sales last year were $185 million.

Until a few years ago, Fasteners was primarily a domestic U.S. company. In 1980, however, it began exporting to several European customers, and sales abroad have grown to about 11 percent of total profits. It had not invested much time on the export division but a recent forecast and study by a management consulting firm convinced the company that its markets abroad would grow substantially within the next 15 years. It would have to make a definite management commitment to international markets in order to capitalize on the potential. The board of directors agreed that they should reorient their emphasis and begin looking at the world as a market. In Western Europe, where 80 percent of their foreign sales existed, the consulting report indicated continued growth; in the Mideast, the Far East, and Latin America, where it had not marketed, the future demand would be even larger than in Europe. One result of the expansion plans would be the need to substantially increase international division personnel. Although the company currently has about 100 employees in the international division, most work in the United States, since they rely heavily on foreign distributors in their European market for sales. Part of the expansion plans would include efforts to establish their own sales and marketing subsidiaries in England, Germany, Italy, and Spain and to continue expansion into new markets with wholly owned divisions wherever feasible. The company has estimated an increase of 200 to 300 new employees in the international division as planned expansion occurs over the next five years. Many of the new employees would be experienced nationals recruited from other international firms within their home countries; others would come from the company's normal recruiting pool, young MBAs, and others.

In discussing long-range development plans for the international division, the issue of equal opportunity for women was raised at one of the board meetings by Judy Sellridge, vice president of personnel. She wanted to know what action the company would take to ensure women an equal opportunity in the company's expansion plans. Fasteners has been totally committed to affirmative action/equal opportunity goals; in fact, Fasteners has taken pride in having, on the average, more women and minority executives than other equal-sized companies within the industry. The president of Fasteners has insisted on strict adherence to affirmative action/equal opportunity guidelines. Ms. Sellridge's question resulted in a lengthy discussion on the issue of equal opportunity in international business. The vice president of the international division questioned whether Fasteners should actively recruit women for the international division when expected career paths would not lead beyond the secretarial level or a position in personnel in the New York corporate offices. He claimed there would be no room in the international division for women executives or for women to represent the company in foreign countries. He also felt that women would be rejected by their foreign contacts. Cultural differences in most other countries of the world do not allow for the equal treatment of women in business efforts. Sellridge countered his point by referring to a recent report that emphasized that while the world, "is not yet quite their oyster," substantial numbers of women managers are beginning to pry open the shell. Women head Latin American operations for the Sunoco overseas subsidiary of Sun Company and for Southeast First Bank of Miami. Women represent General Electric Company in Moscow, and Bank of America in both Tokyo and Beijing. Fasteners' president admitted he had not given much attention to the women's issue in terms of the international division and that there were no women presently in managerial positions in that division. Because of its relatively small size, no problems had arisen; however, with the expected commitment to growth, the question of equal opportunity in the international division must be discussed. Top management split on the issue. The vice president in charge of the international division, who had 25 years of experience in foreign assignments and had been with Fasteners for about five years, opposed the idea of women in any managerial position that would put them in contact with foreign customers. He said their career paths would be shunted to lower levels within the company. He felt there was no future for them in international and he did not want to mislead anyone in order to appear as if the company were complying with the law. Other top management people in domestic operations did not totally agree with this viewpoint. The president was firmly committed to the idea of women in international, but he did not want to override the judgment of those in charge of that division. Basically, the president wanted to find some compromise position that would allow them to hire women for meaningful international management positions and at the same time avoid situations that would be dysfunctional for the division.

Arguments against hiring women for managerial positions in international were based on cultural differences that exist throughout most of the world. In many countries women are not permitted in business, especially not in supervisory or sales positions above the lowest levels. In the Mideast and in some Latin American countries, the woman's role is definitely not in business, and women are not accepted in management positions except in rare situations. The vice president of international had no firsthand experience of how a woman would be received since he had never, as he said, "seen a female executive or anyone above the level of executive secretary in any of the companies I know of." He felt strongly, however, that he could not place a woman in a position to represent Fasteners, to be in a supervisory position of salesmen, to be in sales, or in any position that required contact with locals in another country. To support his position, he asked his assistant to contact other international companies for their experiences with women executives. No company would give concrete figures on how many women were employed in international managerial and sales positions. Because of this reluctance to report hard information, the vice president was suspicious that women did not have equal opportunity in other international divisions either, but since they were all equal opportunity employers they would be reluctant to discuss the issue. Some information on the role of women in business in various countries was available; a brief summary by country or area follows:

Japan and Hong Kong

A 1983 survey of Japanese firms reported 49.9 percent had no women employees in any management ranks.

> A 1982 report on female employment in Japan concluded that Japanese women are more self-effacing in their career ambitions than women in other countries. In a survey of 700 graduate females, 95 percent thought there was "a clear difference of ability and aptitude between men and women."
>
> Thirty-two percent of all business establishments in Japan deny female workers even the chance to be promoted to a responsible position. Only 4.8 percent of all managerial job holders in Japan are women. In government positions, only 0.6 percent of all Japanese public-service employees holding posts of assistant director or higher are women.

Japanese men responded that the reason women were treated as second-class citizens was because they would not stay in a job any longer than they needed to find a good husband; thus, they were not worth having.

One personnel director indicated that while Japanese women were not accepted in Japanese business, the character of the Japanese is such that they would not reject a U.S. woman in a responsible position, at least not obviously.

"In Hong Kong," comments Xerox's China operations director, "Chinese businessmen express amazement, not so much at my job but at the fact that, as a women, I travel and I'm away from home so much."

"Three-quarters of Japanese women are university-educated but only one in four works after graduation. Japanese companies offer no opportunities for women's advancement."

For those in American companies the story is somewhat different. Citicorp is moving more women into higher management positions in Japan. "We are beginning to see more senior women move into slots that would have been unheard of five years ago."

Europe

Article 119 of the Treaty of Rome states, "Each member state shall . . . ensure and . . . maintain the application of the principle of equal remuneration for equal work as between men and women workers."

A European Court order to member countries to comply with Article 119 was met with resistance. One interesting response in Ireland was an advertisement by the government for an *equal pay enforcement officier*, offering different pay rates for men and women.

In Norway, Statoil, the state-owned oil company has allocated $82,000 for training courses and grants for women who wish to compete for higher managerial positions in its technical and economic areas. Further, the company has a policy to choose a woman over a man when two candidates have the same qualifications.

Male resistance to women executives is far stronger in Europe than in the United States. One British advertising executive says, "Of course, there's a place for women in business. They're good at all things that are too boring for machines."

Just eight or nine years ago, women executives were nonexistent except for such female-dominated industries as cosmetics and fashion.

A chief executive of a food company says, "I simply will not have women executives in our firm, but all the same, there is one woman director we deal with at a supplier company who is a superb manager and makes a major contribution to discussions."

European women believe that companies are deliberately barring them from line management positions, such as running a plant or a subsidiary, because women would have problems supervising large numbers of men or women.

In France, the proportion of women in managerial and professional staff positions in the insurance industry rose to 29 percent in 1980 from 13 percent in 1960.

The European Institute of Business Administration (INSEAD) in France has 38 women in its current MBA program. These women represent 15.5 percent of INSEAD's enrollment, more than double that of a year ago.

A French woman executive who made it to the top as president of the firm she inherited said she gets all the qualified women she needs since "women want to work for me because they get such hard times in other French companies." The financial director of her company remarked that she was pregnant when she applied for the post of director of finance and had she been interviewed by a man she never would have gotten the job.

Germany is perhaps the strongest bastion of male chauvinism; German companies always prefer to hire men. One major consulting firm reports that German clients have refused to accept female consultants.

In Spain, women have a long way to go. They still cannot get divorces, and there is no guarantee of equal pay; they have few rights. The position of women and the position of men are best illustrated by a 1978 movie hit called "La Mujer Es Cosa de Hombres" ("Woman Is a Thing of Men").

Most top women executives in Europe are with North American firms—particularly U.S. firms. This is influencing European communities. In Britain banks are increasingly hiring women for key posts, partly because they have seen women performing well in rival U.S. banks.

One U.S. chemical firm has a European branch with a women's equal opportunity program aimed at training and promoting women into administrative functions within the company. While there were some male prejudices initially, there has been progress. For example, in four years, the number of women in junior and middle management positions has risen from 3 to 9 percent of its total European management staff. The firm has placed women process development engineers in Germany, Sweden, and Holland; a project engineer in Holland; attorneys in Spain; and a product-floor manager in Greece.

Latin America and the Mideast

The sex roles in Latin America are just about the same as in Spain—"machismo" is the law.

In Saudi Arabia, women are expected to keep the strict *purdah* (seclusion from all public observation). While Western women are not bound by the strict *purdah*, no woman can drive a car, under penalty of her husband's arrest, and in many places she is cautioned against going about alone in public even in the daytime. Further, Moslem practice in Saudi Arabia forbids men and women to work within sight of each other. Dress is also quite restricted. One businessman called it "Koran chic"; high necklines, arms covered to the wrist, and skirts down to the ankles.

Companies simply assumed that foreign businessmen, accustomed to more patriarchal cultures, would shy away from doing business with U.S. women but they discovered they had been wrong. Recent experience has shown that most foreign businessmen are no more reluctant to do business with an American woman than with an American man. Yet in some parts of the world, the concern is realistic. In Saudi Arabia, a woman would have difficulty even getting a visa.

One bright spot was a study done by Professor Nancy Adler of McGill University. In her study she found that "being foreign was more important than being female."

"Throughout the study, one pattern became particularly clear," she writes, "First and foremost, foreigners are seen as foreigners."

"A foreign woman is not expected to act like the locals. Therefore, the rules governing the behavior of local women and limiting their access to management and to management responsibility do not apply to foreign women." One woman manager told Professor Adler, "I don't think the Japanese could work for a Japanese woman, but they just block it out for foreigners."

Another woman manager in Pakistan said, "There is a double standard between expatriates and local women. The Pakistanis test you, but you enter as a respected person. In India and Pakistan, being a woman helps for marketing and client contact. I got in to see customers because they had never seen a female banker before."

All the information was given to the president of Fasteners, Inc. who remained committed to the principle of equal opportunity. He did not want to jeopardize the effectiveness of the proposed expansion of the international division, but at the same time, he was concerned with four issues.

1. If the five-year goals of the proposed expansion were achieved, the number of U.S. citizens employed in international would equal or be exceeded by those in the domestic division. If no women were employed in the international division above the secretarial or clerk position, would Fasteners, Inc. be in an undesirable position if challenged on equal opportunity?
2. The report from personnel directors indicated that the European Community was beginning to enforce equal opportunity and he was concerned with the impact on Fasteners.
3. Many of the new positions to be created in the next few years would provide opportunities for domestic employees. In fact,

international would look to domestic employees for experienced personnel for foreign assignments. Some of the women presently employed by Fasteners would be qualified. What could the company do if any one of the several qualified women applied for transfers?
4. As international develops, and it becomes clear that the career path to the top must include some international experience, what would the company do when an experienced, qualified woman in the domestic division applied for a transfer and/or promotion to an opening in international?

You have been asked by the president to examine the problem and write a confidential position paper on women in international jobs. You are to deal with positions that require the person to travel for extended periods in foreign countries; permanent positions that require extensive contact with nationals; and positions in direct sales requiring contact with nationals, including supervisory positions over the national sales force. Also, consider problems that may exist for women in dealing primarily on a staff rather than a line position. Basically, the president must know if there would be any real basis for not accepting women in the international division. He pointed out that before any new employees would be ready to move into a foreign-country position they would have to have four or five years of experience. However, since Fasteners, Inc., has experienced women executives in their domestic divisions, there could be requests in the near future for intracompany transfers to positions in international. If the company were to turn down such a request, there would be likelihood of a challenge of the equal opportunity question. It is at that point that management must be able to defend its situation, either by justifying not having female employees or by proceeding with an action plan to provide equal opportunity to women.

A few days after you were given this assignment, Sellridge came by your office and offered some help. In a conversation about the meeting, she agreed that the opportunities for women were not without problems, although she felt attitudes were changing. The attitudes expressed in the board meeting represented conditions that existed at one time but are now softening as companies gain experience with women in international positions. There are women successful in international positions even though problems still exist in specific countries. According to her, biases toward female managers vary depending on the specific foreign country so a blanket negative attitude toward hiring women for overseas assignments would be inappropriate. Although strong biases against women in business may exist in Middle Eastern countries, attitudes toward women in business in Europe and Japan seem to be relatively positive.

She intimated that the material given to you at the board meeting might reflect a more negative position than actually exists. To get a more realistic idea of what the situation really is for women in international business, she suggested you read some of these articles:

Nancy J. Adler, "Expecting International Success: Female Managers Overseas," *Columbia Journal of World Business,* Fall 1984.
Nancy J. Adler, "Women in International Management," *California Management Review,* Summer 1984.
David Nye, "The Female Expat's Promise," *Across the Board,* January 1988, pp. 38–43.
Nancy J. Adler, "Women in Management Worldwide," *International Studies of Management and Organization,* Fall–Winter 1986–87, pp. 1–32.
Yasuko Murota, "Promotion Denied: Plight of Japan's Working Women," *The Asian Wall Street Journal,* February 15, 1988, p. 14.
Sally Solo, "Japan Discovers Woman Power," *Fortune,* June 19, 1989, pp. 153–58.
"Gender Bias in International Business," Chapter 15 in this text.

Case 1–6

NESTLÉ—THE INFANT FORMULA INCIDENT

Nestlé Alimentana of Vevey, Switzerland, one of the world's largest food-processing companies with worldwide sales of over $8 billion, has been the subject of an international boycott. For over 10 years, beginning with a Pan American Health Organization allegation, Nestlé has been directly or indirectly charged with involvement in the death of Third World infants. The charges revolve around the sale of infant feeding formula

which allegedly is the cause for mass deaths of babies in the Third World.

In 1974 a British journalist published a report that suggested that powdered-formula manufacturers contributed to the death of Third World infants by hard-selling their products to people incapable of using them properly. The 28-page report accused the industry of encouraging mothers to give up breast feeding and use powdered milk formulas. The report was later published by the Third World Working Group, a lobby in support of less-developed countries. The pamphlet was entitled, "Nestlé Kills Babies," and accused Nestlé of unethical and immoral behavior.

Although there are several companies who market infant baby formula internationally, Nestlé received most of the attention. This incident raises several issues important to all multinational companies. Before addressing these issues, let's look more closely at the charges by the Infant Formula Action Coalition (INFACT) and others and the defense by Nestlé.

The Charges

Most of the charges against infant formulas focus on the issue of whether advertising and marketing of such products have discouraged breast feeding among Third World mothers and have led to misuse of the products, thus contributing to infant malnutrition and death. Following are some of the charges made:

- A Peruvian nurse reported that formula had found its way to Amazon tribes deep in the jungles of northern Peru. There, where the only water comes from a highly contaminated river—that also serves as the local laundry and toilet—formula-fed babies came down with recurring attacks of diarrhea and vomiting.
- Throughout the Third World, many parents dilute the formula to stretch their supply. Some even believe the bottle itself has nutrient qualities and merely fill it with water. The result is extreme malnutrition.
- One doctor reported that in a rural area, one newborn male weighed 7 pounds. At four months of age, he weighed 5 pounds. His sister, aged 18 months, weighed 12 pounds, the weight one would expect a 4-month-old baby to weigh. She later weighed only 8 pounds. The children had never been breast-fed, and since birth, their diets were basically bottle feeding. For a four-month baby, one tin of formula should have lasted just under three days. The mother said that

one tin lasted two weeks to feed both children.
- In rural Mexico, the Philippines, Central America, and the whole of Africa, there has been a dramatic decrease in the incidence of breast feeding. Critics blame the decline largely on the intensive advertising and promotion of infant formula. Clever radio jingles extoll the wonders of the "white man's powder that will make baby grow and glow." "Milk nurses" visit nursing mothers in hospitals and their homes and provide samples of formula. These activities encourage mothers to give up breast feeding and resort to bottle feeding because it is "the fashionable thing to do or because people are putting it to them that this is the thing to do."

The Defense

The following points are made in defense of the marketing of baby formula in Third World countries:

- First, Nestlé argues that the company has never advocated bottle feeding instead of breast feeding. All its products carry a statement that breast feeding is best. The company states that it "believes that breast milk is the best food for infants and encourages breast feeding around the world as it has done for decades." The company offers as support of this statement one of Nestlé's oldest educational booklets on "Infant Feeding and Hygiene" which dates from 1913 and encourages breast feeding.
- However, the company does believe that infant formula has a vital role in proper infant nutrition as (1) a supplement, when the infant needs nutritionally adequate and appropriate foods in addition to breast milk and, (2) a substitute for breast milk when a mother cannot or chooses not to breast feed.
- One doctor reports, "Economically deprived and thus dietarily deprived mothers

who give their children only breast milk are raising infants whose growth rates begin to slow noticeably at about the age of three months. These mothers then turn to supplemental feedings that are often harmful to children. These include herbal teas, and concoctions of rice water or corn water and sweetened, condensed milk. These feedings can also be prepared with contaminated water and are served in unsanitary conditions."

• Mothers in developing nations often have dietary deficiencies. In the Philippines, a mother in a poor family who is nursing a child produces about a pint of milk daily. Mothers in the United States usually produce about a quart of milk each day. For both the Philippine and U.S. mothers, the milk produced is equally nutritious. The problem is that there is less of it for the Philippine baby. If the Philippine mother doesn't augment the child's diet, malnutrition develops.

• Many poor women in the Third World bottle feed because their work schedules in fields or factories will not permit breast feeding.

• The infant feeding controversy has largely to do with the gradual introduction of weaning foods during the period between three months and two years. The average well-nourished Western woman, weighing 20 to 30 pounds more than most women in less-developed countries, cannot feed only breast milk beyond five or six months. The claim that Third World women can breast feed exclusively for one or two years and have healthy, well-developed children is outrageous. Thus, all children beyond the ages of five to six months require supplemental feeding.

• Weaning foods can be classified as either native cereal gruels of millet or rice, or commercial manufactured milk formula. Traditional native weaning foods are usually made by mixing maize, rice, or millet flours with water and then cooking the mixture.

Other weaning foods found in use are crushed crackers, sugar and water, and mashed bananas.

There are two basic dangers to the use of native weaning foods. First, the nutritional quality of the native gruels is low. Second, microbiological contamination of the traditional weaning foods is a certainty in many Third World settings. The millet or the flour is likely to be contaminated, the water used in cooking will most certainly be contaminated, the cooking containers will be contaminated, and therefore, the native gruel, even after it is cooked, is frequently contaminated with colon bacilli, staph, and other dangerous bacteria. Moreover, large batches of gruel are often made and allowed to sit, inviting further contamination.

• Scientists recently compared the microbiological contamination of a local native gruel with ordinary reconstituted milk formula prepared under primitive conditions. They found both were contaminated to similar dangerous levels.

• The real nutritional problem in the Third World is not whether to give infants breast milk or formula; it is how to supplement mothers' milk with nutritionally adequate foods when they are needed. Finding adequate locally produced, nutritionally sound supplements to mothers' milk and teaching people how to prepare and use them safely is the issue. Only effective nutrition education along with improved sanitation and good food that people can afford will win the fight against dietary deficiencies in the Third World.

The Resolution

In 1974, Nestlé, aware of changing social patterns in the developing world and the increased access to radio and television there, reviewed its marketing practices on a region-by-region basis. As a result, mass media advertising of infant formula began to be phased out immediately in certain markets and, by 1978, was banned worldwide by the company. Nestlé then undertook to carry out more comprehensive health education programs to ensure an understanding of the proper use of their products reached mothers, particularly in rural areas.

"Nestlé fully supports the WHO (World Health Organization) Code. Nestlé will continue to promote breast feeding and ensure that its marketing practices do not discourage breast feeding anywhere. Our company intends to maintain a constructive dialogue with governments and health professionals in all the countries it serves with the sole purpose of servicing mothers and the health of babies."—this quote is from *Nestlé Discusses the Recommended WHO Infant Formula Code.*

In 1977 the Interfaith Center on Corporate Responsibility in New York compiled a case against formula-feeding in developing nations and the Third World Institute launched a boycott against many Nestlé products. Its aim was to halt promotion of infant formulas in the Third World. The Infant Formula Action Coalition (INFACT, successor to the Third World Institute) along with several other world organizations successfully lobbied the World Health Organization (WHO) to draft a code to regulate the advertising and marketing of infant formula in the Third World. In 1981 by a vote of 114–1, (three countries abstained and the United States was the only dissenting vote), 118 member nations of WHO endorsed a voluntary code. The eight-page code urged a worldwide ban on promotion and advertising of baby formula and called for a halt to distribution of free product samples and/or gifts to physicians who promoted the use of the formula as a substitute for breast milk.

In May 1981 Nestlé announced it would support the code and waited for individual countries to pass national codes that would then be put into effect. Unfortunately, very few such codes were forthcoming. By the end of 1983, only 25 of the 157 member nations of the WHO had established national codes.

Accordingly, Nestlé management determined it would have to apply the code in the absence of national legislation and in February 1982, issued instructions to marketing personnel, delineating the company's best understanding of the code and what would have to be done to follow it.

In addition, in May 1982, Nestlé formed the Nestlé Infant Formula Audit Commission (NIFAC) chaired by former Senator Edmund J. Muskie, and asked the commission to review the company's instructions to field personnel to determine if they could be improved to better implement the code. At the same time, Nestlé continued its meetings with WHO and UNICEF to try to obtain the most accurate interpretation of the code.

NIFAC recommended several clarifications for the instructions that it believed would better interpret ambiguous areas of the code; in October 1982, Nestlé accepted those recommendations and issued revised instructions to field personnel.

Other issues within the code, such as the question of a warning statement, were still open to debate. Nestlé consulted extensively with WHO before issuing its label warning statement in October 1983, but there was still not universal agreement with it. Acting on WHO recommendations, Nestlé consulted with firms experienced and expert in developing and field-testing educational materials, so that it could ensure that those materials met the code.

When the International Nestlé Boycott Committee (INBC) listed its four points of difference with Nestlé, it again became a matter of interpretation of the requirements of the code. Here, meetings held by UNICEF proved invaluable, in that UNICEF agreed to define areas of differing interpretation—in some cases providing definitions contrary to both Nestlé's and INBC's interpretations.

It was the meetings with UNICEF in early

1984 that finally led to a joint statement by Nestlé and INBC on January 25. At that time, INBC announced its suspension of boycott activities, and Nestlé pledged its continued support of the WHO code.

Nestlé Supports WHO Code

The company has a strong record of progress and support in implementing the WHO Code, including:

- Immediate support for the WHO Code, May 1981; and testimony to this effect before the U.S. Congress, June 1981.
- Issuance of instructions to all employees, agents, and distributors in February 1982 to implement the code in all Third World countries where Nestlé markets infant formula.
- Establishment of an audit commission, in accordance with Article 11.3 of the WHO Code to ensure the company's compliance with the code. The commission, headed by Edmund S. Muskie, was composed of eminent clergy and scientists.
- Willingness to meet with concerned church leaders, international bodies, and organization leaders seriously concerned with Nestlé's application of the code.
- Issuance of revised instructions to Nestlé personnel, October 1982, as recommended by the Muskie committee to clarify and give further effect to the code.
- Consultation with WHO, UNICEF, and NIFAC on how to interpret the code and how best to implement specific provisions, including clarification by WHO/UNICEF of the definition of children who need to be fed breast milk substitutes, to aid in determining the need for supplies in hospitals.

Nestlé Policies

In the early 1970s Nestlé began to review its infant formula marketing practices on a region-by-region basis. By 1978 the company had stopped all consumer advertising and direct sampling to mothers. Instructions to the field issued in February 1982 and clarified in the revised instructions of October 1982, adopt articles of the WHO Code as Nestlé policy and include:

- No advertising to the general public.
- No sampling to mothers.
- No mothercraft workers.
- No use of commission/bonus for sales.
- No use of infant pictures on labels.
- No point-of-sale advertising.
- No financial or material inducements to promote products.
- No samples to physicians except in three specific situations: a new product, a new product formulation, or a new graduate physician; limited to one or two cans of product.
- Limitation of supplies to those requested in writing and fulfilling genuine needs for breast milk substitutes.
- A statement of the superiority of breast feeding on all labels/materials.
- Labels and educational materials clearly stating the hazards involved in incorrect usage of infant formula, developed in consultation with WHO/UNICEF.

Even though Nestlé stopped consumer advertising, they were able to maintain their share of the Third World infant formula market. By 1988 a call to resume the seven-year boycott was called for by a group of consumer activist members of the Action for Corporate Accountability. The group claimed that Nestlé was distributing free formula through maternity wards as a promotional tactic that undermines the practice of breast feeding. The group claims that Nestlé and others have continued to dump formula in hospitals and maternity wards and that as a result "babies are dying as the companies are violating the WHO resolution."[1]

---

[1] "Boycotts: Activists' Group Resumes Fight against Nestlé, Adds American Home Products," Associated Press, October 5, 1988.

The boycott focus is Taster's Choice Instant Coffee, Coffeemate Nondairy Coffee Creamer, Anacin aspirin, and Advil.

Representatives of Nestlé and American Home Products rejected the accusations and said they were complying with World Health Organization and individual national codes on the subject.

The Issues

Many issues are raised by this incident. Such questions as: How can a company deal with a worldwide boycott of its products? Why did the United States decide not to support the WHO Code? Who is correct, WHO or Nestlé? But, a more important issue concerns the responsibility of a MNC marketing in developing nations. Setting aside the issues for a moment, consider the notion that, whether intentional or not, Nestlé's marketing activities have had an impact on the behavior of many people, that is, Nestlé is a cultural change agent. And, when it or any other company successfully introduces new ideas into a culture, the culture changes and those changes can be functional or dysfunctional to established patterns of behavior. The key issue is—what responsibility does the MNC have to the culture when, as a result of its marketing activities, it causes change in that culture?[2]

---

[2] This case draws from the following: "International Code of Marketing of Breastmilk Substitutes," World Health Organization, Geneva, 1981; INFACT Newsletter, Minneapolis, Minn., February 1979; John A. Sparks, "The Nestlé Controversy—Anatomy of a Boycott," Grove City, Pa., Public Policy Education Fund, Inc.; "Who Drafts a Marketing Code," *World Business Weekly*, January 19, 1981, p. 8; "A Boycott over Infant Formula," *Business Week*, April 23, 1979, p. 137; "The Battle over Bottle-Feeding," *World Press Review*, January 1980, p. 54; "Nestlé and the Role of Infant Formula in Developing Countries: The Resolution of a Conflict," (Nestlé Company, 1985); "The Dilemma of Third World Nutrition," (Nestlé S.A., 1985), 20 pp.; Thomas V. Greer, "The Future of the International Code of Marketing of Breastmilk Substitutes: The Socio-Legal Context," *International Marketing Review*, Spring 1984, pp. 33–41; James C. Baker, "The International Infant Formula Controversy: A Dilemma in Corporate Social Responsibility," *Journal of Business Ethics*, no. 4, 1985, pp. 181–90; Shawn Tully, "Nestlé Shows How To Gobble Markets," *Fortune*, January 16, 1989, p. 75.

Source: An update of "Nestlé in LDCs," case written by J. Alex Murray, University of Windsor, Ontario, Canada, and Gregory M. Gazda and Mary J. Molenaar, University of San Diego. Case originally appeared in the 5th edition of this text.

QUESTIONS

1. What are the responsibilities of companies in this or similar situations?
2. What could Nestlé have done to have avoided the accusations of "killing Third World babies" and still market its products?
3. After Nestlé's experience, how do you suggest it, or any other company, can protect itself in the future?

Case 2–1

MARKETING SWEET CORN TO THE FRENCH

Jean LaRoche of Strasbourg had worked in the United States for over 10 years. While living on Long Island, he acquired a taste for sweet corn on the cob which grew in his own garden. When he first came to the United States he knew there were two American delights he was going to resist, Coca-Cola with meals instead of wine, and iced cold water. He was quick to add a third item to his list when offered corn on the cob at a summer outing. At first, he wasn't too surprised that Americans ate "pig food," after all, they invented the hamburger and ate french fries with catsup, or is it ketchup? He knew about corn; it was grown as animal feed, not fit for human consumption. In fact, he had once tried the field corn grown for animal food and was put off by its toughness and taste. Nevertheless, after repeated entreaties by his Long Island neighbors, and not wanting to continue to refuse their hospitality, he reluctantly tried some real American corn on the cob and has eaten it ever since.

Jean returned to Strasbourg a few years ago and took a supply of his sweet corn seed with him and immediately planted a garden. He has introduced some of his French friends to the wonders of summer sweet corn. Once they agree to taste it, they come back for more. His original 10 rows of corn have grown to nearly a half acre, much of which he sells to friends and neighbors.

Jean being an entrepreneur at heart, has been considering the idea of commercially growing sweet corn and selling it in Europe. After all, he can't keep his friends supplied so why not import the hybrid seed and commission farmers to grow the corn which he will market?

He has made preliminary inquiries and can import the hybrid seed which grows well in France. He sees three different markets: fresh corn during the season; frozen corn kernels throughout the year; and corn cobs pressed into briquettes that burn like charcoal. The idea of corn-cob briquettes came from stories his father used to tell him about how they used corn cobs for heat during the war.

He can get an exclusive contract with a U.S. seed company for the Super Sweet hybrid in which genetic manipulation dramatically retards the conversion of the corn's sugar into starch. Super Sweet varieties contain genes that completely block the sugar-to-starch process on the plant and so retard it after picking, that an ear of corn, properly refrigerated, stays perfectly fresh-tasting for four to five days. This accounts for its super sweetness. The hybrid is about 30 percent more expensive to grow than other types of sweet corn and yields only half as many ears per hectare, about 20,000, as the other hybrids he has tried.

The hardest part of selling sweet corn to Europeans is simply getting them to taste it. You have to constantly fight the misconception that sweet corn is the same as the field corn grown to feed livestock. He has had friends who have tried field corn thinking it was the same as sweet corn. Their response has been that "It's only good for pig food."

He is excited about the prospects of this new business and its potential. In the United States, the average per capita consumption of sweet corn on the cob is 10 ears per person. He does not know how much is sold as frozen kernels but suspects it is considerably higher.

He needs some help in making a preliminary market analysis for his sweet corn business. Using the guidelines in the Appendix— "The Country Notebook: A Guide for Developing a Marketing Plan," prepare a preliminary market analysis for marketing sweet corn in France.

Case 2–2

STARNES-BRENNER MACHINE TOOL COMPANY—TO BRIBE OR NOT TO BRIBE

The Starnes-Brenner Machine Tool Company of Iowa City, Iowa, has a small one-man sales office headed by Frank Rothe in Latino, a major Latin American country. Frank has been in Latino for about 10 years and is retiring this year; his replacement is Bill Hunsaker, one of Starnes-Brenner's top salesmen. Both will be in Latino for about eight months, during which time Frank will show Bill the ropes, introduce him to their principal customers and, in general, prepare him to take over.

Frank has been very successful as a foreign representative in spite of his unique style and, at times, complete refusal to follow company policy when it doesn't suit him. The company hasn't really done much about his method of operation although from time to time he has angered some top company men. As President McCaughey, who retired a couple of years ago, once remarked to a vice president who was complaining about Frank, "If he's making money—and he is (more than any of the other foreign offices)—then leave the guy alone." When McCaughey retired, the new chief immediately instituted organizational changes that gave more emphasis to the overseas operations, moving the company toward a truly worldwide operation into which a loner like Frank would probably not fit. In fact, one of the key reasons for selecting Bill as Frank's replacement, besides Bill's

record as a top salesman, is Bill's capacity as an organization man. He understands the need for coordination among operations and will cooperate with the home office so the Latino office can be expanded and brought into the mainstream.

The company knows there is much to be learned from Frank and Bill's job is to learn everything possible. The company certainly doesn't want to continue some of Frank's practices, but much of his knowledge is vital for continued, smooth operation. Today, Starnes-Brenner's foreign sales account for about 25 percent of the company's total profits, compared with about 5 percent only 10 years ago.

The company is actually changing character from being principally an exporter without any real concern for continuous foreign market representation to worldwide operations where the foreign divisions are part of the total effort rather than a stepchild operation. In fact, Latino is one of the last operational divisions to be assimilated into the new organization. Rather than try to change Frank, the company has been waiting for him to retire before making any significant adjustments in their Latino operations.

Bill Hunsaker is 36 years old with a wife and three children; he is a very good salesman and administrator although he has had no foreign experience. He has the reputation of being fair, honest, and a straight shooter. Some, back at the home office, see his assignment as part of a grooming job for a top position, perhaps eventually the presidency. The Hunsakers are now settled in their new home after having been in Latino for about two weeks. Today is Bill's first day on the job.

When Bill arrived at the office, Frank was on his way to a local factory to inspect some Starnes-Brenner machines that had to have some adjustments made before being acceptable to the Latino government agency buying them. Bill joined Frank for the plant visit. Later, after the visit, we join the two at lunch.

Bill, tasting some chili, remarks, "Boy! this certainly isn't like the chili we have in America."

"No, it isn't, and there's another difference, too . . . the Latinos are Americans and nothing angers a Latino more than to have a 'Gringo' refer to the United States as America as if to say that Latino isn't part of America also. The Latinos rightly consider their country as part of America (take a look at the map) and people from the United States are North Americans at best. So, for future reference, refer to home either as the United States, States, or North America, but, for gosh sakes, not just America. Not to change the subject, Bill, but could you see that any change had been made in those S-27s from the standard model?"

"No, they looked like the standard. Was there something out of whack when they arrived?"

"No, I couldn't see any problem—I suspect this is the best piece of sophisticated bribe-taking I've come across yet. Most of the time the Latinos are more 'honest' about their *mordidas* than this." "What's a *mordida*?" Bill asks. "You know, *kumshaw, dash, bustarella, mordida;* they are all the same: a little grease to expedite the action. *Mordida* is the local word for a slight offering or, if you prefer, bribe," says Frank.

Bill quizzically responds, "Do we pay bribes to get sales?"

"Oh, it depends on the situation but it's certainly something you have to be prepared to deal with." Boy, what a greenhorn, Frank thinks to himself, as he continues, "Here's the story. When the S-27s arrived last January, we began uncrating them and right away the *Jefe* engineer (a government official)—*Jefe,* that's the head man in charge—began extra careful examination and declared there was a vital defect in the machines; he claimed the machinery would be dangerous and thus unacceptable if it wasn't corrected. I looked it over but couldn't see anything wrong so I agreed to have our staff engineer check all the machines and correct any flaws that might exist. Well, the *Jefe* said there wasn't enough time to wait for an engineer to come from the States, that the machines could be adjusted locally, and we could pay him and he would make all the necessary arrangements. So, what do you do? No adjustment his way and there would be an order cancelled; and, maybe there was something out of line, those things have been known to happen. But for the life of me, I can't see that anything had been done since the machines were supposedly fixed. So, let's face it, we just paid a bribe and a pretty darn big bribe at that—about $1,200 per machine—what makes it so aggravating is that that's the second one I've had to pay on this shipment."

"The second?" asks Bill.

"Yeah, at the border when we were transferring the machines to Latino trucks, it was hot and they were moving slow as molasses. It took them over an hour to transfer one machine to a Latino truck and we had 10 others to go. It seemed that every time I spoke to the dock boss about speeding things up, they just got slower. Finally, out of desperation, I slipped him a fistful of pesos and, sure enough, in the next three hours they had the whole thing loaded. Just one of the local customs of doing business. Generally though, it comes at the lower level where wages don't cover living expenses too well."

There is a pause and Bill asks, "What does that do to our profits?"

"Runs them down, of course, but I look at it as just one of the many costs of doing business—I do my best not to pay but when I have to, I do."

Hesitantly Bill replies, "I don't like it, Frank, we've got good products, they're priced right, we give good service, and keep plenty of spare parts in the country, so why should we have to pay bribes to the buyer? It's just no way to do business. You've already had to pay two bribes on one shipment; if you keep it up, the word's going to get around and you'll be paying at every level. Then all the profit goes out the window—you know, once you start, where do you stop? Besides that, where do we stand legally? Perhaps you've missed all the news back in the States about the Wedtech scandal, HUD (Housing & Urban Development) billion dollar rip off, procurement scandals at the Pentagon, and so on. Congress is mad, countries are mad; in fact, the Foreign Bribery Act makes paying bribes like you've just paid illegal. I'd say the best policy is to never start; you might lose a few sales but let it be known that there are no bribes; we sell the best, service the best at fair prices, and that's all."

"You mean the Foreign Corrupt Practices Act, don't you?" Frank asks and continues in a—I'm not really so out of touch—tone of voice, "Haven't some of the provisions of the Foreign Corrupt Practices Act been softened somewhat?"

"Yes, you're right, the provisions on paying a *mordida* or grease have been softened but paying the government official is still illegal, softening or not," replies Bill.

Oh boy! Frank thinks to himself as he replies, "First of all, I've heard about all the difficulty with bribing governments, but what I did was just peanuts compared to Japan and Lockheed. The people we pay off are small and, granted we give good service, but

we've only been doing it for the last year or so. Before that I never knew when I was going to have equipment to sell. In fact, we only had products when there were surpluses stateside. I had to pay the right people to get sales and, besides you're not back in the States any longer. Things are just done different here. You follow that policy and I guarantee that you'll have fewer sales because our competitors from Germany, Italy, and Japan will pay. Look, Bill, everybody does it here; it's a way of life and the costs are generally reflected in the markup and overhead. There is even a code of behavior involved. We're not actually encouraging it to spread, just perpetuating an accepted way of doing business."

Patiently and slightly condescendingly, Bill replies, "I know, Frank, but wrong is wrong and we want to operate differently now. We hope to set up an operation here on a continuous basis; we plan to operate in Latino just like we do in the United States. Really expand our operation and make a long-range market commitment, grow with the country! And, one of the first things we must avoid are unethical. . ."

Frank interrupts, "But really, is it unethical? Everybody does it, the Latinos even pay *mordidas* to other Latinos; it's a fact of life—is it really unethical? I think that the circumstances that exist in a country justify and dictate the behavior. Remember man, 'When in Rome, do as the Romans do.' "

Almost shouting, Bill blurts out, "I can't buy that. We know that our management practices and techniques are our strongest point. Really all we have to differentiate us from the rest of our competition, Latino and others, is that we are better managed and, as far as I'm concerned, graft and other unethical behavior have got to be cut out to create a healthy industry. In the long run, it should strengthen our position. We can't build our futures on illegal and unethical practices."

Frank angrily replies, "Look it's done in the States all the time. What about the big dinners, drinks, and all the other hanky-panky that goes on? Not to mention House Speaker Wright, PACs (Political Action Committee) payments to congressmen, and all those high speaking fees certain congressmen get from special interests. How many congressmen have gone to jail or lost reelection on those kinds of things? What is that, if it isn't *mordida*, the North American way? The only difference is that instead of cash only, in the United States we pay in merchandise and cash."

"That's really not the same and you know it. Besides, we certainly get a lot of business transacted during those dinners even if we are paying the bill."

"Bull, the only difference is that here bribes go on in the open; they don't hide it or dress it in foolish ritual that fools no one. It goes on in the United States and everyone denies the existence of it. That's all the difference—in the United States we're just more hypocritical about it all."

"Look," Frank continues almost shouting, "we are getting off on the wrong foot and we've got eight months to work together. Just keep your eyes and mind open and let's talk about it again in a couple of months when you've seen how the whole country operates; perhaps then you won't be so quick to judge it absolutely wrong."

Frank, lowering his voice, says thoughtfully, "I know it's hard to take; probably the most disturbing aspect of dealing with business problems in underdeveloped countries is the matter of graft. And, frankly, we don't do much advance preparation so we can deal firmly with it. It bothered me at first; but, then I figured it makes its economic contribution, too, since the payoff is as much a part of the economic process as a payroll. What's our real economic role anyway, besides making a profit, of course? Are we developers of wealth, helping to push the country to greater economic growth, or are we missionaries? Or should we be both? I really don't know, but I don't think we can be both simultaneously, and my feeling is that as the company prospers, as higher salaries are paid, and better standards of living are reached, we'll see better ethics. Until then, we've got to operate or leave and, if you are going to win the opposition over, you'd better join them and change them from within, not fight them."

Before Bill could reply, a Latino friend of Frank's joined them and they changed the topic of conversation.

QUESTIONS

1. Is what Frank did ethical? Whose ethics? Latino's or the United States?
2. Are Frank's two different payments legal under the Foreign Corrupt Practices Act as amended by the Omnibus Trade and Competitiveness Act of 1988?
3. Identify the types of payments made in the case; that is, are they lubrication, extortion, or subornation?
4. Frank seemed to imply that there was a difference between what he was doing and what happens in the United States. Is there any difference? Explain.
5. Are there any legal differences between the money paid to the dock workers and the money paid the *jefe* (government official)? Any ethical differences?
6. Frank's attitude seems to imply that a foreigner must comply with all local

customs, but some would say that one of the contributions made by U.S. firms is to change local ways of doing business. Who is right?

7. Should Frank's behavior have been any different had this not been a government contract?

8. If Frank shouldn't have paid the bribe, what should he have done, and what might have been the consequences?

9. What are the company interests in this problem?

10. Explain how this may be a good example of the SRC (self-reference criterion) at work.

11. Do you think Bill will make the grade in Latino? Why? What will it take?

12. How can an overseas manager be prepared to face this problem?

Case 2–3

LICENSING OR JOINT VENTURE

CG Company, hypothetical but representative of U.S. business, possesses advanced technology in the computer graphics sector with important engineering applications. A small enterprise, CG has neither the financial nor the managerial resources to establish its own international sales and service network, let alone production facilities in two target countries, Brazil and France. Qualified, motivated distributors often are difficult to find and, once found, to control. The manufacturer also bears the burden of duty and freight costs. The answer for CG—licensing. Or is it?

CG's knowledge is superior to that of similar companies in Brazil, but the company would get little patent or copyright protection. Its applications would not enjoy top priority in the country; the maximum allowable license would be five years, with a royalty percentage of only 3 percent of net sales after deducting the cost of components supplied by CG. The company estimates that this arrangement would produce only $22,500 in royalties if the local licensee generated $1 million in annual sales. Moreover, the Brazilian government would own 25 percent of royalties as income taxes, and after five years all royalties would cease.

The French situation is more favorable but still not very attractive. After consultation with its government, the French licensee proposes a small down payment and a royalty for four years declining to 2.5 percent in the second half of an eight-year agreement. This proposal reflects a lack of proprietary protection and a fast changing technological situation. Perhaps more important, the French company is committed to distribution and service of other related products, and CG has no assurance that its systems would retain their favored position with the licensee as other products and systems become available.

QUESTIONS

1. List the advantages and disadvantages of licensing or a joint venture for CG.
2. Should CG enter into a licensing arrangement or a joint venture? Write a statement that supports your position.

Case 2–4

DYNAMICS INTERNATIONAL— WRITING A POLICY ON BRIBERY

Concerned about recent revelations of bribery, kickback payoffs, laundered money, and slush funds that companies have been involved in both domestically and internationally, Dynamics International's Board of Directors was surprised to learn they had no policy other than a few general public relations statements on the subject. Although they had not had problems in the United States or abroad—at least none they were aware of—they felt that without a specific set of guidelines, they were setting policy by omission. They realized that some types of unethical or questionable behavior might be avoided if a person faced with a difficult decision had specific guidelines. Their primary concern was with the international situation which they knew would be more difficult to deal with because of the widely variable cultures in which businesses operate.

The board of directors felt this would be a good time to write a policy regarding bribery since it appeared the new Business Practices and Records Act (formerly the Foreign Corrupt Practices Act) which dealt with bribery was being established as the government's position on the subject. The Foreign Corrupt Practices Act (FCPA), passed in 1977, had created a great deal of confusion.

The FCPA made it illegal for companies to bribe foreign officials, candidates, or political parties. Further, the law provided for stiff penalties to be assessed against executives found guilty of having "a reason to know" that a company's independent agents were paying bribes. Immediately after the law was passed, many international companies were uncertain of the interpretation. Did it mean that any payment, even that given to a border guard to have papers processed rapidly, was illegal? Or would the small lubrication payments every executive knew were being paid by most foreign agents expose an international executive that "had reason to know" to U.S. government action? Initially there was a great deal of confusion about the FCPA, but after a few months, the government issued several interpretations that seemed to clarify the issues. The major point of clarification had to do with payments that seemed to be acceptable.

However, the original FCPA was modified in the Omnibus Trade and Competitiveness Act of 1988. Payments to expedite activities that a government agent is legally expected to perform are permitted. Also, criminal penalties for noncompliance are limited to "knowing" instead of "reason to know" as was the case in the original law. Although the law has been modified somewhat and some of the need for interpretation has been eliminated, the board feels the company cannot continue without a definite policy statement.

Dynamics International's foreign business accounts for about 40 percent of total sales and produces an equal amount of profits. It has wholly owned subsidiaries in some countries, and, in other countries, works through a series of agents and middlemen. The countries where the company employs agents are notorious for bribery (primarily the Mideast and Latin America) and management is suspicious their agents may be involved. It is also concerned that some wholly owned subsidiaries might be involved in paying bribes, although not openly.

The first principle to be established is, "What is unethical or unacceptable behavior?" This question is especially important because bribery can range from the relatively innocuous payment of a few cents to a minor official so that he does not take four hours to get papers processed to the extreme of paying millions of dollars to a head of state to ensure preferential treatment for a company. Obviously, a workable policy must effectively deal with all contingencies. Bribery must first be defined and there appear to be limitless variations. The difference between bribery and extortion also should be established. Voluntarily offered payments by someone seeking an unlawful advantage is bribery; payments extracted under duress by someone in authority from a person seeking only what it is lawfully entitled to is extortion. An example of extortion would be a finance minister of a country demanding heavy payments under the threat that millions of dollars of investment would be confiscated. Another variation of bribery that should be defined is the difference between *lubrication* and *subornation*.[1] *Lubrication* involves a relatively small sum of cash, gift, or service made to a low-ranking official in countries where such offerings are not prohibited by law; the purpose being simply to facilitate or expedite the normal, lawful performance of a duty by that official (a practice common in many counties of the world). Subornation, on the other hand, generally involves large sums of money, frequently not properly accounted for, which are designed to entice an official to commit an illegal act of magnitude on behalf of the one paying the bribe. Lubrication payments are requests for a person to do a job more rapidly or more efficiently, whereas subornation is a request for the official to turn his head, not do his job, or to break the law.

A third variation which may appear to be a bribe but may not be, is an agent's fee. A business person uncertain of the rules and regulations may hire an agent to represent the company in a particular country. This would be similar to hiring an agent in the United States, an attorney for example, to file an appeal for a variance in a building code on the basis that the attorney will do a more efficient and thorough job than someone unfamiliar with such procedures. Similar services may be requested of an agent in a foreign country when problems occur. However, a part of the agent's fees may be used to pay bribes, and sometimes it is impossible to determine if the intermediary's fees are being used unlawfully. There are many middlemen, attorneys, agents, distributors, and so forth who may function simply as conduits for illegal payments. The process is further complicated by legal codes which vary from country to country; what is illegal in one country is winked at in another and is legal in a third.

It is obvious from this discussion that the issue of bribery is not absolute and the process of writing a policy on bribery will be intricate. Below are two different codes of ethics from two well-known U.S. companies. Each company considers its codes to be the final word on policy.

---

[1] Hans Schollhammer, "Ethics in an International Business Context," *MSU Business Topics*, Spring 1977, pp. 53–63.

Company A

Some Thoughts to Consider for Ethical Conduct

1. A good name can't be bought; it must be earned . . . from the public, our customers, the government, even our competitors. Without their acceptance of us as an aboveboard corporation, we wouldn't be in business for long.
2. We care about business success, to be sure, but we also care how we achieve that success. At *company A*, "anything goes doesn't go."
3. From boardroom to boiler room, it doesn't require a law degree to know you are doing something that's just plain wrong. If you're genuinely in doubt, ask a company lawyer.
4. Honesty isn't merely the best policy; it's the only policy. Dishonest, immoral, illegal, or unethical conduct is unacceptable in *company A's* way of doing business.
5. Just as a reminder, illegal conduct includes price-fixing, giving or taking bribes or kickbacks, reciprocity, allocating markets, giving improper political contributions, pilferage, and misuse of company funds. It also includes revealing confidential information or accepting confidential information you should not have.
6. Simply ask yourself, Could I do business in complete trust with someone like myself? Make certain that the honest answer is an *unqualified* yes!

Company B

Ethical Business Conduct
Summary of Company Policies

In all instances, it is the policy of the company that its business be conducted in a lawful and ethical manner. The policies which are summarized below need to be understood and followed by every employee who acts on behalf of the company anywhere in the world. They are designed to protect and enhance the company's integrity as an outstanding corporate citizen in every part of the world where it does business. The company does not wish to obtain business which compromises its standards in any way.

Violation of the policies can expose the company and the individuals involved to criminal actions, fines, injunctions, and lawsuits for damages or restitution. Individuals who violate these policies are subject to discharge or other disciplinary action.

It is against company policy for any employee to authorize payment of or to use any funds (either company or personal) for a bribe, kickback, or any other similar payment, whether lawful or unlawful, designed to secure favored treatment for the company. It is equally against company policy to use an intermediary to make any such payment or to disguise any such payment as a commission, refund, or in any other manner. Should you find yourself in any situation where a request is made for a bribe, kickback, or any other payment whose propriety you question, or where you have any knowledge of payments being made to an agent which are in excess of reasonable fees for services rendered, it is your responsibility to report the situation immediately to your manager and to company counsel.

In all countries of the world, it is the policy of all affiliated companies that they do not make political contributions unless they (1) comply with both public policy and law of the country involved; (2) are recommended by the board of directors of the affiliate; (3) are reasonable in amount; (4) are made in approximately equal amounts to the major parties; and (5) are disclosed in advance to company counsel and the company auditor.

Company A's and company B's statements are dissimilar in that one is relatively general, the other more specific. Your task is to evaluate the two statements in terms of their adequacy in covering the kinds of ethical issues that arise internationally and then attempt to write a statement or a policy on bribery for Dynamics International which Dynamics will use as its official policy. Keep in mind that Dynamics International is interested in

pursuing ethical corporate behavior anywhere in the world, but does not want a policy
so rigid it would jeopardize the normal, ethical, and acceptable business practices with
which its operating personnel would be confronted throughout the world.

Case 2–5

GASSELSMANN GmbH MINING AND SMELTING—PAYING RANSOM

Wolf Frankel glanced at the bedside clock as
he reached to answer the telephone. Who
could be ringing at 3 A.M.?

"Herr Frankel? It's James Perez. I'm sorry
to disturb you but we are supposed to report
things like this immediately."

Perez was the second in command in the
South American country where Gasselsmann
GmbH, an aluminum smelting and fabricating
firm based in West Germany, mined most
of its bauxite. Frankel was the firm's director
of international operations.

Perez explained that Lutz Luneberger, the
head of the subsidiary, had been kidnapped
by terrorists.

Frankel was now wide awake. "Go and see
what you can do for Frau Luneberger," he
said. "I'll phone our chief of security and get
him to fly out. Have someone meet him at
the airport tomorrow. And keep me informed
of developments."

Three days later, Perez phoned Frankel to
say that the terrorists had demanded a ransom. "They want food, medical supplies, and
$10 million in cash or they will kill Luneber-
ger," he said.

The security chief also came on the phone
to tell Frankel that the government of the
country was proving difficult to deal with and
suggesting that Frankel himself fly out.

As they drove from the airport, Perez told
Frankel that a priest had been found to act
as intermediary with the terrorists. "But first
we have a meeting with the minister of state
for security," he said.

Frankel knew the minister slightly. He was
unprepared, however, for the uncompromis-
ing line the man took.

"Although you may talk with these people," the minister said, "there is no question
of their demands being met. One cannot compromise with traitors and thugs. You must
realize, also, that if your company gives in
now, in this part of the world, it will open
the flood gates. One cannot afford to be soft
with terrorists."

Frankel's meetings with the intermediary
were attended by a government representative whose presence inhibited free and frank
discussion.

As the weeks passed, Frankel travelled frequently between South America and the corporate headquarters in Dusseldorf. He had
as many problems at home as in the field.
Some members of the board took a hard line,
saying the company should not pay, while
others demanded speedier progress. There
was also the threat of legal action by the family
if the victim was killed.

While attending one of the board meetings,
Frankel received a telex from his security man
saying that he had arranged direct contact
with the terrorists if Frankel wanted to take
advantage of it.

Frankel did. He obtained the approval of
the board to offer the terrorists a ransom of
$1 million if they would drop the request for

food and medical supplies, which could not be delivered without the agreement of the government. The money, however, could be transferred through a Swiss bank.

Frankel flew back to South America and after a week of waiting met the terrorist spokesman secretly. At first he did not seem to be making progress, but after hours of talking the terrorist suddenly agreed to the deal.

Frankel was elated. However, when he got back to his hotel he received a phone call from the minister of state, who asked to see him immediately.

The minister said that he knew all about the cash deal. "In this country, nothing is secret for long. I regret that you have gone behind my back in dealing with these people. The government I represent will not allow this deal to go through. Should you attempt to proceed, we will seize your company's assets."

Frankel believed the minister was bluffing. He did not think the government could afford to alienate other international companies with interests in the country. He said as much to the minister.

"That may be," the minister replied. "But remember, we can make life very difficult for you here, from an operating point of view. You will recall, also, that next year your license to mine and export bauxite comes up for renewal. How would you like to buy your bauxite on the open market?"

That night, Frankel pondered this threat. What should he do? If he paid the money he might save Luneberger's life. But if the company lost its bauxite concession, it would cease to be a fully integrated aluminum concern. That could cost a lot more than the $1 million.

If, however, he did not pay, it was practically certain that Luneberger would be killed.

Source: Adapted from "Dilemma and Decision," *International Management,* October 1979, pp. 8–9.

QUESTIONS

1. How could Frankel save both his colleague and the company?
2. What should the company have done to protect itself against such terrorist acts?
3. What plans could the company make to prepare for any future risks of terrorism?

Case 2–6

WHEN INTERNATIONAL BUYERS AND SELLERS DISAGREE

No matter what line of business you're in, you can't escape sex. That may have been one conclusion drawn by an American exporter of meat products after a dispute with a West German customer over a shipment of pork livers. Here's how the disagreement came about:

The American exporter was contracted to ship "30,000 lbs. of freshly frozen U.S. pork livers, customary merchandisable quality, first rate brands." As the shipment that was prepared met the exacting standards of the American market, the exporter expected the transaction to be completed without any problem.

But when the livers arrived in West Germany, the purchaser raised an objection: "We ordered pork livers of customary merchantable quality—what you sent us consisted of 40 percent sow livers."

"Who cares about the sex of the pig the liver came from?" the exporter asked.

"We do," the German replied. "Here in Germany we don't pass off spongy sow livers as the firmer livers of male pigs. This shipment wasn't merchantable at the price we

expected to charge. The only way we were able to dispose of the meat without a total loss was to reduce the price. You owe us a price allowance of $1,000."

The American refused to reduce the price. The determined resistance may have been partly in reaction to the implied insult to the taste of the American consumer. "If pork livers, whatever the sex of the animal, are palatable to Americans, they ought to be good enough for anyone," the American thought.

It looked as if the buyer and seller could never agree on eating habits.

Source: Copyright © 1968 by Dun & Bradstreet Publications Corp. Reprinted by special permission from the November 1968 issue of *Business Abroad*.

QUESTIONS

1. In this dispute which country's law would apply, that of the United States or of West Germany?
2. If the case were tried in U.S. courts, who do you think would win? In German courts? Why?
3. Draw up a brief agreement which would have eliminated the following problems before they could occur.
   a. Whose law applies.
   b. Whether the case should be tried in U.S. or German courts.
   c. The difference in opinion as to "customary merchandisable quality."
4. Discuss how SRC may be at work in this case.

Case 2–7

HOT CHIPS INC.— MANUFACTURING JOINT VENTURE AND KNOW-HOW LICENSE

Hot Chip, Inc. is the third largest U.S. manufacturer of certain key transistor parts. It has about 22 percent of the domestic market but

has been unsuccessful in its attempts to market its transistor parts in Japan, one of the world's most important markets for the product. To surmount this difficulty, it has entered into a joint venture with Japan Manufacturing (JM), one of Japan's largest industrial combines. They have formed a manufacturing joint venture, JZC, using Hot Chip know-how to produce completed transistors. Hot Chip will have 49 percent of the stock and half of the board of directors. In return for technology, JM will be responsible for the day-to-day operation of JZC. JM has not been in this particular field, but does manufacture a great deal of electronic equipment. Accordingly, the joint venture company will be operating on know-how licensed by Hot Chip.

Hot Chip is concerned because JZC will have lower manufacturing costs than it has in the United States, and JM and JZC may be sources of disruption to Hot Chip's existing marketing arrangements in Australia, New Zealand, the Philippines, Europe, and the United States. Accordingly, Hot Chip has inserted into the agreement with JM a condition that neither JZC nor JM will export the transistor parts to the United States or other designated markets.

QUESTIONS

1. Discuss the legality of the proposed joint venture under U.S. antitrust law. Be certain to consider all ramifications of the agreement.
2. Review the logic of an alliance with a potential competitor.

Case 2–8

EXTRATERRITORIALITY—THE U.S. GOVERNMENT AND MNCs

Background

The General Electric Company (GE), a U.S.-based firm, had contracted in 1981 with three foreign companies in Western Europe to produce rotors for gas turbines using GE technology. These companies were:

John Brown, Ltd., Great Britain
Alsthom Atlantique S.A., France (recently nationalized)
Nuova Pignone, Italy (government-owned)

In addition to these contracts, GE had sold rotors to be used in gas turbines on order to the Soviet Union and to other foreign companies.

Chronological Listing of Events

Late 1981—The Soviet Union offered West Germany low prices for natural gas in exchange for technical assistance and credit arrangements in the construction of a $15 billion pipeline from Siberia to Europe. Other Western European countries were asked to and did join in the plan. Essentially, the European Community (EC) agreed to supply financing below market rates to the Soviets in exchange for a proportion of the technical equipment contracts to build the pipeline.

December 29, 1981—President Ronald Reagan declared an embargo enjoining any U.S. company from exporting gas and oil technological designs and related machinery to the Siberian/Western European pipeline. U.S. firms affected by this embargo included Caterpillar Tractor, International Harvester, Allis Chalmers, Fisher Controls, Inc., Smith International, and Rosemount, Inc. holding contracts estimated at $2.2 billion.

The stated purpose of this embargo was to allow the EC time for the exploration of alternative energy sources that would reduce Western European dependency on the Eastern bloc energy.

June 18, 1982—President Reagan extended the embargo to include foreign subsidiaries of U.S. firms and foreign companies operating under U.S. license. The foreign subsidiaries and licensees included John Brown, Ltd., Alsthom Atlantique S.A., Nuova Pignone, and Dresser France holding contracts worth $1.2 billion.

June 28–29, 1982—The EC compiled a retaliatory list of counter-sanctions at the summer GATT negotiations that included:

1. Offsets to tax breaks the United States provides to foreign subsidies of U.S. companies through domestic international sales corporations.
2. Withdrawal of EC support for the United States push to liberalize world trade in banking and insurance.
3. Further study on imposition of duties on the $9 billion annual farm exports to the EC.

June 30, 1982—The British Trade Secretary signed an order exempting British concerns from having to comply with the U.S. embargo.

July 25, 1982—The French government ordered its companies to ignore the embargo and proceed with shipments to the Soviets.

August 1982—France invoked a 1938 law that allowed the government to "requisition" a company's products or services. French firms failing to "ignore the embargo" faced heavy fines, possible jail sentences, and sei-

zure of requisitioned equipment that the government would then ship to the Soviet Union.

September 1982—Italy issued a statement saying that signed agreements with the Soviet Union would be honored, although Italian firms were not "ordered" to make shipments in fulfillment of these contracts.

October 1982—West Germany, while not taking any legal action, issued a public statement supporting the legal position taken by France.

November 15, 1982—President Reagan withdrew the embargo subsequent to an agreement with Europe on broad strategy to tighten East-West trade. The formal proposal reduced trade credits and technology sales to Moscow in exchange for lifting the ban on U.S. technology exports.

Legal Issues

The legal issues surrounding this situation were indeed complicated since legal disputes existed between governments, between companies and governments, and between two companies.

Foreign licensees of GE had signed contracts agreeing to abide by U.S. export laws (including any new changes) in exchange for U.S. technologies. Second, GE had sold rotor blades for gas turbines to several other European firms holding contracts to provide the Soviet Union with turbines for the pipeline. From the U.S perspective, the existence of these contracts would force all firms involved to honor the embargo.

The European Community accused the United States of acting illegally based on the extraterritoriality issue. The EC argued that the United States had no legal right to abrogate contracts made in Europe between foreign firms and the Soviet Union.

With Great Britain ordering her firms to honor Soviet contracts and ignore the embargo and France threatening her companies with governmental requisitioning, the foreign licensees of GE found themselves caught in the middle. These firms were faced with either breaching contracts with their parent company or breaching contracts with the Soviet Union. They were also faced with punishment by their own governments for violation of governmental orders.

GE chose to maintain a low profile in the conflict. GE could have gone to court in each European country and requested injunctions for breach of contract, forcing its licensees to comply with the U.S. embargo. GE did not do this, however, probably because the Reagan administration lifted the ban before any legal action could be taken and because the negative and far-reaching political and economic impact of this action for GE in future international business dealings was considerable.

The United States acted to apply sanctions against firms that shipped turbines to the Soviet Union after the announcement of the embargo with questionable results.

European Reaction

Because this was a period of severe recession, high unemployment, and runaway inflation, the EC had considered the pipeline project to be the shot-in-the-arm its sagging economy needed. Also, by 1990, the EC had expected the pipeline to be providing 1.1 trillion cubic feet of gas, a tremendous source of energy. The EC stood to lose 20 million hours of labor over the next two years and billions of dollars in revenue from contracts with the Soviets if the embargo was honored.

As a result of the embargo, U.S.-Western European trade relations plunged to the lowest point in a decade. As earlier noted, the EC retaliated against the United States by issuing the list of countersanctions it planned to put into effect.

U.S. Reaction

U.S. multinationals reflected growing nervousness that other industrial products would be included in the embargo and therefore be subject to European retaliation. Rumored targeted industries included computers, heavy machinery, and medical products. GE, its foreign licensees, and the other U.S. firms previously listed had already lost billions of dollars in contracts that could not be completed and at stake were billions of additional dollars in contracts for these other goods.

The embargo also created doubt at home and abroad about U.S. reliability as a supplier to the world market, an image that U.S. multinationals could hardly afford.

Purpose of the Embargo—Economic or Political?

Initially, the Reagan administration said the embargo was put in place to buy Western Europe time to develop alternative energy sources that would reduce its dependency on the Eastern bloc for energy. The administration also said that further U.S. action on easing the sanctions would be influenced by negotiations on curbing the competition in export credit subsidies.

However, the embargo was soon linked to the Soviet repression in Poland. The administration made no attempt to hide the fact that it believed the sanctions would:

1. Force the relaxation of Soviet control over the Eastern-bloc countries, especially Poland, where it wanted martial law ended.
2. Deny the Soviet Union technology that would strengthen its military.
3. Pressure the Soviet Union to divert resources away from its military buildup. If the United States avoided selling any technology that would allow the Soviets to leap ahead economically, it was believed that resources originally allocated to the Soviet

military effort would have to be diverted to the economic sector.

The United States chose to use an economic policy as a tool to enforce a political policy, a sad mistake. When it became clear that the EC would remain firm in its commitment to the pipeline project, the Reagan administration realized it would be impossible to enforce the embargo. The net effect of the U.S. embargo and the EC countersanctions was a growing threat of a worldwide slide to protectionism.

Conclusion

The situation described is a classic example in which a government did not fully appreciate the political and economic importance of an industrial project to the countries involved. The United States essentially tried to inflict its own policies on the EC using its own self-reference criterion. Based on its historical position of world dominance, the United States assumed that the countries in the EC would follow its lead and honor the embargo. The United States, unfortunately, suffered loss of face worldwide when it discovered that this reputation of worldwide dominance was invalid in this situation.

This is also a classic example of the precarious position in which the multinational company can find itself both in its home and host countries. MNCs can easily be subjected to legal jurisdictional disputes and economic sanctions; they can be used by governments as pawns for implementing political policies. Many of these situations are completely beyond the control of MNCs and are made even more complex and of utmost importance due to the millions, even billions of dollars at stake.

Finally, the United States failed to understand that enforcement of economic sanctions on an MNC could have serious backlash effects on the economic system of the imposing country and that this negative impact could be of far greater magnitude than anticipated.

Source: Case material developed by Diane Dieter, Cherryl Hall, and Joe Richardson.

QUESTIONS

1. Identify all the legal questions in this case.
2. Take the role of one (or all) of the following participants and justify the position it took in this case.
   a. The U.S. government
   b. The European Community
   c. The American companies
   d. The European companies
   e. The governments of France, West Germany, Italy, or Great Britain
3. If this situation had involved only the United States government and a U.S. MNC doing business with Russia, would the U.S. government have had an easier time in enforcing the embargo? What if the offending company had been a French subsidiary of a U.S. MNC? What if the goods had to be shipped from the United States?
4. The issue of the government's right and, indeed, need to protect U.S. interests is a difficult one when it involves international trade. Defend either side of the issue.

Case 3–1

MARKETING FLYING DISCS IN MEXICO

A growing recreational activity in the United States is the sport of throwing flying discs. Flying discs, more commonly known by the registered brand name "Frisbee" owned by Whamm-O Corp., are used in games ranging from backyard tossing from one person to another to organized flying disc tournaments on prescribed courses. The most well-known tournaments are sponsored by various regional groups of the National Frisbee Association. Flying discs appeal to all age groups and can be enjoyed with minimum training (if you can throw a paper airplane, you can toss a flying disc) to the most highly trained acrobatic free-style flying-disc athletes, such as those who participate in regional and national tournaments. In the United States, it is estimated that there are over 5 million flying discs in use. The majority are Frisbees, considered the best and only professional flying disc made.

Because of the widespread appeal of flying discs in the United States, three business associates—Roger Blake, owner of a recreational sports store and director of a regional Frisbee Association; Jose Gutierez, a bank vice president employed in the United States but a citizen of Mexico; and Eloise Dunn, a marketing consultant—are considering the possibility of seeking a franchise to manufacture and market flying discs internationally. Preliminary research indicated some marketing of flying discs in several European countries, Great Britain, and Mexico. The success has been spotty; in some cases, outstanding; in others, a growing demand; and in still others; initial sales acceptance but no sustained growth.

Roger Blake and Jose Gutierez approached Eloise Dunn with the idea of organizing a company to market flying discs internationally. At the initial meeting, Blake and Gutierez presented a brief outline of their idea and plans up to that time to Dunn. Briefly, Blake, involved with flying discs since his youth and completely involved as a business person, was certain that the appeal of the flying disc would be as great elsewhere as it has been in the United States if properly marketed. Gutierez indicated that in Mexico active sports participation of all types was widespread, and his own experience with flying discs led him to believe it would appeal to others. Both felt that the flying disc had not been more successful outside the United States because of inadequate marketing rather than lack of interest. They felt that such was the case in those situations with which they were familiar, primarily Germany and Mexico. While use of the flying disc is quickly learned, to gain widespread acceptance, it requires an introduction with a great deal of promotion activity to acquaint people with the new sport. Further, for sustained acceptance of the sport, a continuous marketing program is necessary with adequate publicity, promotion, and distribution. Because of their convictions that proper marketing, both at the introduction and during the growth period, is necessary to successfully introduce the flying disc to a country, the two went to Dunn for marketing expertise.

Roger Blake was experienced with the marketing of flying discs in the United States; besides being regional director of the Frisbee Association and sponsoring and developing several Frisbee tournaments, Blake also had produced and directed a 20-minute film on disc flying. The film was well received by many groups and Blake felt it was an effective promotional device for selling discs to new users. The film dealt with free-style flying disc competitions and was also an excellent illustration of the versatility and general appeal of flying disc games. Since Jose Gutierez was experienced in banking in Mexico and was well connected there, he was primarily interested in exploring the potential for the flying discs in Mexico. Initial investigation revealed that discs had been introduced to Mexico a number of years ago but presently were not being sold there. In fact, the few discs in Mexico were generally found in tourist areas such as Acapulco and Mazatlan and probably were brought down by U.S. citizens on vacation. Gutierez indicated that during a recent two-week vacation in Mazatlan he observed flying discs being used there by Mexican citizens which gave him some assurance that Mexicans would buy flying discs if they were properly marketed. Eloise Dunn agreed to participate in exploring the feasibility of marketing flying discs internationally. Since one of the three was experienced in Mexico, they decided to explore the possibility of acquiring a franchise in Mexico. Dunn agreed to call Ex-O Corp., a major U.S. flying-disc manufacturer, to discuss the possibilities of acquiring a franchise for Mexico.

A call to the international franchisor for flying discs produced the following information: Ex-O Corp. had franchised the manufacture of flying discs in Mexico about six years ago to Alejandro Garcia; the franchisee had not marketed any under the agreement but had purchased four molds and had the exclusive right to market the flying discs in Mexico. Since Garcia had not produced any flying discs within the time limit set by the franchise agreement, the international franchisor considered the contract void. Dunn inquired about the requirements for a current franchise to produce flying discs in Mexico. The international director indicated that the terms of the contract could be negotiated, but would include some initial payment for the right to an exclusive franchise in Mexico, royalty on all items produced, as well as the costs of molds sold exclusively by Ex-O Corp. However, because of the previous experience, he would be reluctant to grant a franchise without a strong commitment by the new franchisee to market the discs effectively. He indicated he would like to see a tentative marketing plan of any potential franchise for Mexico before giving more details. He also suggested that since the former franchisee owned four molds he should be contacted about selling the molds and also about his current situation. The director gave the last-known address and telephone number of Garcia to Dunn.

In a second meeting of the three business associates, Dunn relayed the information acquired from the Ex-O Corp. They agreed to continue the preliminary investigation. Jose Gutierez was returning to Mexico on business and agreed to contact Alejandro Garcia for information on the existing molds. Dunn indicated that if information from Garcia and additional preliminary information on Mexico warranted, they should draft a preliminary marketing plan to present to the Ex-O Corp.

On Gutierez's return to the United States he presented the following facts: Garcia had purchased four molds for the standard promotional flying disc. Garcia's primary business is plastic injection molding; he acquired the flying disc franchise after seeing a promotional flying disc in the United States because he felt it was something he could sell primarily as a promotional piece. The idea was for a company to buy flying discs with a logo printed on them for free distribution as a sales promotion device. His first contact after acquiring the franchise was a major U.S. snack food company. In a contract with this snack food company he produced 50,000 with the company's logo. However, the project never materialized because in Mexico all promotions where merchandise is given away free must be approved by the government. Garcia had bought the molds, produced 50,000 flying discs, but the snack food company could not get a permit to distribute the flying discs. At this juncture, Mr. Garcia gave up the flying disc business. He indicated he tried to market a few, not spending any promotional dollars, but felt he did not know how to market the flying disc and further, could not find anybody who could demonstrate its use. Mr. Garcia said that as far as he knew no one else in Mexico was producing flying discs, that he had not produced any since his contact with the snack food company, that he had no continued interest in producing the flying disc, and that he was willing to sell the molds for $1,000 (U.S.) apiece for a total of $4,000. He stated that the original cost was $3,000 apiece.

Gutierez also reported that Mr. Garcia produced the flying disc at about 30 cents (U.S.). Gutierez brought along a model of one of Garcia's discs and Blake indicated that it was a Regular model, the lowest quality of the line of four. The molds that Garcia has produce a Regular model. Ex-O Corp.'s discs are manufactured in four models: Regular, All-American, Pro, and Super Pro. The basic differences between the models are weight and balance, the Regular is the lightest and the Super Pro the heaviest and best balanced. Ex-O Corp. has also recently introduced a new line it called the World-Class Disc which is differentiated primarily by weight. World Class Discs are gaining in popularity in the United States as flying disc competition increases in importance. Blake believes that as flying disc competition increases in importance and the market becomes more sophisticated, the World Class will become the biggest seller in the United States. He said that the Super Pro and all of the World Class were well balanced and designed in such a way that maximum flexibility in flying styles could be accommodated. For amateur disc flyers, the Regular would be adequate, but as a person develops style and skill, the better engineered and designed models have greater appeal. Although still popular in the U.S.

market, the Regular or promotional discs are not much in demand by experienced disc throwers.

Gutierez also checked pricing in Mexico and found that similar items (toys and other sport items) on the market were priced between 5,250 and 10,500 pesos apiece—about $2.25 and $4.50 (U.S.) at an exchange rate of 2,330 pesos per dollar. He felt that the Pro model or Super Pro model could be sold in Mexico for 15,145 pesos or $6.50 (U.S.). Jose contacted representatives of two major chain stores in Mexico to explain the product and their intentions to introduce it to Mexico through such stores. All indicated they would like a presentation of the product, thought it probably would sell, that they would place small initial orders, and if the product sold well, they would include it as a regular product line in their stores. They did note that there would have to be some sustained demand for them to continue to stock and sell the items. The stores he visited were Comercial Mexicana, similar to Woolco or Target chains, with 26 stores throughout Mexico, and Tiendas Aurerra, comparable to K mart, with 45 stores mainly in the central part of Mexico. He also talked to Puerto de Liverpool, which is similar to the May Co. stores and has four stores in Mexico City. Jose also determined that the flying discs could be imported into Mexico with the 75 percent ad valorem tax; the importation permit would fall under the recreational plastic toys code number 9703A002.

The three associates were optimistic about Gutierez's findings in Mexico and felt that prospects were good for marketing the flying discs there; they also decided that if they proceeded they would definitely have to purchase Garcia's molds in order to prevent possible pirating should they become successful. Further discussion about a marketing plan raised the following questions: What model or models should they sell in Mexico? Roger Blake, because of his experience at the Pro level felt they should not bother with the Regular line but introduce the World Class Disc, Jose Gutierez countered that while the World Class is becoming increasingly successful in the United States (an established market), the Mexican market is new so they should start with the most inexpensive model, gain widespread distribution, then develop the more sophisticated items.

They agreed they would have to buy the molds from Garcia, but should they invest in new molds and manufacture the product in Mexico, an approach which would require substantial investment? Jose assured them he knew someone in the plastics business who could produce from a standard mold in quantities close to 30 cents U.S. Or should they import the flying discs to determine if there was an initial market? Jose Gutierez suggested it might be wise to import flying discs into

in Mexico along with a proposed budget that would exclude the cost of molds purchased from Garcia and the franchise payment to Ex-O. She would formulate the proposal primarily on the information they had already gathered and perhaps some basic information on market characteristics in Mexico.

Consider that you are Eloise Dunn and prepare a tentative marketing plan for the introduction and marketing of flying discs in Mexico. In your plan, answer the following questions: (1) Should they buy the molds? (2) Should they buy Ex-O rights to their discs? and (3) Should the introduction only be in Mexico City or throughout Mexico? Below are media prices to help you put together a budget.

There are five national TV channels in Mexico; their ad prices average for:

(Refers to Column two)

AAA time (19:30 P.M. to 24:00 P.M.)	30 seconds—$632	60 seconds—$1,264 (U.S.)
AA time (17:30 P.M. to 19:30 P.M.)	30 seconds—$437	60 seconds— 874 (U.S.)
A time (24:00 P.M. to 17:30 P.M.)	30 seconds—$300	60 seconds—$ 600 (U.S.)

Mexico and conduct a preliminary test market to get an idea about price, potential demand, and so forth.

Should they go with the Ex-O Corp. or some other manufacturer of flying discs? All agreed that if they were going to the expense of introducing the product, they should go with the recognized brand name which is Ex-O. Also, they reasoned that should they successfully develop a product which was not an Ex-O product, the Ex-O Corp. could come in and sweep the market based on demand that the three associates had generated. Dunn proposed that they put their ideas down in terms of a tentative program, the basis of which they would develop as a presentation to the Ex-O Corp. She reminded them that the Ex-O Corp. did not want to discuss the situation without seeing a proposal of the program for Mexico. The meeting ended with the agreement that Dunn would put together a tentative program for marketing the flying discs

The newspaper ads run on the average for:

1 Page	$1,441 (U.S.)	one day
½ Page	$ 852 (U.S.)	one day
¼ Page	$ 417 (U.S.)	one day

The newspapers are *Novedades, Excelsior, Universal, El Heraldo, El Sol de Mexico*. All these are national newspapers with an average daily circulation of 250,000.

One national newspaper, *Esto*, publishes only sports; its rates are:

1 Page	$565 (U.S.)	one day
½ Page	$282 (U.S.)	one day
¼ Page	$141 (U.S.)	one day

The TV stations and the newspapers have staffs to design ads.

Source: This case is developed on an actual situation but all dates, names, and incidences have been altered to protect the identity of the actual participants.

Case 3–2

CONSULTING FOR BEBE COLA IN LATINO

Bebe Cola, one of the top three soft drink companies in the United States, has contacted you as a consultant with a problem it is experiencing in Latino (a Latin American country). Cola International, a subsidiary of Bebe Cola, Inc., has had operations in Latino since before World War II. Bebe Cola's organization consists of Bebe Cola, Inc., which is the parent company for Bebe Cola USA, the corporation for U.S. sales; and Bebe Cola International for their investments abroad. Bebe Cola International has a partially owned subsidiary in Latino, Bebe Cola Latino. B.C. International owns 49 percent of Bebe Cola Latino, and Latino nationals own 51 percent. As is the case in the United States, B.C. Latino manufactures cola concentrate, which it sells to independently owned bottlers throughout Latino. B.C. Latino owns no bottling plants in Latino. The profit that B.C. Latino makes is solely from the sale of concentrate to bottlers. It is, therefore, extremely important to B.C. Latino, as well as to B.C., Inc., that the bottlers be profitable over the long run. If they do not grow with the market and make proper investments over time, and if market share is lost, B.C. Latino will suffer substantial profit reductions. This relationship is precisely the one that caused B.C. International concern. In an annual review of long-range projections of B.C. Latino, the president of B.C. International became concerned over a study that indicated most of the B.C. bottlers in Latino were operating at near production capacity and that their plans for the next five years did not include sufficient investment in production facilities. After visits with many of the B.C. bottlers, B.C., Inc. found that most

were reluctant to make additional investments because of the continuing profit squeeze facing them.

In Latino nonalcoholic beverages are classified as food and all food is under price control. Soft drinks have had virtually the same price for the past 12 years, but the bottlers' costs, with the exception of sugar, the only other ingredient under price control, have increased. The net result is that over the last 11 years, a very profitable gross margin has dwindled to the point that the more efficient bottlers can realize only a 5 to 10-cent (U.S.) per case profit. This relatively slim profit margin is the major reason given by B.C. bottlers for not planning for future capital investment. Present retail price control for a 12-ounce bottle of B.C. cola (and this price applies to all the colas) is 450 pesos or approximately 20 cents (U.S.). Wholesale prices are approximately: 250 pesos for a 6 ½-ounce bottle, 325 pesos for a 12-ounce bottle, and 525 pesos for a 26-ounce bottle.[1]

This preliminary investigation on the part of B.C. Inc., management was cause for alarm. Even though B.C. shares the cola market equally with Super Cola, the other major cola manufacturer (each has about 48 percent), B.C. management felt that with the market growing, bottlers had to increase their investments in production facilities or they would subsequently lose share of market and suffer reduced profits. B.C., Inc. management could appreciate the reluctance of the Latino bottlers to increase their investments because the production equipment is all produced in the United States and is very expensive. Fur-

---

[1] Convert pesos to U.S. money at a rate of 2,330 pesos to $1.00 (U.S.).

thermore, the equipment carries an import tax of about 50 percent ad valorem. The heavy-duty trucks used to deliver the product are also imported from the United States and have a 100 percent ad valorem tax applied to them. Consequently, an investment in production and delivery facilities in Latino costs about twice as much as it does in the United States.

The immediate response to this problem by B.C.'s management was to look for ways it could assist the Latino bottlers to increase their efficiency. A recent study of production facility utilization among Latino bottlers had been done by the production division and showed that they were perhaps the most efficient bottlers in the whole international company. They were operating, on the average, more than two eight-hour shifts per day, many running very close to 100 percent capacity. The only means to increase production efficiency would be the replacement of present production equipment with high-speed bottling machinery. That alternative would have required a heavy investment which the Latinos weren't willing to make with present profit margins. B.C. management looked elsewhere and considered the possibility of lobbying to have the minimum price for a soft drink raised. This avenue was rapidly discarded since no government official or politician would raise the price of a product so widely used as cola beverages. For example, the per capita consumption of soft drinks in Latino is close to 1,000 eight-ounce bottles per person per year. This compares to about 550 eight-ounce bottles per person per year in the United States. Obviously, soft drink consumption is extremely popular in this country and any politician or government official advocating an increase in the price would incur the wrath of the population. That approach was immediately dropped.

Looking elsewhere for potential solutions, the management decided that distribution patterns utilized by the bottlers might be an avenue for improvement of efficiency. An extensive study of the distribution of soft drinks was conducted. B.C. Cola has now employed you to analyze the data and provide them with suggestions and recommendations. A summary of the highlights of the study follows.

The Cola Market in Latino

The market for soft drinks in Latino is an exceptionally large one. Latinians drink, on the average, about 1,000 to 1,100 eight-ounce equivalent bottles per year per person. Of this amount, about 50 percent are cola-based, the other 50 percent are fruit-flavored drinks. The cola beverage market is about equally divided (approximately 48 percent each) between B.C. Cola and Super Cola. The remaining 4 percent is distributed among four or five other brands including Bubble Cola, Rex Cola, and Latinacola (the only wholly owned Latino cola company). The following comments provide you with some general idea of the characteristics of the market. Where appropriate, U.S. comparisons will be made.

1. Over 90 percent of all sales of bottled soft drinks in the Latino market are made as *cold bottles* in small quantities—one or two bottles at a time. They are either consumed at the point of sale or taken home for immediate use. One of the important characteristics of this market is the high per capita consumption of soft drinks as a refreshment between meals and with meals, both during lunch and dinner. In the United States, about 60 percent of bottled soft drinks are bought in supermarkets in packs of six or eight for consumption in the home. On-premise cold bottle consumption in the United States is only about 15 percent of the market.

Beer is sold in cans, but it does not come under price controls and thus the price can reflect the higher cost of cans. Glass is produced in Latino for bottles by a monopoly or cartel that controls the price of glass which is kept relatively high. While there are an increasing number of supermarkets involved in the distribution of food in Latino, they are still not significant in the distribution of soft drinks. In a major supermarket with floor space of 80,000–90,000 square feet, the beverage section generally contains, of all brands, no more than about 30 or 40 cases. In comparison, a supermarket of equal size in the United States stocks from 300 to 400 cases of soft drinks. Soft drinks are just not bought in packs of six or eight in Latino supermarkets.

2. A large portion of the market does not have adequate refrigeration in the home and depends on small neighborhood stores to provide them with a supply of chilled product. Off-premise consumption in the home follows a pattern similar to the following: A maid or young child is sent before the noon meal to buy one or two bottles to bring home for immediate consumption with the meal. This pattern probably holds true for most of Latino.

3. There is some income distinction in brand preference among consumers. In Latino, four-income classes are generally recognized Class A, with monthly incomes of $2,200 (U.S. equivalent) or more, and class B, with incomes between $1,200 and $2,200 account for about 8 percent of the population. About 30 percent of the population are in class C, earning from $600 to $1,100 per month. The remaining 62 percent are in class D and have incomes below $600.

Super Cola has the status image preferred by class A and B, while B.C.'s image is strongest among classes C and D. Super Cola has had some success trading down to classes C and D while maintaining its upper-class image. B.C. has attempted to trade up to class A and B and follows this strategy in much of its advertising.

4. The predominant method of retail distribution is through small neighborhood stores. (In the United States, the major method of retail distribution is through super-

markets.) Over 90 percent of soft drink sales are made in stores operated by one person, having about 150–200 square feet of selling space, and stocking soft drinks, bread, and a few canned goods. They are found in almost every block, and in some blocks there are two or three. They may be in the middle of the block or on a corner. They play a very important role in the economy and in the distribution of soft drinks. These stores operate on a cash basis and rely on daily or three-times-a-week delivery. There is a problem of keeping them supplied with product. Frequently, even on a daily-delivery basis, stores run out of product before the next delivery. Their lack of cash and small storage capacity prevent them from maintaining adequate inventory.

5. House-to-house selling is employed as a means of distribution in large cities to customers in class A. Because of their high per capita consumption, these households make large purchases, and deliveries are generally made on a once-a-week basis with one-to-two case drop. There is some question as to the profitability of house-to-house delivery. When franchises use this method of distribution, it is generally considered to be more important as a promotional tool than as a profitable distribution method. Many feel that when they have good house-to-house delivery they also have greater total market penetration.

6. A very small percentage of sales is made through vending machines. In most instances, the bottlers own the vending machines. They are placed in high-traffic areas such as factories, service stations, and schools. Vendors are activated by slugs which must be purchased from an attendant. The vendors are generally filled more than once a day.

Presently in Latino, there are two sizes of vendor in general use: one, an upright vendor, has a capacity of about 110 bottles and costs 5,200,000 pesos; the other, a bar type with a top opening, has a capacity of about 200 bottles and costs 3,400,000 pesos. Vendors account for an extremely small part of the total sales.

7. The large number of small accounts means that routes may have as many as 250 accounts to service with a typical case drop of one to two and a half cases serviced daily or three times weekly. In the United States, a route has about 150 accounts with an average case drop of 30 to 50 cases, serviced weekly.

8. Distribution to retail outlets is made by trucks with a driver/salesman and one to three helpers. The driver/salesman has generally had experience as a helper, and is responsible for inventory on the truck and collections. The driver/salesmen are compensated by one of three methods: (1) straight commission, (2) salary plus commission, or (3) commission as an independent agent—an average income is $248 (U.S.) per month. The predominant method of compensation among the plants visited was salary plus commission. Some bottlers sold the driver/salesmen their trucks and dealt with them on an agency basis. The amount of compensation for driver/salesmen varied from franchise to franchise, but in most instances the driver/salesmen earned about twice as much as the helpers, who averaged $200 (U.S.) per month.

The responsibilities of the helpers included sales work. In fact, it appeared in some cases that personal contact with the retailer was most frequently made by helpers. In other words, the lowest-paid person in the sales/delivery team was responsible for the sales function. One franchise recognized this problem and had a system that required that the driver/salesmen visit each customer on the route at least once a week.

Supervisors are used by all franchises, and the number of routes supervised varied from as few as two to as many as five routes per supervisor. The supervisor's responsibility is primarily one of sales and customer contact. They are generally expected to call on accounts to help maintain rate of growth. They are also responsible for allocating promotional monies among the routes, and in some franchises are responsible for promotions with carnival trucks and similar affairs. There seemed to be no pattern as to former employment of supervisors. Some had been salesmen, others had been hired specifically for the position of supervisor.

9. Besides the normal promotion via newspaper, radio, and television, the local bottler spends a great deal of money on in-store displays, painting the stores with Bebe Cola signs, and conducting special events. Most bottlers maintain a supply of tables, chairs, and other equipment which they lend to organizations as a public relations gesture.

10. B.C. is sold in 6½, 12-, 16-, and 26-ounce sizes. The 12- and 16-ounce are the predominant sizes, although there is some growth in the 26-ounce. The 6½-ounce bottle is sold mostly to bars, restaurants, and for special occasions. In the United States, the leading sizes are 16, 22, and 48-ounce. A 12-ounce bottle of B.C. sells at retail for 100 pesos, and the deposit on the bottle is 130 pesos. A very important part of the merchandising of B.C. in Latino is the cost of the glass. The bottler receives very high trippage (20–30 trips) on each of the returnable bottles, but the cost of each bottle is quite high.[2] In the United States, 10 trips per bottle is considered excellent. Thus, in Latino, while the price of glass is high, the high frequency of trips brings the cost per fill down. The general procedure is to charge each retail outlet for the glass as well as the liquid. Any replacement

---

[2] The number of trips means the number of times a bottle is refilled before it is lost or somehow destroyed.

of glass must be paid for by the retailer. Because the glass price is so high, it is frequently used as a promotional device: in some instances, both glass and liquid are given free, and in others, the glass is sold but the liquid is given away. Many bottlers believe that Super Cola gives a large amount of glass away and is extremely competitive at this level. Glass is considered among the bottlers to be one of their most important problems—that is, how to overcome the high cost of glass and to compete with Super Cola which gives glass away. Many feel that their policy of charging for glass is necessary in their operation.

11. Social security payments provide for medical aid plus disability benefits. Total salary is paid while a person is disabled. Any difference between what social security pays and actual salary is made up by the company. The social security program in Latino is similar to that of the United States, but it also provides medical care and disability insurance. Retirement payments are quite low.

12. Many bottlers don't plan for the growth of demand in their area, hence lack facilities for increased production. All of a sudden, demand far outstrips production. It takes approximately 12 months to increase production and in that time a tremendous vacuum can be created.

13. There are 11 chains bottling B.C. Four of them have six plants each, one chain has three plants, two have three plants each, and one has four plants. There are approximately 50 B.C. plants in Latino, 37 of which are in chains (a chain is owned by one company).

14. Super Cola has a larger number of small plants in all of Latino than B.C. has. For example, Super Cola has five plants in the largest cities in Latino versus only two for B.C. Since a larger plant is almost always more efficient than a small one, B.C. is probably more efficient in production than Super Cola.

15. In general, the level of sophistication of managerial techniques used in the operation of franchises is low. There is, however, a very high interest in many plants to experiment with and use modern management methods. Some are beginning to employ new methods. On the average, however, the techniques employed are not fully tested or extremely sophisticated.

Controls such as forecasting, budgeting, market analysis, personnel evaluation, supervision, and motivation are not employed by all. There is growing awareness of the need for some of these more sophisticated management techniques and, as mentioned above, many plants are experimenting with them.

Several of the bottlers visited had recently experienced a situation in which demand far exceeded supply, and for which their managerial efficiency was inadequate. When they passed from a seller's market to a buyer's market, or when Super Cola increased its competition, they immediately found that they could not cope as effectively as they would have liked to.

16. In planning a program for B.C. bottlers, several major characteristics should be considered:

a. Domination of distribution by very small outlets and small sales (1–2½ cases) per account visited.
b. A very high per capita consumption of soft drinks, the majority of which are sold cold.
c. Competition from Super Cola.
d. Price control.
e. All sales on a cash basis.
f. High turnover in ownership of small stores.
g. Lack of depth and breadth in managerial talent.
h. Lack of experience in the use of many basic management tools.

17. A medium-sized plant in Latino manufactures and sells 4 million cases of product per year, a small plant about 2 million cases, and the largest in Latino over 25 million cases per year. In the United States, a small plant is one with a capacity of less than 1 million cases a year, while any plant having a capacity of more than 6 million would be considered very large.

18. The cost of transporting on large flatbed trucks from a production facility to a warehouse averages about 5 pesos per kilometer per case.

19. One of the problems faced by most of the bottlers was a constant out-of-stock situation in the small stores. Even when the market preferred B.C., they would take Super Cola if B.C. wasn't available. The main cause of out-of-stock was that delivery could not be made frequently enough to keep small stores supplied. Most did not have enough money

to carry more than 1–1½ cases at a time. They were also lacking in storage space. Some bottlers tried two deliveries per day, but found the cost too high to continue.

20. The small stores which predominate in the Latino market operate on a cash basis. Very little if any credit is extended by the bottler. One reason given was the high failure rate and high turnover in ownership.

21. The distribution process used in Latino is identical with that in the United States. There is a central bottling plant with warehousing. Trucks are dispatched daily from the plant to the market to call on the various outlets. At the end of the day, or when the route is serviced, they return empty, either for additional product or to be loaded for the following day.

QUESTIONS

1. As a consultant to B.C. International, analyze this case carefully and suggest areas in which distribution efficiencies might be developed.
2. Based on the facts presented in the case, can you suggest a different means of distribution from that presently utilized?
3. Can you suggest improvements in activities other than distribution? Discuss.

Case 3–3

INTERNATIONAL MARKETING OF SERVICES: SHOULD THE GATT CONCEPTS BE EXTENDED TO SERVICES?

Past and current international trade environments explain the United States' recent increased attention to international marketing of services (IMS). Increasing talk of protec-

tionism in Congress, escalating concern with trade deficits, a weakening manufacturing sector, the strategic importance of services to the economy, the mounting activism of the private sector (Coalition of Service Industries), and increasing foreign competition have all played roles in U.S. insistence on including services in the current Uruguay Round of GATT talks. In addition, federal officials have every reason to believe that the impact foreign competition had on the U.S. manufacturing sector a few years ago might be duplicated in the services sector if quality and customer satisfaction are subsumed by complacency.

The extent and variety of the barriers to the international marketing of services indicate the political difficulties of negotiating freer trade in services. Market access may be blocked by technical barriers, unreasonable import licensing requirements (fees, royalties), restrictions on personnel movement, regulation of data transmission (privacy issues), subsidies to domestic businesses (direct or through lower lending rates), denial of issuance of foreign exchange, unreasonable financial requirements (capital structure, tax policies, ownership, and/or financial management), refusing the use of domestic facilities, customs restrictions, government procurement policies, and limits on the use of foreign materials (ad copy, films). The Department of Commerce has compiled a 250-page printout of examples of barriers to free trade in services (see Exhibit 1). Coupled with such problems as political instability, the desire to protect national cultures, and restrictive U.S. laws (the Foreign Corrupt Practices Act, antitrust, and banking laws), these barriers represent a complex problem that defies simple solutions and certainly indicates that not all barriers to trade in services can be removed. Service sectors such as banking and insurance must continue to have a great deal of regulation. *The problem is to sort out the legitimate regulatory interests from the artificial.*

Chronology of Events Leading to the Uruguay Round

The first attempts to deal with trade in services on a multilateral basis can be traced to the post–World War II attempts to liberalize merchandise trade. A brief review of some of the history helps one understand why so little progress has been made. The key events and legislation are summarized in Exhibit 2.

The first GATT was a result of a failed attempt to establish an International Trade Organization (ITO) following World War II. Although the committee preparing the draft of the ITO charter addressed the services issue in dealing with restrictive business practices, the GATT that resulted when the ITO failed to be chartered dealt specifically with only one service, films. The primary thrust of GATT has been and remains liberalization of trade in goods. The preoccupation with achieving this goal has contributed to the neglect of services in the years following World War II.

About the same time as work was being completed on the first GATT, the Organization for European Economic Cooperation (OEEC), which preceded the Organization for Economic Cooperation and Development (OECD), decided to adopt a Code of Liberalization of Current Invisible Operations, and later, a Code of Liberalization of Capital Movement. The OECD took over these codes from the OEEC, and due to its broader membership has become a leading forum for the liberalization of trade in services. The OECD codes, however, appear to be deficient in at least four respects:

1. The membership of the OECD is still too narrow to be representative.
2. All members do not adhere to these particular codes.
3. OECD members regularly violate the codes.
4. The codes themselves tend to treat the symptoms rather than the problems.

In 1972 two reports drew much attention to the need for multilateral negotiations in services: The Rey Report urged action toward the liberalization of trade in the specific service sectors of insurance, tourism, and trans-

EXHIBIT 1 Examples of Regulatory Barriers Affecting Services Trade and Investment

Banking

Canada	Foreign banks limited to no more than 16 percent of total banking system assets (8 percent until 1984)
Mexico	Market closed to foreign banks except through offshore banking facilities
India	Higher taxes on foreign banks
France	Domestic banks have access to subsidized loan funds

Insurance

Bolivia	Foreign insurance companies required to maintain much higher capital reserves
Australia	No new foreign entrants permitted (many other countries have similar restrictions)
Turkey	Some reinsurance must be placed with publicly owned company

Telecommunications

United States	No foreign ownership of basic telecommunications service providers
Japan	Foreign participation limited to joint ventures
Federal Republic of Germany	Public monopoly for all services
France	Public monopoly for all services except information services

Engineering and Construction

United Kingdom	Only British firms eligible for design contracts on North Sea oil projects
Venezuela	Foreign consultants must work through local firms
United States	Embassy construction abroad may be limited to U.S. firms

Shipping

United States	Jones Act restricts coastal shipping to U.S. carriers (many other countries have similar restrictions)

Airlines

Portugal	Government loan guarantees and other financial assistance (many other countries subsidize domestic air carriers)
United States	Government travel restricted to domestic carriers

SOURCES: Office of Technology Assessment; "Selected Problems Encountered by U.S. Service Industries in Trade in Services"; Office of the United States Trade Representative, September 6, 1985, printout.

EXHIBIT 2   Key Events and Legislation Leading to the Uruguay Round

Date	Event or Legislation	Comments
1934	Reciprocal Trade Agreement Act	Gave the president power to change tariffs, incorporated most favored nation principle.
1947	OEEC Code of Liberalization of Current Operations	Invisibles were not necessarily equal to services; excluded key services such as banking, education, and communications.
1948	GATT officially comes into force	With the failure of the International Trade Organization, GATT assumed most of the provisions of the charter.
1956	Treaty of Rome	Liberalized trade in services, mainly in banking and insurance.
1959	OEEC Code of Liberalization of Capital Movements	Dealt with transactions rather than trade; did not give investment freedom.
1972	Rey and McFadzean Reports	Drew attention to the need for multilateral negotiations on services.
1974	Trade Act of 1974	Gave the president negotiating authority for GATT and defined trade as both goods and services.
1975	Tokyo Round	Some progress made on liberalizing trade in services; major impact was to initiate national studies on services.
1982	CSI Formed	The Coalition of Service Industries was formed to lobby, serve as a liaison, and gain international recognition for services.
1982	GATT Ministerial Declaration	Requested national studies on services.
1983	United Nations Conference on Trade and Development IV	Established UNCTAD work program for studies on services.
1984	Trade and Tariff Act of 1984	Established the Service Industries Development Program and the Service Industry Sector Advisory Committee; also included services in GATT Government Procurement Code.
1986	Punta Del Este Declaration	Launched Uruguay Round.
1986–	Uruguay Round	Twin-track discussions; one for goods and one for services.

portation (shipping and air). The McFadzean Report argued for freer trade in capital movements and first suggested multilateral GATT negotiations.

In 1975 the Tokyo Round of GATT talks started after a two-year delay. Services were brought into the discussion in 1980 in preparation for the 1982 GATT ministerial meeting giving no one, including the United States, adequate preparation time. The primary reason for even including services was the aggressive lobbying of the aviation and insurance sectors; oddly enough, the only real progress made in the Tokyo Round addressed films rather than insurance or aviation. Another, almost simultaneous, result of the outcry was the Trade Act of 1974 giving the president authority to negotiate international trade and defining trade as both goods and services. Despite resistance from two U.S. presidents, the developing countries (DCs), and others, international trade in services was discussed at Tokyo. It soon became apparent that a lack of reliable data, theoretical underpinnings, a conceptual framework, and consensus would prevent major decisions. However, delegates agreed to begin gathering data that might allow more fruitful future negotiations. A GATT Ministerial Declaration in 1982 formalized this agreement by requesting National Studies on Trade in Services (NSTS) from those nations interested in addressing the issue of services trade. Another compromise agreed to at the Tokyo Round addressed some services trade issues through changes in the codes on Customs Valuation and Government Procurement. The door was opened for real progress.

National studies were completed by at least 18 of the more developed nations, the EC, and some DCs. Studies from the DCs caused very real concern when the DCs found they did not have adequate data to engage in meaningful negotiations. These national studies represent the first multilateral attempt to document the nature and amount of international trade in services. The United States had completed an earlier study titled *U.S. Service Industries in World Markets: Current Problems and Future Policy Development* (December 1976). Comparable studies were available only from the EC, which leads the world in recognizing the need to examine IMS. The progress toward more liberal trade in services roughly parallels Treaty of Rome (1956) provisions in which the EC partially addressed services issues. The national studies—along with supplemental information from a variety of sources such as the United Nations Conference on Trade and Development—served as the basis for launching the current Uruguay Round of GATT talks in 1986. These talks have continued into 1990.

The Issues

The inclusion of services on the agenda of the Uruguay Round was the source of much controversy. Originally, opposition came from the EC as well as from the DCs lead by Brazil and India. As the EC gathered data, they realized not only that they were the leaders in services trade but also that they stood to gain from liberalization and that they should support the negotiations. Once again, DC concerns that they were neither prepared for nor would necessarily benefit from such discussions were secondary to the more developed nations' desires to liberalize trade in services. A compromise between those opposed to the discussions and those wanting to proceed was reached at Punta Del Este. The compromise called for services to be discussed on a separate track from the normal GATT discussions—the twin track solution. Also, special concessions were to be given to the DCs to encourage their growth and development. The DCs feel that development of their own services is critical to their independence, cultural heritage, national security, and growth. Although the U.S. representa-

tives seemed to think that services were now included in GATT negotiations, other representatives believed that the separate track implied little and guaranteed nothing. This conflict arose because GATT as a forum has always excluded investment issues. The politics involved in foreign direct investment and portfolio investment have traditionally been separated from trade issues. Although it is still not clear what the final outcome will be, it is clear that services have already been included to some extent in GATT and that investment issues cannot be totally separated from trade in services issues.

The discussion of services in the Uruguay Round cannot necessarily immediately lead to more liberal trade in services. Recently, GATT has been a somewhat ineffective forum as barriers to trade become more nontariff in nature and as countries become more sophisticated in bending the rules. Serious questions continue to be raised about GATT's effectiveness at regulating trade in goods or services.

Progress at the GATT negotiations promises to be slow, painful, and extremely limited in scope. Many important issues (investment) are not likely to be addressed and the compromises reached will probably be sector specific. Time, data, and political constraints limit progress.[1] However, the mere fact that the talks are taking place is encouraging. Extending such fundamental GATT concepts as most favored nation status, transparency, nondiscrimination, and national treatment to services is at least being discussed.

---

[1] Marjory Searing, "The Uruguay Round—Up and Running," *Business America*, May 8, 1989, pp. 11–12.

Source: This case was prepared by Professor Gene W. Murdock, College of Commerce and Industry, University of Wyoming, Laramie, Wyoming.

QUESTIONS

1. Why is freer trade in services an important global issue? If it is important, why wasn't it addressed years ago?
2. Is GATT the best mechanism to address issues in services trade? What are its advantages and disadvantages and what are the alternatives?
3. Is trade in services harder to measure and regulate than trade in goods? Why or why not?

SUGGESTED READINGS

Benz, S. F. "Trade Liberalization and the Global Service Economy," *Journal of World Trade Law* 19, March–April 1985, pp. 95–120.

"The Next Trade Crisis May Be Just Around the Corner, America Is Losing Its Edge in Selling Services Overseas," *Business Week* (March 1984), pp. 48–55.

Quinn, James B., and Christopher E. Gagnon. "Will Services Follow Manufacturing into Decline?" *Harvard Business Review* 64, November–December 1986, pp. 95–103.

Riddle, Dorothy I. *Service-led Growth: The Role of the Service Sector in World Development.* New York: Praeger Publishers, 1986.

Sapir, A. "Trade in Services: Policy Issues for the Eighties," *Columbia Journal of World Business* 17, Fall 1982, pp. 77–83.

"Services Also Feeling Sting of Global Barriers," *Marketing News* 21, February 13, 1987, p. 18.

Case 3–4

W. H. SCHWARTZ AND SONS, LTD.

Recently, R. A. Bureau, vice president of marketing and sales of W. H. Schwartz and Sons, Ltd., visited Australia to assess the possibility of Schwartz entering the Australian spice market. Bureau had to consider not only the volume potential of the Australian market but also the strategy the company would use to enter the market, should the situation justify this.

Company History

W. H. Schwartz and Sons, Ltd., is the oldest established spice house in North America, having been founded in the port city of Halifax, Nova Scotia, in 1841. In the early days of the company, the son of the founder was the only salesman, traveling around Nova Scotia by stagecoach in summer and by horse and sleigh in winter. Later, he imported the first bicycle with pneumatic tires from England and traveled throughout Nova Scotia selling his products.

Formed as a family firm, the company is still privately owned and family run. The company was the first in Canada to sell pure spices. Formerly only compound spices, such as ginger mixed with flour and cornmeal, were available. Even though pure spices were more costly than compound spices, Schwartz was able to convince the public that pure spices offered better value than compound spices which lacked strength and flavor. This emphasis on quality has continued throughout the company's history and remains the basis of its worldwide reputation today.

Sales of spices were modest and confined to Nova Scotia until after World War I. Beginning in the 1920s the company expanded both its sales and product line. As the company grew, it acquired in 1930 Canada Spice and Specialty Mills in Saint John, New Brunswick. After this acquisition, the company's product line was extended to include peanut butter, flavoring extracts, and packaged dates and raisins. Later, in 1949, Schwartz purchased the second oldest Canadian spice company, S. W. Ewing, Ltd. Within 10 years this Montreal plant was replaced by a new facility which served all of Quebec, Ontario, and the Western Provinces.

Over the years, the company has demonstrated its ability to adapt to changing market conditions. Although coffee had constituted the bulk of their sales, the line was dropped when it was found that instant coffee was posing a serious challenge. The company adapted to the supermarket revolution by introducing specially designed racks for the display of their spices, and was a forerunner in packaging design, being the first to introduce the apothecary-type glass spice jar. A new merchandising technique was also pioneered by the company. This involved using full-time female staff to service display racks, thus reducing costs and improving retail ser-

EXHIBIT 1   Indicators of the Market Size for Spices: Canada and Australia (Canadian dollars)

Indicator	Canada	Australia
Total population	21,089,000	12,881,964
Annual rate of population increase	1.7 percent	1.9 percent
Net migration gain	127,000	123,000
Percent population between 20 and 40 years of age	33.1 percent	28.3 percent
Percent population 40 years and over	32.0 percent	34.3 percent
Population growth (compared to eight major developed Western economies)	Fastest	Second fastest
Urbanization	22 percent population live in Metro Toronto and Montreal	40 percent population live in Sydney and Melbourne
Gross National Product	$84.5 billion	$52.9 billion
National product per capita	$4,005	$4,107
Per capita disposable income	$2,541	$2,477
Total retail sales—all food products	$7.5 billion	$5.0 billion
Per capita retail food sales	$354	$385
Market size spices at retail	$18.0 million	$10.2 million
Per capita sales spices at retail	$.85	$.78

vicing. So successful was this method that Schwartz's competitors very quickly emulated the pioneering company.

In recent years, Schwartz has further expanded its manufacturing facilities and continues to expand its markets at home and abroad. In 1957, Schwartz entered the British spice market, where its high-quality pure spice was immediately recognized by British cooks. Initial losses were turned around and by 1980 Schwartz had become brand leader. This involved unseating its archrival, the large American McCormick organization from the top spot.

The company now sells in some 50 overseas markets, has gross sales of $27 million, and employs 300 people worldwide. Schwartz is optimistic about its future position in the overseas spice market which accounts for 44 percent of its sales revenues. As one of their managers, commented,'' We have the best quality in the world, the most attractive jar in the world, and the best method of merchandising in the world. How can we fail?''

The Spice Industry

A great deal of the production of the world's spices takes place in the countries of the devel-

EXHIBIT 2   Grocery Product Sales and Population

	Grocery Product Sales	Percent	Population	Percent
Australia	$2,008,575,000	100.0%	12,957,000	100.0%
States				
New South Wales and Australian				
Capital Territory	750,500,000	37.3	4,847,000	37.4
Victoria	578,675,000	28.8	3,564,000	27.5
Queensland	280,450,000	13.9	1,890,000	14.6
South Australia	161,950,000	8.1	1,205,000	9.3
West Australia	173,800,000	8.7	1,063,000	8.2
Tasmania	63,200,000	3.2	388,000	3.0
Urban centers				
Sydney	462,000,000	23.0	2,717,000	21.3
Melbourne	392,000,000	19.5	2,389,000	18.7
Brisbane	n.a.	n.a.	817,000	6.4
Adelaide	n.a.	n.a.	809,000	6.3
Perth	n.a.	n.a.	640,000	5.0

oping world, where, for example, chili peppers, ginger, nutmeg, sesame, cloves, and black and white peppers are grown. Spice production in more developed, nontropical countries consists mostly of herbs such as rosemary, thyme, basil, tarragon, and sage.

The developed nations of the Western world are the most important markets for spices. In most countries, the spice trade is concentrated in the hands of a few importers and spice packers, and processing usually takes place in the importing country. The main users of spices are households and the food industry. In the household sector, only a few spices such as pepper, nutmeg, and paprika are important as the bulk of household consumption is accounted for by these spices. Because most consumers are unfamiliar with spices such as turmeric, coriander, mace, and cardamom, the food industry provides the major market for these spices. In recent years, however, increased travel and

greater numbers of foreign restaurants have led many households to experiment with the more exotic spices. There are, in fact, many spices and the principal companies may sell a hundred or more varieties.

One principal problem of the spice industry is the frequent and wide fluctuations in the prices of most major spices, notably pepper, ginger, and cloves in recent years. These fluctuations are caused by a number of factors including supply irregularities and speculative trading.

The packaging of spices is an important element in the marketing policy of the major packers. Traditional packs involved the use of a cardboard tube sytem with metal or plastic top, and the plastic drum or sachet. Schwartz and McCormick pack the majority of their spices in American-style glass jars. Both companies utilize racks in self-service stores, using their own merchandisers to keep the display stocked. Advertising of spices is

---

EXHIBIT 3 Competitive Data (extracted from the trade journal, *Food Week*, Fast Facts, no. 12)

Fast Facts Herbs and Spices: McCormick Foods describes the market, what it did to it, how the company merchandises its products, and the cooperation it receives from retailers.

Spice consumption rising 20 percent a year without any fall in margins. *In seven years, McCormick Foods has risen from a zero share of the Australian spice market and now claims to be volume market leader.* The company estimates that in 1966, the year it launched in Australia, the market was worth about $2 million, with the average supermarket offering the housewife a range of about 30 spice products. Today the market is worth between $7 and $8 million and the average supermarket offers a range of over 120 items. *Ted McLendon,* managing director of McCormick's in Australia, said:

As world leaders in spices, we introduced the expertise necessary to develop the market and stepped into the quality void that existed. In 1966, our products were distributed by *Socomin,* the *Petersville* company. We opened our own manufacturing plant here and now handle our own sales in Sydney, Melbourne, and Brisbane, with Socomin looking after the other states. In 1985–86 we grew rapidly and now have in excess of 20 percent of the total spice volume sales; our share of the supermarket trade alone would be in excess of 50 percent. We're beginning to concentrate on the smaller food stores and I'm confident that the next two years will see us doubling our sales.

The market is one of the fastest-growing food sectors, with consumption growing annually at about 20 percent. Rivals in growth over the last five years would be frozen foods and soft drinks. And the potential of spices is excellent. On a per capita basis, Australians consume probably less than half the spice intake of Americans. In Australia we're presently marketing 180 products and sizes in three basic ranges—gourmet, regular, and the one-shot aluminum foil pouch range of gravies, sauces, and spice blends. The foil pouch range is our fastest-growing section. It has been available on a limited scale in Australia since 1966 but it is only during the last year that it has really taken off. *One of the major trends* has been the move away from the cardboard tube container to glass or tin. Cardboard is a very poor spice container; in a relatively short period of time it absorbs the essential oils of the spice, leaving the housewife with a flavor-depleted cellulose. That's the major reason we have never used it as a container. Another trend is toward spice blends as distinct from traditional spices.

"*In Australia, spices sell according to areas and there's a lot more to servicing supermarkets than people realize.* We normally start in a supermarket by installing a standard range of products. Over a period of time we study movement and then stock accordingly, planning the right mix for the right area. While we're introducing new products all the time we rarely drop any of the old. Australians are becoming more spice conscious and we haven't yet reached the plateau where we have too many products. From the retailer's point of view, spices are a profit spinner. They don't lend themselves to specializing and we make sure he enjoys a handsome margin and emphasize this point to him. Now we find that more and

---

EXHIBIT 3 *(continued)*

---

more the retailer is beginning to appreciate the value of his spice section. Spices are impulse items and we do a lot of in-store demonstration work, which is quite expensive, to encourage the housewife to purchase.

Fast Facts Herbs and Spices: Master Foods and Somerset Cottage policies.

Van delivery service and merchandising reps help reduce out-of-stocks. *Master Foods has 46 varieties of herbs and spices* and claims the biggest share of the dollar market. Master Foods started a retail van delivery service for herbs and spices and raised sales of some of its products by over 50 percent in a year. One reason it started this service was the many out-of-stocks which retailers suffered when stocking over 100 items. Master Foods says most major chains now stock the company's range. Some use the van delivery service and some the company's merchandising service (company reps bring stock from the store's back room and restock the shelves themselves). Retailers usually carry either a two-shelf spice rack of 18–24 varieties, or a four-shelf rack of 46 varieties. *Master Foods estimates the market to be worth about $6 million at retail prices,* including all herbs, spices, flavored sugar, seasoned salt, curry and mustard powder, pepper, and miscellaneous items such as meat tenderizer and monosodium glutamate. White pepper is the biggest commodity in the market. Parsley flakes, garlic salt, and garnishes are also volume-sellers.

The market is in three segments: (1) health food sales, which include mainly herbs and spices packed by the health food stores in cellophane packs; *(2) cannister and packet sales* of traditional herbs and spices such as peppers, cinnamon, and nutmeg, and *(3) the shaker-pack ranges* produced by Master Foods, McCormick's, and Somerset Cottage. Master Foods says the first two segments provide high sales but low margins. The shaker packs sell fewer units but have the highest dollar sales because of high unit price, and also have the highest margins and highest quality image. The market has good potential for expanding its distribution through butchers, health shops, and delicatessens, apart from grocery outlets. As people become more conscious of herbs and spices, cookbook sales, and the art of cooking, newspaper and women's magazine coverage of the subject are all rapidly increasing. Master Foods says the market is rising at 15–20 percent a year, and should increase its growth rate in the future years. The company is using such promotional materials as a wall chart for the kitchen listing the herbs and spices to use for certain dishes. The increasing number of continental restaurants in capital cities and major towns is making people more conscious of herbs and spices.

John Hemphill, managing director of Hemphill Herbs and Spices, of Dural, N.S.W., says his *Somerset Cottage* range has maintained a steady growth rate in the 15 years he has been in business. There are now also more volume-selling lines. Many people use a jar of chives, onion flakes, garlic powder, or parsley flakes in a week or a fortnight.

We have had a demand for larger sizes in these lines and did introduce them. But they weren't popular with the supermarkets who felt they were too bulky."

Items such as nutmeg, ground ginger, and cinnamon continued to be bought at rare intervals because they last so long. Dried herbs have been the fastest-

EXHIBIT 3   *(concluded)*

such as oregano, sage, and marjoram are just beginning to be noticed and are growing segment of the market.

> Spices have always been around, but herbs really jumping ahead. Certain spices sell better in some areas than others. For instance, in the higher-income suburbs, herbs sell better, and in the poorer areas, items like garlic salt and onion salt sell well.

Other minor brands of spices available in Australia include Lawry's seasoning, Tasty, John Ball, McKenzie's, and Harper's.

EXHIBIT 4   Discussions with Buyers in the Grocery Trade

Meeting 1

McCormick's has approximately 50–60 listings and without doubt had good control of the sections. The stores can adjust listings by deleting items which are listed at the head office. They also have a form on which to request new products. These are then sent to the head office and if the head office receives several requests, they usually list the product. He summarized the effectiveness of McCormick's by the following points:

1. Thorough approach to the market.
2. Good service.
3. Good lines.
4. Good stands and organization of the category for the first time.

Spice Island apparently tried to come into the market a couple of years ago, but were not thorough enough and failed.

The buyer indicated that frankly at this stage, he would not add another range because of the money tied up in relation to the return. This may be a point that would have to be clearly defined. He estimates a return of 6–7 times a year. He also pointed out that McCormick's did good stock rotation and gross profit return was satisfactory at approximately 25–30 percent. He was by no means suggesting that it would be easy or that his store group would even accept another line. He indicated that Master Foods' spices were only being stocked in three of his stores and that they had them for six months and nothing much had come of it. Apparently, Master Foods has been aggressive with its new line for only a couple of years. He did indicate that service and supply might be a bit of a problem with McCormick's and left the door open on the basis that with a proper program, they might well be interested as long as the price was right.

Meeting 2

The buyer indicated that his group is extremely happy with McCormick's. The market was developing satisfactorily and the gross margins were in the region of 30–35 percent. He indicated that specialist stores might be interested in another line of spices.

Apparently, his group tends to be somewhat diffident with suppliers and he was not at all keen to see me, so I was limited to a discussion on the telephone. After discussion with him, he somewhat backed off and suggested that the market might be accessible, but he was not at all optimistic.

EXHIBIT 4   *(concluded)*

Meeting 3

This buyer indicated that the spice section, in his judgment, was becoming proliferated with too many brands. He agreed that there are essentially four elements: the bag; another section which we call the "tube section"; a third section, the regular McCormick-type product; and a fourth section, McCormick's gourmet which is also like Master Foods' product. It was apparent that this buyer intended to thin out the spice section and remove one of the major items, but it will not be McCormick's for whom he has a lot of respect as a result of their selling in the past few years.

He indicated that white pepper is a very big item by far and the tube product sells extremely well. There is a low margin on this line of between 16 and 18 percent. On the other items, there is a 25–30 percent markup. In his opinion, the market is overpriced and really, McCormick's should be selling between 20–25 percent markup.

He indicated that to do in-store demonstrations, which is quite good to move products in the spice section, costs $100 a store for demonstrator space. In addition to that, one has to pay for the demonstrators and the material.

It was obvious this buyer knew his business and was very willing to talk. He indicated by direct question that getting into the spice market may be difficult, but he believed that with the right pricing and promotion that it would not be impossible. However, this is in relation to the fact that the present spice market is probably already overserviced by a number of spice companies.

EXHIBIT 5   Visits to Grocery Stores

Store 1 Spice section is 9 feet—6 feet of McCormick's and 3 feet of Master Foods—4 shelves of each of them.

Store 2 Six feet of shelving—3 of Master Foods and 3 of McCormick's. The gourmet 1½ ounce McCormick's was 55 cents. Cinnamon sticks gourmet were 99 cents.

Store 3 Spice section 6 feet, 3 shelves—1 shelf gourmet and the rest regular McCormick's. Regular peppercorns, 35 cents and gourmet, 53 cents. Regular size is 1¼ ounce and gourmet size is 1⅞ ounce.

Store 4 Spice section has only 1 shelf of gourmet and 2 shelves of regular—6 foot section. The 4-shelf unit has 37 varieties only.

Store 5 Store was approximately 10,000–15,000 square feet in size.

Two brands were represented, primarily Master Foods and McCormick's. The Master Foods shelves were 80 percent empty. A third brand was Somerset Cottage. The shelves were made of metal with shelf dividers. Division of shelves was as follows:

Master Foods:	4 shelves
Somerset Cottage:	3 shelves
McCormick's:	3 shelves

EXHIBIT 5   *(continued)*

The length of the shelves were approximately 3 feet each.
Shelf prices were as follows:

Master Foods:	Ground cinnamon	35 cents
	Sage	28 cents
	White pepper	40 cents
McCormick's:	Garlic salt	33 cents
	Garlic powder	55 cents

The McCormick's products were regular line, not the gourmet line.

Store 6 McCormick's had a 2-foot section; Master Foods a 3-foot section; and Somerset Cottage, a 3-foot section. Again, Master Foods was very poorly serviced, but McCormick's and Somerset Cottage were in better condition. In the case of Master Foods and Somerset Cottage, there were 4 shelves for each and McCormick's had 7 shelves. Prices were as follows:

McCormick's:	Garlic powder	49 cents
	Garlic salt	29 cents
Somerset Cottage:	Garlic powder	55 cents
	Garlic salt	38 cents

Store 7 This was a basement operation, similar to a North American department store gourmet section. This was in downtown Sydney, a part of a complex called Centre Point which is a very upscale shopping center on several levels with stores all around. The food section in the store was quite messy, but may have been due to delivery that day. It had all the makings of a typical downtown store, so did not check prices on spices which might well have been different than the norm.

The spice section was around a pillar and included McCormick's gourmet jars, regular tins and bottles, as well as Master Foods. It looked to me as if organization of the total spice section would not have been amiss in this store.

The Master Foods' and the McCormick's stands were a little more modeled on the English-type stand about 3 feet each with 7 shelves made of tin, though the McCormick's was a gravity-fed metal affair looking like wood. Underneath each stand were two cupboards similar to the U.K. stands that we use. The McCormick's 3-foot stand for the regular McCormick's product was a metal stand of white chrome. The single-shelf McCormick's spice racks containing probably 6 or 7 bottles were also available in this store—priced at $8.95 each.

Store 8 8,000 square feet. Six feet of McCormick's—3 feet regular, 3 feet gourmet, 5 shelves double stacked of the regular and also about 6 feet of baskets of tub products.

Store 9 Five checkouts; this store has about 2,000–3,000 square feet. This store has Master Foods' and McCormick's gourmet, as well as regular—total of about 9 feet.

Store 10 It has 8 checkouts and is approximately 7,000 square foot. It is a clean store, much more like the regular American supermarket.

Nine feet of of spices, 8 shelves high—including McCormick's gourmet, 2 shelves

EXHIBIT 5   *(concluded)*

on the top; Master Foods, 3 shelves; and then baskets, 2 shelves below with the salt underneath. McCormick's gourmet is gravity fed.

Store 11 A little store about 4,000 or 5,000 feet. A small Master Foods spice section—3 feet; only 4 shelves. Also a McCormick's section.

Store 12 About 10,000 square feet. Spice section is about 6 feet, very poorly serviced. McCormick's gourmet and regular.

Store 13 A department store with a food section. The section runs about 500–600 square feet.

   Small spice section, very empty—just the regular McCormick's; 3 foot, 2 shelves, only.

Store 14 There is a 3-foot McCormick's stand with shelves gravity fed of the gourmet and 4 shelves doubled up with the regular underneath.

Store 15 There was a complete gondola, with spices all the way around with gravity fed McCormick's gourmet bottles. Below that were McCormick's regular items.

EXHIBIT 6   The Spice Market at the Retail Level (Australian dollars)

	Bags/tubes	*Regular*	*Gourmet*	*Total $s*
Dollars	3,000,000	2,000,000	1,500,000	6,500,000
Percent	46 percent	31 percent	23 percent	100 percent
Average unit price	19 percent	29 percent	49 percent	—
Trade margin percent	12–16 percent	22 percent	30 percent	20 percent
Volume dozens	1,300,000	575,000	255,000	2,130,000
Percent volume	61 percent	27 percent	12 percent	100 percent
Profit to trade dollars	420,000	440,000	450,000	1,310,000
Profit percent	32 percent	34 percent	34 percent	100 percent

EXHIBIT 7 Cost Price Comparisons—Schwartz and McCormick (Australian dollars)

Spices	Schwartz Regular			McCormick Regular				McCormick Gourmet			
	Ounces	Wholesale Price*	Retail Price at 32 Percent Trade Margin	Ounces	Wholesale Price	Retail Price	Trade Markup (percent)	Ounces	Wholesale Price	Retail Price	Trade Markup (percent)
Black pepper ground	1¼	3.18	0.39	1	2.24	0.25	24%	1½	4.56	0.55	30.9%
Cinnamon ground	1⅛	5.63	0.69	1¼	4.40	0.49	24	1¾	8.20	0.99	31.0
Curry powder mild	1 9/16	2.37	0.29	1⅛	3.16	0.35	26	2	3.72	0.45	31.0
Paprika	1⅜	3.67	0.45	1⅛	3.52	0.39	26	1¾	4.72	0.57	31.0
Bay leaves whole	3/16	7.26	0.89	3/16	3.52	0.39	26	¼	9.68	1.17	31.0
Nutmeg whole	1⅛	4.00	0.49		n.a.			1½	5.56	0.65	28.7
Garlic salt	2 13/16	4.00	0.49	2	2.96	0.33	24	3	4.56	0.55	30.9
Onion salt	2½	4.00	0.49	1¾	2.96	0.33	24	2¾	4.56	0.55	30.9
Black pepper whole	1¼	2.86	0.35	1¼	3.16	0.35	26	1⅞	4.40	0.53	30.8
Parsley	3/16	3.18	0.39	⅛	2.96	0.33	24	¼	4.40	0.53	30.8
Oregano	¼	2.37	0.29		n.a.			7/16	3.72	0.46	31.0
Red pepper	1⅛	2.69	0.33	1	3.52	0.39	26	1⅞	4.40	0.53	30.8
Allspice	1 5/16	5.63	0.69	1½	5.32	0.59	25	1¾	7.36	0.89	31.0

* Price per dozen.

minimal, but various promotions such as spice rack offers and recipe suggestions are frequently used by the major companies.

The Trip to Australia

A variety of information was collected by Bureau on his visit to the Australian market. In overall terms, the vice president felt that Schwartz should contemplate entering the Australian market but had to sell the board of directors on the concept. As well as an entry decision, Bureau had also to think of a marketing strategy which showed the best potential for success in this market. For as his investigations had shown him, the market

was "anticipated to grow approximately 20 percent per year in coming years" (see Exhibit 3), but some industry sources felt that "there was some indication that the spice market was proliferating with too many brands" (see Exhibit 4).

With a board meeting one week away, Bureau began to closely evaluate the data he had collected on the Australian market (see Exhibits 1 through 7).

_____

Source: This case was prepared by Professor Philip Rosson and Janet Forrest of Dalhousie University, Halifax N.S., Canada as a basis for class discussion rather than to illustrate either effective or ineffective handling of an administrative situation.

Case 3–5

A JOB IN RIO DE JANEIRO

Pete Atherton has a difficult decision to make. He is 42 years old and has been with Sentrics, an electronics firm, for 18 years. He has advanced to his present position of sales manager for the Southern California region. He is married with three children—a daughter, 17 years old, who is editor of a high school newspaper and active in many clubs and organizations; a son, 15, who is on the school tennis team; and another son, who is just starting junior high school. His wife, Cathy, is working as a real estate saleswoman in an active real estate market.

Pete has been offered a job as the sales manager for Sentrics in Rio de Janeiro in conjunction with a new plant being built in Brazil. Although Sentrics has plants in Scotland, England, and West Germany, this will be its first plant in Latin America. They need Pete's managerial expertise to assure that the Brazil-

ian sales force effectively sells the product to industrial users. This is especially important since Sentrics is entering the Brazilian market with a direct investment rather than a joint venture, which is a common entry strategy of many of its competitors.

While the company does not require its managers to work abroad in order to be eligible for promotion to top executive positions, the foreign assignment would provide Pete with more visibility than in his present position, since the Brazilian venture would be closely watched. The job itself would be primarily a lateral transfer rather than a promotion, with no increase in salary. However, the company pays the costs for comparable housing and living expenses.

The foreign assignment in Rio would be for at least two years, but probably not more than three years. Although the company has no formal training program for people going abroad, an individual is encouraged to set up an overseas learning experience (i.e., language training, cultural schooling, and so forth) which Sentrics would pay for.

Pete is having a hard time making a decision because of conflicting factors. On the one hand, he would like to go abroad for a few years since he has never been to Brazil. His wife is quite supportive of this new job opportunity but the children do not want to leave their friends and social activities. Also, it would probably be necessary to send the children to an English-speaking school for them to get a comparable education. In fact, his company will pay for them to attend a private

school anywhere Pete wants. What also worries Pete is that he likes Southern California and has made many close friends in the area where he lives. There would be no guarantee he would return to a job in Southern California after his work in Rio. Pete has been putting a decision off, but needs to decide this week about whether to take the sales manager's position in Brazil.

Source: An Update of "A Job in Grenoble," a case written by Gregory M. Gazda and Mary J. Molenaar, University of San Diego, appearing originally in the fifth edition of this text.

QUESTIONS

1. What would you do if you were in Pete's situation? Why?
2. Which factors do you think are the most important ones to consider in making the decision?
3. You have been asked to help Pete get prepared for his journey, if he goes.
   a. List the potential problems he and his family will probably face.
   b. Make a list of things Pete should do to prepare himself for the new position.
   c. Make a list of the things the family should do to prepare to live in Rio de Janeiro for two years or longer.

Case 3–6

FRESHTASTE, INC.—MARKETING MILK STERILIZERS IN JAPAN

Freshtaste, Inc.*, a subsidiary of a U.S. manufacturing firm located in the Pacific Northwest, holds the patents for and a working model of a machine that sterilizes milk. A major advantage of sterilized milk over pasteurized is that once sterilized and properly

* A fictitious company name.

packaged, the milk can be stored at room temperature for up to three months. There are several processes on the market for sterilizing milk, but the Freshtaste process is distinctively different from all others because it produces a sterilized milk with a taste that cannot be distinguished from fresh milk. In fact, the brand name Freshtaste was selected because it highlights the distinctive advantage this process for sterilizing milk has over all others. Other processes produce sterile milk products with a taste that is best described as cooked or slightly burned and which produces a cloying thickness that lingers after the milk is swallowed. A large number of milk drinkers object to that taste sensation. Scientists and food engineers claim the peculiar flavor or after-taste is caused when milk touches a hot surface as it is being sterilized. Milk is sterilized by raising the temperature of the milk to between 135° and 150°C (275° to 302°F) to eliminate all bacteria. When the sterilized milk is vacuum-packed in a manner that shuts out all light and air, the milk can last six weeks to three months at room temperature. Once opened and refrigerated, the milk has twice the shelf life of pasteurized milk.

The Freshtaste process sterilizes the milk as it falls in film-like sheets through a vat. Unlike other sterilizing processes where the milk is boiled and touches hot surfaces, the Freshtaste process prevents the milk from touching any surface hotter than itself. The milk is sterilized by an ultra-high temperature steam virtually while it is in midair. This eliminates the cooked taste that many people find objectionable. Several scientifically run blind taste tests indicate that consumers cannot taste the difference between Freshtaste sterilized milk and regular milk.

A blind taste test in 1980 at the Diary Marketing Forum at a midwestern university showed that 62 percent of the milk tasters incorrectly identified sterile milk as regular, homogenized whole milk and that 54 percent of the evaluators identified regular, homogenized whole milk as a sterile whole milk. On a scale of one (disliked extremely) to nine (liked extremely), the Freshtaste sterile milk had an overall acceptance rating of seven. This rating was the highest acceptance score for any product tested at the Forum in the last several years. The process also can be used for juices and beer or any other liquid. Canned juices currently have a cooked flavor, but we are accustomed to it so we find no objection.

Freshtaste, Inc. has had an operating model of a milk sterilizer for the last three years, but has not been successful in selling the idea to U.S. dairies. Because other sterilizing processes have produced milk with unacceptable flavors and textures, U.S. dairy companies have been reluctant to invest in yet another new process. This reluctance has been reinforced by the technical requirements for the container. The container must be completely airtight for the sterilized milk to have maximum shelf life. To date, the only true airtight containers are sealed cans or glass containers. While the cost of cans for juices has been accepted by consumers over the years, the dairy industry has always opted for the least-expensive containers, first using reusable bottles and now disposable cartons. They have used less-expensive containers to offset the higher cost of refrigeration required to keep the unsterilized milk from spoiling. The use of glass or can containers for sterilized milk would make the product too costly to effectively compete with regular milk even though there are some major cost advantages of sterilized milk. For example, warehousing and delivery costs of fresh milk are the greatest single costs in the industry; the product must be refrigerated from the plant until the customer actually consumes the product. Freshtaste executives say the transportation and energy savings realized from not having to refrigerate during the marketing and distribution of sterilized milk could reduce the total cost of milk in the long run. Since most states require milk to be sold within a few days after it is processed, additional cost savings would result from reduction of spoilage and returns. Pennsylvania, for example, requires milk to be sold within nine days after processing and New York allows only four days; all out-of-date milk (a substantial amount) must be destroyed.

The packaging is a major obstacle. With glass or cans too expensive, the only potentially usable package is a six-layered container constructed of paper, polyethylene, and aluminum foil sold under the name Seal-Pak.[1] This container permits a vacuum-packed process and it is assumed to be completely germ-proof. It has several disadvantages, however: it requires scissors to open, has a nonresealable pouring spout that could create problems for the consumer, and it is about 50 percent more costly than the traditional paper milk containers now in use for fresh milk.

Because of the reasons outlined, Freshtaste, Inc. feels it must wait until an acceptable container is developed to sell equipment in the United States. The use of sterilized milk in the United States may be minimal because of the nationwide network of refrigeration already available for fresh milk handling; thus, the company wants to look elsewhere for potential markets. It feels that markets where the per capita consumption of fresh milk is lower than in the United States but is growing might be effective markets for the introduction of the sterilized milk process. Eventually, the Freshtaste executives feel there will be a market for their equipment in the United States but the time needed for development of that market could be longer than they are willing to invest in at this stage. They are considering marketing the milk machinery in countries with expanding milk consumption.

Initially both Europe and Japan were considered as possible markets for the Freshtaste sterilizer, but it was decided to bypass Europe even though sterilized milk had been introduced in Sweden in 1961 and had spread rapidly to Europe during the mid-1960s. Today, sterilized milk accounts for about 16 percent of total milk consumption in Europe, but the degree of distribution varies considerably according to country. In Italy and West Germany, for example, where the consumption of sterilized milk is fairly high, the production of regular milk is low and most sterilized milk is packaged in paper containers and is available in stores and supermarkets. In other European countries where there are low consumption rates of sterilized milk, such as Britain and Norway, regular fresh milk production is high and is usually bottled and sold on a home-delivery basis. The sterilized milk currently being sold in Europe does not use the Freshtaste process and thus has the distinctive flavor problem that Freshtaste would not have. In Europe, fresh milk is produced in abundance, is reasonably priced, and most of the advantages associated with sterilized milk do not seem to be important. Thus, the decision was made not to enter Europe at this time.

In Japan, however, the situation is different. Consumption rates are increasing, and production of fresh milk is somewhat limited. It appears that there may be some significant advantages in sterilized milk for this market. Exhibit 1 presents some historical data on milk consumption in Japan, the United Kingdom, and the United States.

EXHIBIT 1 Milk Consumption—Japan, United Kingdom, and United States (kg per head per year)

	Japan	United Kingdom	United States
1968	24	147	129
1975	28	142	140
1978	32	139	136
1980	35	135	127
1983	36	133	122
1985	36	131	129

SOURCE: *Eurostat: Basic Statistics of the Community*, 25th ed. (Luxembourg: Statistical Office of the European Community, 1988).

---

[1] A fictitious brand name.

Japanese Market

Prior to World War II, Japan had one of the world's lowest per capita consumption rates of milk. Since World War II, Japanese consumption of milk has increased considerably even though it does not have an extensive dairy industry. On the surface, it seems that Japan offers several opportunities for the successful marketing of Freshtaste sterilizers. For one, there are companies already in Japan with sterilizing equipment that have achieved some degree of acceptance even with the taste problems. Freshtaste executives feel their process is so superior in taste to all others that there would be no real competition. Sterilized milk has been produced in Japan for some years for use on ocean-going ships and on isolated islands. Nestlé Japan first introduced sterilized milk but its share in total milk sales has never been significant (see Exhibits 2 and 3).

One reason for the poor acceptance may

EXHIBIT 2 Diffusion of Sterlized Milk in Europe and Japan

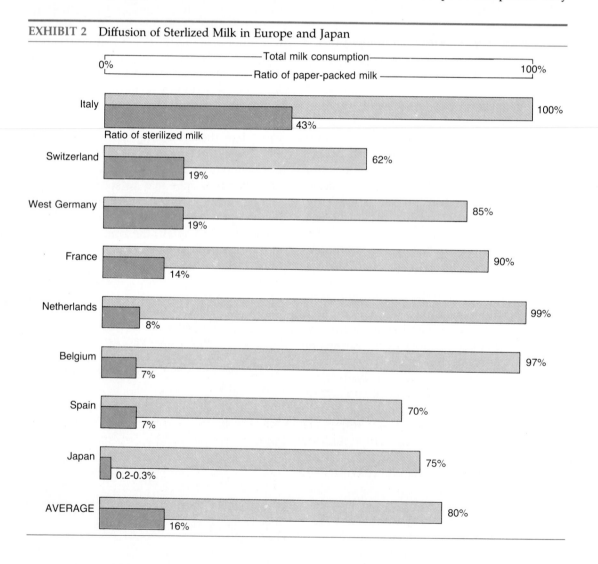

EXHIBIT 3   How Japanese Consumers Buy Milk

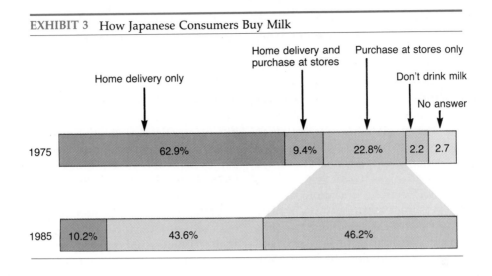

be due to the lack of effective educational advertising. Japanese consumers have shied away from sterilized milk bearing a production date a few weeks old. In addition, milk processors and supermarkets have remained cautious because of the Health and Welfare Administration's regulations affecting all types of milk. Distributors and outlets are required to keep all types of milk, including sterilized milk, at temperatures of 10°C or below.

Even though the diffusion rate for sterilized milk had not been extremely rapid since its introduction, rates of consumption and potential demand for milk appeared so high that Freshtaste, Inc. made a financial commitment in early 1985 to enter the Japanese market. Freshtaste knew that Nagano Consumers Cooperative, Japan's largest dairy farming coop, and Daigaku, Inc., the nation's largest supermarket chain, were to introduce sterilized milk in 1985. They felt that if this introduction was successful it would stimulate demand for sterilized milk. Further, since the Freshtaste sterilizer was so superior to any on the market, the demand created for Freshtaste sterilizers would increase as a result of the Nagano/Daigaku introduction. Additional market planning was underway by Freshtaste, Inc. when a heated controversy over sterilized milk developed in August 1985, with questions ranging from consumer safety to the possible impact on Japan's dairy farming. The Nagano Consumers Cooperative and Daigaku, Inc. triggered the debate when they started full-scale marketing of sterilized milk, in a joint venture with Kimura Milk Industry Company and Seibu Milk Products Company, two of the three largest dairy product companies.

The Consumer's Union of Japan had planned to endorse the sale and consumption of sterilized milk but abruptly changed its mind and came out against the product because of its concern about sterilized milk's safety. The union pointed out that sterilized milk cannot be considered as "fresh milk any longer, but rather is a factory product and high temperatures may alter nutritional quality." Moreover, it worried that ethylene-polymer may be released into the milk from the polyethylene lining used in the container.

Consumer attitudes were mixed: on one hand, many housewives do not see the need for sterilized milk in Japan because almost everyone shops everyday; on the other hand, many housewives expressed the opinion that "sterilized milk is richer than regular milk and is much more convenient because it can be stocked in the packs on the kitchen shelves and opened whenever wanted." The price of sterilized milk is about 10 percent more than regular milk, but it may still be considered more economical because of the lower spoilage rate.

The Consumer Science Association, a federation of 35 consumer organizations, mostly in Tokyo, supported sterilized milk as a means to boost per capita milk consumption, still only one fifth that of Britain. The association had filed a request with the Health and Welfare Administry for removal of the present ordinance requiring all milk to be refrigerated throughout distribution routes and in retail stores so that redundant refrigeration costs could be eliminated.

Diary farmers were also split over the issue of sterilized milk; those in areas neighboring big cities are dead-set against the distribution of sterilized milk. They claimed that since sterilized milk can be shipped long distances without refrigeration, small-scale dairy farming near large urban areas would be all but destroyed by a massive inflow of milk from Hokkaido, the principal dairy farming area of Japan.

The Consumer's Union also claimed that diffusion of sterilized milk from Hokkaido could destroy small dairy farms in other regions, eventually opening the doors to low-priced milk from abroad. Hokkaido has a very sparse population and about 87 percent of all milk produced there is currently sold for processing into butter, cheese, and other milk products which bring lower prices than milk sold for drinking. Thus, if dairy farmers in Hokkaido sterilized their milk they could sell more milk at higher prices to populated areas of Japan, as the market for sterilized milk began to grow.

The opposition to sterilized milk by dairy farmers' cooperatives resulted in one co-op in Kyushu actually cutting shipments 30 percent to Seibu Milk Products Company's local factory in protest against sterilized milk production. The ban was lifted when Seibu Milk Company promised not to increase the quantity of sterilized milk presently being produced. Two other major milk products companies made the same promise to the Central Dairy Council of Agricultural Cooperatives Association.

As the controversy heated up, regional representatives of the Japanese Cooperative Consumer Union, a nationwide federation of 620 consumer cooperatives, met on September 16, 1985, to establish an official policy. The union decided that it would not permit member cooperatives to sell sterilized milk except in special cases. They criticized sterilized milk supporters for neglecting the importance of local, small-scale dairy farming which supplies organic substances indispensable to agriculture. This point will become increasingly more critical as the growing awareness of the alleged harm of overdependence on chemical fertilizers spreads. Moreover, the union said that since the construction of processing plants for sterilized milk required large-scale investment, the distribution of sterilized milk could lead to a big-business monopoly of the dairy industry and hurt consumer interest in the long run.

The Nagano Milk Cooperative is one of the few co-ops that maintains regular home-delivery of fresh milk. One reason they began producing sterilized milk was to relieve employees of early morning deliveries and to lower distribution costs. They expected initially to have to deliver the sterilized milk only once a week and eventually once a month, compared to every-other-day delivery for regular milk at the present time.

Milk specialty stores, whose main business is to make daily home deliveries of bottled milk and some paper-packaged milk, also spoke out against sterilized milk. They claimed the convenience of the present fresh-milk package and the home delivery system had helped spread the milk-drinking habit among the Japanese. Some worried that switching to once-a-week deliveries of sterilized milk would cut down on milk consumption. The fact is that the milk specialty stores have been losing market share ever since supermarkets started selling milk in cartons at lower prices. The distribution of sterilized milk could very well mean the end of milk specialty stores, and they are well aware of this possibility.

To further complicate the issue, the major advantage of sterilized milk, its long shelf life, is wasted because of the ordinance requiring all milk to be refrigerated. The supermarket industry believes, however, that it is only a matter of time before the requirement to refrigerate sterilized milk will be lifted. But, the Health and Welfare Administration and the Administration of Agriculture and Forestry have indicated they would wait and see how well sterilized milk is accepted by consumers before taking any action. As a result of the uproar caused by the different groups, sterilized milk's share of total factory output for milk reached only 2 percent by the end of 1985. (Forecasts before the resistance predicted a 6-to-8 percent share by 1986.)

When the controversy developed over sterilized milk, Freshtaste was about ready to approach a Japanese firm to begin discussing the possibility of a joint venture to introduce the sterilizers into Japan. The company was quite surprised by the reaction of the Japanese. It had not studied the market very thoroughly before getting involved so it decided to terminate all negotiations and to pull back to reexamine the initial decision. You have been asked to reevaluate the situation in Japan and to make a recommendation to the president of Freshtaste, Inc.

The president wants to see a preliminary report on the seriousness of the recent market reaction. Further, in light of the recent developments, he is interested in determining what additional information and research are necessary to complete a thorough feasibility study. The report should include: (1) all the major resistances to the acceptance of sterilized milk and the relative importance of each by consumers, dairy farms, retailers and other distribution middlemen, and milk cooperatives; (2) some general idea of the strategies necessary to overcome the resistances identified in item 1 and to develop a successful marketing program; (3) a rough idea of the time it will take to penetrate the market; and (4) based on your preliminary analysis and the data in items 1, 2, and 3, a recommendation on whether or not the company should even attempt a marketing effort in Japan. Whether your response is to market or not, be prepared to defend your position.

Case 3–7

MEDICO-DEVICES, INC.—OXYGEN CONCENTRATOR

You were recommended to the president of a small company, Medico-Devices, Inc. as someone who could help the company get started in international marketing. You were invited to meet with the president and general sales manager to find exactly what was needed and whether or not you could help. The major points covered at the meeting were as follows:

The Product

The Aire-I oxygen concentrator is basically a simple device. It consists of a motor-powered compressor that forces the ambient air through sieve beds containing a chemical that extracts the nitrogen, dust, and bacteria from room air; it delivers 95-percent pure oxygen at a rate of one to five liters per minute (LPM) to patients who must have oxygen because of some type of respiratory illness.

All oxygen concentrators in the United States are essentially the same except for appearance, compressor, sieve-bed material, or assembly. A basic concentrator consists of the following components:

1. A compressor that must move a minimum of 100 liters of air per minute through the system at 9 to 15 pounds of pressure.
2. An air-cooling device to lower the temperature of the compressed air since the performance level of the molecular sieve is reduced at high operating temperatures.
3. A system of solenoid valves to direct air into the sieve beds so that accumulated nitrogen is purged from the system.
4. A measurement system to regulate oxygen flow for the patient coupled with required alarms to indicate malfunction.

The major advantage Aire-I has over the competition is its aluminum sieve beds designed to eliminate the granulation of the sieve material thus giving it an unlimited life span. PVC is used in competitive units that have an average life of two years. The Medico-Devices sieve beds should last indefinitely if excessive moisture is not allowed to contaminate the material within the beds.

A remote patient control unit allows patients to be 70 feet from the unit yet have all operating controls at their fingertips. A 30-foot nasal cannula (tube) extends the overall distance to 100 feet. Other product features:

1. Operating costs are 60 percent less than competitive products.
2. The Aire-I produces up to 5 liters of 95 percent oxygen per minute.
3. The unit weighs 20 percent less and is 15 percent smaller than other units.
4. All components are accessible and service personnel may enter the components within minutes.
5. Internal adjustments require minimal training.
6. Any component can be replaced within less than an hour of service time.

The Aire-I weighs 94 pounds and operates on 115v, 60Hz (see Exhibit 1 for product specifications). It is designed to operate continuously but needs servicing about every six weeks. Servicing is mostly preventive in nature although the sieve beds may need replacing to ensure maximum output if the concentrator is operated under high humidity conditions. Operating history indicates oxygen output under the most adverse humidity never drops below three liters of 80 percent pure oxygen, although for some patients this would be insufficient oxygen output. Each unit has two sieve beds weighing about three pounds each. Replacement is simple, requiring only the removal of two clamps. The sieve beds contain the chemical that filters the nitrogen out of the ambient air.

Company records show the effective life of a machine to be about three years; that is, after three years, the compressor and motor have a high incidence of malfunction. Company policy is to overhaul machines after three years at the owner's expense. An overhaul generally includes a new compressor and motor and new sieve beds if necessary.

The Problem

Medico-Devices, Inc. is a small manufacturing company. Its product line consists of several medical devices one of which is the oxygen

---

EXHIBIT 1   AIRE-I Oxygen Concentrator

Specifications

Overall System

Output Flow (oxygen enriched air):	0–5 LPM.
Oxygen concentration (±3%):	1–5 LPM 95%.
Power consumption:	330 watts (approx.)

System Operating Pressures:	—Proto-Flo system operates at between 9–11 psig. —Low system pressure means fewer leaks; less purging noise and increased component life.

Main Unit

Dimensions:	Height: 26", Length: 17¼", Width: 18½".
Weight:	94 lbs.
Power Requirements:	115 volts, 60 Hz.
Safety Features:	—Thermal cut-out to prevent overheating of drive motor. —H.E.P.A. filter to provide bacteria-free oxygen. —Warning circuit to indicate power failure. —Warning circuit to indicate when air intake is blocked.
Portability:	Large casters on base and convenient top handle simplify movement of main unit.

Patient Control Unit

Weight:	3 lbs. 6 oz.
Power Requirements:	15 Volt DC
Safety Features:	Bacteria filter provides sterile oxygen.
Indicators:	—Power on/off. —Auxiliary power on. —Power interrupt. —Audible power interrupt warning.
Output Pressure:	5 psig.

A compressor that pushes far beyond expectations. The Aire-I's compressor utilizes a unique low pressure/high flow system. Air volume exceeds 300 litres per minute. The special pump design facilitates easy and fast servicing.

There is something very smart about simple valves. Much of the Aire-I's simplicity is due to its deflector valve, a device which eliminates solenoids and venturi problems. The advanced design integrates the deflector valve with the compressor and motor for peak oxygen production efficiency and rapid nitrogen purging from sieve beds.

Cross-over value. The cross-over valve is also specially designed to ensure balanced sieve beds for improved oxygen production and simplified repairs—if ever needed.

Patients have more control over their lives. The portable patient control unit with controls and patient alerts, includes an audible alarm. It remains within reach of the patient even though he may be as much as 70 feet from the air pumping system. Life is easier for the patient. And oxygen use is safer.

What's good for the patient is good for the dealer. The many design features of the Aire-I which make the unit more convenient, efficient and reliable for patients also result in simplified service requirements. All components are easily accessible. Service time is minimal.

concentrator. The company employs about 150 in manufacturing and has been in business about five years. It has made a modest profit for the last two years. The company has other products but wants to sell only the oxygen concentrator internationally. The company has about 25 percent of the U.S. market (about 20,000 units per year) and has the capacity to produce another 5,000 to 10,000 units in its present facilities. Since the unit is assembled from component parts, production can be increased quickly if demand exceeds present plant capacity. With the exceptions of the cabinet, one special valve, and the sieve beds, the concentrator's parts are available off the shelf from a variety of sources. The basic technology cannot be protected by patents so many small assemblers have been attracted to the market by the initial high margins available in the U.S. market.

Sales have grown rapidly over the last five years but the company believes they have about topped out and forecast sales of 20,000 to 25,000 units per year over the next few years with little growth. Although the total market is projected to grow 10 percent per year, there are many other companies producing the oxygen concentrator that has made price competition so severe the company feels it would be unprofitable to attempt to expand their market share at this time. Medico-Devices's Aire-I is more efficient than others due to the patentable construction of its sieve beds. In spite of its more efficient product and relatively lower costs of manufacturing (the company believes its costs are 10 to 15 percent lower than competitor's), it does not feel it has the resources necessary to engage in a price battle for market share. (See Exhibit 2.)

The strategy is to sell the Aire-I as a premium-priced, quality product, and maintain a market presence while others engage in price competition. When the timing is right,

EXHIBIT 2   Aire-I Costs per Unit (5,000–10,000 units)

Parts	$380
Labor*	260
Quality Control	20
Packaging	15

* Based on labor assembly costs at current average rates of $11.80 per hour including benefits.

the company plans to step up marketing efforts and expand market share slowly. Management realizes this could be a high-risk strategy unless it can enter the European market where margins are high and there is less price competition. The company wants to capture a share of that emerging market while waiting for the U.S. market to settle down; there is evidence that the market is beginning to settle out with 10 companies leaving the market in the last six months.

As a result of its unique design, the Aire-I has a lower operating cost for the patient, requires less maintenance (sieve-bed replacement rarely necessary in the Aire-I versus a two-year replacement for the competition), and has lower overall weight (94 pounds versus 110 pounds for the competition).

The Market

Most patients in the United States using an oxygen concentrator suffer from emphysema (the inability of the lungs to absorb sufficient oxygen from the ambient air requiring their air intake to be enriched with pure oxygen). There are other ailments where oxygen therapy is used but emphysema sufferers are by far the largest users. (Smoking and/or exposure to pollutants are the major causes of emphysema.) If a patient does not use an oxygen concentrator like the Aire-I, oxygen must be supplied from an oxygen cylinder. Convenience is the major advantage of the oxygen concentrator versus an oxygen cylinder. Cylinders are large and have to be replaced on a schedule whereas the Aire-I fits into a cabinet and looks like a piece of furniture. (See Exhibit 3.) If properly maintained, there is no problem of running out of oxygen as is the case with the cylinder. Furthermore, the detachable control station can be moved easily around a room giving the patient more flexibility than offered by a cylinder.

Medical candidates for home use of oxygen are those with heart disease, chronic obstructive pulmonary disease (COPD, which includes emphysema, severe asthma, and bronchitis) or a number of other pulmonary disorders that totally debilitate the patient unless ancillary oxygen is available. The oxygen is delivered to the patient through cannula inserted into the patient's nostrils.

In the United States, the market for patients eligible for home oxygen use is difficult to estimate accurately. However, there are 47 million Americans suffering from some type of lung ailment. In fact, respiratory disorders are the single most common reason people visit their physicians. The total number of persons in the United States suffering from COPD is 16 million. The American Lung Association puts these diseases into three major categories to account for most of that number.

Emphysema	2,000,000
Asthma	6,000,000
Chronic bronchitis	7,100,000

Medical studies indicate that smoking is a major contributor to emphysema. Heavy smokers suffer from some loss of lung function

EXHIBIT 3 The Aire-I

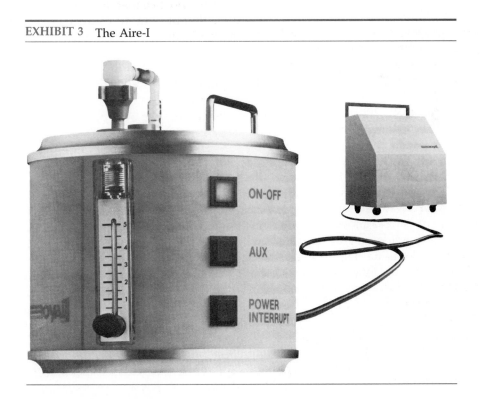

after 15 to 20 years of heavy smoking (heavy smoking is defined as more than one pack of cigarettes per day).

Medico-Devices, Inc. and most other suppliers of concentrators sell directly to distributors who lease or rent to patients. In the United States, there are approximately 11,000 medical-equipment companies handling oxygen concentrators. Trade shows are an important source of contacts for potential customers.

Patients rent the machine from hospitals, pharmacies, respiratory therapists, medical-equipment supply houses, and other companies specializing in medical equipment. In the United States, oxygen can be supplied only if the patient has a prescription for therapeutic oxygen therapy from a medical doctor.

Competition

Domestic prices have been driven down over the last 18 months. Machines comparable to the Aire-I ranged in price from $1,200 to $1,500, f.o.b. manufacturing plant, 18 months ago. Today, prices range from a low of $650 to $980 with average market price at $775, f.o.b. manufacturer. Once marketing and other costs are accounted for, there is little profit at today's market prices.

Company Plans

The company is interested in selling its product in foreign markets. It has no idea where to start selling or how to approach the process. The company does have a medical study that indicates emphysema exists throughout the world in about the same ratio to population distribution as in the United States. The research also revealed that oxygen therapy for emphysema and other COPD is not as widely used elsewhere in the world as in the United States.

The Problem—Part I

Since your first meeting with Medico-Devices was general and they were not sure what they needed, you agreed to present management with some guidelines. The idea is to give the company a format that shows the steps necessary to develop a successful export program, raises questions about exporting, and provides some ideas of the kinds of information (and possible sources) it needs to make a decision. Prepare a report for Medico-Devices.

The Problem—Part II

You have completed the report in Part I and the company is satisfied with your work; it wants you to continue to assist. It has been decided to enter the German market first; like most countries, Germany has its share of people with COPD. Further, oxygen therapy is at the early stages of acceptance within the German medical profession. You have agreed to do a complete market analysis and preliminary marketing plan for the German market for the Aire-I.

The Problem—Part III

Assume two years have elapsed since you completed Parts I and II and the company has had reasonable success in Germany. However, other U.S. companies have also sought markets in Europe and thus have driven the price down. The company must find ways to remain price competitive in both the U.S. market and in Europe. Prices have stabilized in the United States at an average price of $800. Prices in Germany have fallen from an average of $1,700 per unit to $1,050 today. Can you help the company?

Case 3–8

DEVELOPING A KODAK PROMOTIONAL PROGRAM IN JAPAN

Eastman Kodak Company is the largest manufacturer of cameras and other photographic equipment in the United States. Film sales constitute a substantial portion of the firm's $10.6 billion revenue worldwide. For over 30 years, Kodak has been selling film in Japan where sales are lower than in any other nation of its size. There are several reasons for this including tough competition from both Fuji Film and Sakura, who presently dominate the market.

Until 1978 there had been a sharp rise in Kodak's Japanese sales volume of color film in contrast to black and white. However, market share stabilized in 1988 and Kodak's actual share of the lucrative Japanese film market has not increased significantly since 1984. It has about 13 percent of the market, and remains third behind Fuji with 71 percent, and Konica Corporation with 16 percent. The Japanese film market is estimated at $1.77 billion. High tariffs on foreign film helped Fuji but much of the blame must be attributed to slow moving Kodak. In the spring of 1984, Kodak made the commitment to turn things around. The president directed the head of the international photographic division to have his marketing department assess current problems and opportunities and offer alternative solutions that could be put into action within three months. One of the major ideas that came forth was to focus all marketing effort on color film which is more vital to sales than black and white. Also, the following problems were singled out: the price gap that exists between Kodak color film and the competition, the huge advantage Fuji has in retail shelf space, lack of brand awareness, the fear of trial use, and the fact that, in many cases, consumers do not purchase Kodak color film unless it is recommended by the clerk in the shop. With no more than a handful of workers just four years ago and no technical staff to tailor its products to local tastes, sales languished. But Kodak's work force, mostly Japanese nationals, has climbed to 4,000 in the last four years.

Several steps have been taken to remedy the problem. Kodak recently opened a new technical center for customers and distributors, built a $74 million research laboratory, acquired a 10 percent stake in a Japanese camera manufacturer, and bought out the Japanese distributor of several important business products. Further, promotion and public relations people are working overtime to boost Kodak's visibility. A yellow Kodak blimp flies over Tokyo, flashing Kodak neon signs line main thoroughfares, and Kodak sponsors everything from children's judo championships to TV talk shows and an overseas sumo wrestling tournament.[1]

One major objective was to get dealers to promote Kodak color film more positively, thus increasing brand awareness and ultimately sales. To achieve this objective they proposed to narrow the price gap through price reduction, alter the price-value relationship, encourage trial use, and make those with little or no brand loyalty switch to Kodak. The company felt these efforts would be important in getting cooperation from the re-

---

[1] "Kodak Escalates War with Fuji by Opening Japan Lab," *The Asian Wall Street Journal*, October 24, 1988, p. 8.

tailer. With the foregoing in mind, two alternative proposals were made.

The first was a big price reduction to take effect immediately, and last for three months. This reduction was to be much larger than originally suggested and would be offered to the retailer only in exchange for a greater share of shelf space and personal promotion on the retailer's part. It was felt that by doing this the retailer would increase brand awareness of Kodak color film among consumers and alter the price-value relationship by pointing out its superiority. The estimated cost of this solution was $5.2 million.

The other alternative was to initiate a large advertising campaign for the same time period. The idea of a premium promotion campaign was decided on with the title of Kitten Poster Present Campaign. (See Exhibit 1.) The campaign would feature the giving away of a free poster with each roll of film purchased. The poster would be a color picture of five kittens. These kittens were selected because of a Japanese superstition associating this type of kitten with good luck. On the back of the poster would be a character reading with which the consumer could have a lot of fun. Kodak would send to the dealer numerous merchandising setups for store display. Also, a 15-second television commercial was conceptualized along with newspaper and magazine ads that would be run nationally. The total cost of this alternative was estimated at $9.6 million.

After both ideas were explained in full, one of the top international executives voiced the opinion that the idea of the ad campaign was sound but that Japan was an almost hopeless market. Any three-month promotional effort carried out in a market where Kodak possesses only a 15 percent share could not justify spending such a large amount. Also, he stated that since many of the Japanese listen to the advice of the shop clerk, an incentive such

EXHIBIT 1

as a wholesale price reduction would be more than enough initiative to the retailer for personal promotion.

Kodak's head of marketing in Japan spoke on the merits of the advertising campaign. He stated that the Japanese retailer would be delighted with the posters and the colorful merchandising displays because of the attraction they add to the store, whereas a simple price reduction would draw no new customers. The association with picture-taking that the poster would have could significantly increase brand awareness. In addition, he stressed that Kodak has the highest quality color film on the market and that a price reduction could cause some consumers, both at home and abroad, to begin to doubt this if the price was reduced as drastically as planned. It was also pointed out that the Japanese are an aesthetically inclined race; consequently, the retailer would be proud to display and give away the kitten poster. This could very possibly capture those consumers who have no brand loyalty, one of Kodak's major targets.

Source: Based on a case written by Martin R. Walsh.

QUESTIONS

1. Outline all the factors that you think should be considered in deciding between the two alternatives.
2. Based on the information in the case and your response to question 1, which course of action do you recommend Kodak initiate and why?
3. Would a price reduction along with the advertising campaign be a solid idea or not?
4. Based on your analysis of the situation, can you suggest a more effective solution than those proposed by the company? Explain why your proposal would be better.

Case 3–9

THE AMERICAN BEER COMPANY— GOING INTERNATIONAL

The American Beer Company, one of the leading U.S. beer companies, is considering expanding its market coverage to other countries, possibly Germany and Japan.[1] Its major brand of beer—America Beer—currently is exported to these countries in small quantities.

The Company

The American Beer Company brews, packages (under eight different brand names), and sells 50.2 million barrels of beer per year. The company's sales lead its nearest competitor by an estimated 12.9 million barrels.

In 1987 industry sales were flat while American Beer Company sales increased 5.2 per-

---

[1] American Beer Company, Smith Brewing Company, German Beer, and Japan Beer are fictitious company names.

cent achieving record gross sales of $8.3 billion. Since 1979 American Beer has taken 13 share points from its rivals and now has 39.8 percent of the U.S. beer market.

Capital investment plans for new facilities and expansion of existing ones are underway to increase U.S. beer production to 70 million barrels by 1990.

In 1985, the company launched its first international venture by licensing a Canadian brewer to manufacture America Beer for sale in Canada. Although the company is the world's largest brewer, less than 1 percent of its total output is sold overseas.

In 1985 the company entered a distribution arrangement with Britain's second largest brewer to provide it with America Beer. American Beer gained access to the U.K. brewer's retail distribution network and chain of nearly 3,000 (out of 82,000) wholly owned or associated pubs. Because of the growth in demand for lager beer in England, the U.K. brewer wants to sell more lager beer; the arrangement with American Beer provides it with help in the growing take-home market where lager beer is expected to experience rapid growth.

Two major trends exist in the English beer market: a move away from ale to lager beers and the growth of the take-home market. Twenty years ago almost all the beer sold in Great Britain was the traditional brown ale. In 1969, lager accounted for only 3 percent of the market. Today, lager accounts for nearly one third of sales, and its market share has been increasing by 25 percent a year for the last several years making it the fastest-growing part of the market.

More than 90 percent of all beer sold in the U.K. is consumed in pubs and private clubs compared with 30 to 35 percent in the United States. But off-license sales in Britain are growing rapidly and now account for 24 percent of all lager sales. Take-home sales are expected to open up a potentially huge new market for sales to women. Women consume less than 10 percent of the beer in Britain because they still do not frequent pubs.

The company's investments in Great Britain have proved successful because vast numbers of British beer drinkers are asking for lighter lagers instead of the dark ales and stouts for which the country is famous. The market share of lagers, such as America Beer, has grown to 35 percent from 5 percent 15 years earlier. The company's timing in Great Britian was nearly perfect. It was able to capitalize on two major consumer trends: British tastes were changing to a preference for lighter ales; and, the English pub's domination of British beer sales was being eroded by a shift toward buying beer in supermarkets to drink at home in front of the television. English pubs still account for the majority of beer sales but there is a decided trend toward the home market. American Beer is seeking other foreign markets that will prove to be similarly successful.

Statement of Objectives for International Marketing

The company has made a definite decision to explore international markets. As a consequence, it formed American Beer International, Inc. to explore opportunities for export and license production of American Beer Company's beers in international markets. In 1985 overseas business represented less than 2 percent of its total sales that year, but it intends to increase foreign sales to as much as 15 percent of its total business.

The world beer market is four times the size of the U.S. market, representing a significant opportunity for long-term growth. Initially, American Beer International will approach this new market through export of U.S. brewed beers and licensed local production. Where the high delivered price of exports limits volume potential, local production (as in Canada) will allow American Beer International, Inc.'s brands to compete with local beers.

New export and license production agreements will be selectively pursued during the 1990s. Selecting desirable partners and establishing a marketing franchise for American Beer's beers in foreign countries will be carefully developed with an emphasis on long-term success.

Reasons for Going International

Growth in beer consumption is leveling off in the United States while costs are climbing. The strong penetration of the U.S. market by Smith Brewing Co. since it was bought by a major cigarette manufacturer is, of course, a well-known story. American Beer is still the leading brewer with 26 percent of the market but Smith is a close second with 20 percent and Smith has indicated its interest in becoming number one. Continued expansion means taking market share away from someone else. For the last few years, the market in the United States has been relatively flat (see Exhibit 1) and many believe that future expansion of the market will not be great without excessive and unprofitable expenditures. For example, since 1985, American Beer and Smith collectively raised their sales by 12 million barrels (see Exhibit 2), while total beer consumption in the United States increased only slightly. Taking customers from other brands becomes more costly as companies spend more money to protect their market shares.

Tentative Plans

At the moment, American Beer is considering the possibility of entering negotiations with brewers or distributors in Germany and Japan.

In Germany, American Beer is considering an agreement with German Beer, one of the largest German brewers. In this proposed arrangement, German Beer will get a premium beer to help them compete against the Danish, super-premium-priced Tuborg. In return, American Beer will get the rights to distribute German Beer in the United States. The same containers used to ship American's beer to Germany will be used to return German Beer's product to the United States.

In Japan, plans are underway to sell directly to Japan Beers. Japan Beers is a subsidiary of Japan's largest distiller although its beer has only 7 percent of the Japanese beer market. Japan Beer (the fourth largest brewer in Japan) feels that by associating with respected foreign beers, such as American Beer, it will be able to enhance its reputation for domestically produced beers. Japan Beers has been importing American Beer through indirect channels for the last few years and it has sold well in Japan. Japan Beers will import American Beer directly from the company and is considering entering an agreement to brew the beer in Japan under license.

Industry Reactions

Reactions by marketing experts are not very favorable. One big risk is whether or not Germans and Japanese will buy American beer. American beer is very different from most foreign brews. It is fizzier and blander and is meant to be drunk chilled, something al-

EXHIBIT 1 U.S. Beer and Soft Drink Consumption (gallons per capita per year)					
	1985	1986	1987	1988	1989
Beer	23.6	24.3	24.8	24.8	25.2
Soft drinks	37.8	38.9	39.6	40.8	42.3

EXHIBIT 2   American Beer Sales Growth, 1983–1987 (in millions of barrels)

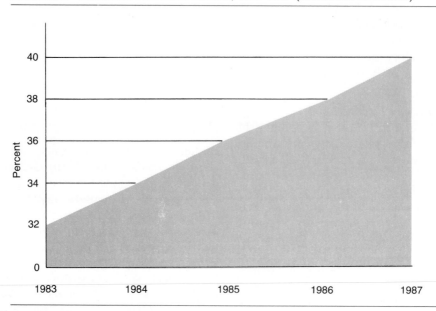

most unknown to foreign tastes. One German newspaper recently described foreign lagers as "imitation continental beer drunk only by refined ladies, people with digestive ailments, tourists and other weaklings." However, this may be true chauvinism at its best.

Problem

Although the company is not necessarily having second thoughts about its tentative moves to enter these two markets, it has not yet spent very much money in market development. However, if it is to establish significant positions in Germany and Japan, a substantial amount of capital will have to be spent in both markets to effectively promote the product. Before it makes a decision to increase marketing expenditures from less than $1 million to over $5 million. American Beer wants to examine its position intensely. As a consultant, you have been asked for an outside opinion. With the following data and other information you can gather, give the company an opinion on its tentative decisions. Make specific recommendations for action.

Industry Statistics

World Beer Production and Market Growth

A recent study in Europe indicated that the European market grew 23 percent since 1975. (See Exhibit 3.) The Netherlands grew 108 percent; the Italian market, 100 percent; Great Britain, Europe's number-two beer consumer, 31 percent; and Germany, only 4 percent. One third of all beer purchased in Europe is consumed at home, and the study says the home market will be the scene of a major clash for market shares during the 1980s (see Exhibits 4 and 5). World beer production increased since 1982; the total volume was up 4.2 percent by 1985 (see Exhibit 6).

Market Data—Germany and Japan

Germany

Germans consume 145.6 liters of beer per capita which amounts to about 38 gallons, com-

EXHIBIT 3 Estimated European Beer Market Growth, 1975–1990 (million hl)

	1975	*1976*	*1977*	*1980*	*1985*	*1990*
Germany	93	96	94	93	95	97
United Kingdom	65	66	65	72	80	85
France	22	24	23	24	26	28
Netherlands	12	14	14	16	20	25
Belgium/Luxembourg	15	15	15	15	15	16
Denmark	9	9	9	9	10	11
Italy	6	7	7	8	10	12
Ireland	6	6	6	6	6	7
Totals	228	237	233	243	262	281

pared to 25 gallons in the United States. (See Exhibits 1 & 7.) U.S. and German consumption patterns are similar. U.S. consumers drink beer in clubs 35 percent of the time and at home 65 percent of the time and so do Germans.

In Germany 1,400 breweries produce 1.6 million gallons of beer each under 5,000 different brands. The market consists of many small breweries; the 10 largest beer groups share only 22 percent of the beer market. The market is fragmented with strong local and regional loyalty. The best-known beer brands in Germany are Beck's, Bitburger Pils, Fuerstenberger Pils, and Lowenbrau. The two best-known imports are Pilsener Urquell (Czechoslovakia) and Tuborg. In 1985 imports accounted for only 1 percent of the total German beer mar-

EXHIBIT 4 Europe Beer Production by Container (1,000 hl)

	Barrels/Tanks	*Percent of Total Production*	*Bottles/Cans*	*Percent of Total Production*
Belgium	5,942	43.0	7,877	57.00
Denmark	711	8.3	7,823	91.67
Germany	27,752	29.4	66,595	70.59
France	4,473	19.6	18,298	80.36
Ireland	5,138	90.8	524	9.25
Italy	292	4.0	7,008	96.00
Luxembourg	285	41.0	410	58.99
Netherlands	3,854	27.6	10,116	72.41
United Kingdom	51,015	78.2	14,222	21.80
Total	99,462	42.8	132,873	57.19

EXHIBIT 5	Top Ten Beer-Producing Countries, 1982–1987	
	Percent Share of World Output	
	1982	*1987*
United States	22.1	22.0
West Germany	11.9	10.3
USSR	7.6	7.9
United Kingdom	8.2	7.6
Japan	5.0	5.0
Brazil	2.2	3.2
Mexico	2.5	2.8
Czechoslovakia	2.8	2.7
East Germany	2.6	2.6
Canada	2.7	2.3
Total	67.6	66.4

EXHIBIT 7	German per Capita Beverage Consumption
Beer	145.6 liters
Wine	24.4
Spirits	2.5
Gaseous drinks	22.1
Mineral water	47.6
Fruit juice	2.0

ket. Important market factors include the following:

Market characteristics. Presently, dark beers account for a larger percentage of beer sales than light. However, there is a growing consumer interest in lighter beers due to the current emphasis on better health and fewer calories. Light beer in Germany is the same as regular beer in the United States.

Although Germans consume 146 liters (310 pints) of beer per person per year, the market has been stagnating since the mid-1970s. Beer consumption has actually decreased slightly, and the actual number of beer-drinking Germans is declining. The smaller brewers are feeling this change. The number of brewers dropped from 1,800 in 1970 to 1,400 in 1982.

In 1989 bottled beer represented 70.6 percent of total domestic beer sales, as compared to 33.8 percent in 1960. Beer accounts for 11 percent of consumer sales of food and beverages. (See Exhibit 8.)

German beer is usually higher in alcohol content and much heavier bodied than U.S. beer. Germans tend to prefer pilsner beer which is a premium type beer. Pilsner beers now make up 56 percent of the total beer

EXHIBIT 6	World Beer Production, 1982–1987			
	Percent Share of Total (1982)	*Percent Share of Total (1985)*	*Percent Growth Rate (1982–1985)*	*Percent Growth Rate (1982–1987)*
Europe	52.4	49.6	3.2	6.8
Americas	33.7	35.1	4.0	17.4
Asia	7.2	8.7	10.3	35.4
Africa	3.7	3.9	9.5	19.6
Australasia	3.0	2.7	−1.6	negligible
Total	100.0	100.0	4.2	12.7

EXHIBIT 8	Beer Sales by Retail Store Group
Hypermarkets/discounters	28%
Chains/coops	25
Independents	30
Small shops	17

market whereas 10 years ago, they accounted for only 25 percent.

Japan

1. *Market characteristics.* Imports have doubled in the past two years while domestic beer sales have risen only 5 percent. In 1989 alone, imports increased by 23.3 percent.

Average consumption per adult was 83.2 bottles of beer in 1985; in 1989, average per capita consumption reached 106.67 bottles per year. Per capita expenditure for alcoholic beverages is 1 percent of annual income. Per capita consumption in 1989 was 36.5 liters.

Men account for most of the beer consumption. As yet, women are not big beer drinkers but they choose it as a gift to give during the summer months. Eighty to 90 percent of the housewives in Japan feel it is almost an obligation to send mid-summer gifts to acquaintances. Beer—especially imported brands—is often chosen for this purpose.

Beer can be obtained in both supermarkets and department stores. The latter is by far the more important of the two, with imported beers being displayed in the gourmet foods section. Vending machines, which in 1989 accounted for $10 billion in sales, sell beer and sake along with traditional items such as coffee and soft drinks. Alcoholic beverages are widely available by vending machine.

Along with imported beers, several well-established domestic breweries exist. The largest, Kirin, commands an unprecedented 62 percent market share. Kirin is so large that is has had to restrict growth for fear of govern-

ment antimonopoly action. Kirin has 12 modern breweries with a total capacity of 20.4 million barrels. Only 9.4 million barrels were sold in 1989. The next largest is Sapporo Breweries, whose market share totals almost 20 percent, followed in size by Asahi and Suntory breweries.

Several imports are presently being marketed in Japan. The leading beer exporters to Japan were the United States with a 38.5 percent share, West Germany with 17.9 percent, and Singapore with 15.5 percent. At the end of 1989, 40 brands of foreign beer were available to the Japanese.

Japanese beer enjoys an international reputation for quality. But beer makers in Japan say they've detected a change in tastes that's spurring the growth of imports. (See Exhibits 9 and 10.) Many Japanese want to recapture the taste of some foreign beer they have tried while traveling overseas.

Imported beers cost about 30 percent more than local brews; and nearly everyone in Japan agrees they don't taste as good as Japanese beer. However, that isn't stopping status-conscious Japanese drinkers, especially young people, from drinking imports in grow-

EXHIBIT 9	Top Ten Brands of Foreign Beer in the Japanese Market (000 cases imported)
Heineken	180
Budweiser	85
Tuborg	80
Guinness	74.7
Lowenbrau	70
Henninger	55
Holsten Bier	51
Schlitz	40
Primo	38
Carlsberg	35

EXHIBIT 10 Major Exporters of Beer to Japan	
United States	38.5%
West Germany	17.9
Singapore	15.5

EXHIBIT 11   Japan's Top Beer Producers (000 kiloliters)

	Production	Market Share
Kirin Brewery	2,767,000 kiloliters	62.1
Sapporo	873,000	19.6
Asahi	517,000	11.6
Suntory	299,000	6.7

ing quantities. Part of the Japanese attitude is that anything foreign has class.

In 1989, 4,480,000 kiloliters of beer were produced by domestic brewers. Japan's imports amounted to 10,000 kiloliters which is equal to about .002 percent of the market.

2. *Domestic competition.* There are currently four major domestic breweries in Japan. Kirin Brewery is the leader with a 62.1 percent share of market (see Exhibit 11).

Case 3–10

LEVI'S—WORLDWIDE ADVERTISING STRATEGY OR LOCALIZED CAMPAIGNS?

The Levi Strauss Company, manufacturer of the famous Levi's jeans and other wearing apparel, markets its products in 70 countries. The company owns and operates plants in 25 countries and has licensees, distributors, and joint ventures in others.

The company is now in the process of evaluating its advertising policy to determine whether to apply a worldwide strategy to all advertising or settle on localized campaigns for each country in which it sells its products.

You have been asked to evaluate its present programs and to make recommendations that will assist management in deciding whether it is better (1) to create advertising campaigns locally or regionally but with a good deal of input and influence from headquarters as they presently do; (2) to allow campaigns to be created independently by local advertising

companies; or (3) to centralize at national headquarters all advertising and develop a consistent worldwide advertising campaign.

You are asked to do the following:

1. Prepare a report listing the pros and cons of each of these three approaches.
2. Make a recommendation about the direction the company should take.
3. Support your recommendation and outline major objectives for whichever approach you recommend.

The following information should be of assistance in completing this assignment:

Company Objectives

In a recent annual report, the following statement of objectives of Levi Strauss International was made:

In addition to posting record sales, [see Exhibit 1] Levi Strauss International continued to advance toward two long-term objectives.

EXHIBIT 1   Sales/Profits ($ millions)

	Total	United States	Europe	Other International
Sales	$2,840	$1,888	$526	$426
Profits	468	314	92	62
Assets	1,375	882	240	253

The first is to develop a solid and continuing base of regular jeans business in markets throughout the world, thus providing a foundation for product diversification into women's-fit jeans, youthwear, menswear, and related tops.

The second objective is to attain the greatest possible self-sufficiency in each of the major geographic areas where Levi Strauss International markets: Europe, Canada, Latin America, and Asia/Pacific. This requires the development of raw material resources and manufacturing in areas where the products are marketed, thus reducing exposure to long supply lines and shipping products across national borders.

Unlike some competitors, Levi Strauss International does not, in its normal markets, seek targets of opportunity, that is, large one-time shipments to customers it may never serve again. Rather, the goal is to develop sustainable and growing shipment levels to long-term customers.

Organization

Western European Group
The company's European operations began in 1959 with a small export business, and, in 1965, an office was opened in Brussels. The company now has 15 European manufacturing plants and marketing organizations in 12 countries. This group includes all Western Europe served by the Continental and Northern European divisions.

The Continental European Division is head-quartered in Brussels and is responsible for operations in Germany, France, Switzerland, the Benelux countries, Spain, and Italy. The Northern European Division is headquartered in London and is responsible for all marketing and production in the United Kingdom and the Scandinavian nations.

Other International Group
The divisions in this group report directly to the president of Levi Strauss International. They are Canada, Latin America, and Asia/Pacific.

The Canadian Division consists of two separate operating units: Levi Strauss of Canada and GWG. Levi Strauss Company is sole owner of GWG which manufactures and markets casual and work garments under the GWG brand.

The Latin American Division traces its origins to 1966 when operations began in Mexico. In the early 1970s, the business was expanded to Argentina, Brazil, and Puerto Rico. In addition to these countries, the division now serves Chile, Venezuela, Uruguay, Paraguay, Peru, Colombia, and Central America. Plans call for the division to explore new markets in Central America and the Andean Region.

The Asia/Pacific Division had its beginning in the 1940s when jeans reached this market through U.S. military exchanges. In 1965 a sales facility was established in Hong Kong. Markets now served include Australia and

Japan, the two largest, as well as Hong Kong, the Philippines, Singapore/Malaysia, and New Zealand. Business in Indonesia and Thailand is handled through licenses. The markets served by this division present opportunity for growth in jeanswear. However, diversification potential in Asia/Pacific is centered in Japan and Australia.

Other Operating Units

One other unit, EXIMCO, not aligned with either Levi Strauss USA or Levi Struass International, reports directly to the president.

EXIMCO has two major responsibilities; market development and joint ventures in Eastern Europe, the USSR, and the People's Republic of China, and directing offshore contract production for the company's division.

Comments

The director of advertising and communications for International shares with you the following thoughts about advertising:

> The success of Levi Strauss International's advertising derived principally from their judging it consistently against three criteria: (1) Is the proposition meaningful to the consumer? (2) Is the message believable? and (3) Is it exclusive to the brand?
>
> A set of core values underlies advertising wherever it is produced and regardless of strategy: honesty/integrity, consistency/reliability, relevance, social responsibility, credibility, excellence, and style. The question remains whether a centralized advertising campaign can be based on this core of values.
>
> Levi Strauss' marketing plans must include 70 countries and recognize the cultural and political differences affecting advertising appeals.
>
> Uniform advertising (i.e., standardized) could ignore local customs and unique

product uses, while locally prepared advertising risks uneven creative work, is likely to waste time and money on preparation, and might blur the corporate image.

Consistency in product image is a priority.

> International advertising now appears in 25 countries. Levi currently uses seven different agencies outside the United States, although one agency handles 80 percent of the business worldwide. In Latin America, it uses four different agencies, and still a different agency in Hong Kong.
>
> Levi is not satisfied with some of the creative work in parts of Latin America. The company wants consistency in Latin American strategy rather than appearing to be a different company in different countries. They are not satisfied with production costs and casting of commercials, and the fact that local agencies are often resistent to outside suggestions to change. They feel there is a knee-jerk reaction in Latin America that results in the attitude that everything must be developed locally.
>
> The risks of too closely controlling a campaign result in uninteresting ads compared with decentralizing all marketing which produces uneven creative quality.

Competition

At the same time that Levi is looking at more centralized control of its advertising, another jeans maker is going in the opposite direction. Blue Bell International's Wrangler jeans company has just ended a six-month review of its international advertising and decided against coordinating its advertising more closely in Europe.

The concept of one idea that will work effectively in all markets is attractive to Wrangler. Yet the disadvantages are just as clear; the individual needs of each market cannot be met, resistance from local managers could be an obstacle, and the management of a centralized advertising campaign would require an organizational structure different from the present one.

To add to the confusion, a leading European jeans manufacturer, the Spanish textile company Y Confecciones Europeas, makers of Louis jeans, recently centralized its marketing through one single advertising agency. Louis, fourth largest jeans maker after Levi, Lee Cooper, and Wrangler, is intent on developing a worldwide international image for its Louis brand.

Review of Current Ads

A review of a selection of Levi advertisements from around the world provided the following notes:

> European television commercials for Levi's were supersexy in appeal, projecting, in the minds of some at headquarters, an objectionable personality for the brand. These commercials were the result of allowing complete autonomy to a sales region.

> Levi's commercials prepared in Latin America projected a far different image than those in Europe. Latin American ads addressed a family-oriented, Catholic market. However, the quality of the creative work was far below the standards set by the company.

> Ads for the United Kingdom, emphasizing that Levi's are an American brand, star an all-American hero, the cowboy, in fantasy wild West settings. In Northern Europe, both Scandinavia and the United Kingdom consumers are buying a slice of America when they buy Levi's.

> In Japan, where an attitude similar to that in the U.K. prevails, a problem confronted Levi's. Local jeans companies had already established themselves as very American. To overcome this, Levi's positioned itself against these brands as legendary Americans jeans with commercials themed "Heroes Wear Levi's," featuring clips of cult figures such as James Dean. These commercials were very effective and carried Levi's from a 35 percent to a 95 percent awareness level in Japan.

> In Brazil, unlike the United Kingdom, consumers are more strongly influenced by fashion trends emanating from the European Continent rather than from America. Thus, the Brazilian-made commercial filmed in Paris featured young people, cool amidst a wild traffic scene—very French. This commercial was intended to project the impression that Levi's are the favored brand among young, trend-setting Europeans.

> Australian commercials showed that creating brand awareness is important in that market. The lines "fit looks tight, doesn't feel tight, can feel comfortable all night" and "a legend doesn't come apart at the seams" highlighted Levi's quality image, and "since 1850 Levi jeans have handled everything from bucking broncos . . ." amplified Levi's unique positioning. This campaign resulted in a 99-percent brand awareness among Australians.[*]

---

[*]Information for this case was taken in part from the following sources: Levi Strauss and Company, Annual Report, 1980, "Exporting a Legend," *International Advertising*, November–December 1981, pp. 2–3, and "Levi Zipping up World Image," *Advertising Age*, September 14, 1981, pp. 35–36.

CASE 3–11

AMERICAN BABY FOODS—A PRELIMINARY REPORT

As assistant to the vice president of marketing for American Baby Foods, you have been given the task of preparing a preliminary report on Japan as a possible market for one of the company's product lines.

The American Baby Food Company, located in Camden, New Jersey, is a well-established manufacturer of a wide line of baby products. Its motto, "Babies are our business . . . our only business," aptly describes the parameters of the firm's activities. The product line is divided into food and nonfood items for the baby. Nonfood items include rubber pants, bibs, bottles, nipples, toys, and other accessory items. Food items are cereals, fruits and vegetables, and strained meat products which meet the dietary requirements for babies 2 to 18 months old. The products are widely used in the United States and Canada and compete to a moderate degree in Europe with the products of Kraft, Heinz, Carnation, and Gerber.

As part of long-range strategy, the company is interested in accelerating its growth outside the U.S. market. The drop in the U.S. birth rate in the early 1960s and approaching zero population growth in the 1980s has caused the company substantial long-range concern. Japan is an appealing market because of concern for diet and, more specifically, increasing population growth.

The product to be considered for marketing in Japan is the line of instant dry cereals that need only water or milk added to make them ready for eating. They can be used as the only food or as a supplement to other foods in a baby's diet until the infant is on a full, varied diet of table food at about 18 months.

The cereals come in 1-ounce, 8-ounce, and 16-ounce packages. The 8-ounce size contains about two weeks' supply of cereal. American Baby Foods produces oatmeal, barley, rice, mixed grains, and high-protein cereals, all to be considered for marketing in Japan.

As is usually the case, the vice president of marketing wants the report yesterday. What the vice president really wants to know is if there is reason to spend additional money to prepare a complete market analysis on Japan. Since this is a hurry-up job, about all you can be expected to do is the following:

1. Make a rough estimate of market demand, immediate and long term.
2. Outline the major marketing problems that will face American Baby Foods in successfully marketing the cereal.
3. Suggest steps that might be taken to overcome the problems.
4. Suggest to the research department the additional information necessary before a thorough market analysis and report can be made.

All the information the research department could dig up on such short notice follows. While there are some real holes in the data, there should be enough information to make a preliminary report. Remember, one of your main tasks is to advise research on what other data you will need.

Population Facts
In 1988, the total population of Japan was approximately 121 million persons and it is expected to be 127 million by 1995. Exhibit 1 shows 1988 population figures for major urban areas of Japan. The birth rate for 1988, according to the Ministry of Welfare, was 19.2 per 1,000 people. A steady but slow increase

EXHIBIT 1 Population—Selected Cities

City	Population (millions)	Percent of Total Population
Tokyo	11.7	10.5%
Osaka	8.5	7.4
Aichi	6.2	5.3
Kanagawa	6.8	5.8

was predicted for the future. Exhibit 2 shows the average number of live births in the major urban areas of Japan for 1988.

Diet

By tradition, a Japanese starts the day with a bowl of mashed soybean soup, pickled horseradish, and seaweed. The rest of the day, a few bits of raw octopus or dried squid accompanied by gobs of the inevitable Asian staple—rice—are the primary diet.

Now, as the Japanese grow in affluence and sophistication, such picturesque eating habits are changing. Today, a typical Japanese breakfast is likely to be toast and coffee. The Japanese diet is rapidly becoming internationalized, primarily westernized. And as the diet changes, more and more U.S. and European

food-processing companies are moving into Japan to take advantage. Among the American companies with established beachheads in Japan are Kellogg (cornflakes), H. J. Heinz (catsup), Del Monte Corporation (tomato juice), General Mills (cake mixes), Libby, McNeil & Libby, Inc. (canned peaches), Corn Products (Knorr packaged soup), McDonald's (fast foods), General Foods (Maxwell House instant coffee), Coca-Cola, Pepsi-Cola, and Canada Dry. Switzerland's food giant, Nestlé, has scored big in Japan with its Nescafé instant coffee.

As an executive of one of the biggest U.S. Food companies says, "Japan should be one of the two fastest-growing food markets in the world this year." (The other is Mexico.) Beyond this, the Japanese are improving their diet as a matter of pride. They are a small people by U.S. standards and they want to become bigger. It's humiliating when a Japanese basketball team is matched against an American basketball team.

Year by year, the Japanese diet is changing. They now eat less rice and more animal and vegetable protein. A Health and Welfare Ministry survey finds the average Japanese intake of animal fat and protein recently exceeded vegetables for the first time ever. "We have become aware of the value of nutrition and

EXHIBIT 2 Live Births (1988)

County	Approximately Annual Average	County	Approximately Annual Average
Tokyo	209,240	Shizuoka	61,060
Kanagawa	128,800	Aichi	120,760
Toyama	18,650	Mie	27,420
Ishikawa	19,720	Shiga	18,300
Fukui	12,950	Kyoto	43,440
Yamanashi	12,120	Osaka	165,560
Nagano	34,150	Hyogo	93,350
Gifu	33,600	Total	987,000

a balanced diet," says the director of one of Japan's biggest cooking schools.

Japanese babies normally are fed milk only until the age of four months, at which time they are given supplemental soft foods prepared in the mother's kitchen. These soft foods are often a mashed mixture of rice, liver, spinach, or other highly nutritional foods saved from the adults' meal. As in many foreign countries, a mortar and pestle are used to grind the food for the babies and small children.

Market Characteristics

There are headaches at the processing level. Many Japanese industries are fragmented, but food is the most fragmented of all—there are almost 100,000 companies engaged in food processing in Japan. Japan has more than 5,000 makers of soy sauce and more than 500 flour milling concerns. U.S. companies would like to spend more on advertising and promotion but are limited by the Japanese government in the amount of money that can be pumped in by the foreign parent. Japanese companies are under no such restrictions, and in some cases, a large manufacturer has almost a monopoly position in a market. Even so, Western food companies are pushing to get into Japan in several ways, and each has its limitations and advantages. Some companies, such as Campbell Soup, do a fair business in Japan through exports. But it's tough to turn a profit this way because of high freight costs and Japanese import duties that range from 15 to 50 percent. A few companies have tried licensing. Kellogg set up a subsidiary to provide technical and sales assistance to Ajinomoto Company, Japan's top maker of seasonings, which produces several varieties of Kellogg dry cereals. And Gerber Products Company licenses its baby food processes and labels to a Japanese group. But, again, profit potential is limited.

U.S. companies that would like to set up their own processing plants in Japan run into

tough restrictions against foreigners controlling Japanese industry. Japan's Ministry of International Trade and Industry has relaxed restrictions a bit, allowing foreign companies to get a controlling interest in certain industries. But the food business categories included in the liberalization were few: beer (it would seem that no outsider could hope to compete against the four Japanese breweries although Anheuser-Busch, Inc. announced it was going to try); monosodium glutamate (Ajinomoto has an impregnable position); and ice (nobody is interested in making ice in Japan).

To be sure, a few of the more successful Western food operations are subsidiaries, owned 100 percent outside Japan. Among them are Nestlé, Coca-Cola, and General Foods. But these were established years back when it was possible to set up subsidiaries capitalized in yen, not dollars; neither the capital nor profits could be repatriated. Few 100 percent ownership deals can be made now.

Most companies have sought out Japanese partners with whom to form joint ventures. Through such ventures, Heinz is linked with Nichiro Fisheries; Corn Products with Ajinomoto; Unilever (the British-Dutch giant) with Hohnen Oil Company; General Mills with Morinaga Confectionery; Libby with Mitsubishi Shoji Kaisha; and Del Monte Corporation with Mitsui and Company and Kikkhoman Shoyu Company; and Budweiser with Sunory. National Dairy Products is studying a deal to have its Kraft brand cheese made in Japan and Corn Products and Ajinomoto introduced a new line of mayonnaise in Japan.

Company Experiences

Most Western companies' efforts to cash in on changing Japanese diets have yielded a mixed bag of profits. As well as differences in tastes and other problems, they are confronted with an excruciating array of restrictions imposed by the Japanese government on foreign companies doing business there.

As a result, U.S. food companies have only a small share of the more than $25 billion that the Japanese spend annually for food and drink (although sales of American agricultural products to Japan—wheat, soybeans, and so forth—run to more than $2.5 billion a year). Food companies are persisting because of the obvious attractions of the Japanese market. Japan is big—over 121 million population—and it growing more Western in its tastes. More important, its fast economic growth rate in recent years has brought more disposable income for food. In 1988, Japan's gross national product was $2,858 billion. Per capita income is expected to top the $20,000 mark, but companies have had mixed results trying to sell processed foods in Japan.

Corn Products has done well with packaged dry soups. General Foods' Maxwell House is battling to hold its estimated 10 percent of the instant coffee market. (Nestlé, which spent heavily in creating a brand image at a time when the instant coffee idea was new to Japan, has 70 percent.) Among European companies, Unilever has run up sizable losses in its venture with Hohnen Oil company. Heinz and Unilever ran into serious difficulties with their Japanese partners and have since been allowed to boost their equity to over 50 percent.

In addition, the American food companies have found scores of other problems. For instance, the Japanese government, to protect domestic manufacturers, restricts foreign companies to producing limited lines of products and imposes ceilings on volume. Foods often have to be adapted to the Japanese palate which may be getting away from traditional dishes but still hasn't accepted Western tastes exactly. Heinz's spaghetti sauce has to be blander than the U.S. product; Corn Products' mayonnaise isn't as sweet as the American. Largely because of the underdevelopment of Japan's milk industry, Kellogg's dry cereals generally are eaten right out of the box as a confection.

Indeed, Japan's limited agriculture poses problems in getting raw materials for foods. Heinz, Del Monte, and Libby are obligated to use domestic tomatoes in their catsup but can only get small quantities. Corn Products' concern over making mayonnaise is how to get a steady supply of fresh eggs.

Food Imports

Japan is not self-sufficient in food production, and its ability to feed itself has declined since the end of World War II. In 1985 Japan imported over 40 percent of all food products consumed, and this trend is likely to continue as the population increases and the land suitable for food production diminishes. Exhibit 3 shows the substantial increases in food imports that have occurred between 1980 and 1989.

Distribution System

Japan has 1.74 million retail and wholesale outlets which employ 8.5 million people. Over 85 percent of the retail outlets are individually or small-family owned and only 5 percent of the retailers have more than $200,000 (U.S. dollars) in sales. There are 292,000 wholesalers, which amount to one wholesaler for every six retail units. There are 83,093 grocery stores serving households which spend about $525 per month each on food.

EXHIBIT 3   Imports of Selected Foods, 1980–1989 (1,000 metric tons)

	1980	1989	Percent of Increase
Cereals	15,803	25,303	60
Vegetables	98	452	361
Fruits	1,182	1,610	36
Meat	220	791	260
Dairy products and milk	561	1,109	98

SOURCE: Japan Institute for Social and Economic Affairs.

Wholesaling in Japan is a major economic factor in distribution. A large percentage of all consumer goods goes through three or more wholesalers between manufacturer and ultimate consumer, with two middlemen being the minimum.

Case 3–12

NATIONAL OFFICE MACHINES— MOTIVATING JAPANESE SALESPEOPLE: STRAIGHT SALARY OR COMMISSION?

National Office Machines of Dayton, Ohio, manufacturers of cash registers, EDP equipment, adding machines, and other small office equipment, has recently entered into a joint venture with Nippon Cash Machines of Tokyo, Japan. Last year, National Office Machines (NOM) had domestic sales of over $1.4 billion and foreign sales of nearly $700 million. Besides the United States, it operates in most of Western Europe, the Mideast, and some parts of the Far East. In the past, it has no significant sales or sales force in Japan although the company was represented there by a small trading company until a few years ago. In the United States, NOM is one of the leaders in the field and is considered to have one of the most successful and aggressive sales forces found in this highly competitive industry.

Nippon Cash Machines (NCM) is an old-line cash register manufacturing company organized in 1882. At one time, Nippon was the major manufacturer of cash register equipment in Japan but it has been losing ground since 1970 even though NCM produces perhaps the best cash register in Japan. Last year's sales were 9 billion yen—125 yen = $1 (U.S.)—a 15 percent decrease over sales the prior year. The fact that it produces only cash registers is one of the major problems;

the merger with NOM will give them much-needed breadth in product offerings. Another hoped-for strength to be gained from the joint venture is managerial leadership which is sorely needed.

Fourteen Japanese companies have products that compete with Nippon, plus several foreign giants such as IBM, National Cash Register, and Unisys of the United States, and Sweda Machines of Sweden. Nippon has a small sales force of 21 men, most of whom have been with the company their entire adult careers. These salesmen have been responsible for selling to Japanese trading companies and to a few large purchasers of equipment.

Part of the joint venture agreement included doubling the sales force within a year, with NOM responsible for hiring and training the new salesmen who must all be young, college-trained Japanese nationals. The agreement also allowed for U.S. personnel in supervisory positions for an indeterminate period of time and retaining the current Nippon sales force.

One of the many sales management problems facing the Nippon/American Business Machines Corporation (NABMC—the name of the new joint venture) was which sales compensation plan to use, that is, should it follow the Japanese tradition of straight salary and guaranteed employment until death with no incentive program, or the U.S. method (very successful for NOM in the United States) of commissions and various incentives based on sales performance, with the ultimate threat of being fired if sales quotas go continuously unfilled?

The immediate response to the problem might well be one of using the tried-and-true U.S. compensation methods since they have worked so well in the United States and are perhaps the kind of changes needed and expected from U.S. management. NOM management is convinced that salespeople selling its kinds of products in a competitive market must have strong incentives to produce. In fact, NOM had experimented on a limited basis in the United States with straight salary about 10 years ago and it was a bomb. Unfortunately, the problem is considerably more complex than it appears on the surface.

One of the facts to be faced by NOM management is the traditional labor-management relations and employment systems in Japan. The roots of the system go back to Japan's feudal era when a serf promised a lifetime of service to his lord in exchange for a lifetime of protection. By the start of Japan's industrial revolution in the 1880s, an unskilled worker pledged to remain with a company all his useful life if the employer would teach him the new mechanical arts. The tradition of spending a lifetime with a single employer survives today mainly because most workers like it that way. There is little chance of being fired, pay raises are regular, and there is a strict order of job-protecting seniority.

Japanese workers at larger companies still are protected from outright dismissal by union contracts and an industrial tradition that some personnel specialists believe has the force of law. Under this tradition, a worker can be dismissed after an initial trial period only for gross cause, such as theft or some other major infraction. As long as the company remains in business, the worker isn't discharged, or even furloughed simply because there isn't enough work to be done.

Besides the guarantee of employment for life, the typical Japanese worker receives many fringe benefits from the company. Just how paternalistic the typical Japanese firm can be is illustrated by a statement from the Japanese Ministry of Foreign Affairs which gives the example of A, a male worker who is employed in a fairly representative company in Tokyo.

> To begin with, A lives in a house provided by his company, and the rent he pays is amazingly low when compared with average city rents. His daily trips between home and factory are paid by the company. A's working hours are from 9 A.M. to 5 P.M. with a break for lunch which he usually takes in the company restaurant at a very cheap price. He often brings home food, clothing, and other miscellaneous articles he has bought at the company store at a discount ranging from 10 percent to 30 percent below city prices. The company store even supplies furniture, refrigerators, and television sets on an installment basis, for which, if necessary, A can obtain a loan from the company almost free of interest.
>
> In case of illness, A is given free medical treatment in the company hospital, and if his indisposition extends over a number of years, the company will continue paying almost his full salary. The company maintains lodges at seaside or mountain resorts where A can spend the holidays or an occasional weekend with the family at moderate prices. . . . It must also be remembered that when A reaches retirement age (usually 55) he will receive a lump-sum retirement allowance or a pension, either of which will assure him a relatively stable living for the rest of his life.

Even though A is only an example of a typical employee, a salesperson can expect the same treatment. Job security is such an expected part of everyday life that no attempt is made to motivate the Japanese salesperson in the same manner as in the United States; as a consequence, selling traditionally has been primarily an order-taking job. Except for the fact that sales work offers some travel, entry to outside executive offices, the opportunity to entertain, and similar side benefits, it provides a young person with little other incentive to surpass basic quotas and drum up new business. The traditional Japanese bonuses (which normally amount to about two or four months' salary over the year) are no larger for salespeople than any other functional job in the company.

As a key executive in a Mitsui-affiliated engineering firm put it recently: "The typical salesman in Japan isn't required to have any particular talent." In return for meeting sales quotas, most Japanese salespeople draw a modest monthly salary, sweetened about twice a year by bonuses. Manufacturers of industrial products generally pay no commission or other incentives to boost their businesses.

Besides the problem of motivation, a foreign company faces other different customs when trying to put together and manage a sales force. Class systems and the Japanese distribution system with its penchant for reciprocity put a strain on the creative talents of the best sales managers, as Simmons, the U.S. bedding manufacturer, was quick to learn. One Simmons executive explained he had no idea of the workings of the class system. Hiring a good person from the lower classes, for instance could be a disaster. If that person called on a client of a higher class, there was a good chance the client would be insulted. There is also a major difference in language among the classes.

In the field, Simmons found itself stymied by the bewildering realities of Japanese marketing, especially the traditional distribution system which operates on a philosophy of reciprocity that goes beyond mere business to the core of the Japanese character. It's involved with *on*, the notion that regards a favor of any kind as a debt that must be repaid. To *wear* another's *on* in business and then turn against that person is to lose face, abhorrent to most Japanese. Thus, the owner of large Western-style apartments, hotels, or de-

velopments buys his beds from the supplier to whom he owes a favor, no matter what the competition offers.

In small department and other retail stores, where most items are handled on consignment, the bond with the supplier is even stronger. Consequently, all sales outlets are connected in a complicated web that runs from the largest supplier, with a huge national force to the smallest local distributor, with a handful of door-to-door salespeople. The system is self-perpetuating and all but impossible to crack from the outside.

However, there is some change in attitude taking place as both workers and companies start discarding traditions for the job mobility common in the United States. Skilled workers are willing to bargain on the strength of their experience in an open labor market in an effort to get higher wages or better job opportunities; in the United States it's called shopping around. And a few companies are showing a willingness to lure workers away from other concerns. A number of companies are also plotting on how to rid themselves of deadwood workers accumulated as a result of promotions by strict seniority.

Toyo Rayon company, Japan's largest producer of synthetic fibers, started reevaluating all its senior employees every five years with the implied threat that those who don't measure up to the company's expectations have to accept reassignment and possibly demotion; some may even be asked to resign. A chemical engineering and construction firm asked all its employees over 42 to negotiate a new contract with the company every two years. Pay raises and promotions go to those the company wants to keep. For those who think they are worth more than the company is willing to pay, the company offers retirement with something less than the $30,000 lump-sum payment the average Japanese worker receives at age 55.

More Japanese are seeking jobs with foreign firms as the lifetime-employment ethic slowly changes. The head of student placement at Aoyama Gakuin University reports that each year the number of students seeking jobs with foreign companies increases. Bank of America, Japan Motorola, Imperial Chemical Industries, and American Hospital Supply are just a few of the companies that have been successful in attracting Japanese students. Just a few years ago, all Western companies were places to avoid.

Even those companies that are successful work with a multitude of handicaps. American companies often lack the intricate web of personal connections that their Japanese counterparts rely on when recruiting. Further, American companies have the reputation for being quick to hire and even quicker to fire, while Japanese companies still preach the virtues of lifelong job security. Those U.S. companies that are successful are offering big salaries and promises of Western-style autonomy. According to a recent study, 20 to 29-year-old Japanese prefer an employer changing environment to a single lifetime employer. They complain that the Japanese system is unfair because pay and promotion is done primarily by seniority rather than ability. Some feel that "if you are really capable, you are better off working with an American company."[1]

A few U.S. companies operating in Japan are experimenting with incentive plans. Marco and Company, a belting manufacturer and Japanese distributor for Power Packing and Seal Company, was persuaded by Power to set up a travel plan incentive for salespeople who topped their regular sales quotas. Unorthodox as the idea was for Japan, Marco went along: the first year, special one-week trips to Far East holiday spots like Hong Kong, Taiwan, Manila, and Macaco were inaugu-

rated. Marcos sales of products jumped 212 percent, and the next year sales were up an additional 60 percent.

IBM also has made a move toward chucking the traditional Japanese sales system (salary plus a bonus but no incentives). For about a year, it has been working with a combination which retains the semiannual bonus while adding commission payments on sales over preset quotas.

"It's difficult to apply a straight commission system in selling computers because of the complexities of the product," an IBM-Japan official said. "Our salesmen don't get big commissions because other employees would be jealous." To head off possible ill-feeling, therefore, some nonselling IBM employees receive monetary incentives.

Most Japanese companies seem reluctant to follow IBM's example because they have doubts about directing older salesmen to go beyond their usual order-taking role. High-pressure tactics are not well-accepted here, and sales channels are often pretty well set by custom and long practice (e.g., a manufacturer normally deals with one trading company, which in turn sells only to customers A, B, C, and D). A salesman or trading company, for that matter, is not often encouraged to go after customer Z and get him away from a rival supplier.

Japanese companies also consider nonsales employees a tough problem to handle. With salesmen deprived of the glamour status often accorded by many top managements in the United States, even Marco executives admit they have a ticklish problem in explaining how salesmen—who are considered to be just another key working group in the company with no special status—rate incentive pay and special earning opportunities.

The Japanese market is becoming more competitive and there is real fear on the part of NOM executives that the traditional system just won't work in a competitive market. On the other hand, the proponents of the incen-

---

[1] Bernard Wysocki, Jr., "Foreign Companies Are Having More Success Recruiting Employees in Japan, Although Some Key Obstacles Remain," *The Wall Street Journal*, January 2, 1985, p. 6.

tive system agree that the system really has not been tested over long periods or even adequately in the short term since it has been applied only in a growing market. In other words, was it the incentive system that caused the successes achieved by the companies or was it market growth? Especially there is doubt since other companies following the traditional method of compensation and employee relations also have had sales increases during the same period.

The problem is further complicated for Nippon/American because it will have both new and old salespeople. The young Japanese seem eager to accept the incentive method but older ones are hesitant. How do you satisfy both since you must, by agreement, retain all the sales staff?

A recent study done by the Japanese government on attitudes of youth around the world suggests that younger Japanese may be more receptive to U.S. incentive methods

EXHIBIT 1 Life Goals

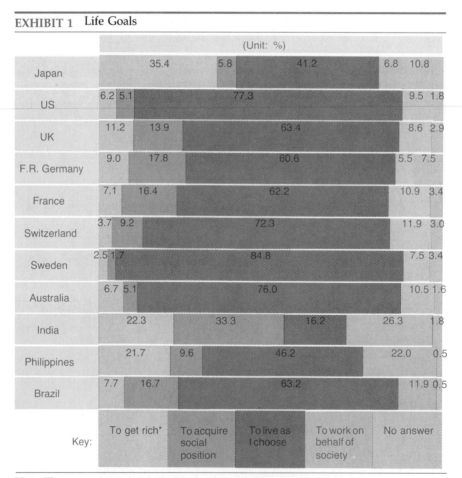

(Unit: %)

	To get rich*	To acquire social position	To live as I choose	To work on behalf of society	No answer
Japan	35.4	5.8	41.2	6.8	10.8
US	6.2	5.1	77.3	9.5	1.8
UK	11.2	13.9	63.4	8.6	2.9
F.R. Germany	9.0	17.8	60.6	5.5	7.5
France	7.1	16.4	62.2	10.9	3.4
Switzerland	3.7	9.2	72.3	11.9	3.0
Sweden	2.5	1.7	84.8	7.5	3.4
Australia	6.7	5.1	76.0	10.5	1.6
India	22.3	33.3	16.2	26.3	1.8
Philippines	21.7	9.6	46.2	22.0	0.5
Brazil	7.7	16.7	63.2	11.9	0.5

Note: The respondents were asked to choose one answer.

*The literal translation of the question asked the Japanese pollees is close to "to be well-off economically." Had the Japanese respondents been asked the more blunt "to get rich," probably fewer of them would have chosen this alternative.

SOURCE: Prime Minister's Office: "How Youth See Life," *Focus Japan*

than one would anticipate. In a study done by the Japanese Prime Minister's Office there were some surprising results when Japanese responses were compared with responses of similar aged youths from other countries. Exhibit 1 summarizes some of the information gathered on life goals. One point that may be of importance in shedding light on the decision NOM has to make is a comparison of Japanese attitudes with young people in 11 other countries—the Japanese young people are less satisfied with their home life, school, and working situations, and are more passive in their attitudes toward social and political problems. Further, almost a third of those employed said they were dissatisfied with their present jobs primarily because of

low income and short vacations. Asked if they had to choose between a difficult job with responsibility and authority, 64 percent of the Japanese picked the former, somewhat less than the 70–80 percent average in other countries.

Another critical problem lies with the non-sales employees; traditionally, all employees on the same level are treated equally whether sales, production, or staff. How do you encourage competitive, aggressive salesmanship in a market unfamiliar to such tactics, and how do you compensate salespeople to promote more aggressive selling in the face of tradition-bound practices of paternalistic company behavior?

QUESTIONS

1. What should they offer—incentives or straight salary? Support your answer.
2. If incentives are out, how do you motivate salespeople and get them to aggressively compete?
3. Design a U.S.-type program for motivation and compensation of salespeople. Point out where difficulties may be encountered with your plan and how the problems are to be overcome.
4. Design a pay system you think would work, satisfying old salespeople, new salespeople, and other employees.
5. Discuss the idea that perhaps the kind of motivation and aggressiveness found in the United States is not necessary in the Japanese market.
6. Develop some principles in motivation which could be applied by an international marketer in other countries.

Case 3–13

SELLING AMERICAN TOURIST ATTRACTIONS TO FOREIGN TOURISTS

Regionalizing the American touristic geography for foreign visitors is a major goal of the United States Travel and Tourism Administration.

The idea of grouping states, cities, and distinct areas of the country into touristic regions is not new. Some regional arrangements are based on historical heritage, others derive their common interest from geography, and still others are founded on economic considerations. Some, such as the Foremost West or the Old West Trail Foundation or Travel South have formal organizational and management structures; others, such as America's Heartland, the Great Lakes Region or the New England Region carry out cooperative promotional programs under the auspices of state and local tourism officials.

Regionalization makes sense for three principal reasons. First, the pooled resources of a region make it possible to carry out promotional programs of sufficient magnitude to make an impact in international markets. Second, segmenting a very large country into areas of manageable size helps demonstrate the diversity of the United States and helps groups of states develop a touristic identity. Third, regionalizing helps focus and measure the economic benefits of tourism more efficiently.

Cooperative marketing programs range from consumer advertising to tour product development projects to travel trade or foreign travel writer familiarization to regional marketing conferences.[1]

Exporting Tourism

Until recently, very few industrial, political, or economic leaders thought of the travel industry's international trade potential. The fact is, hardly any one considered its economic potential at all. Travel was always something that people did for fun or because they had to, but it was rarely thought of as either a big or a serious business.

Fortunately, those attitudes are all changing. The change is occurring partly because the industry itself is beginning to recognize

---

[1] Excerpted from Max J. Allen, "Regional Cooperative Marketing Programs in Tourism," *Business America*, February 15, 1988, p. 6.

its position and partly because the industry's economic statistics are too big to be ignored.

From a cottage industry full of mom-and-pop operations has sprung one of America's—and one of the world's—largest industries:

- Nationwide, the travel industry is the second largest employer, the third largest retail industry, and the largest invisible export for the United States in the services sector.
- The late futurist Herman Kahn predicted that by the year 2010, tourism will be the world's largest industry.
- In 1987 expenditures in the United States by U.S. and foreign travelers were in the $300 billion range.
- Those figures do not reflect the sales by companies which supply the tourism industry.
- Globally, tourism increasingly is a major source of foreign-exchange earnings for many countries and is, therefore, a priority in world trade.
- The World Tourism Organization estimates that international tourism receipts worldwide reached $150 billion.

When we look at the several reasons why tourism is important, we must realize that tourists, collectively, are temporary, additional populations which require food, shelter, water, transportation, and other public utilities. Their demand for the services of the restaurant, hotel, and transport industries creates a secondary round of demand for the products and services of related industries, such as petroleum, agriculture, livestock, meat packing, food processing, fishing, construction, appliance manufacturing, banking, and retail trade.

In short, tourism is a basic industry—not in the sense that economists would use the term, but in the sense that tourism stimulates nontourist industries. In fact, there is probably scarcely a company whose products and sales are not, and will not continue to be, affected by tourism, its growth, and the changing composition of the U.S. travel market.

Increasingly, that market is not just domestic. While travel by Americans within America is undoubtedly the larger share of the industry's activity, tourism from abroad is growing rapidly, and we can no longer take for granted selling only to one market. U.S. companies need to diversify and explore new markets to maintain a competitive edge.

Japanese tourists, for example, are traveling throughout the United States and are the largest group of foreign visitors to New York. These Japanese visitors, like all foreign tourists, consume and purchase American manufactured goods while they are traveling here. In 1986, 1.7 million Japanese visitors spent more than $1.6 billion on U.S. goods and services in the United States. In 1987, 2.1 million Japanese visitors put an estimated $2.1 billion into the U.S. economy. U.S. tourism revenues from Japanese visitors in 1988 were expected to reach $2.8 billion. To complete the picture, the U.S. travel account with Japan enjoyed a $1.2 billion surplus in 1987.

All of this means that American industries outside the travel industry—from steel and banking to textiles and agriculture—benefit from tourism. For example, foreign visitor demand for rental cars translates into demand for U.S.-manufactured steel, glass, plastic, and automotive parts. The foreign visitor's need for currency exchange services generates business for banks. His use of U.S. hotels and restaurants translates into sales not only for the lodging and food service industries but also into sales for the textile, furniture, flatware, agriculture, fishing, and beverage industries. Foreign visitors patronizing U.S. hotels and restaurants use U.S.-manufactured towels, linens, beds, chairs, telephones, tables, and china; they consume foods and beverages produced by the American farmer, fisherman, enologist, brewer, and distiller.

Visitors from abroad who use the services of U.S. carriers contribute to demand for U.S.-manufactured aircraft and telecommunications equipment.

No other economic activity affords business the growth potential that tourism does, and no other medium of exposure provides the opportunities for selling American products that the U.S. travel industry provides.[2]

World Tourism

In the last ten years, tourism has emerged as the fastest-growing component of world trade in services (Exhibit 1). In 1985 it accounted for nearly $96 billion, or roughly 28 percent, of the world's $345 billion in earnings from trade in services.

This represents an increase of about $58 billion,[3] or 153 percent, since 1976. During the same interval, trade in service as a whole rose only 126 percent; world receipts from "other goods, services and income,"[4] 122 percent; revenues from "other transportation,"[5] 112 percent; and income from shipment, 111 percent.

The fastest growth in tourism receipts has occurred in Asia and the European developing countries (Cyprus, Greece, Hungary, Malta, Portugal, Romania, and Turkey), not in the industrial nations (Exhibit 2). Asia's tourism revenues have increased more than

---

[2] Excerpted from Donna F. Tuttle, "Why Export U.S. Tourism Services?" *Business America*, February 15, 1988, pp. 3–4.

[3] Data in Exhibits 1, 2, 3, and 4 are expressed in Special Drawing Right (SDRs), a unit of account used by the International Monetary Fund, *not* U.S. dollars. The conversion rate for U.S. dollars per SDR was 1.0153 in 1985.

[4] May include such items as reinsurance transactions, commissions, and fees for management, communications, and technical services.

[5] May include such items as landing fees and port disbursements.

EXHIBIT 1   Growth of International Services 1976–1985 Transactions (millions of SDRs)

Services Category	1976	1985	Percent Change
Shipment	23.2	49.2	+111.0
Other transportation	30.5	64.8	+112.0
Tourism	37.4	94.5	+153.0
Other private goods, services and income	59.3	131.4	+122.0
Total	150.5	339.0	+126.0

Note: An SDR is a unit of account used by the International Monetary Fund. Its value is based on the value of a basket of currencies and fluctuates accordingly. In 1985, the conversion rate for U.S. dollars per SDR was 1.0153; therefore, the figures above should be multiplied by that rate to obtain the dollar value of the 1985 figures.

1985 data for countries that did not report 1976 data and 1976 data for countries that did not report 1985 data were excluded to achieve a valid comparison; therefore, the figures may not agree precisely with those reported by the IMF. Countries whose figures were excluded for comparative purposes include China, India, Saudi Arabia, and Yugoslavia, all of which are major tourism destinations.

SOURCE: International Monetary Fund, *Balance of Payments Statistics Yearbook*, 37 part 2, 1986.

330 percent, and the European developing countries over 285 percent.

Growth of this magnitude has been fueled by expanding international travel and has been made possible by increased accommodation capacity. International tourist arrivals worldwide rose by more than 112 million, from 220.7 million to almost 330 million, between 1976 and 1985, or more than 50 percent (Exhibit 3). At the same time, more than 1.2 million new rooms were added to the world's accommodation capacity (Exhibit 4).

East Asia has experienced the most rapid growth in international tourist arrivals, 290 percent. The region's accommodation capacity has increased by almost 250,000 rooms,

or nearly 50 percent, and now totals more than 768,000.

Of the world's regions, North America has recorded the smallest growth in international tourist arrivals, less than 7 percent, due partially to the high value of the U.S. dollar between 1982 and 1985 and to stepped-up competition for the tourist market from other regions. Despite this lackluster performance, however, more new hotel rooms—roughly a half million—have been built in North America in the last ten years than in any other world region.

As world travel has grown and expenditures on travel-related services have risen, the tourism share of world trade in services has expanded, except in the Middle East and the developing countries of the Western Hemisphere (Exhibit 5). Even in those regions, tourism remains a major component of overall trade in services, 26 percent for the Middle

EXHIBIT 2   Growth of Tourism Receipts by Region 1976–1985 (millions of SDRs)

	1976	1985	Percent Change
World	37.4	94.5	+153.0
Industrial countries	29.3	69.8	+138.0
Developing countries	8.1	24.7	+205.0
Africa	.8	2.5	+213.0
Asia	1.6	6.9	+331.0
Europe	1.5	5.8	+287.0
Middle East	.6	1.8	+200.0
Western Hemisphere	3.5	7.7	+120.0

Note: 1985 data for countries that did not report 1976 data and 1976 data for countries that did not report 1985 data were omitted to achieve a valid comparison; therefore, the figures may not agree precisely with those reported by the IMF. Countries whose figures had to be omitted for comparative purposes include China, India, Saudi Arabia, and Yugoslavia, all of which are major tourism destinations.

SOURCE: International Monetary Fund, *Balance of Payments Statistics Yearbook*, 37 part 2, 1986.

EXHIBIT 3 Trends in International Tourist Arrivals 1976–1985 (millions)

	Arrivals		Percent Change
	1976	1985	
World	220.7	333.0	51.0
Africa	4.4	9.1	107.0
North America	30.5	32.5	6.6
Central and South America and the Caribbean	13.8	20.3	47.0
East Asia and the Pacific	9.5	37.0	289.5
Europe	157.8	224.5	42.3
Middle East	3.8	7.1	87.0
South Asia	1.7	2.5	47.0

Note: Totals are for members of the World Tourism Organization, whose membership is not identical to that of the International Monetary Fund.

SOURCE: World Tourism Organization, *Tourism Compendium, 1981 Edition,* Table 2, International Tourist Arrivals by Region, 1950–1980, p. 32; and World Tourism Organization, *Tourism Compendium, 7th ed. 1986,* World and Regional Totals, pp. 154–93.

East and 39 percent for Latin America. As a share of trade in services, tourism has expanded the most rapidly in Asia, from less than 19 percent in 1976 to nearly 29 percent in 1985.

Interestingly, tourism accounts for a greater share of the developing countries' receipts from traded services—more than one third—than of the industrialized nations'. It represents almost half of the European developing countries' exchange earnings from services and more than two fifths of the services revenues of the developing countries in the Western Hemisphere.

In 1985, the most recent year for which International Monetary Fund data are available, seven developing countries (Singapore, Thailand, Greece, Portugal, Turkey, Israel, and Mexico) earned more than $1 billion each from tourism. Singapore earned over $1.7 billion, and Mexico more than $2.9 billion. Sixteen developing countries earned more than $500 million.

For a number of countries in all regions of the world, tourism, together with passenger fare receipts, represents the single largest component of trade in services. For 18 countries which earn at least $500 million annually from international tourism, tourism and passenger fare receipts account for at least 42 percent of total income from traded services. For nine of the 18, the tourism/fare receipts' share of services income is 50 percent—or higher (Exhibit 6).

Executives outside the tourism industry are examining these figures for two reasons:

• The tourism sector, especially the hotel industry, is a heavy purchaser of the output of other industries.
• The figures indicate the countries and regions where tourism is growing and when there may be business opportunities as a result.

Tourism stimulates nontourist industries, such as agriculture; fishing; meat-packing; food processing; brewing and distilling; bottling; floriculture; construction; and appliance, furniture, and linen manufacture. Demand for hotel rooms can create, in turn, demand for the services of contractors, which generates secondary demand for steel, bricks, lumber, tile, marble, glass, plumbing and air conditioning systems, elevator cars, carpets, and a variety of other goods. Similarly, tourist demand for restaurant meals creates business not only for restaurants, but also for producers and packagers of fresh and frozen foods, butchers, dairies, and ultimately, for manufacturers of farm implements and fertilizers.

As the value of the U.S. dollar comes down, U.S. products such as these can be expected

EXHIBIT 4   Accommodation Capacity by World Region 1981–1986

| | Hotel Rooms | | |
	1981	1985	Percent Change
World	8,701,423	9,931,874	+14.1
East Asia and the Pacific	523,285	768,815	+46.9
Africa	157,983	202,341	+28.1
North	69,809	93,270	+33.6
Other	88,174	109,071	+23.7
Europe	4,671,810	5,062,748	+8.4
East	267,993	284,052	+6.0
North	570,885	819,562	+43.6
South	1,798,789	1,902,324	+5.8
West	2,003,993	2,023,769	+1.0
Middle East	74,438	100,031	+34.4
Americas	3,202,362	3,701,798	+15.6
North	2,334,770	2,786,104	+19.3
Central and South	786,118	819,623	+4.3
Caribbean	81,474	96,071	+17.9
South Asia	71,545	96,141	+34.4

SOURCE: World Tourism Organization, *Compendium of Tourism Statistics*, 7th ed. (Madrid: 1986), pp. 162–93.

to become more price-competitive in the international marketplace.[6]

European Travel Trends

Travel between the United States and Europe is the largest and most important component of U.S. international trade in tourism with other countries (excluding Canada and Mexico).

Four in ten visitors to America from overseas countries are European, and fully half of U.S. citizens traveling to overseas destinations are bound for Europe. Some of the statistical highlights of European visitors to the United States follow in Exhibits 7 through 14:[7]

With such strong prospects for U.S. international tourism one would think that states, city convention and visitor bureaus, airlines, hotels, car rental firms, and major tourist attractions, among others, would begin new promotional programs abroad or expand existing ones. This has occurred to some extent, but the majority of industry organizations have been slow to react to the potential wait-

[6] Excerpted from Donna F. Tuttle, "Whether Your Business Is Tourism or Not, Tourism Is Your Business," *Business America*, February 16, 1987, pp. 3–7.

[7] Don Wynegar, "The U.S.-Europe Travel Market: The Atlantic Connection," *Business America*, February 16, 1987, pp. 13–18; Exhibits 10 through 14 from Jean Getman O'Brien, "Is the U.S. Travel Industry Competitive?" *Business America*, February 15, 1988, pp. 10–12.

EXHIBIT 5   World Foreign Exchange Earnings from Trade in Services and Tourism's Share of Trade in Services 1985 (millions of SDRs)

	Total Trade in Services	Shipment	Other Transportation	Travel	Other Private Goods, Services, and Income	Tourism's Trade in 1985	Share of Services 1976
World	339.9	49.2	64.8	94.5	131.4	27.8	24.9
Industrial countries	267.9	40.5	51.7	69.8	105.9	26.1	23.4
Developing countries	72.0	8.7	13.1	24.7	25.5	34.3	32.0
Africa	8.3	1.1	1.9	2.5	2.8	30.1	27.1
Asia	24.1	3.4	3.9	6.9	9.9	28.6	18.8
Europe	13.0	1.3	1.7	5.8	4.2	44.6	43.0
Middle East	7.0	1.0	1.4	1.8	2.8	25.7	29.0
Western Hemisphere	19.6	1.9	4.2	7.7	5.8	39.3	44.3

SOURCE: International Monetary Fund, *Balance of Payments Statistics Yearbook*, 37, part 2, 1986, Tables C–3, C–4, C–5, and C–10.

EXHIBIT 6 Tourism and Passenger Fare Share of Total Trade in Services for 18 Selected Countries 1985 (millions of SDRs)

Country	Merchandise Receipts	Tourism Receipts	Passenger Fare Receipts	Shipment Receipts	Other Transportation Receipts	Receipts from Other Goods, Services and Receipts	Total Services Income	Tourism and Passenger Fare Percent of Total Service Income
Australia	21,960	1,050	482	281	1,079	504	3,396	45.1%
Austria	16,650	4,409	—	620*	69	3,601	8,699	50.7
Bahamas	292	8550	8	—	104	99	1,061	80.9
Canada	88,741	3,567†	—	684	457	3,607	8,315	42.9
China	24,729	964	267	854	355	441	2,881	42.7
Greece	4,223	1,396	8	62	189	921	2,576	54.5
Indonesia	18,180	540	—	—	41	191	772	69.9‡
Israel	6,489	1,092	238	607	174	811	2,922	45.5
Italy	76,507	8,625	965	2,919	1,083	5,972	19,564	44.1
Jordan	776	510	292	78	97	160	1,137	44.9
Malaysia	14,909	594	221	388	225	513	1,941	42.0
Mexico	21,541	2,882	336	—	207	2,234	5,659	56.9
Portugal	5,589	1,108	80	90	243	398	1,919	61.9
Spain	23,649	7,962	896	927	1,475	1,345	12,614	70.2
Switzerland	36,497	3,124	933	373	—	3,406	7,835	51.8
Thailand	6,957	1,153	24	334	98	245	1,854	64.5
Turkey	8,101	1,075	—	598	60	810	2,543	42.3‡
Tunisia	1,675	550	119	101	27	79	876	74.4

* Includes railway passenger fares.
† Includes passenger fares.
‡ reflects tourism share only.

SOURCE: International Monetary Fund, *Balance of Payments Statistics Yearbook*, 37, parts 1 and 2, 1986.

EXHIBIT 7   European Arrivals in the USA Preliminary 1986 Estimates (thousands)

Source	1986 Arrivals	Percent Change 1986/1985	Percent of Total European Arrivals
Total Europe	3,707	+28%	100.0%
Western Europe	3,624	+28	97.8
United Kingdom	1,140	+32	30.8
W. Germany	650	+28	17.5
France	440	+31	11.9
Italy	260	+19	7.0
Switzerland	183	+23	4.9
Netherlands	165	+26	4.5
Sweden	139	+24	3.7
Spain	106	+18	2.9
Ireland	95	+40	2.6
Belgium	80	+29	2.2
Norway	79	+28	2.1
Denmark	70	+26	1.9
Other W. Europe	217	+20	5.9
Eastern Europe	83	+24	2.2
Poland	54	+29	1.5
Hungary	15	+12	0.4
Other E. Europe	16	+33	0.4

SOURCE: U.S. Travel and Tourism Administration.

EXHIBIT 8   Projections for European Travel to the United States in 1987 (thousands)

Origin	1987 Arrivals	Percent Change 1987/1986
Total Europe	4,060	9%
United Kingdom	1,247	9
West Germany	734	11
France	472	7
Italy	283	8
Switzerland	205	12
Netherlands	185	13
Other Europe	934	7

SOURCE: U.S. Travel and Tourism Administration, Department of Commerce.

ing for them in the international marketplace. Why?

The U.S. Travel and Tourism Administration (USTTA) is seriously concerned with this question, as the agency's mission is to encourage and assist U.S. enterprise to promote their tourism products in foreign markets. There is research to show that many American organizations are not marketing abroad because:

- The domestic market generates such large revenues that it overshadows the potential to do business internationally.
- Tourism officials don't know their organization has market potential overseas.
- People think foreign visitors will travel only to U.S. gateway cities.

EXHIBIT 9   Market Characteristics Profiles of European Visitors to the United States in 1984

	Europeans to the USA		*Europeans to the USA*		*Europeans to the USA*
Seasonality		**Use of prepaid inclusive package**		**Port of entry**	
First quarter	17%	Yes	17%	New York	46%
Second quarter	27	No	83	Chicago	6
Third quarter	34	**Type and size of traveling party***		Los Angeles	8
Fourth quarter	22			Boston	7
Purpose of trip*		Traveling alone	44%	Miami	5
Business	39%	Family group	35	San Francisco	5
Attend convention	10	Business group	12	Other	23
Vacation, holiday	41	Mixed business/ family, other	9	**Lodging in the United States***	
Visit friends	16	Average party size (persons)	1.5	Hotel, motel	78
Visit relatives	20	**Age of visitors**		Private home	42
Study	4	Children under 18	6%	Other	10
Other	3	Male adults	66%	Average nights in hotel	9.7
Means of booking air trip*		Female adults	29%	Average nights in private home	21.5
Travel agent	70%	Average age of Male adults (years)	41.1	**Transportation in the United States***	
Self	12	Average age Female adults (years)	39.1	Domestic airlines	51%
Company travel department	20			Rented auto	45
Other	6	**Annual household income**		Private auto	38
Information sources*		Average (U.S. $)	$36,293	City bus/subway	23
Travel agency	62%	Median (U.S. $)	$27,791	Intercity bus	16
Airline	18	**Length of trip**		Intercity train	7
Government sources	3	Average nights away from home	26.4	Other	13
Friends, relatives	23			**Number of U.S. states**	
Newspapers, magazines	7	Average nights in the United States	22.7	One state	41%
Other	13			Two states	25
Type of airline ticket		Median nights away from home	15.0	Three states	15
First class	5			Four or more states	19
Executive, business	20	Median nights in the United States	14.0	**U.S. destinations visited**	
Economy, tourist	71			*New England*	14%
Other	4			Massachusetts	10
				Boston	8

EXHIBIT 9   *(concluded)*

	Europeans to the USA		*Europeans to the USA*		*Europeans to the USA*
Eastern Gateway	45%	Michigan	4	*Pacific Islands*	3%
New York	42	Ohio	4	Hawaii	3
New York City	39	*Mountain West*	5%	*Atlantic Islands*	1%
New Jersey	6	Frontier West	17	Trip expenditures[†]	
George Wash-	22%	Arizona	8	Per capita total	$2,084
ington Country		Grand Can-	6	Per capita in the	$1,026
Washington,	15	yon		United States	
D.C.		Texas	7	Domestic	$197
Pennsylvania	7	Dallas/Ft.	3	transportation	(19%)
Philadelphia	4	Worth		Lodging	$333
The South	27	Houston	3		(32%)
Florida	18	Far West	35	Food, bever-	$243
Miami	7	California	33	ages	(24%)
Orlando	8	Los Angeles	19	Gifts, souve-	$121
Louisiana	5	San Fran-	18	nirs, pur-	(12%)
New Orleans	5	cisco		chases	
Great Lakes Country	17%	San Diego	5	Entertainment	$82 (8%)
Illinois	8	Yosemite	5	Other	$49 (5%)
Chicago	7	Nevada	9		
		Las Vegas	8		

* Multiple responses; percentages add to more than 100 percent.

[†] Data on Europeans' expenditures developed from respondents' recall of actual spending. Information was gathered aboard sampled international flights departing in the USA.

SOURCE: U.S. Travel and Tourism Administration.

- Public and private sector groups believe it costs hundreds of thousands of dollars, or more, to successfully penetrate a foreign market.
- U.S. firms and government agencies do not have an international marketing plan or don't want to invest the resources, and/or feel they don't have the expertise to develop one.
- Tourism officials don't know how to join with other organizations in their region to develop and implement cooperative international marketing programs.[8]

The Problem

Prepare a program to increase the number of foreign tourist visits to a region in the United States. Your task:

---

[8] Excerpted from Richard Seely, "USTTA's Cooperative Marketing Program Stimulates New Business," *Business America*, February 16, 1987, p. 11.

EXHIBIT 10   United States-Europe Travel Dollar Account 1985 (millions)

	U.S. Travel Receipts	Percent of Total	U.S. Travel Payments	Percent of Total	Balance
Total W. Europe	$2,263	100.0%	$5,457	100.0%	−3,194
United Kingdom	435	19.2	1,645	30.1	−1,210
France	305	13.5	770	14.1	−465
Germany	539	23.8	672	12.3	−133
Italy	135	6.0	619	11.3	−484
Switzerland	n.a.	n.a.	369	6.8	n.a.
Spain	n.a.	n.a.	229	4.2	n.a.
Austria	n.a.	n.a.	191	3.5	n.a.
Netherlands	132	5.8	168	3.1	−36
Greece	n.a.	n.a.	148	2.7	n.a.
Ireland	n.a.	n.a.	138	2.5	n.a.
Denmark	n.a.	n.a.	120	2.2	n.a.
Belgium-Luxembourg	n.a.	n.a.	94	1.7	n.a.
Norway	n.a.	n.a.	92	1.7	n.a.
Sweden	n.a.	n.a.	88	1.6	n.a.
Portugal	n.a.	n.a.	36	0.7	n.a.
Other W. Europe	n.a.	n.a.	78	1.4	n.a.

SOURCE: Bureau of Economic Analysis, U.S. Department of Commerce.

EXHIBIT 11   United States Share of World International Tourism, Expenditures and Receipts 1980–1986

	Percent	
Year	Expenditures	Receipts
1980	10.0%	10.4%
1981	11.4	12.7
1982	13.3	13.1
1983	15.0	12.1
1984	16.7	11.8
1985	17.1	11.6
1986	14.9	10.6

SOURCE: International Monetary Fund, *Balance of Payments Statistics Year,book* 38, part 2, 1987, based on Table C-5, pp. 50–51.

1. Select a region (a city, tourist area within a state, or a multiple state region such as the Pacific Northwest or Rocky Mountain West in the United States) that has potential as a destination for foreign tourists.
2. Analyze the region as to why a foreign tourist would want to visit the region.
3. Select a foreign target market (i.e., country or countries) to which you want to appeal.
4. Determine the attractiveness and/or potential problems of your region to visitors from target market selected in item 3.
5. Develop a marketing plan to sell your region to tourists in the target market. Your marketing plan should be designed to:

   a. Convince a foreign tourist travel

EXHIBIT 12 World Residents' Spending on Foreign Travel (1981–1986) (millions of SDRs)*

	1981	1985	Percent Change	1986	Percent Change
Total	86,063	95,100	+10.5	100,412	+ 5.6
Industrial countries	61,282	72,739	+18.7	81,683	+12.3
West Europe	42,115	44,382	+ 5.4	53,886	+21.4
North America	13,233	21,380	+61.6	19,592	− 8.4
Japan, Australia, New Zealand	5,935	6,979	+17.6	8,205	+17.6
Developing countries	24,781	22,360	− 9.8	18,729	−16.2
Africa	3,133	2,287	−27.0	2,026	−11.4
Asia	4,282	8,025	+87.4	6,769	−15.7
Europe	1,161	1,517	+30.7	1,569	+ 3.4
Middle East	5,542	4,377	−21.0	3,031	−30.8
W. Hemisphere	10,663	6,154	−42.3	5,334	−13.3
Oil exporters	7,988	4,840	−39.4	2,871	−40.7
Non-oil exporters	16,793	17,521	+ 4.3	15,858	− 9.5

* A Special Drawing Right (SDR) is an International Monetary Fund reserve asset created in 1969 whose value is determined on the basis of changes in the value of a basket of currencies, including the U.S. dollar. In 1986, the official conversion rate (period average) was 1.1732 U.S. dollars per SDR; in 1981, 1.1792; in 1985, 1.0153.

SOURCE: International Monetary Fund, *Balance of Payments Statistics Yearbook* 38, part 2, 1987, Table C-5, Travel, pp. 50–51.

EXHIBIT 13 Regional Comparison of Developing Country Residents' Spending on Foreign Travel: Share Attributable to Each Region

	Percent		
	1981	1985	1986
Total	100.0%	100.0%	100.0%
Africa	12.6	10.2	10.8
Asia	17.3	35.9	36.1
Europe	4.7	6.8	8.4
Middle East	22.4	19.6	16.2
W. Hemisphere	43.0	27.5	28.5
Oil exporters	32.2	21.6	15.3
Non-oil exporters	67.8	78.4	84.7

SOURCE: International Monetary Fund, *Balance of Payments Statistics Yearbook* 38, part 2, 1987, Table C-5, Travel, pp. 50–51.

EXHIBIT 14 The Source of U.S. International Tourism Receipts 1981–1986 (percent and millions of U.S. dollars)

	1981	1982	1983	1984	1985	1986
Total	*$12,913*	*$12,393*	*$11,408*	*$11,386*	*$11,675*	*$12,913*
Western Hemisphere	5,517	4,892	3,726	3,391	3,567	3,712
Percent of total	42.7%	39.5%	32.7%	29.8%	30.6%	28.7%
Canada	$ 2,672	$ 2,624	$ 3,168	$ 3,116	$ 3,049	$ 3,185
Percent of total	20.7%	21.2%	27.8%	27.4%	26.1%	24.7%
Western Europe	$ 2,549	$ 2,476	$ 2,157	$ 2,227	$ 2,263	$ 2,924
Percent of total	19.7%	20.0%	18.9%	19.6%	19.4%	22.6%
Japan	$ 949	$ 1,084	$ 1,128	$ 1,287	$ 1,418	$ 1,614
Percent of total	7.3%	8.7%	9.9%	11.3%	12.1%	12.5%
Other Asia/Africa	$ 875	$ 918	$ 841	$ 929	$ 936	$ 985
Percent of total	6.8%	7.4%	7.4%	8.2%	8.0%	7.6%
Australia/New Zealand/ South Africa	$ 351	$ 399	$ 388	$ 436	$ 442	$ 493
Percent of total	2.7%	3.2%	3.4%	3.8%	3.8%	3.8%

SOURCE: U.S. Department of Commerce, Bureau of Economic Analysis, *Survey of Current Business* 67, no. 96 (September 1987), Table X, pp. 50–55, and selected earlier issues.

wholesaler to include your region as a part of its touristic product line.[9]

---

[9] Travel wholesalers assemble large blocks of travel space on commercial transportation lines, hotel rooms, and entertainment packages that they offer to travel agents to sell at a commission. For example, a one-week trip to London with hotel, meals, and entertainment package for $1,000 you might purchase from a U.S. travel agent has been assembled and purchased in bulk and at a discount by a travel/tourist wholesaler and then offered to retail travel agents to sell to tourists.

b. Propose an advertising campaign directed specifically to potential tourists in the target market. The advertising campaign should include suggestions for relevant promotional themes designed to create interest in your region as a tourist destination point and cause potential foreign tourists to visit a local travel agent for information and eventually to buy a travel/tourist package to the region.

Case 3–14

RALLYSPORT INTERNATIONAL— PROMOTING RACQUETBALL IN JAPAN

Racquetball grew from an obscure sport played in just a few cities in the United States to the fastest-growing participatory sport on the American scene. In 1975 there were fewer than 30 private court clubs in the entire nation featuring racquetball. By 1985 every major city had a number of clubs devoted exclusively to racquetball or to racquetball and squash. Rallysport International was started in 1975 by Dana Edwards to capitalize on the trend. It was his expressed intention that Rallysport International would become "the McDonald's of the racquetball world." To do so, Rallysport developed several sets of plans, a packaged marketing and promotional program, an entire management and management control system, and subsidiaries devoted to court construction and supervisory management. The company's plans called for a three-state expansion: the first in prime markets throughout the United States; the second into less-desirable but substantial markets in the

United States; the third into developed countries outside the United States.

Three five-year plans were developed; 1975 to 1985—Phase I, 1985 to 1990—Phase II, 1990 to 1995—Phase III (International). During the second five-year plan, however, Edwards observed that competition in the United States was growing so quickly that the company would not have enough time to establish its primacy in domestic market categories and decided to enter the international markets before they became saturated. Tobby Lewis, the company's development manager, was given responsibility for determining whether first to enter Japan or Germany, the company's two target markets, His research led him to the conclusion that the character of the game was ideally fitted to the Japanese who, he said, "are competitive, fast, sports oriented, and tuned into American athletics." He also pointed out that expensive land costs and relative lack of urban land made the racquetball business ideal for Japan because it took so little space. A few squash courts exist in Japan and are considered very exclusive. This is because they are fully enclosed heavy construction which is expensive and unusual in Japan.

I. A. Savant and Company was hired to conduct a market study of the Japanese market and make general recommendations concerning market entry. The company discovered that there are some 115 million Japanese spread among some 40 million households, 90 percent of whom classified themselves as middle class. Sixty percent of the national population inhabit an area adjacent to three major cities. Tokyo, Nagoya, and Osaka, which essentially constitute one major metropolitan area. Savant's conclusion was that the metro market alone could support at least 24 racquet clubs, averaging 10 courts each. That would represent only one club per 1 million households. Their report pointed out that the average per capita income in 1989 was 3,156,174 yen per year ($1.00 = 143 yen), two thirds of which came from the male head of household's regular monthly income, 20 percent from a semiannual bonus, 6 percent from wives, 3 percent from other family members, and 3 percent from other sources. Although those figures are considerably lower than the per capita income in the United States, Savant pointed out that Japanese like new things, are particularly addicted to U.S. products and activities (although that attraction may have eroded somewhat in recent years), and that Japanese had shown consistent ability to spend on products that were meaningful to them while saving in other areas. Approximately 20 percent of the population is in the 20-to-35-year age bracket which is considered to be a prime market for racquetball in the United States. The consultant saw no reason to question the acceptance of the game in Japan. Volleyball is extremely popular with housewives who have formed many large leagues.

Tobby Lewis developed an overall plan for invading the Japanese market. He first recommended that at least four clubs be built simultaneously for the following reasons. (1) The market is segmented, and should be tested thoroughly. Therefore one club would be built in a purely business location, one in a business-residential combination area, and two in residential areas—one close in, and one further out. One of the locations was to be in the Kanto region where the head offices of most major Japanese companies are located. (2) Advertising expenditures must be heavy enough to make strong initial impact—one club alone could not support heavy advertising in such a high-cost market. (3) Rallysport's Japanese joint venture partners are prepared to finance four clubs. (4) Building four clubs establishes a market presence making market entry difficult for other firms. (5) Because of the immense demand potential, each of the four clubs should be immediately profitable.

Savant did foresee some problems. One is that many industrial companies have extensive recreational programs for their employees so that those employees might not be in the market for private recreation. The second problem was that the clubs need to be operated 10 to 11 hours per day to function profitably. Clubs in the United States often operate above that range, but Savant suggested that there were some cultural questions to be considered. Counteracting these issues, the consultant suggested, was a recent survey showing that the target youth market had four primary interests—music, sports, fashion, and travel. The same study pointed out that youth were particularly concerned with health and environmental problems and that the nation's general shift to a five-day week had placed more emphasis on sports and recreation.

The primary contributions of Rallysport International were to be promotional programs, developmental activities, managerial systems, and construction advice. Among other activities, Edwards and Lewis structured an advertising and promotional campaign plan for review by their Japanese joint-venture partner, a major financial institution with extensive experience in industrial goods but limited involvement in the consumer arena. Because the international expansion is of such importance to the company, the board of directors was asked to review the total development program before showing it to the Japanese partner. At the board meeting when it was reviewed, Dave Irwin raised several questions; specifically he mentioned his concern about the cultural fit of the game. He also suggested that the promotional program made basic assumptions about the way the Japanese market would react. He personally questioned, although he admitted he did not know the answers, whether the promotional program was appropriate for the Japanese market or whether it reflected U.S. thinking patterns. He therefore recommended that someone thoroughly familiar with the Japanese culture be asked to review the promotion plan to try to identify problem areas and inconsistencies. He was particularly concerned that Rallysport not present a program that would cause the company to lose face when it was presented to the Japanese partner.

Following are the main items included in the advertising and promotional plan devised by Dana Edwards and Tobby Lewis:

Rallysport - International

Promotion

1. All clubs will tie into the Rallysport name: Rallysport-Tokyo, Rallysport-Osaka, and so forth.
2. Club use will be restricted to members only. (In the United States, some have restricted and some have open-member policies.)
3. Members will be charged a flat monthly fee rather than hourly rate (both systems are used in the United States).
4. Primary target market will be white-collar workers, 25- to 35-years old, upper-middle income.
5. Secondary target market will be Japanese housewives and female office employees.
6. Low-cost, one-month trial memberships will be widely used.
7. Celebrities will be widely used in promotion. A championship U.S. racquetball player may be utilized, or we may tie-in with someone such as Sadeharu Oh and the Yomiuri Giants (leading baseball player and team in Japan, presently endorse Sogo department stores, Toshiba watches, Nichiban plastic bandages, Kyo-Komachi rice cakes, and Pepsi-Cola. Oh and the Giants would be very expensive, perhaps as much as 30 million yen per year for full tie-in).

Advertising

1. Themes: Three types of advertising are widely used in Japan—follow-the-leader advertising, celebrity tie-ins, and mood advertising. Rally will use the celebrity mode.
2. Multiple themes: Different themes will be used for each market segment, but all will tie to some general themes. The three major market segments to be appealed to will be middle-management executives, clerical workers, and housewives.
3. Overall theme: ''Economical Fun and Health with America's Fastest Growing Sport.''

4. Subthemes: Exclusive Clubs; a New Sport; Health and Fitness—stressing cardiovascular benefits; "You Don't Have to Leave the City to Have Fun"; "Easy to Learn, After Just One Hour You Can Have Fun."
5. Campaign will utilize heavy copy and active photography which will explain the game, its benefits, and popularity in the United States. Above all, stress fun.

Media Policy and Timing

1. Timing: A significant segment of the budget will be devoted to a long build-up, teaser-type campaign to establish interest and familiarity and, hopefully, encourage membership presales.
2. Budget allocation: Twenty percent of the total budget will be used for endorsements and for exhibitions by endorsers of the new clubs. Forty percent of the budget will be devoted to television commercials utilizing 60-second spots rather than the more typical 15-second spots. The 60-second spots will give time to show plenty of action and

explain the game and benefits of club membership. Twenty-five percent of the budget will be devoted to newspapers, spread between the nationwide dailies, which reach some 90 percent of all households, or local dailies, which reach over 40 percent of the market, and sports newspapers such as those owned by Chunichi Shimbum. Ten percent of the budget will be allocated to develop publicity in television, newspapers, and magazines and 5 percent to direct mail. Overall media expenditures in Japan are as follows: 35 percent television, 31 percent newspapers, 6 percent magazines, 6 percent direct mail, 5 percent radio, 17 percent outdoor and all other.

Graphics

Graphics will emphasize racquetball play. They will focus on (1) celebrities who are sponsored by the company, (2) American players in tournament competition, and (3) playing women or husband and wife combinations showing the game's broad appeal.

QUESTIONS

1. You have been appointed promotional consultant. Analyze the general promotion policy, the budget, advertising themes, and the graphics approach.
2. What other areas or activities should be included in the promotional advertising program?
3. Evaluate other aspects of the proposal.
4. Who else should review this proposal before it is presented to the joint-venture partner?

Case 3–15

SOCIAL RESPONSIBILITY AND ETHICS IN INTERNATIONAL MARKETING DECISIONS: TWO SITUATIONS[1]

Strategic decisions move a company toward its stated goals and perceived success. Strategic decisions also reflect the firm's social responsibility and ethical values on which such decisions are made. They reflect what is considered important and what a company wants to achieve.

Mark Pastin, writing on the function of ethics in business decisions, observes:

> There are fundamental principles, or ground rules, by which organizations act. Like the ground rules of individuals, organizational ground rules determine **which actions are possible** for the organization and **what the actions mean.** Buried beneath the charts of organizational responsibility, the arcane strategies, the crunched numbers, and the political intrigue of every firm are sound rules by which the game unfolds. [emphasis author's][2]

The following situations reflect different strategic decisions by multinational firms and imply the social responsibility and ethical values that become the ground rules for the decisions. Read each situation carefully to assess the ground rules that guide each firm's decisions.

Internationalizing the Sweatshop[3]

KADER Enterprise Ltd., Hong Kong's largest toy maker, manufactures toys under contract for a variety of U.S. companies. Teddy Ruxpin bears, Mickey and Minnie Mouse dolls, Ghostbusters, Big HollerTot toy trains, Rambo dolls, and Mattel's Rainbow Brite dolls are all manufactured by KADER under contract to U.S. companies. KADER's factories are located in China's special economic zones. KADER employs 12,000 mainland Chinese who typically work 14-hour days, seven days a week to produce toys for the American market. Chinese law officially bans hiring youths under 17 and forcing people to work more than eight hours a day, six days a week. The law is hard to enforce, however, because economic reforms that promote foreign investment are pitted against those of Chinese labor unions.

In some economic zones, Chinese investigators have discovered 10-year-old children making toys, electronic gear, garments, and artificial flowers. The children work 14 to 15 hours a day for $10 to $31 a month and often have to sleep two or three to a bed in dormitories.

Hong Kong law forbids youths under 15 from working; and women are not allowed to work more than 10 hours a day, including overtime. Thus Shekou—the best managed of four economic zones set up to attract foreign investment and just 50 minutes by hydro-

---

[1] This case was prepared by John Garnand and Philip Cateora, University of Colorado-Boulder, 1989.

[2] Mark Pastin, *The Hard Problems of Management* (San Francisco: Jossey-Bass Publishers, 1986), p. 24.

---

[3] Adapted from Dinah Lee and Rose Brady, "Long, Hard Days-At Pennies an Hour," *Business Week,* October 31, 1988, pp. 46–47.

foil from Hong Kong—looks inviting to firms like KADER. "We can work these girls all day and all night, while in Hong Kong it would be impossible," says a KADER executive. "We couldn't get this kind of labor even if we were willing to meet Hong Kong wage levels."

Recently, working hours have grown even more oppressive. To meet the holiday demand for Ghostbusters, Big Holler trains and Mickey Mouse dolls, the workers at the KADER plant were ordered to put in one or two 24-hour shifts each month with only two meal breaks per shift.

Such working conditions are not limited to toy manufacturing. In the largest special economic zone, Shenzhen, mainland investigators dismissed almost 500 workers under age 16 in 22 factories. Some electronics and garment factories were employing girls as young as 10 for 14-hour days at $21 a month.

By these standards, KADER's toy plant offers mainland Chinese workers acceptable working conditions. At Shekou, the 2,600 employees, mostly women from 17 to 25 years old, sleep six to a room in their own beds in a company dormitory. They eat two regular meals a day and earn $31 a month in local currency, plus 12 cents an hour overtime.

For overtime work, including the 24-hour marathon shifts, KADER pays its workers in highly prized Hong Kong dollars, which are hard currency in China. While that is a powerful incentive, workers who refuse overtime can be blacklisted from getting extra hours in the future. Such tactics are illegal under China's provincial labor law. KADER's chairman claims he was not aware that mandatory overtime and 24-hour shifts were the rule at his plant. He asserted that if compulsory overtime existed, it would be stopped. But the plant manager claims U.S. buyers know about the harsh conditions because they monitor production during the 24-hour shifts. He notes that Chinese unions have also complained about working conditions, but "I just disregard them."

Most of KADER's U.S. customers reached for comment said they were not aware of the situation. "Because KADER is a subcontractor you don't have much to say," says an operations vice president of one U.S. company that purchases toys from KADER. Other U.S. executives say they thought conditions at the plant were good. As one executive remarked, "The Chinese employees are bright and happy and productive. I never gave it the slightest thought that they were overworked. We would be shocked if the allegations made against KADER are true." A Hong Kong executive with an American toy vendor acknowledges that U.S. companies may not know that pregnant women faint on the shop floor and that tremendous pressure is put on the workers to get orders filled.

Chinese authorities have stepped up pressure on KADER to reduce its long hours, but the company is resisting. "We told them, this is the toy business. If you don't allow us to do things our way, we'll close down our Chinese factories and move to Thailand."[4]

Exporting U.S. Cigarette Consumption

In the United States, 600 billion cigarettes are sold annually, but sales are shrinking rapidly. Unit sales have been dropping at about 1 to 2 percent a year, and sales have been down by almost 5 percent in the last 6 years. The U.S. Surgeon General's campaign against smoking and the concern Americans have about general health have led to the decline in tobacco consumption.

Recently, a major U.S. tobacco company signed a joint-venture agreement with the

---

[4] Ibid., p. 47.

Chinese government to produce cigarettes in China. The $21 million factory will employ 350 people and produce 2.5 billion cigarettes annually when fully operational.[5]

China, with more than 200 million smokers, produces and consumes about 1.4 trillion cigarettes per year, more than any other country in the world. The company projects that about 80 percent of the cigarettes produced under the joint venture will be for the domestic market, with the remainder for export.

By using China's low-cost labor, this factory will put cigarettes within easy reach of 1.1 billion consumers. The tobacco company estimates that China has more smokers than the United States has people. Just 1 percent of that 1.4 trillion cigarette market would increase the U.S. tobacco company's overseas sales by 15 percent and would be worth as much as $300 million in added revenue.

C. Everett Coop, the recently retired U.S. Surgeon General, was quoted in a recent news conference as saying, "Companies' claims that science cannot say with certainty that tobacco causes cancer were flat-footed lies" and that "sending cigarettes to the Third World was the export of death, disease, and disability." The World Health Organization has launched a "World No-Smoking Day." However, WHO's antismoking budget totals about $2 million—while the tobacco companies spend $2 billion on advertising in one year.[6]

Europeans are also becoming increasingly concerned about the hazards of cigarette smoking. At a recent conference in Madrid, one research report revealed that tobacco was responsible for killing 800,000 Europeans a year and that 100 million others alive today will die of tobacco-related causes if smoking continues at its current rate. Tobacco companies operating in Spain and other European countries have agreed to pull television and radio spots and to limit advertising in other media.[7]

At a time when most industrialized countries are discouraging smoking, the tobacco industry is avidly courting consumers throughout the developing world, using catchy slogans, obvious image compaigns, and single cigarette sales that fit a hard-pressed customer's budget. The reason is clear: the Third World is an expanding market. Indonesia's per capita cigarette consumption quadrupled from 1973 to 1981. Kenya's consumption rises 8 percent annually. In pursuing Third World markets, tobacco companies operate unburdened by many of the restraints they face in the West. Radio and television advertising is generally unrestricted, and cigarette packages do not have to carry health warnings.

In Gambia, smokers have sent in cigarette box tops to qualify for a chance on a new car. In Argentina, smoking commercials fill 20 percent of television advertising time. And in crowded African cities, billboards that link smoking to the good life tower above the sweltering shantytowns. Latin American tobacco consumption rose by more than 24 percent over a 10-year period. In the same period it rose by 4 percent in North America.

Third World governments often stand to profit from tobacco sales, as well. Brazil collects 75 percent of the retail price of cigarettes in taxes, some $100 million a month. Tobacco is Zimbabwe's largest cash crop. China's state-owned tobacco industry took in $5 billion last year.

---

[5] "RJ Reynolds-China Venture Begins to Produce Cigarettes," *The Journal of Commerce*, October 31, 1988, p. 5a.

[6] Margaret Carlson, "A Doctor Prescribes Hard Truth," *Time*, April 24, 1989, pp. 82–83.

[7] "Smoke Alarms," *Europe*, January/February 1989, pp. 7–8.

Critics claim that sophisticated promotions in unsophisticated societies entice people who can not afford the necessities of life to spend money on a luxury, and a dangerous one at that.

The sophistication theme runs throughout the smoking ads. In Kinshasa, Zaire, billboards depict a man in a business suit stepping out of a black Mercedes as a chauffeur holds the door. In Nigeria, promotions for Graduate brand cigarettes show a university student in his cap and gown. Those for Gold Leaf cigarettes have a barrister in a white wig and the slogan, "A very important cigarette for very important people." In Kenya, a magazine ad for Embassy cigarettes shows an elegant executive officer with three young men and women equivalent to American yuppies. Some women in Africa, in their struggle for women's rights, defiantly smoke cigarettes as a symbol of freedom.

Every cigarette manufacturer is in the image business, and tobacco companies say their promotional slant is both reasonable and common. They point out that in the Third World a lot of people cannot understand what is written in the ads anyway, so the ads zero in on the more understandable visual image.

The scope of promotional activity is enormous. In Kenya, a major tobacco company is the fourth-largest advertiser. Tobacco-sponsored lotteries bolster sales in some countries by offering as prizes expensive goods that are beyond most people's budgets. Gambia has a population of just 640,000, but in 1987 a tobacco company lottery attracted 1.5 million entries (each sent in on a cigarette box top) when it raffled off a Renault car.

Another source of concern is the tar and nicotine content of cigarettes. A 1979 study found three major U.S. brands with filters had 17 milligrams of tar in the U.S., 22.3 in Kenya, 29.7 in Malaysia and 31.1 in South Africa. Another brand with filters had 19.1 milligram of tar in the U.S., 28.8 in South Africa and 30.9 in the Philippines.

Although cigarette companies deny they sell higher tar and nicotine cigarettes in the Third World, one British tobacco company does concede that some of its brands sold in developing countries contain more tar and nicotine than those sold in the United States and Europe. This firm leaves the tar and nicotine levels decisions to its foreign subsidiaries, which tailor their products to local tastes. The firm says that Third World smokers are used to smoking their own locally made product, which might have several times more tar and nicotine.

Smokers from the poorest countries often buy cigarettes one at a time and consume fewer than 20 a day. However, even these small quantities represent a serious drain on resources in a country like Zimbabwe, where average monthly earnings are the equivalent of $70 U.S. and a single cigarette costs the equivalent of about 2 U.S. cents.

A study published in the *Lancet*, the British medical journal, reported that Bangladesh smokers spent about 20 percent of their income on tobacco. It asserted that smoking only five cigarettes a day in a poor household in Bangladesh might lead to a monthly dietary deficiency.

It is hard to judge how smoking may be affecting Third World health. In Kenya, for instance, the cause of death is certified by a physician in only one in ten cases. Some statistics do suggest an increase in smoking-related diseases in Shanghai. According to the World Health Organization, lung cancer doubled between 1963 and 1975, a period that followed a sharp increase in smoking in the 1950s.

Generally, smoking is not a big concern of governments beset by debt, internal conflict, drought, or famine. It is truly tragic, but the worse famine becomes, the more people smoke—just as with war, when people who are worried want to smoke. "In any case," says one representative of a international tobacco company, "People in developing countries don't have a long enough life expectancy to worry about smoking-related problems. You can't turn to a guy who is going to die at age 40 and tell him that he might not live up to 2 years extra at age 70." As for promoting cigarettes in the Third World, "If there is no ban on TV advertising, then you aren't going to be an idiot and impose restrictions on yourself," says the representative, ". . . and likewise, if you get an order and you know that they've got money, no one is going to turn down the business."[8]

Assessing the Ethics of Strategic Decisions

It is quickly apparent that ethics is not a simplistic "right" or "wrong" determination. Eth-

The complexity of ethical decisions is compounded in the international setting—comprising different cultures, different perspectives of right and wrong, and different legal requirements. Clearly, when U.S. companies conduct business in an international setting, the ground rules become further complicated by the values, customs, traditions, and ethics of the host countries who have developed their own ground rules for conducting business.

Three prominent American ethicists have developed a *framework* to view ethical implications of strategic decisions by American firms. They identify three ethical principles that can guide American managers in assessing the ethical implications of their decisions and the degree to which these decisions reflect these ethical principles or ground rules. They suggest asking, "Is the corporate strategy acceptable according to the following ethical ground rules?"

Principles	*Question*
* Utilitarian ethics (Bentham, Smith)	Does the corporate strategy optimize the "common good" or benefits of all constituencies?
* Rights of the parties (Kant, Locke)	Does the corporate strategy respect the rights of the individuals involved?
* Justice or fairness (Aristotle, Rawls)	Does the corporate strategy respect the canons of justice or fairness to all parties involved?

ical ground rules are complex, tough to sort out and to set priorities, tough to articulate, and tough to use. It is also apparent that they are inescapable.

---

[8] Steve Mufson, "Smoking Section: Cigarette Companies Develop Third World as a Growth Market," *The Wall Street Journal*, July 5, 1985, p. 1.

These questions can help uncover the ethical ground rules embedded in the two situations (sweatshops and tobacco consumption) described earlier. These questions lead to an ethical analysis of the degree to which these strategies are *beneficial* or *harmful* to the parties, and ultimately, whether they are "right" or "wrong" strategies, or whether the *consequences* of these strategies are ethical or so-

EXHIBIT 1   A Decision Tree for Incorporating Ethical and Social Responsibility
Issues Into Multinational Business Decisions

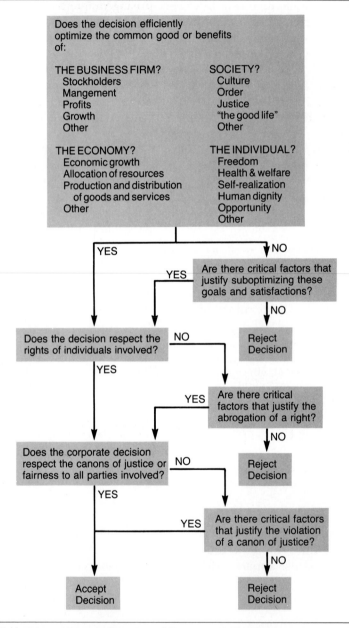

SOURCE: This decision tree is an adaptation of Figure 1, "A Decision Tree for Incorporating
Ethics into Political Behavior Decisions," in Gerald F. Cavanagh, Dennis J. Moberg, and
Manuel Velasquez, "The Ethics of Organizational Politics," *Academy of Management Review*,
1981, pp. 368, and Exhibit 1: The Value Hierarchy—A Model for Management Decision, in
Wilmar F. Bernthal, "Value Perspectives in Management Decisions," *Journal of the Academy
Management*, December 1962, p. 196.

cially responsible for the parties involved.[9] These ideas are incorporated in the decision tree in Exhibit 1.

Laczniak and Naor discuss the complexity of international ethics or, more precisely, the ethical assumptions which underlie strategic decisions for multinationals. They suggest that multinationals can develop *consistency* in their policies by using federal law as a baseline for appropriate behavior as well as respect for the host country's general value structure. They conclude with four recommendations for multinationals:

1. Expand *codes of ethics* to be worldwide in scope.
2. Expressly consider ethical issues when developing worldwide corporate strategies.
3. If the firm encounters major ethical dilemmas, consider withdrawal from the problem market.
4. Develop periodic ethics-impact statements, including impacts on host parties.[10]

---

[9] Gerald F. Cavanagh, Dennis J. Moberg, and Manuel Velasquez, "The Ethics of Organizational Politics," Academy of Management Annual Meeting Address, 1981.

[10] Gene R. Laczniak and Jacob Naor, "Global Ethics: Wrestling with the Corporate Conscience," *Business* (July, August, September 1985).

QUESTIONS

1. Using the model in Exhibit 1 as a guide, assess the ethical and social responsibility implications of each of the situations presented.
2. Can you recommend alternative strategies or solutions to these dilemmas? Are they feasible? What is the price of ethical behavior?

Bibliography

Part I

Baker, James C.; John K. Ryans, Jr.; and Donald Howard, eds. *International Business Classics.* Lexington, Mass: Lexington Books, 1988.

Barfield, Claude E., and John H. Makin, eds. *Trade Policy and U.S. Competitiveness.* Washington, D.C.: American Enterprise Institute for Public Research, 1987.

Bartels, Robert. *Global Development and Marketing.* Columbus, Ohio: Grid, 1981.

Berenbeim, Ronald E. *Operating Foreign Subsidiaries: How Independent Can They Be?* Report No. 836. New York: The Conference Board, 1983.

Bertrand, Kate. "North of the Border, Up Trade Reform Way. . ." *Business Marketing,* February 1988, p. 26.

Copeland, Lennie, and Lewis Griggs. *Going International.* New York: Random House, 1985.

Curran, John. "What Foreigners Will Buy Next." *Fortune,* February 13, 1989, pp. 94–97.

Dymsza, William A. "Global Strategic Planning: A Model and Recent Development." *Journal of International Business Studies,* Fall 1984, pp. 169–83.

"Europe Gets Ready for 1992." *Fortune,* February 1, 1988, pp. 81–84.

Fields, George. *From Bonsai to Levi's.* New York: Macmillan, 1983.

"For Sale: America." *Time,* September 14, 1987, pp. 52–62.

Friedman, David. *The Misunderstood Miracle: Industrial Development and Political Change in Japan.* Ithaca, N.Y.: Cornell University Press, 1988.

Hollerman, Leon. *Japan, Disincorporated: The Economic Liberalization Process.* Stanford, Calif: Hoover Institution Press, 1988.

"International Direct Investment: Global Trends and the U.S. Role," *U.S. Department of Commerce,* 1988, p. 180.

"The Issue Globalists Don't Talk About." *International Management,* September 1987, pp. 37–40.

Kelley, Bill. "The New Wave from Europe." *Sales & Marketing Management,* November 1987, pp. 45–50.

Kin, W. Chan, and Philip K. Y. Young. *The Pacific Challenge in International Business.* Ann Arbor, Mich.: UMI Research Press, 1987.

Kocher, Eric. *International Jobs.* Rev. ed. Reading, Mass.: Addison-Wesley Publishing, 1984.

Lawson, Eugene K., ed. *U.S.-China Trade: Problems and Prospects.* New York: Praeger Publishing, 1988.

Levitt, Theodore. "The Globalization of Markets." *Harvard Business Review,* May–June 1983, pp. 92–102; and From the Editor (Theodore Levitt), "The Pluralization of Consumption." *Harvard Business Review,* May–June 1988, pp. 7–8.

Littler, Sir Geoffrey. "Europe, 1992." *Speaking of Japan,* March 1989, pp. 15–19.

Magaziner, Ira C., and Mark Patinkin. "Fast Heat: How Korea Won the Microwave War." *Harvard Business Review,* January–February 1989, pp. 83–92.

"Major Foreign Acquisitions of the 1980s." *Fortune,* February 13, 1989, p. 96.

"More U.S. Companies Are Selling Operations to Foreign Concerns." *The Wall Street Journal,* February 24, 1988, p. 1.

Moskowitz, Milton. *The Global Marketplace: 102 of the Most Influential Companies Outside America.* New York: Macmillan, 1987.

"The Omnibus Trade and Competitiveness Act of 1988." *The International Division, U.S. Department of Commerce.* Washington, D.C., 1988.

"The 100 Largest U.S. Multinationals." *Forbes,* July 25, 1988, pp. 248–50.

"Outlook for the Community Economy Is Bright: The Commission's Forecasts for 1990 and Revisions for 1989." *Europe,* April 1989, pp. 26–27.

Porter, Michael E. "Changing Patterns of International Competition." *California Management Review,* Winter 1986, pp. 9–40.

"The Selling of America (cont'd)." *Fortune,* May 22, 1988, pp. 54–64.

Spence, A. Michael, and Heather A. Hazard, eds. *International Competitiveness.* Cambridge, Mass: Ballinger Publishing, 1988.

Taylor, Alex, III. "The U.S. Gets Back in Fighting Shape." *Fortune,* April 24, 1989, pp. 42–48.

Tolchin, Martin. *Buying into America: How Foreign Money Is Changing the Face of Our Nation.* New York: Times Books, 1988.

Tully, Shawn. "Europe Gets Ready for 1992." *Fortune,* February 1, 1988, pp. 81–84.

"The Coming Boom in Europe." *Fortune,* April 10, 1989, pp. 108–14.

Van Wolferen, Karel. "The Enigma of Japanese Power." *Fortune,* May 8, 1989, pp. 150–53.

Walter, Ingo, ed., and Tracy Murray, assoc. ed. *Handbook of International Management.* New York: John Wiley & Sons, 1988.

Part II

Adler, Nancy J. *International Dimensions of Organizational Behavior.* Boston, Mass: Kent Publishing, 1986.

Aggarwal, M. R. *New International Economic Order: Interdependence and Southern Development.* New York: Envoy Press, 1987.

Anthropology and International Business. Williamsburg, Va.: Department of Anthropology, College of William and Mary, 1986.

Berney, K. "Finding the Ethical Edge." *Nation's Business,* August 1987, pp. 18–24.

Bond, Kenneth. "To Stay or Leave: The Moral Dilemma of Divestment of South African Assets." *Journal of Business Ethics,* January–February 1988, pp. 9–18.

Debt-Equity Swaps: How to Tap an Emerging Market. New York: Business International Corp., 1987.

Graham, John L. "Foreign Corrupt Practices: A Manager's Guide." *Columbia Journal of World Business,* Fall 1983, pp. 89–94.

————. *Smart Bargaining: Doing Business with the Japanese.* Cambridge, Mass.: Ballinger Publishing, 1984.

Hall, Edward T. *The Silent Language.* New York: Doubleday, 1959.

————. *Beyond Culture.* New York: Anchor Press/Doubleday, 1976.

Harris, Philip R. *Managing Cultural Differences.* Houston, Texas: Gulf Publishing, 1987.

Kelley, Lance; Arthur Whatley; and Reginald Worthley. "Assessing the Effects of Culture on Management Attitudes—A Three-Culture Test." *Journal of International Business Studies,* Summer 1987, pp. 17–31.

Khan, Mohsin S. "Islamic Interest-Free Banking: A Theoretical Analysis." *International Monetary Fund Papers,* March 1988, p. 1.

Kline, John M. *International Codes and Multinational Business: Setting Guidelines for International Business Operations.* Westport, Conn.: Quorum Books, 1985.

Laaksonen, Oiva. *Management in China during and after Mao in Enterprises, Government, and Party.* New York: W. De Gruyter, 1988.

Levinson, Marc. "Is Strategic Trade Fair Trade?" *Across the Board,* June 1988, pp. 47–51.

Lodge, George C., and Ezra F. Vogel. *Ideology and National Competitiveness: An Analysis of Nine Countries.* Boston: Harvard Business School Press, 1987.

Mansfield, Mike. "The Century of the Pacific." *Speaking of Japan,* March 1989, pp. 20–24.

Mennes, L. B. M., and Jacob Kol, eds. *European Trade Policies and the Developing World*. New York: Croom Helm, 1988.

Moran, Theodore H. *Multinational Corporations*. Lexington, Mass.: Lexington Books, 1985.

Mossman, Jennifer, ed. *Encyclopedia of Geographic Information Sources, International Volume*. Detroit, Mich: Gale Research Co., 1988.

"New Boom for North American Exports: Summary of the U.S. Canada Free-Trade Agreement." *Export Today*, September–October 1987, pp. 57–62.

Ohmae, Kenichi. "The Triad World View." *Journal of Business Strategy*, Spring 1987, pp. 8–19.

Okahashi, Sumio. "The Myth of Universality." *Speaking of Japan*, February 1989, pp. 1–4.

Paul, Karen, ed. *Business Environment and Business Ethics: The Social, Moral, and the Political Dimensions of Management*. Cambridge, Mass: Ballinger Publishing, 1987.

Pollio, Gerald, and Charles H. Riemenschneider. "The Coming Third World Investment Revival." *Harvard Business Review*, March–April 1988, pp. 114–18, 122–24.

Raddock, David D. *Assessing Corporate Political Risk: A Guide for International Businessmen*. Totowa, N.J.: Rowman & Littlefield, 1986.

Reeder, John A. "When West Meets East: Cultural Aspects of Doing Business in Asia." *Business Horizons*, January–February, 1987, pp. 69–74.

Teichman, Judith A. *Policymaking in Mexico: From Boom to Crisis*. Boston: Allen & Unwin, 1988.

Teng, Weizao, and N. T. Wang, eds. *Transnational Corporations and China's Open Door Policy*. Lexington, Mass: Lexington Books, 1988.

Terpstra, Vern, and David, Kenneth. *The Cultural Environment of International Business*. 2d ed. Cincinnati: South-Western Publishing, 1985.

Thomas, Harmon C. *A Study of Trade Among Developing Countries, 1950–1980: An Appraisal of the Emerging Pattern*. New York: Elsevier–North Holland, 1988.

Ting, Wenlee. *Multinational Risk Assessment and Management: Strategies for Investment and Marketing Decisions*. New York: Quorum Books, 1988.

Tung, Rosalie L. *Business Negotiations with the Japanese*. Lexington, Mass.: D.C. Heath, 1984.

Van Mesdag, Martin. "Winging It in Foreign Markets." *Harvard Business Review*, January–February 1987, pp. 71–74.

Whitehill, Arthur M. "American Trade Deficit: The Human Problems." *Business Horizons*, January–February 1988, pp. 18–23.

Williams, Gwyneth. *Third-World Political Organizations: A Review of Developments*. Atlantic Highlands, N.J.: Humanities Press International, 1987.

Zimmerman, Mark. *How to Do Business with the Japanese*. New York: Random House, 1985.

Part III

Aronson, Jonathan David. *When Countries Talk: International Trade in Telecommunications Services.* Cambridge, Mass: Ballinger Publishing, 1988.

Basche, James R. *Eliminating Barriers to International Trade and Investment in Services.* New York: The Conference Board, 1986.

Bello, Daniel C., and Nicholas C. Williamson. "The American Export Trading Company: Designing a New International Marketing Institution." *Journal of Marketing,* Fall 1985, pp. 60–69.

Bolt, James F. "Global Competitors: Some Criteria for Success." *Business Horizons,* January–February 1988, pp. 34–41.

Bornschier, Volker. *Transnational Corporations and Underdevelopment.* New York: Praeger Publishers, 1985.

Cavusgil, S. Tamer, "Unraveling the Mystique of Export Pricing." *Business Horizons,* May–June 1988, pp. 54–63.

Choudhry, Yusuf A. "Pitfalls in International Marketing Research: Are You Speaking French Like a Spanish Cow?" *Akron Business and Economic Review,* Winter 1986, pp. 18–28.

Cohen, Stephen S., and John Zysman. "Countertrade, Offsets, Barter, and Buybacks." *California Management Review,* Winter 1986, pp. 41–56.

Contractor, Farok, and Peter Lorange, eds. *Cooperative Strategies in International Business.* Lexington, Mass: Lexington Books, 1988.

Elderkin, Kenton W. *Creative Countertrade: A Guide to Doing Business Worldwide.* Cambridge, Mass: Ballinger Publishing, 1987.

Friedmann, Roberto. "Psychological Meaning of Products: A Simplification of Standardization vs. Adaptation Debate." *Columbia Journal of World Business,* Summer 1986, pp. 97–104.

Gordon, John S. *Profitable Exporting: A Complete Guide to Marketing Your Products Abroad.* New York: John Wiley & Sons, 1988.

Hite, Robert E., and Cynthia Frazier. "International Advertising Strategies of Multinational Corporations." *Journal of Advertising Research,* August–September 1988, p. 16.

Huszagh, Sandra M., and Hiram C. Barksdale. "International Barter and Countertrade: An Exploratory Study." *Academy of Marketing Science,* Spring 1986, pp. 21–27.

Jackson, John Howard. *International Competition in Services: A Constitutional Framework.* Washington, D.C.: American Enterprise Institute for Policy Research, 1988.

Johansson, Johny K., and Ikujiro Nonaka. "Market Research the Japanese Way." *Harvard Business Review,* May–June 1987, pp. 16–22.

Kacker, Madhav P. "The Metamorphosis of European Retailing." *European Journal of Marketing,* Vol. 22, no. 8, 1988, pp. 15–22.

Link, Gordon L. "Global Advertising: An Update." *Journal of Consumer Marketing,* Spring 1988, pp. 69–74.

Lipman, Joanne. "Ad Fad—Marketers Turn Sour on Global Sales Pitch Harvard Guru Makes." *The Wall Street Journal,* May 12, 1988, p. 1.

Mahini, Amir. *Making Decisions in Multinational Corporations: Managing Relations with Sovereign Governments.* New York: John Wiley & Sons, 1988.

"1992—Europe without Frontiers—The Single Market, E.C. Institutions and Easy Access to Rest of Europe Make It a Mecca for International Business." *Europe,* April 1989, pp. 14–47.

"1992 Will Change the Transatlantic Relationship." *Europe,* April 1989, pp. 14–47.

Noyelle, Thierry J. *International Trade in Business Services: Accounting, Advertising, Law, and Management Consulting.* Cambridge, Mass: Ballinger Publishing, 1988.

Onkvisit, Sak, and John J. Shaw. "Marketing Barriers in International Trade." *Business Horizons,* May–June 1988, pp. 64–72.

Peebles, Dean M., and John K. Ryans, Jr. *Management of International Advertising.* Boston: Allyn & Bacon, 1984.

"Protecting American Intellectual Property Abroad." *Business America,* October 27, 1986, pp. 2–7.

Santoro, Elaine. "Telemarketing Globalized." *Direct Marketing,* June 1987, pp. 102–6, 110.

Schuller, Frank C. *Venturing Abroad: Innovation by U.S. Multinationals.* New York: Quorum Books, 1988.

"Service Exports: The Silent Revolution." *Europe Today,* April 1989, pp. 5–8.

Swasy, Alecia. "After Early Stumbles, P&G Is Making Inroads Overseas." *The Wall Street Journal,* February 9, 1989, p. B1.

Taqi, S. J. *Sales Force Management in Europe.* Geneva: Business International S.A., 1988.

Walter, Ingo. *Global Competition in Financial Services: Market Structure, Protection, and Trade Liberalization.* Cambridge, Mass: Ballinger Publishing, 1988.

White, Lawrence J. *International Trade in Ocean Shipping Services: The United States and the World.* Cambridge, Mass: Ballinger Publishing 1988.

Part IV

Bartlett, Christopher A., and Sumantra Ghoshal. "Organizing for Worldwide Effectiveness: The Transnational Solution." *California Management Review,* Fall 1988, pp. 54–74.

Dyment, John J. "Strategies and Management Controls for Global Corporations," *Journal of Business Strategy,* Spring 1987, pp. 20–26.

Evans, Thomas G. *Foreign Exchange Risk Management under Statement 52.* Stamford, Conn: Financial Accounting Standards Board of the Financial Accounting Foundation, 1986.

Feldstein, Martin, ed. *International Economic Cooperation.* Chicago: University of Chicago Press, 1988.

Finlayson, Jock A. *Managing International Markets: Developing Countries and the Commodity Trade Regime.* New York: Columbia University Press, 1988.

Ghoshal, S. "Global Strategy: An Organizing Framework." *Strategic Management Journal,* October 1987, pp. 425–40.

"Managing Now for the 1990s." *Fortune,* September 26, 1988, p. 45.

Savona, Paulo, and George Sutija, eds. *Eurodollars and International Banking.* New York: St. Martin's Press, 1985.

Strategic Cost Reduction: How International Companies Achieve Cost Leadership. Geneva: Business International S. A., 1987.

"3M's Global Marketing Plan: How a New Package Helped Its Worldwide Reorganization." *Business International,* July 13, 1987, pp. 217–18.

Trade Finance: Current Issues and Developments. Washington, D.C.: U.S. Department of Commerce, 1988.

Vernon, Raymond. *Beyond Globalism: Remaking American Foreign Economic Policy.* New York: Free Press, 1989.

Viner, Aron. *The Emerging Power of Japanese Money.* Homewood, Ill.: Dow Jones-Irwin, 1988.

Name Index

Subject Index

Avon Products, Inc.
  direct marketing, 590
  international trade, 8

B

Back translation, 388
Balance of payments, 39–44
  definition, 39–40
  statement of, 41
    current account, 41, 42
Balance of trade, 41–44
Barbados, 266
Barter, 558
Barter houses, 563
Belgium
  advertising, 475, 480
  European market groups, 256
  GNP per person, 230
  import tax, 648
  industrial corporations, 36
  life expectancy, 230
  political parties, 146
  population, 228, 230
Belgium, Key to the Common Market,
  381
Belize, 266
Benelux nations, 252
Benin, 269
Bill of lading, 637–38
  clean or foul, 638
Bills of exchange, 665, 667–69
Black & Decker Manufacturing
  Company, 333
Blocked accounts, 57
Blocked currency, 54
Bolivia
  inflation, 267
  Latin-American market groups,
    266
  LLDCs, 267
Botswana, 673
Boycott, 52–53, 630
Brazil
  advertising, 465, 475, 476, 491
  boycotts, 52
  business customs, 101, 122–23
  countertrading, 673
  discouraging of foreign
    manufacturing, 167
  economic development, 287, 292–
    93
  economic indicators, 294
  family income, 223
  GNP per person, 230
  import restrictions, 159
  industrialization, 34
  inflation, 662
  infrastructure, 296

Brazil—*Cont.*
  life expectancy, 230
  living standards, 324
  Latin-American Integration
    Association, 266
  market indicators, 321
  monetary import restrictions, 55
  more-developed countries, 267
  100 largest industrial corporations,
    36
  political risks in financing trade,
    670–71
  population, 230
  price controls, 159
  product adaptation, 418
  trading companies, 600
Brazilian Coffee Institute (IBC), 555
Bretton Woods Agreement, 671–72
Bribery, 127–32
  Foreign Corrupt Practices Act, 200
  political payoffs, 174–75
Bristol-Myers Company, 581
Britain; *see* United Kingdom,
British Broadcasting Corporation,
  477
British Commonwealth of Nations,
  246, 253–54
Britone, 283
Broker
  foreign country middleman, 609
  home country middleman, 603
Brunei, 271
Bulgaria, 311 n
Bureau for International Registration
  of Trademarks, 195
Burkine Faso, 269, 270
Burroughs Company, 499
Business America, 378
Business customs, 100–132
  adaptation, 100–102
  adiaphora, 103, 104–5
  authority, 107–11
  communications, 114–17, 135–42
  ethics, 127–32
  exclusives, 103, 105
  imperatives, 103
  management objectives, 111–14
  modes of doing business, 107–27
  negotiations, 123–28, 140–43
  relation to culture, 105
Business ethics, 127–32
  bribery, 127–32
Business Index, 396
Business International, 179, 626
*Business International, Worldwide
  Economic Indicators*, 397
*Business International Master Key
  Index*, 396
Business Periodical Index, 396

Business services, 451–57
  competition, 456
  growth of U.S. services, 452
  market environment for, 454–57
  types of transactions, 451
Buy American Act of 1933, 52
Buy-back agreement, 561
Buying offices, 603–4

C

Cameroon, 269
  African market groups, 269, 270
Campbell Soup Company, 415, 419,
  423–24
Canada
  climate and topography, 213
  economic nationalism, 150
  industrial corporations, 36
  GNP per person, 230
  investment in United States, 6
  life expectancy, 230
  market indicators, 321
  marketing laws, 197–98
  population, 230
  television advertising, 480
  trade agreement with United
    States; *see* United States and
    Canada Free Trade
    Agreement
Canadian American Commercial
  Arbitration Commission, 188
Canon Company, 370
Cape Verde, 269
Capital account (balance of payment
  statement), 41
Capital investment, 661
Capital requirements
  market penetration, 658
  working capital, 658
Caribbean Community and
  Common Market (CARICOM),
  265–66, 268
Carnation Milk, 5
Carrefour, 284
Casablanca Group, 269
Cash-in-advance, 669
Caterpillar Tractor company, 205
  dealers, 609
CBS Records, 5
Central African Republic, 269, 270
Central American Common Market
  (CACM), 246, 247, 252
Centralized organization, 693, 694,
  708
Certificate of origin, 637
C&F (cost and freight), 639
Chad, 269
Chamber of Commerce, U.S., 379